PROSE AND POETRY OF AMERICA

The Prose and Poetry Series

PROSE AND POETRY JOURNEYS

PROSE AND POETRY ADVENTURES

PROSE AND POETRY FOR ENJOYMENT

PROSE AND POETRY FOR APPRECIATION

PROSE AND POETRY OF AMERICA

PROSE AND POETRY OF ENGLAND

PROSE AND POETRY OF THE WORLD

AGNES L. McCARTHY

Head of the English Department and Director of Curriculum,

Faribault High School, Faribault, Minnesota

Prose and Poetry

❖❖❖❖❖❖❖❖❖❖❖❖❖❖❖❖❖❖❖❖❖❖❖❖

DESIGN BY STEFAN SALTER

ILLUSTRATIONS BY FRITZ KREDEL

DELMER RODABAUGH

Associate Professor of English, Long Beach State College,

Long Beach, California

Fifth Edition

THE L. W. SINGER COMPANY, INC.

SYRACUSE, NEW YORK

The editors and the publisher acknowledge with thanks the permission
to use copyrighted selections as indicated by footnotes
on the pages where the selections begin.

Cover Design: "Daniel Boone Escorting a Band of Pioneers into the Western
Country." Painting by George Caleb Bingham.
From the collection of Washington University, St. Louis, Missouri.

PREFACE

In preparing the fifth edition of PROSE AND POETRY OF AMERICA, the editors have kept in mind the important role of American literature in educating young Americans for life in our democracy. They have also been mindful of the many problems that arise in meeting the needs of students of all degrees of ability and literary aptitude. These considerations have greatly influenced the choice of selections, the organization of the book, and the amount and kind of the teaching and study helps that have been provided.

An examination of any part of the book will show that the selections reflect youth and youthful interests. For example, while all of the short stories included in the modern section are by outstanding American writers, almost all of the principal characters are young people—the majority of high school age. In the drama unit, mystery and adventure are prominent. In biography, the principle of American free enterprise is presented in episodes from the youth of successful Americans who rose from humble beginnings. Even in the essays and articles there is a strong appeal to American youth. In poetry, always a challenge to the editors of high school literature texts, the young people themselves have done the choosing. The poems in all three sections of the book have been tested in the classroom and have been found to be popular and teachable.

Probably the most distinctive feature of PROSE AND POETRY OF AMERICA is its or-

ganization. The book is divided into three approximately equal sections. Within each section are smaller units, each organized to develop the broad objectives of the main sections. Consequently, there are three kinds of organization: type, historical theme, and author. While *ideas* are emphasized throughout the book, rather than form or the chronological development of American literature, the three kinds of organization help to focus attention successively on three important aspects of a good literature program.

There are definite advantages in beginning with modern literature, and arranging it by literary types. Because high school students like to read about contemporary people and problems, the modern material captures initial interest. The type arrangement helps to insure some basic knowledge of literary form which will be helpful in discussing and evaluating selections in all sections of the book. An understanding of the distinctive features of each literary type is best acquired while students are dealing with content, ideas, and concepts that are close to them. Whenever the type recurs in subsequent units, this basic knowledge can be reviewed and refined.

The second section of the book is organized by themes which are roughly chronological. Here an attempt is made to develop through literature an understanding and appreciation of the great periods or movements that have contributed to the growth of American democracy.

These historical units serve as a framework for presenting as much of a core of chronological American literature as seems desirable at the high school level. The themes are broad and mainly historical because the editors believe that study of minor literary trends and periods properly belongs at the college level. In high school, a knowledge of successive stages of American history and of the development of American ideals is of primary importance.

It will be noted that in each of these historical units, contemporary material about the period has been included. In the early periods of American history, the amount of really good literature produced, particularly that of interest to young people, is not equal to the importance of those periods historically. However, there is good modern writing which can help students to understand the times and appreciate the aims and ideals of the people of those early days. In each historical grouping the modern material is placed at the beginning to arouse interest and to set the stage for writing done during the period.

The third section of the book, *Masters of American Literature*, is made up of the work of important American writers of the nineteenth century. The selections are grouped according to authors, and these are arranged chronologically. The writers represented have so profoundly influenced or interpreted American life or thought that their work has become a part of our literary heritage. Here they are singled out for special attention.

The aids needed for effective teaching and learning are included in the text of PROSE AND POETRY OF AMERICA. As in the choice of selections, the kind and arrangement of study helps were determined by the objectives of each section and by the particular problems or difficulties posed by each piece of literature. Each of the three main sections and each of the smaller units begins with a brief motivating introduction. In addition, each selection has its own introduction to arouse interest, to provide necessary background, and to direct reading.

Biographical sketches of authors are placed where they are most usable—with the selections. In the modern and historical sections they are brief, including only what will help in understanding and appreciating the literature. However, in the section *Masters of American Literature* biographies include critical evaluation of the author's work and emphasize his contributions to American literature.

Following each selection are questions, vocabulary exercises, and suggested activities. These are varied in kind and difficulty to fit the selection and to provide for differences in classes and individuals. There are also end-of-unit questions, language arts activities and projects, and lists for further reading.

Throughout the book, understanding and appreciation of America and American ideals are stressed. However, the growth of ability to read good literature with discrimination, and the cultivation of a lifelong interest in reading for enjoyment, are also major aims. These objectives can be achieved only by providing rich and satisfying experiences with literature in school. The editors believe that the selections, the organization, and the study materials in PROSE AND POETRY OF AMERICA contribute to those ends.

CONTENTS

CONTENTS

CONTENTS

II. A FREE PEOPLE BUILDS A NATION

FOOTHOLD IN THE WILDERNESS

STRUGGLE FOR INDEPENDENCE

FRONTIERS TO THE WEST

CONTENTS

III. MASTERS OF AMERICAN LITERATURE

CONTENTS

CONTENTS BY TYPES

CONTENTS BY TYPES

LYRIC POETRY

CONTENTS BY TYPES

DOUBLEDAY BOOK SHOP, 655 FIFTH AVENUE, NEW YORK, NEW YORK

MODERN AMERICAN LITERATURE

The literature of any country reflects the land and the people from which it comes. American writers, like other Americans, have been influenced by the forces that mold character and thought in a democratic society. As they grew up they absorbed such American traditions as respect for the rights of the individual, freedom of speech and religion, and the spirit of competitive free enterprise. In addition to this common all-American heritage, each acquired the distinctive qualities of a particular region of America and of a small area of that region. Each one's personality was shaped not only by national ideals but by a neighborhood, by social and economic conditions, and by family relationships. American writers are therefore as different from one another as are the different regions of the broad and varied country they live in.

What is true of the writers is also true of their writing. In the foreword to a recent book Mr. E. B. White said: "Whoever sets pen to paper writes of himself whether knowingly or not." Therefore, Americans write of America, and each one writes of the particular segment of America that he knows. Even when his subject is far removed from his own land and its people, he writes as an American. What he is will determine what he looks for in life and how he interprets it. Because our literature is colored by American attitudes, by an American sense of values, it reflects the many different aspects of life in a democracy.

The modern selections in the first section of this book are of different literary types. They represent various sections of the country, and touch upon almost every feature of American life. They picture the land and the people of North and South, East and West and Middle West. They show city, small town, and country life. The authors you will read are from many of the different national backgrounds that make up America. The characters you will meet are also of diverse national origin and of various social levels. They are young, old, and in between. A few are rich, some are poor, but most are neither. Among them are farmers, mechanics, artists, cowboys. They meet with adventure and romance, humor and tragedy. Reading about them should help you to a better understanding of life in our democracy today—for, taken all together they represent the people of America.

SHORT STORIES

A TYPICALLY AMERICAN FORM OF LITERATURE

Of all forms of literature the short story is most American, for it was developed in America. Like people everywhere, the citizens of our country in its early days liked a good story. They brought up their children on old tales and ballads which had come from Europe. However, almost from the beginning there was a difference in the kind of stories Americans enjoyed. The tempo of life in the New World was less leisurely than that in the Old World. The majority of Americans, then as now, had little time or inclination for the long, rambling tales that were popular in Europe. Even in the first half of the nineteenth century when the novels of James Fenimore Cooper, Nathaniel Hawthorne, and Herman Melville were being read widely both at home and abroad, it was the short tales appearing in the new magazines that won most favor in America. Since then the demand for entertaining short stories has steadily increased until today there are twenty times as many short stories as novels published in the United States each year. It is particularly important, therefore, that Americans learn to evaluate short stories in order to select wisely the most worth-while from the great number available, and also to get the most enjoyment possible from those that they read.

THE DEVELOPMENT OF THE SHORT STORY

Some examples of the earliest fiction in America from which the modern short story developed were the tales written by Washington Irving, in the years between 1819 and 1824. A number of them had their setting in the state of New York. They differed from most later short stories in that they were written in an easy-going, leisurely style which gave opportunity for comments about the quaint customs and ideas of the Hudson Valley Dutch; and for extended descriptions of picturesque aspects of the New York landscape. You are no doubt familiar with "Rip Van Winkle" and "The Legend of Sleepy Hollow," for they have become classics of American literature. In the *Masters of American Literature* section of this book you will have an opportunity to read two other famous tales by Irving: "The Stout Gentleman" and "The Devil and Tom Walker." You will notice that their style and construction are in sharp contrast to that of the stories by other authors who followed Irving.

The first examples of the more typical American short story were written in the 1830's and 1840's by Edgar Allan Poe and Nathaniel Hawthorne. In their unusual situations and strange characters these stories had some of the romantic qualities of Irving's tales. However, they resemble modern short stories in their carefully constructed plots and the unity of effect or impression which they create. In fact it was Poe who first defined the short story as a particular type of literature. He believed that as a work of art the short story should create *a single definite emotion or impression,* and that every word should contribute something toward that effect. As you will discover when you read "The Masque of the Red Death" and "The Cask of Amontillado" the effect produced by Poe's own stories was usually one of horror or terror. Many of Poe's stories were highly dramatic, skillfully building up suspense step by step until they reached an exciting (and usually horrifying) conclusion. Both Poe and Hawthorne created fascinating characters, although those in Poe's stories were often unbalanced or warped individuals—in keeping with his fantastic plots and weird settings. Hawthorne was more interested in the moral problems, and the deeper thoughts and emotions, of normal people. Like modern writers he tried to interpret human nature for his readers. His stories were sometimes almost as strange as Poe's, because "normal" human life, beneath the surface, is a great deal more complex and strange than we ordinarily realize. In spite of an air of mystery and unreality, Hawthorne's stories are frequently very much like present-day stories in their psychological approach to the study of human behavior.

The next important step in the development of the short story was taken by a group of *local color* writers, represented in this book by Bret Harte. Each of these writers tried to get into his stories the color and atmosphere of a particular region and of groups or classes of people who lived there. There were stories about life in the New England village, on the Southern plantation, and in the California town or mining camp. While some local color authors succeeded in giving a true picture of segments of American life, others, like Bret Harte, helped to build up or keep alive romantic misconceptions about sections of our country. This they did by emphasizing peculiarities of so-called *typical* people. Because human beings are too complex, too individual, to be tagged and catalogued by region or group, the characters of many local color stories are not true-to-life people. They are stock characters or *stereotypes* cut to a pattern. Nevertheless, the local color movement made a significant contribution to the American short story because it awakened Americans—writers and readers alike—to the great variety of environments and the many different kinds of people in their own land.

One more important movement to leave its mark on the short story was the rise of *realism* in literature. Instead of looking for romantic peculiarities in people and their surroundings, realistic writers found interest and drama in the everyday lives of very ordinary people. In order to create a true and complete picture of life these writers included in their stories commonplace and sometimes ugly details that would have been passed over by romantic writers. Two good examples of early realistic stories in this book are Stephen Crane's "A Mystery of Heroism" in the section called *A Time of Crisis*, and Hamlin Garland's "Among the Corn Rows" in *Frontiers to the West*. Not only the settings and the characters of these stories, but their plots, are realistic. The authors do not try to astonish their readers with a series of fantastic or unusual events. The stories build up to a climax, but it is such a climax as might often occur in real life. The richness of actual experience—not the excitement of a make-believe situation—is what interests the authors.

THE SHORT STORY OF TODAY

As you read the modern short stories in the following pages, you will find that our writers of today have been influenced by most earlier developments in this type of literature. Although they are not primarily local color stories, nearly every one gives a glimpse of what life is like in a particular region of America. For example, much of the interest of "Two Soldiers" comes from the fact that the speaker has the characteristics of a Mississippi farm lad; and both "The Secret Life of Walter Mitty" and "The Gift of the Magi" are snapshots of city life.

Most modern stories are realistic—picturing people you might actually meet, and scenes that you might actually see, in modern America. You will discover that some stories have plots somewhat like Poe's—consisting of an unusual series of events that are carefully arranged to lead to a dramatic conclusion. However, in most of them the characters' "adventures" are entirely possible and believable. There is usually one central episode or situation which is dramatic and important, but as in the ups and downs of real life there is not always a thrilling climax.

A feature that is to be found in all these stories is *singleness of effect*. One mood, one strong impression, is produced by each; and the plot, the characters, and the setting are carefully combined to give this desired effect. To modern authors, as to Edgar Allan Poe, a short story is a work of art which must be perfectly designed and in which every detail—almost every word—must be exactly right.

6

TWO SOLDIERS

WILLIAM FAULKNER

The two soldiers in this story are poor farm boys from the Deep South. One of them is only nine years old; yet he shows the same kind of loyalty and courage as does his older brother who leaves home to join the army. You will enjoy the younger boy's account of how they both went to war.

Me and Pete would go down to Old Man Killegrew's and listen to his radio. We would wait until after supper, after dark, and we would stand outside Old Man Killegrew's parlor window, and we could hear it because Old Man Killegrew's wife was deaf, and so he run the radio as loud as it would run, and so me and Pete could hear it plain as Old Man Killegrew's wife could, I reckon, even standing outside with the window closed.

And that night I said, "What? Japanese? What's a pearl harbor?" and Pete said, "Hush."

And so we stood there, it was cold, listening to the fellow in the radio talking, only I couldn't make no heads nor tails out of it. Then the fellow said that would be all for a while, and me and Pete walked back up the road to home, and Pete told me what it was. Because he was nigh twenty and he had done finished the Consolidated[1] last June and he knowed a heap: about them Japanese dropping bombs on Pearl Harbor and that Pearl Harbor was across the water.

"Across what water?" I said. "Across that Government reservoy up at Oxford?"[2]

"Naw," Pete said. "Across the big water. The Pacific Ocean."

We went home. Maw and Pap was already asleep and me and Pete laid in bed, and I still couldn't understand where it was, and Pete told me again— the Pacific Ocean.

"What's the matter with you?" Pete said. "You're going on nine years old. You been in school now ever since September. Ain't you learned nothing yet?"

"I reckon we ain't got as fer as the Pacific Ocean yet," I said.

We was still sowing the vetch[3] then that ought to been all finished by the fifteenth of November, because Pap was still behind, just like he had been ever since me and Pete had knowed him. And we had firewood to git in, too, but every night me and Pete would go down to Old Man Killegrew's and stand outside his parlor window in the cold and listen to his radio; then we would come back home and lay in bed and Pete would tell me what it was. That is, he would tell me for a while. Then he wouldn't tell me. It was like he didn't want to talk about it no more. He would tell me to shut up because he wanted to go to sleep, but he never wanted to go to sleep.

[1] CONSOLIDATED—A school in which the students are from several school districts.

[2] OXFORD—A town in northern Mississippi.

[3] VETCH—A plant belonging to the same family as peas and beans, often cultivated for forage, and to help renew the soil.

"Two Soldiers" by William Faulkner from the *Saturday Evening Post* of March 28, 1942 published by The Curtis Publishing Company, copyright, 1942, by The Curtis Publishing Company, reprinted by permission of Harold Ober Associates.

He would lay there, a heap stiller than if he was asleep, and it would be something, I could feel it coming out of him, like he was mad at me, or like he was worried about something, and it wasn't that neither, because he never had nothing to worry about. He never got behind like Pap, let alone stayed behind. Pap give him ten acres when he graduated from the Consolidated, and me and Pete both reckoned Pap was durn glad to get shut of at least ten acres, less to have to worry about himself; and Pete had them ten acres all sowed to vetch and busted out and bedded for the winter, and so it wasn't that. But it was something. And still we would go down to Old Man Killegrew's every night and listen to his radio, and they was at it in the Philippines now, but General MacArthur was holding um. Then we would come back home and lay in the bed, and Pete wouldn't tell me nothing or talk at all. He would just lay there still as an ambush and when I would touch him, his side or leg would feel hard and still as iron, until after a while and I would go to sleep.

Then one night—it was the first time he had said nothing to me except to jump on me about not chopping enough wood at the wood tree where he was cutting—he said, "I got to go."

"Go where?" I said.

"To that war," Pete said.

"Before we even finish gettin' in the firewood?"

"Firewood, heck," Pete said.

"All right," I said. "When we going to start?"

But he wasn't even listening. He laid there, hard and still as iron in the dark. "I got to go," he said. "I jest ain't going to put up with no folks treating the Unity States that way."

"Yes," I said. "Firewood or no firewood, I reckon we got to go."

This time he heard me. He laid still again, but it was a different kind of still.

"You?" he said. "To a war?"

"You'll whup the big uns and I'll whup the little uns," I said.

Then he told me I couldn't go. At first I thought he just never wanted me tagging after him, like he wouldn't leave me go with him when he went sparking them girls of Tull's. Then he told me the Army wouldn't leave me go because I was too little, and then I knowed he really meant it and that I couldn't go nohow noways. And somehow I hadn't believed until then that he was going himself, but now I knowed he was and that he wasn't going to leave me go with him a-tall.

"I'll chop the wood and tote the water for you-all then!" I said. "You got to have wood and water!"

Anyway, he was listening to me now. He wasn't like iron now.

He turned onto his side and put his hand on my chest because it was me that was laying straight and hard on my back now.

"No," he said. "You got to stay here and help Pap."

"Help him what?" I said. "He ain't never caught up nohow. He can't get no further behind. He can sholy take care of this little shirttail of a farm while me and you are whupping them Japanese. I got to go too. If you got to go, then so have I."

"No," Pete said. "Hush now. Hush." And he meant it, and I knowed he did. Only I made sho from his own mouth. I quit.

"So I just can't go then," I said.

"No," Pete said. "You just can't go. You're too little, in the first place, and in the second place—"

"All right," I said. "Then shut up and leave me to go to sleep."

So he hushed then and laid back. And I laid there like I was already asleep, and pretty soon he was asleep and I knowed it was the wanting to go to the war that had worried him and kept him awake, and now that he had decided to go, he wasn't worried any more.

The next morning he told Maw and Pap. Maw was all right. She cried.

"No," she said, crying, "I don't want him to go. I would rather go myself in his place, if I could. I don't want to save the country. Them Japanese could take it all and keep it, so long as they left me and my family and my children alone. But I remember my brother Marsh in that other war. He had to go to that one when he wasn't but nineteen and our mother couldn't understand it

then any more than I can now. But she told Marsh if he had to go, he had to go. And so, if Pete's got to go to this one, he's got to go to it. Jest don't ask me to understand why."

But Pap was the one. He was the feller. "To the war?" he said. "Why I don't see a bit of use in that. You ain't old enough for the draft, and the country ain't being invaded. Our President in Washington, D. C., is watching the conditions and he will notify us. Besides, in that other war your ma just mentioned, I was drafted and sent clean to Texas and was held there nigh eight months until they finally quit fighting. It seems to me that that, along with your Uncle Marsh who received a actual wound on the battlefields of France, is enough for me and mine to have to do to protect the country, at least in my lifetime. Besides, what'll I do for help on the farm with you gone? It seems to me I'll get mighty far behind."

"You been behind as long as I can remember," Pete said. "Anyway I'm going. I got to."

"Of course he's got to go," I said. "Them Japanese—"

"You hush your mouth!" Maw said, crying. "Nobody's talking to you! Go and get Ma a armful of wood! That's what you can do!"

So I got the wood. And all the next day, while me and Pete and Pap was getting in as much wood as we could in that time because Pete said how Pap's idea of plenty of wood was one more stick laying against the wall that Maw ain't put on the fire yet, Maw was getting Pete ready to go. She washed and mended his clothes and cooked him a shoe box of vittles. And that night me and Pete laid in the bed and listened to her packing his grip and crying, until after a while Pete got up in his nightshirt and went back there, and I could hear them talking, until at last Maw said, "You ought to go, and so I want you to go. But I don't understand it, and I won't never, and so don't expect me to." And Pete come back and got into bed again and laid again still and hard as iron on his back, and then he said, and he wasn't talking to me, he wasn't talking to nobody: "I got to go. I just got to."

"Sho you got to," I said. "Them Japanese—" He turned over hard, he kind of surged over onto his side, looking at me in the dark.

"Anyway, you're all right," he said. "I expected to have more trouble with you than with all the rest of them put together."

"I reckon I can't help it neither," I said. "But maybe it will run a few years

longer and I can get there. Maybe someday I will jest walk in on you."

"I hope not," Pete said. "Folks don't go to wars for fun. A man don't leave his maw crying just for fun."

"Then why are you going?" I said.

"I got to," he said. "I just got to. Now you go on to sleep. I got to ketch that early bus in the morning."

"All right," I said, "I hear tell Memphis is a big place. How will you find where the Army's at?"

"I'll ask somebody where to go to join it," Pete said. "Go on to sleep now."

"Is that what you'll ask for? Where to join the Army?" I said.

"Yes," Pete said. He turned onto his back again. "Shut up and go to sleep."

We went to sleep. The next morning we et breakfast by lamplight because the bus would pass at six o'clock. Maw wasn't crying now. She jest looked grim and busy, putting breakfast on the table while we et it. Then she finished packing Pete's grip, except he never wanted to take no grip to the war, but Maw said decent folks never went nowhere, not even to a war, without a change of clothes and something to tote them in. She put in the shoe box of fried chicken and biscuits and she put the Bible in, too, and then it was time to go. We didn't know until then that Maw wasn't going to the bus. She jest brought Pete's cap and overcoat, and still she didn't cry no more, she jest stood with her hands on Pete's shoulders and she didn't move, but somehow, and just holding Pete's shoulders, she looked as hard and fierce as when Pete had turned toward me in the bed last night and tole me that anyway I was all right.

"They could take the country and keep the country, as long as they never bothered me and mine," she said. Then she said, "Don't never forget who you are.

You ain't rich and the rest of the world outside of Frenchman's Bend never heard of you. But your blood is good as any blood anywhere, and don't you never forget it."

Then she kissed him, and then we was out of the house, with Pap toting Pete's grip whether Pete wanted him to or not. There wasn't no dawn even yet, not even after we had stood on the highway by the mailbox, awhile. Then we seen the lights of the bus coming and I was watching the bus until it come up and Pete flagged it, and then, sho enough, there was daylight—it had started while I wasn't watching. And now me and Pete expected Pap to say something else foolish, like he done before, about how Uncle Marsh getting wounded in France and that trip to Texas Pap had taken in 1918 ought to be enough to save the Unity States in 1942, but he never. He done all right too. He jest said, "Goodby, Son. Always remember what your ma told you and write her whenever you find the time." Then he shaken Pete's hand, and Pete looked at me a minute and put his hand on my head and rubbed my head durn nigh hard enough to wring my neck off and jumped into the bus, and the feller wound the door shut and the bus begun to hum; then it was moving, humming and grinding and whining louder and louder; it was going fast, with two little red lights behind it that never seemed to get no littler, but jest seemed to be running together until pretty soon they would touch and jest be one light. But they never did, and then the bus was gone, and even like it was, I could have pretty nigh busted out crying, nigh to nine years old and all.

Me and Pap went back to the house. All that day we worked at the wood tree, and so I never had no good chance until about middle of the afternoon. Then I

taken my slingshot and I would have liked to took all my bird eggs, too, because Pete had give me his collection and he holp me with mine, and he would like to git the box out and look at them as good as I would, even if he was nigh twenty years old. But the box was too big to tote a long ways and have to worry with, so I just taken the shikepoke [4] egg, because it was the best un, and wropped it up good into a matchbox and hid it and the slingshot under the corner of the barn. Then we et supper and went to bed, and I thought then how if I would 'a' had to stayed in that room and that bed like that even for one more night, I jest couldn't 'a' stood it. Then I could hear Pap snoring, but I never heard no sound from Maw, whether she was asleep or not, and I don't reckon she was. So I taken my shoes and drapped them out the window, and then I clumb out like I used to watch Pete do when he was still jest seventeen and Pap wouldn't leave him out, and I put on my shoes and went to the barn and got the slingshot and the shikepoke egg and went to the highway.

It wasn't cold, it was jest durn confounded dark, and that highway stretched on in front of me like, without nobody using it, it had stretched out half again as fer just like a man does when he lays down, so that for a time it looked like full sun was going to ketch me before I had finished them twenty-two miles to Jefferson. But it didn't. Daybreak was jest starting when I walked up the hill into town. I could smell breakfast cooking in the cabins and I wished I had thought to brought me a cold biscuit, but that was too late now. And Pete had told me Memphis was a piece beyond Jefferson, but I never knowed it was

[4] SHIKEPOKE—A variant of shitepoke, a kind of heron.

no eighty miles. So I stood there on that empty square, with daylight coming and coming and the street lights still burning and that Law[5] looking down at me, and me still eighty miles from Memphis, and it had took me all night to walk jest twenty-two miles, and so, by the time I got to Memphis at that rate, Pete would 'a' done already started for Pearl Harbor.

"Where do you come from?" the Law said. And I told him again. "I got to git to Memphis. My brother's there."

"You mean you ain't got any folks around here?" the Law said. "Nobody but that brother? What are you doing way off down here and your brother in Memphis?"

And I told him again, "I got to git to Memphis. I ain't got no time to waste talking about it and I ain't got time to walk it. I got to git there today."

"Come on here," the Law said.

We went down another street. And there was the bus, jest like when Pete got into it yestiddy morning, except there wasn't no lights on it now and it was empty. There was a regular bus dee-po like a railroad dee-po, with a ticket counter and a feller behind it, and the Law said, "Set down over there," and I set down on the bench, and the Law said, "I want to use your telephone," and he talked into the telephone a minute and put it down and said to the feller behind the ticket counter, "Keep your eye on him. I'll be back as soon as Mrs. Habersham can arrange to get herself up and dressed." He went out. I got up and went to the ticket counter.

"I want to go to Memphis," I said.

"You bet," the feller said. "You set down on the bench now. Mr. Foote will be back in a minute.

"I don't know no Mr. Foote," I said.

[5] LAW—A policeman.

"I want to ride that bus to Memphis."

"You got some money?" he said. "It'll cost seventy-two cents."

I taken out the matchbox and unwropped the shikepoke egg. "I'll swap you this for a ticket to Memphis," I said.

"What's that?" he said.

"It's a shikepoke egg," I said. "You never seen one before. It's worth a dollar. I'll take seventy-two cents fer it."

"No," he said, "the fellers that own that bus insist on a cash basis. If I started swapping tickets for bird eggs and livestock and such, they would fire me. You go and set down on the bench now, like Mr. Foote—"

I started for the door, but he caught me, he put one hand on the ticket counter and jumped over it and caught up with me and reached his hand out to ketch my shirt. I whupped out my pocketknife and snapped it open.

"You put a hand on me and I'll cut it off," I said.

I tried to dodge him and run at the door, but he could move quicker than any grown man I ever see, quick as Pete almost. He cut me off and stood with his back against the door and one foot raised a little, and there wasn't no other way to get out. "Get back on that bench and stay there," he said.

And there wasn't no other way out. And he stood against the door. So I went back to the bench. And then it seemed like to me that dee-po was full of folks. There was that Law again, and there was two ladies in fur coats and their faces already painted. But they still looked like they had got up in a hurry and they still never liked it, a old one and a young one, looking down at me.

"He hasn't got an overcoat!" the old one said. "How in the world did he ever get down here by himself?"

"I ask you," the Law said. "I couldn't

get nothing out of him except his brother is in Memphis and he wants to get back up there."

"That's right," I said. "I got to git to Memphis today."

"Of course you must," the old one said. "Are you sure you can find your brother when you get to Memphis?"

"I reckon I can," I said. "I ain't got but one and I have knowed him all my life. I reckon I will know him again when I see him."

The old one looked at me. "Somehow he doesn't look like he lives in Memphis," she said.

"He probably don't," the Law said. "You can't tell though. He might live anywhere, overhalls or not. This day and time they get scattered overnight from hope to breakfast; boys and girls, too, almost before they can walk good. He might have been in Missouri or Texas either yestiddy, for all we know. But he don't seem to have any doubt his brother is in Memphis. All I know to do is send him up there and leave him look."

"Yes," the old one said.

The young one set down on the bench by me and opened a hand satchel and taken out a artermatic writing pen and some papers.

"Now, honey," the old one said, "we're going to see that you find your brother, but we must have a case history for our files first. We want to know your name and your brother's name and where you were born and when your parents died."

"I don't need no case history neither," I said. "All I want is to git to Memphis. I got to git there today."

"You see?" the Law said. He said it almost like he enjoyed it. "That's what I told you."

"You're lucky, at that, Mrs. Habersham," the bus feller said. "I don't think he's got a gun on him, but he can open that knife fast enough to suit any man."

But the old one just stood there looking at me.

"Well," she said. "Well. I really don't know what to do."

"I do," the bus feller said. "I'm going to give him a ticket out of my own pocket, as a measure of protecting the company against riot and bloodshed. And when Mr. Foote tells the city board about it, it will be a civic matter and they will give me a medal too. Hey, Mr. Foote?"

But nobody paid him no mind. The old one still stood looking down at me. She said "Well," again. Then she taken a dollar from her purse and give it to the bus feller. "I suppose he will travel on a child's ticket, won't he?"

"Wellum," the bus feller said, "I just don't know what the regulations would be. Likely I will be fired for not crating him and marking the crate Poison. But I'll risk it."

Then they were gone. Then the Law come back with a sandwich and give it to me.

"You're sure you can find that brother?" he said.

"I ain't yet convinced why not," I said. "If I don't see Pete first, he'll see me. He knows me too."

Then the Law went out for good, too, and I et the sandwich. Then more folks come in and bought tickets, and then the bus feller said it was time to go, and I got into the bus just like Pete done, and we were gone.

I seen all the towns. I seen all of them. When the bus got to going good, I found out I was jest about wore out for sleep. But there was too much I hadn't never saw before. We run out of Jefferson and run past fields and woods, then we would run into another town and out of that un and past fields and woods again, and then into another town with stores and gins [6] and water tanks, and we run along by the railroad for a spell and I seen the signal arm move, and then some more towns, and I was jest about plumb wore out for sleep, but I couldn't resk it. Then Memphis begun. It seemed like, to me, it went on for miles. We would pass a patch of stores and I would think that was sholy it and the bus would even stop. But it wouldn't be Memphis yet and we would go on again past water tanks and smokestacks on top of the mills, and if they was gins and sawmills, I never knowed there was that many and I never seen any that big, and where they got enough cotton and logs to run um I don't know.

Then I seen Memphis. I knowed I was right this time. It was standing up into the air. It looked like about a dozen whole towns bigger than Jefferson was set up on the edge in a field, standing up into the air higher than ara [7] hill in all Yoknapatawpha County. Then we was in it, with the bus stopping every few feet, it seemed like to me, and cars rushing past on both sides of it and the streets crowded with folks from ever'where in town that day, until I didn't see how there could 'a' been nobody left in Mis'sippi a-tall to even sell me a bus ticket, let alone write out no case histories. Then the bus stopped. It was another bus dee-po, a heap bigger than the one in Jefferson. And I said, "All right. Where do folks join the Army?"

"What?" the bus feller said.

And I said it again, "Where do folks join the Army?"

[6] GINS—Cotton gins; machines which remove the seeds from the cotton.   [7] ARA—Any.

"Oh," he said. Then he told me how to get there. I was afraid at first I wouldn't ketch on how to do in a town as big as Memphis. But I caught on all right. I never had to ask but twice more. Then I was there, and I was durn glad to git out of all them rushing cars and shoving folks and all that racket fer a spell, and I thought, it won't be long now, and I thought how if there was any kind of a crowd there that had done already joined the Army, too, Pete would likely see me before I seen him. And so I walked into the room. And Pete wasn't there.

He wasn't even there. There was a soldier with a big arrerhead on his sleeve, writing, and two fellers standing in front of him, and there was some more folks there, I reckon. It seems to me I remember some more folks there.

I went to the table where the soldier was writing, and I said, "Where's Pete?" and he looked up and I said, "My brother. Pete Grier. Pete—where is he?"

"What?" the soldier said. "Who?"

And I told him again. "He joined the Army yestiddy. He's going to Pearl Harbor. So am I. I want to ketch him. Where you all got him?" Now they were all looking at me, but I never paid them no mind. "Come on," I said. "Where is he?"

The soldier had quit writing. He had both hands spraddled out on the table. "Oh," he said. "You're going, too, hah?"

"Yes," I said. "They got to have wood and water. I can chop it and tote it. Come on. Where's Pete?"

The soldier stood up. "Who let you in here?" he said. "Go on. Beat it."

"Durn that," I said. "You tell me where Pete—"

I be dog if he couldn't move faster than the bus feller even. He never come over the table, he come around it, he was on me almost before I knowed it, so that I jest had time to jump back and whup out my pocketknife and snap it open and hit one lick, and he hollered and jumped back and grabbed one hand with the other and stood there cussing and hollering.

One of the other fellers grabbed me from behind, and I hit at him with the knife, but I couldn't reach him.

Then both of the fellers had me from behind, and then another soldier come out of a door at the back. He had on a belt with a britching strop over one shoulder.

"What's this?" he said.

"That little son cut me with a knife!" the first soldier hollered. When he said that I tried to git at him again, but both them fellers was holding me, two against one, and the soldier with the backing strop said, "Here, here. Put your knife up, feller. None of us are armed. A man don't knife-fight folks that are barehanded." I could begin to hear him then. He sounded jest like Pete talked to me. "Let him go," he said. They let me go. "Now what's all the trouble about?" And I told him. "I see," he said. "And you come up to see if he was all right before he left."

"No," I said. "I came to—"

But he had already turned to where the first soldier was wropping a handkerchief around his hand.

"Have you got him?" he said. The first soldier went back to the table and looked at some papers.

"Here he is," he said. "He enlisted yestiddy. He's in a detachment leaving this morning for Little Rock." He had a watch stropped on his arm. He looked at it. "The train leaves in about fifty minutes. If I know country boys, they're probably all down there at the station right now."

"Get him up here," the one with the backing strop said. "Phone the station. Tell the porter to get him a cab. And you come with me," he said.

It was another office behind that un, with jest a table and some chairs. We set there while the soldier smoked, and it wasn't long; I knowed Pete's feet soon as I heard them. Then the first soldier opened the door and Pete come in. He never had no soldier clothes on. He looked jest like he did when he got on the bus yestiddy morning, except it seemed to me like it was at least a week, so much had happened, and I had done had to do so much traveling. He come in and there he was, looking at me like he hadn't never left home, except that here we was in Memphis, on the way to Pearl Harbor.

"What in durnation are you doing here?" he said.

And I told him, "You got to have wood and water to cook with. I can chop it and tote it for you-all."

"No," Pete said. "You're going back home."

"No, Pete," I said. "I got to go too. I got to. It hurts my heart, Pete."

"No," Pete said. He looked at the soldier. "I jest don't know what could have happened to him, lootenant," he said. "He never drawed a knife on anybody before in his life."

He looked at me. "What did you do it for?"

"I don't know," I said. "I jest had to. I jest had to git here. I jest had to find you."

"Well, don't you never do it again, you hear?" Pete said. "You put that knife in your pocket and you keep it there. If I ever again hear of you drawing it on anybody, I'm coming back from

wherever I am at and whup the fire out of you. You hear me?"

"I would pure cut a throat if it would bring you back to stay," I said. "Pete," I said. "Pete."

"No," Pete said. Now his voice wasn't hard and quick no more, it was almost quiet, and I knowed now I wouldn't never change him. "You must go home. You must look after Maw, and I am depending on you to look after my ten acres. I want you to go back home. To-day. Do you hear?"

"I hear," I said.

"Can he get back home by himself?" the soldier said.

"He come up here by himself," Pete said.

"I can get back, I reckon," I said. "I don't live in but one place. I don't reckon it's moved."

Pete taken a dollar out of his pocket and give it to me. "That'll buy your bus ticket right to our mailbox," he said. "I want you to mind the lootenant. He'll send you to the bus. And you go back home and you take care of Maw and look after my ten acres and keep that durn knife in your pocket. You hear me?"

"Yes, Pete," I said.

"All right," Pete said. "Now I got to go." He put his hand on my head again. But this time he never wrung my neck. He just laid his hand on my head a minute. And then I be dog if he didn't lean down and kiss me, and I heard his feet and then the door, and I never looked up and that was all, me setting there, rubbing the place where Pete kissed me and the soldier throwed back in his chair, looking out the window and coughing. He reached into his pocket and handed something to me without looking around. It was a piece of chewing gum.

"Much obliged," I said. "Well, I

reckon I might as well start back. I got a right fer piece to go."

"Wait," the soldier said. Then he telephoned again and I said again I better start back, and he said again, "Wait. Remember what Pete told you."

So we waited, and then another lady come in, old, too, in a fur coat, too, but she smelled all right, she never had no artermatic writing pen nor no case history neither. She come in and the soldier got up, and she looked around quick until she saw me, and come and put her hand on my shoulder light and quick and easy as Maw herself might 'a' done it.

"Come on," she said. "Let's go home to dinner."

"Nome," I said. "I got to ketch the bus to Jefferson."

"I know. There's plenty of time. We'll go home and eat dinner first."

She had a car. And now we was right down in the middle of all them other cars. We was almost under the busses, and all them crowds of people on the street close enough to where I could have talked to them if I had knowed who they was. After a while she stopped the car. "Here we are," she said, and I looked at it, and if all that was her house, she sho

had a big family. But all of it wasn't. We crossed a hall with trees growing in it and went into a little room without nothing in it but a Negro dressed up in a uniform a heap shinier than them soldiers had, and the Negro shut the door, and then I hollered, "Look out!" and grabbed, but it was all right; that whole little room jest went right on up and stopped and the door opened and we was in another hall, and the lady unlocked a door and we went in, and there was another soldier, an old feller, with a britching strop, too, and a silver-colored bird on each shoulder.

"Here we are," the lady said. "This is Colonel McKellogg. Now, what would you like for dinner?"

"I reckon I'll jest have some ham and eggs and coffee," I said.

She had done started to pick up the telephone. She stopped. "Coffee?" she said. "When did you start drinking coffee?"

"I don't know," I said. "I reckon it was before I could remember."

"You're about eight, aren't you?" she said.

"Nome," I said. "I'm eight and ten months. Going on eleven months."

She telephoned then. Then we set

there and I told them how Pete had jest left that morning for Pearl Harbor and I had aimed to go with him, but I would have to go back home to take care of Maw and look after Pete's ten acres, and she said how they had a little boy about my size, too, in a school in the East. Then a Negro, another one, in a short kind of shirttail coat, rolled a kind of wheelbarrer in. It had my ham and eggs and a glass of milk and a piece of pie, too, and I thought I was hungry. But when I taken the first bite I found out I couldn't swallow it, and I got up quick.

"I got to go," I said.

"Wait," she said.

"I got to go," I said.

"Just a minute," she said. "I've already telephoned for the car. It won't be but a minute now. Can't you drink the milk even? Or maybe some of your coffee?"

"Nome," I said. "I ain't hungry. I'll eat when I git home." Then the telephone rung. She never even answered it.

"There," she said. "There's the car." And we went back down in that 'ere little moving room with the dressed-up Negro. This time it was a big car with a soldier driving it. I got into the front with him. She give the soldier a dollar. "He might get hungry," she said. "Try to find a decent place for him."

"O.K., Mrs. McKellogg," the soldier said.

Then we was gone again. And now I could see Memphis good, bright in the sunshine, while we was swinging around it. And the first thing I knowed, we was back on the same highway the bus run on this morning—the patches of stores and them big gins and sawmills, and Memphis running on for miles, it seemed like to me, before it begun to give out. Then we was running again between the fields and woods, running fast now, and

except for that soldier, it was like I hadn't never been to Memphis a-tall. We was going fast now. At this rate, before I knowed it we would be home again, and I thought about me riding up to Frenchman's Bend in this here big car with a soldier running it, and all of a sudden I begun to cry. I never knowed I was fixing to, and I couldn't stop it. I set there by that soldier, crying. We was going fast.

◇◆◇◆◇◆◇◆◇◆◇◆◇◆◇◆◇◆◇◆◇◆◇◆◇◆◇

FOR UNDERSTANDING

1. What did you learn about the situation at the beginning of the story and about the two boys themselves as they listened to the Killegrews' radio?

2. How were the boys different from their parents? Considering Pete's background, is there any way to explain his interest in world affairs and his industry in cultivating his ten acres? Is the younger boy more like Pete or his parents?

3. Why do you suppose Pete had such a difficult time making up his mind to go to war? Was it lack of patriotism or concern about leaving his parents and his younger brother? Support your opinion by definite references to the story.

4. What did you learn about Pete from the way he treated his little brother? How can you account for his gruffness when the younger boy wanted to go to war with him?

5. What is revealed about the boys' parents in the way they react to Pete's announcement that he is going to war? What seems to be the father's real reason for not wanting Pete to go? What further insight into Maw's character do you get from her preparations for Pete's leaving and her advice to him when they part?

6. Why didn't Pete have the trouble he expected to have in leaving the little boy? When did you first suspect that the younger boy was going to war too?

7. What characteristics of the younger boy came out in his encounter with "the

Law" on his trip to Memphis? Why do you think the people he came in contact with were so willing to help him?

8. Why was the little boy satisfied to go home after Pete's talk with him? Why do you think the author named the story "Two Soldiers"?

A STORY IN THE FIRST PERSON

"Two Soldiers" is written in the first person. That is, one of the characters is the narrator and tells the story in his own words.

1. From the standpoint of making an interesting and entertaining story, what advantage can you see in having the younger boy as narrator? Where does the humor depend upon his language or point of view rather than upon what actually happened?

2. Often, first person stories demand more of the reader than other types of narrative. In this story, for example, because of the youth and inexperience of the boy who told the story, it was necessary for you to read between the lines and interpret what he said in the light of your own knowledge and experience. Find passages in which the boy did not completely understand the situations and events he told about.

3. Tell why you think this story was more, or less, effective because it was told in the first person.

WILLIAM FAULKNER (Born 1897)

William Faulkner is an author from the Deep South. He was born in New Albany, Mississippi, attended Mississippi University, and served as a lieutenant with the Canadian Flying Force in World War I. He has lived for many years on a farm near Oxford, Mississippi.

Mr. Faulkner's writing is usually extremely realistic and frequently concerns abnormal characters. *The Sound and the Fury*, one of his most important novels, is the story of the decay of a Southern family as seen through the eyes of the idiot son Benjy. "Two Soldiers" and a recent novel, *Intruder in the Dust*, are evidence that he can also create wholesome characters. In 1949 he was awarded the Nobel Prize for literature for a "forceful and independently artistic contribution to modern American fiction."

◇◇◇◇◇

I CAN'T BREATHE

RING LARDNER

You will probably recognize in Aunt Jule's niece a resemblance to heart-breakers closer home. For while there are not many girls quite so silly as this one, most of them have at least some of her characteristics. And the boys? Well, few who read the story have not been singed at least once like Walter, or Gordon, or Frank.

July 12

I am staying here at the Inn for two weeks with my Uncle Nat and Aunt Jule and I think I will keep a kind of a diary while I am here to help pass the time and so I can have a record of things that happen though goodness knows there isn't likely to anything happen, that is, anything exciting with Uncle Nat and Aunt Jule making the plans as they are both at least 35 years old and maybe older.

Dad and Mother are abroad to be gone a month and me coming here is supposed to be a recompense for them not taking me with them. A fine recompense to be left with old people that come to a place like this to rest. Still it would be a heavenly place under different conditions, for instance, if Walter were here, too. It would be heavenly if he were here, the very thought of it makes my heart stop.

I can't stand it. I won't think about it. This is our first separation since we have been engaged, nearly 17 days. It will be 17 days tomorrow. And the hotel orchestra at dinner this evening played that old thing "Oh how I miss you tonight" and it seemed as if they must be playing it for my benefit though, of course, the person in that song is talking about how they miss their mother though, of course, I miss Mother, too, but a person gets used to missing their mother and it isn't like Walter or the person you are engaged to.

But there won't be any more separations much longer. We are going to be married in December even if Mother does laugh when I talk to her about it because she says I am crazy to even think of getting married at 18.

She got married herself when she was 18, but of course that was "different," she wasn't crazy like I am, she knew whom she was marrying. As if Walter were a policeman or a foreigner or something. And she says she was only engaged once while I have been engaged at least five times a year since I was 14, of course, it really isn't as bad as that and I have really only been really what I call engaged six times altogether, but is get-

ting engaged my fault when they keep insisting and hammering at you and if you didn't say yes they would never go home.

But it is different with Walter. I honestly believe if he had not asked me I would have asked him. Of course I wouldn't have, but I would have died. And this is the first time I have ever been engaged to be really married. The other times when they talked about when should we get married I just laughed at them, but I hadn't been engaged to Walter ten minutes when he brought up the subject of marriage and I didn't laugh. I wouldn't be engaged to him unless it was to be married. I couldn't stand it.

Anyway Mother may as well get used to the idea because it is "No Foolin'" this time and we have got our plans all made and I am going to be married at home and go out to California and Hollywood on our honeymoon. December, five months away. I can't stand it. I can't wait.

There were a couple of awfully nice looking boys sitting together alone in the dining room tonight. One of them wasn't so much, but the other was cute. And he—

There's the dance orchestra playing "Always," what they played at the Biltmore the day I met Walter. "Not for just an hour, not for just a day." I can't live. I can't breathe.

July 13

This has been a much more exciting day than I expected under the circumstances. In the first place I got two long night letters, one from Walter and one from Gordon Flint. I don't see how Walter ever had the nerve to send his, there was everything in it and it must have been horribly embarrassing for him while the telegraph operator was reading it over and counting the words to say nothing of embarrassing for the operator.

But the one from Gordon was a kind of a shock. He just got back from a trip around the world, left last December to go on it and got back yesterday and called up our house and Helga gave him my address, and his telegram, well it was nearly as bad as Walter's. The trouble is that Gordon and I were engaged when he went away, or at least he thought so, and he wrote to me right along all the time he was away and sent cables and things and for a while I answered his letters, but then I lost track of his itinery and couldn't write to him any more and when I got really engaged to Walter I couldn't let Gordon know because I had no idea where he was besides not wanting to spoil his trip.

And now he still thinks we are engaged and he is going to call me up tomorrow from Chicago and how in the world can I explain things and get him to understand because he is really serious and I like him ever and ever so much and in lots of ways he is nicer than Walter, not really nicer but better looking and there is no comparison between their dancing. Walter simply can't learn to dance, that is really dance. He says it is because he is flat-footed, he says that as a joke, but it is true and I wish to heavens it wasn't.

All forenoon I thought and thought and thought about what to say to Gordon when he calls up and finally I couldn't stand thinking about it any more and just made up my mind I wouldn't think about it any more. But I will tell the truth though it will kill me to hurt him.

I went down to lunch with Uncle Nat and Aunt Jule and they were going out to play golf this afternoon and were insisting that I go with them, but I told them I had a headache and then I had a terrible time getting them to go without me. I didn't have a headache at all and just wanted to be alone to think about Walter and besides when you play with Uncle Nat he is always correcting your stance or your swing or something and always puts his hands on my arms and shoulders to show me the right way and I can't stand it to have old men touch me, even if they are your uncle.

I finally got rid of them and I was sitting watching the tennis when that boy that I saw last night, the cute one, came and sat right next to me and of course I didn't look at him. So we got to talking and he is even cuter than he looks, the most original and wittiest person I believe I ever met and I haven't laughed so much in I don't know how long.

For one thing he asked me if I had heard Rockefeller's song and I said no and he began singing "Oil alone." [1] Then he asked me if I knew the orange juice song and I told him no again and he said it was "Orange juice sorry you made me cry." [2] I was in hysterics before we had been together ten minutes.

His name is Frank Caswell and he has been out of Dartmouth a year and is 24 years old. That isn't so terribly old, only two years older than Walter and three years older than Gordon. I hate the name Frank, but Caswell is all right and he is cute.

He was out in California last winter and visited Hollywood and met everybody in the world and it is fascinating to listen to him. He met Norma Shearer [3] and he said he thought she was the prettiest thing he had ever seen. What he

[1] "OIL ALONE"—A pun on the song "All Alone," by Irving Berlin.
[2] "ORANGE JUICE . . ."—Another pun, this time on the song "I'm Sorry I Made You Cry."
[3] NORMA SHEARER—A famous Hollywood actress during the twenties and thirties.

said was "I did think she was the prettiest girl in the world, till today." I was going to pretend I didn't get it, but I finally told him to be sensible or I would never be able to believe anything he said.

Well, he wanted me to dance with him tonight after dinner and the next question was how to explain how we had met each other to Uncle Nat and Aunt Jule. Frank said he would fix that all right and sure enough he got himself introduced to Uncle Nat when Uncle Nat came in from golf and after dinner Uncle Nat introduced him to me and Aunt Jule and we danced together all evening, that is *not* Aunt Jule. They went to bed, thank heavens.

He is a heavenly dancer, as good as Gordon. One dance we were dancing and for one of the encores the orchestra played "In a cottage small by a waterfall" and I simply couldn't dance to it. I just stopped still and said "Listen, I can't bear it, I can't breathe" and poor Frank thought I was sick or something and I had to explain that that was the tune the orchestra played the night I sat at the next table to Jack Barrymore[4] at Barney Gallant's.

I made him sit out the encore and wouldn't let him talk till they got through playing it. Then they played something else and I was all right again and Frank told me about meeting Jack Barrymore. Imagine meeting him. I couldn't live.

I promised Aunt Jule I would go to bed at eleven and it is way past that now, but I am all ready for bed and have just been writing this. Tomorrow Gordon is going to call up and what will I say to him? I just won't think about it.

July 14

Gordon called up this morning from

[4] JACK BARRYMORE—John Barrymore (1882–1942) a famous star of stage and screen.

Chicago and it was wonderful to hear his voice again though the connection was terrible. He asked me if I still loved him and I tried to tell him no, but I knew that would mean an explanation and the connection was so bad that I never could make him understand so I said yes, but I almost whispered it purposely, thinking he wouldn't hear me, but he heard me all right and he said that made everything all right with the world. He said he thought I had stopped loving him because I had stopped writing.

I wish the connection had been decent and I could have told him how things were, but now it is terrible because he is planning to get to New York the day I get there and heaven knows what I will do because Walter will be there, too. I just won't think about it.

Aunt Jule came in my room just after I was through talking to Gordon, thank heavens. The room was full of flowers. Walter had sent me some and so had Frank. I got another long night letter from Walter, just as silly as the first one. I wish he would say those things in letters instead of night letters so everybody in the world wouldn't see them. Aunt Jule wanted me to read it aloud to her. I would have died.

While she was still in the room, Frank called up and asked me to play golf with him and I said all right and Aunt Jule said she was glad my headache was gone. She was trying to be funny.

I played golf with Frank this afternoon. He is a beautiful golfer and it is thrilling to watch him drive, his swing is so much more graceful than Walter's. I asked him to watch me swing and tell me what was the matter with me, but he said he couldn't look at anything but my face and there wasn't anything the matter with that.

He told me the boy who was here with

him had been called home and he was glad of it because I might have liked him, the other boy, better than himself. I told him that couldn't be possible and he asked me if I really meant that and I said of course, but I smiled when I said it so he wouldn't take it too seriously.

We danced again tonight and Uncle Nat and Aunt Jule sat with us a while and danced a couple of dances themselves, but they were really there to get better acquainted with Frank and see if he was all right for me to be with. I know they certainly couldn't have enjoyed their own dancing, no old people really can enjoy it because they can't really *do* anything.

They were favorably impressed with Frank I think, at least Aunt Jule didn't say I must be in bed at eleven, but just not to stay up too late. I guess it is a big surprise to a girl's parents and aunts and uncles to find out that the boys you

go around with are all right, they always seem to think that if I seem to like somebody and the person pays a little attention to me, why he must be a convict or a policeman or a drunkard or something queer.

Frank had some more songs for me tonight. He asked me if I knew the asthma song and I said I didn't and he said "Oh, you must know that. It goes yes, sir, asthma baby." [5] Then he told me about the underwear song. "I underwear my baby is tonight." He keeps you in hysterics and yet he has his serious side, in fact he was awfully serious when he said good night to me and his eyes simply shone. I wish Walter were more like him in some ways, but I mustn't think about that.

[5] YES, SIR, ASTHMA BABY—Another "play" on a song title, "Yes, Sir, That's My Baby." The underwear song in the next line comes from "I Wonder Where My Baby Is Tonight."

July 15

I simply can't live and I know I'll never sleep tonight. I am in a terrible predicament or rather I won't know whether I really am or not till tomorrow and that is what makes it so terrible.

After we had danced two or three dances, Frank asked me to go for a ride with him and we went for a ride in his car and finally he told me he loved me and I said not to be silly, but he said he was perfectly serious and he certainly acted that way. He asked me if I loved anybody else and I said yes and he asked if I didn't love him more than anybody else and I said yes, but only because I thought he wouldn't remember it anyway and the best thing to do was humor him under the circumstances.

Then all of a sudden he asked me when I could marry him and I said, just as a joke, that I couldn't possibly marry him before December. He said that was a long time to wait, but I was certainly worth waiting for and he said a lot of other things and maybe I humored him a little too much, but that is just the trouble, I don't know.

I was absolutely sure he would forget the whole thing. If he doesn't remember anything about it, of course I am all right. But if he does remember and if he took me seriously, I will simply have to tell him about Walter and maybe about Gordon, too. And it isn't going to be easy. The suspense is what is maddening and I know I'll never live through this night.

July 16

I can't stand it, I can't breathe, life is impossible. Frank remembered everything about last night and firmly believes we are engaged and going to be married in December. His people live in New York and he says he is going back when I do and have them meet me.

Of course it can't go on and tomorrow I will tell him about Walter or Gordon or both of them. I know it is going to hurt him terribly, perhaps spoil his life and I would give anything in the world not to have had it happen. I hate so to hurt him because he is so nice besides being so cute and attractive.

He sent me the loveliest flowers this morning and called up at ten and wanted to know how soon he could see me and I hope the girl wasn't listening in because the things he said were, well, like Walter's night letters.

And that is another terrible thing, today I didn't get a night letter from Walter, but there was a regular letter instead and I carried it around in my purse all this afternoon and evening and never remembered to read it till ten minutes ago when I came up in the room. Walter is worried because I have only sent him two telegrams and written him one letter since I have been here. He would be a lot more worried if he knew what has happened now, though of course it can't make any difference because he is the one I am really engaged to be married to and the one I told Mother I was going to marry in December and I wouldn't dare tell her it was somebody else.

I met Frank for lunch and we went for a ride this afternoon and he was so much in love and so lovely to me that I simply did not have the heart to tell him the truth, I am surely going to tell him tomorrow and telling him today would have just meant one more day of unhappiness for both of us.

He said his people had plenty of money and his father had offered to take him into partnership and he might accept, but he thinks his true vocation is journalism with a view to eventually writing novels and if I was willing to undergo a few hardships just at first we would probably both be happier later on if he was doing something he really liked. I didn't know what to say, but finally I said I wanted him to suit himself and money wasn't everything.

He asked me where I would like to go on my honeymoon and I suppose I ought to have told him my honeymoon was all planned, that I was going to California, with Walter, but all I said was that I had always wanted to go to California and he was enthusiastic and said that is where we would surely go and he would take me to Hollywood and introduce me to all those wonderful people he met there last winter. It nearly takes my breath away to think of it, going there with someone who really knows people and has the entrée.

We danced again tonight, just two or three dances, and then went out and sat in the tennis court, but I came upstairs early because Aunt Jule had acted kind of funny at dinner. And I wanted to be alone, too, and think, but the more I think the worse it gets.

Sometimes I wish I were dead, maybe that is the only solution and it would be best for everyone concerned. I *will* die if things keep on the way they have been. But of course tomorrow it will be all over, with Frank I mean, for I must tell him the truth no matter how much it hurts us both. Though I don't care how much it hurts me. The thought of hurting him is what is driving me mad. I can't bear it.

July 18

I have skipped a day. I was busy every minute of yesterday and so exhausted when I came upstairs that I was tempted to fall into bed with all my clothes on. First Gordon called me up from Chicago to remind me that he would be in New York the day I got there and that when he comes he wants me all to himself all the time and we can make plans for our wedding. The connection was bad again and I just couldn't explain to him about Walter.

I had an engagement with Frank for lunch and just as we were going in another long distance call came, from Walter this time. He wanted to know why I haven't written more letters and sent him more telegrams and asked me if I still loved him and of course I told him yes because I really do. Then he asked me if I had met any men here and I told him I had met one, a friend of Uncle Nat's. After all it was Uncle Nat who introduced me to Frank. He reminded me that he would be in New York on the 25th which is the day I expect to get home, and said he would have theater tickets for that night and we would go somewhere afterwards and dance.

Frank insisted on knowing who had kept me talking so long and I told him it was a boy I had known a long while, a very dear friend of mine and a friend of my family's. Frank was jealous and kept asking questions till I thought I would go mad. He was so serious and kind of cross and gruff that I gave up the plan of telling him the truth till some time when he is in better spirits.

I played golf with Frank in the afternoon and we took a ride last night and I wanted to get in early because I had promised both Walter and Gordon that I would write them long letters, but Frank wouldn't bring me back to the Inn till I had named a definite date in December. I finally told him the 10th and he said all right if I was sure that wasn't a Sunday. I said I would have to look it up, but as a matter of fact I know the 10th falls on a Friday because the date Walter and I have agreed on for our wedding is Saturday the 11th.

Today has just been the same thing over again, two more night letters, a long-distance call from Chicago, golf and a ride with Frank, and the room full of flowers. But tomorrow I am going to tell Frank, and I am going to write Gordon a long letter and tell him, too, because this simply can't go on any longer. I can't breathe, I can't live.

July 21

I wrote to Gordon yesterday, but I didn't say anything about Walter because I don't think it is a thing a person ought to do by letter. I can tell him when he gets to New York and then I will be sure that he doesn't take it too hard and I can promise him that I will be friends with him always and make him promise not to do anything silly, while if I told it to him in a letter there is no telling what he would do, there all alone.

And I haven't told Frank because he hasn't been feeling well, he is terribly sunburned and it hurts him terribly so he can hardly play golf or dance, and I want him to be feeling his best when I do tell him, but whether he is all right or not I simply must tell him tomorrow because he is actually planning to leave here on the same train with us Saturday night and I can't let him do that. Life is so hopeless and it could be so wonderful.

It is only half past ten, the earliest I

have gone to bed in weeks, but I am worn out and Frank went to bed early so he could put cold cream on his sunburn.

Listen, diary, the orchestra is playing "Limehouse Blues." The first tune I danced to with Merle Oliver, two years ago. I can't stand it. And how funny that they should play that old tune tonight of all nights, when I have been thinking of Merle off and on all day, and I hadn't thought of him before in weeks and weeks. I wonder where he is, I wonder if it is just an accident or if it means I am going to see him again. I simply mustn't think about it or I'll die.

July 22

I knew it wasn't an accident. I knew it must mean something, and it did.

Merle is coming here today, here to this Inn, and just to see me. And there can only be one reason. And only one answer. I knew that when I heard his voice calling from Boston. How could I ever have thought I loved anyone else? How could he ever have thought I meant it when I told him I was engaged to George Morse?

A whole year and he still cares and I still care. That shows we were always intended for each other and for no one else. I won't make *him* wait till December. I doubt if we even wait till Dad and Mother get home. And as for a honeymoon I will go with him to Long

Beach or the Bronx Zoo, wherever he wants to take me.

After all, this is the best way out of it, the only way. I won't have to say anything to Frank, he will guess when he sees me with Merle. And when I get home Sunday and Walter and Gordon call me up, I will invite them both to dinner and Merle can tell them himself. With two of them there it will only hurt each one half as much as if they were alone.

The train is due at 2:40, almost three hours from now. I can't wait. And what if it should be late? I can't stand it.

◇◇◇◇◇◇◇◇◇◇◇◇◇◇◇◇◇◇◇◇◇◇◇◇

DIARY OF A GLAMOUR GIRL

1. What did you learn about the girl in the story from the first entry in her diary? Consider how she wrote as well as what she said. What did you find out about her age, her idea of a good time, and her activities before she joined Aunt Jule and Uncle Nat?

2. How can you account for her popularity with the boys? How long did it take her to "get engaged" to Frank? By July 21 how many fiancés did she have? How many on the twenty-second? Do you think she really did marry Merle?

3. What is your opinion of the boys in the story? How did Frank's sense of humor impress you? For which boy do you feel most sorry?

4. Often people reveal their real natures most unfavorably and quite unconsciously. As you read the diary of this glamour girl, what seem to you to be the fundamental weaknesses in her character? Do you think she will outgrow her undesirable traits?

5. The dance steps, songs, and jokes of the 1920's probably seem strange to you. How would these details be different in a story with a present-day setting? Show why

these differences are superficial rather than basic.

FORM AND STYLE

1. Why was the diary a particularly appropriate form for this story? Would the girl be as likely to reveal her true personality if she expected someone to read what she had written?

2. How does the style of writing suggest the personality of the girl? How are the run-on sentences and the grammatical errors appropriate in this story?

3. Show how each entry helps to further the plot. Why is it effective to end the story before Merle Oliver arrives?

4. The purpose of satire is "to hold up to ridicule *vice, folly,* or *incapacity.*" By direct reference to the story, show how Mr. Lardner made the girl appear ridiculous (*a*) in general intelligence (or lack of it), (*b*) in habits of thinking and attitudes toward life, (*c*) in character.

RING LARDNER (1885–1933)

Ringgold Wilmer Lardner is somehow an incongruous name for a humorist and satirist. Its euphony, however, was soon dropped for "Ring" Lardner, a name which became famous in sporting news. Although his mother wanted him to be a minister and his father an engineer, Ring chose his own field, leaving the Armour Institute of Technology in Chicago for a job as a reporter in South Bend. From there he moved to the Chicago *Tribune.* For seven years he went to two hundred baseball games a year and "Lardner's Ringlish," his racy baseball vernacular, became famous in newspaper articles and in the "You Know Me, Al" sketches. For a while he wrote songs for a quartet of baseball players. Literary critics finally accepted his work with its sardonic humor. His *How to Write Short Stories* in 1924 enjoyed real success. His sudden death in 1935 was a serious loss to American humor.

THE SECRET LIFE
OF WALTER MITTY

JAMES THURBER

At the beginning this story is a little confusing when Walter Mitty changes from his secret life to his outer life and back again. All of us are somewhat like the daydreaming hero of this very funny but rueful little sketch. We can't blame him for preferring his imaginary self to his real one.

"We're going through!" The Commander's voice was like thin ice breaking. He wore his full-dress uniform, with the heavily braided white cap pulled down rakishly over one cold gray eye. "We can't make it, sir. It's spoiling for a hurricane, if you ask me." "I'm not asking you, Lieutenant Berg," said the Commander. "Throw on the power lights! Rev her up to 8,500! We're going through!" The pounding of the cylinders increased: ta-pocketa-pocketa-pocketa-*pocketa-pocketa*. The Commander stared at the ice forming on the pilot window. He walked over and twisted a row of complicated dials. "Switch on No. 8 auxiliary!" he shouted. "Switch on No. 8 auxiliary!" repeated Lieutenant Berg. "Full strength in No. 3 turret!" shouted the Commander. "Full strength in No. 3 turret!" The crew, bending to their various tasks in the huge, hurtling eight-engined Navy hydroplane, looked at each other and grinned. "The Old Man'll get us through," they said to one another. "The Old Man ain't afraid of anything!". . .

"Not so fast! You're driving too fast!" said Mrs. Mitty. "What are you driving so fast for?"

"Hmm?" said Walter Mitty. He looked at his wife, in the seat beside him, with shocked astonishment. She seemed grossly unfamiliar, like a strange woman who had yelled at him in a crowd. "You were up to fifty-five," she said. "You know I don't like to go more than forty. You were up to fifty-five." Walter Mitty drove on toward Waterbury in silence, the roaring of the SN202 through the worst storm in twenty years of Navy flying fading in the remote, intimate airways of his mind. "You're tensed up again," said Mrs. Mitty. "It's one of your days. I wish you'd let Dr. Renshaw look you over."

Walter Mitty stopped the car in front of the building where his wife went to have her hair done. "Remember to get those overshoes while I'm having my hair done," she said. "I don't need overshoes," said Mitty. She put her mirror back into her bag. "We've been all through that," she said, getting out of the car. "You're not a young man any longer." He raced the engine a little. "Why don't you wear your gloves? Have

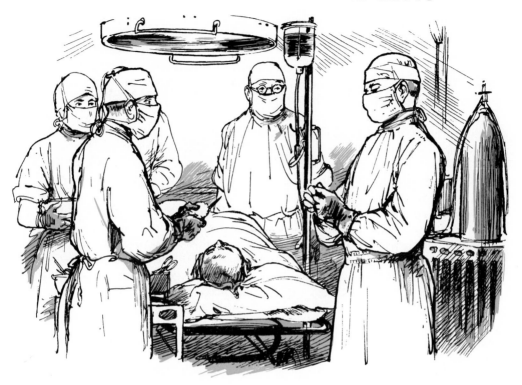

you lost your gloves?" Walter Mitty reached in a pocket and brought out the gloves. He put them on, but after she had turned and gone into the building and he had driven on to a red light, he took them off again. "Pick it up, brother!" snapped a cop as the light changed, and Mitty hastily pulled on his gloves and lurched ahead. He drove around the streets aimlessly for a time, and then he drove past the hospital on his way to the parking lot.

. . ."It's the millionaire banker, Wellington McMillan," said the pretty nurse. "Yes?" said Walter Mitty, removing his gloves slowly. "Who has the case?" "Dr. Renshaw and Dr. Benbow, but there are two specialists here, Dr. Remington from New York and Dr. Pritchard-Mitford from London. He flew over." A door opened down a long, cool corridor and Dr. Renshaw came out. He looked distraught and haggard. "Hello, Mitty," he said. "We're having the devil's own time with McMillan, the millionaire banker and close personal friend of Roosevelt. Obstreosis of the ductal tract. Tertiary. Wish you'd take a look at him." "Glad to," said Mitty.

In the operating room there were whispered introductions: "Dr. Remington, Dr. Mitty. Dr. Pritchard-Mitford, Dr. Mitty." "I've read your book on streptothricosis," said Pritchard-Mitford, shaking hands. "A brilliant performance, sir." "Thank you," said Walter Mitty. "Didn't know you were in the States, Mitty," grumbled Remington. "Coals to Newcastle, bringing Mitford and me up here for a tertiary." "You are very kind," said Mitty. A huge, complicated machine, connected to the operating table, with many tubes and wires, began at this moment to go pocketa-pocketa-pocketa.

"The new anesthetizer is giving way!" shouted an interne. "There is no one in the East who knows how to fix it!" "Quiet, man!" said Mitty, in a low, cool voice. He sprang to the machine, which was now going pocketa-pocketa-queep-pocketa-queep. He began fingering delicately a row of glistening dials. "Give me a fountain pen!" he snapped. Someone handed him a fountain pen. He pulled a faulty piston out of the machine and inserted the pen in its place. "That will hold for ten minutes," he said. "Get on with the operation." A nurse hurried over and whispered to Renshaw, and Mitty saw the man turn pale. "Coreopsis has set in," said Renshaw nervously. "If you would take over, Mitty?" Mitty looked at him and at the craven figure of Benbow, who drank, and at the grave, uncertain faces of the two great specialists. "If you wish," he said. They slipped a white gown on him; he adjusted a mask and drew on thin gloves; nurses handed him shining . . .

"Back it up, Mac! Look out for that Buick!" Walter Mitty jammed on the brakes. "Wrong lane, Mac," said the parking-lot attendant, looking at Mitty closely. "Gee. Yeh," muttered Mitty. He began cautiously to back out of the lane marked "Exit Only." "Leave her sit there," said the attendant. "I'll put her away." Mitty got out of the car. "Hey, better leave the key." "Oh," said Mitty, handing the man the ignition key. The attendant vaulted into the car, backed it up with insolent skill, and put it where it belonged.

They're so cocky, thought Walter Mitty, walking along Main Street; they think they know everything. Once he had tried to take his chains off, outside New Milford, and he had got them wound around the axles. A man had had to come out in a wrecking car and

unwind them, a young, grinning garageman. Since then Mrs. Mitty always made him drive to a garage to have the chains taken off. The next time, he thought, I'll wear my right arm in a sling; they won't grin at me then. I'll have my right arm in a sling and they'll see I couldn't possibly take the chains off myself. He kicked at the slush on the sidewalk. "Overshoes," he said to himself, and he began looking for a shoe store.

When he came out into the street again, with the overshoes in a box under his arm, Walter Mitty began to wonder what the other thing was his wife had told him to get. She had told him twice before they set out from their house for Waterbury. In a way he hated these weekly trips to town—he was always getting something wrong. Kleenex, he thought, Squibb's, razor blades? No. Tooth paste, toothbrush, bicarbonate, carborundum, initiative and referendum? He gave it up. But she would remember it. "Where's the what's-its-name?" she would ask. "Don't tell me you forgot the what's-its-name." A newsboy went by shouting something about the Waterbury trial.

. . . "Perhaps this will refresh your memory." The District Attorney suddenly thrust a heavy automatic at the quiet figure on the witness stand. "Have you ever seen this before?" Walter Mitty took the gun and examined it expertly. "This is my Webley-Vickers 50.80," he said calmly. An excited buzz ran around the courtroom. The Judge rapped for order. "You are a crack shot with any sort of firearms, I believe?" said the District Attorney, insinuatingly. "Objection!" shouted Mitty's attorney. "We have shown that the defendant could not have fired the shot. We have shown that he wore his right arm in a sling on the night of the fourteenth of July." Walter Mitty raised his hand briefly and the bickering attorneys were stilled. "With any known make of gun," he said evenly, "I could have killed Gregory Fitzhurst at three hundred feet *with my left hand*." Pandemonium broke loose in the courtroom. A woman's scream rose above the bedlam and suddenly a lovely, dark-haired girl was in Walter Mitty's arms. The District Attorney struck at her savagely. Without rising from his chair, Mitty let the man have it on the point of the chin. "You miserable cur!". . .

"Puppy biscuit," said Walter Mitty. He stopped walking and the buildings of Waterbury rose up out of the misty courtroom and surrounded him again. A woman who was passing laughed. "He said 'Puppy biscuit,'" she said to her companion. "That man said 'Puppy biscuit' to himself." Walter Mitty hurried on. He went into an A & P, not the first one he came to but a smaller one farther up the street. "I want some biscuit for small, young dogs," he said to the clerk. "Any special brand, sir?" The greatest pistol shot in the world thought a moment. "It says 'Puppies Bark for It' on the box," said Walter Mitty.

His wife would be through at the hairdresser's in fifteen minutes, Mitty saw in looking at his watch, unless they had trouble drying it; sometimes they had trouble drying it. She didn't like to get to the hotel first; she would want him to be there waiting for her as usual. He found a big leather chair in the lobby, facing the window, and he put the overshoes and the puppy biscuit on the floor beside it. He picked up an old copy of *Liberty* and sank down into the chair. "Can Germany Conquer the World Through the Air?" Walter Mitty looked at the pictures of bombing planes and of ruined streets.

. . ."The cannonading has got the wind up in young Raleigh, sir," said the sergeant. Captain Mitty looked up at him through tousled hair. "Get him to bed," he said wearily, "with the others. I'll fly alone." "But you can't, sir," said the sergeant anxiously. "It takes two men to handle that bomber and the Archies are pounding the air. Von Richtman's circus is between here and Saulier." "Somebody's got to get that ammunition dump," said Mitty. "I'm going over. Spot of brandy?" He poured a drink for the sergeant and one for himself. War thundered and whined around the dugout and battered at the door. There was a rending of wood, and splinters flew through the room. "A bit of a near thing," said Captain Mitty carelessly. "The box barrage is closing in," said the sergeant. "We only live once, Sergeant," said Mitty, with his faint, fleeting smile. "Or do we?" He poured another brandy and tossed it off. "I never see a man could hold his brandy like you, sir," said the sergeant. "Begging your pardon, sir." Captain Mitty stood up and strapped on his huge Webley-Vickers automatic. "It's forty kilometers through hell, sir," said the sergeant. Mitty finished one last brandy. "After all," he said softly, "what isn't?" The pounding of the cannon increased; there was the rat-tat-tatting of machine guns, and from somewhere came the menacing pocketa-pocketa-pocketa of the new flame throwers. Walter Mitty walked to the door of the dugout humming "Auprès de Ma Blonde." He turned and waved to the sergeant. "Cheerio!" he said. . . .

Something struck his shoulder. "I've been looking all over this hotel for you,"

said Mrs. Mitty. "Why do you have to hide in this old chair? How did you expect me to find you?" "Things close in," said Walter Mitty vaguely. "What?" Mrs. Mitty said. "Did you get the what's-its-name? The puppy biscuit? What's in that box?" "Overshoes," said Mitty. "Couldn't you have put them on in the store?" "I was thinking," said Walter Mitty. "Does it ever occur to you that I am sometimes thinking?" She looked at him. "I'm going to take your temperature when I get you home," she said.

They went out through the revolving doors that made a faintly derisive whistling sound when you pushed them. It was two blocks to the parking lot. At the drugstore on the corner she said, "Wait here for me. I forgot something. I won't be a minute." She was more than a minute. Walter Mitty lighted a cigarette. It began to rain, rain with sleet in it. He stood up against the wall of the drugstore, smoking. . . . He put his shoulders back and his heels together. "To the devil with the handkerchief," said Walter Mitty scornfully. He took

one last drag on his cigarette and snapped it away. Then, with that faint, fleeting smile playing about his lips, he faced the firing squad; erect and motionless, proud and disdainful, Walter Mitty the Undefeated, inscrutable to the last.

◇◇◇◇◇◇◇◇◇◇◇◇◇◇◇◇◇◇◇◇◇◇◇◇◇◇◇◇◇

FOR UNDERSTANDING

1. Explain why at the beginning of the story Walter Mitty's daydream caused him to drive too fast. In his imagined life as a navy commander he was *confident, decisive,* and *highly capable.* Explain how these same characteristics appeared in his "life" as a famous surgeon.

2. The actual Walter Mitty is like many of Thurber's heroes—a confused little man who sometimes finds it difficult to cope with the simplest of everyday problems. Give two or more examples of Mitty's inability to do things right.

3. The power of Thurber's story comes from the fact that it is about *us.* At times modern life will seem complicated and bewildering to almost anyone. Describe two occasions when you have felt flustered and bewildered—for instance, handling an auto-

mobile or other machine, or even trying to get the right bus.

4. The daydreaming parts of the story are also about us. Give several examples of the daydreams that might be indulged in by children or by people of your own age—not necessarily by you yourself.

5. What sort of differences in Walter Mitty's daily life might cause him to do less daydreaming?

GETTING INSIDE A CHARACTER'S MIND

"The Secret Life of Walter Mitty" is full of clever, realistic touches that show how a person's thoughts operate. An example is the way Walter Mitty's imagination gives only a *vague, fleeting impression* of the things he naturally doesn't know much about. In the first daydream the instrument board appears only as "a row of complicated dials." In the second daydream the operating room contains "a huge, complicated machine . . . with many tubes and wires." The patient is supposed to have "obstreosis of the ductal tract"—a made-up ailment which nevertheless sounds very impressive.

The story contains many other carefully planned details that show the workings of a person's mind.

1. In the first daydream the motors go "pocketa-pocketa-pocketa." Explain how this same noise is worked into two other daydreams.

2. An imaginary career as a surgeon is suggested to Mitty's mind by the fact that he has just driven by a hospital on his way to a parking lot. What actual event sets him to imagining that he is on trial in a courtroom? What makes him imagine he is Captain Mitty, about to go out on a bombing raid?

3. After buying his overshoes, Mitty couldn't remember what else he wanted to buy. Which detail from his daydream reminded him that he needed puppy biscuit?

4. Explain how the *actuality* and the *dream-situation* are intermingled as Mitty stands waiting for his wife at the end of the story.

JAMES THURBER (1894–1961)

For many years James Thurber was a noted contributor to the *New Yorker* magazine. Americans take delight in both his writings and his cartoons, for in his characters they recognize themselves— rather dismayed and uncertain people on whom, in Walter Mitty's words, "Things close in." Thurber's people are mainly men. He seems to feel that women are more domineering, better adapted to the rough seas of life, than the mere male, and a little frightening.

Thurber was born in Ohio and educated at Ohio State University. His humorous autobiography, *My Life and Hard Times*, gives the impression that during his youth both he and his family underwent as many weird mishaps as the characters in his stories. Two of his best known books are *Fables for Our Time* and an extremely funny and imaginative fairy tale, *The White Deer*. *The Thurber Carnival* is an excellent sampling of some of his most distinguished work.

THE HACK DRIVER

*Sinclair Lewis was well acquainted with the people to be met on the Main
Streets all across America. Here he takes us on a day's tour of the typical
small town of New Mullion, and introduces us to what is called a town
"character"—a fellow as wholesome and individualistic as a sharp-flavored
country apple.*

I dare say there's no man of large affairs, whether he is bank president or
senator or dramatist, who hasn't a sneaking love for some old rumhound in a
frightful hat, living back in a shanty and
making his living by ways you wouldn't
care to examine too closely. (It was the
Supreme Court justice speaking. I do
not pretend to guarantee his theories or
his story.) He may be a Maine guide,
or the old garageman who used to keep
the livery stable, or a perfectly useless
innkeeper who sneaks off to shoot ducks
when he ought to be sweeping the floors,
but your pompous big-city man will contrive to get back and see him every year,
and loaf with him, and secretly prefer
him to all the highfalutin leaders of the
city.

There's that much truth, at least, to
this Open Spaces stuff you read in advertisements of wild and woolly Western
novels. I don't know the philosophy of
it; perhaps it means that we retain a
decent simplicity, no matter how much
we are tied to Things, to houses and
motors and expensive wives. Or again it
may give away the whole game of civilization; may mean that the apparently
civilized man is at heart nothing but a
hobo who prefers flannel shirts and bristly
cheeks and cussing and dirty tin plates to
all the trim, hygienic, forward-looking life

our womenfolks make us put on for
them.

When I graduated from law school I
suppose I was about as artificial and idi-
otic and ambitious as most youngsters.
I wanted to climb, socially and financially. I wanted to be famous, and dine
at large houses with men who shuddered
at the Common People who don't dress
for dinner. You see, I hadn't learned
that the only thing duller than a polite
dinner is the conversation afterward,
when the victims are digesting the dinner and accumulating enough strength
to be able to play bridge. Oh, I was a
fine young calf! I even planned a rich
marriage. Imagine then how I felt when,
after taking honors and becoming fifteenth assistant clerk in the magnificent
law firm of Hodgins, Hodgins, Berkman,
and Taupe, I was set not at preparing
briefs but at serving summonses! Like a
cheap private detective! Like a mangy
sheriff's officer! They told me I had to
begin that way and, holding my nose, I
feebly went to work. I was kicked out of
actresses' dressing rooms, and from time
to time I was righteously beaten by large
and indignant litigants.[1] I came to know,

[1] LITIGANTS (lĭt'ĭ·găntz). Those involved
in a lawsuit.

"The Hack Driver" from *Selected Short Stories of
Sinclair Lewis*, copyright, 1923, by Sinclair Lewis,
reprinted by permission of Doubleday & Company, Inc.

and still more to hate, every dirty and shadowy corner of the city. I thought of fleeing to my home town, where I could at once become a full-fledged attorney-at-law. I rejoiced one day when they sent me out forty miles or so to a town called New Mullion, to serve a summons on one Oliver Lutkins. This Lutkins had worked in the Northern Woods, and he knew the facts about a certain timberland boundary agreement; we needed him as a witness, and he had dodged service.

When I got off the train at New Mullion, my sudden affection for sweet and simple villages was dashed by the look of the place, with its mud-gushing streets and its rows of shops either paintless or daubed with a sour brown. Though it must have numbered eight or nine thousand inhabitants, New Mullion was as littered as a mining camp. There was one agreeable-looking man at the station—the expressman. He was a person of perhaps forty, red-faced, cheerful, thick; he wore his overalls and denim jumper as though they belonged to him; he was quite dirty and very friendly, and you knew at once that he liked people and slapped them on the back out of pure easy affection.

"I want," I told him, "to find a fellow named Oliver Lutkins."

"Him? I saw him 'round here 'twa'n't an hour ago. Hard fellow to catch, though—always chasing around on some phony business or other. Probably trying to get up a poker game in the back of Fritz Beineke's harness shop. I'll tell you, boy— Any hurry about locating Lutkins?"

"Yes. I want to catch the afternoon train back." I was as impressively secret as a stage detective.

"I'll tell you. I've got a hack. I'll get out the old boneshaker and we can drive around together and find Lutkins. I know most of the places he hangs out."

He was so frankly friendly, he so immediately took me into the circle of his affection, that I glowed with the warmth of it. I knew, of course, that he was drumming up business, but his kindness was real, and if I had to pay hack fare in order to find my man, I was glad that the money would go to this good fellow. I got him down to two dollars an hour; he brought from his cottage, a block away, an object like a black piano box on wheels.

He didn't hold the door open, certainly he didn't say: "Ready, sir." I think he would have died before calling anybody "sir." When he gets to Heaven's gate he'll call St. Peter "Pete," and I imagine the good saint will like it. He remarked, "Well, young fellow, here's the handsome equipage," and his grin— well, it made me feel that I had always been his neighbor. They're so ready to help a stranger, those villagers. He had already made it his own task to find Oliver Lutkins for me.

He said, and almost shyly: "I don't want to butt in on your private business, young fellow, but my guess is that you want to collect some money from Lutkins —he never pays anybody a cent; he still owes me six bits on a poker game I was fool enough to get into. He ain't a bad sort of a Yahoo, but he just naturally hates to loosen up on coin of the realm. So if you're trying to collect any money off him, we better kind of, you might say, creep up on him and surround him. If you go asking for him—anybody can tell you come from the city, with that trick Fedora [2] of yours—he'll suspect something and take a sneak. If you want me to, I'll go into Fritz Beineke's and

[2] FEDORA—A soft felt hat.

35

ask for him, and you can keep out of sight behind me."

I loved him for it. By myself I might never have found Lutkins. Now, I was an army with reserves. In a burst I told the hack driver that I wanted to serve a summons on Lutkins; that the fellow had viciously refused to testify in a suit where his knowledge of a certain conversation would clear up everything. The driver listened earnestly—and I was still young enough to be grateful at being taken seriously by any man of forty. At the end he pounded my shoulder (very painfully) and chuckled: "Well, we'll spring a little surprise on Br'er Lutkins."

"Let's start, driver."

"Most folks around here call me Bill. Or Magnuson, William Magnuson, fancy carting and hauling."

"All right, Bill. Shall we tackle this harness shop—Beineke's?"

"Yes, jus' likely to be there as anywheres. Plays a lot of poker, and a great hand at bluffing." Bill seemed to admire Mr. Lutkins' ability as a scoundrel; I fancied that if he had been sheriff he would have caught Lutkins with fervor and hanged him with affection.

At the somewhat gloomy harness shop we descended and went in. The room was odorous with the smell of dressed leather. A scanty sort of man, presumably Mr. Beineke, was selling a horse collar to a farmer.

"Seen Nolly Lutkins around today? Friend of his looking for him," said Bill, with treacherous heartiness.

Beineke looked past him at my shrinking alien self; he hesitated, and owned: "Yuh, he was in here little while ago. Guess he's gone over to the Swede's to get a shave."

"Well, if he comes in, tell him I'm looking for him. Might get up a little game of poker. I've heard tell that

Lutkins plays these here immoral games of chance."

"Yuh, I believe he's known to sit in on Authors," Beineke growled.

We sought the barbershop of "the Swede." Bill was again good enough to take the lead, while I lurked at the door. He asked not only the Swede but two customers if they had seen Lutkins. The Swede decidedly had not; he raged: "I ain't seen him, and I don't want to, but if you find him you can just collect the dollar thirty-five he owes me!" One of the customers thought he had seen Lutkins "hiking down Main Street, this side of the hotel."

"Well, then," Bill concluded, as we labored up into the hack, "his credit at the Swede's being *ausgewent*, he's probably getting a scrape at Heinie Gray's. He's too darn lazy to shave himself."

At Gray's barbershop we missed Lutkins by only five minutes. He had just left—presumably for the poolroom. At the poolroom it appeared that he had merely bought a "pack" of cigarettes and gone on. Thus we pursued him, just behind him but never catching him, for an hour, till it was past one and I was hungry. Village born as I was and in the city often lonely for good coarse country wit, I was so delighted by Bill's cynical opinions on the barbers and clergymen and doctors and draymen of New Mullion that I scarcely cared whether I found Lutkins or not.

"How about something to eat?" I suggested. "Let's go to a restaurant and I'll buy you a lunch."

"Well, ought to go home to the old woman. I don't care much for these restaurants—ain't but four of 'em and they're all rotten. Tell you what we'll do. Like nice scenery? There's an elegant view from Wade's Hill. We'll get the old woman to put us up a lunch—she

won't charge you but half a dollar, and it'd cost you that for a greasy feed at the cafe—and we'll go up there and have a Sunday-school picnic."

I knew that my friend Bill was not free from guile; I knew that his hospitality to the Young Fellow from the City was not altogether a matter of brotherly love. I was paying him for his time; in all I paid him for six hours (including the lunch hour!) at what was then a terrific price. But he was no more dishonest than I, who charged the whole thing up to the Firm, and it would have been worth paying him myself to have his presence. His country serenity, his natural wisdom, was a refreshing bath to the city-twitching youngster. As we sat on the hilltop, looking across orchards and a creek which slipped among the willows, he talked of New Mullion, gave a whole gallery of portraits. He was cynical yet tender. Nothing had escaped him, yet there was nothing, no matter how ironically he laughed at it, which was beyond his understanding and forgiveness. In ruddy color he painted the rector's wife who, when she was most in debt, most loudly gave the responses of what he called the "Episcopalopian church." He commented on the boys who came home from college in "ice-cream pants," and on the lawyer who, after years of torrential argument with his wife, would put on either a linen collar or a necktie, but never both. He made them live. In that day I came to know New Mullion better than I did the city and to love it better.

If Bill was ignorant of universities and of urban ways, yet much had he traveled in the realm of jobs. He had worked on railroad section gangs, in harvest fields, and contractors' camps, and from his adventures he had brought back a philosophy of simplicity and laughter. He strengthened me. Nowadays, thinking of Bill, I know what people mean (though I abominate the simpering phrase) when they yearn over "real he-men."

We left that placid place of orchards and resumed the search for Oliver Lutkins. We could not find him. At last Bill cornered a friend of Lutkins and made him admit that "he guessed Oliver's gone out to his ma's farm, three miles north."

We drove out there, mighty with strategy.

"I know Oliver's ma. She's a terror. She's a cyclone," Bill sighed. "I took a trunk out for her once, and she pretty near took my hide off because I didn't treat it like it was a crate of eggs. She's somewheres about nine feet tall and four feet thick and quick's a cat, and she sure manhandles the Queen's English. I'll bet Oliver has heard that somebody's on his trail, and he's sneaked out there to hide behind Ma's skirts. Well, we'll try bawling her out. But you better let me do it, boy. You may be great at Latin and geography, but you ain't educated in cussing." We drove into a poor farm-yard; we were faced by an enormous and cheerful old woman. My guardian stockily stood before her and snarled, "Remember me? I'm Bill Magnuson, the expressman. I want to find your son Oliver. Friend of mine here from the city got a present for him."

"I don't know anything about Oliver, and I don't want to," she bellowed.

"Now you look here. We've stood for just about enough plenty nonsense. This young man is the attorney general's provost, and we got legal right to search any and all premises for the person of one Oliver Lutkins."

Bill made it sound terrific, and the Amazon seemed impressed. She retired into the kitchen and we followed. From the low old range, turned by years of heat into a dark silvery gray, she snatched a sadiron,[3] and she marched on us, clamoring, "You just search all you want to —providin' you don't mind getting burnt to a cinder." She bellowed, she swelled, she laughed at our nervous retreat.

"Let's get out of this. She'll murder us," Bill groaned and, outside: "Did you see her grin? She was making fun of us. Can you beat that for nerve?"

I agreed that it was *lèse majesté.*[4]

We did, however, make adequate search. The cottage had but one story. Bill went around it, peeking in at all the windows. We explored the barn and the stable; we were reasonably certain that Lutkins was not there. It was nearly time for me to catch the afternoon train, and Bill drove me to the station. On the way to the city I worried very little over my failure to find Lutkins. I was too absorbed in the thought of Bill Magnuson. Really, I considered returning to New Mullion to practice law. If I had found Bill so deeply and richly human, might I not come to love the yet uncharted Fritz Beineke and the Swede barber and a hundred other slow-spoken, simple, wise neighbors? I saw a candid and happy life beyond the neat learnings of universities and law firms. I was excited, as one who has found a treasure.

But if I did not think much about Lutkins, the office did. I found them in a state, next morning; the suit was ready to come to trial; they had to have Lutkins; I was a disgrace and a fool. That morning my eminent legal career

---

[3] SADIRON—Flatiron.
[4] *Lèse majesté* (lāz mä'zhĕs'tā')—An offense which shows disrespect for a king or other important personage.

almost came to an end. The Chief did everything but commit mayhem; he somewhat more than hinted that I would do well at ditch-digging. I was ordered back to New Mullion, and with me they sent an ex-lumbercamp clerk who knew Lutkins. I was rather sorry, because it would prevent my loafing again in the gorgeous indolence of Bill Magnuson.

When the train drew in at New Mullion, Bill was on the station platform, near his dray. What was curious was that the old dragon, Lutkins' mother, was there talking to him, and they were not quarreling but laughing.

From the car steps I pointed Bill out to the lumbercamp clerk, and in young hero worship I murmured: "There's a fine fellow, a real man."

"Meet him here yesterday?" asked the clerk.

"I spent the day with him."

"He help you hunt for Oliver Lutkins?"

"Yes, he helped me a lot."

"He must have! He's Lutkins himself!"

But what really hurt was that when I served the summons Lutkins and his mother laughed at me as though I were a bright boy of seven, and with loving solicitude they begged me to go to a neighbor's house and take a cup of coffee.

"I told 'em about you, and they're dying to have a look at you," said Lutkins joyfully. "They're about the only folks in town that missed seeing you yesterday."

<><><><><><><><><><><><><><><><><><><><><>

FOR UNDERSTANDING

1. The main point of this story is the tremendous joke played on the narrator. How was each person in town able to catch on to the joke quickly enough not to reveal who the hack driver was? How was the barber's remark humorous? Why was it particularly funny to go out to the farm to question the old lady? Would the last remark in the story make the victim feel better or worse?

2. An especially pleasing feature of the yarn is the way everybody enters into the trick on the outsider. The entire incident is the kind that might be remembered for years in the town and retold many times, with listeners slapping their knees in delight. But the joke is on the reader, too. How do the opening paragraphs tend to mislead him? Did you begin to guess the outcome before you reached the end? What clues might make a reader suspect what is happening?

3. Until the very end, the story *seems* to be an appreciation of the good things about small-town life; and it actually is this, to a great extent. Summarize the differences in character between the "citified" young lawyer and the hack driver. Why could one say that the hack driver was getting more out of life than the young man?

4. Give an example of a good-humored practical joke you have heard about—preferably a joke played by a large group of conspirators.

SINCLAIR LEWIS (1885–1951)

Sinclair Lewis is best known for his novels. Until 1920 he was a writer who had attracted little attention, but in that year the best-seller *Main Street* brought him both praise and censure. It is a realistic story of life in a small town very much like Lewis' birthplace, Sauk Center, Minnesota. Many of his later books have also been subjects of controversy. Some readers admire his vigorous attacks on smugness and shallow-mindedness in American life, while others object to his biting satire as being one-sided. His two most popular novels after *Main Street* were *Babbitt*, picturing a "typical" prosperous businessman, and *Arrowsmith*, in which the main character is a brilliant medical scientist.

Lewis' novels have the simplest of plots.

Each one is merely "a slice of life," telling the big things and the trivial things that happen to the principal character. By filling his chapters with great heaps of closely observed details, Lewis makes himself a sort of photographer of the American scene. In particular, he knows exactly how Americans *talk*. Although the long conversations in his books can become tiresome, they are probably the most successful reproductions of actual speech ever made by an American author.

In his later life Lewis traveled a great deal. Some of his books have become very popular in Europe. In 1930 he was awarded the Nobel Prize for distinction in world literature—the first American to receive this honor.

◇◇◇◇◇

PAUL'S CASE

WILLA CATHER

In studying a person who is ill or in trouble, a doctor, social worker, or psychologist often compiles a record of all available information which might throw some light on the ailment or the problem. Such a record is called a case history.

The story you are about to read has many characteristics of a case history. It deals with a boy who has been suspended from school, and presents information about his personality, his home life, and his associates which should help an alert reader to understand why he behaved as he did. Unfortunately, none of the people who came in contact with Paul were able to interpret the facts in the case and help the boy to a satisfactory solution of his problem.

It was Paul's afternoon to appear before the faculty of the Pittsburgh High School to account for his various misdemeanors. He had been suspended a week ago, and his father had called at the principal's office and confessed his perplexity about his son. Paul entered the faculty room suave and smiling. His clothes were a trifle outgrown, and the tan velvet on the collar of his open overcoat was frayed and worn; but for all that there was something of the dandy about him, and he wore an opal pin in his neatly knotted black four-in-hand, and a red carnation in his buttonhole. This latter adornment the faculty somehow felt was not properly significant of the contrite spirit befitting a boy under the ban of suspension.

Paul was tall for his age and very thin, with high, cramped shoulders and a narrow chest. His eyes were remarkable for a certain hysterical brilliancy, and he continually used them in a conscious theatrical sort of way, peculiarly offensive in a boy. The pupils were abnormally large, as though he were addicted to belladonna, but there was a glassy glitter about them which that drug does not produce.

When questioned by the principal as to why he was there, Paul stated, politely enough, that he wanted to come back to school. This was a lie, but Paul was quite accustomed to lying; found it, indeed, indispensable for overcoming friction. His teachers were asked to state their respective charges against him, which they did with such a rancor and aggrievedness as evinced that this was not a usual case. Disorder and impertinence were among the offences named, yet each of his instructors felt that it was scarcely possible to put into words the real cause of the trouble, which lay in a sort of hysterically defiant manner of the boy's; in the contempt which they all knew he felt for them, and which he seemingly made not the least effort to conceal. Once, when he had been making a synopsis of a paragraph at the blackboard, his English teacher had stepped to his side and attempted to guide his hands. Paul had started back with a shudder and thrust his hands violently behind him. The astonished woman could scarcely have been more hurt and embarrassed had he struck at her. The insult was so involuntary and definitely personal as to be unforgettable. In one way and another he had made all his teachers, men and women alike, conscious of the same feeling of physical aversion. In one class he habitually sat with his hand shading his eyes; in another he always looked out of the window during the recitation; in another he made a running commentary on the lecture, with humorous intent.

His teachers felt this afternoon that his whole attitude was symbolized by his shrug and his flippantly red carnation flower, and they fell upon him without mercy, his English teacher leading the pack. He stood through it smiling, his pale lips parted over his white teeth. (His lips were continually twitching, and he had a habit of raising his eyebrows that was contemptuous and irritating to the last degree.) Older boys than Paul had broken down and shed tears under that ordeal, but his set smile did not once desert him, and his only sign of discomfort was the nervous trembling of the fingers that toyed with the buttons of his overcoat, and an occasional jerking of the other hand which held his hat. Paul was always smiling, always glancing about him, seeming to feel that people might be watching him and trying to detect something. This conscious expression, since it was as far as possible from boyish mirthfulness, was usually attributed to insolence or "smartness."

As the inquisition proceeded, one of his instructors repeated an impertinent remark of the boy's, and the principal asked him whether he thought that a courteous speech to make to a woman. Paul shrugged his shoulders slightly and his eyebrows twitched.

"I don't know," he replied. "I didn't mean to be polite or impolite, either. I guess it's a sort of way I have, of saying things regardless."

The principal asked him whether he didn't think that a way it would be well to get rid of. Paul grinned and said he guessed so. When he was told that he could go, he bowed gracefully and went out. His bow was like a repetition of the scandalous red carnation.

His teachers were in despair, and his drawing master voiced the feeling of them all when he declared there was something about the boy which none of them understood. He added, "I don't really believe that smile of his comes altogether from insolence; there's something sort of haunted about it. The boy is not strong, for one thing. There is something wrong about the fellow."

The drawing master had come to realize that, in looking at Paul, one saw only his white teeth and the forced animation of his eyes. One warm afternoon the boy had gone to sleep at his drawing board, and his master had noted with amazement what a white, blue-veined face it was; drawn and wrinkled like an old man's about the eyes, the lips twitching even in his sleep.

His teachers left the building dissatisfied and unhappy; humiliated to have felt so vindictive toward a mere boy, to have uttered this feeling in cutting terms, and to have set each other on, as it were, in the gruesome game of intemperate reproach. One of them remembered having seen a miserable street cat set at bay by a ring of tormentors.

As for Paul, he ran down the hill whistling the "Soldiers' Chorus" from *Faust*,[1] looking wildly behind him now and then to see whether some of his teachers were not there to witness his lightheartedness. As it was now late in the afternoon and Paul was on duty that evening as usher at Carnegie Hall, he decided that he would not go home to supper.

When he reached the concert hall the doors were not yet open. It was chilly outside, and he decided to go up into the picture gallery—always deserted at this hour—where there were some of Raffaelli's[2] gay studies of Paris streets and an airy blue Venetian scene or two that always exhilarated him. He was delighted to find no one in the gallery but the old guard, who sat in the corner, a newspaper on his knee, a black patch over one eye

and the other closed. Paul possessed himself of the place and walked confidently up and down, whistling under his breath. After a while he sat down before a blue Rico and lost himself. When he bethought him to look at his watch, it was after seven o'clock, and he rose with a start and ran downstairs, making a face at Augustus Caesar, peering out from the cast room, and an evil gesture at the Venus of Milo as he passed her on the stairway.

When Paul reached the ushers' dressing room half a dozen boys were there already, and he began excitedly to tumble into his uniform. It was one of the few that at all approached fitting, and Paul thought it very becoming—though he knew the tight, straight coat accentuated his narrow chest, about which he was exceedingly sensitive. He was always excited while he dressed, twanging all over to the tuning of the strings and the preliminary flourishes of the horns in the music room; but tonight he seemed quite beside himself, and he teased and plagued the boys until, telling him that he was crazy, they put him down on the floor and sat on him.

Somewhat calmed by his suppression, Paul dashed out to the front of the house to seat the early comers. He was a model usher. Gracious and smiling he ran up and down the aisles. Nothing was too much trouble for him; he carried messages and brought programs as though it were his greatest pleasure in life, and all the people in his section thought him a charming boy, feeling that he remembered and admired them. As the house filled, he grew more and more vivacious and animated, and the color came to his cheeks and lips. It was very much as though this were a great reception and Paul were the host. Just as the musicians came out to take their places,

---

[1] *Faust* (foust)—An opera by Charles Gounod about a philosopher who sells his soul to the devil in return for youth and power.
[2] RAFFAELLI—Pronounced rä′fä′ĕ′lē′.

his English teacher arrived with checks for the seats which a prominent manufacturer had taken for the season. She betrayed some embarrassment when she handed Paul the tickets, and a *hauteur* [3] which subsequently made her feel very foolish. Paul was startled for a moment, and had the feeling of wanting to put her out; what business had she here among all the fine people and gay colors? He looked her over and decided that she was not appropriately dressed and must be a fool to sit downstairs in such togs. The tickets had probably been sent her out of kindness, he reflected, as he put down a seat for her, and she had about as much right to sit there as he had.

When the symphony began, Paul sank into one of the rear seats with a long sigh of relief and lost himself as he had done before the Rico. It was not that sym-

phonies, as such, meant anything in particular to Paul, but the first sigh of the instruments seemed to free some hilarious spirit within him; something that struggled there like the Genius in the bottle found by the Arab fisherman.[4] He felt a sudden zest of life; the lights danced before his eyes and the concert hall blazed into unimaginable splendor. When the soprano soloist came on, Paul forgot even the nastiness of his teacher's being there, and gave himself up to the peculiar intoxication such personages always had for him. The soloist chanced to be a German woman, by no means in her first youth, and the mother of many children; but she wore a satin gown and a tiara, and she had that undefinable air

---

[3] *Hauteur* (hô·tûr´)—Arrogance.

[4] GENIUS . . . ARAB FISHERMAN—In one of the tales from the *Arabian Nights*, a fisherman releases a Genii which had been confined in a bottle for hundreds of years.

of achievement, that world-shine upon her, which always blinded Paul to any possible defects.

After a concert was over, Paul was often irritable and wretched until he got to sleep—and tonight he was even more than usually restless. He had the feeling of not being able to let down, of its being impossible to give up this delicious excitement which was the only thing that could be called living at all. During the last number he withdrew and, after hastily changing his clothes in the dressing room, slipped out to the side door where the singer's carriage stood. Here he began pacing rapidly up and down the walk, waiting to see her come out.

Over yonder the Schenley, in its vacant stretch, loomed big and square through the fine rain, the windows of its twelve stories glowing like those of a lighted cardboard house under a Christmas tree. All the actors and singers of any importance stayed there when they were in the city, and a number of the big manufacturers of the place lived there in the winter. Paul had often hung about the hotel, watching the people go in and out, longing to enter and leave schoolmasters and dull care behind him forever.

At last the singer came out, accompanied by the conductor, who helped her into her carriage and closed the door with a cordial *auf wiedersehen* [5]—which set Paul to wondering whether she were not an old sweetheart of his. Paul followed the carriage over to the hotel, walking so rapidly as not to be far from the entrance when the singer alighted and disappeared behind the swinging glass doors which were opened by a Negro in a tall hat and a long coat. In the moment that the door was ajar, it seemed to Paul that he, too, entered. He seemed to feel himself

go after her up the steps, into the warm, lighted building, into an exotic, a tropical world of shiny, glistening surfaces and basking ease. He reflected upon the mysterious dishes that were brought into the dining room, the green bottles in buckets of ice, as he had seen them in the supper party pictures of the Sunday supplement. A quick gust of wind brought the rain down with sudden vehemence, and Paul was startled to find that he was still outside in the slush of the gravel driveway; that his boots were letting in the water and his scanty overcoat was clinging wet about him; that the lights in front of the concert hall were out, and that the rain was driving in sheets between him and the orange glow of the windows above him. There it was, what he wanted—tangibly before him, like the fairy world of a Christmas pantomime; as the rain beat in his face, Paul wondered whether he were destined always to shiver in the black night outside, looking up at it.

He turned and walked reluctantly toward the car tracks. The end had to come sometime; his father in his night clothes at the top of the stairs, explanations that did not explain, hastily improvised fictions that were forever tripping him up, his upstairs room and its horrible yellow wallpaper, the creaking bureau with the greasy plush collar box, and over his painted wooden bed the pictures of George Washington and John Calvin,[6] and the framed motto, "Feed My Lambs," which had been worked in red worsted by his mother, whom Paul could not remember.

Half an hour later, Paul alighted from the Negley Avenue car and went slowly down one of the side streets off the main

[5] *Auf wiedersehen* (ouf′ vē′dĕr·zā′ĕn). German for "farewell."

[6] JOHN CALVIN—A sixteenth-century reformer and theologian whose doctrine became known as Calvinism.

thoroughfare. It was a highly respectable street, where all the houses were exactly alike, and where businessmen of moderate means begot and reared large families of children, all of whom went to Sabbath school and learned the shorter catechism, and were interested in arithmetic; all of whom were as exactly alike as their homes, and of a piece with the monotony in which they lived. Paul never went up Cordelia Street without a shudder of loathing. His home was next the house of the Cumberland minister. He approached it tonight with the nerveless sense of defeat, the hopeless feeling of sinking back forever into ugliness and commonness that he had always had when he came home. The moment he turned into Cordelia Street he felt the waters close above his head. After each of these orgies of living, he experienced all the physical depression which follows a debauch; the loathing of respectable beds, of common food, of a house permeated by kitchen odors; a shuddering repulsion for the flavorless, colorless mass of everyday existence; a morbid desire for cool things and soft lights and fresh flowers.

The nearer he approached the house, the more absolutely unequal Paul felt to the sight of it all; his ugly sleeping chamber; the cold bathroom with the grimy zinc tub, the cracked mirror, the dripping spigots; his father, at the top of the stairs, his hairy legs sticking out from his nightshirt, his feet thrust into carpet slippers. He was so much later than usual that there would certainly be inquiries and reproaches. Paul stopped short before the door. He felt that he could not be accosted by his father tonight; that he could not toss again on that miserable bed. He would not go in. He would tell his father that he had no carfare, and it was raining so hard he had gone home

with one of the boys and stayed all night.

Meanwhile, he was wet and cold. He went around to the back of the house and tried one of the basement windows, found it open, raised it cautiously, and scrambled down the cellar wall to the floor. There he stood, holding his breath, terrified by the noise he had made; but the floor above him was silent, and there was no creak on the stairs. He found a soapbox, and carried it over to the soft ring of light that streamed from the furnace door, and sat down. He was horribly afraid of rats, so he did not try to sleep, but sat looking distrustfully at the dark, still terrified lest he might have awakened his father. In such reactions, after one of the experiences which made days and nights out of the dreary blanks of the calendar, when his senses were deadened, Paul's head was always singularly clear. Suppose his father had heard him getting in at the window and had come down and shot him for a burglar? Then, again, suppose his father had come down, pistol in hand, and he had cried out in time to save himself, and his father had been horrified to think how nearly he had killed him? Then, again, suppose a day should come when his father would remember that night and wish there had been no warning cry to stay his hand? With this last supposition Paul entertained himself until daybreak.

The following Sunday was fine; the sodden November chill was broken by the last flash of autumnal summer. In the morning Paul had to go to church and Sabbath school, as always. On seasonable Sunday afternoons the burghers of Cordelia Street usually sat out on their front "stoops," and talked to their neighbors on the next stoop, or called to those across the street in neighborly fashion.

The men sat placidly on gay cushions placed upon the steps that led down to the sidewalk, while the women, in their Sunday "waists," sat in rockers on the cramped porches, pretending to be greatly at their ease. The children played in the streets; there were so many of them that the place resembled the recreation grounds of a kindergarten. The men on the steps—all in their shirt sleeves, their vests unbuttoned—sat with their legs well apart, their stomachs comfortably protruding, and talked of the prices of things, or told anecdotes of the sagacity of their various chiefs and overlords. They occasionally looked over the multitude of squabbling children, listened affectionately to their high-pitched, nasal voices, smiling to see their own proclivities reproduced in their offspring, and interspersed their legends of the iron kings with remarks about their sons' progress at school, their grades in arithmetic, and the amounts they had saved in their toy banks.

On this last Sunday of November, Paul sat all the afternoon on the lowest step of his "stoop," staring into the street, while his sisters, in their rockers, were talking to the minister's daughters next door about how many shirtwaists they had made in the last week, and how many waffles someone had eaten at the last church supper. When the weather was warm and his father was in a particularly jovial frame of mind, the girls made lemonade, which was always brought out in a red glass pitcher, ornamented with forget-me-nots in blue enamel. This the girls thought very fine, and the neighbors joked about the suspicious color of the pitcher.

Today Paul's father, on the top step, was talking to a young man who shifted a restless baby from knee to knee. He happened to be the young man who was daily held up to Paul as a model, and after whom it was his father's dearest hope that he would pattern. This young man was of a ruddy complexion, with a compressed, red mouth, and faded, near-sighted eyes, over which he wore thick spectacles, with gold bows that curved about his ears. He was clerk to one of the magnates of a great steel corporation, and was looked upon in Cordelia Street as a young man with a future. There was a story that, some five years ago—he was now barely twenty-six—he had been a trifle "dissipated," but in order to curb his appetites and save the loss of time and strength that a sowing of wild oats might have entailed, he had taken his chief's advice, oft reiterated to his employees, and at twenty-one had married the first woman whom he could persuade to share his fortunes. She happened to be an angular schoolmistress, much older than he, who also wore thick glasses, and who had now borne him four children, all nearsighted, like herself.

The young man was relating how his chief, now cruising in the Mediterranean, kept in touch with all the details of the business, arranging his office hours on his yacht just as though he were at home, and "knocking off work enough to keep two stenographers busy." His father told, in turn, the plan his corporation was considering, of putting in an electric railway plant at Cairo. Paul snapped his teeth; he had an awful apprehension that they might spoil it all before he got there. Yet he rather liked to hear these legends of the iron kings that were told and re-told on Sundays and holidays; these stories of palaces in Venice, yachts on the Mediterranean, and high play at Monte Carlo [7] appealed to his fancy, and he was interested in the triumphs of cash boys

[7] MONTE CARLO—A gambling resort near the border of Italy and France.

who had become famous, though he had no mind for the cash boy stage.

After supper was over, and he had helped to dry the dishes, Paul nervously asked his father whether he could go to George's to get some help in his geometry, and still more nervously asked for carfare. This latter request he had to repeat, as his father, on principle, did not like to hear requests for money, whether much or little. He asked Paul whether he could not go to some boy who lived nearer, and told him that he ought not to leave his school work until Sunday; but he gave him the dime. He was not a poor man, but he had a worthy ambition to come up in the world. His only reason for allowing Paul to usher was that he thought a boy ought to be earning a little.

Paul bounded upstairs, scrubbed the greasy odor of the dishwater from his hands with the ill-smelling soap he hated, and then shook over his fingers a few drops of violet water from the bottle he kept hidden in his drawer. He left the house with his geometry conspicuously under his arm, and the moment he got out of Cordelia Street and boarded a downtown car, he shook off the lethargy of two deadening days, and began to live again.

The leading juvenile of the permanent stock company which played at one of the downtown theaters was an acquaintance of Paul's, and the boy had been invited to drop in at the Sunday night rehearsals whenever he could. For more than a year Paul had spent every available moment loitering about Charley Edwards' dressing room. He had won a place among Edwards' following not only because the young actor, who could not afford to employ a dresser, often found him useful, but because he recognized in

Paul something akin to what churchmen term "vocation." [8]

It was at the theater and at Carnegie Hall that Paul really lived; the rest was but a sleep and a forgetting. This was Paul's fairy tale, and it had for him all the allurement of a secret love. The moment he inhaled the gassy, painty, dusty odor behind the scenes, he breathed like a prisoner set free, and felt within him the possibility of doing or saying splendid, brilliant things. The moment the cracked orchestra beat out the overture from *Martha*, or jerked at the serenade from *Rigoletto*,[9] all stupid and ugly things slid from him, and his senses were deliciously, yet delicately fired.

Perhaps it was because, in Paul's world, the natural nearly always wore the guise of ugliness, that a certain element of artificiality seemed to him necessary in beauty. Perhaps it was because his experience of life elsewhere was so full of Sabbath-school picnics, petty economies, wholesome advice as to how to succeed in life, and the unescapable odors of cooking, that he found this existence so alluring, these smartly clad men and women so attractive, that he was so moved by these starry apple orchards that bloomed perennially under the limelight.

It would be difficult to put it strongly enough how convincingly the stage entrance of that theater was for Paul the actual portal of Romance. Certainly none of the company ever suspected it, least of all Charley Edwards. It was very like the old stories that used to float about London of fabulously rich Jews, who had subterranean halls, with palms, and fountains, and soft lamps, and richly apparelled women who never saw the

[8] "VOCATION"—A calling.
[9] *Martha . . . Rigoletto* (rĭg'ȯ·lĕt'ō)— These are both operas. The first is by Friedrich von Flotow, the second by Giuseppe Verdi.

disenchanting light of London day. So, in the midst of that smoke-palled city, enamored of figures and grimy toil, Paul had his secret temple, his wishing carpet, his bit of blue-and-white Mediterranean shore bathed in perpetual sunshine.

Several of Paul's teachers had a theory that his imagination had been perverted by garish fiction; but the truth was, he scarcely ever read at all. The books at home were not such as would either tempt or corrupt a youthful mind, and as for reading the novels that some of his friends urged upon him—well, he got what he wanted much more quickly from music; any sort of music, from an orchestra to a barrel organ. He needed only the spark, the indescribable thrill that made his imagination master of his senses, and he could make plots and pictures enough of his own. It was equally true that he was not stage-struck—not, at any rate, in the usual acceptation of that expression. He had no desire to become an actor, any more than he had to become a musician. He felt no necessity to do any of these things; what he wanted was to see, to be in the atmosphere, float on the wave of it, to be carried out, blue league after blue league, away from everything.

After a night behind the scenes, Paul found the schoolroom more than ever repulsive; the bare floors and naked walls; the prosy men who never wore frock coats, or violets in their buttonholes; the women with their dull gowns, shrill voices, and pitiful seriousness about prepositions that govern the dative. He could not bear to have the other pupils think, for a moment, that he took these people seriously; he must convey to them that he considered it all trivial, and was there only by way of a joke, anyway. He had autographed pictures of all the members of the stock company which he showed his classmates, telling them the most incredible stories of his familiarity with these people, of his acquaintance with the soloists who came to Carnegie Hall, his suppers with them and the flowers he sent them. When these stories lost their effect and his audience grew listless, he would bid all the boys good-by, announcing that he was going to travel for awhile; going to Naples, to California, to Egypt. Then, next Monday, he would slip back, conscious and nervously smiling; his sister was ill, and he would have to defer his voyage until spring.

Matters went steadily worse with Paul at school. In the itch to let his instructors know how heartily he despised them and how thoroughly he was appreciated elsewhere, he mentioned once or twice that he had no time to fool with theorems; adding—with a twitch of the eyebrows and a touch of that nervous bravado which so perplexed them—that he was helping the people down at the stock company; they were old friends of his.

The upshot of the matter was that the principal went to Paul's father, and Paul was taken out of school and put to work. The manager at Carnegie Hall was told to get another usher in his stead; the doorkeeper at the theater was warned not to admit him to the house; and Charley Edwards remorsefully promised the boy's father not to see him again.

The members of the stock company were vastly amused when some of Paul's stories reached them—especially the women. They were hard-working women, most of them supporting indolent husbands or brothers, and they laughed rather bitterly at having stirred the boy to such fervid and florid inventions. They agreed with the faculty and with his father, that Paul's was a bad case.

The eastbound train was ploughing through a January snowstorm; the dull dawn was beginning to show gray when the engine whistled a mile out of Newark. Paul started up from the seat where he had lain curled in uneasy slumber, rubbed the breath-misted window glass with his hand, and peered out. The snow was whirling in curling eddies above the white bottom lands, and the drifts lay already deep in the fields and along the fences, while here and there the long dead grass and dried weed stalks protruded black above it. Lights shone from the scattered houses, and a gang of laborers who stood beside the track waved their lanterns.

Paul had slept very little, and he felt grimy and uncomfortable. He had made the all-night journey in a day coach because he was afraid if he took a Pullman he might be seen by some Pittsburgh businessman who had noticed him in Denny & Carson's office. When the whistle woke him, he clutched quickly at his breast pocket, glancing about him with an uncertain smile. But the little, clay-bespattered Italians were still sleeping, the slatternly women across the aisle were in openmouthed oblivion, and even the crumby, crying babies were for the nonce stilled. Paul settled back to struggle with his impatience as best he could.

When he arrived at the Jersey City station, he hurried through his breakfast, manifestly ill at ease and keeping a sharp eye about him. After he reached the Twenty-third Street station, he consulted a cabman, and had himself driven to a men's furnishing establishment which was just opening for the day. He spent upward of two hours there, buying with endless reconsidering and great care. His new street suit he put on in the fitting room; the frock coat and dress clothes he had bundled into the cab with his new shirts. Then he drove to a hatter's and a shoe house. His next errand was at Tiffany's, where he selected silver mounted brushes and a scarf pin. He would not wait to have his silver marked, he said. Lastly, he stopped at a trunk shop on Broadway, and had his purchases packed into various traveling bags.

It was a little after one o'clock when he drove up to the Waldorf, and, after settling with the cabman, went into the office. He registered from Washington; said his mother and father had been abroad, and that he had come down to await the arrival of their steamer. He told his story plausibly and had no trouble, since he offered to pay for them in advance, in engaging his rooms; a sleeping room, sitting room, and bath.

Not once, but a hundred times Paul had planned this entry into New York. He had gone over every detail of it with Charley Edwards, and in his scrapbook at home there were pages of description about New York hotels, cut from the Sunday papers.

When he was shown to his sitting room on the eighth floor, he saw at a glance that everything was as it should be; there was but one detail in his mental picture that the place did not realize, so he rang for the bellboy and sent him down for flowers. He moved about nervously until the boy returned, putting away his new linen and fingering it delightedly as he did so. When the flowers came, he put them hastily into water, and then tumbled into a hot bath. Presently he came out of his white bathroom, resplendent in his new silk underwear, and playing with the tassels of his red robe. The snow was whirling so fiercely outside his windows that he could scarcely see across the street; but within, the air was deliciously soft and fragrant. He put the violets and jonquils on the

taboret [10] beside the couch, and threw himself down with a long sigh, covering himself with a Roman blanket. He was thoroughly tired; he had been in such haste, he had stood up to such a strain, covered so much ground in the last twenty-four hours, that he wanted to think how it had all come about. Lulled by the sound of the wind, the warm air, and the cool fragrance of the flowers, he sank into deep, drowsy retrospection.

It had been wonderfully simple; when they had shut him out of the theater and concert hall, when they had taken away his bone, the whole thing was virtually determined. The rest was a mere matter of opportunity. The only thing that at all surprised him was his own courage— for he realized well enough that he had always been tormented by fear, a sort of

apprehensive dread that, of late years, as the meshes of the lies he had told closed about him, had been pulling the muscles of his body tighter and tighter. Until now, he could not remember a time when he had not been dreading something. Even when he was a little boy, it was always there—behind him, or before, or on either side. There had always been the shadowed corner, the dark place into which he dared not look, but from which something seemed always to be watching him—and Paul had done things that were not pretty to watch, he knew.

But now he had a curious sense of relief, as though he had at last thrown down the gauntlet [11] to the thing in the corner.

Yet it was but a day since he had been sulking in the traces; but yesterday after-

[10] TABORET (tăb'ô·rĕt)—A small table.

[11] GAUNTLET (gônt'lĕt)—A challenge.

noon that he had been sent to the bank with Denny & Carson's deposit, as usual —but this time he was instructed to leave the book to be balanced. There was above two thousand dollars in checks, and nearly a thousand in the bank notes which he had taken from the book and quietly transferred to his pocket. At the bank he had made out a new deposit slip. His nerves had been steady enough to permit of his returning to the office, where he had finished his work and asked for a full day's holiday tomorrow, Saturday, giving a perfectly reasonable pretext. The bankbook, he knew, would not be returned before Monday or Tuesday, and his father would be out of town for the next week. From the time he slipped the bank notes into his pocket until he boarded the night train for New York, he had not known a moment's hesitation.

How astonishingly easy it had all been; here he was, the thing done; and this time there would be no awakening, no figure at the top of the stairs. He watched the snowflakes whirling by his window until he fell asleep.

When he awoke, it was four o'clock in the afternoon. He bounded up with a start; one of his precious days gone already! He spent nearly an hour in dressing, watching every stage of his toilet carefully in the mirror. Everything was quite perfect; he was exactly the kind of boy he had always wanted to be.

When he went downstairs, Paul took a carriage and drove up Fifth Avenue toward the park. The snow had somewhat abated; carriages and tradesmen's wagons were hurrying soundlessly to and fro in the winter twilight; boys in woolen mufflers were shoveling off the doorsteps; the avenue stages made fine spots of color against the white street. Here and there on the corners were stands, with whole flower gardens blooming behind glass windows, against which the snowflakes stuck and melted; violets, roses, carnations, lilies of the valley—somehow vastly more lovely and alluring that they blossomed thus unnaturally in the snow. The park itself was a wonderful stage winter piece.

When he returned, the pause of the twilight had ceased, and the tune of the streets had changed. The snow was falling faster, lights streamed from the hotels that reared their many stories fearlessly up into the storm, defying the raging Atlantic winds. A long, black stream of carriages poured down the avenue, intersected here and there by other streams, tending horizontally. There were a score of cabs about the entrance of his hotel, and his driver had to wait. Boys in livery were running in and out of the awning stretched across the sidewalk, up and down the red velvet carpet laid from the door to the street. Above, about, within it all, was the rumble and roar, the hurry and toss of thousands of human beings as hot for pleasure as himself, and on every side of him towered the glaring affirmation of the omnipotence of wealth.

The boy set his teeth and drew his shoulders together in a spasm of realization; the plot of all dramas, the text of all romances, the nerve-stuff of all sensations was whirling about him like the snowflakes. He burnt like a faggot in a tempest.

When Paul came down to dinner, the music of the orchestra floated up the elevator shaft to greet him. As he stepped into the thronged corridor, he sank back into one of the chairs against the wall to get his breath. The lights, the chatter, the perfumes, the bewildering medley of color—he had, for a moment, the feeling of not being able to stand it. But only for a moment; these were his own people, he told himself. He went slowly about the corridors, through the writing rooms, smoking rooms, reception rooms, as though he were exploring the chambers of an enchanted palace, built and peopled for him alone.

When he reached the dining room he sat down at a table near a window. The flowers, the white linen, the many-colored wine glasses, the gay toilettes of the women, the low popping of corks, the undulating repetitions of the "Blue Danube" from the orchestra, all flooded Paul's dream with bewildering radiance. When the roseate tinge of his champagne was added—that cold, precious, bubbling stuff that creamed and foamed in his glass—Paul wondered that there were honest men in the world at all. This was what all the world was fighting for, he reflected; this was what all the struggle was about. He doubted the reality of his past. Had he ever known a place called Cordelia Street, a place where fagged-looking businessmen boarded the early car? Mere rivets in a machine they seemed to Paul—sickening men, with combings of children's hair always hanging to their coats, and the smell of cooking in their clothes. Cordelia Street— ah, that belonged to another time and country! Had he not always been thus, had he not sat here night after night, from as far back as he could remember, looking pensively over just such shimmering textures, and slowly twirling the stem of a glass like this one between his thumb and middle finger? He rather thought he had.

He was not in the least abashed or lonely. He had no especial desire to meet or to know any of these people; all he demanded was the right to look on and conjecture, to watch the pageant. The mere stage properties were all he contended for. Nor was he lonely later in the evening, in his loge at the Opera. He was entirely rid of his nervous misgivings, of his forced aggressiveness, of the imperative desire to show himself different from his surroundings. He felt now that his surroundings explained him. Nobody questioned his purple; he had only to wear it passively. He had only to glance down at his dress coat to reassure himself that here it would be impossible for anyone to humiliate him.

He found it hard to leave his beautiful sitting room to go to bed that night, and sat long watching the raging storm from his turret window. When he went to sleep, it was with the lights turned on in his bedroom, partly because of his old timidity, and partly so that, if he should wake in the night, there would be no wretched moment of doubt, no horrible suspicion of yellow wallpaper, or of Washington and Calvin above his bed.

On Sunday morning the city was practically snowbound. Paul breakfasted late, and in the afternoon he fell in with a wild San Francisco boy, a freshman at Yale, who said he had run down for a "little flyer" over Sunday. The young man offered to show Paul the night side of the town, and the two boys went off together after dinner, not returning to the hotel until seven o'clock the next morning. They had started out in the confiding warmth of a champagne friendship, but their parting in the elevator was singularly cool. The freshman pulled himself together to make his train, and Paul went to bed. He awoke at two o'clock in the afternoon, very thirsty and dizzy, and rang for ice water, coffee, and the Pittsburgh papers.

On the part of the hotel management, Paul excited no suspicion. There was this to be said for him, that he wore his spoils with dignity and in no way made himself conspicuous. His chief greediness lay in his ears and eyes, and his excesses were not offensive ones. His dearest pleasures were the gray winter twilights in his sitting room; his quiet enjoyment of his flowers, his clothes, his wide divan, his cigarette, and his sense of power. He could not remember a time when he had felt so at peace with himself. The mere release from the necessity of petty lying, lying every day and every day, restored his self-respect. He had never lied for pleasure, even at school, but to make himself noticed and admired, to assert his difference from other Cordelia Street boys; and he felt a good deal more manly, more honest even, now that he had no need for boastful pretensions, now that he could, as his actor friends used to say, "dress the part." It was characteristic that remorse did not occur to him. His golden days went by without a shadow, and he made each as perfect as he could.

On the eighth day after his arrival in New York, he found the whole affair exploited in the Pittsburgh papers, exploited with a wealth of detail which indicated that local news of a sensational nature was at a low ebb. The firm of Denny & Carson announced that the boy's father had refunded the full amount of his theft, and that they had no intention of prosecuting. The Cumberland minister had been interviewed, and expressed his hope of yet reclaiming the motherless lad, and Paul's Sabbath-school teacher declared that she would spare no effort to that end. The rumor had reached Pittsburgh that the boy had been seen in a New York hotel, and his father had gone East to find him and bring him home.

Paul had just come in to dress for din-

ner; he sank into a chair, weak in the knees, and clasped his head in his hands. It was to be worse than jail, even; the tepid waters of Cordelia Street were to close over him finally and forever. The gray monotony stretched before him in hopeless, unrelieved years; Sabbath school, Young People's Meeting, the yellow-papered room, the damp dishtowels; it all rushed back upon him with sickening vividness. He had the old feeling that the orchestra had suddenly stopped, the sinking sensation that the play was over. The sweat broke out on his face, and he sprang to his feet, looked about him with his white, conscious smile, and winked at himself in the mirror. With something of the childish belief in miracles with which he had so often gone to class, all his lessons unlearned, Paul dressed and dashed whistling down the corridor to the elevator.

He had no sooner entered the dining room and caught the measure of the music, than his remembrance was lightened by his old elastic power of claiming the moment, mounting with it, and finding it all-sufficient. The glare and glitter about him, the mere scenic accessories had again, and for the last time, their old potency. He would show himself that he was game, he would finish the thing splendidly. He doubted, more than ever, the existence of Cordelia Street, and for the first time he drank his wine recklessly. Was he not still himself, and in his own place? He drummed a nervous accompaniment to the music and looked about him, telling himself over and over that it had paid.

He reflected drowsily, to the swell of the violin and the chill sweetness of his wine, that he might have done it more wisely. He might have caught an outbound steamer and been well out of their clutches before now. But the other side of the world had seemed too far away and too uncertain then; he could not have waited for it; his need had been too sharp. If he had to choose over again, he would do the same thing tomorrow. He looked affectionately about the dining room, now gilded with a soft mist. Ah, it had paid indeed!

Paul was awakened next morning by a painful throbbing in his head and feet. He had thrown himself across the bed without undressing, and had slept with his shoes on. His limbs and hands were lead-heavy, and his tongue and throat were parched. There came upon him one of those fateful attacks of clearheadedness that never occurred except when he was physically exhausted and his nerves hung loose. He lay still and closed his eyes and let the tide of realities wash over him.

His father was in New York; "stopping at some joint or other," he told himself. The memory of successive summers on the front stoop fell upon him like a weight of black water. He had not a hundred dollars left; and he knew now, more than ever, that money was everything, the wall that stood between all he loathed and all he wanted. The thing was winding itself up; he had thought of that on his first glorious day in New York, and had even provided a way to snap the thread. It lay on his dressing table now; he had got it out last night when he came blindly up from dinner—but the shiny metal hurt his eyes, and he disliked the look of it, anyway.

He rose and moved about with a painful effort, succumbing now and again to attacks of nausea. It was the old depression exaggerated; all the world had become Cordelia Street. Yet somehow he was not afraid of anything, was absolutely calm; perhaps because he had looked into the dark corner at last, and

knew. It was bad enough, what he saw there—but somehow not so bad as his long fear of it had been. He saw everything clearly now. He had a feeling that he had made the best of it, that he had lived the sort of life he was meant to live, and for half an hour he sat staring at the revolver. But he told himself that was not the way, so he went downstairs and took a cab to the ferry.

When Paul arrived at Newark, he got off the train and took another cab, directing the driver to follow the Pennsylvania tracks out of the town. The snow lay heavy on the roadways and had drifted deep in the open fields. Only here and there the dead grass or dried weed stalks projected, singularly black, above it. Once well into the country, Paul dismissed the carriage and walked, floundering along the tracks, his mind a medley of irrelevant things. He seemed to hold in his brain an actual picture of everything he had seen that morning. He remembered every feature of both his drivers, the toothless old woman from whom he had bought the red flowers in his coat, the agent from whom he had got his ticket, and all of his fellow passengers on the ferry. His mind, unable to cope with vital matters near at hand, worked feverishly and deftly at sorting and grouping these images. They made for him a part of the ugliness of the world, of the ache in his head, and the bitter burning on his tongue. He stopped and put a handful of snow into his mouth as he walked, but that, too, seemed hot. When he reached a little hillside where the tracks ran through a cut some twenty feet below him, he stopped and sat down.

The carnations in his coat were drooping with the cold, he noticed; all their red glory over. It occurred to him that all the flowers he had seen in the show

windows that first night must have gone the same way, long before this. It was only one splendid breath they had, in spite of their brave mockery at the winter outside the glass. It was a losing game in the end, it seemed, this revolt against the homilies [12] by which the world is run. Paul took one of the blossoms carefully from his coat and scooped a little hole in the snow, where he covered it up. Then he dozed a while, from his weak condition, seeming insensible to the cold.

The sound of an approaching train woke him, and he started to his feet, remembering only his resolution, and afraid lest he should be too late. He stood watching the approaching locomotive, his teeth chattering, his lips drawn away from them in a frightened smile; once or twice he glanced nervously sidewise, as though he were being watched. When the right moment came, he jumped. As he fell, the folly of his haste occurred to him with merciless clearness, the vastness of what he had left undone. There flashed through his brain, clearer than ever before, the blue of Adriatic water, the yellow of Algerian sands.

He felt something strike his chest— his body was being thrown swiftly through the air, on and on, immeasurably far and fast, while his limbs gently

[12] HOMILIES—Rules of conduct.

relaxed. Then, because the picture-making mechanism was crushed, the disturbing visions flashed into black, and Paul dropped back into the immense design of things.

◇◇◇◇◇◇◇◇◇◇◇◇◇◇◇◇◇◇◇◇◇◇◇◇◇◇◇◇

INTERPRETING THE FACTS
OF THE CASE

1. What clues to Paul's personality are there in the description of his dress and manner when he appeared before the faculty?

2. What specific charges did the teachers bring against Paul? Do you think the offenses named were serious enough to justify a special meeting? Which, if any, seem petty and might not necessarily mean that Paul was abnormal in any way? Which seem to you serious enough to justify the concern of the faculty?

3. Do you think the teachers were fair and objective in considering the case, or were they prejudiced? Point out passages to support your opinion.

4. How did the teachers interpret Paul's attitude and behavior during the hearing? What other interpretation is possible? For example, what besides insolence might account for the fact that he was continually smiling? Why were the teachers unhappy at the close of the hearing?

5. What did you discover about Paul after he left the school? What is revealed by his visit to the art gallery and his excitement before the concert began? In addi-

tion to the fact that he had a vivid imagination, what do you find out about Paul from his experience outside the opera singer's hotel?

6. Contrast Paul's imaginary visit to the hotel with his memory of his own home. How does the difference between the two help to explain his unhappiness? What good things might another type of person have been able to see in Paul's neighborhood, his home, and his family?

7. In view of Paul's lying and other objectionable behavior at school, do you think his father did the right thing in taking him away from his job at Carnegie Hall and forbidding him to see his theatrical friends? Can you suggest any better way of handling the situation?

8. What were the weaknesses in Paul's character that led to the tragedy of his life? How could a boy with his tastes and interests have satisfied his natural desire for beauty and refinement and still have led the life of a normal high-school student? How might he have used his imagination and his longing for a different type of life constructively?

FACING REALITY

All normal people retreat into a dream world at times to escape from the trials and frustrations of everyday life. The well-adjusted person, though he tries to improve his circumstances and environment, does not run away from reality. Sensitive people like Paul need help to see that no amount of pretending really removes the distasteful and unpleasant side of living. They need help to see that the only lasting way to make life more bearable is to find a way to make the real world more like the ideal world. The following questions will help you understand how the tragedy of Paul's case resulted from his attempt to live in his dream world and escape entirely from his real life.

1. Many sensitive boys and girls grow up in uncongenial surroundings, yet become happy, well-adjusted people. What indica-

tions are there throughout the story that Paul was abnormal in his continued refusal to accept reality?

2. All businesses have "cash boys," boys who do the routine jobs while preparing for better positions. Do you see anything significant in the statement that Paul "was interested in the triumphs of cash boys who had become famous, though he had no mind for the cash boy stage"?

3. Often those who love music or the theater have youthful ambitions to become musicians or actors. The author says of Paul: "He had no necessity to do any of these things; what he wanted was to see, to be in the atmosphere, float on the wave of it, to be carried blue league after blue league, away from everything." Why is a person with such desires bound to be disillusioned and disappointed in life?

4. You have seen what kind of dream world Paul preferred. Can you suggest how he could have been helped to make a bridge between his dream world and the real world? How could he have been helped to do something about his dreams? For example, how could he have satisfied his desires to become a part of the world of art without being an artist? How did his father and teachers hinder any adjustment along these lines? What kind of help could they have given him?

THE POINT OF VIEW

At the beginning of the story when he appears before the high school faculty, we have a chance to see Paul through the eyes of others. Most of the time, however, we look at things from Paul's viewpoint. That is, we know what Paul is seeing and feeling and thinking.

Try to imagine how this story might have been written from the point of view of one of the minor characters: the principal, one of the teachers, Paul's father, or Charley Edwards. In deciding how your viewpoint character would react to Paul's case, you will first have to determine what kind of person he or she is. Put yourself in that person's place and write Paul's story from another point of view. You may or may not choose to use the first person.

WILLA CATHER (1876–1947)

Although she was born in Virginia, Willa Cather spent her childhood in Nebraska where she grew up with the children of pioneer Germans, Scandinavians, and Bohemians. Tutored at home and steeped in the English classics, Miss Cather had no formal education until she went to high school. Later she attended the University of Nebraska and wrote regularly for the college newspaper. At various times she was an English teacher, a magazine editor, and a free-lance writer before she concentrated on writing as a career.

Although Miss Cather had absorbed the culture of two continents through her reading and travels, most of her best writing is based upon memories of her childhood. Probably her best loved novel is *My Antonia*, the story of a Bohemian immigrant girl in Nebraska. No doubt the inspiration for "Paul's Case" came from her teaching days in Pittsburgh. Another important contribution to American literature is her novel about the early missionaries in New Mexico, *Death Comes for the Archbishop*.

◇◇◇◇◇

THE GIFT OF THE MAGI

O. HENRY

The custom of giving gifts at Christmas is said to have originated with the Magi, or wise men, who carried gold, frankincense, and myrrh to the Christ Child at Bethlehem. The fact that the following story takes place on Christmas Eve is a clue to the significance of the title. However, you will have to read to the very end of the story to appreciate fully the resemblance between the Magi of long ago and a young couple in New York at the turn of the century.

One dollar and eighty-seven cents. That was all. And sixty cents of it was in pennies. Pennies saved one and two at a time by bulldozing the grocer and the vegetable man and the butcher until one's cheeks burned with silent imputation of parsimony that such close dealing implied. Three times Della counted it. One dollar and eighty-seven cents. And the next day would be Christmas.

There was clearly nothing to do but flop down on the shabby little couch and howl. So Della did it. Which instigates the moral reflection that life is made up of sobs, sniffles, and smiles, with sniffles predominating.

While the mistress of the home is gradually subsiding from the first stage to the second, take a look at the home. A furnished flat at eight dollars per week. It did not exactly beggar description, but it certainly had that word on the lookout for the mendicancy squad.

In the vestibule below was a letter box into which no letter would go, and an electric button from which no mortal finger could coax a ring. Also appertaining thereunto was a card bearing the name "Mr. James Dillingham Young."

The "Dillingham" had been flung to the breeze during a former period of prosperity when its possessor was being paid thirty dollars per week. Now, when the income was shrunk to twenty dollars, the letters of "Dillingham" looked blurred, as though they were thinking seriously of contracting to a modest and unassuming D. But whenever Mr. James Dillingham Young came home and reached his flat above, he was called "Jim" and greatly hugged by Mrs. James Dillingham Young, already introduced to you as Della. Which is all very good.

Della finished her cry and attended to her cheeks with the powder rag. She stood by the window and looked out dully at a gray cat walking a gray fence in a gray back yard. Tomorrow would be Christmas Day, and she had only one dollar and eighty-seven cents with which to buy Jim a present. She had been saving every penny she could for months, with this result. Twenty dollars a week doesn't go far. Expenses had been greater than she had calculated. They always are. Only one dollar and eighty-seven cents to buy a present for Jim. Her Jim. Many a happy hour she had spent planning something nice for him. Something fine and rare and sterling—something just a little bit near to being worthy of the honor of being owned by Jim.

There was a pier-glass [1] between the windows of the room. Perhaps you have seen a pier-glass in an eight-dollar flat. A very thin and very agile person may, by observing his reflection in a rapid se-

[1] PIER-GLASS—A long, narrow mirror.

quence of longitudinal strips, obtain a fairly accurate conception of his looks. Della, being slender, had mastered the art.

Suddenly she whirled from the window and stood before the glass. Her eyes were shining brilliantly, but her face had lost its color within twenty seconds. Rapidly she pulled down her hair and let it fall to its full length.

Now, there were two possessions of the James Dillingham Youngs in which they both took a mighty pride. One was Jim's gold watch that had been his father's and his grandfather's. The other was Della's hair. Had the Queen of Sheba lived in the flat across the airshaft, Della would have let her hair hang out the window some day to dry just to depreciate her majesty's jewels and gifts. Had King Solomon been the janitor, with all his treasures piled up in the basement, Jim would have pulled out his watch every time he passed, just to see him pluck at his beard from envy.

So now Della's beautiful hair fell about her, rippling and shining like a cascade of brown waters. It reached below her knee and made itself almost a garment for her. And then she did it up again nervously and quickly. Once she faltered for a minute and stood still while a tear or two splashed on the worn red carpet.

On went her old brown jacket; on went her old brown hat. With a whirl of skirts and with the brilliant sparkle still in her eyes she fluttered out the door and down the stairs to the street.

Where she stopped the sign read: "Mme. Sofronie. Hair Goods of All Kinds." One flight up Della ran, and collected herself, panting. Madame, large, too white, chilly, hardly looked the "Sofronie."

"Will you buy my hair?" asked Della.

"I buy hair," said Madame. "Take yer

claiming its value by substance alone and not by meretricious ornamentation—as all good things should do. It was even worthy of The Watch. As soon as she saw it she knew that it must be Jim's. It was like him. Quietness and value—the description applied to both. Twenty-one dollars they took from her for it, and she hurried home with the eighty-seven cents. With that chain on his watch Jim might be properly anxious about the time in any company. Grand as the watch was, he sometimes looked at it on the sly on account of the old leather strap that he used in place of a chain.

When Della reached home her intoxication gave way a little to prudence and reason. She got out her curling irons and lighted the gas and went to work repairing the ravages made by generosity added to love. Which is always a tremendous task, dear friends—a mammoth task.

Within forty minutes her head was covered with tiny, close-lying curls that made her look wonderfully like a truant schoolboy. She looked at her reflection in the mirror long, carefully, and critically.

"If Jim doesn't kill me," she said to herself, "before he takes a second look at me, he'll say I look like a Coney Island chorus girl. But what could I do—oh! what could I do with a dollar and eighty-seven cents?"

At seven o'clock the coffee was made and the frying pan was on the back of the stove hot and ready to cook the chops.

Jim was never late. Della doubled the fob chain in her hand and sat on the corner of the table near the door that he always entered. Then she heard his step on the stair way down on the first flight, and she turned white for just a moment. She had a habit of saying little silent

hat off and let's have a sight at the looks of it."

Down rippled the brown cascade.

"Twenty dollars," said Madame, lifting the mass with a practiced hand.

"Give it to me quick," said Della.

Oh, and the next two hours tripped by on rosy wings. Forget the hashed metaphor. She was ransacking the stores for Jim's present.

She found it at last. It surely had been made for Jim and no one else. There was no other like it in any of the stores, and she had turned all of them inside out. It was a platinum fob chain, simple and chaste in design, properly pro-

prayers about the simplest everyday things, and now she whispered: "Please, God, make him think I am still pretty."

The door opened and Jim stepped in and closed it. He looked thin and very serious. Poor fellow, he was only twenty-two—and to be burdened with a family! He needed a new overcoat and he was without gloves.

Jim stopped inside the door, as immovable as a setter at the scent of quail. His eyes were fixed upon Della, and there was an expression in them that she could not read, and it terrified her. It was not anger, nor surprise, nor disapproval, nor horror, nor any of the sentiments that she had been prepared for. He simply stared at her fixedly with that peculiar expression on his face.

Della wriggled off the table and went for him.

"Jim, darling," she cried, "don't look at me that way. I had my hair cut off and sold it because I couldn't have lived through Christmas without giving you a present. It'll grow out again—you won't mind, will you? I just had to do it. My hair grows awfully fast. Say 'Merry Christmas!' Jim, and let's be happy. You don't know what a nice—what a beautiful, nice gift I've got for you."

"You've cut off your hair?" asked Jim, laboriously, as if he had not arrived at that patent fact yet even after the hardest mental labor.

"Cut it off and sold it," said Della. "Don't you like me just as well, anyhow? I'm me without my hair, ain't I?"

Jim looked about the room curiously.

"You say your hair is gone?" he said, with an air almost of idiocy.

"You needn't look for it," said Della. "It's sold, I tell you—sold and gone, too. It's Christmas Eve, boy. Be good to me, for it went for you. Maybe the hairs of my head were numbered," she went on

with a sudden seriousness, "but nobody could ever count my love for you. Shall I put the chops on, Jim?"

Out of his trance Jim seemed quickly to wake. He enfolded his Della. For ten seconds let us regard with discreet scrutiny some inconsequential object in the other direction. Eight dollars a week or a million a year—what is the difference? A mathematician or a wit would give you the wrong answer. The Magi brought valuable gifts, but that was not among them. This dark assertion will be illuminated later on.

Jim drew a package from his overcoat pocket and threw it upon the table.

"Don't make any mistake, Della," he said, "about me. I don't think there's anything in the way of a haircut or a shave or a shampoo that could make me like my girl any less. But if you'll unwrap that package you may see why you had me going a while at first."

White fingers and nimble tore at the string and paper. And then an ecstatic scream of joy; and then, alas! a quick feminine change to hysterical tears and wails, necessitating the immediate employment of all the comforting powers of the lord of the flat.

For there lay The Combs—the set of combs, side and back, that Della had worshiped for long in a Broadway window. Beautiful combs, pure tortoise shell, with jeweled rims—just the shade to wear in the beautiful vanished hair. They were expensive combs, she knew, and her heart had simply craved and yearned over them without the least hope of possession. And now they were hers, but the tresses that should have adorned the coveted adornments were gone.

But she hugged them to her bosom, and at length she was able to look up with dim eyes and a smile and say: "My hair grows so fast, Jim!"

And then Della leaped up like a little singed cat and cried, "Oh, oh!"

Jim had not yet seen his beautiful present. She held it out to him eagerly upon her open palm. The dull precious metal seemed to flash with a reflection of her bright and ardent spirit.

"Isn't it a dandy, Jim? I hunted all over town to find it. You'll have to look at the time a hundred times a day now. Give me your watch. I want to see how it looks on it."

Instead of obeying, Jim tumbled down on the couch and put his hands under the back of his head and smiled.

"Della," said he, "let's put our Christmas presents away and keep 'em a while. They're too nice to use just at present. I sold the watch to get the money to buy your combs. And now suppose you put the chops on."

The Magi, as you know, were wise men —wonderfully wise men—who brought gifts to the Babe in the manger. They invented the art of giving Christmas presents. Being wise, their gifts were no doubt wise ones, possibly bearing the privilege of exchange in case of duplication. And here I have lamely related to you the uneventful chronicle of two foolish children in a flat who most unwisely sacrificed for each other the greatest treasures of their house. But in a last word to the wise of these days let it be said that of all who give gifts these two were the wisest. Of all who give and receive gifts, such as they are wisest. Everywhere they are wisest. They are the Magi.

◇◇◇◇◇◇◇◇◇◇◇◇◇◇◇◇◇◇◇◇◇◇◇◇◇◇◇◇◇

THE GIFT AND THE GIVER

1. What details date this story so that you know that it could not have happened recently? On the other hand, explain how the central idea or theme is not dated and could apply to people at any time. What might a present-day Della and Jim sacrifice for each other?

2. Under the circumstances do you think the Youngs should have given each other more practical gifts? For example, Della might have given Jim a pair of gloves. In your opinion, what should one consider in giving and receiving gifts?

3. In what way can the Magi's gift of gold, frankincense, and myrrh be compared to the watch chain and the combs? Tell why you do or do not agree with the author when he says, ". . . of all who give gifts these two were the wisest."

4. How does the author's style of writing contribute to the humor of the story? For example, instead of stating simply that the Youngs were not as well off financially as they once had been, he makes a humorous comparison between their reduced circumstances and the blurred appearance of the "Dillingham" in their name on the letter box. Find another example of the same type of humor.

THE SURPRISE ENDING

"The Gift of the Magi" is a good example of the surprise-ending story which made O. Henry famous. In this type of story the plot is more important than character development. In order to produce a clever ending the author sometimes manipulates characters and events in an unnatural way. The result, particularly in less skillful hands than O. Henry's, is often artificial, or *contrived*.

1. How do Della's actions at the beginning of the story, the description of the flat, and the dreary view from the window help to make the outcome of the story seem believable? What reason can you see for mentioning the card on the letter box? Does it throw any light on the Youngs which might help to explain their buying expensive gifts for each other later on?

2. The author began early in the story to make the surprise at the end seem right

and logical. Show how his description of the length and beauty of Della's hair serves a double purpose in the development of the plot. How does that passage account for Jim's gift as well as make Della's possible?

USING WORDS EFFECTIVELY

1. O. Henry was fond of using high-sounding words. Test your knowledge of the italicized words in the following phrases from the story by substituting for each an appropriate common synonym.

  a. silent *imputation* of *parsimony*
  b. the *mendicancy* squad
  c. *appertaining thereunto* was a card
  d. not by *meretricious ornamentation*

How did your rephrasing change the tone or flavor of the passage? Can you see any reason for the use of such pretentious words in telling a simple story like "The Gift of the Magi"?

2. A metaphor is a figure of speech in which a comparison between two unlike things is suggested or implied without the use of the words *like* or *as*. Sometimes speakers and writers produce humor unintentionally when they become entangled in their metaphors. Here, O. Henry purposely used a mixed or, as he expressed it, *hashed* metaphor. To dramatize how quickly time passed for Della he said: "Oh, and the next two hours tripped by on rosy wings." Obviously, *tripped* and *wings* do not belong together. In what two ways can this metaphor be straightened out? Find in the story at least one example of effective use of figurative language, either simile or metaphor.

O. HENRY (1862–1910)

The life of William Sydney Porter, who in prison took the name of O. Henry, was spiced with the ironic twists he doted on in his own stories. Born in Greensboro, North Carolina, he left school at fifteen to work in a drugstore. Later he went to Texas where he became a teller in an Austin bank. When an examiner discovered irregularities in the records, Porter foolishly fled to South America. Hearing that his wife was dying, he returned to Austin, stood trial for embezzlement, and was sentenced to a term in prison. Actually he seems not to have been guilty of fraud but of careless bookkeeping. It was in prison that he began writing short stories.

Upon his release he went to New York where he agreed to a contract with the *New York World* for a story a week at a hundred dollars a story. Then began his eternal struggle with editors, for O. Henry was notorious for his late copy, waiting until the last possible moment before submitting his "propitiatory fragments" as he called them. Although he wrote more than six hundred pieces in his writing career, his stories with a New York background have been most successful. Some of the best are contained in *The Four Million*. At forty-seven he died of tuberculosis, the disease that had threatened him since boyhood.

O. Henry was a master of the art of surprise and is quoted as having given this formula for writing stories: "Be concise and familiar, and punch when your adversary is off guard. This stuns him, and you may then disappear."

FLIGHT

JOHN STEINBECK

One day Pepé was a simple, carefree boy on his mother's farm; the next, he was a man fleeing for his life in a hostile mountain wilderness. Here, as in most of John Steinbeck's writing, you will find a realistic but sympathetic treatment of America's poor and lowly. You will also get a vivid picture of the mountain country in the section of California near Monterey, where the author was born.

About fifteen miles below Monterey, on the wild coast, the Torres family had their farm, a few sloping acres above a cliff that dropped to the brown reefs and to the hissing white waters of the ocean. Behind the farm the stone mountains stood up against the sky. The farm buildings huddled like little clinging aphids [1] on the mountain skirts, crouched low to the ground as though the wind might blow them into the sea. The little shack, the rattling, rotting barn were gray-bitten with sea salt, beaten by the damp wind until they had taken on the color of the granite hills. Two horses, a red cow and a red calf, half a dozen pigs, and a flock of lean, multi-colored chickens stocked the place. A little corn was raised on the sterile slope, and it grew short and thick under the wind, and all the cobs formed on the landward sides of the stalks.

Mama Torres, a lean, dry woman with ancient eyes, had ruled the farm for ten years, ever since her husband tripped over a stone in the field one day and fell full length on a rattlesnake. When one is bitten on the chest there is not much that can be done.

Mama Torres had three children, two undersized black ones of twelve and fourteen, Emilio and Rosy, whom Mama kept fishing on the rocks below the farm when the sea was kind and when the truant officer was in some distant part of Monterey County. And there was Pepé,[2] the tall smiling son of nineteen, a gentle, affectionate boy, but very lazy. Pepé had a tall head, pointed at the top, and from its peak, coarse black hair grew down like a thatch all around. Over his smiling little eyes Mama cut a straight bang so he could see. Pepé had sharp Indian cheek bones and an eagle nose, but his mouth was as sweet and shapely as a girl's mouth, and his chin was fragile and chiseled. He was loose and gangling, all legs and feet and wrists, and he was very lazy. Mama thought him fine and brave, but she never told him so. She said, "Some lazy cow must have got into thy father's family, else how could I have a son like thee." And she said, "When I carried thee, a sneaking lazy coyote came out of the brush and looked at me one day. That must have made thee so."

Pepé smiled sheepishly and stabbed at the ground with his knife to keep the blade sharp and free from rust. It was his inheritance, that knife, his father's

[1] APHIDS ($\bar{a}'$fĭdz)—A kind of plant insect.

[2] PEPÉ—Pronounced pā·pā'.

knife. The long heavy blade folded back into the black handle. There was a button on the handle. When Pepé pressed the button, the blade leaped out ready for use. The knife was with Pepé always, for it had been his father's knife.

One sunny morning when the sea below the cliff was glinting and blue and the white surf creamed on the reef, when even the stone mountains looked kindly, Mama Torres called out the door of the shack, "Pepé, I have a labor for thee."

There was no answer. Mama listened. From behind the barn she heard a burst of laughter. She lifted her full long skirt and walked in the direction of the noise.

Pepé was sitting on the ground with his back against a box. His white teeth glistened. On either side of him stood the two black ones, tense and expectant. Fifteen feet away a redwood post was set in the ground. Pepé's right hand lay limply in his lap, and in the palm the big black knife rested. The blade was closed back into the handle. Pepé looked smiling at the sky.

Suddenly Emilio cried, "Ya!"

Pepé's wrist flicked like the head of a snake. The blade seemed to fly open in mid-air, and with a thump the point dug into the redwood post, and the black handle quivered. The three burst into excited laughter. Rosy ran to the post and pulled out the knife and brought it back to Pepé. He closed the blade and settled the knife carefully in his listless palm again. He grinned self-consciously at the sky.

"Ya!"

The heavy knife lanced out and sunk into the post again. Mama moved forward like a ship and scattered the play.

"All day you do foolish things with the knife, like a toy-baby," she stormed. "Get up on thy huge feet that eat up shoes. Get up!" She took him by one loose shoulder and hoisted at him. Pepé grinned sheepishly and came halfheartedly to his feet. "Look!" Mama cried. "Big lazy, you must catch the horse and put on him thy father's saddle. You must ride to Monterey. The medicine bottle is empty. There is no salt. Go thou now. Peanut! Catch the horse."

A revolution took place in the relaxed figure of Pepé. "To Monterey, me? Alone? Sí,[3] Mama."

She scowled at him. "Do not think, big sheep, that you will buy candy. No, I will give you only enough for the medicine and the salt."

Pepé smiled. "Mama, you will put the hatband on the hat?"

She relented then. "Yes, Pepé. You may wear the hatband."

His voice grew insinuating, "And the green handkerchief, Mama?"

"Yes, if you go quickly and return with no trouble, the silk handkerchief will go. If you make sure to take off the handkerchief when you eat so no spot may fall on it. . . ."

"Sí, Mama. I will be careful. I am a man."

"Thou? A man? Thou art a peanut."

He went into the rickety barn and brought out a rope, and he walked agilely enough up the hill to catch the horse.

When he was ready and mounted before the door, mounted on his father's saddle that was so old that the oaken frame showed through torn leather in many places, then Mama brought out the round black hat with the tooled leather band, and she reached up and knotted the green silk handkerchief about his neck. Pepé's blue denim coat was much darker than his jeans, for it had been washed much less often.

Mama handed up the big medicine bottle and the silver coins. "That for

[3] *Sí* (sē)—Spanish for *yes*.

the medicine," she said, "and that for the salt. That for a candle to burn for the papa. That for *dulces*[4] for the little ones. Our friend Mrs. Rodriguez[5] will give you dinner and maybe a bed for the night. When you go to the church say only Paternosters and only twenty-five Ave Marias.[6] Oh! I know, big coyote. You would sit there flapping your mouth over Aves all day while you looked at the candles and the holy pictures. That is not good devotion to stare at the pretty things."

The black hat, covering the high pointed head and black thatched hair of Pepé, gave him dignity and age. He sat the rangy horse well. Mama thought

how handsome he was, dark and lean and tall. "I would not send thee now alone, thou little one, except for the medicine," she said softly. "It is not good to have no medicine, for who knows when the toothache will come, or the sadness of the stomach. These things are."

"Adiós, Mama," Pepé cried. "I will come back soon. You may send me often alone. I am a man."

"Thou art a foolish chicken."

He straightened his shoulders, flipped the reins against the horse's shoulder and rode away. He turned once and saw that they still watched him, Emilio and Rosy and Mama. Pepé grinned with pride and gladness and lifted the tough buckskin horse to trot.

When he had dropped out of sight over a little dip in the road, Mama turned to the black ones, but she spoke

[4] *Dulces* (dōōl′säs)—Sweets.
[5] RODRIGUEZ—Pronounced rô·drĕ′gäs.
[6] PATERNOSTERS . . . AVE MARIAS. The first is Latin for Our Father, the opening words of the Lord's Prayer; the second refers to the prayers to the Virgin Mary.

to herself. "He is nearly a man now," she said. "It will be a nice thing to have a man in the house again." Her eyes sharpened on the children. "Go to the rocks now. The tide is going out. There will be abalones [7] to be found." She put the iron hooks into their hands and saw them down the steep trail to the reefs. She brought the smooth stone *metate* [8] to the doorway and sat grinding her corn to flour and looking occasionally at the road over which Pepé had gone. The noonday came and then the afternoon, when the little ones beat the abalones on a rock to make them tender and Mama patted the tortillas to make them thin. They ate their dinner as the red sun was plunging down toward the ocean. They sat on the doorsteps and watched the big white moon come over the mountain-tops.

Mama said, "He is now at the house of our friend Mrs. Rodriguez. She will give him nice things to eat and maybe a present."

Emilio said, "Some day I too will ride to Monterey for medicine. Did Pepé come to be a man today?"

Mama said wisely, "A boy gets to be a man when a man is needed. Remember this thing. I have known boys forty years old because there was no need for a man."

Soon afterwards they retired, Mama in her big oak bed on one side of the room, Emilio and Rosy in their boxes full of straw and sheepskins on the other side of the room.

The moon went over the sky and the surf roared on the rocks. The roosters crowed the first call. The surf subsided to a whispering surge against the reef. The moon dropped toward the sea. The roosters crowed again.

[7] ABALONES (ăb′á·lō′nēz)—Shellfish.
[8] *Metate*—Pronounced mâ·tä′tä.

The moon was near down to the water when Pepé rode on a winded horse to his home flat. His dog bounced out and circled the horse yelping with pleasure. Pepé slid off the saddle to the ground. The weathered little shack was silver in the moonlight and the square shadow of it was black to the north and east. Against the east the piling mountains were misty with light; their tops melted into the sky.

Pepé walked wearily up the three steps and into the house. It was dark inside. There was a rustle in the corner.

Mama cried out from her bed. "Who comes? Pepé, is it thou?"

"Sí, Mama."

"Did you get the medicine?"

"Sí, Mama."

"Well, go to sleep, then. I thought you would be sleeping at the house of Mrs. Rodriguez." Pepé stood silently in the dark room. "Why do you stand there, Pepé? Did you drink wine?"

"Sí, Mama."

"Well, go to bed then and sleep out the wine."

His voice was tired and patient, but very firm. "Light the candle, Mama. I must go away into the mountains."

"What is this, Pepé? You are crazy." Mama struck a sulphur match and held the little blue burr until the flame spread up the stick. She set light to the candle on the floor beside her bed. "Now, Pepé, what is this you say?" She looked anxiously into his face.

He was changed. The fragile quality seemed to have gone from his chin. His mouth was less full than it had been, the lines of the lips were straighter, but in his eyes the greatest change had taken place. There was no laughter in them any more, nor any bashfulness. They were sharp and bright and purposeful.

He told her in a tired monotone, told

her everything just as it had happened. A few people came into the kitchen of Mrs. Rodriguez. There was wine to drink. Pepé drank wine. The little quarrel—the man started toward Pepé and then the knife—it went almost by itself. It flew, it darted before Pepé knew it. As he talked, Mama's face grew stern, and it seemed to grow more lean. Pepé finished. "I am a man now, Mama. The man said names to me I could not allow."

Mama nodded. "Yes, thou art a man, my poor little Pepé. Thou art a man. I have seen it coming on thee. I have watched you throwing the knife into the post, and I have been afraid." For a moment her face had softened, but now it grew stern again. "Come! We must get you ready. Go. Awaken Emilio and Rosy. Go quickly."

Pepé stepped over to the corner where his brother and sister slept among the sheepskins. He leaned down and shook them gently. "Come, Rosy! Come, Emilio! The mama says you must arise."

The little black ones sat up and rubbed their eyes in the candlelight. Mama was out of bed now, her long black skirt over her nightgown. "Emilio," she cried. "Go up and catch the other horse for Pepé. Quickly, now! Quickly." Emilio put his legs in his overalls and stumbled sleepily out the door.

"You heard no one behind you on the road?" Mama demanded.

"No, Mama. I listened carefully. No one was on the road."

Mama darted like a bird about the room. From a nail on the wall she took a canvas water bag and threw it on the floor. She stripped a blanket from her bed and rolled it into a tight tube and tied the ends with string. From a box beside the stove she lifted a flour sack half full of black stringy jerky.[9] "Your father's black coat, Pepé. Here, put it on."

Pepé stood in the middle of the floor watching her activity. She reached behind the door and brought out the rifle, a long 38–56, worn shiny the whole length of the barrel. Pepé took it from her and held it in the crook of his elbow. Mama brought a little leather bag and counted the cartridges into his hand. "Only ten left," she warned. "You must not waste them."

Emilio put his head in the door. "'Qui 'st 'l caballo,[10] Mama."

"Put on the saddle from the other horse. Tie on the blanket. Here, tie the jerky to the saddle horn."

Still Pepé stood silently watching his mother's frantic activity. His chin looked hard, and his sweet mouth was drawn and thin. His little eyes followed Mama about the room almost suspiciously.

Rosy asked softly, "Where goes Pepé?"

Mama's eyes were fierce. "Pepé goes on a journey. Pepé is a man now. He has a man's thing to do."

Pepé straightened his shoulders. His mouth changed until he looked very much like Mama.

At last the preparation was finished. The loaded horse stood outside the door. The water bag dripped a line of moisture down the bay shoulder.

The moonlight was being thinned by the dawn and the big white moon was near down to the sea. The family stood by the shack. Mama confronted Pepé. "Look, my son! Do not stop until it is dark again. Do not sleep even though you are tired. Take care of the horse in order that he may not stop of weariness.

---

[9] JERKY—Dried beef.
[10] 'Qui 'st 'l caballo (kēst'l kä·bä'yō)—Here is the horse.

Remember to be careful with the bullets —there are only ten. Do not fill thy stomach with jerky or it will make thee sick. Eat a little jerky and fill thy stomach with grass. When thou comest to the high mountains, if thou seest any of the dark watching men, go not near to them nor try to speak to them. And forget not thy prayers." She put her lean hands on Pepé's shoulders, stood on her toes and kissed him formally on both cheeks, and Pepé kissed her on both cheeks. Then he went to Emilio and Rosy and kissed both of their cheeks.

Pepé turned back to Mama. He seemed to look for a little softness, a little weakness in her. His eyes were searching, but Mama's face remained fierce. "Go now," she said. "Do not wait to be caught like a chicken."

Pepé pulled himself into the saddle. "I am a man," he said.

It was the first dawn when he rode up the hill toward the little canyon which let a trail into the mountains. Moonlight and daylight fought with each other, and the two warring qualities made it difficult to see. Before Pepé had gone a hundred yards, the outlines of his figure were misty; and long before he entered the canyon, he had become a gray, indefinite shadow.

Mama stood stiffly in front of her doorstep, and on either side of her stood Emilio and Rosy. They cast furtive glances at Mama now and then.

When the gray shape of Pepé melted into the hillside and disappeared, Mama relaxed. She began the high, whining keen [11] of the death wail. "Our beautiful—our brave," she cried. "Our protector, our son is gone." Emilio and Rosy moaned beside her. "Our beautiful— our brave, he is gone." It was the formal wail. It rose to a high piercing whine

[11] KEEN—A wailing dirge for the dead.

and subsided to a moan. Mama raised it three times and then she turned and went into the house and shut the door.

Emilio and Rosy stood wondering in the dawn. They heard Mama whimpering in the house. They went out to sit on the cliff above the ocean. They touched shoulders. "When did Pepé come to be a man?" Emilio asked.

"Last night," said Rosy. "Last night in Monterey." The ocean clouds turned red with the sun that was behind the mountains.

"We will have no breakfast," said Emilio. "Mama will not want to cook." Rosy did not answer him. "Where is Pepé gone?" he asked.

Rosy looked around at him. She drew her knowledge from the quiet air. "He has gone on a journey. He will never come back."

"Is he dead? Do you think he is dead?"

Rosy looked back at the ocean again. A little steamer, drawing a line of smoke sat on the edge of the horizon. "He is not dead," Rosy explained. "Not yet."

Pepé rested the big rifle across the saddle in front of him. He let the horse walk up the hill and he didn't look back. The stony slope took on a coat of short brush so that Pepé found the entrance to a trail and entered it.

When he came to the canyon opening, he swung once in his saddle and looked back, but the houses were swallowed in the misty light. Pepé jerked forward again. The high shoulder of the canyon closed in on him. His horse stretched out its neck and sighed and settled to the trail.

It was a well-worn path, dark soft leaf-mold earth strewn with broken pieces of sandstone. The trail rounded the shoulder of the canyon and dropped steeply into the bed of the stream. In the shallows the water ran smoothly, glinting in the first morning sun. Small round stones on the bottom were as brown as rust with sun moss. In the sand along the edges of the stream the tall, rich wild mint grew, while in the water itself the cress, old and tough, had gone to heavy seed.

The path went into the stream and emerged on the other side. The horse sloshed into the water and stopped. Pepé dropped his bridle and let the beast drink of the running water.

Soon the canyon sides became steep and the first giant sentinel redwoods guarded the trail, great round red trunks bearing foliage as green and lacy as ferns. Once Pepé was among the trees, the sun was lost. A perfumed and purple light lay in the pale green of the underbrush. Gooseberry bushes and blackberries and tall ferns lined the stream, and overhead the branches of the redwoods met and cut off the sky.

Pepé drank from the water bag, and he reached into the flour sack and brought out a black string of jerky. His white teeth gnawed at the string until the tough meat parted. He chewed slowly and drank occasionally from the water bag. His little eyes were slumberous and tired, but the muscles of his face were hard set. The earth of the trail was black now. It gave up a hollow sound under the walking hoofbeats.

The stream fell more sharply. Little waterfalls splashed on the stones. Five-fingered ferns hung over the water and dripped spray from their finger tips. Pepé rode half over in his saddle, dangling one leg loosely. He picked a bay leaf from a tree beside the way and put it into his mouth for a moment to flavor the dry jerky. He held the gun loosely across the pommel.

Suddenly he squared in his saddle, swung the horse from the trail and kicked it hurriedly up behind a big redwood tree. He pulled up the reins tight against the bit to keep the horse from whinnying. His face was intent and his nostrils quivered a little.

A hollow pounding came down the trail, and a horseman rode by, a fat man with red cheeks and a white stubble beard. His horse put down its head and blubbered at the trail when it came to the place where Pepé had turned off. "Hold up!" said the man and he pulled up his horse's head.

When the last sound of the hoofs died away, Pepé came back into the trail again. He did not relax in the saddle any more. He lifted the big rifle and swung the lever to throw a shell into the chamber, and then he let down the hammer to half cock.

The trail grew very steep. Now the redwood trees were smaller and their tops were dead, bitten dead where the wind reached them. The horse plodded on; the sun went slowly overhead and started down toward the afternoon.

Where the stream came out of a side canyon, the trail left it. Pepé dismounted and watered his horse and filled up his water bag. As soon as the trail had parted from the stream, the trees were gone and only the thick brittle sage and manzanita and chaparral edged the trail. And the soft black earth was gone, too, leaving only the light tan broken rock for the trail bed. Lizards scampered away into the brush as the horse rattled over the little stones.

Pepé turned in his saddle and looked back. He was in the open now: he could be seen from a distance. As he ascended the trail the country grew more rough and terrible and dry. The way wound about the bases of great square rocks.

Little gray rabbits skittered in the brush. A bird made a monotonous high creaking. Eastward the bare rock mountaintops were pale and powder-dry under the dropping sun. The horse plodded up and up the trail toward a little V in the ridge which was the pass.

Pepé looked suspiciously back every minute or so, and his eyes sought the tops of the ridges ahead. Once on a white barren spur, he saw a black figure for a moment, but he looked quickly away, for it was one of the dark watchers. No one knew who the watchers were, nor where they lived, but it was better to ignore them and never to show interest in them. They did not bother one who stayed on the trail and minded his own business.

The air was parched and full of light dust blown by the breeze from the eroding mountains. Pepé drank sparingly from his bag and corked it tightly and hung it on the horn again. The trail moved up the dry shale hillside, avoiding rocks, dropping under clefts, climbing in and out of old water scars. When he arrived at the little pass he stopped and looked back for a long time. No dark watchers were to be seen now. The trail behind was empty. Only the high tops of the redwoods indicated where the stream flowed.

Pepé rode on through the pass. His little eyes were nearly closed with weariness, but his face was stern, relentless and manly. The high mountain wind coasted sighing through the pass and whistled on the edges of the big blocks of broken granite. In the air, a red-tailed hawk sailed over close to the ridge and screamed angrily. Pepé went slowly through the broken jagged pass and looked down on the other side.

The trail dropped quickly, staggering among broken rock. At the bottom of the slope there was a dark crease, thick with brush, and on the other side of the crease a little flat, in which a grove of oak trees grew. A scar of green grass cut across the flat. And behind the flat another mountain rose, desolate with dead rocks and starving little black bushes. Pepé drank from the bag again for the air was so dry that it encrusted his nostrils and burned his lips. He put the horse down the trail. The hoofs slipped and struggled on the steep way, starting little stones that rolled off into the brush. The sun was gone behind the westward mountain now, but still it glowed brilliantly on the oaks and on the grassy flat. The rocks and the hillsides still sent up waves of the heat they had gathered from the day's sun.

Pepé looked up to the top of the next dry withered ridge. He saw a dark form against the sky, a man's figure standing on top of a rock, and he glanced away quickly not to appear curious. When a moment later he looked up again, the figure was gone.

Downward the trail was quickly covered. Sometimes the horse floundered for footing, sometimes set his feet and slid a little way. They came at last to the bottom where the dark chaparral was higher than Pepé's head. He held up his rifle on one side and his arm on the other to shield his face from the sharp brittle fingers of the brush.

Up and out of the crease he rode, and up a little cliff. The grassy flat was before him, and the round comfortable oaks. For a moment he studied the trail down which he had come, but there was no movement and no sound from it. Finally he rode out over the flat, to the green streak, and at the upper end of the damp he found a little spring welling out of the earth and dropping into a dug basin before it seeped out over the flat.

Pepé filled his bag first, and then he let the thirsty horse drink out of the pool. He led the horse to the clump of oaks, and in the middle of the grove, fairly protected from sight on all sides, he took off the saddle and the bridle and laid them on the ground. The horse stretched his jaws sideways and yawned. Pepé knotted the lead rope about the horse's neck and tied him to a sapling among the oaks, where he could graze in a fairly large circle.

When the horse was gnawing hungrily at the dry grass, Pepé went to the saddle and took a black string of jerky from the sack and strolled to an oak tree on the edge of the grove, from under which he could watch the trail. He sat down in the crisp dry oak leaves and automatically felt for his big black knife to cut the jerky, but he had no knife. He leaned back on his elbow and gnawed at the tough strong meat. His face was blank, but it was a man's face.

The bright evening light washed the eastern ridge, but the valley was darkening. Doves flew down from the hills to the spring, and the quail came running out of the brush and joined them, calling clearly to one another.

Out of the corner of his eye Pepé saw a shadow grow out of the bushy crease. He turned his head slowly. A big spotted wildcat was creeping toward the spring, belly to the ground, moving like thought.

Pepé cocked his rifle and edged the muzzle slowly around. Then he looked apprehensively up the trail and dropped the hammer again. From the ground beside him he picked an oak twig and threw it toward the spring. The quail flew up with a roar and the doves whistled away. The big cat stood up: for a long moment he looked at Pepé with cold yellow eyes, and then fearlessly walked back into the gulch.

The dusk gathered quickly in the deep valley. Pepé muttered his prayers, put his head down on his arm and went instantly to sleep.

The moon came up and filled the valley with cold blue light, and the wind swept rustling down from the peaks. The owls worked up and down the slopes looking for rabbits. Down in the brush of the gulch a coyote gabbled. The oak trees whispered softly in the night breeze.

Pepé started up, listening. His horse had whinnied. The moon was just slipping behind the western ridge, leaving the valley in darkness behind it. Pepé sat tensely gripping his rifle. From far up the trail he heard an answering whinny and the crash of shod hoofs on the broken rock. He jumped to his feet, ran to his horse and led it under the trees. He threw on the saddle and cinched it tight for the steep trail, caught the unwilling head and forced the bit into the mouth. He felt the saddle to make sure the water bag and the sack of jerky were there. Then he mounted and turned up the hill.

It was velvet dark. The horse found the entrance to the trail where it left the flat, and started up, stumbling and slipping on the rocks. Pepé's hand rose up to his head. His hat was gone. He had left it under the oak tree.

The horse had struggled far up the trail when the first change of dawn came into the air, a steel grayness as light mixed thoroughly with dark. Gradually the sharp snaggled edge of the ridge stood out above them, rotten granite tortured and eaten by the winds of time. Pepé had dropped his reins on the horn, leaving direction to the horse. The brush grabbed at his legs in the dark until one knee of his jeans was ripped.

Gradually the light flowed down over

the ridge. The starved brush and rocks stood out in the half light, strange and lonely in high perspective. Then there came warmth into the light. Pepé drew up and looked back, but he could see nothing in the darker valley below. The sky turned blue over the coming sun. In the waste of the mountainside, the poor dry brush grew only three feet high. Here and there, big outcroppings of unrotted granite stood up like moldering houses. Pepé relaxed a little. He drank from his water bag and bit off a piece of jerky. A single eagle flew over, high in the light.

Without warning Pepé's horse screamed and fell on its side. He was almost down before the rifle crash echoed up from the valley. From a hole behind the struggling shoulder, a stream of bright crimson blood pumped and stopped and pumped and stopped. The

hoofs threshed on the ground. Pepé lay half stunned beside the horse. He looked slowly down the hill. A piece of sage clipped off beside his head and another crash echoed up from side to side of the canyon. Pepé flung himself frantically behind a bush.

He crawled up the hill on his knees and one hand. His right hand held the rifle up off the ground and pushed it ahead of him. He moved with the instinctive care of an animal. Rapidly he wormed his way toward one of the big outcroppings of granite on the hill above him. Where the brush was high he doubled up and ran, but where the cover was slight he wriggled forward on his stomach, pushing the rifle ahead of him. In the last little distance there was no cover at all. Pepé poised and then he darted across the space and flashed around the corner of the rock.

72

He leaned panting against the stone. When his breath came easier he moved along behind the big rock until he came to a narrow split that offered a thin section of vision down the hill. Pepé lay on his stomach and pushed the rifle barrel through the slit and waited.

The sun reddened the western ridges now. Already the buzzards were settling down toward the place where the horse lay. A small brown bird scratched in the dead sage leaves directly in front of the rifle muzzle. The coasting eagle flew back toward the rising sun.

Pepé saw a little movement in the brush far below. His grip tightened on the gun. A little brown doe stepped daintily out on the trail and crossed it and disappeared into the brush again. For a long time Pepé waited. Far below he could see the little flat and the oak trees and the slash of green. Suddenly his eyes flashed back at the trail again. A quarter of a mile down there had been a quick movement in the chaparral. The rifle swung over. The front sight nestled in the V of the rear sight. Pepé studied for a moment and then raised the rear sight a notch. The little movement in the brush came again. The sight settled on it. Pepé squeezed the trigger. The explosion crashed down the mountain and up the other side, and came rattling back. The whole side of the slope grew still. No more movement. And then a white streak cut into the granite of the slit and a bullet whined away and a crash sounded up from below. Pepé felt a sharp pain in his right hand. A sliver of granite was sticking out from between his first and second knuckles and the point protruded from his palm. Carefully he pulled out the sliver of stone. The wound bled evenly and gently. No vein nor artery was cut.

Pepé looked into a little dusty cave in the rock and gathered a handful of spider web, and he pressed the mass into the cut, plastering the soft web into the blood. The flow stopped almost at once.

The rifle was on the ground. Pepé picked it up, levered a new shell into the chamber. And then he slid into the brush on his stomach. Far to the right he crawled, and then up the hill, moving slowly and carefully, crawling to cover and resting and then crawling again.

In the mountains the sun is high in its arc before it penetrates the gorges. The hot face looked over the hill and brought instant heat with it. The white light beat on the rocks and reflected from them and rose up quivering from the earth again, and the rocks and bushes seemed to quiver behind the air.

Pepé crawled in the general direction of the ridge peak, zigzagging for cover. The deep cut between his knuckles began to throb. He crawled close to a rattlesnake before he saw it, and when it raised its dry head and made a soft beginning whirr, he backed up and took another way. The quick gray lizards flashed in front of him, raising a tiny line of dust. He found another mass of spider web and pressed it against his throbbing hand.

Pepé was pushing the rifle with his left hand now. Little drops of sweat ran to the ends of his coarse black hair and rolled down his cheeks. His lips and tongue were growing thick and heavy. His lips writhed to draw saliva into his mouth. His little dark eyes were uneasy and suspicious. Once when a gray lizard paused in front of him on the parched ground and turned its head sideways he crushed it flat with a stone.

When the sun slid past noon he had not gone a mile. He crawled exhaustedly a last hundred yards to a patch of high sharp manzanita, crawled desperately, and when the patch was reached he wriggled in among the tough gnarly trunks and dropped his head on his left arm. There was little shade in the meager brush, but there was cover and safety. Pepé went to sleep as he lay and the sun beat on his back. A few little birds hopped close to him and peered and hopped away. Pepé squirmed in his sleep, and he raised and dropped his wounded hand again and again.

The sun went down behind the peaks and the cool evening came, and then the dark. A coyote yelled from the hillside, Pepé started awake and looked about with misty eyes. His hand was swollen and heavy; a little thread of pain ran up the inside of his arm and settled in a pocket in his armpit. He peered about and then stood up, for the mountains were black and the moon had not yet risen. Pepé stood up in the dark. The coat of his father pressed on his arm. His tongue was swollen until it nearly filled his mouth. He wriggled out of the coat and dropped it in the brush, and then he struggled up the hill, falling over rocks and tearing his way through the brush. The rifle knocked against stones as he went. Little dry avalanches of gravel and shattered stone went whispering down the hill behind him.

After a while the old moon came up and showed the jagged ridgetop ahead of him. By moonlight Pepé traveled more easily. He bent forward so that his throbbing arm hung away from his body. The journey uphill was made in dashes and rests, a frantic rush up a few yards and then a rest. The wind coasted down the slope rattling the dry stems of the bushes.

The moon was at meridian when Pepé came at last to the sharp backbone of the ridgetop. On the last hundred yards of the rise no soil had clung under the wearing winds. The way was on solid rock. He clambered to the top and looked down on the other side. There was a draw like the last below him, misty with moonlight, brushed with dry struggling sage and chaparral. On the other side the hill rose up sharply and at the top the jagged rotten teeth of the mountain showed against the sky. At the bottom of the cut the brush was thick and dark.

Pepé stumbled down the hill. His throat was almost closed with thirst. At first he tried to run, but immediately he fell and rolled. After that he went more carefully. The moon was just disappearing behind the mountains when he came to the bottom. He crawled into the heavy brush feeling with his fingers for water. There was no water in the bed of the stream, only damp earth. Pepé laid his gun down and scooped up a handful of mud and put it in his mouth, and then he spluttered and scraped the earth from his tongue with his finger, for the mud drew at his mouth like a poultice. He dug a hole in the stream bed with his fingers, dug a little basin to catch water; but before it was very deep his head fell forward on the damp ground and he slept.

The dawn came and the heat of the day fell on the earth, and still Pepé slept. Late in the afternoon his head jerked up. He looked slowly around. His eyes were slits of wariness. Twenty feet away in the heavy brush a big tawny mountain lion stood looking at him. Its long thick tail waved gracefully, its ears were erect with interest, not laid back dangerously. The lion squatted down on its stomach and watched him.

Pepé looked at the hole he had dug in the earth. A half inch of muddy water had collected in the bottom. He tore the sleeve from his hurt arm, with his teeth ripped out a little square, soaked it in the water and put it in his mouth. Over and over he filled the cloth and sucked it.

Still the lion sat and watched him. The evening came down but there was no movement on the hills. No birds visited the dry bottom of the cut. Pepé looked occasionally at the lion. The eyes of the yellow beast drooped as though he were about to sleep. He yawned and his long thin red tongue curled out. Suddenly his head jerked around and his nostrils quivered. His big tail lashed. He stood up and slunk like a tawny shadow into the thick brush.

A moment later Pepé heard the sound, the faint far crash of horses' hoofs on gravel. And he heard something else, a high whining yelp of a dog.

Pepé took his rifle in his left hand and he glided into the brush almost as quietly as the lion had. In the darkening evening he crouched up the hill toward the next ridge. Only when the dark came did he stand up. His energy was short. Once it was dark he fell over the rocks and slipped to his knees on the steep slope, but he moved on and on up the hill, climbing and scrabbling over the broken hillside.

When he was far up toward the top, he lay down and slept for a little while. The withered moon, shining on his face, awakened him. He stood up and moved up the hill. Fifty yards away he stopped and turned back, for he had forgotten his rifle. He walked heavily down and poked about in the brush, but he could not find his gun. At last he lay down to rest. The pocket of pain in his armpit had grown more sharp. His arm seemed to swell out and fall with every heartbeat. There was no position lying down

where the heavy arm did not press against his armpit.

With the effort of a hurt beast, Pepé got up and moved again toward the top of the ridge. He held up his swollen arm away from his body with his left hand. Up the steep hill he dragged himself, a few steps and a rest, and a few more steps. At last he was nearing the top. The moon showed the uneven sharp back of it against the sky.

Pepé's brain spun in a big spiral up and away from him. He slumped to the ground and lay still. The rock ridge-top was only a hundred feet above him.

The moon moved over the sky. Pepé half turned on his back. His tongue tried to make words, but only a thick hissing came from between his lips.

When the dawn came, Pepé pulled himself up. His eyes were sane again. He drew his great puffed arm in front of him and looked at the angry wound. The black line ran up from his wrist to his armpit. Automatically he reached in his pocket for the big black knife, but it was not there. His eyes searched the ground. He picked up a sharp blade of stone and scraped at the wound, sawed at the proud flesh [12] and then squeezed the green juice out in big drops. Instantly he threw back his head and whined like a dog. His whole right side shuddered at the pain, but the pain cleared his head.

In the gray light he struggled up the last slope to the ridge and crawled over and lay down behind a line of rocks. Below him lay a deep canyon exactly like the last, waterless and desolate. There was no flat, no oak trees, not even heavy brush in the bottom of it. And on the other side a sharp ridge stood up, thinly brushed with starving sage, littered

[12] PROUD FLESH—New tissue growing over an open wound.

with broken granite. Strewn over the hill there were giant outcroppings, and on the top the granite teeth stood out against the sky.

The new day was light now. The flame of the sun came over the ridge and fell on Pepé where he lay on the ground. His coarse black hair was littered with twigs and bits of spider web. His eyes had retreated back into his head. Between his lips the tip of his black tongue showed.

He sat up and dragged his great arm into his lap and nursed it, rocking his body and moaning in his throat. He threw back his head and looked up into the pale sky. A big black bird circled nearly out of sight, and far to the left another was sailing near.

He lifted his head to listen, for a familiar sound had come to him from the valley he had climbed out of; it was the crying yelp of hounds, excited and feverish, on a trail.

Pepé bowed his head quickly. He tried to speak rapid words, but only a thick hiss came from his lips. He drew a shaky cross on his breast with his left hand. It was a long struggle to get to his feet. He crawled slowly and mechanically to the top of a big rock on the ridge peak. Once there, he arose slowly, swaying to his feet, and stood erect. Far below he could see the dark brush where he had slept. He braced his feet and stood there, black against the morning sky.

There came a ripping sound at his feet.

A piece of stone flew up and a bullet droned off into the next gorge. The hollow crash echoed up from below. Pepé looked down for a moment and then pulled himself straight again.

His body jarred back. His left hand fluttered helplessly toward his breast. The second crash sounded from below. Pepé swung forward and toppled from the rock. His body struck and rolled over and over, starting a little avalanche. And when at last he stopped against a bush, the avalanche slid slowly down and covered up his head.

◇◇◇◇◇◇◇◇◇◇◇◇◇◇◇◇◇◇◇◇◇◇◇◇◇◇◇◇◇◇◇

FOR UNDERSTANDING

1. Why was Pepé pleased at the prospect of going to Monterey alone? What can you learn about him from his plans for the trip?

2. What kind of woman was Mama? Find evidence to show that she was a good mother to her children in spite of the fact that she kept them out of school to fish. What is revealed about her and about Pepé in her instructions to him as he set out on his errand?

3. How was Pepé affected by what happened in Monterey? Show how the change in him was reflected in his appearance and his actions when he returned to the farm.

4. What character traits does Mama show during the preparations for the flight? In what way was her attitude toward Pepé different from what it was earlier in the story? Compare her advice to him as he set out for the mountains with her admoni-

tions when he started for Monterey. Which statements were directed to a thoughtless boy? Which to a responsible man? Do you think she loved him less because of what he had done? How can you explain her apparent lack of feeling when he left her?

5. How well did Pepé conduct himself on his flight into the mountains? When was he wise and resourceful? In what instances did he betray panic or lack of self-control? What mistakes did he make, if any?

6. What do you think Mama meant when she said: "A boy gets to be a man when a man is needed. I have known boys forty years old because there was no need for a man"? How is the truth of her statement borne out in the story? In what way was Pepé's need to be a man different from what his mother probably expected?

THE STORYTELLER'S CRAFT

1. Notice how the author used language effectively to help you visualize the setting and the people and to sense the mood.

a. What is there about the description of the farm to suggest the tragic development of the story?

b. The following quotation is from a picture of nature when the family was happy before Pepé went to Monterey: ". . . the sea below the cliff was glinting and blue and the white surf creamed on the reef, . . . even the stone mountains looked kindly." Find other passages in which the fortunes or feelings of the people are reflected in the landscape.

c. What deft touches in the description of Pepé's appearance and actions make him stand out vividly as an individual?

d. Find the passage in which specific details, picturesque comparisons, or accurate choice of words most effectively made you feel the heat, or thirst, or pain that Pepé endured during his flight.

2. The actions of an individual in good fiction must be consistent with his character and personality. How does Pepé's playing with the knife early in the story help the reader to understand how a simple, gentle boy might kill a man? When did you first suspect that Pepé would be unsuccessful in his attempt to escape? What was there in his character, the situation, and events leading up to the conclusion that made his death a right and logical ending for the story?

JOHN STEINBECK (Born 1902)

The birthplace of John Steinbeck was Salinas, California. He comes from a mixed German and Irish ancestry. His father was county treasurer of Salinas for many years. Over sixty years ago his mother taught in the little red brick schoolhouse of the Big Sur among the jagged cliffs and mountains. John Steinbeck was with the first surveying party to go into the Big Sur; and it is against the rugged background of that country that he has done much of his writing.

Steinbeck attended Stanford University intermittently; he traveled about the country doing odd jobs, and later went to New York where he was a reporter for a New York newspaper. He returned to California where his first three books were published. These were not very successful; but with the publishing two years later of his *Tortilla Flat*, he gained his first recognition. *Grapes of Wrath* and *The Moon Is Down* helped carry him along in his career to fame.

Mr. Steinbeck enjoys the simple, quiet life of his ranch home in California. He is a tall man with fair hair, a moustache, blue eyes, and a deep, slow voice.

For Broader Understanding

1. How do modern American short stories differ from early tales like "Rip Van Winkle" and "The Legend of Sleepy Hollow"?

2. What is meant by a *local color* story? What contribution did that type of story make to the development of American literature? Which stories in this unit are, at least in part, local color stories? How many sections of America are represented here? Choose one story and show that the characters and events belong particularly to one area or region.

3. The rise of realism made a lasting impression on the American short story. Remember that the realists wrote about the everyday happenings of ordinary people. They attempted to present life exactly as they saw it, including commonplace, ugly, and even unpleasant details. See if you can point out specific examples of realistic writing in the stories of this unit.

4. Many modern short-story writers are most interested in interpreting or explaining human behavior. Which of the stories you have read most clearly illustrate this concern with showing why people behave as they do?

5. Next to the characters, plot is probably the most important element of the short story. Some writers are more concerned with plot than they are with the development or interpretation of character. Choose one story in which the plot is particularly original. Show how events build up to a climax, or high point, and then move swiftly to a solution of the conflict. In which stories is plot less important than characters, impression, or ideas?

6. An artistic short story should have *unity*. Unity is achieved generally by having *one* principal character and centering the action around *one* incident, conflict, or problem. Everything in the story should contribute to *one* effect, impression, or mood. Show how the principle of unity applies to any one of the stories you have read.

7. There are several teen-age boys and girls among the characters in these stories. Which seem to you fairly representative of American young people? Which, if any, are exaggerated in order to satirize certain teen-age characteristics from an adult point of view? Which teen-age character did you admire most? Tell why.

READING, SPEAKING, AND WRITING ACTIVITIES

With the help of your teacher and the librarian, make a class collection of modern short stories. Your sources should include back numbers of several magazines that feature short stories. After each student has read several stories of his choice, the class might organize in various ways to report on, discuss, and evaluate the reading.

1. *Stories by a particular author.* Are they confined to one general type? How are they alike? How different? What aspects of American life do they reflect or interpret?

2. *Stories from various issues of one magazine.* See *Scholastic, Seventeen, The Atlantic, Harper's, The New Yorker, The Saturday Evening Post,* and others. To what special interests or to what type of reader do the stories appeal? Are they of good quality as judged by criteria developed during discussion of stories in this book?

3. *Adventure stories, or stories in which plot or action is important.* Is the action believable? Give examples of originality, surprise or trick endings, development of suspense.

4. Write a sketch of the character who interested you most in the stories you read. You might begin with the person's appearance. Then select two or three outstanding character traits and show how each is revealed by the action or dialogue of the story.

5. Write an original short story. Begin with the central character and create a situ-

ation which will bring out the personality and character traits of that person. If you cannot think of an interesting character around which to build your story, you might choose a minor character in one of the stories you have read. Here are some possibilities: one of the parents in "Two Soldiers"; Walter, Gordon, or Frank in "I Can't Breathe"; or Oliver Lutkins' mother in "The Hack Driver." Skim through the stories for other possibilities.

FOR FURTHER READING

STEPHEN VINCENT BENÉT, *Tales Before Midnight* (Rinehart). The author's fine craftsmanship and lyrical prose are evident in these unusual stories.

ANGUS BURRELL and BENNETT CERF, editors, *The Fireside Book of Famous American Short Stories* (Random). Beginning with Irving and coming down to the present, this collection contains a particularly good representation of modern authors.

WILLA CATHER, *Youth and the Bright Medusa* (Knopf). These stories show Miss Cather's adeptness at characterizing people of sensitive temperament.

KENDELL FOSTER CROSSEN, editor, *Future Tense* (Greenberg). This collection of tales of the future offers unusual entertainment and some startling ideas.

PAUL ENGLE and HANSFORD MARTIN, editors, *Prize Stories, 195–: The O. Henry Awards* (Doubleday). A collection of stories from current magazines is published annually in memory of the noted author O. Henry. Prizes are awarded to the ones which in the editors' judgment are the best for that year.

MARTHA FOLEY, editor, *The Best American Short Stories* 195– (Houghton). Miss Foley's annual collection of outstanding stories, together with the *Prize Stories* mentioned above, offers an opportunity to enjoy some of the best present-day writing.

OWEN FRANK, editor, *Teen-Age Companion* (Lantern). An excellent collection of magazine stories, these tales range in subject matter from cowboys to mountain climbing.

O. HENRY, *Best Short Stories of O. Henry,* selected by Bennett Cerf and Van H. Cartmell (Sun Dial) and *The Four Million* by O. Henry (Doubleday). Here are more stories by the master of the surprise ending.

PAUL JENSON, editor, *The Fireside Book of Flying Stories* (Simon & Schuster). Stories of the air, both fiction and fact, by Lindbergh, Michener, Nordhoff and Hall, all contribute to your information and pleasure.

RING LARDNER, *Roundup* (Scribner). Lardner's keen portrayal of the American scene shows genuine insight as he follows the everyday happenings of all sorts of people—boxers, musical comedy stars, and a host of others.

SCOTT MEREDITH, editor, *Bar 2 Roundup of Best Western Stories* (Dutton). This is a real "roundup" of some thrill-packed westerns. It includes Frank O'Rourke's "The Last Shot."

FRED LEWIS PATTEE, editor, *Century Readings in the American Short Story* (Appleton). This collection contains many of the best local color stories written in the middle and late nineteenth century.

HARRY SHAW and RUTH DAVIS, *Americans One and All* (Harper). Here are twenty-four stories, each concerning a different nationality. Taken together, they enrich our appreciation of America.

ERNESTINE TAGGARD, editor, *Here We Are* (McBride). In this collection you will find such famous authors as Sinclair Lewis, John Steinbeck, Dorothy Canfield Fisher, and many others.

HARRY R. WARFEL and HARRISON G. ORIANS, editors, *American Local Color Stories* (American). If you enjoy stories of local color you will like this collection. Through such writers as Bret Harte, Zona Gale, and Stephen Crane the reader can trace the interesting development of this type of story.

WILLIAM ROBERT WUNSCH and EDNA ALBERS, editors, *Thicker Than Water* (Appleton). The best of American writers contribute to this fine collection of stories on family life. The reader is sure to find some of his own personal experiences here.

DRAMA

THE GROWTH OF THE AMERICAN THEATER

Drama in one form or another is probably the most popular kind of entertainment in America today. Successful plays run for months or years on Broadway and then go on tour and play to packed houses throughout the country. Some even cross the ocean and are enthusiastically received in European capitals. Little theaters in our big cities and small towns make really good drama available to thousands of communities. And, of course, the motion picture, radio, and television bring dramatic entertainment—good, bad, and mediocre—into every neighborhood and almost every home.

This love of the theater is nothing new in America. During the nineteenth century, New York and other large cities had theaters where companies performed plays by European and American writers. Traveling troupes took plays into the new towns farther west, and showboats sailed up and down the rivers and canals, making one-night stands in the water-front towns far in the interior of the country. The types of entertainment offered ranged from Shakespeare to minstrel shows, sometimes a combination of both. Actors frequently doubled as singers and dancers while scenery was being shifted between acts. It was a hard life but good training for those who survived. Many great families in the American theater like the Booths, the Drews, and the Barrymores rose to fame in those early days.

Considering how much Americans of the 1800's enjoyed the theater, it is hard to understand why there were no great American plays produced until well into the twentieth century. As late as World War I foreign plays were considered far superior to any written in this country. Popular plays were generally either *farces* with stock comic characters or *melodramas* with heartless villains and beautiful weeping heroines. The plots of the latter followed a familiar romantic pattern leading to the usual happy ending. Before the final curtain the hero had rescued the heroine or paid off the mortgage, and the villain was led off the stage by the sheriff or a policeman. Today we laugh at those overly-dramatic and sentimental plays. When they were produced, however, people took them seriously; and audiences wept with the heroine, cheered the hero, and hissed the villain.

One form of dramatic entertainment that reached a high level of quality in the early part of the twentieth century was *vaudeville*. A vaudeville performance consisted of short skits, usually humorous, intermixed with songs, acrobatic stunts, and sometimes tricks of magic. Some of our modern radio and television shows put on programs similar to the old vaudeville. But Americans of an earlier generation declare regretfully that vaudeville is dead, and that the theater is not what it used to be.

Perhaps the passing of the old vaudeville is to be regretted. But our regular stage plays, in the early twentieth century, were raised to a higher level than ever before by the "Little Theater" movement. Dissatisfied with the quality of most commercially successful plays, idealistic young actors and artists organized their own theater companies. They worked hard and with little money, painting their own scenery and making their own stage equipment. Some of these little theaters were connected with the newly created drama departments of universities and colleges. Many of their productions were one-act plays by unknown authors who had startling new ideas. One such little theater group was the Provincetown Players in Massachusetts, who set up their stage in an unused fish house. Another was the Washington Square Players in New York. Some of the Washington Square Players later organized the tremendously successful Theater Guild. From the little theaters have come some of our best actors and many fine plays. America's most famous playwright, Eugene O'Neill, gained his first success with his short plays written for the Provincetown Players. "In the Zone," which you will read in the following pages, is a good example of O'Neill's work. Susan Glaspell's play "Trifles" was also first acted by little theater players.

As time went on, the commercial theaters themselves were transformed by the new movement. The public learned to enjoy more intellectual and more genuinely dramatic plays. It was found that realistic plots as well as the old-style romantic stories could be successful at the box office. All sorts of original experiments were tried in stagecraft and lighting. Playwrights themselves continued to experiment. Eugene O'Neill became the first American playwright to win international recognition by being awarded the Nobel Prize. In the biography unit in this text you will read about George Gershwin's great music-drama of Negro life, *Porgy and Bess*, which was a sensational hit in 1935. It will doubtless become a landmark in the de-

velopment of a peculiarly American type of drama. Some of our dramatists, like English playwrights in Shakespeare's time, are writing plays in poetic form. You will be
able to examine one such experiment in dramatic verse when you read the selection
from Maxwell Anderson's *Valley Forge*. In the space of thirty years, the United
States has risen from an inferior position in the field of dramatic art to one of leadership.

Motion pictures brought a new type of drama to America. And while a great many
photoplays have been inferior, appealing to immature people, many have been very
fine. For instance, "In the Zone" is one of four of Eugene O'Neill's plays which were
combined into a superb motion picture called *The Long Voyage Home*. Radio
and television are still newer media of mass production of dramatic entertainment.
While both use adaptations of regular stage plays, they also create a market for new
plays written especially for each type of presentation. There have been excellent
radio and television dramatizations of famous novels and short stories. An example
of this new drama may be seen in the suspense-filled story "Footfalls."

Some people have pessimistically argued that films, radio, and television would be
the death of legitimate drama. However, such fears seem unfounded. New York is
full of theaters which play to capacity audiences, performing old plays and new.
The more successful shows play elsewhere in the nation for a year or two longer. It
is true that only a few of these Broadway plays can be called great drama. The high
cost of a modern production guarantees that no play will be acted unless it seems
likely to please a large proportion of the theater-going public—and in general the
public prefers amusing entertainment to high dramatic art. Perhaps some of the
finest things that have come to the stage in our time are the great musical shows
like *Oklahoma!* and *South Pacific*, which are popular entertainment of a splendidly
rich and exciting kind. All types of theatrical productions are, on the average, far
superior to those of a few generations ago; and most of the really successful plays
are intelligent and thought-provoking to a degree that would have astonished your
great-grandparents.

DRAMA AS A TYPE OF LITERATURE

In order to discuss plays intelligently and to understand the reviews that appear in
newspapers and magazines, you should know something about drama as a type of
literature. For the same reasons it will also be helpful to acquire some of the technical vocabulary used by playwrights, drama critics, and theater patrons.

Plays of all kinds are classified as drama. Technically speaking, a drama is a piece
of literature designed to be acted rather than read. It is a work of art created by
the writer, the actors, and the watching audience. Like a concert it comes into existence each night it is played to a houseful of people—and each night it disappears
the moment the curtain falls on the final scene. The first English plays were merely

acted, but they early found their way into manuscript or printed record. Today we can follow the author's words on the page and "act" his play in our own minds. It is therefore possible for you to enjoy plays that you cannot see on the stage.

Drama should present a section of life in rapid, vivid action. Unlike novels and short stories it is dependent for expression on actors and their voices, gestures, movements, and reactions. Characterization must be developed swiftly through dialogue and action, and the play usually moves rapidly toward its conclusion. Drama, like fiction, centers around a plot—that is, a succession of events which make up the general scheme of the story. A thread of happenings, the *rising action*, leads to the big dramatic moment, the *climax*. This moment is the turning point of the plot. It is followed by the *falling action*, which leads to the solution, or *denouement*. Both characters and plot are developed in harmony with the *setting*—that is, with the place and time of the story.

Dramas fall into two main classifications according to their action. If we think of the plot of a play as a conflict between two opposing forces, such as between man and a personal weakness, or between man and his environment, the outcome of the conflict determines the classification. If in the struggle the man is victorious, the play is a *comedy*; if he is overcome by the opposing forces, it is a *tragedy*. You will see that a comedy is not necessarily funny and that tragedy does not always end in bloodshed or death. Modern tragedy usually ends with a man's failure to make peace with his universe or with himself.

Given characters, plot, and setting, the final test of a play is that it must act. The playwright must so handle his materials that dialogue and action tell his story in a lifelike fashion. "Actability" is not easy to define, but it is easily recognized once the players take to the stage. It is the most important element of any drama.

READING PLAYS WITH UNDERSTANDING

In order to enjoy reading a play, you should remember that the dramatist intended that you should see and hear it. Therefore, as you read you should try to create the play in your imagination. To do that you will have to pay particular attention to the directions for setting, staging, acting, and interpretation that are included in the printed text of the play. You should also remember that character and plot are revealed entirely through dialogue and action. Therefore, you will need to be alert to discover clues to character traits in every speech and movement. Everything in the play is there for a purpose. Lighting suggests mood or atmosphere. Sound is important, particularly in radio plays. Camera directions should help you to visualize a scene in a television play as it would appear on the screen of your set at home. With a little practice in creative reading, you will find that reading a good play is more rewarding than seeing a poor play performed. Of course, there is no substitute for actually seeing a first-rate company put on a really good play.

IN THE ZONE

EUGENE O'NEILL

IN THE ZONE *was written at the time of the First World War, but you will discover that its theme is as appropriate today as it was then.*

Because action as well as speech is important in portraying character and unfolding the plot of a play, you will need to pay particular attention to the stage directions that are included in the text. These directions take the place of the descriptions and running narrative in a story. They accompany the dialogue and often make it understandable. You will notice, for example, that IN THE ZONE *has explicit directions at the beginning and at the end of the play. In fact, the reaction of the audience is more dependent upon what the men* DO *as the curtain falls than upon what they* SAY.

CHARACTERS

SMITTY
DAVIS
SWANSON
SCOTTY
IVAN — *Seamen on the British Tramp Steamer, Glencairn*
PAUL
JACK
DRISCOLL
COCKY

SCENE: *The seamen's forecastle. On the right above the bunks three or four portholes covered with black cloth can be seen. On the floor near the doorway is a pail with a tin dipper. A lantern in the middle of the floor, turned down very low, throws a dim light around the place. Five men,* SCOTTY, IVAN, SWANSON, SMITTY, *and* PAUL, *are in their bunks apparently asleep. It is about ten minutes to twelve on a night in the fall of the year 1915.*

SMITTY *turns slowly in his bunk and, leaning out over the side, looks from one to another of the men as if to assure himself that they are asleep. Then he climbs carefully out of his bunk and stands in the middle of the forecastle fully dressed, but in his stocking feet, glancing around him suspiciously. Reassured, he leans down and cautiously pulls out a suitcase from under the bunk in front of him.*

Just at this moment DAVIS *appears in the doorway, carrying a large steaming coffeepot in his hand. He stops short when he sees* SMITTY. *A puzzled expression comes over his face, followed by one of suspicion, and he retreats farther back in the alleyway, where he can watch* SMITTY *without being seen.*

All the latter's movements indicate a fear of discovery. He takes out a small bunch of keys and unlocks the suitcase, making a slight noise as he does so. SCOTTY *wakes up and peers at him over the side of the bunk.* SMITTY *opens the suitcase and takes out a small black tin box, carefully places this under his mattress, shoves the suitcase back under the bunk, climbs into his bunk again, closes his eyes and begins to snore loudly.*

DAVIS (*enters the forecastle, places the coffeepot beside the lantern, and goes from one to the other of the sleepers and shakes them vigorously, saying to each in a low voice*): Near eight bells, Scotty. Arise and shine, Swanson. Eight bells, Ivan.

[SMITTY *yawns loudly with a great pretense of having been dead asleep. All of the rest of the men tumble out of their bunks, stretching and gaping, and commence to pull on their shoes. They go one by one to the cupboard near the open door, take out their cups and spoons, and sit down together on the benches. The coffeepot is passed around. They munch their biscuits and sip their coffee in dull silence.*]

DAVIS (*suddenly jumping to his feet—nervously*). Where's that air comin' from?

[*All are startled and look at him wonderingly.*]

SWANSON (*a squat, surly-faced Swede—grumpily*). What air? I don't feel nothing.

DAVIS (*excitedly*). I kin feel it—a draft. (*He stands on the bench and looks around—suddenly exploding.*) Square-head! (*He leans over the upper bunk in which PAUL is sleeping and slams the porthole shut.*) I got a good notion to report him. Serve him bloody well right! What's the use o' blindin' the ports when that thick-head goes an' leaves 'em open?

SWANSON (*yawning—too sleepy to be aroused by anything—carelessly*). Dey don't see what little light go out yust one port.

SCOTTY (*protestingly*). Dinna be a loon, Swanson! D'ye no ken the dangerr o' showin' a licht[1] wi' a pack o' submarrines lyin' aboot?

[1] LICHT (lĭkt)—Light.

IVAN (*shaking his shaggy ox-like head in an emphatic affirmative*). Dot's right, Scotty. I don' li-ike blow up, no, by devil!

SMITTY (*his manner slightly contemptuous*). I don't think there's much danger of meeting any of their submarines, not until we get into the war zone, at any rate.

DAVIS (*he and SCOTTY look at SMITTY suspiciously—harshly*). You don't, eh? (*He lowers his voice and speaks slowly.*) Well, we're in the war zone right this minit if you wants to know.

[*The effect of this speech is instantaneous. All sit bolt upright on their benches and stare at DAVIS.*]

SMITTY. How do you know, Davis?

DAVIS (*angrily*). 'Cos Drisc heard the First send the Third below to wake the skipper when we fetched the zone—bout five bells, it was. Now whata y' got to say?

SMITTY (*conciliatingly*). Oh, I wasn't doubting your word, Davis; but you know they're not pasting up bulletins to let the crew know when the zone is reached—especially on ammunition ships like this.

IVAN (*decidedly*). I don't li-ike dees voyage. Next time I ship on windjammer Boston to River Plate, load with wood only so it float, by golly!

SCOTTY (*looking at SMITTY, who is staring at the doorway in a dream, his chin on his hands. Meaningly*). It is no the submarrines only we've to fear, I'm thinkin'.

DAVIS (*assenting eagerly*). That's no lie, Scotty.

SWANSON. You mean the mines?

SCOTTY. I wasna thinkin' o' mines eitherr.

DAVIS. There's many a good ship blown up and at the bottom of the sea, what never hit no mine or torpedo.

SCOTTY. Did ye neverr read of the

Gerrman spies and the dirrty work they're doin' all the war?

[*He and* DAVIS *both glance at* SMITTY, *who is deep in thought and is not listening to the conversation.*]

DAVIS. An' the clever way they fool you!

SWANSON. Sure; I read it in paper many time.

DAVIS. Well— (*He is about to speak but hesitates and finishes lamely.*) You got to watch out, that's all I says.

[JACK *enters. He is a young American with a tough, good-natured face. He wears dungarees and a heavy jersey.*]

JACK. Eight bells, fellers.

IVAN (*stupidly*). I don' hear bell ring.

JACK. No, and yuh won't hear any ring, yuh boob— (*Lowering his voice unconsciously.*) now we're in the war zone.

SWANSON (*anxiously*). Is the boats all ready?

JACK. Sure; we can lower 'em in a second.

DAVIS. A lot o' good the boats'll do, with us loaded deep with all kinds o' dynamite and stuff the like o' that! If a torpedo hits this hooker [2] we'll all be goners b'fore you could wink your eye.

JACK. They ain't goin' to hit us, see? That's my dope. Whose wheel is it?

IVAN (*sullenly*). My wheel. (*He lumbers out.*)

JACK. And whose lookout?

SWANSON. Mine, I tink. (*He follows* IVAN.)

JACK (*scornfully*). A lot of use keepin' a lookout! We couldn't run away or fight if we wanted to. (*To* SCOTTY *and* SMITTY.) Better look up the bo'sun or the Fourth, you two, and let 'em see you're awake.

[SCOTTY *goes to the doorway and turns to wait for* SMITTY, *who is still in*

² HOOKER—Any clumsy craft.

the same position, head on hands, seemingly unconscious of everything. JACK *slaps him roughly on the shoulder and he comes to with a start.*]

Aft and report, Duke! What's the matter with yuh—in a dope dream?

[SMITTY *goes out after* SCOTTY *without answering.* JACK *looks after him with a frown.*]

He's a queer guy. I can't figger him out.

DAVIS. Nor no one else. (*Lowering his voice—meaningly.*) An' he's liable to turn out queerer than any of us think if we ain't careful.

JACK (*suspiciously*). What d'yuh mean?

[*They are interrupted by the entrance of* DRISCOLL *and* COCKY.]

COCKY (*protestingly*). Blimey if I don't fink I'll put in this 'ere watch ahtside on deck.

[*He and* DRISCOLL *go over and get their cups.*]

I down't want to be caught in this 'ole if they 'its us. (*He pours out coffee.*)

DRISCOLL (*pouring his*). Divil a bit ut wud matther where ye arre. Ye'd be blown to smithereens b'fore ye cud say your name.

[*He sits down, overturning as he does so the untouched cup of coffee which* SMITTY *had forgotten and left on the bench. They all jump nervously as the tin cup hits the floor with a bang.* DRISCOLL *flies into an unreasoning rage.*]

Who left this cup where a man 'ud sit on ut?

DAVIS. It's Smitty's.

DRISCOLL (*kicking the cup across the forecastle*). Does he think he's too much av a gentleman to put his own away loike the rist av us? If he does I'm the bye'll beat that noshun out av his head.

COCKY. Be the airs 'e puts on you'd

think 'e was the Prince of Wales. Wot's 'e doin' on a ship, I arsks yer? 'E ain't now good as a sailor, is 'e?—dawdlin' abaht on deck like a chicken wiv 'is 'ead cut orf!

JACK. Hey, Davis, what was you sayin' about Smitty when they come in?

DAVIS (*with a great air of mystery*). I'll tell you in a minit. I want to wait an' see if he's comin' back. (*Impressively.*) You won't be callin' him all right when you hears what I seen with my own eyes. (*He adds with an air of satisfaction.*) An' you won't be feelin' no safer, neither.

[*They all look at him with puzzled glances full of a vague apprehension. SCOTTY enters.*]

SCOTTY (*in awed tones*). Mon, but it's clear outside the nicht! Like day.

DAVIS (*in low tones*). Where's Smitty, Scotty?

SCOTTY. Out on the hatch starin' at the moon like a mon half-daft.

DAVIS. Kin you see him from the doorway?

SCOTTY (*goes to doorway and carefully peeks out*). Aye, he's still there.

DAVIS. Keep your eyes on him for a moment. I've got something I wants to tell the boys and I don't want him walkin' in in the middle of it. Give a shout if he starts this way.

SCOTTY (*with suppressed excitement*). Aye, I'll watch him. And I've somethin' myself to tell aboot his Lordship.

DRISCOLL (*impatiently*). Out wid ut! You're talkin' more than a pair av auld women wud be standin' in the road, and gittin' no further along.

DAVIS. Listen! You 'member when I went to git the coffee, Jack?

JACK. Sure, I do.

DAVIS. Well, I brings it down here same as usual and got as far as the door there when I sees him.

JACK. Smitty?

DAVIS. Yes, Smitty! He was standin' in the middle of the fo'c'stle there (*pointing*) lookin' around sneakin'-like at Ivan and Swanson and the rest 's if he wants to make certain they're asleep.

[*He pauses significantly, looking from one to the other of his listeners. SCOTTY is nervously dividing his attention between SMITTY on the hatch outside and DAVIS' story, fairly bursting to break in with his own revelations.*]

JACK (*impatiently*). What of it?

DAVIS. Listen! He was standin' right there—(*pointing again*) in his stockin' feet—no shoes on, mind, so he wouldn't make no noise!

JACK (*spitting disgustedly*). Aw!

DAVIS (*not heeding the interruption*). I seen right away somethin' on the queer was up so I slides back into the alleyway where I kin see him but he can't see me. After he makes sure they're all asleep he goes in under the bunks there—bein' careful not to raise a noise, mind!—an' takes out his bag there.

[*By this time everyone, JACK included, is listening breathlessly to his story.*]

Then he fishes in his pocket an' takes out a bunch o' keys an' opens it.

SCOTTY (*unable to keep silent longer*). Mon, didn't I see him do that same thing wi' these two eyes. 'Twas just that moment I woke and spied him.

DAVIS (*surprised, and a bit nettled to have to share his story with anyone*). Oh, you seen him, too, eh? (*To the others.*) Then Scotty kin tell you if I'm lyin' or not.

DRISCOLL. An' what did he do whin he'd the bag opened?

DAVIS. He bends down and reaches out his hand sort o' scared-like, like it was somethin' dang'rous he was after, an' feels round in under his duds—hidden in under his duds an' wrapped up in 'em, it was—an' he brings out a black iron box!

COCKY (*looking around him with a frightened glance*). Blimey!

[*The others likewise betray their uneasiness, shuffling their feet nervously.*]

DAVIS. Ain't that right, Scotty?

SCOTTY. Right as rain, I'm tellin' ye!

DAVIS (*to the others with an air of satisfaction*). There you are! (*Lowering his voice.*) An' then what d'you suppose he did? Sneaks to his bunk an' slips the black box in under his mattress —in under his mattress, mind!

JACK. And it's there now?

DAVIS. Course it is!

[JACK *starts toward* SMITTY'S *bunk.* DRISCOLL *grabs him by the arm.*]

DRISCOLL. Don't be touchin' ut, Jack!

JACK. Yuh needn't worry. I ain't goin' to touch it.

[*He pulls up* SMITTY'S *mattress and looks down. The others stare at him, holding their breaths. He turns to them, trying hard to assume a careless tone.*]

It's there, aw right.

COCKY (*miserably upset*). I'm gointer 'op it aht on deck.

[*He gets up but* DRISCOLL *pulls him down again.* COCKY *protests.*]

It fair guvs me the trembles sittin' still in 'ere.

DRISCOLL (*scornfully*). Are ye frightened, ye toad? 'Tis a fine thing fur grown men to be shiverin' loike childer at a bit av a black box. (*Scratching his head in uneasy perplexity.*) Still, ut's queer, the looks av ut.

DAVIS (*sarcastically*). A bit of a black box, eh? How big d'you think them— (*He hesitates.*)—things has to be—big as this fo'c'stle?

JACK (*in a voice meant to be reassuring*). I'll bet it ain't nothin' but some coin he's saved got locked up in there.

DAVIS (*scornfully*). That's likely, ain't it? Then why does he act so s'picious? He's been on ship near two year, ain't he? He knows there ain't no thiefs in this fo'c'stle, don't he? An' you know 's well 's I do he didn't have no money when he came on board an' he ain't saved none since. Don't you? (JACK *doesn't answer.*) Listen! D'you know what he done after he put that thing in under his mattress?—an' Scotty'll tell you if I ain't speakin' truth. He looks round to see if anyone's woke up—

SCOTTY. I clapped my eyes shut when he turned round.

DAVIS. An' then he crawls into his bunk an' shuts his eyes, an' starts in snorin', pretendin' he was asleep, mind!

SCOTTY. Aye, I could hear him.

DAVIS. An' when I goes to call him I don't even shake him. I just says, "Eight bells, Smitty," in a'most a whisper-like, an' up he gets yawnin' an' stretchin' fit to kill hisself as if he'd been dead asleep.

DRISCOLL (*shaking his head*). Ut looks bad, divil a doubt av ut.

DAVIS (*excitedly*). An' now I come to think of it, there's the porthole. How'd it come to git open, tell me that? I know'd well Paul never opened it. Ain't he grumblin' about bein' cold all the time?

SCOTTY. The mon that opened it meant no good to this ship, whoever he was.

JACK (*sourly*). What porthole? What're yuh talkin' about?

DAVIS (*pointing over* PAUL'S *bunk*). There. It was open when I come in. I felt the cold air on my neck an' shut it. It would'a been clear's a lighthouse to any sub that was watchin'—an' we s'posed to have all the ports blinded! Who'd do a dirty trick like that? It wasn't none of us, nor Scotty here, nor Swanson, nor Ivan. Who would it be, then?

COCKY (*angrily*). Must'a been 'is Lordship.

DAVIS. For all's we know he might'a been signallin' with it. They does it like that by winkin' a light. Ain't you read how they gets caught doin' it in London an' on the coast?

COCKY (*firmly convinced now*). An' wot's 'e doin' aht alone on the 'atch—keepin' 'isself clear of us like 'e was afraid?

DRISCOLL. Kape your eye on him, Scotty.

SCOTTY. There's no move oot o' him.

JACK (*in irritated perplexity*). But ain't he an Englishman? What'd he wanta—

DAVIS. English? How d'we know he's English? 'Cos he talks it? That ain't no proof. Ain't you read in the papers how all them German spies they been catchin' in England has been livin' there for ten, often as not twenty years, an' talks English as good's anyone? An' look here, ain't you noticed he don't talk natural? He talks it too good, that's what I mean. He don't talk exactly like a toff, does he, Cocky?

COCKY. Not like any toff as I ever met up wiv.

DAVIS. No; an' he don't talk it like us, that's certain. An' he don't look English. An' what d'we know about him when you come to look at it? Nothin'! He ain't ever said where he comes from or why. All we knows is he ships on here in London 'bout a year b'fore the war starts, as an A. B.[3]—stole his papers most lik'ly—when he don't know how to box the compass, hardly. Ain't that queer in itself? An' was he ever open with us like a good shipmate? No; he's always had

[3] A. B.—Able-bodied; able seaman.

that sly air about him 's if he was hidin' somethin'.

DRISCOLL (*slapping his thigh—angrily*). Divil take me if I don't think ye have the truth av ut, Davis.

DAVIS. An' the name he calls hisself—Smith! I'd risk a quid[4] of my next payday that his real name is Schmidt, if the truth was known.

JACK (*evidently fighting against his own conviction*). Aw, say, you guys give me a pain! What'd they want puttin' a spy on this old tub for?

DAVIS (*shaking his head sagely*). They're deep ones, an' there's a lot o' things a sailor'll see in the ports he puts in ought to be useful to 'em. An' if he kin signal to 'em an' they blows us up it's one ship less, ain't it? (*Lowering his voice and indicating* SMITTY's *bunk.*) Or if he blows us up hisself.

DRISCOLL (*furiously*). No man at all cud be puttin' up wid the loike av this—an' I'm not wan to be fearin' anything or any man in the worrld'll stand up to me face to face; but this divil's trickery in the darrk— (*He starts for* SMITTY's *bunk.*) I'll throw ut out wan av the portholes an' be done wid ut. (*He reaches toward the mattress.*)

SCOTTY (*grabbing his arm—wildly*). Arre ye daft, mon?

DAVIS. Don't monkey with it, Drisc. I knows what to do. Bring the bucket o' water here, Jack, will you?

[JACK *gets it and brings it over to* DAVIS.]

An' you, Scotty, see if he's back on the hatch.

SCOTTY (*cautiously peering out*). Aye, he's sittin' there the noo.

DAVIS. Sing out if he makes a move. Lift up the mattress, Drisc—careful now!

[DRISCOLL *does so with infinite caution.*]

[4] QUID—A coin, the sovereign, worth about five dollars.

89

Take it out, Jack—careful—don't shake it now; Here—put it in the water—easy! There, that's fixed it!

[*They all sit down with great sighs of relief.*]

DRISCOLL (*slapping* DAVIS *on the back*). Good wurrk for ye, Davis. (*He spits on his hands aggressively.*) An' now what's to be done wid that black-hearted thraitor?

COCKY (*belligerently*). Guv 'im a shove in the marf [5] and 'eave 'im over the side!

DAVIS. An' serve him right!

JACK. Aw, say, give him a chance. Yuh can't prove nothin' till yuh find out what's in there.

DRISCOLL (*heatedly*). Is ut more proof ye'd be needin' afther what we've seen an' heard? Then listen to me—an' ut's Driscoll talkin'—if there's divilmint in that box an' we see plain 'twas his plan to murrdher his own shipmates that have served him fair— (*He raises his fist.*) I'll choke his rotten hearrt out wid me own hands, an' over the side wid him, and one man missin' in the mornin'.

DAVIS. An' no one the wiser. He's the balmy kind what commits suicide.

COCKY. They 'angs spies ashore.

JACK (*resentfully*). If he's done what yuh think I'll croak him myself. Is that good enough for yuh?

DRISCOLL (*looking down at the box*). How'll we be openin' this, I wonder?

SCOTTY (*from the doorway—warningly*). He's standin' up.

DAVIS. We'll take his keys away from him when he comes in. Quick, Drisc! You an' Jack get beside the door and grab him.

[*They get on either side of the door.* DAVIS *snatches a small coil of rope from one of the upper bunks.*]

This'll do for me an' Scotty to tie him.

[5] MARF—Mouth.

SCOTTY. He's turnin' this way—he's comin'! (*He moves away from door.*)

DAVIS. Stand by to lend a hand, Cocky.

COCKY. Righto.

[*As* SMITTY *enters the forecastle he is seized roughly from both sides and his arms pinned behind him. At first he struggles fiercely, but seeing the uselessness of this, he finally stands calmly and allows* DAVIS *and* SCOTTY *to tie up his arms.*]

SMITTY (*when they have finished—with cold contempt*). If this is your idea of a joke I'll have to confess it's a bit too thick for me to enjoy.

COCKY (*angrily*). Shut yer marf, 'ear!

DRISCOLL (*roughly*). Ye'll find ut's no joke, me bucko, b'fore we're done wid you. (*To* SCOTTY.) Kape your eye peeled, Scotty, and sing out if anyone's comin'.

[SCOTTY *resumes his post at the door.*]

SMITTY (*with the same icy contempt*). If you'd be good enough to explain—

DRISCOLL (*furiously*). Explain, is ut? 'Tis you'll do the explainin'—an' quick, or we'll know the reason why. (*To* JACK *and* DAVIS.) Bring him here, now.

[*They push* SMITTY *over to the bucket.*] Look here, ye murrdherin' swab. D'you see ut?

[SMITTY *looks down with an expression of amazement which rapidly changes to one of anguish.*]

DAVIS (*with a sneer*). Look at him! S'prised, ain't you? If you want to try your dirty spyin' tricks on us you've gotter git up earlier in the mornin'.

SMITTY (*trying to restrain his growing rage*). What— What do you mean? That's only— How dare— What are you doing with my private belongings?

DRISCOLL (*shouting*). What is ut, ye swine? Will you tell us to our faces? What's in ut?

SMITTY (*biting his lips—holding himself in check with a great effort*). Nothing but— That's my business. You'll please attend to your own.

DRISCOLL. Oho, ut is, is ut? (*Shaking his fist in* SMITTY'S *face.*) Talk aisy now if ye know what's best for you. Your business, indade! Then we'll be makin' ut ours, I'm thinkin'. (*To* JACK *and* DAVIS.) Take his keys away from him an' we'll see if there's one'll open ut, maybe.

[SMITTY *struggles with all of his strength and keeps them busy for a few seconds.*]

JACK (*taking a small bunch of keys from* SMITTY'S *pocket*). Here yuh are, Drisc.

DRISCOLL (*taking them*). We'll soon be knowin'. (*He takes the pail and sits down, placing it on the floor between his feet.*)

[SMITTY *again tries to break loose but he is too tired and is easily held back against the wall.*]

SMITTY (*breathing heavily and very pale*). Cowards!

JACK (*with a growl*). Nix on the rough talk, see! That don't git yuh nothin'.

DRISCOLL (*looking at the lock on the box in the water and then scrutinizing the keys in his hand*). This'll be ut, I'm thinkin'. (*He selects one and gingerly reaches his hand in the water.*)

SMITTY (*his face grown livid—chokingly*). Don't you open that box, Driscoll. If you do, I'll kill you if I have to hang for it.

DRISCOLL (*pausing—his hand in the water*). Whin I open this box I'll not be the wan to be kilt, me sonny bye! I'm no dirty spy.

SMITTY (*his voice trembling with rage. His eyes are fixed on* DRISCOLL'S *hand*). Spy? What are you talking about? I only put that box there so I could get it

quick in case we were torpedoed. Are you all mad? Do you think I'm— (*Chokingly.*) You stupid curs. You cowardly dolts!

[DAVIS *claps his hand over* SMITTY'S *mouth.*]

DAVIS. That'll be enough from you!

[DRISCOLL *takes the dripping box from the water and starts to fit in the key.* SMITTY *springs forward furiously, almost escaping from their grasp, and drags them after him halfway across the forecastle.*]

SMITTY (*raging*). Cowards! Rotten curs! (*He is thrown to the floor and held there.*) Cowards! Cowards!

DRISCOLL. I'll shut your dirty mouth for you. (*He goes to his bunk and pulls out a big wad of waste* [6] *and comes back to* SMITTY.)

SMITTY. Cowards! Cowards!

DRISCOLL (*with no gentle hands slaps the waste over* SMITTY'S *mouth*). That'll teach you to be misnamin' a man, ye sneak. Have ye a handkerchief, Jack?

[JACK *hands him one and he ties it tightly around* SMITTY'S *head over the waste.*]

That'll fix your gab. Stand him up, now, and tie his feet, too, so he'll not be movin'.

[*They do so and leave him with his back against the wall near* SCOTTY. *Then they all sit down beside* DRISCOLL, *who again lifts the box out of the water and sets it carefully on his knees. He picks out the key, then hesitates, looking from one to the other uncertainly.*]

We'd best be takin' this to the skipper, d'you think, maybe?

JACK (*irritably*). This is our game and we c'n play it without no help.

DRISCOLL (*boldly*). Here goes, thin!

[6] *Waste*—Cotton material used for mattress filling.

91

[*He slowly turns the key in the lock. The others instinctively turn away. He carefully pushes the cover back on its hinges and looks at what he sees inside with an expression of puzzled astonishment. The others crowd up close. Even* SCOTTY *leaves his post to take a look.*]

What is ut, Davis?

DAVIS (*mystified*). Looks funny, don't it? Somethin' square tied up in a rubber bag. Maybe it's dynamite—or somethin' —you can't never tell.

JACK. Aw, it ain't got no works so it ain't no bomb, I'll bet.

DAVIS (*dubiously*). They makes them all kinds, they do.

JACK. Open it up, Drisc.

DAVIS. Careful now!

[DRISCOLL *takes a black rubber bag resembling a large tobacco pouch from the box and unties the string which is wound tightly around the top.*

He opens it and takes out a small packet of letters also tied up with string. He turns these over in his hands and looks at the others questioningly.]

JACK (*with a broad grin*). On'y letters! (*Slapping* DAVIS *on the back.*) Yuh're a swell Sherlock Holmes, ain't yuh? Letters from his best girl too, I'll bet.

[DRISCOLL *commences untying the packet. There is a muffled groan of rage and protest from* SMITTY.]

DAVIS (*triumphantly*). There! Listen to him! Look at him tryin' to git loose! Ain't that proof enough? He knows well we're findin' him out. Listen to me! Love letters, you says, Jack, 's if they couldn't harm nothin'. Listen! I was reading in some magazine in New York on'y two weeks back how some German spy in Paris was writin' love letters to some woman spy in Switzerland who sent 'em on to Berlin, Germany. To read 'em you wouldn't s'pect nothin'—just mush and all. (*Impressively.*) But they had a way o' doin' it—a sneakin' way. They had a piece o' plain paper with pieces cut out of it an' when they puts it on top o' the letter they sees on'y the words what tells them what they wants to know. An' the Frenchies gets beat in a fight all on account o' that letter. (*Seeing his audience is again all with him.*) An' even if these letters of his do sound all right they may have what they calls a code. You can't never tell. (*To* DRISCOLL, *who has finished untying the packet.*) Read one of 'em, Drisc. My eyes is weak.

DRISCOLL (*takes the first one out of its envelope and bends down to the lantern with it. He turns up the wick to give him a better light.*) I'm no hand to be readin' but I'll try ut.

[*Again there is a muffled groan from* SMITTY *as he strains at his bonds.*]

DAVIS (*gloatingly*). Listen to him! He knows. Go ahead, Drisc!

DRISCOLL (*his brow furrowed with concentration*). Ut begins: Dearest Man— (*His eyes travel down the page.*) An' thin there's a lot av blarney tellin' him how much she misses him now she's gone away to singin' school—an' how she hopes he'll settle down to rale worrk an' not be skylarkin' around now that she's away loike he used to before she met up wid him—and ut ends: "I love you betther than anythin' in the worrld. You know that, don't you, dear? But b'fore I can agree to live out my life wid you, you must prove to me that the black shadow—I won't menshun uts hateful name but you know what I mean—which might wreck both our lives, does not exist for you. You can do that, can't you, dear? Don't you see you must for my sake?" (*He pauses for a moment—then adds gruffly.*) Uts signed: "Edith."

[*At the sound of the name* SMITTY, *who has stood tensely with his eyes shut as if he were undergoing torture during the reading, makes a muffled sound like a sob and half turns his face to the wall.*]

JACK (*sympathetically*). What's the use of readin' that stuff even if—

DAVIS (*interrupting him sharply*). Wait! Where's that letter from, Drisc?

DRISCOLL. There's no address on the top av ut.

DAVIS. What'd I tell you? Look at the postmark, Drisc—on the envelope.

DRISCOLL. The name that's written is Sidney Davidson, wan hundred an'—

DAVIS. Never mind that. O' course it's a false name. Look at the postmark.

DRISCOLL. There's a furrin stamp on ut by the looks av ut. The mark's blurred so it's hard to read. (*He spells it out laboriously.*) B-e-r—the nixt is an l, I think—i—an' an n.

DAVIS (*excitedly*). Berlin! What did I tell you? I knew them letters was from Germany.

COCKY (*shaking his fist in* SMITTY's *direction*). Rotten 'ound!

[*The others look at* SMITTY *as if this last fact had utterly condemned him in their eyes.*]

DAVIS. Give me the letter, Drisc. Maybe I kin make somethin' out of it. (DRISCOLL *hands the letter to him.*) You go through the others, Drisc, and sing out if you sees anythin' queer.

[*He bends over the first letter as if he were determined to figure out its secret meaning.* JACK, COCKY, *and* SCOTTY *look over his shoulder with eager curiosity.* DRISCOLL *takes out some of the other letters, running his eyes quickly down the pages. He looks curiously over at* SMITTY *from time to time, and sighs frequently with a puzzled frown.*]

93

DAVIS (*disappointedly*). I gotter give it up. It's too deep for me, but we'll turn 'em over to the perlice when we docks at Liverpool to look through. This one I got was written a year before the war started, anyway. Find anythin' in yours, Drisc?

DRISCOLL. They're all the same as the first—lovin' blarney, an' how her singin' is doin', an' the great things the Dutch teacher says about her voice, an' how glad she is that her Sidney bye is worrkin' harrd an' makin' a man av himself for her sake.

[SMITTY *turns his face completely to the wall.*]

DAVIS (*disgustedly*). If we on'y had the code!

DRISCOLL (*taking up the bottom letter.*) Hullo! Here's wan addressed to this ship—*S.S. Glencairn,* ut says—whin we was in Cape Town sivin months ago— (*Looking at the postmark.*) Ut's from London.

DAVIS (*eagerly*). Read it!

[*There is another choking groan from* SMITTY.]

DRISCOLL (*reads slowly—his voice becomes lower and lower as he goes on*). Ut begins wid simply the name Sidney Davidson—no dearest or sweetheart to this wan. "Ut is only from your chance meetin' wid Harry—whin you were drunk —that I happen to know where to reach you. So you have run away to sea loike the coward you are because you knew I had found out the truth—the truth you have covered over with your mean little lies all the time I was away in Berlin and blindly trusted you. Very well, you have chosen. You have shown that your drunkenness means more to you than any love or faith av mine. I am sorry—for I loved you, Sidney Davidson—but this is the end. I lave you—the mem'ries; an' if ut is any satisfaction to you I lave yu the real-i-zation that you have wrecked my loife as you have wrecked your own. My one remainin' hope is that nivir in God's worrld will I ivir see your face again. Good-by. Edith."

[*As he finishes there is a deep silence, broken only by* SMITTY's *muffled sobbing. The men cannot look at each other.* DRISCOLL *holds the rubber bag limply in his hand and some small white object falls out of it and drops noiselessly on the floor. Mechanically* DRISCOLL *leans over and picks it up, and looks at it wonderingly.*]

DAVIS (*in a dull voice*). What's that?

DRISCOLL (*slowly*). A bit av a dried-up flower—a rose, maybe.

[*He drops it into the bag and gathers up the letters and puts them back. He replaces the bag in the box, and locks it and puts it back under*

SMITTY's *mattress. The others follow him with their eyes. He steps softly over to* SMITTY *and cuts the ropes about his arms and ankles with his sheath knife, and unties the handkerchief over the gag.* SMITTY *does not turn around but covers his face with his hands and leans his head against the wall. His shoulders continue to heave spasmodically but he makes no further sound.*]

DRISCOLL (*stalks back to the others—there is a moment of silence, in which each man is in agony with the hopelessness of finding a word he can say—then* DRISCOLL *explodes*). Are we never goin' to turn in fur a wink av sleep?

[*They all start as if awakening from a bad dream and gratefully crawl into their bunks, shoes and all, turning their faces to the wall, and pulling their blankets up over their shoulders.* SCOTTY *tiptoes past* SMITTY *out into the darkness. . . .* DRISCOLL *turns down the light and crawls into his bunk as the curtain falls.*]

◇◇◇◇◇◇◇◇◇◇◇◇◇◇◇◇◇◇◇◇◇◇◇◇

FOR UNDERSTANDING

1. Do you think Smitty's shipmates were spiteful or malicious men eager to make trouble for him, or were their actions based upon justifiable suspicions? Were they acting reasonably, or were they driven by fear?

2. Why were Smitty's actions easily misunderstood? Which of the men were most suspicious of him? How did they make known their suspicions to the audience and to each other without Smitty's suspecting their remarks? Which of the men were most reluctant to believe that there was something wrong? How were they convinced that Smitty was dangerous?

3. Is the general action of the play plausible? Do you think such an incident might take place on board a ship in time of war? Are the characters true to life? Point out passages which make some of them stand out as individuals with particular human characteristics, either good or bad.

4. What is the theme or basic idea of the play? What problem in human relations does it present? Does the playwright suggest any solution? If so, what is it?

INTERPRETING DIALOGUE AND ACTION IN A PLAY

1. How is the action of the plot started before the dialogue begins? What mood or atmosphere is produced by the actions of Smitty and those who see him? What did you learn about the personality of each character from his first actions?

2. What did the first few speeches reveal about the position of the ship and about her cargo? What further information about the characters did you learn from their first words?

3. Why did O'Neill not have the letters read while Smitty was absent? How did the action of the men and of Smitty during the reading add to the effectiveness of the play? How does the dramatist indicate the men's change of attitude as the truth about Smitty is revealed?

4. Do you like the way the play ends? What effect did Driscoll's last speech have on the men? How do you think that speech would affect an audience? What is significant about the way the men crawl into their bunks? What do you think will be the relations between Smitty and his shipmates for the rest of the voyage?

EUGENE O'NEILL (1888–1953)

Eugene O'Neill was born in a Broadway hotel while his father was playing the lead in *The Count of Monte Cristo.* As a child, he accompanied his parents on theatrical tours, and later he became a member of his father's company. Suspended after his first year at Princeton, Mr. O'Neill became in rapid succession secretary for a New York mail-order house, a gold prospector in Honduras, an assistant manager of his father's theatrical corporation, and a vagabond seaman, sailing on voyages, loitering around water fronts, and picking up material for the plays he would one day write.

After a fight against tuberculosis in 1912, he decided to become a professional playwright. *Beyond the Horizon* won him applause and the Pulitzer Prize. Then came a succession of successful plays, most of them showing an interest in moral and social problems. *Marco Millions* is a criticism of American smugness and materialism. *Dynamo* and *Days Without End* show much thought on the deeper problems of life and religion. After 1936 when he was awarded the Nobel Prize, there was a ten-year period when he published nothing. In 1946, *The Iceman Cometh* opened on Broadway and became the most talked-of play of the season. It is a tragedy of the down-and-outer, presented with stark but compelling realism.

There is no doubt that Eugene O'Neill is America's greatest dramatist. His plays have been translated into several languages and have been frequently produced abroad. He experimented extensively with dramatic form and was recognized before his death as a great influence on the theater of our time.

◇◇◇◇◇

FOOTFALLS

WILBUR DANIEL STEELE

(ADAPTED FOR TELEVISION BY HEDDA ROWAN)

Television has created new demands for drama, particularly for one-act plays that can be produced within the limits of the usual broadcast period. In addition to scripts written expressly for television, many favorite stories and stage plays have been adapted for the new medium. The following play is the television version of a famous American short story by Wilbur Daniel Steele. The original story is a weird tale of murder and revenge powerfully told. Even if you have read the story, you will enjoy having it brought to life as it might appear on your television set at home.

Because this is a television play, camera directions are important. Watch the close-ups particularly for dramatic effects and clues to plot development. As the title suggests, sound is also important, for the principal character is blind.

FOOTFALLS

Camera opens on full shot of a dilapidated clapboard house of the past century. New England fishing-village style. We see a neat street with colonial houses, a church, etc.

Camera moves in for a close-up of the sign on door: "Boaz, Cobbler." Camera goes through door into the shop. It is one room with two rear windows and a rear door. Camera picks up BOAZ at work. He is blind. He pounds on a shoe on a last.[1] He blindly but surely finds the right nails. Intermittently he pauses as sound of footsteps comes up.

Camera picks up several people going past his shop, then we see only the feet —a young girl in high heels, a child running, a man's confident stride in well-designed shoes. At this last shot, BOAZ jumps up, tense, gripping the iron last, listening hard as a blind man listens. The footsteps pass. He sits, a slight moan escaping from him. He shakes his head as if to remove an obsessive thought. He goes back to pounding the last, more fiercely than before.

LORENZO *enters the shop, carrying several pairs of boots. He is a fisherman— Portuguese—and dressed as one. He shuts the door behind him. The hammering does not stop.* BOAZ *speaks first.*

BOAZ. What do you want, Lorenzo?

[1] *Last*—A metal form shaped like a human foot.

LORENZO. For a blind man, you see very well.

BOAZ. What do you want?

LORENZO. I heard your hammer. So I thought to come in.

[BOAZ *continues with hammer. Pause. Finally*—]

BOAZ. So?

LORENZO. So I have . . . boots for you to patch up. Mine and Federico's, too. Federico . . . he would not come. (*Tosses boots on bench.*)

BOAZ. Tomorrow they will be ready.

LORENZO. You make him very sad, Boaz. Federico is very sad about you. (*Silence.*) Boaz, my friend, listen to me. We are all your friends.

BOAZ. Do not try to be kind. I don't want your kindness. (*He stops hammering.*)

LORENZO. This way a man cannot live. Everyone needs—

BOAZ. I need nobody. Nobody. Not you. Not the others. Now go. Leave me to my work.

LORENZO. Boaz! Just to sit here? Never to go out?

BOAZ. Never will I go out. I wait. I listen. What if I should let him pass? What if I let . . . that dog . . . slip by?

LORENZO. This will bring no good to you. I speak from my heart. Day and night to pound and pound your hammer . . .

BOAZ. Yes. I pound. I pound these shoes. And do you know—when there are no more shoes, I pound on the iron last, on and on . . . I want to keep them strong . . . my hands and arms should be powerful and strong.

LORENZO. Everyone says, after so many years, Boaz now will forget his son, Manuel.

BOAZ. How do you know what I have to forget? I still wait. Do you hear? That dog will come. He will come back!

Do you hear? He will come back!

LORENZO. I'm sorry, Boaz. I did not mean to bring this . . . distress; to remind you . . . I was just thinking of the other days. When everything was different. The shop was full of laughter. You were happy then, you would come singing. I was just remembering . . .

[*Dissolve to: Four young men sitting, singing a sea chanty.* FEDERICO, ALFREDO, LORENZO, JOSEPH—*all fishermen.* BOAZ—*younger, stronger, erect—stops his hammering to join in. Chanty ends in laughter.*]

FEDERICO. Come, come, Boaz—why do you fix it too good, my friend? This way shoes last too long. You lose your business, eh?

BOAZ. A minute more . . . I like it to be right, yes.

FEDERICO. Many thanks. But I cannot wait. I . . .

LORENZO. His feet have the itch . . . that one . . .

ALFREDO. And where, my fine Federico, is your itch leading you? . . . Where?

JOSEPH. Tell us! Tell us!

LORENZO. His ears get red. Look. Like a girl's. (*Laughter.*)

FEDERICO. Joke. Go on. Have your joke.

LORENZO. What we want to know is what your so big hurry is?

BOAZ. A girl, Federico? Which one? We are all friends, no?

ALFREDO. Maria, maybe? Maria with the twinkling ankle and the good legs? Sure, I think it is the one.

FEDERICO. You can laugh. Go ahead. Boaz, my boot. I don't have to listen to these—

BOAZ. Do not mind them, Federico. Already, they have a wife. They are strong and young. And they know how to fish and tell loud jokes, but truly they

envy you. Here. Here is your boot. Go. Run, run to your Maria.

FEDERICO. How much, Boaz?

BOAZ. Today, half price, eh? Because it is spring, and we are all friends, and there is no evil in the world? (*Laughter.*) Now you can all go. I have work to do. Except, Lorenzo. His boots I have yet to fix.

JOSEPH. We go . . . we go . . . we have work, too.

[*They exit except* ALFREDO *and* LORENZO.]

BOAZ. Alfredo, you did not go?

ALFREDO. For a blind man you see very well. I go! Till tomorrow, Boaz— (*He exits.*)

BOAZ. Wait—someone is here . . . (*He pauses, listens intently.*)

[*Camera close-up of* MANUEL's *feet walking.*]

Manuel? Is it you, Manuel?

[MANUEL *appears through draped doorway leading to back of house.*]

MANUEL. Hello, Pop.

BOAZ. He look good, Manuel? Nice clothes—they fit him good, no?

LORENZO. Tell us, do you go for Consuela to take her for a ride in the park?

MANUEL. I've got other things on my mind.

LORENZO. How about coming out with me tomorrow on the boat? There are too many fish this year—work for everyone.

BOAZ. He is still a boy, Lorenzo.

LORENZO. What do you say, Manuel?

MANUEL. I got other things on my mind.

LORENZO. And till then your old poppa skins his fingers hammering day and night. Trying to save a few dollars.

MANUEL. Pop? He likes to work. He's just made that way, see?

BOAZ. Enough, enough. There is plenty of time yet for Manuel, and work.

He is a good boy. Go, Manuel, go. Have a good time.

MANUEL. OK, Pop. Say Pop, you got five bucks to spare? It's something . . .

BOAZ. Don't explain to the old man. Sure. Here's money. And more if you need it.

MANUEL. That's swell. Thanks, Pop. (*Gives* BOAZ *an affectionate squeeze on his shoulder.*) I got to go now. (*Gives* LORENZO *a scornful look.*)

BOAZ. You be home midnight for sure.

MANUEL. Sure. Sure. Don't worry about me. (*He exits.*)

BOAZ. Manuel, he is a good boy.

LORENZO. You are a good father to him, Boaz. Sometimes I think you are too good. When he was a little boy, that was one thing. Now he is a grown man. My father would throw me two cents on the day he got paid and to me it was great luck. And today, why to-day . . . I am a good fisherman, that's what!

BOAZ. Manuel, he have plenty of time to work. Besides, he . . . he is not too stout.

LORENZO. You, yourself, you are not too stout.

BOAZ. Money? I do not worry about it. Here I make my living. I own my own house. Even I have a boarder who pays me well.

LORENZO. Mister Wood? Hah! With such a rich job at the bank, he should pay you well!

BOAZ. He has the upstairs of the house. Manuel and I . . . we live down here. On Saturdays he pays me five dollars . . . I cannot complain. (*Pause.*) Wait! . . . someone comes . . .

[*Close-up of* MR. WOOD *walking. Legs and feet only, coming from outside of shop. His hand, manicured, opens the door, showing jeweled cuff links.*]

BOAZ. It is you, Mister Wood?

[*Close-up of* WOOD—*a gentleman, impeccably dressed, well-groomed, diamond tie pin.*]

WOOD. Good evening, Boaz. Still working at this hour?

BOAZ. Work, work, work. What else is there for me? (*Laughs.*) This is my friend, Lorenzo, here.

LORENZO. Very pleased to make your acquaintance, Mr. Wood. (*Embarrassed.*) Now I go. My wife, she waits for me. . . . Good-by, Mr. Wood.

BOAZ. Your boots—here!

[LORENZO *rushes out.*]

BOAZ. There is nothing wrong, Mr. Wood? Your room? Everything is OK, eh?

WOOD. Fine. Fine, Boaz. Just one thing I want to ask. The lock on the door. It's . . . I might say . . . a little weak. Would it trouble you to get me a stronger one? Not that I have any valuables to speak of, you know, but . . .

BOAZ (*disturbed*). A new lock? But no one goes up there. No one but Manuel . . . and I. But sure, if you say so. Alfredo is good lockmaker. Tomorrow, it is done.

WOOD. Fine. Well—I have some reading to do—(*Picks up brief case and book.*)

BOAZ (*attempting to make conversation*). Always you are reading, Mr. Wood.

WOOD. It's my one hobby. It might do your son good to try a bit of reading instead of—I mean, haven't you ever thought of having Manuel learn the trade?

BOAZ. Shoemaking is good enough only for a blind man.

WOOD. Oh, I don't know. At least it's better than doing nothing at all.

BOAZ (*after a pause*). Manuel, he ain't too stout, you know. (*Loud.*) Manuel is a good boy!

WOOD. Yes, I suppose so. . . . Well, I'll be running along now. You'll see about the lock, then?

BOAZ. Tomorrow . . .

[WOOD *exits.* BOAZ *is upset. He gets up, pokes up stove, returns to last, starts pounding, stops* . . .]

BOAZ (*aloud, to himself—bitter, afraid*). He speak against Manuel. He speak against my boy. . . . A new lock? . . . A strong one, eh? Why? Ignorant Boaz, he want to know why? So . . . So . . . let it be. (BOAZ *stops work. Walks to clock without glass, touches the hands. It's ten o'clock. He walks tiredly to a washstand across the room. Blindly pours water into basin. Washes his face, goes to cot in another corner, lies down, pulls blanket over himself. He does not sleep, but stares with his blind eyes. Finally he closes his eyes for sleep.*)

[*Cut to Wood's room. He is just closing the door. He turns the key. Adjusts another lock. He removes his coat, studies his face in mirror, puts on his dressing gown, sits down, fills his pipe, starts reading.*

Sound of bright whistling. Cut to MANUEL *coming into shop. The clock points to* 2 A.M. MANUEL, *noisy, bumps into a chair.* BOAZ *stirs, awakes.*]

MANUEL. It's only me, Pop. Go back to sleep.

BOAZ. What time is it, Manuel?

MANUEL. Two o'clock. I'm late, Pop. Some of the fellows got in a card game. I won. Here's your five bucks back. (*Puts it in his hand.*)

BOAZ. Such money I do not want. Take it. (BOAZ *tosses it on the floor.*)

MANUEL. What's the matter, Pop? What you mad about? What'd I do?

BOAZ. Such money I do not want. Dirty money. (*Gently now.*) You make me very sad, Manuel.

MANUEL. Ah, Pop. Don't start that again!

BOAZ. It's not honest—such money.

MANUEL. What are you talking about? I didn't cheat, did I?

BOAZ. If you don't work, you cheat. Federico, Lorenzo—their money is all right. They work for it.

MANUEL. And you know what I think about your Federicos and Lorenzos; fools, suckers. Look at them. Working like dogs, what've they got? Look at you, yes, skinning your fingers—and for what?

BOAZ (*sadly puzzled*). What do you want, Manuel? You are not a boy any more. What do you want?

MANUEL. I don't know, Pop. I don't know. Except it's not what Federico got —or you—it's something more. . . . It's like I gotta get out of something or find something . . . y'know?

BOAZ (*groping*). Sure . . . sure . . . you want something . . . you don't know what.

MANUEL. Just give me time, Pop. I'll find it. Wait and see.

BOAZ. Sure. Sure, there is plenty of time for work. You are not too stout yet.

MANUEL (*gently*). Go to sleep now, Pop, it's late.

BOAZ. You are a good boy, Manuel.

MANUEL. Quit the kidding, Pop.

BOAZ. You go to sleep too, eh?

[BOAZ *gets back into bed, pulls the blanket up.* MANUEL *watches.* BOAZ *closes his eyes.* MANUEL *picks up the crumpled five dollar bill, straightens it out, puts it in his pocket. He exits.*

Dissolve to the next day, WOOD *entering cobbler shop. He carries bulging brief case, books. Room is empty.* WOOD *calls.*]

WOOD. Hello? Boaz? . . .

[*From behind the drape,* BOAZ *enters.*

The drape remains open, revealing MANUEL, *eating in the kitchen beyond.*]

Sorry, I didn't mean to interrupt. I'll come back later—

BOAZ. No . . . no. You are early from the bank. Everything all right, Mr. Wood?

WOOD. Fine. I just thought I'd pay you earlier this week. I have business out of town tomorrow. Be back Saturday, though.

[BOAZ *is standing on one side of his work table.* WOOD *is fumbling with his brief case, trying to get it open on the other side of the work bench. It sticks.*]

I have the money right here . . . what a nuisance . . . it's stuck.

[*Finally opens brief case; as he does so a large wad of bills falls out, hits Boaz's hand.*]

Oh . . . sorry. Clumsy of me.

[BOAZ *feels for the money, picks it up in his hand, feeling the amount. He turns toward* MANUEL. WOOD *returns roll to brief case and draws out his wallet, also from brief case.*]

Here's your money, Boaz. That makes us up to date.

BOAZ (*low, tense*). That was very much money, Mr. Wood.

WOOD. Yes, very much. Government money. It's for the breakwater workings. I'm to deliver it tomorrow. Payroll, you know. Have to get an early start, you know. Well—Good night!

[*Sound of footsteps going out. Camera follows* WOOD *out.* BOAZ *remains motionless listening after him. Camera picks up* MANUEL, *eating, apparently absorbed.* BOAZ *finally enters, sits down at table.* BOAZ *knows as a blind man knows that* MANUEL *has seen the money.* MANUEL *speaks without looking up from table.*]

MANUEL. What'd the old boy want?

BOAZ. Nothing. Just paid his rent. Nothing.

MANUEL. Oh.

BOAZ (*searching*). Maybe you go out and see the boys tonight? Go and buy them all a drink, eh?

MANUEL. What's the matter, Pop? Trying to get rid of me? I'm just gonna stay home and take it easy.

[*Camera cuts to* MR. WOOD *in his room. He is wearing his dressing gown. Brief case, carelessly tossed on table, money exposed.*

Cut to MANUEL *lying on cot, reading. He gets up, crosses room, gets tooth-pick.*

Cut to BOAZ *sitting in chair, tense, alert to every sound. He jumps forward at each movement. He listens acutely as we get alternate close-ups of footsteps of* WOOD *and* MANUEL. BOAZ *gets up. He touches the clock. It's nine o'clock. He sits again. He is like an animal, waiting, crouched, waiting, expectant.*

WOOD *puts his head out of his door.*]

WOOD. Manuel! Hey, down there! You still up?

MANUEL. Yeah. Ain't sleepy.

WOOD. Neither am I. Say, do you like to play cards?

MANUEL. What kind? Rummy? Poker?

WOOD. What do you say to having a game of poker, then? If you're not sleepy.

[*Camera follows* MANUEL *upstairs to Wood's room. Cut to* BOAZ *sitting tense, drawn, fearful.*]

BOAZ (*whispers, almost a prayer*). Do not stay there, Manuel. Do not stay. Do not stay. (*He gets up, crosses room, comes back to chair.*)

BOAZ. Come down, Manuel. . . . Come down where you belong. There is no good for you up there.

[*Camera cuts to* MANUEL *and* WOOD *playing cards. There is a bottle of wine. They're concentrating on the game.*

Cut back to clock. It is one o'clock.

Cut to BOAZ *listening to the sounds— of glasses, footsteps, of cards thrown down and a loud laugh. Silence. Then sound of scuffle. A thud. Silence, then only the sound of the clock ticking. Finally footsteps, footfalls going down the stairs from Wood's room.*

Close-up of feet on stairs. You can't tell whether it is MANUEL *or* WOOD. *Sound of door closing. Footsteps disappear. Smoke begins to pour into the room.* BOAZ *stumbles about.*]

BOAZ (*whimpering*). Manuel, my boy . . . Manuel . . .

[*Dissolve through fire effect to police-men and others standing about.*]

POLICEMAN. Sorry about the house, Boaz. Only thing left is this room.

BOAZ. The body?

POLICEMAN. It's Mr. Wood all right— even though the body's burnt to a crisp. He still had the cuff links and the diamond pin. Must have been all dressed up.

LORENZO. Funny he couldn't have got away.

POLICEMAN. He couldn't get away because he was murdered.

LORENZO. Murdered?

POLICEMAN. The back of his skull was smashed with this andiron . . . feel of it, Boaz. You recognize it?

BOAZ. Yes. . . . It is mine.

POLICEMAN. Boaz—where is Manuel? (*Silence.*) Answer me, Boaz. Where is Manuel?

BOAZ. Yes, where is Manuel?

POLICEMAN. Come now, Boaz, when did you see him last?

BOAZ. At supper.

POLICEMAN. The bank has already informed us that Mr. Wood had fifty thousand dollars in cash. Payroll for Government workings. Tell us, you knew about this money?

BOAZ. Yes. Yes, I knew of it.

POLICEMAN. And did Manuel know?

BOAZ. Manuel?

POLICEMAN. Come on, Boaz. Out with it.

BOAZ. Yes. Perhaps . . . perhaps Manuel, he know.

POLICEMAN TWO. And you know that Manuel is gone, and the money too is gone?

BOAZ. Yes, I know that Manuel is gone.

POLICEMAN. Do you think you can save him this way, Boaz! We will find him out. That is all for now.

BOAZ (close-up). That is all, you say? That is all? Now I have lost everything. My house. My son. Even my honor. You do not think I would like to live. But I live. I work. One day he shall come back again, in the dark night to have a look . . . Till then I wait . . . I listen . . . I wait for his step.

[Camera dissolve. We come back to BOAZ with LORENZO standing near him as in opening scene.]

BOAZ. He will come back! Do you hear! He will come back!

LORENZO. Boaz, my friend . . .

BOAZ (lifting his head). Are you still here?

LORENZO. Are you all right? Sure? You were starting so . . . like . . .

BOAZ. It's nothing. Forget it.

LORENZO. When will the boots be ready?

BOAZ. Tomorrow.

LORENZO (leaving). Nothing you need, Boaz?

BOAZ. Nothing.

[LORENZO exits. BOAZ starts to work, stops, goes to water basin, picks up pitcher and pours water, then stops, stunned. He is listening to the sound of footfalls coming closer.

Close-up of footsteps coming up stairs to cobbler shop. BOAZ returns to work bench, starts pounding on a shoe, waiting. Footsteps pause. Close-up of doorknob being turned. Door opens. Silence. Then—]

BOAZ. What . . . what can I do for you?

[Close-up of WOOD, bearded. He cannot be recognized.]

WOOD. You are a cobbler?

BOAZ. Yes. My . . . name is Boaz. You . . . you are a stranger here?

WOOD. Yes. I was just passing through, thought I'd look around. My shoes could use a pair of heels. . . .

BOAZ. I am a little deaf. . . . I cannot hear. . . . Would you come . . . closer?

WOOD. I said I have a pair of shoes— You mend shoes?

BOAZ. Yes. That is my job.

WOOD. I thought if you could do them at once . . .

BOAZ. I'm sorry—I still do not hear. You left the door open. I will shut it.

[He closes door. WOOD walks toward door.]

WOOD. On the other hand, I don't think there's enough time today. I'll— (Tries to open door. It's locked.) It's locked! The door's locked! What are you trying to—

BOAZ (hard). It takes a long time for a blind man to learn to keep his doors locked to strangers. A long time, but then he learns even if he is ignorant as Boaz.

WOOD. What are you talking about? Let me out of here. You're making a mistake. (*He tries to pull open the door.*)

BOAZ. It will not open. I have a strong lock.

WOOD. You're crazy. I'll have you arrested. I'll . . . (*He has his back against door as* BOAZ *slowly approaches him.*)

BOAZ. You thought, how would he know me, it is so long, and you thought to come and smell around like the dirty dog that you are. But the old fool did not forget, no, Boaz did not forget.

WOOD. Don't touch me. Let me go!

[BOAZ *has him by the shoulder. They struggle, Boaz's hands around Wood's neck.*]

BOAZ. I have waited a long time. Do not be so frightened. Death is not so bad. You taught me, too . . . that killing is not always bad. I just put my hands around your neck so . . .

WOOD. Help! Help!

BOAZ. And so . . . and so . . . I have trained my hands well, eh? They are strong and powerful, they have been waiting for this. . . . Perhaps I choke you too fast. Perhaps I should let you die slowly, you dog. Nine years I waited for you to come; nine years I waited for you to come; nine years I listened to every step that went by, every day, every night. I dreamed of this. A thousand times, I choked you . . . just so . . . as I do now.

[*While* BOAZ *speaks there is a pounding on the door, growing louder and more insistent. Now the camera moves in for a close-up as* BOAZ *drops the body and stands staring down at it with a blind man's eyes. Door crashes open.* POLICEMEN, LORENZO, *and* FEDERICO *rush into the shop.*]

POLICEMAN. What goes on here?

LORENZO. It's Boaz . . . with a dead man.

POLICEMAN. Stand back, stand back all of you.

[*They all approach the body.*]

BOAZ. Is it . . . he, that dog?

FEDERICO. Manuel?

LORENZO. You mean Manuel?

BOAZ. No, not Manuel. Manuel was a good boy; no, it was my boy that was burned. It was that dog who called my boy upstairs, that dog who killed my boy. He put his clothes on my boy, and he set my house on fire. I know all the time. Because when I heard those feet go away. I knew they were the feet of that one from the bank. No, it was not my boy that went away. Not the footsteps of my Manuel. You fools! Did you think I was waiting for my own boy? Manuel was a good boy. Old Boaz, he knew. Yes, a good boy.

[*Camera moves in for a close-up of Boaz's face. His expression is happy and triumphant.*]

◇◇◇◇◇◇◇◇◇◇◇◇◇◇◇◇◇◇◇◇◇◇◇◇◇◇

THE STORY BEHIND THE PLAY

1. What kind of man was Boaz before Mr. Wood came into his life? Show how your judgment is based upon his attitude toward his work, his relationship with his son, and his friendship with the fishermen who come to his shop.

2. What were your first impressions of Manuel? What details helped to build up and confirm your opinion? Were you influenced by Boaz's repeated statements that his son was "a good boy"? What attitude toward Manuel was revealed by Boaz's *actions*? Point out specific passages to support your opinion. What was the son's feeling for his father? Tell why you think so.

3. Why did Mr. Wood ask for a lock for his door? How did you interpret his request

when it was first made? How did it take on a different meaning for you when you finished the play?

4. On the day following his request for the lock, why did Mr. Wood open his brief case in front of Boaz? What was his apparent reason at the time? What different reason is revealed by subsequent events?

5. When did you first suspect that the murdered man was Manuel and not Wood? When do you think Boaz first suspected? Now that you have read the play, re-examine his speeches and actions for evidence. Do you think he ever did believe that Manuel was a murderer?

6. Does the plot of the story seem possible to you? What in Boaz's character and background might help to account for the way he took to avenge the murder of his son? What had his blindness and his occupation to do with the development of the plot? Why didn't he confide in his friends or tell the authorities of his suspicions instead of waiting for nine years for the murderer to return? Does it seem likely to you that the murderer would risk a return visit to the shop?

CAMERA AND SOUND EFFECTS

1. How much could you learn about Boaz from what the camera shows before the dialogue begins? What purpose does Lorenzo serve? What additional information is revealed by his conversation with Boaz? How does his presence lead to the flashback to earlier days?

2. How does the camera first pick up Mr. Wood? What do the close-ups emphasize that will be important later on in the play?

3. When Mr. Wood leaves to go to his room after the brief-case incident, the script says: "Sound of footsteps going out. Camera follows Wood out. Boaz remains motionless listening after him." Where else do camera and sound effects concentrate on footsteps?

4. When Wood returns to the shop after nine years, the close-up directions tell the reader that the bearded man is Wood. What had you been led to believe about Wood up to that point? Presumably, since the script also says that the man can not be recognized, a viewer would have to guess the stranger's identity. Who else might he be? Why would the play have more suspense for a viewer than for a reader? What other advantages would there be to seeing the play on the television screen?

CHECK THE SOURCE

If you have not read "Footfalls" as it was originally written by Wilbur Daniel Steele, plan to read it soon. Compare the two endings and tell why you like one better than the other. Which is more original? Which has greater suspense? How well has the story's eerie atmosphere been preserved in the play?

WILBUR DANIEL STEELE

(Born 1886)

Although he was born in Greensboro, North Carolina, Wilbur Daniel Steele was educated in Denver, Colorado, and traveled extensively in this country and abroad. He originally wanted to be an artist and studied art in the Museum of Fine Arts in Boston, in New York, and in Paris. For a time he lived in the artists' colony in Provincetown, Massachusetts. The scene of most of his writing is the eastern seacoast.

During World War I Steele served as a correspondent. After the war he began to write novels and plays but was most successful with short stories. In 1925 he was honored by the O. Henry Memorial Award Committee for the excellence of his short stories over a period of three years. His best stories are original and well constructed. He likes to show the drama in ordinary lives like those of the Portuguese fishermen in "Footfalls."

TRIFLES

SUSAN GLASPELL

This play starts out like an ordinary murder mystery with an investigation at the scene of the crime by the county attorney and the sheriff. However, you will discover that it is a most unusual play in many respects. For one thing, the principal character never appears on the stage; yet she becomes more vivid and real than any of the people portrayed by the actors in the cast.

CHARACTERS

GEORGE HENDERSON, *County Attorney*
HENRY PETERS, *Sheriff*
LEWIS HALE, *a neighboring farmer*
MRS. PETERS
MRS. HALE

SCENE: *The kitchen in the now abandoned farmhouse of* JOHN WRIGHT: *a gloomy kitchen, and left without having been put in order—unwashed pans under the sink, a loaf of bread outside the breadbox, a dish towel on the table—other signs of incompleted work. At the rear the outer door opens and the* SHERIFF *comes in followed by the* COUNTY ATTORNEY *and* HALE. *The* SHERIFF *and* HALE *are men in middle life; the* COUNTY ATTORNEY *is a young man; all are much bundled up and go at once to the stove. They are followed by the two women— the* SHERIFF'S *wife first. She is a slight, wiry woman, a thin nervous face.* MRS. HALE *is larger and would ordinarily be called more comfortable looking, but she is disturbed now and looks fearfully about as she enters. The women have come in slowly, and stand close together near the door.*

COUNTY ATTORNEY (*rubbing his hands*). This feels good. Come up to the fire, ladies.

MRS. PETERS (*after taking a step forward*). I'm not—cold.

SHERIFF (*unbuttoning his overcoat and stepping away from the stove as if to mark the beginning of official business*). Now, Mr. Hale, before we move things about, you explain to Mr. Henderson just what you saw when you came here yesterday morning.

COUNTY ATTORNEY. By the way, has anything been moved? Are things just as you left them yesterday?

SHERIFF (*looking about*). It's just the same. When it dropped below zero last night I thought I'd better send Frank out this morning to make a fire for us— no use getting pneumonia with a big case on, but I told him not to touch anything except the stove—and you know Frank.

COUNTY ATTORNEY. Somebody should have been left here yesterday.

SHERIFF. Oh—yesterday. When I had to send Frank to Morris Center for that man who went crazy—I want you to know I had my hands full yesterday. I knew you could get back from Omaha by today and as long as I went over everything here myself—

COUNTY ATTORNEY. Well, Mr. Hale,

"Trifles" from *Plays* by Susan Glaspell, copyright, 1920, 1948, by Susan Glaspell. Reprinted by permission of Dodd, Mead & Company.

tell just what happened when you came here yesterday morning.

HALE. Harry and I had started to town with a load of potatoes. We came along the road from my place and as I got here I said, "I'm going to see if I can't get John Wright to go in with me on a party telephone." I spoke to Wright about it once before and he put me off, saying folks talked too much anyway, and all he asked was peace and quiet—I guess you know about how much he talked himself; but I thought maybe if I went to the house and talked about it before his wife, though I said to Harry that I didn't know as what his wife wanted made much difference to John—

COUNTY ATTORNEY. Let's talk about that later, Mr. Hale. I do want to talk about that, but tell now just what happened when you got to the house.

HALE. I didn't hear or see anything, I knocked at the door, and still it was all quiet inside. I knew they must be up, it was past eight o'clock. So I knocked again, and I thought I heard somebody say, "Come in." I wasn't sure, I'm not sure yet, but I opened the door—this door (*Indicating the door by which the two women are still standing.*) and there in that rocker—(*Pointing to it.*) sat Mrs. Wright.

[*They all look at the rocker.*]

COUNTY ATTORNEY. What—was she doing?

HALE. She was rockin' back and forth. She had her apron in her hand and was kind of—pleating it.

COUNTY ATTORNEY. And how did she —look?

HALE. Well, she looked queer.

COUNTY ATTORNEY. How do you mean —queer?

HALE. Well, as if she didn't know what she was going to do next. And kind of done up.

COUNTY ATTORNEY. How did she seem to feel about your coming?

HALE. Why, I don't think she minded —one way or other. She didn't pay much attention. I said, "How do, Mrs. Wright, it's cold, ain't it?" And she said, "Is it?"—and went on kind of pleating at her apron. Well, I was surprised; she didn't ask me to come up to the stove, or to set down, but just sat there, not even looking at me, so I said, "I want to see John." And then she—laughed. I guess you would call it a laugh. I thought of Harry and the team outside, so I said a little sharp, "Can't I see John?" "No," she says, kind o' dull-like. "Ain't he home?" says I. "Yes," says she, "he's home." "Then why can't I see him?" I asked her, out of patience. "'Cause he's dead," says she. "Dead?" says I. She just nodded her head, not getting a bit excited, but rockin' back and forth. "Why—where is he?" says I, not knowing what to say. She just pointed upstairs—like that. (*Himself pointing to the room above.*) I got up, with the idea of going up there. I walked from there to here—then I says, "Why, what did he die of?" "He died of a rope round his neck," says she, and just went on pleatin' at her apron. Well, I went out and called Harry. I thought I might— need help. We went upstairs and there he was lyin'—

COUNTY ATTORNEY. I think I'd rather have you go into that upstairs, where you can point it all out. Just go on now with the rest of the story.

HALE. Well, my first thought was to get that rope off. It looked . . . (*Stops, his face twitches.*) but Harry, he went up to him, and he said, "No, he's dead all right, and we'd better not touch anything." So we went back downstairs. She was still sitting that same way. "Has anybody been notified?" I asked. "No,"

says she, unconcerned. "Who did this, Mrs. Wright?" said Harry. He said it businesslike—and she stopped pleatin' of her apron. "I don't know," she says. "You don't know?" says Harry. "No," says she. "Weren't you sleepin' in the bed with him?" says Harry. "Yes," says she, "but I was on the inside." "Somebody slipped a rope round his neck and strangled him and you didn't wake up?" says Harry. "I didn't wake up," she said after him. We must 'a looked as if we didn't see how that could be, for after a minute she said, "I sleep sound." Harry was going to ask her more questions but I said maybe we ought to let her tell her story first to the coroner, or the sheriff, so Harry went fast as he could to Rivers' place, where there's a telephone.

COUNTY ATTORNEY. And what did Mrs. Wright do when she knew that you had gone for the coroner?

HALE. She moved from that chair to this one over here (*Pointing to a small chair in the corner.*) and just sat there with her hands held together and looking down. I got a feeling that I ought to make some conversation, so I said I had come in to see if John wanted to put in a telephone, and at that she started to laugh, and then she stopped and looked at me—scared.

[*The COUNTY ATTORNEY, who has had his notebook out, makes a note.*]

I dunno, maybe it wasn't scared. I wouldn't like to say it was. Soon Harry got back, and then Dr. Lloyd came, and you, Mr. Peters, and so I guess that's all I know that you don't.

COUNTY ATTORNEY (*looking around*). I guess we'll go upstairs first—and then out to the barn and around there. (*To the SHERIFF.*) You're convinced that there was nothing important here—that is, nothing that would point to any motive.

SHERIFF. Nothing here but kitchen things.

[*The* COUNTY ATTORNEY, *after again looking around the kitchen, opens the door of a cupboard closet. He gets up on a chair and looks on a shelf. Pulls his hand away, sticky.*]

COUNTY ATTORNEY. Here's a nice mess.

[*The women draw nearer.*]

MRS. PETERS (*to the other woman*). Oh, her fruit; it did freeze. (*To the* AT- TORNEY.) She worried when it turned so cold. She said the fire'd go out and her jars would break.

SHERIFF. Well, can you beat the women! Held for murder and worryin' about her preserves.

COUNTY ATTORNEY. I guess before we're through she may have something more serious than preserves to worry about.

HALE. Well, women are used to worrying over trifles.

[*The two women move a little closer together.*]

COUNTY ATTORNEY (*with the gallantry of a young politician*). And yet, for all their worries, what would we do without the ladies?

[*The women do not unbend. He goes to the sink, takes a dipperful of water from the pail and, pouring it into a basin, washes his hands. Starts to wipe them on the roller towel, turns it for a cleaner place.*] Dirty towels! (*Kicks his foot against the pans under the sink.*) Not much of a housekeeper, would you say, ladies?

MRS. HALE (*stiffly*). There's a great deal of work to be done on a farm.

COUNTY ATTORNEY. To be sure. And yet (*With a little bow to her.*) I know there are some Dickson County farm- houses which do not have such roller towels. (*He gives it a pull to expose its full length again.*)

MRS. HALE. Those towels get dirty awful quick. Men's hands aren't always as clean as they might be.

COUNTY ATTORNEY. Ah, loyal to your sex, I see. But you and Mrs. Wright were neighbors. I suppose you were friends, too.

MRS. HALE (*shaking her head*). I've not seen much of her of late years. I've not been in this house—it's more than a year.

COUNTY ATTORNEY. And why was that? You didn't like her?

MRS. HALE. I liked her all well enough. Farmers' wives have their hands full, Mr. Henderson. And then—

COUNTY ATTORNEY. Yes?

MRS. HALE (*looking about*). It never seemed a very cheerful place.

COUNTY ATTORNEY. No—it's not cheer- ful. I shouldn't say she had the home- making instinct.

MRS. HALE. Well, I don't know as Wright had, either.

COUNTY ATTORNEY. You mean that they didn't get on very well?

MRS. HALE. No, I don't mean any- thing. But I don't think a place'd be any cheerfuller for John Wright's being in it.

COUNTY ATTORNEY. I'd like to talk more of that a little later. I want to get the lay of things upstairs now. (*He goes to the left, where three steps lead to a stair door.*)

SHERIFF. I suppose anything Mrs. Pe- ters does'll be all right. She was to take in some clothes for her, you know, and a few little things. We left in such a hurry yesterday.

COUNTY ATTORNEY. Yes, but I would like to see what you take, Mrs. Peters, and keep an eye out for anything that might be of use to us.

MRS. PETERS. Yes, Mr. Henderson.

[*The women listen to the men's steps*

on the stairs, then look about the kitchen.]

MRS. HALE. I'd hate to have men coming into my kitchen, snooping around and criticizing. (*She arranges the pans under sink which the* LAWYER *had shoved out of place.*)

MRS. PETERS. Of course it's no more than their duty.

MRS. HALE. Duty's all right, but I guess that deputy sheriff that came out to make the fire might have got a little of this on. (*Gives the roller towel a pull.*) Wish I'd thought of that sooner. Seems mean to talk about her for not having things slicked up when she had to come away in such a hurry.

MRS. PETERS (*who has gone to a small table in the left rear corner of the room, and lifted one end of a towel that covers a pan*). She had bread set. (*Stands still.*)

MRS. HALE (*eyes fixed on a loaf of bread beside the breadbox, which is on a low shelf at the other side of the room. Moves slowly toward it*). She was going to put this in there. (*Picks up loaf, then abruptly drops it. In a manner of returning to familiar things.*) It's a shame about her fruit. I wonder if it's all gone. (*Gets up on the chair and looks.*) I think there's some here that's all right, Mrs. Peters. Yes—here; (*Holding it toward the window.*) this is cherries, too. (*Looking again.*) I declare I believe that's the only one. (*Gets down, bottle in her hand. Goes to the sink and wipes it off on the outside.*) She'll feel awful bad after all her hard work in the hot weather. I remember the afternoon I put up my cherries last summer. (*She puts the bottle on the big kitchen table, center of the room. With a sigh, is about to sit down in the rocking chair. Before she is seated realizes what chair it is; with a slow look at it, steps back. The chair which she has touched rocks back and forth.*)

MRS. PETERS. Well, I must get those things from the front room closet. (*She goes to the door at the right, but after looking into the other room, steps back.*) You coming with me, Mrs. Hale? You could help me carry them.

[*They go into the other room; reappear,* MRS. PETERS *carrying a dress and skirt,* MRS. HALE *following with a pair of shoes.*]

MRS. PETERS. My, it's cold in there. (*She puts the clothes on the big table, and hurries to the stove.*)

MRS. HALE (*examining the skirt*). Wright was close. I think maybe that's why she kept so much to herself. She didn't even belong to the Ladies Aid. I suppose she felt she couldn't do her part, and then you don't enjoy things when you feel shabby. She used to wear pretty clothes and be lively, when she was Minnie Foster, one of the town girls singing in the choir. But that—oh, that was thirty years ago. This all you was to take in?

MRS. PETERS. She said she wanted an apron. Funny thing to want, for there isn't much to get you dirty in jail, goodness knows. But I suppose just to make her feel more natural. She said they was in the top drawer in this cupboard. Yes, here. And then her little shawl that always hung behind the door. (*Opens stair door and looks.*) Yes, here it is. (*Quickly shuts door leading upstairs.*)

MRS. HALE (*abruptly moving toward her*). Mrs. Peters?

MRS. PETERS. Yes, Mrs. Hale?

MRS. HALE. Do you think she did it?

MRS. PETERS (*in a frightened voice*). Oh, I don't know.

MRS. HALE. Well, I don't think she did. Asking for an apron and her little shawl. Worrying about her fruit.

MRS. PETERS (*starts to speak, glances up, where footsteps are heard in the room above. In a low voice*). Mr. Peters says it looks bad for her. Mr. Henderson is awful sarcastic in a speech and he'll make fun of her sayin' she didn't wake up.

MRS. HALE. Well, I guess John Wright didn't wake when they was slipping that rope under his neck.

MRS. PETERS. No, it's strange. It must have been done awful crafty and still. They say it was such a—such a funny way to kill a man, rigging it all up like that.

MRS. HALE. That's just what Mr. Hale said. There was a gun in the house. He says that's what he can't understand.

MRS. PETERS. Mr. Henderson said coming out that what was needed for the case was a motive; something to show anger, or—sudden feeling.

MRS. HALE (*who is standing by the table*). Well, I don't see any signs of anger around here. (*She puts her hand on the dish towel which lies on the table, stands looking down at table, one half of which is clean, the other half messy.*) It's wiped to here. (*Makes a move as if to finish work, then turns and looks at loaf of bread outside the breadbox. Drops towel. In that voice of coming back to familiar things.*) Wonder how they are finding things upstairs. I hope she had it a little more redd-up up there. You know, it seems kind of *sneaking.* Locking her up in town and then coming out here and trying to get her own house to turn against her!

MRS. PETERS. But Mrs. Hale, the law is the law.

MRS. HALE. I s'pose 'tis. (*Unbuttoning her coat.*) Better loosen up your things, Mrs. Peters. You won't feel them when you go out.

[MRS. PETERS *takes off her fur tippet, goes to hang it on hook at back of* room, *stands looking at the under part of the small corner table.*]

MRS. PETERS. She was piecing a quilt. (*She brings the large sewing basket and they look at the bright pieces.*)

MRS. HALE. It's log cabin pattern. Pretty, isn't it? I wonder if she was goin' to quilt it or just knot it?

[*Footsteps have been heard coming down the stairs. The* SHERIFF *enters followed by* HALE *and the* COUNTY ATTORNEY.]

SHERIFF. They wonder if she was going to quilt it or just knot it!

[*The men laugh, the women look abashed.*]

COUNTY ATTORNEY (*rubbing his hands over the stove*). Frank's fire didn't do much up there, did it? Well, let's go out to the barn and get that cleared up.

[*The men go outside.*]

MRS. HALE (*resentfully*). I don't know as there's anything so strange, our takin' up our time with little things while we're waiting for them to get the evidence. (*She sits down at the big table smoothing out a block with decision.*) I don't see as it's anything to laugh about.

MRS. PETERS (*apologetically*). Of course they've got awful important things on their minds. (*Pulls up a chair and joins* MRS. HALE *at the table.*)

MRS. HALE (*examining another block*). Mrs. Peters, look at this one. Here, this is the one she was working on, and look at the sewing! All the rest of it has been so nice and even. And look at this! It's all over the place! Why, it looks as if she didn't know what she was about!

[*After she has said this they look at each other, then start to glance back at the door. After an instant* MRS. HALE *has pulled at a knot and ripped the sewing.*]

MRS. PETERS. Oh, what are you doing, Mrs. Hale?

MRS. HALE (*mildly*). Just pulling out a stitch or two that's not sewed very good. (*Threading a needle.*) Bad sewing always made me fidgety.

MRS. PETERS (*nervously*). I don't think we ought to touch things.

MRS. HALE. I'll just finish up this end. (*Suddenly stopping and leaning forward.*) Mrs. Peters?

MRS. PETERS. Yes, Mrs. Hale?

MRS. HALE. What do you suppose she was so nervous about?

MRS. PETERS. Oh—I don't know. I don't know as she was nervous. I sometimes sew awful queer when I'm just tired.

[MRS. HALE *starts to say something, looks at* MRS. PETERS, *then goes on sewing.*]

Well, I must get these things wrapped up. They may be through sooner than we think. (*Putting apron and other things together.*) I wonder where I can find a piece of paper, and string.

MRS. HALE. In that cupboard, maybe.

MRS. PETERS (*looking in cupboard*). Why, here's a bird cage. (*Holds it up.*) Did she have a bird, Mrs. Hale?

MRS. HALE. Why, I don't know whether she did or not—I've not been here for so long. There was a man around last year selling canaries cheap, but I don't know as she took one; maybe she did. She used to sing real pretty herself.

MRS. PETERS (*glancing around*). Seems funny to think of a bird here. But she must have had one, or why would she have a cage? I wonder what happened to it.

MRS. HALE. I s'pose maybe the cat got it.

MRS. PETERS. No, she didn't have a cat. She's got that feeling some people have about cats—being afraid of them. My cat got in her room and she was real upset and asked me to take it out.

MRS. HALE. My sister Bessie was like that. Queer, ain't it?

MRS. PETERS (*examining the cage*). Why, look at this door. It's broke. One hinge is pulled apart.

MRS. HALE (*looking too*). Looks as if someone must have been rough with it.

MRS. PETERS. Why, yes. (*She brings the cage forward and puts it on the table.*)

MRS. HALE. I wish if they're going to find any evidence they'd be about it. I don't like this place.

MRS. PETERS. But I'm awful glad you came with me, Mrs. Hale. It would be lonesome for me sitting here alone.

MRS. HALE. It would, wouldn't it? (*Dropping her sewing.*) But I tell you what I do wish, Mrs. Peters. I wish I had come over sometimes when *she* was here. I—(*Looking around the room.*)—wish I had.

MRS. PETERS. But of course you were awful busy, Mrs. Hale—your house and your children.

MRS. HALE. I could've come. I stayed away because it weren't cheerful—and that's why I ought to have come. I—I've never liked this place. Maybe because it's down in a hollow and you don't see the road. I dunno what it is, but it's a lonesome place and always was. I wish I had come over to see Minnie Foster sometimes. I can see now— (*Shakes her head.*)

MRS. PETERS. Well, you mustn't reproach yourself, Mrs. Hale. Somehow we just don't see how it is with other folks until—something turns up.

MRS. HALE. Not having children makes less work—but it makes a quiet house, and Wright out to work all day, and no company when he did come in. Did you know John Wright, Mrs. Peters?

MRS. PETERS. Not to know him; I've

seen him in town. They say he was a good man.

MRS. HALE. Yes—good; he didn't drink, and kept his word as well as most, I guess, and paid his debts. But he was a hard man, Mrs. Peters. Just to pass the time of day with him— (*Shivers.*) Like a raw wind that gets to the bone. (*Pauses, her eye falling on the cage.*) I should think she would 'a wanted a bird. But what do you suppose went with it?

MRS. PETERS. I don't know, unless it got sick and died.

[*She reaches over and swings the broken door, swings it again, both women watch it.*]

MRS. HALE. You weren't raised round here, were you?

[MRS. PETERS *shakes her head.*]
You didn't know—her?

MRS. PETERS. Not till they brought her yesterday.

MRS. HALE. She—come to think of it, she was kind of like a bird herself—real sweet and pretty, but kind of timid and—fluttery. How—she—did—change. (*Silence; then as if struck by a happy thought and relieved to get back to everyday things.*) Tell you what, Mrs. Peters, why don't you take the quilt in with you? It might take up her mind.

MRS. PETERS. Why, I think that's a real nice idea, Mrs. Hale. There couldn't possibly be any objection to it, could there? Now, just what would I take? I wonder if her patches are in here—and her things.

[*They look in the sewing basket.*]

MRS. HALE. Here's some red. I expect this has got sewing things in it. (*Brings out a fancy box.*) What a pretty box. Looks like something somebody would give you. Maybe her scissors are in here. (*Opens box. Suddenly puts her hand to her nose.*) Why—

[MRS. PETERS *bends nearer, then turns her face away.*]

There's something wrapped up in this piece of silk.

MRS. PETERS. This isn't her scissors.

MRS. HALE (*lifting the silk*). Oh, Mrs. Peters—it's—

[MRS. PETERS *bends closer.*]

MRS. PETERS. It's the bird.

MRS. HALE (*jumping up*). But, Mrs. Peters—look at it! Its neck! Look at its neck! It's all—other side *to.*

MRS. PETERS. Somebody—wrung—its —neck.

[*Their eyes meet. A look of growing comprehension, of horror. Steps are heard outside.* MRS. HALE *slips box under quilt pieces, and sinks into her chair. Enter* SHERIFF *and* COUNTY ATTORNEY. MRS. PETERS *rises.*]

COUNTY ATTORNEY (*as one turning from serious things to little pleasantries*). Well, ladies, have you decided whether she was going to quilt it or knot it?

MRS. PETERS. We think she was going to—knot it.

COUNTY ATTORNEY. Well, that's interesting, I'm sure. (*Seeing the bird cage.*) Has the bird flown?

MRS. HALE (*putting more quilt pieces over the box*). We think the—cat got it.

COUNTY ATTORNEY (*preoccupied*). Is there a cat?

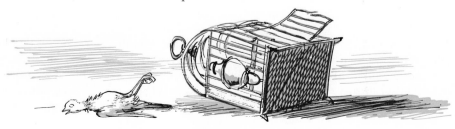

[MRS. HALE *glances in a quick covert way at* MRS. PETERS.]

MRS. PETERS. Well, not now. They're superstitious, you know. They leave.

COUNTY ATTORNEY (*to* SHERIFF PETERS, *continuing an interrupted conversation*). No sign at all of anyone having come from the outside. Their own rope. Now let's go up again and go over it piece by piece. (*They start upstairs.*) It would have been someone who knew just the—

[MRS. PETERS *sits down. The two women sit there not looking at one another, but as if peering into something and at the same time holding back. When they talk now it is in the manner of feeling their way over strange ground, as if afraid of what they are saying, but as if they cannot help saying it.*]

MRS. HALE. She liked the bird. She was going to bury it in that pretty box.

MRS. PETERS (*in a whisper*). When I was a girl—my kitten—there was a boy took a hatchet, and before my eyes— and before I could get there— (*Covers her face an instant.*) If they hadn't held me back I would have—(*Catches herself, looks upstairs where steps are heard, falters weakly.*)—hurt him.

MRS. HALE (*with a slow look around her*). I wonder how it would seem never to have had any children around. (*Pause.*) No, Wright wouldn't like the bird—a thing that sang. She used to sing. He killed that, too.

MRS. PETERS (*moving uneasily*). We don't know who killed the bird.

MRS. HALE. I knew John Wright.

MRS. PETERS. It was an awful thing was done in this house that night, Mrs. Hale. Killing a man while he slept, slipping a rope around his neck that choked the life out of him.

MRS. HALE. His neck. Choked the life out of him. (*Her hand goes out and rests on the bird cage.*)

MRS. PETERS (*with rising voice*). We don't know who killed him. We don't know.

MRS. HALE (*her own feeling not interrupted*). If there'd been years and years of nothing, then a bird to sing to you, it would be awful—still, after the bird was still.

MRS. PETERS (*something within her speaking*). I know what stillness is. When we homesteaded in Dakota, and my first baby died—after he was two years old, and me with no other then—

MRS. HALE (*moving*). How soon do you suppose they'll be through, looking for the evidence?

MRS. PETERS. I know what stillness is. (*Pulling herself back.*) The law has got to punish crime, Mrs. Hale.

MRS. HALE (*not as if answering that*). I wish you'd seen Minnie Foster when she wore a white dress with blue ribbons and stood up there in the choir and sang. (*A look around the room.*) Oh, I wish I'd come over here once in a while! That was a crime! That was a crime! Who's going to punish that?

MRS. PETERS (*looking upstairs*). We mustn't—take on.

MRS. HALE. I might have known she needed help! I know how things can be —for women. I tell you, it's queer, Mrs. Peters. We live close together and we live far apart. We all go through the same things—it's all just a different kind of the same thing. (*Brushes her eyes, noticing the bottle of fruit, reaches out for it.*) If I was you I wouldn't tell her her fruit was gone. Tell her it ain't. Tell her it's all right. Take this in to prove it to her. She—she may never know whether it was broke or not.

MRS. PETERS (*takes the bottle, looks about for something to wrap it in; takes petticoat from the clothes brought from the other room, very nervously begins winding this around the bottle. In a false voice*). My, it's a good thing the men couldn't hear us. Wouldn't they just laugh! Getting all stirred up over a little thing like a—dead canary. As if that could have anything to do with— with—wouldn't they laugh!

[*The men are heard coming downstairs.*]

MRS. HALE (*under her breath*). Maybe they would—maybe they wouldn't.

COUNTY ATTORNEY. No, Peters, it's all perfectly clear except a reason for doing it. But you know juries when it comes to women. If there was some definite thing. Something to show—something to make a story about—a thing that would connect up with this strange way of doing it—

[*The women's eyes meet for an instant. Enter HALE from outer door.*]

HALE. Well, I've got the team around. Pretty cold out there.

COUNTY ATTORNEY. I'm going to stay here a while myself. (*To the SHERIFF.*) You can send Frank out for me, can't you? I want to go over everything. I'm not satisfied that we can't do better.

SHERIFF. Do you want to see what Mrs. Peters is going to take in?

[*The ATTORNEY goes to the table, picks up the apron, laughs.*]

COUNTY ATTORNEY. Oh, I guess they're not very dangerous things the ladies have picked out. (*Moves a few things about, disturbing the quilt pieces which cover the box. Steps back.*) No, Mrs. Peters doesn't need supervising. For that matter, a sheriff's wife is married to the law. Ever think of it that way, Mrs. Peters?

MRS. PETERS. Not—just that way.

SHERIFF (*chuckling*). Married to the law. (*Moves toward the other room.*) I just want you to come in here a minute,

George. We ought to take a look at these windows.

COUNTY ATTORNEY (*scoffingly*). Oh, windows!

SHERIFF. We'll be right out, Mr. Hale.

[HALE *goes outside. The* SHERIFF *follows the* COUNTY ATTORNEY *into the other room. Then* MRS. HALE *rises, hands tight together, looking intensely at* MRS. PETERS, *whose eyes make a slow turn, finally meeting* MRS. HALE'S. *A moment* MRS. HALE *holds her, then her own eyes point the way to where the box is concealed. Suddenly* MRS. PETERS *throws back quilt pieces and tries to put the box in the bag she is wearing. It is too big. She opens box, starts to take bird out, cannot touch it, goes to pieces, stands there helpless. Sound of a knob turning in the other room.* MRS. HALE *snatches the box and puts it in the pocket of her big coat. Enter* COUNTY ATTORNEY *and* SHERIFF.]

COUNTY ATTORNEY (*facetiously*). Well, Henry, at least we found out that she was not going to quilt it. She was going to—what is it you call it, ladies?

MRS. HALE (*her hand against her pocket*). We call it—knot it, Mr. Henderson.

[*Curtain.*]

WEIGHING THE EVIDENCE

1. Why were Mrs. Hale and Mrs. Peters able to uncover and evaluate evidence which the men missed? How did the women react toward the men's scornful attitude toward Mrs. Wright's interest in her canned fruit? Why was a cracked fruit jar no *trifle* to the women?

2. What was the first piece of evidence which the women discovered? How did their actions show that they understood its

significance? Show how their interest in trifles led them to further discoveries.

3. Why did the discovery of the dead bird cause Mrs. Peters to recall her feelings toward the boy who killed her kitten years ago? How did that memory affect her attitude toward Mrs. Wright? What other past experience from her own life helped Mrs. Peters to understand Mrs. Wright? What memories influenced Mrs. Hale? Why did she say: "Oh, I wish I'd come over here once in a while"? What did she mean when she said: "We all go through the same things—it's all just a different kind of the same thing"?

4. This play was adapted by Susan Glaspell from her short story "A Jury of Her Peers." Explain the significance of that title. Who were the jury? Why were they the peers, or equals, of the accused woman? What was their verdict?

THE PLAYWRIGHT'S CRAFT

1. The principal charm of most plays is that they let us see living people in action. However, the most alive person in this play, Minnie Foster Wright, is not seen at all. How is her appearance and personality revealed in what Mrs. Hale and Mrs. Peters say as they concern themselves with the *trifles* they find in the farmhouse? What did you find out from them about Minnie Foster as a young girl? What details helped you to visualize her in later years?

2. What is revealed about Mr. Wright's personality in Mr. Hale's account of how he discovered the murder? What does Mrs. Hale say that helps to complete the characterization?

3. Since plays are meant to be acted, stage directions often suggest a great deal. For example, when the men scoff at Mrs. Wright's worrying about her canned fruit, the stage directions say: "The two women move a little closer together." What is the significance of that action? How does it show what the women are thinking? How does it further the development of the plot? Find other examples of stage directions that

are equally as important as dialogue in conveying meaning.

4. There is considerable dramatic irony in this play. That is, there are actions and speeches which have an entirely different meaning for the audience from what they have for the actors. For example, after the women have found the dead bird, the county attorney says: "If there was some definite thing. Something to show—something to make a story about—a thing that would connect up with this strange way of doing it—" What does the audience know that makes his speech and his determination to continue the search ironic? Later, when the sheriff asked him whether he wanted to examine the things Mrs. Peters was taking to Mrs. Wright, he said: "Oh, I guess they're not very dangerous things the ladies have picked out." Point out the irony in that statement. What is ironic about the title of the play?

SUSAN GLASPELL (1882–1948)

Susan Glaspell began writing as a newspaper reporter, and later wrote successful short stories and novels. However, her chief interest was the theater. With her husband, George Cram Cook, she helped establish an experimental Little Theater group in Massachusetts called the Provincetown Players. This group played an important part in the development of the theater in America. It was the Provincetown Players who produced the early plays of Eugene O'Neill and other unknown playwrights who were later to become famous. Miss Glaspell served them in several capacities. She was actress, playwright, and producer. Her unusually fine biography of her husband, *The Road to the Temple*, is in part the story of the Provincetown Players.

Miss Glaspell did a great deal of writing for the theater besides *Trifles*, which some critics consider the greatest one-act play written in America. *Suppressed Desires* is probably her most popular comedy. Her full-length drama, *Alison's House*, won the Pulitzer Prize in 1931.

For Broader Understanding

1. Compared with that of other countries, what was the position of American drama during the nineteenth century? Describe the types and the quality of the plays that were popular then. Name some important actors and actresses, or whole theatrical families, that came out of that period. Are any still acting today? If so, who are they, and in what plays have they recently appeared?

2. What determines whether a play is a tragedy, a comedy, a farce, or a melodrama? Which type do you think is most popular with the general public? Classify each of the plays in this unit according to the types mentioned. How would you classify the general run of motion pictures? How would you classify the daytime serials, the Westerns, and the mystery and crime thrillers that appear on radio and television? Name a popular play of each of these types.

3. What is meant by the Little Theater movement? Why was it started? How did it affect the development of drama in America? Why were one-act plays particularly suitable for Little Theater production?

4. How has the invention of the motion picture, radio, and television affected drama in America? What important stage plays can you name that have been adapted for one or another of these mass media? Can you name any important novels or short stories that have been dramatized for the movies, radio, or television? How was the dramatized version different from the original story? Is there any way to account for the changes in the dramatization if there were some? In answering the questions compare in *number* and in *educational background* those who would read the story with those who would see the dramatization.

5. What types of dramatic production have achieved a high degree of excellence in America? Can you name an outstanding example of each? Tell about some trends in American drama in recent years.

6. How should one read a play silently in order to get the most pleasure and enjoyment? Tell why it is important to read descriptions of characters, settings, and stage directions even though the play will not be acted. Why is dialogue more important in a play than in a novel or short story?

LISTENING AND VIEWING ACTIVITIES

There are opportunities to enjoy good drama in every community in America. In connection with this unit, the class should explore possibilities to see and listen to some dramatic productions. Following are a few suggestions.

1. If a suitable play is showing at a nearby theater or college campus, or if an outstanding motion picture is showing at a local theater, the class might plan to attend in a group.

2. Recordings of famous American plays like *Abe Lincoln in Illinois* or outstanding music-dramas like *Porgy and Bess* and *South Pacific* can be brought into class for enjoyment, discussion, and evaluation.

3. Groups of students might prepare to read aloud for the class scenes from plays they have enjoyed. One student could explain the situation and summarize the action leading up to the scene.

SPEAKING ACTIVITIES

1. Prepare a report on a famous American actor or actress. If possible, read one complete biography in addition to other sources you might use. The following people would be interesting subjects for reports: The Barrymores, Otis or Cornelia Otis Skinner, Joseph Jefferson, Edwin or John Wilkes Booth, Helen Hayes, Marie Dressler.

2. Make a report on a leading American dramatist. You might include selected readings from the plays as well as informa-

tion about the playwright. Eugene O'Neill, Maxwell Anderson, and Thornton Wilder are possible subjects.

3. Report on the development of motion pictures in America. If films or filmstrips of early pictures are available, use them to add interest to your report.

WRITING ACTIVITIES

1. If you have seen or read a nineteenth-century melodrama, write a burlesque of such a play. Include in your cast of characters the usual stereotypes, and invent a thrill-packed sentimental plot. A group might present the finished play to the class or, if you like, you might write a radio play and make a tape-recording.

2. Write a radio or television dramatization of a favorite short story. Be sure to make the best possible use of the techniques of the media you choose in creating atmosphere and mood. Before you write your own, study several plays of the type you plan to write. Notice how the authors indicate sound, camera, and background music.

3. Write a critical review of a stage play, motion picture, radio play, or television play, that you have seen recently. In preparation read professional reviews in the theater sections of several newspapers and magazines. Your review should include evaluations of two or more of the following: the play itself, the casting and acting, and such technical aspects as stage setting, lighting, and sound or photography.

FOR FURTHER READING

MARY COYLE CHASE, *Harvey* (Oxford). A Pulitzer Prize winner, this humorous play about an invisible rabbit piled up a staggering record of performances in New York.

NORMAN CORWIN, *Untitled and Other Radio Dramas* (Holt). Each of these fine plays is followed by a description of its broadcast performance.

ESTHER E. GALBRAITH, editor, *Plays Without Footlights* (Harcourt). This book tells how to produce a play. The dramas have been chosen for their literary worth and their appeal to students.

RUTH GORDON, *Years Ago* (Viking). A prominent modern actress tells about her girlhood years and her parents' difficulties with their stage-struck daughter.

J. ROGER GOW and HELEN JEANETTE HANLON, editors, *Five Broadway Plays* (Harper). Of special interest is the hilarious hit play "Junior Miss," a comedy by Chodorov and Fields about a teen-ager.

GEORGE KELLY, *The Show-Off* (French). At once funny and realistic, this superb comedy gives the adventures of a back-slapping, go-getting braggart and his family.

HOWARD LINDSAY and RUSSEL CROUSE, *State of the Union* (Random). Concerned with contemporary politics, this play traces the career of a young business executive who is being groomed for the Presidency.

ARTHUR MILLER, *Death of a Salesman* (Viking). This work is a criticism of the "get ahead in the world" ideal. The main character is forced to face the reality of what his whole adult life has been, and to recognize its shabbiness.

EUGENE O'NEILL, *Beyond the Horizon.* This play can be found in O'Neill's *Collected Plays* (Liveright). By telling the story of two brothers' lives, O'Neill investigates man's dreams and disappointments and discusses the question of what true happiness is.

ROBERT SHERWOOD, *Abe Lincoln in Illinois* (Scribner). This absorbing drama tells of Lincoln's early life in New Salem and of his political activities up to the year 1861 when he sets out for Washington as president-elect of the United States.

THORNTON WILDER, *Our Town* (Coward-McCann). Grover's Corners, a small New England town, is the setting for this unusual, thought-filled drama about life and death.

HERMAN WOUK, *The Caine-Mutiny Court Martial* (Doubleday). Mr. Wouk has adapted for the stage the last portion of his best-selling novel. The mental disintegration of the hated Captain Queeg as he faces his examiners will grip the reader.

BIOGRAPHY

In recent years biography has become almost as popular as fiction in America. Most best-seller lists include some biographical writing, and motion pictures based on the careers of scientists, musicians, statesmen, or athletes rival musical comedies as box-office attractions. When you consider that we read stories and novels and go to plays primarily because we are interested in people, it should not be difficult for you to understand the attraction of biographies, which are, after all, true stories about real people. There is double appeal in this type of literature. In the first place, we are naturally curious. We like to know about other people—what they are like, what they have done, where they have been. There are few quirks of personality and few places that we cannot explore by reading biography. In the second place, since we all have problems to solve and adjustments to make in life, we like to read of another's successes and failures. They give us guidance and inspiration for our own lives.

CHANGING PATTERNS OF BIOGRAPHY

However, biography was not always so widely read as it is today. In fact, before 1900 there were comparatively few biographies in America worth reading. One outstanding exception was Benjamin Franklin's *Autobiography*, written in the eighteenth century, but still fascinating to modern readers. You will have a chance to sample it later in this book. If you were to examine some of the other biographies written before 1900, you would readily see why they failed to interest the average reader. Most of them were typical dull "lives" of national heroes. George Washington was naturally a favorite subject. Generally, the author attempted to give a complete history of the great man "from the cradle to the grave," sparing no insignificant or uninteresting detail. Furthermore, the early biographer was usually a prejudiced writer. He felt that he must glorify his hero by praising his virtues and concealing the faults and weaknesses that are present to some degree in all human beings. The result was a lifeless character, too good to be true and lacking in human warmth and appeal.

Early in the twentieth century there was a revolt against the hero-worship type of biography. Then, instead of emphasizing virtues, some writers went to the opposite extreme. They seemed to delight in tearing down the reputations of good and great men by ferreting out hidden scandals, publicizing unfortunate mistakes, and playing up weaknesses and failures. Leaders in this movement were known as the "debunkers." Of course, their biographies were just as one-sided and untrue as those of the earlier period. For as any real student of human nature knows, people are neither all good nor all bad but something in between. The good biography presents a well-rounded picture of a real human being.

Just recently biography has had a re-birth. It is now recognized as a literary art worthy of the efforts of the best writers. Modern American biographers include the famous poet Carl Sandburg, whose great biography of Abraham Lincoln is represented in the section A *Time of Crisis*; the talented Catherine Drinker Bowen, whose biographies of great Americans read like fiction; and scholarly historians like Allan Nevins and Douglas Southall Freeman, whose books are carefully documented histories of their subjects and of the times in which they lived. These writers realize that their readers are entitled to information as accurate as may be attained, enlivened by sidelights of human interest. Good modern biographers are able to combine the painstaking research of the historian with many of the techniques of the novelist.

THE BIOGRAPHER'S CRAFT

You can see that it is not easy to write biography. First, the author must spend a great deal of time—often years—studying records, reading letters and diaries, and interviewing people. When he has finally collected every available bit of information, he must select from his great mass of material the events and incidents which will reveal what he believes is significant about the character of his subject, and about the times in which he lived. If the writer is doing a fictionalized biography, he must know his subject so well as to be able to imagine what the person would do and say and even think in a particular circumstance. If the author is too close to his subject, it is hard to keep an unprejudiced viewpoint. If he is too far removed in time, it is hard to get trustworthy information. If a man writes about himself, as the author of an autobiography does, he must look into his own life and evaluate his own experiences in order to select those which were most influential in shaping his personality and determining the course of his life. Then he must avoid the unpleasant extremes of boastfulness and false modesty. Surely a good modern biographer must possess an unusual combination of talents. In selecting biographies to read and in evaluating biographical material you will do well to consider the author's qualifications for the job he is doing.

REPRESENTATIVE MODERN BIOGRAPHIES

The three selections in the following section reflect significant and distinctly different aspects of American life. They also represent three types of modern biography. "High School Days" is the autobiography of the prominent American novelist, Edna Ferber. You will see how the author has selected from her girlhood days in a small Midwestern town experiences which help us to understand her, her family and friends, and the place where she grew up and went to school. In "The Real American Folk Song" you will find an example of the fictionalized biography so popular today. This one, a typical American success story, reads like a novel. In "Henry Ford Builds a Horseless Carriage," you have the scholarly "life" of a great American industrialist, showing a man in relation to his work and his times. Throughout subsequent sections in this book you will have further opportunities to read other outstanding examples of each type of biography.

◇◇◇◇◇

HIGH SCHOOL DAYS

EDNA FERBER

Looking back on her high-school days in Appleton, Wisconsin, in the early 1900's Edna Ferber says: "Always I have felt sorry for boys and girls who haven't spent the first sixteen years of their lives in a small American town."

Viewed objectively, Appleton as Miss Ferber recreates it was a typical Midwestern town of an earlier period. There was the high school with its happy mixture of German, Irish, Jewish, and Bohemian students. There was Ferber's general store, managed by the enterprising Mrs. Ferber because the father of the family was ill and blind. There was also the Sherman House, where the traveling salesmen sat in the plate-glass windows in the evenings. There were no automobiles, no movies, and no television. Until you have read the selection, you may wonder why the author considered her home town an ideal place to be young in.

A vast collection of sentimental slosh has been written about dear old school days. Since I never had a college education I am in no position to speak for the Higher Learning. When I graduated from the Ryan High School of Appleton, Wisconsin, at the age of seventeen, my formal education was finished. But the ancient ramshackle firetrap was not merely the place in which I and my classmates had spent four years grubbing away at algebra, geometry, economics, English, and physics. We had had four miraculous years of the most exhilarating and heartening fun. I have never seen a public school like it. It was, for us, a clubhouse, a forum, a social center, a playground, a second home. We danced, flirted, played tennis there; learned to think and speak on our feet, learned a sense of honor and fair play, learned, in the best sense of the word, freedom of thought and conduct. On Saturday mornings I used to wake up with a sinking feeling because there was no school that day. By ten o'clock Saturday morning I and my crowd would be over at the high school playing tennis, roaming the dim echoing halls, so strangely quiet now in contrast to the clattering heels and din of talk on weekdays. We sprawled on the grass and talked; we had dates in the cool shade of the side porch, we rehearsed school plays, practiced for contests.

There's no explaining the spirit that permeated that school. Its equipment was of the shabbiest and most archaic. It will seem fantastic to the point of madness when I say that when I visited Oxford many years later and saw the splendor of its spirit shining through its worn corridors and ancient rooms I was reminded of that shabby, dim high school in a small Wisconsin town.

Much of this quality of inner splendor must have been due to the influence of the school principal, Ralph Pringle. The man himself was a shy soft-spoken fellow, round-faced behind his spectacles. I don't know where he came by his modern ideas. Modern schools were not even in fashion then. No one ever told him or us that we were being educated in a strange departure from the usual school code. But I know that in those four years we were encouraged to think and act for ourselves; we were in an atmosphere where debate, oratory, theatricals, and scholarships were considered more important than athletics. The system was almost purely one of honor. We were allowed to come and go almost at will. Pringle's little private office boasted the only decent mirror in the school—there was no proper coatroom or dressing room—and we used to drift into that office and airily primp before that mirror with as much freedom as though it were our own room. Public speaking was stressed. After four years at Ryan the shyest and awkwardest of boys and girls had learned a certain composure and ease on the platform.

Being a piece-speaking fool, this was, of course, just my cup of tea. In my sophomore year I entered the Wisconsin State Declamatory Contest held each May. The contest was a weeding-out process from which the survivors went to Madison, the state capital, for the final fray. The two local Appleton high schools chose three speakers each. Of these six, one was chosen to enter the district high-school contest in which cities of a certain section of the state were represented. At this contest again one was chosen to represent the districts at the state contest. Wisconsin is a great state for public speakers; an articulate state, probably because its students are urged to express themselves in public. I

selected as my recitation a short story entitled "The Story of Patsy," by Kate Douglas Wiggin. It wasn't particularly suited to declamation, and neither, it appeared, was I, for at Madison I came off second in the contest, to my fury. I am too vain to accept second best. . . .

In my last year at Ryan High I again entered the state declamatory contest. My recitation was Richard Harding Davis' "The Littlest Girl," a story about a stage child. I loved it, probably because it was of the theater. Its opening line: "It was at the end of the first act of the first night of the *Sultana*, and there were over a dozen children in front of the footlights—" and I was off like a whippet.

I won first place at Madison. Curiously enough, this event always was given a great deal of publicity in the newspapers of the state. Appleton was de-

lirious. I returned from Madison to find the entire high school and most of the town at the depot, together with the two complete fire engine companies who had been called to control the gigantic blaze of the bonfire which had been lighted in the school athletic field just a block away. The Ryan High School boys had swiped dry goods boxes and packing crates from the rear of every store on College Avenue, including Ferber's, where they definitely felt justified in helping themselves. The bonfire in celebration of the state-contest victory now threatened to become a conflagration. I was rather uncomfortably ridden to the bonfire on the shoulders of two husky football boys, and endeavored to appear shy and deprecating, but I was bursting with my own importance. My father and mother had stayed up until after midnight to hear the news the night before; the high-school bell had been rung to waken all the local burghers out of their sleep. The school presented me with an inscribed loving cup, a dear possession which I still cherish. I was happy, elated, almost (but not quite) self-confident. The bristling resentful little girl of the Ottumwa, Iowa,[1] days disappeared now for months at a time.

For the rest, I was not a good student except in the studies which came naturally to me—English, history, economics. Algebra, geometry, physics were not difficult merely—they were impossible for me. I think I was given passing grades in these studies only because of a rather broad-minded tendency of the school faculty following my victory in the state contest. Otherwise I still would be a permanent member of the senior class at Appleton High School. The simplest problem in algebra today would floor me, and if I had to extract a square root or die, then death would have no sting.

Contests and high-school Forum Debating Society appearances, together with leading lady parts in school plays, gave me assurance. We presented *A Scrap of Paper*, and my role demanded that I faint in the second act. I set about learning how to faint with real limpness and dramatic effect. I had seen various leading ladies faint in professional performances, and few of them had convinced me. I wanted to go down with that crumpling of the muscles and joints which only the relaxed and unconscious body can achieve. The elocution teacher essayed to teach me the trick, but I wasn't satisfied. My mother, busy at the store, had a way of calling up the house on the telephone to learn how things were with the household, and how I was

faring after school hours. My sister Fannie, three years my senior, had graduated and was deep in other concerns, though she was managing the household as well.

The telephone rang. I had been busy rehearsing myself, and I resented the interruption, knowing that it was probably merely my mother.

"What are you doing?" this rather terrific lady demanded, it being a moment of pause in the business of the store.

"I'm fainting," I answered, tartly, impatient of the intrusion.

"What!" shouted my mother.

"I'm fainting!" I yelled, louder than ever, and hung up. The play had been discussed at home. I assumed she would understand. I didn't, as a matter of fact, give it a thought. I had a mattress spread on the floor of my bedroom, and I was flopping like a tenpin at three-minute intervals. It wasn't until my mother arrived, breathless, wild-eyed, and generally frantic, that I realized the construction she had put on my two-word extracurriculum report.

At that time I was a plump, stocky, and ugly girl in eyeglasses perched atop a high-bridged nose inherited from my father. It was a feature which gave his countenance dignity and strength. It was overpowering on my round-cheeked face. I was self-conscious about my plainness; this was aggravated by the fact that my sister Fannie was very handsome, with great lustrous dark eyes and a fine figure. She was exquisitely clever with fabrics and line and color. She could make dresses, make and trim hats; she had great feeling for the indefinable thing known as style. She was running the household and taking daily instruction in millinery in the workroom of a local milliner. I remember my awe and envy of a terrific piece of headgear she produced at this time, and which she wore perched modishly atop her pompadour. A pancake made of yards and yards and yards of pleated chiffon, a rose coquetting from beneath its brim. This, together with a form-hugging fawn broadcloth suit (homemade) caused the boys outside the Sherman House to sit up.

As my hair at that time was a black thick wiry bush, and as I played a good deal of bad tennis, I was accidentally given the nickname of Fluff. "Get the ball, Fluff!" someone on the side lines yelled as I sped toward a trick serve on the Ryan High-School courts. And Fluff I remained for years, even into my Milwaukee newspaper-reporter days, when my plumpness and eyeglassed severity made the name quite out of character. Later, in Milwaukee, that nickname was abandoned and I found myself known as Weber [2] to my *Journal* office friends for a reason which I'll later make clear. And Weber or Web I still am to certain Chicago and New York friends. I rather cherish these nicknames of my girlhood, my young womanhood, my later years. Fluff—Boots—Weber. Nicknames are fond names. We do not give them to people we dislike.

Curiously enough, plain though I was I never lacked a beau. I must have been good company. When there was a dance, a hayrack ride, a picnic, an excursion, I was invited by the current swain. His name never was Loeb or Hammel. The Jewish boys of my age and Esther's [3] didn't take us out. They yearned rather toward the Gentile girls (though there was little enough distinction between us in Appleton). I was squired by Tom Monaghan or Arnold Knuppel or Frank (Pat) Murphy. And I had a fine time. As to health, I was sound and had endurance, with muscular strength and a deep well of nervous energy. But I was inclined toward anemia, low blood pressure, and low thyroid. These should have served to retard me in anything requiring energy or concentration, but ambition and a kind of fury to succeed triumphed over them. I was able then, as now, to sleep eight or nine hours without waking; to walk five or six miles without tiring. I awoke alert and refreshed, I liked to drink water and to eat three meals a day, and to dance. You can't be ill on that unless you break your neck.

At home we had a maid of all work, supervised by Fannie, but the omniscient Julia [4] ruled the roost, though she was busy now earning the living for all of us. We were encouraged to cook. At Ryan I had joined the weekly cooking class, where I learned a good deal about the principles of cookery. The dishes we essayed were, however, a shade too smothered in cream sauce for my taste. Goy cooking, we called it. Ours was richer, more sophisticated food. My mother was fond of telling that when she came, a bride, to Kalamazoo, she thought that the longer an egg boiled the softer it grew. She knew better than this now, but she had no real gift for cookery. She used to do a prodigious amount of preserving, pickling, and canning, however, standing over the stove in the evening or early morning, before and after store hours, stirring, bottling, straining juices. The house would be fragrant with the delicious scent of boiling berries or peaches or quinces; or with the mouthwatering smell of vinegar and spice. In the cellar there were hundreds of Mason jars, row on row along the shelves, showing scarlet and golden and purple and

[2] WEBER—When the author gave her name, people often thought she said Weber. At last her fellow workers began calling her by this name.

[3] ESTHER—A school chum.

[4] JULIA—Miss Ferber's mother.

green; stone crocks of dill pickles, put up in brine with dill and grape leaves in layers; barrels of apples, bins of vegetables, besides such tantalizers as piccalilli, chowchow, corn relish, watermelon pickle, cucumber slices. But of cooking my mother did none except to make an occasional strudel. This famous Hungarian dainty she probably had learned early in her marriage, in deference to her husband's taste. I don't know how she conquered it, for it is a difficult dish, and no relation to the flabby, heavy mass of dough encountered in restaurants under the name of strudel. She got out the baking board and the rolling pin only on very special occasions. The dough must be stretched so thin that it was transparent as tissue paper. A fraction of a fraction of an inch more and it must have split. Over this glaze of dough were sprinkled nuts, citron, raisins, cinnamon, brown sugar, lumps of butter. Then, ever so cautiously, it was rolled in a long papyrus, over and over, and coiled like a white snake into a well-greased pan. This delectable dessert emerged crisp and crackling on the outside, melting and toothsome on the inside. Eaten with whipped cream it was a Hungarian's dream.

We even baked homemade bread in our household of Appleton days. I am glad that I can remember the great yellow crock plump with white dough, covered over with a clean checked tablecloth and left to rise (or raise) overnight in a snug warm spot behind the kitchen stove or near the furnace radiator. In the morning the half-filled crock of the night before was running over at the top. Kneaded and shaped into plump loaves, butter-swabbed and slid into the hot oven, the bread emerged delicious beyond description. The very scent of fresh-baked dough is one of the most tantalizing in the world, in a class with the aroma of hot coffee on a cold winter morning, or broiling bacon in the woods.

Fannie and I cooked the pot roasts, the potted chickens, the stuffed turkeys, the devil's-food cakes, the stuffed breast of veal. The back yard yielded refreshing desserts in the summertime—iced and sugared bowls of raspberries, currants, sweet cherries. Years later, after her marriage, my sister wrote *Fannie Fox's Cook Book*, published by Little, Brown & Company (Advt.), and I still think it is one of the best cookbooks of its day. I wrote a food-choked introduction to it, enviously.

Always I have felt sorry for boys and girls who haven't spent the first sixteen years of their lives in a small American town. There one finds a nice balance of leisure and society which makes for richness in living. Just to sit on the front porch and watch the town go by is something of an education. You knew the wives who were bad housekeepers, because their husbands went home to noonday dinner carrying a little moist brown paper packet that was the meat for the meal. We knew when a boy came courting, and when he and his girl had quarreled, and he came no more, or only, perhaps, as a silent loping figure stealing past after dark for a hungry glimpse of his lost love through the unshaded small-town windows. The local drayman drove rattling home to dinner at twelve in his faded overalls and battered hat. On Sunday, in suave black, he ushered at the fashionable Congregational church, and passed the contribution box. The Congregational church boasted a choir of one hundred male voices, and the Sunday evening services were a dazzling success the year round. Every one of us had a beau in the choir. We would listen, entranced, to the shrill of his tenor or the rumble of his bass. Then we would dawdle a little on our way out after the service, in order to give him time to stampede his way out of the choir jam, dash through the Sunday-school room and out to the line-up at the front door. Two by two we paired off to stroll into the summer night or to walk, blissfully oblivious of the northern cold and ice, across town to our homes.

The swells of the town belonged to the Episcopalian church presided over by a pink-cheeked youthful rector named Selden P. Delany. I often attended evensong with my school friend Eva Hogue, because I loved the theatrical quality of the service; the white-robed choirboys, the very high-church goings-on, the incense, the ceremony. Then, one day, Mrs. Delany, the rector's mother, confided to my mother that they had noticed my visits to the church and that they did so hope that they would be able to convert me.

My attendance ceased.

By now the store was beginning to flourish under the active management of my mother. By active I mean to convey a kind of fury. She was up before seven. She wore shirtwaists and skirts, and she returned from a Chicago buying trip with the first short skirt that Appleton had ever seen on a grown woman. It just cleared the ground. The more conservative wives and mothers raised a disapproving eye at this, and our next-door neighbor took her aside to warn her that no nice woman would appear on the street thus with her ankles showing. But the determined feet under the ground-clearing gray cloth skirt marched their way down to the store and back twice a day, daily, just the same. And presently every woman in Appleton followed her initiative. Women did not use make-up in that day. My mother's skin was sallow. Rouge was considered definitely fast, but Julia kept in her dresser drawer a cotton rose leaf dyed a brilliant red, and this she used to brush on her cheekbones to give the skin a faint flush of pink. Heaven knows for whom; just wholesome vanity. A touch of defiance, too, directed at life.

When first she had taken hold of the business there used to be a caller at the store whose appearance froze the blood in her veins. This grim visitor was the head of the First National Bank of Appleton; a shrewd, kindly-enough man with an eye to business. Affable though he was, he knew that my father's insurance had been mortgaged, that there were mounting doctor's bills, that money had been borrowed.

Into the store he would stroll, his greeting polite and even cheery. "Good morning, good morning, Mrs. Ferber!" He would stand a moment, balancing airily from toe to heel, taking a large speculative view of the shop and its shelves and bins of goods. Then he would begin to stroll ruminatively down one aisle and up the next, his shrewd little eyes seeing and appraising everything. He would hum a little absent-minded tune as he walked, picking up a piece of china to glance at its pattern, turning over a charming Limoges [5] plate, all guileless rosebuds on creamy white, to note the maker's mark on the back; tapping a water pitcher with judicial knuckles, staring approvingly at a smart little toilet set of ebony brushes with silver ornaments. He would put each piece down carefully after his inspection, proceeding step by step to the lamps, the hardware, the stockings, the toys.

"Very pretty. Ve-ry pretty indeed. Hmm." And so, his hands behind his back, still humming, out the screen door

[5] LIMOGES—Pronounced lē mōzh'.

into the sunshine of College Avenue, leaving desperation behind him.

But now those visits had ceased. I heard an endless amount of talk about business, and hated it. My mother was, I suppose, an unhappy woman at that time, and I must have heard something of this, too. Marriage seemed to me to be less than a desirable state of being. Perhaps it was then I decided that I would have none of it. Sometimes, when I have a nightmare, I dream that it is Christmas time at the store, the aisles are packed and feverish, drafts of icy Wisconsin December air stream through the constantly opening front door, and I am saying to a mill girl or to some townswoman, "What can I show you?"

At Christmas time we all helped. My school friends used to ask if they could clerk, for the fun of it. I loathed it— the rush, the noise, the rather senseless selecting of gifts. It must be accountable for my feeling about Christmas all these years. It depresses me, I don't enjoy it, I tell myself it is because I like making gifts when I feel inclined, or when the right object strikes me, and not when the calendar dictates.

Mill hands, farmers' wives, Lawrence University professors, East End society, middle-class householders—my mother talked to everyone. Rather, they talked to her. Sitting there, in a business lull, on a stool in a corner up front beneath the bookshelves, Julia Ferber was a sort of small-town sibyl. She had pansylike eyes, a sympathetic and compelling way. Practically everyone told her everything. To the slick young traveling men she was a sort of mother confessor. Theirs wasn't an easy life. These drummers, living in second-rate small-town hotels, unpacking and packing their samples, vying with one another for business, eating greasy hotel food, were lonely for their wives

and children, or for their girls. In the evening, after the day's work, they would sit in the plate-glass windows of the Sherman House, or outside on benches in summertime. The town girls would flounce by—good middle-class girls to whom these rather grubby little men from the world outside their home town represented who knows what of romance and adventure.

These would lean an elbow on the showcase in the store, push their smart saw-edged sailor hats back from their brows, open their hearts, show the picture in the front of their watch or wallet, and Tell All. Their love affairs, their business worries, their marital difficulties, their grievances against the firm back East.

"Why, that's terrible!" she would say. "If I were you . . ." Her advice usually was sound. Sometimes if they were broke she lent them a few dollars, but not much. She hadn't it to spare. They always paid her back.

I heard and saw a great deal of this, and absorbed its meaning and character and atmosphere without being conscious of it. When she went to Chicago on her buying trips she visited the big German and French importing houses from whom she bought foreign china, glassware, toys. The salesmen often tried a flirtation or invited her to dinner and the theater, but she would have none of them. Dead tired at the end of a day spent in the wholesale district, making decisions on which depended the success or failure of the next six business months, she would go home and tumble into bed at the Neumanns'.[6] Her three brothers and her sister, all unmarried, lived together in a comfortable house on the south side of Chicago. Of five children,

[6] NEUMANNS'—The home of Julia Ferber's family.

my mother was the only one who married.

The margin between loss and gain was so slender in those days of her first taking hold that there was something miraculous in her maintaining the balance at all. She tried little harmless tricks that represented the difference between a hundred dollars' gain or loss on the week. Two glass punch bowls that had cost a dollar each at wholesale in Chicago could be rented out, together with silver ladles that had been wedding presents to the Kalamazoo bride, every day in the week for college parties, club meetings, whist [7] parties, dances, and lodge shindigs. Nothing escaped her. Cracked or chipped dishes could be sold to the farmers' wives to be used in threshing or harvest time. Once, on a buying trip, she came across hundreds of discarded paperbound copies of *Sappho*. She bought the lot for almost nothing, had them dusted off, stacked them luridly in the window, from which they vanished like hot cakes for twenty-five cents apiece. *Sappho* was considered a very daring book indeed in those days. Rather pitiful little tricks, and touchingly desperate, but legitimate. She had an incredible eye for a bargain. At the famous importing house of Borgfeldt she happened upon a great bin with shelves full of dusty grimy china figures, evidently neglected and forgotten. They were from five inches to a foot high; religious figures, in colors, representing all the saints, the Pietà,[8] the cradle in the manger.

"How much?" she demanded of the salesman.

"Those!" He stared, vaguely surprised.

"Oh, you don't want those, Mrs. Ferber. That's a discarded lot of china stuff."

"How much for the lot?"

Shipped back to Appleton, dusty and shelfworn, in their bedding of straw and paper, they were given a bath in soap and water—hundreds of these small figures. Beneath the grime they emerged fine examples of foreign workmanship, their blue and gold and crimson and purple and white brilliant and fadeless as the color found in the cathedrals of Europe. Saints, angels, and cherubim gleamed fresh-cheeked and rosy in the window. Father Fitzmaurice's parishioners made a clean sweep of them in less than twenty-four hours. Only four hundred dollars. But no million-dollar Wall Street coup [9] ever brought such a feeling of quiet triumph.

Some of this I used in the novel *Fanny Herself*. Much of the material used in the Emma McChesney stories [10] stemmed from these days when my eyes and ears were wide open, and my mind as porous as a sponge.

The farm women and their husbands and their hard, often tragic, lives emerged from the old yellow trunk when I started to write *So Big*,[11] many years later. In those days there was no whirling into town in fifteen minutes in the Ford, to go to the movies and buy a Coca-Cola and the evening paper. The Wisconsin farmer started for town on Saturday before daybreak, the great farm horses, shaggy of mane and fetlock, clop-clopping down the dirt road or snow ruts, with the farmer, his wife, the day's market produce and such children as could be spared from the farm work piled into

---

[7] WHIST—A card game similar to bridge.

[8] PIETÀ (pyā·tä′)—In art a representation of the Virgin Mary mourning over the Crucified Christ. Usually she is depicted as holding the body on her knees.

[9] COUP (kōō)—A brilliant stroke; stratagem.

[10] EMMA McCHESNEY STORIES—Emma, the heroine of these stories, was a traveling saleswoman.

[11] *So Big*—A novel about a woman who struggled to make her small farm a success.

the buckboard. Calves, pigs, vegetables, chickens, corn, oats, children arrived in town half frozen in the winter, baked in the summer. At noon on Saturday you would see the farm wagons thick in the barnyard of the Farmers Rest Hotel on Morrison Street, and the smell of frying pork and potatoes and cabbage and pipe tobacco floated out from the open doors and windows. To the Ferber family it would have seemed very odd indeed to have to purchase at Appleton grocers' or butchers' in the ordinary way such supplies as chickens, ducks, butter, eggs, corn, peas, beets, beans, apples, and the like. The farmers preferred to trade in these commodities for articles of wearing apparel and household necessity. Stockings, china, kitchenware, glassware made the exchange. A farm wagon would drive up to the door of the Ferber house on North Street and the kitchen table would immediately take on the look of a Hans Holbein [12] still life.

The farmers' wives were wrinkled and old long before their time. It was a bitter, hard life. Such ready money as the farmers had went into farm machinery and livestock and repairs. There were no radios then, no washing machines, no electricity, no automobiles in the Wisconsin farmhouse. In winter the farmer's wife would be wrapped in a huge shapeless fringed shawl, but the husband would be snug in a sheepskin or even a buffalo-hide coat. Sometimes the women tried to furbish their mashed little hats with red cotton roses bobbing grotesquely atop them. Invariably the women had bad teeth, with great gaps where molars were missing. Often the comparatively well-to-do had new and improbable sets of gleaming blue-white china store teeth. The women, at thirty,

looked like crones of sixty. Back-breaking work, childbearing, and the monotony of farm life took their toll of young red-cheeked farm girls. Julia Ferber would talk to them as they waited in the store for their husbands to call for them.

"How many children?"

"Well, I had ten a'ready. And I never had no doctor, neither, time they was born."

"Who helped you?"

"Neighbor woman, she helped. We never had no doctor in our house, yet."

"How many of your children are living, Mrs. Koepke?"

"I got two boys and one girl, she ain't so strong, her back."

If the farmers came to Ferber's store for their threshing dishes and chamber pots, the social East End set soon learned that the whist prizes, the china, the glassware, and novelties were distinctive. They were bought from importers, and had the foreign craftsman's touch. These, too, confided in Julia Ferber, strangely enough. My husband—my children—my gowns—my hopes—my fears. There was a little strain of mischief in her, and she sometimes used to guy [13] these people gently; people who bragged too much. She called it "blowing."

"You don't say!" she would exclaim, murderously, as they recounted their importance or their social exploits. "That's perfectly LOVE-ly!"

Of the clerks in the store there were two who were more than employees; they were warmhearted friends and helpers. One was Martha Gresens. Martha not only clerked, but on dull days, or when the streets were locked in drifts of snow, you found her up in the broad balcony, where the sleds and tricycles and such heavy toys were kept, sewing on dresses

[12] HANS HOLBEIN (hôl′bīn)—A famous sixteenth-century artist.

[13] GUY—Make fun of.

for me or Fannie. Martha was an accomplished needlewoman. She actually made my high-school graduation dress—a dream dress in my opinion, made of white point d'esprit [14] with row after row of narrow white satin ribbon. A sensational dress.

Arthur Howe, an Irish boy, gangling, red-wristed and witty, was clerk, handyman, and delivery. He was a born actor, with a devastating gift of mimicry. Fortunately, Appleton's dignitaries never heard or saw Arthur's miraculous imitations. Toward my father Arthur was patience itself. He took him on long walks—too long—when he delivered goods. Sometimes he made those deliveries trailing after him a child's size painted wooden cart, the blind man at his side. They must have made a touching and grimly comic picture. Mercifully, perhaps, it didn't strike us so, or the townspeople.

The eyes were very bad now. He could still see just a glimmering little. There never had come to him the compensation that the blind usually have—a heightening of the remaining senses as one sense grows weak and weaker. He never became reconciled to blindness, he fought it and bitterly resented it. He would start out alone when we weren't looking, and then would begin a rather wild hunt, with a clutching of fear at our vitals. For usually, when the pain came upon him, he would grow dizzy and faint. Never, in those years, could I see a little crowd collected anywhere on the street that I failed to feel that clutch of sick apprehension. I would break into a little run, afraid to look but elbowing through the throng to look and peer until I saw whether what I feared was true or not.

[14] POINT D'ESPRIT (pwăN d'ĕs'prē′)—A kind of lace.

He spent longer and longer hours on the front porch at home, and with this we were content. There was between us a mild joke. At an Elks convention in Appleton some years back the lodge members had gone up and down the streets shouting the Elks convention formula greeting of "Hello, Bill!" All that week I had greeted my father, facetiously, with the stock, "Hello, Bill" and Bill he remained to me thereafter. He, from my early childhood, had called me Pete. I was, I suppose, a self-assertive and boyish little girl. So, then, there was this mild joke between us.

"Hello, Bill!" I would greet him.

"Hello, Pete! What you reading?"

"Dickens."

"Dickens! I thought you'd read that."

It was sad when he lost his taste for smoking. Ever since I could remember he had loved to smoke mild pale-brown dapper cigars. As sight slipped from him his enjoyment of this solace went with it. The smoker usually is unaware that he watches the smoke from cigar, cigarette, or pipe, and is soothed by it as by the narcotic. It must have been so in his case. As he held his cigar between his teeth a little puzzled disappointed look would come into his face. He would take the cigar from his lips and look at it, sorrowfully, as one would survey a treacherous trusted friend. He would quietly put it down, the smoke would curl futilely for a while, then die. The fragrant weed would be a dead stinking thing, fit only for the ash can. When a friend or a chance traveling man offered him a cigar he would shake his head sadly. "No. I used to love to smoke. But now I can't see it. No sir, I don't enjoy smoking any more. I don't know why."

Now the four happy years at Ryan High School were over. Curiously enough, I not only had been happy—

131

I had known I was happy. I used to say to myself, "Edna, you're having a wonderful time. You're having the time of your life."

Perhaps the bitter years of early childhood had taught me that. It is true that all my life (perhaps this was, unconsciously, the writer's double reaction) I have been able to have a sensation and to analyze myself while having it. It makes enjoyment doubly keen, and pain doubly sharp, and it is, incidentally, deathly hard on romance.

After winning the Wisconsin State Declamatory Contest just before graduation in June my mind was made up. I would go away to the Northwestern University School of Elocution, in Evanston, Illinois. I don't think my imagination leaped so far as to encompass the distance between this elocutionary course and the professional stage, but I must have had this stored away somewhere in the back of my mind.

My announcement of this resolution caused a family whirlwind. I had no money of my own. I was seventeen. We, a family of four, were bound together in ties even closer than those of the average Jewish family. The blind man leaned on me, and I felt a great protective pity for him as he stumbled so clumsily through life. My mother was working like a man. My sister, pretty, gentle, talented in her own way, was too tied to the house and its duties. I tried to stand out against it all, but I was still too young and too tenderhearted and too weak. The matter of pocket money or some such matter came up, was threshed out, led to high words.

In a white-hot rage I, saying nothing to the family, marched down to the office of the *Appleton Daily Crescent* and had a blistering talk with Sam Ryan, its editor. He, owner of this well-run small-town paper, had heard of my work on the high-school paper. Then, too, I had written a piece describing the confirmation service at Temple Emanu-El that year, and the *Crescent* had printed it. Too, the winning of the state contest had put me, so far as that small community was concerned, in something of the position of the college athlete who easily gets a job selling bonds in a broker's office.

My business with Sam Ryan concluded, I then marched home bursting with spite and announced that I had signed a contract with Sam Ryan to work for three dollars a week as a reporter on the *Appleton Crescent*. The fact that I was not of legal age, and that any contract must therefore be void, never occurred to any of us.

Well, there I was, a girl reporter. I didn't want to be a writer. I never had wanted to be a writer. I couldn't even use a typewriter, never having tried. The

stage was my one love. To this moment I feel sure (but not so sure as I once did) that I would have been The Actress of my day. I go to the theater because I love it; I write plays for the theater because I love it. I am still wrapped in my childish dream, and I never see such gifted girls as Katharine Cornell, Helen Hayes, Ruth Gordon, Lynn Fontanne that I do not feel sure I could do much better than they if only I were up there playing the part. Perhaps one reason why I've never acted is the fear of showing myself up to myself as a fraud after all these resentful years.

At any rate, then, at seventeen my writing career accidentally began. It was brewed in a storm. I don't remember a day since then when I haven't been writing, in all sorts of circumstances, happy and wretched, ill or well, traveling or at home. Writing has brought me friends and fortune and happiness and world-wide interests.

But to this day I regard myself as a blighted Bernhardt.[15]

[15] BERNHARDT—Sarah Bernhardt, a famous French actress.

◇◆◇◆◇◆◇◆◇◆◇◆◇◆◇◆◇◆◇◆◇◆◇◆◇◆◇◆◇

FOR UNDERSTANDING

1. What made the old Ryan High School good in spite of the fact that it was an "ancient, ramshackle firetrap" with shabby and archaic equipment? What qualities made Miss Ferber compare it to the famous Oxford University in England?

2. What kind of man was the principal, Mr. Pringle? Miss Ferber says that he had modern ideas about education. In explaining what she means she says: ". . . we were encouraged to think and act for ourselves; were in an atmosphere where debate, oratory, theatricals, and scholarship were considered more important than athletics."

How well does what she admired in her school apply to the average American high school today? How accurately does it describe your school?

3. Can you see why Miss Ferber would appreciate a high school like the one she attended? Why was it particularly suited to a girl with her special interests and abilities? What type of student would not find it congenial?

4. Besides her school what else in Appleton contributed to Miss Ferber's education and enjoyment? What are some of the things she mentions as being good about small-town life?

5. What were Miss Ferber's early ambitions for a career? How did she happen to become a writer instead? What talents and preparation did she have for each career?

THE ART OF AUTOBIOGRAPHY

In this chapter about her high-school days, Miss Ferber did not attempt to tell everything that she did or everything that happened to her during that period of her life. Instead, she selected significant incidents from which the reader could build up a picture of her character and personality, the town, its people, and the times.

1. What were you able to learn about the author's personality and special interests from her account of the state declamation contest? What does that incident reveal about the school and the community?

2. Besides adding a touch of humor, what does her story about rehearsing for the school play tell you about her ambitions and her character and about her mother's personality?

3. Why do you suppose she chose to tell about the family's interest in food and cooking? What does that passage reveal about the Ferbers' family life and background?

4. Which incidents show Mrs. Ferber's independence and resourcefulness? Which reveal the relationship between the author and her father? Which help to explain her success as a writer?

PICTURESQUE WORDS

You know that writers often use striking comparisons or figures of speech to express what they have to say vividly and colorfully. Many common words are picturesque because they originated in apt comparisons. For example in the sentence describing the high school Miss Ferber refers to the building as a "ramshackle firetrap." The word *ramshackle*, which means *falling apart* or *rickety*, comes from *ransack*, which means *to search*. A *ramshackle* building, therefore, would have the appearance of one that had been thoroughly searched—literally torn apart or weakened by searchers.

Look up the origins or literal meanings of the italicized words in the following phrases taken from the selection and compare them with present meanings. Explain how each word is in itself a figure of speech.

1. *grubbing* away at algebra
2. I answered *tartly*
3. a rose *coquetting* from beneath the brim
4. such *tantalizers* as piccalilli
5. he would begin to stroll *ruminatively*

EDNA FERBER (Born 1887)

Edna Ferber was born in Kalamazoo, Michigan, but her parents moved to Appleton, Wisconsin, where Edna went to high school. At seventeen she began her successful literary career as a reporter on the *Appleton Daily Crescent*. Later she worked for the *Milwaukee Journal* and for the *Chicago Tribune*.

Almost from the time when she published her first story at twenty-three, Edna Ferber has been an important American writer. Her clever and entertaining short stories have always been popular, and her novels interpreting American life have repeatedly made the best-seller lists. Several of her novels, including *So Big* and *Cimarron*, have been made into plays and movies. *Show Boat* became the basis for the Broadway musical hit for which Jerome Kern wrote some of his most famous songs. In collaboration with George Kaufman Miss Ferber also contributed to the American theater such well-known plays as *Dinner at Eight*, *Stage Door*, and *The Land Is Bright*.

❖❖❖❖

THE REAL AMERICAN
FOLK SONG

DAVID EWEN

George Gershwin, famous composer of popular music, called himself a "typical self-made American." Certainly there was little in his background or environment to account for his musical success. He was born in Brooklyn of immigrant parents and grew up on the lower East Side of New York where he absorbed the atmosphere of American city life with the very air he breathed. His parents, who were industrious and intelligent, made a good home for George and his older brother, Ira. It was to give Ira the cultural advantages of a musical education that a piano was brought into the Gershwin apartment when George was twelve years old. Almost before its wrappings had been removed, George amazed his mother by playing the new piano. His parents were so impressed with the younger boy's musical ability that they decided to give him lessons along with Ira.

George probably learned little from his earliest teachers. However, there was one man, Charles Hambitzer, himself an accomplished concert pianist and composer, who recognized the boy's genius and gave him the encouragement and inspiration he needed. There was only one respect in which the distinguished teacher was disappointed in his promising pupil: the boy failed to show the proper scorn for ragtime, the popular music of the day. In fact, George loved ragtime because it seemed to him to express the America of his generation better than classical music ever could. He decided that what he wanted to do more than anything else was to compose really good popular music that would be sung and played and loved by people everywhere.

The headquarters for the kind of music that George hoped to write was "Tin Pan Alley," a district in New York where the publishers of popular music had their offices. To get as close as possible to the music of America, George left school at sixteen and became a piano player for a music publishing company in the "Alley." There he played and sang and listened to all types of popular music, including a new variety of ragtime called jazz. From the first, Gershwin and jazz seemed made for each other. It was through jazz that he was best able to interpret the America that he knew; and because he was a great musician, he was instrumental in making jazz respectable and acceptable as serious American music.

Before he died at the age of thirty-eight, George Gershwin had realized his early ambition to write good American music that would be popular with all kinds of people. Since his death, his songs, musical comedies, and symphonic compositions have become part of America's musical heritage. Among the most famous is the well-loved RHAPSODY IN BLUE, which was written at the request of Paul Whiteman for a jazz concert at Aeolian Hall in New York. Probably his greatest achievement was PORGY AND BESS. In the following chapter from THE STORY OF GEORGE GERSHWIN David Ewen tells how that first real American folk opera came to be written.

135

Ever since his early one-act experiment in opera, seen for just one night at the *Scandals*,[1] Gershwin had been ambitious to write an American opera—an opera whose libretto and music would arise from strictly American backgrounds and experiences. Earlier in his career he put off fulfilling his ambition until he should acquire more experience in the writing of serious music. To Jerome Kern he once said wistfully: "I wonder if I'm ready to write an opera. I have some talent—and a great deal of nerve."

But after he had become the successful composer of two rhapsodies, a piano concerto, a symphonic poem, and an overture, he felt that perhaps the time had come for the writing of his largest and greatest work. He began hunting for an appropriate libretto. For a while, he thought of writing music for a Yiddish play called *The Dybbuk* which had been translated into English and had enjoyed a successful run in New York. But an Italian composer had the exclusive opera rights to that play, and the project had to be forgone. Then he thought of using some text with the setting of a large American city (the "melting pot" of all races and creeds) with a typical American family as principal characters. He found nothing that answered these conditions—nothing, that is, which would have lent itself to musical treatment. And he waited for the proper book to come along.

The urge to write an opera—perhaps the first *real* American opera—became more and more irresistible. He was further spurred on by the encouragement of his many friends and admirers. He had been performed at Aeolian Hall, Carnegie Hall, Symphony Hall in Boston, Lewisohn Stadium, and other American concert auditoriums. Why not at the Metropolitan Opera House? The idea exhilarated Gershwin—for it would mean the greatest artistic triumph of all.

He remembered a Theater Guild play he had seen in New York. It was by DuBose Heyward and its title was *Porgy*. It told of the love of a crippled Negro beggar in Charleston, South Carolina, for a girl named Bess. The play had moved him—as it had moved capacity audiences for about a year—because of its American flavor, its simplicity, its picturesque background. George also recalled that at the time he saw the play he had met the author and said to him, "Some day, when I learn how, I'd like to write an opera about Porgy."

Why not an opera about Porgy? Richard Wagner had written an opera about the love of Tristan for Isolde; Debussy about that of Pelléas for Mélisande.[2] Suddenly Gershwin realized that the love of humble Porgy for Bess was in its own way as eloquent and as touching as those of other opera heroes. Why should he not write an American love story with a Negro setting and Negro characters? It could become an American folk opera, with an American setting, rich with American musical lore. In the opera-pageant of great lovers, why should not Porgy and Bess join Tristan and Isolde, and Pelléas and Mélisande?

Once he knew what his libretto would be, Gershwin became restive, impatient to set to work upon what he knew must be his most ambitious undertaking. There was the problem of whipping together a suitable libretto from the original play. But that could be left to DuBose Heyward himself, in collabora-

---

[1] *Scandals*—A Broadway revue for which Gershwin wrote the music.

[2] WAGNER . . . MÉLISANDE—The proper nouns here are pronounced as follows: Wagner (väg′nẽr); Isolde (ĭ·sōld′); Debussy (dẽ·bü′sẽ′); Pelléas (pĕ′lā′ȧs′); Mélisande (mȧ′lē′zäɴd′).

tion with George's brother Ira, who would also write the song lyrics. Impatiently, George dropped all other work, brushed aside about a quarter of a million dollars' worth of contracts, and began to sketch the broad outlines of his opera.

The musical ideas did not come easily, for what Gershwin wanted was something richer and deeper than jazz music. He wanted his music to interpret a race, its nobility and naïveté, its heroism and cruelty, its savagery and tenderness. Such music, he felt at last, could not be plucked out of the atmosphere of New York City as the *Rhapsody* and the *Concerto* had been. He must familiarize himself with the local color of South Carolina, live with the folk music of the Negro until it became a part of him, come to know Negro people well and personally.

He abandoned his luxurious duplex apartment on East 72nd Street, took the train for the South, and rented a shack in the bleak setting of the waterfront near Charleston.

"Under the baking suns of July and August," DuBose Heyward recalled later, "we established ourselves on Folly Island, a small barrier island ten miles from Charleston. James Island, with its large population of primitive Gullah Negroes, lay adjacent, and furnished us with a laboratory in which to test our theories, as well as an inexhaustible source of folk material.

"The most interesting discovery to me, as we sat listening to their spirituals, or watched a group shuffling before a cabin or a country store, was that to George it was more like a homecoming than an exploration. The quality in him which had produced the *Rhapsody in Blue*, in the most sophisticated city in America, found its counterpart in the impulse behind the music and bodily rhythms of the simple Negro peasant of the South.

"The Gullah Negro prides himself on what he calls 'shouting.' This is a complicated rhythmic pattern beaten out by feet and hands as an accompaniment to the spirituals, and is indubitably an African survival. I shall never forget the night when, at a Negro meeting on a remote sea island, George started shouting with them—and eventually to their huge delight stole the show from their champion 'shouter.' I think that he is probably the only white man in America who could have done it.

"Another night as we were about to enter a dilapidated cabin that had been taken as a meeting house by a group of Negro Holy Rollers,[3] George caught my arm and held me. The sound that had arrested him was one to which, through long familiarity, I attached no special importance. But now, listening to it with him, and noticing his excitement, I began to catch its extraordinary quality. It consisted of perhaps a dozen voices raised in loud rhythmic prayer. The odd thing about it was that while each had started at a different time, upon a different theme, they formed a clearly defined rhythmic pattern, and that this, with the actual words lost, and the inevitable pounding of the rhythm, produced an effect almost terrifying in its primitive intensity. Inspired by the extraordinary effect, George wrote six simultaneous prayers producing a terrifying primitive invocation to God in the face of hurricane."

Having saturated himself with Negro music and ritual in Charleston, George could write music for his opera rich with Negroid flavors and colors. His melodies assumed the naïve patterns, and expressed the simple joys and pathos, of

[3] HOLY ROLLERS—A minor religious sect known for its emotionalism.

137

the spiritual. His street cries reproduced the strange and haunting intervals intoned by vendors of fish and cakes in Catfish Row. His rhythms assumed the barbarous and savage passion of the "shouting" Gullahs. He was writing folk music of a race, and writing it with such authenticity that, in its final form, it seemed to be the work not of an American born and raised in city streets but that of several generations of Negroes who had passed these melodies from father to son.

Gershwin worked for eleven months on the score of his opera, writing part of it in South Carolina and other parts in various sections of the country from upper New York to Florida. Another nine months were consumed in orchestrating it. Finally, the opera was finished. Gershwin handled the seven hundred pages of closely written music—and he felt it was good.

It had been contracted for by the Theater Guild, which had produced the original play. Rouben Mamoulian, who had directed the original dramatic production, was once again called upon to supervise.

Mamoulian has eloquently described his first impressions of Gershwin's music to the opera as he heard George himself play it on the piano.

"It was rather amusing how we were trying to be nonchalant and poised that evening, yet we were trembling with excitement. The brothers handed me a tall highball, and put me in a comfortable leather armchair. George sat down at the piano, while Ira stood over him like a guardian angel. George's hands went up in the air about to strike the shining keys. Halfway down, he changed his mind, turned to me and said, 'Of course, Rouben, you must understand it is very difficult to play the score. As a

matter of fact, it's really impossible. Can you play Wagner on the piano? Well, this is just like Wagner.' I assured George that I understood. Up went his nervous hands again, and the next second I was listening to the opening piano music of the opera.

"I found it so exciting, so full of color and so provocative in its rhythm, that after this first piano section was over, I jumped out of my armchair and interrupted George to tell him how much I liked it. Both brothers were as happy as children to hear words of praise—though heaven knows they should have been used to them by then. When my explosion was over and they went back to the piano, they both blissfully closed their eyes before they continued with the lovely 'Summertime' song. George played with the most beatific smile on his face. He seemed to float on the waves of his own music, with the southern sun shining on him. Ira sang—he threw his head back with abandon, his eyes closed, and sang like a nightingale. In the middle of the song George couldn't bear it any longer and took over the singing from him. To describe George's face while he sang 'Summertime' is something that is beyond my capacity as a writer. *Nirvana* [4] might be the word. So it went on. George was the orchestra and sang half the parts. Ira sang the other half. Ira was also frequently the audience.

"It was touching to see how he, while singing, would become so overwhelmed with admiration for his brother that he would look from him to me with half-open eyes and pantomime with a soft gesture of the hand, as if saying, 'He did it. Isn't it wonderful? Isn't *he* wonderful?' George would frequently take his

[4] *Nirvana* (nĭr·vä′nȧ)—A state of oblivion brought on by great joy or ecstasy.

eyes away from the score and watch me covertly, and my reaction to the music, while pretending that he wasn't really doing it at all. It was far into the night before we finished with the opera, and sometimes I think that in a way this was the best performance of it I ever heard. We all felt exultantly happy. The next morning both George and Ira had completely lost their voices; for two days they couldn't talk, they only whispered. I shall never forget that evening—the enthusiasm of the two brothers about the music, their anxiety to do it justice, their joy at its being appreciated, and with it all their touching devotion to each other. It is one of those rare, tender memories one so cherishes in life."

Then began the round of rehearsals, with Todd Duncan and Anne Brown heading an all-Negro cast, and Alexander Smallens conducting. For several weeks, George knew all the frustrations, the heartbreak, and (gradually) the exhilaration of seeing his work emerge into life. He was gentle and soft-spoken, offering his criticisms quietly, rarely losing patience. When rehearsals went well, he would sit in the back of the darkened auditorium, his eyes closed as he drank in the music. But there were times when things did not go smoothly, and he would then pace the aisles nervously, the muscles of his face taut.

At last the performance was in shape; even Gershwin was satisfied. The Boston tryout, on September 30, 1935, was highly successful; at the end of the performance the audience rose to its feet to cheer the composer. Then came the New York première—at the Alvin Theater on October 10.

Many in that first-night audience were puzzled by what they saw and heard. Some complained that this was not really an opera but some hybrid product com-

PHOTOGRAPH BY VANDAMM

bining elements of the musical comedy with those of opera. Others considered it too realistic for the make-believe world of the music-drama: who ever heard of a crap game in an opera—and a crap game treated musically through a respectable fugue?[5]

Perhaps it was still too early for the audience to realize that they were witnessing something new—an American folk opera, treated with American realism and flavor. It had always been the fate of opera—when it attempted to strike for new directions—to be misunderstood by audiences who heard it for the first time. Eighteenth-century listeners said of Gluck's *Orfeo*[6] that it was not an opera because the composer sought new avenues for dramatic expression. In the same manner the nineteenth century criticized Debussy, Wagner, Charpentier.[7] And the twentieth was now complaining about Gershwin's work.

As a serious opera—so some critics said —*Porgy and Bess* had numerous dramatic and musical weaknesses: the various numbers, both solo and ensemble, were loosely assembled; there were pages that lacked artistic conviction; the recitatives were sometimes awkward. "The work," wrote Olin Downes, "does not utilize all the resources of the operatic composer or pierce very often to the depth of the simple and pathetic drama." But, in a second critical article about the work, Mr. Downes realized that "this is an opera with real melodies in it. . . . In his own way and according to his own lights, Mr. Gershwin has taken a substantial

step, and advanced the cause of native opera."

But if, at its opening performance, *Porgy and Bess* had not received the acclaim it deserved, it was not to be permanently denied its due measure of fame. It was revived in 1938 in Los Angeles and San Francisco with the original New York cast, and was acclaimed by both cities. In 1937 the David Bispham Silver Medal was awarded to *Porgy and Bess* as an outstanding native achievement in the field of opera. Early in 1942 it was revived in New York and it proved sensationally successful, one of the most substantial hits of the dramatic season, enjoying the longest run ever had by a "revival." The Music Critics' Circle of New York singled it out as the most important musical "revival" of the year.

Porgy and Bess is an opera about America, with the simplicity, beauty, tender humor, wistfulness, and pathos of great folk art. Gershwin himself called it, appropriately, a folk opera. "I have been asked why it is so called," he wrote. "The explanation is a simple one. *Porgy and Bess* is a folk tale. Its people naturally would sing folk music. When I first began work on the music I decided against the use of original folk material because I wanted the music to be all of one piece. Therefore I wrote my own spirituals and folk songs. But they are still folk music—and therefore, being operatic in form, *Porgy and Bess* becomes a folk opera."

It is now recognized that it is one of the most successful examples of native American opera. For two centuries, American composers have written operas; but rarely have they written American operas. The texts they used were frequently remote from American experiences. Even when composers wrote op-

---

[5] FUGUE (fūg)—A musical composition in which the central theme is interwoven with a number of minor melodies. The dominant melody is sometimes lost, but always reappears.

[6] GLUCK'S (glŏŏk) *Orfeo*—The complete title is *Orfeo ed Euridice*.

[7] CHARPENTIER—Pronounced shàr'pän'tyā'.

eras about American subjects—like Walter Damrosch in *The Scarlet Letter*, or Victor Herbert in *Natoma*, or Charles Wakefield Cadman in *Shanewis*—the music was but a pale imitation of European models. But Gershwin's opera could have been written only by an American; and its music has roots deeply embedded in American soil.

◇◇◇◇◇◇◇◇◇◇◇◇◇◇◇◇◇◇◇◇◇◇◇◇◇◇

FOR UNDERSTANDING

1. Why hadn't Gershwin attempted to write an opera earlier in his career? What made him believe that he might finally be ready?

2. Why was the story of Porgy ideal for an American opera? How did it provide an opportunity to use native American music? In what ways did Gershwin hope to make the music of his opera different from jazz?

3. Why couldn't Gershwin get ideas and inspiration for the music for *Porgy* from the Negroes in and around New York? What made the people of the islands near Charleston particularly good sources of the atmosphere and rhythms that were needed for the opera? What did Gershwin have in common with those people that made them accept him as one of themselves?

4. What was revealed about Gershwin's character and personality in each of the following: his long preparation for writing *Porgy*? his associations with the Negroes of James Island? his relationship with his brother?

AN AMERICAN FOLK OPERA

1. What is Gershwin's explanation of the term "folk opera"? What makes the story of Porgy and Bess a folk tale?

2. What is the difference between *original* folk music and the folk music of *Porgy and Bess*? Why didn't Gershwin use original folk music?

3. What is the difference between *Porgy and Bess* and other operas written by American composers? For example, what makes *Porgy* more thoroughly American than other operas that are also based upon American subjects?

4. If someone in the class has an album of recordings of *Porgy and Bess*, you might arrange to play some of the songs. See if you can recognize in them the characteristics and qualities of real American folk music.

FOR YOUR MUSIC VOCABULARY

You may have learned the meaning of some musical terms just from reading this chapter of the biography of a composer. Make your own definition of each of the italicized words in the following quotations. Then check with the glossary or with a dictionary to be sure you have the exact meanings. Try using each word in an original sentence.

1. There was the problem of whipping together a suitable *libretto* from the original play.

2. Gershwin worked for eleven months on the *score* of his opera. . . .

3. . . . the various numbers, both solo and *ensemble*, were loosely assembled; there were pages that lacked artistic conviction; the *recitatives* were sometimes awkward.

DAVID EWEN (Born 1907)

A free-lance writer for over twenty-five years, Mr. Ewen is said to have written and sold more books on music than anyone anywhere. Born in Austria, he came to America to study at the College of the City of New York, and while in college, published his first book. In the years following, thirty more books, on every phase of musical activity, have appeared. His work has been translated into eight languages and includes such best sellers as *Music for the Millions*, *Dictators of the Baton*, and *The Complete Book of Twentieth-Century Music*.

HENRY FORD BUILDS A HORSELESS CARRIAGE

ALLAN NEVINS

The following selections are from the biography FORD: THE TIMES, THE MAN, THE COMPANY, *by Allan Nevins written in collaboration with Frank Ernest Hill. They deal with a man and with events that were to have a profound effect on America and Americans.*

Today we accept, without thinking about it, the constant use of the automobile in our daily existence. We also accept the power and speed, the beauty, and the comfort of our automobiles rather matter-of-factly. Yet without the work of men like Henry Ford who revolutionized manufacturing methods our pleasures, our habits, our business and commerce would be so different as to be almost unrecognizable.

It all began when young Henry Ford decided to leave his father's farm permanently and take a job in Detroit as engineer for the Edison Illuminating Company. Ford's real interest was not electricity and lighting, but he felt that in the fast-growing town of Detroit he could learn the mechanical principles, and find the technically experienced helpers he needed to achieve his ambition—the manufacture of a "horseless carriage." Ford did more than realize this ambition. He not only made one of the earliest practical motorcars; but by inventing and using MASS PRODUCTION methods he was able to sell his Model T automobile at prices that a vast number of Americans could afford to pay. Competing manufacturers adopted similar methods—and the motor age was born.

No less important than mass production of the automobile is the fact that hundreds of other products are now manufactured according to the same plan. Efficient methods and large-volume production create low prices; low prices, in turn, create a larger market which enables prices to be lowered still further; and the American people have luxuries and conveniences which in other countries are enjoyed only by the rich.

The date of the first passage reprinted here from Allan Nevins' biography is 1896. It describes some of Ford's early experiences with his machine, on which he was working every night after a full day as a power plant engineer. In the second passage, Ford demonstrates the improvements made on his second car.

The general character of the carriage as it developed toward final form showed originality and anticipated later Ford practice. In contrast with King's wagon [1] it was strikingly small and light—the lightest vehicle of its type yet produced. The entire machine without fuel would, when complete, weigh only five hundred pounds. Seeing it in pictures or at the Henry Ford Museum in Dearborn we can imagine a man picking it up, a feat quite possible if the motor were removed. It ran on bicycle-type wheels with pneumatic tires. The frame Ford and Bishop [2] constructed, getting the necessary materials as the work progressed. Their car was less like a buggy than any other model to date, even the seat being a bicycle saddle; but when later this was removed and a light carriage seat for two substituted, with a straight dashboard, it had more of the buggy look.

Ford provided two speeds, one ten and one twenty miles an hour, and a neutral gear. Changes were effected by a clutch lever which tightened or loosened a belt. Pulled back, this lever put the car in low; erect, in neutral; forward, in high. Later the belt was discarded and gear shifts substituted. The motor had a flywheel, spun in neutral to start the engine. To stop, the machine was again put in neu-

tral and the brake applied: for a while the car had none, but a foot-brake was soon provided. There was no reverse.

The builder procured materials from various Detroit firms. "Most of the iron work," he testified in 1904, "was got from a firm by the name of Barr & Dates; they were located at that time on the corner of Park Place and State Street, Detroit. The wheels I made; the seat I got from the Wilson Carriage Company, and from C. A. Strelinger & Co. bolts and screws and nuts; I made the handle myself; I don't know where I got the balance wheel from; I made the pattern and got it cast; I made the sparking device; the springs from the Detroit Steel and Spring Co." King contributed four intake valves which he had discarded in the process of building his four-cylinder motor. When Ford speaks of making something himself, quite obviously he includes the work of Bishop, Huff, and Cato done under his supervision; as we shall see, a number of the metal parts were made later by a fourth assistant.

According to King, Ford was sometimes hard-pressed for money with which to buy the materials he needed, and his credit at "a local house" (presumably Strelinger's) was only fifteen dollars. Charles T. Bush, then an employee of that firm, seemed unaware of any such restriction when telling years later of Ford's relationship with the house, and Barthel [3] did not think that Henry was ever hard-pressed

[1] KING'S WAGON—Charles B. King, inventor and industrial designer, had demonstrated a motor-driven carriage or wagon on the streets of Detroit in March, 1896. He advised and encouraged Ford in his experiments.

[2] BISHOP—Like Ford, "Jim" Bishop was an employee of the Edison Illuminating Company of Detroit. He was one of Ford's helpers after regular work hours.

[3] BARTHEL—Oliver Barthel was King's assistant.

financially. "He was working, he had his pay coming in." Although Clara Ford [4] mentions no limitations on credit, she recalled that the materials for the car ate up all the family's surplus above expenses. "It seemed as if we would never have any for ourselves." Telling Henry's sister Margaret about drawing out money needed for the quadricycle, she recalled wondering more than once if she would ever live to see the bank balance restored. "Her only concern then," said Mrs. Ruddiman,[5] "was the immediate one that Henry needed parts for his work. She wanted to be sure that there was sufficient money in the bank to pay for them." These comments indicate that building the little carriage was a financial strain on the family. No wonder; King, by no means hard-pressed for money, had been forced to suspend activities because experimentation was too costly, and the Duryeas [6] ran through three sets of backers.

Ford went on working, happy to see his dream taking tangible form. The other occupant of the double house was Felix Julien, who of course was entitled to use half of the little brick shed in which the carriage was being constructed. A friendly man of advanced years, he soon became much interested in it, perceived that the half of the building being used as a shop cramped Ford's activities, and insisted finally on tearing down the brick partition which divided the shed, storing his own wood and coal in his house, and thus giving his neighbor more room. He would then sit and watch the

[4] CLARA FORD—Henry Ford's wife.
[5] MRS. RUDDIMAN—Ford's sister, Mrs. Margaret Ford Ruddiman.
[6] THE DURYEAS—Frank and Charles Duryea had made the first public run of a gasoline automobile in America in September, 1893, in Springfield, Massachusetts. After some improvements, the machine was able to travel a distance of nearly twenty miles.

progress of the work. There were few other observers—King, perhaps, and Barthel and Cato. In this period Clara's cousin Nettie Bryant Scott and her sister, Kate Bryant, were sometimes staying with the Fords. Clara puzzled both girls by making nightly visits to the little shed, always alone. "Henry is making something, and maybe some day I'll tell you," she told them. "Well," recalled Mrs. Scott, "she didn't tell us. Of course after a little while the car came out, and we found out what it was."

The last days of May, 1896, saw the quadricycle almost completed. Ford and Bishop were working every night. "We often wondered when Henry Ford slept," remarked Charles T. Bush of the Strelinger company, "because he was putting in long hours working [at the Edison plant] and when he went home at night he was always experimenting or reading." Clara worried about his loss of sleep, but did not let him guess that she feared that his efforts might culminate in a breakdown. For the last forty-eight hours before the vehicle was ready he hardly slept at all. Finally, early on the morning of June 4—between 2 and 4 A.M.—the task was finished, and the builder was ready to take his car out for a trial run.*

At this moment, however, he discovered a fact almost as disconcerting as Robinson Crusoe's realization that he had

* Simonds writes (Henry Ford, 52) that the first trial was made in May. This is doubtful if we accept King's evidence that the chain for the drive arrived late that month, although a belt could have been employed at first. Ford, Huff, and Bishop for years asserted that the car had been operated in 1893, but eventually the Ford Motor Company accepted the year 1896 instead, and Bishop fixed the date as June 4 and the time as 4 A.M. Samuel S. Marquis, who probably quoted Ford or Mrs. Ford says (Henry Ford: An Interpretation, 26) that the car was ready at 2 A.M. Barthel and King both agree that June 4, 1896, was the date, and that Bishop was present. (Author's note)

built his boat too far from the shore to permit its being launched. For while the machine was in the shed, now that it was finished it was too big to go through the door! Faced with this unexpected situation, Ford did not hesitate; he seized an ax and knocked down a sufficient part of the brick wall to permit his first car to emerge. Mrs. Ford, who had sat up on this as on many other nights, came out with an umbrella, for it was raining. Jim Bishop was on hand with his bicycle, ready to ride ahead of the quadricycle and warn any drivers of horse-drawn vehicles of its coming—if indeed any other vehicles were met with at such an early hour—and to be at hand in case of accident. Henry put the clutch lever in neutral and spun the flywheel. When the motor came to life, he climbed to the bicycle seat, seized the steering rod, put the car in low, and started off. The quadricycle bumped slowly along the cobble-

stones of the alley and into the street beyond, with Bishop pedaling ahead of it. Ford steered it down Grand River Avenue to Washington Boulevard, master at last of a horseless vehicle moving under its own power. Then suddenly the car stopped.

Ford called to Bishop. The two discovered that a spring actuating one of the "ignitors" had failed. They went to the nearby Edison plant and got a new one. Meanwhile, some guests from the old Cadillac Hotel had gathered about the little car and "wondered what kind of an infernal machine this thing was, and who was crazy enough to spend a lot of time and money on such a contraption." Ford and Bishop, putting in the new spring, started the car. They decided it was operating well, and drove back to 58 Bagley, leaving an amazed knot of spectators behind them, and on arrival "both went off to bed for a few winks of sleep."

Clara then served breakfast and the two men reported for work as usual.

Ford was exultant. He had made only a short run, but it crowned his years of planning and his recent months of night work. He knew that the little machine would go farther the next time.

One fact he apparently did not know, nor did his friend Charles B. King. In the preceding November George B. Selden of Rochester, New York, had finally obtained his long-delayed patent for a "road-carriage." In time both Detroiters, and Ford in particular, would be made sharply aware of this fact, for Selden was to claim that his patent covered all gasoline-driven vehicles developed since 1879, and manufactured after the issue of the patent. He would soon take steps to enforce that contention.[7]

The initial run of the little car was not reported in the Detroit papers, and Ford was satisfied to be unnoticed, for he was not yet ready for a public demonstration. Indeed, his immediate concern was to repair the break in the shed which he had made in order to get the car out. He arranged with two bricklayers at the Edison plant to restore the wall and the door to their original condition. They had hardly begun work when the owner of the house, Wreford, appeared to collect the June rent. When he saw the broken wall he became angry and excited. Ford tried to quiet him, explaining that everything would be restored exactly as it had been, but Wreford kept demanding, "What did you do it for?"

"I had to get my car out to see if it would run," Ford replied.

Wreford forgot his anger.

"You ran it?"

"Yes, sir."

"Let me see it."

Ford showed him the car. The landlord forgot about the wall for a few minutes, then suddenly remembered it.

"Say!" he exclaimed. "If these fellows put the wall back up, how are you going to get your car out again? I've got an idea. Tell those bricklayers to leave that opening and then you can put in swinging doors. That will let you in and out."

Thus perhaps the first garage door in the United States was planned. When years later Ford restored the little shop as an exhibit in Greenfield Village the right-hand door was still wider than the other.

It was long assumed that the first car made by Ford remained, except for the addition of a seat and two water-jackets, much the same as it was when taken out for its initial run. This was not the fact. Evidence recently uncovered shows that the quadricycle was practically rebuilt in the months following that event.

David M. Bell, an American of Scottish birth (1864), had worked in Detroit at the carriage trade and at the Pullman shop in the city, but in July, 1896, found himself out of employment. He was told that a mechanic was wanted at the Edison Company, where he should report to a man named Ford. Bell sought out the chief engineer, and told him that he wanted a job as a blacksmith.

"What kind of a blacksmith are you?" Ford asked him.

Bell explained that although he had been working for the Pullman Car Company, he was really a carriage blacksmith.

"Oh, a carriage blacksmith," echoed Ford. He eyed the applicant a moment and then remarked crisply: "You come to work." Bell was really an answer to a prayer. Ford had many changes to make

[7] CONTENTION—Selden claimed royalties for the rights to his patent, which Ford refused to pay. In 1911 Ford's engine was declared fundamentally different from Selden's.

in his car, and in Bell found exactly the workman he needed.

He soon took the new employee down into the basement shop next door to the Edison building. There Bell saw the quadricycle, which Ford had brought from 58 Bagley. As originally constructed, nearly all the vehicle (apart from motor, axles, wheels, and steering rod) was of wood. "There were no metal parts in it," Bell recalled in 1953. Ford explained that he wanted new and sturdier wheels, a seat with metal railing, metal elements in the undercarriage, particularly for the drive, and a new all-metal steering rod and mechanism. The two men rigged up a forge and Bell was busy for weeks, doubtless mostly at night and on week ends. He made a device for shaping the metal wheel spokes and under Ford's direction fashioned the other parts for the front wheels. (The smaller rear wheels seem to have been left unchanged.) He substituted iron pipe for the mechanical elements beneath the body, and made a much improved steering mechanism. After Bell had taken measurements Ford returned the car to Bagley Avenue, took the various parts as Bell fashioned them, and rebuilt the car himself, doubtless with Huff's and Bishop's aid. Bell noticed that Ford did little work himself. "I never saw Mr. Ford make anything. He was always doing the directing." In Bishop, Huff, Cato, and Bell he had at least four highly capable workers to carry out his ideas and supply certain improvements of their own.

The car was now greatly strengthened, and Ford could carry a passenger on the seat beside him. He soon began to push out of the city with the quadricycle. Nettie Bryant Scott saw it at Greenfield, and always thought that this run to Clara's old home was the first extended trip made. Margaret Ford Ruddiman remembered its arrival at the Ford farm in Springwells-Dearborn, and has painted a vivid picture of the occasion:

My first sight of the little car was as it came along what is now Ford Road. The wheels on one side were high in the center of the road. Henry had built the car in such a way that the distance between the wheels was less than that of wagons and carriages so drove in this way on a road which had a rut. Clara and Edsel [8] were on the front seat with him and all of them were sitting on the slanted seat. I remember Edsel was a very small boy in dresses at this time and he was held tightly by his mother on her lap. . . . I well remember the peculiar sensation of what seemed to be a "great speed" and the sense of bewilderment I felt when I first rode in this carriage which moved without a horse. . . . After I had ridden in the car I wondered more than ever at the cool confidence and nerve which Clara displayed in trusting herself and Edsel to Henry's little car for the first ride into the country.

William Ford would not take a ride that first day. "He examined the machine, listened to Henry's explanations, but wouldn't get into the car. Father was a conservative farmer. . . . He saw no reason why he should risk his life at that time for a brief thrill from being propelled over the road in a carriage without horses."

Although Mrs. Ruddiman did not recall Charles B. King's presence, King has intimated that he was the passenger who accompanied Ford on the first trip to the farm:

I remember the day Henry Ford and I drove out to his father's farm to show off Henry's new quadricycle. Henry was as proud as could be when we swung through the farm gates. His father was a serious

[8] EDSEL—After he grew up, Edsel Ford (1893–1943) became an important executive in his father's firm.

old fellow, a deacon and a justice of the peace and so on, and he came out of the house and just stood and stared at us. Some of the neighbors came by and stared too. I could see that old Mr. Ford was ashamed of a grown-up man like Henry fussing over a little thing like a quadricycle. We'd gone and humiliated him in front of his friends. Henry stood it as long as he could, then he turned to me and said, in a heartbroken way, "Come on, Charlie, let's you and me get out of here."

Trips to Greenfield and Dearborn seem to have been only a few of those that the little car made. They convinced Ford that he needed a cooling system, for the motor heated up and bits of solder dropped from it. He brazed water-jackets around the cylinders and supplied a tank to which the water could return to be cooled. Meanwhile, he drove to Belle Isle and about town. He asserted later that hundreds of people in Detroit must have seen him with the car. On one occasion, writes W. A. Simonds, Henry and Clara were spinning along Grand Boulevard at a point where a slight uphill grade gave them anxiety. A boy on a bicycle just ahead of them, even more worried as to what the strange carriage would do, fell off and rolled under the wheels. "Both Mr. and Mrs. Ford scrambled out to see whether he had been hurt—as luckily he hadn't—and the world's first automobile accident ended without a casualty." * Jim Bishop usually preceded the car on a bicycle and saw that all horses were firmly held by their drivers.

Undoubtedly the car frightened a number of horses, and caused protests. Fortunately the man about to become mayor,

* Simonds, *Henry Ford*, 54. It was of course not the first accident. Aside from some in Europe, which certainly dated back to the 1880's, Frank Duryea on November 2, and Elwood Haynes on November 28, 1895, both disabled their cars trying to avoid collisions. (Author's note)

William C. Maybury, was an old family friend. He came to the shop to see the car—a visit which would flower into an active interest in its inventor several years later. When elected, Maybury stood ready to give his younger friend a blessing. "I had to get a special permit from the mayor," said Ford himself in 1923, "and thus for a time enjoyed the distinction of being the only licensed chauffeur in America." Simonds says it was only a verbal permit, but at any rate it pleased the builder.

He enjoyed the sensation the machine made. Sometimes he would leave it by the road in Belle Isle Park, station himself behind bushes, and listen to the comments of the curious crowds that gathered. Curiosity also brought its annoyances. "If I stopped my machine anywhere," Ford himself later recalled, "a crowd was around it before I could start up again. If I left it alone for even a minute some inquisitive person always tried to run it. Finally, I had to carry a chain and chain it to a lamppost whenever I left it anywhere." Ford occasionally offered rides to friends and of course to such associates as Bishop, Huff, King, and Barthel. One acquaintance, E. G. Graham, has described his sensations as he drove with Ford one day on Woodward Avenue:

A man ran across the street to the west in front of us, and Henry deliberately clanged the gong and chased him. . . . I recollect there was quite a cloud of smoke well in the air behind us, and we hadn't gone far before there were twenty-five to fifty bicyclists following us. We circled around—I do not remember where—until finally we reached Lafayette Street, going west, and when we got fairly close to Fourth Street Mr. Ford instructed me when we turned the corner to jump out and run and open the door of the stable so that the car could be driven in before the crowd of bicyclists overtook us. This was done, and Mr. Ford just snapped the padlock in the hasp when around the corner they came and one of them said, "Mister, can you tell us where that horseless carriage went?" Henry replied, "Yes, right up that alley," and away they went up the alley to the east. Mr. Ford gave one of his humorous chuckles, and we walked back to the Edison station.

A ride in the quadricycle was definitely an adventure, spiced with its builder's love for a joke. . . .

[*In the following passage, Ford has resigned from his job with the Edison Illuminating Company and has helped to organize the Detroit Automobile Company. In 1899, the date of the first events told about in this section, the newly created firm has only hopes and plans, but by 1900 it is actually ready to offer a car for sale.*]

Henry Ford was superintendent of the Detroit Automobile Company, and a small stockholder. He seems to have signed over his patents to the Company and turned enthusiastically to making his first commercial model. Only a few changes and it would be ready.

On leaving the Edison Company the inventor tried to take with him David M. Bell, who had helped him remodel the quadricycle and had also worked on the second car.

"Dave, you'll grow with the business," he urged.

"What business?" the ingenious carriage blacksmith demanded.

He had no intention of leaving the security of the Edison Company for a horseless carriage even if Ford—as he saw it—was foolish enough to do so.*

The Detroit Automobile Company

* So Bell states in his *Reminiscences.* (Author's note)

signed a three-year lease on the building recently vacated by the Detroit Motor Company. "The draftsmen . . . have already taken possession of one of the upper floors under Henry Ford," announced the *Free Press* on August 19, "who will be superintendent of the works. The company expects to have the plant in operation as soon as the machinery can be gotten into place, and by October 1 it is expected to have one or two automobiles completed." Before the end of August Strelinger sold the organization a Snyder drill, a grinder, a blower, a Horton drill chuck, lathe tools, and innumerable smaller items.

One of the stockholders, Frank R. Alderman, the secretary for the new company and its spokesman, radiated confidence. "We have several new devices in connection with the construction of our automobiles," he volunteered, "on which patents are now pending, which will make them as near perfect as they can be made. We have solved the problem of overcoming the bad odor by securing perfect combustion, and with our improved method of applying the power to the rear axle [not at all new to Frank Duryea or to Daimler in Europe] and of keeping all the machinery hidden from sight, we will have a fine motor carriage. We expect to have a hundred to a hundred and fifty men employed before the year is past. We have secured a three-year lease of the building with the privilege of purchasing the property after that time if we desire."

Thus the stockholders were really enthusiasts. As if by magic they saw their dingy little shop quarters expanding into acres of machine tools and assembly floors, all their own, disgorging automobiles for a motor-mad public. The magic would work in time, even beyond their expectations, but not for them.

Still, the Detroit Automobile Company

was a lively firm that fall. Ford did not produce a car for them by October 1, or even by December 1—dates which Alderman suggested—but he actually had one ready early in the new year. The Detroit *Journal* announced on January 12, 1900:

FIRST AUTOMOBILE OF THE DETROIT CO.
READY TOMORROW

The vehicle took the form of a delivery wagon. This was doubtless to emphasize the practical possibilities of the machine as well as its serviceability as a pleasure car. The new and improved automobile, the *Journal* announced, would be exhibited at the first annual meeting of the Company, to be held the following day.

"The body is built like any of the better class of its kind drawn about town by horses," ran the article, "and the whole thing is so constructed as to almost wholly conceal the motive power.

"The machinery, which is to do away with the horse as a drawer of wagons about the cities, looks like a very delicate piece of work, and doubtless is so in conception, but there the delicacy seems to end, as strength is one of its chief characteristics. The whole wagon will weigh about twelve hundred pounds, the motor taking up about five hundred of this. [Despite his passion for lightness, Ford had found more weight necessary.] This weight, while it might at first seem considerable, is really very little compared with others, one of which was recently seen doing good work about the city with something over three thousand pounds of its own weight to carry. Many of the parts are made of gun metal, this material being considered the most durable of all for gear wheels, etc. The caps and the large case for the flywheel are of aluminum, which partly accounts for the light weight."

The axles were of nickel steel, which was expensive but unusually durable, and the Company boasted that because of the materials used and the "perfection of its manufacture," the car would be good fifteen years from the date of its completion. That the delivery wagon was only one model was shown by the statement that seven more cars "of different kinds" were under construction. As to the rate of production, by March 1 the shop would turn out ten a month, with a goal of two a day as its next objective. The price was to be one thousand dollars. A catalogue, according to the article, showed "ever [y] imaginable kind of useful and ornamental conveyance, all of which can be run by women and children"! If an owner used his car six days a week for an average of thirty-six miles a day, operation would cost him only twenty-eight dollars a year.

The postmaster of Detroit had agreed to use the vehicle for several days, and the *Journal* predicted that cars would soon carry the mails regularly. A final sentence emphasized the aesthetic. "The Detroit Automobile Co. claims for its machine that it will emit no odor, and that it will make less noise than the ordinary vehicle drawn by a horse."

This glowing article seems deeply impregnated with wishful thinking. If catalogues, praise, and the big vision could carry Henry Ford into commercial production at high gear, his associates were wafting him there, but the dream and the reality were still remote from each other. Alderman, Murphy, and their associates seemed now to be thinking of the car as a completed job and using it as a multiple of accomplishment. Ford, wrestling with unsolved problems, knew better. The mail test, scheduled for "next week," did not take place for more than a month. To be sure, the result was hailed as a triumph, the car making the trip in a quarter of the time required by horse and wagon. However, the shop was encountering difficulties, and such performances did not speed up regular production. Neither did the announcement that a number of "phaeton automobiles" [9] would be ready in a short time.

We can only guess at the causes for delay in the shop. One factor may have been that the "heavier parts" were being manufactured elsewhere, and sometimes arrived late. Another may have been the inexperience of the men in assembling a car, and their constant discovery of shortcomings in the parts delivered by other firms, and in the car design. "You would be surprised," Alderman told a reporter in February, "at the amount of detail about an automobile." They had been delayed for weeks over a spring or a small gear. "To show the trials of the automobile builder, let me say that we lost a week simply because we found that the steering rod apparatus would bind in a certain way, on account of a little screw and a small catch. One of the screws was about one-sixteenth of an inch too long; and as there were a lot of other screws in the plate, it took us a long time to locate the trouble. It was only after we had spent about fifty dollars that we found where the trifling hitch came." It seems safe to say that if seven machines were under way early in 1900, most of them were in the planning stage.

William W. Pring, who was later to work for Ford and already knew him, was at the Olds plant in 1899, and tested that company's new cars. He recalled seeing Ford, evidently that summer, operating his own machine, and once in his "curved-dash Olds" ran a race with

Henry. "I beat him. He could only go about twenty-five miles an hour." Not long after, Ford asked Pring to come and work for him.

"Well," countered the Olds employee, "have you got me something [to do] building this car?"

Ford replied: "I've got one and a half started."

This seems to have been in the fall of 1899. The Detroit Automobile Company plant, as Pring recalled it, had space in the same building as the C. R. Wilson Body Works. Perhaps Alderman had rented a part of the structure of this organization. "They [Wilson] had the back part of it and Ford had the front part downstairs." The Wilson firm was making bodies for Olds. Ford's working force, as Pring recalled it, consisted of the overseer, George Abbott, the blacksmith, George Wetterich, the electrician, Arvy Wilson, and two laborers. Actually others were employed, including William Boyer, Ed (Edward S.) Huff, and John Thomas. Pring makes no mention of the men engaged in drafting, noted by the Detroit papers, among whom was Boyer.

Even before the "delivery wagon" made its mail runs, an enterprising reporter for the News-Tribune had taken a ride in it. His observations were reported on the front page of the second section of the paper under a three-column head:

SWIFTER THAN A RACE-HORSE IT FLEW
OVER THE ICY STREETS
Thrilling Trip on the First Detroit-Made Automobile, When Mercury Hovered About Zero.

A pen-and-ink illustration, with the caption "Showing How Easily an Automobile May Be Steered Out of Danger," depicted a car with two occupants being swung aside from the path of a team of horses.

---

[9] "PHAETON AUTOMOBILES"—A type of automobile having an open body and two cross seats.

The reporter related how he had gone at five degrees above zero to ride in the new car "which will soon be seen in the regular service of one of the largest firms on Woodward Avenue." He commented favorably on its appearance: "Smooth-covered, box-topped, with black enamel sides, red wheels, and running gear, nothing but the absence of the proverbial horse revealed that the motive power was to come from within." From the seat, to the reporter's surprise, no machinery was visible except the brake pedal and steering levers. The engine and other running parts were "placed practically under the floor." He commented on the use of aluminum, and the lightness and compactness of the mechanical units. "There was really little or nothing to show that there was an engine aboard at all." Ford, discovering that he had no gasoline, filled the tank, which held three gallons—"enough to run the automobile one hundred miles or more at the rate of a cent a mile." He assured the reporter that the running gear was sturdy, and that the machine weighed thirteen hundred pounds "complete."

Ford then gave a few jerks at the starter, explaining that this pulled a charge into the cylinder. He pressed an electric "switch handle" and the engine came to life. "She's ready!" he announced.

"But you didn't touch a match to something or other?" asked his passenger, evidently for the benefit of the News-Tribune's readers.

"No necessity," answered Ford with a smile. "The ignition is by electricity. Didn't you see me touch the switch up there? That fires the gas, and the puff you heard was the explosion."

As a man opened the factory door, the machine rolled out. With "incomparable swiftness" it picked up speed and glided into the snowy, windblown streets. It didn't mind the near-zero temperature in the least. "It flew along with the very poetry of motion." Ford first took the car out on a country road, rutted and partially snow-covered, and went at about eight miles an hour "with a dreamlike smoothness. There was none of the bumping common even to a street car." Then Ford warned his passenger to expect some speed.

"Hold on tight!" he counseled. "When we strike the asphalt we will have a run."

"How fast?"

"Twenty-five miles an hour."

"Hold on. I get out!"

Naturally he didn't. There was a sharp clang—clang of the car's bell as the driver warned a milk wagon he was approaching.

The horse pricked up his ears, his eye gleamed ominously; he shivered as though about to run away. His driver applied the whip.

"Ever frighten horses?" asked the visitor, wonderingly.

"Depends on the horse. A low-bred, ignorant horse, yes; a high-born fellow, no. There's as much difference between horses as between dogs. Some are wise, some otherwise. The other day I was passing down in front of the Majestic Building in the big crush; along came a man with a speeding cart and racer. Alderman, who was with me, told me to slack down, as there would surely be trouble. The racer came flying right by us and merely gave a side glance. He was too wise to show any emotion."

When they reached the boulevard, Ford shifted the lever and picked up speed. And, declared the reporter, he now heard a noise new in history—the noise of the automobile.

There has always been at each decisive period in this world's history some voice, some note, that represented for the time being the prevailing power.

There was a time when the supreme cry of authority was the lion's roar.

Then, came the voice of man.

After that, it was the crackle of fire.

By and by, it was the hammering of the stone ax.

Then, it was the slapping of the oars in the Roman galleys.

Next it was the voice of the wind against sails.

It came at last to speak with a loud report, such as announced the reign of gunpowder.

The roar of dynamite was a long time later.

The shriek of the steam whistle for several generations has been the compelling power of civilization.

And now, finally, there was heard in the streets of Detroit the murmur of this newest and most perfect of forces, the automobile, rushing along at the rate of twenty-five miles an hour.

What kind of a noise is it?

That is difficult to set down on paper.

It was not like any other sound ever heard in this world. It is not like the puff! puff! of the exhaust of gasoline in a river launch; neither is it like the cry! cry! of a working steam engine; but a long, quick, mellow gurgling sound, not harsh, not unmusical, not distressing; a note that falls with pleasure on the ear. It must be heard to be appreciated. And the sooner you hear its newest chuck! chuck! the sooner you will be in touch with civilization's latest lisp, its newest voice.

They "rushed" along, presumably at twenty or twenty-five miles an hour. The reporter saw a heavily-laden brewery wagon loom up, and cried "Look out!" but the driver "turned gracefully to the right." The passenger, now really alarmed, wanted to get out, but Ford said "Nonsense!" As he dodged a pedestrian, he announced he would show how

quickly his vehicle would stop. "I'll wager a race horse going a mile in 1:40 cannot be hauled up in less than one-sixteenth of a mile; we'll do it in six feet." He did. The reporter wanted to know how long it would take to learn to drive.

"Oh, depends," replied Ford. "Have you any sense about machinery?"

"Little."

"Well, in a few days, maybe in a few hours—there's little to learn. Ride a bicycle? It's the same thing."

"But," remonstrated his guest, "that puffing! Isn't she liable to blow up?"

"Nothing to blow up!"

"But we are sitting on top of three gallons of gasoline!"

"That's nothing. It's perfectly safe. There's no fire about here. And then, we're in the open air."

They passed a harness shop. "His trade is doomed!" Ford announced.

The clanging of street car gongs mingled with the sound of the auto bell, adding a new noise to the alarms of daily life. But she slid over the earth with infinite ease; and careened in and out among trucks, delivery wagons, carriages and bicycles; and everywhere people had a welcoming smile and an expression of delight. The new "chuck! chuck!" the newest voice of civilization, sounded like rare music in their ears—a music as yet involved with the delight of absolute novelty.

"The horse is doomed," said the passenger.

At that moment the auto whizzed past a poor team attached to a truck.

"That's the kind," said Ford. "Those horses will be driven from the land. Their troubles will soon be over."

And the "chuck! chuck!" of the new voice sounded for the first time in the strange horses' ears.

Meanwhile the auto had slipped like a sunbeam around the corner.

The account gives us a vivid glimpse of

Ford as a demonstrator, and of his driving habits—he was always to drive with a slap-dash confidence that later worried employees of the Ford Motor Company. It gives us some sense of familiarity with the improved model of Ford's second car. Particularly it recreates for us the wonder and exhilaration which the first passengers in such vehicles knew.

◇◇◇◇◇◇◇◇◇◇◇◇◇◇◇◇◇◇◇◇◇◇◇◇◇◇◇◇◇◇

A QUADRICYCLE ON THE STREETS OF DETROIT

1. The word "quadricycle" suggests that Ford's first automobile seemed more like a bicycle than a carriage. Find passages that give hints of the structure of the machine, and then tell all the ways you can in which it resembled a bicycle.

2. Why did Ford sometimes chain his automobile to a lamppost when he wanted to leave it for any length of time? Describe an incident in connection with the machine which proves that Ford sometimes showed a sense of humor.

3. Explain how it happened that the first garage door in the United States was constructed. What were the details of "the world's first automobile accident"?

4. Give evidence that some people were doubtful of the worth of Ford's automobile. What do you suppose Ford's reason was for frequently driving it in parts of the city where it would be seen by many people? Do you think he was glad to have the reporter for the *News-Tribune* take a ride with him?

5. Explain the meaning of the words *quadricycle, tricycle, bicycle,* and *motorcycle.* There is also a machine known as a *monocycle.* What would it be like, judging from its name?

INTERPRETING THE TIMES AND THE MAN

Most good biographies do more than tell the personal story of their "subject." They analyze and interpret his work—for of course, a person's accomplishments in his chosen occupation are an extremely important part of his life. In addition, a good biography re-creates the time a man lived in so that his activities may be more fully understood. This is especially true of the books of Mr. Nevins, who is as much a *historian* as he is a *biographer.* To him Henry Ford, for all his genius, was partly a product of his time and place—and Ford's career was important not merely as the adventures of one man but as a shaping influence on American civilization.

1. In the 1890's, both the booming little city of Detroit and the country as a whole seemed to have reached a high peak in the use of machinery. Steamships and railroads had been in use for several generations. Homes and streets were beginning to be lighted by electricity. Gasoline motors were being put to work in a variety of ways. Bicycles were seen everywhere. Yet this was only a beginning. To manufacture and work the machines, thousands of mechanics and engineers were needed—and these men were constantly seeking to develop still newer machines. Even in the short passage you have read from the life of Henry Ford, it is evident that other men, also, were trying to make a "horseless carriage." Name at least two of these men. Just after describing Ford's first run in his automobile, the author mentions a rival inventor who had already taken out a patent on a "road-carriage." What was his name? Explain what effect his patent might later have had on Henry Ford's career.

2. The reader of this biography is never allowed to forget Ford's *surroundings* as he worked—that is, the city of Detroit. At one point "the old Cadillac Hotel" is mentioned. This hotel was named after an early French explorer, Antoine de la Mothe Cadillac. What special significance does its name have for us? Mention at least three other specific buildings, business firms, or locations in Detroit that are mentioned in the selection. In what notable event did "Jim" Bishop play a part?

3. The author often makes clear *what person* is the source of a particular piece of information on Henry Ford. Quote two examples of sentences which identify the source of the information that is to follow.

"THE NEWEST VOICE OF CIVILIZATION"

1. The imaginative reporter who "wrote up" his ride with Henry Ford declared that the people of Detroit were listening to "the newest voice of civilization." Reread his quick sketch of the history of the world. In deciding which "voice" represented each period of history, on what did he base his decision? Quote an expression in which he tried to tell his readers what the voice of the automobile was like. What sound or sounds would you name as the representative "voices" of civilization today? Explain the reasons for your choice.

2. Summing up the newspaper article, the biographer says it captures for us "the wonder and exhilaration which the first passengers in such vehicles knew." What details of the automobile ride seem to have most delighted and impressed the newspaper reporter? What was the exhilarating speed at which the automobile "rushed" along?

ALLAN NEVINS (Born 1890)

After graduating from the University of Illinois, Allan Nevins taught English at his alma mater for a year while taking his Master's degree. Next he became the *New York Evening Post's* youngest editor. During his years there he earned a reputation for unusual industriousness, turning out editorials in such number and on such a wide range of topics that his colleagues declared he would have been able to carry on the entire editorial page by himself. Altogether, Mr. Nevins worked nineteen years on the *Post* and two other New York papers, the *Sun* and the *World*—but twice he obtained leave of absence to teach history, once at Cornell University and once at Columbia University.

Mr. Nevins has been just as industrious in historical scholarship as he was in his journalistic work. Two of his most important books are *The American States During and After the Revolution* and *Frémont, Pathfinder of the West*. He has written several biographies of men who played important roles in our country's development. Two of these—biographies of Grover Cleveland and Hamilton Fish, the secretary of state under President Grant—were awarded Pulitzer Prizes. With Henry Steele Commager, another historian at Columbia, Nevins published *The Heritage of America*. It is a collection of first-hand narratives of American life from the discovery of the New World down to the 1930's.

Throughout his career, Mr. Nevins has been keenly aware of the important influence on our history of the growth of our great business and manufacturing firms. He showed this awareness in his book *John D. Rockefeller: The Heroic Age in American Business*, and showed it again in his recent biography of Henry Ford. In preparing the latter book, he made use of the wealth of materials that are now available for the first time in the Ford Archives at Dearborn, Michigan. Mr. Nevins was particularly interested in studying the many tape recordings contained in the Archives—oral reminiscences by older employees and executives of the Ford Motor Company. This type of historical record, made possible by modern scientific progress, will enrich the knowledge that future generations will have of life in the twentieth century.

For Broader Understanding

1. Why were early American biographies —those written before 1900—not generally popular? What was usually the author's purpose in writing a biography? What kinds of people were chosen as subjects?

2. What were the "debunkers"? What contribution did they make to the development of modern biography? How was their method sometimes abused?

3. What techniques are used by modern authors to make biography not only more readable, but also more reliable? Point out examples of the use of these techniques in the biographies in this unit.

4. What is meant by fictionalized biography? Do you think a biographer has the right to invent incidents and speeches in order to make his book more interesting? How can a biography be essentially "true" even though it has some elements of fiction?

5. Which biography in this unit would you say is probably the best *documented*? Explain what the term means. Find an example of documentation and explain why you think it is or is not important.

6. Explain how a good biographer works. What interests and abilities must he have? What are some of the difficulties and problems of writing biography and autobiography?

7. The great American writer and thinker Ralph Waldo Emerson said: "There is properly no History; only Biography." How do you interpret this quotation? In what respects are the biographies in this unit historical? What could one learn about American life, culture, or ideals from reading any one of them?

BIOGRAPHICAL SOURCES

1. We read literary biographies like those in this unit for the pleasure and entertainment we get from becoming intimately acquainted with interesting people and their times. Sometimes, however, we simply want biographical facts about an important person. Find out what biographical reference books are available in your library. Compare the *type* and *amount* of information given about a particular person in two or more reference works.

2. Use the card catalogue in your library to compile a bibliography of *entire books* and *parts of books* available about a particular person. Compare at least two books.

READING AND SPEAKING ACTIVITIES

1. One proof of the popularity of biography is the number of radio and television programs based upon the lives of famous people. To aid in preparing a list of such programs for the class bulletin board, students might want to examine the radio and television reviews and previews in such magazines as *Senior Scholastic, Saturday Review,* and *Time,* and the entertainment page of the Sunday newspaper. Groups or individuals can then report on particular programs.

2. Today there are fascinating biographies of people who have been successful in many different professions and occupations. For individual reading, students interested in a particular vocation might choose a biography about a person in that line of work. Reports should include answers to the following questions: What interests and abilities did the person have that contributed to success? What hardships and disagreeable aspects of the work are revealed in the book? What rewards and satisfactions? Each point should be illustrated by references.

3. In reporting on individual reading, you might pretend that you are the person whose biography you read. Select from the book one interesting experience and prepare to tell it to the class as if it had happened to you. Another student might introduce the distinguished visitor, giving sufficient background material so that the incident can be understood and appreciated.

WRITING ACTIVITIES

1. Write a short autobiography. Do not attempt to tell everything that ever happened to you. Select incidents that affected your life in some way, or those that reveal something about yourself or your environment.

2. In her autobiography, Edna Ferber includes many thumbnail sketches of people she knew during her high-school days. There were the members of her family, the high-school principal, and the people who worked in the store. The reader gets to know these people by reading about what they did and said. For example, you formed an opinion of Mr. Pringle from his effect upon the school, and you learned to know Mrs. Ferber as you watched her managing her business and her family. Try writing a similar sketch of a member of your own family or of someone else you know well.

3. Choose some person who was important in the history of your community and write a short biography of him. Give the main facts of his personal life, including exact dates when possible; the activities that made him prominent in your city or town; and whatever you can learn about his character and personality. Be sure to use reliable sources.

FOR FURTHER READING

CATHERINE DRINKER BOWEN, *Yankee from Olympus* (Little). One of the influential statesmen of our time was Oliver Wendell Holmes, associate justice of the United States Supreme Court from 1902 to 1932. This biography is a fine appreciation of a wise and great man.

AGNES DE MILLE, *Dance to the Piper* (Little). This American ballerina has created dances for the music-dramas "Oklahoma" and "Carousel." With wit and honesty she reveals what it costs in time, money, courage, and endurance to become a dancer.

FRANK GRAHAM, *Lou Gehrig: A Quiet Hero* (Putnam). Readers interested in sports and sports' heroes will want to read this story of a Yankee baseball star and his courageous battle against a crippling disease.

HERMANN HAGEDORN, *The Roosevelt Family of Sagamore Hill* (Macmillan). This life of Theodore Roosevelt and his family at their home in Oyster Bay is full of interesting personalities.

EMMETT KELLY, *Clown* (Prentice). The sad-faced clown of Ringling Brothers–Barnum and Bailey Circus relates his experiences in the circus world. His description of the great circus fire in Hartford, Connecticut, is especially interesting.

J. ALVIN KUGELMAS, *Ralph J. Bunche: Fighter for Peace* (Messner). Scholar and statesman, Mr. Bunche has brought credit to his race and country.

GLADYS MALVERN, *Curtain Going Up! The Story of Katharine Cornell* (Messner). This book is an excellent biography of the theater's "first lady."

BELLAMY PARTRIDGE, *Country Lawyer* (McGraw). Here is a realistic portrait of a shrewd country lawyer and the small American town where he lived and worked.

CONSTANCE ROURKE, *Davy Crockett* (Harcourt). This account of the life of one of America's best-known soldiers and frontiersmen also gives extensive information about the folklore that surrounds his name.

ROBERT SHERWOOD, *Roosevelt and Hopkins* (Harper). Brilliant and unconventional, Harry Hopkins became the confidential adviser of President Franklin Roosevelt. This book is a double biography of Hopkins and the President during the time of their closest association.

KEN SMITH, *The Willy Mays Story* (Greenberg). Baseball fans will enjoy this life of the Giants' popular centerfielder.

IRVING STONE, *Immortal Wife* (Doubleday). John Charles Frémont was an important figure in the exploration and settlement of the West. His wife, Jessie Benton Frémont, did much to advance his career.

ANTONINA VALLENTIN, *The Drama of Albert Einstein* (Doubleday). A close friend of Einstein reveals the great scientist's personality through many anecdotes.

ESSAYS AND JOURNALISM

CURRENT INTEREST IN NONFICTION

Americans are naturally curious. They are constantly looking for information on all kinds of subjects. They want to know what is happening in the world, why things are the way they are, and what makes them go. Their interest in how to do and make things has built up a whole new "do-it-yourself" industry. Their desire to understand science, history, and world affairs has resulted in fascinating documentary films and entertaining, informative television and radio programs. This same urge to find out all they can about the world they live in has led the American people to turn more and more to nonfiction reading material. There they can find not only information and knowledge but also the stimulation and satisfaction that comes from contact with the thoughts and ideas of interesting people.

Among the various types of nonfiction are such widely different forms as history, travel, essays, diaries, letters, magazine articles, speeches, and newspaper writing. Of these forms, essays and biographies have most often been considered literature. The quality of writing, however, is the principal consideration in determining what is literature and what is not. Thus, unusual orations, radio talks, letters, and even news stories and editorials may be of such high quality that they are placed above ordinary writing in the expanding body of lasting literature. Since in this book biography is considered separately, the following pages will be devoted to different types of essays and a variety of the kinds of writing usually called journalism.

SOME TYPES OF THE ESSAY

It is not easy to define an essay. Perhaps the closest one can come is to say that it is an attempt to put on paper some ideas on a chosen subject which interests the writer and which he hopes will interest the reader. He may be in earnest or he may be joking. He may tell a little story or assume an impersonal aloofness. It is as though the reader were able to sit down with the writer and listen to him tell about his experiences, as he would tell them to a friend, commenting on them and digressing to make observations on whatever interests him. To know what a person thinks and how he feels is to know him better than we know most of our friends. All that we require of the essayist is that he follow a train of thought to something like a conclusion, and that along the way he point out to us some new ideas.

It has been the custom to classify essays as *formal* or *familiar*. In the formal essay, the author has taken his subject seriously. He is definitely trying to instruct or to convince the reader. His style is therefore dignified, and perhaps impersonal. Emerson's "Self-Reliance," which you will find in the unit *Masters of American Literature* in this book, and Herbert Hoover's "The Miracle of America" in this section are essays of the formal type.

The informal or familiar essay is lighter in subject and style. It may range all the way from the humor of Clarence Day's "Father Opens My Mail" to Mr. E. B. White's clever and thought-provoking comments on minor items in the day's news. The easy, conversational type of the informal essay reached its peak during the nineteenth century. The first two decades of the twentieth century also produced some essayists of delightful style; but today the type of writing called the essay is being broadened to include, or possibly is being replaced by, the discussion articles—articles about contemporary affairs, interesting places or personalities, and matters of opinion or belief.

MODERN TRENDS IN JOURNALISM

Journalism covers a wide field ranging from news items to articles and editorials very similar to the essay. Generally, the difference between an article and an essay is that the article is more factual and informative. It may also be entertaining and thoughtful. Pure news stories are often written rapidly and seldom last longer than the newspapers in which they appear. However, an occasional piece, such as those written by Ernie Pyle for *Yank*, the Army magazine, is so well written that it is reprinted and preserved in anthologies as an example of excellent writing in a particular field. Feature writers, columnists, and editorial writers are more likely than news reporters to write literary material. Many of our finest writers like John Mason Brown, Bennett Cerf, and E. B. White were formerly newspapermen.

Another important type of journalistic writing is criticism of all kinds. Leading magazines and newspapers devote pages or sections to reviews of books, drama, motion pictures, and radio and television programs. These reviews serve a double purpose— they help readers, viewers, and listeners to choose wisely what they will read, see, and hear, and in so doing they play an important part in forming the thought and taste of the American people. An example of this type of writing is Quentin Reynolds' review of Charles Lindbergh's book *The Spirit of St. Louis.*

Newspapers and magazines also offer many interesting short pieces that are difficult to classify, but which have a wide appeal to readers. Among these are jokes, quips, and sayings that appear as fillers or as special columns in such magazines as *The Reader's Digest* and *The Saturday Evening Post.* Cartoons are often scattered among the pages to add spice and interest to many leading magazines of various types. Among the most famous are those which have appeared in *The New Yorker.* Because humor is a very personal matter and depends largely on the background and experience of each individual not everyone enjoys all of the work of outstanding American cartoonists. However, some cartoons have a very wide appeal because they point up the humor in familiar situations. For example, most American young people are accustomed to asking for the use of the family car. They will therefore appreciate the problem of the witch's daughter in Charles Addams' cartoon in this book. In a way the art of the cartoonist is similar to that of the poet; he presents a situation and assumes that whoever looks at his drawing will have the necessary background and perception to "get the point."

With increased interest in nonfiction have come changes in the various types of writing included in that group. The essayists and the journalists have taken on some of the tricks of the writers of fiction and biography. Sometimes it is difficult to tell whether a piece of writing is properly classified as a story, a biography, or an essay. For example, you will discover in "Father Opens My Mail" characteristics of all three types. It has the narrative interest of the short story; it is biography because it is about real people; it is a familiar essay because of the interesting and amusing comments that Mr. Day makes on his experiences.

There are examples of this modern trend even in Mr. Hoover's "The Miracle of America," a discussion which shows America to Americans as the wonderful country it really is. Here in using personal experiences to illustrate and illuminate ideas, the author introduces narrative interest. Other examples are "The Heraldry of the Range," in which information on cattle brands is enlivened by amusing anecdotes, and "The Case of the Eleven Blue Men," a news article written in the style of a detective story.

FATHER OPENS MY MAIL

CLARENCE DAY

One of the most entertaining of all the many books about American family life is Clarence Day's LIFE WITH FATHER. It became the basis for a hit play on Broadway, a successful motion picture, and finally, a popular television program. No wonder the members of the Day family, who lived in New York in the late 1800's, are better known to many present-day Americans than they were to some of their own neighbors.

In the following selection from LIFE WITH FATHER, Clarence Jr., the oldest of the four red-headed boys, tells about the trials he inherited with his father's name.

There was a time in my boyhood when I felt that Father had handicapped me severely in life by naming me after him, "Clarence." All literature, so far as I could see, was thronged with objectionable persons named Clarence. Percy was bad enough, but there had been some good fighters named Percy. The only Clarence in history was a duke who did something dirty at Tewkesbury, and who died a ridiculous death afterwards in a barrel of malmsey.[1]

As for the Clarences in the fiction I read, they were horrible. In one story, for instance, there were two brothers, Clarence and Frank. Clarence was a "vain, disagreeable little fellow," who was proud of his curly hair and fine clothes, while Frank was a "rollicking boy who was ready to play games with anybody." Clarence didn't like to play games, of course. He just minced around looking on.

[1] THE ONLY CLARENCE . . . MALMSEY— This is a reference to George, Duke of Clarence, who is said to have killed Edward Plantaganet at the Battle of Tewkesbury. Imprisoned on charges of treason, he was found drowned in a barrel of malmsey wine.

One day when the mother of these boys had gone out, this story went on, Clarence "tempted" Frank to disobey her and fly their kite on the roof. Frank didn't want to, but Clarence kept taunting him and daring him until Frank was stung into doing it. After the two boys went up to the roof, Frank got good and dirty, running up and down and stumbling over scuttles, while Clarence sat there, giving him orders, and kept his natty clothes tidy. To my horror, he even spread out his handkerchief on the trap door to sit on. And to crown all, this sneak told on Frank as soon as their mother came in.

This wasn't an exceptionally mean Clarence, either. He was just run-of-the-mill. Some were worse.

So far as I could ever learn, however, Father had never heard of these stories, and had never dreamed of there being anything objectionable in his name. Quite the contrary. And yet as a boy he had lived a good rough-and-tumble boy's life. He had played and fought on the city streets, and kept a dog in Grandpa's stable, and stolen rides to Greenpoint Ferry on the high, lurching bus. In the summer he had gone to West Springfield and had run down Shad Lane through the trees to the house where Grandpa was born, and had gone barefoot and driven the cows home just as though he had been named Tom or Bill.

He had the same character as a boy, I suppose, that he had as a man, and he was too independent to care if people thought his name fancy. He paid no attention to the prejudices of others, except to disapprove of them. He had plenty of prejudices himself, of course, but they were his own. He was humorous and confident and level-headed, and I imagine that if any boy had tried to make fun of him for being named Clarence, Father would simply have laughed and told him he didn't know what he was talking about.

I asked Mother how this name had ever happened to spring up in our family. She explained that my great-great-grandfather was Benjamin Day, and my great-grandfather was Henry, and consequently my grandfather had been named Benjamin Henry. He in turn had named his eldest son Henry and his second son Benjamin. The result was that when Father was born there was no family name left. The privilege of choosing a name for Father had thereupon been given to Grandma, and unluckily for the Day family she had been reading a novel, the hero of which was named Clarence.

I knew that Grandma, though very like Grandpa in some respects, had a dreamy side which he hadn't, a side that she usually kept to herself, in her serene, quiet way. Her romantic choice of this name probably made Grandpa smile, but he was a detached sort of man who didn't take small matters seriously, and who drew a good deal of private amusement from the happenings of everyday life. Besides, he was partly to blame in this case, because that novel was one he had published himself in his magazine.

I asked Mother, when she had finished, why I had been named Clarence too.

It hadn't been her choice, Mother said. She had suggested all sorts of names to Father, but there seemed to be something wrong with each one. When she had at last spoken of naming me after him, however, he had said at once that that was the best suggestion yet—he said it sounded just right.

Father and I would have had plenty of friction in any case. This identity of names made things worse. Every time that I had been more of a fool than he liked, Father would try to impress on me my responsibilities as his eldest son, and above all as the son to whom he had given his name, as he put it. A great deal was expected, it seemed to me, of a boy who was named after his father. I used to envy my brothers, who didn't have anything expected of them on this score at all.

I envied them still more after I was old enough to begin getting letters. I then discovered that when Father "gave" me his name he had also, not unnaturally, I had to admit, retained it himself, and when anything came for Clarence S. Day he opened it, though it was sometimes for me.

He also opened everything that came addressed to Clarence S. Day, Jr. He didn't do this intentionally, but unless the "Jr." was clearly written, it looked like "Esq." and anyhow Father was too accustomed to open all Clarence Day letters to remember about looking carefully every time for a "Jr." So far as mail and express went, I had no name at all of my own.

For the most part nobody wrote to me when I was a small boy except firms whose advertisements I had read in the *Youth's Companion* and to whom I had written requesting them to send me their circulars. These circulars described remarkable bargains in magicians' card outfits, stamps and coins, pocketknives, trick spiders, and imitation fried eggs, and they seemed interesting and valuable to me when I got them. The trouble was that Father usually got them and at once tore them up. I then had to write for such circulars again, and if Father got the second one too, he would explode with annoyance. He became particularly indignant one year, I remember, when he was repeatedly urged to take advantage of

a special bargain sale of false whiskers. He said that he couldn't understand why these offerings kept pouring in. I knew why, in this case, but at other times I was often surprised myself at the number he got, not realizing that as a result of my postcard request my or our name had been automatically put on several large general mailing lists.

During this period I got more of my mail out of Father's wastebasket than I did from the postman.

At the age of twelve or thirteen, I stopped writing for these childish things and turned to a new field. Father and I, whichever of us got at the mail first, then began to receive not merely circulars but personal letters beginning:

DEAR FRIEND DAY:

In reply to your valued request for one of our Mammoth Agents' Outfits, kindly forward post-office order for $1.49 to cover cost of postage and packing, and we will put you in a position to earn a large income in your spare time with absolutely no labor on your part, by taking subscriptions for *The Secret Handbook of Mesmerism*, and our *Tales of Blood* series.

And one spring, I remember, as the result of what I had intended to be a secret application on my part, Father was assigned "the exclusive rights for Staten Island and Hoboken of selling the Gem Home Popper for Pop Corn. Housewives buy it at sight."

After Father had stormily endured these afflictions for a while, he and I began to get letters from girls. Fortunately for our feelings, these were rare, but they were ordeals for both of us. Father had forgotten, if he ever knew, how silly young girls can sound, and I got my first lesson in how unsystematic they were. No matter how private and playful they meant their letters to be, they forgot to put "Jr." on the envelope every once in so often. When Father opened these letters, he read them all the way through, sometimes twice, muttering to himself over and over: "This is very peculiar. I don't understand this at all. Here's a letter to me from some person I never heard of. I can't see what it's about." By the time it had occurred to him that possibly the letter might be for me, I was red and embarrassed and even angrier at the girl than at Father. And on days when he had read some of the phrases aloud to the family, it nearly killed me to claim it.

Lots of fellows whom I knew had been named after their fathers without having such troubles. But although Father couldn't have been kinder-hearted or had any better intentions, when he saw his name on a package or envelope it never dawned on him that it might not be for him. He was too active in his habit to wait until I had a chance to get at it. And as he was also single-minded and prompt to attend to unfinished business, he opened everything automatically and then did his best to dispose of it.

This went on even after I grew up, until I had a home of my own. Father was always perfectly decent about it, but he never changed. When he saw I felt sulky, he was genuinely sorry and said so, but he couldn't see why all this should annoy me, and he was surprised and amused that it did. I used to get angry once in a while when something came for me which I particularly hadn't wished him to see and which I would find lying, opened, on the hall table marked "For Jr.?" when I came in; but nobody could stay angry with Father—he was too utterly guiltless of having meant to offend.

He often got angry himself, but it was mostly at things, not at persons, and he didn't mind a bit (as a rule) when persons got angry at him. He even declared, when I got back from college, feeling dignified, and told him that I wished he'd be more careful, that he suffered from these mistakes more than I did. It wasn't *his* fault, he pointed out, if my stupid correspondents couldn't remember my name, and it wasn't any pleasure to him to be upset at his breakfast by finding that a lunatic company in Battle Creek had sent him a box of dry bread crumbs, with a letter asserting that this rubbish would be good for his stomach. "I admit I threw it into the fireplace, Clarence, but what else could I do? If you valued this preposterous concoction, my dear boy, I'm sorry. I'll buy another box for you today, if you'll tell me where I can get it. Don't feel badly! I'll buy you a barrel. Only I hope you won't eat it."

In the days when Mrs. Pankhurst and her friends were chaining themselves to lampposts in London, in their campaign for the vote, a letter came from Frances Hand trustfully asking "Dear Clarence" to do something to help Woman Suffrage—speak at a meeting, I think. Father got red in the face. "Speak at one of their meetings!" he roared at Mother. "I'd like nothing better! You can tell Mrs. Hand that it would give me great pleasure to inform all those crackpots in petticoats exactly what I think of their antics."

"Now, Clare," Mother said, "you mustn't talk that way. I like that nice Mrs. Hand, and anyhow this letter must be for Clarence."

One time I asked Father for his opinion of a low-priced stock I'd been watching. His opinion was that it was not worth anything. I thought this over, but I still wished to buy it, so I placed a scale order with another firm instead of with Father's office, and said nothing about it. At the end of the month this other firm sent me a statement, setting forth each of my little transactions in full, and of course they forgot to put the "Jr." at the end of my name. When Father opened the envelope, he thought at first in his excitement that this firm had actually opened an account for him without being asked. I found him telling Mother that he'd like to wring their necks.

"That must be for me, Father," I said, when I took in what had happened.

We looked at each other.

"You bought this stuff?" he said incredulously. "After all I said about it?"

"Yes, Father."

He handed over the statement and walked out of the room.

Both he and I felt offended and angry.

We stayed so for several days, too, but we then made it up.

Once in a while when I got a letter that I had no time to answer I used to address an envelope to the sender and then put anything in it that happened to be lying around on my desk—a circular about books, a piece of newspaper, an old laundry bill—anything at all, just to be amiable, and yet at the same time to save myself the trouble of writing. I happened to tell several people about this private habit of mine at a dinner one night—a dinner at which Alice Duer Miller and one or two other writers were present. A little later she wrote me a criticism of Henry James and ended by saying that I needn't send her any of my old laundry bills because she wouldn't stand it. And she forgot to put on the "Jr."

"In the name of—," Father said bleakly, "this is the worst yet. Here's a woman who says I'd better not read *The Golden Bowl*, which I have no intention whatever of doing, and she also warns me for some unknown reason not to send her my laundry bills."

The good part of all these experiences, as I realize now, was that in the end they drew Father and me closer together. My brothers had only chance battles with him. I had a war. Neither he nor I relished its clashes, but they made us surprisingly intimate.

◇◇◇◇◇◇◇◇◇◇◇◇◇◇◇◇◇◇◇◇◇◇◇◇◇

SEEING THE FUNNY SIDE

1. Besides the mix-up in getting mail, what other disadvantages were there for Clarence in being named after his father?

2. Clarence Jr. said that there would have been friction between him and his father even if they had not had the same name. What was there about the personalities of each that made misunderstandings inevitable?

3. How did Mr. Day's personality contribute to the humor of the essay? How might a less serious-minded or more understanding father have reacted differently to the letters that he opened by mistake? How did Clarence explain his father's apparent lack of consideration?

4. As Clarence Jr. looked back upon the incidents that he told about in this essay, he found them amusing. Why did he fail to see anything funny about them when they happened? Can you think of experiences in your own life which seemed tragic at the time but which are amusing now when you recall them? How can you explain your change in attitude?

WHAT'S IN A NAME?

1. Why didn't Clarence Jr. like his name? If you can, tell how your attitude toward a particular name was influenced by a person you knew or a book you read.

2. How did Clarence Jr. explain the fact that his father saw nothing objectionable in the name that he himself disliked so thoroughly? What difference in their personalities is revealed by their contrasting attitudes toward the name?

3. What advantages or disadvantages can you see in naming children for their parents or other close relatives as the Days did?

CLARENCE DAY (1874–1935)

Son of a prosperous Wall Street broker and grandson of the founder of the *New York Sun*, Clarence Day joined the navy to escape a career in business. Afflicted early in life with arthritis, he spent thirty-six years as an invalid and turned to writing to lessen the boredom. *Life with Father*, written during his last year of life, became a best seller. There is hardly a literate American today who is not familiar with "Father's" booming voice and "Mother's" frantic attempts at budget-balancing. It has been said that Clarence Day's "literary ability, intellectual integrity, and cheerful, courageous, human spirit charmed all who knew him, either personally or through his books."

"Mom, can I have the broom tonight?"

Cartoon by Charles Addams.   Reproduced by permission.   Copyright 1954, The New Yorker Magazine, Inc.

"I heard of the craziest thing the other day. An unlisted *telephone*."

"Guess what began in the gloaming, and busily all the night has been heaping field and highway with a silence deep and white."

THE MIRACLE OF AMERICA

HERBERT HOOVER

The question, "After the Presidency, what?" seems to have been answered most successfully by our thirty-first president, Herbert Hoover, for he continues to be one of our most distinguished public servants. He works so quietly that many Americans are scarcely aware of his activities, but abroad, wherever there has been misery and famine, his name is known and loved. He is a man who has seen the miracle of America at work in his own life and who works tirelessly to make it come true in the lives of others. Here he explains why the miracle is possible only in a free country.

During the last score of years our American form of civilization has been deluged with criticism. It comes from our own people who deplore our undoubted faults and genuinely wish to remedy them. It comes from our political parties by their denunciations in debate of our current issues. It arises from the forthright refusal of the American people to wash their dirty linen in secret. It comes from our love of sensational incidents where villainy is pursued by law and virtue triumphs. It comes from intellectuals who believe in the American system but who feel that our moral and spiritual greatness has not risen to the level of our industrial accomplishments.

Criticism also comes from our native Communists who want to overturn the system. And from the fuzzy-minded totalitarian liberals who believe that their creeping collectivism can be adopted without destroying personal liberty and representative government. It comes bitterly and daily from the governments behind the Iron Curtain and their officials and even from the press of the western European nations that we are trying to help.

Altogether we seem to be in a very, very bad way and engaged in our decline and fall. Criticism is no doubt good for our national soul—if it does not discourage us entirely.

Perhaps the time has come for Americans to take a little stock and think something good about themselves.

We could point out that our American system has perfected the greatest productivity of any nation on earth; that our standard of living is the highest in the world. We could point to our constantly improving physical health and lengthening span of life. We could mention the physical condition of our youth as indicated somewhat by our showing in the recent Olympic games.

In the cultural field, we could point out that with only about six per cent of the world's population we have more youth in high schools and institutions of higher learning, more musical and literary organizations, more libraries and proba-

"The Miracle of America" by Herbert Hoover, as reprinted in *Woman's Home Companion*, November 1948 issue, copyright, 1948, The Crowell-Collier Publishing Co., used by their permission and that of the author.

bly more distribution of the printed and spoken word than all the other ninety-four per cent put together.

On the moral and spiritual side, we have more hospitals and charitable institutions than all of them. And we could suggest that we alone, of all nations, fought in two world wars and asked no indemnities, no acquisition of territory, no domination over other nations. We could point to an advancement of the spirit of Christian compassion such as the world has never seen, and prove it by the tons of food and clothes and billions of dollars we have made as gifts in saving hundreds of millions from famine and governments from collapse.

Much as I feel deeply the lag in spots which do not give equal chance to our Negro population, yet I cannot refrain from saying that our twelve million Negroes probably own more automobiles than all the two hundred million Russians or the three hundred million Negroes under European governments in Africa.

All of which is not boasting, but just fact. And we could say a good deal more.

Whatever our faults may be, our critics do not grasp the sense of a word which is daily on our lips—America. From its intangible meanings spring the multitude of actions, ideals, and purposes of our people. Recently I had an occasion to say something on that subject which I can summarize here.

America means far more than a continent bounded by two oceans. It is more than pride of military power, glory in war or in victory. It means more than vast expanse of farms, of great factories or mines, magnificent cities or millions of automobiles and radios. It is more even than the traditions of the great tide westward from Europe which pioneered the conquest of a continent. It is more than our literature, our music, our poetry. Other nations have these things also.

What we have in addition, the intangible we cannot describe, lies in the personal experience and the living of each of us rather than in phrases, however inspiring.

Perhaps without immodesty I can claim to have had some experience in what *American* means. I have lived many kinds of American life. After my early boyhood in an Iowa village, I lived as the ward of a country doctor in Oregon. I lived among those to whom hard work was the price of existence. The opportunities of America opened up to me the public schools. They carried me to the professional training of an American university. I began by working with my own hands for my daily bread. I have tasted the despair of fruitless search for a job. I know the kindly encouragement of a humble boardinghouse keeper.

I have conducted the administration of great industries with their problems of production and the well-being of their employees.

I have seen America in contrast with many nations and races. My profession took me into many foreign lands under many kinds of government. I have worked with their great spiritual leaders and their great statesmen. I have worked in governments of free men, of tyrannies, of Socialists, and of Communists. I have met with princes, kings, despots, and desperadoes.

I have seen the squalor of Asia, the frozen class barriers of Europe. I was not a tourist. I was associated in their working lives and problems. I had to deal with their social systems and their governments. And outstanding everywhere to these great masses of people there was a hallowed word—America.

To them it was the hope of the world.

Every homecoming was for me a re-affirmation of the glory of America. Each time my soul was washed by the relief from the grinding poverty of other nations, by the greater kindliness and frankness which comes from acceptance of equality and the wide-open opportunity to all who want a chance. It is more than that. It is a land of self-respect born alone of free men.

In later years I participated on behalf of America in a great war. I saw untold misery and revolution. I have seen liberty die and tyranny rise. I have seen human slavery again on the march.

I have been repeatedly placed by my countrymen where I had need to deal with the hurricanes of social and economic destruction which have swept the world. I have seen bitter famine and the worst misery that the brutality of war can produce.

I have had every honor to which any man could aspire. There is no place on the whole earth except here in America where all the sons of man could have this chance in life.

The meaning of our word *America* flows from one pure source. Within the soul of America is the freedom of mind and spirit in man. Here alone are the open windows through which pours the sunlight of the human spirit. Here alone human dignity is not a dream but a major accomplishment.

At the time our ancestors were proclaiming that the Creator had endowed all mankind with rights of freedom as the children of God, with a free will, the German philosophers, Hegel and others, and later, Karl Marx, were proclaiming a satanic philosophy of agnosticism and that the rights of man came from the state. The greatness of America today comes from one philosophy, the despair of Europe from the other.

But there are people in our country today who would compromise in these fundamental concepts. They scoff at these tested qualities in men. They never have understood and never will understand what the word *America* means. They explain that these qualities were good while there was a continent to conquer and a nation to build. They say that time has passed. No doubt the land frontier has passed. But the frontiers of science and better understanding of human welfare are barely opening.

This new land of science with all its high promise cannot and will not be conquered except by men and women inspired by these same concepts of free spirit and free mind.

And it is those moral and spiritual qualities which rise alone in free men which will fulfill the meaning of the word *American*. And with them will come centuries of further greatness to our country.

◇◇◇◇◇◇◇◇◇◇◇◇◇◇◇◇◇◇◇◇◇◇◇◇◇◇◇◇◇◇◇

TEST YOUR UNDERSTANDING

1. According to Mr. Hoover, from what different sources does criticism of America come? Which type of criticism does he seem to feel is justifiable? Which critics are sincere but misguided? Which deliberately aim at the destruction of American ideals?

2. Review some of the good things about America to which Mr. Hoover calls attention. Which do you consider most valuable?

3. The author admits that much of what he finds good about America is also found in other countries. However, he believes that we in America have something in addition. How does he use experiences from his own life to show what that "something" is?

4. Mr. Hoover believes that the difference between the American way of life and that of some Euroepan countries is based upon a fundamental difference in philosophy. What is the basic philosophy of American democracy? What is the philosophy upon which totalitarian governments are based?

APPLYING THE AUTHOR'S IDEAS

1. People are said to "wash their dirty linen" when they reveal personal faults and family scandals by quarreling. Can you give examples from current happenings or from history to illustrate what Mr. Hoover calls "the forthright refusal of the American people to wash their dirty linen in secret"? What is it that we gain from publicizing our national faults? Are there any dangers in this practice?

2. The public enjoys seeing the villain "get his just deserts" in popular modern fiction—stories, movies, and television—as well as in old-fashioned melodrama. Mr. Hoover refers to this general desire to see criminals tracked down and punished when he speaks of "our love of sensational incidents where villainy is pursued by law and virtue triumphs." Give an example of exposure of graft or corruption in national affairs which may have been motivated, at least in part, by the public's satisfaction in seeing wrong-doers brought to justice.

3. What is the reasoning of those who believe that the principles upon which our nation was founded are not practical for a modern society? In your own words give Mr. Hoover's answer to those people. What conditions today does he say are parallel to those which challenged early Americans?

FOR YOUR POLITICAL
VOCABULARY

In order to read understandingly about politics and about the ideas and ideals upon which governments are founded, you should make sure of the exact meanings of the italicized words in the following sentences taken from Mr. Hoover's essay.

1. And [criticism comes] from the fuzzy-minded *totalitarian liberals* who believe that their creeping *collectivism* can be adopted without destroying personal liberty and *representative government*.

2. I have worked in governments of free men, of *tyrannies*, of *Socialists*, and of *Communists*.

HERBERT HOOVER (Born 1874)

Herbert Hoover's life is a real success story. He was born in Iowa, but lived his later boyhood years in Oregon. His parents died when he was very young; but with the help of relatives and his own industry, he succeeded in getting an excellent education. He took his bachelor's degree from Leland Stanford University in California. He became an engineer and did so well in his profession that he had made himself financially independent by the time he reached middle age. He has therefore been able to give most of his time to working for others.

In 1914 and 1915, Hoover served as chairman of the American Relief Commission in London. For the next four years he was chairman of the Relief Commission to Belgium, and from 1917 to 1919 he was American Food Administrator. The great task of feeding European orphans after the First World War was carried on under his direction; and he spent much of his time in the devastated countries. In 1929 he became the thirty-first president of the United States. Through a period of acute financial depression he served ably and honestly. When he left office four years later, it was to continue work with his many activities in behalf of social welfare. When the Second World War broke out, his duties as Food Administrator and as a Commissioner of Relief again assumed chief importance. Since the end of the war he has been one of the trusted advisors of the government, particularly in matters of efficiency and economy.

NOTES ON OUR TIMES

E. B. WHITE

Here are some observations on the modern American scene by a man whom many people consider the foremost essayist of our time. Mr. White is a versatile writer who has produced many fine essays, stories, and humorous poems. You will surely want to read more of his writing than can be represented here. The following brief sketches are typical of his contributions to the editorial pages of the NEW YORKER magazine, with which he has been associated for many years. In his writing, journalism rises to the level of literature.

Notice how the author selects bits of the day's news and presents them in such a way that we take a more critical look at ourselves and our life today.

COWBOY

We recommend to historians the steer wrestler who has been commuting between Chicago and New York by plane, in order to throw steers in the rodeos of both cities. In this pendulous [1] cowboy, if cowboy is the word for him, our century comes to a sort of head: the winged ranch hand, his eye on two steers at once, and the steers a thousand miles apart yet capable of being thrown by the winged, neither steer needing to be thrown, each existing only to be thrown. The cowboy rises from the head of the fallen animal, dusts the seat of his pants, walks stiff-legged to the waiting airliner. The spectators, yearning for the open West and its herds of cattle on the ranges, rise from their mezzanine seats, stiff-legged, dust off their unfulfilled desires, walk to the exits.

[1] PENDULOUS—Swinging back and forth.

"Cowboy" from *The Second Tree from the Corner* by E. B. White, copyright, 1948, by E. B. White. Reprinted by permission of Harper & Brothers.

"The Home" from *The Second Tree from the Corner* by E. B. White, copyright, 1944, by E. B. White. Reprinted by permission of Harper & Brothers.

THE HOME

Homemaking reared its chintzy [1] little head the other day when the ladies of the American Home Economics Association decided that maybe the Home should rate a Cabinet position, to be called the Department of the American Home. It is a noble idea and would unquestionably attract the wrong people. If we had a Secretary of the Home, like a Secretary of State or a Secretary of Commerce, she would probably be a lady whose emphasis would be upon vitamins and lampshades. She would be against mice. The American Home, given Cabinet status, would continue to move (as it has moved in the last few years) in the wrong direction. The American Kitchen would become more and more stagy and unlivable; the American Cellar would finally and for-

[1] CHINTZY—"Arty"; the allusion is to people who are given to prettifying their homes with curtains made of chintz (colorful printed cloth).

ever emerge as a rumpus room, above ground; the Home as a whole would tend to become collapsible, transparent, mobile, washable, sterile, and devoid of human life.

Home is too delicate an organism to be federalized. The eviction [2] of even so small a thing as a mouse threatens its balance; the absence of a hummingbird from the delphiniums can destroy its tone. Some of the most vital and dependable homes we have ever been in were ones in which the economics were deplorable; some of the barest of homes were ones which, physically, were the answer to an economist's dream. Home was quite a place when people stayed there, but Home Economics is just another in the long line of activities that take ladies away. Of the home economists we have met in our lifetime, all had one trait in common: not one of them was at home.

[2] EVICTION—Putting out, forcing to leave the house or property.

MRS. WIENCKUS

The Newark police arrested a very interesting woman the other day—a Mrs. Sophie Wienckus—and she is now on probation after being arraigned as disorderly. Mrs. Wienckus interests us because her "disorderliness" was simply her capacity to live a far more self-contained life than most of us can manage. The police complained that she was asleep in two empty cartons in a hallway. This was her preferred method of bedding down. All the clothes she possessed she had on—several layers of coats and sweaters. On her person were bankbooks showing that she was ahead of the game to the amount of $19,799.09. She was a working woman—a domestic—and, on

"Mrs. Wienckus" from *The Second Tree from the Corner* by E. B. White, copyright, 1951, by E. B. White. Reprinted by permission of Harper & Brothers.

the evidence, a thrifty one. Her fault, the Court held, was that she lacked a habitation.

"Why didn't you rent a room?" asked the magistrate. But he should have added parenthetically "(and the coat hangers in the closet and the cord that pulls the light and the dish that holds the soap and the mirror that conceals the cabinet where lives the aspirin that kills the pain)." Why didn't you rent a room "(with the rug that collects the dirt and the vacuum that sucks the dirt and the man that fixes the vacuum and the fringe that adorns the shade that dims the lamp and the desk that holds the bill for the installment on the television set that tells of the wars)?" We feel that the magistrate oversimplified his question.

Mrs. Wienckus may be disorderly, but one pauses to wonder where the essential disorder really lies. All of us are instructed to seek hallways these days (except school children, who crawl under the desks), and it was in a hallway that they found Mrs. Wienckus, all compact. We read recently that the only hope of avoiding inflation [1] is through ever increasing production of goods. This to us is always a terrifying conception of the social order —a theory of the good life through accumulation of objects. We lean toward the order of Mrs. Wienckus, who has eliminated everything except what she can conveniently carry, whose financial position is solid, and who can smile at Rufus Rastus Johnson Brown. [2] We salute a woman whose affairs are in such excellent order in a world untidy beyond all belief.

[1] INFLATION—A time of high prices, when there seems danger that money will become almost valueless.
[2] RUFUS RASTUS JOHNSON BROWN—A shiftless character in an old song. He is faced with the problem of what to do "when the rent comes 'round."

HOW DOES MODERN LIFE LOOK TO YOU?

1. How does Mr. White make the rodeo cowboy's life seem futile and ridiculous? Explain how this cowboy is definitely a product of our times. How does the author comment indirectly on the people in the rodeo audience? What are they seeking? Mention some other forms of entertainment in which modern Americans have become passive spectators rather than active participants.

2. How can you tell in the first sentence of "The Home" that the author is being mildly satirical about professional "homemakers"? He says that the proposed cabinet post would undoubtedly attract the *wrong* people. Whom would he probably consider the *right* people for such a position? What does he find lacking in modern American home life?

3. How do you suppose most people would react to reading the story of Mrs. Wienckus as it might have appeared in the daily paper? Do you think they would believe that her right to live as she pleased had been unjustly interfered with by the police? Show how Mr. White uses her story to call attention to the burdensome complexities of modern living. Do you think that he is really advocating that we all live like Mrs. Wienckus? Give arguments both for and against Mr. White's belief that the good life cannot be achieved by the accumulation of material things.

E. B. WHITE (Born 1899)

Elwyn Brooks White was born in Mount Vernon, New York. In 1921, shortly after his graduation from Cornell University, he went to New York where he began his literary career by writing for an advertising firm. Later he became a member of the staff of the *New Yorker*. In those early years his editorials, sketches and essays, and poems helped to give that magazine the reputation for literary excellence which it still maintains. His writing is both wise and witty—and he shows a warm good will toward the human race.

Mr. White has done much writing in addition to his work for the *New Yorker*. One notable series of essays, based upon his experiences when he took a holiday from city life to be a farmer in Maine, appeared first in *Harper's Magazine*. In 1942 the essays were published as a book under the title of *One Man's Meat*. It was awarded the Limited Editions Club's Gold Medal for being the book "most likely to attain the stature of a classic." Other important works include *Here Is New York*, published in 1949, and a recent miscellaneous collection of his writing titled *The Second Tree from the Corner*.

❖❖❖❖❖

THE HERALDRY OF
THE RANGE

J. FRANK DOBIE

The practice of using marks or symbols for identification did not originate with the branding of cattle on our western plains. As a matter of fact, people

"The Heraldry of the Range" from *On the Open Range* by J. Frank Dobie. Reprinted by permission of the author.

carved or burned crude signs on their personal belongings long before they learned to write.

Probably the most complicated system of using symbols for identification was the one developed by the knights of the Middle Ages to decorate their shields and helmets. In England those elaborate medieval trade-marks were —and still are—designed by the College of Heralds. That is why the art or science of making and explaining coats of arms is known as heraldry.

Here Frank Dobie discusses the heraldry of the cattle country of America. In reading his essay you will pick up some curious bits of information about cattle brands. You will also enjoy the flavor of the West in the cowboy anecdotes that are included in the selection.

The other day a ranchman out in West Texas whose brand is T Half Circle announced that the United States Patent Office had registered it as a trade-mark. In as much as many cattle raisers nowadays sell their product by mail, the owner's brand on an animal being a guaranty of its standard breeding, other cowmen are likely to have their brands registered as trade-marks. A brand is just that—a trade-mark—though it is also much more, and to it is attached all the sentiment and connotation once borne by coats of arms.

Primarily it is a means of identification, whether against thieves or among honest men, on the owner's home range or far away. If names and addresses were not so long, they would be branded on cattle. A brand is a seal that stands for a name; and somewhere, with name and address, every legal brand is recorded, just as with the purchaser's name are recorded the make and engine number of every automobile, somewhere.

The range is branded with brands, and branded deep. The knowledge of brands is a special knowledge, and the language expressing that knowledge is a special language, hieroglyphic as well as utilitarian; familiarity with it stamping ranch people far more genuinely than such purchasable equipment as boots and spurs.

At a one-teacher school out in the mesquite the Friday-afternoon session usually closed with recitations. A frequent recitation began with the well-known injunction to the little star:

> Twinkle, twinkle, little star!
> How I wonder what you are,
> Up above the world so high
> Like a diamond in the sky.

One of the school urchins was the son of a rancher who ran the Diamond P brand —◈. That was the only diamond the lad knew, and he confesses now that he used to study the stars by the hour, trying to catch one of them assuming the diamond shape so familiar to him on the sides of cows and at the hot end of a branding iron. He knew the language of brands better than he knew the language of jewels and poetry.

The brand fixes its language to everything pertaining to it. The chuck wagon of the Olmos—Elms—Ranch is seldom called the Olmos wagon, but is almost invariably referred to as the "A Dot wagon," ⋀ being the ranch brand. The cow crowd working on the Withers range is customarily referred to not as the

Withers outfit but as the "Pig Pen out-fit"; the Pig Pen, made thus—⊨—being the Withers brand. A cowboy rides a "Double Circle horse," which is branded ◎. Another cowboy is "one of the Spur hands." A herd in the distance "looks like a Long L herd."

A ranch may be named for its owner, as the Kokernut Ranch; it may be named after a creek or some other topographical unit on it, as the San Francisco Ranch; it may derive its name from some event in local history, as the Wagon Sheet Ranch, where a camper once drove off, absent-mindedly leaving his wagon sheet behind; or, as more often, a ranch may derive its name from something in nature pertaining to the place of its location, as the Seven Oaks and the Cochina—Hog. The famous Jingle-Bob outfit took its name from an earmark—the jingle-bob— a deep split that left the lower half of the ear flopping down. But the greater number of ranches by far take their names simply from the ranch brand—the J A ranch—⅄—the pitchfork—ψ—the Hundred and One—|O|.

The very owner of a ranch sometimes loses his name in his brand. There was W 6 Wright of the Nueces, who considered it a great joke when he found that he had signed the bond of a man indicted for stealing some W6 yearlings— Wright's own brand. There is Diamond and a Half Hud of the plains, who signs his checks as W. D. Hudson and gives ⋈ as his brand. There is the S M S Kid, who has not been a kid for forty years, but who is still helping to burn ⅗⋀⅗ on white-faced calves. Colonel B. H. Campbell, a prominent cowman of the Indian Territory[1] who for a time managed the great X I T Ranch of Texas, gave for his brand B͞Q. It was read as "Barbeque,"

and "Barbeque Campbell" has been a household word all over the Southwest for half a century.

As a means of identification the brand envelops all things else on the range. An incident related by Walter Billingsley of San Antonio well illustrates this fact.

"In 1884," he says, "I took a herd of King Ranch steers from South Texas to Cheyenne, Wyoming. Everything went all right until we crossed the South Platte and reached Fort Sidney, Nebraska. While we held the herd a few miles out from town, I let a bunch of the boys go in to see the sights. Five of them laid out and did not report for work next morning. I rode in, found them, and fired them on the spot. I owed them one hundred and twenty dollars apiece. I had no money to pay them off, and I did not know a soul in Sidney.

"My first move was to see the banker. Says I to him: 'I'm trail boss for the King Ranch, owned by Captain Richard King and known from Canada to the Rio Grande. I've fired five of the sorriest cowboys that ever rode out of Texas. They are due six hundred dollars, and when they get it they will make you fine citizens and spend it all right here. I want to leave them with you, and I want to draw on Wright and Beverley at Dodge City for the six hundred dollars. Will you cash my draft?'

"'Well,' says the banker, 'you look all right and I am satisfied you are all right, but can't you get somebody to identify you?'

"'I'm where I never was before and where I never expect to be again,' I replied, 'and I don't see a soul in town that I know.'

"The banker seemed awful anxious to accommodate me, and I sure did not want to hire those cowboys back just because I couldn't pay them off. I just

[1] INDIAN TERRITORY—Part of the territory that became the state of Oklahoma.

wasn't going to give them the whip hand over me that way.

" 'Suppose you look around a little and see if you can't strike somebody you know,' the banker concluded, 'and then come back.'

"I went out. My mind was made up. I rounded up the men I'd fired and said, 'Follow me and get your money.'

"We galloped to camp. 'Load up and hitch up,' I says to the cook, 'and follow me.'

"Then I called the horse wrangler. 'Drive up that *remuda* [2] of saddle horses,' I says to him, 'and follow the chuck wagon.'

"When we were all ready we struck a high trot for town, and a sight we must have made—me in the lead, those five sorry cowboys after me, then the chuck wagon with six mules hitched to it, and then one hundred and fifty saddle horses with the *remudero* and a couple of other hands driving them. I drew up at the bank and the outfit halted.

" 'Come here!' I yelled to the banker, who was already at the door. 'Come out here and look at my identification!'

"He came a-laughing.

" 'Now,' says I, 'I guess you know what the King Ranch brand is—Running W on the side and K on the jaw. Well, there's one hundred and fifty saddle horses branded K W. There's a wagon with K W branded on the side boards, branded on the chuck box, branded all over everything. Look at the cook's saddle on that near wheel mule, and you'll see K W on it. In fact, everything and everybody in this outfit is branded K W.'

"The banker was impressed all right. He shelled out the six hundred dollars right away. I paid off the quitters; they

[2] *remuda* (rĕ·mū′dà)—The string of saddle horses from which the daily mounts were chosen. The man in charge of the *remuda* was the *remudero*.

Strays Found and Sold.

The following is a list of the brands on strays, proceeds of which have been remitted to the Secretary of the Wyoming Stock Growers Association.

THE BETTMANN ARCHIVE

unsaddled right there, turned their horses into the *remuda*, took their bedding out of the wagon, and the Running W outfit rolled its tail on for Cheyenne."

The average cowhand is so conscious of brands that in season and out of season, appropriately and inappropriately, consciously and unconsciously, he brands whatever he comes across. He whittles brands on sticks; he burns them into the planks of branding chutes, on pasture gates, on the anchor posts of windmill towers. He smears them with axle grease across the doors of barns and garages. He paints them with charcoal on the rock walls of canyons in which he has made a campfire. He carves them into his spur straps, leggings, and saddle—above all, into his boot tops. "My pistol belt," says an old trail driver, "had brands on it representing ranges from Chihuahua to Montana." More pistols were etched with cattle brands than were ever notched for dead victims. Many a cook has stenciled the ranch coat of arms into the top crust of that gala-day treat—a wild-plum cobbler. Ranch boys are incorrigible when it comes to carving brands on their desks at school. They play ranch, and with baling wire for running irons brand oak balls, the sawed-off tips of horns, spools, and other objects used to represent cattle and horses. Unconscious of or callous to any cruelty, cowboys will mark and brand a buck deer they have roped, a coyote, or anything else.

An old-time, dyed-in-the-wool cowman took pride in nothing more than in his memory for brands, and good cowmen still take the same pride. There are hotel clerks who never forget a face, scholars who never falter on a date, and automobile salesmen who hold in mind the engine number of every car sold or inspected. One must marvel with Mark Twain at the memory of a trained Mississippi River steamboat pilot. But the memory of a top brandman surpasses any other kind of memory I have ever met or heard of. It is more than memory; it is an instinct for cattle. Still riding the range are men who can count a hundred

head of mixed cattle as they string along, and then from memory classify them and give every brand correctly.

Some of the cattle inspectors operating today in stockyards and on the range can recognize, with only an occasional reference to their brand books, literally thousands of brands. They say that Lod Calohan, head inspector for the Texas and Southwestern Cattle Raisers' Association at the Kansas City stockyards, can tell what brand an animal had on it by tasting the beef. An incident recalled by him will illustrate this genius for brands.

"A cow," he said, "was shipped to the Kansas City market by two ranchmen in partnership at Big Bend, Colorado. She was so branded up that she looked like a map of Jerusalem. I had to shear her to make out all the brands. Then I had to trace down her history to tell which was the holding brand—the brand of her last legitimate owner. One of the brands, together with the earmarks, told me that she had been calved in Arizona. Carrying this Arizona brand, she had been driven into New Mexico, where three successive owners branded her. Then she passed into Colorado, where a fifth owner burned his brand on about the only vacant space left on her hide. The shippers had not known whether the cow belonged to them or the man in the moon. She was in their herd and they sent her to market. The brand of that fifth owner—the Colorado man—happened to be one of the fifteen thousand represented by the association for which I work, and the money for which the cow was sold was sent to him."

Deciphering and remembering the letters, figures, curves, and other configurations that make up brands is not enough. The thoroughgoing rangeman is a master of brand nomenclature, on the esoteric principles [3] of which somebody ought to write a grammar. Generally, be it said, brands read from top to bottom and from left to right. Many brands—probably a majority of them—are so simple that nearly anybody can call them properly. The brand H4 can be nothing else than H Four; H⊳ will easily be conceived to be the H Triangle. But only the initiated denominate ⊥ as Lazy H, or Ɛ as Crazy Three. Any letter "too tired to stand up" is "lazy"; though if it is merely in an oblique position and not on its back, it is "tumbling." ⊤ or ⊥ is Tumbling T.

A letter with curves at the ends is often said to be "running." The most noted illustration of this principle is the Running W brand, ⋎⋏⋎, of the million-acre King Ranch, which, however, Mexicans call La Viborita—Little Snake. A letter or figure with "wings" to it is "flying"—thus, W is the "Flying W."

Brands "walk," "drag," "swing," and "rock" as well as they "run" or "fly." Ɛ is the Walking F and A is the Walking A. The projection at the bottom of the figure makes ⁊ the Drag Seven. L suspended from a curve, ⌐L, becomes the Swinging L. Many brands are on rockers, as the Rocking H—H . But if the rocker is unjoined, then it is a half or quarter circle; so ⌣H⌣ is H Half Circle. One of the most historic brands of the West is the Rocking Chair—⌣ .

Sometimes a brand rests on a "bench," as ⊥, the Y Bench. V-shaped prongs attached to some part of a letter make it forked. Ƨ is Forked S, but ⅄ is not Forked N; it is Forked Lightning.

A straight mark is usually a bar, but if it is very long or leaning at an angle to the normal horizontal position, it is apt

to be called a slash, and ⊢ is Bradded Dash. The \/ is called Cut and Slash. John Chisum, of Jingle-Bob fame, branded twenty thousand calves a year with a straight line running from shoulder to tail, and that bar was known all over the cattle country as the Fence Rail. A brand burner added to it thus—⎯o⎯—and the result was known both as Knot on the Rail and Bug on the Rail. The Kellog boys in the Big Bend of Texas branded N on the shoulder and K on the hip, connected with a bar, but instead of being called N Bar K, the brand is called N Chain K. o—o might be O Bar O, but it isn't. It is Hobble O, for it resembles a pair of horse hobbles.

The identical brand may go by one name in one section and by another name in another section. The great Laureles—Laurel Leaf—Ranch on the Rio Grande gave the Laurel Leaf brand, but the same insignia three hundred miles north on the San Saba went under the name of Flowering Lucy—a patent corruption of flower-de-luce, itself a degeneration from *fleur-de-lis*. A flattened O may be Goose Egg, Mashed O, or Link. ☐ is both Box and Block.

One time a rancher out on the Pecos started a new brand configured thus—ᛋ . Somebody asked him what he called it. "*Quién sabe?*" [4] he replied—Who knows? And as the Quién Sabe brand it was known ever afterward. Looking through a mixed herd of cattle or a brand book, one might note many brands of apparently *quién sabe* nature, but somehow the range men have usually found a name for the most nameless device.

Some brands, because of the oddity of the device or name, became better known than certain simpler brands much more widely used. Such a brand was ⌣⌣. Originally it was known as Pot Hooks.

[4] *Quién sabe*—Pronounced kyĕn sä′bä.

It was run on the Colorado River, Texas, by McAulay and Clampitt. In the drought of 1884 their herd of ten thousand cattle was reduced to five thousand, and they moved farther west into the Green Valley country. Here the brand took the name of Straddle Bug. It began on the shoulder and ended at the rear of the animal's thigh. It was said: "The only way for a cow thief to burn the Straddle Bug out was to burn up the brute wearing it."

Though new brands are constantly being recorded over the entire range country, the most interesting and original belong to the past, though many of them are still in use. Just when brands were introduced to the world would be difficult to say. The claim has often been made that Cortés, conqueror of Mexico, originated branding not only in America but in the world. He may have branded first in America, but certainly not in the world. It is said that a tomb twenty-five hundred years old has been uncovered in Thebes bearing among other mural decorations the representation of a cow tied down and a man branding her with a geometric design. The tomb must have been that of an Egyptian cattle king. When Chaucer's pilgrims set out on their immortal journey from London to Canterbury more than five hundred years ago, some of them probably rode on rented horses. At least, horses kept for rent at that time were, says the great historian, Jusserand—who cites authority for the statement—"branded in a prominent manner, so that unscrupulous travelers should not be tempted to quit the road and appropriate the steeds." Indeed, Will C. Barnes has traced branding in England back to the eighth century. In 1643, before the cattle industry in the Southwest was born, the New Haven, Connecticut, code stipulated how horses should be branded in order to prevent trouble between rival claimants of "horses running together in the woods."

A brand might spring forth full-grown without premeditation, but with most cowmen choosing a brand has always been a more serious matter than naming a baby. The practical cowman wants a brand that is plain and easily read. He wants it large enough that it cannot be blotched or run out by cow thieves, and at the same time not so large that it will ruin the value of a hide. In the old days it was more important than it is now to have a brand that does not lend itself to being run into another brand. The Straddle Bug, already described, well illustrates the fulfillment of this latter requisite.

While such consideration always entered into the selection of brands by real cowmen, at the same time many a brand expresses personality and autobiography. With elegant simplicity, Mrs. Katie Barr spelled out her whole name in KT—K T Bar. Jack Barber approached his last name with merely B̄R̄. Pete Coffin had both his jest and his name in ⊕. A man by the name of Hightower ran HiR.

Some names naturally lend themselves to this sort of rebus brand better than others. Without any pictorial effect at all, John M. Doak was satisfied with DOK for his brand, but L. J. Story felt that he must tell the whole story, and he did with STORY—an absurdly long brand. Napoleon Daniel embodied in a brand his nickname—BONY. Ingenious but a little puzzling was Mr. Float's brand, ꟼᵒ, which does spell FLOT.

Often, rather than a name, the brand expresses some sort of idea. J. C. Studer was a blacksmith working for the Santa Fe Railroad when it was built across the Texas Panhandle. He fell in love with the country, invested his savings in land

and cattle, and out of respect for his trade adopted ⏚, an anvil, as his brand. One of the ship captains, Thomas Decrow, who used to sail in the Gulf of Mexico, quit the sea for ranching, but he could not forget the old seafaring life, and his Ship's Anchor brand—↵⊶—was a tribute to the memory. The famous John Marsh, of California, who, before the acquisition of California by the United States, was raising cattle for hides that were shipped at two dollars apiece, branded his herds with the same emblem.

There are legendary tales about brands, as there are about everything else with which man has had a vital connection. One of the most widely known of these legends tells how the "Four Sixes"— 6666—originated.

Back in the early days a young cowboy by the name of Burk Burnett, who was just getting his start in cattle, rode into the village of Fort Worth one morning bent on indulging his skill in the favorite game of the range—poker. At one of the many gaming tables, then wide open to the public, he invested in a sombrero [5] full of chips. At first he lost heavily; then the game became variable; about midnight his luck had changed, and by daylight he had a barrelful of money.

One of his opponents was desperate. "Burk," he said, "I'm broke, but I'll play my ranch and cattle against your pile." "You've made a bet," was the reply.

On the deal Burk Burnett drew two sixes. He discarded three other cards, keeping the pair. Then he drew two more sixes. The four sixes won the ranch. Immediately, the story goes on, Burnett rebranded the cattle he had won with his lucky number—6666. In time he increased his holdings until he had three hundred thousand acres in the Indian Territory stocked with Four Sixes

[5] SOMBRERO—A broad-brimmed hat.

cattle, besides an enormous ranch in North Texas. An oil field came in on his land and a boom city named Burkburnett sprang up. When his widow died, only a few years ago, she left several million dollars to Texas Christian University—probably the best poker hand that a Christian institution ever drew.

When queried himself as to how he came to select the 6666 brand, Burk Burnett used to smile and say that in the beginning of his career he thought that if he should ever have 6666 cattle he would be a considerable cowman. Another account, vouched for by Burk Burnett's own nephew and range boss, is that Burnett bought out a small stock of cattle branded with four sixes and adopted the brand as his own. Whatever the facts, the poker story has fastened itself upon the imagination of thousands of recounters and will live for a long time. And Burk Burnett believed in his brand!

Occasionally the romance of lovers has expressed itself in brands. O. Henry wrote a story—"Hearts and Crosses"—on the theme that probably had its basis in fact. At a round-up out on the plains Asa Jones saw a heifer wearing on her left side ᴰᴼᴸᴸʸ, but Dolly was so far away that she probably never glimpsed this expression of a lovelorn cowboy. On the frontier, where pretty girls were exceedingly rare, a cowman by the name of Plunkett —so an old tale goes—one time brought his daughter fair to live at the ranch. Her name was Lilybel, she said, but the cowboys called her Lil, and before long they were vying with one another in branding all the mavericks they could put their ropes on with LIL. The L I L brand became a herd not to sneeze at. Meantime Lilybel went on encouraging the rustics and writing to the dude back East to whom she was engaged. She married him, and her husband became owner of all the wealth created by his rivals.

No account of brands would be complete without consideration of the art of burning out brands. It was an art that reached the height of development during the days of open range, but it is by no means lost yet. Before the practice of counterbranding went out, a thief might void a brand by running a bar through it or by counterbranding the animal—as if it had been legitimately sold—and then putting his own brand on it. Again, he might rub out the owner's brand by taking a hot smoothing iron and burning all that part of an animal's hide covered by a brand. This was called blotching, or blotting. The result would be an enormous scar or blotch, through which the original lines were apt still to be visible. In any case, the blotch was evidence that the animal had been stolen, though not always could it be ascertained from whom stolen.

The most common practice by far was, and is yet, to run the original brand into something else.

One of the oldest chestnuts [6] in the cow country is the I See You Too story. A ranchman somewhere started the IC brand. Before long he noticed in his herd some cattle wearing ICU. Not to be outdone, he did a little doctoring himself, and then the whole herd wore the ICU2 brand. A similar bromide is of the fellow who started with B4 for a brand. A longhorn [7] neighbor presently claimed that cattle branded B4U were his. The king of brand alterers then rode in, and presently nobody could find on the range anything that was not branded B4U2.

Could brands be subtracted from as

[6] CHESTNUTS—Old stories or jokes.
[7] LONGHORN—Cattle with long horns.

well as added to, the problem of the brand burner would be much simpler; but in brands, as in Scripture, what is writ is writ. Running the 7P into Seven Up appears simple, the result looking like this 7P. But in order to make a new brand that is plausible out of an old one, the original must be reburned so that it will appear to be of the same age as the additional lines. If the old brand is burned at all deeply, it will not heal neatly, like the newer portion, and thus will stick out like a sore thumb. To obviate this give-away, thieves sometimes run the branding iron over the old brand with a piece of wet blanket between iron and flesh. No matter what means are employed, the practiced eye of a good cowman can usually detect a flaw that reveals the trick. If the evidence is not conclusive, there is one infallible method of detecting whether or not the original brand has been mutilated. That is to kill the animal and examine the hide from the underside. From this surface the original brand invariably shows as distinct from the made-over brand. Many times in trial courts hides have thus been produced as evidence against cow thieves.

The classic story of brand burning has, fittingly, to do with the largest ranch the United States of America has known—the X I T, the three million acres of which were granted by the state of Texas to the Capital Syndicate in exchange for the present granite capitol building at Austin. Wherever men talk of brands—and that is wherever range cattle graze—the story of the Star Cross burn is told. "I bet," confesses an old hand, "that when I was punching cattle on the plains I spent not less than a solid month of time trying to figure out some way in which the X I T brand could be burned. I've seen cowboys figure in the sand for hours, demonstrating various devices."

EWING GALLOWAY

One time, however, the yarn goes, a clever range rider solved the problem. He revealed his secret to no one; he never blurred a brand. He was an artist. Nevertheless, he was finally brought to trial. The evidence was conclusive that he had built up from nothing a herd of cattle branded Star Cross, ⛥, but the prosecuting attorney was unable to inform the jury how X I T could be altered into that symbol, and so the rustler was freed. The X I T people were helpless. They offered him five thousand dollars if he would tell them how he achieved the Star Cross and would quit burning it on cow brutes.

Another prong of the story told by J. Evetts Haley, in his remarkable history of the X I T Ranch of Texas, discloses the legendary rustler's secret. The branding iron used to make the Capital Syndicate brand was, says Haley, a straight bar five inches long. With two applications the X could be made, with one the I, and with two more the T. Haste on the part of the man doing the branding or the squirming of the calf on the ground often resulted in a brand far from even or symmetrical. One day a rustler who had been doing a lot of figuring on the ground sighted such a brand. It was made thus: ✗I⊤. According to an old saying, all that was necessary to start a herd on the open range was a rope, a running iron, and nerve. The rustler had all three. He traced the X and the I and the crooked T into an almost perfect star cross— ⛥ .

Among the thousands of Syndicate cattle were many other warped brands. That rustler must have ridden until he got them all. He is still riding. Whatever the story, it is safe to assert that in the range country more time has been consumed trying to run—on paper or in the sand—X I T into a five-pointed Texas star inclosing a cross than within the same region has ever been consumed on cross-word puzzles or laddergrams.

Although brand burning forms a lurid and picturesque feature in the history of the range, its extent has often been over-emphasized. After all, a great majority of range men were honest, and the brands on cattle, as a general rule, served the purpose for which they have always been designed—that is, to identify and maintain ownership.

If branding could be avoided it would be avoided. Humane societies have pro-tested against the practice; experiments have been conducted with chemical com-positions purporting to make an indelible but painless mark. But no substitute has been found for branding. Anyhow, branding is not unduly cruel, and the re-sultant pain is of short duration. As long as there are ranches, there will be brands —and that will be until millions and millions of acres of rocks and arid soil are made fertile and moist. The heraldry of the range is not obsolete; it is not even obsolescent.

◇◇◇◇◇◇◇◇◇◇◇◇◇◇◇◇◇◇◇◇◇◇◇◇◇◇◇◇◇

FOR UNDERSTANDING

✶1. What are the practical reasons for branding cattle? How is the importance of brands in a cattle country illustrated by the incident of the cattle man who needed to borrow six hundred dollars to pay the cowboys he had fired? What other cow-boy anecdote shows specialized knowledge about brands or intense interest in them?

2. How much of the language of brands can you remember from the essay? How does one read a brand? What is meant by such terms as *lazy, crazy,* and *running* when applied to letters in a brand? Can you recall at least one brand that spells out a complete word, possibly the owner's name? Can you draw or describe a brand that has a name in no way suggested by its appear-ance? Tell how such a brand came to be named.

✶3. What are the characteristics of a good brand? What things must be taken into consideration in adopting a new one?

✶4. Explain how the practice of branding is a natural outgrowth of the section of the country where it originated. Why does Mr. Dobie believe that there is little pos-sibility of the heraldry of the range becom-ing obsolete?

WORDS FOR BRANDS—OLD AND NEW

The following words name identifying marks of one kind or another. Make sure of the exact meaning of each and then use it to fill in the appropriate blank in the sentences below.

emblem   crest   trade-mark   hallmark

1. The eagle is an _____ of the United States.
2. On the silver was stamped the _____ that guaranteed its quality.
3. The family _____ was embroidered on all her linen.
4. He found that the _____ which he wanted to use for his invention had already been patented.

J. FRANK DOBIE (Born 1888)

When Mr. Dobie writes of the Texas ranges, he is right at home with his subject. He was born on a ranch in Live Oak County. After his schooling in Texas, which included degrees at Southwestern University, he continued his education at Columbia and at Cambridge Universities. During the Second World War he served with the United States Army, lecturing at Shrevenham American University in Eng-land as well as to American troops in Ger-many.

He is now living in Austin, Texas, and writing for numerous magazines. His fa-vorite subject is the American Southwest. Representative titles from his works are *A Guide to Life and Literature of the South-west, A Texan in England,* and *Coronado's Children.*

THE CASE OF THE ELEVEN
BLUE MEN

BERTON ROUECHÉ

You would scarcely expect to find material for a detective story in the files of the New York Department of Health. Nevertheless, that is where Mr. Berton Roueché, a writer for THE NEW YORKER *magazine, uncovered this fascinating mystery. The weird title of the article and the style of writing suggest a Sherlock Holmes type of yarn. As a matter of fact, there is a mystery here as baffling as any that confronted that famous sleuth. The fact that this tale is not fiction but a true account of the work of modern medical detectives adds to its interest.*

At about eight o'clock on Monday morning, September 25, 1944, a ragged, aimless old man of eighty-two collapsed on the sidewalk on Dey Street, near the Hudson Terminal. Innumerable people must have noticed him, but he lay there alone for several minutes, dazed, doubled up with abdominal cramps, and in an agony of retching. Then a policeman came along. Until the policeman bent over the old man, he may have supposed that he had just a sick drunk on his hands; wanderers dropped by drink are common in that part of town in the early morning. It was not an opinion that he could have held for long. The old man's nose, lips, ears, and fingers were sky blue. The policeman went to a telephone and put in an ambulance call to Beekman-Downtown Hospital, half a dozen blocks away. The old man was carried into the emergency room there at eight-thirty. By that time, he was unconscious and the blueness had spread over a large part of his body. The examining physician attributed the old man's morbid color to cyanosis, a condition that usually results from an insufficient supply of oxygen in the blood, and also noted that he was diarrheic and in a severe state of shock. The course of treatment prescribed by the doctor was conventional. It included an instant gastric lavage,[1] heart stimulants, bed rest, and oxygen therapy. Presently, the old man recovered an encouraging, if painful, consciousness and demanded, irascibly and in the name of God, to know what had happened to him. It was a question that, at the moment, nobody could answer with much confidence.

For the immediate record, the doctor made a free-hand diagnosis of carbon-monoxide poisoning—from what source,

---

[1] GASTRIC LAVAGE—Washing out of the stomach.

"The Case of the Eleven Blue Men" from *Eleven Blue Men and Other Narratives of Medical Detection* by Berton Roueché, copyright, 1948, by Berton Roueché, reprinted by permission of Little, Brown & Company. Originally published in *The New Yorker*.

whether an automobile or a gas pipe, it was, of course, pointless even to guess. Then, because an isolated instance of gas poisoning is something of a rarity in a section of the city as crammed with human beings as downtown Manhattan, he and his colleagues in the emergency room braced themselves for at least a couple more victims. Their foresight was promptly and generously rewarded. A second man was rolled in at 10:25. Forty minutes later, an ambulance drove up with three more men. At 11:20, two others were brought in. An additional two arrived during the next fifteen minutes. Around noon, still another was admitted. All of these nine men were also elderly and dilapidated, all had been in misery for at least an hour, and all were rigid, cyanotic, and in a state of shock. The entire body of one, a bony, seventy-three-year-old consumptive named John Mitchell, was blue. Five of the nine, including Mitchell, had been stricken in the Globe Hotel, a sunless, upstairs flophouse at 190 Park Row, and two in a similar place, called the Star Hotel, at 3 James Street. Another had been found slumped in the doorway of a condemned building on Park Two, not far from City Hall Park, by a policeman. The ninth had keeled over in front of the Eclipse Cafeteria, at 6 Chatham Square. At a quarter to seven that evening, one more aged blue man was brought in. He had been lying, too sick to ask for help, on his cot in a cubicle in the Lion Hotel, another flophouse, at 26 Bowery, since ten o'clock that morning. A clerk had finally looked in and seen him.

By the time this last blue man arrived at the hospital, an investigation of the case by the Department of Health, to which all outbreaks of an epidemiological nature must be reported, had been under way for five hours. Its findings thus far had not been illuminating. The investigation was conducted by two men. One was the Health Department's chief epidemiologist, Dr. Morris Greenberg, a small, fragile, reflective man of fifty-seven, who is now acting director of the Bureau of Preventable Diseases; the other was Dr. Ottavio Pellitteri, a field epidemiologist, who, since 1946, has been administrative medical inspector for the Bureau. He is thirty-six years old, pale, and stocky, and has a bristling black mustache. The other afternoon, when I was in Dr. Greenberg's office, the pair of them told me about the case. Their recollection of it is, understandably, vivid. The derelicts were the victims of a type of poisoning so rare that only ten previous outbreaks of it had been recorded in medical literature. Of these, two were in the United States and two in Germany; the others had been reported in France, England, Switzerland, Algeria, Australia, and India. Up to September 25, 1944, the largest number of people stricken in a single outbreak was four. That was in Algeria, in 1926.

The Beekman-Downtown Hospital telephoned a report of the occurrence to the Health Department just before noon. As is customary, copies of the report were sent to all the Department's administrative officers. "Mine was on my desk when I got back from lunch," Dr. Greenberg said to me. "It didn't sound like much. Nine persons believed to be suffering from carbon-monoxide poisoning had been admitted during the morning, and all of them said that they had eaten breakfast at the Eclipse Cafeteria, at 6 Chatham Square. Still, it was a job for us. I checked with the clerk who handles assignments and found that Pellitteri had gone out on it. That was all I wanted to know. If it amounted to anything, I knew he'd phone me before making a written report. That's an arrangement we have here. Well, a couple of hours later I got a call from him. My interest perked right up."

"I was at the hospital," Dr. Pellitteri told me, "and I'd talked to the staff and most of the men. There were ten of them by then, of course. They were sick as dogs, but only one was in really bad shape."

"That was John Mitchell," Dr. Greenberg put in. "He died the next night. I understand his condition was hopeless from the start. The others, including the old boy who came in last, pulled through all right. Excuse me, Ottavio, but I just thought I'd get that out of the way. Go on."

Dr. Pellitteri nodded. "I wasn't at all convinced that it was gas poisoning," he continued. "The staff was beginning to doubt it, too. The symptoms weren't quite right. There didn't seem to be any of the headache and general dopiness that you get with gas. What really made me suspicious was this: only two or three of the men had eaten breakfast in the cafeteria at the same time. They had straggled in all the way from seven o'clock to ten. That meant that the place would have had to be full of gas for at least three hours, which is preposterous. It also indicated that we ought to have had a lot more sick people than we did. Those Chatham Square eating places have a big turnover. Well, to make sure, I checked with Bellevue, Gouverneur, St. Vincent's, and the other downtown hospitals. None of them had seen a trace of cyanosis. Then I talked to the sick men some more. I learned two interesting things. One was that they had all got sick right after eating—within thirty minutes. The other was that all but one had eaten oatmeal, rolls, and coffee. He ate just oatmeal. When ten men eat the same thing in the same place on the same day and then all come down with the same illness. . . . I told Greenberg that my hunch was food poisoning."

"I was willing to rule out gas," Dr. Greenberg said. A folder containing data on the case lay on the desk before him. He lifted the cover thoughtfully, then let it drop. "And I agreed that the oatmeal sounded pretty suspicious. That was as far as I was willing to go. Common, ordinary, everyday food poisoning —I gathered that was what Pellitteri had in mind—wasn't a very satisfying answer. For one thing, cyanosis is hardly symptomatic of that. On the other hand, diarrhea and severe vomiting are, almost invariably. But they weren't in the clinical picture, I found, except in two or three of the cases. Moreover, the incubation periods—the time lapse between eating and illness—were extremely short. As you probably know, most food poisoning is caused by eating something that has been contaminated by bacteria. The usual offenders are the staphylococci [2]—they're mostly responsible for boils and skin infections and so on—and the salmonella.[3] The latter are related to the typhoid organism. In a staphylococcus case, the first symptoms rarely develop in under two hours. Often, it's closer to five. The incubation period in the other ranges from twelve to thirty-six hours. But here we were with something that hit in thirty minutes or less. Why, one of the men had got only as far as the sidewalk in front of the cafeteria before he was knocked out. Another fact that Pellitteri had dug up struck me as very significant. All of the men told him that the illness had come on with extraordi-

[2] STAPHYLOCOCCI—Pronounced stăf′ĭ·lô·kŏk′sī.

[3] SALMONELLA—Pronounced săl′mô·nĕl′à.

nary suddenness. One minute they were feeling fine, and the next minute they were practically helpless. That was another point against the ordinary food-poisoning theory. Its onset is never that fast. Well, that suddenness began to look like a lead. It led me to suspect that some drug might be to blame. A quick and sudden reaction is characteristic of a great many drugs. So is the combination of cyanosis and shock."

"None of the men were on dope," Dr. Pellitteri said. "I told Greenberg I was sure of that. Their pleasure was booze."

"That was O.K.," Dr. Greenberg said. "They could have got a toxic dose of some drug by accident. In the oatmeal, most likely. I couldn't help thinking that the oatmeal was relevant to our problem. At any rate, the drug idea was very persuasive."

"So was Greenberg," Dr. Pellitteri remarked with a smile. "Actually, it was the only explanation in sight that seemed to account for everything we knew about the clinical and environmental picture."

"All we had to do now was prove it," Dr. Greenberg went on mildly. "I asked Pellitteri to get a blood sample from each of the men before leaving the hospital for a look at the cafeteria. We agreed he would send the specimens to the city toxicologist, Dr. Alexander O. Gettler, for an overnight analysis. I wanted to know if the blood contained methemoglobin.[4] Methemoglobin is a compound that's formed only when any one of several drugs enters the blood. Gettler's report would tell us if we were at least on the right track. That is, it would give us a yes-or-no answer on drugs. If the answer was yes, then we could go on from there to identify the particular drug. How we would go about that

[4] METHEMOGLOBIN—Pronounced mĕt·hē′-mô·glō′bĭn.

would depend on what Pellitteri was able to turn up at the cafeteria. In the meantime, there was nothing for me to do but wait for their reports. I'd theorized myself hoarse."

Dr. Pellitteri, having attended to his bloodletting with reasonable dispatch, reached the Eclipse Cafeteria at around five o'clock. "It was about what I'd expected," he told me. "Strictly a horse market, and dirtier than most. The sort of place where you can get a full meal for fifteen cents. There was a dance hall on one side, a cigar store on the other, and the 'L' overhead. Incidentally, the Eclipse went out of business a year or so after I was there, but that had nothing to do with us. It was just a coincidence. Well, the place looked deserted and the door was locked. I knocked, and a man came out of the back and let me in. He was one of our people, a health inspector for the Bureau of Food and Drugs, named Weinberg. His bureau had stepped into the case as a matter of routine, because of the reference to a restaurant in the notification report. I was glad to see him and to have his help. For one thing, he had put a temporary embargo on everything in the cafeteria. That's why it was closed up. His main job, though, was to check the place for violations of the sanitation code. He was finding plenty."

"Let me read you a few of Weinberg's findings," Dr. Greenberg said, extracting a paper from the folder on his desk. "None of them had any direct bearing on our problem, but I think they'll give you a good idea of what the Eclipse was like—what too many restaurants are like. This copy of his report lists fifteen specific violations. Here they are: 'Premises heavily infested with roaches. Fly infestation throughout premises. Floor defective in rear part of dining room. Kitchen

walls and ceiling encrusted with grease and soot. Kitchen floor encrusted with dirt. Refuse under kitchen fixtures. Sterilizing facilities inadequate. Sink defective. Floor and walls at serving tables and coffee urns encrusted with dirt. Kitchen utensils encrusted with dirt and grease. Storage-cellar walls, ceiling, and floor encrusted with dirt. Floor and shelves in cellar covered with refuse and useless material. Cellar ceiling defective. Sewer pipe leaking. Open sewer line in cellar.' Well . . ." He gave me a squeamish smile and stuck the paper back in the folder.

"I can see it now," Dr. Pellitteri said. "And smell it. Especially the kitchen, where I spent most of my time. Weinberg had the proprietor and the cook out there, and I talked to them while he prowled around. They were very co-operative. Naturally. They were scared to death. They knew nothing about gas in the place and there was no sign of any, so I went to work on the food. None of what had been prepared for breakfast that morning was left. That, of course, would have been too much to hope for. But I was able to get together some of the kind of stuff that had gone into the men's breakfast, so that we could make a chemical determination at the Department. What I took was ground coffee, sugar, a mixture of evaporated milk and water that passed for cream, some bakery rolls, a five-pound carton of dry oatmeal, and some salt. The salt had been used in preparing the oatmeal. That morning, like every morning, the cook told me, he had prepared six gallons of oatmeal, enough to serve around a hundred and twenty-five people. To make it, he used five pounds of dry cereal, four gallons of water—regular city water—and a handful of salt. That was his term—a handful. There was an open gallon can of salt standing on the stove. He said the handful he'd put in that morning's oatmeal had come from that. He refilled the can on the stove every morning from a big supply can. He pointed out the big can—it was up on a shelf—and as I was getting it down to take with me, I saw another can, just like it, near by. I took that one down, too. It was also full of salt, or, rather, something that looked like salt. The proprietor said it wasn't salt. He said it was saltpetre—sodium nitrate—that he used in corning beef and in making pastrami.[5] Well, there isn't any harm in saltpetre. But I wrapped it up with the other loot and took it along, just for fun. The fact is, I guess, everything in that place looked like poison."

After Dr. Pellitteri had deposited his loot with a Health Department chemist, Andrew J. Pensa, who promised to have a report ready by the following afternoon, he dined hurriedly at a restaurant in which he had confidence and returned to Chatham Square. There he spent the evening making the rounds of the lodging houses in the neighborhood. He had heard at Mr. Pensa's office that an eleventh blue man had been admitted to the hospital, and before going home he wanted to make sure that no other victims had been overlooked. By midnight, having covered all the likely places and having rechecked the downtown hospitals, he was satisfied. He repaired to his office and composed a formal progress report for Dr. Greenberg. Then he went home and to bed.

The next morning, Tuesday, Dr. Pellitteri dropped by the Eclipse, which was still closed but whose proprietor and staff he had told to return for questioning. Dr. Pellitteri had another talk with the proprietor and the cook. He also had a few inconclusive words with the rest of the cafeteria's employees—two dishwashers, a busboy, and a counterman. As he was leaving, the cook, who had apparently passed an uneasy night with his conscience, remarked that it was possible that he had absent-mindedly refilled the salt can on the stove from the one that contained saltpetre. "That was interesting," Dr. Pellitteri told me, "even though such a possibility had already occurred to me, and even though I didn't know whether it was important or not. I assured him that he had nothing to worry about. We had been certain all along that nobody had deliberately poisoned the old men." From the Eclipse, Dr. Pellitteri went on to Dr. Greenberg's office, where Dr. Gettler's report was waiting.

"Gettler's test for methemoglobin was positive," Dr. Greenberg said. "It had to be a drug now. Well, so far so good. Then we heard from Pensa."

"Greenberg almost fell out of his chair when he read Pensa's report," Dr. Pellitteri observed cheerfully.

"That's an exaggeration," Dr. Greenberg said. "I'm not easily dumfounded. We're inured to the incredible around here. Why, a few years ago we had a case involving some numskull who stuck a fistful of potassium-thiocyanate[6] crystals, a very nasty poison, in the coils of an office water cooler, just for a practical joke. However, I can't deny that Pensa rather taxed our credulity. What he had found was that the small salt can and the one that was supposed to be full of sodium nitrate both contained sodium

[5] PASTRAMI (päs·trä′mĭ)—A highly seasoned Italian dish.

[6] POTASSIUM-THIOCYANATE—Pronounced pô·tăs′ĭ·ŭm-thī′ô·sī′á·nāt.

nitrite. The other food samples, incidentally, were O.K."

"That also taxed my credulity," Dr. Pellitteri said.

Dr. Greenberg smiled. "There's a great deal of difference between nitrate and nitrite," he continued. "Their only similarity, which is an unfortunate one, is that they both look and taste more or less like ordinary table salt. Sodium nitrite isn't the most powerful poison in the world, but a little of it will do a lot of harm. If you remember, I said before that this case was almost without precedent—only ten outbreaks like it on record. Ten is practically none. In fact, sodium-nitrite poisoning is so unusual that some of the standard texts on toxicology don't even mention it. So Pensa's report was pretty startling. But we accepted it, of course, without question or hesitation. Facts are facts. And we were glad to. It seemed to explain everything very nicely. What I've been saying about sodium-nitrite poisoning doesn't mean that sodium nitrite itself is rare. Actually it's fairly common. It's used in the manufacture of dyes and as a medical drug. We use it in treating certain heart conditions and for high blood pressure. But it also has another important use, one that made its presence at the Eclipse sound plausible. In recent years, and particularly during the war, sodium nitrite has been used as a substitute for sodium nitrate in preserving meat. The government permits it but stipulates that the finished meat must not contain more than one part of sodium nitrite per five thousand parts of meat. Cooking will safely destroy enough of that small quantity of the drug." Dr. Greenberg shrugged.

"Well, Pellitteri had had the cook pick up a handful of salt—the same amount, as nearly as possible, as went into the oatmeal—and then had taken this to his office and found that it weighed approximately a hundred grams. So we didn't have to think twice to realize that the proportion of nitrite in that batch of cereal was considerably higher than one to five thousand. Roughly, it must have been around one to about eighty before cooking destroyed part of the nitrite. It certainly looked as though Gettler, Pensa, and the cafeteria cook between them had given us our answer. I called up Gettler and told him to run a specific test for nitrites on his blood samples. He had, as a matter of course, held some blood back for later examination. His confirmation came through in a couple of hours. I went home that night feeling pretty good."

Dr. Greenberg's serenity was a fugitive one. He awoke on Wednesday morning troubled in mind. A question had oc-

curred to him that he was unable to ignore. "Something like a hundred and twenty-five people ate oatmeal at the Eclipse that morning," he said to me, "but only eleven of them got sick. Why? The undeniable fact that those eleven old men were made sick by the ingestion of a toxic dose of sodium nitrite wasn't enough to rest on. I wanted to know exactly how much sodium nitrite each portion of that cooked oatmeal had contained. With Pensa's help again, I found out. We prepared a batch just like the one the cook had made on Monday. Then Pensa measured out six ounces, the size of the average portion served at the Eclipse, and analyzed it. It contained two and half grains of sodium nitrite. That explained why the hundred and fourteen other people did not become ill. The toxic dose of sodium nitrite is three grains. But it didn't explain how each of our eleven old men had received an additional half grain. It seemed extremely unlikely that the extra touch of nitrite had been in the oatmeal when it was served. It had to come in later. Then I began to get a glimmer. Some people sprinkle a little salt, instead of sugar, on hot cereal. Suppose, I thought, that the busboy, or whoever had the job of keeping the table salt shakers filled, had made the same mistake that the cook had. It seemed plausible. Pellitteri was out of the office—I've forgotten where—so I got Food and Drugs to step over to the Eclipse, which was still under embargo, and bring back the shakers for Pensa to work on. There were seventeen of them, all good-sized, one for each table. Sixteen contained either pure sodium chloride or just a few inconsequential traces of sodium nitrite mixed in with the real salt, but the other was point thirty-seven per cent nitrite. That one was enough. A spoonful of that salt contained a bit more than half a grain."

"I went over to the hospital Thursday morning," Dr. Pellitteri said. "Greenberg wanted me to check the table-salt angle with the men. They could tie the case up neatly for us. I drew a blank. They'd been discharged the night before, and God only knew where they were."

"Naturally," Dr. Greenberg said, "it would have been nice to know for a fact that the old boys all sat at a certain table and that all of them put about a spoonful of salt from that particular shaker on their oatmeal, but it wasn't essential. I was morally certain that they had. There just wasn't any other explanation. There was one other question, however. Why did they use so *much* salt? For my own peace of mind, I wanted to know. All of a sudden, I remembered Pellitteri had said they were all heavy drinkers. Well, several recent clinical studies have demonstrated that there is usually a subnormal concentration of sodium chloride in the blood of alcoholics. Either they don't eat enough to get sufficient salt or they lose it more rapidly than other people do, or both. Whatever the reasons are, the conclusion was all I needed. Any animal, you know, whether a mouse or a man, tends to try to obtain a necessary substance that his body lacks. The final question had been answered."

◇◇◇◇◇◇◇◇◇◇◇◇◇◇◇◇◇◇◇◇◇◇◇◇◇◇◇◇◇◇

SCIENTIFIC SLEUTHING

1. What was there about the old man who collapsed on Dey Street that set him apart from the ordinary sick drunk that was frequently found in that neighborhood? How did the hospital physicians diagnose his condition? What led them to expect that they would soon have more patients with similar symptoms?

2. Why were the Department of Health

doctors unable to tell at once what kind of epidemic they were dealing with? What made Dr. Pellitteri doubt that the men were suffering from gas poisoning? How did he trace the source of the illness to oatmeal?

3. Why was Dr. Greenberg unwilling to believe that the mysterious epidemic was caused by ordinary food poisoning? How did he conclude that some drug must be to blame?

4. What conditions did Dr. Pellitteri find when he inspected the Eclipse Cafeteria? Describe his procedure in attempting to trace the source of the poison. What did he learn from questioning the employees?

5. Why were Dr. Greenberg and Dr. Pellitteri shocked by the report of the chemist who had analyzed the samples of food from the cafeteria? Explain the similarities and differences between sodium *nitrate* and sodium *nitrite*. How did the doctors account for the presence of sodium nitrite in the Eclipse Cafeteria?

6. Why wasn't Dr. Greenberg satisfied to consider the case solved after he discovered that sodium nitrite had been used to make the oatmeal? What finally convinced him that it was possible for one hundred and fourteen men to eat the oatmeal without ill effects? How did he explain the extra dose of the eleven men who turned blue?

STORIES IN THE NEWS

1. How did the author's manner of telling this factual story make it more interesting? What did he add that was probably not included in the Department of Health records of the case? In addition to the use of direct quotations what was there about the way the article was written that made it seem more like fiction than like the report of a scientific investigation?

2. Since this story was the result of an actual happening, it very likely appeared as a news article in the daily paper at the time of the investigation. Use the information in the article and write the story as it might have appeared in the newspaper. Have an interesting headline and a lead paragraph that tells *who, what, when, where,* and *why.*

3. Find a news article in the daily paper which might make an interesting detective story. Try to write the story adding details, using direct quotations, and building up to a climax as Mr. Roueché did in his story.

WORDS WITH A SCIENTIFIC FLAVOR

1. To give his article a scientific flavor, the author used many technical terms. In most cases where the unusual words are not actually defined, there are strong clues to their meaning in the context, that is, in the way they are used. Check with the dictionary after you have used context clues to figure out the meaning of the italicized words in the following sentences:

a. The examining physician attributed the old man's *morbid* color to cyanosis, a condition that usually results from an insufficient supply of oxygen in the blood . . .

b. The undeniable fact that those eleven old men were made sick by the *ingestion* of a toxic dose of sodium nitrite wasn't enough to rest on.

2. There are often familiar elements in a new word to help you determine its meaning. For example, two unusual words in the article you just read are *epidemiological* and *toxicologist*. No doubt you recognize the similarity between those words and such common words as *biological* and *biologist*. If you also know the meaning of the words *epidemic* and *toxic*, you should be able to see that *epidemiological* means pertaining to epidemics and that a *toxicologist* is one who specializes in the study of poisons. Find at least one other unfamiliar scientific term. See if you can guess its meaning by using context clues or recognizing familiar elements before turning to the dictionary.

BERTON ROUECHÉ (Born 1910)

Berton Roueché's writing career began at the University of Missouri. After graduation he became a reporter on the *Kansas City Star* and in 1944 a staff writer for the *New Yorker* magazine. His articles on people, places, and medicine are well known. In 1950 he was the recipient of the Lasker Foundation Award for Medical Reporting.

Mr. Roueché is the author of a novel, *Black Weather*, and *The Greener Grass*, a collection of profiles and short pieces. His medical articles of which "The Case of the Eleven Blue Men" is one have appeared in the *New Yorker*.

◇◇◇◇◇

THE BOLD VICTORY OF A MAN ALONE

QUENTIN REYNOLDS

People who like books generally like to read about books. That is why most newspapers and many leading magazines have whole sections or departments of book reviews. In fact there are magazines like THE SATURDAY REVIEW that are primarily devoted to book reviews and other articles and features of interest to those who buy and read books. The NEW YORK TIMES BOOK REVIEW and the NEW YORK HERALD-TRIBUNE BOOKS are two other such magazines that are well known. Each is a part of the Sunday edition of a nationally prominent newspaper. If you have not yet discovered that reading about books can be enjoyable as well as profitable, you should probably do some exploring in that field.

Here is a review of a book that many high-school students have enjoyed— Charles Lindbergh's THE SPIRIT OF ST. LOUIS. You will discover that, like all good reviewers, Mr. Reynolds does more than just summarize the contents of the book: he tells you what he thinks of it and why he thinks so.

. . . At last we have a book that explains and humanizes Lindbergh; that brings him into the company of his fellow mortals. The book is *The Spirit of St. Louis,* and it is of course written by the one man who really knows Lindbergh —himself. He spent fourteen years in the writing of it; the years were well spent.

Were this merely a personal account of his almost miraculous flight it would have interest, but not much significance. But this is far more than that; this is a frank and fascinating autobiography that

"The Bold Victory of a Man Alone" by Quentin Reynolds from *The New York Times Book Review,* September 13, 1953, reprinted by permission of the author.

destroys the myth of the phlegmatic, nerveless airman, impervious to doubt and to the uncertainties that plague lesser mortals. Lindbergh had his moments of doubt and fear, when fourteen hours out of Roosevelt Field ice appeared on the wings of his plane and when black thunderheads loomed ahead. "They [thunderheads] are barbaric in their methods. They lash you with their hailstones, poison you with freezing mist." No, Lindbergh during that flight was not merely a robot-like figure at the stick, he was not the supremely confident master of his plane and of his destiny. Was he on the right course? "Am I heading for Africa instead of Europe?" he asked himself in desperate anxiety.

His book is written in the present tense, a happy choice, for somehow this style sustains the tension of the flight and enables the reader to feel himself a stowaway aboard the plane, sharing the dangers, the uncertainties, and the eventual triumph. It takes quite a bit of literary skill to sustain the first person singular, present indicative, throughout five hundred pages, but take the word of this awed and amazed reader, Lindbergh writes as well as he flies, and the interest and suspense never lessen.

What did Lindbergh think about during those long, lonely hours of flight? There were long periods of calm weather when the gallant plane needed only the light touch of his hand on the stick to maintain course. In an effort to combat the insidious and at times overwhelming desire to sleep, Lindbergh reviewed his childhood in Little Falls, Minnesota, his lack of interest in college; his intense obsession with flying; his years of barnstorming, wing-walking, and exhibition parachute jumping. Lindbergh uses what the films call the flashback method

and he uses it far more effectively than do most movie-makers. He brings to life the hitherto shadowy figures of the men who taught him to fly, of his pals who flew the mail routes with him, of his parents and his uncles and above all of his grandfather. Grandfather Lindbergh, a true pioneer, occasionally worked in a sawmill to earn a little "hard" money. One day he stumbled, fell against the spinning saw and half severed his left arm. It was three days before a doctor came, but the doughty old Swede was still alive. The doctor amputated the arm.

"My grandfather lived despite shock, infection, and loss of blood. Lying on his bed, in great pain, he demanded to see his left arm before it was buried in the garden. It was brought to him in a small rough-board coffin. Taking the fingers in those of his right hand, he said slowly, in broken English, 'You have been a good friend to me for fifty years. But you can't be with me any more. So good-by. Good-by, my friend.'"

Lindbergh reminisces about his father —the Congressman to his constituents but a rather wonderful and wise companion to his young son. He taught Charles to shoot and swim. "I became his partner," the Lindbergh of 1927 says proudly. They had adventures together quite as remarkable at the time as the desperate flying venture the grown-up son was engaged in now. There was the time they made a rowboat voyage from the headwaters of the Mississippi right down the river to their farm at Little Falls. At night, as bass sizzled in the frying pan, the Congressman would talk to his son about tariffs, monopoly, and the "money trust."

"I sometimes wonder if he [Father] doesn't spend too much time thinking about problems he doesn't have to

EWING GALLOWAY

solve. . . . But of course my father isn't like other men. There are moments when I feel he can see into the future, as though he were living, today, in years ahead; as though it's my life to come that he dwells in rather than his own.

" 'Money can't draw such high interest rates indefinitely,' Father continues. 'A man who has a mortgage on his land at ten or twelve per cent doesn't have a fair chance. If the farmers don't organize, big business will take everything they've got. This country belongs to the people, but they haven't learned how to run it. The trouble is that people don't have any way of getting at the truth.'

"Father's concerned about the war, too. He says special interests would like to get us in it, and that propaganda is already under way. 'We're making too many foreign loans,' he tells me; and, 'the trouble with war is that it kills the best and youngest men.' "

Did his father's words shape Lindbergh's own course in 1940, when to the dismay of so many of his admirers he joined the isolationists? He doesn't say; he's too busy dodging thunderheads and fighting sleep. And then it's smooth sailing again and his mind wanders back to the eleven schools he attended from Washington, D. C., to Redondo Beach, California, "and there's not one that I enjoyed." Oh, there was one exception, he recalls. He graduated as top man in the Army flying school in Texas, and when his wings were pinned on his chest they "were like a silver passport to the realm of light."

He never knew it then, but every hour he spent unraveling the mystery of words like "Mercator," "gnomonic," "polyconic," "variation" was bringing him closer to "I love the sky and flying more than anything else on earth," he tells himself—and that's his credo.

Flying through the long, solitary night toward Europe, Lindbergh forced his sleep-obsessed mind to check and re-check his course, and gradually his will strengthened and sluggishly at first his body responded—and then he was awake again and wondering if the dream could possibly come true. It had been born one moon-clear night while flying the mail from St. Louis to Chicago. Why couldn't he fly a plane non-stop from one hemisphere to another as he was now flying from one city to another? Raymond Orteig had announced a prize of twenty-five thousand dollars to anyone making a New York–Paris flight. Why wasn't that feasible? The dream wouldn't be denied. He enlisted the support of nine St. Louis friends and they became touched by the dream—and eventually they helped him buy the beautifully de-signed plane he was flying now. He could never repay them for their incredi-ble faith. He might fail, but it wouldn't be their fault nor would it be the fault of this lovely plane. He himself repre-sented the intangible element. Could he stay awake; could he find the coast of Ireland and then France? Then ahead he sees specks which grow into fishing smacks. He's only six hundred miles from Paris. He speeds on.

"Time is no longer endless, or the horizon destitute of hope. The strain of take-off, storm, and ocean lies behind. There'll be no second night above the clouds, no more grappling with misty walls of ice. . . . Life is real. It always was real. . . . My mind is able to com-mand, and my body follows out its or-ders with precision. . . . Yesterday I walked on Roosevelt Field; today I'll walk on Le Bourget."

And six hours later he achieved his destiny. . . .

◇◇◇◇◇◇◇◇◇◇◇◇◇◇◇◇◇◇◇◇◇◇◇◇◇◇◇◇◇◇◇

EXAMINING A CRITICAL REVIEW

1. It is obvious from the first paragraph that this is a favorable review. What, in particular, does Mr. Reynolds like about the book?

2. The reviewer says that *The Spirit of St. Louis* is a *significant* book because it destroys a popular myth about Lindbergh. What kind of man was the mythical Lind-bergh? What kind of person is the real Lindbergh who is revealed in the book? Show how the author uses direct quotations from the book to illustrate the human char-acteristics of Lindbergh.

3. How does the author of the review reveal the type of material contained in the book? How much of the actual contents of the book does he tell? How much of the review is his opinion or evaluation of the book? How much is quoted directly from the book? What particular point is the reviewer trying to illustrate by each quo-tation? Are his quotations well chosen in each case?

4. Find passages in which the reviewer discusses the form and style of the book. Why does he think that Lindbergh was right to tell his story in the present tense? Do you usually like books written in "the first person singular, present indicative"? Give reasons for your answer, if you can.

SUGGESTED ACTIVITIES

1. For further reading, make a collection of magazines that contain book reviews and of the book pages or sections of as many newspapers as are available. Sample as many different sources as possible in carry-ing out the following activities.

a. Find and compare different reviews of the same book. How well do the reviewers agree? In what particulars do they dis-agree? Which reviewer supports his opin-ions most convincingly?

b. Select at least one unfavorable review for careful reading. What does the reviewer criticize in the book? What reasons or concrete evidence does he give to support his unfavorable opinions? Does he find anything to praise in the book?

2. After you have read several reviews, choose two or three books that you would like to read. Copy exactly the title, author, publisher, and price, and make a brief annotation for each. Compare your choices with those of other members of the class. You might compile a list of general favorites to present to your school librarian or the librarian of the local public library as suggestions for purchase.

3. Write a critical review of a book you have read recently. Remember to avoid summarizing the entire contents of the book. Instead, imitate the professional reviewers by giving opinions or evaluations and supporting each by specific reference to the book. Try to use at least one direct quotation to illustrate a point you wish to make.

FOR YOUR VOCABULARY

Because book reviews are written by and for people who read extensively, they sometimes contain words not in the average student's vocabulary. Test your own knowledge of words by trying to define the itali-cized words in the following phrases from the review you just read. If you are in doubt about any, check with the dictionary.

   a. the *phlegmatic,* nerveless airman, *impervious* to doubt
   b. the *insidious* and at times overwhelming desire to sleep
   c. the *doughty* old Swede
   d. the Congressman to his *constituents*

QUENTIN REYNOLDS (Born 1902)

Quentin Reynolds was born in New York and educated at Brown University, Brooklyn Law School, and the University of Western Ontario. He began his writing career as a sports writer for the *New York World.* Originally, he planned to work his way through law school by working on newspapers, but the writing urge became stronger than his desire to become a lawyer. As a reporter for International News Service he became one of America's ace war correspondents. His adventures in getting in and out of war-torn countries have been enjoyed by many. From 1933 to 1935 he was associate editor for *Collier's.* It was in *Collier's* that many of his short stories first appeared. Among his books are *London Diary,* 1941; *Dress Rehearsal,* 1943; and *The Wright Brothers,* 1950. He is now editor of *United Nations World* and lives in New York City.

◇◇◇◇◇

For Broader Understanding

1. Although there is no clear-cut distinction between *essays* and *articles,* we usually think of the two as different. Briefly describe the difference. Consider *the author's aim, the topic he writes about,* and *the attitude he takes toward his subject.*

2. Which selections in this unit would you call *essays,* and which would you call *articles?* Compare your answers with those of other members of the class.

3. Most essays and articles are a mixture of *entertainment* and *information.* Think over the ones in this unit, and state which are mainly for entertainment and which are mainly informative. What one selection would you name as having the *most serious* purpose—that is, to improve the reader in some way, or to make him think more clearly on some important subject? Explain why you named this particular selection.

4. Name one or more selections that are interesting not because they are of direct importance in our own affairs, but because *they discuss the adventures of a fellow human being in life.* In each, *which details stand out in your mind as most interesting?*

CLASS ACTIVITIES

1. Make a class collection of favorite cartoons for a bulletin board display. The cartoons can be grouped according to subject or artist. Some members of the class might try drawing original cartoons showing familiar situations in the home or school life of young Americans.

2. The interest of the American people in information and ideas is reflected in the increasingly large amount of nonfiction that is being published. This same interest is also reflected in radio and television programs. Let the class work in groups to compile lists of programs that might be considered similar in content and appeal to articles and essays. These might include news commentaries, interviews, panels, and travelogues. Indicate the class favorites on the lists, and plan to see or listen to those with which you are not familiar.

3. Study the nonfiction articles in one issue of a popular magazine to see *what reader interests* the magazine appeals to. Some prominent ones might be adventure, the international situation, national problems, personal happiness or success, unusual or amusing people. Which two or three kinds of reader interest are given most attention in this particular magazine? How do the advertisements also reflect interests of readers? Report on such magazines as *Collier's, The Saturday Evening Post, The Reader's Digest, The Atlantic, Harper's,* or *The New Yorker.*

4. Reread "Father Opens My Mail" and then imitate Clarence Day, the author, by writing an essay on some painful or funny childhood experience. You could start by saying "I am still embarrassed when I remember—" or "I still get angry when I remember—"

FOR FURTHER READING

GEORGE MATTHEW ADAMS, *Better Than Gold* (Duell). Here are essays by a well-known newspaperman on subjects from first editions to anger, dogs, and pencils.

JOHN MASON BROWN, *As They Appear* (McGraw). An excellent dramatic critic, Mr. Brown here discusses present-day drama with his customary wit and common sense.

WILL CUPPY, *How to Tell Your Friends from the Apes* (Liveright). These wise-cracking essays on prehistoric man, the animal kingdom, and ourselves are scientifically accurate, but they are written for sheer fun.

JOSEPH WOOD KRUTCH, *Best of Two Worlds* (Sloane). These quiet personal essays on such varied subjects as cats, mice, solitude, and frogs are both thoughtful and humorous.

JAMES THURBER, *The Thurber Carnival* (Harper). Many of Mr. Thurber's most hilarious sketches are collected in this book. Other excellent books by the same author are *The Owl in the Attic and Other Perplexities; The Middle-Aged Man on the Flying Trapeze;* and *My World—and Welcome to It.*

Other collections of essays you may enjoy are the following:

ROBERT BENCHLEY, *Benchley or Else!* and *Roundup* (Harper).

CLARENCE DAY, *Life with Father, Life with Mother,* and *This Simian World* (Knopf).

WALTER EATON, *On Yankee Hilltops* (Wilde).

DON MARQUIS, *Best of Don Marquis* (Doubleday).

HELEN and GEORGE PAPASHVILY, *Thanks to Noah* (Harper) and *Dogs and People* (Lippincott).

ERNIE PYLE, *Here Is Your War, Brave Men,* and *Last Chapter* (Holt).

LOUIS L. SNYDER and RICHARD B. MORRIS, *A Treasury of Great Reporting* (Simon & Schuster).

ELWYN BROOKS WHITE, *One Man's Meat* and *Quo Vadimus? or The Case for the Bicycle* (Harper).

POETRY

"I HEAR AMERICA SINGING"

Poetry is the oldest kind of literature, the parent stock from which the other kinds grew. And poetry is as intimately woven into the texture of life today, in the twentieth century, as ever it was in the history of man—although we are often hardly conscious of its presence. Some of our most common, familiar sayings—"Good night; sleep tight" and "An apple a day keeps the doctor away"—imitate the form of poetry. The "singing commercials" we hear on the radio, and our innumerable popular songs, are combinations of verse and music. In "America" and "The Star-Spangled Banner," two poets of the nineteenth century still influence our attitude toward the nation we live in. And our customs of divine worship would be quite different without the well-known prayers we say and the hymns we sing—some of them very fine poetry indeed.

Poetry is not only the oldest but the *most personal and individual* form of literature. The poet expresses his inmost mind, his intricate and subtle thoughts and emotions, more fully than the storyteller or the dramatist can. In this fact we see one reason why so much excellent poetry—of so many different kinds—is produced in modern America. Poetry is highly individual; and it is *in free countries* that individualism is cherished and encouraged to grow. In countries that are ruled by tyrannical governments, most of the population live in ignorance and misery, and they are crushed into a common mold. Only where there is hope and freedom can each man's particular talent assert itself. The lively, stimulating environment of democratic America calls forth the creative energies of our people. As you will see when you read the following poems in this book, modern America is rich in poets—and for each one, our birthright of "the pursuit of happiness" is a different thing.

Sometimes our poets try to give the feeling, the atmosphere, of particular places in America, as Carl Sandburg does in "Chicago" and as Robert Frost does in a number of poems. At other times the poet expresses his conclusions about human life, or the attitudes by which he lives—again, as in some of Frost's poems, and as in Edna St. Vincent Millay's "First Fig." Another kind of poetry can be seen in Sandburg's "Window," which is like a quick, bold pencil sketch of a single scene. Edwin Arlington Robinson and Edgar Lee Masters give us character descriptions of some of the interesting people to be met among the great multitudes that make up America. You will read rebellious poems of protest; poems of devotion to our nation and its ideals; and poems that are written just for fun, or that make witty observations on life as one author has experienced it. When the famous poet Walt Whitman wrote, "I hear America singing, the varied carols I hear," he was referring to what he could hear *in his imagination.* But since Whitman's time, poets have sprung up everywhere in the nation—people who are very different from one another in background, in education, and in their interests and ideas—to sing the "varied carols" that Whitman only dreamed of. Reading the poets represented in this section, you will learn their fears and their hopes, hear their words of distress or joy, share their feelings and see with their eyes. Taken all together, their songs are the many-voiced chorus of American life today.

THE CHARACTERISTICS OF POETRY

People sometimes suppose that "If it rhymes, it's poetry, and if it doesn't, it isn't." This, of course, is far from the case. Rhyme was not used in ancient Greek and Roman poetry, and in modern times, also, much poetry is unrhymed. True poetry, first of all, *must present some significant thought or experience or impression*—must make the reader "see" something really worth while that he never saw before. Second, the poet's way of expressing his thought *must be in some way distinguished or striking.* The poet is an artist with words, and the way he expresses his thought is no less important than the thought itself. Compare, for example, the first line of Carl Sandburg's "Chicago"—"Hog Butcher for the World"—with this prose sentence from an encyclopedia: "Chicago is the greatest livestock market and meat-

packing center of the world." The prose sentence states a well-known and important fact—and that is all. Sandburg's vivid line of poetry suggests, as it is intended
to do, coarseness and vigor and strength.

These two basic requirements of poetry—freshness of vision and power of artistic
expression—are so closely related to each other that they can hardly be separated.
The way something is said can make us understand it more fully, more intensely,
than before, even when the thought is somewhat familiar to us.

What we have just said about the characteristics of poetry is also true of good
prose writing. In fact there is no sharp line between poetry and fine prose. An
oration by such a man as Patrick Henry or Abraham Lincoln, or a superbly written
short story, may approach the level of poetry. We recognize this fact when we occasionally speak of a powerful work of literature as "a prose poem." However, there
are certain additional features of poetry that are customarily accepted as marking it off
from prose. Poetry is expected to delight the *ear* as well as the mind. It does so,
mainly, by means of the ornament of *rhythm*—whether the somewhat irregular and
varied rhythm of "free verse" or the exact and regular rhythm called "meter." Many
poems, but by no means all, use also the ornament of *rhyme*—which pleases us by
the repetition of sounds at the ends of words. Another familiar ornament, but less
widely used, is *alliteration*—the repetition of sounds at the beginnings of words. It
should be remembered that rhythm, rhyme, and alliteration, although they are the more
obvious features of poetry, are not the ones of prime importance. A piece of writing
which uses these typical ornaments or devices, but fails the two basic tests mentioned
earlier, is more properly called *verse* than *poetry*.

One other characteristic frequently found in poetry is *the use of figurative language*.
When the poet Edwin Markham, speaking of a poor, downtrodden peasant, says,
". . . on his back the burden of the world," he does not mean that the peasant literally has a weight on his back. He means that the man is bowed with toil and misery, that other people—"the world"—live on the results of his labor. Imaginative
figures of speech like this one are used in prose writing as well as in poetry, and they
are frequently used in ordinary spoken language also. But they are used most often
in poetry, and many times it is by means of them that the poet awakens us to a new
understanding, startles us into "seeing."

POETRY IN AMERICA

The basic characteristics of poetry, and also its traditional ornaments, had been
established centuries before the first white men came to America. Our earliest poets,
therefore, used a European form of literature in writing about American subjects.
William Cullen Bryant's "To a Waterfowl" and Henry Wadsworth Longfellow's
"The Arsenal at Springfield," in the last unit of this book, are typical examples of
our poets' attempts to adapt an older style of writing to scenes in America. Then in
the middle of the nineteenth century appeared a poet—Walt Whitman—who de-

clared that the New World should have a new kind of poetry. In almost all his poems, Whitman discarded rhyme. He discarded also regular, exact meter and substituted uneven, swinging, chant-like rhythms which sounded more like natural speech than the traditional poetry did. Whitman used many of the words and expressions—sometimes very forceful and colorful—that were heard in everyday conversation rather than the dignified, formal language that had become usual in poetry. This had not been done before except in humorous dialect poems. As a result of Whitman's new ideas his poems were burly, vigorous, even noisy, as compared to the often "pretty" and usually quiet and restrained poems by earlier writers. The contrast can be seen by comparing the opening line of one of Bryant's poems—"Whither, midst falling dew"—with the opening line of a poem by Whitman—"Why, who makes much of a miracle?"

Although Whitman's poems drew attention, for a long time they had little influence on other poets. Near the end of the nineteenth century several authors showed a tendency toward greater freedom of style in verse. Among them was Stephen Crane, who was, however, better known as a writer of fiction than of poetry. In 1914 Carl Sandburg's slangy, informal poem "Chicago" made the general public aware of the new "free verse" movement. The movement reached its height in the early 1920's, attracting nearly all the poets of that period. It is impossible to say how much the free verse poets owed to Whitman—for one thing, the movement was European as well as American—but they all looked back to Whitman as a pioneer. Even though some critics objected that free verse, also called by its French name *vers libre*, was nothing but prose chopped up to look like poetry, for a while it seemed that rhyme and exact meter would never be in fashion again.

After a few years, free verse was no longer new and there was a swing in the other direction. Americans discovered once more the excellence of poets like Edwin Arlington Robinson and Robert Frost. You will see, when you examine their poems, that both writers preferred the more traditional style. Some younger writers agreed with them, others with the free verse group. Today, a number of poets compose both rhymed and unrhymed poems. Often they use regular meter and yet they move, when they please, into more casual rhythms. The most talented poets are not concerned about whether their styles are "modern" or "traditional," but about whether their writing has real worth. The various movements in poetry have left their mark, however. Sandburg is a loyal follower of Walt Whitman, and Edgar Lee Masters' character sketches are written in free verse. You will find that Frost, Robinson, and all our poets use natural, conversational language when it suits their purpose. In subject matter, too, poetry is more varied than was formerly the case. One poem in this section, "Miniver Cheevy," is about a drunkard; one is a disgusted comment on men ("They make me sick, they make me tired"); and one is on a tragic accident with a buzz-saw. The old belief that certain kinds of topics, and no others, are "poetic"— a belief that was never shared by the great poets of any nation—is gone. American poetry is the richer for its disappearance.

The Death of the Hired Man

ROBERT FROST

You will learn about the hired man by eavesdropping on a conversation between the farmer and his wife. What those two people say will not only
reveal a great deal about the old man but also about Mary and Warren
themselves.

Because most of the poem is conversation, you will need to watch the
quotation marks. Notice that what Silas and Warren said to each other in
an earlier conversation is set off by single quotation marks.

Mary sat musing on the lamp-flame at the table
Waiting for Warren. When she heard his step,
She ran on tiptoe down the darkened passage
To meet him in the doorway with the news
And put him on his guard. "Silas is back." 5
She pushed him outward with her through the door
And shut it after her. "Be kind," she said.
She took the market things from Warren's arms
And set them on the porch, then drew him down
To sit beside her on the wooden steps. 10

"When was I ever anything but kind to him?
But I'll not have the fellow back," he said.
"I told him so last haying, didn't I?
'If he left then,' I said, 'that ended it.'
What good is he? Who else will harbor him 15
At his age for the little he can do?
What help he is there's no depending on.
Off he goes always when I need him most.
'He thinks he ought to earn a little pay,
Enough at least to buy tobacco with, 20
So he won't have to beg and be beholden.'
'All right,' I say, 'I can't afford to pay
Any fixed wages, though I wish I could.'
'Someone else can.' 'Then someone else will have to.'

I shouldn't mind his bettering himself   25
If that was what it was. You can be certain,
When he begins like that, there's someone at him
Trying to coax him off with pocket money—
In haying time, when any help is scarce.
In winter he comes back to us. I'm done."   30

"Sh! not so loud: he'll hear you," Mary said.

"I want him to: he'll have to soon or late."

"He's worn out. He's asleep beside the stove.
When I came up from Rowe's I found him here,
Huddled against the barn door fast asleep,   35
A miserable sight, and frightening, too—
You needn't smile—I didn't recognize him—
I wasn't looking for him—and he's changed.
Wait till you see."

                    "Where did you say he'd been?"

"He didn't say. I dragged him to the house,   40
And gave him tea and tried to make him smoke.
I tried to make him talk about his travels.
Nothing would do: he just kept nodding off."

"What did he say? Did he say anything?"

"But little."   45

            "Anything? Mary, confess
He said he'd come to ditch the meadow for me."

"Warren!"

            "But did he? I just want to know."

"Of course he did. What would you have him say?
Surely you wouldn't grudge the poor old man
Some humble way to save his self-respect.   50
He added, if you really care to know,
He meant to clear the upper pasture, too.
That sounds like something you have heard before?
Warren, I wish you could have heard the way
He jumbled everything. I stopped to look   55
Two or three times—he made me feel so queer—
To see if he was talking in his sleep.

He ran on Harold Wilson—you remember—
The boy you had in haying four years since.
He's finished school, and teaching in his college.   60
Silas declares you'll have to get him back.
He says they two will make a team for work:
Between them they will lay this farm as smooth!
The way he mixed that in with other things.
He thinks young Wilson a likely lad, though daft   65
On education—you know how they fought
All through July under the blazing sun,
Silas upon the cart to build the load,
Harold along beside to pitch it on."

"Yes, I took care to keep well out of earshot."   70

"Well, those days trouble Silas like a dream.
You wouldn't think they would. How some things linger!
Harold's young college boy's assurance piqued him.
After so many years he still keeps finding
Good arguments he sees he might have used.   75
I sympathize. I know just how it feels
To think of the right thing to say too late.
Harold's associated in his mind with Latin.
He asked me what I thought of Harold's saying
He studied Latin like the violin   80
Because he liked it—that an argument!
He said he couldn't make the boy believe
He could find water with a hazel prong—
Which showed how much good school had ever done him.
He wanted to go over that. But most of all   85
He thinks if he could have another chance
To teach him how to build a load of hay—"

"I know, that's Silas' one accomplishment.
He bundles every forkful in its place,
And tags and numbers it for future reference,   90
So he can find and easily dislodge it
In the unloading. Silas does that well.
He takes it out in bunches like big birds' nests.
You never see him standing on the hay
He's trying to lift, straining to lift himself."   95

"He thinks if he could teach him that, he'd be
Some good perhaps to someone in the world.
He hates to see a boy the fool of books.
Poor Silas, so concerned for other folk,

And nothing to look backward to with pride, 100
And nothing to look forward to with hope,
So now and never any different."

Part of a moon was falling down the west,
Dragging the whole sky with it to the hills.
Its light poured softly in her lap. She saw 105
And spread her apron to it. She put out her hand
Among the harplike morning-glory strings,
Taut with the dew from garden bed to eaves,
As if she played unheard the tenderness
That wrought on him beside her in the night. 110
"Warren," she said, "he has come home to die:
You needn't be afraid he'll leave you this time."

"Home," he mocked gently.

                            "Yes, what else but home?
It all depends on what you mean by home.
Of course he's nothing to us, any more 115
Than was the hound that came a stranger to us
Out of the woods, worn out upon the trail."

"Home is the place where, when you have to go there,
They have to take you in."

                            "I should have called it
Something you somehow haven't to deserve." 120

Warren leaned out and took a step or two,
Picked up a little stick, and brought it back
And broke it in his hand and tossed it by.
"Silas has better claim on us, you think,
Than on his brother? Thirteen little miles 125
As the road winds would bring him to his door.
Silas has walked that far no doubt today.
Why didn't he go there? His brother's rich,
A somebody—director in the bank."

"He never told us that." 130

                            "We know it though."

"I think his brother ought to help, of course.
I'll see to that if there is need. He ought of right
To take him in, and might be willing to—

He may be better than appearances.
But have some pity on Silas. Do you think   135
If he'd had any pride in claiming kin
Or anything he looked for from his brother,
He'd keep so still about him all this time?"

"I wonder what's between them."

                          "I can tell you.
Silas is what he is—we wouldn't mind him—   140
But just the kind that kinsfolk can't abide.
He never did a thing so very bad.
He don't know why he isn't quite as good
As anyone. He won't be made ashamed
To please his brother, worthless though he is."   145

"I can't think Si ever hurt anyone."

"No, but he hurt my heart the way he lay
And rolled his old head on that sharp-edged chair back.
He wouldn't let me put him on the lounge.
You must go in and see what you can do.   150
I made the bed up for him there tonight.
You'll be surprised at him—how much he's broken.
His working days are done; I'm sure of it."

"I'd not be in a hurry to say that."

"I haven't been. Go, look, see for yourself.   155
But, Warren, please remember how it is:
He's come to help you ditch the meadow.
He has a plan. You mustn't laugh at him.
He may not speak of it, and then he may.
I'll sit and see if that small sailing cloud   160
Will hit or miss the moon."

                         It hit the moon.
Then there were three there, making a dim row,
The moon, the little silver cloud, and she.
Warren returned—too soon, it seemed to her,
Slipped to her side, caught up her hand, and waited.   165

"Warren," she questioned.

                        "Dead," was all he answered.

FOR UNDERSTANDING

1. Why did Mary want to talk to Warren before he went into the house? Where did their conversation take place?

2. Under what conditions had Silas left Warren to work for someone else? Why had Warren needed help particularly at the time? Do you think Warren was justified in not wanting to take Silas back?

3. Why did the old man tell Mary that he had come back to ditch the meadow for Warren? Why did Mary accept the excuse when she knew that Silas was ill and unable to work? How was Warren able to guess what Silas had said? What does the incident reveal about each of the three people in the poem?

4. What do you learn about Silas from the talk about Harold Wilson? What had Harold found in life that Silas had missed? In what way was Silas Harold's superior? How did the old man hope to give his life some meaning through Harold? What does Mary's account of the relationship between Silas and Harold tell you about her own personality? Have you ever shared with her and Silas the experience of knowing what you should have said when the time for saying it has passed?

5. Compare the two definitions of home given in lines 118–120. Which do you like better? What others do you know?

6. Why had Silas never talked about his brother? How did Mary explain the relationship between the two brothers? Why do you think it likely that relatives would be more critical of a man like Silas than strangers would be?

7. When do you think Warren decided to allow Silas to stay? What were Warren's feelings toward Silas from the start? How were they different from Mary's?

THE POET'S CRAFT

There are some good examples in this poem of Robert Frost's ability to help us see beauty and significance in commonplace scenes and actions.

1. In Warren's account of how Silas built a load of hay, lines 88–95, what accurate choice of words and picturesque comparisons help you to visualize the old man as he worked and to appreciate the skill that it takes to build a load properly?

2. What is most effective and original about the description of Mary sitting on the steps in the moonlight? Point out at least one good figure of speech in that passage, lines 103–112.

ROBERT FROST (1875–1963)

Robert Frost, who was to become famous for his poems about rural New England, was born in San Francisco. However, at the death of his father when Robert was only ten, his mother took him and his sister to live with their grandfather in Lawrence, Massachusetts. There on his grandfather's farm the boy began to store up the impressions of New England farm life that were to appear in his poems.

When he finished high school in Lawrence, Robert and another tied for top honors and both were named valedictorian. The other student, Elinor White, later became his wife. Robert made two attempts to get a college education, first at Dartmouth following his graduation from high school and then at Harvard after he was married, but he disliked formal study and never received a degree. He began to write early and had a poem published when he was only seventeen, but though he continued to write regularly, he received little recognition for the next twenty years. He tried various ways of making a living. He was a mill hand, shoemaker, journalist, and teacher. Finally, his grandfather bought him a farm in New Hampshire where he lived for twelve years, farming and writing and occasionally supplementing his income by teaching.

In 1912 he sold his farm and went to England with his wife and four children. It was there that *A Boy's Will*, his first volume of verse, was published. That book and *North of Boston* which followed it the next year were immediately successful, and Frost became regarded as an important poet both in England and in America. In later life he was awarded the Pulitzer Prize four times: in 1923 for *New Hampshire*, in 1930 for his *Collected Poems*, in 1936 for *A Further Range*, and in 1942 for *A Witness Tree*. He was a member of the staff at Amherst College, and at the University of Michigan, and at Boston University. He also taught at the Breadloaf School of English in Vermont. His *Complete Poems* was published in 1949.

Robert Frost was one of America's best loved contemporary poets. His verse had the calm, cool tone of the New England character—and he had the Yankee trick of saying much in a brief phrase. He wrote about familiar experiences using the everyday language of ordinary people. However, he used his simple material with the skill of an artist. His poems have deeper meanings than appear on the surface, and he used his common words in a most uncommon way so that they take on beauty and significance in his verse. The feeling produced by many an unassuming little poem will come back to mind, long after it is first read, with the sharpness that is a sign of true literary power.

◇◇◇◇◇

Birches

ROBERT FROST

There are memories connected with familiar things. A line of bending birch trees reminds this New England farmer of a favorite boyhood sport.

When I see birches bend to left and right
Across the line of straighter darker trees,
I like to think some boy's been swinging them.
But swinging doesn't bend them down to stay.
Ice storms do that. Often you must have seen them   5
Loaded with ice a sunny winter morning
After a rain. They click upon themselves
As the breeze rises, and turn many-colored
As the stir cracks and crazes their enamel.
Soon the sun's warmth makes them shed crystal shells   10
Shattering and avalanching on the snow-crust—
Such heaps of broken glass to sweep away
You'd think the inner dome of heaven had fallen.
They are dragged to the withered bracken by the load,
And they seem not to break; though once they are bowed   15

So low for long, they never right themselves:
You may see their trunks arching in the woods
Years afterwards, trailing their leaves on the ground
Like girls on hands and knees that throw their hair
Before them over their heads to dry in the sun.   20
But I was going to say when truth broke in
With all her matter-of-fact about the ice storm
I should prefer to have some boy bend them
As he went out and in to fetch the cows—
Some boy too far from town to learn baseball,   25
Whose only play was what he found himself,
Summer or winter, and could play alone.
One by one he subdued his father's trees
By riding them down over and over again
Until he took the stiffness out of them,   30
And not one but hung limp, not one was left
For him to conquer. He learned all there was
To learn about not launching out too soon
And so not carrying the tree away
Clear to the ground. He always kept his poise   35
To the top branches, climbing carefully
With the same pains you use to fill a cup
Up to the brim, and even above the brim.
Then he flung outward, feet first, with a swish,
Kicking his way down through the air to the ground.   40

So I was once myself a swinger of birches;
And so I dream of going back to be.
It's when I'm weary of considerations,
And life is too much like a pathless wood
Where your face burns and tickles with the cobwebs   45
Broken across it, and one eye is weeping
From a twig's having lashed across it open.
I'd like to get away from earth awhile
And then come back to it and begin over.

May no fate wilfully misunderstand me   50
And half grant what I wish and snatch me away
Not to return. Earth's the right place for love:
I don't know where it's likely to go better.
I'd like to go by climbing a birch tree,
And climb black branches up a snow-white trunk   55
Toward Heaven, till the tree could bear no more,
But dipped its top and set me down again.
That would be good both going and coming back.
One could do worse than be a swinger of birches.

FOR UNDERSTANDING AND

APPRECIATION

1. What memories of his boyhood come to the poet when he sees birch trees bent over at the top? Just what did the boy do with the trees that was fun? What skill did the sport require?

2. What specific details help you to visualize the birches covered with ice? What poetic comparison, or simile, suggests the appearance of trees that have been permanently bowed?

3. Beginning with line 41, what comparison does the poet make between life and a wood? What in life is symbolized by the cobweb and the twig? What has swinging on birches to do with the desire to escape for a while from the wood, or life?

❖❖❖❖❖

Mending Wall

ROBERT FROST

When the early New England farmers cleared their rocky soil, they put the stones to practical use by building stone fences or walls between the fields. Here Mr. Frost describes the annual spring mending of the wall between two neighbors.

Something there is that doesn't love a wall,
That sends the frozen ground swell under it,
And spills the upper boulders in the sun;
And makes gaps even two can pass abreast.
The work of hunters is another thing: 5
I have come after them and made repair
Where they have left not one stone on a stone,
But they would have the rabbit out of hiding,
To please the yelping dogs. The gaps I mean,
No one has seen them made or heard them made,   10
But at spring mending-time we find them there.
I let my neighbor know beyond the hill;
And on a day we meet to walk the line
And set the wall between us once again.
We keep the wall between us as we go.   15
To each the boulders that have fallen to each.
And some are loaves and some so nearly balls
We have to use a spell to make them balance:

"Stay where you are until our backs are turned!"
We wear our fingers rough with handling them,   20
Oh, just another kind of outdoor game,
One on a side. It comes to little more:
There where it is we do not need the wall:
He is all pine and I am apple orchard.
My apple trees will never get across   25
And eat the cones under his pines, I tell him.
He only says, "Good fences make good neighbors."
Spring is the mischief in me, and I wonder
If I could put a notion in his head:
"Why do they make good neighbors? Isn't it   30
Where there are cows? But here there are no cows.
Before I built a wall I'd ask to know
What I was walling in or walling out,
And to whom I was like to give offense.
Something there is that doesn't love a wall,   35
That wants it down." I could say "Elves" to him,
But it's not elves exactly, and I'd rather
He said it for himself. I saw him there
Bringing a stone grasped firmly by the top
In each hand, like an old-stone savage armed.   40
He moves in darkness as it seems to me,
Not of woods only and the shade of trees.
He will not go behind his father's saying,
And he likes having thought of it so well
He says again, "Good fences make good neighbors."   45

FENCES AND NEIGHBORS

1. What evidence does the poet give to support his statement: "Something there is that doesn't love a wall"? What is the difference between the holes nature makes and those made by hunters? What seems to be the farmer's feeling about hunters?

2. What was the difference between the attitudes of the two men in the poem toward keeping the fence mended? Why was this particular fence not needed?

3. What truth was there in the saying one of the men had learned from his father? Under what conditions would good fences make good neighbors? Why has the saying lost its wisdom for the farmers in the poem? Can you think of other sayings or practices which might once have been wise but which are now outmoded and no longer apply?

4. What kind of man is the neighbor who mends the wall without asking himself why he does it? What type of people might he represent generally? What besides his appearance would suggest "an old-stone savage armed"? Contrast him with the man who says:

"Before I built a wall I'd ask to know
What I was walling in or walling out
And to whom I was like to give offense."

What kind of person do you think he represents?

BROADER MEANINGS

What do you think the wall might symbolize in human affairs? Name several kinds of figurative walls that separate *neighbors* from each other. How are the walls kept in repair?

◇◇◇◇◇

Fire and Ice

ROBERT FROST

Like all good poetry the following poem suggests more than it actually says. The first sentence states a simple fact. What the remaining two tell you will depend upon the associations which you have for the terms used by the poet.

Some say the world will end in fire,
Some say in ice.
From what I've tasted of desire
I hold with those who favor fire.
But if it had to perish twice,
I think I know enough of hate
To say that for destruction ice
Is also great
And would suffice.

DEPARTMENTAL

FOR UNDERSTANDING

1. Heat and cold are often used in connection with human emotions. We speak of *fiery* temper and *cold* disdain. What emotion is represented here by fire? What is symbolized by ice?

2. Literally, the world might end in fire from an explosion from within or from collision with another planet. In a less literal sense, how might it end in fire? What relationship can you see between human desires and the destruction of the world by fire?

3. What is the scientific basis for believing that the world may end in ice? If cold is a symbol for hate, what might bring about the destruction of the world by ice?

◇◇◇◇◇

Departmental

ROBERT FROST

You do not have to know much about specialization in an ant hill to enjoy this poem. If you have ever watched the businesslike activities of a few stray ants, you must have seen incidents like those described here. You may even have made humorous comparisons similar to Mr. Frost's between the busy insects and people in our own highly organized society.

An ant on the tablecloth
Ran into a dormant moth
Of many times his size.
He showed not the least surprise.
His business wasn't with such. 5
He gave it scarcely a touch,
And was off on his duty run.
Yet if he encountered one
Of the hive's enquiry squad
Whose work is to find out God 10
And the nature of time and space,
He would put him onto the case.
Ants are a curious race;
One crossing with hurried tread
The body of one of their dead 15
Isn't given a moment's arrest—

Seems not even impressed.
But he no doubt reports to any
With whom he crosses antennae,
And they no doubt report 20
To the higher up at court.
Then word goes forth in Formic:
"Death's come to Jerry McCormic,
Our selfless forager Jerry.
Will the special Janizary 25
Whose office it is to bury
The dead of the commissary
Go bring him home to his people.
Lay him in state on a sepal.
Wrap him for shroud in a petal. 30
Embalm him with ichor of nettle.

22. FORMIC—*Formica* is the Latin word for ant.
25. JANIZARY—A Turkish soldier.
31. ICHOR—The fluid that took the place of blood in the veins of the gods.

This is the word of your
   Queen."
And presently on the scene
Appears a solemn mortician;
And taking formal position   35
With feelers calmly atwiddle,
Seizes the dead by the middle,

And heaving him high in air,
Carries him out of there.
No one stands round to stare.   40
It is nobody else's affair.

It couldn't be called ungentle.
But how thoroughly departmental.

FOR ENJOYMENT

1. It is not uncommon to compare people to insects. No doubt you know someone who is *busy as a bee* and someone else who is a *social butterfly*. Here Mr. Frost reverses the process and humorously compares ants to people. In what respect are the two alike? What actions does the poet describe to illustrate the similarity?

2. What absurd associations add to the humor of the poem? For example, what is the chief business of the enquiry squad? Point out other ridiculous statements. In themselves, there is nothing humorous about the words *Janizary* and *ichor*. What makes them funny here?

3. Can you see any connection between the form of the poem and its subject? What do the short lines suggest? Why is the poem continuous rather than broken up into stanzas?

Stopping by Woods on a Snowy Evening

ROBERT FROST

Here a New England farmer on a country road stops his horse for a few minutes to enjoy the peace and beauty of a winter scene. You may read into this simple poem more than just a lovely picture.

Whose woods these are I think I know.
His house is in the village though;
He will not see me stopping here
To watch his woods fill up with snow.

My little horse must think it queer   5
To stop without a farmhouse near
Between the woods and frozen lake
The darkest evening of the year.

He gives his harness bells a shake
To ask if there is some mistake.   10
The only other sound's the sweep
Of easy wind and downy flake.

The woods are lovely, dark, and deep,
But I have promises to keep,
And miles to go before I sleep,   15
And miles to go before I sleep.

FOR UNDERSTANDING AND APPRECIATION

1. Sound is important in this poem. Notice how the sound of the harness bells emphasizes by contrast the quiet of *easy wind* and *downy flake*. Point out other words or phrases which suggest peace and quiet by their sound as well as their sense.

2. What definite and accurate references make the poem realistic as well as poetic?

3. A road is often used to symbolize life. If the road is life in this poem, what might be represented by the wood where the traveler pauses? What could be symbolized by the miles yet to go and the promises that must be kept? What might be the sleep at the end of the journey?

◇◇◇◇◇

"*Out, Out——*"

ROBERT FROST

The unusual title of this poem comes from Shakespeare's play MACBETH. *Long ago in Scotland Macbeth pondered the brevity of human life and expressed his ideas on the subject in one of the most famous passages in all of Shakespeare's writing. In one line life is compared to a lighted candle which may be snuffed out in an instant. Macbeth's exact words are: "Out, out, brief candle!"*

Every hour of every day the same truth is brought home to someone somewhere. Here Robert Frost takes an illustration from a peaceful Vermont farmyard.

> The buzz saw snarled and rattled in the yard
> And made dust and dropped stove-length sticks of wood,
> Sweet-scented stuff when the breeze drew across it.
> And from there those that lifted eyes could count
> Five mountain ranges one behind the other   5
> Under the sunset far into Vermont.
> And the saw snarled and rattled, snarled and rattled,
> As it ran light, or had to bear a load.
> And nothing happened: day was all but done.
> Call it a day, I wish they might have said   10
> To please the boy by giving him the half hour
> That a boy counts so much when saved from work.

His sister stood beside them in her apron
To tell them "Supper." At the word, the saw,
As if to prove saws knew what supper meant, 15
Leaped out at the boy's hand, or seemed to leap—
He must have given the hand. However it was,
Neither refused the meeting. But the hand!
The boy's first outcry was a rueful laugh,
As he swung toward them holding up the hand 20
Half in appeal, but half as if to keep
The life from spilling. Then the boy saw all—
Since he was old enough to know, big boy
Doing a man's work, though a child at heart—
He saw all spoiled. "Don't let him cut my hand off— 25
The doctor, when he comes. Don't let him, sister!"
So. But the hand was gone already.
The doctor put him in the dark of ether.
He lay and puffed his lips out with his breath.
And then—the watcher at his pulse took fright. 30
No one believed. They listened at his heart.
Little—less—nothing!—and that ended it.
No more to build on there. And they, since they
Were not the one dead, turned to their affairs.

FOR UNDERSTANDING

1. How does the boy's youth help to emphasize the idea suggested by the title? What details make him seem very much alive and human before the accident? How do the last two lines of the poem reinforce the idea of the swiftness with which a human life can be blotted out?

2. Robert Frost found the material for this poem in rural New England. What incident might a modern city poet use for a poem on the same theme?

3. One pupil might read aloud the passage beginning "Out, out . . ." in *Macbeth*, Act v, Scene 5, and contrast Shakespeare's thoughts on the brevity of life with Frost's thought.

THE POET'S CRAFT

1. There is a dramatic contrast between the familiar peaceful setting and sudden tragedy. What specific references help you to visualize the scene in the farmyard? How does the sister in her apron add to the comfort and security of the picture?

2. Which words in lines 1 and 7 suggest by their own sound the sound of the saw? Read lines 7 and 8 aloud and notice how the sound combines with the meaning to help you hear and see the saw at work.

3. How is the saw personified; that is, how are its actions made to seem human, with human motives and feelings behind them? Point out some specific words or phrases.

Chicago

CARL SANDBURG

When "Chicago" first appeared in 1914 it was both praised and condemned. POETRY, the magazine that published it, awarded it a two hundred dollar prize for being the best American poem of the year. On the other hand, there were some who said that it was too coarse and ugly to be poetry at all. How you react to it will depend upon your own conception of poetry.

Carl Sandburg considered a great industrial city a good subject for a poem. He believed too that the most effective words and phrases to convey impressions and pictures of a modern city should come from the speech of people living in the city at the time rather than from a special literary language that he called "book language." Notice how words, pictures, and rhythms work together in this poem to create an impression of this American city.

> Hog Butcher for the World,
> Toolmaker, Stacker of Wheat,
> Player with Railroads and the Nation's Freight Handler;
> Stormy, husky, brawling,
> City of the Big Shoulders: 5
>
> They tell me you are wicked and I believe them, for I have seen your
>   painted women under the gas lamps luring the farm boys.
> And they tell me you are crooked and I answer: Yes, it is true I have
>   seen the gunman kill and go free to kill again.
> And they tell me you are brutal and my reply is: On the faces of
>   women and children I have seen the marks of wanton hunger.
> And having answered so I turn once more to those who sneer at this
>   my city, and I give them back the sneer and say to them:
>
> Come and show me another city with lifted head singing so proud to
>   be alive and coarse and strong and cunning.   10
> Flinging magnetic curses amid the toil of piling job on job, here is a
>   tall bold slugger set vivid against the little soft cities;
> Fierce as a dog with tongue lapping for action, cunning as a savage
>   pitted against the wilderness,

Bareheaded,
Shoveling,
Wrecking,
Planning,
Building, breaking, rebuilding,
Under the smoke, dust all over his mouth, laughing with white teeth,
Under the terrible burden of destiny laughing as a young man laughs,
Laughing even as an ignorant fighter laughs who has never lost a battle,
Bragging and laughing that under his wrist is the pulse, and under his
    ribs the heart of the people,
                    Laughing!
Laughing the stormy, husky, brawling laughter of Youth, half-naked,
    sweating, proud to be
Hog Butcher, Toolmaker, Stacker of Wheat, Player with Railroads,
    and Freight Handler to the Nation.

15

20

IMPRESSIONS OF A CITY

1. In the opening five lines of the poem the poet pictures Chicago as a giant worker. What types of work are represented? Which types are not mentioned? What general impression of Chicago did you get from the first stanza?

2. In the following lines what unfavorable aspects of life in a great city are presented? What admirable characteristics follow? Do you think good and evil are equally represented? Which does the poet believe to be stronger? Point out at least one passage to support your opinion.

3. Sandburg is a staunch believer in the democratic way of life. Point out evidence in this poem that he admired the common people and had faith in their future.

THE POET'S CRAFT

1. Notice the words and phrases that Sandburg used to describe the giant that he created to represent Chicago. Which suggest power and strength? Which suggest pride? What is symbolized by the dust on the giant's mouth and by his laughter?

2. The total impression of Chicago is suggested by a series of images or pictures. Which show evil and crime? Which suggest power and energy? Which represents the planning and scheming that goes on?

3. Point out examples of slang words and phrases that are characteristic of Sandburg's poetry. Show that each is appropriate because it fits the subject and helps to convey the impression which the poet is trying to create.

CARL SANDBURG (Born 1878)

Carl Sandburg was born in Galesburg, Illinois. His parents were Swedish immigrants who had had very little education. It seemed only natural that Carl should leave school at thirteen to go to work. Before he was seventeen he had been a driver of a milk wagon, porter in a barber shop, and truck operator in a brick kiln. Later he traveled through the West, riding "blind baggage," washing dishes in hotels, selling stove polish, and working in the harvest fields. He served in the army for eight months during the Spanish American War. When the war ended he returned to Galesburg and worked his way through Lombard College. There, in addition to making a good scholastic record, he was captain of the basketball team and editor-in-chief of the annual. Following graduation he worked at various jobs before becoming an editorial writer for the *Chicago Daily News*.

In the meantime, he had been writing poetry about the places and people he knew best: the prairies and towns and the farm hands and industrial workers of the Middle West. *Chicago Poems*, published in 1916; *Cornhuskers*, which appeared in 1918; and *Smoke and Steel*, which won him half the Pulitzer Prize in 1920—all marked him as the poet of the working man and of industrial America. *The People, Yes*, published in 1936, shows his admiration for the common man and his faith in democracy. Besides writing original poetry, Carl Sandburg has helped to preserve and popularize American folk songs in *The American Songbag*, which was published in 1927. He has also written stories for children and an exceptionally fine biography of Abraham Lincoln. The second section of that biography, *Abraham Lincoln: The War Years*, was awarded the Pulitzer Prize for history in 1940. Sandburg's autobiography, *Always the Young Strangers*, was published in 1952.

Carl Sandburg is a modernist in his use of free verse and in his experimentation with words and rhythms. He is a man of intense vigor and his language is sometimes coarse and even brutal. However, he has his quiet moods in which he traces word paintings as delicate and flawless as frost on glass, and he is capable of great tenderness as is demonstrated in his prose tales for children and in the lyrical passages of his biography of Abraham Lincoln.

Aside from his poetry Mr. Sandburg is a colorful personality. Even in recent years he has traveled around the country with his guitar delighting audiences by singing folk songs and reading from his own poems.

Clean Curtains

CARL SANDBURG

The appearance of clean curtains in the windows of a ramshackle tenement house may seem a strange subject for a poem. However, poetry is where you find it, and Carl Sandburg found the inspiration for many of his poems in the crowded city streets of Chicago.

New neighbors came to the corner house at Congress and Green Streets.

The look of their clean white curtains was the same as the rim of a nun's bonnet.

One way was an oyster-pail factory, one way they made candy, one way paper boxes, strawboard cartons.

The warehouse trucks shook the dust of the ways loose and the wheels whirled dust—there was dust of hoof and wagon wheel and rubber tire —dust of police and fire wagons—dust of the winds that circled at midnight and noon listening to no prayers.

"O, Mother, I know the heart of you," I sang passing the rim of a nun's
    bonnet—O white curtains—and people clean as the prayers of Jesus here
    in the faded ramshackle at Congress and Green.   5

Dust and the thundering trucks won—the barrages of the street wheels and
    the lawless wind took their way—was it five weeks or six the little mother,
    the new neighbors, battled and then took away the white prayers in the
    windows?

FOR UNDERSTANDING

1. How does the poet describe the new neighbors? Do you think it is possible to judge people as he apparently does by the kind of curtains they hang in their windows?

2. What do you think had happened to the people in the house at the corner of Congress and Green Streets when the curtains disappeared from the windows? Did the family move from the neighborhood? What other explanation is possible?

3. What general idea about the relationship between people and their environment is suggested in this poem? What do the clean white curtains symbolize? What is represented by the dust and the lawless wind?

THE POET'S CRAFT

1. Why does the poet mention particular factories in describing the location of the house? Why would it be less effective if he had merely said that the corner of Congress and Green Streets was an industrial neighborhood?

2. What original comparison or simile is used to describe the curtains in the second line? Point out the suggested comparison or metaphor in the last line. How are the curtains like a prayer? What do they seem to be asking?

3. How does the sound contribute to the image or picture in the stanza about the dust? Read the stanza aloud and emphasize the jarring sound in line 1 and the whirling sound in the first part of line 2.

Limited

CARL SANDBURG

In addition to giving an impression of speed and power, this poem about a modern streamliner suggests a general truth about life.

I am riding on a limited express, one of the crack trains of the nation.
Hurtling across the prairie into the blue haze and dark air go fifteen all-
    steel coaches holding a thousand people.
(All the coaches shall be scrap and rust and all the men and women laugh-
    ing in the diners and sleepers shall pass to ashes.)
I ask a man in the smoker where he is going and he answers: "Omaha."

FINDING SUGGESTED MEANINGS

1. What thought is suggested by the train load of people speeding over the country? What will eventually become of the train and the people? What general truth about life is symbolized in this short poem?

2. What type of person is represented by the man in the smoker? How do his thoughts contrast with those of the poet? Can you see anything ironic in his saying that he was going to Omaha? That is, in the light of the thought expressed earlier in the poem, what is his real destination? Explain the double meaning of the title of the poem.

◇◇◇◇◇

Window

CARL SANDBURG

This one-sentence poem is merely an impression of what a poet saw from a railway car window at night.

Night from a railroad car window
Is a great, dark, soft thing
Broken across with slashes of light.

"Window" from *Chicago Poems* by Carl Sandburg, copyright, 1916, by Henry Holt and Company, Inc., copyright, 1944, by Carl Sandburg, reprinted by permission of the publishers.

◇◇◇

POETIC COMPARISONS

1. How does the suggested comparison help to give an impression of dark and speed at the same time? Why does the poet use a vague word like *thing* to refer to night rather than name a specific object? What are the slashes of light? Why is *slashes* a better word than *spots* or *patches*?

2. Try writing a one-sentence poem similar to this one in which the entire poem is a suggested comparison or metaphor giving your own impression of something you have seen or experienced.

Flammonde

EDWIN ARLINGTON ROBINSON

You will not find Tilbury Town on any map, for it is an imaginary town peopled by the characters of Mr. Robinson's poems. Yet it is probably safe to say that it has more famous citizens than any other town its size in all of the New England states. One of the most popular of its inhabitants was not a native of the town. He had moved there rather late in life from places unknown. You will enjoy meeting the mysterious Mr. Flammonde.

The man Flammonde, from God knows
   where,
With firm address and foreign air,
With news of nations in his talk
And something royal in his walk,
With glint of iron in his eyes,   5
But never doubt, nor yet surprise,
Appeared, and stayed, and held his head
As one by kings accredited.

Erect, with his alert repose
About him, and about his clothes,   10
He pictured all tradition hears
Of what we owe to fifty years.
His cleansing heritage of taste
Paraded neither want nor waste;
And what he needed for his fee   15
To live, he borrowed graciously.

He never told us what he was,
Or what mischance, or other cause,
Had banished him from better days
To play the Prince of Castaways.   20
Meanwhile he played surpassing well
A part, for most, unplayable;
In fine, one pauses, half afraid
To say for certain that he played.

23. IN FINE—In conclusion.
"Flammonde" from *Collected Poems* by Edwin Arlington Robinson, copyright, 1944, by Edwin Arlington Robinson, and used with the permission of The Macmillan Co., publishers.

For that, one may as well forego   25
Conviction as to yes or no;
Nor can I say just how intense
Would then have been the difference
To several, who, having striven
In vain to get what he was given,   30
Would see the stranger taken on
By friends not easy to be won.

Moreover, many a malcontent
He soothed and found munificent;
His courtesy beguiled and foiled   35
Suspicion that his years were soiled;
His mien distinguished any crowd,
His credit strengthened when he bowed;
And women, young and old, were fond
Of looking at the man Flammonde.   40

There was a woman in our town
On whom the fashion was to frown;
But while our talk renewed the tinge
Of a long-faded scarlet fringe,
The man Flammonde saw none of
   that,   45
And what he saw we wondered at—
That none of us, in her distress,
Could hide or find our littleness.

There was a boy that all agreed
Had shut within him the rare seed   50

Of learning. We could understand,
But none of us could lift a hand.
The man Flammonde appraised the
    youth,
And told a few of us the truth;
And thereby, for a little gold,   55
A flowered future was unrolled.

There were two citizens who fought
For years and years, and over nought;
They made life awkward for their friends,
And shortened their own dividends.   60
The man Flammonde said what was
    wrong
Should be made right; nor was it long
Before they were again in line,
And had each other in to dine.

And these I mention are but four   65
Of many out of many more.
So much for them. But what of him—
So firm in every look and limb?
What small satanic sort of kink
Was in his brain? What broken
    link   70
Withheld him from the destinies
That came so near to being his?

What was he, when we came to sift
His meaning, and to note the drift
Of incommunicable ways   75
That make us ponder while we praise?
Why was it that his charm revealed
Somehow the surface of a shield?
What was it that we never caught?
What was he, and what was he not?   80

How much it was of him we met
We cannot ever know; nor yet
Shall all he gave us quite atone
For what was his, and his alone;
Nor need we now, since he knew
    best,   85
Nourish an ethical unrest:
Rarely at once will nature give
The power to be Flammonde and live.

We cannot know how much we learn
From those who never will return,   90
Until a flash of unforeseen
Remembrance falls on what has been.
We've each a darkening hill to climb;
And this is why, from time to time
In Tilbury Town, we look beyond   95
Horizons for the man Flammonde.

FOR UNDERSTANDING

1. What was there about Flammonde that aroused the interest and curiosity of the townspeople? Why did they respect him? What showed his good taste and refinement?

2. What is the first suggestion in the poem of a flaw in Flammonde's character? How did he make a living? Why did people continue to trust him in spite of the mystery surrounding his past?

3. In what respects was Flammonde a better man than other people in the town? What character traits are revealed by the following: his attitude toward the woman who was frowned upon by others, his efforts in aiding the boy with talent, and his settling the quarrel between the two citizens?

4. How do you think the people of Tilbury Town would have treated Flammonde if they had known for certain that there was something dishonorable in his past? Support your opinion by references to the poem or by reasons based upon what you know about human nature.

5. What general truth is expressed in the last stanza? How is it illustrated by the portrait of Flammonde which the poet has painted in the poem?

HOMONYMS AND SYNONYMS

1. Homonyms are words which are pronounced alike but which have different meanings and sometimes different spellings.

You no doubt know at least one homonym for each of the italicized words in the following lines describing Flammonde. Check with the dictionary for the pronunciation as well as for the appropriate meaning.

a. With firm *address* and foreign *air*
b. His *mien* distinguished any crowd

2. A synonym is a word that means the same, or almost the same, as another word. From the two words listed below each of the following phrases choose the one which you think is the better synonym for the italicized word as it is used in the verse.

a. Moreover, many a *malcontent*
   (grumbler, agitator)
b. He soothed and found *munificent*
   (generous, lavish)
c. His courtesy *beguiled* and foiled
   (deceived, charmed)
d. Suspicion that his years were *soiled*
   (dirty, disgraced)

EDWIN ARLINGTON ROBINSON

(1869–1935)

Edwin Arlington Robinson was born in Head Tide, Maine, but he grew up in Gardiner, a typical New England town which served as a model for the fictitious Tilbury Town of "Flammonde." Even as a small boy Robinson was interested in poetry, and he began to write early. However, he destroyed most of what he wrote while he was in school. When he finished school in Gardiner he entered Harvard, but at the end of two years he was called home by his father's illness and never returned to graduate. During the next five years he published two volumes of verse which attracted little attention.

It was while he was living in New York, trying desperately to make enough money so that he could continue to write, that he came to the attention of President Theodore Roosevelt. The President had been favorably impressed by some of Robinson's poems, and knowing that the poet was having a hard time, helped him get a position in the New York Customs House. His salary there made it possible for him to go on writing, but he said himself that he gave the government very poor service. In 1911 he decided to give all his time to writing.

It was not until 1916 when he published *The Man Against the Sky* that Robinson was generally acknowledged as an outstanding American poet. However, recognition came fast after that. In 1921 his *Collected Poems* was awarded the Pulitzer Prize. He was to receive the prize two more times before he died.

In *Merlin*, *Lancelot*, and *Tristram* he retold some of the old Arthurian legends. The rest of his poetry is mostly about the ordinary happenings of everyday life. He was particularly interested in interpreting character, especially the characters of people who were apparent failures in life. He wrote his poetry in the language of modern speech, but he kept the traditional verse forms.

◇◇◇◇◇

Miniver Cheevy

EDWIN ARLINGTON ROBINSON

You may recognize some of the characteristics of a friend or neighbor, or even of yourself, in Miniver Cheevy, who continually "sighed for what was not."

MINIVER CHEEVY

Miniver Cheevy, child of scorn,
  Grew lean while he assailed the sea-
    sons;
He wept that he was ever born,
  And he had reasons.

Miniver loved the days of old   5
  When swords were bright and steeds
    were prancing;
The vision of a warrior bold
  Would set him dancing.

Miniver sighed for what was not,
  And dreamed, and rested from his la-
    bors;   10
He dreamed of Thebes and Camelot,
  And Priam's neighbors.

Miniver mourned the ripe renown
  That made so many a name so fra-
    grant;
He mourned Romance, now on the
    town,   15
  And Art, a vagrant.

Miniver loved the Medici,
  Albeit he had never seen one;
He would have sinned
    incessantly
  Could he have been one.   20

Miniver cursed the commonplace,
  And eyed a khaki suit with
    loathing;
He missed the medieval grace
  Of iron clothing.

Miniver scorned the gold he sought,   25
  But sore annoyed was he without it;
Miniver thought, and thought, and
    thought,
  And thought about it.

Miniver Cheevy, born too late,
  Scratched his head and kept on think-
    ing;   30
Miniver coughed, and called it fate,
  And kept on drinking.

FOR ENJOYMENT

1. Why wasn't Miniver able to find beauty and romance in modern life?

2. Tell why you think Miniver would or would not have been successful and happy in the days "when knights were bold." What passages indicate that his ideas of "the good old days" were romantic or idealistic rather than realistic?

IRONIC HUMOR

Irony is a figure of speech in which words have an intended meaning that is the op-posite of the literal meaning. In a situation or event there is irony when the circum-stance or happening is the opposite of what might logically be expected. You will en-joy this poem more if you can recognize the irony in the following passages.

1. He missed the medieval grace
  Of iron clothing.

2. Miniver scorned the gold he sought
  But sore annoyed was he without it.

3. Miniver coughed and called it fate,
  And kept on drinking.

The Man with the Hoe

EDWIN MARKHAM

The poem THE MAN WITH THE HOE was inspired by Millet's painting which shows a peasant of the days before the French Revolution leaning against the handle of his hoe. For Markham, who was interested in social reform, and particularly in the rights of the laboring man, the picture had special significance. He saw in the French peasant a symbol of all the toilers of the world down through the ages who have been exploited and degraded by their fellow men.

> *God created man in his own image*
> *In the image of God created He him.*
> *—Genesis*

Bowed by the weight of centuries he leans
Upon his hoe and gazes on the ground,
The emptiness of ages in his face,
And on his back the burden of the world.
Who made him dead to rapture and despair,   5
A thing that grieves not and that never hopes,
Stolid and stunned, a brother to the ox?
Who loosened and let down this brutal jaw?
Whose was the hand that slanted back this brow?
Whose breath blew out the light within this brain?   10

Is this the thing the Lord God made and gave
To have dominion over sea and land;
To trace the stars and search the heavens for power;
To feel the passion of eternity?
Is this the dream He dreamed who shaped the suns   15
And marked their ways upon the ancient deep?
Down all the caverns of hell to their last gulf
There is no shape more terrible than this—
More tongued with cries against the world's blind greed—
More filled with signs and portents for the soul—   20
More packed with danger to the universe.

"The Man with the Hoe" by Edwin Markham, reprinted by permission of Virgil Markham.

What gulfs between him and the seraphim!
Slave of the wheel of labor, what to him
Are Plato and the swing of Pleiades?
What the long reaches of the peaks of song,   25
The rift of dawn, the reddening of the rose?
Through this dread shape the suffering ages look;
Time's tragedy is in that aching stoop;
Through this dread shape humanity betrayed,
Plundered, profaned, and disinherited,   30
Cries protest to the Powers that made the world,
A protest that is also prophecy.

O masters, lords and rulers in all lands,
Is this the handiwork you give to God,
This monstrous thing distorted and soul-quenched?   35

24. PLATO—A Greek writer and philosopher (427–347 B.C.).
24. PLEIADES (plē′yá·dēz)—The seven daughters of Atlas and Pleione who were transformed
into a group of stars.

How will you ever straighten up this shape;
Touch it again with immortality;
Give back the upward looking and the light;
Rebuild in it the music and the dream;
Make right the immemorial infamies,   40
Perfidious wrongs, immedicable woes?

O masters, lords and rulers in all lands,
How will the future reckon with this man?
How answer his brute question in that hour
When whirlwinds of rebellion shake all shores?   45
How will it be with kingdoms and with kings—
With those who shaped him to the thing he is—
When this dumb terror shall rise to judge the world,
After the silence of the centuries?

POETRY AND SOCIAL PROBLEMS

When "The Man with the Hoe" was published in the *San Francisco Examiner* in 1899, it created a great deal of comment and was quoted and reprinted all over the world. Its success is a good illustration of the power of literature to arouse public opinion to the need for social reform. This one poem probably did more for the cause of labor than pages of cold facts about low wages, long hours, and poor working conditions. Notice how the poet tried to *arouse the feelings* of his readers against a social injustice rather than to *appeal to them with facts and logical reasons.*

1. Why did Mr. Markham preface the poem with a quotation from the Bible? How were you affected by the contrast between man as he was created by God and the man in the picture as the poet described him? Point out effective phrases in the description of the man. For example, how does the poet describe his expression and his lack of feeling? What words tell of his lack of hope or inspiration? How would you answer the four questions at the end of the first stanza?

2. In lines 22–26, how does the poet symbolize the kinds of satisfaction that are lost to "the slave of the wheel of labor"? In your own words tell what those satisfactions or interests are. How have they been denied to the laboring man?

3. How would you answer the questions in lines 36–41? What has been done since this poem was written to improve the condition of those symbolized by the "man with the hoe"?

4. In the last eight lines what did the poet predict about "the man with the hoe," or those he represents? What events might be symbolized by the "whirlwind hour"? How would you answer the questions asked in this stanza?

FOR DISCUSSION

The right to work and the satisfactions that come from honest labor and from a job well done have long been recognized as being among life's greatest blessings. How can it be work, then, that is responsible for the condition of "the man with the hoe"? Under what circumstances does work become oppressive and degrading as it is pictured here? What other forces besides toil and drudgery have contributed to the misery and degradation of the underprivileged people of the world?

EDWIN MARKHAM (1852–1940)

Edwin Markham was the child of pioneer parents who were among Oregon's early settlers. His mother was the earliest woman writer in Oregon. As a growing boy Edwin knew hardship and hard work. He worked at farming, blacksmithing, and ranching. Encouraged by a teacher who recognized his poetic possibilities, Markham read widely and later became a teacher in the California schools.

Among the most pressing social problems at the beginning of the century were those involving the rights of labor. Markham's sympathies were wholly on the side of labor. It was while he was principal of a school in Oakland in 1899 that he published "The Man with the Hoe," the poem that made him famous. The widespread recognition which it received is evidence of the influence writers can wield in forming public opinion. "Lincoln, the Man of the People" is another remarkably fine poem, which appeared in 1901. Markham continued to write throughout his long life, and in 1932, on his eightieth birthday, published *New Poems: Eighty Songs at Eighty.*

❖❖❖❖❖

Blue Squills

SARA TEASDALE

One lifetime is scarcely long enough to enjoy the beauty in familiar things. Here a poet hopes to outwit time by carrying into eternity something of the joy she experienced in seeing a bed of blue flowers and a blossoming tree.

How many million Aprils came
    Before I ever knew
How white a cherry bough could be,
    A bed of squills, how blue!

And many a dancing April   5
    When life is done with me,
Will lift the blue flame of the
      flower
    And the white flame of the tree.

Oh, burn me with your beauty, then,
    Oh, hurt me, tree and flower,   10
Lest in the end death try to take
    Even this glistening hour.

O shaken flowers, O shimmering trees,
    O sunlit white and blue,
Wound me, that I through endless
      sleep   15
    May bear the scar of you.

◇◇

FOR APPRECIATION

1. The word *million* in the first line of the poem is not intended to be taken literally. What do we learn about the poet's *present* attitude from her emphasis on all the *past* Aprils when she was unaware of cherry blossoms and squills?

2. What is the meaning of the last two stanzas? How could one be burned by beauty? What things are actually marked or branded by burning? Why does the poet wish to be *burned* by the beauty of the flowers and the trees?

SARA TEASDALE (1884–1933)

Sara Teasdale had a rare gift of words, coupled with a simplicity of idea, which makes her verse charming. She was born into a wealthy Missouri family and led a life of comparative ease and quiet—traveling, writing, and reading. Miss Teasdale began writing verse at college where she wrote translations from the French. She soon adopted a pleasant style of her own, and her original verse was eagerly accepted by numerous magazines. Later she became the editor of a magazine. With the publication of *Love Songs* in 1917, her reputation was established. Many of her lilting, rhythmic poems have been set to music.

❖❖❖❖❖

I Shall Not Care

SARA TEASDALE

Sara Teasdale is best known for her love poems. Probably this one can be more accurately described as a poem about the loss of love.

When I am dead and over me bright
    April
  Shakes out her rain-drenched hair,
Though you should lean above me bro-
    ken-hearted,
  I shall not care.

I shall have peace, as leafy trees are peace-
    ful
  When rain bends down the bough;
And I shall be more silent and cold-
    hearted
  Than you are now.

◇◇◇

THE POET'S CRAFT

1. Why do you think the poet chose April rather than some other month for the word pictures presented? What dramatic contrast is provided by putting April and death together?

2. How is April personified in the first stanza? What picture or image is used to suggest peace?

3. What is ironic about the situation suggested in the poem? To whom is the poem addressed? What is evidently the relationship between that person and the poet? What contrast is there between the real situation and the one imagined?

◇◇◇◇◇◇◇◇◇◇◇◇◇◇◇◇◇◇◇◇◇◇◇

Recuerdo

EDNA ST. VINCENT MILLAY

The vital quality of her verse and a sophisticated view of life made Edna
St. Vincent Millay a popular poet with the young people of her generation.
Among her many poems about the joys and sorrows of young lovers is this
one of a carefree pair who spent the entire night riding back and forth across
the Hudson River on a ferryboat.

> We were very tired, we were very merry—
> We had gone back and forth all night on the ferry.
> It was bare and bright, and smelled like a stable—
> But we looked into a fire, we leaned across a table,
> We lay on the hilltop underneath the moon; 5
> And the whistles kept blowing, and the dawn came soon.

> We were very tired, we were very merry—
> We had gone back and forth all night on the ferry;
> And you ate an apple, and I ate a pear,
> From a dozen of each we had bought somewhere; 10
> And the sky went wan, and the wind came cold,
> And the sun rose dripping, a bucketful of gold.

We were very tired, we were very merry,
We had gone back and forth all night on the ferry.
We hailed, "Good morrow, Mother!" to a shawl-covered head,   15
And bought a morning paper, which neither of us read;
And she wept, "God bless you!" for the apples and the pears,
And we gave her all our money but our subway fares.

FOR ENJOYMENT

1. The title of this poem means *I re-member*. What details stand out vividly in the speaker's mind? Which memories are vague?

2. Although nothing is said directly about the feeling of the young people for each other, how do you know that they were very much in love? Which lines suggest that they were indifferent to their surroundings? Which show that they were unconcerned about what they ate and about the affairs of the rest of the world?

3. Why do you suppose the old woman wept when she thanked them for the apples and the pears?

EDNA ST. VINCENT MILLAY

(1892–1950)

Edna St. Vincent Millay was born in Rockland, Maine. She began to write when she was very young and won an award for poetry from *St. Nicholas* magazine when she was only fourteen. At nineteen she wrote "Renascence," one of her finest poems. Her first volume of poetry, which included "Renascence" and took its name from that poem, was published the year she was graduated from Vassar College.

After graduation Miss Millay lived for a time in New York. There she wrote short stories and poems and enjoyed the society of other poets and artists in Greenwich Village. Later she joined the Provincetown Players as a writer and actress. Among her plays is the libretto for *The King's Hench-man*, an opera for which Deems Taylor composed the music. Her volumes of verse include A *Few Figs from Thistles, Second April, The Harp-Weaver and Other Poems, There Are No Islands Any More*, and *Collected Sonnets*. The *Harp-Weaver* was awarded the Pulitzer Prize for poetry in 1923.

Moriturus

EDNA ST. VINCENT MILLAY

Edna St. Vincent Millay wrote passionately about love and beauty and the joy of living. She also wrote several poems about death which, like most of her poetry, reveal an unconventional and rebellious spirit. These stanzas from a rather long poem are typical of her attitude.

234

Withstanding Death
  Till Life be gone,
I shall treasure my breath,
  I shall linger on.

I shall bolt my door   5
  With a bolt and a cable;
I shall block my door
  With a bureau and a table;

With all my might
  My door shall be barred.   10
I shall put up a fight,
  I shall take it hard.

With his hand on my mouth
  He shall drag me forth,
Shrieking to the south   15
  And clutching at the north.

FOR DISCUSSION

1. What is your opinion of the attitude toward death expressed in the poem? Is it courageous or cowardly? Give reasons for your opinion.

2. Death is personified in the poem, that is, given the characteristics of a person. What kind of person is death here? Point out passages that suggest character traits.

3. Death is represented in various ways in art and literature. Common symbols are a skeleton, a reaper with a scythe, and an angel. How would you symbolize death?

4. Is it shameful to fear death? Do you think those individuals who get a great deal out of life are most reluctant to die? What is your attitude toward people who say that dying is a simple matter?

First Fig

EDNA ST. VINCENT MILLAY

We sometimes hear the expression—usually spoken in disapproval—"He's burning the candle at both ends." In the following poem Miss Millay picks up this popular expression, explores its full meaning, and also states a philosophy of life. Since a lighted candle is often used to symbolize a person's life, you should have little difficulty interpreting the figurative language.

My candle burns at both ends;
It will not last the night;
But ah, my foes, and oh, my friends—
It gives a lovely light!

FOR UNDERSTANDING

1. Explain the symbolism in the poem. If the candle represents the speaker's life, how can it be burned at both ends? What does the night stand for? What is symbolized by the light?

2. What kind of person do you think the speaker is? How would she probably be regarded by the *friends* addressed in the poem? What do you suppose the *foes* would think about her?

3. What do you think of the philosophy expressed here? How could it be interpreted to mean something rather selfish and shallow? Can you see how it might mean something generous and fine? Is there anything in the poem to indicate how it should be interpreted?

4. Would you rather live a long, uneventful life or a short, colorful, exciting life? Which one do you think the majority of people would choose, and what evidence can you give?

◇◇◇◇◇

General William Booth Enters into Heaven

VACHEL LINDSAY

William Booth was the founder of the Salvation Army, a religious organization that began as a missionary project in the slums of London and continues to serve the poor and the outcasts of society. No doubt you have seen members of the Army marching in uniform or holding street-corner services. You may have heard them sing "The Blood of the Lamb," one of their favorite hymns which is used as a sort of refrain in the following poem.

Vachel Lindsay, who displayed considerable missionary zeal himself in his efforts to spread the "gospel of beauty," had great admiration for the work of the Salvation Army. He wrote "General William Booth Enters into Heaven" soon after Booth died in 1912. It was intended to honor the memory of a great man. As you read, try to visualize a typical Salvation Army parade led by William Booth himself beating the big drum, and made up of all those who had been saved through his efforts.

(To be sung to the tune of "The Blood of the Lamb" with indicated instrument.)

I

(Bass drum beaten loudly.)
Booth led boldly with his big bass drum—
(Are you washed in the blood of the Lamb?)
The Saints smiled gravely and they said: "He's come."
(Are you washed in the blood of the Lamb?)
Walking lepers followed, rank on rank,   5
Lurching bravos from the ditches dank,
Drabs from the alleyways and drug fiends pale—
Minds still passion-ridden, soul-powers frail—
Vermin-eaten saints with moldy breath,
Unwashed legions with the ways of Death—   10
(Are you washed in the blood of the Lamb?)

  (Banjos.)
Every slum had sent its half-a-score
The round world over. (Booth had groaned for more.)
Every banner that the wide world flies
Bloomed with glory and transcendent dyes.   15
Big-voiced lasses made their banjos bang,
Tranced, fanatical, they shrieked and sang—
"Are you washed in the blood of the Lamb?"
Hallelujah! It was queer to see
Bull-necked convicts with that land make free.   20
Loons with trumpets blowed a blare, blare, blare
On, on upward thro' the golden air!
(Are you washed in the blood of the Lamb?)

II

(Bass drum slower and softer.)
Booth died blind and still by Faith he trod.
Eyes still dazzled by the ways of God.   25
Booth led boldly, and he looked the chief
Eagle countenance in sharp relief,
Beard a-flying, air of high command
Unabated in that holy land.

  (Sweet flute music.)
Jesus came from out the courthouse door,   30
Stretched his hands above the passing poor.
Booth saw not, but led his queer ones there
Round and round the mighty courthouse square.
Yet in an instant all that blear review
Marched on spotless, clad in raiment new.   35

The lame were straightened, withered limbs uncurled
And blind eyes opened on a new, sweet world.

   (*Bass drum louder.*)

Drabs and vixens in a flash made whole!
Gone was the weasel-head, the snout, the jowl!
Sages and sibyls now, and athletes clean,   40
Rulers of empires, and of forests green!

   (*Grand chorus of all instruments. Tambourines to the
     foreground.*)

The hosts were sandaled, and their wings were fire!
(Are you washed in the blood of the Lamb?)
But their noise played havoc with the angel choir.
(Are you washed in the blood of the Lamb?)   45
O, shout Salvation! It was good to see
Kings and princes by the Lamb set free.
The banjos rattled and the tambourines
Jing-jing-jingled in the hands of queens.

   (*Reverently sung, no instruments.*)

And when Booth halted by the curb for prayer   50
He saw his Master thro' the flag-filled air.
Christ came gently with a robe and crown
For Booth the soldier, while the throng knelt down.
He saw King Jesus. They were face to face,
And he knelt a-weeping in that holy place.   55
Are you washed in the blood of the Lamb?

FOR UNDERSTANDING

1. What different types of outcasts and down-and-outers are represented in the parade following General Booth as he enters Heaven?

2. What opinion did you form of Booth from the word picture at the beginning of part II? What did he look like? What kind of person was he? What did you learn about him from the reference to his blindness?

3. How people visualize Heaven depends upon their own religious experiences and their ideas of what is good and beautiful. How is the picture of Heaven presented here in keeping with the teaching and practices of the Salvation Army? Why would the drum, the tambourine, and the banjo be more likely to represent heavenly music for the people of Booth's army than the harp would, for example? Why is the courthouse more appropriate here than the usual throne of God?

MUSIC IN POETRY

Vachel Lindsay attached a great deal of importance to the use of sound in poetry. He was skillful in employing the various poetic sound effects and sometimes suggested musical accompaniment for his poems. He believed that poetry should be chanted in the manner of the old minstrels rather than read.

1. Notice how the sound of a drum is suggested by the rhythm and by the sound of the words in the first line of the poem. Read the line to emphasize the drum sound and marching rhythm. How do you think the hymn line in parentheses should be read?

2. Repetition is a common device used to produce music in poetry. Point out examples of the repetition of lines, phrases, and words in this poem. *Rhyme* is the repetition of the same end sound in different words. How does Lindsay use rhyme here? Another type of repetition used in poetry is *alliteration*, that is, the repetition of the same beginning consonant in words coming close together. Notice the repetition of words beginning with *b* in the first line. Find other examples.

3. Lindsay was also fond of the poetic sound effect called *onomatopoeia*. Onomatopoetic words are those that imitate the sounds they name. The italicized words in the following lines are examples:

Big-voiced lasses made their banjos *bang*,
Tranced, fanatical, they *shrieked* and sang—

As you read the words in the line, try to emphasize their sound effect. Can you point out other examples of *onomatopoeia*?

4. Practice reading the entire poem as you think Vachel Lindsay might have read it himself. You might arrange to play recordings of Lindsay's reading of some of his poems if the records are available.

NICHOLAS VACHEL LINDSAY

(1879–1931)

Because he couldn't get a job as an artist, coal shoveler, or newspaper reporter, Vachel Lindsay one day in New York tried begging. It worked; and so, discouraged at his failure as an artist, he made two trips through the country reciting his verses in exchange for lodging and food. Later he gathered his poems into a little pamphlet, *Rhymes to Be Traded for Bread*, which he distributed as he made his way across the continent.

Lindsay was a versatile writer, employing various verse forms and writing on many subjects. Much of his work deals with the loveliness of nature and "the gospel of beauty." His most famous poems, however, are those that use a peculiar rhythm, a kind of syncopated sound, "an infectious blend of rhyme, religion, and ragtime." Although all poetry may well be read aloud, Lindsay's poetry practically demands oral reading. In the years just before his death he was a popular lecturer and chanted his poems to many appreciative audiences. He also made recordings of some of his poems.

❖❖❖❖❖

Kansas

VACHEL LINDSAY

Vachel Lindsay tramped through Kansas when he toured the West reciting his poems in exchange for food and lodging. He came to know the transient workers who followed the harvest and who became strong and free and happy for at least one month in the year while they gathered in the wheat crop. In this poem you will feel with the harvest hand the strain of work under a hot sun, the joy of good food and companionship, and the peace that comes with rest at the end of a hard day.

Oh, I have walked in Kansas
Through many a harvest field,
And piled the sheaves of glory there
And down the wild rows reeled:

Each sheaf a little yellow sun,   5
A heap of hot-rayed gold;
Each binder like Creation's hand
To mold suns, as of old.

Straight overhead the orb of noon
Beat down with brimstone breath: 10
The desert wind from south and west
Was blistering flame and death.

Yet it was gay in Kansas,
A-fighting that strong sun;
And I and many a fellow tramp   15
Defied that wind and won.

And we felt free in Kansas
From any sort of fear,
For thirty thousand tramps like us
There harvest every year.   20

She stretches arms for them to come,
She roars for helpers then,
And so it is in Kansas
That tramps, one month, are men.

We sang in burning Kansas   25
The songs of Sabbath-school,
The "Day Star" flashing in the East,
The "Vale of Eden" cool.

We sang in splendid Kansas
"The flag that set us free"—   30
That march of fifty thousand men
With Sherman to the sea.

We feasted high in Kansas
And had much milk and meat.
The tables groaned to give us power   35
Wherewith to save the wheat.

Our beds were sweet alfalfa hay
Within the barn-loft wide.
The loft doors opened out upon
The endless wheat-field tide.   40

I loved to watch the windmills spin
And watch that big moon rise.
I dreamed and dreamed with lids half-
    shut,
The moonlight in my eyes.

For all men dream in Kansas   45
By noonday and by night,
By sunrise yellow, red and wild
And moonrise wild and white.

The wind would drive the glittering
    clouds,
The cottonwoods would croon,   50
And past the sheaves and through the
    leaves
Came whispers from the moon.

FOR APPRECIATION

1. In spite of the heat and the hard work, why were the tramps happy while they were harvesting the wheat? In what way were they free? Free from what? What specific pleasures and satisfactions did they enjoy?

2. How is the mood of the last three stanzas different from that of the rest of the poem? What ideas are suggested by the following line: "For all men dream in Kansas"? What dreams do you think might come to the tramp who had worked in the wheat fields? What opportunities might he see in a state like Kansas that would be lacking in the older and more settled communities of the East and South?

THE POET'S CRAFT

1. What word pictures or images in the first three stanzas contribute to the impres-

sion of extreme heat? Include images of sound and feeling as well as those of sight. Which words or phrases in the second stanza make the wheat itself seem to radiate heat? How is the intense heat of the sun and the wind suggested in the third stanza?

2. Contrast the images in the last stanza with those of the third stanza. Which word suggests cool rather than hot light? What choice of words make the wind seem welcome and soothing rather than oppressive as in the third stanza?

3. Review the section on "Music in Poetry" in the study helps for the preceding poem. Then see how many examples of poetic sound effects you can find in this poem.

⬦⬦⬦⬦⬦

Yet Do I Marvel

COUNTÉE CULLEN

Because this poem builds up to a climax, you will have to read to the very end to understand the significance of the title. Notice that while there are fourteen lines in the poem, as there are in all sonnets, there are only three sentences. Be sure to read by sentences and not by lines.

> I doubt not God is good, well-meaning, kind,
> And did He stoop to quibble could tell why
> The little buried mole continues blind,
> Why flesh that mirrors Him must some day die;
> Make plain the reason tortured Tantalus   5
> Is baited by the fickle fruit, declare
> If merely brute caprice dooms Sisyphus
> To struggle up a never-ending stair.
> Inscrutable His ways are, and immune
> To catechism by a mind too strewn   10
> With petty cares to slightly understand
> What awful brain compels His awful hand.
> Yet do I marvel at this curious thing:
> To make a poet black and bid him sing.

5. TANTALUS—This mythological character was punished in Hades by being plunged up to the chin in water with the finest fruits hanging over his head, but both fruit and water receded whenever he tried to slake his thirst or satisfy his hunger.

7. SISYPHUS—A character in mythology who was condemned to roll to the top of a steep hill a huge stone that always rolled down again as he almost reached the top.

UNDERSTANDING A SONNET

The poem you have just read follows a particular form or pattern of poetry called a *sonnet*. While there are interesting variations which distinguish different kinds of sonnets, particularly in the rhyme scheme, they all follow the same general pattern. A sonnet always has fourteen lines. There is usually a distinct change in thought between the first eight lines, called the *octave*, and the last six, called the *sestet*. Frequently, as in this poem, the most important idea, to which the rest of the poem builds up, is contained in the last two lines of the sestet.

While it is not necessary to know the names of the different parts of a sonnet in order to enjoy it, understanding the main divisions may help you to get the meaning. Knowing how a sonnet is built will also give you some appreciation of the poet's skill in fitting his idea into a restricted form.

1. In the first eight lines the poet mentions examples of cruelty and injustice. What two examples does he take from nature? What are two from mythology? What types of human suffering do the last two symbolize? In these lines what is the poet's attitude toward the part God plays in the apparent injustices of life?

2. In the last six lines what change is there in the poet's attitude toward the ways of God? What explanation is offered for failure to understand the injustices mentioned earlier in the poem?

3. What injustice is mentioned in the last two lines? Why is it more impressive coming after the examples given and the questions raised in the first eight lines, and the explanation suggested in the first four lines of the *sestet*? What is the force of the word *yet* which introduces the concluding lines? Explain the irony in those lines. What conditions in society make it hard for a black poet to sing?

RHYTHM AND RHYME

1. All sonnets have the same rhythm, that is, the same pattern of accented and unaccented syllables. If you were to exaggerate the rhythm in the first line of "Yet Do I Marvel" you would read it like this:

Ĭ doubt˘ nŏt God˘ ĭs good,˘

wĕll mean˘ ĭng, kind˘ .

You will notice that there are five accented syllables in the line. A line of poetry with five accented syllables is called a *pentameter* line. When each accented syllable is preceded by an unaccented syllable, as it is in this poem, the line is *iambic pentameter*. This rhythmic pattern is the one most commonly used in English poetry. Practice reading other lines of the poem stressing the accented syllables.

2. In examining the rhyme pattern of this sonnet, it will help to assign a letter to each rhyming sound at the end of a line. For example, if *a* stands for *kind* at the end of the first line, all end words that rhyme with *kind* will be represented by *a*. Since *why*, the word at the end of the second line, does not rhyme with *kind*, it and all words that rhyme with it will be represented by *b*. If you follow the system through the fourteen lines of the sonnet, you will have the following picture of the rhyme scheme of "Yet Do I Marvel": *a,b,a,b, c,d,c,d,e,e,f,f,g,g.* Try representing the rhyme scheme of one other short poem.

COUNTÉE CULLEN (1903–1946)

When Countée Cullen was only twenty-two years old he published a volume of poems that immediately gave him a place among contemporary poets. His early life was spent in New York City, his birthplace. He attended public schools and was graduated from New York University. Later he went to Harvard. He taught French in a New York junior high school until 1945. Mr. Cullen said of himself, "Most things I write, I do for the sheer love of the music in them. A number of times I have said that I wanted to be a poet and known as such and not as a Negro poet. Somehow or other, however, I find my poetry of itself treating of the Negro, of his joys and his sorrows—mostly the latter."

EWING GALLOWAY

America the Beautiful

KATHARINE LEE BATES

In the summer of 1893 Katharine Lee Bates made a trip to the summit of Pike's Peak in Colorado. She said that while she was on the mountaintop and stood "looking out over the sealike expanse of fertile country spreading away so far under ample skies" the opening lines of this hymn came to her.

The song has become a favorite hymn in our own country "from sea to shining sea"; and we are told that it has been adopted by the Australians who merely substitute the name of their island continent for the name America.

"America the Beautiful" by permission of Estate of Katharine L. Bates.

O beautiful for spacious skies,
  For amber waves of grain,
For purple mountain majesties
    Above the fruited plain!
      America! America!   5
  God shed His grace on thee,
And crown thy good with brotherhood
  From sea to shining sea!

O beautiful for pilgrim feet,
  Whose stern, impassioned stress   10
A thoroughfare for freedom beat
  Across the wilderness!
    America! America!
  God mend thine every flaw,
Confirm thy soul in self-control,   15
  Thy liberty in law!

O beautiful for heroes proved
  In liberating strife,
Who more than self their country loved,
  And mercy more than life!   20
    America! America!
  May God thy gold refine,
Till all success be nobleness,
  And every gain divine!

O beautiful for patriot dream   25
  That sees beyond the years
Thine alabaster cities gleam
  Undimmed by human tears!
    America! America!
  God shed His grace on thee,   30
And crown thy good with brotherhood
  From sea to shining sea.

FOR UNDERSTANDING AND APPRECIATION

1. In the first stanza what specific things about America are singled out as being good and beautiful? What is the prayer at the end of the stanza?

2. What different aspect of America is praised in the second stanza? Who were the pilgrims referred to? How did they make a thoroughfare or road for freedom? What do you think is meant by the last two lines of the stanza? In what document did our forefathers confirm liberty in law? What has self-control to do with liberty?

3. How often before 1893, when this poem was written, had Americans proved their patriotism in "liberating strife"? Name the specific wars. When and where have Americans fought for freedom since those words were first written?

4. What ideals and future hopes are expressed for our country in the poem? What specific prayers? Are those hopes and prayers as fitting today as when the poem was written?

5. Mention the qualities that make the song appeal to all sections of the country. Why do you think it continues to be a favorite among our national songs?

KATHARINE LEE BATES (1859–1929)

Katharine Lee Bates, an American teacher and writer, was born at Falmouth, Massachusetts. One of the earliest graduates of Wellesley College, she later taught in the Department of English for about forty years. In her spare time she edited English classics for school texts, and wrote some verse, plays, and stories for young people. Her name will long be remembered for her poem, "America the Beautiful."

George Gray

EDGAR LEE MASTERS

George Gray in this poem and Lucinda Matlock in the one following are characters from Masters' SPOON RIVER ANTHOLOGY. The book is a collection of poetic sketches of people who are supposed to have lived and died in the imaginary town of Spoon River, Illinois. As the characters speak from their graves in the cemetery, they reveal their real natures. Here George Gray comments on his own monument.

I have studied many times
The marble which was chiseled for me—
A boat with a furled sail at rest in a harbor.
In truth it pictures not my destination
But my life.   5
For love was offered me and I shrank from its disillusionment;
Sorrow knocked at my door, but I was afraid;
Ambition called to me, but I dreaded the chances.
Yet all the while I hungered for meaning in my life.
And now I know that we must lift the sail   10
And catch the winds of destiny
Wherever they drive the boat.
To put meaning in one's life may end in madness,
But life without meaning is the torture
Of restlessness and vague desire—   15
It is a boat longing for the sea and yet afraid.

"George Gray" from *Spoon River Anthology* by Edgar Lee Masters, and reprinted by permission of his estate.

◇◇

FOR UNDERSTANDING

1. What was the carving on George Gray's monument intended to symbolize? What do the boat and the sea stand for? Why was the boat represented in the harbor with furled sail?

2. How does George himself interpret the monument? What was his attitude toward life while he was living? How would he live differently if he were to have another chance?

3. Explain the metaphor or poetic comparison suggested in lines 10–13. What is compared to a boat? What are the winds that drive it? How can one "lift the sail"? Give the meaning of the last four lines in your own words.

EDGAR LEE MASTERS (1869–1950)

Edgar Lee Masters was born in Kansas, but spent his boyhood in Illinois not far from the Spoon River, which he later made famous in his poetry. Encouraged by one of his high-school English teachers, Masters read widely in all types of literature and later at Knox College, Illinois, developed a taste for foreign languages, particularly Greek. He published a few poems which attracted little or no attention and then began the practice of law in Chicago. He did not lose his interest in writing, however, and at the suggestion of a friend he read the *Greek Anthology*, a collection of brief poetic sketches. Using this idea, he wrote the *Spoon River Anthology*, a collection of sketches which are the confessions after death of some two hundred men and women of a small Midwest town. The publication of this book produced a furore in literary circles and established Masters' reputation. Described as "broad-shouldered and of athletic build, having the earmarks of his profession and none of the mannerisms ascribed to poets," he was an interesting figure in the literary world of New York City where he lived for many years. One of his best works is his sympathetic biography of his poet friend—*Vachel Lindsay, A Poet in America*. His autobiography, *Across Spoon River*, is a remarkable commentary on his life and times.

❖❖❖❖❖

Lucinda Matlock

EDGAR LEE MASTERS

Lucinda Matlock who was a pioneer in Spoon River has a message for modern Americans.

I went to dances at Chandlerville,
And played snap-out at Winchester.
One time we changed partners,
Driving home in the moonlight of middle June,
And then I found Davis.   5
We were married and lived together for seventy years,
Enjoying, working, raising the twelve children,
Eight of whom we lost
Ere I had reached the age of sixty.
I spun, I wove, I kept the house, I nursed the sick,   10
I made the garden, and for holiday
Rambled over the fields where sang the larks,
And by Spoon River gathering many a shell,
And many a flower and medicinal weed—

"Lucinda Matlock" from *Spoon River Anthology* by Edgar Lee Masters, and reprinted by permission of his estate.

Shouting to the wooded hills, singing to the green valleys.   15
At ninety-six I had lived enough, that is all,
And passed to a sweet repose.
What is this I hear of sorrow and weariness,
Anger, discontent, and drooping hopes?
Degenerate sons and daughters,   20
Life is too strong for you—
It takes life to love Life.

THE GOOD LIFE IN SPOON RIVER

1. What kind of person was Lucinda? What is revealed about her personality in the first five lines of the poem? What natural pleasures did she enjoy? How did she meet the responsibilities and sorrows of life? How did she regard death?

2. Why does Lucinda refer to her descandants as *degenerate?* What does she find lacking in them? Explain the meaning of the last two lines.

3. Contrast Lucinda's attitude toward life with that of George Gray while he was alive. How well did her life fit his later philosophy?

A WOMAN'S WORLD

1. Compare the life of a woman of Lucinda Matlock's time with the life of a woman today. Which would require greater courage and energy? In which is there greater opportunity for service? What advantages do you see in each? Which do you think would be more satisfying?

2. What do you think Lucinda would be like if she were alive today? What hardships would she be spared? How would she find pleasure and recreation? How could she use her talents and her energy? Do you think she would have been happy in today's world?

In Flanders Fields

JOHN McCRAE

This is the poem that made the red poppy of Flanders the symbol of remembrance for soldiers who served in World War I. The British and Belgians made their first resistance against the Germans in the fields of Flanders in 1914. The casualties were great. In a second battle a year later, Colonel McCrae observed that Nature had laid her healing hand upon the military cemeteries. Wild red poppies were growing between the rows of white

"In Flanders Fields" by John McCrae. Reprinted by permission of D. E. Kilgour.

crosses *that marked the graves of the dead.* Colonel McCrae *expressed the thoughts that occurred to him there from the point of view of the dead soldiers.*

EWING GALLOWAY

In Flanders fields the poppies blow
Between the crosses, row on row,
    That mark our place, and in the sky,
    The larks still bravely singing, fly,
Scarce heard amid the guns below.   5

We are the Dead. Short days ago
We lived, felt dawn, saw sunset
    glow,

Loved, and were loved, and now we lie
    In Flanders fields.

Take up our quarrel with the foe!   10
To you from failing hands we throw
    The torch; be yours to hold it high!
    If ye break faith with us who die
We shall not sleep, though poppies grow
    In Flanders fields.   15

FOR APPRECIATION

1. What details made you aware of the dramatic contrast between the natural beauty of the scene and the tragedy of war? What joys of living are mentioned to make you feel the sacrifice of the dead soldiers?

2. Explain the symbolism in the third stanza. What do you think is meant by the torch? To whom is the challenge ad-

dressed? How can the torch be held high? Who is "the foe"? Do you think it is necessarily a particular enemy, or could it be interpreted to mean a general type of danger?

THE POET'S CRAFT

In this poem John McCrae used an intricate poetic pattern called a *rondeau*. A rondeau uses only two rhymes throughout the poem. Here they are words to rhyme with *blow* and words to rhyme with *sky*. How are they arranged? (Use the method for showing a rhyme scheme described in the questions following "Yet Do I Marvel" on page 241.) A rondeau also makes use of a refrain. What is the refrain in this poem? Though a rondeau is a difficult form to use, John McCrae did not sacrifice meaning to form. The delicate melody serves only as a suitable setting for the thought.

1. Notice that the sentences are not twisted to make the rhyming words come at the end of the line. Show that each word fits the meaning and falls naturally in the right place.

2. Point out instances where the poet carried the thought over into the middle of the next line to keep the rhyme from being too pronounced.

3. Notice how the refrain is woven smoothly into the thought of the poem so that it does not seem to be tacked on for the sake of form or sound.

JOHN McCRAE (1872–1918)

John McCrae's fame as a writer rests almost entirely upon the single poem, "In Flanders Fields," described by one critic as "the most famous set of verses written in English during the Great War." A physician of Montreal, McCrae enlisted as a medical officer in the Canadian Army and served as a lieutenant-colonel in charge of medicine at Boulogne. "In Flanders Fields" was written during the second battle of Ypres and was first published anonymously in an English magazine, *Punch*. McCrae's death of pneumonia occurred in France in 1918.

◇◇◇◇◇

The Purple Cow

GELETT BURGESS

These four lines of pure nonsense are among the most frequently quoted stanzas of American verse.

I never saw a Purple Cow,
I never hope to see one;
But I can tell you, anyhow,
I'd rather see than be one.

"The Purple Cow" from *Burgess Nonsense Book* by Gelett Burgess, published by Liveright Publishing Corp., and used with their permission.

◇◇◇

FOR ENJOYMENT

1. How would you explain the popularity of this rhyme? What ridiculous picture does it suggest?

2. Using the same rhythm and rhyme scheme try composing a stanza of nonsense verse. Make a class collection of favorite humorous verse. Include some limericks in your collection.

GELETT BURGESS (1866–1951)

There seems to be little in Gelett Burgess' background to account for his successful career as a humorist. He was born in Boston and was graduated from the Massachusetts Institute of Technology. For three years after he left college he worked as a draftsman for the Pacific Railway. Later he was an instructor of topographical drawing at the University of California.

After he left the university Mr. Burgess became interested in a small magazine called the *Wave*, to which he contributed humorous verse. Later he helped to launch the *Lark*. It was in the first issue of the *Lark* that "The Purple Cow" originally appeared. Since then it has been reprinted countless times. Although he wrote successful novels and mystery stories, Burgess is best known as a humorist. One of his amusing books is *Why Men Hate Women*.

❖❖❖❖❖

Experience

DOROTHY PARKER

Experience taught Dorothy Parker to classify men according to three interesting types.

Some men break your heart in two,
Some men fawn and flatter,
Some men never look at you;
And that cleans up the matter.

❖❖

FOR ENJOYMENT

1. What makes this poem humorous? Why are the three classifications obviously ridiculous? How do they reflect a very prejudiced and personal point of view? Does the poem tell you anything about men, or does it reveal something about women?

2. Read the poem substituting the word *girls* for *men*. Is it equally true from a different point of view? What kind of person is the speaker in each case? What age do you think the speaker is?

DOROTHY PARKER (Born 1893)

Dorothy Parker was born in West End, New Jersey, and was educated in private schools in New Jersey and New York. While she is best known for her clever and witty light verse, she has also written exceptionally fine short stories and successful motion picture scenarios. In 1929 she won the O. Henry Memorial Prize for "Big Blonde," probably her most famous story.

Among her volumes of poetry are *Enough Rope*, *Death and Taxes*, and *Not So Deep As a Well*.

Men

DOROTHY PARKER

Judging from the number of poems Dorothy Parker has written about men, one is forced to conclude that she must have spent considerable time and thought studying the subject. However, if you are romantically inclined you will probably be unwilling to accept her evaluation.

They hail you as their morning star
Because you are the way you are.
If you return the sentiment,
They'll try to make you different;
And once they have you, safe and sound,
They want to change you all around.

Your moods and ways they put a curse on;
They'd make of you another person.
They cannot let you go your gait;
They influence and educate.
They'd alter all that they admired.
They make me sick, they make me tired.

FOR ENJOYMENT

1. What particularly annoying inconsistency in men's behavior is Dorothy Parker complaining about? How much truth do you think there is in what she says?

2. Do you think that the tendency to make over other people is confined to men, or are women equally guilty?

Résumé

DOROTHY PARKER

This satirical poem is addressed to the chronic complainer who can find nothing worth living for. You will see that Dorothy Parker has little sympathy for the type.

Razors pain you;
Rivers are damp;
Acid stains you;
And drugs cause cramp.

Guns aren't lawful;
Nooses give;
Gas smells awful;
You might as well live.

FOR APPRECIATION

1. How can you tell that this poem is to be taken as light satire? What marks the comments about the various methods of committing suicide as too trivial to be taken seriously?

2. To say that "Rivers are damp" is to make an obvious understatement. Rivers are decidedly *wet*. To someone contemplating suicide they would be more than wet. Point out other examples of humorous understatement.

3. What reason for staying alive does the poet suggest to the disgruntled person? Why is it obviously ridiculous?

❖❖❖❖❖

For Broader Understanding

1. What are the most common ornaments of poetry by which we distinguish it from prose? Explain the difference between true *poetry* and mere *verse*.

2. You have just been reading a number of famous *modern* poems. Thinking them over, how would you sum up the differences between modern and traditional poetry, that is, poetry by such American writers as Longfellow, Emerson, and Whittier? In your answer consider the choice of language, the style (conversational or formal?), and the subject matter.

3. Name four poems which in your opinion bring out American ideals, or reveal typical American attitudes. For each, tell what the attitude or ideal is and explain how it is brought out in the poem. Give proof that the subject you are discussing really is typical of Americans.

4. Think over the poems you have read which express a certain philosophy, or outlook on life, held by the author. It can be on some deep, weighty matter, or on something comparatively trivial. Choose two of these which made a strong impression on you—whether because you emphatically agree, or because you think the author is mistaken. For each poem, give reasons in support of or in opposition to the author's point of view.

5. Different poems appeal to different people—although among readers of broad experience there is fairly general agreement as to which poems are "good." Decide which two or three poems in this section of the book stand out most prominently in your memory. Then try to determine what feature of each poem made the strongest impression on you. It may be a strikingly original way of saying something, or it may be the tuneful way some thought is expressed. For fun, in class discussion compare your choices to those of other students, and see whether the class can agree on its own list of "best" modern poems.

SPEAKING AND LISTENING
   ACTIVITIES

1. Your teacher may wish to ask each student to bring one poem (not in the textbook) to read to the class. To do a good job, select a poem you especially like—for instance, because of its ideas, music, form, or humor. You should practice reading it aloud beforehand.

2. There are many good recordings of poems read by their authors or by professional readers. If any are available, play them in class. Notice how the reader keeps the rhythm of the poem without making it "sing-song."

3. Carl Sandburg is one of the most widely known of modern poets. Find and read a number of his poems that are not in this text. Read also several discussions of his poetry. From these, and from your own acquaintance with his poems, form an opinion of *his aims as an author* and *his ideas*

about American life. Make a report to the class on this topic, and read aloud a poem by Sandburg which you especially like.

WRITING ORIGINAL POEMS

1. As a class project, try writing an imitation of one poem you have studied. For instance, imitate Sandburg's "Chicago" in a free-verse poem characterizing your own city or town. Or imitate Edgar Lee Masters' brief sketches of people, choosing some familiar "character type"—for example, some particular type of student often met in high school. Make up a name for him, and in the poem make him as real as possible. In the actual writing, after the class has chosen a subject appoint one student to write lines of verse or brief descriptive bits on the blackboard as various students suggest them. Then arrange and combine these into a completed poem.

2. Some students may want to try to write an original poem, either humorous or serious. A simple *scene* or *situation*, an *idea*, a *person*, or *something you don't like* are topics that may inspire a poem. Try to use some striking comparisons, and make the sound suggest the mood or sense of the poem.

FOR FURTHER READING

Joseph Auslander and Frank E. Hill, editors, *The Winged Horse* (Doubleday). Great poets of all ages—and poetry itself—are the subjects of this book. The student who likes to read but thinks he "doesn't care for poetry" will find it fascinating.

Stephen Vincent Benét, *John Brown's Body* (Rinehart). In a novel told in poetic form, one of America's famous poets gives the adventures of several people during the War Between the States.

Robert Frost, *Complete Poems of Robert Frost* (Holt). Students will enjoy poems like "Mowing," "The Pasture," and "The Tuft of Flowers."

Max T. Hohn, editor, *Stories in Verse* (Odyssey). This is an excellent collection

of short narrative poems. Mr. Hohn also points out details about the poet's craft in a way that much increases the reader's enjoyment.

Edgar Lee Masters, *Spoon River Anthology* (Macmillan). Sometimes grim and tragic, these famous "epitaphs" uttered by the people buried in the Spoon River cemetery give a frank picture of some Americans.

F. O. Matthiessen, editor, *The Oxford Book of American Verse* (Oxford). A brilliant critic has chosen these examples of modern poetic art.

Edwin Arlington Robinson, *Collected Poems of Edwin Arlington Robinson* (Macmillan). Most students will enjoy Robinson's brief portraits of the people in his imaginary "Tilbury Town."

Louis Untermeyer, *The Forms of Poetry* (Harcourt). In a highly readable little book, Mr. Untermeyer explains the technical details of poetry and gives examples.

Louis Untermeyer, editor, *Modern American Poetry* (Harcourt). In this anthology Mr. Untermeyer presents some well-known poems and discusses each writer.

Here are more volumes of poetry to enjoy.

Franklin P. Adams, editor, *Innocent Merriment* (Garden City) and *The Melancholy Lute* (Viking), a collection of Adams' own verse.

William Rose Benét, *With Wings As Eagles: Poems and Ballads of the Air* (Dodd).

Countée Cullen, *On These I Stand* (Harper).

Rolfe Humphries, editor, *New Poems by American Poets* (Ballantine).

Vachel Lindsay, *Johnny Appleseed and Other Poems* and *Collected Poems* (Macmillan).

Edna St. Vincent Millay, *Renascence and Other Poems* (Harper).

Ogden Nash, *The Face Is Familiar, Parents Keep Out*, and *Versus* (Little).

Dorothy Parker, *Not So Deep As a Well* (Viking).

Lew Sarett, *Slow Smoke* (Holt).

Sara Teasdale, *Collected Poems* (Macmillan).

A FREE PEOPLE
BUILDS A NATION

Through literature you can gain an understanding of a nation and its people that you can acquire in no other way. No doubt your study of history has given you considerable knowledge about America's great men, her political parties, her wars, and her industrial development. All these matters are of great importance, of course. But your understanding of America's past is incomplete if you know only historical facts. You need also to understand the motives, ideals, and emotions of those who took part in the various events.

By reading the literature of America from the beginning we can see, bit by bit, the characteristics of our people being formed—as one watches the building of a house, or the day by day growth of a flower. It was through their experiences—fighting for their liberty, building new towns and cities, crossing the great plains in covered wagons and then spanning them with railroads—that our ancestors came to be different from the English or the French. The thoughts they had as they did these things have come down to us in the songs, poems, and public speeches that make up most of our early literature.

We can "relive" the experiences of earlier Americans not only *through their own writings* but *through books written by modern Americans.* Present-day authors can realize, by their study of old records like newspapers, diaries, and letters, what it felt like to establish a home in Massachusetts; or to shiver with cold in General Washington's camp at Valley Forge, waiting for spring to come. A good author has the imagination and skill to invent details which will illustrate the facts he has learned. He can *dramatize* for us the information he has gathered—can make us understand it in a way we were unable to understand it before. With the help of such authors we can re-create past periods of history in our own minds.

There are particular periods and movements in our history which have been more productive of literature than others—movements which stir the imagination because they are the ones that had most to do with developing our typical American attitudes. One such movement was the fight of the earliest settlers to win a foothold in the wilderness. Another was the struggle against British tyranny which was begun by thirteen little colonies—and was finished by thirteen free and independent states. Still another was the long, slow, irresistible migration in search of new homes and a better life, always in one direction—west.

In the following pages you will find literature which illustrates these and other periods of our past history. You can "see" and live the events that hammered and molded us. By realizing how America was made, you will know better what America is. That knowledge will increase your pride in American traditions and ideals.

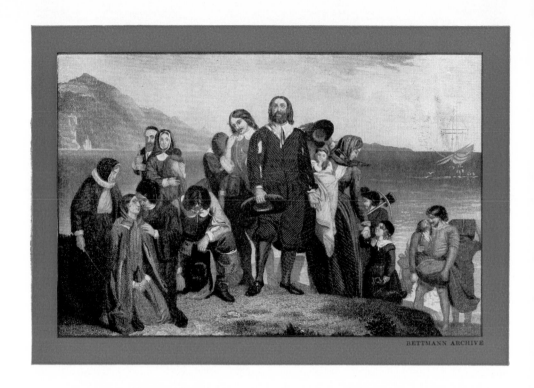

FOOTHOLD IN THE WILDERNESS

Colonial America—As Seen by Modern Writers

As modern writers look back at American history, the first important movement that captures their imaginations is the growth of colonies along the eastern coast of our continent. First came the Virginia settlement, then the Pilgrims in Massachusetts, then others until there were thirteen in all. In poem and story the authors represented here will help you to "relive" that early time. You will find that selections like "Croatan" and "The Lady of the Tomahawk" express, more fully than mere historical records do, the feelings of the first hardy adventurers—their love of the mysterious new land, their constant expectation of hearing the war-whoop of attacking Indians, their sense that they were beginning a strange, untried kind of life. Realizing that the great nation of America was eventually to develop out of the colonies, present-day authors naturally look for typical American characteristics in the colonists. Stephen Vincent Benét's *Western Star* shows that the early voyagers to our shores came for a variety of reasons. Among them were idealism; love of adventure; a desire for easy wealth; and distaste for the conditions they had known in the old country. But all these different motives had one thing in common, the urge *to assert oneself, to better oneself.* Perhaps this hopefulness and vigor is the most valuable part of our heritage from the first settlers in the American wilderness.

Look What You Did, Christopher!

OGDEN NASH

*Mr. Nash's thumbnail sketch of how America began is an appropriate intro-
duction to the Colonial period. These stanzas from his poem are a humorous reminder of facts everybody knows—that America was discovered almost
by accident, and that immigrants afterward flocked to the new land in such
numbers that finally they constituted a full-sized nation.*

In fourteen hundred and ninety-two
Somebody sailed the ocean blue.
Somebody borrowed the fare in Spain
For a business trip on the bounding main.
And to prove to people, by actual test, 5
You could get to the East by traveling
  West.
Somebody said, Sail on! Sail on!
And studied China and China's lingo,
And cried from the bow, There's China
  now!
And promptly bumped into San Do-
  mingo. 10
Somebody murmured, Oh dear, oh dear!
I've discovered the Western Hemisphere.

And that, you may think, my friends, was
  that.
But it wasn't. Not by a fireman's hat.

Well enough wasn't left alone, 15
And Columbus was only a cornerstone.
There came the Spaniards,
There came the Greeks,
There came the Pilgrims in leather breeks.
There came the Dutch, 20
And the Poles and Swedes,
The Persians, too
And perhaps the Medes,
The Letts the Lapps and the Lithuanians,
Regal Russians, and ripe Roumanians.
There came the French 26
And there came the Finns,
And the Japanese
With their friendly grins.
The Tartars came, 30
And the Terrible Turks—
In a word, humanity shot the works.
And the country that should have been
  Cathay
Decided to be
The U. S. A. . . . 35

◇◇

FOR UNDERSTANDING

1. In the first section of the poem, point
out two statements that are based on fact
but are humorous because of the absurd
way they are expressed. Point out one example of humor in the second section which
you particularly like.

2. From reading the poem one might
suppose immigration to America began at
once after Columbus' voyage. How long
was it, in fact, before permanent settlements were made? How does the second
section convey the idea that immigrants
came in great numbers, swelling our country's population very rapidly? What nationalities are named in the poem that did
not actually come to America, or came only
in very small numbers? Why did the poet
include these?

3. History textbooks usually say Columbus was trying to reach India, but in this poem he is trying to reach China. The explanation is that in Columbus' time "India" was a name loosely applied to all parts of the Orient. Look up and explain the word "Cathay." Where is San Domingo? What continents are included in the Western Hemisphere?

4. Explain how *both* sections of the poem suggest that Columbus would be surprised to know what he had done.

OGDEN NASH (Born 1902)

One of America's most original humor-ists, Ogden Nash has been publishing verse in magazines for over twenty years. The titles of two of his books—*Free Wheeling,* and *Hard Lines*—suggest his happy independence of ordinary rules of poetry. He constantly uses slang; he makes wild puns; and he is likely to rhyme "tarantulas" with "Los Angeles." If he feels like it, he will produce a long hit-or-miss line that doesn't have any meter at all—but the next line manages somehow to overtake it, and to come up with a rhyme. Mr. Nash seems able to write on any subject in the world, and his many "fans" are delighted that his material is inexhaustible.

◇◇◇◇◇

CROATAN

JIM KJELGAARD

The "lost colony" of Roanoke Island is one of the unsolved mysteries of American history. The island is off the coast of what is now North Carolina. Sir Walter Raleigh sent 117 settlers there under John White in 1587. Governor White's own granddaughter, Virginia Dare, was the first English child born in America. White sailed back to England for further supplies and equipment, but when he returned in 1591 the colonists had completely disappeared, leaving only the single word "Croatan" carved on a tree. Some people believe they went away with a friendly tribe of Indians, for later settlers found a mixed people living inland who called themselves Croatans.

The following story is an imaginative guess as to what happened to little Virginia Dare and the rest of the Roanoke colony. In making his guess, the author has kept in mind the mixed attitudes of the first white men in America —those who expected easy wealth, those who were homesick for England, and those who fell in love with the rich, fertile New World.

Flight after flight of little green-winged teal dipped out of the sky to settle on the slough.[1] Their flapping wings churned the water into a froth, and those already on the slough scarcely moved aside as others sought to enter. It seemed, Tom Weston thought, that there was no water

"Croatan" from *Buckskin Brigade* by Jim Kjelgaard, copyright, 1947, by Jim Kjelgaard. Reprinted by permission of Holiday House.

[1] SLOUGH (sloo)—A marshland creek.

at all, but only successive layers of teal, with the final row of bobbing heads and restlessly moving wings on top. But newcomers always found a place.

The teal were harbingers of cold weather. Last year their vanguard had arrived on the fifteenth of October, two months after Governor White had sailed to England—supposedly to return within nine months with more people and more things for them to work with. Not that there was any real need of that. If a hundred men and a dozen women couldn't support themselves on an island like this, then only the Lord could help them.

When the colonists had first arrived, they had expected both to be welcomed and to find plentiful stores waiting. But the savages who inhabited this Roanoke Island—or at least came to it whenever they aroused enough ambition to paddle —had destroyed or carried off the stores and killed the fifteen men left to guard them. That had been an unpleasant shock to the men and women who had landed on this island fifteen months ago, in the year of Our Lord, 1587. And that shock was their principal trouble.

Well, maybe it wasn't. Most of them had listened to glowing tales of great wealth and easy living when they had embarked for this new colony of Virginia. Everything, they had been told, would be waiting for them and they had only to lift a hand now and again in order to ensure themselves a richer and finer life than they had ever known before. Because nothing had been waiting for them, and there had been no one to tell them exactly what to do, they didn't even want to lift that hand.

A great horde of teal swooped down and somehow crowded in among those on the slough. There was a mighty quacking gabbling, and Tom rose suddenly from the log behind which he had been crouching. As he did so his right hand was whirling a crude, homemade bolo [2] —four buckskin thongs attached to holes in pierced shells. There was a deafening roar of wings, and an immense splashing to the water. The bolo sailed into a veritable horde of ducks, and when it dropped to the slough five of the little teal were entangled in its serpentine coils. Tom waded out to retrieve his kill, dropped them behind the log on top of the twenty-three he had already captured, and again concealed himself until the settling teal came in closer.

He lay indolently, letting the sun caress his back and warm his legs. Of course that warm sun wouldn't last very long; frost would follow the teal within six weeks. When the great black-necked, white-throated geese appeared you could be certain that frost would come almost within a day. It didn't make much difference. There were no crops to kill because those who should have been planting had instead passed their time on the shore watching for the ship from England. When that came there would be no need of crops because there would be food in plenty.

What the colonists should have known, but did not, was that the ship wasn't coming. It was impossible to look across the Atlantic Ocean and see that Elizabeth's England was again at war with Spain. John White had said that he would be back and the colonists had been watching for him since spring. Now it was October, and the earliest a ship could come was next April or May. No captain cared to risk his sailing vessel in the Atlantic while it was lashed by storms.

If only the colonists would work, and look to that which was all about them for their own salvation! But they would

[2] BOLO—An Indian weapon used as a kind of lasso.

not, and now their confusion and hopelessness would be multiplied tenfold. Ananias Dare, son-in-law of John White, husband of Eleanor, and acting governor of the colony while John White was away, had died yesterday. He had done as well as he could, but Ananias had been ailing for the past six months and a sick man could not carry out his own orders. Now that he was gone, and no authority reigned, there was bound to be bickering. All most of the colonists could think of was getting back to England, and the fool ideas they had for getting there. . . .

Tom rose to throw his bolo again, and added three more ducks to his catch. He could stay here all day, and all tomorrow, and the colony could still eat all the ducks he was able to catch. But somebody had to hunt, and they depended on him because he was better equipped than any other to get along in this new land. He had been self-supporting since he was eight, when his father had been cast into debtor's prison. Some of the methods he had employed in order to eat had proved useful, if not lawful. He had poached many a rabbit and grouse from manor estates and taken many a trout from the gentry's streams. He'd been tinker, pedlar, and vagabond, by turn. But fortunately he had become a cobbler's apprentice in London when John White stopped in to be fitted for a new pair of boots. Tom had listened, wide-eyed and openmouthed, while White spoke of the second Virginia colony that Sir Walter Raleigh was organizing. Offered an opportunity to join, Tom had signed on two minutes later.

And, somehow, the land was all John White had said it was and very much more. Where, in England, could you stop at a slough and kill as many ducks as you wished? Where in England, outside your own guild and social circle, could you consider yourself equal to any other man? Where could you walk anywhere at all, and be warned away by no keeper or bailiff? This Virginia had something England never would have. An unclothed man here, with no possessions other than those to be found at hand, was better off than—well, at least better than a cobbler's apprentice in London. Tom grinned wryly. He had been on the verge of thinking himself better off than an English lord, but he had no basis of comparison for that. Anyhow, under no conditions, was he going back. He must have been born to live a life like this. Maybe he was half savage.

But the savages got along all right. Only the wealthiest Englishmen ate as sumptuously as they did, and no Englishman was more free. The savages had the right idea. They worked when they felt like it, and loafed when they didn't. And nobody was more stealthy in a forest or more quiet in a thicket. They killed their deer, caught their fish, and even tilled their fields after a fashion. But certainly no savage would work in a London cobbler's shop from the first light of day until the last of night. That sort of life was fit only for those who liked it; probably almost any man on Roanoke would choose it in preference to what he had. But not Tom Weston.

He threw his bolo again, and retrieved the ducks entangled in it. Snatches of a hymn drifted to his ears. The colonists should be finished with the burial by this time, and Ananias Dare resting in his forest grave.

He, the hunter, would probably be branded a heretic and a hopeless savage for not attending the funeral. But he was a heretic anyway for counseling that the colonists get busy and help themselves. And it was far more important to help those living than to attend the funeral of even a man like Ananias Dare. Tom knelt, and slipped the heads of the teal through loops on a buckskin thong. Two of the fattest he separated from the pile, and tucked inside his leather jerkin.[3]

He started toward the settlement.

He broke out of the forest into a small natural clearing that swept to the sea. The huge, unwieldy skeleton of a quarter-finished sloop, made of adze-hewn timbers, was as prominent as a beacon fire on the east side of the island. Tom regarded it caustically. Simon Fernando, the pilot who had brought them over, was supervising the building of that sloop. Most of the men in the colony, who looked upon it as a means of going somewhere else—preferably back to England, but anywhere so long as they didn't have to remain here—worked on it from time to time. Tom sniffed audibly. Simon Fernando was a Spaniard, and the fact that Englishmen would listen to his plans at all was an indication of the low estate to which the colony had fallen.

Smoke from a lackadaisical fire drifted up through a wooden rack and curled lazily around three huge fish that somebody had caught. Beside them was a great pile of wild grapes, drying in the sun. Still desperately hoping that a ship from England would come, at least some of the colonists were awakening to the probability that it would not, and were starting out to gather a reserve of food.

They should have started in the spring. But better late than never. And nobody was going to starve anyway. Fish were easy to catch, there would be geese and some species of ducks all winter, and they still had three guns with which to bring down deer and bear. There were only half a dozen charges for each gun, but they could fashion bows and arrows when that was gone. The Indians killed big

[3] JERKIN—A short coat; a jacket.

game with such tackle, and anything an Indian could do a white man could do.

Tom dropped his string of ducks in the center of the square formed by the bark-thatched huts. A fresh-faced young woman wearing clothes that she had patiently fashioned from deer skins looked up from her cooking fire and smiled.

"Fresh barley bread and greens for a brace of those fowl, young huntsman," she called. "Is it a trade?"

"It is that, Molly," Tom's white teeth flashed in a smile. "Here's two of the best for you and your John."

Clutching the two teal, Molly Gibbes disappeared into her hut. Other colonists gathered around. Old Granny Desmond, who at seventy-one still hadn't been too old to try something new, hobbled over and held up a pewter mug in her stained hands.

"Tom Weston, you've been gone since afore dawn!" she scolded. "Huntin' for idle folk too lazy to work! Here's a summat to drink. The juice o' wild grapes won't touch a pint of English ale, but 'twill serve, if a body's thirsty. I've been pressin' it out all day."

"Thank'ee, Granny. And here's a duck for you. A fat one, too."

"Give it to those in need of it," Granny Desmond sniffed disdainfully.

"I'll give them where I please, you toothless old dame," Tom answered with a grin. "Don't worry, Granny; it will eat as tender as any suckling pig."

Molly Gibbes had come out of her hut and was staring at the sea. She took a tentative step toward the sloop, then walked up to touch Tom's elbow.

"There's trouble afoot, Tom, and I fear my John's temper. Look yonder."

Tom swung on his heel to stare at the little knot of men clustered about the sloop. John Gibbes, a square-jawed farmer, who was one of Tom's few friends

in the colony, was backed against the skeleton of the ship. Simon Fernando, his head belligerently lowered and his expressive Latin hands gesturing, stood directly in front of him.

Dropping the ducks, Tom strode hurriedly down to the sloop. At a softly spoken word from one of the men behind him, Fernando turned away from John Gibbes. The slow-thinking, slow-talking farmer's face was red with anger, and his thick forefinger trembled as he pointed it at the Spaniard.

"I am a freeman here, and till my land at no man's order. No Spanish sailor will provision his ship with *my* grain, governor or no!"

"And why not?" Simon Fernando purred. "Was I not chosen your new leader this very day? Will not my ship provide passage for all who have—how you say—co-operated?"

"No," Tom interrupted. "Firstly, if by chance this ship is finished, I doubt it will float. Secondly, it would hold but a score of souls. You delude the rest with false promises. You know full well our labor were better spent in making needful preparations against the winter."

Practical and true as they were, his words only angered the little group behind Simon Fernando. All of them wanted to go back to England, and they'd have been loyal to anything that promised even a faint hope of getting there. They believed in Fernando because they wished to. Even though only a dozen people might go in his sloop, those nearest Simon would be among them. But here were two who would not.

Side by side, they walked back to the village, the ex-poacher who had found a free hunter's paradise, and the former leaseholder whose only landlord now was nature. John Gibbes was a stolid, un-imaginative farmer, whose only loves had been his wife and the soil that his ances-tors had tilled for countless generations. But he had found a new soil with neither rents nor restrictions, poor and unproduc-tive though it was, and the harvest he had coaxed from it with patient skill he regarded as his rightful possession.

"So you would cling to your rocky fields, John?" Tom asked. "I could make you a hunter, if you would but try."

"Farming is in my blood," the older man replied. "'Tis all I know. Poor as this soil is, I would not change my lot."

Tom stopped suddenly. "This little island will soon become too small for Fernando's unruly crew and us. I have a plan. Meet me tonight at the little bay on the west shore. It's the bay with the three big sycamores in a line. Tell Molly I have asked you to hunt with me to-morrow."

Before the mystified Gibbes could an-swer, Tom turned on his heel and left him.

He walked to the last building, knocked softly, and when a feminine voice an-swered, he rolled the skin door aside and entered. Light streamed through the un-glassed windows to reveal in soft outline the neat interior. There were joint-stools and a carved chest from England, and English pots and kettles hung from hooks set in the stone fireplace. Fresh rushes had been strewn on the smooth earthen floor. There were traces of tears in the eyes of the young woman who knelt be-fore the hearth. She rose to her feet.

"Oh, it's you, Mr. Weston."

"Yes, Mrs. Dare. I—I just stopped by."

"You are always welcome."

"I'm sorry about Ananias," Tom mum-bled. "It was not right that he had to be taken."

"It was God's will," Eleanor Dare said softly. "How are the rest accepting it?"

Tom hesitated, then said bluntly, "They have chosen Simon Fernando in your husband's place."

Eleanor Dare nodded. "'Tis no sur-prise. Is there anything I can do for you, Mr. Weston?"

"Could I—er—see the baby?"

"Mr. Weston! You, the woods-runner, to take an interest in my babe! How long has this affair of the heart been in progress?"

"Since she was born."

"Virginia should be flattered!" Eleanor Dare laughed. "How many English girls, think you, have an admirer when they're scarce a twelvemonth old."

She went to the rear of the room, bent over a crude, homemade trundle bed, and lifted a golden-haired, chubby-cheeked child from its feather mattress. Tom shrank away.

"What! Afraid to touch her?" Eleanor Dare smiled. She held out the baby to-ward him.

"Uh—oh, no," Tom said lamely. "I just wanted to look at her. And to give her—you, that is—these birds." He pulled the two teal from his jerkin and laid them on the hearth. "And if there's aught I can do, if you need help. . . ."

"I won't forget," Eleanor Dare said soberly. "And thank you, Mr. Weston."

A round, yellow-orange moon rose to shine through the tall trees. The quaver-ing whicker of a raccoon floated softly as the call of a ghost through the darkness. From somewhere out in the forest came a shrill scream. Tom walked on, unheed-ing and unafraid. The night woods were no more dangerous than those of the day, and when a grouse clucked sleepily in a tree he paused with one hand on the hilt of his knife. Slowly he walked two steps backward, his head bent. But he had to dodge and twist about, stepping from place to place, before he saw the grouse that had clucked and seven others silhouetted against the moon on the limb of a gum tree. Cautiously he withdrew the knife from its belt sheath, and poised, grasping its tip with thumb and forefinger.

But he slid the knife back into its sheath. He had no other, and there was too much danger of loss involved in throwing it at night. Very slowly, making no noise, he withdrew the bolo. He threw that, and when it dropped to earth there was a sodden thud and a frantic beating of wings as a grouse dropped with it.

Tom picked up his game. Grouse were fine eating, much better than teal, and for a moment he thought of Eleanor Dare and her baby. But it was too late to return to the settlement now. He hadn't spent a night there in six months, anyway, because he liked the forest better. It was good to be away from people who seemed always at cross purposes and never satisfied.

Suddenly he stepped out of the trees onto a beach. The shining moon danced on the water, painting it with rich gold that little waves were trying to wash away. A raft of ducks—not teal but bigger, ocean-faring ducks—cast a shadow as they drifted across a patch of moonlight.

Tom walked to the base of a huge tree whose low-sweeping branches almost touched the water, and stooped to lift long streamers of moss from a canoe. Moss was a much better covering than almost anything else because it stayed green. Withered foliage was a certain give-away to anyone who knew what should and should not be. Carefully he laid the moss at the side of his canoe, noting each piece so that it could be re-placed, and examined the little craft that had taken so many painful days of labor.

Sixteen feet long, the canoe was fashioned from a single tree trunk, the ends of which had been shaped with adze and knife. The inside of the log had been burned out, and then scraped clean with the adze, to form a heavy but serviceable craft. An outrigger, a piece of buoyant dead log supported on green sticks, prevented the canoe's tipping even in rough water. A paddle lay under it.

Satisfied, Tom re-covered the canoe, then gathered a pile of tinder and struck a spark into it with his flint and steel. The tinder glowed, sparkled, and climbed into leaping flame. Tom added more wood. When the fire was blazing he dressed his grouse, rolled the unplucked bird in wet mud, plastered more mud about it with his fingers, and buried it in the fire to cook. When it was done the feathers would come away with the mud pack.

For half an hour he fed the fire, then suddenly stiffened in the act of adding more wood. Somebody was coming. Silently he stepped away from the fire and slunk behind the bole of a tree. His fingers curled about the hilt of his knife.

But it was John Gibbes who, a moment later, broke out of the trees and stood peering about in the light of the fire. His russet doublet, leather breeches, and coarse kersey stockings looked oddly out of place in such wild surroundings. Tom grinned in the darkness.

"It's a poor hunter you'd make, John, with those great boots of yours. You sound like a west-country ox."

The farmer started, then smiled his slow smile. "That's as may be. But I've brought a loaf of my goodwife's bread, and a bit of souse. You'd hunt a long time in your plagued woods to find the like."

"Molly's bread is more than welcome, but there's something better than pickled fish."

Tom raked the grouse from the fire, cracked the mud packing from it, and broke the steaming bird in half. He laid both halves on the projecting root of a tree, and when they had cooled gave one to John Gibbes. They ate in silence, and after they had finished Tom sat staring over the moon-dappled sea at the dark, mysterious mainland. There was a great swamp just across the water over which he gazed. But what was beyond the swamp? Well, he was ready to find out at last.

"John," he asked suddenly. "What does England have that you miss here?"

"Well," John Gibbes said ponderously, "well, kindred souls, you might say, for one. A mug of ale at the ordinary,[4] now, and friends to drink it with! There's farmers enough on this island but the land is poor, and that Spaniard fellow has made 'em shiftless. There's not a real husbandman left in the lot."

"But suppose there were a thousand farmers here?"

"They could never live on this god-forsaken land," the practical Gibbes replied.

"But there's more land beyond."

"Aye, a wilderness."

"It may be," Tom admitted. "And if it were, I would not care. But you are a tiller of the soil, and want your neighbor to be, likewise. Suppose your neighbors had red skins?"

"What do you mean?"

"I mean that these savages on the mainland cannot live wholly by hunting. I know not where they get their crops. But they must have some."

"Do you mean there may be farmers

4 ordinary—A tavern where meals are served; the dining room in a tavern or inn.

yonder?" John Gibbes asked, and for the first time there was a note of enthusiasm in his voice.

"I warrant there are. At least, I have fashioned a canoe, and mean to find out. Will you go with me?"

The sun broke over the trees, poured itself down on the water, and broke into a thousand little shimmering jewels as a breeze danced across the river in front of them. With John Gibbes, an apprehensive but stalwart passenger, Tom had paddled his dugout canoe over the water separating Roanoke from the swampland and turned north along the swamp's borders. It had still been dark when he entered the mouth of what he had known was either a lagoon or river. Now, when he scooped up water in his hand and tasted it, he knew they had come into a river.

He drove the crude craft toward the bank, where they could be ready to disembark and run into the shelter of the trees if anything happened which made such a course necessary. But it was a peaceful river, a wild and primitive place which, judging by outward appearances, had not been disturbed since the beginning of time. Trees crowded to its very edge, and trailing vines interlaced them to dangle their ends in the water. A pair of cranes, snow-white save for a smooth red crest, lumbered awkwardly out of the water and flapped slowly away.

"Tom, look you there! What is that ugly thing?"

There was a note of amazement and incredulity in John Gibbes' voice, but no fear. Tom looked at the fourteen-foot, greenish black creature that floated on top of the river. It submerged until only its little balls of eyes showed above the water. Involuntarily Tom reached for his knife, then let the puny weapon slide back into the sheath. John White, who had sailed along the borders of this land —Croatan, he had called it—had said that many strange things inhabited it. He had spoken truly!

Tom drove the dugout forward, cleaving the water with long, clean strokes of his paddle, and watching the dark, tree-fringed shore on either side. Ahead of them a little sandspit jutted into the river, and on it a herd of deer stood gazing curiously at the dugout. Their heads outthrust and their long ears alert, they stamped their feet as though in cadence to the rippling wake that curled from the stern of the canoe. A million birds seemed to call among the trees, and an unconcerned black bear watched the dugout slide past. This was a forgotten land of unimaginable plenty, a place where a man might find anything, and live forever without need, fear, or restraint.

"Tom, do you note the blackness of the soil, and how lush the vegetation? 'Tis the richness of the river silt, I reckon."

With a jerk Tom's thoughts were dragged out of the clouds and back to the passenger in his dugout. He saw unfettered opportunity, John Gibbes saw fertile land. But that was the way it should be. This land had everything to offer. It was a challenge to the man who had never known contentment elsewhere, and a promise to him who wished only to till its soil. Neither Roanoke nor England itself had that.

The river narrowed, and Tom edged the canoe away from the bank. Nothing had appeared to dispute their way. It was almost inconceivable that, in so wealthy a land, there should be no one to enjoy it. He drove the canoe around a bend in the river, and almost before he was aware of it the trees

to his left gave way to a big clearing.

In the center of the clearing was a small village of bark-thatched huts, surrounded by fields of standing corn. Pumpkins yellowed on the vine among the cornstalks. Nearer the huts were other fields that bore, Tom guessed, the new world crop which Ananias Dare had described as potatoes.

Not until then did he notice the half-dozen men who had been sitting indolently on the bank of the river. Almost imperceptibly, dipping his paddle as lightly as possible, Tom edged the canoe toward the center of the river. Attired only in breechcloths, moccasins, and necklaces or armbands, the savages had risen to stare curiously. One turned to gesture toward the village. More men and boys, even women with babies tied to their backs, streamed down to the river's edge.

"Let us land," said John Gibbes in sudden excitement. "They do not appear unfriendly."

Tom swung the canoe around cautiously. You never could tell about new people. There was always the possibility of a trick, and he had no wish to step into a trap. But none of the Indians were armed, and who gained anything without venturing? Tom hesitated another second, and then drove the canoe toward shore with long, deep strokes of his paddle.

The dugout grated softly on the river bank. John Gibbes stepped out, and without hesitation started toward a group of squaws who had stopped work in the cornfield to stare at the strange visitors. Tom followed, and the remainder of the village's population trooped amicably by his side.

Gibbes turned to him, held out a handful of the rich, black earth, and crumbled it between his fingers.

"There's naught like this in all England," he said reverently.

Tom turned to look at the forests that hemmed in the little clearing, and his own excitement leaped higher. This, assuredly, was the place for a man. He could go as far as his own strength and courage would take him, the only obstacle his own indolence. This was an unbelievable land. Probably not even Governor White had known of its existence. If the Roanoke colonists had only been brought here, instead of being settled on a tiny island shut in by salt water!

Gibbes had been kneeling in the dirt, his stolid face red from excitement and the unaccustomed effort of trying to express himself by signs. Suddenly he leaped to his feet, the moldy remnants of a fish skeleton in his hands.

"Tom," he exclaimed, "I do believe these benighted heathens are real farmers. Look! They must fertilize with dead fish; there's a skeleton in every hill of this turkey-wheat."

Tom laughed. "As I live, the savages think you're hungry! See, they wish us to go to their huts."

John Gibbes was still looking back over his shoulder as the Indians led them away. Bearskin mats were spread before the largest hut, and as they sat down, an old squaw brought bark slabs on which lay sizzling hot venison steaks. Smaller dishes contained fish, potatoes, a mixture of beans and corn, and fresh berries. The white men, sitting cross-legged like their hosts, gorged themselves until they could eat no more.

"Well, friend Gibbes," said Tom at last, "what think you of this land of Croatan?"

"If I could but find a way, I'd move here tomorrow."

"Would Molly come?"

"She goes where I go, and gladly, too."

"Yes," said Tom thoughtfully, "and Granny Desmond would come. If Mistress Dare would listen to us, mayhap some of the fools who now think of naught but England could be persuaded, too. . . ."

It was mid-afternoon when they again reached Roanoke Island. It had been a hard crossing, for even on the inland side of the island there had been a nasty little cross-chop to the waves, and an uneasy swell on the normally placid water. As they beached the dugout and pulled it up to its hiding place, Tom noted a thin, thread-like V-line of geese winging its way southward. The coming of the geese meant that storm or cold, or both, were on the way.

As they approached the settlement, a man's voice, frantic with excitement, carried to them.

"A ship! A ship! At last a ship!"

Tom stopped, felt John Gibbes stop behind him, and for a brief space stood perfectly still. The rattling hammer of a woodpecker seemed unnaturally loud. Then, again, came a joyous shout.

"She's heaving to! She's heaving to!"

On the dead run, they broke into the clearing, to see a knot of colonists gathered on the beach, staring out to sea. Sure enough, there was a ship out there, a great, war-rigged ship with furling sails. The sun winked from the brass culverins on her main deck, and the polished rail on the poop. But the flag restlessly snapping in the rising wind was the red and yellow banner of Spain!

Tom knocked softly on the door of the hut.

"Who is there?"

"Tom Weston."

"Come in."

Tom stooped to enter, and dropped the

deerskin covering in place behind him. Eleanor Dare was sitting before the fire, with the baby on her lap. The child stretched its arms toward Tom, and gurgled. There was a muffled shouting from those gathered on the beach. Eleanor Dare spoke almost gaily.

"Well, Mr. Weston, which shall it be now: more colonists to hunt for, or a return to England?"

"Neither, I think," Tom said bluntly. "That ship flies the Spanish flag."

Eleanor Dare looked searchingly at him, and then glanced down at her baby. For a moment she was silent.

"I can only suspect what that means," she said at last. "But I think a Spanish ship would not dare approach an English colony unless something were amiss."

"I'll not be a prisoner of Spain, Mistress," Tom said hotly.

"No more will I," was the cool reply. "But what can we do? This little settlement is helpless."

"John Gibbes and I have just returned from a land across the water—the place that your father called Croatan. There is safety there for us. If I send Granny Desmond and Molly Gibbes here to you, will you take all the guns and whatever else you can carry, and meet John Gibbes at the north path? He knows where my canoe is. Hold it in readiness. If the Spaniards mean trouble, John will take you to the place we found yesterday, where friendly savages will give you shelter. Will you trust us?"

"I trust you," Eleanor Dare said. "But what of yourself?"

"I propose to talk with the others; perchance I can persuade them to hide on the island until the Spaniards go."

Tom stepped from the hut and walked slowly down to the beach. Granny Desmond hobbled to his side and spoke soberly in his ear.

"What d'ye make of it, Tom?"

"Little enough, Granny. Take Molly Gibbes and go to Mistress Dare's. She will tell you what's to be done."

The waves were crashing up on the beach now, showing their white teeth and falling back again like angry dogs. Tom walked up to Simon Fernando. The big, bearded man looked at him with malice.

"So," he said, "the Adam of our little island paradise! I regret that you have no Eve to stay with you, Master Weston. Naturally, one who loves this place so much will not choose to leave it, eh?"

"Fernando, listen to me."

"Listen to you! For more than a twelvemonth we have heard you sing the praises of this Roanoke. Sing them to yourself henceforth!"

Tom mastered his temper with difficulty. "That's a Spanish ship," he said loudly, for all to hear. "Who knows whether it comes in peace or war? Better to hide until we are sure, than be prisoners."

Simon Fernando lashed out with his fist and caught Tom a tremendous blow on the cheek. Tom staggered backward, and tasted the blood that oozed from a cut lip. He looked toward the sea, and saw small boats putting out from the ship.

Without a backward glance he walked toward the forest. At the beginning of the north path he met Eleanor Dare, who carried a gun in her hands.

"You should not be here," he cried fiercely.

"I am not accustomed to being ordered about, Mr. Weston," she said with composure. "And, if need be, two can fight better than one. Granny Desmond and Molly are watching my babe, and I have been watching you. Your venture met with ill success, I fear."

The ship's boats touched land, and the murmur of many voices came from the

beach. A voice spoke loudly and authoritatively in Spanish.

"He called them English pigs and commanded them to silence," Eleanor Dare translated in a whisper. Her eyes flashed. "Spain and England are at war, and he says their great armada has already destroyed the English fleet. He lies, the rogue! Hawkins and Drake and Raleigh defeated by those lisping lapdogs? Never!"

They slipped back into the forest as a detachment of Spanish marines marched up toward the settlement and began to attack the huts with the colonists' own mattocks and adzes. There came the sound of rending bark and falling timbers. A man yelled. Another voice—a strangely familiar one—spoke in Spanish. There was a reply in the same tongue.

"That was Simon Fernando!" Eleanor Dare said contemptuously. "He said others remained on the island, and was told they could starve here. The ship must get off ere the storm strikes."

An hour later, when they dared come out of their hiding place, they found the huts in ruins and the beach deserted. The Spanish ship was already a spread of white sails putting out to sea. As they watched, a powerful gust of wind swept across her, and she heeled dangerously.

"There goes my lord Raleigh's second venture," said Eleanor Dare sadly. "Would you still have us go, too?"

"We must wait for the storm to pass,"

Tom replied, "and gather whate'er we can from these ruins. Next time, the Spaniards will not find us so easily."

"True, Mr. Weston." Eleanor Dare's eyes were clouded. "But could an English ship find us, either? God send there may be one, some day."

Tom looked to the westward, the unbounded land where there were none but them to carry Raleigh's dream.

"I can promise only this," he said gently. "There will be some to follow us, and we can point the way."

He stepped to a tree and with the point of his knife carved one word:

C R O A T A N

FOR UNDERSTANDING

1. According to the author, what became of the people of the Lost Colony?

2. What attracted Tom most to the land near Roanoke? What attracted John Gibbes? Why do you suppose most of their fellow colonists refused to follow them?

3. In 1588, the year of this story, the long quarrel between Spain and England became an open war when Spain sent her great Armada (navy) against the English. Explain how this historical fact is used in the plot of "Croatan." What do you think would later happen to the colonists who sided with Simon Fernando?

4. How are the feelings of Tom and of John Gibbes similar to the feelings of the later pioneers who pushed farther and farther west until the whole American conti-

nent was settled? Explain what message the word "Croatan" was supposed to convey to later Englishmen.

JIM KJELGAARD (1910–1958)

Mr. Kjelgaard (pronounced Kĕl'gärd) was born in New York City, but his family moved to the Pennsylvania mountain country while he was a child. As a boy he seized every opportunity to go on fishing and hiking expeditions—and in his writing, too, he deals with outdoor scenes. He has published articles, short stories, and a number of books. His story "Croatan" is from the book *Buckskin Brigade*, a series of tales which trace the history of American frontiersmen all the way to the West coast.

❖❖❖❖

Western Star

STEPHEN VINCENT BENÉT

The first permanent English colonies were at Jamestown (1607) and Plymouth (1620). WESTERN STAR is a poetic narrative about these early settlements in Virginia and Massachusetts. The brave men and women who took up a new life there developed, in their battle with the wilderness, a sturdy independence which was eventually to lead to the founding of our nation.

The following passages are excerpts from the long poem. As can be seen in the first few lines, the author keeps in mind the characteristics of LATER Americans. He finds in the colonists the same traits and habits which have become traditional in Americans and have made our country what it is.

Americans are always moving on.
It's an old Spanish custom gone astray,
A sort of English fever, I believe,
Or just a mere desire to take French leave,
I couldn't say. I couldn't really say.   5
But, when the whistle blows, they go away.
Sometimes there never was a whistle blown,
But they don't care, for they can blow their own
Whistles of willow-stick and rabbit-bone,
Quail-calling through the rain   10
A dozen tunes but only one refrain,
"We don't know where we're going, but we're on our way!"
—Bird-whistles, sleepy with Virginia night,
Veery and oriole,

Lines from *Western Star* by Stephen Vincent Benét, published by Rinehart & Company, Inc., copyright, 1943, by Rosemary Carr Benét. Reprinted by permission of Brandt & Brandt.

Calling the morning from the Chesapeake   15
To rise, in pomp, with redbud at her breast,
The whistles of the great trains going west,
Lonely, at night, through cold Nebraska towns,
The chunking of the bullfrogs in the creek
Where the forgotten wampum slowly drowns,   20
Cow-horn and turkey-call,
And last, purest of all,
The spell of peace, the rapture of the ear,
The water-music mounting into light,
The hermit thrush that is New England's soul—   25
These are the notes they hear.

Americans, what are Americans?
I went downtown as I had done before.
I took my girl to town
To buy a calico gown,   30
I traded in my pelts at Offut's store.
And then, when I came back, the folks were gone,
Warm ashes on the hearth, but nothing more.
And, if you ask me just what made them go,
And what they thought they'd find by going there,   35
Why, you can ask the horses, or the Ford,
Hauling its gipsy children through the mud,
With the wry klaxon croaking "Going on!"
And the tame rooster on the running board.
But I don't know—I do not really know.   40
I think it must be something in the blood.
Perhaps it's only something in the air.

Oh, paint your wagons with "Pike's Peak or Bust!"
Pack up the fiddle, rosin up the bow,
Vamoose, skedaddle, mosey, hit the grit!   45
(We pick our words, like nuggets, for the shine,
And, where they didn't fit, we make them fit,
Whittling a language out of birch and pine.)
We're off for Californ-iay,
We're off down the wild O-hi-o!   50
And every girl on Natchez bluff
Will cry as we go by-o! . . .

There was a wind over England, and it blew.
(Have you heard the news of Virginia?)
A west wind blowing, the wind of a western star,   55
To gather men's lives like pollen and cast them forth,
Blowing in hedge and highway and seaport town,

Whirling dead leaf and living, but always blowing,
A salt wind, a sea wind, a wind from the world's end,
From the coasts that have new, wild names, from the huge unknown. . . .   60

They landed and explored.
It was the first flood of Virginia spring,
White with new dogwood, smelling of wild strawberries,
Warm and soft-voiced, cornflower-skied and kind.
And they were ravished with it, after the sea,   65
And half-forgot their toils, half-forgot the gold,
As they went poking and prying a little way
In childish wonderment.
A handful of men in hot, heavy, English gear,
With clumsy muskets, sweating but light at heart,   70
Staring about them, dubiously but ravished,
As a flying-squirrel leapt from a swaying branch
And a gray opossum squeaked and scuttled away.
Oh, the fair meadows, the goodly trees and tall,
The fresh streams running in silver through the woods!   75
'Twas a land, a land!
                        They blest themselves and were gay.
And that very evening,
As they were going back to the anchored ships,
The savages came down on them from the hills,
Creeping like bears through the grass, with bows in their mouths,   80
And the sudden arrows flew in the goodly wood,
The first ambush, the first taste of Indian war.
They stood it and fired blind musket-shots through the dusk
But Captain Archer was wounded in both hands,
A sailor named Morton hurt, and the attackers   85
Neither hurt, nor, it seemed, dismayed, for they bore the lagging
Rattle of musket-shots disdainfully,
And melted back, like spirits, into the wood.
And there were the wounded men and the evening star,
The balmy night, the strange country, the shot arrows,   90
And it was not a dream.
                        So they went back to their ships,
And that same night opened their Pandora's box
And saw the names of their council—
                        Christopher Newport,
Gosnold and Ratcliffe, the captains of the three ships,
John Martin, George Kendall, Edward-Maria Wingfield,   95

92. PANDORA'S BOX—A box which, according to Greek mythology, contained all human ills.
When Pandora, out of curiosity, opened it, the evils escaped, and have plagued mankind ever since.
Here, the colonists are compared to Pandora because they did not know who their officers were to
be until they opened their sealed orders after the landing.   Some of the officers soon proved to be
incapable men.

And the chimera-prisoner, John Smith.
A ticklish business, for Smith was under arrest.
They would not admit him, though they were soon to use him,
John Smiths being somewhat difficult to bind. . . .

Let us turn for a moment to another figure,   100
Who, of all of them, shines with a clear steadfast light,
Robert Hunt, the minister of God,
So ill when they lay at the Downs that no man thought
He would live the voyage, yet living because he must,
Being God's servant, to conciliate,   105
Appease, soften the hearts of angry men
And show the true, calm courage of the true priest
Through the hard winter and the starving time.
He will lose the few poor books of his scant library
In Jamestown fire—aye, all but the clothes on his back,   110
"Yet none did ever hear him repine of his loss,"
And those who rail
At others, call him still "Good Master Hunt."
For the rest complained. He did not. They marveled at him.
And we may marvel, too, and, marveling, praise.   115
Peace to your steadfast heart, good Master Hunt,
And may the wild Virginia earth lie lightly
Upon the pure devotion of your name.

Now there was a month of peace and settlement,
A rich May month with each new day yet more fair   120
And the smiling, shimmering country bursting with spring,
As they went up and down, explored the waterways,
Found oysters and strawberries and turkey-eggs,
And, everywhere, the colored clouds of the birds.
They had never seen such birds, they had never seen   125
A finer river, a land more delectable.
There were Indians but the Indians were friendly.
The Werowance of Paspahegh sent them a deer,
The Werowance of Rappahannock came
With his train, all goodly men, to the waterside   130
—An Indian dandy, playing on a reed flute,
Painted in crimson and blue, with a deer's hair crown—
Oh, the fine, wild noise of the flute and the courtly savage!
It was like a masque and a stage play and yet true,
When he led them through the woods and showed them his town. 135
It was like a strong enchantment, a waking dream
And the drums in the forest said, "We watch, we watch.

96. CHIMERA (kī·mēr′á)—A fantastically shaped monster in Greek mythology. Here the word
implies that John Smith had a strange, unbelievable career.

They are white men with thundersticks but they are few."
The loops of the grapevine whispered, "They are few.
Perhaps we will fight them, perhaps we will give them corn.   140
It is hard to know. This is new. It is hard to know."

They settled, at last, some thirty miles upriver,
Where the flood was deep. They could moor their ships to the trees
Of that small peninsula, islanded at high water.
It was May fourteenth when they started to clear the ground,   145
Build the essential fort, the essential church,
And by then, no doubt, they thought themselves seasoned men.
They had lived through the voyage, survived one brush with Indians,
Found other Indians friendly and well-disposed,
They had tasted the fruits of the land and found them sweet   150
As the fair, enchanting weather that warmed their hearts,
Though the sun was hotter, now. It was with good cheer
That they got their goods ashore from the ships at last,
Stretched a sail for a church roof between two tall trees,
Saw Wingfield elected President of the Council   155
And slept on the low-lying, ominous shore.

And we would all have done better—no doubt of that.
We would not have squatted down in a fever-marsh

Just as the mosquitoes bred and the heat began.
(The Pilgrims did not—and yet the Pilgrims died.)   160
We would have known which Indians were friendly.
(Let's hope we know as much of the Martians.)
We'd not have quarreled and wrangled—with a crew
Made of ex-soldiers, fledgling aviators,
Truck drivers, furniture salesmen, drugstore clerks,   165
Machinists, workmen, a radio announcer
And a sprinkling of nice clean boys from Yale or Harvard.
We'd have known the Martian birds and the Martian beasts
And how to hunt them and trap them. We'd have known
The ways of the Martian climate and all the ropes.   170
In fact, we would have done wonders.
                              They were there.
They were there and raising a fort in the smiling wilderness,
While Newport and Smith went exploring up the river
As far as the Falls of the James—and returned to hear
The news of the sudden, breath-taking attack   175
When only the ships' guns had saved the settlement.
One moment, they had been working, and the next
The hazel arrows had rained from the thick coverts,
The Indian yell gone up.
                    And, when it had passed,
There were seventeen of them hurt, and one boy dead,   180
And again the clumsy muskets had done no harm.
They had had to run for them, stored in the dry-fats,
And 'twas hard to shoot men slipping from tree to tree.
But they'd be warier now, build a palisade,
Keep closer watch. They did so with toil and sweat.   185
But, beyond the fort were the weeds and the long grass,
The thick, primeval cover—and enemies
Who did not stand in battalia to be butchered
But crept like the forest vines.
                    It daunted a man.
Step beyond the fort—aye, but ten paces beyond,   190
As Eustace Clovell, gentleman, did one day,
Unarmed, on a pleasant Sunday—they heard him running,
They heard his voice crying hoarsely out "Arm! Arm!"
But he stumbled into the fort with six arrows in him,
Died eight days later.
                    And so it was, day after day.   195
A man would be killed or hurt or the arrows fall

---

162. MARTIANS—Looking back over the past, we can see the mistakes made by the colonists at
Jamestown, but Benét points out that if we were to form an expedition to colonize Mars, we would
probably not act more wisely, since we know approximately as much about Mars as the colonists
knew about America.

Like fierce, spring raindrops out of the smiling sky,
But, when you fired at the forest, there was nothing.
Nevertheless, at last they had their fort,
A few thatched cabins, a sturdy palisade,   200
Corn sown and growing, a tiny supply of grain,
A cargo of wood and sweet-smelling sassafras
For the ships to take home to England.
                            And when the ships sailed
At the end of June, as they must, and the last spars
Dwindled down the river, were mixed with the trees   205
At the curve of a river-bend, there was no more England.
And the men who watched were like men lost on the moon. . . .

And now, to Jamestown,
The wildfowl came, and the first cool days of fall,
And John Smith went exploring.   210
He is one of the first Americans we know,
And we can claim him, though not by the bond of birth,
For we've always bred chimeras.
                            And he was one,
This bushy-bearded, high-foreheaded, trusting man
Who could turn his hand to anything at a pinch,   215
Bragging, canny, impatient, durable
And fallen in love with the country at first sight.
For that is something which happens or does not.
It did to him.
                    You can see the difference in Percy,
Who is always the Englishman among the natives,   220
And never sheds his skin or his English ways,
A good man, an excellent colonial-governor
But not this skin-changing stepchild of Ulysses,
On fire, yes, fed or fasting, to see new things,
Explore, map out, taste, venture, enjoy, astound   225
And look, look, look with a fly's remembering eye,
A child's delight in marvels, a liar's gorgeousness,
And the patient, accurate pen that mapped two great coasts.
This is how they roast corn.
                        This is how their women are painted.
These are the birds, the beasts—oh, look and see!   230
This is a beast that they call aroughcan,
Much like a badger but useth to live in trees,
This is their beaver, big as a water dog,
This is the toadfish, swelling in the air,

219. PERCY—George Percy, son of the 8th Earl of Northumberland, was a member of the original band of colonists. Later, in the absence of the governor, he served as deputy governor of the colony.
223. ULYSSES—The hero of *The Odyssey*, which recounts his amazing voyages and adventures.
231. AROUGHCAN—Raccoon.

And here I did—oh, the marvelous things I did! 235
But the maps that I draw are true, and when I see
Without myself in the picture, I see and know.
This is their language. I will write it down.
"Kekaten pokahuntas—" and the rest,
"Bid Pocahontas bring hither two little baskets 240
And I will give her white beads to make her a chain."
And, in between, I will get men working again,
Shame the lazy, master the sulky, heave
My shoulder to the sticking wheel of Jamestown
And make it groan and turn till it grinds the corn. 245
And didn't I do it well? There is no one like me!

No, my chimera—and yet, we'll see you again,
In many shapes, before the long tale is told,
The braggarts who, somehow, carried out the brag,
The stepchildren of Ulysses, many-deviced, 250
"And it was proved to his face that he begged in Ireland
Like a rogue without a license," says Wingfield angrily.
Well, perhaps he did. I wouldn't doubt it at all.
For such things occur to chimeras—and if he did,
The people he begged from got their money's worth 255
And goggled, hearing the tale, as we goggle yet.
For this man was always alive to his fingertips.
He would not lie down and die and he will not still.
There were tears on the faces of the men sick for home?
Good God, how could men behave so, in a new world, 260
With a bay to explore, an aroughcan to see,
An Indian king or a possum to talk about?
How could one weep for the Christmases of England
When we never feasted more or had better fare
Than in the dry smoky houses of Kecoughtan? 265
How could men be sick at heart,
With a savage chief to visit and beguile,
Or a wild child-princess, bursting out of the woods,
Her train of girls behind her, shouting and screaming,
With deerhorns set on their foreheads—a Bacchant rout, 270
Led by the nonpareil, the daring child,
Who was to die a Christian and a lady
And leave her slight bones in the English earth
And her son's sons to know Virginia still,
Such being the fate.
                    And they were to meet again, 275
Years later, in England, the lady Rebecca Rolfe

270. BACCHANT ROUT—Wild, unrestrained revelry or merry-making.
271. THE NONPAREIL (nŏn'pá·rĕl')—The unequalled or peerless one. This was a name applied
to Pocahontas, in admiration of her beauty, when she came to England after marrying John Rolfe.

And Captain Smith—a strange meeting—strange and sad,
The Indian princess in her fine English clothes
And the bearded, baldish Ulysses, both nine years older
And one very soon to die as caged things will   280
Just when they seem acclimated to the cage.
When he came to see her, she turned away her face,
Would not talk for hours, talked a little at last
In her new-learned English. He must still call her "child."
She would always call him "father" and be his countryman.   285
"And always they did tell us that you were dead.
But your countrymen will lie much."

                          You hear the words
Evenly spoken, without bitterness,
Mere fact she had learned with other white men's facts.
But there is a bitter sadness about that meeting   290
And Ulysses, for once, said little.

                        He had advised
Sagely and humbly, writing to the Queen,
That the little princess be royally entertained,
For she had a great spirit and could move her people.
Well, it had been done—and there was his nonpareil   295
—The red-winged blackbird of Virginia's woods
—The young, wild child—

                    There was his nonpareil
In her fine clothes, coughing.
"Bid Pocahontas bring hither two little baskets
And I will give her white beads to make her a chain."   300
He left the room and never saw her again.
He was outward bound—to chart the New England coast
From Cape Cod to Penobscot.
Two thousand miles of it in an open boat.
And so, by incredible labors, make the map   305
That drew men's minds to New England—the laborious
Chimera, who could not look at the land and lie,
Only about himself and other men,
Who doubted gentlemen's hearts but never the goal
And, in the end, could say with a flat claim   310
Superbly boastful and precisely just,
"These colonies being, in some sort, my children."
He had none out of his body, for all the tales.
He had no fortune out of the lands he mapped,
Not even a twelve-pound knighthood—but they came,   315
Gorged on his books, believing truth and lies,
They settled Massachusetts and Virginia,
And where they settled, he had been before.

You can see why he maddened others and does so still.
But, spent and old, he believed to his last breath   320
That this was a good country.
We have had others since, and born in the land,
Who blessed it only while they could milk it dry
And, that being done with, cursed it in the street,
Though they were not at Jamestown or the wars   325
But lived more easily than men at Jamestown,
In fact, lived very well.
                    I may be wrong.
But, thinking of some well-dressed gentlemen
And well-fed ladies I have met at times
Who spent their years despairing of the Republic   330
And trying ways to beat an income-tax,
I think I can hear the comment of Captain Smith
Clear from St. Sepulchre's, the biting voice,
The huge chimera-scorn. . . .

Dickon Heron's heart was bursting his ribs.   335
He had talked with one of the men who were to sail

335. DICKON HERON—A character introduced earlier in the poem. He is a poor apprentice boy in
London.

And a knight, no less. It was too good to be true,
Though Master Knapp had grumbled about the cloak-lining.
"Aye, Sir Gilbert Hay—but who is Sir Gilbert Hay?
These farthing knights with long swords and empty pockets!   340
Well, take him the stuff—but see that you get the price
And no clipped money, neither!"
                                    He had the price
But that was not the dazing thing. It seemed the knight
Had marked him down in the shop for a stirring youth
And, being bound for Virginia, much deplored   345
That such lads must rust in London, when all men knew
The golden prizes waiting in the new land
For those with spirit. But there, 'twas none of his care.
Though, oddly enough, he had need of a trusty boy,
"Having pensioned my former fellow, a tried, good servant   350
And saved my life more than once in the bogs of Ireland,
But, if truth be told, too old for this sort of work,
Though he begged to go."
                                    Perhaps Dickon would look about him.
"I could take a country fellow from mine estate
But I've a fancy now for a Londoner   355
As brisker."
                    Dickon listened with glowing eyes
While the shrewd, remembering part of his mind took in
The shabby lodging, the splendid plum-colored hose,
The hard mouth and bitter eyes of Sir Gilbert Hay.
"If he hath an estate," thought Dickon, "I'm a Dutchman   360
And Master Knapp is lucky to get his price,
For the purse is lean—and already he smells of wine."
But it did not matter. Nothing mattered but this,
Knave or honest, he was bound for Virginia
And needed a likely lad.
                                    "Aye sir," said Dickon,   365
In the false, respectful voice that he knew by heart,
"If your worship will trust me, your worship shall have his will."
He didn't dare to wink, though he thought of it,
But his heart beat so that it almost stifled him. . . .

And the ships weighed anchor and put to sea,   370
Six from London, from Plymouth three,
A notable venture, a lusty crew
With Gates and Somers and Newport, too,
And a bold eight hundred jammed aboard
To win Virginia with spade and sword.   375
Their sails were white in the blue May air.
—But Dickon sailed with Delaware,

Nine months later, grumbling at fate,
For the gold would be found and he came too late. . . .
And then he was sick, and then was sicker,   380
And his knight swore vilely and called for liquor.
"Fine, brisk weather," the sailors said,
But Dickon groaned as he held his head
—And woke, one morning, shaken and wan
To find that he had his sea-legs on   385
And could think of dinner and not begin
To feel the sweat creep out on his skin
At the first rank whiff of the salted meat.
He was born and bred to the London street.
He had no knowledge, except of men,   390
But it served him now, and it would again
As he looked about with his sparrow's eye
At rearing billow and tossing sky,
The whipping sheet and the breaker curled
And all of the whole new, strange sea-world,   395
Thinking, "This is a venture where some will die
But I'll take some pains that it be not I.". . .

Dickon Heron looked around
His three rough acres of granted ground
And rested a moment on his hoe   400
At the end of a tobacco row.
—A queer, wild plant with a bitter leaf
And the lusty appetite of a thief,
But Master Rolfe thought it worth the trying,
And he'd try anything new but dying.   405

He was three years older as years are told,
But old for Virginia, ages old,
For he'd seen them come and he'd seen them die,
The raw men out of each new supply,
And now he was one of the seasoned few   410
That Death had given a stroke or two,
Tried with the cold fit and the hot,
With bleak starvation and arrow-shot,
And then let go, with an air that said,
"Remember me, while you eat your bread."   415

"Aye, I remember you," Dickon thought
"And shall while my bones remember aught,
Remember my first cold wintertide
When a hundred and fifty of us died
And our Governor found that an eastbound ship   420
Was the one sure cure for Jamestown pip.

And, faith, by the time that he got aboard,
There was little left of the noble lord!
And I'll remember Sir Gilbert Hay,
With his sunken eyes and his beard gone gray,   425
Calling for dice with his last breath,
The dog-wolf, snarling back at Death,
And swearing he'd leave me a thousand pound
If I saw him buried in clean, dry ground.
And he lied. And he knew that I knew he lied.   430
But I watched beside him until he died,
For do I not owe him my fortune here?"
He smiled at that and the smile was queer,
Neither embittered nor desperate
But the flirt of a sparrow's head at Fate. . . .   435

She was a sturdy ship, with her double-decks,
High-sterned, slow-sailing, chunky, hard to wear out,
Long in the wine-trade, smelling of it still,
And known for that as a "sweet" ship, meaning a healthy one.
They steered her hundred and eighty tons with a whipstaff.   440
And she'd trudged the seas for years,
Slow, roomy, durable, smelling of salt and wine,
—A housewife of a ship, not a gallant lady,
Who would groan at storms but get through them and get home,
Like a housewife plodding, market basket in hand—   445
The *Mayflower*—a common name for ships—
With Christopher Jones of Harwich for her master.
—And what he thought of the voyage, heaven knows,
His business being to sail the ship across,
Land his queer passengers somewhere and return home,   450
But that was his last voyage, though he knew it not,
For he died ten months after getting back to England,
Neither Puritan nor rogue, but the mere seaman
Who had done his seaman's task and gotten his death
And brought his ship home to sail under other captains.   455
For that is the chance of the sea.
                      And the trudging housewife
Went on with her work, and plodded from port to port
Till she met the end of every laboring ship,
Though we do not know what it was.
                      We only know
They appraised her, later—at least we think it was she—   460
And valued her at a hundred and sixty pounds,
Including fifteen pounds for a suit of worn sails.

Now she meets Atlantic, and labors in the gray seas.

And, for those aboard,
We think of them all of one stamp, which they were not.   465
There were a hundred and one of them all told
But only thirty-five from the Leyden church.
The rest were drawn from London and Southampton
And drawn sometimes, as needs must, from the sort of folk
Willing to stake their lives and seven years   470
Against a possible future and free land.
They did their best at the choosing, no doubt of that.
They chose Miles Standish, the little chimney soon fired,
Who was to be their buckler in the wilderness;
They picked up young John Alden at the last moment,   475
For he was a cooper and a hopeful youth;
But there were a number, neither saints nor Puritans,
Who grumbled even while they were still on board
At being ruled by the small band of Zion's men
And swore they would have their liberties, once ashore,   480
For the patent held for Virginia but not New England.
And, hearing them, Zion's leaders thought it well
To draw a compact, binding their own together
In a lawful government for the town to be.
—And that was to be a cornerstone, in time,   485
Of something they never visioned from first to last.
But they did not know it then. How could they know it?
They were taking emergency measures in an emergency;
They were founding Zion, not the United States.
—And the seed is sown, and it grows in the deep earth,   490
And from it comes what the sower never dreamed.

Let us count them now, the beginnings of New England.
There were thirty-eight grown men,
From Brewster and Carver, both of them in their fifties,
To young John Alden and the other bachelors,   495
Eighteen married women, three of them with child,
Twenty boys, eleven girls
(And seven of these were parish waifs from London
Or seem to have been and no one knows why they came,
But five of the seven died ere they were grown),   500
Nine servants, five men hired for various tasks,
Including two sailors who would stay but a year,
A spaniel dog and a great mastiff bitch.
And that is the roll. You could write the whole roll down

467. LEYDEN—A city in Holland. Some of the Pilgrims had settled there, seeking freedom of worship, before deciding to go to America.
476. COOPER—A man who makes barrels or casks.
479. ZION'S MEN—The Puritans, who hoped to establish an ideal community. Zion is a Biblical name for heaven or a heavenly city—that is, a city governed according to God's law.

On a single sheet of paper, yes, even the dogs.   505
—And, when you have written them down, you write New England.

So think of them through the sixty-five long days
Of tempest and fair weather, of calm and storm,
They were not yet Pilgrim Fathers in steeple-hats,
Each with an iron jaw and a musketoon,   510
They were not Pilgrim Mothers, sure of their fame.
They were men and women and children, cramped in a ship,
Bound for an unknown land and wondering.
The godly prayed, the ungodly spat overside,
The sailors jeered now and then at the pious speeches,   515
The Billington boys behaved like limbs of Satan,
And the three pregnant women walked the decks
Or lay in their cabins, wondering at night
What hour their pains would strike and what would be born.
In fact, there were human beings aboard the *Mayflower*,   520
Not merely ancestors.
               And yet there is
An unforced, almost childish sweetness about the whole
—The sweetness they could muster with their rigor,
The honey of the iron, the naïve
Devoted, confident wonder that made them pilgrims.   525
Were they sick? They staggered up to the decks and the air
And so felt better. Did the tempest break
And the ship's planks strain and leak? They braced the main beam
With an iron jackscrew they'd brought, and all was well.
They might long for the bliss of God and groan at His judgments,   530
But they brought with them butter and pease and beer
And the scurvy did not strike and the voyage was healthy. . . .

There is no time to grieve now, there is no time.
There is only time for the labor in the cold,
As we build the city of Zion, in the cold.   535
As we cast the lots for the houses, plan the street,
On the hill's slope, where the Indian cornfield grew,
For there, God be thanked, is cleared ground.
               And, a furlong away,
There is still the forest, there is the endless forest,
And we build, and as we build,   540
We stand between forest and sea as between two paws.

Now tell the tale of the second torment,
Not by fever and heat but by wind and frost,
The slow long torment of the northern god,
The god of the Norther and the knife of stone,   545

The god with the gull's beak, dipping it in their hearts.
He gave them an open winter, as if in bounty,
But it was not enough.
            They were tradesmen and husbandmen,
Shoemakers, weavers, printers, a few servants,
They were strong enough and most were used to hard fare   550
But, till the voyage, they had been living in towns.
And now they began to die.
               There was the fierce
New climate, the scanty food and the great toil
And the sickness came—not the fever of the marsh,
But scurvy at last and the sicknesses of the cold,   555
Striking impartially on ship and shore
Through the bleak first months of the New England year
When the new year lies and wails like a weakling child
In the cold cave, the dark cave, the cave of January,
And you cannot believe the earth will ever grow warm   560
Or the brooks run out to the sunlight.
                  It was a grim
Business of backbreak labor in whirling snow
In the gusty, heart-chilling rain. They could faint and die
But the wood must be cut and gathered, the fire kept lit,
And there was the time when their common house caught fire.   565
The flame did not reach the powder, for God was with them. . . .

Write it on iron,
Write it on iron and New England rock,
The story of those four months when they built the town,
For they built it with the dying and the dead.   570
They built it upon the bones of fourteen women
Who had come for life, not death.
They built it upon the bones of the friends they knew.

And her husband lived but Rose Standish was to die,
A pretty name, Rose Standish, a pretty name,   575
And her bold little man went nursing sick and dying
With patient and fiery care all winter through,
Though he had not been a Puritan,
Cleansing the filth of sickness, tending the fires,
Cooking and sweeping, making them eat and drink   580
And breathing his own quick stubborn life in them
And yet could not save his Rose. . . .

               And, when it was done,
There were four living women out of eighteen,
The colony cut in half, four households wiped out,

Wife, husband, child, and servant, four spared completely.   585
(And one was the Billingtons and one the Brewsters,
So read that fate as you will.)
                    And, of the rest,
There were nearly as many children alive as men,
Though some were orphans, now,
But the women, dead and living, had saved the children,   590
Saved all but six, saved Peregrine, born in the land,
Saved the child born on the sea and named Oceanus
And Samuel Fuller who was but a sucking child,
And the pitiful, tiny clump of houses stood
Where the Indian corn had grown,   595
And the winter broke and they looked at each other's faces,
Remembering their dead,
And the birds sang very sweetly, that cold Spring.

It is done. The dice have been cast,
The wave has gone west at last   600
That will turn back no more,
Against the painted year.
There are houses standing here
That were not standing before.

Now the long, crooked coast lies open, now the fishermen find the Banks. 605

A handful here and a handful,
A scrabble of hard-won ground
And nothing sure that they know.
The South and the North are begun,
The green corn blooms in the sun,   610
The clearings grow. . . .

End the song, end the song,
For now the flood goes west, the rushing tide,
The rushing flood of men,
Hundred on hundred, crowding the narrow ships.   615
Massachusetts begins, and Providence Plantations,
Connecticut begins, Virginia spreads out.
There are Swedes by the Delaware, Scotchmen after Dunbar,
They whip the first Quaker bloodily through the street.
Exile, rebel, men against fortune, all   620
Who are driven forth, who seek new life and new hope
As the wheel of England turns, they are coming now
To the exile's country, the land beyond the star.

618. SCOTCHMEN AFTER DUNBAR—In 1650, an army of the Scotch followers of King Charles II of
England were defeated at the village of Dunbar by the Puritan forces under Oliver Cromwell. Afterwards, many of the conquered men fled to America, seeking refuge.

(Remember that till you die. Remember that.
Remember the name of the outcast and the stranger.   625
Remember that when you say
"I will have none of this exile and this stranger
For his face is not like my face and his speech is strange."
You have denied America with that word
Though your fathers were the first to settle the land.)   630
A rolling, resistless wave of seeking men,
Settling and planting, creeping along the coast,
Pushing up river-valleys to the new ground,
Winthrop and Hooker and Williams—Father John White
Who prayed to all the angels of the Americas,   635
(For they must be there) as they settled Maryland.
There was a wind over England and it blew.
There was a wind through the nations, and it blew.
Strong, resistless, the wind of the western star,
The wind from the coasts of hope, from the barely-known,   640
And, under its blowing, Plymouth and Jamestown sink
To the small, old towns, the towns of the oldest graves,
Notable, remembered, but not the same.
This was where we planted—aye—but the corn has grown,
The corn has grown to a rustling yellow field,   645
And a trembling hand writes down,
"This year, thirty persons still living of the old stock."
Standish—Brewster—the names fade out with the wind—
The names ring fainter, the names of the first, the bold,
"This year twelve persons still living of the old stock."   650
They have gotten their children. They sleep in Burial Hill.
They sleep by the Jamestown church. They sleep well and long.
Though their seed be increased, they know their seed no more.
This last, this seventieth year,

"Two persons living that came in the first ships"   655
Of the old stock . . . the old stock . . .
There are two . . . there are none at last . . .
Of the old stock . . . the old stock . . .

And the west wind blew in the faces of Dickon's sons
And they looked to the West and searched it with their eyes,   660
And there was the endless forest and the sharp star.

◇◇

FOR UNDERSTANDING

1. The first sixty lines are from the Prelude to the poem. What characteristics of Americans are mentioned in these lines? Give illustrations of these characteristics from history or from present-day life.

2. What pleasing and attractive features of the new land were noticed by the Virginia colonists? Name two mistakes that they made in the first days of the settlement.

3. What is Dickon Heron's opinion of Sir Gilbert Hay? Why is Dickon willing to take service with him? What characteristics does Dickon have? What reasons could be given for saying that Dickon is better off, after three years in Jamestown, than when he was in London?

4. How did the Pilgrims' reasons for coming to America differ from those of the Virginia settlers? Two Pilgrims mentioned briefly in the poem are Miles Standish and John Alden. What well-known story about these two men is told in "The Courtship of Miles Standish," by Henry Wadsworth Longfellow?

5. Why does the author say, "In fact, there were human beings aboard the *Mayflower*, not merely ancestors"? What do you think was responsible for the "almost childish sweetness" in the character of most of the Pilgrims?

6. What chief difficulties did the Pilgrims have? With what season of the year does the author end his story of the Pilgrims? Explain why this is an appropriate climax.

7. Near the end of the poem the author says, "Now the long, crooked coast lies open, now the fishermen find the Banks." This is a reference to the Grand Banks, a shoal east of Newfoundland which swarms with schools of fish—and which began to be visited every year by English fishing fleets soon after the first colonies were founded. Explain why the discovery and use of the Grand Banks would have an effect on American history. Then explain what is implied by this remark a few lines earlier:

"The dice have been cast,
    The wave has gone west at last
    That will turn back no more."

8. In the line "The South and the North are begun," the author implies that he has described the beginning of both parts of our great nation. How is this true? Name three *southern* colonies of the original thirteen; then name three *northern* colonies.

9. Quote a line or two in which the author refers to the gradual dying out of the first generation of settlers in both colonies, which will leave the land in the possession of people born here.

HOW THE FIRST COLONISTS
SHAPED THE DEVELOP-
MENT OF AMERICA

1. Find and reread the passage in which the Pilgrims "draw a compact"—that is, draw up an agreement as to how the colony is to be governed. Explain why they thought it necessary to adopt such an agreement. Explain what the author is hinting when he comments, "And the seed is sown

288

. . . and from it comes what the sower never dreamed."

2. Discuss the possibility that the *motives* and the *characteristics* of the earliest settlers may have had important effects on American history.

3. The last three lines of the poem speak of *Dickon's* sons, instead of the sons of some highborn colonist. Why is it appropriate to the whole history of our nation to close the poem by referring to the descendants of a poor, lower-class boy? What valuable qualities might you expect to find in such people?

4. What hint as to the future development of America is contained in the line, "And they looked to the West and searched it with their eyes"? What reason do you suppose the author had for calling his poem *Western Star?* In answering, explain how the title is appropriate both to the earliest settlers and to their descendants for many generations afterward. It will be helpful to turn back to the early part of the poem and read the passage beginning, "There was a wind over England, and it blew."

PUTTING YOURSELF IN THEIR PLACE

Looking back to a past historical event, we find it hard to realize *what it was like then.* We read of errors made by earlier people, and feel smugly superior—forgetting that we have the advantage of "hindsight," of knowing the results of their actions. An imaginative writer of history can help us overcome our narrow-minded attitude by comparing new problems "then" with new and confusing problems today.

1. Find and reread the passage which compares the Jamestown colonists to space-travelers who have just arrived on Mars. This comparison makes us realize how strange the Virginia coast seemed to Englishmen and why they made many blunders. Why does the author imagine such a mixed crew in the space ship? What is meant by *fledgling* aviators? What corresponded to them in the Jamestown colony? What cor-

responded to the "nice clean boys from Yale or Harvard"? Explain the meaning of the line, "In fact, we would have done wonders."

2. In the eighteenth and nineteenth centuries, two much-discussed medical treatments were in use. One was inserting blood from a sick cow into the body of a human being: it was supposed to protect him from smallpox. Another was opening a vein of the arm of an invalid and draining off some of his blood: it was supposed to rid his body of unwholesome substance, so that he could regain his vigor. Both treatments were hotly criticized, and also defended. Which was right? Recently there has been much debate over adding fluoride to drinking water, with the idea of preventing tooth decay. Is this a debate between foolish people on the one side, and intelligent people on the other? How will we find out who is right?

3. Were the people wise or foolish who invested money in Columbus' voyage? Would it be wise or foolish to invest money in a rocket journey to Mars?

STEPHEN VINCENT BENÉT

(1898–1943)

Among our modern authors none seems more typically American than Stephen Vincent Benét. Most of his writing deals with America's past. He wrote of the great and small men of history. He took humorous pride in tracing one line of his ancestry back to a mythical Mexican bandit. Actually, Stephen was born in Pennsylvania of old colonial stock. His father was an army man; and while Stephen was young, the family moved from army post to army post. The boy loved it. He became well acquainted with the country itself and with its history and traditions. He had access to many old military records which he loved to pore over.

With such a background, it is not surprising that Benét centered nearly all his best writing on American history and American ideals. He published his first book when he was seventeen. Four years later, he graduated from Yale. Later he studied for a time in Paris. It was there that he wrote his famous *John Brown's Body*—a narrative poem about the War Between the States. For this work he was awarded the Pulitzer Prize. He wrote a number of excellent short stories on historical subjects, and made one of them, "The Devil and Daniel Webster," into a one-act folk opera. He planned to write a great epic poem dealing with the westward movement in America, but did not live to complete it. *Western Star*, the first section of this poem, was published in the year of his death.

◇◇◇◇◇

The Lady of the Tomahawk

ROBERT P. TRISTRAM COFFIN

As the settlements spread farther inland, they were exposed to bloody Indian raids. Sometimes the red men massacred all their victims; sometimes they took them away as prisoners. There are many early tales of white people held captive by the Indians—but none more strange than the one told here. Hannah Dustin was an actual historical character who lived in Haverhill, in northern Massachusetts. In 1697 she performed the deed described in this poem.

Hannah was a lady,
  She had a feather bed,
And she'd worked Jonah and the whale
  Upon the linen spread,
She did her honest household part   5
To give our land a godly start.

Red Injuns broke the china
  Her use had never flawed,
They ripped her goose tick up with knives
  And shook the down abroad.   10
They took her up the Merrimac
With only one shirt to her back.

10. DOWN—The soft bird feathers used for making feather beads.

Hannah Dustin pondered
  On her cupboard's wrongs,
Hannah Dustin duly mastered   15
  The red-hot Injun songs.
She lay beside her brown new mates
Remembering the Derby plates.

She got the chief to show her
  How he aimed his blow   20
And cut the white man's crop of hair
  And left the brains to show.
The Lord had made her quick to learn
The way to carve or chop or churn.

The moon was on the hilltop,   25
  Sleep was on the waves,
Hannah took the tomahawk
  And scalped all twenty braves.
She left her master last of all,
And at the ears she shaved his poll.   30

Homeward down the river
  She paddled her canoe.
She went to her old cellar-place
  To see what she could do.

She found some bits of plate that
  matched,   35
What plates she could she went and
  patched.

She built her chimney higher
  Than it had been before,
She hung her twenty sable scalps
  Above her modest door.   40
She sat a-plucking new gray geese
For new mattresses in peace.

FOR UNDERSTANDING

1. The *reality* of Mrs. Dustin's experience was hideous, although the *story* as told in this poem does not seem hideous. The Indians murdered her youngest child while she looked on helplessly. Her own act of retaliation seems ferocious nowadays, when we stop to think of it. She killed each one of the sleeping warriors with a single blow of the hatchet—silently, so as not to wake the others. Taking the scalps, for which the Colonial government would pay a bounty, was an afterthought.

Because the event happened so long ago, and because it became a hand-me-down tale which was known even to little children, Mr. Coffin has decided that it can be regarded humorously. How has he inserted humor into his description of the raid on Hannah Dustin's home? What is humorous about Hannah's thoughts during her captivity? Point out other bits of humor—including the author's choice of words and phrases.

2. Read one stanza aloud, rather rapidly. How is the rhythmic swing of the verse well suited to the humorous atmosphere of the poem?

3. Explain "the linen spread"; "the china her use had never flawed"; "her goose tick."

4. What two kinds of damage to Hannah's belongings are mentioned in the second stanza? How are both of these brought into the story again at the end of the poem? The author seems to suggest that Hannah's main grievance is that the Indians have disrupted her tidy housekeeping. How does he connect her *ability to scalp the Indians* with her *housekeeping abilities?*

FOR A SPECIAL REPORT

For a report to the class, look up additional details of Mrs. Dustin's life. The school librarian or public librarian will help you to find the information.

ROBERT P. TRISTRAM COFFIN
(1892–1955)

Mr. Coffin was a professor of English at his alma mater, Bowdoin College, which was also the college of Nathaniel Hawthorne and Henry Wadsworth Longfellow. He was a well-known lecturer and critic as well as a poet. His literary career was merely an avocation—a diversion from his teaching profession—but he wrote several volumes of verse, and in 1936 he won the Pulitzer Prize for poetry. His works include essays, some biography, novels, and an autobiography. In his poetry he creates a feeling of contentment and satisfaction with common events, the simple relations of everyday living. Many of his poems deal with picturesque Maine folk, or Maine history and legend.

Colonial America—As Seen by the Men Who Were There

The "men who were there," that is, the settlers of the early colonies, were too busy keeping themselves alive to produce a large body of literature. Their writings were most often of the kind that was directly useful—reports and records, descriptions of the country, legal and governmental documents. Equally useful were works like *The New England Primer* and *The Bay Psalm Book*, the one for teaching children to read and the other for the Sunday worship service which was so prominent a feature of New England life. Two elements, the *practical* and the *sternly religious*, are especially characteristic of Colonial literature.

CAPTAIN SMITH AND POCAHONTAS

From THE GENERALL HISTORIE OF VIRGINIA

JOHN SMITH

Pocahontas, beautiful daughter of the great Indian chief Powhatan, is one of the famous persons in early American history. In 1613 Pocahontas was held in Jamestown to insure the safety of some colonists whom the Indians had captured. Soon she became friendly with the whites, became converted to Christianity, and married John Rolfe with whom she went to England. Some prominent Virginia families are descended from Pocahontas and Rolfe.

In the following selection, written in England years after Pocahontas' death, Captain John Smith tells a story about meeting the Indian princess and about having his life saved by her in 1608 when she was a little girl. Historians are doubtful about the specific details of this well-known tale, for in his books Smith sometimes exaggerated his adventures. However, the main story—his expedition into the forest and his captivity—is true.

The next voyage hee[1] proceeded so farre that with much labour by cutting of trees insunder he made his passage; but when his Barge could passe no farther, he left her in a broad bay out of danger of shot, commanding none should goe a shore till his returne: himselfe with two English and two Salvages went up higher in a Canowe; but hee was not long absent, but his men went a shore, whose want of government gave both occasion and opportunity to the Salvages to surprise one *George Cassen,* whom they slew, and much failed not[2] to have cut of [f] the boat and all the rest.

Smith, little dreaming of that accident, being got to the marshes at the rivers head, twentie myles in the desert,[3] had his two men slaine (as is supposed) sleeping by the Canowe, whilst himselfe by fowling sought them victuall: who finding he was beset with 200. Salvages, two of them hee slew, still defending himselfe with the ayd of a Salvage his guid[e], whom he bound to his arme with his garters, and used him as a buckler,[4] yet he was shot in his thigh a little and had many arrowes that stucke in his cloathes but no great hurt, till at last they tooke him prisoner. . . .

He demanding for their Captaine, they shewed him *Opechankanough,* King of *Pamaunkee,* to whom he gave a round Ivory double compass Dyall. Much they

[1] HEE—John Smith himself, the author.
[2] MUCH FAILED NOT—Came very near.
[3] DESERT—Wilderness.
[4] BUCKLER—Shield.

293

NATIONAL GALLERY OF ART, WASHINGTON, D. C.

At last they brought him to *Meronoco-moco*, where was *Powhatan*, their Emperor. Here more than two hundred of those grim Courtiers stood wondering at him, as he had beene a monster; till *Powhatan* and his trayne had put themselves in their greatest braveries. Before a fire upon a seat like a bedsted, he sat covered with a great robe, made of *Rarowcun*[5] skinnes, and all the tayles hanging by. On either hand did sit a young wench of 16 or 18 yeares, and along on each side the house, two rowes of men, and behind them as many women, with all their heads and shoulders painted red: many of their heads bedecked with the white downe of Birds; but every one with something, and a great chayne of white beads about their necks.

At his entrance before the King, all the people gave a great shout. The Queene of *Appamatuck* was appointed to bring him water to wash his hands, and another brought him a bunch of feathers, in stead of a Towell, to dry them: having feasted him after their best barbarous manner they could, a long consultation was held; but the conclusion was, two great stones were brought before *Powhatan*. Then as many as could layd hands on him, dragged him to them, and thereon laid his head, and being ready with their clubs, to beate out his braines, *Pocahontas* the Kings dearest daughter, when no intreaty could prevaile, got his head in her armes, and laid her owne upon his to save him from death: whereat the Emperour was contented he should live to make him hatchets, and her bells, beads, and copper; for they thought him as well of all occupations as themselves. For the King himselfe will make his owne robes, shooes, bowes, arrowes, pots; plant, hunt, or doe any thing so well as the rest.

[5] RAROWCUN—Raccoon.

marvailed at the playing of the Fly and Needle, which they could see so plainely and yet not touch it, because of the glasse that covered them. But when he demonstrated by that Globe-like Jewell, the roundnesse of the earth and skies, the spheare of the Sunne, Moone, and Starres, and how the Sunne did chase the night round about the world continually; the greatnesse of the Land and Sea, the diversitie of Nations, varietie of complexions, and how we were to them *Antipodes*, and many other such like matters, they all stood as amazed with admiration.

Notwithstanding, within an houre after they tyed him to a tree, and as many as could stand about him prepared to shoot him: but the King holding up the Compass in his hand, they all laid downe their Bowes and Arrowes, and in a triumphant manner led him to *Orpaks*, where he was after their manner kindly feasted, and well used. . . .

They say he bore a pleasant shew,
But sure his heart was sad.
For who can pleasant be, and rest,
That lives in feare and dread:
And having life suspected, doth
It still suspected lead.

Two days after, *Powhatan*, having disguised himselfe in the most fearefullest manner he could, caused Captain *Smith* to be brought forth to a great house in the woods, and there upon a mat by the fire to be left alone. Not long after, from behind a mat that divided the house, was made the most dolefullest noyse he ever heard; then *Powhatan*, more like a devill then a man, with some two hundred more as blacke as himselfe, came unto him and told him now they were friends, and presently he should goe to *James* towne, to send him two great gunnes, and a gryndstone, for which he would give him the Country of *Capahowosick*, and for ever esteeme him as his sonne *Nantaquoud.*

So to *James* towne with 12 guides Powhatan sent him. That night they quartered in the woods, he still expecting (as he had done all this long time of his imprisonment) every houre to be put to one death or other, for all their feasting. But almightie God (by his divine providence) had mollified the hearts of those sterne *Barbarians* with compassion. The next morning betimes they came to the Fort, where *Smith*, having used the Salvages with what kindnesse he could, he shewed *Rawhunt, Powhatans* trusty servant, two demi-Culverings [6] and a millstone to carry *Powhatan:* they found them somewhat too heavie; but when they did see him discharge them, being loaded with stones, among the boughs of a great tree loaded with Isickles, the yce and branches came so tumbling downe, that the poore Sal-

[6] DEMI-CULVERINGS—Cannons.

vages ran away halfe dead with feare. But at last we regained some conference with them, and gave them such toyes; and sent to *Powhatan*, his women, and children such presents, as gave them in generall full content.

◇◇◇◇◇◇◇◇◇◇◇◇◇◇◇◇◇◇◇◇◇◇◇◇◇◇◇◇◇

FOR UNDERSTANDING

1. What seems to have been the purpose of Smith's journey up the river? How does he make clear in his narrative that the three companions who lost their lives had only themselves to blame? What impression is given of Smith's own conduct during the battle with the Indians?

2. How does Smith make use of his knowledge, gained as a sailor, of astronomy and geography?

3. Describe in your own words the dramatic way in which Pocahontas saves Smith from death. How is Smith of service to Pocahontas during his captivity?

4. What difference between white and Indian customs is brought out in Smith's remarks about being employed by the Indians to make metal tools and ornaments? Make a list of the details of Indian life recorded by Smith.

5. Smith apparently agreed to send Powhatan two cannons and a grindstone. Can you find evidence that Smith had a sly suspicion that he would not actually have to send these things? What did he substitute for the grindstone? Why do you suppose, after he was safe in Jamestown, he went through the motions of fulfilling his promise to Powhatan?

6. This whole narrative might have been entitled "The Many Narrow Escapes I Have Had." How many times does Smith's life seem to be in danger?

JOHN SMITH (1580–1631)

John Smith's writings are our chief source of information about the Jamestown colony, but they are not altogether accurate. We must take Smith for what he was—a brave, hardy, active fellow who was also something of a braggart and trouble-maker. According to his own stories, before he went to America he had a strange career as a soldier of fortune. He was a hero in a war between Christians and Turks, he was captured and sent to Constantinople as a slave, and he escaped through the help of the Turkish empress, who had fallen in love with him. After further adventures he got back to England in 1604.

Next, Smith sailed with the Virginia colonists. On board ship, he was accused of mutiny and was treated as a prisoner. Upon disembarking at Jamestown, the colonists opened their sealed orders and were embarrassed to find Smith named as a member of the governing council. Soon he was leading expeditions into the forest, both to learn more about the country and to raid the Indian villages for corn. After his capture by Powhatan's tribe, and his release, he was temporarily in danger of being executed because he had lost two of the men in his exploring party. However, after the Indians became more dangerous Smith was elected President of the colony because of his aggressiveness and his stout, cheerful attitude in time of trouble. It was during this time that he gave his famous order, "He who will not work shall not eat," and punished disobedient men by pouring a can of cold water up their sleeves. In 1609 he was badly hurt by an exploding bag of gunpowder—purposely set off to kill him, said Smith—and returned to England.

Smith continued to engage in colonizing ventures. He made one more trip to America, this time farther north, conducting an exploration for a company of London merchants who were interested in New World products. It was he who gave the upper coast region its name of "New England." In his later life he wrote a number of books defending and praising his own acts.

It was mainly from his own writings that Smith's great reputation grew. Nevertheless, he is one of the authentic heroes of early America.

◇◇◇◇◇

The Bay Psalm Book

THE BAY PSALM BOOK (1640) is a landmark in American literature because it is the first book, except for a brief almanac, published in the British colonies. However, its importance to the colonists themselves was of a different kind. As its title suggests, it was the hymnbook used by the entire Massachusetts Bay Colony—and therefore performed an important function in Puritan life.

The Puritan settlers felt that songs in praise of God were an essential part of divine service. At the same time they believed it would be wrong to sing hymns from any source but the Bible. Accordingly, the compilers of THE BAY PSALM BOOK made their translations of the Psalms as literally accurate *as they could.   In arranging the Psalms to fit familiar church tunes they destroyed the original beauty and dignity of the language.   Some sentences are so distorted that they require a second reading to get the meaning.*

23 A PSALME OF DAVID

The Lord to mee a shepheard is, want therefore shall not I.

2 Hee in the folds of tender-grasse, doth cause mee downe to lie:
To waters calme me gently leads (3) Restore my soule doth hee:
he doth in paths of righteousnes: for his names sake leade mee.

4 Yea though in valley of deaths shade I walk, none ill I'le feare:
because thou art with mee, thy rod and staffe my comfort are.

5 For mee a table thou hast spread, in presence of my foes:
thou dost annoynt my head with oyle, my cup it over-flowes.

6 Goodnes & mercy surely shall all my dayes follow mee:
and in the Lords house I shall dwell so long as dayes shall bee.

FOR UNDERSTANDING

1. In versifying the Twenty-third Psalm, the authors have sometimes been forced to change the normal word order of sentences. Poets often do this—but do not usually have to go to such extremes. Point out two examples of "turned-around" phrases. In the last line, "so long as dayes shall bee" has been substituted for the "forever" in the King James version of the Bible. Explain why this change was made.

2. The Psalm is written in traditional ballad-meter. A regular ballad stanza has four lines, and rhymes *a b c b*. The stressed or emphasized syllables in a ballad-stanza are as follows:

> First line—4 stresses
> Second line—3 stresses
> Third line—4 stresses
> Fourth line—3 stresses

The first *two* lines of the Twenty-third Psalm correspond exactly to this *four*-line ballad stanza, which was the poetic form best known to Englishmen. Show the correspondence by naming the stressed syllables in the first two lines. Then read these lines aloud, exaggerating the stresses.

3. In the King James Bible the Twenty-third Psalm is printed as if it were prose, but it is a very fine unrhymed poem just as it stands. For comparison, have one member of the class repeat or read aloud the King James version of the psalm, and then read aloud *The Bay Psalm Book* version.

4. State in your own words the central idea of the Twenty-third Psalm. Then explain how the early Puritans in America might have felt that this idea was particularly comforting to people in their situation.

IT'S NOT GREAT POETRY

The Bay Psalm Book is a good sample of the earliest literature of New England. Nearly all the older writings are sober and religious in subject matter. Of course they use old-fashioned spelling, and old word forms like "doth" which we seldom see except in the Bible. They are somewhat stiff and awkward, for early New Englanders were doers, not writers. Above all, these earliest writings have little beauty in them, but are intended to serve an important practical purpose—keeping the colonists united as worshipers according to the Puritan faith.

The authors of *The Bay Psalm Book* expressed their practical, rather than artistic, aim in these words: "God's altar needs not our polishing." Explain how this remark is applicable to the purpose for which they wrote their book. What does it imply as to the beauty and music of their poetry?

From what you know of Puritanism, explain how this remark could apply more broadly to Puritan beliefs about ornament and ceremony in places of worship.

❖❖❖❖❖

The New England Primer

In England the word "primer" originally meant a prayer book for the use of lay members of congregations. Later, primers of similar subject matter were prepared especially for children, to teach them to read and at the same time to give them religious instruction. The New England Primer is true to its religious ancestry. Besides the letters of the alphabet and lists of easily learned words, its contents include two catechisms. One of these was prepared by the Reverend John Cotton, the spiritual leader of Puritan Boston.

A — In Adam's Fall, We sinned all.

B — Heaven to find, The Bible mind.

C — Christ crucify'd, For Sinners dy'd.

D — The Deluge drown'd The Earth around.

E — Elijah hid, By Ravens fed.

F — The Judgment made Felix afraid.

G — As runs the Glass, Our Life doth pass

H — My Book and Heart Must never part.

J — Job feels the Rod, Yet blesses GOD.

K — Proud Korah's Troop Was swallow'd up.

L — Lot fled to Zoar, Saw fiery Shower On Sodom pour.

M — Moses was he Who Israel's Host Led thro' the Sea.

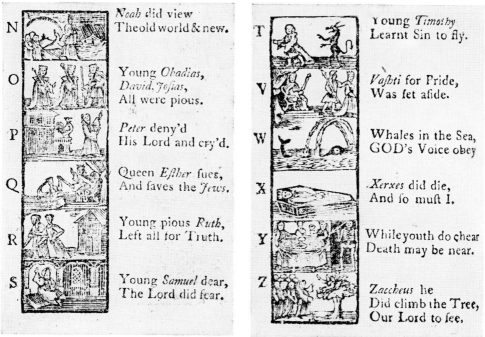

Noah did view
The old world & new.

Young *Obadias,*
David, Josias,
All were pious.

Peter deny'd
His Lord and cry'd.

Queen *Esther* sues,
And saves the *Jews.*

Young pious *Ruth,*
Left all for Truth.

Young *Samuel* dear,
The Lord did fear.

Young *Timothy*
Learnt Sin to fly.

Vashti for Pride,
Was set aside.

Whales in the Sea,
GOD's Voice obey

Xerxes did die,
And so must I.

While youth do chear
Death may be near.

Zaccheus he
Did climb the Tree,
Our Lord to see.

A. S. W. ROSENBACH COLLECTION OF EARLY AMERICAN CHILDREN'S BOOKS OF THE FREE LIBRARY OF PHILADELPHIA

Among other materials in the book are the Lord's Prayer and several religious poems.

The PRIMER is believed to have been first published in 1683, in Boston. No first edition has survived, but the book was republished more than forty times. It is estimated that about two million copies were printed. For several generations of people in early New England, the PRIMER truly was the "first" book both in religion and literature.

FOR UNDERSTANDING

1. Puritan children were given lessons in religion and morality at the same time they were taught the alphabet. Explain briefly the Bible story referred to in the verse accompanying three of the letters—for instance, M, N, and R. Point out two examples of verses which do not refer to Bible characters but still teach a moral idea.

2. Examine the crude woodcut illustrations. They show that art had not advanced very far in seventeenth-century Bos-ton. Which one reveals the Puritans' method of measuring time? Do you find any pictures of Biblical events which look more like the seventeenth century than like the time of the Bible?

3. Appoint a member of the class to bring a modern ABC book for children. In class discussion compare this book to the selection from the *New England Primer*—considering illustrations, attractiveness to young children, and difficulty of understanding the material. What changes in teaching methods do you see?

SINNERS IN THE HANDS
OF AN ANGRY GOD

JONATHAN EDWARDS

Some Puritan preachers emphasized God's punishment of sinners more than they did the love and mercy expressed in the teachings of Jesus. "Fire and brimstone" preaching was common in early New England but was less typical after 1700. However, during the "Great Awakening," a revivalistic movement that swept over the colonies in the 1730's and 1740's, some of the sermons of the famous Jonathan Edwards were even more full of warnings and denunciations than the sermons of earlier ministers. "Sinners in the Hands of an Angry God," from which this selection is taken, was so overpowering that when Edwards delivered it on Sunday, July 8, 1741, members of the congregation wept and some became almost hysterical from fear.

The God that holds you over the pit of hell much as one holds a spider or some loathsome insect over the fire, abhors you, and is dreadfully provoked; his wrath towards you burns like fire; he looks upon you as worthy of nothing else but to be cast into the fire; he is of purer eyes than to bear to have you in his sight; you are ten thousand times so abominable in his eyes as the most hateful and venomous serpent is in ours. You have offended him infinitely more than ever a stubborn rebel did his prince: and yet it is nothing but his hand that holds you from falling into the fire every moment. 'Tis ascribed to nothing else, that you did not go to hell the last night; that you was suffered to awake again in this world after you closed your eyes to sleep; and there is no other reason to be given why you have not dropped into hell since you arose in the morning, but that God's hand has held you up. There is no other reason to be given why you have not gone to hell since you have sat here in the house of God, provoking his pure eyes by your sinful wicked manner of attending his solemn worship. Yea, there is nothing else that is to be given as a reason why you do not this very moment drop down into hell.

O sinner! Consider the fearful danger you are in. 'Tis a great furnace of wrath, a wide and bottomless pit, full of the fire of wrath, that you are held over in the hand of that God whose wrath is provoked and incensed as much against you as against many of the damned in hell. You hang by a slender thread, with the flames of divine wrath flashing about it, and ready every moment to singe it and burn it asunder; and you have no interest in any Mediator, and nothing to lay hold of to save yourself, nothing to keep off the flames of wrath, nothing of your own, nothing that you ever have done, nothing that you can do, to induce God to spare you one moment. . . .

It is *everlasting* wrath. It would be dreadful to suffer this fierceness and wrath of Almighty God one moment; but you must suffer it to all eternity: there will be no end to this exquisite, horrible misery. When you look forward you shall see a long forever, a boundless duration before you, which will swallow up your thoughts and amaze your soul; and you will absolutely despair of ever having any deliverance, any end, any mitigation, any rest at all; you will know certainly that you must wear out long ages, millions of millions of ages, in wrestling and conflicting with this almighty, merciless vengeance; and then when you have so done, when so many ages have actually been spent by you in this manner, you will know that all is but a point to what remains. So that your punishment will indeed be infinite. Oh, who can express what the state of a soul in such circumstances is! All that we can possibly say about it gives but a very feeble, faint representation of it; it is inexpressible and inconceivable, for "who knows the power of God's anger?"

How dreadful is the state of those that are daily and hourly in danger of this great wrath and infinite misery! But this is the dismal case of every soul in this congregation that has not been born again, however moral and strict, sober and religious, they may otherwise be. Oh, that you would consider it, whether you be young or old! There is reason to think that there are many in this congregation now hearing this discourse, that will actually be the subjects of this very misery to all eternity. We know not who they are, or in what seats they sit, or what thoughts they now have. It may be they are now at ease and hear all these

things without much disturbance, and are now flattering themselves that they are not the persons, promising themselves that they shall escape. If we knew that there was one person, and but one, in the whole congregation, that was to be the subject of this misery, what an awful thing it would be to think of! If we knew who it was, what an awful sight would it be to see such a person! How might all the rest of the congregation lift up a lamentable and bitter cry over him! But alas! instead of one, how many is it likely will remember this discourse in hell! And it would be a wonder, if some that are now present should not be in hell in a very short time, before this year is out. And it would be no wonder if some persons that now sit here in some seats of this meetinghouse in health, and quiet and secure, should be there before tomorrow morning. Those of you that finally continue in a natural condition, that shall keep out of hell longest, will be there in a little time! Your damnation does not slumber; it will come swiftly and, in all probability, very suddenly upon many of you. You have reason to wonder that you are not already in hell. 'Tis doubtless the case of some that heretofore you have seen and known, that never deserved hell more than you and that heretofore appeared as likely to have been now alive as you. Their case is past all hope; they are crying in extreme misery and perfect despair. But here you are in the land of the living and in the house of God, and have an opportunity to obtain salvation. What would not those poor, damned, hopeless souls give for one day's such opportunity as you now enjoy!

And now you have an extraordinary opportunity, a day wherein Christ has flung the door of mercy wide open, and stands in the door calling and crying with a loud voice to poor sinners; a day wherein many are flocking to him and pressing into the Kingdom of God. Many are daily coming from the east, west, north, and south; many that were very likely in the same miserable condition that you are in, are in now a happy state, with their hearts filled with love to him that has loved them and washed them from their sins in his own blood, and rejoicing in hope of the glory of God. How awful is it to be left behind at such a day! To see so many others feasting, while you are pining and perishing! To see so many rejoicing and singing for joy of heart, while you have cause to mourn for sorrow of heart and howl for vexation of spirit! How can you rest for one moment in such a condition? Are not your souls as precious as the souls of the people at Suffield,[1] where they are flocking from day to day to Christ?

[1] SUFFIELD—Edwards preached this sermon in Enfield, Connecticut. Suffield was a town near by.

FOR UNDERSTANDING

1. Edwards' sermon is based on the doctrine of *Calvinism*—that is, on the teachings of the famous French preacher, John Calvin—which was accepted by many, though not all, of the Puritan churches. One point in Calvinistic doctrine was that the human race is so completely unworthy, judged by divine standards, that no person is able to bring about any real improvement in himself except through God's mercy and help. Find two comments in the sermon which express this point of view.

2. The sermon is designed to frighten its hearers with the fear of hell. Which passage would you choose as especially vivid and eloquent in awakening such fear?

3. Summarize in your own words the remarks which show that the sermon was a part of a revival movement—an attempt to bring about a greater earnestness in religion in each congregation.

JONATHAN EDWARDS (1703–1758)

The Reverend Jonathan Edwards was one of the most learned men in the colonies. As a boy he showed signs of scientific genius in his investigations of insects, of the rainbow, and of possible explanations for the existence of different colors. He delved into philosophical questions about the human mind and the nature of beauty. While a student at Yale, he read with understanding and delight the book *On the Human Understanding*, by the great English thinker John Locke. After his graduation from Yale, he spent further years in theological study, and eventually became pastor of the Congregationalist Church at Northampton, Massachusetts.

Edwards was a prominent defender of the "Great Awakening" against charges that it was only a mass hysteria, an epidemic of senseless emotional outbursts. He declared that the movement was "a surprising work of God" which should be welcomed. His congregation supported him, but disagreement arose a few years later when Edwards maintained that there was no true conversion to Christianity except "supernatural" conversion. Like the earlier Puritans, he insisted that no person should be admitted to church fellowship merely because of belief in God, and obedience to divine commandments; to be saved, he must have direct inner experience of God's glory. After much controversy, Edwards was dismissed from the pastorate he had held for over twenty years, and went to the little town of Stockbridge, Massachusetts, on the western frontier, as pastor and missionary to the Indians. He continued to study and write. In 1758 he was appointed president of Princeton. Five weeks later, as a result of taking the new and still very crude vaccination treatment against smallpox, he died.

For Broader Understanding

1. Explain the various motives that brought the first explorers and settlers to America, and give examples from your reading. From what countries did the settlers come?

2. Which were the earliest of the thirteen colonies? Describe the dangers and hardships faced by the colonists.

3. What chief characteristics and ideas of the early settlers are brought out in the literary selections you have read? Discuss the effect the new life in America would have on them and their descendants.

4. Give the main facts of the life of Pocahontas. What book of Colonial times tells about her?

5. Explain why *The Bay Psalm Book* and *The New England Primer* might be described as books of practical usefulness. Describe these early works of American literature.

6. What sort of ideas did Jonathan Edwards emphasize in his preaching?

CLASS PROJECTS

1. *Thanksgiving.* The Puritans originated Thanksgiving. One student may look up and report briefly on how the day was celebrated in Colonial times. Then the class may make a list of all the things we associate with Thanksgiving *in modern times.* Include sports events, and all the traditional foods.

2. *A Colonial Exhibit.* Bring books containing pictures of Colonial homes and furniture. Some students may be able to bring actual examples of Colonial tools, firearms, china, or household utensils. Include a good picture of a spinning wheel.

3. *Different Nationalities Represented in the Thirteen Colonies.* Appoint one student to draw a large map of the thirteen colonies. Class members should find out from what nation the settlers in each colony came, and write the names on the appropriate part of the map.

SPEAKING AND WRITING ACTIVITIES

The following topics make interesting subjects for reports.

The Voyage of Leif Ericson to America.

Puritan Ideas About Proper Behavior. Include a description of *stocks* and *ducking stools* used for punishment, and describe Sunday worship.

New England Beliefs About Witchcraft.

Longfellow's Poem, "The Courtship of Miles Standish." One student may review the poem for the class, and read some of the more dramatic passages aloud.

The Virginia Colonists and the Massachusetts Colonists. Give the main dates and facts concerning each settlement, and describe the ways in which the two were different from each other.

The Life Story of John Smith. Look for information on how he governed Jamestown.

The Pilgrims, and Their Voyage on the Mayflower.

Roger Williams and the Founding of Rhode Island.

Anne Bradstreet, Poet.

The Writings of Cotton Mather. Give the titles of several works of this New England author and tell briefly what each was about.

FOR FURTHER READING

GLEASON L. ARCHER, *With Axe and Musket at Plymouth* (American Historical Society). This history of the Colonial period offers a vivid and dramatic picture of the people who lived at that time.

HERBERT BEST, *Long Portage* (Viking). Young Philip Dearborn ran away from New York to join Rogers' Rangers in the French and Indian War. French spies, Indian attacks, rough and ready rangers, and good historical background make this a book for the reader who likes plenty of action.

THOMAS BOYD, *Shadow of the Long Knives* (Scribner). This novel tells of a frontiersman who travels through the Ohio country when no other white men are there. At the beginning of the American Revolution he is serving as a scout at Fort Detroit.

LE GRAND CANNON, JR., *Look to the Mountain* (Holt). Life in New England is pictured with warmth and understanding in this story of the men and women who settled and developed a northern New Hampshire town.

WILLIAM C. LANGDON, *Everyday Things in America* (Scribner). Profusely illustrated, this is a storehouse of information on everything the colonists used in their daily living.

ELIZABETH PAGE, *Wilderness Adventure* (Rinehart). A young girl is captured by Indians. The search of the five men who set out from Virginia to find her is filled with adventure and suspense.

ELSIE SINGMASTER, *A High Wind Rising* (Houghton). The early German settlers in the interior of Pennsylvania were greatly exposed to Indian raids. The "high wind" is the coming of the French and Indian War and the death and destruction these settlers faced.

GRACE ZARING STONE, *The Cold Journey* (Morrow). Stories of colonists captured by Indians are related in this book based on the actual Indian massacre at Deerfield, Massachusetts.

CLIFFORD M. SUBLETTE, *The Bright Face of Danger* (Little, Brown). Francis Havenell's father is killed in America. He sets out from England to search for the murderer and in doing so joins in Bacon's rebellion against the Crown.

FLORENCE M. UPDEGRAFF, *Blue Dowry* (Harcourt). The scene of this book is a Connecticut farm in the days just before the Revolution, when a girl is torn by loyalty both to her English father and her American mother.

GEORGE F. WILLISON, editor, *The Pilgrim Reader* (Doubleday). Here are accounts, written by the Pilgrims themselves, of the Pilgrim movement in 1620 from England to America. The whole is a story of courage and endurance.

STANLEY YOUNG, *Mayflower Boy* (Rinehart). Giles Hopkins is a central figure in this account of the first dangerous months of America's settlement.

◇◇◇◇◇

HISTORY IN REVIEW

MILESTONES	TRENDS IN AMERICAN LIFE	LITERATURE
1607–1733—Founding of the thirteen colonies	Pioneering in the wilderness forms the new American character, a strange mixture of intolerance and passionate love of freedom	1624—John Smith's *Generall Historie of Virginia* published in England
1619—First Negro slaves brought to America; Virginia House of Burgesses created		1640—*The Bay Psalm Book*
1664—Surrender of Dutch colonies to the English	North and South become differentiated. Northerners live on small farms, and clustered in villages; Southerners develop a gracious life on plantations	1650—Anne Bradstreet publishes first volume of original verse in New England
1692—Salem witchcraft trials		1683—*The New England Primer*
1698–1748—Frontier warfare between colonists and French and Indians		1704—First colonial newspaper published in Boston
1735—Freedom of press furthered by trial of John Peter Zenger	Founding of Harvard University, William and Mary, Yale	1730—Franklin's *Pennsylvania Gazette*
1754–1760—Colonists are allies of British in French and Indian War	Indians driven farther inland	1733–1758—Franklin's *Poor Richard's Almanac* published annually
	British win eastern area of present U. S. from French; settlers push farther westward	
1765—Stamp Act passed by Parliament	The idea of colonial union takes root through Franklin's proposal to Albany Congress	1741—Jonathan Edwards' "Sinners in the Hands of an Angry God"
	Trade flourishes despite the Navigation Acts	

STRUGGLE FOR INDEPENDENCE

The American Revolution—As Seen by Modern Writers

In the writings of the twentieth-century authors in this section you will see the colonists stoutly resisting the tyranny of King George III, and re-enacting their terrible eight years' struggle against British military might. Looking back at the Revolutionary War, modern American writers have a double reason for finding it an inspiring period. Not only are they thrilled by the exciting events of the Revolution, but they are deeply conscious of what the patriots of 1776 won for us and all Americans. Our independence as a nation; our freedom to act as we please so long as we do not harm the freedom of others; and our Constitution, the basic organization of our democratic government—all these we owe to the courageous men and women of Revolutionary times. These modern plays, biographies, and stories bring out the noble ideals of Revolutionary leaders—men like John Adams of Boston and George Washington of Virginia. To know those men, to understand their dream of justice and of laws that would be fair to all, is to realize again the high purposes to which our nation is dedicated.

Ballad for Americans

JOHN LATOUCHE

"Ballad for Americans" is a cantata for baritone and chorus, with music by Earl H. Robinson. After it was first broadcast in 1939, it was applauded by music-hall audiences from coast to coast. In those tense years just before Pearl Harbor, the "Ballad" voiced the re-awakened patriotism, and sense of unity, of Americans. It centers on the figure of Uncle Sam—a fellow of every religion, every race, every trade. The opening lines, which are given below, carry us back to our "Year One." In their triumphant, thumping rhythm speaks a nation which is proud of its history but not oversolemn about it.

In seventy-six the sky was red
Thunder rumbling overhead
Bad King George couldn't sleep in his
    bed
And on that stormy morn
Ol' Uncle Sam was born.   5

Chorus: Some birthday!
Ol' Sam put on a three-cornered hat
And in a Richmond church he sat
And Patrick Henry told him that
While America drew breath   10
It was "Liberty or Death."

Chorus: Hum—Hum—What kind of
    hat is a three-cornered hat?

8. IN A RICHMOND CHURCH HE SAT—Here, "Uncle Sam" is the convention of Virginia patriots at Richmond, in 1775. On this occasion Patrick Henry delivered his famous oration.

One voice from chorus: Did they all
    believe in liberty in those days?
Nobody—who was anybody—believed it
Ev'rybody—who was anybody—they
    doubted it—   15
Nobody had faith
Nobody, Nobody but Washington
        Tom Paine
        Benjamin Franklin
        Chaim Salomon
        Crispus Attucks
        Lafayette   22
        Nobodies.

20. CHAIM SALOMON—Chaim or Haym Salomon, a Jewish merchant in Philadelphia, raised two million dollars for the nearly bankrupt Revolutionary government.

21. CRISPUS ATTUCKS—Of Negro and Indian blood, Crispus Attucks was the first person killed in the Boston Massacre, and therefore the first American to die in the struggle for freedom.

22. LAFAYETTE—The Marquis de Lafayette, a French nobleman, out of enthusiasm for the principle of self-government served as an officer under Washington.

FOR UNDERSTANDING

1. To appreciate the vigor of the lines, read them aloud. Your teacher may wish to appoint two members of the class to recite the song, one person as "soloist" and one as "chorus." As you listen, notice how the repetition of rhyme sound—*red, overhead, bed*—builds up a feeling of climax.

2. The author is deliberately informal in his way of talking about the birth of the American republic. For instance, "seventy-six" is a slangy way of referring to an important year in history. Point out other ex-

pressions that add a flavor of informality and fun. This manner of speaking about the nation or about government matters is typical of Americans. What kind of "person" do you imagine when you hear the familiar name "Uncle Sam"? What homely name have we adopted for the executive mansion in our nation's capital? Give examples of two or more widely known nicknames for American presidents.

3. The stormy sky and the thunder mentioned in the poem are references to the Revolutionary War, which had already begun in 1776. What "King George" is being referred to, and why do Americans consider him "bad"? Why is this particular year named as the date Uncle Sam was born?

4. Among the "nobodies" who believed in liberty was Tom Paine—a self-educated British workman who came to America and wrote pamphlets in support of the Revolution. Of the other patriots mentioned in the song, which ones might have been considered "nobodies" until 1776? How does the list of Revolutionary leaders illustrate the fact that America is made up of people who differ greatly in background?

JOHN LATOUCHE (Born 1917)

Because John Latouche showed unusual literary talent while he was still a high-school student in Virginia, his family sent him to a private school in New York where he could receive special training. Then he attended Columbia University, where he was active in student dramatic productions. Since writing "Ballad for Americans" he has written lyrics for a number of songs and musical plays, including *Cabin in the Sky*. He is the author of a travel book, *Congo*.

◇◇◇◇◇

JOHN ADAMS AND THE BOSTON MASSACRE

FROM *John Adams and the American Revolution*

CATHERINE DRINKER BOWEN

Angry feeling ran high in Boston in the year 1770. British troops had been sent to control the unruly Americans and to enforce the hated Townshend Acts. Seeing the soldiers on the streets enraged the Americans more than ever. Then—the Boston Massacre.

We remember this historic event, but usually forget that the soldiers were victims of a situation for which they were not to blame. The following selection gives the facts of the tragedy, and shows that the soldiers actually had no choice but to fire when they did. The selection also shows the integrity and courage of a great American, John Adams. It was dangerous

to speak up for the soldiers, hated as they were. Adams himself felt hatred
—not for the soldiers, but for the highhanded policy that had caused them
to be sent to Boston. He insisted on every man's rights before the law.

There was a layer of ice on the ground that morning; during the day a few inches of snow fell. In the afternoon the sky cleared, and with sunset a young moon appeared over Beacon Hill, shining very bright, throwing shadows along the streets. Parties of boys, apprentices, soldiers, stood about; there seemed more than the usual crowd, cursing and jeering. From Murray's barracks, in Water Street, a party of ten or twelve soldiers emerged, armed with clubs and cutlasses. They were out for a stroll, they said. A small crowd of citizens collected near the wooden church on Brattle Square. Most of them had canes and heavy cudgels which they struck and clashed together noisily.

At a little after eight o'clock, Captain Goldfinch of the Army crossed King Street on his way to Murray's barracks. A sentinel was stationed as usual on the corner by the Custom House. As the Captain passed, a barber's boy whistled through his fingers and called out—with embellishments—that the Captain owed his master for dressing his hair. The sentinel gave chase, whacked the boy with the butt of his musket. The boy set up a howl calculated to raise the dead. By now the crowd before Murray's barracks had begun scuffling with the soldiers on guard, pelting them with snowballs and ice. Captain Goldfinch ordered his men within, shut the yard gate, and promised the crowd that no more soldiers would be let out that night. . . .

At a little after nine a crowd moved toward King Street from the direction of Royal Exchange Lane. As they reached the sentinel by the Custom House, some-

one shouted, "Here is the soldier that struck the barber's boy!"

"Kill the soldier, kill the coward, kill him, knock him down!" voices cried. The sentinel, backing up the steps of the Custom House, shoved the rammer down his musket and primed it. Chunks of wood were thrown at him; pieces of ice, sharp-edged and heavy. The sentinel, dodging for his life, shouted for help. Captain Preston of the main guard heard him from Murray's barracks, sent a file of seven men across the square, headed by a very young, very flustered officer. The eight crossed the icy cobbles on the trot, pushed the crowd aside with threats from their bayonets, and formed a half-circle round the sentry box. The crowd continued to jeer and hurl ice. Captain Preston himself appeared, ordered his men to prime and load.

There were now nine soldiers on the steps, counting Preston. The crowd before them numbered perhaps a hundred, whooping, cursing, whistling piercingly between their fingers and throwing anything that came to hand—clubs, oyster shells, icy snowballs. The big ropewalker —the man who had put the question last Friday on Gray's wharf—was much in evidence with his friends. "You cowards!" the crowd yelled at the soldiers. "Let's see you fire! . . . You dare not fire. . . . Lobsters![1] . . . Bloody backs! . . . Let's burn the sentry box. . . . Come on boys. . . . *Lobsters!* Who buys lo-obsters tonight?"

One of the soldiers, struck by a missile,

[1] LOBSTERS!—Jeering Bostonians called the soldiers by this nickname, alluding to the color of their uniforms.

lost his footing and fell; his gun flew out of his hand. No one heard the order to fire, though many afterward swore they heard it and that it came from Captain Preston. The eight soldiers, one after another, fired their muskets into the crowd. When the smoke cleared, five men lay sprawled on the snow—three dead, the others mortally wounded. For a brief moment the crowd seemed frozen motionless, silent with horror. Then the stillness was broken by the thud and rattle of rammers as the soldiers pounded a new charge down the muzzles of their guns.

Captain Preston ordered his men to withdraw across the street. The people surged forward, dragged their dead to cover, carried the wounded men away. Drums began to beat; soldiers from the 29th Regiment marched into the square, formed two platoons around the main guard. A third company took up position by the northeast corner of the State House and at command, dropped to one knee in the position for street firing.

Suddenly, all over the city, bells began to ring the alarm. The streets were full of men carrying cudgels, knives, any weapon they could find, running toward Dock Square. The cry of "fire" was drowned in another cry: "To arms! *Town-born, turn out!*" In his house at the north end of town, Governor Hutchinson [2] heard the bell in the Brick Church nearby. Almost before he could reach his front door, men were on the steps, breathless with news. The Governor must come immediately to King Street,

[2] GOVERNOR HUTCHINSON—Acting Governor Hutchinson was American-born, but had received his office by royal appointment. For this reason he was considered the representative of the British government, and the mob made its protests to him.

"or the town will be all in blood." Making his way with difficulty to the market place in Dock Square, Hutchinson found himself in a pushing, dense, excited throng, all carrying cutlasses or heavy sticks and calling for guns, muskets. Hutchinson did his best to make himself heard, climbed the steps of a dwelling house, and tried to compel attention from the people. He was pushed roughly into the street; almost fell, heard his name spoken with a curse.

From a nearby doorway, friendly hands reached out, drew Hutchinson to safety. The Governor let himself be led through the house, then slipped out and into King Street by a private way. The square was jammed with people, apparently waiting for Hutchinson, expecting him. He was forced bodily into the State House, up the stairs to the Council Chamber, and out onto the balcony. In the moonlight he faced a seething, roaring, angry mass that filled the square and one side of the street. On the other side the soldiers stood or kneeled, their muskets primed and pointed. Behind Hutchinson the lighted windows threw him boldly into silhouette. The crowd, sighting him, was silent; on their upturned faces the moon shone almost bright as day. Hutchinson stood a moment and waited.

"Go home," he said at last. "Let the law settle this thing! Let the law have its course. I myself will live and die by the law. Let you also keep to this principle. Blood has been shed; awful work was done this night. Tomorrow there will be an inquiry. . . ."

Next morning early, John [3] walked to his office by the State House door. Already the streets were full of people. Many were obviously from the country;

they carried muskets; their clothes in bundles were tied ludicrously to the barrels. Someone must have sent for them in the night, John thought. He remembered hearing Molineux, the new captain of the liberty boys, say something about dispatching expresses to Roxbury and Dorchester to warn the countryside.

In front of John's office a little crowd was waiting. Benjamin Edes of the *Gazette* was there, Crafts the painter and Swift of the North Enders. John took them inside with him. "How many were killed last night?" he asked quickly. "Four," Ben Edes replied. "One was Sam Gray, the ropewalker that started the fight Friday morning on the docks. Crispus Attucks was killed, the big mulatto. You must have seen him around town, Mr. Adams. The two others were simply standing in the street looking on —one a lad of seventeen. Patrick Carr the Irishman is dying at his house of a gunshot wound. Dr. Warren is with him. Captain Preston is in jail. They have been questioning him all night; there is no doubt he gave the command to fire."

"When the crowd dispersed at three this morning," Edes went on, "we tried to countermand the order we had sent the Sons [4] in the neighboring towns, asking for help and arms. But we were too late. The people are flocking to town; have you seen them, with bundles on their muskets?"

"Get them out of town," John replied roughly. "Get them home. Where is Sam Adams? We had best organize a citizens' watch for tonight. There will be more trouble when the sun goes down."

[3] JOHN—John Adams, then thirty-five years old and a well-known champion of the American claims.

[4] THE SONS—The Sons of Liberty was an organization devoted to securing the full privileges of English citizenship for the colonists.

He had scarcely finished speaking when there was a rapid knock at the street door. A man stumbled in, his clothes torn, tears streaming down his face. John recognized him immediately as Mr. Forester, a friend of the British officers—surely, the last person John expected to see in his office at such a moment and in such a condition. Around town Forester was known as "the Irish Infant," a good-natured man who liked to take his dram at the British Coffee House. John spoke quickly to Ben Edes, who moved at once to help clear the office, get the men out of the door and off the stoop. John turned the key in the lock.

Forester, breathing hard, sat down and was silent a moment, struggling for composure. He came directly from Captain Preston in prison, he said at last. He bore a message, a solemn message from a very unfortunate man. Preston's life was in danger; he desperately needed a lawyer. No one would help him. Preston was in terrible condition, bruised all over, his face and eyes swollen and black. Since three this morning they had questioned him; he had had no sleep all night. None of them had slept, Forester added, his fingers twisting nervously. Preston's examiners were trying to make him say it was he who had given the fatal order to fire into the crowd. . . .

"As God is my witness," Forester said, gripping the arms of his chair, his eyes wide with distress, "as God is my witness, Preston is an innocent man! His soldiers were defending their lives from the mob. . . . Mr. Adams, were you in King Street last night? Did you see what happened?"

John shook his head shortly, made no answer. "Why are you here, Mr. Forester?" he said at last.

"They will try Preston within ten days," Forester said. "He has no one to defend him. Mr. Adams, would you consider—will you take his case?"

Forester almost sobbed; the words came out in a rush. Already this morning he had called on three of the crown lawyers—naturally, he went first to them. They would not defend Preston, would not even touch the case. Mr. Auchmuty, the admiralty judge, was the only one who would listen. Auchmuty said he would act for Preston on one condition: if John Adams of the people's faction would serve as counsel with him. "After that I went to Mr. Josiah Quincy, Junior, next door to you," Forester continued. "The eight soldiers are in jail, too, for murder. Mr. Quincy gave the same answer as Auchmuty. He will defend Captain Preston if you will act with him."

Forester raised his eyes wildly; John watched him without speaking. . . . So the crown lawyers would not defend Preston! Their own man, and they dared not. They were afraid of the mob. Thousands would be on the streets today, hundreds had already gathered round the stone jail. Coming down Queen Street this morning, John had heard a name called again and again, in a kind of roaring chant. Now he knew the name had been Preston. . . .

Color rose in John's face. So far, he had felt nothing but anxiety, a great dread and horror that such things could come to pass in his own town, his own country. Now, suddenly, he was angry. Here in Massachusetts Bay, where the English law gave everyone fair judgment by trial of his peers—here a man, an Englishman, lay in jail in peril of his life, and the bar denied him counsel! Auchmuty the Younger—John knew him well. He had lately been named Judge of Admiralty for all New England. He was a confirmed, even a bitter Tory and very much of a swell, driving his own coach and four, trading blatantly on the reputation of his distinguished father. He was not a college graduate; John had little respect for his knowledge of the law. (Jeremiah Gridley, John remembered now, had been openly scornful on the subject.) Yet Auchmuty was an able advocate in his way, a good jury lawyer, quick with his tongue and capable of an eloquent appeal. With someone behind him to bolster his dramatics by sound legal props, Auchmuty might do well for Preston. No doubt all the judges would be scared to death of the mob—except Hutchinson, who would naturally refuse to serve anyway. As for Josiah Quincy, at twenty-six, he was a clever lawyer and a very eloquent man. But he was furiously impulsive, apt to let his feelings run away with him in court. As likely as not he would rise at the trial and orate to the bench on the meaning of "liberty."

Forester was talking. "Captain Preston is innocent," he repeated. Tears rolled down his face. "You will excuse me, Mr. Adams . . . Before God in heaven, Preston acted in self-defense! He is an innocent man."

"That," John said coldly, "must be ascertained at his trial."

Forester drew a long, shuddering breath and sat upright; he seemed afraid to speak. Outside in the street the clamor increased; the square before the State House was filling with people. A man ran heavily past the window; there were shouts. There flashed through John's mind the scene at Salem courthouse last autumn. . . . An old woman, gray-haired, haggard, accused of murder. *Ordeal by touch.* The people would have hanged her, not on evidence but on superstition. . . .

I will take this case, John thought suddenly. *I will defend Preston if it is the last thing I do. . . .* And he would use no tricks of the trade. No sophistry,[5] no lurid adjectives. No trembling voice or pointing of the finger at a hypnotized jury. Fact, evidence, and the law would try Captain Preston. There were things at stake greater than a man's life—greater than nine men's lives, for if he defended Preston he must *ipso facto*[6] defend the soldiers with him. And if what he had gathered since morning were true, this would prove as important a case as had been tried in any court of any country in the world.

John was suddenly swept with emotion, almost with awe, at the thing he had undertaken. The implications of it staggered him, towered higher than he could see. He got up, cleared his throat. "If Captain Preston," he said, "thinks he cannot have a fair trial without my help, then he shall have it. Here is my hand."

Forester sprang forward, seized John's hand and wrung it. Then he dug in three different pockets and brought up, after some struggle, a single guinea. He held it out. "A retaining fee," he said, his face entirely serious. John took the money with equal seriousness, bowed gravely. If he never received another cent for this most difficult, perhaps impossible task, both men knew the coin was binding. Avoiding a second wringing of the hand, John opened the door, bade Forester good morning, and saw him down the steps.

The crowd by the door had increased; they pressed forward. "It's the Irish Infant," someone said. "It's him all right!" Benjamin Edes of the *Gazette* stepped out; close behind him was Swift of the North End gang. "What's the Irish Infant coming to *you* for, Mr. Adams?" Swift asked roughly.

5 SOPHISTRY—Cleverly false arguments.
6 *Ipso facto*—By that very fact.

John stood on the steps; his eyes went from face to face. "Forester came to me from the jail," he said. "Ben Edes, you may tell whom you please that I have agreed to act as counsel for Captain Preston, who is held for murder. You may say also that I shall defend the British soldiers lying in the stone jail under capital charges."

There was a murmur from the little crowd. The sweat trickled down from his armpits but John stood a moment longer, rocking on his heels. His hands were behind his back, his coattails bunched forward; if he was afraid he did not show it. The light of battle was in his eye; he looked ready to take on all comers. "If you desire more information," he finished abruptly, "you will know where to find me." He turned, stepped into his office, and shut the door.

✧✧✧✧✧✧✧✧✧✧✧✧✧✧✧✧✧✧✧✧✧✧✧

FOR UNDERSTANDING

As he had promised, John Adams defended Captain Preston and his soldiers—and won his case. All the rest of his life, he was sometimes accused of having shown Tory, or pro-British, sympathies. But his deed helped to raise the American rebellion far above mere hatred and blind mob-violence; and it had caused justice to be done.

1. Explain why eight armed soldiers gathered on the steps of the Custom House. If the facts are correct as given in this selection, why would soldiers on duty be forced to fire on the crowd? Afterward, how did the soldiers get away?

2. What did Governor Hutchinson promise the crowd that gathered before the State House?

3. Why would the "crown lawyers"—men who favored the British side—not defend the soldiers? In John Adams' opinion, there were reasons for accepting the case

which were "greater than a man's life—greater than nine men's lives." What were they? Explain the significance of the coin which was offered to Adams, and which he accepted. That is, how did the act of accepting the coin give the other man a firm assurance that Adams would carry out the promise he had just made?

FICTIONIZED BIOGRAPHY

In this selection, all the important events are literally true, but the *conversations*, and of course John Adams' *thoughts*, are invented by Mrs. Bowen, the author. They are as true to Adams' character and ideas as she can make them, after close study of his autobiography, his letters, and his private diary. She can be sure Adams would have talked over the massacre with his friends, but must guess at what was said.

1. Does the author think Adams felt frightened, standing on the steps of his law office, when he announced that he would act as defense attorney? This dramatic scene is imaginary, though something very much like it *might* have happened. Explain why it would be *true to the general situation.*

2. Reread the conversation between John Adams and the "Irish Infant"—a man who came to ask him to defend the British soldiers. Why is it likely that this man might actually have said the things the author has him say? Do you think *his appearance* and his *frightened state of mind* are both plausible? Explain.

FOR BROADER MEANINGS

The mob itself was the cause of the deaths that occurred. Its *actions* are to be blamed. They were the unwise expression of a *resentment of tyranny* which is worthy of high praise. John Adams—who was later to be a signer of the Declaration of Independence, and the second president of the United States—disapproved of the mob action but approved the resistance to tyranny.

1. Adams probably thought the soldiers

were blameless. Do you think he would have wanted them to be defended in court if he had believed otherwise?

2. Do you think that in the long run Adams would be more respected or less respected because of his defense of the accused men? Remembering this action, why would people be more likely to believe the Declaration of Independence was justified when they learned John Adams supported it?

3. Explain how the history of our country might have been very different if, in its first years, there had not been men in the government like John Adams. Do you believe the nation has preserved Adams' love of justice? What support can you give for your answer?

SPECIAL REPORTS TO THE CLASS

1. Using several sources of information, report on the main events of Adams' life. Pay special attention to his services to the American Revolution. Be sure to discuss the offices he held before his term as president.

2. Report on the trial of Captain Preston and the soldiers. If possible, use several sources of information. One of the best is pages 378–406 of the book from which this selection is taken.

CATHERINE DRINKER BOWEN
(Born 1897)

Catherine Drinker Bowen was born in Pennsylvania, where her father was for many years president of Lehigh University. Her family was interested in music, and in her youth she studied for a time at the Peabody Conservatory of Music in Baltimore. Then came marriage, travel, and writing. She began by writing articles on yachting, for Mrs. Bowen is a sailing enthusiast. She has published several books on music and noted musicians.

Her book *Yankee from Olympus* quickly became famous. It is a life of Oliver Wendell Holmes—not the poet and essayist, but his son, the professor of law who became a famous justice of the Supreme Court. The book was praised as a fascinating and intelligent interpretation of Holmes's career. It was also criticized because it goes beyond the actually known facts—presenting thoughts and conversations which are based on true knowledge, but are imaginary. Instead of a biography, it might be called a fine historical novel about a real person. *John Adams and the American Revolution* follows the same plan. The books are also alike in that each one centers on the hero's boyhood, his marriage, and the earlier part of his mature career.

AN ADVENTURE
AT NEWPORT

ELIZABETH PAGE

*Because he could speak French, young Captain Peyton Howard was ap-
pointed aide to General Lafayette. Peyton was mindful of the debt his
country owed to France. He was aware that French money, ships, and soldiers had come to the American colonists to help them in their fight against
England; he was also aware that French political ideas had helped to inspire
the Declaration of Independence; but it was only by accident that he discovered the charm of a French girl and the warm human qualities of the
great Frenchman he served.* THE TREE OF LIBERTY, *in which the following episode occurs, is a novel about the growth of the American idea of
freedom.*

As he rode out of Providence on that fine
July morning in 1780 with the Marquis
de Lafayette, Captain Peyton Howard
had a thrilling sense of impending adventure. It was useless to argue it away.
It was there. Of course, there was his
commission, the reward of a year's difficult work, and his new uniform of blue
with buff facings, buff trousers and high
black boots. Decent clothing was unusual enough to be an adventure these
days. And there was this assignment to
keep the Marquis in touch with the Commander-in-chief [1] during the meeting at
Newport with the leaders of the French
fleet and the division of regiments just
landed from France. At the outset it
had seemed to promise only the usual
dull routine; but Monsieur de Lafayette
had a reputation for sudden daring action, and Peyton had hoped from the beginning something might happen. And
now there was this rumor that the British
fleet had been cruising around Newport
and was still lying off Block Island. If it
were true, then this visit of consultation
might well develop into a real excitement.

The nearer they came to Bristol ferry
the plainer it was that the authorities at
least believed the rumor. Squads of
minutemen were hurrying along the road;
and here and there one of them, remembering some glimpse of Lafayette at the
abortive siege of Newport two years before or just guessing the identity of the
foreign-looking youngster in the Continental general's uniform, would raise a
cry of "Three cheers for the markiss!"

[1] THE COMMANDER-IN-CHIEF—General George
Washington.

Lafayette always laughed and waved his hat in answer to the cheers. But it was not until they reached the ferry where a sizeable concentration of troops was encamped, some on the mainland and some plainly visible across on Butt's Hill, that they heard the first real news. The British fleet was indeed at Block Island, a call had been sent out to the militia of Massachusetts and Connecticut, and General Heath was already in Newport with five thousand men. The French regiments had been landed and the French fleet was anchored across the main channel. The second battle of Newport might be expected to begin at any time.

Peyton looked at the young Frenchman beside whom he was standing and saw his eyes brightening and his nostrils stirring. . . .

As they neared Newport he saw with satisfaction the Massachusetts militiamen busily strengthening the fortifications left by the British. Every sign pointed to impending battle and it did not occur to him, until the Marquis broke in on his thoughts, that as courier [2] he might not even see it begin.

"If they are right," Lafayette was saying, "if the fighting must be here instead of at New York, you may have a hard ride before you, Captain Howard. With so great a change in the General's plans I may be forced to ask you to start back with a message tonight."

Even as he murmured his acceptance of his usual duty Peyton's mind rejected the disagreeable possibility which did not fit his mood. He knew something real was going to happen this time. Once in town they sought out the headquarters of the Count de Rochambeau, and while Lafayette waited for the sentry to make

known his arrival he gave Peyton a few hurried instructions.

"There is an inn near the center of town, the White Horse, Captain Howard. Will you kindly take lodgings there for us both? We may be here several days, though there is the chance that I—"

A group of brilliantly dressed officers burst through the open door of the house and swarmed down the steps to claim him, with bows, embraces, and a flood of French too swift for Peyton to follow. When he could free himself the Marquis turned to his waiting courier.

"A council of war is in progress, Captain Howard, so may I suggest a few hours' rest? I must ask you to report for duty at nightfall, at the White Horse."

"I am here to serve you, sir," said Peyton.

"Ah, no!" Lafayette spoke quickly, his Gallic extravagance [3] increased by the presence of his friends. "We both serve His Excellency—and the need of the hour."

Peyton secured rooms at the back of the White Horse overlooking a little green lawn, but when he had seen to the proper care of the horses he found quiet intolerable. Transferring his saddle to a plug from the inn livery, he rode slowly out to see the town. There were two cobbled streets that paralleled the harbor, and he explored them both. Since the hoods on his stirrups hid his misshapen foot,[4] there was nothing to detract from the strength which months of hard riding had added to the grace of his lean, tall figure, or from the unique distinction which his somber eyes with their lifting brows gave to his face. More than once

[2] COURIER—Official messenger.

[3] HIS GALLIC EXTRAVAGANCE—His typically French habit of expressing his thoughts with a flourish.

[4] HIS MISSHAPEN FOOT—Peyton has a club-foot.

a girl turned her head to look after him. This involuntary flattery added to his sense of well-being. He found himself smiling.

There was little on these streets to suggest a threatened town. Gaily-dressed French officers made legs [5] and bowed at each other as they met. If one was accompanied by a lady the flourishes amounted to extravagance. Peyton found them very amusing, but in time he tired even of them. Then he followed the road from the harbor up Castle Hill and turned north along its flank to where he could get a view over meadows scarred with entrenchments from Easton's Pond to Narragansett Bay and dotted with the tents of the French. To the west were the clustered roofs of the town, and the harbor, with a crooked arm of land shutting it off from the passage to the open sea. It was a wonderful view of fields and water, of islands and wooded shore. He sat drinking it in while the shadows grew longer.

The sun was just setting when he reached the town again, and wishing to enjoy the final loveliness of day, he turned out on the pier, the clop-clop of the horse's hoofs sounding hollow on the wooden flooring. Sunshine still lingered on the forested crest of the Canonicut shore, but Goat and Rose Islands were already in shadow. One of the French ships, the *Duc de Bourgogne*, anchored high up the channel, was a purple shape on a sea of silver. Brown fishing boats were coming in for the night and on one, hove-to near at hand, men were singing as they lowered the sail. Peyton stayed until the three lanterns on the poop of the *Duc de Bourgogne* were lit and below them rosy fingers trembled on the darkening water. Nightfall had come,

and reluctantly he turned toward shore. It was then he heard the voices. A woman was crying out in French.

"À *moi! Que Dieu nous aide!* [6] À *moi! À—*"

There was a sound as if a hand had been clapped over her mouth, and another woman spoke. This voice was young, urgent.

"*Tais-toi, madame, je te prie! Monsieur le Capitaine s'amuse.*" [7]

Wheeling his horse, Peyton clattered along the edge of the wharf, peering in the direction of the sounds until he could make out a ship's boat being held motionless by four rowers about three oar's lengths from the landing stage of the pier. In the stern seat was a burly man and on the middle thwart between the oarsmen were the cloaked figures of the women. The younger was speaking again, this time in English.

"But surely you jest, monsieur. I am stranger there. I must insist that you take us *immédiatement*—how you say— along the side!"

"'Tain't a bit o' use your insistin', miss. I know you have a purse full o' gold in the front of that dress o' yourn, but if you was—"

Peyton waited to hear no more. Whipping out his pistol he shouted across the water.

"Hola! You, there! Bring those ladies at once alongside here, before I shoot. I have you covered and the distance is excellent!"

"Thunderation!" remarked the burly man. "Stow your pistol, sir, you're barkin' up the wrong tree entirely."

"Right or wrong," declared Peyton

[5] MADE LEGS—To "make a leg" is to thrust one leg out behind in order to make a bow.

[6] À *moi! Que Dieu nous aide!* (ä mwà kĕ dyû nōōz ĕd)—Help! May Heaven aid us!
[7] *Tais-toi, madame . . . s'amuse* (tā twà mä′dàm′ zhà tá prē mē·syû′ lá kà′pē′tĕn′ sä′-müs′)—Hush, madam, I pray you! The captain is joking.

F·KREDEL

firmly, "I mean what I say. Bring them alongside here and be quick about it, or I'll blow your head out from in under your hat!"

"Mon Dieu!" moaned the older woman and the younger moved as if she put an arm about her.

With a few brisk strokes the sailors brought the boat up and Peyton, dismounting, hurried down the stair to help the ladies to the stage. When the burly man leaped ashore after them he once more presented his pistol, but to his surprise the circle of light from the lamppost at the stairfoot showed him an honest, weather-beaten face in a half-moon of gray beard, and blue eyes under shaggy brows where amusement was gaining the upper hand over annoyance.

"I'll hev to tell you, young man, you've showed more gumption than you hev

sense, if your idee was to please the young lady. The very last thing she wanted was to be set on shore."

Puzzled and somewhat dashed, Peyton turned to the two women and summoned his best French.

"Madame, mademoiselle, I am completely at your service. I supposed from Madame's call for aid that this fellow was annoying you. If I am mistaken I beg a thousand pardons. But if there is the least need of my assistance I am yours to command."

The answer was such a torrent of voluble French from both at once that he was obliged to throw up his hands and beg for mercy.

"I can understand if you will do me the kindness to speak slowly. After all, I am only an American."

At a slower pace then, the tale came

out. The tall young lady was the daughter of the Vicomte d'Estivet, just arrived with her companion, Madame Goureaud, from Boston on the schooner of Monsieur le Capitaine Otterby. They had entered the harbor and dropped anchor, but when Mademoiselle d'Estivet had desired to be taken to le *Duc de Bourgogne* that she might seek her father, Monsieur le Capitaine refused to put her alongside.

"He makes difficulties, monsieur, and would put me down in this town," the young lady finished in English. "I am stranger here. I do not desire to encounter the town only when I have the escort of monsieur my father."

"They won't neither of 'em take any stock in what I say," put in Captain Otterby, "but mebbe they'll listen to you. Stands to reason we couldn't get aboard one o' them ships 'thout a pass or somethin', and anyway, a man-o'-war ain't the place for a lady."

Peyton nodded.

"The captain is right, mademoiselle. You would need a pass to board the ship. But Monsieur le Comte de Rochambeau has his headquarters here in town; and it is likely that all the officers are also ashore, either here or with their troops in the camps."

"Then, monsieur, will you conduct me to the Count at once?"

Peyton hesitated. It would be the natural conclusion to the episode, but somehow he was not anxious to have the episode conclude. He had not yet seen her face, shadowed as it was by the hood of her cloak. And also there was Lafayette, waiting, perhaps, even now.

"I am yours to command, mademoiselle," he said, "yet if I might make a suggestion?"

She sighed impatiently but gave assent.

"It is late, and I am unknown in Newport. There would probably be delay. But at an inn not three steps from here I am meeting the Marquis de Lafayette and he—"

"De Lafayette! Madame, *est-ce que tu entends?* [8] Lafayette has been in my father's house, monsieur. You are right, we will depend on his aid."

His design had succeeded, but as he led the way up the stair Peyton jeered inwardly at himself. If she had noticed his uniform the young lady was undoubtedly thinking his lameness an interesting disability due to a wound. Now, thanks to his cleverness, she would see him in a lighted room, and the face he was so oddly curious about would wear the expression with which he was only too familiar, a faint repulsion veiled, but not hidden, by politeness. He took the bridle of his horse and limped by her side in silence, his zest for the adventure gone. He would place her under the protection of the Marquis and disappear.

But at the White Horse they found the Marquis had not yet arrived. It seemed more than likely he had been kept at headquarters for dinner, and might not come until very late. Captain Otterby suggested that the ladies return with him to the ship, and try again in the morning. This was Peyton's chance, of course, to withdraw gracefully from the situation, but with the perverseness that he admitted afterward had characterized his behavior from the beginning he found himself urging the girl to stay at the inn. In the crowded common room she had drawn her hood further forward, as if to shelter her face from staring eyes, and he had not seen it yet.

"It is surely possible for you and Madame Goureaud to have comfortable

[8] *Est-ce que tu entends?* (ĕs kĕ tü än′ tän′)—Do you understand?

rooms here," he declared, and mine host with a beaming face supported him. "If you go back to the ship and Monsieur le Marquis should have to leave early, you might miss him, and that would be a pity."

"I can serve a little supper for you, ladies, in your room in less time than you can think," added the innkeeper.

This seemed to decide the young lady, for she turned to Peyton.

"You will honor us at supper, monsieur, and you, too, Monsieur le Capitaine?"

But Otterby begged to be excused. He had business to attend to, and he must get back on board.

"I'll hev the men bring your baggage at once, miss," he said. "I can leave you 'thout a mite o' worry under the protection of sich a fire-eatin' young colonel."

Peyton laughed deprecatingly.

"Only a captain, sir. Captain Peyton Howard at your service."

Captain Otterby bowed and left them. The young lady followed the innkeeper up the stair still without dropping her hood, so it was not until he bowed before her at suppertime that Peyton saw her face. It was an unusual face, as he had suspected, and quite un-American in contour and the set of large, hazel eyes. Some might say it was too thin, for there was more than a suggestion of cheekbones and a firm sweep of jaw, but the lovely curves of the wide mouth and the intelligence of the brilliant glance gave it undeniable charm. It was above all a frank face, and Peyton suddenly did something he had never done in all his life before. When he led her to her chair he thrust out the ugly lump of his crippled foot where she could not help but see.

Adrienne d'Estivet caught her breath.

"It was not a wound then, monsieur,"

she exclaimed softly. "You are always lame?" She raised her eyes with a look of wonder. "Monsieur, you are magnificent! There were five strong men in that boat when you called us to land."

Peyton laughed in his relief.

"You forget my pistol, mademoiselle. Gunpowder levels great odds."

But she shook her head.

"Between one man and two or even three, perhaps, monsieur. Not between one and five."

Madame Goureaud murmured an enthusiastic assent. They would not have it otherwise. He had been a hero, at least, in his intent; but they all laughed merrily over their mutual misunderstandings.

"I make certain you are a highwayman, monsieur," confessed Madame Goureaud, "and I nearly die of fright."

It was easy to expand in such an atmosphere and before the meal was over they were on a footing of genuine friendliness. Passing lightly over his work as military courier, Peyton talked to her of Virginia, halting often and feeling for the correct phrase, of Albemarle Hall, Elm Hill, and the tree-shadowed streets of Williamsburg. And fluently, with flashing wit, she told him of life in Paris at the Hôtel d'Estivet [9] where, for a year and more, young as she was, she had been hostess to her father's friends, the Marquis de Condorcet, the Duc de La Rochfoucauld [10] and the rest.

"They are philosophers, my father's friends, and they meet, oh, several times in the week, to discuss the writings of Monsieur Rousseau and *The Social Con-*

[9] HÔTEL D'ESTIVET (ô'tĕl' dĕs'tē'vā')—The mansion of the Estivet family.
[10] CONDORCET (kôn'dôr'sĕ'), LA ROCHFOUCAULD (là rôsh'fōō'kō')—These are names of actual persons who are famous in the history of French thought.

tract.[11] They consider the rights of men, and whether it will ever be possible to return to that state of nature where all are free. It is very instructive to hear them talk."

"And madame your mother?" asked Peyton.

Her face grew sober.

"I do not remember my mother, monsieur, she died so long ago, but monsieur my father tells me she was very intelligent. He despairs that I will ever be so intelligent as my mother, although he has always guided my instruction himself."

"I see. And that is why he has summoned you here?"

Whatever his reasons, Peyton thought the Vicomte strangely lacking in the intelligence he so much admired. Adrienne laughed delightedly.

"But, monsieur! My father does not know I am here. He thinks me safe in the Convent du Boissy where he left me."

"You have come without his knowledge! In heaven's name, why?"

In his surprise Peyton had spoken in English, and now he blushed furiously and bit his lip in vexation that he had been betrayed into so impertinent a question. But with a little gesture that accepted his confusion as an apology Adrienne d'Estivet answered also in English.

"Monsieur, you will never believe me, but it is absolutely because Mère Joseph d'Arimathé has—how you say—a wart on her nose."

"Mère Joseph d'Arimathé?" Peyton repeated stupidly.

"But yes, monsieur, the abbess of the Convent du Boissy."

Du Boissy, it seemed, was a small foundation, noted for the piety and the education of its sisterhood, which explained the Vicomte's choice of the house for his daughter's asylum during his absence, but the discipline of the school was very strict. Young Adrienne d'Estivet, fresh from more than a year of participation in a philosophical salon,[12] was treated like an immature child. Her books were taken from her and needlework which she detested was placed in her hands. She was bidden to combat with long seasons of prayer the questioning of her mind.

"I could have endured it, monsieur, for after all my father had placed me there, but they spied on me. By day and night. You have no idea, monsieur, what it was like. A door opens without noise. One thinks one is alone, and yet one knows one is observed. I turn and there is the shadow of a black veil and the white nose with that wart. It withdraws and the door shuts again without a sound. Always the black shadow with the white nose and that wart. I begin to dream of it. In vain I tell myself that they are but watching to see I obey, that I do not read or discuss with the other young ladies, or do the things forbidden. I cannot sleep. At night I lie in my cell watching my door to see will it open, will that white nose appear. The wart on it makes it so horrible. At last I say to myself, it is better to seek my father and give him a little surprise, than it is to stay and go mad. Besides, monsieur, even a woman enjoys an adventure. Nothing will ever happen in the Convent

---

[11] MONSIEUR ROUSSEAU (mē·syü′ rōō′sō′) AND *The Social Contract*—In 1762 the French philosopher Jean-Jacques Rousseau published *The Social Contract*, a book which declared that governments are unjust unless they derive their powers from the consent of the governed.

[12] A PHILOSOPHICAL SALON—A salon is a drawing room. The word is also used for repeated meetings of distinguished guests, such as writers or artists, at the home of some noted person.

du Boissy. The sisters are too good and too strict."

"But how did you ever get away?"

"That, monsieur, I am keeping as a secret to whisper in the ear of my daughter if I ever have to leave her in a convent. It was very clever, and I think it would always work. The Hôtel d'Estivet was closed, but I went to my dear Goureaud who was living with her sister and who was just as *triste* [13] as I. Were you not, *chère madame?*" [14]

Madame Goureaud cast her merry black eyes to heaven and called the saints to witness to the extent of her *tristesse*. She had gone with her young lady to the Vicomte's agent, of whom Adrienne had demanded part of the collected rents to defray the expense of the journey. With a sinfulness that she was ready to admit she gave the poor man to understand that the Vicomte had sent for her.

"I was very much surprised that he had no letter of instructions. I could only suppose it had been lost on the so dangerous sea. He was not certain that he could act without the word of monsieur my father, but I was so very certain that the Vicomte would be angry at any delay that at last he consented to conduct us to Le Havre, and to secure passage to Boston on a ship of Monsieur Hancock. At Boston we learn that the French fleet is at Newport. But Monsieur le Capitaine Otterby has also a ship of Monsieur Hancock. So it is very simple. In the one little office everything arranges itself, and the same afternoon we embark for Newport. The rest, monsieur, you know."

Although it was long after midnight when Lafayette came in, Peyton was waiting for him. The Marquis listened, now with sympathy in his large gray eyes and now with gay laughter, while his aide poured out the story of Mademoiselle d'Estivet. His answer, when Peyton was done, was prompt and decisive.

"But, of course, we will help her. Adrienne d'Estivet—yes, I remember. An odd-looking young thing—almost as odd as I am myself," he added, passing his hand over his own strangely retreating forehead, "but with charm, oh, decidedly, with charm. Captain Howard, did it occur to you in hearing her exploits that such independence will be wasted in France?"

"Monsier le Marquis," Peyton admitted with a faint heightening of his color, "you read my thoughts."

"Aha! So that's it. My dear Howard, you can always count me to further an *amour*. [15] I shall be filled with business tomorrow, and with infinite regret I shall leave the affair in your hands. You will proceed to headquarters and find out where is Monsieur le Vicomte, and then you will conduct Mademoiselle to her father, that being a proceeding which will give you more of the young lady's companionship than the more sensible arrangement of bringing her father here. And to make you *persona grata* [16] to Papa you must have some means of solving all his difficulties in his daughter's arrival—now what—?" He stared anxiously at Peyton who maintained a hopeful silence. "I have it! Before you do anything at all, before Mademoiselle awakes, you must ride out to the encampment of the Bourbonnais. You'll find them in the woods north of town. Ask for my brother-in-law, the Vicomte de Noailles. He will be very sleepy and very annoyed, but he will give you a letter to Miss

[13] *Triste* (trĭst)—Sad.
[14] *Chère madame* (shâr mȧ′dȧm′)—Dear madam.

[15] AN *amour* (ä′mōōr′)—A love affair.
[16] *Persona grata* (pēr·sō′nȧ grā′tȧ)—An acceptable person, a welcome person.

Mollie Robinson, if you appeal to him as one lover to another. She has the heart of an angel, and she will persuade her father to take your Adrienne into a home more suited to her situation than the White Horse. *Voilà, mon enfant!* [17] which is, in American, as you should know: Go in and win!"

It all worked out according to their plan. After the early morning dash to the camp of the Bourbonnais, Peyton carried the Marquis' invitation to the ladies, asking them to join him at breakfast, and at table with an utterly convincing air of distress the young Frenchman explained his inability to serve as escort to the daughter of his friend, but placed his aide, Captain Howard, at her disposal for the day. Then, having given Peyton an introduction to open the doors at headquarters, he left them with every appearance of a man overburdened with affairs.

"*Il est gentil, n'est-ce pas!*" [18] sighed Madame Goureaud.

"The girls at the convent would die of envy if they knew of this breakfast," Adrienne told Peyton. "Le Marquis de Lafayette is all the rage at Paris. You cannot believe, monsieur. Even I shone with the reflection of glory because he has visited at the house of my father."

At the headquarters a great amount of time was consumed as they were passed from room to room, in the ceremonies of greeting which convention seemed to require; but at last they learned that Monsieur le Vicomte d'Estivet was attached to the grenadiers of Soissons who had been sent out to man the fort and entrenchments at the entrance of the harbor. There was a holiday excursion across to the fort in a small boat over

water sparkling under the July sun, with gulls circling before and behind them like a guard of honor. The fishing boats had put out to sea again but the great French vessel swung at its moorings with gun ports closed. It was wash day and lines of shirts fluttered from the stays like white signal flags.

"The world seems to me very gay," Adrienne remarked, "but perhaps it is just because I so soon shall see my father."

Looking across at Peyton on the seat opposite hers, she came to the conclusion that she liked Americans. Monsieur le Capitaine Howard was not as gay as Monsieur le Marquis, but his manner was easy, entirely as it should be. Peyton caught her glance and smiled at her, for he was thinking that hazel eyes with long black lashes were the most beautiful eyes in the world. His smile, the girl told herself, was charming. Decidedly she need not be ashamed to introduce him to her father.

The introduction was effected in a bare room of the barracks inside the fort. A white uniform with facings of rose and a rose colored plume on the hat tossed on a stool looked almost frivolous in contrast with the grim surroundings, but there was nothing frivolous about the Vicomte. Spare almost to emaciation, he looked as if the fire of his spirit had burned away all superfluities even of the flesh. Only on Mr. Jefferson's face had Peyton ever seen that same expression of avid intelligence; but the wise eyes of the Frenchman under their jutting brows, unlike Mr. Jefferson's, were sad. The intimate friends of such a man would naturally be philosophers.

His evident joy in receiving his daughter was tempered as the Marquis had foreseen, even in its first moments, by something like consternation, which

[17] *Voilà, mon enfant!* (vwà'là'môn än' fän') —There you are, my boy!

[18] *Il est gentil, n'est-ce pas!* (ēl ĕ zhän'tē' nĕs·pä')—He is splendid, isn't he!

Peyton hastened to allay, as soon as he was introduced, by presenting the letter to Miss Robinson. Monsieur de Lafayette wished to assure the Vicomte that the young lady, a friend of the Vicomte de Noailles, would be a charming companion for his daughter, and her home a congenial place in which to stay.

"I am ready to conduct you both thither, Monsieur le Vicomte," Peyton concluded. "It shall not be necessary for Mademoiselle to pass a second night at an inn."

"Lafayette must have been born wise," remarked the Vicomte, "for he certainly has not lived long enough to acquire such understanding of a father's anxiety. We shall wait upon Mademoiselle Robinson this afternoon, but now, monsieur, you must honor us with your presence at —Adrienne, how is it one says *déjeuner?*" [19]

"Lunch, monsieur *mon père.*" [20]

"Aha! lunch. How could I forget! It bites the air, that word. Monsieur le Capitaine, you will honor us there?"

The Vicomte's fellow officers shared the almost universal European curiosity in regard to General Washington, and when Captain Howard let it be known that his grandfather had served at Great Meadow and also at the first attempt on Fort Duquesne, they kept him talking through most of the meal. Peyton was fluent and unselfconscious, launched as he was in praise of the man whom he revered nearly to the point of idolatry, as did most of the officers and men of the Continental Line. If there was something touching on extravagance in his attitude toward his Chief, it served only to recommend him to his warmhearted hosts.

[19] *Déjeuner* (dā′zhǔ′nā′)—Breakfast or lunch.
[20] *Mon père* (mòn pâr)—My father.

Monsieur d'Estivet, therefore, was already favorably impressed with the young American officer when the time came for the return to Newport, and in the boat he made room for Peyton by his side on the seat opposite his daughter and Madame Goureaud, that he might prolong their conversation. He was curious to know if these young Americans were aware of the wide implications of the experiment on which they were embarked.

"You make it very clear that your Monsieur Washington is a great man, monsieur," he said as the boat slid away from the shore. "With such a leader and such a cause you will win your war. But when it is won, what then?"

"Then, monsieur," cried Peyton, "we shall be ready to begin!"

The Vicomte raised his brows.

"To begin? What?"

"You see, monsieur, we aim to set up a state which shall be for all men equally, none privileged, none greater than his neighbor. My French is so poor, monsieur, it is difficult to explain, but the task is new. We must feel our way. There are abuses to be swept away, but we dare not remove old props until we have set in new ones."

"Ah!" The Vicomte's tone held surprised satisfaction. "You are awake to the necessity to preserve even while you destroy?"

"That's what makes it difficult, monsieur. It would be easy just to destroy."

"You will pardon my saying it, Monsieur le Capitaine, but your ideas are surprising in one so young. I had given up expecting youth to be farsighted."

A light came into Peyton's fine eyes.

"I am fortunate in my father, monsieur. And my father's best friend is Monsieur Thomas Jefferson."

The Vicomte smiled.

"You explain everything and you double my curiosity to hear more."

Plied with questions, Peyton unfolded the plan of action as it was developing in Virginia, conscious not only of the Vicomte's interest but of Adrienne d'Estivet's absorbed face. He could scarcely believe his eyes when the town wharf loomed before them. As they came out on the street the Vicomte laid a hand apologetically on his arm.

"I hope you can pardon the number of my questions, Monsieur le Capitaine, but you cannot conceive the excitement one feels when ideals one has cherished for years in the study are put to the test of the market place."

"Indeed, monsieur," Peyton assured him earnestly, "to meet you has been a great privilege for me. I only wish I had talked less and had given you a chance to say more. We have great need of your accumulation of wisdom."

"Monsieur, it is fortunate your duties will call you elsewhere soon. Otherwise, you would find me importuning your constant company. It is a great mistake, to encourage any old man to talk—and an old man who calls himself a philosopher is the greatest pest of all!"

"If I can only remain in Newport, Monsieur le Vicomte, I shall hold myself subject to your call."

"My daughter has already whispered that you are a brave young man," declared the Vicomte, and they sealed their friendship with laughter.

Miss Mollie Robinson had been prepared for their coming by the Vicomte de Noailles. She greeted them with sweet Quaker gravity, through which a warm friendliness made itself felt. She had given up her own room to Adrienne, because, as she said, it had a view of the fort across the harbor.

"She can put a candle in her window each night," she told the Vicomte, "and thee will know she is well. I thought it would make thee both feel more secure."

Then she went on to say there was to be a dance that evening at Colonel Crary's, and though she did not dance herself, she had secured an invitation for Mademoiselle d'Estivet and for Captain Howard, whom Monsieur de Lafayette had agreed to release from any military duties. Adrienne clapped her hands with pleasure at this, but Peyton felt his heart slowly sinking into his misshapen boot.[21] How could the Marquis have deprived him of his only excuse? What could he say now?

"Miss Robinson," he began, "you are more than kind, but—"

[21] HIS HEART SLOWLY SINKING INTO HIS MISSHAPEN BOOT—Being a cripple, Peyton cannot dance.

He sought for words, his face reddening. Gracefully the Vicomte came to his aid.

"Monsieur le Capitaine has been too kind to us already," he said. "He has devoted himself since early morning to our affairs, when I do not doubt there has been business of his own which he has neglected."

Eagerly Peyton caught at the straw.

"Business! Yes, that's it—though it has been the greatest pleasure of my life to serve you, mademoiselle."

Under his eyes her face was changing from a warm and living thing to a politely smiling mask.

"I quite understand, monsieur. Please do not think to derange yourself further. I have the escort of monsieur my father."

"To be sure you have, mademoiselle," he agreed nervously. "And you will go and have a good time?"

"But of course, monsieur!" Her tone was cool and mocking.

"Mademoiselle, please don't misunderstand—"

"How could I, monsieur? As my father says, you have been very kind. And so—monsieur." She swept him a curtsey.

"Mademoiselle." He bowed and escaped as soon as he could.

Once outside he felt a driving need to be alone. He turned the corner, climbed Castle Hill, and limped back and forth for hours along its northern flank. Darkness came. Lights inside turned the tents below him to glowing shapes. He paused in his pacing and took refuge from his angry thoughts in looking at them. They were like dying embers, fire within veiled in gray. A rising breeze brought the sound of spinet, flute, and viol from the town. The dance had begun.

The flute was still wailing when he dropped down the harbor road to the White Horse. It was late and the usual crowd had gone home as he had hoped, but Lafayette was sitting at a table talking with the host, and at sight of Peyton he jumped up.

"Ah, Captain," he said, "you are home earlier than I hoped, and it is well, for—I could not spoil your day, of course—but there is a dispatch that should have been on its way before now. Still—you look tired, *mon enfant*—do you think you can—"

"Certainly, Monsieur le Marquis. I—I shall be glad of the excuse to ride. I'll get my horse."

He would have gone, but Lafayette caught him by the arm.

"Not so fast! Not so fast! How was the dance? She is divine, *n'est-ce pas?*"

"I did not go to the dance, monsieur. Is the dispatch here, or shall I find it in your room?"

"It's in my room. I'll bring— Not go to the dance! But why?"

"I should think, Monsieur le Marquis," Peyton burst out, the last shred of his patience giving way, "that would be fairly obvious!"

He turned once more to the door but again the young Frenchman put himself in his path.

"My dear fellow! This is absurd. Do you mean you did not go because—" He put his hands on Peyton's shoulders. "*Mon cher!* [22] She would not be her father's daughter if she did not think of a man's head and not his heels!"

"Monsieur, surely you know the custom—I was counting on you to explain—that a lady dances with her escort all evening. I cannot dance—and I could not spoil her first American party."

"*Sacré bleu!*" [23] Lafayette sat down

[22] *Mon cher* (môɴ shâr)—My dear fellow!
[23] *Sacré bleu!* (sȧ′krā′ blü)—This is a mild oath.

suddenly. "I had forgotten your savage custom—excuse me, *mon cher,* but you see yourself how savage it is— You count on me to explain! But didn't you explain?"

Peyton shook his head obstinately.

"I never speak of—this," he said.

"Oh, *mon Dieu!*" The Marquis was exasperated. "He never speaks—and I waste my time on such— Here, Monsieur Innkeeper, bring us paper, a pen, ink, quick! You don't speak, you say? You can write, then. Write her a letter now, and make it ardent, if you value her friendship. I shall take it to that dance and give it to her myself."

He stood impatiently beating a tattoo with one foot while Peyton wrote, and he delivered the note after his aide had ridden away with the dispatches. He traced the house by the throb of the music, and obtained entrance by the simple expedient of giving his name at the door. There was no house in America that was not open to the Marquis de Lafayette. He found the Vicomte d'Estivet and stood chatting with him until Adrienne joined them. When he could with courtesy, he offered her his arm and drew her into a corner, where he handed her the folded paper.

"It is a message of great importance which I was asked to bring to Mademoiselle d'Estivet," he said.

He watched her while she read, watched the bright color sweep up to her eyes, up to her hair. Adrienne looked at him with a smile as she folded the note.

"I think, Monsieur le Marquis, that your Captain Howard is a very foolish man."

Gilbert Motier de Lafayette made a leg and swept her a profound bow.

"I doubt, mademoiselle," he said gaily, "if you could find a greater fool in all

America. *Mais,*[24] *il est gentil, n'est-ce pas?*"

[24] *Mais* (mā). But.

◇◇◇◇◇◇◇◇◇◇◇◇◇◇◇◇◇◇◇◇◇◇◇◇◇◇◇◇◇◇◇

FOR UNDERSTANDING

1. What mistaken idea does Peyton have, at first, about the argument that is going on in the rowboat? Explain why it is out of the question for Adrienne to be taken to her father's ship.

2. What arrangements had Adrienne's father made for her when he came to America? How can we tell that Adrienne is a lively, adventurous person?

3. Explain why Adrienne becomes offended during the conversation about the dance. What former American custom at dances must we know about in order to understand the full reason for Peyton's "impoliteness"? How does the author make clear that Adrienne will accept his apology?

4. How does the story give a clearer understanding of the reason French leaders like Lafayette were interested in helping the American revolutionists?

FOR FURTHER READING

Students who are especially interested in American history will enjoy reading more of Elizabeth Page's *The Tree of Liberty*. It is a long, thoughtful book—tracing the story of a Virginia family from Colonial days through the events of the Revolution, and on to the time when migration into Ohio and beyond was a clearly established trend. The story ends in 1806, the year the Lewis and Clark Expedition brought back from Oregon news of vast habitable areas in the interior of America. Much of the action in *The Tree of Liberty* centers on the conflict between Thomas Jefferson's and Alexander Hamilton's political ideas, both of which have been influential in our country's development.

Adolph Latzko's *Lafayette, a Life* is a

good book for additional information on the great French patriot and friend of liberty.

ELIZABETH PAGE (Born 1889)

Early in life Elizabeth Page was influenced toward an interest in America that went beyond the boundaries of her native Vermont. As a child she was taken on trips to Oklahoma, where some of her relatives were missionaries, and she has worked with the famous medical missionary, Sir Wilfred Grenfell, in Newfoundland. The stimulus for her first book, *Wagons West,* and for her first reading about the American past, was a series of letters written by her great-uncle about his journey across the plains in 1849.

Miss Page was educated at Vassar College and at Columbia University. Her novels are careful historical studies that show deep understanding of men, movements, and ideas in American history. Her most recent book, *Wilderness Adventure,* has its setting in the year 1742.

❖❖❖❖❖

VALLEY FORGE

MAXWELL ANDERSON

The Revolutionary War seemed all but lost in the winter of 1777–1778, when Washington's troops were encamped at Valley Forge, Pennsylvania. Both the British and the Americans were waiting for milder weather—but the British were living comfortably in Philadelphia while, huddled together in crude shacks, Washington's men endured starvation, sickness, and cold. In his play VALLEY FORGE, *Maxwell Anderson recreates those dark days. The following excerpt shows the idealism and determination that carried Washington and his army through the winter.*

SCENE: *A bunkhouse at Valley Forge in January, 1778. The building is of logs, long, low, and windowless. At the right is an entrance door, at the left a stone fireplace. Between the two, bunks are built against the wall in double tiers, constructed entirely of saplings, about twelve in all. Logs are heaped at the fireplace and a few cut logs are used as seats. A washstand also stands not far from the*

fire, built of hewn timber, and a table, similarly made, is placed not far from the center of the room. The bunks are filled, over the sapling bottoms, with straw and pine needles, covered with what blankets the men have. It is evening; some candles burn on the table, and about half the bunks are occupied.

SPAD, *a round and red-faced Virginian, sits at the table with his tin of food.* TEAGUE, *wearing hunter's clothes, leans at the doorway, a man of fifty-five, lean and corded.* ALCOCK, *a beefy man, wear-*

ing a blanket, is sitting on one of the log ends. MASON *sits on one of the bunks. Teague's son,* NICK, *kneels to adjust his leggings.*

MASON. There was a Hessian Johnny [1] here today with leather boots on—looking for a job as a general—or maybe commander-in-chief. He stayed long enough to soak in a few fair-sized impressions and then took out for Philadelphia to join up with General Howe. [2]

SPAD. They eat over in Philadelphia.

MASON. Sure, the big-hearted patriots of Pennsylvania—we fight for their liberty and they carry their butter and eggs to Philadelphia in a steady stream to feed King George's troops. And you can't stop 'em. Shoot 'em dead and you can't stop 'em.

ALCOCK. King George pays cash and we pay in continentals. [3] Did you ever meet up with a Quaker [4] that didn't prefer a guinea in the hand to any amount of liberty in the bush? You can shoot 'em, hang 'em, give 'em the water cure, rip their guts out and fill 'em up with old iron, they go right on selling hogs to the English.

TEAGUE. I'm no Quaker, Son, and I'll fill anybody up with old iron that says I'd sell out to General Howe! We're going home, that's all.

ALCOCK. All right, all right. You've

read the orders: the new penalty for desertion is seventy-five lashes on the bare back, well laid on—or hanging if there's treason connected with it. Don't get caught, that's all.

TEAGUE. I've never been caught yet.

ALCOCK. How often have you taken French leave?

TEAGUE. Whenever there's nothing to do here I go home.

ALCOCK. All right.

[*The door opens and* LIEUTENANT CUTTING *comes in. He is somewhat better dressed than the men and wears a neatly cocked and corded hat. A dog follows him in and goes to the plate of food which* ALCOCK *has set beside him on the floor.*]

CUTTING. What dog's that?

ALCOCK. He came in with you, Leftenant. [5]

CUTTING. The cur's been following me all the way from the King of Prussia Inn.

SPAD. You'd better avast from that mess, pup. It'll poison you. . . .

A VOICE (*outside*). Hey, boy, what regiment's this?

ANOTHER VOICE (*outside*). Who goes?

FIRST VOICE. You keep kind of an offhand guard here, soldier. If you must know it's Lieutenant Colonel Lucifer Tench, and I asked you a question.

SECOND VOICE. First Virginia.

TENCH. Good (*He enters.*) I didn't know whether that was a sentry you had out there or a prehistoric animal. He's standing with his feet in his hat and a blanket over his ears, making no sense whatever.

[*Two or three of the men rise or half-rise out of respect.*] Sit down! Sit down and put your feet in your hats if that's the latest fashion.

---

[1] A HESSIAN JOHNNY—A Hessian fellow, evidently a freelance professional soldier from the province of Hesse in Germany.

[2] GENERAL HOWE—William Howe, the British commander-in-chief.

[3] IN CONTINENTALS—In paper money issued by the Continental Congress. Lack of confidence in the new government made the bills almost worthless.

[4] A QUAKER—Because they were firmly opposed to all wars, some Quakers insisted on continuing to trade with the British even during the American Revolution. Alcock's opinion of the Quakers is unfair, but it is the opinion a soldier would naturally have.

[5] LEFTENANT—Lieutenant. In England the pronunciation is "leftenant." Americans formerly pronounced the word the same way.

MASON. We've lost a couple of sentries with frostbite this month, sir, and the boys' shoes are none too good.

TENCH. I'm sorry to hear it, because I'm looking for a squad with passable footwear. How many able-bodied men in your company, Leftenant?

CUTTING. Seventy-two this morning.

TENCH. How many with guns, shoes, and equipment for a little stroll across country in the snow?

CUTTING. Twenty-eight—or thereabout.

ALCOCK. Put me in! I'm going if I go in my shirttails!

CUTTING. Twenty-eight.

TENCH. Twenty-eight! It'll have to do. This is a raid on the hay islands below Darby under the personal supervision of the Commander-in-chief. We have information that Sir William Howe is running short of horse-fodder in Philadelphia and will shortly make an attempt to bring in the forage which was stored last fall on the islands of the Delaware. We mean to get there first with a party of horse to cut off his approach, and a small party of pioneers to salvage the hay for ourselves or else dump it in the river. This company is made up of the kind of men we need for the work—hunters, farmers, fishermen, outdoor fellows and equal to anything.

SPAD. Right.

CUTTING. When are we supposed to start?

TENCH. Tonight. We must be there by three in the morning. Draw four days' rations for each man. We may be gone some time.

CUTTING. We don't start tonight, though.

TENCH. You heard the order, I believe!

CUTTING. With my compliments, sir, it happens the thing is impossible. We've drawn the last ration for this regiment, such as it was. If that dog keeps it on his stomach he'll probably go to meet his Maker before morning.

TENCH. The supplies for your regiment were sufficient for ten more days.

CUTTING. On paper, yes. But when they rolled out the last twenty barrels the meat was spoiled. As for the flour, they baked the remains of it this morning. . . .

[*The door opens and an* AIDE *appears.*]

THE AIDE. General Washington wishes to know if this matter is arranged, Colonel. He's in haste to reach General Wayne—

TENCH. Will you say to General Washington that I've encountered unexpected difficulties, and would be glad if he could step in for a moment—I'll tell him myself.

[*He turns and goes out, followed by the* AIDE. *There is tension in the air. One or two of the men adjust their clothes. A tall, dark* FRENCH OFFICER *of nineteen or twenty enters in resplendent uniform.* WASHINGTON *comes in after him in shabby boots, a long, much-worn cloak, and an old cocked hat.* TENCH *re-enters. The men have all risen.*]

WASHINGTON. I'm distressed to hear of this shortage of supplies, Lieutenant, but happily we are not entirely without resource. A long-expected wagon train began to arrive this evening, and though the first wagons are loaded only with munitions there are eighteen long tons of flour and pork bringing up the rear, and it should be possible to victual your expedition by the time you can put yourselves in marching order.

CUTTING. We shall make our preparations at once then. Is this the train which was sent on from Fishkill by General Putnam, sir?

WASHINGTON. It is. Though how you

may have learned of that I'm at a loss to conceive.

CUTTING. I supped this evening with General Conway, who had received a letter from Putnam. And if the information in the letter is correct I very much fear you will be disappointed of your expectations in regard to the salt pork and flour. Putnam was unable to locate mules or wagons to accommodate the food allotment.

WASHINGTON. Unable—?

CUTTING. Completely unable, as he said.

WASHINGTON. You have information that the food was not sent?

CUTTING. So it would seem.

[A pause.]

WASHINGTON. When did the letter arrive?

CUTTING. I believe yesterday.

WASHINGTON (to Tench). Can there be truth in this?

TENCH. As a matter of fact the bills of lading failed to cover the food supplies, but I supposed them in error—

WASHINGTON. I should like to hope this report was erroneous, but some little experience with the commissary department has taught me to credit any amount of ill news from that quarter. It sticks in my crop a little, let me add, that I should receive important intelligence in a manner so singularly circuitous. General Putnam writes, not to me, but to General Conway, and General Conway conveys his intelligence, not to me, but to a junior officer with whom he has supped. Quite by chance I encounter this officer and in the course of conversation these little military details are relayed to me—

CUTTING. Sir, I hope I have not offended—

WASHINGTON. Not in the least, sir. I am in your debt for the information, and can only congratulate you and General Conway on the celerity with which you receive dispatches which have not been vouchsafed [6] to the Commander-in-chief. (He turns to Tench.) The expedition will be postponed or assigned to some other company better prepared to move. Meanwhile food must be obtained for this regiment if we have to cut steaks off the members of the Board of War. They're all prime, I've noticed. (He has turned to go.)

LAFAYETTE (looking at the dog's collar). General, would you care to know whose dog this is?

WASHINGTON. We're in haste, Marquis.

LAFAYETTE. Yes, but the inscription on this collar reads: Rover, Sir William Howe. This rover has roved all the way from Philadelphia. It is General Howe's dog.

ALCOCK. I was planning to skin him—and now I'll eat him.

WASHINGTON. I might have known by the fat on his ribs he was no local product. We must see that he's returned. Have you pen and ink here?

SPAD. Yes, sir. (He sets an inkhorn and quill on the table.)

WASHINGTON. Lucifer!

[TENCH crosses to take dictation at the table.]

"Sir Wm. Howe, British Headquarters, Philadelphia.

Dear Sir: The bearer of this note will return to you a dog of which you appear to be the owner, since he wears your name on his collar. May I say that I was the more astonished to find him at Valley Forge because I believed the desertions to be going the other way. G. Washington." Choose a reliable man and send him to Philadelphia with a flag. The animal is to be delivered to the

[6] VOUCHSAFED—Granted, given.

General himself with this note and my compliments. (*Indicating* ALCOCK.) This is a man I know. Would the errand amuse you?

ALCOCK. I'm easy to amuse, General, but the fact is I haven't any britches.

WASHINGTON. Well, that can hardly be considered a defect of character. Choose a messenger, Lieutenant.

CUTTING. Yes, sir.

SPAD. I'd like to carry the note, sir.

WASHINGTON. If it's agreeable to your officer.

CUTTING. Certainly.

WASHINGTON. Then take good care of the brute, and my thanks. (*He hands the note to* SPAD.)

TEAGUE. General Washington!

WASHINGTON. Deliver both into Howe's hands.

TEAGUE. General Washington!

MASON. Hark quiet, you fool!

WASHINGTON. What is it?

TEAGUE. These here new regulations about men going home. Going home without leave. They say it's seventy-five lashes if they catch you now. Why is that?

WASHINGTON. The traditional penalty for desertion is shooting at sunrise. We've been more lenient here.

TEAGUE. But look, General Washington, it don't make sense. It don't stand to reason—

NICK. Do you want to talk your neck into a rope?

WASHINGTON. Let him say what's on his mind.

TEAGUE. Well, here it is: I'm going hungry here and my woman's going hungry at home. You let me go home for the winter, and you won't have to feed me, and that relieves the commissary; I rustle some wild meat for the younguns and the old woman, and they don't starve and I don't starve. More'n that, every-body knows there's two or three thousand men gone home already for that same reason, and if they was here now they'd be chewing the bark off the second-growth birch like so many cottontails. I don't hold it against you and I don't hold it against anybody because I don't know who in thunder to hold it against, but there's nothing to eat here.

ALCOCK. Stow it, will you? The dog ate the stuff, and he isn't dead yet.

TEAGUE. It ain't that I'm afraid of a good fight. A good fight's ham and eggs to me. Me and my boy here, we make for home every winter when the grub gets scarce, and we come back every spring when the fighting starts. We're coming back next spring, and every spring, till we chase the redcoats clear out of Chesapeake Bay, and across the Atlantic Ocean and right up a lamppost in London town! Fighting's fine, but sitting here and starving down to a hide and buttons—I don't savvy it.

WASHINGTON. What is your name, sir?

TEAGUE. Teague, sir. Teague's my name.

WASHINGTON. Well, Master Teague, if they catch you they'll give you seventy-five lashes, and that's a good deal to take and live. On the other hand you're quite right from your own angle, and if I were you I'd feel as you do. But this you should know, sir: if you go home, and we all go home this winter, you won't need to bother about coming back in the spring. There'll be no fighting to come back to. General Howe will march out of Philadelphia and take over these states of ours. If he knew now how many have deserted, how many are sick, how many unfit for duty on account of the lack of food and clothes and munitions, he'd come out in force and wring our necks one by one, and the neck of our sickly little revolution along with us. So far we've kept him pinned in Philadelphia by sheer bluster and bluff and show of arms. We've raided his supplies and cut off his shipping and captured his food trains and so bedeviled him generally that he thinks there's still an army here. But every able-bodied man, every man that owns a pair of dungarees for his legs and brogans for his feet, has to look like ten men if this nation's coming through the winter alive. What are we in this war for? Are we tired of it? Do we want to quit?

THE MEN. No, sir. No.

WASHINGTON. I can't blame you if you sound a bit halfhearted about it.

TEAGUE. I'm not halfhearted about it! Not me! I'm fighting to keep King George out of my backyard! I moved west three times to get away from his tax collectors, and every time they caught up to me! I'm sick of tax collectors, that's why I'm in it!

WASHINGTON. Then it may be you're here in error, and the sooner you discover it the better. You'll get death and taxes under one government as well as another. But I'll tell you why I'm here, and why I've hoped you were here, and why it's seemed to me worth while to stick with it while our guns rust out for lack of pow-der, and men die around me for lack of food and medicine and women and children sicken at home for lack of clothing and the little they need to eat—yes, while we fight one losing battle after another, and retreat to fight again another year, and yet another and another, and still lose more than we win, and yet fight on while our hair grows gray and our homes break up in our absence, and the best and youngest among us give their blood to swell spring freshets and leave their bones and marrow to flesh the hills. This is no lucky war for me. I thought it was at first. I wanted to astound the world as a military leader, but my head's grayer now and I've had enough of that. What I fight for now is a dream, a mirage, perhaps, something that's never existed and will never exist unless we can make it and put it here—the right of free-born men to govern themselves in their own way. Now men are mostly fools, as you're well aware. They'll govern themselves like fools. There are probably more fools to the square inch in the Continental Congress than in the Continental Army, and the percentage runs high in both. But we've set our teeth and trained our guns against the hereditary right of arbitrary kings, and if we win it's curfew for all the kings of the world. . . . It may not be

PHOTO BY CHARLES PHELPS CUSHING

worth the doing. . . . It's for you to decide, Master Teague—you, and your son, and the rest of you. This is your fight more than mine. I don't know how long the Congress means to keep me where I am nor how long you mean to stay with me. If you desert they may catch you and they may not, but the chances are they won't, for the sentries are men as you are—hungry, shivering, miserable, and inclined to look the other way. Make your own decision. But if we lose you—if you've lost interest in this cause of yours—we've lost our war, lost it completely, and the men we've left lying on our battlefields died for nothing whatever—for a dream that came too early— and may never come true. (*He pauses, looks round at the men, then at the officers.*) We mark time here, gentlemen, and there's much to do. (*He goes to the door, followed by* LAFAYETTE *and the* AIDE.) Tench!

TENCH. I'll follow you in a moment, sir.

[WASHINGTON, LAFAYETTE, *and the* AIDE *go out.* TEAGUE *and* NICK *look at each other briefly.*]

TEAGUE. I guess the old woman'll get along. She's brought in her own bear meat before.

NICK. Well, it's all right with me. (*He straightens up, deliberately takes in another hole in his belt, crosses to a bunk, and lies back.*)

SCENE 2

SCENE: *Washington's headquarters. The parlor of a colonial house. Windows and an entrance door to the left; to the rear a fireplace and a door to dining room. A small desk is placed at the right, and rather formal chairs are spaced about the room. A large map hangs on the rear wall, showing Philadelphia, the Delaware below the city, and Valley Forge.* TENCH *is seated at the desk.* GENERALS VARNUM *and* STIRLING *are seated near him.* LAFAYETTE *is leaning at the rear doorway and* WASHINGTON *stands near the window, occasionally pacing back and forth.*

WASHINGTON. It's not accident,
as you may have thought, that you four
    are here tonight.
There's a question I ask myself so often
    now
I must ask it of someone else. The reports before us
show us we've neither food nor clothes
    nor arms
for the maintenance of an army, nor defense
if we're attacked. In my last letter to
    Congress
I told them we must either starve or
    dissolve
unless they sent instant aid. I've written
    before
almost as urgently, receiving replies—
friendly, cajoling, evasive, full of advice,
mostly unworkable, and a thin stream of
    goods,
sufficient, say, for half a regiment,
and we've foraged for the rest. They're
    sending tomorrow
two commissioners to investigate; by the
    time
we've satisfied these stool-wits [7] that we're
    dying
the men who have gumption left to arise
    and walk
will have walked away, and we'll muster
    nobody here
but the sick and naked. It's begun already.
Great bands of marauders shift away from
    camp
and range the country like brigands.
    Some thousand or two

[7] STOOL-WITS—Men who make investigations and reports instead of acting.

have put out for home; it's reckoned another thousand
has crossed the lines to Howe. One-third of our soldiers,
and those the most able-bodied, have gone—the remainder—
how they hold out, or why, I don't know. We can't blame them
if they follow their fellows. Now when our army's gone,
as it seems to be going, Sir William Howe, who's waited
for just this chance, will stroll out in his fat-haunched way
to round us in and we're done for. My question's simply:
Does this end the adventure? Is the revolution over,
or is it worth trying to hold on into spring
when at least there's food to be had? It will cost lives,
by hundreds, perhaps by thousands. What it means to me
to say this, I think you know. I ask General Varnum,
as first in rank, to speak first.
   VARNUM. Sir, I'm a soldier. If I were in command
of the Continental Army, I'd say now
we can't go on. But I'm not in command.
I'm a soldier, and I take orders. And what I say
as a soldier, one who takes orders, is, now God help you,
you who bear this burden, to find some way
to command though we feed on dust and carrion,
and wear no pelts but our own, that we stick it out—
What orders you give
May there be men left to follow!
   WASHINGTON. And you, General Stirling?
   STIRLING. I'll string along with Varnum.

It's not on my conscience, I know, and it is on yours
if men die in a dead cause. As a way to die
it's early and unpleasant, and may come to nothing,
but I think you underestimate the number
who'll see it through with you, if you give the word,
till we've eaten the wolves extinct.
   WASHINGTON. Enough, you think,
to hold the English till spring?
   STIRLING. No!
There would be enough—
now here I take up a sore subject, and one perhaps
there's no place for in this conference— but there'd be enough
and then to spare, if those moth-eaten drones
who've served abroad, and spread their dog-eared commissions
in every company, to prove they've been in a war—
if they were dumped in the Schuylkill through the ice
till they'd mixed their brandy with water.
   WASHINGTON. Let's stay with our subject.
There are many with us who served in England and France,
and in Germany, too, before this war. There are some
of irreplaceable value—
   STIRLING. And some,
who'd sell the cannon out of Valley Forge
for three Spanish dollars, paper! . . .
   TENCH. This country'd come to you
with open arms if you said to them once for all:
I'll take just this and that, and I'll take it now
when it's needed! One word, one breath from you and you'd blow
the Congress from here to Maine!

WASHINGTON. A dictator?

TENCH. Why,
are you so afraid of words? It's that or
lose.

WASHINGTON. Has it escaped you, sir,
that we fight this war
against usurpation of power? Should I
usurp
the powers of Congress, which gave me
what power I have,
I'd have nothing left to fight for.

TENCH. I beg your pardon!
We're in rebellion against the King of
England,
or so I thought.

WASHINGTON. It happens that our Congress
is the heart of what we fight for, good or
bad,
and I uphold it. Now, keeping that in
mind,
is it possible to go on?

TENCH. No, it is not.
Last night there was mutiny in the Eighteenth; they objected
to their food, and little blame to them.
The riot
was quelled only by scouring out the
larders
of neighboring battalions. This will happen again
and spread. . . .
. . . I'm not a pious man;
I'm a soldier, as Varnum says he is, and a
soldier's business
is to fight when he has to, run away when
he can,
eat if he can get it, drink as much as
there is,
and stay alive. I'll fight for the man I
believe in,
but if I'm to fight to make Congress
permanent
they can take their revolution and stick
it back
in the bung it came from!

WASHINGTON. That's plainly said.

TENCH. If it's too plain I'm sorry.

STIRLING. Well, but pause a moment,
my gentle Lucifer;[8] there's treason
enough
without our adding to it.

TENCH. If I speak treason,
make the most of it! The whole war
is treason to King George! It all depends
on the point of view, and whether you
win!

VARNUM. But still
this war's for liberty; and the government
we've set up freely for ourselves, we're
here
to defend it—for nothing else.

TENCH. Well, when it comes
to governments you'll have to let me out.
They're all alike, and have one business,
governments,
and it's to plunder. This new one we've
set up
seems to be less efficient than the old style
in its methods of plundering folk, but
give them time;
they'll learn to sink their teeth in what
you've got
and take it from you. Forget the cause!
I'll fight
while I'm fed and paid, and I haven't
seen much lately
of either one.

WASHINGTON. This is new.

TENCH. I've read your letters
to Congress, and read their replies, and
they've sickened me
of our war for freedom!

WASHINGTON. Marquis?

LAFAYETTE. I'm loath to speak,
gentlemen, in this conference. I shall
offend,
I know, being but a young man, alien,

[8] LUCIFER—This is Tench's first name. It is
also the name of the angel that rebelled against
Heaven.

the scion [9] of an old kingdom, *ancien regime* [10]
in word and manner.

WASHINGTON. The more reason we should hear you.

STIRLING. Let's have it, lad.

LAFAYETTE. Shall I begin by saying
something you know, but may have forgotten? This world
you have cut from a wilderness is a new world, brighter
with sun in summer, colder with winter cold
than the world I knew. The air's strange-sharp, the voice
rings here with a hard ring. I find no man
but looks you in the eye and says his thought
in your teeth, and means it. This was not known before
on this star we inhabit. Europe has thirty kings
and a hundred million slaves. But here in this land
each man's a king, and walks like a king, each woman
bears herself regally, like a queen. You will find
this is not easy to throw away. The air
of this coast has fired your blood, and while three among you,
no more than three, hold hard against the old masters,
the kingdoms lessen and dwindle. They've felt your breath
and feared it, in the old world. Lose! Now the gods
in heaven hear me, you cannot lose! Bow down

and humble yourselves if you can! It's not in you to bow
nor to speak humbly. It's a trick you've never learned
and cannot learn in this air! . . .
. . . The name of Washington
is magical in France. It conjures up
all we have hoped to dare, all our young men
have deemed worth dying for. . . .
. . . We have set ourselves
to send you men, money, ships. The little king
may scream, and cling to his velvet furniture
and stamp on his powdered wig, still he's dragged along
with Beaumarchais [11] and before the end of spring
you will have these men, money, and ships.

STIRLING. The end of spring.

LAFAYETTE. You cannot wait. I know it. Not possibly.
Yet if you knew what dreams and faith rest on you,
You would do this impossible. . . .

VARNUM. Yes, but the question's not what we want to do
but what we can.

WASHINGTON. What's on hand?

TENCH. We might scratch up
by equalizing, three or four days' provision
for every corps.

WASHINGTON. Three days!
As for our high purpose,
we have it still, but the men, the men are mortal
and die around us so fast the heaviest work's
to bury the dead. Our slopes are honeycombed

---

[9] SCION (sī'ŭn)—Descendant.

[10] *Ancien regime* (än'syäN′ rå'zhēm′)—The old order. Although the Marquis de Lafayette is a friend of democracy, he is a product of the aristocratic tradition which the American Revolutionists are fighting to overthrow.

[11] BEAUMARCHAIS (bō'már'shĕ′)—The assumed name of Pierre Caron, French playwright and political leader, who favored giving aid to the American colonies.

with digging graves. The wards are crammed with sick
lying on logs without blankets. No medicine,
no food, no care; the farms around us swept
board-clean of grain this thirty miles. It's the men;
the men are human. They chop green wood for fires,
and shiver over them, stand their watch by night,
and drill by day, go to sleep supperless
and watch each other sicken. A stench goes up,
but whether it's from the living, dying or dead
it's too late to care. The lines of war we keep,
one middling wind would blow them with the leaves and heap them in the gullies. Gentlemen,
looking back over what you've offered— each one of you
has said in his own way—even Lafayette—
there's no immediate hope. And since I agree
that this is true—we should make our preparations
to break up camp and give over. We should—and yet—
since it's begun
and we're in it deep, while we have men and arms
and a government behind us and a gambler's stake
in what's to happen, we must still stand here
and take things as they come.
    LAFAYETTE. This is the man
we heard of overseas!
    WASHINGTON. If you heard of a martyr
I fear I'll disappoint you. I'd rather live
and have my fun in my time, before my face hardens
into a mountain crag. I have no taste
for being stood into a hero: St. George and the dragon,
one foot on tyranny's neck, a long spontoon [12]
glittering in my gripe! What's the king to me?
A customer for tobacco. But we have three days.
And the order's given. We gamble our three days
on a change of luck and face what brand of hell's
reserved for madmen.
    [*The officers rise.*]
    TENCH. Our usual brand of hell,
only more of it.
    VARNUM. It will come to complete disaster,
very likely.
    STIRLING. And yet, if you'd said, "We quit, tonight,"
I'd have walked to the other side of the glen
and blown my brains out.
    TENCH. You'd have taken a drink
and then another, and said, "All right, we quit."
And so would I.
    WASHINGTON. All commanders
meet here at five in the morning.
    STIRLING. At five? The night's
half-shot already.
    WASHINGTON. At five.
    TENCH. Drink one less bottle
and you'll come out plumb at five. Good night.
    WASHINGTON. Good night, sir. . . .

[12] SPONTOON—A broad-bladed weapon used in the eighteenth and nineteenth centuries.

◇◇◇◇◇◇◇◇◇◇◇◇◇◇◇◇◇◇◇◇◇◇◇◇◇◇◇◇◇◇

FOR UNDERSTANDING

1. How is it shown that Washington's men are not receiving proper food? that

some of Washington's officers fail to keep him informed about whether the army is receiving supplies?

2. Explain why Teague feels, at first, that it is right to leave the army and go home. Quote a remark by Washington which shows that he sympathizes with Teague's point of view. If Teague were caught, would Washington soften the punishment for his desertion? Explain the reason Washington gives to show why it is necessary for the men to stay at Valley Forge.

3. In his second long speech, Washington describes the almost hopeless situation of the American army. Quote the expression in which he states, in a few words, the American dream—the dream that makes him keep on fighting.

4. How does Washington's action concerning the dog show the courtesy with which opposing generals treated each other in this period of history? The joking message which Washington dictates shows the pleasant, human side of his character. What is the joke? Point out other ways in which the author uses the dog to add humor to this rather grim, solemn story.

5. In the second scene—talking confidentially to the officers who work most closely with him—Washington seems more uncertain than in the first scene about what he should do. He apparently thinks he might hold out until spring, although at great cost to his men. Explain why he is not sure that he should do so.

6. Why is Washington unswervingly loyal to Congress even though he agrees with his advisers that Congress has acted unwisely?

7. What qualities does Lafayette find in American life that he has not found in Europe? What hope does he hold out for the Americans if they can keep up the fight a little longer?

8. In this play, Washington is the hero but the heroic spirit of his soldiers and his officers is also emphasized. How does the author make clear that the men are more determined in the fight for independence than would appear from their attitudes?

FOR BROADER MEANINGS

1. If it is true, as Lafayette says, that a new, rather unruly attitude of sturdy self-respect grew up in the American colonies, what caused it? That is, why did the Americans—who were, after all, of European background—begin to feel like free men even while they were still under the rule of a European government?

2. Washington says, "Men are mostly fools . . . They'll govern themselves like fools," but he still prefers democracy to the rule of kings. Explain why self-government is desirable even if we accept Washington's remark as being wholly true.

3. Near the end of the complete play *Valley Forge*, Washington says:

This liberty will look easy by and by,
When nobody dies to get it.

The play was written to make us realize the value of freedom by remembering what it cost earlier Americans. Give examples from modern history which prove that American citizens are still as worthy of freedom as were the men at Valley Forge. See how many examples the class can think of in *other countries* of heroic defense against foreign tyranny.

MAXWELL ANDERSON (1888–1959)

Born in Pennsylvania, Mr. Anderson was a prominent Broadway playwright for many years. He attended the University of North Dakota, then taught English in California while taking graduate work at Stanford University. He began his literary career as a writer of articles and poems. Many of his dramas are, like *Valley Forge*, written at least partly in poetic form.

Anderson's first "hit" was the vigorous and very funny war play *What Price Glory?* It was written in collaboration with Lawrence Stallings and was first performed in 1924. In 1933 Anderson's *Both Your Houses* won the Pulitzer Prize for its powerful denunciation of graft in American politics.

BETTMANN ARCHIVE

The American Revolution—As Seen by the Men Who Were There

You will notice that some of the literature which was written during the Revolutionary period does not itself deal with the Revolution. For example, Benjamin Franklin's *Autobiography* and his *Poor Richard's Almanac* are not directly connected with the question of freedom from British rule. However, such works suggest the independent spirit of hard-working American artisans and businessmen. Respecting their own tough self-reliance, proud to stand on their own feet, they were not to be awed by the commands of kings and aristocrats. Other examples of the literature of Revolutionary times are ballads like "Yankee Doodle" which were sung by the patriots; Patrick Henry's fiery speech calling for the defense of liberty; and famous documents of statecraft like the Declaration of Independence and Washington's Farewell Address. You will discover that the literature often strikes a high, heroic note. It is an excited, and at the same time a serious and thoughtful, literature. Americans well knew they were living in a time that called for great deeds. Determined to see their brave struggle through to the end, they were also determined to plan their new government so wisely that the liberty they had won would be preserved for all time.

EARLY LIFE AND
SELF-EDUCATION

BENJAMIN FRANKLIN

These incidents from the early life of Franklin show in him even as a young boy the many-sided curiosity and the enterprise that were later to distinguish his career.

Josiah, my father, married young, and carried his wife with three children into New England, about 1682. The conventicles [1] having been forbidden by law, and frequently disturbed, induced some considerable men of his acquaintance to remove to that country, and he was prevailed with to accompany them thither, where they expected to enjoy their mode of religion with freedom. By the same wife he had four children more born there, and by a second wife ten more, in all seventeen; of which I remember thirteen sitting at one time at his table, who all grew up to be men and women, and married; I was the youngest son, and the youngest child but two, and was born in Boston, New England. My mother, the second wife, was Abiah Folger, daughter of Peter Folger, one of the first settlers of New England, of whom honorable mention is made by Cotton Mather, in his church history of that country, as *"a godly, learned Englishman,"* if I remember the words rightly. I have heard that he wrote sundry small occasional pieces, but only one of them was printed, which I saw now many years since.

My elder brothers were put apprentices to different trades. I was put to the grammar school at eight years of age, my

[1] CONVENTICLES—Religious meetings.

father intending to devote me to the service of the Church. My early readiness in learning to read (which must have been very early, as I do not remember when I could not read), and the opinion of all his friends, that I should certainly make a good scholar, encouraged him in this purpose of his. My Uncle Benjamin, too, approved of it, and proposed to give me all his shorthand volumes of sermons, I suppose as a stock to set up with. I continued, however, at the grammar school not quite one year, though in that time I had risen gradually from the middle of the class of that year to be the head of it, and was removed into the next class above it. But my father, in the meantime, from a view of the expense of a college education, which having so large a family he could not well afford, altered his first intention, took me from the grammar school, and sent me to a school for writing and arithmetic, kept by a then famous man, Mr. George Brownell, very successful in his profession generally, and that by mild, encouraging methods. Under him I acquired fair writing pretty soon, but I failed in the arithmetic, and made no progress in it. At ten years old I was taken home to assist my father in his business, which was that of a tallow chandler and soap boiler; a business he was not bred to, but had assumed on his arrival in New England, and on finding his dyeing trade would not maintain his family. Accordingly, I was employed in cutting wick for the candles, filling the dipping mold and the molds for cast candles, attending the shop, going of errands, etc.

I disliked the trade, and had a strong inclination for the sea, but my father declared against it; however, living near the water, I was much in and about it, learned early to swim well, and to manage boats; and when in a boat or canoe with other boys, I was commonly allowed to govern,[2] especially in any case of difficulty; and upon other occasions I was generally a leader among the boys, and sometimes led them into scrapes, of which I will mention one instance, as it shows an early public spirit, though not then justly conducted.[3]

There was a salt marsh that bounded part of the millpond, on the edge of which, at high water, we used to stand to fish for minnows. By much trampling, we had made it a mere quagmire. My proposal was to build a wharf there fit for us to stand upon, and I showed my comrades a large heap of stones, which were intended for a new house near the marsh, and which would very well suit our purpose. Accordingly, in the evening, when the workmen were gone, I assembled a number of my playfellows, and working with them diligently like so many emmets[4] sometimes two or three to a stone, we brought them all away and built our little wharf. The next morning the workmen were surprised at missing the stones, which were found in our wharf. Inquiry was made after the removers; we were dis-

covered and complained of; several of us were corrected by our fathers; and, though I pleaded the usefulness of the work, mine convinced me that nothing was useful which was not honest.

To return: I continued thus employed in my father's business for two years, that is, till I was twelve years old; and my brother John, who was bred to that business, having left my father, married, and set up for himself at Rhode Island, there was all appearance that I was destined to supply his place, and become a tallow chandler. But my dislike to the trade continuing, my father was under apprehensions that if he did not find one for me more agreeable, I should break away and get to sea, as his son Josiah had done, to his great vexation. He therefore sometimes took me to walk with him, to see joiners,[5] bricklayers, turners, braziers,[6] etc., at their work, that he might observe my inclination, and endeavor to fix it on some trade or other on land. It has ever since been a pleasure to me to see good workmen handle their tools; and it has been useful to me, having learned so much by it as to be able to do little jobs myself in my house when a workman could not readily be got, and to construct little machines for my experiments, while the intention of making the experiment was fresh and warm in my mind. My father at last fixed upon the cutler's trade, and my uncle Benjamin's son Samuel, who was bred to that business in London, being about that time established in Boston, I was sent to be with him some time on liking. But his expectations of a fee[7] with me displeasing my father, I was taken home again.

---

[2] GOVERN—Steer.
[3] JUSTLY CONDUCTED—Turned in the right direction.
[4] EMMETS—Ants.

[5] JOINERS—Woodworkers, especially those who make doors and stairs, and do other things where "joining" is necessary.
[6] BRAZIERS—Workers in brass.
[7] FEE—Payment for teaching Benjamin.

From a child I was fond of reading, and all the little money that came into my hands was ever laid out in books. Pleased with the *Pilgrim's Progress*, my first collection was of John Bunyan's works in separate little volumes. I afterward sold them to enable me to buy R. Burton's *Historical Collections*; they were small chapmen's books,[8] and cheap, 40 or 50 in all. My father's little library consisted chiefly of books on divinity, most of which I read, and have since often regretted that, at a time when I had such a thirst for knowledge, more proper books had not fallen in my way. Plutarch's *Lives*[9] there was in which I read abundantly, and I still think that time spent to great advantage. There was also a book of De Foe's, called an *Essay on Projects*,[10] and another of Dr. Mather's, called *Essays To Do Good*, which perhaps gave me a turn of thinking that had an influence on some of the principal future events of my life.

This bookish inclination at length determined my father to make me a printer, though he had already one son (James) of that profession. In 1717 my brother James returned from England with a press and letters to set up his business in Boston. I liked it much better than that of my father, but still had a hankering for the sea. To prevent the apprehended effect of such an inclination, my father was impatient to have me bound to my brother. I stood out some time, but at last was persuaded, and signed the indentures when I was yet but twelve years old. I was to serve as an apprentice till I was twenty-one years of age, only I was to

be allowed journeyman's wages during the last year. In a little time I made great proficiency in the business, and became a useful hand to my brother. I now had access to better books. An acquaintance with the apprentices of booksellers enabled me sometimes to borrow a small one, which I was careful to return soon and clean. Often I sat up in my room reading the greatest part of the night, when the book was borrowed in the evening and to be returned early in the morning, lest it should be missed or wanted.

And after some time an ingenious tradesman, Mr. Matthew Adams, who had a pretty[11] collection of books, and who frequented our printing house, took notice of me, invited me to his library, and very kindly lent me such books as I chose to read. I now took a fancy to poetry, and made some little pieces; my brother, thinking it might turn to account, encouraged me, and put me on composing occasional ballads.[12] One was called "The Lighthouse Tragedy," and contained an account of the drowning of Captain Worthilake, with his two daughters: the other was a sailor's song, on the taking of *Teach* (or Blackbeard) the pirate. They were wretched stuff, and when they were printed he sent me about the town to sell them. The first sold wonderfully, the event being recent, having made a great noise.[13] This flattered my vanity; but my father discouraged me by ridiculing my performances, and telling me versemakers were generally beg-

---

[8] CHAPMEN'S BOOKS—Books sold by peddlers.

[9] PLUTARCH'S *Lives*—A famous series of biographies of distinguished Greeks and Romans.

[10] *Essay on Projects*—The projects treated were insurance companies, banks, and other commercial institutions.

[11] PRETTY—Very good.

[12] OCCASIONAL BALLADS—In colonial times it was the custom of printers to get out on the "occasion" of any unusual event a "ballad," or piece of rough-and-ready poetry, telling about the happening. These were sold on the streets. They were the "extras" of the day.

[13] HAVING MADE A GREAT NOISE—Having been noised abroad.

gars. So I escaped being a poet, most probably a very bad one; but as prose writing has been of great use to me in the course of my life, and was a principal means of my advancement, I shall tell you how, in such a situation, I acquired what little ability I have in that way.

There was another bookish lad in the town, John Collins by name, with whom I was intimately acquainted. We sometimes disputed, and very fond we were of argument, and very desirous of confuting one another, which disputatious turn, by the way, is apt to become a very bad habit, making people often extremely disagreeable in company by the contradiction that is necessary to bring it into practice; and thence, besides souring and spoiling the conversation, is productive of disgusts and, perhaps, enmities where you may have occasion for friendship. I had caught it by reading my father's books of dispute about religion. Persons of good sense, I have since observed, seldom fall into it, except lawyers, university men, and men of all sorts that have been bred at Edinborough.[14]

A question was once started between Collins and me, of the propriety of educating the female sex in learning, and their abilities for study. He was of opinion that it was improper, and that they were naturally unequal to it. I took the contrary side, perhaps a little for dispute's sake. He was naturally more eloquent, had a ready plenty of words; and sometimes, as I thought, bore me down more by his fluency than by the strength of his reasons. As we parted without settling the point, and were not to see one another again for some time, I sat down to put my arguments in writing, which I

copied and sent to him. He answered, and I replied. Three or four letters had passed, when my father happened to find my papers and read them. Without entering into the discussion, he took occasion to talk to me about the manner of my writing; observed that, though I had the advantage of my antagonist in correct spelling and pointing,[15] I fell far short in elegance of expression, in method, and in perspicuity. I saw the justice of his remarks, and thence grew more attentive to the manner in writing, and determined to endeavor at improvement.

About this time I met with an odd volume of the *Spectator*.[16] I had never before seen any of them. I bought it, read it over and over, and was much delighted with it. I thought the writing excellent, and wished, if possible, to imitate it. With this view I took some of the papers, and, making short hints[17] of the sentiment in each sentence, laid them by a few days, and then, without looking at the book, tried to complete the papers again, by expressing each hinted sentiment at length, and as fully as it had been expressed before, in any suitable words that should come to hand. Then I compared my *Spectator* with the original, discovered some of my faults, and corrected them. But I found I wanted a stock of words, or a readiness in recollecting and using them, which I thought I should have acquired before that time if I had gone on making verses; since the continual occasion for words of the same import, but of different length, to suit

[15] POINTING—Punctuation.

[16] *Spectator*—The *Spectator* was a light periodical published for about two years by the English writers, Joseph Addison and Richard Steele. The chief feature of the leaflets was a series of essays on manners and affairs. The essays were later bound in volumes and were known as the *Spectator Papers*. It was one of these volumes that Franklin had discovered.

[17] HINTS—Notes.

[14] BRED AT EDINBOROUGH—A fling at the Scotch who are popularly believed to enjoy arguing.

the measure, or of different sound for the rhyme, would have laid me under a constant necessity of searching for variety, and also have tended to fix that variety in my mind, and make me master of it. Therefore I took some of the tales and turned them into verse; and, after a time, when I had pretty well forgotten the prose, turned them back again. I also sometimes jumbled my collections of hints into confusion, and after some weeks endeavored to reduce them into the best order, before I began to form the full sentences and complete the paper. This was to teach me methods in the arrangement of thoughts. By comparing my work afterwards with the original, I discovered many faults and amended them; but I sometimes had the pleasure of fancying that, in certain particulars of small import, I had been lucky enough to improve the method or the language, and this encouraged me to think I might possibly in time come to be a tolerable English writer, of which I was extremely ambitious. My time for these exercises and for reading was at night, after work or before it began in the morning, or on Sundays, when I contrived to be in the printing house alone, evading as much as I could the common attendance on public worship which my father used to exact on me when I was under his care, and which indeed I still thought a duty, though I could not, as it seemed to me, afford time to practice it.

◇◇◇◇◇◇◇◇◇◇◇◇◇◇◇◇◇◇◇◇◇◇◇◇◇◇◇

FOR UNDERSTANDING

1. Cotton Mather described Benjamin Franklin's grandfather as a "godly, learned Englishman." Why would the same expression apply equally well to Benjamin's father? Why did Benjamin Franklin's father leave England for America?

2. Explain how Franklin was continuing in the tradition of his ancestors when he became a leader in the revolt against the tyranny of the English government.

3. Franklin's writings have been published all over the world in several languages. What was the earliest incident that showed in him an inclination to become a writer? How did his dispute with a friend lead to practice in writing? Explain what steps Franklin took, without stimulus from any outside source, to improve himself as a writer.

4. In later life Franklin conducted several notable scientific experiments and also made some practical inventions, such as his famous stove. How does this selection show that he had early acquaintance with trades and craftsmanship?

5. Franklin made his greatest contribution to American history as a statesman and diplomat during the time of the Revolution. How does his early life show his tendency to be a leader and organizer?

6. If you are not already informed, look up an explanation of the practice of apprenticeship. Explain the following terms: *apprentice, journeyman, master, indenture.*

A SELF-MADE MAN

1. Give reasons why according to modern standards Franklin was given rather a poor start in life. In your answer, consider the terms of the apprenticeship to his brother, and the amount of schooling Franklin was given.

2. At the age of seventeen, Franklin had a disagreement with his brother and ran away to Philadelphia where he got a job in a printing shop. Six years later he had his own press and began to publish the *Pennsylvania Gazette*, which gradually made him a well-known person in the colonies. The above selection shows that even as a boy he made full use of his few opportunities for self-improvement, particularly in educating himself. Name four books that he read. Explain three different ways by which he obtained books.

3. It has been jokingly said that first Franklin improved himself; then he improved the city of Philadelphia by starting such projects as a public library, a city police force, and a city hospital; and then he went on to the improvement of the political condition of the American colonies. How was his boyish prank with the building stones an example of "public spirit," although it was a misguided one?

FOR YOUR VOCABULARY

Franklin was a *versatile* man. That is, he was *many-sided, able to do many kinds of things*. Another example of a versatile genius was Leonardo Da Vinci, the great Renaissance painter who was also an architect, musician, engineer, and scientist. Thomas Jefferson was also versatile.

Each of these men could "turn his hand to almost anything," and the word *versatile* is derived from a Latin word meaning *to turn*. The word *versus* means *turned against*, as when one athletic team is matched against another. Another word from the same root is *version*. It can mean *a translation*, as when we speak of a *version* of the Bible; or it can mean *an account or description from a different point of view*, as when we ask someone to give his version of something he saw happen. Explain how both meanings of *version* are connected with the idea of *a turning*.

What kind of turning takes place when you *invert* something? when you *reverse* your direction? Using a dictionary, explain which side of a coin is the *reverse* and which is the *obverse*.

BENJAMIN FRANKLIN (1706–1790)

It is often said that Benjamin Franklin typifies the age in which he lived. But it is also true that Franklin had those qualities which would make him thrive in any age. He was intelligent and ambitious. He had shrewd common sense, and an understanding of human nature. Above all, he was a tireless worker. As we read the list of his achievements, we are divided in wonder between the *variety* of his abilities and the prodigious *amount* he accomplished. How could one man possibly do so many things so well? Consider a partial list:

Although he had only two years of schooling, for twenty-five years he circulated the most popular piece of reading matter throughout the colonies—*Poor Richard's Almanac*.

He founded the school that later became the University of Pennsylvania.

He invented the Franklin stove which pointed the way to our modern systems of heating by radiation.

He identified electricity and proposed a theory in explanation of it to which scientists have returned, naming the "particles" Franklin talked about "electrons."

He organized in Philadelphia an efficient paying postal system which became the model for the postal system of the United States.

He organized the first police force in the colonies, the first fire company, the first state militia, and established the first public library.

Self-taught, he became our most pleasing and successful representative in London and Paris.

He was the only American to sign the four great documents of his age—the Declaration of Independence, the Treaty of Alliance with France, the Peace Treaty with Great Britain, and the Constitution of the United States.

Such a list reveals four sides of Franklin's nature. He was a *practical* man—one who knew how to make his ideas work; an *inquisitive* scientist; a *persistent* reformer and improver; and a *statesman*. As if this were not enough, Franklin had two other valuable characteristics. He was a genial, good-humored man who had a considerable reputation as a humorist; and he had a knack of getting along with people. This last characteristic was important when, representing the colonies in England, Franklin had to make the force of his personality felt by the highborn gentlemen whose political favor he needed. It was important again when he served as ambassador to France. There, it was good form in court circles to adopt a gracefully flirtatious manner toward the ladies. The elderly, homely Franklin became a gallant "beau"—and succeeded in getting French aid for the American Revolution. One thing that helped him was the fact that intellectual brilliance was fashionable among ladies of the French nobility.

The key to Franklin's achievements may be found in the most readable of his works, his *Autobiography*. In it he reveals himself as a clear-headed, methodical man. He could set a course for himself, and keep it. Because he was in control of himself at all times, he was able to control others. Past eighty, he was, when we see him holding in line the quarreling delegates to the Constitutional Convention. Throughout the period of the Revolution he was—next to Washington—the best known and the most revered man in America.

◈◈◈◈◈

Sayings from
POOR RICHARD'S ALMANAC

BENJAMIN FRANKLIN

An almanac is an elaborate calendar to which is added weather forecasts, astronomical facts, and miscellaneous information like tables of weights and measures. Benjamin Franklin's almanac, which he issued under the name of Richard Saunders, was a best seller during the twenty-five years he published it. Like other publishers of almanacs, Franklin made weather predictions for the entire year—but he did not expect his readers to take them very seriously. In one preface "Richard Saunders" explained with mock gravity that every one of his prophecies would come true "IN SOME PLACE OR OTHER on this little diminutive globe of ours."

What distinguished Franklin's almanac were the proverbs and witty sayings with which he filled up the blank spaces in each edition. Some were invented by Franklin himself, but most of them were bits of concentrated wisdom which he took from the literature of many nations—often improving them. Although they dealt with every imaginable subject, it was noticeable that they especially emphasized the good common-sense virtues of honesty, self-respect, and hard work. Over the years, the character of their imaginary author, Poor Richard, was built up as that of a shrewd, thrifty countryman with a gift for homespun humor. By thousands of people he was—and still is—quoted with delight.

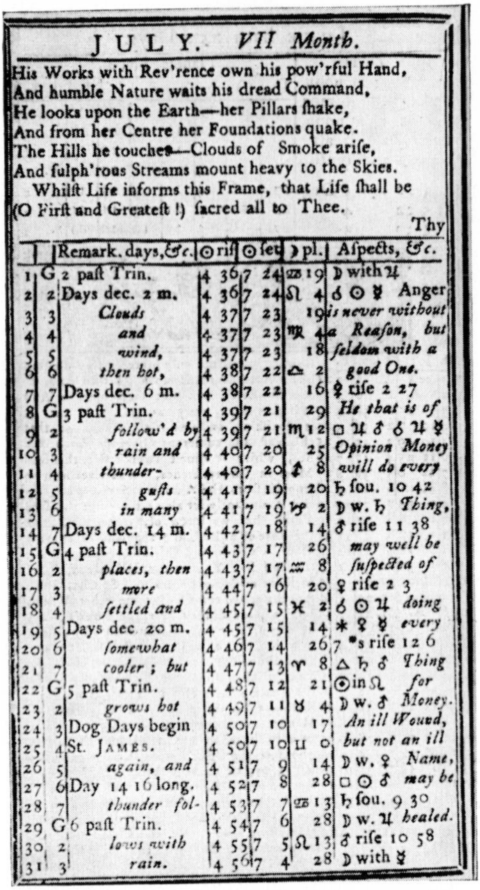

JULY. *VII Month.*

His Works with Rev'rence own his pow'rful Hand,
And humble Nature waits his dread Command,
He looks upon the Earth—her Pillars ſhake,
And from her Centre her Foundations quake.
The Hills he touches—Clouds of Smoke ariſe,
And ſulph'rous Streams mount heavy to the Skies.
Whilſt Life informs this Frame, that Life ſhall be
(O Firſt and Greateſt !) ſacred all to Thee.

Thy

		Remark. days, &c.	☉ riſ	☉ ſet	☽ pl.	Aſpects, &c.
1	G	2 paſt Trin.	4 36	7 24	♋ 19	☽ with ♃
2	2	Days dec. 2 m.	4 36	7 24	♌ 4	☌ ☉ ☿ Anger
3	3	*Clouds*	4 37	7 23	19	*is never without*
4	4	*and*	4 37	7 23	♍ 4	*a Reaſon, but*
5	5	*wind,*	4 37	7 23	18	*ſeldom with a*
6	6	*then hot,*	4 38	7 22	♎ 2	*good One.*
7	7	Days dec. 6 m.	4 38	7 22	16	♀ riſe 2 27
8	G	3 paſt Trin.	4 39	7 21	29	*He that is of*
9	2	*follow'd by*	4 39	7 21	♏ 12	□ ♃ ♂ ☌ ♃ ☿
10	3	*rain and*	4 40	7 20	25	*Opinion Money*
11	4	*thunder-*	4 40	7 20	♐ 8	*will do every*
12	5	*guſts*	4 41	7 19	20	♄ ſou. 10 42
13	6	*in many*	4 41	7 19	♑ 2	☽ w. ♄ *Thing,*
14	7	Days dec. 14 m.	4 42	7 18	14	♂ riſe 11 38
15	G	4 paſt Trin.	4 43	7 17	26	*may well be*
16	2	*places, then*	4 43	7 17	♒ 8	*ſuſpected of*
17	3	*more*	4 44	7 16	20	♀ riſe 2 3
18	4	*ſettled and*	4 45	7 15	♓ 2	☌ ☉ ♃ *doing*
19	5	Days dec 20 m.	4 45	7 15	14	✱ ♀ ☿ *every*
20	6	*ſomewhat*	4 46	7 14	26	7 *s riſe 12 6
21	7	*cooler ; but*	4 47	7 13	♈ 8	△ ♄ ♂ *Thing*
22	G	5 paſt Trin.	4 48	7 12	21	☉ in ♌ *for*
23	2	*grows hot*	4 49	7 11	♉ 4	☽ w. ♂ *Money.*
24	3	Dog Days begin	4 50	7 10	17	*An ill Wound,*
25	4	St. JAMES.	4 50	7 10	♊ 0	*but not an ill*
26	5	*again, and*	4 51	7 9	14	☽ w. ♀ *Name,*
27	6	Day 14 16 long.	4 52	7 8	28	□ ☉ ♂ *may be*
28	7	*thunder fol-*	4 53	7 7	♋ 13	♄ ſou. 9 30
29	G	6 paſt Trin.	4 54	7 6	28	☽ w. ♃ *healed.*
30	2	*lows with*	4 55	7 5	♌ 13	♂ riſe 10 58
31	3	*rain.*	4 56	7 4	28	☽ with ☿

Keep thy shop, and thy shop will keep thee.

Early to bed, and early to rise, makes a man healthy, wealthy, and wise.

God helps them that help themselves.

The worst wheel of the cart makes the most noise.

It is hard for an empty sack to stand upright.

Honesty is the best policy.

Haste makes waste.

You may talk too much on the best of subjects.

Silks and satins put out the kitchen fire.

A Plowman on his legs is higher than a Gentleman on his knees.

A good Example is the best Sermon.

Laziness travels so slowly that Poverty soon overtakes him.

Beware of little Expences, a small leak will sink a great ship.

FOR UNDERSTANDING

1. Find two or more of Poor Richard's sayings that emphasize *industriousness.*

2. Nearly all of the sayings cast new light on the topics they discuss—make us see them in a different, more vivid way. Even the familiar "Honesty is the best policy" is more subtle than it first seems, for it recommends honesty as *good business sense.* The one on *laziness* dramatizes what happens to the man who doesn't attend to his job. Can you explain how the proverb about *the worst wheel of the cart* is to be applied to human beings? The proverb about the *empty sack* is much more complex. It is based on one of Franklin's favorite ideas—that thrift and prosperity actually improve moral character, because people who have enough to live on are not tempted to cheat. Explain why the empty sack won't stand up as firmly as the full sack. What kind of human being does each sack represent?

3. The proverb about *silks and satins* warns housewives not to buy luxuries that are beyond the family budget. Explain how such luxuries "put out the kitchen fire." The *Gentleman on his knees* is kneeling before the king, thus showing that in reality he is a kind of slave. What is implied by saying that the *Plowman* is higher?

4. "Haste makes waste" is a very simple proverb which is pleasing because the two words sound somewhat alike. The similarity in the *sounds* helps to persuade us that there is a similarity in *what the sounds stand for.* "Keep thy shop, and thy shop will keep thee" is constructed on the same principle though more elaborately. The *second half* of the proverb is merely the *first half* turned around. We readily accept the suggestion that when the one happens, the other happens also. What does the proverb mean?

SPEECH IN THE VIRGINIA CONVENTION

PATRICK HENRY

In 1775 the differences between the colonies and England had become critical. Petitions sent to the king from individual colonies had been received with contempt. A petition sent by the First Continental Congress had achieved no result. Benjamin Franklin—who was in England on a peacemaking mission for Pennsylvania, New Jersey, and Massachusetts—was having a stormy time of it and was about to set sail for home.

In Virginia the House of Burgesses had been dissolved by the royal governor, but a Provincial Convention met at Richmond. At this convention Patrick Henry introduced a resolution to form a militia which would protect the liberties of Virginians. He further proposed "that this colony be immediately put into a posture of defense."

When some of the conservative delegates spoke against such a drastic move, the fiery young lawyer replied with one of the most memorable speeches ever delivered. Says Tyler in his LIFE OF PATRICK HENRY, "He commenced somewhat calmly, but the smothered excitement began more and more to play upon his features and thrill in the tones of his voice . . . His voice rose louder and louder, until the walls of the building, and all within them, seemed to shake and rock in its tremendous vibrations . . . Men leaned forward and their eyes glared like the speaker's. His last exclamation, 'Give me liberty or give me death!' was like the shout of the leader which turns back the rout of battle." Parts of the speech are given here.

Mr. President:

No man thinks more highly than I do of the patriotism, as well as abilities, of the very worthy gentlemen [1] who have just addressed the house. But different men often see the same subject in different lights; and, therefore, I hope it will not be thought disrespectful to those gentlemen, if, entertaining as I do, opinions of a character very opposite to theirs, I shall speak forth my sentiments freely, and without reserve. . . .

I have but one lamp by which my feet are guided, and that is the lamp of experience. I know of no way of judging of the future but by the past. And judging by the past, I wish to know what there has been in the conduct of the British ministry for the last ten years, to justify those hopes with which gentlemen have

[1] WORTHY GENTLEMEN—The gentlemen who had opposed Henry's resolution.

been pleased to solace themselves and the house. Is it that insidious smile with which our petition has been lately received? Trust it not, sir: it will prove a snare to your feet. Suffer not yourselves to be betrayed with a kiss.[2] Ask yourselves how this gracious reception of our petition comports with those warlike preparations [3] which cover our waters and darken our land. Are fleets and armies necessary to a work of love and reconciliation? Have we shown ourselves so unwilling to be reconciled that force must be called in to win back our love? Let us not deceive ourselves, sir. These are the implements of war and subjugation— the last arguments to which kings resort. I ask, sir, what means this martial array, if its purpose be not to force us to submission? Can gentlemen assign any other

[2] BETRAYED WITH A KISS—Judas betrayed Christ with a kiss.
[3] WARLIKE PREPARATIONS—Although the French and Indian Wars had ended in 1763, British troops remained in the colonies. A fifty-gun ship had been sent to Boston Harbor, and two regiments of soldiers had been quartered in Boston.

possible motive for it? Has Great Britain any enemy in this quarter of the world, to call for all this accumulation of navies and armies? No, sir, she has none. They are meant for us: they can be meant for no other. They are sent over to bind and rivet upon us those chains which the British ministry have been so long forging. And what have we to oppose to them? Shall we try argument? Sir, we have been trying that for the last ten years.[4] Have we anything new to offer upon the subject? Nothing. We have held the subject up in every light of which it is capable; but it has been all in

[4] FOR THE LAST TEN YEARS—The Navigation Acts, which forbade the colonies to trade with any other nation than England, were heatedly resented. By smuggling, many colonists evaded the restrictions of the Acts. Beginning in 1763, George III's prime minister attempted to enforce the laws more vigorously. Writs of Assistance were issued—permitting officers to search the homes of the colonists for smuggled goods. A standing army of English soldiers was maintained in the colonies. To help pay the cost, new taxes were imposed. During this whole time, the colonists had tried by petition and by argument to have the laws changed.

vain. Shall we resort to entreaty and humble supplication? What terms shall we find which have not been already exhausted? Let us not, I beseech you, sir, deceive ourselves longer.

Sir, we have done everything that could be done to avert the storm which is now coming on. We have petitioned; we have remonstrated; we have supplicated; we have prostrated ourselves before the throne, and have implored its interposition to arrest the tyrannical hands of the ministry and Parliament. Our petitions have been slighted; our remonstrances have produced additional violence and insult; our supplications have been disregarded; and we have been spurned with contempt from the foot of the throne![5] In vain, after these things, may we indulge the fond hope of peace and reconciliation. There is no longer any room for hope. If we wish to be free, if we mean to preserve inviolate those inestimable privileges for which we have been so long contending, if we mean not basely to abandon the noble struggle in which we have been so long engaged, and which we have pledged ourselves never to abandon until the glorious object of our contest shall be obtained—we must fight! I repeat it, sir, we must fight! An appeal to arms and to the God of Hosts is all that is left us!

They tell us, sir, that we are weak—unable to cope with so formidable an adversary. But when shall we be stronger? Will it be the next week, or the next year? Will it be when we are totally disarmed, and when a British guard shall be stationed in every house? Shall we gather strength by irresolution and inaction? Shall we acquire the means of effectual resistance by lying supinely on our backs, and hugging the delusive phantom of hope until our enemies shall have bound us hand and foot? Sir, we are not weak, if we make the proper use of those means which the God of nature hath placed in our power. Three millions of people, armed in the holy cause of liberty, and in such a country as that which we possess, are invincible by any force which our enemy can send against us. Besides, sir, we shall not fight our battles alone. There is a just God who presides over the destinies of nations, and who will raise up friends to fight our battles for us.[6] The battle, sir, is not to the strong alone; it is to the vigilant, the active, the brave. Besides, sir, we have no election.[7] If we were base enough to desire it, it is now too late to retire from the contest. There is no retreat but in submission and slavery! Our chains are forged! Their clanking may be heard on the plains of Boston![8] The war is inevitable—and let it come! I repeat it, sir, let it come!

It is in vain, sir, to extenuate the matter. Gentlemen may cry, Peace, Peace—but there is no peace. The war is actually begun! The next gale that sweeps from the north[9] will bring to our ears the clash of resounding arms! Our brethren are already in the field! Why stand we here idle? What is it that gentlemen wish? What would they have? Is life so dear, or peace so sweet, as to be purchased at the price of chains and slavery? Forbid it, Almighty God! I know not what course others may take; but as for me, give me liberty or give me death!

[5] SPURNED . . . FROM THE FOOT OF THE THRONE—The speaker here refers to the various petitions that had been sent to the king, with no result.

[6] WILL RAISE UP FRIENDS TO FIGHT OUR BATTLES FOR US—France did join the colonies against England.

[7] ELECTION—Choice.

[8] ON THE PLAINS OF BOSTON—This is a reference to the British troops in Boston, and to the Boston Massacre—in which redcoats fired on a civilian mob—which had occurred in 1770.

[9] THE NEXT GALE THAT SWEEPS FROM THE NORTH—A month after this speech, the battles of Lexington and Concord were fought.

FOR UNDERSTANDING

1. How does Henry show courtesy to the opposing speakers? What excuse does he give for expressing disagreement with them?

2. What argument does he use to show that "this gracious reception of our petition" is insincere and misleading? How does he attempt to convince his listeners that British troops could not have been sent to America for "any other possible motive" than to subdue the colonists?

3. Why did it seem, in the face of facts, hopeless for the colonies to take up arms against Britain? From your knowledge of American history, explain why the Americans were able to win the unequal war which Patrick Henry was instrumental in starting.

4. What sentences indicate Henry's strong religious faith? Find a sentence, besides the last one, which indicates his devotion to the principle of liberty. How was Henry, whether or not he later took part in the actual fighting of the Revolutionary War, endangering his life by his insistence on liberty?

MATTERS OF STYLE

1. At what point does the speech begin to show Henry's rising emotion? Quote the earliest sentence which is an excited exclamation rather than a direct factual statement.

2. A *rhetorical question* is a question having an obvious answer, like "Do we want to lose everything we have worked for?" It is asked only to make clear or emphasize a point. Point out a passage in which Henry's speech gathers intensity by asking a series of rhetorical questions. Choose two of these questions and explain how the only possible answer is one that supports Henry's argument.

3. Turn back to the early part of the speech and explain how "warlike preparations" could be said to "cover our waters." How could they "darken our land"?

4. The speech is not merely an impassioned oration, but has a logical development. Show its structure by stating in your own words (*a*) the objections which Patrick Henry realizes might be made to his proposal; and (*b*) the reply or replies with which he sweeps away each objection in turn.

PATRICK HENRY (1736–1799)

Patrick Henry was one of the liberty-loving orators who set the flame of liberty burning. He was born in Hanover County, Virginia, of Scotch and Welsh descent. After a somewhat irregular schooling he decided to study law and was licensed in 1760. His natural fire and stormy eloquence made him almost immediately successful.

In 1765 he became a member of the House of Burgesses. Insignificant and unknown, he created a furor by offering a resolution declaring that only the Burgesses and the Governor had the right to impose taxes in Virginia—that all attempts of the British Parliament to tax the colonies were unconstitutional. During the stormy debate that followed, he cried, "Caesar had his Brutus, Charles the First his Cromwell, and George the Third—" At this moment he was interrupted by cries of "Treason! Treason!" He finished his sentence, "—may profit by their example," and added, "If this be treason, make the most of it!" His resolution was adopted, and Patrick Henry was recognized as a power in the colony.

Thereafter he took an active part in all the discussions, continuing a member of the House of Burgesses until it was dissolved. He was sent as a delegate to the First Continental Congress at Philadelphia in 1774. Back home again, he made his defiant speech, "Give me liberty or give me death!"—and was proclaimed an outlaw by the royal governor, Lord Dunmore. But Lord Dunmore was soon forced to flee to England, and Henry himself became governor of Virginia. For the rest of his life he continued active in governmental matters. To him goes much of the credit for the incorporation of the Bill of Rights into the Constitution.

Yankee Doodle

REVOLUTIONARY BALLAD

The tune of "Yankee Doodle" was a rollicking old melody known all through the European countries. It is said that at least some of the stanzas were written by someone in the British army and that other stanzas were invented later—all of them in derision of the awkward, gaping Yankee boys from the backwoods. But the American troops liked the tune, and by 1775 it had become a favorite camp and marching song.

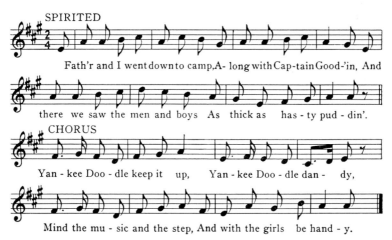

SPIRITED

Fath'r and I went down to camp, A-long with Cap-tain Good-'in, And there we saw the men and boys As thick as has-ty pud-din'.

CHORUS

Yan-kee Doo-dle keep it up, Yan-kee Doo-dle dan-dy, Mind the mu-sic and the step, And with the girls be hand-y.

Fath'r and I went down to camp,
  Along with Captain Good'in,
And there we saw the men and boys
  As thick as hasty puddin'.

CHORUS: *Yankee Doodle keep it up,* 5
       Yankee Doodle dandy,
       Mind the music and the step,
       And with the girls be handy.

And there we see a thousand men,
  As rich as Squire David; 10
And what they wasted ev'ry day,
  I wish it could be savèd.

And there was Captain Washington
  Upon a slapping stallion,
A-giving orders to his men; 15
  I guess there was a million.

And then the feathers on his hat,
  They look'd so very fine, ah!
I wanted peskily to get
  To give to my Jemima. 20

And there I see a swamping gun,
  Large as a log of maple,
Upon a mighty little cart;
  A load for father's cattle.

4. HASTY PUDDIN'—A thick pudding or mush made by boiling wheat flour in milk or water.

And every time they fired it off,   25
  It took a horn of powder;
It made a noise like Father's gun
  Only a nation louder.

And there I see a little keg,
  Its head all made of leather,   30
They knocked upon't with little sticks,
  To call the folks together.

And Cap'n Davis had a gun,
  He kind o' clapt his hand on't

And stuck a crooked stabbing-iron   35
  Upon the little end on't.

The troopers, too, would gallop up
  And fire right in our faces;
It scared me almost half to death
  To see them run such races.   40

It scared me so I hooked it off,
  Nor stopped, as I remember,
Nor turned about till I got home,
  Locked up in Mother's chamber.

FOR UNDERSTANDING

1. Point out expressions that suggest the inexperienced Yankee boy's amazement over the sights to be seen at a military camp. The eighth stanza describes what happens when the command "Fix bayonets!" is given. Which phrase suggests the snappy military way in which the bayonet is attached to the musket all in one motion?

2. Point out three expressions which use simple, homely comparisons in picturing equipment which the country lad had never seen before. Point out three expressions which seem intended to make fun of backwoods dialect. What details of colonial life do we learn from the song—details about food or dress or customs?

3. The last two stanzas make it seem that the boy is badly frightened. However, what methods of fighting did the frontier youths know that helped them beat the British soldiers? Explain why the British did not understand such methods.

4. What characteristics of the tune of "Yankee Doodle" make it a good marching song?

"YOU'RE IN THE ARMY NOW"

It is likely that when the American soldiers sang "Yankee Doodle" they thought of it as ridiculing not the whole American army but the newcomers who were not used to military life. Give two or more examples of humorous stories that are told in our own day to show the simple-mindedness of the "rookie"—that is, the new recruit.

THE DECLARATION OF INDEPENDENCE

THOMAS JEFFERSON

Legend has it that as John Hancock, the first signer of the Declaration of Independence, wrote his name in bold letters he remarked that King George would be able to read it without his spectacles; and as Benjamin Franklin signed he declared, "We must hang together or we will hang separately."

Perhaps these men joked in order to help keep up everyone's courage, for the document being signed was no less than formal defiance of the British government—written by Thomas Jefferson and adopted by the Congress of the thirteen colonies on July 4, 1776. If America lost the war, the signers could expect to be hunted down as traitors to England.

The idea that men have inalienable rights, and that any ruling authority which destroys those rights should be abolished, had long been familiar to political writers in Europe and America. However, this was the first time in history an actual government had been founded on such a doctrine. The Declaration was both an announcement that the colonists no longer considered themselves Englishmen, and an indication that America was to be a new kind of nation. It has been called "the best known and the noblest of American state papers."

When in the Course of human events, it becomes necessary for one people to dissolve the political bands which have connected them with another, and to assume among the Powers of the earth, the separate and equal station to which the Laws of Nature and of Nature's God entitle them, a decent respect to the opinions of mankind requires that they should declare the causes which impel them to the separation.

We hold these truths to be self-evident, that all men are created equal, that they are endowed by their Creator with certain inalienable Rights, that among these are Life, Liberty, and the pursuit of Happiness. That to secure these rights, Governments are instituted among Men, deriving their just powers from the consent of the governed. That whenever any Form of Government becomes destructive of these ends, it is the Right of the People to alter or to abolish it, and to institute a new Government, laying its foundation on such principles and organizing its powers in such form, as to them shall seem most likely to effect their Safety and Happiness. Prudence, indeed, will dictate that Governments long established should not be changed for light and transient causes; and accordingly all experience hath shown, that mankind are more disposed to suffer, while evils are sufferable, than to right themselves by abolishing the forms to which they are accustomed. But when a long train of abuses and usurpations, pursuing invariably the same Object, evinces a design to reduce them under absolute Despotism, it is their right, it is their duty, to throw off such Government, and to provide new Guards for their future security.

Such has been the patient sufferance of these Colonies; and such is now the necessity which constrains them to alter their former Systems of Government. The history of the present King of Great Britain is a history of repeated injuries and usurpations; all having in direct object the establishment of an absolute Tyranny over these States. To prove this, let Facts be submitted to a candid world.

[*Here follows the list of injustices suffered by the colonies.*]

In every stage of these Oppressions We have Petitioned for Redress in the most humble terms: Our repeated Petitions have been answered only by repeated injury. A Prince, whose character is thus marked by every act which may define a Tyrant, is unfit to be the ruler of a free People.

Nor have We been wanting in attention to our British brethren. We have warned them from time to time of attempts by their legislature to extend an unwarrantable jurisdiction over us. We have reminded them of the circumstances of our emigration and settlement here. We have appealed to their native justice and magnanimity, and we have conjured them by the ties of our common kindred to disavow these usurpations, which would inevitably interrupt our connections and correspondence. They too have been deaf to the voice of justice and of consanguinity.[1] We must, therefore, acquiesce in the necessity which denounces our Separation, and hold them, as we hold the rest of mankind, Enemies in War, in Peace, Friends.

We, therefore, the Representatives of the United States of America, in General Congress Assembled, appealing to the Supreme Judge of the world for the rectitude of our intentions, do, in the Name, and by Authority of the good People of these Colonies, solemnly publish and declare, That these United Colonies are, and of Right ought to be Free and Independent States; that they are Absolved from all Allegiance to the British Crown, and that all political connection between them and the State of Great Britain, is and ought to be totally dissolved; and that as Free and Independent States, they have full Power to levy War, conclude Peace, contract Alliances, establish Commerce, and to do all other Acts and Things which Independent States may of right do. And for the support of this Declaration, with a firm reliance on the Protection of Divine Providence, we mutually pledge to each other our Lives, our Fortunes, and our sacred Honor.

◇◇◇◇◇◇◇◇◇◇◇◇◇◇◇◇◇◇◇◇◇◇◇◇◇◇◇◇◇◇◇

FOR UNDERSTANDING

1. The members of the Continental Congress showed "decent respect to the opinions of mankind" by stating carefully and fully their reasons for the Declaration of Independence. Why would it be of great practical importance to create a favorable impression of what they were doing—both on foreign nations and on the population at home?

2. What is meant by "self-evident"? From what source does Jefferson say men derive their rights? Explain why naming this source was important in discussing resistance to the established government.

3. "All men are created equal" clearly cannot refer to equal ability. Neither can it refer to income, for industrious persons deserve the wealth they earn. Explain what the sentence really means. Then give two examples of how in your own community the laws protect this equality.

[1] CONSANGUINITY   (kŏn′săng·gwĭn′ĭ·tĭ)— Blood relationship.

4. Does Jefferson think governments should be lightly overthrown? What justifies a change in government?

5. Show how the Declaration of Independence is organized as a logical, connected argument which leads to an inescapable conclusion. These headings will help:

a. The only rightful government is one which . . .

b. The government of the present King of Great Britain has . . .

c. Our requests that this be changed have . . .

d. Therefore, our conclusion is . . .

FOR APPRECIATION OF STYLE

Find the next-to-last sentence of the Declaration and read it aloud. Can you explain why listening to it gives one a strong impression of the dignity and importance of the action Congress was taking?

FOR SPECIAL REPORTS

1. Where is the original copy of the Declaration of Independence kept? Can it be seen by the public? What precautions are taken to preserve it from harm?

2. Bring to class and exhibit a copy of the Declaration which includes a list of the signers. Name the signers whose names would be familiar to anyone who has studied American history, and tell briefly about the careers of any two (except Franklin and Jefferson).

3. Give a talk on how Independence Day is celebrated. Of course some Americans treat it as just "a day off." But what customs do you know of that set it apart from other holidays, and link it to July 4, 1776?

THOMAS JEFFERSON (1743–1826)

It is curious that Thomas Jefferson, who of all our statesmen was most completely devoted to the cause of the common man, should have been born of an aristocratic family and have enjoyed all the advantages of wealth and culture. He was born near Charlottesville, Virginia, of a prominent plantation-owning family. He went to William and Mary College where he took, first, the regular academic subjects, and then five years of law. When he entered the Virginia House of Burgesses in 1769, he began an unbroken series of activities for the people and their government which culminated in his fulfillment of two terms as President of the United States. He was a member of every assembly and convention of the Virginia colony, and when he became delegate to the Continental Congress in 1775, he had won the respect of men north and south. Young and old turned to him as the logical man to draft the Declaration of Independence. If he had never written anything else, that one document could stand a tribute to his genius.

Jefferson did write a great deal more, though chiefly letters and papers of state. In quieter times, he would have preferred to stay at home and occupy himself with managing his splendid estate—but no man ever served the public interest more unselfishly. As a lover of freedom, Jefferson exerted himself to shape laws that would forever prevent the establishment of a monarchy in the United States. His foreign policy as President was one of peace, and aloofness from the affairs of European nations. It was he who authorized the Louisiana Purchase from France—more than doubling the territory of our country. He worked long and earnestly for the cause of universal education as a necessary bulwark of liberty. He was one of the first leading Americans to protest against the practice of slavery. In 1806 he recommended to Congress the prohibition of slave trade. He planned and built his beautiful home at the Monticello plantation, and designed the Virginia state capitol as well as some of the buildings in Washington. His love of Greek and Roman styles of architecture created a tradition in the design of government buildings.

After he had retired from public life, he devoted his time to establishing the University of Virginia.

None of the other great men of Revolutionary times except Franklin was so many-sided and productive as Jefferson. In high idealism and earnest purpose he may be compared to his fellow Virginian, George Washington. Jefferson was a spokesman for the rights of man, and he devoted his life to securing those rights in actual fact for the citizens of America.

◇◇◇◇◇

Nathan Hale

REVOLUTIONARY BALLAD

On a September dawn in 1776 Nathan Hale died at the orders of General Howe. His special mission had failed. He had lost the life he had risked. But the enemy were not done with him. In hanging a spy they created a hero and a legend. The story has come down to us in many forms, but particularly typical of Revolutionary times is the following ballad version.

The breezes went steadily through the tall pines,
    A-saying "Oh! hu-ush!" a-saying "Oh! hu-ush!"
As stilly stole by a bold legion of horse,
    For Hale in the bush, for Hale in the bush.

"Keep still!" said the thrush, as she nestled her young   5
    In a nest by the road, in a nest by the road;
"For the tyrants are near, and with them appear
    What bodes us no good, what bodes us no good."

The brave captain heard it, and thought of his home
    In a cot by the brook, in a cot by the brook;   10
With mother and sister and memories dear,
    He so gaily forsook, he so gaily forsook.

Cooling shades of the night were coming apace,
    The tattoo had beat, the tattoo had beat;
The noble one sprang from his dark lurking-place   15
    To make his retreat, to make his retreat.

He warily trod on the dry rustling leaves
   As he passed through the wood, as he passed through the wood,
And silently gained his rude launch on the shore,
   As she played with the flood, as she played with the flood.   20

The guards of the camp on that dark dreary night,
   Had a murderous will, had a murderous will;
They took him and bore him afar from the shore,
   To a hut on the hill, to a hut on the hill.

No mother was there, nor a friend who could cheer,   25
   In that little stone cell, in that little stone cell;
But he trusted in love from his Father above—
   In his heart all was well, in his heart all was well.

An ominous owl with his solemn bass voice
   Sat moaning hard by, sat moaning hard by: 30
"The tyrant's proud minions most gladly rejoice,
   For he must soon die, for he must soon die."

The brave fellow told them, no thing he restrained—
   The cruel gen'ral; the cruel gen'ral!
His errand from camp, of the ends to be gained,   35
   And said that was all, and said that was all.

They took him and bound him and bore him away,
   Down the hill's grassy side, down the hill's grassy side.
'Twas there the base hirelings, in royal array,
   His cause did deride, his cause did deride.   40

Five minutes were given, short moments, no more,
   For him to repent, for him to repent.
He prayed for his mother—he asked not another—
   To heaven he went, to heaven he went.

The faith of a martyr the tragedy showed,   45
   As he trod the last stage, as he trod the last stage.
And Britons still shudder at gallant Hale's blood,
   As his words do presage, as his words do presage:

"Thou pale king of terrors, thou life's gloomy foe,
   Go frighten the slave, go frighten the slave;   50
Tell tyrants, to you their allegiance they owe—
   No fears for the brave, no fears for the brave!"

FOR UNDERSTANDING

1. Look up the story of Nathan Hale. In the ballad version who are "the brave captain"; "the cruel general"; "the tyrant"; "the base hirelings in royal array"? What details of the actual event are not mentioned in the poem? What details has the poet added that histories omit? What do you think was the purpose of adding them here?

2. Although the penalty Hale paid was the one always paid by captured spies according to military custom, the poet takes the attitude that it was a wicked deed to execute him. Find one or more phrases that reveal this attitude. Why do you suppose the death penalty is imposed on spies? Under what circumstances would Hale, when captured behind enemy lines, have been treated merely as a soldier and been imprisoned instead of hanged?

3. Who are the "bold legion of horse" mentioned in the first stanza? What was their errand? What do you think is the meaning of "the tattoo had beat," in line 14?

4. Why would the "Britons still shudder at gallant Hale's blood"? What is the meaning of "presage" in line 48?

5. Who is speaking in the last stanza? Explain the meaning of the stanza.

◇◇◇◇◇

FAREWELL ADDRESS

GEORGE WASHINGTON

For eight years Washington had been president of the young republic. He knew the dangers, external and internal, that still threatened it. To help meet those dangers, in his "Farewell Address" he laid down some carefully thought-out principles of procedure. His advice was thoroughly practical, based on fact and experience. After a century and a half, it still repays thoughtful study.

Because the address is long, dwelling much on matters of especial interest in 1796, a condensation is presented here.

Friends and Fellow Citizens: The period for a new election of a citizen to administer the executive government of the United States being not far distant, and the time actually arrived when your thoughts must be employed in designating the person who is to be clothed with that important trust, it appears to me proper, especially as it may conduce to a more distinct expression of the public voice, that I should now apprise you of the resolution I have formed, to decline being considered among the number of those out of whom a choice is to be made.

I rejoice that the state of your concerns, external as well as internal, no longer renders the pursuit of inclination incompatible with the sentiment of duty or propriety; and am persuaded, whatever partiality may be retained for my services, that, in the present circumstances [1] of our country, you will not disapprove my determination to retire. . . .

II

Here, perhaps, I ought to stop. But a solicitude for your welfare, which cannot end but with my life, and the apprehension of danger natural to that solicitude, urge me, on an occasion like the present, to offer to your solemn contemplation, and to recommend to your frequent review, some sentiments which are the result of much reflection, of no inconsiderable observation, and which appear to me all-important to the permanency of your felicity as a people. These will be offered to you with the more freedom, as you can only see in them the disinterested warnings of a parting friend, who can possibly have no personal motive to bias his counsel. Nor can I forget, as an encouragement to it, your indulgent reception of my sentiments on a former and not dissimilar occasion. [2]

Interwoven as is the love of liberty with every ligament of your hearts, no recommendation of mine is necessary to fortify or confirm the attachment.

The unity of government, which constitutes you one people, is also dear to you. [3] It is justly so; for it is a main pillar in the edifice of your real independence, the support of your tranquility at home, your peace abroad; of your safety; of your prosperity; of that very liberty which you so highly prize.

For this you have every inducement of sympathy and interest. Citizens, by birth or choice, of a common country, that country has a right to concentrate your affections. [4] The name of America, which belongs to you, in your national capacity, must always exalt the just pride of patriotism, more than any appellation [5] derived from local discriminations. With slight shades of difference, you have the same religion, manners, habits, and political principles. You have in a common cause fought and triumphed together; the independence and liberty you possess are the work of joint counsels and joint efforts, of common dangers, sufferings and successes.

[Here Washington warns against parties based on geographical divisions; enlarges on the necessity of union; urges respect for existing laws; declares that any attempt to act contrary to existing laws is destructive of government; and pleads against the "spirit of innovation."]

III

I have already intimated to you the danger of parties in the State, with particular reference to the founding of them

[1] PRESENT CIRCUMSTANCES—By 1796, "external as well as internal" affairs had somewhat improved. For example, treaties had been concluded with England and with Spain, Hamilton's financial system had restored the national credit, the collapse of the Whiskey Rebellion had strengthened the hand of the federal government, and while party animosity was still bitter there was, nevertheless, discernible a stronger national spirit.

[2] FORMER AND NOT DISSIMILAR OCCASION—An allusion to Washington's resignation of his commission at the close of the war at Annapolis, December 23, 1783, when he said: "I resign with satisfaction the appointment I accepted with diffidence. . . . My gratitude for . . . the assistance I have received from my countrymen increases with every review of the momentous contest."

[3] UNITY . . . ALSO DEAR TO YOU—By 1796 the strong feeling of local patriotism which had threatened the complete adoption of the Constitution had considerably diminished.

[4] TO CONCENTRATE YOUR AFFECTIONS—That is, to demand that your affections be centered upon it.

[5] APPELLATION—Name. Washington alludes to the pride which some of his contemporaries took in being called Virginians or New Yorkers, and so on.

on geographical discrimination. Let me now take a more comprehensive view, and warn you in the most solemn manner against the baneful effects of the spirit of party, generally.

This spirit, unfortunately, is inseparable from our nature, having its root in the strongest passions of the human mind. It exists under different shapes in all governments, more or less stifled, controlled, or repressed; but in those of the popular form it is seen in its greatest rankness, and is truly their worst enemy.

The alternate domination of one faction over another, sharpened by the spirit of revenge, natural to party dissension, which in different ages and countries has perpetrated the most horrid enormities,[6] is itself a frightful despotism. But this leads at length to a more formal and permanent despotism. The disorders and miseries which result gradually incline the minds of men to seek security and repose in the absolute power of an individual; and sooner or later the chief of some prevailing faction, more able or more fortunate than his competitors, turns this disposition to the purposes of his own elevation, on the ruins of public liberty.

Without looking forward to an extremity of this kind (which nevertheless ought not to be entirely out of sight), the common and continued mischiefs of the spirit of party are sufficient to make it the interest and duty of a wise people to discourage and restrain it.

IV

It is important, likewise, that the habits of thinking in a free country should inspire caution in those intrusted with its administration, to confine themselves within their respective constitutional

[6] MOST HORRID ENORMITIES—Washington had in mind very likely the excesses to which party rivalry led in the French Revolution.

spheres, avoiding in the exercise of the powers of one department to encroach upon another.[7] The spirit of encroachment tends to consolidate the powers of all the departments in one, and thus to create, whatever the form of government, a real despotism. A just estimate of that love of power, and proneness to abuse it, which predominates in the human heart, is sufficient to satisfy us of the truth of this position. The necessity of reciprocal checks[8] in the exercise of political power, by dividing and distributing it into different depositories and constituting each the guardian of the public weal against invasions by the others, has been evinced by experiments ancient and modern, some of them in our country and under our own eyes.[9] To preserve them must be as necessary as to institute them. If, in the opinion of the people, the distribution or modification of the constitutional powers be in any particular wrong, let it be corrected by an amendment in the way which the Constitution designates. But let there be no change by usurpation; for, though this, in one instance, may be the instrument of good, it is the customary weapon by which free governments are destroyed. The precedent must always greatly overbalance in permanent

[7] TO CONFINE . . . ENCROACH UPON ANOTHER—Washington here alludes, of course, to the danger which would follow upon permitting one department of the government, for example, the executive, to usurp the powers of the legislative and judicial branches.

[8] RECIPROCAL CHECKS—Washington here refers to such constitutional checks as the following examples: (1) the President may make no appointments to office without the advice and consent of the Senate; (2) the laws made by Congress may be declared unconstitutional by the Supreme Court; (3) the President is given the power of veto.

[9] IN OUR OWN COUNTRY AND UNDER OUR OWN EYES—Those things in our Constitution which have worked especially well had been in operation in various colonial governments before the separation from England.

evil any partial or transient benefit which the use can at any time yield.

v

Of all the dispositions and habits which lead to political prosperity, religion and morality are indispensable supports. In vain would that man claim the tribute of patriotism, who should labor to subvert these great pillars of human happiness, these firmest props of the duties of men and citizens. The mere politician equally with the pious man ought to respect and to cherish them. A volume could not trace all their connections with private and public felicity. Let it simply be asked, Where is the security for property, for reputation, for life, if the sense of religious obligation desert the oaths, which are the instruments of investigation in courts of justice? And let us with caution indulge the supposition that morality can be maintained without religion.

Whatever may be conceded to the influence of refined education on minds of peculiar structure, reason and experience[10] both forbid us to expect that national morality can prevail in exclusion of religious principle.

It is substantially true that virtue or morality is a necessary spring of popular government. The rule, indeed, extends with more or less force to every species of free government. Who that is a sincere friend to it can look with indifference upon attempts to shake the foundation of the fabric?

Promote, then, as an object of primary importance, institutions for the general diffusion of knowledge. In proportion as the structure of a government gives force to public opinion, it is essential that public opinion should be enlightened.

VI

Observe good faith and justice towards all nations; cultivate peace and harmony with all. Religion and morality enjoin this conduct; and can it be that good policy does not equally enjoin it? It will be worthy of a free, enlightened, and at no distant period a great nation, to give to mankind the magnanimous and too novel example of a people always guided by an exalted justice and benevolence.

In the execution of such a plan, nothing is more essential than that permanent, inveterate antipathies against particular nations, and passionate attachments[11] for others, should be excluded;

[10] EXPERIENCE—Washington no doubt had in mind the attempt made by the French Revolutionists to abolish both God and religion and to set up a rule of reason.

[11] ANTIPATHIES . . . ATTACHMENTS—Washington here alludes to the pro-British sympathies of the Federalists and the pro-French sympathies of the Republicans which had heightened the bitter party strife of his two administrations.

and that, in place of them, just and amicable feelings towards all should be cultivated.

So likewise, a passionate attachment of one nation for another produces a variety of evils. Sympathy for the favorite nation, facilitating the illusion of an imaginary common interest in cases where no real common interest exists, and infusing into one the enmities of the other, betrays the former into a participation in the quarrels and wars of the latter, without adequate inducement or justification.

The great rule of conduct for us, in regard to foreign nations, is, in extending our commercial relations, to have with them as little political connection as possible. So far as we have already formed engagements, let them be fulfilled with perfect good faith. Here let us stop.

Europe has a set of primary interests, which to us have none, or a very remote relation. Hence she must be engaged in frequent controversies, the causes of which are essentially foreign to our concerns. Hence, therefore, it must be unwise in us to implicate ourselves, by artificial ties, in the ordinary vicissitudes of her politics, or the ordinary combinations and collisions of her friendships or enmities.

Our detached and distant situation invites and enables us to pursue a different course. If we remain one people, under an efficient government, the period is not far off when we may defy material injury from external annoyance; when we may take such an attitude as will cause the neutrality we may at any time resolve upon, to be scrupulously respected; when belligerent nations, under the impossibility of making acquisitions upon us, will not lightly hazard the giving us provocation; when we may choose peace or war, as our interest, guided by justice, shall counsel.

Why forego the advantages of so peculiar a situation? Why quit our own to stand upon foreign ground? Why, by interweaving our destiny with that of any part of Europe, entangle our peace and prosperity in the toils of European ambition, rivalship, interest, humor, or caprice?

It is our true policy to steer clear of permanent alliances with any portion of the foreign world; so far, I mean, as we are now at liberty to do it; for let me not be understood as capable of patronizing infidelity to existing engagements. I hold the maxim no less applicable to public than to private affairs, that honesty is always the best policy. I repeat it, therefore, let those engagements be observed in their genuine sense. But, in my opinion, it is unnecessary and would be unwise to extend them.

Taking care always to keep ourselves, by suitable establishments, on a respectable defensive posture, we may safely trust to temporary alliances for extraordinary emergencies.

VII

In offering to you, my countrymen, these counsels of an old and affectionate friend, I dare not hope they will make the strong and lasting impression I could wish; that they will control the usual current of the passions, or prevent our nation from running the course which has hitherto marked the destiny of nations. But, if I may even flatter myself that they may be productive of some partial benefit, some occasional good; that they may now and then recur to moderate the fury of party spirit, to warn against the mischiefs of foreign intrigue, to guard against the impostures of pretended patriotism; this hope will be a full

recompense for the solicitude for your welfare, by which they have been dictated.

Though, in reviewing the incidents of my administration, I am unconscious of intentional error, I am nevertheless too sensible of my defects not to think it probable that I may have committed many errors. Whatever they may be, I fervently beseech the Almighty to avert or mitigate the evils to which they may tend. I shall also carry with me the hope that my country will never cease to view them with indulgence; and that, after forty-five years of my life dedicated to its service with an upright zeal, the faults of incompetent abilities will be consigned to oblivion, as myself must soon be to the mansions of rest.

◇◇◇◇◇◇◇◇◇◇◇◇◇◇◇◇◇◇◇◇◇◇◇◇◇◇◇◇◇◇◇

FOR UNDERSTANDING

PART I

There is no doubt that if Washington had desired, he could have been the first king instead of the first president of his country, but he decisively rejected such a possibility. What connection can you see between his opposition to *founding a monarchy* and his decision *not to be a candidate for a third term?* How closely has America followed his precedent in regard to a third term? Discuss the arguments for and against the wisdom of this precedent. Quote the sentence in which Washington says he is not neglecting his country in deciding not to be a candidate.

PART II

What reason does Washington mention for hoping that his countrymen will listen to his advice? What other reasons could be given? What advice does he say it is *not* necessary to give? Had the unity of government, which he considers so essential, always been "dear" to the thirteen states? Discuss the extent to which Americans today have "the same religion, manners, habits, and political principles." Name one or more "common dangers," besides the obvious one of war, against which the whole nation has sometimes united.

PART III

Explain in your own words the dangers that Washington sees in political parties. In spite of his advice, our country has been politically divided for a long time into two rival parties. Discuss the question of whether we have been able to avoid the "spirit of revenge." What proof can you give that Republicans and Democrats, unlike the European political parties Washington was thinking of, agree on some matters? What points could be made in favor of a division into political parties?

PART IV

What general tendency in human nature, according to Washington, must be restrained by "reciprocal checks" in the various departments of government? Can you give an instance from American history when either the judiciary or the executive exercised more power than was intended by the makers of the Constitution? Do you think there is a tendency in the world today toward all-powerful central governments, or toward the diffusion of powers and direct popular government? Cite examples in support of your answer.

PART V

What is the American doctrine of the relation of the church and the state? Has history any examples of nations which have been hostile toward religion? With what results? What nation or nations today can you name that have adopted an attitude toward religion which is radically different from most? What, in your judgment, will be the outcome of this attitude? Washington would probably approve of the vast increase in popular education since his day. Explain his reason for favoring such an increase.

PART VI

Washington says that in addition to *religion* and *morality, good policy* urges us to live in peace with other nations. What active steps are being taken in the world today to prevent war? What proof can you give that the United States has followed Washington's advice, avoiding war whenever it was possible to do so? Are we, as a people, prone to any special likes or dislikes in our attitudes toward foreign nations? Have we ever disregarded Washington's advice, "interweaving our destiny with that of any part of Europe"? Explain why our situation is no longer as "detached and distant" from Europe as when Washington uttered these words. In spite of this, what parts of his advice on international affairs do you think it would be wise to apply in the world situation today?

PART VII

Washington's statement that he has spent forty-five years in his country's service indicates that his public career began as early as 1751. What responsibilities, besides the presidency, had he had? Besides fulfilling his duties as a military leader and as president, what less obvious services did he render his country? What other American statesmen would you name as nearly equal to Washington, and why?

FOR CLASS DISCUSSION: THE ADDRESS AS A WHOLE

Have we chiefly followed, or chiefly ignored, the counsels given in Washington's address? Which points need re-emphasis today? What amendments to his advice do you think Washington would make if he were living today? Explain the unforeseen developments of the last century and a half that would cause him to make these amendments. If Washington were alive now and in his prime, what chief problems of the nation do you think he would concern himself with, and what solutions would he seek?

GEORGE WASHINGTON
(1732–1799)

Aside from his high intelligence and his ability as a leader of men, one of Washington's outstanding traits was his long-suffering patience. Not that he was a benign, superhuman being. It was sometimes hard for him to rule his temper when a military operation was bungled, or when politicians squabbled—and on occasion his anger could be thunderous. But he had a dignity and nobility of character that called out the best in the men who worked with him in establishing the young republic.

Washington's early life was not one of ease, although he belonged to a family of wealthy Virginia planters. His father left his property to the children of his first wife —George's half-brothers. The father died when George was eleven, and the mother moved to Fredericksburg where she lived apparently in modest, if not straitened, circumstances. After a few years of schooling, George received the opportunity to be surveyor of the vast lands of Lord Fairfax. The work was a valuable experience—especially in the ways of the frontier. During the French and Indian Wars he served as commander of colonial soldiers, in aid of the British regular army. He learned much about conducting war in the American wilderness—a knowledge which the British officers never gained.

Then came a short period of peaceful life as a country gentleman. Washington married; his half-brother Lawrence died, and Washington inherited the splendid estate of Mount Vernon. But he served in the Virginia House of Burgesses, and was elected to both Continental Congresses. When the Revolutionary War began, recognizing his military experience his fellow-patriots elected him commander-in-chief of the Continental Army. He had to fight as best he could against professionally trained British troops—with inadequate equipment, and armies whose personnel was constantly changing because the soldiers had enlisted for only short periods. But Washington was a superb commander. A famous early exploit of the war was the crossing of the Delaware. On Christmas night, 1776, Washington and his troops slipped silently across the river in small boats and captured a sleeping British garrison at Trenton, New Jersey. This victory, followed quickly by another at Princeton, put heart into the discouraged Americans at a time when the Revolution might have failed.

The Continental Congress did a poor job of supplying food, clothing, and pay for the troops, and sometimes it interfered disastrously with Washington's conduct of the war. The Congress was a convention of the representatives of thirteen nations, rather than the united legislature of a single nation. Its mismanagement was so bad that some of Washington's officers urged him to defy civilian authority, and set himself up as a military dictator. Washington would not do this. He informed Congress that it could remove him from command if it wished, but that until then he must have full control over military strategy. His greatness as a general showed itself conspicuously during the ordeal of the winter at Valley Forge in 1778. Somehow, Washington kept his men together—and by spring, he had created a well-drilled, disciplined army. From then on, he was able to take the offensive. Within two years the British were beaten in the north and west, and their final surrender came at Yorktown, Virginia, in 1781.

After the war, Washington became the first president of the United States. His wisdom and integrity were badly needed. The country was weak and impoverished, the government was in debt, there was no stable currency, and a new war between England and France created a serious problem of foreign policy. In two terms as chief executive, Washington guided the nation through its first perilous years. He refused a third term, and returned to Mount Vernon—where, within three years, he died. He richly deserved the love and trust expressed in the memorial tribute, "First in war, first in peace, and first in the hearts of his countrymen."

For Broader Understanding

1. Name two selections in this unit *by modern authors* which bring out the ideals for which our forefathers fought. What famous men are pictured in these selections? Choose one Revolutionary leader who was forced to make a difficult decision, and explain what it was.

2. Name two heroes mentioned in the selections whom we seldom hear about today, and tell what each contributed to the American struggle for independence.

3. Mention three pieces of literature produced in Revolutionary times which deal either with the war or with the problems of the American nation. In each, what ideas are expressed about our country or our government which we uphold today?

4. Name one literary selection produced near the time of the Revolution which does not deal directly with the colonists' struggle for freedom. Explain how this work of literature helps modern Americans understand the *characteristics* of the colonists which caused them to demand their freedom.

5. Which two or three pieces of literature of Revolutionary times are most famous today? That is, which ones has every American *heard about* even though he may actually know very little about them? Selecting one of these, tell one particular thing about it which would be desirable for every American to know.

READING AND SPEAKING ACTIVITIES

Find information on one of the following topics and make a report to the class.

1. *Famous Men.* Report briefly on one of these leaders: Samuel Adams; John Paul Jones; Chaim (or Haym) Salomon; Robert Morris; Ethan Allen.

2. *"The Star-Spangled Banner."* Where was Francis Scott Key, and what was happening, when he wrote our national anthem? In your report, read some of the lines which refer specifically to the circumstances under which the song was written.

3. *Novels About the Revolution.* Choose a novel from any good reading list about the period. Prepare a report in which you bring out the following:

a. Historical facts, and information about living conditions, customs, social attitudes, political situations. How are these presented differently from the way they would be presented in a history or reference book?

b. Interesting sidelights on historical characters which make them more human or appealing.

c. Incidents which show idealism, courage, or heroism, or otherwise make a strong emotional appeal. Evaluate the book as a piece of literature and as a reliable source of information.

WRITING ACTIVITIES

Write a report on one of the following topics. Use several sources of information.

Thomas Paine and His Pamphlet "Common Sense." Give the main facts of Paine's life, and tell what ideas were expressed in his famous and influential pamphlet.

Philip Freneau and His Poems. Read "The Wild Honey Suckle" and "The Indian Burying-Ground" and summarize the thought of each. What part did Freneau play in the war?

The Hartford Wits. Who were the most important of the Hartford Wits (also called the Connecticut Wits)? What political aims did they have in their writings? Name two or more of their principal works.

Joel Barlow's "The Hasty Pudding." Read at least a part of this humorous poem and describe it in your report. Quote one or two short passages which you find amusing.

Charles Brockden Brown and "Wieland." Find out what the major events are in the plot of this strange novel, and summarize them. Name some of Brown's other works.

The Federalist. When were the *Fed-*

eralist papers published, what were the major ideas expressed in them, and what was the situation in America that caused them to be written? Who were the authors?

◇◇◇◇◇◇◇◇◇◇◇◇◇◇◇◇◇◇◇◇◇◇◇◇◇◇◇◇◇◇

FOR FURTHER READING

ALFRED HOYT BILL, *Valley Forge: The Making of an Army* (Harper). A decisive moment in American history is re-created here.

STEPHEN BONSAL, *When the French Were Here* (Doubleday). The French participation in the Yorktown siege, and their subsequent stay in America, is well told.

MARISTAN CHAPMAN, *Rogue's March* (Lippincott). A fine description of the battle of King's Mountain is given here. The plot concerns a Colonial soldier and the daughter of an ardent Tory.

ESTHER FORBES, *Paul Revere and the World He Lived In* (Houghton). This delightfully written biography of the silversmith, powder maker, etcher, and hero is also an interesting account of Boston, birthplace of our liberty.

PHILIP GUEDALLA, *Fathers of the Revolution* (Putnam). Twelve of the men who played a part in the American Revolution are pictured here in portraits drawn with wit and wisdom.

BRUCE LANCASTER, *Guns of Burgoyne* (Stokes). Burgoyne's expedition and defeat at Saratoga are told from the point of view of a young Hessian soldier. There is swift action and good interpretation of American character.

NATHAN SCHACHNER, *The Founding Fathers* (Putnam). The first twelve years of the United States were an exciting test to determine whether the new form of government was to survive. Meet the men of genius and talent who accomplished the miracle.

◇◇◇◇◇

HISTORY IN REVIEW

MILESTONES	TRENDS IN AMERICAN LIFE	LITERATURE
1765—Stamp Act	The fierce spirit of liberty manifests itself in the War for Independence from England, but this same spirit makes it difficult for Americans to unite afterward until the Constitution is adopted	1733–1758—Franklin's *Poor Richard's Almanac* published annually
1769—Daniel Boone crosses Cumberland Gap into Kentucky		1775—Patrick Henry's Speech in the Virginia Convention; "Yankee Doodle"
1770—Boston Massacre		
1773—Boston Tea Party		1776—Thomas Paine's *Common Sense*; Thomas Jefferson writes Declaration of Independence
1775—Battle of Concord and Lexington begins Revolution	Pioneering west of the Appalachians continues and increases; the nation fills out its borders to the Mississippi	
1776—Declaration of Independence, July 4		1777 (?)—Revolutionary ballad "Nathan Hale"
1777–1778—American victory in Battle of Saratoga; Washington's army winters at Valley Forge; France comes to aid of colonies	Eli Whitney's cotton gin brings prosperity to the South	1786–1809—Poems of Philip Freneau
	Transportation improves with the invention of the steamboat	1796—Washington's Farewell Address
1781—Cornwallis surrenders at Yorktown, ending Revolutionary War; Articles of Confederation ratified		1798—Charles B. Brown's *Wieland*, first important American novel
1789—Adoption of Constitution; Washington becomes president		1809—Washington Irving's *The Knickerbocker History of New York*
1803—Louisiana Purchase		1814—Francis Scott Key's "The Star-Spangled Banner"
1812–1815—War of 1812 against England	After the War of 1812 America is more securely established as a nation. An "Era of Good Feeling" in America follows the war	1817—William Cullen Bryant's "Thanatopsis"
		1818—Franklin's *Autobiography*

FRONTIERS TO THE WEST

The Westward Frontier—As Seen by Modern Writers

The romance, adventure, and hardships of frontier life are reflected in the prose and poetry of this unit. As you read, you can follow American scouts and pioneers on the great trek west across the North American continent. Almost as soon as the first colonists had become established along our eastern seaboard, a few adventurous souls began to explore the unknown land beyond the western boundaries of the early settlements. Vachel Lindsay tells us that it was "in the days of President Washington" when Johnny Appleseed "blew West" across the Appalachians on his way to Ohio and Indiana. From that time until the outbreak of the War Between the States there were continuous streams of expeditions into new and often hostile territory. In 1848, when gold was discovered in California, those streams became a flood.

However, the conquest of the continent was not complete when Americans had finally reached the Pacific coast. In between the two oceans were rivers to be explored, forests to be cleared, and rich lands to be brought under cultivation. Except for the years when both North and South were completely occupied by war, the

Westward Movement continued on into the twentieth century. Hordes of settlers swarmed across the great plains of the Middle West, breaking the land and building towns—particularly along the navigable rivers. Through the poems, stories, and biographies included in the following pages, you can share in one of the greatest adventures in the history of our country.

You will meet three types of American pioneers in the poems by present-day writers. There is William Sycamore, typical frontier hunter and restless adventurer, continually moving farther west as the settlements grew and the land was fenced. There are the strong, silent men and women pictured by Edgar Lee Masters in "Rutherford McDowell." They represent the permanent settlers who had the patience and the strength of character to withstand the hardships and discouragements encountered in establishing homes on the frontier. Then there is Johnny Appleseed, the visionary and idealist, working unselfishly for future generations. Each in his own way contributed to the building of America, and each possessed character traits which have always been, and still are, highly prized by Americans.

◇◇◇◇◇

The Ballad of William Sycamore

STEPHEN VINCENT BENÉT

In this vigorous ballad William Sycamore tells the story of his life on the Western frontier in pioneer days. As you read, you will discover that he possessed many of the same sturdy qualities that brought his ancestors to America and made it possible for them to establish an independent nation in the New World.

My father, he was a mountaineer,
His fist was a knotty hammer;
He was quick on his feet as a running
  deer,
And he spoke with a Yankee stammer.

My mother, she was merry and brave, 5
And so she came to her labor,

With a tall green fir for her doctor grave
And a stream for her comforting neighbor.

And some are wrapped in the linen fine,
And some like a godling's scion;   10
But I was cradled on twigs of pine
And the skin of a mountain lion.

And some remember a white, starched
  lap
And a ewer with silver handles;

10. SCION (sī'ŭn)—Son, heir.
14. EWER (ū'ĕr)—A wide-mouthed jug.

"The Ballad of William Sycamore" from *Selected Works of Stephen Vincent Benét*, published by Rinehart & Company, Inc., copyright, 1922, by Stephen Vincent Benét. Reprinted by permission of Brandt & Brandt.

But I remember a coonskin cap   15
And the smell of bayberry candles.

The cabin logs, with the bark still rough,
And my mother who laughed at trifles,
And the tall, lank visitors, brown as snuff,
With their long, straight squirrel
    rifles.   20

I can hear them dance, like a foggy song,
Through the deepest one of my slumbers,
The fiddle squeaking the boots along
And my father calling the numbers.

The quick feet shaking the puncheon
    floor,   25
And the fiddle squealing and squealing,
Till the dried herbs rattled above the
    door
And the dust went up to the ceiling.

24. NUMBERS—Dance steps.
31. "MONEY MUSK"—An old dance tune.

There are children lucky from dawn till
    dusk,
But never a child so lucky!   30
For I cut my teeth on "Money Musk"
In the Bloody Ground of Kentucky!

When I grew tall as the Indian corn,
My father had little to lend me,
But he gave me his great, old powder
    horn   35
And his woodsman's skill to befriend me.

With a leather shirt to cover my back,
And a redskin nose to unravel
Each forest sign, I carried my pack
As far as a scout could travel.   40

Till I lost my boyhood and found my
    wife,
A girl like a Salem clipper!

32. BLOODY GROUND—A name applied to
Kentucky because of conflicts with the Indians
which took place there.

A woman straight as a hunting knife
With eyes as bright as the Dipper!

We cleared our camp where the buffalo
    feed,   45
Unheard-of streams were our flagons;
And I sowed my sons like the apple seed
On the trail of the Western wagons.

They were right, tight boys, never sulky
    or slow,
A fruitful, a goodly muster.   50
The eldest died at the Alamo.
The youngest fell with Custer.

The letter that told it burned my hand.
Yet we smiled and said, "So be it!"
But I could not live when they fenced
    my land,   55
For it broke my heart to see it.

I saddled a red, unbroken colt
And rode him into the day there;
And he threw me down like a thunder-
    bolt
And rolled on me as I lay there.   60

46. FLAGON—A pitcher with handles and
spout; also its contents.

The hunter's whistle hummed in my ear
As the city men tried to move me,
And I died in my boots like a pioneer
With the whole wide sky above me.

Now I lie in the heart of the fat, black
    soil,   65
Like the seed of a prairie thistle;
It has washed my bones with honey and
    oil
And picked them clean as a whistle.

And my youth returns, like the rains of
    Spring,
And my sons, like the wild geese fly-
    ing;   70
And I lie and hear the meadow lark
    sing
And have much content in my dying.

Go play with the towns you have built
    of blocks,
The towns where you would have bound
    me!
I sleep in my earth like a tired fox,   75
And my buffalo have found me.

PORTRAIT OF A PIONEER

1. What kind of people were William Sycamore's father and mother? See if you can find suggestions of their character and personality as well as of their physical characteristics.

2. Why did William Sycamore consider himself lucky in spite of his hardships and privations? What happy memories did he have of his childhood and youth?

3. What did he seem to admire most about the girl he married? Which of her characteristics would be equally prized in a modern wife?

4. What can you learn about William Sycamore's character from the way he received the news of his sons' death? Why was his own death a suitable ending for the kind of life he had led?

THE POET'S CRAFT

Throughout "The Ballad of William Sycamore" there are effective figures of speech which make the story vivid and colorful and frequently add a touch of humor. Since William Sycamore is supposed to be telling his own story, all such poetic comparisons must be made from the point of view of a pioneer. For example, when he describes his father in the first stanza William says: "He was quick on his feet *as a running deer*." In the fifth stanza he speaks of ". . . the tall, lank visitors, brown *as snuff*." Point out other examples and tell why you think each is effective and appropriate.

STEPHEN VINCENT BENÉT

For further information on this famous author, see pages 289–290.

Rutherford McDowell

EDGAR LEE MASTERS

When the photographer Rutherford McDowell lived in Spoon River, Wisconsin, the frontier days were over. It was the grandchildren and the great-grandchildren of the pioneers who came to him to have their pictures taken. However, in the course of his work, he did have occasion to study the faces of some of the early settlers and compare them with those of their descendants. The differences that he noted should be of concern to modern Americans.

They brought me ambrotypes
Of the old pioneers to enlarge.
And sometimes one sat for me—
Some one who was in being
When giant hands from the womb of
    the world   5
Tore the republic.
What was it in their eyes?—
For I could never fathom
That mystical pathos of drooped eyelids,
And the serene sorrow of their eyes.   10
It was like a pool of water,
Amid oak trees at the edge of a forest,
Where the leaves fall,
As you hear the crow of a cock
From a far-off farmhouse, seen near the
    hills   15

Where the third generation lives, and the
    strong men
And the strong women are gone and for-
    gotten.
And these grandchildren and great-grand-
    children
Of the pioneers!
Truly did my camera record their faces,
    too,   20
With so much of the old strength gone,
And the old faith gone,
And the old mastery of life gone,
And the old courage gone,
Which labors and loves and suffers and
    sings   25
Under the sun!

"Rutherford McDowell" from *Spoon River Anthology* by Edgar Lee Masters, and reprinted by permission of his estate.

◇◇◇

FOR UNDERSTANDING

1. In your own words tell what Rutherford McDowell saw in the faces of the old pioneers. What do you think caused the sorrow in their eyes that puzzled him?

2. In lines 11 through 17 the poet tries to put into a word picture of the landscape the same qualities that he saw in the pioneer faces. How well do you think he succeeded? What is suggested by the pool, the trees, the falling leaves, and the cock?

3. What did the photographer find lacking in the faces of the great-grandchildren of the pioneers? How would you account for the differences between the faces of the pioneers and those of their descendants? Do you think that faces reveal character? Do you agree with the implication that Americans lack character today? If not, give evidence to show that modern Americans do have character.

In Praise of Johnny Appleseed

VACHEL LINDSAY

Among the early pioneers who crossed the Appalachians and moved West was a young man who was to become one of the most interesting figures in American folklore. His real name was John Chapman, but because he distributed appleseeds to the pioneers, he became known as Johnny Appleseed. Born in Massachusetts at the time of the Revolution, he moved first to Pennsylvania and from there on West, planting and tending apple trees wherever he went. In 1847, when he was seventy-three years old, he died in Fort Wayne, Indiana. To this day there are orchards in Ohio and Indiana supposed to have been started by Johnny Appleseed.

Vachel Lindsay combines fact and legend in his tribute to Johnny Appleseed. Although the long poem has been somewhat abridged you can follow Johnny on his strange mission through the wilderness and sense something of the vision of the future that inspired him and other idealists among the pioneers to follow the sun "to the farthest West." Notice how the humorous pictures in the introductory part of the poem suggest the power and sweep of the Westward Movement. Everybody and everything were going West!

In the days of President Washington,
The glory of the nations,
Dust and ashes,
Snow and sleet,
And hay and oats and wheat,   5
Blew west,
Crossed the Appalachians,
Found the glades of rotting leaves, the soft deer-pastures,
The farms of the far-off future
In the forest.   10
Colts jumped the fence,
Snorting, ramping, snapping, sniffing,
With gastronomic calculations,
Crossed the Appalachians,
The east walls of our citadel,   15
And turned to gold-horned unicorns,

To be read like old leaves on the elm tree of Time, Sifting soft winds with sentence and rhyme.

Feasting in the dim, volunteer farms of the forest.
Stripedest, kickingest kittens escaped,
Caterwauling "Yankee Doodle Dandy."
Renounced their poor relations,   20
Crossed the Appalachians,
And turned to tiny tigers
In the humorous forest.
Chickens escaped
From farmyard congregations,   25
Crossed the Appalachians,
And turned to amber trumpets
On the ramparts of our Hoosiers' nest and citadel,
Millennial heralds
Of the foggy mazy forest.   30
Pigs broke loose, scrambled west,
Scorned their loathsome stations,
Crossed the Appalachians,
Turned to roaming, foaming wild boars
Of the forest.   35
The smallest, blindest puppies toddled west
While their eyes were coming open,
And, with misty observations,
Crossed the Appalachians,
Barked, barked, barked   40
At the glowworms and the marsh lights and the lightning bugs,
And turned to ravening wolves
Of the forest.
Crazy parrots and canaries flew west,
Drunk on Maytime revelations,   45
Crossed the Appalachians,
And turned to delirious, flower-dressed fairies
Of the lazy forest.
Haughtiest swans and peacocks swept west,
And, despite soft derivations,   50
Crossed the Appalachians.
And turned to blazing warrior souls
Of the forest,
Singing the ways
Of the Ancient of Days.   55
And the "Old Continentals
In their ragged regimentals,"
With bard's imaginations,
Crossed the Appalachians.
And   60
A boy
Blew west,

And with prayers and incantations,
And with "Yankee Doodle Dandy,"
Crossed the Appalachians,   65
And was "young John Chapman,"
Then
"Johnny Appleseed, Johnny Appleseed,"
Chief of the fastnesses, dappled and vast,
In a pack on his back,   70
In a deer-hide sack,
The beautiful orchards of the past,
The ghosts of all the forests and the groves—
In that pack on his back,
In that talisman sack,   75
Tomorrow's peaches, pears, and cherries,
Tomorrow's grapes and red raspberries,
Seeds and tree-souls, precious things,
Feathered with microscopic wings,
All the outdoors the child heart knows,   80
And the apple, green, red, and white,
Sun of his day and his night—
The apple allied to the thorn,
Child of the rose.
Porches untrod of forest houses   85
All before him, all day long,
"Yankee Doodle" his marching song;
And the evening breeze
Joined his psalms of praise
As he sang the ways   90
Of the Ancient of Days.
Leaving behind august Virginia,
Proud Massachusetts, and proud Maine.
Planting the trees that would march and train
On, in his name to the great Pacific,   95
Like Birnam wood to Dunsinane,
Johnny Appleseed swept on,
Every shackle gone,
Loving every sloshy brake,
Loving every skunk and snake,   100
Loving every leathery weed,
Johnny Appleseed, Johnny Appleseed,
Master and ruler of the unicorn-ramping forest,
The tiger-mewing forest,
The rooster-trumpeting, boar-foaming, wolf-ravening forest,   105
The spirit-haunted, fairy-enchanted forest,

96. BIRNAM WOOD TO DUNSINANE—In Shakespeare's *Macbeth* the soldiers of Malcolm advanced to Dunsinane carrying branches from Birnam wood.

Stupendous and endless,
Searching its perilous ways
In the name of the Ancient of Days.

II. The Indians Worship Him, but He Hurries On

Painted kings in the midst of the clearing   110
Heard him asking his friends the eagles
To guard each planted seed and seedling.
Then he was a god, to the red man's dreaming;
Then the chiefs brought treasures grotesque and fair—
Magical trinkets and pipes and guns,   115
Beads and furs from their medicine-lair—
Stuck holy feathers in his hair.
Hailed him with austere delight.
The orchard god was their guest through the night. . . .

But he left their wigwams and their love.   *While you*   120
By the hour of dawn he was proud and stark,   *read, hear*
Kissed the Indian babes with a sigh,   *the hoof-*
                                                   beats of deer
Went forth to live on roots and bark,   *in the snow.*
                                                   And see, by
Sleep in the trees, while the years howled by.   *their track,*
                                                   bleeding
                                                   footprints
                                                   we know.
Calling the catamounts by name,   125
And buffalo bulls no hand could tame.
Slaying never a living creature,
Joining the birds in every game,
With the gorgeous turkey gobblers mocking,
With the lean-necked eagles boxing and shouting;   130
Sticking their feathers in his hair—
Turkey feathers,
Eagle feathers,
Trading hearts with all beasts and weathers
He swept on, winged and wonder-crested,   135
Bare-armed, barefooted, and bare-breasted. . . .

III. Johnny Appleseed's Old Age

Long, long after   *To be read*
When settlers put up beam and rafter,   *like faint*
                                                   hoofbeats
They asked of the birds: "Who gave this fruit?   *of fawns*
                                                   long gone
                                                   From respectable
Who watched this fence till the seeds took root?   *pasture, and*   140
                                                   park and
Who gave these boughs?" They asked the sky,   *lawn,*
                                                   And heart-
And there was no reply.   *beats of*
                                                   fawns that
But the robin might have said,   *are coming*
                                                   again
"To the farthest West he has followed the sun,   *When the*
                                                   forest, once
His life and his empire just begun."   *more, is the*   145
                                                   master of
Self-scourged, like a monk, with a throne for wages, *men.*

379

Stripped, like the iron-souled Hindu sages,
Draped like a statue, in strings like a scarecrow,
His helmet-hat an old tin pan,
But worn in the love of the heart of man,   150
More sane than the helm of Tamerlane!
Hairy Ainu, wild man of Borneo, Robinson Crusoe—Johnny Appleseed!
And the robin might have said,
"Sowing, he goes to the far, new West,
With the apple, the sun of his burning breast—   155
The apple allied to the thorn,
Child of the rose."
Washington buried in Virginia,
Jackson buried in Tennessee,
Young Lincoln, brooding in Illinois,   160
And Johnny Appleseed, priestly and free,
Knotted and gnarled, past seventy years,
Still planted on in the woods alone.
Ohio and young Indiana—
These were his wide altar stone,   165
Where still he burnt out flesh and bone.
Twenty days ahead of the Indian, twenty years ahead of the white man,
At last the Indian overtook him, at last the Indian hurried past him;
At last the white man overtook him, at last the white man hurried past him;
Many cats were tame again,   170
Many ponies tame again,
Many pigs were tame again,
Many canaries tame again;
And the real frontier was his sunburnt breast. . . .

And the dew on the grass and his own cold tears   175
Were one in brooding mystery,
Though death's loud thunder came upon him,
Though death's loud thunder struck him down—
The boughs and the proud thoughts swept through the thunder,
Till he saw our wide nation, each State a flower,   180
Each petal a park for holy feet,
With wild fawns merry on every street,
With wild fawns merry on every street,
The vista of ten thousand years, flower-lighted and complete.

Hear the lazy weeds murmuring, bays and rivers whispering, 185
From Michigan to Texas, California to Maine;
Listen to the eagles screaming, calling,

151. HELM OF TAMERLANE (tăm'ēr·lān)—The helmet of Tamerlane, an early Mongol conqueror famous for his cruelty.
152. AINU (ĭ'noo)—A primitive race in Japan who have a great wealth of hair and heavy beards.

"Johnny Appleseed, Johnny Appleseed,"
There by the doors of old Fort Wayne.

In the four-poster bed Johnny Appleseed built,   190
Autumn rains were the curtains, autumn leaves were the quilt.
He laid him down sweetly, and slept through the night,
Like a bump on a log, like a stone washed white,
There by the doors of old Fort Wayne.

FOR UNDERSTANDING AND APPRECIATION

1. Which of the many things that crossed the Appalachians seemed most amusing to you? Find specific words that suggest characteristic appearance and actions of the different animals and birds described. Which words have a humorous effect? Tell why, if you can. For example, neither the word *gastronomic* nor *calculations* is humorous in itself. Why, then, are they amusing as they are used in line 13?

2. How could Johnny Appleseed carry the "orchards of the past" and the fruit of the future in the sack on his back?

3. Find the lines which tell that Johnny Appleseed loved and protected the wildlife that he found in the wilderness. Why do you think the poet made particular mention of *sloshy brake, skunk, snake,* and *leathery weed* as examples of what Johnny loved in nature?

4. Why was Johnny Appleseed revered by the Indians? What led them to believe that he was a god, or at least a medicine man?

5. What were the reactions of the settlers when they found apple orchards growing in the woods?

6. Explain the figurative language in the last six lines of the poem. What was the four-poster bed that Johnny Appleseed built? Have you ever heard the expression "like a bump on a log"? How is it generally used? Do you think it is appropriate as it is used here? What is the *sleep* referred to?

BROADER MEANINGS

1. The following lines are from Part III which tells about Johnny Appleseed's old age:

"To the farthest West he has followed the sun,
His life and his empire just begun."

Since Johnny Appleseed's life was actually drawing to a close and the trees he had planted were full grown, the lines are obviously not literally true. How, then, would you interpret the passage? In what ways had "His life and his empire just begun"?

2. What lines suggest that Johnny Appleseed is a dedicated person with one great purpose? What was his vision of America's future? How much of his dream has been fulfilled? Point out passages which show that, like all people, Johnny saw things in the light of his own interests and experiences.

VACHEL LINDSAY (1879–1931)

For further information on this famous author, see page 239.

The Westward Frontier—As Seen by the Men Who Were There

Naturally, there are some aspects of pioneer life which can be most vividly described by the men who were actually there. In the second section of this unit are realistic selections which re-create places and people that their authors really knew. In "Among the Corn Rows" you will feel something of the heartbreaking drudgery that Hamlin Garland experienced as a boy on his father's pioneer farm in the Midwest. You will visit a California mining town with Bret Harte, who himself lived in places like Poker Flat and Sandy Bar. You will know the terror that grips a man alone in the frozen Yukon country where Jack London prospected for gold. And you will enjoy the fun and excitement of a steamboat ride down the great Mississippi with the American humorist, Mark Twain, as pilot. Finally, you can review the spirit of the western frontiersmen, and get a glimpse of the great Westward Movement as a whole, by reading Walt Whitman's "Pioneers, O Pioneers."

AMONG THE CORN ROWS

HAMLIN GARLAND

The early writers about the settling of the West played up the adventure and excitement of pioneer life. Their heroes were often picturesque frontiersmen in coonskin caps who tamed the wilderness by blazing new trails and fighting hostile Indians. To Hamlin Garland, who had grown up on pioneer farms in the Middle West, the tales of those writers seemed misleading. At any rate he knew that they failed to tell the whole truth about life on the frontier, and he resolved to present the other side of the picture. His characters were the hard-working farmers who followed the scouts and explorers west and tried to establish permanent homes.

As you read "Among the Corn Rows," you will discover that until Rob Rodemaker appeared, there was very little romantic adventure in the life of Julia Peterson.

A cornfield in July is a sultry place. The soil is hot and dry; the wind comes across the lazily murmuring leaves laden with a warm, sickening smell drawn from the rapidly growing, broad-flung banners of the corn. The sun, nearly vertical, drops a flood of dazzling light upon the field over which the cool shadows run, only to make the heat seem the more intense.

Julia Peterson, faint with hunger, was toiling back and forth between the corn rows, holding the handles of the double-shovel corn plough, while her little brother Otto rode the steaming horse. Her heart was full of bitterness, her face flushed with heat, and her muscles aching with fatigue. The heat grew terrible. The corn came to her shoulders, and not a breath seemed to reach her, while the sun, nearing the noon mark, lay pitilessly upon her shoulders, protected only by a calico dress. The dust rose under her feet, and as she was wet with perspiration it soiled her till with a woman's instinctive cleanliness, she shuddered. Her head throbbed dangerously. What matter to her that the kingbird pitched jovially from the maples to catch a wandering bluebottle fly, that the robin was feeding its young, that the bobolink was singing? All these things, if she saw them, only threw her bondage to labor into greater relief.

Across the field, in another patch of corn, she could see her father—a big, gruff-voiced, wide-bearded Norwegian—at work also with a plough. The corn must be ploughed, and so she toiled on, the tears dropping from the shadow of the ugly sunbonnet she wore. Her shoes, coarse and square-toed, chafed her feet; her hands, large and strong, were browned, or, more properly, *burnt*, on the backs by the sun. The horse's harness "*creak*-cracked" as he swung steadily and patiently forward, the moisture pouring from his sides, his nostrils distended.

"Among the Corn Rows" from *Main-Travelled Roads* by Hamlin Garland. Reprinted by permission of Constance Garland Doyle and Isabel Garland Lord

The field bordered on a road, and on the other side of the road ran a river—a broad, clear, shallow expanse at that point, and the eyes of the boy gazed longingly at the pond and the cool shadow each time that he turned at the fence.

"Say, Jule, I'm goin' in! Come, can't I? Come—say!" he pleaded, as they stopped at the fence to let the horse breathe.

"I've let you go wade twice."

"But that don't do any good. My legs is all smarty, 'cause ol' Jack sweats so." The boy turned around on the horse's back and slid back to his rump. "I can't stand it!" he burst out, sliding off and darting under the fence. "Father can't see."

The girl put her elbows on the fence and watched her little brother as he sped away to the pool, throwing off his clothes as he ran, whooping with uncontrollable delight. Soon she could hear him splashing about in the water a short distance up the stream, and caught glimpses of his little shiny body and happy face. How cool that water looked! And the shadows there by the big basswood! How that water would cool her blistered feet. An impulse seized her, and she squeezed between the rails of the fence, and stood in the road looking up and down to see that the way was clear. It was not a main-traveled road; no one was likely to come; why not?

She hurriedly took off her shoes and stockings—how delicious the cool, soft velvet of the grass! and sitting down on the bank under the great basswood, whose roots formed an abrupt bank, she slid her poor blistered, chafed feet into the water, her bare head leaned against the huge tree trunk.

And now, as she rested, the beauty of the scene came to her. Over her the wind moved the leaves. A jay screamed far off, as if answering the cries of the boy. A kingfisher crossed and recrossed the stream with dipping sweep of his wings. The river sang with its lips to the pebbles. The vast clouds went by majestically, far above the treetops, and the snap and buzzing and ringing whir of July insects made a ceaseless, slumberous undertone of song solvent[1] of all else. The tired girl forgot her work. She began to dream. This would not last always. Someone would come to release her from such drudgery. This was her constant, tenderest, and most secret dream. *He* would be a Yankee, not a Norwegian. The Yankees didn't ask their wives to work in the field. He would have a home. Perhaps he'd live in town—perhaps a merchant! And then she thought of the drug clerk in Rock River who had looked at her—A voice broke in on her dream, a fresh, manly voice.

"Well, by jinks! if it ain't Julia! Just the one I wanted to see!"

The girl turned, saw a pleasant-faced young fellow in a derby hat and a cutaway suit of diagonals.[2]

"Bob Rodemaker! How come—"

She remembered her situation and flushed, looked down at the water, and remained perfectly still.

"Ain't you goin' to shake hands? Y' don't seem very glad t' see me."

She began to grow angry. "If you had any eyes, you'd see."

Rob looked over the edge of the bank, whistled, turned away. "Oh, I see! Excuse *me*! Don't blame yeh a bit, though. Good weather f'r corn," he went on,

[1] SOLVENT (sŏl'vĕnt)—Here used in the sense of blending these sounds and blotting out all others.

[2] DIAGONALS—A twilled fabric with diagonal ridges or stripes.

looking up at the trees. "Corn seems to be pretty well forward," he continued, in a louder voice, as he walked away, still gazing into the air. "Crops is looking first-class in Boomtown. Hello! This Otto? H'yare, y' little scamp! Get on to that horse agin. Quick, 'r I'll take y'r skin off an' hang it on the fence. What y' been doin'?"

"Ben in swimmin'. Jimminy, ain't it fun! When 'd y' get back?" said the boy, grinning.

"Never you mind!" replied Rob, leaping the fence by laying his left hand on the top rail. "Get on to that horse." He tossed the boy up on the horse and hung his coat on the fence. "I s'pose the ol' man makes her plough, same as usual?"

"Yup," said Otto.

"Dod ding a man that'll do that! I don't mind if it's necessary, but it ain't necessary in his case." He continued to mutter in this way as he went across the other side of the field. As they turned to come back, Rob went up and looked at the horse's mouth. "Gettin' purty near of age. Say, who's sparkin' Julia now—anybody?"

"Nobody 'cept some ol' Norwegians. She won't have them. Por wants her to, but she won't."

"Good f'r her. Nobody comes t' see her Sunday nights, eh?"

"Nope; only 'Tias Anderson an' Ole Hoover; but she goes off an' leaves 'em."

"Chk!" said Rob, starting old Jack across the field.

It was almost noon, and Jack moved reluctantly. He knew the time of day as well as the boy. He made this round after distinct protest.

In the meantime, Julia, putting on her shoes and stockings, went to the fence and watched the man's shining white shirt as he moved across the cornfield.

There had never been any special tenderness between them, but she had always liked him. They had been at school together. She wondered why he had come back at this time of the year, and wondered how long he would stay. How long had he stood looking at her? She flushed again at the thought of it. But he wasn't to blame; it was a public road. She might have known better.

She stood under a little popple [3] tree, whose leaves shook musically at every zephyr, and her eyes, through half-shut lids, roved over the sea of deep-green, glossy leaves, dappled here and there by cloud shadows, stirred here and there like water by the wind; and out of it all a longing to be free from such toil rose like a breath, filling her throat and quickening the motion of her heart. Must this go on forever, this life of heat and dust and labor? What did it all mean?

The girl laid her chin on her strong red wrists and looked up into the blue spaces between the vast clouds—aerial mountains dissolving in a shoreless azure sea. How cool and sweet and restful they looked! If she might only lie out on the billowy, snow-white, sunlit edge! The voices of the driver and the ploughman recalled her, and she fixed her eyes again upon the slowly nodding head of the patient horse, on the boy turned half about on his saddle, talking to the white-sleeved man, whose derby had bobbed up and down quite curiously, like the horse's head. Would she ask him to dinner! What would her people say?

"Phew! it's hot!" was the greeting the young fellow gave as he came up. He smiled in a frank, boyish way, as he hung his hat on the top of a stake and looked up at her. "D' y' know, I kind o' enjoy gettin' at it again? Fact. It ain't no work for a girl, though," he added.

[3] POPPLE—Dialect for poplar.

385

"When 'd you get back?" she asked, the flush not yet out of her face. Rob was looking at her thick, fine hair and full Scandinavian face, as rich as a rose in color, and did not reply for a few seconds. She stood with her hideous sunbonnet pushed back on her shoulders. A kingbird was chattering overhead.

"Oh, a few days ago."

"How long y' goin' t' stay?"

"Oh, I d' know. A week, mebbe."

A far-off halloo came pulsing across the shimmering air. The boy screamed "Dinner!" and waved his hat with an answering whoop, then flopped off the horse like a turtle off a stone into water. He had the horse unhooked in an instant and had flung his toes up over the horse's back, in act to climb on, when Rob said:

"H'yare, young fellow! wait a minute. Tired?" he asked the girl, with a tone that was more than kindly. It was almost tender.

"Yes," she replied, in a low voice. "My shoes hurt me."

"Well, here y' go," he replied, taking his stand by the horse, and holding out his hand like a step. She colored and smiled a little as she lifted her foot into his huge, hard, sunburned hand.

"Oop-a-daisy!" he called. She gave a spring and sat on the horse like one at home there.

Rob had a deliciously unconscious, abstracted, businesslike air. He really left her nothing to do but enjoy his company, while he went ahead and did precisely as he pleased.

"We don't raise much corn out there, an' so I kind o' like to see it once more."

"I wish I didn't have to see another hill of corn as long as I live!" replied the girl, bitterly.

"Don't know as I blame yeh a bit. But, all the same, I'm glad you was working in it today," he thought to himself, as he walked beside her horse toward the house.

"Will you stop to dinner?" she inquired bluntly, almost surlily. It was evident there were reasons why she didn't mean to press him to do so.

"You bet I will," he replied; "that is, if you want I should."

"You know how we live," she replied evasively. "If you can stand it, why—" She broke off abruptly.

Yes, he remembered how they lived in that big, square, dirty, white frame house. It had been three or four years since he had been in it, but the smell of the cabbage and onions, the penetrating, peculiar mixture of odors, assailed his memory as something unforgettable.

"I guess I'll stop," he said, as she hesitated. She said no more, but tried to act as if she were not in any way responsible for what came afterward.

"I guess I c'n stand f'r one meal what you stand all the while," he added.

As she left them at the well and went to the house he saw her limp painfully, and the memory of her face so close to his lips as he helped her down from the horse gave him pleasure at the same time that he was touched by its tired and gloomy look. Mrs. Peterson came to the door of the kitchen, looking just the same as ever. Broad-faced, unwieldly, flabby, apparently wearing the same dress he remembered to have seen her in years before—a dirty drab-colored thing—she looked as shapeless as a sack of wool. Her English was limited to, "How de do, Rob?"

He washed at the pump, while the girl, in the attempt to be hospitable, held the clean towel for him.

"You're purty well used up, eh?" he said to her.

"Yes; it's awful hot out there."

"Can't you lay off this afternoon?"

"No. *He* won't listen to that."

"Well, let me take your place."

"No; there ain't any use o' that."

Peterson, a brawny, wide-bearded Norwegian, came up at this moment and spoke to Rob in a sullen, gruff way.

"Hallo, whan yo' gaet back?"

"Today. He ain't *very* glad to see me," said Rob, winking at Julia. "He ain't b'ilin' over with enthusiasm; but I c'n stand it, for your sake," he added, with amazing assurance; but the girl had turned away, and it was wasted.

At the table he ate heartily of the "bean swaagen," which filled a large wooden bowl in the center of the table, and which was ladled into smaller wooden bowls at each plate. Julia had tried hard to convert her mother to Yankee ways, and had at last given it up in despair. Rob kept on safe subjects, mainly asking questions about the crops of Peterson, and when addressing the girl, inquired of the schoolmates. By skillful questioning, he kept the subject of marriage uppermost, and seemingly was getting an inventory of the girls not yet married or engaged.

It was embarrassing for the girl. She was all too well aware of the difference between her home and the home of her schoolmates and friends. She knew that it was not pleasant for her "Yankee" friends to come to visit her when they could not feel sure of a welcome from the tireless, silent, and grim-visaged old Norse, if, indeed, they could escape insult. Julia ate her food mechanically, and it could hardly be said that she enjoyed the brisk talk of the young man, his eyes were upon her so constantly and his smile so obviously addressed to her.

Isn't this normal?

She rose as soon as possible and, going outside, took a seat on a chair under the trees in the yard. She was not a coarse or dull girl. In fact, she had developed so rapidly by contact with the young people of the neighborhood that she no longer found pleasure in her own home. She didn't believe in keeping up the old-fashioned Norwegian customs, and her life with her mother was not one to breed love or confidence. She was more like a hired hand. The love of the mother for her "Yulyie" was sincere though rough and inarticulate, and it was her jealousy of the young "Yankees" that widened the chasm between the girl and herself—an inevitable result.

Rob followed the girl out into the yard and threw himself on the grass at her feet, perfectly unconscious of the fact that this attitude was exceedingly graceful and becoming to them both. He did it because he wanted to talk to her, and the grass was cool and easy; there wasn't any other chair, anyway.

"Do they keep up the ly-ceum [4] and the sociables same as ever?"

"Yes. The others go a good 'eal, but I don't. We're gettin' such a stock round us, and Father thinks he needs me s' much, I don't get out often. I'm gettin' sick of it."

"I sh'd think y' would," he replied, his eyes on her face.

"I c'd stand the churnin' and housework, but when it comes t' workin' outdoors in the dirt an' hot sun, gettin' all sunburned and chapped up, it's another thing. An' then it seems as if he gets stingier 'n' stingier every year. I ain't had a new dress in—I d'-know-how-long. He says it's all nonsense, an' Mother's just about as bad. *She* don't want a new

[4] LY-CEUM—This is the way Rob pronounced lyceum (lī·sē′ŭm), an organization designed to promote cultural interests.

dress, an' so she thinks I don't." The girl was feeling the influence of a sympathetic listener and was making up for the long silence. "I've tried t' go out t' work, but they won't let me. They'd have t' pay a hand twenty dollars a month f'r the work I do, an' they like cheap help; but I'm not goin' t' stand it much longer, I can tell you that."

Rob thought she was very handsome as she sat there with her eyes fixed on the horizon, while these rebellious thoughts found utterance in her quivering, passionate voice.

"Yulie! Kom haar!" roared the old man from the well.

A frown of anger and pain came into her face. She looked at Rob. "That means more work."

"Say! let me go out in your place. Come, now; what's the use—"

"No; it wouldn't do no good. It ain't t'-day's much; it's every day, and—"

"*Yulie!*" called Peterson again, with a string of impatient Norwegian. "Batter yo' kom pooty quick."

"Well, all right, only I'd like to—" Rob submitted.

"Well, good-by," she said, with a little touch of feeling. "When d' ye go back?"

"I don't know. I'll see y' again before I go. Good-by."

He stood watching her slow, painful pace till she reached the well where Otto was standing with the horse. He stood watching them as they moved out into the road and turned down toward the field. He felt that she had sent him away; but still there was a look in her eyes which was not altogether—

He gave it up in despair at last. He was not good at analyses of this nature; he was used to plain, blunt expressions. There was a woman's subtlety here quite beyond his reach.

He sauntered slowly off up the road

after his talk with Julia. His head was low on his breast; he was thinking as one who is about to take a decided and important step.

He stopped at length, and, turning, watched the girl moving along the deeps of the corn. Hardly a leaf was stirring; the untempered sunlight fell in a burning flood upon the field; the grasshoppers rose, snapped, buzzed, and fell; the locust uttered its dry, heat-intensifying cry. The man lifted his head.

"It's a shame!" he said, beginning rapidly to retrace his steps. He stood leaning on the fence, awaiting the girl's coming very much as she had waited his on the round he had made before dinner. He grew impatient at the slow gait of the horse, and drummed on the rail while he whistled. Then he took off his hat and dusted it nervously. As the horse got a little nearer he wiped his face carefully, pushed his hat back on his head, and climbed over the fence, where he stood with elbows on the middle rail as the girl and boy and horse came to the end of the furrow.

"Hot, ain't it?" he said, as she looked up.

"Jimminy Peters, it's awful!" puffed the boy. The girl did not reply till she swung the plough about after the horse and set it upright into the next row. Her powerful body had a superb swaying motion at the waist as she did this—a motion which affected Rob vaguely but massively.

"I thought you'd gone," she said gravely, pushing back her bonnet till he could see her face dewed with sweat, and pink as a rose. She had the high cheekbones of her race, but she had also their exquisite fairness of color.

"Say, Otto," asked Rob, alluringly, "wan' to go swimmin'?"

"You bet," replied Otto.

"Well, I'll go round if—"

The boy dropped off the horse, not waiting to hear any more. Rob grinned, but the girl dropped her eyes, then looked away.

"Got rid o' him mighty quick. Say, Julyie, I hate like thunder t' see you out here; it ain't right. I wish you'd—I wish—"

She could not look at him now, and her bosom rose and fell with a motion that was not due to fatigue. Her moist hair matted around her forehead gave her a boyish look.

Rob nervously tried again, tearing splinters from the fence. "Say, now, I'll tell yeh what I came back here for—t' git married; and if you're willin' I'll do it tonight. Come, now, whaddy y' say?"

"What've *I* got t' do 'bout it?" she finally asked, the color flooding her face, and a faint smile coming to her lips. "Go ahead. I ain't got anything—"

Rob put a splinter in his mouth and faced her. "Oh, looky here, now, Julyie! you know what I mean. I've got a good claim out near Boomtown—a *rattlin'* good claim; a shanty on it fourteen by sixteen —no tarred paper about it, and a suller to keep butter in, and a hundred acres o' wheat just about ready to turn now I need a wife."

Here he straightened up, threw away the splinter, and took off his hat. He was a very pleasant figure as the girl stole a look at him. His black laughing eyes were especially earnest just now. His voice had a touch of pleading. The popple tree over their heads murmured applause at his eloquence, then hushed to listen. A cloud dropped a silent shadow down upon them, and it sent a little thrill of fear through Rob, as if it were an omen of failure. As the girl remained silent, looking away, he began, man-fashion, to desire her more and more, as he feared to lose her. He put his hat on the post again and took out his jack-knife. Her calico dress draped her supple and powerful figure simply but naturally. The stoop in her shoulders, given by labor, disappeared as she partly leaned upon the fence. The curves of her muscular arms showed through her sleeve.

"It's all-fired lonesome f'r me out there on that claim, and it ain't no picnic f'r you here. Now, if you'll come out there with me, you needn't do anything but cook f'r me, and after harvest we can git a good layout o' furniture, an' I'll lath and plaster the house and put a little hell [ell] in the rear." He smiled, and so did she. He felt encouraged to say: "An' there we be, as snug as y' please. We're close t' Boomtown, an' we can go down there to church sociables an' things, and they're a jolly lot there."

The girl was still silent, but the man's simple enthusiasm came to her charged with passion and a sort of romance such as her hard life had known little of. There was something enticing about this trip to the West.

"What'll my folks say?" she said at last.

A virtual surrender, but Rob was not acute enough to see it. He pressed on eagerly:

"I don't care. Do you? They'll jest keep y' ploughin' corn and milkin' cows till the day of judgment. Come, Julyie, I ain't got no time to fool away. I've got t' get back t' that grain. It's a whoppin' old crop, sure's y'r born, an' that means sompin purty scrumptious in furniture this fall. Come, now." He approached her and laid his hand on her shoulder very much as he would have touched Albert Seagraves or any other comrade. "Whaddy y' say?"

She neither started nor shrunk nor looked at him. She simply moved a step

away. "They'd never let me go," she replied bitterly. "I'm too cheap a hand. I do a man's work an' get no pay at all."

"You'll have half o' all I c'n make," he put in.

"How long c'n you wait?" she asked, looking down at her dress.

"Just two minutes," he said, pulling out his watch. "It ain't no use t' wait. The old man'll be jest as mad a week from now as he is today. Why not go now?"

"I'm of age in a few days," she mused, wavering, calculating.

"You c'n be of age tonight if you'll jest call on old Squire Hatfield with me."

"All right, Rob," the girl said, turning and holding out her hand.

"That's the talk!" he exclaimed, seizing it. "And now a kiss, to bind the bargin, as the fellah says."

"I guess we c'n get along without that."

"No, we can't. It won't seem like an engagement without it."

"It ain't goin' to seem like one, anyway," she answered, with a sudden realization of how far from her dreams of courtship this reality was.

"Say, now, Julyie, that ain't fair; it ain't treatin' me right. You don't seem to understand that I *like* you, but I do."

Rob was carried quite out of himself by the time, the place, and the girl. He had said a very moving thing.

The tears sprang involuntarily to the girl's eyes. "Do you mean it? If y' do, you may."

She was trembling with emotion for the first time. The sincerity of the man's voice had gone deep.

He put his arm around her almost timidly, and kissed her on the cheek, a great love for her springing up in his heart. "That settles it," he said. "Don't cry, Julyie. You'll never be sorry for it.

Don't cry. It kind o' hurts me to see it."

He hardly understood her feelings. He was only aware that she was crying, and tried in a bungling way to soothe her. But now that she had given way, she sat down in the grass and wept bitterly.

"Yulyie!" yelled the vigilant old Norwegian, like a distant foghorn.

The girl sprang up; the habit of obedience was strong.

"No; you set right here, and I'll go round," he said. "Otto!"

The boy came scrambling out of the wood, half dressed. Rob tossed him upon the horse, snatched Julia's sunbonnet, put his own hat on her head, and moved off down the corn rows, leaving the girl smiling through her tears as he whistled and chirped to the horse. Farmer Peterson, seeing the familiar sunbonnet above the corn rows, went back to his work, with a sentence of Norwegian trailing after him like the tail of a kite—something about lazy girls who didn't earn the crust of their bread, etc.

Rob was wild with delight. "Git up there, Jack! Hay, you old corncrib! Say, Otto, can you keep your mouth shet if it puts money in your pocket?"

"Jest try me 'n' see," said the keen-eyed little scamp.

"Well, you keep quiet about my bein' here this afternoon, and I'll put a dollar on y'r tongue—hay?—what?—understand?"

"Show me y'r dollar," said the boy, turning about and showing his tongue.

"All right. Begin to practise now by not talkin' to me."

Rob went over the whole situation on his way back, and when he got in sight of the girl his plan was made. She stood waiting for him with a new look on her face. Her sullenness had given way to a peculiar eagerness and anxiety to believe in him. She was already living that free life in a far-off wonderful country. No more would her stern father and sullen mother force her to tasks which she hated. She'd be a member of a new firm. She'd work, of course, but it would be because she wanted to, and not because she was forced to. The independence and the love promised grew more and more attractive. She laughed back with a softer light in her eyes, when she saw the smiling face of Rob looking at her from her sunbonnet.

"Now you mustn't do any more o' this," he said. "You go back to the house an' tell y'r mother you're too lame to plough any more today, and it's gettin' late, anyhow. Tonight!" he whispered quickly. "Eleven! Here!"

The girl's heart leaped with fear. "I'm afraid."

"Not of *me*, are yeh?"

"No, I'm not afraid of you, Rob."

"I'm glad o' that. I—I want you—to *like* me, Julyie; won't you?"

"I'll try," she answered, with a smile.

"Tonight, then," he said, as she moved away.

"Tonight. Good-by."

"Good-by."

He stood and watched her till her tall figure was lost among the drooping corn leaves. There was a singular choking feeling in his throat. The girl's voice and face had brought up so many memories of parties and picnics and excursions on far-off holidays, and at the same time suggestions of the future. He already felt that it was going to be an unconscionably long time before eleven o'clock.

He saw her go to the house, and then he turned and walked slowly up the dusty road. Out of the mayweed the grasshoppers sprang, buzzing and snapping their dull red wings. Butterflies, yellow and white, fluttered around moist places in the ditch, and slender, striped water snakes glided across the stagnant pools at sound of footsteps.

But the mind of the man was far away on his claim, building a new house, with a woman's advice and presence.

It was a windless night. The katydids and an occasional cricket were the only sounds Rob could hear as he stood beside his team and strained his ear to listen. At long intervals a little breeze ran through the corn like a swift serpent, bringing to his nostrils the snappy smell of the growing corn. The horses stamped uneasily as the mosquitoes settled on their shining limbs. The sky was full of stars, but there was no moon.

"What if she don't come?" he thought. "Or *can't* come? I can't stand that. I'll go to the old man an' say, 'Looky here—' Sh!"

He listened again. There was a rustling in the corn. It was not like the fitful movement of the wind; it was

steady, slower, and approaching. It ceased. He whistled the wailing, sweet cry of the prairie chicken. Then a figure came out into the road—a woman—Julia!

He took her in his arms as she came panting up to him.

"Rob!"

"Julyie!"

A few words, the dull tread of swift horses, the rising of a silent train of dust, and then—the wind wandered in the growing corn, the dust fell, a dog barked down the road, and the katydids sang to the liquid contralto of the river in its shallows.

⬦⬦⬦⬦⬦⬦⬦⬦⬦⬦⬦⬦⬦⬦⬦⬦⬦⬦⬦⬦⬦⬦⬦⬦

FOR UNDERSTANDING

1. Besides the heavy work and long hours, what made Julia's life on the farm particularly hard to bear? Why was marriage her only hope of release? How did she picture the man who she hoped would rescue her from her drudgery?

2. Is there any way to explain Mr. Peterson's apparent lack of feeling for his family? What is there in the story to show that it was not laziness on his part that caused him to work his children so hard? Can you think of possible circumstances or conditions in his early life that might have made him overly determined to make the most of his new opportunities? How might life in the New World be more difficult for him than for the "Yankees" whom Julia admired?

3. In what respects did Rob Rodemaker measure up to Julia's ideal suitor? How was he different? Do you think he really loved Julia, or was he merely looking for a strong, healthy wife who would be able to work hard on his own farm? Refer to the story to support your opinion.

4. Do you think Julia had a good chance for a happy married life with Rob? What

character and personality traits did each have that would contribute to the success or failure of their marriage? Where in the story are those traits revealed?

THE REALISTIC STORY

Writers of realistic fiction believe that there is interest and significance in the everyday lives of ordinary people. Furthermore, realists believe that a writer should tell the whole truth about life as he sees it —including the commonplace, and even the ugly and the unpleasant. The following questions will help you to find examples of realism in "Among the Corn Rows."

1. Find an example of realistic description in the story. Point out some of the commonplace details which make you feel that the author had actually experienced what he wrote about. Are there any passages which seem to you ugly, unpleasant, or repulsive?

2. In order to make the conversation natural, the author used many contractions and sometimes tried to spell words as the speaker would pronounce them. The following is a typical sample of the dialogue: "This Otto? H'yare, y' little scamp! Get on to that horse agin. Quick, 'r I'll take y'r skin off an' hang it on the fence." Do you think this attempt to write realistic conversation was successful? Recently, even realistic writers merely *suggest* the way the people talk by using a few re-spellings and common contractions. Which method do you prefer? Which is easier to read?

3. Courtship is a popular subject of fiction writers. Romantic authors idealize the love-making with noble sentiments and pretty speeches. Usually their stories end with marriage, and the implication is that the lovers "lived happily ever afterwards." How is the courtship in "Among the Corn Rows" different from the typical romantic type? For example, consider Rob's proposal. How is it more realistic than romantic? What other examples of realism can you find in Rob's courtship?

SUGGESTED ACTIVITIES

1. The story you have just read is Part II of "Among the Corn Rows." Part I, which you can find in Hamlin Garland's volume of stories and sketches titled *Main-Travelled Roads*, shows Rob on his claim farther west before he returned home to find a wife. You might like to read the story for a special report to the class.

2. Try writing a sequel to "Among the Corn Rows." You might tell what happened at the Peterson farm when Julia's elopement was discovered, or you might tell about Julia and Rob in their new home. Make your story true to the personalities of the characters as they were revealed in "Among the Corn Rows."

HAMLIN GARLAND (1860–1940)

Hamlin Garland was the first American author to write with complete realism about the West. Because he was born in Wisconsin and lived on pioneer farms in Iowa and North Dakota, he was a true son of the "Middle Border" about which he wrote. He worked part time on the farm while he attended Cedar Valley Seminary at Osage, Iowa. He taught school for a time and later took up a claim in North Dakota.

It was with the two hundred dollars he received from mortgaging his claim that he went to Boston to begin his literary career. There he lived and worked in dismal attic rooms, miserable and half-starved. Out of the eight dollars a week that he earned, a part went home to support his father and mother, who had had two years of crop failure on their North Dakota farm.

Garland could have written and sold romantic, sentimental stories about the West, but he was determined to write the whole truth about the country that he knew, and he refused to write anything that was not honest and true to life as he saw it. When someone asked him why he did not write something that would sell, he is reported to have said: "We have had enough of those lies."

Although Mr. Garland wrote both poetry

and prose, he is best known for his books that are largely autobiographical. Among the most significant are *A Son of the Middle Border*, *A Daughter of the Middle Border*, which won the Pulitzer Prize in 1921, and *Trail Makers of the Middle Border*. His prose is as down to earth and natural as the country about which he wrote.

◇◇◇◇◇

THE OUTCASTS OF POKER FLAT

BRET HARTE

Because Bret Harte lived in California during the gold rush period, his western stories are based on first-hand knowledge. He had actually seen the wild places he described, and he drew his characters from the interesting and unusual people he met in frontier towns and mining camps. No wonder his stories reflect a colorful picture of the Old West. As a matter of fact, they were so popular in their own day that they were influential in the development of a new type of American story. Following the author's example, writers in other sections of the country attempted to present in their stories the picturesque aspects of American life that they found in their own regions. These stories were called local color stories.

As you read "The Outcasts of Poker Flat" see whether you think Bret Harte succeeded in using his experiences and his observation to give a realistic picture of the setting of his story and to create characters who are true-to-life individuals rather than mere western types.

As Mr. John Oakhurst, gambler, stepped into the main street of Poker Flat on the morning of the twenty-third of November, 1850, he was conscious of a change in its moral atmosphere since the preceding night. Two or three men, conversing earnestly together, ceased as he approached, and exchanged significant glances. There was a Sabbath lull in the air, which, in a settlement unused to Sabbath influences, looked ominous.

Mr. Oakhurst's calm, handsome face betrayed small concern in these indications. Whether he was conscious of any predisposing cause was another question. "I reckon they're after somebody," he reflected; "likely it's me." He returned to his pocket the handkerchief with which he had been whipping away the red dust of Poker Flat from his neat boots, and quietly discharged his mind of any further conjecture.

"The Outcasts of Poker Flat" by Bret Harte. Reprinted by permission of Houghton Mifflin Company.

In point of fact, Poker Flat was "after somebody." It had lately suffered the loss of several thousand dollars, two valuable horses, and a prominent citizen. It was experiencing a spasm of virtuous reaction quite as lawless and ungovernable as any of the acts that had provoked it. A secret committee had determined to rid the town of all improper persons. This was done permanently in regard to two men who were then hanging from the boughs of a sycamore in the gulch, and temporarily in the banishment of certain other objectionable characters. I regret to say that some of these were ladies.

Mr. Oakhurst was right in supposing that he was included in this category. A few of the committee had urged hanging him as a possible example and a sure method of reimbursing themselves from his pockets of the sums he had won from them. "It's agin justice," said Jim Wheeler, "to let this yer young man from Roaring Camp—an entire stranger—carry away our money." But a crude sentiment of equity residing in the breasts of those who had been fortunate enough to win from Mr. Oakhurst overruled this narrower local prejudice.

Mr. Oakhurst received his sentence with philosophic calmness, none the less coolly that he was aware of the hesitation of his judges. He was too much of a gambler not to accept fate. With him life was at best an uncertain game, and he recognized the usual percentage in favor of the dealer.

A body of armed men accompanied the deported wickedness of Poker Flat to the outskirts of the settlement. Besides Mr. Oakhurst, who was known to be a coolly desperate man, and for whose intimidation the armed escort was intended, the expatriated party consisted of a young woman familiarly known as "The Duchess"; another who had won the title of "Mother Shipton"; and "Uncle Billy," a suspected sluicerobber[1] and confirmed drunkard.

The cavalcade provoked no comments from the spectators, nor was any word uttered by the escort. Only when the gulch which marked the uttermost limit of Poker Flat was reached, the leader spoke briefly and to the point. The exiles were forbidden to return at the peril of their lives.

As the escort disappeared, their pent-up feelings found vent in a few hysterical tears from the Duchess, some bad language from Mother Shipton, and a Parthian volley[2] of expletives from Uncle Billy. The philosophic Oakhurst alone remained silent. He listened calmly to Mother Shipton's desire to cut somebody's heart out, to the repeated statements of the Duchess that she would die in the road, and to the alarming oaths that seemed to be bumped out of Uncle Billy as he rode forward.

With the easy good humor characteristic of his class, he insisted upon exchanging his own riding horse, "Five-Spot," for the sorry mule which the Duchess rode. But even this act did not draw the party into any closer sympathy. The young woman readjusted her somewhat draggled plumes with a feeble, faded coquetry; Mother Shipton eyed the possessor of "Five-Spot" with malevolence, and Uncle Billy included the whole party in one sweeping anathema.[3]

The road to Sandy Bar—a camp that,

[1] SLUICEROBBER—One who stole gold from the troughs used to separate the gold from the gravel or sand.

[2] PARTHIAN VOLLEY—A parting shot. The expression comes from the military tactics of the ancient Parthians who while riding away from the enemy turned in the saddle to fire arrows at them.

[3] ANATHEMA (á·nǎth'ê·má)—A curse.

not having as yet experienced the re-generating influences of Poker Flat, consequently seemed to offer some invitation to the emigrants—lay over a steep mountain range. It was distant a day's severe travel. In that advanced season the party soon passed out of the moist, temperate regions of the foothills into the dry, cold, bracing air of the Sierras. The trail was narrow and difficult. At noon the Duchess, rolling out of her saddle upon the ground, declared her intention of going no farther and the party halted.

The spot was singularly wild and impressive. A wooded amphitheater, surrounded on three sides by precipitous cliffs of naked granite, sloped gently toward the crest of another precipice that overlooked the valley. It was, undoubtedly, the most suitable spot for a camp, had camping been advisable. But Mr. Oakhurst knew that scarcely half the journey to Sandy Bar was accomplished, and the party were not equipped or provisioned for delay. This fact he pointed out to his companions curtly, with a philosophic commentary on the folly of throwing up their hand before the game was played out.

But they were furnished with liquor, which in this emergency stood them in place of food, fuel, rest, and prescience.[4] In spite of his remonstrances, it was not long before they were more or less under its influence. Uncle Billy passed rapidly from a bellicose state into one of stupor, the Duchess became maudlin, and Mother Shipton snored. Mr. Oakhurst alone remained erect, leaning against a rock, calmly surveying them.

Mr. Oakhurst did not drink. It interfered with a profession which required coolness, impassiveness, and presence of mind, and, in his own language, he

[4] PRESCIENCE (prē'shǐ·ĕns)—Foresight, prudence.

"couldn't afford it." As he gazed at his recumbent fellow exiles, the loneliness begotten of his pariah[5] trade, his habits of life, his very vices, for the first time seriously oppressed him. He bestirred himself in dusting his black clothes, washing his hands and face, and other acts characteristic of his studiously neat habits, and for a moment forgot his annoyance.

The thought of deserting his weaker and more pitiable companions never perhaps occurred to him. Yet he could not help feeling the want of that excitement which, singularly enough, was most conducive to that calm equanimity for which he was notorious. He looked at the gloomy walls that rose a thousand feet sheer above the circling pines around him, at the sky ominously clouded, at the valley below, already deepening into shadow; and, doing so, suddenly he heard his own name called.

A horseman slowly ascended the trail. In the fresh, open face of the newcomer Mr. Oakhurst recognized Tom Simson, otherwise known as "The Innocent," of Sandy Bar. He had met him some months before over a "little game," and had, with perfect equanimity, won the entire fortune—amounting to some forty dollars—of that guileless youth. After the game was finished, Mr. Oakhurst drew the youthful speculator behind the door and thus addressed him: "Tommy, you're a good little man, but you can't gamble worth a cent. Don't try it over again." He then handed him his money back, pushed him gently from the room, and so made a devoted slave of Tom Simson.

There was a remembrance of this in his boyish and enthusiastic greeting of Mr. Oakhurst. He had started, he said, to go to Poker Flat to seek his fortune.

[5] PARIAH (pá·rī'á)—Despised; outcast.

"Alone?" No, not exactly alone; in fact (a giggle), he had run away with Piney Woods. Didn't Mr. Oakhurst remember Piney? She that used to wait on the table at the Temperance House? They had been engaged a long time, but old Jake Woods had objected, and so they had run away, and were going to Poker Flat to be married, and here they were. And they were tired out, and how lucky it was they had found a place to camp, and company.

All this the Innocent delivered rapidly, while Piney, a stout, comely damsel of fifteen, emerged from behind the pine tree, where she had been blushing unseen, and quickly rode to the side of her lover.

Mr. Oakhurst seldom troubled himself with sentiment, still less with propriety; but he had a vague idea that the situation was not fortunate. He retained, however, his presence of mind sufficiently to kick Uncle Billy, who was about to say something, and Uncle Billy was sober enough to recognize in Mr. Oakhurst's kick a superior power that would not bear trifling.

He then endeavored to dissuade Tom Simson from delaying further, but in vain. He even pointed out the fact that there was no provision, nor means of making a camp. But, unluckily, the Innocent met this objection by assuring the party that he was provided with an extra mule loaded with provisions, and by the discovery of a rude attempt at a log house near the trail. "Piney can stay with Mrs. Oakhurst," said the Innocent, pointing to the Duchess, "and I can shift for myself."

Nothing but Mr. Oakhurst's admonishing foot saved Uncle Billy from bursting into a roar of laughter. As it was, he felt compelled to retire up the canyon until he could recover his gravity. There

397

he confided the joke to the tall pine trees, with many slaps of his leg, contortions of his face, and the usual profanity. But when he returned to the party, he found them seated by a fire—for the air had grown strangely chill and the sky overcast—in apparently amicable conversation.

Piney was actually talking in an impulsive girlish fashion to the Duchess, who was listening with an interest and animation she had not shown for many days. The Innocent was holding forth, apparently with equal effect, to Mr. Oakhurst and Mother Shipton, who was actually relaxing into amiability.

"Is this yer a picnic?" said Uncle Billy, with inward scorn, as he surveyed the sylvan group, the glancing firelight, and the tethered animals in the foreground.

Suddenly an idea mingled with the alcoholic fumes that disturbed his brain. It was apparently of a jocular nature, for he felt impelled to slap his leg again and cram his fist into his mouth.

As the shadows crept slowly up the mountain, a slight breeze rocked the tops of the pine trees and moaned through their long and gloomy aisles. The ruined cabin, patched and covered with pine boughs, was set apart for the ladies. As the lovers parted, they unaffectedly exchanged a kiss, so honest and sincere that it might have been heard above the swaying pines. The frail Duchess and the malevolent Mother Shipton were probably too stunned to remark upon this last evidence of simplicity, and so turned without a word to the hut. The fire was replenished, the men lay down before the door, and in a few minutes were asleep.

Mr. Oakhurst was a light sleeper. Toward morning he awoke benumbed and cold. As he stirred the dying fire, the wind, which was now blowing strongly,

brought to his cheek that which caused the blood to leave it—snow!

He started to his feet with the intention of awakening the sleepers, for there was no time to lose. But turning to where Uncle Billy had been lying, he found him gone. A suspicion leaped to his brain, and a curse to his lips. He ran to the spot where the mules had been tethered—they were no longer there. The tracks were already rapidly disappearing in the snow.

The momentary excitement brought Mr. Oakhurst back to the fire with his usual calm. He did not waken the sleepers. The Innocent slumbered peacefully, with a smile on his good-humored freckled face; Piney slept beside her frailer sisters as sweetly as though attended by celestial guardians; and Mr. Oakhurst, drawing his blanket over his shoulders, stroked his mustaches and waited for the dawn. It came slowly in a whirling mist of snowflakes that dazzled and confused the eye. What could be seen of the landscape appeared magically changed. He looked over the valley, and summed up the present and future in two words, "Snowed in!"

A careful inventory of the provisions, which, fortunately for the party, had been stored within the hut, and so escaped the felonious fingers of Uncle Billy, disclosed the fact that with care and prudence they might last ten days longer.

"That is," said Mr. Oakhurst *sotto voce* [6] to the Innocent, "if you're willing to board us. If you ain't—and perhaps you'd better not—you can wait till Uncle Billy gets back with provisions."

For some occult reason, Mr. Oakhurst could not bring himself to disclose Uncle Billy's rascality, and so offered the

[6] *Sotto voce* (sōt′tô vō′chä)—In an undertone.

hypothesis that he had wandered from the camp and had accidentally stampeded the animals. He dropped a warning to the Duchess and Mother Shipton, who of course knew the facts of their associate's defection.

"They'll find out the truth about us *all* when they find out anything," he added significantly, "and there's no good frightening them now."

Tom Simson not only put all his worldly store at the disposal of Mr. Oakhurst, but seemed to enjoy the prospect of their enforced seclusion. "We'll have a camp for a week, and then the snow'll melt, and we'll all go back together."

The cheerful gaiety of the young man and Mr. Oakhurst's calm infected the others. The Innocent, with the aid of pine boughs, extemporized a thatch for the roofless cabin, and the Duchess directed Piney in the rearrangement of the interior with a taste and tact that opened the blue eyes of that provincial maiden to their fullest extent.

"I reckon now you're used to fine things at Poker Flat," said Piney.

The Duchess turned away sharply to conceal something that reddened her cheeks through their professional tint, and Mother Shipton requested Piney not to "chatter." But when Mr. Oakhurst returned from a weary search for the trail, he heard the sound of happy laughter echoed from the rocks. He stopped in some alarm, and his thoughts first naturally reverted to the whiskey, which he had prudently cached. "And yet it don't somehow sound like whiskey," said the gambler. It was not until he caught sight of the blazing fire through the still blinding storm, and the group around it, that he settled to the conviction that it was "square fun."

Whether Mr. Oakhurst had cached his cards with the whiskey as something debarred the free access of the community, I cannot say. It was certain that, in Mother Shipton's words, he "didn't say 'cards' once" during that evening. Haply the time was beguiled by an accordion, produced somewhat ostentatiously by Tom Simson from his pack. Notwithstanding some difficulties attending the manipulation of this instrument, Piney Woods managed to pluck several reluctant melodies from its keys, to an accompaniment by the Innocent on a pair of bone castanets.

But the crowning festivity of the evening was reached in a rude camp-meeting hymn, which the lovers, joining hands, sang with great earnestness and vociferation. I fear that a certain defiant tone and Covenanters' [7] swing to its chorus, rather than any devotional quality, caused it speedily to infect the others, who at last joined in the refrain:

"I'm proud to live in the service of
the Lord,
And I'm bound to die in His army."

The pines rocked, the storm eddied and whirled above the miserable group, and the flames of their altar leaped heavenward, as if in token of the vow.

At midnight the storm abated, the rolling clouds parted, and the stars glittered keenly above the sleeping camp. Mr. Oakhurst, whose professional habits had enabled him to live on the smallest possible amount of sleep, in dividing the watch with Tom Simson somehow managed to take upon himself the greatest part of that duty. He excused himself to the Innocent by saying that he had "often been a week without sleep."

"Doing what?" asked Tom.

[7] COVENANTERS (kŭv'ĕ·năn·tērz)—Seventeenth-century Scotsmen who signed a Covenant resisting Anglican Church rule. Their religious fervor was best shown in their hymn singing.

"Poker!" replied Oakhurst sententiously. "When a man gets a streak of luck, he don't get tired. The luck gives in first. Luck," continued the gambler reflectively "is a mighty queer thing. All you know about it for certain is that it's bound to change. And it's finding out when it's going to change that makes you. We've had a streak of bad luck since we left Poker Flat—you come along, and slap you get into it, too. If you can hold your cards right along you're all right. For," added the gambler, with cheerful irrelevance,

" 'I'm proud to live in the service of the
    Lord,
And I'm bound to die in His army.' "

The third day came, and the sun, looking through the white-curtained valley, saw the outcasts divide their slowly decreasing store of provisions for the morning meal. It was one of the peculiarities of that mountain climate that its rays diffused a kindly warmth over the wintry landscape, as if in regretful commiseration of the past. But it revealed drift on drift of snow piled high around the hut—a hopeless, uncharted, trackless sea of white lying below the rocky shores to which the castaways still clung.

Through the marvelously clear air the smoke of the pastoral village of Poker Flat rose miles away. Mother Shipton saw it, and from a remote pinnacle of her rocky fastness hurled in that direction a final malediction. It was her last vituperative attempt, and perhaps for that reason was invested with a certain degree of sublimity. It did her good, she privately informed the Duchess. "Just you go out there and cuss, and see."

She then set herself to the task of amusing "the child," as she and the Duchess were pleased to call Piney. Piney was no chicken, but it was a soothing and original theory of the pair thus to account for the fact that she didn't swear and wasn't improper.

When night crept up again through the gorges, the reedy notes of the accordion rose and fell in fitful spasms and longdrawn gasps by the flickering campfire. But music failed to fill entirely the aching void left by insufficient food, and a new diversion was proposed by Piney—storytelling. Neither Mr. Oakhurst nor his female companions caring to relate their personal experiences, this plan would have failed too, but for the Innocent.

Some months before he had chanced upon a stray copy of Mr. Pope's ingenious translation of The Iliad.[8] He now proposed to narrate the principal incidents of that poem—having thoroughly mastered the argument and fairly forgotten the words—in the current vernacular of Sandy Bar. And so for the rest of that night the Homeric demigods again walked the earth. Trojan bully and wily Greek wrestled in the winds, and the great pines in the canyon seemed to bow to the wrath of the son of Peleus.[9]

Mr. Oakhurst listened with quiet satisfaction. Most especially was he interested in the fate of "Ash-heels," as the Innocent persisted in denominating the "swift-footed Achilles."

So, with small food and much of Homer and the accordion, a week passed over the heads of the outcasts. The sun again forsook them, and again from leaden skies the snowflakes were sifted over the land. Day by day closer around them drew the snowy circle, until at last they looked from their prison over drifted

[8] MR. POPE'S . . . Iliad—The eighteenth-century English poet, Alexander Pope, made a translation of the Greek epic poem, The Iliad. The story was about the Trojan War.
[9] SON OF PELEUS (pē'lūs)—Achilles (á·kĭl'-ēz), the hero of The Iliad.

walls of dazzling white, that towered twenty feet above their heads. It became more and more difficult to replenish their fires, even from the fallen trees beside them, now half hidden in the drifts. And yet no one complained.

The lovers turned from the dreary prospect and looked into each other's eyes, and were happy. Mr. Oakhurst settled himself coolly to the losing game before him. The Duchess, more cheerful than she had been, assumed the care of Piney.

Only Mother Shipton—once the strongest of the party—seemed to sicken and fade. At midnight on the tenth day she called Oakhurst to her side. "I'm going," she said, in a voice of querulous weakness, "but don't say anything about it. Don't waken the kids. Take the bundle from under my head, and open it."

Mr. Oakhurst did so. It contained Mother Shipton's rations for the last week, untouched. "Give 'em to the child," she said, pointing to the sleeping Piney.

"You've starved yourself," said the gambler.

"That's what they call it," said the woman querulously, as she lay down again, and, turning her face to the wall, passed quietly away.

The accordion and the bones were put aside that day, and Homer was forgotten. When the body of Mother Shipton had been committed to the snow, Mr. Oakhurst took the Innocent aside, and showed him a pair of snowshoes, which he had fashioned from the pack saddle.

"There's one chance in a hundred to save her yet," he said, pointing to Piney; "but it's there," he added, pointing toward Poker Flat. "If you can reach there in two days she's safe." "And you?" asked Tom Simson.

"I'll stay here," was the curt reply.

The lovers parted with a long embrace. "You are not going, too?" said the Duchess, as she saw Mr. Oakhurst apparently waiting to accompany him.

"As far as the canyon," he replied. He turned suddenly and kissed the Duchess, leaving her pallid face aflame, and her trembling limbs rigid with amazement.

Night came, but not Mr. Oakhurst. It brought the storm again and the whirling snow. Then the Duchess, feeding the fire, found that someone had quietly piled beside the hut enough fuel to last a few days longer. The tears rose to her eyes, but she hid them from Piney.

The women slept but little. In the morning, looking into each other's faces, they read their fate. Neither spoke, but Piney, accepting the position of the stronger, drew near and placed her arm around the Duchess' waist. They kept this attitude for the rest of the day. That night the storm reached its greatest fury, and, rending asunder the protecting vines, invaded the very hut.

Toward morning they found themselves unable to feed the fire, which gradually died away. As the embers slowly blackened, the Duchess crept closer to Piney, and broke the silence of many hours: "Piney, can you pray?" "No, dear," said Piney simply. The Duchess, without knowing exactly why, felt relieved, and, putting her head upon Piney's shoulder, spoke no more. And so reclining, the younger and purer pillowing the head of the other upon her breast, they fell asleep.

The wind lulled as if it feared to waken them. Feathery drifts of snow, shaken from the long pine boughs, flew like white-winged birds, and settled about them as they slept. The moon through the rifted clouds looked down upon what had been the camp. But all human stain, all trace of earthly travail, was hidden beneath the spotless mantle mercifully flung from above.

They slept all that day and the next, nor did they waken when voices and footsteps broke the silence of the camp. And when pitying fingers brushed the snow from their wan faces, you could scarcely have told from the equal peace that dwelt upon them which was she that had sinned. Even the law of Poker Flat recognized this, and turned away, leaving them still locked in each other's arms.

But at the head of the gulch, on one of the largest pine trees, they found the deuce of clubs pinned to the bark with a bowie knife. It bore the fol-

lowing, written in pencil in a firm hand:

BENEATH THIS TREE
LIES THE BODY
OF
JOHN OAKHURST,
WHO STRUCK A STREAK OF BAD LUCK
ON THE 23D OF NOVEMBER 1850,
AND
HANDED IN HIS CHECKS
ON THE 7TH DECEMBER, 1850.

And pulseless and cold, with a derringer by his side and a bullet in his heart, though still calm as in life, beneath the snow lay he who was at once the strongest and yet the weakest of the outcasts of Poker Flat.

FOR UNDERSTANDING

1. Why did the people of Poker Flat suddenly decide to get rid of Mr. Oakhurst and the other "improper persons"? From what the author says about the real motives of the members of the committee, what can you conclude about the moral standards of the citizens of Poker Flat?

2. What is revealed about the personalities of the four outcasts from the way each behaved when the group was left alone outside Poker Flat? Which seemed then to be the strongest character? Which the weakest? Which seemed to you the most objectionable?

3. What hints are there early in the story that in spite of their evil ways there was

some good in most of the characters? For example, what admirable characteristics did Mr. Oakhurst display even before Tom and Piney appeared on the scene? What is the first suggestion of good in the Duchess and in Mother Shipton? Show how association with Tom and Piney revealed capacity for kindness and generosity in the outcasts. Which character seemed to you to show no admirable traits? Do you think that Bret Harte is right in implying that there is good in nearly everyone—even in people like the outcasts of Poker Flat?

4. Explain the last sentence of the story. In what ways had Mr. Oakhurst shown himself to be the strongest of the outcasts? When did he prove himself to be also the weakest?

THE LOCAL COLOR STORY

Bret Harte wrote his western stories for the people back East. His readers were primarily interested in the aspects of the West that were different from their own settled part of the country. To satisfy them, Harte and the other local color writers played up the unusual and the picturesque in both the landscape and the characters of their stories. Therefore, while local color stories give the atmosphere and flavor of a particular region, they do not present a completely realistic picture.

1. How can you identify the location and the period of this story in the very first paragraph? What details in that paragraph and in the following one further suggest the color and atmosphere of the Old West?

2. How do the names of places and people contribute to the local color? What other specific words and phrases in the narrative or in the dialogue have a distinctly western flavor?

3. Point out other passages that describe the country as Bret Harte must have known it. How much of his picture of the West do you consider authentic and realistic? Can you find parts that seem to you idealistic or romantic?

4. Considering other western stories that you have read and western movies that you have seen, pick out the characters in this story that represent types generally found in western fiction. Are they mere stock characters or *stereotypes*, or do they have individual personalities? Support your opinion by specific references to the story.

HOW WOULD YOU HAVE SAID IT?

Although Bret Harte tried to reproduce in his dialogue the ordinary language that was actually used by the people of the region he wrote about, he was fond of unusual words and high sounding phrases when he was speaking for himself.

First make sure that you know the exact meaning of the italicized words in the following phrases from the story. Then try to restate the phrase in simpler language.

1. a crude *sentiment* of *equity*
2. the *expatriated* party
3. his *recumbent* fellow exiles
4. the *felonious* fingers of Uncle Billy
5. her last *vituperative* attempt
6. in the current *vernacular*
7. with *malevolence*

FRANCIS BRET HARTE [1836–1902]

Bret Harte, an Easterner strayed West, immortalized the eccentricities of Californians of the gold rush period. Harte was an expert showman, playing upon the emotions and sympathies of his audience with all the dexterity of a Hollywood impresario. At one time the *Atlantic Monthly* offered him ten thousand dollars for twelve contributions, unusual recompense for short-story writing at that time.

Harte's career was interesting and varied, beginning in Albany, New York; continuing in San Francisco, Germany, and Scotland; and ending in London. At eighteen he went to California by way of Panama and after various odd jobs settled in San Francisco as a printer. As editor of the *Overland Monthly*, he adopted a policy which made him famous. He conceived the idea of making his magazine a mirror of the stirring events about him and he depicted the romance and picturesqueness of the California gold rush of 1849. His later stories never rivaled the success of these first ones. In 1880 he became United States consul at Glasgow, Scotland, and after a term there moved to London where he spent the rest of his life trying to recapture his waning popularity as a writer.

TO BUILD A FIRE

JACK LONDON

The Klondike gold rush, 1897–1899, was the beginning of a further movement of the American people—this time in a northwestern direction. Gold-seekers swarmed along the Yukon Trail from upper Canada all the way across Alaska. As a result the region became better known. The Alaskan fishing industry was enormously expanded, settlements increased, and farming was begun in some parts of the territory. Today, motorists can travel as far as Fairbanks on the famous Alcan Highway, and Alaska seems likely to become the forty-ninth state of the Union.

When the adventurous Jack London joined the stampede to the Yukon he found no gold, but the short stories about the Far North that he wrote immediately afterward gave him his first fame. "To Build a Fire" shows us what it means to travel alone over the snow at temperatures far below zero. It is a fight to the finish—man against the brutal cold.

Day had broken cold and gray, exceedingly cold and gray, when the man turned aside from the main Yukon trail and climbed the high earth bank, where a dim and little-traveled trail led eastward through the fat spruce timberland. It was a steep bank, and he paused for breath at the top, excusing the act to himself by looking at his watch. It was nine o'clock. There was no sun nor hint of sun, though there was not a cloud in the sky. It was a clear day, and yet there seemed an intangible pall over the face of things, a subtle gloom that made the day dark, and that was due to the absence of sun. This fact did not worry the man. He was used to the lack of sun. It had been days since he had seen the sun, and he knew that a few more days must pass before that cheerful orb, due south, would just peep above the sky line and dip immediately from view.

The man flung a look back along the way he had come. The Yukon lay a mile wide and hidden under three feet of ice. On top of this ice were as many feet of snow. It was all pure white, rolling in gentle undulations where the ice jams of the freeze-up had formed. North and south, as far as his eye could see, it was unbroken white, save for a dark hairline that curved and twisted from around the spruce-covered island to the south, and that curved and twisted away into the north, where it disappeared behind another spruce-covered island. This dark hairline was the trail—the main trail—that led south five hundred miles to the Chilkoot Pass, Dyea, and salt water; and that led north seventy miles to Dawson, and still on to the north a thousand miles to Nulato, and finally to St. Michael on Bering Sea, a thousand miles and half a thousand more.

"To Build a Fire" by Jack London. Reprinted by permission of Charmian K. London.

But all this—the mysterious, far-reaching hairline trail, the absence of sun from the sky, the tremendous cold, and the strangeness and weirdness of it all—made no impression on the man. It was not because he was long used to it. He was a newcomer in the land, a *chechaquo*, and this was his first winter. The trouble with him was that he was without imagination. He was quick and alert in the things of life, but only in the things, and not in the significances. Fifty degrees below zero meant eighty-odd degrees of frost. Such fact impressed him as being cold and uncomfortable, and that was all. It did not lead him to meditate upon his frailty as a creature of temperature, and upon man's frailty in general, able only to live within certain narrow limits of heat and cold, and from there on it did not lead him to the conjectural field of immortality and man's place in the universe. Fifty degrees below zero stood for a bite of frost that hurt and that must be guarded against by the use of mittens, ear flaps, warm moccasins, and thick socks. Fifty degrees below zero was to him just precisely fifty degrees below zero. That there should be anything more to it than that was a thought that never entered his head.

As he turned to go on, he spat speculatively. There was a sharp, explosive crackle that startled him. He spat again. And again, in the air, before it could fall to the snow, the spittle crackled. He knew that at fifty below spittle crackled on the snow, but this spittle had crackled in the air. Undoubtedly it was colder than fifty below—how much colder he did not know. But the temperature did not matter. He was bound for the old claim on the left fork of Henderson Creek, where the boys were already. They had come over across the divide from the Indian Creek country, while he had come the roundabout way to take a look at the possibilities of getting out logs in the spring from the islands in the Yukon. He would be in to camp by six o'clock; a bit after dark, it was true, but the boys would be there, a fire would be going, and a hot supper would be ready. As for lunch, he pressed his hand against the protruding bundle under his jacket. It was also under his shirt, wrapped up in a handkerchief and lying against the naked skin. It was the only way to keep the biscuits from freezing. He smiled agreeably to himself as he thought of those biscuits, each cut open and sopped in bacon grease, and each inclosing a generous slice of fried bacon.

He plunged in among the big spruce trees. The trail was faint. A foot of snow had fallen since the last sled had passed over, and he was glad he was without a sled, traveling light. In fact, he carried nothing but the lunch wrapped in the handkerchief. He was surprised, however, at the cold. It certainly was cold, he concluded, as he rubbed his numb nose and cheekbones with his mittened hand. He was a warm-whiskered man, but the hair on his face did not protect the high cheekbones and the eager nose that thrust itself aggressively into the frosty air.

At the man's heels trotted a dog, a big native husky, the proper wolf dog, gray-coated and without any visible or temperamental difference from its brother, the wild wolf. The animal was depressed by the tremendous cold. It knew that it was no time for traveling. Its instinct told it a truer tale than was told to the man by the man's judgment. In reality, it was not merely colder than fifty below zero; it was colder than sixty below, than seventy below. It was seventy-five below zero. Since the freezing point is thirty-two above zero, it meant that one hundred and seven degrees of frost obtained. The dog did not know anything about thermometers. Possibly in the brain there was no sharp consciousness of a condition of very cold such as was in the man's brain. But the brute had its instinct. It experienced a vague but menacing apprehension that subdued it and made it slink along at the man's heels, and that made it question eagerly every unwonted movement of the man, as if expecting him to go into camp or to seek shelter somewhere and build a fire. The dog had learned fire, and it wanted fire, or else to burrow under the snow and cuddle its warmth away from the air.

The frozen moisture of its breathing had settled on its fur in a fine powder of frost, and especially were its jowls, muzzle, and eyelashes whitened by its crystaled breath. The man's red beard and mustache were likewise frosted, but more solidly, the deposit taking the form of ice and increasing with every warm, moist breath he exhaled. Also the man was chewing tobacco, and the muzzle of ice held his lips so rigidly that he was unable to clear his chin when he expelled the juice. The result was that a crystal beard of the color and solidity of amber was increasing its length on his chin. If he fell down it would shatter itself, like glass, into brittle fragments. But he did not mind the appendage. It was the penalty all tobacco chewers paid in that country, and he had been out before in two cold snaps. They had not been so cold as this, he knew, but by the spirit thermometer at Sixty Mile he knew they had been registered at fifty below and at fifty-five.

He held on through the level stretch of woods for several miles, crossed a wide flat of boulders, and dropped down a bank to the frozen bed of a small stream.

This was Henderson Creek, and he knew he was ten miles from the forks. He looked at his watch. It was ten o'clock. He was making four miles an hour, and he calculated that he would arrive at the forks at half past twelve. He decided to celebrate that event by eating his lunch there.

The dog dropped in again at his heels, with a tail drooping discouragement, as the man swung along the creek bed. The furrow of the old sled trail was plainly visible, but a dozen inches of snow covered the marks of the last runners. In a month no man had come up or down that silent creek. The man held steadily on. He was not much given to thinking, and just then particularly he had nothing to think about save that he would eat lunch at the forks and that at six o'clock he would be in camp with the boys. There was nobody to talk to; and, had there been, speech would have been impossible because of the ice muzzle on his mouth. So he continued monotonously to chew tobacco and to increase the length of his amber beard.

Once in a while the thought reiterated itself that it was very cold and that he had never experienced such cold. As he walked along he rubbed his cheekbones and nose with the back of his mittened hand. He did this automatically, now and again changing hands. But rub as he would, the instant he stopped his cheekbones went numb, and the following instant the end of his nose went numb. He was sure to frost his cheeks; he knew that, and experienced a pang of regret that he had not devised a nose strap of the sort Bud wore in cold snaps. Such a strap passed across the cheeks, as well, and saved them. But it didn't matter much, after all. What were frosted cheeks? A bit painful, that was all; they were never serious.

Empty as the man's mind was of thoughts, he was keenly observant, and he noticed the changes in the creek, the curves and bends and timber jams, and always he sharply noted where he placed his feet. Once, coming around a bend, he shied abruptly, like a startled horse, curved away from the place where he had been walking, and retreated several paces back along the trail. The creek, he knew, was frozen clear to the bottom—no creek could contain water in that arctic winter—but he knew also that there were springs that bubbled out from the hillsides and ran along under the snow and on top of the ice of the creek. He knew that the coldest snaps never froze these springs, and he knew likewise their danger. They were traps. They hid pools of water under the snow that might be three inches deep, or three feet. Sometimes a skin of ice half an inch thick covered them, and in turn was covered by the snow. Sometimes there were alternate layers of water and ice skin, so that when one broke through he kept on breaking through for a while, sometimes wetting himself to the waist.

That was why he had shied in such panic. He had felt the give under his feet and heard the crackle of a snow-hidden ice skin. And to get his feet wet in such a temperature meant trouble and danger. At the very least it meant delay, for he would be forced to stop and build a fire, and under its protection to bare his feet while he dried his socks and moccasins. He stood and studied the creek bed and its banks, and decided that the flow of water came from the right. He reflected a while, rubbing his nose and cheeks, then skirted to the left, stepping gingerly and testing the footing for each step. Once clear of the danger, he took a fresh chew of tobacco and swung along at his four-mile gait.

In the course of the next two hours he came upon several similar traps. Usually the snow above the hidden pools had a sunken candied appearance that advertised the danger. Once again, however, he had a close call; and once, suspecting danger, he compelled the dog to go on in front. The dog did not want to go. It hung back until the man shoved it forward, and then it went quickly across the white, unbroken surface. Suddenly it broke through, floundered to one side, and got away to firmer footing. It had wet its forefeet and legs, and almost immediately the water that clung to it turned to ice. It made quick efforts to lick the ice off its legs, then dropped down in the snow and began to bite out the ice that had formed between the toes. This was a matter of instinct. To permit the ice to remain would mean sore feet. It did not know this. It merely obeyed the mysterious prompting that arose from the deep crypts of its being. But the man knew, having achieved a judgment on the subject, and he removed the mitten from his right hand and helped tear out the ice particles. He did not expose his fingers more than a minute, and was astonished at the swift numbness that smote them. It certainly was cold. He pulled on the mitten hastily, and beat the hand savagely across his chest.

At twelve o'clock the day was at its brightest. Yet the sun was too far south on its winter journey to clear the horizon. The bulge of the earth intervened between it and Henderson Creek, where the man walked under a clear sky at noon and cast no shadow. At half past twelve, to the minute, he arrived at the forks of the creek. He was pleased at the speed he had made. If he kept it up, he would certainly be with the boys by six. He unbuttoned his jacket and shirt and drew

forth his lunch. The action consumed no more than a quarter of a minute, yet in that brief moment the numbness laid hold of the exposed fingers. He did not put the mitten on, but, instead, struck the fingers a dozen sharp smashes against his leg. Then he sat down on a snow-covered log to eat. The sting that followed upon the striking of his fingers against his leg ceased so quickly that he was startled. He had had no chance to take a bite of biscuit. He struck the fingers repeatedly and returned them to the mitten, baring the other hand for the purpose of eating. He tried to take a mouthful, but the ice muzzle prevented. He had forgotten to build a fire and thaw out. He chuckled at his foolishness, and as he chuckled he noted the numbness creeping into the exposed fingers. Also he noted that the stinging which had first come to his toes when he sat down was already passing away.

He wondered whether the toes were warm or numb. He moved them inside the moccasins and decided that they were numb.

He pulled the mitten on hurriedly and stood up. He was a bit frightened. He stamped up and down until the stinging returned into the feet. It certainly was cold, was his thought. That man from Sulphur Creek had spoken the truth when telling how cold it sometimes got in the country. And he had laughed at him at the time! That showed one must not be too sure of things. There was no mistake about it, it *was* cold. He strode up and down, stamping his feet and threshing his arms, until reassured by the returning warmth. Then he got out matches and proceeded to make a fire. From the undergrowth, where high water of the previous spring had lodged a supply of seasoned twigs, he got his firewood. Working carefully from a small beginning, he soon had a roaring fire, over which he thawed the ice from his face and in the protection of which he ate his biscuits. For the moment the cold of space was outwitted. The dog took satisfaction in the fire, stretching out close enough for warmth and far enough away to escape being singed.

When the man had finished, he filled his pipe and took his comfortable time over a smoke. Then he pulled on his mittens, settled the ear flaps of his cap firmly about his ears, and took the creek trail up the left fork. The dog was disappointed and yearned back toward the fire. The man did not know cold. Possibly all the generations of his ancestry had been ignorant of cold, of real cold, of cold one hundred and seven degrees below freezing point. But the dog knew; all its ancestry knew, and it had inherited the knowledge. And it knew that it was not good to walk abroad in such fearful cold. It was the time to lie snug in a hole in the snow and wait for a curtain of cloud to be drawn across the face of outer space whence this cold came. On the other hand, there was no keen intimacy between the dog and the man. The one was the toil-slave of the other, and the only caresses it had ever received were the caresses of the whiplash and of harsh and menacing throat sounds that threatened the whiplash. So the dog made no effort to communicate its apprehension to the man. It was not concerned in the welfare of the man; it was for its own sake that it yearned back toward the fire. But the man whistled, and spoke to it with the sound of whiplashes, and the dog swung in at the man's heels and followed after.

The man took a chew of tobacco and proceeded to start a new amber beard. Also, his moist breath quickly powdered with white his mustache, eyebrows, and lashes. There did not seem to be so many springs on the left fork of the Henderson, and for half an hour the man saw no signs of any. And then it happened. At a place where there were no signs, where the soft, unbroken snow seemed to advertise solidity beneath, the man broke through. It was not deep. He wet himself halfway to the knees before he floundered out to the firm crust.

He was angry, and cursed his luck aloud. He had hoped to get into camp with the boys at six o'clock, and this would delay him an hour, for he would have to build a fire and dry out his footgear. This was imperative at that low temperature—he knew that much; and he turned aside to the bank, which he climbed. On top, tangled in the underbrush about the trunks of several small spruce trees, was a high-water deposit of dry firewood—sticks and twigs, principally, but also larger portions of seasoned branches and fine, dry, last year's grasses. He threw down several large pieces on top of the snow. This served for a foundation and prevented the young flame from drowning itself in the snow it otherwise would melt. The flame he got by touching a match to a small shred of birch bark that he took from his pocket. This burned even more readily than paper. Placing it on the foundation, he fed the young flame with wisps of dry grass and with the tiniest dry twigs.

He worked slowly and carefully, keenly aware of his danger. Gradually, as the flame grew stronger, he increased the size of the twigs with which he fed it. He squatted in the snow, pulling the twigs out from their entanglement in the brush and feeding directly to the flame. He knew there must be no failure. When it is seventy-five below zero a man must not fail in his first attempt to build a fire—that is, if his feet are wet. If his feet are dry, and he fails, he can run along the trail for half a mile and restore his circulation. But the circulation of wet and freezing feet cannot be restored by running when it is seventy-five below. No matter how fast he runs, the wet feet will freeze the harder.

All this the man knew. The old-timer on Sulphur Creek had told him about it the previous fall, and now he was appreciating the advice. Already all sensation had gone out of his feet. To build the fire, he had been forced to remove his mittens, and the fingers had quickly gone numb. His pace of four miles an hour had kept his heart pumping blood to the surface of his body and to all the extremities. But the instant he stopped, the action of the pump eased down. The cold of space smote the unprotected tip of the planet, and he, being on that unprotected tip, received the full force of the blow. The blood of his body recoiled before it. The blood was alive, like the dog, and like the dog it wanted to hide away and cover itself up from the fearful cold. So long as he walked four miles an hour, he pumped that blood, willy-nilly, to the surface; but now it ebbed away and sank down into the recesses of his body. The extremities were the first to feel its absence. His wet feet froze the faster, and his exposed fingers numbed the faster, though they had not yet begun to freeze. Nose and cheeks were already freezing, while the skin of all his body chilled as it lost its blood.

But he was safe. Toes and nose and cheeks would be only touched by the frost, for the fire was beginning to burn with strength. He was feeding it with twigs the size of his finger. In another minute he would be able to feed it with branches the size of his wrist, and then

he could remove his wet footgear, and, while it dried, he could keep his naked feet warm by the fire, rubbing them at first, of course, with snow. The fire was a success. He was safe. He remembered the advice of the old-timer on Sulphur Creek, and smiled. The old-timer had been very serious in laying down the law that no man must travel alone in the Klondike after fifty below. Well, here he was; he had had the accident; he was alone; and he had saved himself. Those old-timers were rather womanish, some of them, he thought. All a man had to do was to keep his head, and he was all right. Any man who was a man could travel alone. But it was surprising the rapidity with which his cheeks and nose were freezing. And he had not thought his fingers could go lifeless in so short a time. Lifeless they were, for he could scarcely make them move together to grip a twig, and they seemed remote from his body and from him. When he touched a twig he had to look and see whether or not he had hold of it. The wires were pretty well down between him and his finger ends.

All of which counted for little. There was the fire, snapping and crackling and promising life with every dancing flame. He started to untie his moccasins. They were coated with ice; the thick German socks were like sheaths of iron halfway to the knees; and the moccasin strings were like rods of steel all twisted and knotted as by some conflagration. For a moment he tugged with his numb fingers, then, realizing the folly of it, he drew his sheath knife.

But before he could cut the strings, it happened. It was his own fault, or, rather, his mistake. He should not have built the fire under the spruce tree. He should have built it in the open. But it had been easier to pull the twigs from the brush and drop them directly on the fire. Now the tree under which he had done this carried a weight of snow on its boughs. No wind had blown for weeks, and each bough was fully freighted. Each time he had pulled a twig he had communicated a slight agitation to the tree—an imperceptible agitation, so far as he was concerned, but an agitation sufficient to bring about the disaster. High up in the tree one bough capsized its load of snow. This fell on the boughs beneath, capsizing them. This process continued, spreading out and involving the whole tree. It grew like an avalanche, and it descended without warning upon the man and the fire, and the fire was blotted out! Where it had burned was a mantle of fresh and disordered snow.

The man was shocked. It was as though he had just heard his own sentence of death. For a moment he sat and stared at the spot where the fire had been. Then he grew very calm. Perhaps the old-timer on Sulphur Creek was right. If he had only had a trail mate he would have been in no danger now. The trail mate could have built the fire. Well, it was up to him to build the fire over again, and this second time there must be no failure. Even if he succeeded, he would most likely lose some toes. His feet must be badly frozen by now, and there would be some time before the second fire was ready.

Such were his thoughts, but he did not sit and think them. He was busy all the time they were passing through his mind. He made a new foundation for a fire, this time in the open, where no treacherous tree could blot it out. Next he gathered dry grasses and tiny twigs from the high-water flotsam. He could not bring his fingers together to pull them out, but he was able to gather them by the handful.

In this way he got many rotten twigs and bits of green moss that were undesirable, but it was the best he could do. He worked methodically, even collecting an armful of the larger branches to be used later when the fire gathered strength. And all the while the dog sat and watched him, a certain yearning wistfulness in its eyes, for it looked upon him as the fire provider, and the fire was slow in coming.

When all was ready, the man reached in his pocket for a second piece of birch bark. He knew the bark was there, and, though he could not feel it with his fingers, he could hear its crisp rustling as he fumbled for it. Try as he would, he could not clutch hold of it. And all the time, in his consciousness, was the knowledge that each instant his feet were freezing. This thought tended to put him in a panic, but he fought against it and kept calm. He pulled on his mittens with his teeth, and threshed his arms back and forth, beating his hands with all his might against his sides. He did this sitting down, and he stood up to do it; and all the while the dog sat in the snow, its wolf brush of a tail curled around warmly over its forefeet, its sharp wolf ears pricked forward intently as it watched the man. And the man, as he beat and threshed his arms and hands, felt a great surge of envy as he regarded the creature that was warm and secure in its natural covering.

After a time he was aware of the first faraway signals of sensation in his beaten fingers. The faint tingling grew stronger till it evolved into a stinging ache that was excruciating, but which the man hailed with satisfaction. He stripped the mitten from his right hand and fetched forth the birch bark. The exposed fingers were quickly going numb again. Next he brought out his bunch of sulphur matches. But the tremendous cold had already driven the life out of his fingers. In his effort to separate one match from the others, the whole bunch fell in the snow. He tried to pick it out of the snow, but failed. The dead fingers could neither touch nor clutch. He was very careful. He drove the thought of his freezing feet, and nose, and cheeks, out of his mind, devoting his whole soul to the matches. He watched, using the sense of vision in place of that of touch, and when he saw his fingers on each side the bunch, he closed them—that is, he willed to close them, for the wires were down, and the fingers did not obey. He pulled the mitten on the right hand, and beat it fiercely against his knee. Then, with both mittened hands, he scooped the bunch of matches, along with much snow, into his lap. Yet he was no better off.

After some manipulation he managed to get the bunch between the heels of his mittened hands. In this fashion he carried it to his mouth. The ice crackled and snapped when by a violent effort he opened his mouth. He drew the lower jaw in, curled the upper lip out of the way, and scraped the bunch with his upper teeth in order to separate a match. He succeeded in getting one, which he dropped on his lap. He was no better off. He could not pick it up. Then he devised a way. He picked it up in his teeth and scratched it on his leg. Twenty times he scratched before he succeeded in lighting it. As it flamed he held it with his teeth to the birch bark. But the burning brimstone went up his nostrils and into his lungs, causing him to cough spasmodically. The match fell into the snow and went out.

The old-timer on Sulphur Creek was right, he thought in the moment of controlled despair that ensued: after fifty below, a man should travel with a partner. He beat his hands, but failed in exciting any sensation. Suddenly he bared both hands, removing the mittens with his teeth. He caught the whole bunch between the heels of his hands. His arm muscles, not being frozen, enabled him to press the hand heels tightly against the matches. Then he scratched the bunch along his leg. It flared into flame, seventy sulphur matches at once! There was no wind to blow them out. He kept his head to one side to escape the strangling fumes, and held the blazing bunch to the birch bark. As he so held it, he became aware of sensation in his hands. His flesh was burning. He could smell it. Deep down below the surface he could feel it. The sensation developed into pain that grew acute. And still he endured it, holding the flame of the matches clumsily to the bark that would not light readily because his own burning hands were in the way, absorbing most of the flame.

At last, when he could endure no more, he jerked his hands apart. The blazing matches fell sizzling into the snow, but the birch bark was alight. He began laying dry grasses and the tiniest twigs on the flame. He could not pick and choose, for he had to lift the fuel between the heels of his hands. Small pieces of rotten wood and green moss clung to the twigs, and he bit them off as well as he could with his teeth. He cherished the flame carefully and awkwardly. It meant life, and it must not perish. The withdrawal of blood from the surface of his body now made him begin to shiver, and he grew more awkward. A large piece of green moss fell squarely on the little fire. He tried to poke it out with his fingers, but his shivering frame made him poke too far, and he disrupted the nucleus of the little fire, the burning grasses and tiny twigs separating and scattering. He tried to poke them together again, but, in spite of the tenseness of the effort, his shivering got away with him, and the twigs were hopelessly scattered. Each twig gushed a puff of smoke and went out. The fire-provider had failed. As he looked apathetically about him, his eyes chanced on the dog, sitting across the ruins of the fire from him, in the snow, making restless, hunching movements, slightly lifting one forefoot and then the other, shifting its weight back and forth on them with wistful eagerness.

The sight of the dog put a wild idea into his head. He remembered the tale of the man, caught in a blizzard, who killed a steer and crawled inside the carcass, and so was saved. He would kill the dog and bury his hands in the warm body until the numbness went out of them. Then he could build another fire. He spoke to the dog, calling it to him; but in his voice was a strange note of fear that frightened the animal, who had never known the man to speak in such way before. Something was the matter, and its suspicious nature sensed danger— it knew not what danger, but somewhere, somehow, in its brain arose an apprehension of the man. It flattened its ears down at the sound of the man's voice, and its restless, hunching movements, and the liftings and shiftings of its forefeet became more pronounced; but it would not come to the man. He got on his hands and knees and crawled toward the dog. This unusual posture again excited suspicion, and the animal sidled mincingly away.

The man sat up in the snow for a moment and struggled for calmness. Then he pulled on his mittens, by means of his teeth, and got upon his feet. He glanced down at first in order to assure himself that he was really standing up, for the absence of sensation in his feet left him unrelated to the earth. His erect position in itself started to drive the webs of suspicion from the dog's mind; and when he spoke peremptorily with the sound of whiplashes in his voice, the dog rendered its customary allegiance and came to him. As it came within reaching distance, the man lost control. His arms flashed out to the dog, and he experienced genuine surprise when he discovered that his hands could not clutch, that there was neither bend nor feeling in the fingers. He had forgotten for the moment that they were frozen and that they were freezing more and more. All this happened quickly, and before the animal could get away, he encircled its body with his arms. He sat down in the snow, and in this fashion held the dog, while it snarled and whined and struggled.

But it was all he could do, hold its body encircled in his arms and sit there. He realized that he could not kill the dog. There was no way to do it. With his helpless hands he could neither draw nor hold his sheath knife nor throttle the animal. He released it, and it plunged wildly away, with tail between its legs, and still snarling. It halted forty feet away and surveyed him curiously, with ears sharply pricked forward. The man looked down at his hands in order to locate them, and found them hanging on the ends of his arms. It struck him as curious that one should have to use his eyes in order to find out where his hands were. He began threshing his arms back and forth, beating the mittened hands against his sides. He did this for five minutes, violently, and his heart pumped enough blood up to the surface to put a stop to his shivering. But no sensation was aroused in the hands. He had an impression that they hung like weights on the ends of his arms, but when he tried to run the impression down, he could not find it.

A certain fear of death, dull and oppressive, came to him. This fear quickly became poignant as he realized that it was no longer a mere matter of freezing his fingers and toes, or of losing his hands and feet, but that it was a matter of life and death, with the chances against him. This threw him into a panic, and he turned and ran up the creek bed along the old dim trail. The dog joined in behind and kept up with him. He ran blindly, without intention, in fear such as he had never known in his life. Slowly, as he plowed and floundered through the snow, he began to see things again—the banks of the creek, the old timber jams, the leafless aspens, and the sky. The running made him feel better. He did not shiver. Maybe, if he ran on, his feet would thaw out; and, anyway, if he ran far enough he would reach the camp and the boys. Without doubt he would lose some fingers and toes and some of his face; but the boys would take care of him, and save the rest of him when he got there. And at the same time there was another thought in his mind that said he would never get to the camp and the boys; that it was too many miles away, that the freezing had too great a start on him, and that he would soon be stiff and dead. This thought he kept in the background and refused to consider. Sometimes it pushed itself forward and demanded to be heard, but he thrust it back and strove to think of other things.

It struck him as curious that he could run at all on feet so frozen that he could not feel them when they struck the earth and took the weight of his body. He seemed to himself to skim along above the surface, and to have no connection with the earth. Somewhere he had once seen a winged Mercury, and he wondered if Mercury felt as he felt when skimming over the earth.

His theory of running until he reached camp and the boys had one flaw in it: he lacked the endurance. Several times he stumbled, and finally he tottered, crumpled up, and fell. When he tried to rise, he failed. He must sit and rest, he decided, and next time he would merely walk and keep on going. As he sat and regained his breath, he noted that he was feeling quite warm and comfortable. He was not shivering, and it even seemed that a warm glow had come to his chest and trunk. And yet, when he touched his nose or cheeks, there was no sensation. Running would not thaw them out. Nor would it thaw

out his hands and feet. Then the thought came to him that the frozen portions of his body must be extending. He tried to keep this thought down, to forget it, to think of something else; he was aware of the panicky feeling that it caused, and he was afraid of the panic. But the thought asserted itself, and persisted, until it produced a vision of his body totally frozen. This was too much, and he made another wild run along the trail. Once he slowed down to a walk, but the thought of the freezing extending itself made him run again.

And all the time the dog ran with him, at his heels. When he fell down a second time, it curled its tail over its forefeet and sat in front of him, facing him, curiously eager and intent. The warmth and security of the animal angered him, and he cursed it till it flattened down its ears appeasingly. This time the shivering came more quickly upon the man. He was losing in his battle with the frost. It was creeping into his body from all sides. The thought of it drove him on, but he ran no more than a hundred feet, when he staggered and pitched headlong. It was his last panic. When he had recovered his breath and control, he sat up and entertained in his mind the conception of meeting death with dignity. However, the conception did not come to him in such terms. His idea of it was that he had been making a fool of himself, running around like a chicken with its head cut off—such was the simile that occurred to him. Well, he was bound to freeze anyway, and he might as well take it decently. With this new-found peace of mind came the first glimmerings of drowsiness. A good idea, he thought, to sleep off to death. It was like taking an anesthetic. Freezing was not so bad as people thought. There were lots worse ways to die.

He pictured the boys finding his body next day. Suddenly he found himself with them, coming along the trail and looking for himself. And, still with them, he came around a turn in the trail and found himself lying in the snow. He did not belong with himself any more, for even then he was out of himself standing with the boys and looking at himself in the snow. It certainly was cold, was his thought. When he got back to the States, he could tell the folks what real cold was. He drifted on from this to a vision of the old-timer on Sulphur Creek. He could see him quite clearly, warm and comfortable, and smoking a pipe.

"You were right, old hoss; you were right," the man mumbled to the old-timer of Sulphur Creek.

Then the man drowsed off into what seemed to him the most comfortable and satisfying sleep he had ever known. The dog sat facing him and waiting. The brief day drew to a close in a long, slow twilight. There were no signs of a fire to be made, and, besides, never in the dog's experience had it known a man to sit like that in the snow and make no fire. As the twilight drew on, its eager yearning for the fire mastered it, and with a great lifting and shifting of forefeet, it whined softly, then flattened its ear down in anticipation of being chidden by the man. But the man remained silent. Later, the dog whined loudly. And still later it crept close to the man and caught the scent of death. This made the animal bristle and back away. A little longer it delayed, howling under the stars that leaped and danced and shone brightly in the cold sky. Then it turned and trotted up the trail in the direction of the camp it knew, where were other food providers and fire providers.

FOR UNDERSTANDING

1. What is lacking in the man that makes him unfit to survive in the northern wilderness? What advantage does the dog have over the man?

2. Mention two or more details in the story that impress on us how cold it is.

3. What is the first unlucky accident that the man has? After this piece of bad luck, what mistake does he make in building his fire? Explain why, after this fire is put out, he is unable to build a new one.

4. Which wins the contest—man or nature? What finally happens to the dog, and how does this emphasize the outcome of the contest?

THE STORYTELLER'S ART

1. Early in the story, why does the author talk so much about *fifty* degrees below zero before revealing that the temperature is actually much lower? How does the extreme cold hamper the man in building a fire to dry himself? Mention several ways the cold further hampers him in trying to save himself after this fire is destroyed.

2. By giving many small details of the man's activities, the author makes us feel as if we are *there*, experiencing the story ourselves. Mention three such details—ones that are not very important, but make the story more realistic.

3. Near the beginning, how does the manner of the dog suggest to us that the man is in danger? How do the man's thoughts add to our feeling that he is in danger, even though he himself does not realize it?

4. There is a point not far beyond the middle of the story where the man seems to realize—for a moment, at least—that it's all over and that he will die. From there on we merely follow, with horror and fascination, his more and more desperate struggles. Quote the words in which we are told of the man's sudden glimpse of what his fate will be.

FOR FURTHER READING

1. The poem "Angus McGregor," by Lew Sarett, deals with the same subject that Jack London treats in "To Build a Fire"—that is, the struggle of a traveler against the fierce Arctic cold. One student might be appointed to find the poem and read it to the class, pointing out expressions in it that emphasize the cold and desolation of the Far North.

2. Jack London's *The Call of the Wild* and *White Fang* are highly dramatic novels about the North. They are good books for supplementary reading. In each, the hero is a dog.

3. London's short story "An Odyssey of the North" is a strange tale of conflict and revenge, of Eskimo against invading white man.

4. Irving Stone's *Sailor on Horseback* is a good biography of Jack London. Students who read this book will find that Jack's own experiences on the road and in the Klondike are as exciting as any in his novels.

JACK LONDON (1876–1916)

Jack London specialized in dramatic tales of adventure—of primitive, violent struggles between man and man, or between man and nature. He himself had led a strange life. He grew up along the Oakland, California, waterfront. At fifteen he bought a sloop and robbed oyster beds. Then he shipped as a seaman on a world cruise, worked as a laborer, enrolled in the University of California—but left after one semester to go back to work. Following an unsuccessful trip after Yukon gold he began publishing short stories in the *Overland Monthly* and the *Atlantic Monthly*. During the remainder of his life he turned out an amazing number of stories and novels, which made him wealthy; traveled to the South Seas and other parts of the globe; and spent his last years—unhappy ones—on his great ranch in California.

SCENES ON THE MISSISSIPPI

MARK TWAIN (SAMUEL L. CLEMENS)

Today Hannibal, Missouri, is a town of railroad shops and foundries. A century ago it was one of the centers of a more romantic trade—the Mississippi River traffic. Railroads had not yet arrived in the deep interior of America, and the main artery of commerce and travel was the great river-highway. The life of a town like Hannibal eddied about the landing where the steamboats docked. To boys, the river meant adventure, and far-off cities that they longed to see.

Samuel Clemens came to this town as a child. His teens found him busy in print shops and newspaper offices there and in the East. But as a young man he came back to fulfill the ambition of his boyhood—to become a steamboat pilot. His LIFE ON THE MISSISSIPPI, from which this selection is taken, gives a dramatic account of cub pilot days.

EARLY AMBITION

When I was a boy, there was but one permanent ambition among my comrades in our village on the west bank of the Mississippi River. That was, to be a steamboatman. We had transient ambitions of other sorts, but they were only transient. When a circus came and went, it left us all burning to become clowns; the first Negro minstrel show that ever came to our section left us all suffering to try that kind of life; now and then we had a hope that, if we lived and were good, God would permit us to be pirates. These ambitions faded out, each in its turn; but the ambition to be a steamboatman always remained.

Once a day a cheap, gaudy packet [1] arrived upward from St. Louis, and another downward from Keokuk. [2] Before these events, the day was glorious with expectancy; after them, the day was a dead and empty thing. Not only the boys, but the whole village, felt this. After all these years I can picture that old time to myself now, just as it was then: the white town drowsing in the sunshine of a summer's morning; the streets empty, or pretty nearly so; one or two clerks sitting in front of the Water Street stores, with their splint-bottomed chairs tilted back against the walls, chins on breasts, hats slouched over their faces, asleep—with shingle shavings enough around to show what broke them down; a sow and a litter of pigs loafing along the sidewalk, doing a good business in

[1] PACKET—A mail boat traveling on a regular schedule. It carried passengers and freight as well as mail.

[2] KEOKUK (kē′ŏ·kŭk)—Keokuk, Iowa, sixty miles above Hannibal on the Mississippi.

"Scenes on the Mississippi" from *Life on the Mississippi* by Mark Twain. Reprinted by permission of Harper & Brothers.

417

watermelon rinds and seeds; two or three lonely little freight piles scattered about the "levee"; a pile of "skids" on the slope of the stone-paved wharf, and the fragrant town drunkard asleep in the shadow of them; two or three wood flats [3] at the head of the wharf, but nobody to listen to the peaceful lapping of the wavelets against them; the great Mississippi, the majestic, the magnificent Mississippi, rolling its mile-wide tide along, shining in the sun; the dense forest away on the other side; the "point" above the town, and the "point" below, bounding the river-glimpse and turning it into a sort of sea, and withal a very still and brilliant and lonely one.

Presently a film of dark smoke appears above one of those remote "points"; instantly a Negro drayman, famous for his quick eye and prodigious voice, lifts up the cry, "S-t-e-a-m-boat a-comin'!" and the scene changes! The town drunkard stirs, the clerks wake up, a furious clatter of drays follows, every house and store pours out a human contribution, and all in a twinkling the dead town is alive and moving. Drays, carts, men, boys, all go hurrying from many quarters to a common center, the wharf. Assembled there, the people fasten their eyes upon the coming boat as upon a wonder they are seeing for the first time. And the boat *is* rather a handsome sight, too. She is long and sharp and trim and pretty; she has two tall, fancy-topped chimneys, with a gilded device of some kind swung between them; a fanciful pilothouse, all glass and "gingerbread," perched on top of the "texas" deck [4] behind them; the paddleboxes are gorgeous

with a picture or with gilded rays above the boat's name; the boiler deck, the hurricane deck, and the texas deck are fenced and ornamented with clean white railings; there is a flag gallantly flying from the jack staff; the furnace doors are open and the fires glaring bravely; the upper decks are black with passengers; the captain stands by the big bell, calm, imposing, the envy of all; great volumes of the blackest smoke are rolling and tumbling out of the chimneys—a husbanded grandeur created with a bit of pitch pine just before arriving at a town; the crew are grouped on the forecastle; the broad stage [5] is run far out over the port bow, and an envied deck hand stands picturesquely on the end of it with a coil of rope in his hand; the pent steam is screaming through the gauge cocks; the captain lifts his hand, a bell rings, the wheels stop; then they turn back, churning the water to foam, and the steamer is at rest. Then such a scramble as there is to get aboard, and to get ashore, and to take in freight and to discharge freight, all at one and the same time; and such a yelling and cursing as the mates facilitate it all with! Ten minutes later the steamer is under way again, with no flag on the jack staff and no black smoke issuing from the chimneys. After ten more minutes the town is dead again, and the town drunkard asleep by the skids once more.

My father was a justice of the peace, and I supposed he possessed the power of life and death over all men, and could hang anybody that offended him. This was distinction enough for me as a general thing; but the desire to be a steamboatman kept intruding, nevertheless. I first wanted to be a cabin boy, so that I could come out with a white apron on

[3] FLATS—Flat-bottomed boats.

[4] "TEXAS" DECK—The *texas* was a structure on the top deck containing the officers' quarters. The cabins on steamboats were named after states of the union. The officers' cabin was the *texas* because it was largest.

[5] BROAD STAGE—The landing stage, or gangplank.

and shake a tablecloth over the side, where all my old comrades could see me; later I thought I would rather be the deck hand who stood on the end of the stage plank with the coil of rope in his hand, because he was particularly conspicious. But these were only daydreams —they were too heavenly to be contemplated as real possibilities.

By and by one of our boys went away. He was not heard of for a long time. At last he turned up as apprentice engineer or "striker" on a steamboat. This thing shook the bottom out of all my Sunday-school teachings. That boy had been notoriously worldly, and I just the reverse; yet he was exalted to this eminence, and I left in obscurity and misery. There was nothing generous about this fellow in his greatness. He would always manage to have a rusty bolt to scrub while his boat tarried at our town, and he would sit on the inside guard and scrub it, where we all could see him and envy him and loathe him. And whenever his boat was laid up he would come home and swell around the town in his blackest and greasiest clothes, so that nobody could help remembering that he was a steamboatman; and he used all sorts of steamboat technicalities in his talk, as if he were so used to them that he forgot common people could not understand them. He would speak of the "labboard" side of a horse in an easy, natural way that would make one wish he was dead. And he was always talking about "St. Looy" like an old citizen; he would refer casually to occasions when he was "coming down Fourth Street," or when he was "passing by the Planter's House," or when there was a fire and he took a turn on the brakes of "the old Big Missouri"; and then he would go on and lie about how many towns the size of ours were burned down

there that day. Two or three of the boys had long been persons of consideration among us because they had been to St. Louis once and had a vague general knowledge of its wonders, but the day of their glory was over now. They lapsed into a humble silence, and learned to disappear when the ruthless "cub" engineer approached. This fellow had money, too, and hair oil. Also an ignorant silver watch and a showy brass watch chain. He wore a leather belt and used no suspenders. If ever a youth was cordially admired and hated by his comrades, this one was. No girl could withstand his charms. He "cut out" every boy in the village. When his boat blew up at last, it diffused a tranquil contentment among us such as we had not known for months. But when he came home the next week, alive, renowned, and appeared in church all battered up and bandaged, a shining hero, stared at and wondered over by everybody, it seemed to us that the partiality of Providence for an undeserving reptile had reached a point where it was open to criticism.

This creature's career could produce but one result, and it speedily followed. Boy after boy managed to get on the river. The minister's son became an engineer. The doctor's and the postmaster's sons became "mud clerks"; the wholesale liquor dealer's son became a barkeeper on a boat; four sons of the chief merchant, and two sons of the county judge, became pilots. Pilot was the grandest position of all. The pilot, even in those days of trivial wages, had a princely salary—from a hundred and fifty to two hundred and fifty dollars a month, and no board to pay. Two months of his wages would pay a preacher's salary for a year. Now some of us were left disconsolate. We could not get on the river—at least our parents would not let us.

So, by and by, I ran away. I said I would never come home again till I was a pilot and could come in glory. But somehow I could not manage it. I went meekly aboard a few of the boats that lay packed together like sardines at the long St. Louis wharf, and humbly inquired for the pilots, but got only a cold shoulder and short words from mates and clerks. I had to make the best of this sort of treatment for the time being, but I had comforting daydreams of a future when I should be a great and honored pilot, with plenty of money, and could kill some of these mates and clerks and pay for them.

I TAKE A FEW EXTRA LESSONS

During the two or two and a half years of my apprenticeship I served under many pilots, and had experience of many kinds of steamboatmen and many varieties of steamboats; for it was not always convenient for Mr. Bixby [6] to have me with him, and in such cases he sent me with somebody else. I am to this day profiting somewhat by that experience; for in that brief, sharp schooling, I got personally and familiarly acquainted with about all the different types of human nature that are to be found in fiction, biography, or history. The fact is daily borne in upon me that the average shore employment requires as much as forty years to equip a man with this sort of an education. When I say I am still profiting by this thing, I do not mean that it has constituted me a judge of men—no, it has not done that, for judges of men are born, not made. My profit is various in kind and degree, but the

feature of it which I value most is the zest which that early experience has given to my later reading. When I find a well-drawn character in fiction or biography I generally take a warm personal interest in him, for the reason that I have known him before—met him on the river.

The figure that comes before me oftenest, out of the shadows of that vanished time, is that of Brown, of the steamer *Pennsylvania*. He was a middle-aged, long, slim, bony, smooth-shaven, horse-faced, ignorant, stingy, malicious, snarling, fault-hunting, mote-magnifying tyrant. I early got the habit of coming on watch with dread at my heart. No matter how good a time I might have been having with the off-watch below, and no matter how high my spirits might be when I started aloft, my soul became lead in my body the moment I approached the pilothouse.

I still remember the first time I ever entered the presence of that man. The boat had backed out from St. Louis and was "straightening down." I ascended to the pilothouse in high feather, and very proud to be semiofficially a member of the executive family of so fast and famous a boat. Brown was at the wheel. I paused in the middle of the room, all fixed to make my bow, but Brown did not look around. I thought he took a furtive glance at me out of the corner of his eye, but as not even this notice was repeated, I judged I had been mistaken. By this time he was picking his way among some dangerous "breaks" abreast the woodyards; therefore it would not be proper to interrupt him; so I stepped softly to the high bench and took a seat.

There was silence for ten minutes; then my new boss turned and inspected me deliberately and painstakingly from

[6] MR. BIXBY—Horace Bixby, the pilot who has taken Samuel as a cub and who is teaching him to be a pilot.

head to heel for about—as it seemed to me—a quarter of an hour. After which he removed his countenance and I saw it no more for some seconds; then it came around once more, and this question greeted me:

"Are you Horace Bixby's cub?"

"Yes, sir."

After this there was a pause and another inspection. Then:

"What's your name?"

I told him. He repeated it after me. It was probably the only thing he ever forgot; for although I was with him many months he never addressed himself to me in any other way than "Here!" and then his command followed.

"Where was you born?"

"In Florida, Missouri."

A pause. Then:

"Dern sight better stayed there!"

By means of a dozen or so pretty direct questions, he pumped my family history out of me.

The leads were going now in the first crossing. This interrupted the inquest. When the leads had been laid in he resumed:

"How long you been on the river?"

I told him. After a pause:

"Where'd you get them shoes?"

I gave him the information.

"Hold up your foot!"

I did so. He stepped back, examined the shoe minutely and contemptuously, scratching his head thoughtfully, tilting his high sugar-loaf hat well forward to facilitate the operation, then ejaculated, "Well, I'll be dod derned!" and returned to his wheel.

What occasion there was to be dod derned about it is a thing which is still as much of a mystery to me now as it was then. It must have been all of fifteen

minutes—fifteen minutes of dull, home-sick silence—before that long horse-face swung around upon me again—and then what a change! It was as red as fire, and every muscle in it was working. Now came this shriek:

"Here! You going to set there all day?"

I lit in the middle of the floor, shot there by the electric suddenness of the surprise. As soon as I could get my voice I said apologetically: "I have had no orders, sir."

"You've had no *orders*! My, what a fine bird we are! We must have *orders*! Our father was a *gentleman*—owned slaves—and *we've* been to *school*. Yes, *we* are a gentleman, *too*, and got to have *orders*! Orders, is it? ORDERS is what you want? Dod dern my skin, *I'll* learn you to swell yourself up and blow around *here* about your dod-derned *orders*! G'way from the wheel!" (I had approached it without knowing it.)

I moved back a step or two and stood as in a dream, all my senses stupefied by this frantic assault.

"What you standing there for? Take that ice pitcher down to the texas-tender! Come, move along, and don't you be all day about it!"

The moment I got back to the pilot-house Brown said:

"Here! What was you doing down there all this time?"

"I couldn't find the texas-tender; I had to go all the way to the pantry."

"Derned likely story! Fill up the stove."

I proceeded to do so. He watched me like a cat. Presently he shouted:

"Put down that shovel! Derndest numskull I ever saw—ain't even got sense enough to load up a stove."

All through the watch this sort of thing went on. Yes, and the subsequent watches were much like it during a stretch of months. As I have said, I soon got the habit of coming on duty with dread. The moment I was in the presence, even in the darkest night, I could feel those yellow eyes upon me, and knew their owner was watching for a pretext to spit out some venom on me. Preliminarily he would say:

"Here! Take the wheel."

Two minutes later:

"*Where* in the nation you going to? Pull her down! Pull her down!"

After another moment:

"Say! You going to hold her all day? Let her go—meet her! meet her!"

Then he would jump from the bench, snatch the wheel from me, and meet her himself, pouring out wrath upon me all the time.

George Ritchie was the other pilot's cub. He was having good times now; for his boss, George Ealer, was as kind-hearted as Brown wasn't. Ritchie had steered for Brown the season before; consequently, he knew exactly how to entertain himself and plague me, all by the one operation. Whenever I took the wheel for a moment on Ealer's watch, Ritchie would sit back on the bench and play Brown, with continual ejaculations of "Snatch her! Snatch her! Derndest mud-cat I ever saw!" "Here! Where are you going *now*? Going to run over that snag?" "Pull her *down*! Don't you hear me? Pull her *down*!" "There she goes! *Just* as I expected! I *told* you not to cramp that reef. G'way from the wheel!"

So I always had a rough time of it, no matter whose watch it was; and sometimes it seemed to me that Ritchie's good-natured badgering was pretty nearly as aggravating as Brown's dead-earnest nagging.

I often wanted to kill Brown, but this

would not answer. A cub had to take everything his boss gave, in the way of vigorous comment and criticism; and we all believed that there was a United States law making it a penitentiary offense to strike or threaten a pilot who was on duty. However, I could *imagine* myself killing Brown; there was no law against that; and that was the thing I used always to do the moment I was abed. Instead of going over my river [7] in my mind, as was my duty, I threw business aside for pleasure, and killed Brown. I killed Brown every night for months; not in old, stale, commonplace ways, but in new and picturesque ones—ways that were sometimes surprising for freshness of design and ghastliness of situation and environment.

Brown was *always* watching for a pretext to find fault; and if he could find no plausible pretext, he would invent one. He would scold you for shaving a shore, and for not shaving it; for hugging a bar, and for not hugging it; for "pulling down" when not invited, and for *not* pulling down when not invited; for firing up without orders, and for waiting *for* orders. In a word, it was his invariable rule to find fault with *everything* you did; and another invariable rule of his was to throw all his remarks to you into the form of an insult.

One day we were approaching New Madrid, bound down and heavily laden. Brown was at one side of the wheel, steering; I was at the other, standing by to "pull down" or "shove up." He cast a furtive glance at me every now and then. I had long ago learned what that meant; viz., he was trying to invent a trap for me. I wondered what shape it

[7] GOING OVER MY RIVER IN MY MIND—Reviewing, for future use, all the details of the stretch of river that had just been traveled. Pilots had to know all the shoals, snags, and safe channels, because there were no markers.

was going to take. By and by he stepped back from the wheel and said in his usual snarly way:

"Here! See if you've got gumption enough to round her to."

This was simply *bound* to be a success; nothing could prevent it; for he had never allowed me to round the boat to before; consequently, no matter how I might do the thing, he could find free fault with it. He stood back there with his greedy eye on me, and the result was what might have been foreseen: I lost my head in a quarter of a minute, and didn't know what I was about; I started too early to bring the boat around, but detected a green gleam of joy in Brown's eye, and corrected my mistake. I started around once more while too high up, but corrected myself again in time. I made other false moves, and still managed to save myself; but at last I grew so confused and anxious that I tumbled into the very worst blunder of all—I got too far *down* before beginning to fetch the boat around. Brown's chance was come.

His face turned red with passion; he made one bound, hurled me across the house with a sweep of his arm, spun the wheel down, and began to pour out a stream of vituperation upon me which lasted till he was out of breath. In the course of this speech he called me all the different kinds of hard names he could think of, and once or twice I thought he was even going to swear—but he had never done that, and he didn't this time. "Dod dern" was the nearest he ventured to the luxury of swearing, for he had been brought up with a wholesome respect for future fire and brimstone.

That was an uncomfortable hour; for there was a big audience on the hurricane deck. When I went to bed that night, I killed Brown in seventeen different ways —all of them new.

BROWN AND I EXCHANGE COMPLIMENTS

Two trips later I got into serious trouble. Brown was steering; I was "pulling down." My younger brother appeared on the hurricane deck, and shouted to Brown to stop at some landing or other, a mile or so below. Brown gave no intimation that he had heard anything. But that was his way: he never condescended to take notice of an underclerk. The wind was blowing; Brown was deaf (although he always pretended he wasn't), and I very much doubted if he had heard the order. If I had had two heads, I would have spoken; but as I had only one, it seemed judicious to take care of it; so I kept still.

Presently, sure enough, we went sailing by that plantation. Captain Klinefelter appeared on the deck, and said:

"Let her come around, sir, let her come round. Didn't Henry tell you to land here?"

"No, sir!"

"I sent him up to do it."

"He *did* come up; and that's all the good it done, the dod-derned fool. He never said anything."

"Didn't *you* hear him?" asked the captain of me.

Of course I didn't want to be mixed up in this business, but there was no way to avoid it; so I said: "Yes, sir."

I knew what Brown's next remark would be, before he uttered it. It was:

"Shut your mouth! You never heard anything of the kind."

I closed my mouth, according to instructions. An hour later Henry entered the pilothouse, unaware of what had been going on. He was a thoroughly inoffensive boy, and I was sorry to see him come, for I knew Brown would have no pity on him. Brown began, straightway:

"Here! Why didn't you tell me we'd got to land at that plantation?"

"I did tell you, Mr. Brown."

"It's a lie!"

I said:

"You lie, yourself. He did tell you."

Brown glared at me in unaffected surprise; and for as much as a moment he was entirely speechless; then he shouted to me:

"I'll attend to your case in a half a minute!" then to Henry, "And you leave the pilothouse; out with you!"

It was a pilot law, and must be obeyed. The boy started out, and even had his foot on the upper step outside the door, when Brown, with a sudden access of fury, picked up a ten-pound lump of coal and sprang after him; but I was between, with a heavy stool, and I hit Brown a good honest blow which stretched him out.

I had committed the crime of crimes— I had lifted my hand against a pilot on duty! I supposed I was booked for the penitentiary sure, and couldn't be booked any surer if I went on and squared my long account with this person while I had the chance; consequently I stuck to him and pounded him with my fists a considerable time. I do not know how long, the pleasure of it probably made it seem longer than it really was; but in the end he struggled free and jumped up and sprang to the wheel: a very natural solicitude, for, all this time, here was this steamboat tearing down the river at the rate of fifteen miles an hour and nobody at the helm! However, Eagle Bend was two miles wide at this bankfull stage, and correspondingly long and deep; and the boat was steering herself straight down the middle and taking no chances. Still, that was only luck—a body *might* have found her charging into the woods.

Perceiving at a glance that the *Pennsylvania* was in no danger, Brown gathered up the big spyglass, war-club fashion, and ordered me out of the pilot-house with more than Comanche bluster. But I was not afraid of him now; so, instead of going, I tarried, and criticized his grammar. I reformed his ferocious speeches for him, and put them into good English, calling his attention to the advantage of pure English over the bastard dialect of the Pennsylvania collieries whence he was extracted. He could have done his part to admiration in a cross fire of mere vituperation, of course; but he was not equipped for this species of controversy; so he presently laid aside his glass and took the wheel, muttering and shaking his head; and I retired to the bench. The racket had brought everybody to the hurricane deck, and I trembled when I saw the old captain looking up from amid the crowd.

I said to myself, "Now I *am* done for!" for although, as a rule, he was so fatherly and indulgent toward the boat's family, and so patient of minor shortcomings, he could be stern enough when the fault was worth it.

I tried to imagine what he *would* do to a cub pilot who had been guilty of such a crime as mine, committed on a boat guard-deep with costly freight and alive with passengers. Our watch was nearly ended. I thought I would go and hide somewhere till I got a chance to slide ashore. So I slipped out of the pilot-house, and down the steps, and around to the texas-door, and was in the act of gliding within, when the captain confronted me! I dropped my head, and he stood over me in silence a moment or two, then said impressively:

"Follow me."

I dropped into his wake; he led the way to his parlor in the forward end of the texas. We were alone, now. He closed the after door; then moved slowly to the forward one and closed that. He sat down; I stood before him. He looked at me some little time, then said:

"So you have been fighting Mr. Brown?"

I answered meekly:

"Yes, sir."

"Do you know that that is a very serious matter?"

"Yes, sir."

"Are you aware that this boat was plowing down the river fully five minutes with no one at the wheel?"

"Yes, sir."

"Did you strike him first?"

"Yes, sir."

"What with?"

"A stool, sir."

"Hard?"

"Middling, sir."

"Did it knock him down?"

"He—he fell, sir."

"Did you follow it up? Did you do anything further?"

"Yes, sir."

"What did you do?"

"Pounded him, sir."

"Pounded him?"

"Yes, sir."

"Did you pound him much? that is, severely?"

"One might call it that, sir, maybe."

"I'm deuced glad of it! Hark ye, never mention that I said that. You have been guilty of a great crime; and don't you ever be guilty of it again, on this boat. But—lay for him ashore! Give him a good sound thrashing, do you hear? I'll pay the expenses. Now go—and mind you, not a word of this to anybody. Clear out with you! You've been guilty of a great crime, you whelp!"

I slid out, happy with the sense of a close shave and a mighty deliverance;

and I heard him laughing to himself and slapping his fat thighs after I had closed his door.

When Brown came off watch he went straight to the captain, who was talking with some passengers on the boiler deck, and demanded that I be put ashore in New Orleans—and added:

"I'll never turn a wheel on this boat again while that cub stays."

The captain said:

"But he needn't come round when you are on watch, Mr. Brown."

"I won't even stay on the same boat with him. One of us has got to go ashore."

"Very well," said the captain, "let it be yourself," and resumed his talk with the passengers.

During the brief remainder of the trip I knew how an emancipated slave feels, for I was an emancipated slave myself.

A SECTION IN MY BIOGRAPHY

In due course I got my license. I was a pilot now, full-fledged. I dropped into casual employments; no misfortunes resulting, intermittent work gave place to steady and protracted engagements. Time drifted smoothly and prosperously on, and I supposed—and hoped—that I was going to follow the river the rest of my days, and die at the wheel when my mission was ended. But by and by the war came, commerce was suspended, my occupation was gone.

I had to seek another livelihood. So I became a silver miner in Nevada; next, a newspaper reporter; next, a gold miner in California; next, a reporter in San Francisco; next, a special correspondent in the Sandwich Islands; next, a roving correspondent in Europe and the East; next, an instructional torchbearer on the lecture platform; and, finally, I became a scribbler of books, and an immovable fixture among the other rocks of New England.

In so few words have I disposed of the twenty-one slow-drifting years that have come and gone since I last looked from the windows of a pilothouse.

◇◇◇◇◇◇◇◇◇◇◇◇◇◇◇◇◇◇◇◇◇◇◇◇◇◇◇

FOR UNDERSTANDING

1. What caused Sam Clemens and the other boys in his town to decide to become clowns, or performers in a minstrel show? What temporary, and not very serious, ambitions do you know of among modern boys and girls? Explain why the boys' desire to be steamboat pilots was deeper and more permanent than their other ambitions.

2. In describing the transformation of the town when the steamboat docked, Twain tries to give us the exact feeling of the old-time river days. Point out details that humorously emphasize the peaceful laziness of the little country town. Give two details that show the town waking up. How can we tell that the steamboat people like to "put on a show" for the crowd that has gathered to watch them?

3. Brown's treatment of young Sam Clemens shows that the pilot was a small-minded person who enjoyed bullying those under his authority. How does the story make clear that it was impossible to satisfy Brown? Knocking down the pilot was a dangerous, if not criminal, thing to do. What particularly outrageous act of Brown's caused Sam Clemens to strike the pilot?

4. A delightful thing about much of Twain's writing is his exuberance, or overflowing high spirits. This quality shows itself in humorous exaggerations, and in colorful expressions that show how much he enjoys what he is telling. For example, he says "I hit Brown *a good honest blow*." Point out two other examples of vigorous, picturesque sentences.

FOR FURTHER KNOWLEDGE OF THE MISSISSIPPI RIVER ERA

1. Appoint one student to find books containing photographs of river steamboats, for demonstration in class. He should be prepared to answer questions on their construction and size.

2. Arrange for someone to sing, or read aloud, "Old Man River." A phonograph recording might be used, for there are several recordings of parts of *Show Boat*, the musical comedy for which this song was written. What characteristics of the Mississippi River and of river life are stressed in the song?

3. Appoint a student to look up the poem "Jim Bludso," by John Hay. In his report to the class he should explain the characteristics of the hero, who is a river pilot, and also the information contained in the poem about steamboat racing. He might conclude by reading the poem aloud.

DESCRIBING A "BIG" EVENT

In any town, or school, there are "big" moments like the arrival of the steamboat in Mark Twain's home town. Examples are an annual parade, a traditional ceremony of some kind, or the moment the home team runs out on the football field. As a basis for an original composition, choose an event that is familiar to most class members. In class discussion, decide what *details* should go into a description of such an event. In working out the list of details, imitate Mark Twain by including what would be observed *before* the big moment, and what would be observed *during* the moment.

FOR FURTHER READING

Edna Ferber, *Show Boat*. This is a novel about the floating theaters which used to travel the river, giving performances at every town. The heroine, to her misfortune, marries one of the professional gamblers who ride the passenger steamers. The novel was later made into a successful operetta.

Darwin Teilhet, *Steamboat on the River.* This novel is about the perilous trip of the little steamer "Talisman," in 1832, up the Mississippi, the Illinois, and the Sangamon rivers to Springfield, Illinois. Young Abra-

ham Lincoln, then a backwoods storekeeper, is one of the minor characters.

MARK TWAIN (1835–1910)

For further information on this famous author, see Samuel L. Clemens, page 707.

◇◇◇◇◇

From *Pioneers! O Pioneers!*

WALT WHITMAN

Walt Whitman was the American poet who wrote most frequently and enthusiastically of the pioneers who opened up the West. Here he expresses the vigor and the excitement of the Westward Movement. He is writing about the whole migration, not any one special part of it.

Come, my tan-faced children,
Follow well in order, get your weapons ready;
Have you your pistols? have you your sharp-edged axes?
    Pioneers! O pioneers!

For we cannot tarry here,   5
We must march, my darlings, we must bear the brunt of danger,
We, the youthful sinewy races, all the rest on us depend,
    Pioneers! O pioneers!

O you youths, western youths,
So impatient, full of action, full of manly pride and friendship,   10
Plain I see you, western youths, see you tramping with the foremost,
    Pioneers! O pioneers!

Have the elder races halted?
Do they droop and end their lesson, wearied, over there beyond the seas?
We take up the task eternal, and the burden, and the lesson,   15
    Pioneers! O pioneers!

All the past we leave behind;
We debouch upon a newer, mightier world, varied world,
Fresh and strong the world we seize, world of labor and the march,
    Pioneers! O pioneers!   20

18. DEBOUCH (dē·bōōsh′)—March out into an open area.

We detachments steady throwing,
Down the edges, through the passes, up the mountains steep,
Conquering, holding, daring, venturing, as we go, the unknown ways,
      Pioneers! O pioneers!

We primeval forests felling,   25
We the rivers stemming, vexing we and piercing deep the mines within;
We the surface broad surveying, we the virgin soil upheaving,
      Pioneers! O pioneers!

Colorado men are we,
From the peaks gigantic, from the great sierras and the high plateaus,   30
From the mine and from the gully, from the hunting trail we come,
      Pioneers! O pioneers!

From Nebraska, from Arkansas,
Central inland race are we, from Missouri, with the continental blood intervein'd;
All the hands of comrades clasping, all the Southern, all the Northern,   35
      Pioneers! O pioneers!

O resistless, restless race!
O beloved race in all! O my breast aches with tender love for all!
O I mourn and yet exult—I am rapt with love for all,
      Pioneers! O pioneers!   40

Raise the mighty mother mistress,
Waving high the delicate mistress, over all the starry mistress (bend your heads all),
Raise the fang'd and warlike mistress, stern, impassive, weapon'd mistress,
      Pioneers! O pioneers!

See, my children, resolute children,   45
By those swarms upon our rear, we must never yield or falter,
Ages back in ghostly millions, frowning there behind us urging,
      Pioneers! O pioneers!

On and on the compact ranks,
With accessions ever waiting, with the places of the dead quickly fill'd,   50
Through the battle, through defeat, moving yet and never stopping,
      Pioneers! O pioneers!

O to die advancing on!
Are there some of us to droop and die? has the hour come?
Then upon the march we fittest die, soon and sure the gap is fill'd,   55
      Pioneers! O pioneers!

26. STEMMING—Stopping or damming up.
26. VEXING—Disturbing the soil, tossing it about.

All the pulses of the world,
Falling in, they beat for us, with the western movement beat;
Holding single or together, steady moving to the front, all for us,
    Pioneers! O pioneers!   60

   Life's involv'd and varied pageants,
All the forms and shows, all the workmen at their work,
All the seamen and the landsmen, all the masters with their slaves,
    Pioneers! O pioneers! . . .

   O you daughters of the West!   65
O you young and elder daughters! O you mothers and you wives!
Never must you be divided, in our ranks you move united,
    Pioneers! O pioneers!

   Minstrels latent on the prairies!
(Shrouded bards of other lands! you may sleep—you have done your work)   70
Soon I hear you coming warbling, soon you rise and tramp amid us,
    Pioneers! O pioneers!

   Not for delectations sweet;
Not the cushion and the slipper, not the peaceful and the studious;
Not the riches safe and palling, not for us the tame enjoyment,   75
    Pioneers! O pioneers!

   Do the feasters gluttonous feast?
Do the corpulent sleepers sleep? have they lock'd and bolted doors?
Still be ours the diet hard, and the blanket on the ground,
    Pioneers! O pioneers!   80

   Has the night descended?
Was the road of late so toilsome? did we stop discouraged, nodding on our way?
Yet a passing hour I yield you, in your tracks to pause oblivious,
    Pioneers! O pioneers!

   Till with sound of trumpet,   85
Far, far off the daybreak call—hark! how loud and clear I hear it wind;
Swift! to the head of the army!—swift! spring to your places,
    Pioneers! O pioneers!

73. DELECTATIONS (dē′lĕk·tā′shŭnz)—Pleasures.
78. CORPULENT (kôr′pū·lĕnt)—Stout, fat.

◇◇◇

FOR UNDERSTANDING
   1. According to the poet, what are the chief characteristics of the men who settle the West? Find a phrase which shows that he considers them superior to the inhabitants of European nations.

2. What details of *industrial development* of the new lands are referred to?

3. How does Whitman make clear that the heroes of this poem are not from any one locality in America?

4. It may surprise you to be told that the "fang'd and warlike mistress" in line 43 is the American flag. Reread the stanza in which this line occurs. What phrase or phrases show that some sort of flag or banner is being referred to? How can we tell that it is the *American* flag?

5. In a sense the Westward Movement had its beginning when Europeans first crossed the Atlantic to American shores. Afterward, the movement continued to be European as well as American. Immigrants came to America and immediately took up homesteads in the West. The prosperity of America and her growing industries made it possible for many additional immigrants to find jobs in the eastern cities. To millions of downtrodden people in the old countries, America offered hope and opportunity. In which lines does Whitman seem to hint at these facts?

6. Near the end of the poem Whitman speaks of people who live luxuriously and tamely. Who are these people, in your opinion?

7. What time of day is described in the final stanza? Explain how the *last two* stanzas suggest that some of the recent settlements in the West have not been very successful, but that in Whitman's opinion the movement will go on in spite of this fact?

WALT WHITMAN (1819–1892)

For further information on this famous author, see pages 694–695.

◈◈◈◈◈

For Broader Understanding

1. What different motives led people to leave their homes and friends to face the dangers and hardships of life on the western frontier? For example, what prompted the various characters in the selections of this unit to go West? To what extent did each find what he wanted?

2. Judging by the people in these stories and poems, what personal qualities or character traits were common to most pioneers? Consider two such unlike people as William Sycamore and Johnny Appleseed. In what ways were they alike? Compare and contrast them in the following respects: (*a*) reasons for moving West (*b*) ability to endure hardships (*c*) courage and resourcefulness (*d*) love of adventure (*e*) attitude toward nature (*f*) idealism or desire to serve humanity (*g*) faith in the future of the country. Which of their common qualities are also shared by other characters in the unit?

3. The first three poems in this unit present the Westward Movement as seen by present-day writers. In the remaining selections we see the movement through the eyes of the "men who were there." Which group of writers makes pioneering more attractive? Give specific illustrations of the difference in attitude, if you think there is a difference.

4. Explain the difference between *local color* and *realism* in fiction about the Westward Movement. Cite examples of each type of writing in the stories of this unit and, if possible, name some also in your individual reading about *Frontiers to the West*. Name one writer who made important contributions to the development of each kind of writing.

5. In spite of the hardships and privations of life on the frontier, there were pleasures and satisfactions in pioneering. What amusement and entertainment did the early settlers have which we no longer enjoy, or which we enjoy to a limited extent? Are there any which we have attempted to preserve or which we have revived? Besides fun

or entertainment, what other rewards or satisfactions come to pioneers in any field?

SPEAKING AND WRITING ACTIVITIES

1. Prepare a report on a famous scout or pioneer not included in this unit. Read from at least three sources, including, if possible, one full-length biography. The class might enjoy hearing about Davy Crockett, Sam Houston, Buffalo Bill, Daniel Boone, Narcissa Whitman, Jessie Frémont, or Rachel Jackson.

2. You may have heard people speak enthusiastically about "the good old days" when life was less complicated and more serene than it is today. From your reading and discussion decide whether you think you would like to have lived in pioneer times. Then write your own evaluation of "the good old days." Try to limit your composition to one phase of frontier life. Make your points by comparing conditions then and now. Draw on class and individual reading for illustrations to make your paper colorful and interesting. Following are some possible topics though you may prefer others: "Farming Then and Now," "Fun on the Frontier," "Home Life in the Good Old Days," "Social Life on the Frontier," and "How the Pioneers Dressed."

3. Many western stories, movies, and radio and television programs have plots based upon a familiar formula. The people in these "Westerns" are not individuals but stock characters, or *stereotypes*, representing typical "western" characters. Write a "take-off" or burlesque of such a story or play. Be sure to have the usual hero, heroine, villain, and sheriff among your characters. Make the plot as "typical" as you can, and have the characters act and speak as Western fans expect such characters to act and speak.

FOR FURTHER READING

A. B. GUTHRIE, *The Way West* (Sloane). This dramatic account of westward passage describes the experiences of one pioneer band as they journey from Missouri to Oregon.

EDWARD EGGLESTON, *The Hoosier Schoolmaster* (Grosset). Ralph Hartsook, a young Indiana schoolteacher, learns to meet unusual situations with courage and a sense of humor. The book provides a good look at the customs and thoughts of a day gone by.

JOHAN BOJER, *The Emigrants* (Appleton). This story of Norwegian pioneer settlers in America tells of their struggle with cold winters, droughts, locusts, and loneliness. The growth of their settlement is inspiring.

FRANCIS PARKMAN, *The Oregon Trail* (Modern Library). The author's first-hand experiences with Indians and prairie settlers are well told.

ROSE WILDER LANE, *Let the Hurricane Roar* (Longmans). Young homesteaders in the Dakotas find courage beyond their expectations as they face a host of perils.

BRET HARTE, *Bret Harte's Stories of the Old West* (Houghton). These are some of Mr. Harte's most exciting pioneer stories.

MAY LAMBERTON BECKER, compiler, *Golden Tales of the Prairie States* and *Golden Tales of the Far West* (Dodd). Both books are excellent anthologies about pioneer life.

THEODORE ROOSEVELT, *Stories of the Great West* (Appleton). A great American sketches the development of the West from the days of Daniel Boone to the time of the great western ranches.

DONALD C. PEATTIE, *Forward the Nation* (Putnam). In lyrical prose Mr. Peattie tells the story of the Indian girl guide Sacajawea and the Lewis and Clark expedition through the wilderness to the Pacific.

LUCIEN HUBBARD, *Rivers to the Sea* (Simon & Schuster). Here is a lively picture of steamboat travel on the Ohio and Mississippi rivers.

CONRAD RICHTER, *The Trees* (Knopf). The effect of the forest upon the pioneer settlers is shown in this novel of atmosphere which gives a fine picture of the frontier. *The Fields* and *The Sea of Grass* are also vivid descriptions of frontier life by Mr. Richter.

EDNA FERBER, *Cimarron* (Grosset). Oklahoma's newspaperman Yancey brings democracy to the Indians and to his neighbors in a lively story of the frontier.

EVERETTE DICK, *The Sod House Frontier* (Appleton). A wealth of material on frontier life in Kansas, Nebraska, and the Dakotas can be found here.

MONTE BARRETT, *Tempered Blade* (Bobbs-Merrill). This is the story of James Bowie who invented the Bowie knife and died a hero at the Alamo. Here we see Texas in turmoil and are shown conditions that led to the break with Mexico.

◇◇◇◇◇

HISTORY IN REVIEW

MILESTONES	TRENDS IN AMERICAN LIFE	LITERATURE
1819—Florida purchased from Spain	New England becomes a center of high intellectual culture, and of trade and manufacture	
1820—Missouri Compromise; this and two later compromises temporarily avert war by keeping an equal number of slave and free states	With the election of Andrew Jackson, a "man of the people," the "West" gets its first taste of political power	1823–1841—*The Leatherstocking Tales* of James Fenimore Cooper 1827—Poe's *Tamerlane and Other Poems*
1823—Monroe Doctrine; expression of U. S. disapproval of European intervention in the Americas	"Johnny Appleseed" sows orchards through Ohio, Indiana, Illinois	1837—Emerson's oration "The American Scholar"; Hawthorne's *Twice-Told Tales*
1836—Battle of Alamo; Texas wins its independence from Mexico		1841—Emerson's *Essays, First Series* which contains "Self-Reliance" and "Compensation"
1845—Texas admitted to the Union	Immigration from Europe sharply increases	1845—Poe's *The Raven, and Other Poems*
1846–1848—Mexican War	Admission of new states to the Union emphasizes sectional differences over slavery and helps bring on the War Between the States	
1846—Treaty with England establishes our Northwest boundary		1847–1848—Longfellow's *Evangeline*; Lowell's *The Vision of Sir Launfal*
1849—California Gold Rush	Extension of railroads to Middle West	
1853–1854—Commodore Perry opens trade relations with Japan		1850–1858—Hawthorne's *The Scarlet Letter* and *The House of the Seven Gables*; Melville's *Moby Dick*; Thoreau's *Walden*; Longfellow's *Tales of a Wayside Inn*
1861–1865—War Between the States		
1862—Homestead Act passed		
1867—Purchase of Alaska	After the war homesteaders settle the Great Plains region. Great cattle ranches flourish in Western states. Era of big business begins, and huge industrial cities rise in the East. Communication and transportation develop. Social welfare movements arise. From America's new status as an important world power comes a growing feeling of optimism and national pride	1866—Whittier's *Snowbound*
1873—Panic due to inflation, speculation, and overexpansion		1870—*The Luck of Roaring Camp and Other Sketches* by Bret Harte
1889—Oklahoma opened to settlement		1884—Mark Twain's *The Adventures of Huckleberry Finn*
1890–1912—Admission of last states to the Union—Wyoming, Idaho, Utah, Oklahoma, New Mexico, Arizona		1890–1892—Publication of Emily Dickinson's *Poems*; Garland's *Main-Travelled Roads*; final edition of Whitman's *Leaves of Grass*
1898—Spanish-American War; U. S. gains possession of Hawaiian Islands and Philippines		

A TIME OF CRISIS

The War Between the States—As Seen by Modern Writers

Like some gigantic natural catastrophe, the War Between the States, 1861–1865, changed the course of many thousands of lives. Directly or indirectly it affected the fortunes of all the people then living in our nation. For a time it interrupted the great movement westward which had begun three generations before—just as it interrupted all other forms of progress. The war came partly because of conflicts between the economic interests of Northern industrialists and those of the agricultural South. It came also because of two important disputes about the nature of our political order

—whether in a democracy men and women could be held in slavery; and whether individual states could secede, or withdraw, from a nation which had begun as a voluntary union of individual states. These were fundamental questions, and they shook our republic to its foundations. When good will and wise statesmanship could postpone them no longer, they were finally answered on the battlefields of Bull Run, Shiloh, and Gettysburg.

The sheer size of the conflict gives it power over our imaginations. Although the war took place within the borders of one country, the number of troops engaged and the number of campaigns made it like a "world war." Other nations looked on fascinated while two great armies fought each other to the point of exhaustion. The outcome of the fighting, many people believed, would show whether a country could survive without the rule of a king—not only America, but any country on earth. In modern poetry, and especially in modern fiction, biography, and history, we see this mighty and fateful drama played over again.

The tragic experience of the war remains deeply embedded in the memories of Americans—as can be seen by the large amount of literature that continues to be written about it nearly a hundred years later. Our modern authors find the war especially dramatic because it was not fought thousands of miles away and beyond an ocean, but in American streets and fields. They make us remember the sacrifice and the heroism of both sides. In stories like Stephen Crane's "A Mystery of Heroism" they give us realistic pictures of the battlefields. The two greatest leaders in this time of crisis, Abraham Lincoln in the North and Robert E. Lee in the South, are brought to life here in selections from biographies by Carl Sandburg and Douglas Southall Freeman, and in poems by Stephen Vincent Benét and Vachel Lindsay.

❖❖❖❖❖

Abraham Lincoln

STEPHEN VINCENT BENÉT

Lincoln's greatness could not be known until, as President during the War Between the States, he was called on to face a task such as no other American statesman had faced. Certainly the people of Lincoln's home town did not, beforehand, suspect him of greatness. In the following poem the author imagines what the people in Springfield, Illinois, saw when they looked at Abe Lincoln.

Lincoln was a long man.
He liked out of doors.
He liked the wind blowing
And the talk in country stores.

He liked telling stories,   5
He liked telling jokes.
"Abe's quite a character,"
Said quite a lot of folks.

Lots of folks in Springfield
Saw him every day,   10
Walking down the street
In his gaunt, long way.

Shawl around his shoulders,
Letters in his hat.
"That's Abe Lincoln."   15
They thought no more than that.

Knew that he was honest,
Guessed that he was odd,
Knew he had a cross wife
Though she was a Todd.   20

Knew he had three little boys
Who liked to shout and play,
Knew he had a lot of debts
It took him years to pay.

Knew his clothes and knew his house.   25
"That's his office, here.
Blame good lawyer, on the whole,
Though he's sort of queer.

"Sure, he went to Congress, once,
But he didn't stay.   30
Can't expect us all to be
Smart as Henry Clay.

"Need a man for troubled times?
Well, I guess we do.
Wonder who we'll ever find?   35
Yes—I wonder who."

That is how they met and talked,
Knowing and unknowing.
Lincoln was the green pine.
Lincoln kept on growing.   40

FOR UNDERSTANDING

1. What characteristic of Lincoln would make him well liked by neighbors and acquaintances? What details suggest that his appearance was somewhat laughable?

2. Find two or more expressions in the poem which indicate that Springfield people had no especially high opinion of Lincoln. Can you find *one* of their opinions in which there is a hint of his greatness—although they themselves do not realize it?

3. The last two lines of the poem may mean that Lincoln was not yet really a great man at the time he lived in Springfield. They also suggest something about the *rate of development* of some men of genius. Perhaps Lincoln did not seem as sure of himself, as mature, as well established in life, as other men did at the same age. How does the author suggest that this immaturity is a sign of Lincoln's superiority?

4. How is the author justified in saying that the people of Springfield were "knowing and unknowing"?

LINCOLN SPEAKS AT GETTYSBURG

CARL SANDBURG

Lincoln's Gettysburg Address is one of the great speeches of American literature. Yet it is only ten sentences long and was delivered in the last five minutes of a three-hour program. Legend and history are not in complete agreement about when and where Lincoln wrote his brief, eloquent message, and there are conflicting reports about how it was received by those who heard it. In the following selection from ABRAHAM LINCOLN: THE WAR YEARS *Carl Sandburg gives his account of the events leading up to the ceremonies at Gettysburg and tells us just what happened there. Since Carl Sandburg probably knows more about Lincoln than any man now living, his version should be very close to the truth.*

As you read see if you can discover the qualities that make Sandburg's biography so appealing to modern readers. Notice that even in this short selection the author combines historical accuracy, a sympathetic understanding of his subject, and the ability to write colorful and moving prose.

A printed invitation came to Lincoln's hands notifying him that on Thursday, November 19, 1863, exercises would be held for the dedication of a National Soldiers' Cemetery at Gettysburg. The same circular invitation had been mailed to senators, congressmen, the governors of Northern States, members of the Cabinet, by the commission of Pennsylvanians who had organized a corporation through which Maine, New Hampshire, Vermont, Massachusetts, Rhode Island, Maryland, Connecticut, New York, New Jersey, Pennsylvania, Delaware, West Virginia, Ohio, Indiana, Illinois, Michigan, Wisconsin, and Minnesota were to share the cost of a decent burying ground for the dust and bones of the Union and Confederate dead.

In the helpless onrush of the war, it was known, too many of the fallen had lain as neglected cadavers rotting in the open fields or thrust into so shallow a resting place that a common farm plow caught in their bones. Now by order of Governor Curtin of Pennsylvania seventeen acres had been purchased on Cemetery Hill, where the Union center stood its colors on the second and third of July, and plots of soil had been allotted each state for its graves.

The sacred and delicate duties of

orator of the day had fallen on Edward Everett. An eminent cultural figure, perhaps foremost of all distinguished American classical orators, he was born in 1794, had been United States Senator, Governor of Massachusetts, member of Congress, Secretary of State under Fillmore, Minister to Great Britain, Phi Beta Kappa poet at Harvard, professor of Greek at Harvard, president of Harvard. . . .

Serene, suave, handsomely venerable in his sixty-ninth year, a prominent specimen of Northern upper-class distinction, Everett was a natural choice of the Pennsylvania commissioners, who sought an orator for a solemn national occasion. When in September they notified him that the date of the occasion would be October 23, he replied that he would need more time for preparation, and the dedication was postponed till November 19.

Lincoln meanwhile, in reply to the printed circular invitation, sent word to the commissioners that he would be present at the ceremonies. This made it necessary for the commissioners to consider whether the President should be asked to deliver an address when present. Clark E. Carr of Galesburg, Illinois, representing his state on the Board of Commissioners, noted that the decision of the Board to invite Lincoln to speak was an afterthought. "The question was raised as to his ability to speak upon such a grave and solemn occasion. . . . Besides, it was said that, with his important duties and responsibilities, he could not possibly have the leisure to prepare an address. . . . In answer . . . it was urged that he himself, better than anyone else, could determine as to these questions, and that, if he were invited to speak, he was sure to do what, under the circumstances, would be right and proper."

And so on November 2 David Wills of Gettysburg, as the special agent of Governor Curtin and also acting for the several states, by letter informed Lincoln that the several states having soldiers in the Army of the Potomac who were killed, or had since died at hospitals in the vicinity, had procured grounds for a cemetery and proper burial of their dead. "These grounds will be consecrated and set apart to this sacred purpose by appropriate ceremonies on Thursday, the nineteenth instant. I am authorized by the governors of the various states to invite you to be present and participate in these ceremonies, which will doubtless be very imposing and solemnly impressive. It is the desire that after the oration, you, as Chief Executive of the nation, formally set apart these grounds to their sacred use by a few appropriate remarks.". . .

Lamon [1] noted that Lincoln wrote part of his intended Gettysburg address at Washington, covered a sheet of foolscap paper with a memorandum of it, and before taking it out of his hat and reading it to Lamon he said that it was not at all satisfactory to him, that he was afraid he would not do himself credit nor come up to public expectation. He had been too busy to give it the time he would like to. . . .

Various definite motives besides vague intuitions may have guided Lincoln in his decision to attend and speak even though half his Cabinet had sent formal declinations in response to the printed circular invitations they had all received. Though the Gettysburg dedication was to be under interstate auspices, it had tremendous national significance for Lincoln because on the platform would be the state governors whose co-operation with him was of vast importance. Also a slander and a libel had been widely mouthed and printed that on his visit to the battlefield of Antietam [2] nearly a year before he had laughed obscenely at his own funny stories and called on Lamon to sing a cheap comic song. Perhaps he might go to Gettysburg and let it be seen how he demeaned himself on a somber landscape of sacrifice. . . .

When Lincoln boarded the train for Gettysburg on November 18, his best chum in the world, Tad, [3] lay sick abed and the doctors not sure what ailed him. The mother still remembered Willie [4] and was hysterical about Tad. But the President felt imperative duty called him to Gettysburg.

[1] LAMON—Ward Hill Lamon, Lincoln's law partner in Danville, Illinois. When Lincoln was elected president, Lamon became his private secretary. Later he wrote a book entitled *Recollections of Abraham Lincoln*.

[2] ANTIETAM—Pronounced ăn·tē′tăm.

[3] TAD—Lincoln's son.

[4] WILLIE—Another son who had died.

Provost Marshall General James B. Fry as a War Department escort came to the White House, but the President was late in getting into the carriage for the drive to the station. They had no time to lose, Fry remarked. Lincoln said he felt like an Illinois man who was going to be hanged, and as the man passed along the road on the way to the gallows the crowds kept pushing into the way and blocking passage. The condemned man at last called out, "Boys, you needn't be in such a hurry to get ahead, there won't be any fun till I get there."

Flags and red-white-and-blue bunting decorated the four-car special train. Aboard were the three cabinet members, Nicolay and Hay, army and navy representatives, newspapermen, the French and Italian Ministers and attaches. [5] The rear third of the last coach had a drawing room, where from time to time the President talked with nearly everyone aboard as they came and went. Henry Clay Cochrane, lieutenant of the Marines, noted:

"I happened to have a *New York Herald* and offered it to Mr. Lincoln. He took it and thanked me, saying, 'I like to see what they say about us.' The news was about Burnside at Knoxville, Grant and Sherman at Chattanooga, and Meade on the Rapidan, all expecting trouble. He read for a little while and then began to laugh at some wild guesses of the paper about pending movements. It was pleasant to see his sad face lighted up. He was looking sallow, sunken-eyed, thin, careworn and very quiet. He returned the paper remarking among other things that when he had first passed over that road on his way to Congress in 1847, he noticed square-rigged vessels up

[5] ATTACHES (ăt′á·shāz′)—Members of diplomatic staffs; assistants to an ambassador.

the Patapsco River as far as the Relay House and now there seemed to be only small craft.

"At the Calvert Street Station Secretary Seward began to get uneasy as we approached Baltimore. Upon reaching the Calvert Street Station in Baltimore all was quiet, less than two hundred people assembled, among them women with children in arms. They called for the President. He took two or three of the babies up and kissed them which greatly pleased the mothers. General Schenck and staff joined us and soon after the President went forward in the car and seated himself with a party of choice spirits, among whom was Mayor Frederick W. Lincoln of Boston, not a kinsman. They told stories for an hour or so, Mr. Lincoln taking his turn and enjoying it. Approaching Hanover Junction, he arose and said, 'Gentlemen, this is all very pleasant, but the people will expect me to say something to them tomorrow, and I must give the matter some thought.' He then returned to the rear room of the car.". . .

At sundown the train pulled into Gettysburg and Lincoln was driven to the Wills residence, Seward to the Harper home fronting on the public square. A sleepy little country town of thirty-five hundred was overflowing with human pulses again. Private homes were filled with notables and nondescripts. Hundreds slept on the floors of hotels. Military bands blared till late in the night serenading whomsoever. The weather was mild and the moon up for those who chose to go a-roaming. When serenaders called on the President for a speech, he made again one of those little addresses saying there was nothing to say. "In my position it is sometimes important that I should not say foolish things. (A voice: "If you can help it.") It very

often happens that the only way to help it is to say nothing at all. Believing that is my present condition this evening, I must beg of you to excuse me from addressing you further."

The crowd didn't feel it was much of a speech. They went next door with the band and blared for Seward. He spoke so low that Hay could not hear him, but he opened the stopgaps of patriotic sentiment, saying in part, "I thank my God for the hope that this is the last fratricidal war which will fall upon the country which is vouchsafed to us by Heaven—the richest, the broadest, the most beautiful, the most magnificent, and capable of a greater destiny than has ever been given to any part of the human race." What more could a holiday crowd ask for on a fair night of moonlit November? Seward gave them more and closed: "Fellow citizens, good night." It was good night for him but not for them. They serenaded five other speakers. . . .

At dinner in the Wills home that evening Lincoln met Edward Everett, a guest under the same roof, and Governor Curtin and others. About ten o'clock he was in his room, with paper and pencil ready to write, when he sent a colored servant down for Judge Wills to come up. Still later, about eleven o'clock, he sent the colored servant down again for Judge Wills, who came up and heard Lincoln request to see Mr. Seward. Judge Wills offered to go and bring Seward from next door at the Harpers'. "No, I'll go and see him," said Lincoln, who gathered his sheets of paper and went for a half hour with his Secretary of State.

Whether Seward made slight or material alterations in the text on the sheets was known only to Lincoln and Seward. It was midnight or later that Lincoln

Address delivered at the dedication of the cemetery at Gettysburg.

Four score and seven years ago our fathers brought forth on this continent, a new nation, conceived in Liberty, and dedicated to the proposition that all men are created equal.

Now we are engaged in a great civil war, testing whether that nation, or any nation so conceived and so dedicated, can long endure. We are met on a great battle field of that war. We have come to dedicate a portion of that field, as a final resting place for those who here gave their lives that that nation might live. It is altogether fitting and proper that we should do this.

But, in a larger sense, we can not dedicate — we can not consecrate — we can not hallow — this ground. The brave men, living and dead, who struggled here, have consecrated it, far above our poor power to add or detract. The world will little note, nor long remember what we say here, but it can never forget what they did here. It is for us the living, rather, to be dedicated here to the unfinished work which they who fought here have thus far so nobly advanced. It is rather for us to be here dedicated to the great task remaining before us — that from these honored dead we take increased devotion to that cause for which they gave the last full measure of devotion — that we here highly resolve that these dead shall not have died in vain — that this nation, under God, shall have a new birth of freedom — and that government of the people, by the people, for the people, shall not perish from the earth.

Abraham Lincoln.

November 19, 1863.

went to sleep, probably perfectly clear in his mind as to what his speech would be the next day. The one certainty was that his "few appropriate remarks," good or bad, would go to an immense audience. Also he slept better for having a telegram from Stanton reporting there was no real war news and "On inquiry Mrs. Lincoln informs me that your son is better this evening."

Fifteen thousand, some said thirty thousand or fifty thousand people were on Cemetery Hill for the exercises the next day when the procession from Gettysburg arrived afoot and horseback representing the United States Government, the army and navy, governors of states, mayors of cities, a regiment of troops, hospital corps, telegraph-company representatives, Knights Templar, Masonic Fraternity, Odd Fellows, and other benevolent associations, the press, fire departments, citizens of Pennsylvania and other states. They were scheduled to start at ten o'clock and at that hour of the clock Lincoln in a black suit, high silk hat, and white gloves came out of the Wills residence and mounted a horse. A crowd was on hand and he held a reception on horseback. At eleven the parade began to move. The President's horse seemed small for him, as some looked at it. Clark E. Carr, just behind the President, believed he noticed that the President sat erect and looked majestic to begin with and then got to thinking so that his body leaned forward, his arms hung limp, and his head bent far down. . . .

The march of the procession of military and civic bodies began. "Mr. Lincoln was mounted upon a young and beautiful chestnut horse, the largest in the Cumberland Valley," wrote Lieutenant Cochrane. This seemed the first occasion that anyone had looked at the President mounted with a feeling that just the right horse had been picked to match his physical length. "His towering figure surmounted by a high silk hat made the rest of us look small," thought Cochrane. . . .

The march was over in fifteen minutes. But Mr. Everett, the orator of the day, had not arrived. Bands played till noon. Mr. Everett arrived. . . .

The United States House chaplain, the Reverend Thomas H. Stockton, offered a prayer while the thousands stood with uncovered heads. . . .

Benjamin B. French, officer in charge of buildings in Washington, introduced the Honorable Edward Everett, orator of the day, who rose, bowed low to Lincoln, saying, "Mr. President." Lincoln responded, "Mr. Everett."

The orator of the day then stood in silence before a crowd that stretched to limits that would test his voice. Beyond and around were the wheat fields, the meadows, the peach orchards, long slopes of land, and five and seven miles farther the contemplative blue ridge of a low mountain range. His eyes could sweep them as he faced the audience. He had taken note of it in his prepared and rehearsed address. "Overlooking these broad fields now reposing from the labors of the waning year, the mighty Alleghenies dimly towering before us, the graves of our brethren beneath our feet, it is with hesitation that I raise my poor voice to break the eloquent silence of God and Nature. But the duty to which you have called me must be performed—grant me, I pray you, your indulgence and your sympathy.". . .

Northern cities would have been trampled in conquest but for "those who sleep beneath our feet," said the orator. He gave an outline of how the war began, traversed decisive features of the three days' battles at Gettysburg, discussed the doctrine of state sovereignty and denounced it, drew parallels from European history, and came to his peroration [6] quoting Pericles on dead pa-

triots: "The whole earth is the sepulcher of illustrious men." The men of nineteen sister states had stood side by side on the perilous ridges. "Seminary Ridge, the Peach-Orchard, Cemetery, Culp, and Wolf Hill, Round Top, Little Round Top, humble names, henceforward dear and famous—no lapse of time, no distance of space, shall cause you to be forgotten." He had spoken for an hour and fifty-seven minutes, some said a trifle over two hours, repeating almost word for word an address that occupied nearly two newspaper pages, as he had written it and as it had gone in advance sheets to many newspapers.

Everett came to his closing sentence without a faltering voice: "Down to the latest period of recorded time, in the glorious annals of our common country there will be no brighter page than that which relates the battles of Gettysburg." It was the effort of his life and embodied the perfections of the school of oratory in which he had spent his career. His erect form and sturdy shoulders, his white hair and flung-back head at dramatic points, his voice, his poise, and chiefly some quality of inside goodheartedness, held most of his audience to him, though the people in the front rows had taken their seats three hours before his oration closed.

The Baltimore Glee Club sang an ode written for the occasion by Benjamin B. French, who had introduced Everett to the audience. The poets Longfellow, Bryant, Whittier, Lowell, George Boker, had been requested but none found time to respond with a piece to be set to music. . . .

Having read Everett's address, Lincoln knew when the moment drew near for him to speak. He took out his own manuscript from a coat pocket, put on his steel-bowed glasses, stirred in his

[6] PERORATION—The concluding part of a speech. Pericles (pĕr'ĭ·klēz), whom Everett quoted, was a statesman in ancient Athens.

chair, looked over the manuscript, and put it back in his pocket. The Baltimore Glee Club finished. The specially chosen Ward Hill Lamon rose and spoke the words "The President of the United States," who rose, and holding in one hand the two sheets of paper at which he occasionally glanced, delivered the address in his high-pitched and clear-carrying voice. The *Cincinnati Commercial* reporter wrote, "The President rises slowly, draws from his pocket a paper, and, when commotion subsides, in a sharp, unmusical treble voice, reads the brief and pithy remarks." Hay wrote in his diary, "The President, in a firm, free way, with more grace than is his wont, said his half dozen words of consecration." Charles Hale of the *Boston Advertiser*, also officially representing Governor Andrew of Massachusetts, had notebook and pencil in hand, took down the slow-spoken words of the President, as follows:

Fourscore and seven years ago, our fathers brought forth upon this continent a new nation, conceived in liberty and dedicated to the proposition that all men are created equal.

Now we are engaged in a great civil war, testing whether that nation—or any nation, so conceived and so dedicated—can long endure.

We are met on a great battlefield of that war. We are met[7] to dedicate a portion of it as the final resting place of those who have given their lives that that nation might live.

[7] WE ARE MET—In the final draft of his speech Lincoln wrote "we have come" instead of repeating "we are met" a second time.

It is altogether fitting and proper that we should do this.

But, in a larger sense, we cannot dedicate, we cannot consecrate, we cannot hallow, this ground. The brave men, living and dead, who struggled here, have consecrated it, far above our power [8] to add or to detract. The world will very little note nor long remember what we say here; but it can never forget what they did here.

It is for us, the living, rather, to be dedicated here, to the unfinished work that they have thus far so nobly carried on. It is rather for us to be here dedicated to the great task remaining before us; that from these honored dead we take increased devotion to that cause for which they here gave the last full measure of devotion; that we here highly resolve that these dead shall not have died in vain; that the nation shall, under God, have a new birth of freedom, and that government of the people, by the people, for the people, shall not perish from the earth.

.   .   .   .

The *New York Tribune* and many other newspapers indicated "(Applause.)" at five places in the address and "(Long continued applause.)" at the end. The applause, however, according to most of the responsible witnesses, was formal and perfunctory, a tribute to the occasion, to the high office, to the array of important men of the nation on the platform, by persons who had sat as an audience for three hours. Ten sentences had been spoken in five minutes, and some were surprised that it should end before the orator had really begun to get his outdoor voice.

A photographer had made ready to record a great historic moment, had bustled about with his dry plates, his black box on a tripod, and before he had his head under the hood for an exposure,

the President had said "by the people, for the people" and the nick of time was past for a photograph. . . .

According to Lamon, Lincoln himself felt that about all he had given the audience was ordinary, garden-variety dedicatory remarks, for Lamon wrote that Lincoln told him just after delivering the speech that he had regret over not having prepared it with greater care. "Lamon, that speech won't *scour*. It is a flat failure and the people are disappointed." On the farms where Lincoln grew up as a boy when wet soil stuck to the moldboard of a plow they said it didn't "scour."

The nearby *Patriot and Union* of Harrisburg took its fling: "The President succeeded on this occasion because he acted without sense and without constraint in a panorama that was gotten up more for the benefit of his party than for the glory of the nation and the honor of the dead. . . . We pass over the silly remarks of the President; for the credit of the nation we are willing that the veil of oblivion shall be dropped over them and that they shall no more be repeated or thought of.". . .

The *Philadelphia Evening Bulletin* said that thousands who would not read the elaborate oration of Mr. Everett would read the President's few words "and not many will do it without a moistening of the eye and a swelling of the heart." The *Detroit Advertiser and Tribune* said Mr. Everett had nobly told the story of the battle, "but he who wants to take in the very spirit of the day, catch the unstudied pathos that animates a sincere but simple-minded man, will turn from the stately periods of the professed orator to the brief speech of the President." The *Providence Journal* reminded readers of the saying that the hardest thing in the world is to make a

[8] OUR POWER—This phrase usually reads "our poor power." In delivering his address Lincoln unintentionally omitted it.

good five-minute speech: "We know not where to look for a more admirable speech than the brief one which the President made at the close of Mr. Everett's oration. . . . Could the most elaborate and splendid oration be more beautiful, more touching, more inspiring, than those thrilling words of the President? They had in our humble judgment the charm and power of the very highest eloquence.". . .

Everett's opinion of the speech he heard Lincoln deliver was written in a note to Lincoln the next day and was more than mere courtesy: "I should be glad if I could flatter myself that I came as near to the central idea of the occasion in two hours as you did in two minutes." Lincoln's immediate reply was: "In our respective parts yesterday, you could not have been excused to make a short address, nor I a long one. I am pleased to know that, in your judgment, that little I did say was not entirely a failure.". . .

After the ceremonies at Gettysburg Lincoln lunched with Governor Curtin, Mr. Everett, and others at the Wills home, held a reception that had not been planned, handshaking nearly an hour, looking gloomy and listless but brightening sometimes as a small boy or girl came in line, and stopping one tall man for remarks as to just how high up he reached. At five o'clock he attended a patriotic meeting in the Presbyterian church, walking arm-in-arm with old John Burns, and listening to an address by Lieutenant Governor-elect Anderson of Ohio. At six-thirty he was on the departing Washington train. . . .

The ride to Washington took until midnight. Lincoln was weary, talked little, stretched out on one of the side seats in the drawing room and had a wet towel laid across his eyes and forehead.

He had stood that day, the world's foremost spokesman of popular government, saying that democracy was yet worth fighting for. He had spoken as one in mist who might head on deeper yet into mist. He incarnated the assurances and pretenses of popular government, implied that it could and might perish from the earth. What he meant by "a new birth of freedom" for the nation could have a thousand interpretations. The taller riddles of democracy stood up out of the address. It had the dream touch of vast and furious events epitomized for any foreteller to read what was to come. He did not assume that the drafted soldiers, substitutes, and bounty-paid privates had died willingly under Lee's shot and shell, in deliberate consecration of themselves to the Union cause. His cadences sang the ancient song that where there is freedom men have fought and sacrificed for it, and that freedom is worth men's dying for. For the first time since he became President he had on a dramatic occasion declaimed, howsoever it might be read, Jefferson's proposition which had been a slogan of the Revolutionary War—"All men are created equal"—leaving no other inference than that he regarded the Negro slave as a man. His outwardly smooth sentences were inside of them gnarled and tough with the enigmas of the American experiment.

Back at Gettysburg the blue haze of the Cumberland Mountains had dimmed till it was a blur in a nocturne. The moon was up and fell with a bland golden benevolence on the new-made graves of soldiers, on the sepulchers of old settlers, on the horse carcasses of which the onrush of war had not yet permitted removal. The *New York Herald* man walked amid them and ended the story he sent his paper: "The air, the trees, the graves are silent. Even the

relic hunters are gone now. And the soldiers here never wake to the sound of reveille."

In many a country cottage over the land, a tall old clock in a quiet corner told time in a tick-tock deliberation. Whether the orchard branches hung with pink-spray blossoms or icicles of sleet, whether the outside news was seedtime or harvest, rain or drought, births or deaths, the swing of the pendulum was right and left and right and left in a tick-tock deliberation.

The face and dial of the clock had known the eyes of a boy who listened to its tick-tock and learned to read its minute and hour hands. And the boy had seen years measured off by the swinging pendulum, and grown to man size, had gone away. And the people in the cottage knew that the clock would stand there and the boy never again come into the room and look at the clock with the query, "What is the time?"

In a row of graves of the Unidentified the boy would sleep long in the dedicated final resting place at Gettysburg. Why he had gone away and why he would never come back had roots in some mystery of flags and drums, of national fate in which individuals sink as in a deep sea, of men swallowed and vanished in a man-made storm of smoke and steel.

The mystery deepened and moved with ancient music and inviolable consolation because a solemn Man of Authority had stood at the graves of the Unidentified and spoken the words "We cannot consecrate—we cannot hallow—this ground. The brave men, living and dead, who struggled here, have consecrated it far above our poor power to add or detract. . . . From these honored dead we take increased devotion to that cause for which they gave the last full measure of devotion."

To the backward and forward pendulum swing of a tall old clock in a quiet corner they might read those cadenced words while outside the windows the first flurry of snow blew across the orchard and down over the meadow, the beginnings of winter in a gun-metal gloaming to be later arched with a star-flung sky.

<hr/>

FOR UNDERSTANDING

1. What were Edward Everett's qualifications for being the principal orator at the dedication ceremonies? Why do you suppose Sandburg makes a point of telling how long it took Everett to prepare his speech?

2. Why did Sandburg tell in such detail what Lincoln did and said during the journey from Washington and in Gettysburg before the speech? What light is shed on Lincoln's character by the joke he told on the way to the train, the speech he made

to the serenaders, and his going next door to speak to Mr. Seward instead of having Seward come to him?

3. What concrete evidence did Sandburg give to show that Edward Everett gave a very good speech at Gettysburg? How did his success affect Lincoln's chance to make a good impression on the audience?

4. What was Lincoln's own evaluation of his speech? How would you explain the unfavorable opinion printed in the *Harrisburg Patriot and Union*? Can you point out one statement in that article that was particularly ironic? Contrast that review with those in the *Philadelphia Evening Bulletin* and the *Detroit Advertiser and Tribune*. What statement about speeches in general was made in the *Providence Journal*? If you agree with the statement, why do you think it is true?

5. In what way did Lincoln's reply to Everett's note show courtesy and consideration for others?

CONSIDERING THE SPEECH ITSELF

In the paragraph following the one about the trip back to Washington, Sandburg points out some of the things that make the Gettysburg Address a great speech. His comments should help you to a better understanding and appreciation of what Lincoln said. Find the passages in the speech that are referred to and explain what you think they mean.

1. For example, what do you think might be some of the "thousand interpretations" for the phrase "a new birth of freedom"? Which interpretation do you prefer?

2 What do you consider some of the "taller riddles of democracy"? Where are they referred to in the speech?

3. What were the "vast and furious events" that were "epitomized" in the speech? How does Lincoln show that the ceremonies at Gettysburg were related to the struggle for independence and to the ideals upon which the country was founded?

4. Sandburg says of Lincoln: "He did not assume that the drafted soldiers, substitutes, and bounty-paid privates had died willingly under Lee's shot and shell, in deliberate consecration of themselves to the Union cause." If you agree with Sandburg tell why you think the speech would have been less effective if Lincoln had represented the soldiers as eager to die for their country.

5. In referring to the speech, Sandburg mentions Lincoln's *cadences*—that is, his rhythmical language—and his "smooth sentences." Read the speech aloud or listen to someone else read it, and see if you can hear the cadences and sense the smoothness of the sentences. How do the rhythm, the type of sentence, and the choice of words fit the solemn theme and the lofty ideas of the speech?

FOR YOUR VOCABULARY

1. Examine the following pairs of words taken from the selection. Decide which, if any, are synonyms, or near synonyms; which are antonyms; and which belong to neither classification. Use the dictionary to check meanings of words about which you have any doubt.

a. serene	suave
b. imposing	impressive
c. dedication	consecration
d. slander	libel
e. notables	nondescripts

2. Show that you understand the exact meanings of the words in the pairs above that are neither synonyms nor antonyms by using each in an original sentence.

CARL SANDBURG (Born 1878)

For further information on this famous author, see pages 220–221.

Abraham Lincoln Walks at Midnight

VACHEL LINDSAY

It was from Springfield, Illinois, that Lincoln went to the White House in 1861, and after his assassination it was in Springfield that he was buried. Vachel Lindsay, born in this same town, found that Lincoln was often in his thoughts. When Lindsay thought about crises in modern history, and about the problems and misfortunes of the common people of the world, he remembered the great leader who had been concerned with such matters. It was almost like having a vision of Lincoln pacing the streets, still weighed down with the cares of mankind.

It is portentous, and a thing of state
That here at midnight, in our little town,
A mourning figure walks, and will not rest,
Near the old courthouse pacing up and down.

Or by his homestead, or in shadowed yards   5
He lingers where his children used to play,
Or through the market, on the well-worn stones
He stalks until the dawn-stars burn away.

A bronzed, lank man! His suit of ancient black,
A famous high top hat and plain worn shawl   10
Make him the quaint great figure that men love,
The prairie lawyer, master of us all.

He cannot sleep upon his hillside now.
He is among us—as in times before!
And we who toss and lie awake for long,   15
Breathe deep, and start, to see him pass the door.

His head is bowed. He thinks of men and kings.
Yea, when the sick world cries, how can he sleep?

1. IT IS PORTENTOUS—The expression means both "It is a thing to marvel at" and "It is for a reason."

Too many peasants fight, they know not why;
Too many homesteads in black terror weep.   20

The sins of all the war lords burn his heart.
He sees the dreadnaughts scouring every main.
He carries on his shawl-wrapped shoulders now
The bitterness, the folly and the pain.

He cannot rest until a spirit-dawn   25
Shall come—the shining hope of Europe free:
The league of sober folk, the Workers' Earth,
Bringing long peace to Cornland, Alp, and Sea.

It breaks his heart that kings must murder still,
That all his hours of travail here for men   30
Seem yet in vain. And who will bring white peace
That he may sleep upon his hill again?

FOR UNDERSTANDING

1. From earliest times the idea has existed that the spirits of the dead sometimes return—unable to forget whatever thing most concerned them in life. Have you ever heard or read a story about such a return from the grave? Where was it supposed to have occurred? What scene or past event was supposed to explain the appearance of the spirit?

2. This poem was written in 1914. Why might we imagine that in that year the spirit of Lincoln would be disturbed? Thinking of the circumstances of Lincoln's life, give reasons why he would be particularly concerned over the fate of the *ordinary people* like peasants and workers? There are several reasons.

3. What details of Lincoln's appearance are similar to details in Benét's poem "Abraham Lincoln"?

4. Line 15 speaks of "we who toss and lie awake," but the poet does not give any reason for their restlessness. What reason can you guess?

LINDSAY'S SYMBOLIC USE OF "LIGHT" AND "DARKNESS"

Ghosts are supposed to appear at night, and in this poem the time is midnight. The second stanza tells when Lincoln's spirit—as is usual in supernatural tales—will leave. However, in this poem *night* has also a deeper meaning. It is a symbol of war and the suffering caused by war. And just as Lincoln's spirit cannot cease from walking until the night is over, so, in a deeper sense, it cannot have permanent rest until the darkness of war has ended forever. Find two expressions in lines 25–28 which associate the idea of *peace* with the idea of *light*. Is this association made again in the final stanza? Can you see a new reason for one particular expression in line 20?

R. E. LEE

DOUGLAS SOUTHALL FREEMAN

Second highest in his class at West Point, young Robert E. Lee had quickly made a name for himself first as an army engineer and afterward as a cavalry officer. He possessed high character, shining ideals, and military genius. As war approached, both sides, North and South, wanted the services of this man who was the most brilliant soldier of his age.

Lee owed loyalty to the American Army, and he also owed loyalty to his own state of Virginia. Decision was forced on him early in 1861. The Federal government, following the advice of Lee's old friend and commander General Winfield Scott, made him a colonel. Within days, the Confederate government offered to make him a brigadier general—the highest rank in the Southern Army. In the first of the following selections from the biography by Douglas Southall Freeman, you will learn Lee's feelings during this fateful time, and you will learn also of his unwavering determination to follow what he believed to be his highest duty.

After the long years of slow promotion the honors were coming fast—a colonelcy in one army and a like offer of a generalship in the rival service, all in a breath! There is no record of any reply by Lee to this tender from the new Confederacy. It is probable that he ignored the offer, and it is certain that he was not lured by the promise of high position. He owned allegiance to only two governments, that of Virginia and that of the Union, and there could be no thought of a third so long as these two did not conflict and Virginia did not throw in her destiny with the Confederate States.

For a few days it seemed as if the conflict of allegiance might be avoided. As late as April 3 the expectation was general that Fort Sumter [1] would be evacuated and a clash avoided. On April 4 a test vote in the Virginia convention showed a majority of two-to-one against secession. Lee would not despair of the Union. He was for forbearance to the last, recognizing no necessity for recourse to arms. The maintenance of slavery meant nothing to him. He felt that if he owned all the slaves in the South he would cheerfully give them up to pre-

[1] FORT SUMTER—This Federal fort, in Charleston harbor, South Carolina, was blockaded by the Confederate forces. President Lincoln seemed uncertain whether to take military action against the states which began to secede from the Union immediately after he was elected. However, he could not ignore an attack on Fort Sumter—and on the other hand the Confederates were not willing to tolerate a garrison of Federal soldiers within their borders.

serve the Union. He would hold to the army and to the flag as long as he could in honor do so. But during those days of suspense, Lee was confirmed in his point of view. He had been determined from the outset that he would adhere to Virginia and defend her from any foe. Now, fully, he realized that though he considered secession neither more nor less than revolution, he could not bring himself to fight against the states that regarded secession as a right. He could not think of himself as fighting with the South against the Union, unless Virginia's defense were involved, but neither, as the possibility seemed to be brought nearer, could he reconcile himself to fighting with the Union against the South. "That beautiful feature of our landscape," he said sadly one day, as he pointed to the Capitol across the Potomac, "has ceased to charm me as much as formerly. I fear the mischief that is brewing there."

This was Lee's state of mind when, on April 7, his old comrade of Mexican days,[2] P. G. T. Beauregard, took a decisive step at Charleston, South Carolina, where he was then in command of the Confederate forces. Believing that Fort Sumter was about to be reinforced, Beauregard ordered supplies of fresh food cut off from the Federal garrison. The next day, April 8, a confidential messenger from President Lincoln announced to Governor Pickens of the Palmetto State[3] that Sumter would be revictualed[4] by United States ships. On the instant all the passions that had been rising since 1830 in South Carolina suddenly overflowed, and at daylight on April 12 the

bombardment of Fort Sumter began. On the 14th Sumter surrendered without the loss of a single life on either side. The next day, to a nation that had gone mad, Lincoln issued his proclamation calling for seventy-five thousand volunteers "to suppress combinations" and "to cause the laws to be duly executed."

The North and the South were arrayed, and blows had passed, though no blood had yet been shed—what would the border states do? What would be the action of Virginia? For the answer, Lee turned his eyes from Sumter to Richmond, where the convention was still in session. He was at a distance and knew little of the inner workings of that body. All his information was derived from the newspapers, which were too excited to be explicit.

Late on April 16, or on the 17th, he heard that the Virginia convention had gone into secret session. That was the only news from Richmond; but from Washington, on the 17th, there arrived a letter and a message. The letter bore Scott's[5] signature and requested Lee to call at his office on the 18th. The message was conveyed in a note from a Washington cousin, John Lee. It was that Francis P. Blair, Sr., a publicist of Lee's acquaintance, formerly editor of The Congressional Globe, desired Lee to meet him the next morning at his house in Washington.

What was afoot now? Were the two calls related? The answer, in its entirety, Lee did not learn during his lifetime. He never realized how anxious some men high in office and influence had been to save his services to the United States Army. In addition to what General Scott had done, Francis P. Blair, Sr., father of Colonel Lee's Missouri friend,

[2] MEXICAN DAYS—A reference to the Mexican War (1846–48).
[3] PALMETTO STATE—A nickname for South Carolina.
[4] REVICTUALED (rē·vǐt′ld)—Resupplied with food.
[5] SCOTT—General Winfield Scott, Lieutenant General in the United States Army.

Montgomery Blair, had been at work. He had been to President Lincoln, who had authorized him to "ascertain Lee's intentions and feelings." Blair had also discussed the subject with Secretary Cameron [6] and had been directed by him to make a proposition to Lee. It was to explain this that Blair had sent the message to Arlington. [7]

Duly on the morning of April 18 Lee rode over the bridge and up to the younger Blair's house on Pennsylvania Avenue, directly opposite the State, War, and Navy Building, where he found the old publicist awaiting him. They sat down behind closed doors. Blair promptly and plainly explained his reason for asking Lee to call. A large army, he said, was soon to be called into the field to enforce the federal law; the President had authorized him to ask Lee if he would accept the command.

Command of an army of seventy-five thousand, perhaps one hundred thousand men; opportunity to apply all he had learned in Mexico; the supreme ambition of a soldier realized; the full support of the government; many of his ablest comrades working with him; rank as a major general—all this may have surged through Lee's mind for an instant, but if so, it was only for an instant. Then his Virginia background and the mental discipline of years asserted themselves. He had said: "If the Union is dissolved and the government disrupted, I shall return to my native state and share the miseries of my people and save in defence will draw my sword on none." There he stood, and in that spirit, after listening to all Blair had to say, he made the fateful reply that is best given in his own

[6] SECRETARY CAMERON—Simon Cameron, Secretary of War.
[7] ARLINGTON—Lee's home across the Potomac from Washington, D. C.

simple account of the interview: "I declined the offer he made me to take command of the army that was to be brought into the field, stating as candidly and as courteously as I could, that though opposed to secession and deprecating war, I could take no part in an invasion of the Southern States." That was all, as far as Lee was concerned. He had long before decided, instinctively, what his duty required of him, and the allurement of supreme command, with all that a soldier craved, did not tempt him to equivocate for an instant or to see if there were not some way he could keep his own honor and still have the honor he understood the President had offered him. Blair talked on in a futile hope of converting Lee, but it was to no purpose.

Bidding farewell to Blair, Lee went directly to Scott's office. He sensed Scott's deep interest in his action, and as soon as he arrived he told him what Blair had offered and what he had answered. "Lee," said Scott, deeply moved, "you have made the greatest mistake of your life; but I feared it would be so."

Deep as was the difference between the two men on a public question that made personal enemies of many lifelong friends, Scott did not stop with this sad observation, but expressed the belief that if Lee were going to resign he ought not to delay. "There are times," Scott is reported to have said, "when every officer in the United States service should fully determine what course he will pursue and frankly declare it. No one should continue in government employ without being actively employed." And again, "I suppose you will go with the rest. If you purpose to resign, it is proper that you should do so at once; your present attitude is equivocal."

This added a complication that Lee pondered as he left his old commander

for the last time. He loved the army and the Union too well to leave either until he was in honor compelled to do so. Though willing to resign rather than to fight against the South, he had clung to the hope that he would not have to act unless Virginia seceded and the people voted affirmatively on an ordinance of secession. But Scott had now said that he should not remain in the army if he was unwilling to perform active duty. Those seventy-five thousand soldiers, of whom Blair had talked, would not have been asked of the states if they had not been intended for early service in the field. And if they were so intended, Lee, as an officer of the army, might be called upon immediately for duty he could not conscientiously perform. Then he would have to resign under orders. That was a disgrace to any soldier.

As his brother Smith was on duty in Washington, Lee stopped to discuss this new question with him. They could come to no immediate conclusion on it and parted in the expectation of meeting again before either of them took any action. At length, over the route he had so often traveled, Lee rode out of Washington, across the bridge and up the quiet hills to the home whose white columns he could see for most of the way. He was never again to make that journey in that same fashion. The next time he was to cross the Potomac, it was to be upstream, from the South, with bands playing and a victorious, a cheering army around him.

But he did not leave his problem behind him as he turned his back on his country's capital. He carried it with him; he wrestled with it. Was his position equivocal? Ought he to resign at once, regardless of what Virginia did? He felt that Scott was right, but his own mind was so opposed to secession, and his devotion to the Union and to the army proved so strong, now it was put to the test, that he delayed the actual writing of his resignation, hoping against hope.

All this time he had not known what had happened after the Virginia convention had gone into secret session on the 16th. *The Washington Star* of April 18 contained an unverified report that the Virginia convention had passed an ordinance of secession and had caused three ships to be sunk at the mouth of the Elizabeth River, but *The Alexandria Gazette* of the same day contained a dispatch from Richmond, dated April 17, 5:00 P.M., affirming that the convention was still in secret session and that no ordinance withdrawing the state from the Union had been passed.

The next morning, April 19, Lee went into Alexandria on business, and there he read the news he had hoped he would never see: Virginia had seceded! To his mind that meant the wreck of the nation, "the beginning of sorrows," the opening of a war that was certain to be long and full of horrors. But of all that he thought and felt in the first realization that his mother state had left the Union, his only recorded observation is one he made to a druggist when he went into a shop to pay a bill. "I must say," he remarked sadly, "that I am one of those dull creatures that cannot see the good of secession."

If Lee had any doubt of the truth of the report in the Alexandria paper that morning, it was soon removed. That afternoon, *The Washington Star* took the news for granted. By nightfall on the 19th, Lee had no alternative to believing it. When other hopes had failed him before this time, Lee had told himself that secession could not become an accomplished fact until the voters of Vir-

ginia had passed on the ordinance of secession, as they had specifically reserved the right to do, but now Lee's judgment told him that war would not wait on a referendum.[8] Virginia would certainly consider that her safety required the seizure of Federal depots within her borders. Had not Texas similarly provided for a referendum on secession, and had not he, with his own eyes, seen how the Texas committee of safety had committed an act of war by seizing United States property without waiting for the people to confirm or disavow the ordinance of the convention? The Federal government, for its part, would certainly take prompt action since the state just across the river from its capital had left the Union. As one of the senior field officers in Washington, he might be summoned at any hour to defend Washington by invading Virginia—which he could not do. Duty was plain. There could be no holding back. The time had come. All the Lees had been Americans, but they had been Virginians first. From Richard the emigrant [9] onward, the older allegiance had been paramount with each of them until the Revolution came. Had not his own father called Virginia "my native country"? In a crisis that seemed in his day to threaten the Union, had not "Light-Horse Harry" [10] said: "Should my efforts . . . be unavailing, I shall lament my country's fate and acquiesce in my country's will . . ."? Now revolu-

[8] REFERENDUM (rĕf'ĕr·ĕn'dŭm)—A special ballot by voters on a proposed measure.

[9] RICHARD THE EMIGRANT—Richard Lee, the first of the family to come to America, remained loyal to the British ruling family after the Puritans executed Charles I in 1649.

[10] LIGHT-HORSE HARRY—General Henry Lee, hero of the American Revolution and the father of R. E. Lee. In 1798, when Virginia seemed about to secede from the newly formed nation, "Light-Horse Harry" opposed such action but at the same time announced that he would stand by his native state, whatever its decision.

R. E. LEE

tion and the older allegiance were the same. The son must be as the sire. Washington, his great model, had embraced a revolutionary cause. Dearly as Lee loved the Union, anxious as he was to see it preserved, he could not bear arms against the South. Virginia had seceded and doubtless would join the South; her action controlled his; he could not wait for the uncertain vote of the people when war was upon him. So after midnight on the 19th he sat down and wrote this letter, not more than fifteen hours after he had received positive information that Virginia had seceded:

> Arlington, Virginia
> (Washington City P.O.)
> 20 April 1861.
>
> Hon. Simon Cameron
> Secty of War
> Sir:
> I have the honor to tender the resignation of my commission as Colonel of the 1st Regt. of Cavalry.
> Very resp'y Your Obedient Servant.
> R. E. Lee
> Col. 1st Cav'y.

His resignation was not prompted by passion, nor did it carry with it resentment against the Union he left. On the contrary, if there was any resentment, it was against the authors, Northern and Southern, of the consummate wickedness of bringing about division within the Union. There was a pang and a heartache at the separation from brother officers whose patriotism he had seen vindicated in the hardships of campaigning and in the dangers of battle. He was willing to defend Virginia, whatever her allegiance, but he did not desire to fight against the flag under which he had served. If he must see the Union wrecked by men who would not forbear and plead for justice through constitutional means, if he must tear himself

from the service of a nation of which he had been proud, then the hope of his heart was that he might never again be called to draw a sword which only Virginia could command. It was in this spirit that he wrote farewell to General Scott, that loyal old friend, who had admired him, taught him, and advanced him. He penned this letter:

> Arlington, Va., April 20, 1861.
> General:
> Since my interview with you on the 18th inst.[11] I have felt that I ought no longer to retain my commission in the Army. I therefore tender my resignation, which I request you will recommend for acceptance. I would have presented it at once, but for the struggle it has cost me to separate myself from a service to which I have devoted all the best years of my life and all the ability I possessed.
> During the whole of that time—more than a quarter of a century—I have experienced nothing but kindness from my superiors and a most cordial friendship from my comrades. To no one, General, have I been as much indebted as to yourself for uniform kindness and consideration, and it has always been my ardent desire to meet your approbation. I shall carry to the grave the most grateful recollections of your kind consideration, and your name and fame will always be dear to me.
> Save in defence of my native State, I never desire again to draw my sword.
> Be pleased to accept my most earnest wishes for the continuance of your happiness and prosperity, and believe me, most truly yours,
> R. E. Lee.

He came downstairs when he had finished the letters. Mrs. Lee was waiting for him. She had heard him pacing in the room above her and had thought she had heard him fall on his knees in prayer. "Well, Mary," he said calmly, "the ques-

[11] INST.—Instant; a word used with dates in referring to the current month.

tion is settled. Here is my letter of resignation and a letter I have written General Scott."

She understood. Months later she wrote a friend, "My husband has wept tears of blood over this terrible war, but as a man of honor and a Virginian, he must follow the destiny of his state." The other members of the family understood, also. Arlington became as still and gloomy as if a death had occurred, because as one of his daughters confided to a kinswoman the following Sunday, "the army was to him home and country." Rooney, who hastened to consult his father as soon as the state seceded, was in deep depression as he saw how jubilant the people were. They had lost their senses, he held, and had no conception of what a terrible mistake they were making. Custis [12] was no believer in secession. Had he been able to dictate policy, he said, he would have called the movement revolution and would forthwith have seized and fortified Arlington Heights.

Lee dispatched his resignation to General Scott that morning, probably by special messenger, and before night it had been forwarded to the Secretary of War.

After he had sent off the paper, he sat down to explain his act to his sister, Mrs. Marshall, and to his brother Smith. Mrs. Marshall's husband was Unionist in his sympathies. Her son Louis was now a captain in the United States Army. She herself sided with her husband and son, though she could not quite forget her Virginia uprearing. Lee took her situation into account and wrote her as tactfully as he could:

Arlington, Virginia, April 20, 1861.
My Dear Sister:
I am grieved at my inability to see you.

[12] CUSTIS—Lee's son Custis was an officer in the United States Army.

. . . I have been waiting for a "more convenient season," which has brought to many before me deep and lasting regret. Now we are in a state of war which will yield to nothing. The whole South is in a state of revolution, into which Virginia, after a long struggle, has been drawn; and, though I recognize no necessity for this state of things, and would have forborne and pleaded to the end for a redress of grievances, real or supposed, yet in my own person I had to meet the question whether I should take part against my native state.

With all my devotion to the Union and the feeling of loyalty and duty of an American citizen, I have not been able to make up my mind to raise my hand against my relatives, my children, my home. I have therefore resigned my commission in the Army, and save in defence of my native state, with the sincere hope that my poor services may never be needed, I hope I may never be called on to draw my sword. I know you will blame me; but you must think as kindly of me as you can, and believe that I have endeavored to do what I thought right.

To show you the feeling and struggle it has cost me, I send you a copy of my letter of resignation. I have no time for more. May God guard and protect you and yours and shower upon you everlasting blessings, is the prayer of your devoted brother,
R. E. Lee.

He had left Smith Lee on the 18th with the understanding that they would confer again regarding their course of action. He therefore wrote to explain why he had resigned before consulting with him further:

Arlington, Virginia, April 20, 1861.
My Dear Brother Smith:
The question which was the subject of my earnest consultation with you on the 18th inst., has in my own mind been decided. After the most anxious inquiry as to the correct course for me to pursue, I concluded to resign, and sent in my resigna-

tion this morning. I wished to wait until the Ordinance of Secession should be acted on by the people of Virginia; but war seems to have commenced, and I am liable at any time to be ordered on duty, which I could not conscientiously perform. To save me from such a position and to prevent the necessity of resigning under orders, I had to act at once, and before I could see you again on the subject, as I had wished. I am now a private citizen, and have no other ambition than to remain at home. Save in defence of my native state, I have no desire ever again to draw my sword. I send you my warmest love.

Your affectionate brother,
R. E. Lee.

Lee gave no advice to Smith regarding his own course, nor did he counsel Custis, who was as loath as he to quit the service of the United States. "Tell Custis," he subsequently wrote, "he must consult his own judgment, reason and conscience as to the course he may take. I do not wish him to be guided by my wishes or example. If I have done wrong, let him do better. The present is a momentous question which every man must settle for himself and upon principle."

When he took up his daily paper, *The Alexandria Gazette*, it was to discover that others beside himself were interested in the action he had taken. For an editorial article read as follows:

It is probable that the secession of Virginia will cause an immediate resignation of many officers of the Army and Navy from this State. We do not know, and have no right to speak for or anticipate the course of Colonel Robert E. Lee. Whatever he may do, will be conscientious and honorable. But if he should resign his present position in the Army of the United States, we call the immediate attention of our State to him, as an able, brave, experienced officer—no man his superior in all that constitutes the soldier and the gentleman—no

man more worthy to head our forces and lead our army. There is no man who would command more of the confidence of the people of Virginia, than this distinguished officer; and no one under whom the volunteers and militia would more gladly rally. His reputation, his acknowledged ability, his chivalric character, his probity,[13] honor, and—may we add, to his eternal praise—his Christian life and conduct—make his very name a "tower of strength." It is a name surrounded by revolutionary and patriotic associations and reminiscences.

It was not a pleasant article for a modest man to read, and it was disquieting, besides, with its assurance that some, at least, were looking to him to lead the army of Virginia, against the Union and the old flag, if war came. . . . He could only pray it would not.

During the day Lee saw his neighbor and friend, John B. Daingerfield, and showed him a copy of his letter of resignation. The rest of that fateful 20th of April was doubtless spent at Arlington. Nothing of consequence occurred except the receipt, late in the evening, of a letter from Judge John Robertson, of Richmond. The judge was then in Alexandria and asked for an interview the next day. Lee set one o'clock as the hour and offered to meet him in town. Meantime, Lee waited and pondered. Surrounded by objects familiar through thirty years of tender association, and with his invalid wife in her chair, he must have realized that if hostilities came, war and invasion would soon bring Arlington within the lines of the Union Army. The Federals could not long permit so commanding a position, so close to the capital, to remain unguarded. But in none of his letters prior to his resignation and in none of his reported conversation is there even a hint that he had any selfish regard for the fate of Arlington,

[13] PROBITY (prŏb′ĭ·tĭ)—Honesty.

either in delaying his resignation until Virginia's secession, or in deciding to leave the army when he did.

Sunday morning, April 21, dressed in civilian clothes, Lee went into Alexandria with one of his daughters to attend service at Christ Church. The town was wild. Overwhelmingly Southern in their sentiment, the people rejoiced at the secession of Virginia as if it meant deliverance from bondage. In their enthusiasm they fancied they were repeating the drama of 1776 and that the spirit of a Washington gave its benediction to a new revolution.

In all this rejoicing Lee took no part. His resignation was not generally known as yet, though his neighbors and friends had been waiting to see what he would do. His sorrow, his sense of the fitness of things, and his knowledge that war would be long and terrible kept him from any statement of his action. In the church, as he prayed, it must have been for his divided country. When the Psalter for the morning of the twenty-first day was read, he doubtless felt there was more than coincidence in these verses and the responses:

13 What time as they went from one nation to another: from one kingdom to another people;
14 He suffered no man to do them wrong; but reproved even kings for their sakes. . . .

At length the service was over. The congregation stopped to talk of the inevitable theme, and then straggled slowly into the churchyard. When Lee reached the open air he became engaged in serious conversation with three men, who were unknown to the congregation and whose identity has never been established. His neighbors and friends thought the strangers were commissioners from the

governor of Virginia, but it seems more probable that they were companions of Judge Robertson, who explained that the judge had gone to Washington and had been detained there but would soon arrive to keep his appointment. Lee had not been in communication with the state convention or with the governor. He had no information as to the military plans. Perhaps the visitors acquainted him with what had happened and intimated that his service was desired by his mother state, but in Judge Roberston's absence there could have been nothing official. Lee waited and chatted several hours and then, concluding that Robertson would not return, rode back to Arlington.

That evening a messenger arrived at the mansion with a letter from Robertson. He apologized for his delay and—this was the important item—invited Lee, in the name of the governor, to repair to Richmond for conference with the chief executive. Lee realized, of course, that this meant participation in the defense of Virginia, but he did not hesitate an hour. The very reason that had impelled him to resign from the United States Army, his allegiance to Virginia, prompted him to sit down at once and to write an answer to Robertson. Virginia's action in withdrawing from the Union carried him with her, and if she called him now it was his duty to obey. In a few words he notified the governor's representative that he would join him in Alexandria the next day in time to take the train for Richmond. There was no questioning, no holding back, no delay. The road from Arlington, though lit with glory, led straight to Appomattox.[14] But Lee never re-

[14] APPOMATTOX (ăp'ô·măt'ŭks)—General Lee's surrender at Appomatox, Virginia, in 1865 marked the final defeat of the Confederate cause.

gretted his action, never even admitted that he had made a choice. With the war behind him, with the South desolate and disfranchised, and with her sons dead on a hundred battlefields, he was to look back with soul unshaken and was to say: "I did only what my duty demanded. I could have taken no other course without dishonor. And if it all were to be done over again, I should act in precisely the same manner."

[*In the third winter of the war things were beginning to go badly with the Army of Northern Virginia, commanded by General Lee. Even under his leadership the army could not stand up forever against superior numbers. Food and other supplies were becoming scarce. Yet the fighting spirit of the men remained high. There were several reasons for their good morale—their memory of earlier victories, their sense of humor, their religious faith. And there was still another cause—*]

Lee himself was a force no less potent in preserving the morale of the army. His methods were as simple as they were effective. They reflected his own character and his interest in the welfare of the men entrusted to him, and in no sense did they bespeak any ordered, calculating analysis of what would or would not inspire soldiers. He rode frequently among the camps, alone or attended by only one or two staff officers. Sometimes the men would cheer him; more often they received him with a silence that was almost reverent. Yet they never hesitated to bring him their complaints, in the knowledge that he would always receive them as friends in a common cause. During the Gettysburg campaign, as Lee stood by a road along which a column

of half-exhausted men were marching under a singeing sun, a stout private broke ranks and approached him. Some of the staff turned the man back, but Lee told them to let him come to him. "What is it you want?" he said kindly. The soldier, who was perspiring in streams, answered quickly, "Please, General, I don't want much, but it's powerful wet marching this weather. I can't see for the water in my eyes. I came aside to this old hill to get a rag or something to wipe the sweat out of my eyes." Lee immediately took out his handkerchief and handed it to him. "Will this do?" he inquired. "Yes, my Lordy, that indeed!" the man exclaimed. "Well, then," Lee answered encouragingly, "take it with you, and back quick to ranks; no straggling this march, you know, my man." General Sorrel, who witnessed this typical incident, said in comment on it, "Lee's talk and manner with the soldier were inimitable [15] in their encouraging kindness."

John H. Worsham recalled that after the campaign of 1864 opened, Lee chanced again to be by the roadside, mounted on Traveller [16] while some of his veterans were on the march. "As our column approached him," he wrote, "an old private stepped out of ranks and advanced to General Lee. They shook hands like acquaintances and entered into a lively conversation. As I moved on I looked back, and the old man had his gun in one hand and the other hand on Traveller's neck, still talking."

Lee was as simple with the farmers of the countryside as he was with his soldiers. On one of the advances of the army, a farmer rode up to bivouac [17] where Lee was sitting and addressed him as "colonel," not guessing his identity.

[15] INIMITABLE (ĭn·ĭm'ĭ·tá·b'l)—Matchless.
[16] TRAVELLER—Lee's famous saddle horse.
[17] BIVOUAC (bĭv'wăk)—Encampment.

Lee put him at his ease and chatted with him for some time. At length the planter told the "colonel" that he had come to the army in the hope of seeing General Lee and wondered if it was possible for him to do so. "I am General Lee," his host replied, "and I am most happy to have met you." While he was on the Rappahannock,[18] a soldier called at Lee's tent, with his wife. Lee invited the couple in and soon learned all about them by friendly questions. "She was from Abbeville district, South Carolina," he enthusiastically wrote Mrs. Lee that night. "Said she had not seen her husband for more than two years, and, as he had written to her for clothes, she herself thought she would bring them on. It was the first time she had traveled by railroad, but she got along very well by herself. She brought an entire suit of her own manufacture for her husband. She spun the yarn and made the clothes herself. She clad her three children in the same way, and had on a beautiful pair of gloves she had made for herself. Her children she had left with her sister. . . . She was very pleasing in her address and modest in her manner, and was clad in a nice, new alpaca. I am certain she could not have made that. . . . She, in fact, was an admirable woman. Said she was willing to give up everything she had in the world to attain our independence, and the only complaint she made of the conduct of our enemies was their arming our servants against us. Her greatest difficulty was to procure shoes. She made them for herself and children of cloth with leather soles. She sat with me about ten minutes and took her leave—another mark of sense—and made no request for herself or husband."

With the courtesy he showed this woman, he welcomed all visitors, humble in station or exalted in rank. Only those who came to appeal from the verdict of courts-martial and those who importuned him for promotion found access to him difficult. If an officer wrote him in protest at the elevation of someone else, or in complaint of his failure to receive recognition, Lee would turn the paper over to one of his staff with the request, " 'Suage him,[19] Colonel; 'suage him." If he could avoid it without discourtesy, he would not grant an interview to such an officer. Once, after a man with a grievance had insisted on seeing him, Lee came out of his quarters with a flushed face and exclaimed to Colonel Venable, "Why did you permit that man to come to my tent and make me show my temper?"

Lee's respect for the individuality of his men extended to their wants and their duties. He was quick to defend them against discrimination and against imposition. The sutlers[20] who set themselves up at Orange Courthouse during the winter were, in the main, a grasping lot, and they became so exorbitant in their charges that the men rose against them and plundered their wares. In plaintive indignation the sutlers hurried to General Lee to ask protection for the future. He heard their protests with his wonted patience and ended by putting this question to them: "You think that the boys treated you badly?" The sutlers were of one mind: "Outrageously, General," they insisted, "outrageously." Lee looked at them: "Had you not, then, better set up shop somewhere else?" They did. On the other hand, he investigated every just grievance, and when a prisoner complained to him that the

[18] RAPPAHANNOCK (răp′á·hăn′ŭk)—A river in Virginia.

[19] 'SUAGE HIM—Assuage him—that is, appease or soothe him.

[20] SUTLERS (sŭt′lẽrz)—Followers of an army who sell liquor, food, etc., to the soldiers.

soldiers had abused and taunted him, Lee was instant in his reproof.

The spiritual needs of his men he supplied, also, as best he could. Some of his generals, less religious in nature than he, fell into the habit of making Sunday a time for reviews and festivities. Two of the chaplains came to Lee and tactfully asked that military duties on the Sabbath Day be reduced to the necessary minimum. Lee made no promises but let the conversation drift to the progress of the revivals.[21] One of the clergymen noted that as they told Lee of what was happening, "we saw his eye brighten and his whole countenance glow with pleasure." When the ministers rose to leave, the spokesman stated, "I think it right that I should say to you, General, that the chaplains of this army have a deep interest in your welfare, and that some of the most fervent prayers we offer are in your behalf." Lee flushed, and tears came into his eyes. He choked for a moment and then, with the directness that would have been cant[22] in a soul

less simple than his, he replied, "Please thank them for that, sir. I warmly appreciate it. And I can only say that I am nothing but a poor sinner, trusting in Christ alone for salvation, and need all the prayers they can offer for me." The next day he issued a general order for the better observance of the Sabbath. He went regularly to church, and not infrequently, when his duties did not press too heavily, he attended the chaplains' meetings.

His regard for his men was, of course, known to them, and when coupled with their respect for him as a soldier, it produced in them something akin to the idolatry of youth for greatness. After one of his battles, Lee met a soldier who was coming from the front with a shattered right arm. "I grieve for you, my poor fellow," Lee said, "can I do anything for you?" The soldier answered, "Yes, sir, you can shake hands with me, General, if you will consent to take my left hand." Lee grasped his powder-stained hand warmly—with an admiration he made no effort to conceal.

Late in the winter a scout arrived at headquarters with newspapers and reports of a heavy eastward movement of troop trains along the Baltimore and

[21] REVIVALS—During the winter of 1863–64, revival meetings were held in the Confederate army camps. A great many soldiers became church members.
[22] CANT (kănt)—Insincere religious phrases.

Ohio. The scout, who was only a boy in years, had ridden one horse to death in order to reach Lee speedily and was close to collapse. Lee listened to him and left him for a moment to issue an order. When he returned, he found that the boy had toppled over from his camp-stool and had fallen half on the General's cot, in the deep sleep of exhaustion. Lee covered him, walked out of the tent, tied the flap and left him alone until his cramped position caused him to awaken, two hours later. Then the General supplied him with food and saw to it that he received proper care. Incidents of this sort became known to the army and explain in part why it was that in March, 1864, when he was in Richmond, the men who were waiting at the transportation office heard of his presence in the city and with many a "God-bless-him," inquired where they could see him. But perhaps the best tribute to him was paid one night when some of the infantry were discussing *The Origin of Species*, which had been published less than four years. Darwinism had its warm advocates,[23] but one soldier refused to accept the arguments. "Well, boys," he said, "the rest of us may have developed from monkeys; but I tell you none less than God could have made such a man as 'Marse Robert.' "[24]

[23] ITS WARM ADVOCATES—Its backers, those who agreed with Darwin's theory of evolution.
[24] 'MARSE ROBERT'—"Master Robert," an affectionate nickname for General Lee.

◇◇◇◇◇◇◇◇◇◇◇◇◇◇◇◇◇◇◇◇◇◇◇◇◇◇◇◇◇◇

FOR UNDERSTANDING

1. What was Lee's attitude toward slavery? toward preserving the union? At the beginning of this selection, Lee had just been made a colonel in the United States Army. At almost the same time he was offered a high rank in the Confederate Army. What was the only condition under which he would be willing to fight for the Confederate government?

2. What incident brought about actual war between North and South? What was Lee's feeling about the outbreak of war?

3. On April 18, 1861, Colonel Lee was offered a much higher post in the United States Army than that of colonel. What was it? Explain why he felt it necessary to refuse the offer.

4. What action did Lee take the next day after learning that Virginia had joined other states in seceding from the Union? Explain why this action was difficult for him to take. Why do you suppose his letter to General Scott was so much longer, and so much more detailed, than his letter to the Secretary of War?

5. On Sunday evening, April 21, private citizen Robert E. Lee received an invitation to go to Richmond for a conference with the governor of Virginia. What would the conference be about? Did Lee accept the invitation?

6. In deciding what he would do, Lee was guided by one loyalty which was stronger than all others for him. What was it? Looking back after the war was over, did he feel that he had made an unwise decision?

7. Give two examples of Lee's thoughtful and kindly treatment of the common soldiers in his army. What evidence can you give that the soldiers realized that they could approach the general and expect to be received in a friendly manner?

8. The soldier who had lost his right arm in battle, and who felt apologetic about shaking hands with General Lee with his left hand, showed in an extreme form the reverent attitude of the Southern troops toward their leader. Mention another incident which showed a similar attitude.

BIOGRAPHERS' USE OF SOURCE MATERIALS

By the use of *source materials*, modern biographers and historians restudy past events and try to understand them more fully than they were understood by earlier writers. Some of the materials used by Douglas Southall Freeman in his life of Lee were government records; old newspapers; letters; diaries; and the testimony of people who participated in the War Between the States and wrote down their experiences from memory. Using such sources, Mr. Freeman was able to reconstruct some periods of Robert E. Lee's life day by day. In the full-length biography, footnotes show the reader the source of each item of information. The book gives us an authoritative picture of Lee's mind and character; of the time in which he lived; and of the specific events in which Lee played a part.

1. Give two examples of *personal letters* used in the biography. To whom was each letter written, and what was its subject?

2. Give one example of a *letter to a government official* used in the biography. What was it about?

3. What attitude of Virginians toward Lee does Mr. Freeman show by quoting from *The Alexandria Gazette?*

4. On April 19, 1861, Lee learned that Virginia had seceded from the Union. On the same day he remarked to a druggist that he could not "see the good of secession." How do you suppose Lee's words to the druggist are known?

DOUGLAS SOUTHALL FREEMAN

(1886–1953)

Douglas Southall Freeman's father had been a private in Lee's army, and all his life the son was interested in the history of the War Between the States. He was trained as a scholar, receiving his doctor's degree in history at Johns Hopkins University in 1908. He entered newspaper work, and in 1915 became editor of the Richmond, Virginia, *News Leader*—a position he held many years.

The first notable work Freeman did as a historian was to edit the confidential army dispatches from General Lee to President Jefferson Davis. His work with these important papers, never before published, made him an authority on strategy and operations of the war. After nineteen years of research and writing, Freeman published his four-volume *R. E. Lee.* Recognized at once as the outstanding book on its subject, the biography won its author the Pulitzer Prize in 1934.

His lectures, his duties as an officer of numerous organizations and educational institutions, and his work on the *News Leader* made great demands on Freeman's time. For years, besides doing his editorial work he made two daily newscasts for his paper. Yet by strict budgeting of his day, by hard work, and by phenomenal energy he was able to continue studying and writing. *Lee's Lieutenants*, on the brilliant generals who served under Lee, is one of his greatest books. The last years of his life were spent in finishing his life of Washington, of which Volumes I and II, *Young Washington*, had been published in 1948.

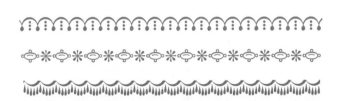

A MYSTERY OF HEROISM

STEPHEN CRANE

The people in this story do not seem to be "story book" characters. They talk, act, and think just as any of us would in the same situation. Furthermore, the scene seems very real. The little, commonplace details, as well as the big, important ones, stand out and catch our attention as if we had taken shelter from cannon fire, along with the soldiers of A Company, against the side of a hill. Notice how the author "builds up" the total picture out of many specific sights and sounds—for each, using the expression that precisely describes it. Selecting one small episode from the War Between the States, he lets us experience all the sensations of battle.

The dark uniforms of the men were so coated with dust from the incessant wrestling of the two armies that the regiment almost seemed a part of the clay bank which shielded them from the shells. On the top of the hill a battery was arguing in tremendous roars with some other guns, and to the eye of the infantry the artillerymen, the guns, the caissons, the horses, were distinctly outlined upon the blue sky. When a piece was fired, a red streak as round as a log flashed low in the heavens, like a monstrous bolt of lightning. The men of the battery wore white duck trousers, which somehow emphasized their legs; and when they ran and crowded in little groups at the bidding of the shouting officers, it was more impressive than usual to the infantry.

Fred Collins, of A Company, was saying: "Thunder! I wisht I had a drink. Ain't there any water here?" Then somebody yelled: "There goes th' bugler!"

As the eyes of half the regiment swept in one machinelike movement, there was an instant's picture of a horse in a great convulsive leap of a death wound and a rider leaning back with a crooked arm and spread fingers before his face. On the ground was the crimson terror of an exploding shell, with fibers of flame that seemed like lances. A glittering bugle swung clear of the rider's back as fell headlong the horse and the man. In the air was an odor as from a conflagration.

Sometimes they of the infantry looked down at a fair little meadow which spread at their feet. Its long green grass was rippling gently in a breeze. Beyond it was the gray form of a house half torn to pieces by shells and by the busy axes of soldiers who had pursued firewood. The line of an old fence was now dimly marked by long weeds and by an occasional post. A shell had blown the well house to fragments. Little lines of gray smoke ribboning upward from some embers indicated the place where had stood the barn.

From beyond a curtain of green woods there came the sound of some stupendous scuffle, as if two animals of the size of islands were fighting. At a distance there were occasional appearances of swift-moving men, horses, batteries, flags, and with the crashing of infantry volleys were heard, often, wild and frenzied cheers. In the midst of it all Smith and Ferguson, two privates of A Company, were engaged in a heated discussion which involved the greatest questions of the national existence.

The battery on the hill presently engaged in a frightful duel. The white legs of the gunners scampered this way and that, and the officers redoubled their shouts. The guns, with their demeanors of stolidity and courage, were typical of something infinitely self-possessed in this clamor of death that swirled around the hill.

One of a "swing" team [1] was suddenly smitten quivering to the ground, and his maddened brethren dragged his torn body in their struggle to escape from this turmoil and danger. A young soldier astride one of the leaders swore and fumed in his saddle and furiously jerked at the bridle. An officer screamed out an order so violently that his voice broke and ended the sentence in a falsetto shriek.

The leading company of infantry regiment was somewhat exposed, and the colonel ordered it moved more fully under the shelter of the hill. There was the clank of steel against steel.

A lieutenant of the battery rode down and passed them holding his right arm carefully in his left hand. And it was as if this arm was not at all a part of him, but belonged to another man. His sober and reflective charger went slowly. The officer's face was grimy and perspiring, and his uniform was tousled as if he had been in direct grapple with an enemy. He smiled grimly when the men stared at him. He turned his horse toward the meadow.

Collins, of A Company, said: "I wisht I had a drink. I bet there's water in that there ol' well yonder!"

"Yes; but how you goin' to git it?"

For the little meadow which intervened was now suffering a terrible onslaught of shells. Its green and beautiful calm had vanished utterly. Brown earth was being flung in monstrous handfuls. And there was a massacre of the young blades of grass. They were being torn, burned, obliterated. Some curious fortune of the battle had made this gentle little meadow the object of the red hate of the shells, and each one as it exploded seemed like an imprecation [2] in the face of a maiden.

The wounded officer who was riding across this expanse said to himself: "Why, they couldn't shoot any harder if the whole army was massed here!"

A shell struck the gray ruins of the house, and as, after the roar, the shattered wall fell in fragments, there was a noise which resembled the flapping of shutters during a wild gale of winter. Indeed, the infantry paused in the shelter of the bank appeared as men standing upon a shore contemplating a madness of the sea. The angel of calamity had under its glance the battery upon the hill. Fewer white-legged men labored about the guns. A shell had smitten one of the pieces, and after the flare, the smoke, the dust, the wrath of this blow were gone, it was possible to see white legs stretched horizontally upon the ground. And at that interval to the rear where it is the business of battery horses to stand with their noses to the fight, awaiting the command to drag their guns out of the destruction, or into it, or wheresoever these incomprehensible humans demanded with whip and spur— in this line of passive and dumb spec-

[1] "SWING" TEAM—The second pair of six horses when hitched one pair behind another.

[2] IMPRECATION—A curse.

tators, whose fluttering hearts yet would not let them forget the iron laws of man's control of them—in this rank of brute-soldiers there had been relentless and hideous carnage. From the ruck [3] of bleeding and prostrate horses, the men of the infantry could see one animal raising its stricken body with its forelegs and turning its nose with mystic and profound eloquence toward the sky.

Some comrades joked Collins about his thirst. "Well, if yeh want a drink so bad, why don't yeh go git it?"

"Well, I will in a minnet, if yeh don't shut up!"

A lieutenant of artillery floundered his horse straight down the hill with as little concern as if it were level ground. As he galloped past the colonel of the infantry, he threw up his hand in swift salute. "We've got to get out of that," he roared angrily. He was a black-bearded officer, and his eyes, which resembled beads, sparkled like those of an insane man. His jumping horse sped along the column of infantry.

The fat major, standing carelessly with his sword held horizontally behind him and with his legs far apart, looked after the receding horseman and laughed. "He wants to get back with orders pretty quick, or there'll be no batt'ry left," he observed.

The wise young captain of the second company hazarded to the lieutenant colonel that the enemy's infantry would probably soon attack the hill, and the lieutenant colonel snubbed him.

A private in one of the rear companies looked out over the meadow, and then turned to a companion and said, "Look there, Jim!" It was the wounded officer from the battery, who some time before had started to ride across the meadow, supporting his right arm carefully with

[3] RUCK—An entangled mass.

his left hand. This man had encountered a shell, apparently, at a time when no one perceived him, and he could now be seen lying face downward with a stirruped foot stretched across the body of his dead horse. A leg of the charger extended slantingly upward, precisely as stiff as a stake. Around this motionless pair the shells still howled.

There was a quarrel in A Company. Collins was shaking his fist in the faces of some laughing comrades. "Dern yeh! I ain't afraid t' go. If yeh say much, I will go!"

"Of course, yeh will! You'll run through that there medder, won't yeh?"

Collins said, in a terrible voice: "You see now!"

At this ominous threat his comrades broke into renewed jeers.

Collins gave them a dark scowl, and went to find his captain. The latter was conversing with the colonel of the regiment.

"Captain," said Collins, saluting and standing at attention—in those days all trousers bagged at the knees—"Captain, I want t' get permission to go git some water from that there well!"

The colonel and the captain swung about simultaneously and stared across the meadow. The captain laughed. "You must be pretty thirsty, Collins?"

"Yes, sir, I am."

"Well—ah," said the captain. "Can't you wait?"

"No, sir."

The colonel was watching Collins' face. "Look here, my lad," he said, in a pious sort of voice—"Look here, my lad"—Collins was not a lad—"don't you think that's taking pretty big risks for a little drink of water?"

"I dunno," said Collins uncomfortably. Some of the resentment toward his companions, which perhaps had forced him

into this affair, was beginning to fade. "I dunno w'ether 'tis."

The colonel and the captain contemplated him for a time.

"Well," said the captain finally.

"Well," said the colonel, "if you want to go, why, go."

Collins saluted. "Much obliged t' yeh."

As he moved away the colonel called after him. "Take some of the other boys' canteens with you, an' hurry back."

"Yes, sir, I will."

The colonel and the captain looked at each other then, for it had suddenly occurred that they could not for the life of them tell whether Collins wanted to go or whether he did not.

They turned to regard Collins, and as they perceived him surrounded by gesticulating comrades, the colonel said: "Well, by thunder! I guess he's going."

Collins appeared as a man dreaming. In the midst of the questions, the advice, the warnings, all the excited talk of his company mates, he maintained a curious silence.

They were busy preparing him for his ordeal. When they inspected him carefully, it was somewhat like the examination that grooms give a horse before a race; and they were amazed, staggered, by the whole affair. Their astonishment found vent in strange repetitions.

"Are yeh sure a-goin'?" they demanded again and again.

"Certainly I am," cried Collins at last, furiously.

He strode sullenly away from them. He was swinging five or six canteens by their cords. It seemed that his cap would not remain firmly on his head, and often he reached and pulled it down over his brow.

There was a general movement in the compact column. The long animal-like thing moved slightly. Its four hundred eyes were turned upon the figure of Collins.

"Well, sir, if that ain't th' derndest thing! I never thought Fred Collins had the blood in him for that kind of business."

"What's he goin' to do, anyhow?"

"He's goin' to that well after water."

"We ain't dyin' of thirst, are we? That's foolishness."

"Well, somebody put him up to it, an' he's doin' it."

"Say, he must be a desperate cuss."

When Collins faced the meadow and walked away from the regiment, he was vaguely conscious that a chasm, the deep valley of all prides, was suddenly between him and his comrades. It was provisional, but the provision was that he return as a victor. He had blindly been led by quaint emotions, and laid himself under an obligation to walk squarely up to the face of death.

But he was not sure he wished to make a retraction, even if he could do so without shame. As a matter of truth, he was sure of very little. He was mainly surprised.

It seemed to him supernaturally strange that he had allowed his mind to maneuver his body into such a situation. He understood that it might be called dramatically great.

However, he had no full appreciation of anything, excepting that he was actually conscious of being dazed. He could feel his dulled mind groping after the form and color of this incident. He wondered why he did not feel some keen agony of fear cutting his sense like a knife. He wondered at this, because human expressions had said loudly for centuries that men should feel afraid of certain things, and that all men who did not feel this fear were phenomena [4]—heroes.

He was, then, a hero. He suffered that disappointment which we would all have if we discovered that we were ourselves capable of those deeds which we most admire in history and legend. This, then, was a hero. After all, heroes were not much.

No, it could not be true. He was not a hero. Heroes had no shames in their lives, and, as for him, he remembered borrowing fifteen dollars from a friend and promising to pay it back the next day, and then avoiding that friend for ten months. When, at home, his mother had aroused him for the early labor of his life on the farm, it had often been his fashion to be irritable, childish, diabolical; and his mother had died since he had come to the war.

He saw that, in this matter of the well, the canteens, the shells, he was an intruder in the land of fine deeds.

He was now about thirty paces from his comrades. The regiment had just turned its many faces toward him.

From the forest of terrific noises there suddenly emerged a little uneven line of men. They fired fiercely and rapidly at distant foliage on which appeared little puffs of white smoke. The spatter of skirmish firing was added to the thunder of the guns on the hill. The little line of men ran forward. A color sergeant fell flat with his flag as if he had slipped on ice. There was hoarse cheering from this distant field.

Collins suddenly felt that two demon fingers were pressed into his ears. He could see nothing but flying arrows, flaming red. He lurched from the shock of this explosion, but he made a mad rush

[4] PHENOMENA (fĕ·nŏm'ĕ·nà)—Used here in the sense of surprising, unusual.

for the house, which he viewed as a man submerged to the neck in a boiling surf might view the shore. In the air little pieces of shell howled, and the earthquake explosions drove him insane with the menace of their roar. As he ran the canteens knocked together with a rhythmical tinkling.

As he neared the house, each detail of the scene became vivid to him. He was aware of some bricks of the vanished chimney lying on the sod. There was a door which hung by one hinge.

Rifle bullets called forth by the insistent skirmishers came from the far-off bank of foliage. They mingled with the shells and the pieces of shells until the air was torn in all directions by hootings, yells, howls. The sky was full of fiends who directed all their wild rage at his head.

When he came to the well, he flung himself face downward and peered into its darkness. There were furtive silver glintings some feet from the surface. He grabbed one of the canteens, and, unfastening its cap, swung it down by the cord. The water flowed slowly in with an indolent gurgle.

And now, as he lay with his face turned away, he was suddenly smitten with terror. It came upon his heart like the grasp of claws. All the power faded from his muscles. For an instant he was no more than a dead man.

The canteen filled with a maddening slowness, in the manner of all bottles. Presently he recovered his strength and addressed a screaming oath to it. He leaned over until it seemed as if he intended to try to push water into it with his hands. His eyes as he gazed down into the well shone like two pieces of metal, and in their expression was a great appeal and a great curse. The stupid water derided him.

There was the blaring thunder of a shell. Crimson light shone through the swift-boiling smoke and made a pink reflection on part of the wall of the well. Collins jerked out his arm and canteen with the same motion that a man would use in withdrawing his head from a furnace.

He scrambled erect and glared and hesitated. On the ground near him lay the old well bucket, with a length of rusty chain. He lowered it swiftly into the well. The bucket struck the water and then, turning lazily over, sank. When with hand reaching tremblingly over hand, he hauled it out, it knocked often against the walls of the well and spilled some of its contents.

In running with a filled bucket, a man can adopt but one kind of gait. So, through this terrible field over which screamed practical angels of death, Collins ran in the manner of a farmer chased out of a dairy by a bull.

His face went staring white with anticipation—anticipation of a blow that would whirl him around and down. He would fall as he had seen other men fall, the life knocked out of them so suddenly that their knees were no more quick to touch the ground than their heads. He saw the long blue line of the regiment, but his comrades were standing looking at him from the edge of an impossible star. He was aware of some deep wheel-ruts and hoofprints in the sod beneath his feet.

The artillery officer who had fallen in this meadow had been making groans in the teeth of the tempest of sound. These futile cries, wrenched from him by his agony, were heard only by shells, bullets. When wild-eyed Collins came running, this officer raised himself. His face contorted and blanched from pain, he was about to utter some great beseeching cry. But suddenly his face straightened, and he called: "Say, young man, give me a drink of water, will you?"

Collins had no room amid his emotions for surprise. He was mad from the threats of destruction.

"I can't!" he screamed, and in his reply was a full description of his quaking apprehension. His clothes made it appear that he had been dragged over the ground by the heels. He ran on.

The officer's head sank down, and one elbow crooked. His foot in its brass-bound stirrup still stretched over the body of his horse, and the other leg was under the steed.

But Collins turned. He came dashing back. His face had now turned gray, and in his eyes was all terror. "Here it is! here it is!"

The officer was as a man gone in drink.

His arm bent like a twig. His head dropped as if his neck were of willow. He was sinking to the ground, to lie face downward.

Collins grabbed him by the shoulder. "Here it is. Here's your drink. Turn over. Turn over, man!"

With Collins hauling at his shoulder, the officer twisted his body and fell with his face turned toward that region where lived the unspeakable noises of the swirling missiles. There was the faintest shadow of a smile on his lips as he looked at Collins. He gave a sigh, a little primitive breath like that from a child.

Collins tried to hold the bucket steadily, but his shaking hands caused the water to splash all over the face of the dying man. Then he jerked it away and ran on.

The regiment gave him a welcoming

470

roar. The grimed faces were wrinkled in laughter.

His captain waved the bucket away. "Give it to the men!"

The two genial, skylarking young lieutenants were the first to gain possession of it. They played over it in their fashion.

When one tried to drink, the other teasingly knocked his elbow. "Don't, Billie! You'll make me spill it," said the one. The other laughed.

Suddenly there was an oath, the thud of wood on the ground, and a swift murmur of astonishment among the ranks. The two lieutenants glared at each other. The bucket lay on the ground empty.

◇◇◇◇◇◇◇◇◇◇◇◇◇◇◇◇◇◇◇◇◇◇◇◇◇◇◇◇◇◇◇

FOR UNDERSTANDING

1. Fred Collins seemed a hero to his fellow soldiers because he braved danger to go for a drink of water. At first he had no intention of doing such a thing. Explain how his conversation with the other men led him step by step to the decision to risk his life. The two officers from whom he gained permission could not tell whether Private Collins wanted to go or not. What do you think? Explain the conflict of feelings in Collins which makes it possible that Collins himself did not know whether he wanted to go.

2. Reread the description of Collins' thoughts during his dangerous journey to the well. Why did it seem to him that he was not really a hero? Any soldier who is willing to risk enemy fire might properly be called a hero. However, the best type of heroism is shown when someone displays high courage in reaching a *very important* goal. Explain why Collins' act falls short of this standard. What do the last few paragraphs of the story make us feel about his act? On the other hand, what one very brave and fine thing did he do? Was he frightened or calm at that moment?

3. How does the author emphasize that the soldiers in the story are ordinary, "real life" people? Look for evidence in the conversation and actions of the officers as well as of the enlisted men.

4. Point out two passages that best show the fury or destructiveness of the battle.

5. We are not told outright what war is being fought, or which army is being described. Can you find any evidence that it is the Union Army of the War Between the States?

STEPHEN CRANE'S GIFT OF THE "PERFECT PHRASE"

Stephen Crane is famous for being able to "say it exactly right." In the first paragraph he says, "On top of the hill a battery was *arguing in tremendous roars with some other guns.*" Explain what details of the battle are brought out by the italicized words.

A lieutenant rides by "holding his right arm carefully in his left hand. And it was as if this arm was not at all a part of him, but belonged to another man." What is the author saying about the way this arm lay in the hand that was holding it?

As Collins ran back toward safety, it seemed that "his comrades were standing *looking at him from the edge of an impossible star.*" What feelings in Collins' mind are revealed by the italicized words?

Select other expressions that seem especially exact or vivid. Compare the choices made by different members of the class, and by vote decide which two are best.

NATURALISTIC WRITING

The expression *naturalism*, when it refers to writing, means both the use of many exact, realistic details and a certain attitude on the part of the author. Naturalistic writers look upon human beings somewhat as biologists look upon plants and animals. They seem to think human beings are ruled by events, that they do not really make their own decisions but merely react helplessly to the things that happen in their immediate environment. In his books Stephen Crane often shows such an attitude.

1. How is it suggested that the men of A Company are helpless in the situation in which we see them? What does the bombardment of the little meadow (where there are no troops) suggest in regard to whether the enemy artillerymen are *really* in control of their own actions?

2. How was Collins "forced" to start after the water? Did anyone force him? Why would he find it "impossible" to turn back after he had started, no matter how much he might wish to do so?

3. Did anyone want the water to be wasted? Would Collins have carried back a bucket of water if he had expected it to be wasted?

ARMY TERMS

See which of the following military expressions you can explain without looking them up; then check their meanings in your dictionary.

infantry	caissons
artillery	canteens
battery	skirmishers

WRITING PROJECTS

1. Stephen Crane speaks of "that disappointment which we would all have if we discovered that we were ourselves capable of those deeds which we most admire in history and legend." In a small way, such a disappointment has been felt by most of us.

Write a brief composition describing your former feelings about the honors and privileges enjoyed by "wonderful" older students—then the let down when you reached the same age and didn't feel any more important than before.

2. Imitate Stephen Crane by writing a description, not more than three sentences long, of some vivid detail of a scene, or some single happening like falling down hard on an icy sidewalk. Before writing, think hard about the experience. What, exactly, did you feel or see? Then try to put into words precisely what you felt or saw. You may want to use an imaginative comparison to get your thought across.

STEPHEN CRANE (1871–1900)

Before he had actually had any personal experience of war, Stephen Crane wrote one of the finest war novels of all time, *The Red Badge of Courage*. The book concentrates on what one typical soldier, Private Henry Fleming, sees and experiences in the War Between the States. We follow the soldier everywhere he goes, know his inmost emotions and fears, and become so absorbed that we feel as if we had been fighting the war instead of reading about it.

Crane was a devoted student of literary art all his life. After finishing two years of college he went to New York to start his career as author and newspaper reporter. His first novel—its printing paid for partly with money borrowed from his brother—did not sell. Then, after study of war accounts, and painstaking toil to perfect his writing, he published *The Red Badge of Courage* in 1895. Its instant success assured his literary reputation. For the rest of his short life, Crane was engaged as a war correspondent by various American and English periodicals. He was sent to report a Cuban revolution. The ship he was on sank, and with other passengers Crane was in a lifeboat two days before being rescued. From this experience he wrote his most famous short story, "The Open Boat." He reported the Greco-Turkish War, and went back to Cuba a second time to report the Spanish-American War. After finally seeing battle at first hand, he was happy to be able to say to a friend, "*The Red Badge of Courage* is all right."

Crane's later books include novels; volumes of short stories and other brief sketches; and two collections of free verse poems. In his later years, because he sometimes wrote of the New York slums and of social outcasts, he was falsely accused of leading a dissipated life and even of being a drug addict. He was a tall, lanky man of frail constitution. Worn down by the exposure and the strenuous activity of a war correspondent's life, he died of tuberculosis in 1900.

The War Between the States—As Seen by the Men Who Were There

Although much fiction was written about the War Between the States at the time of the fighting and immediately afterward, most of it is forgotten today. One of the most famous novels of the period was *Uncle Tom's Cabin*, by Harriet Beecher Stowe —a book that appeared nine years before the war, and was influential in arousing antislavery feeling in the North. Like many a novel of the time, *Uncle Tom's Cabin* is oversentimental; and at many points the story is one-sided in its unfavorable picture of conditions on the Southern plantations. Even so, it is an exciting and colorful novel which still finds readers. A more gifted author, Ambrose Bierce, actually served in the war. Later he drew on his experiences for a book of gripping stories, *Tales of Soldiers and Civilians*. He is represented here by "A Horseman in the Sky."

The finest literature produced during the war period was not fiction, but oratory and poetry. Modern readers in general care little for the oratory of a bygone day, but they find inspiration in the "Gettysburg Address" and the "Second Inaugural Address"

473

of Abraham Lincoln. Quiet, thoughtful, and noble, Lincoln's addresses have the simplicity of great poetry—and of a great mind. In poetry, some of the best work inspired by the war was that of Walt Whitman—who is represented by four poems in the following pages. Also represented are three poets of the South, Abram Joseph Ryan, Henry Timrod, and Sidney Lanier. Timrod and Lanier were typical of many brilliant young men whose lives and careers were ruined by the war. Their best remembered poems express the sadness of defeat, and also the courage and strength of the South in the dark years that followed. And finally, a very different type of poetry that has come down to us from the war is the marching songs with which both the Blue and the Gray kept up their spirits. The song that seems most likely to live—if only because of its catchy, quickstep tune—is "Dixie."

◇◇◇◇◇

Dixie

DANIEL EMMETT

Nobody is sure how the term "Dixie Land" originated. One theory says it refers to the Mason-Dixon line between North and South. At any rate, "Dixie" has meant "the South" ever since the Confederate armies stepped along to the tune that bears this name. "Dixie" was first sung in a Broadway minstrel show shortly before the War Between the States began. Then it traveled to New Orleans as a song in a comic play—just in time to be adopted by the Louisiana regiments, who spread it among their fellow soldiers everywhere. As you read it, don't ponder seriously over its meaning. Read it rapidly, to appreciate its brisk, cheerful rhythm.

> I wish I was in de land ob cotton,
> Old times dar am not forgotten;
>   Look away, look away, look away, Dixie Land!
> In Dixie Land whar I was born in,
> Early on one frosty mornin',
>   Look away, look away, look away, Dixie Land!
>
> CHORUS:
>
> *Den I wish I was in Dixie! Hooray! Hooray!*
> *In Dixie's Land we'll take our stand, to lib an' die in Dixie.*
> *Away! away! away down South in Dixie.*
> *Away! away! away down South in Dixie.*

474

Ole missus marry "Will-de-weaber";
Willum was a gay deceaber;
   Look away, look away, look away, Dixie Land!
But when he put his arm around her,
He smiled as fierce as a forty-pounder;
   Look away, look away, look away, Dixie Land!

His face was sharp as a butcher's cleaber;
But dat did not seem to greab her;
   Look away, look away, look away, Dixie Land!
Old missus acted de foolish part,
And died for a man dat broke her heart;
   Look away, look away, look away, Dixie Land!

Now here's a health to de next old missus,
An' all the gals dat want to kiss us;
   Look away, look away, look away, Dixie Land!
But if you want to drive 'way sorrow,
Come hear dis song tomorrow;
   Look away, look away, look away, Dixie Land!

Dar's buckwheat cakes and Injin batter,
Makes you fat or a little fatter;
   Look away, look away, look away, Dixie Land!
Den hoe it down an' scratch your grabble,
To Dixie's land I'm bound to trabble;
   Look away, look away, look away, Dixie Land!

FOR UNDERSTANDING

Several stanzas of this song are only good-natured nonsense—but for some reason, singing nonsensical songs is a good way to express gaiety and high spirits. This was why "Dixie" appealed to the young soldiers marching off to meet the Yankees, and appealed also to the friends who cheered them on their way. The song is permanently established as the beloved "national anthem" of the South.

1. What expressions in the first stanza suggest the patriotic feelings of Southerners? in the chorus? Notice that in the chorus, three of the lines give much the same effect as cheering, in unison, for the land of Dixie.

2. Ask class members who are musically talented to sing the song. Afterward, the whole class should try it.

DANIEL EMMETT (1815-1905)

Daniel Decatur Emmett organized the first traveling minstrel troupe in the world. He wrote songs for his show, and helped to sing them himself. Emmett was an uneducated man who had joined the United States Army at seventeen, and afterward played in circus bands, before he started his minstrel show. Besides "Dixie," he wrote "Old Dan Tucker" and several other songs that won popularity.

Beat! Beat! Drums!

WALT WHITMAN

Like his fellow Americans North and South, the poet Walt Whitman realized that 1861 was a fateful year. After decades of peace and increasing prosperity, American life was shaken to its foundations by the outbreak of the War Between the States. In this poem, Whitman expresses the tension and distracting excitement of that time. For dramatic effect, he pictures the disturbance as being caused by the loud, alarming noise of military drums.

Beat! beat! drums!—Blow! bugles! blow!
Through the windows—through doors—burst like a ruthless force,
Into the solemn church, and scatter the congregation;
Into the school where the scholar is studying;
Leave not the bridegroom quiet—no happiness must he have now with
    his bride;   5
Nor the peaceful farmer any peace, plowing his field or gathering his
    grain;
So fierce you whirr and pound, you drums—so shrill you bugles blow.

Beat! beat! drums!—Blow! bugles! blow!
Over the traffic of cities—over the rumble of wheels in the streets:
Are beds prepared for sleepers at night in the houses? No sleepers
    must sleep in those beds;   10
No bargainers' bargains by day—no brokers or speculators—would
    they continue?

Would the talkers be talking? would the singer attempt to sing?
Would the lawyer rise in the court to state his case before the judge?
Then rattle quicker, heavier drums—you bugles wilder blow.

Beat! beat! drums!—Blow! bugles! blow!   15
Make no parley—stop for no expostulation;
Mind not the timid—mind not the weeper or prayer;
Mind not the old man beseeching the young man;
Let not the child's voice be heard, nor the mother's entreaties;
Make even the trestles to shake the dead, where they lie awaiting the
    hearses,   20
So strong you thump, O terrible drums—so loud you bugles blow.

20. TRESTLES—Frames upon which coffins are placed.

FOR UNDERSTANDING

1. Throughout the poem, the sound of drums and bugles is used as a metaphor for the war itself. Glance through the poem for passages that emphasize the urgent violence of this sound. Which one do you think expresses it most vividly?

2. What clues does the poem give as to whether the author himself approves of the war? Explain how they show his attitude.

3. In thinking of a general situation, for instance the coming of a war, a literary artist almost instinctively tries to make it more real to himself by imagining concrete situations. Whitman at once thinks of the farmer leaving his field and the lawyer leaving his case. How will the drums "scatter the congregation"? Which of Whitman's many examples do you think shows the disruptive force of the war in its most extreme form?

WALT WHITMAN (1819–1892)

For information on the life of this famous poet, see pages 694–695.

◇◇◇◇◇

Come Up from the Fields, Father

WALT WHITMAN

This simply worded poem makes us share in the suffering which war can bring to people far behind the lines. During the War Between the States, Walt Whitman volunteered for duty as a nurse in the government hospital in Washington. He was often called on to write letters home for men who were wounded, perhaps fatally. In this poem, in imagination he follows such a letter to an Ohio farm.

Come up from the fields, Father, here's a letter from our Pete;
And come to the front door, Mother—here's a letter from thy dear
son.

Lo, 'tis autumn;
Lo, where the trees, deeper green, yellower and redder,
Cool and sweeten Ohio's villages, with leaves fluttering in the moderate wind;
Where apples ripe in the orchards hang, and grapes on the trellis'd vines;
(Smell you the smell of the grapes on the vines?
Smell you the buckwheat, where the bees were lately buzzing?)

5

Above all, lo, the sky, so calm, so transparent after the rain, and with
    wondrous clouds;
Below, too, all calm, all vital and beautiful—and the farm prospers
    well.   10

Down in the fields all prospers well;
But now from the fields come, Father—come at the daughter's call;
And come to the entry, Mother—to the front door come, right away.

Fast as she can she hurries—something ominous—her steps trembling;
She does not tarry to smoothe her hair, nor adjust her cap.   15
Open the envelope quickly;
Oh, this is not our son's writing, yet his name is sign'd;
Oh, a strange hand writes for our dear son—O stricken mother's soul!
All swims before her eyes—flashes with black—she catches the main
    words only;
Sentences broken—*gunshot wound in the breast, cavalry skirmish,*
    taken to hospital,   20
At present low, but will soon be better.

Ah, now, the single figure to me,
Amid all teeming and wealthy Ohio, with all its cities and farms,
Sickly white in the face, and dull in the head, very faint,
By the jamb of a door leans.   25
Grieve not so, dear Mother (the just-grown daughter speaks through
    her sobs;
The little sisters huddle around, speechless and dismay'd);
See, dearest Mother, the letter says Pete will soon be better.

Alas, poor boy, he will never be better (nor maybe needs to be better,
    that brave and simple soul);
While they stand at home at the door, he is dead already;   30
The only son is dead.

But the mother needs to be better;
She, with thin form, presently dressed in black,
By day her meals untouch'd—then at night fitfully sleeping, often
    waking,
In the midnight waking, weeping, longing with one deep longing,   35
O that she might withdraw unnoticed—silent from life, escape and
    withdraw,
To follow, to seek, to be with her dear dead son.

FOR UNDERSTANDING

1. How does the country scene contrast with the news brought in the letter? Whit-man was alert to all the sights and sounds of the outdoors. Choose two phrases which seem especially effective in picturing the place or the time of year.

2. Whitman's imagination enacts the drama in full detail—not only the setting, but the steps by which the news is disclosed. How is the father summoned? Who opens the letter? What is the earliest indication that the news is bad?

3. Restate the meaning of lines 22–25 in your own words. What do they show us about the poet? In these lines he expresses his *own* feelings about the mother. In which lines does he put into words the grief which is in *her* mind?

4. Reread line 29 and explain "nor maybe needs to be better."

5. Whitman made a deliberate effort to use fresh, living language such as is heard in conversation rather than found in books. In the first line, the homely name "Pete" instead of some more high-sounding name shows Whitman's belief that simple, familiar terms have their own dignity. What expression in line 2 is so commonplace that you would not expect to find it in a poem?

6. On the other hand, in Whitman's poems these everyday expressions are mixed with conventional "poetic" terms. Point out three words or longer expressions which are more typical of *poetry* than of ordinary speaking and writing.

⬦⬦⬦⬦⬦

As Toilsome I Wander'd Virginia's Woods

WALT WHITMAN

This poem, like the preceding one, is about one of the many tragedies of the War Between the States. However, this time the poet gives us only a glimpse of a story. The poem is a record of a brief experience—something the poet saw—which sticks in his memory. If the poem is successful, the experience will stick in the reader's memory also.

As toilsome I wander'd Virginia's woods,
To the music of rustling leaves, kicked by my feet (for 'twas autumn),
I marked at the foot of a tree the grave of a soldier,
Mortally wounded he, and buried on the retreat (easily all could I understand);
The half of a midday hour, when up! no time to lose—yet this sign left,   5
On a tablet scrawled and nailed on the tree by the grave,
Bold, cautious, true, and my loving comrade.

Long, long I muse, then on my way go wandering;
Many a changeful season to follow, and many a scene of life;

Yet at times through changeful season and scene, abrupt, alone, or in the
   crowded street,   10
Comes before me the unknown soldier's grave—comes the inscription
   rude in Virginia's woods,
Bold, cautious, true, and my loving comrade.

FOR UNDERSTANDING

1. The poet makes no comment on what he saw in the Virginia woods. However, what thoughts does the poem bring to our minds about war and about the attitudes of soldiers toward each other?

2. Whitman says that this one sight— the tablet, or piece of board, with the inscription on it—still comes to his mind sometimes. In "Come Up from the Fields, Father," what one sight does he make the most important detail in the poem?

EMPHASIZING IMPORTANT
  DETAILS

It is *the words on the tablet* that Whitman wishes to emphasize. In the first sec-tion of the poem, he does not give the details of the experience in the order in which they would naturally occur. He would have seen and read the tablet *before* reconstructing in his mind what happened on the day the soldier was killed. But in telling about it he saves *the words* until last. They are the climax of this passage.

In the second section, this arrangement is followed again. Everything that precedes the last line is a build-up to that line. And by giving the words *twice* in this brief poem, Whitman emphasizes them more strongly.

Read the poem aloud, noticing this effect of *climax*. When you reach the last line of each section, read it slowly and with emphasis.

ANECDOTES OF LINCOLN

Even during Lincoln's lifetime, people repeated hundreds of stories illustrating his wit and humor. Some are anecdotes Lincoln is supposed to have told. As a traveling "circuit lawyer" he heard all the amusing yarns that circulated in the Illinois backwoods. At night, sitting in the lobbies of little prairie-town hotels, he loved to swap stories with his fellow lawyers. Later, in political life, he would often illustrate some point he wanted to make with "That reminds me of the story . . ." —going on to tell an anecdote that perfectly fitted what he wanted to express.

Sometimes Lincoln's humor showed itself in an unexpected witty remark— like the time two of his friends got into a dispute about how long a man's legs should be in proportion to the rest of his body. They asked Lincoln to settle the argument. He replied that a man's legs ought to be "at least long enough to reach from him to the ground." Through all the tragic years of the War Between the States, one thing that helped Lincoln to keep his sanity was his irrepressible sense of fun.

In many a prairie cabin by candlelight as the snowdrifts piled, and another crock of apples was passed to those who sat by the wood fire, the tale had been told of Abe Lincoln driving a two-horse team on a road heavy with mud. It was sunset time and Abe had his back to the sunset. And he met another driver with a two-horse wagon. Both knew that whoever turned out would be up to the hubs in mud, almost sure to get stuck in the mud. "Turn out," the other fellow called. "Turn out yourself," called Abe. The other fellow refused. Then Abe, with his back to the sunset, began to rise from his seat in the wagon, rising and rising, his tall shape getting longer and longer against the setting sun, as he was saying, "If you don't turn out I'll tell you what I'll do." And the other fellow hollered: "Don't go any higher. I'll turn out." And after he had struggled through and passed by Lincoln, he called back, "Say, what would you have done if I hadn't turned out?" Lincoln answered, "I'd've turned out myself." *

[*To describe the way he felt about having to bear the terrible responsibility of the War Between the States, Lincoln told a story about James and John, two mischievous boys who let a dangerous hog out of its pen.*]

"The hog went straight for the boys and drove John up a tree. Then the hog went for the seat of James's trousers, and the only way the boy could save himself was by holding on to the hog's tail. The hog would not give up his hunt nor the boy his hold. After they had made a good many circles around the tree, the boy's courage began to give out, and he

shouted to his brother, 'I say, John, come down quick, and help me *let this hog go.*' . . . That is exactly my case. I wish someone would come and help me let this hog go." †

[*After Lincoln took office in 1861, it seemed that everybody in the country thought the new administration should give him a job. These office-seekers were so numerous and so determined that they hindered the work of government. Sometimes, when they managed to see the President himself, he got rid of them in short order.*]

. . . A delegation called on Mr. Lincoln to ask the appointment of a gentleman as Commissioner to the Sandwich Islands. They presented their case as earnestly as possible, and, besides his fitness for the place, they urged that he was in bad health, and a residence in that balmy climate would be of great benefit to him. The President closed the interview with this discouraging remark:

"Gentlemen, I am sorry to say that there are eight other applicants for that place, and they are all sicker than your man." ‡

† From *Abraham Lincoln: The War Years*, Volume 1, by Carl Sandburg, copyright, 1939, by Harcourt, Brace and Company, Inc., and used by their permission.
‡ From *Reminiscences of Abraham Lincoln by Distinguished Men of His Time*, edited by Allen Thorndike Rice.

◇◇◇◇◇◇◇◇◇◇◇◇◇◇◇◇◇◇◇◇◇◇◇◇◇◇◇◇

FOR UNDERSTANDING

1. Lincoln's dispute with the other driver illustrates his humor and resourcefulness in holding his own in the rough frontier environment of early Illinois. Even the victim might get a laugh out of the way Lincoln had outsmarted him. The story is the kind of yarn that folks like to repeat about someone they remember with affection. Notice that Lincoln's *ungainly appearance* gets into

* From *Abraham Lincoln: The Prairie Years*, Volume 1, by Carl Sandburg, copyright, 1926, by Harcourt, Brace and Company, Inc.; renewed by Carl Sandburg. Used by permission of Harcourt, Brace and Company, Inc.

the story. How does it play an important part in making Lincoln's opponent give in?

2. Lincoln's story about the hog expressed the frightened, overwhelmed feeling brought by the outbreak of the War Between the States. Furthermore, it precisely described Lincoln's situation. He hardly knew whether *he was running the war* or *the war was in control of him*. Explain how the boy's ridiculous-sounding remark conveys this idea.

3. In the third story, Lincoln does not attempt to explain that in a well-run government, important jobs are filled on the basis of the applicants' abilities—not their needs. Just the same, Lincoln's reply to his visitors is like a spotlight revealing the fundamental absurdity of their point of view. Think about his comment, and then tell how it shows that his visitors have used an absurd argument.

ABRAHAM LINCOLN (1809–1865)

Abraham Lincoln, born February 12, 1809, in Kentucky, stands today one of the great men of history. The story of his humble birth, his struggle with poverty, his intellectual curiosity that could not be satisfied, his slow rise to political power with its culmination in the highest office in the United States—these are facts known to every American; yet each retelling seems but to cause us to cherish more deeply the memory of this unusual man. When Lincoln was eight years of age his father moved from Kentucky to Indiana, where the family lived until Lincoln was twenty-one. He then moved with his father to Illinois, with which state he was ever after associated.

A trip down the Mississippi River to New Orleans in 1831 gave Lincoln a glimpse of slavery and fixed in him a lifelong hatred of the institution. The next year he began to study law and in 1834 was elected to the Illinois legislature.

The slavery question had become involved with nearly every phase of politics. Slave and anti-slave states fought over admission of territories, over the tariff; suspicion grew, and peace was constantly menaced. The Missouri Compromise of 1820, fixing the line between slave and free states at 36°30' north latitude, probably saved the young republic by allowing it forty years of unchecked growth before the dispute reached the stage of actual conflict. However, with each decade the question of the spread, or else the destruction, of slavery became more clearly unavoidable. Holding the balance of power between the two sections took all the juggler tricks the statesmen and politicians could master. In 1858 Lincoln said in a speech accepting the Republican nomination for United States Senator, " 'A house divided against itself cannot stand.' I believe this government cannot endure permanently half slave and half free. I do not expect the Union to be dissolved—I do not expect the house to fall—but I do expect it will cease to be divided."

In the Lincoln-Douglas debates during the campaign that followed, Lincoln had many opportunities to put before the public his ideas of Union and slavery. Defeated by Douglas for the senatorship, he had nevertheless made himself so popular that he was nominated for president by the Republican party in its National Convention at Chicago two years later. The facts of his life from this time on are a part of history and are well known. However, one thing we often forget is that during most of Lincoln's presidency he was not recognized as an outstanding statesman. Educated people thought him an ignorant, stupid man who was dangerously unfit for his position. When he first took office, his policy of moderation toward the seceding states enraged Northern extremists. Lincoln refused to fight until the Confederate government's attack on Fort Sumter, a Federal garrison, left him no choice. Some of the same fire-eating Abolitionists who had called him a coward now learned what Lincoln had understood all along—the horror and tragedy of war—and this time they denounced him because he would not ask for peace, on whatever terms the South would grant.

Lincoln was able to see the war through

to a successful conclusion only because of the support given him by rank-and-file voters. They sensed "Old Abe's" nobility of mind, his compassion, his sheer intelligence —and at last the "intellectual leaders" of the country realized that the common people's judgment had been better than their own. Lincoln has become the American who, not even Washington excepted, is closest to the nation's heart and love.

◇◇◇◇◇

SECOND INAUGURAL ADDRESS

ABRAHAM LINCOLN

When Lincoln spoke to the nation on beginning his second term in March, 1865, there were signs that the war might soon be over. A naval blockade had choked off the foreign trade without which the South could not continue the fight. The Northern armies, having slowly been built up to overwhelming size, by their massive weight were pushing General Lee's and General Johnston's armies before them. The very fact that Lincoln had been triumphantly re-elected was equally important. Supporting him, the North gave notice that—contrary to the hopes of Confederate leaders—it had made up its mind to fight the war to the end.

Lincoln's long ordeal was all but over, his most bitter critics would soon be silenced by victory. The speech he made in this moment of success was humble and sober. Among the few public addresses of his presidency—all of them marked by nobility of thought and language—the "Second Inaugural Address" is one of the greatest. The rhythms of his closing words beat on in the world's memory. They speak to us of Lincoln's earnestness and dignity, and of his heart.

Fellow-countrymen:

At this second appearing to take the oath of the presidential office, there is less occasion for an extended address than there was at first. Then a statement, somewhat in detail, of a course to be pursued, seemed fitting and proper. Now, at the expiration of four years, during which public declarations have been constantly called forth on every point and phase of the great contest which still absorbs the attention and engrosses the energies of the nation, little that is new could be presented. The progress

BETTMANN ARCHIVE

of our arms, upon which all else chiefly depends, is as well known to the public as to myself; and it is, I trust, reasonably satisfactory and encouraging to all. With high hope for the future, no prediction in regard to it is ventured.

On the occasion corresponding to this four years ago, all thoughts were anxiously directed to an impending civil war. All dreaded it—all sought to avert it. While the inaugural address was being delivered from this place, devoted altogether to saving the Union without war, insurgent agents were in the city seeking to destroy it without war—seeking to dissolve the Union, and divide effects, by negotiation. Both parties deprecated[1] war; but one of them would make war rather than let the nation survive; and the other would accept war rather than let it perish. And the war came.

[1] DEPRECATED—Expressed disapproval of.

One-eighth of the whole population were colored slaves, not distributed generally over the Union, but localized in the southern part of it. These slaves constituted a peculiar and powerful interest. All knew that this interest was, somehow, the cause of the war. To strengthen, perpetuate, and extend this interest was the object for which the insurgents would rend the Union, even by war; while the government claimed no right to do more than to restrict the territorial enlargement of it.[2]

Neither party expected for the war the magnitude or the duration which it has already attained. Neither anticipated that the cause of the conflict might

[2] GOVERNMENT CLAIMED . . . ENLARGEMENT OF IT—Before the outbreak of war Lincoln said he had no right "to interfere with the institution of slavery in the states where it exists." However, he expressed the belief that Congress could legally ban its extension to new territories.

cease [3] with, or even before, the conflict itself should cease. Each looked for an easier triumph and a result less fundamental and astounding. Both read the same Bible, and pray to the same God; and each invokes His aid against the other. It may seem strange that any men should dare to ask a just God's assistance in wringing their bread from the sweat of other men's faces; but let us judge not, that we be not judged. The prayers of both could not be answered—that of neither has been answered fully.

The Almighty has his own purposes. "Woe unto the world because of offenses! [4] for it must needs be that offenses come; but woe to that man by whom the offense cometh." If we shall suppose that American slavery is one of those offenses which in the providence of God, must needs come, but which, having continued through his appointed time, He now wills to remove, and that He gives to both North and South this terrible war, as the woe due to those by whom the offense came, shall we discern therein any departure from those divine attributes which the believers in a living God always ascribe Him? Fondly do we hope —fervently do we pray—that this mighty scourge of war may speedily pass away. Yet, if God wills that it continue until all the wealth piled by the bondman's two hundred and fifty years of unrequited toil shall be sunk, and until every drop of blood drawn with the lash shall be paid by another drawn with the sword, as was said three thousand years ago, still it must be said, "The judgments of the Lord [5] are true and righteous altogether."

[3] CAUSE OF THE CONFLICT MIGHT CEASE— Slavery was abolished by the Emancipation Proclamation on January 1, 1863.

[4] "WOE UNTO THE WORLD BECAUSE OF OFFENSES!"—This, and the remainder of the quotation, is from Matthew 18.

[5] "THE JUDGMENTS OF THE LORD . . ."— This quotation is from the 19th Psalm.

With malice toward none; with charity for all; with firmness in the right, as God gives us to see the right, let us strive on to finish the work we are in; to bind up the nation's wounds; to care for him who shall have borne the battle, and for his widow and his orphan—to do all which may achieve and cherish a just and lasting peace among ourselves, and with all nations.

◇◇◇◇◇◇◇◇◇◇◇◇◇◇◇◇◇◇◇◇◇◇◇◇◇◇

FOR UNDERSTANDING

1. Many times during the War Between the States Lincoln must have gone over and over in his mind its causes, the justifications for the stand taken by each side, and the question of whether he himself had acted rightly. In the "Second Inaugural Address" he fixes the minds of his listeners on the same subject. Does he say the war will soon be over? How does he explain the outbreak of a war neither side wanted? The *direct* reason for the war was disagreement over whether a state could secede from the Union. Quote a passage in which Lincoln says that the *underlying* reason was disagreement over the question of slavery.

2. The fourth paragraph inquires into, rather than explains, the puzzling fact that both sides prayed to God for victory. What is meant by saying that neither side has had its prayers answered fully?

3. The fifth paragraph expresses the idea that the war is in some way a judgment of God. Is it said to be a judgment on one side alone? Find expressions that speak of the war as a calamity. The quotations from the Bible help to raise the discussion to a high, solemn level. People sometimes speak of Lincoln as an uneducated "rail-splitter," a clever country lawyer—forgetting that he read many books, and all his life pondered over the teachings of the Bible. The wording of this paragraph, like the wording of all Lincoln's orations, has a Biblical ring. In making his final quotation from the Bible,

what is Lincoln saying about God's treatment of the American nation?

4. The last paragraph rises to the height of great poetry. Read it aloud to appreciate its power. In it, where do you find an expression of sorrow? of forgiveness? of determination? of gratitude for service? Notice that it contains no hint of hatred or vengefulness. Find out and explain what plan Lincoln intended to follow for the reunion of North and South.

FOR FURTHER READING

Students who like any kind of rigid, step-by-step logical reasoning will enjoy reading Lincoln's "Cooper Union Speech." Delivered in New York early in 1860 this speech helped to interest Eastern Republicans in Lincoln and was thus instrumental in winning him the nomination for president. In it, Lincoln defends his belief that Congress had the power to limit slavery to the states where it then existed, and refutes one argument in favor of slavery—that "Our forefathers understood this question better than we." Lincoln accepts this remark as a starting-point and goes on to investigate *what* our forefathers thought about slavery. He attempts to prove that nearly all the makers of the Constitution opposed slavery, although they postponed abolishing it. His conclusion, of course, is that to follow the beliefs of the Founding Fathers is to adopt the Republican Party's platform on slavery.

❖❖❖❖❖

A HORSEMAN IN THE SKY

AMBROSE BIERCE

The following story centers around a young man who, although he is from Virginia, is a soldier in the Union Army. He is on guard duty—a post of great responsibility. To fail his duty might cost the lives of hundreds of men. The story tells about a terrible decision he must make, and reminds us what an unnatural and tragic thing war is.

One sunny afternoon in the autumn of the year 1861 a soldier lay in a clump of laurel by the side of a road in western Virginia. He lay at full length upon his stomach, his feet resting upon the toes, his head upon the left forearm. His extended right hand loosely grasped his rifle. But for the somewhat methodical disposition of his limbs and a slight rhythmic movement of the cartridge box at the back of his belt he might have been thought to be dead. He was asleep at his post of duty. But if detected he would be dead shortly afterward, death being the just and legal penalty of his crime.

The clump of laurel in which the criminal lay was in the angle of a road which after ascending southward a steep acclivity [1] to that point turned sharply to the west, running along the summit for perhaps one hundred yards. There it turned

[1] ACCLIVITY ($\check{a} \cdot$ klĭv′ĭ$\cdot$tĭ)—A slope or hillside.

486

southward again and went zigzagging downward through the forest. At the salient [2] of that second angle was a large flat rock, jutting out northward, overlooking the deep valley from which the road ascended. The rock capped a high cliff; a stone dropped from its outer edge would have fallen sheer downward one thousand feet to the tops of the pines. The angle where the soldier lay was on another spur of the same cliff. Had he been awake he would have commanded a view, not only of the short arm of the road and the jutting rock, but of the entire profile of the cliff below it. It might well have made him giddy to look.

The country was wooded everywhere except at the bottom of the valley to the northward, where there was a small natural meadow, through which flowed a stream scarcely visible from the valley's rim. This open ground looked hardly larger than an ordinary dooryard, but was really several acres in extent. Its green was more vivid than that of the inclosing forest. Away beyond it rose a line of giant cliffs similar to those upon which we are supposed to stand in our survey of the savage scene, and through which the road had somehow made its climb to the summit. The configuration [3] of the valley, indeed, was such that from this point of observation it seemed entirely shut in, and one could but have wondered how the road which found a way out of it had found a way into it, and whence came and whither went the waters of the stream that parted the meadow more than a thousand feet below.

No country is so wild and difficult but men will make it a theater of war; concealed in the forest at the bottom of that

military rat trap, in which half a hundred men in possession of the exits might have starved an army to submission, lay five regiments of Federal infantry. They had marched all the previous day and night and were resting. At nightfall they would take to the road again, climb to the place where their unfaithful sentinel now slept, and descending the other slope of the ridge fall upon a camp of the enemy at about midnight. Their hope was to surprise it, for the road led to the rear of it. In case of failure, their position would be perilous in the extreme; and fail they surely would should accident or vigilance apprise [4] the enemy of the movement.

The sleeping sentinel in the clump of laurel was a young Virginian named Carter Druse. He was the son of wealthy parents, an only child, and had known such ease and cultivation and high living as wealth and taste were able to command in the mountain country of western Virginia. His home was but a few miles from where he now lay. One morning he had risen from the breakfast table and said, quietly but gravely: "Father, a Union regiment has arrived at Grafton. I am going to join it."

The father lifted his leonine head, looked at the son a moment in silence, and replied: "Well, go, sir, and whatever may occur do what you conceive to be your duty. Virginia, to which you are a traitor, must get on without you. Should we both live to the end of the war, we will speak further of the matter. Your mother, as the physician has informed you, is in a most critical condition; at the best she cannot be with us longer than a few weeks, but that time is precious. It would be better not to disturb her."

So Carter Druse, bowing reverently to

[2] SALIENT (sā'lĭ·ĕnt)—A projection; a jutting out.
[3] CONFIGURATION—Shape; form.

[4] APPRISE (ă·prīz')—Acquaint; inform.

his father, who returned the salute with a stately courtesy that masked a breaking heart, left the home of his childhood to go soldiering. By conscience and courage, by deeds of devotion and daring, he soon commended himself to his fellows and his officers; and it was to these qualities and to some knowledge of the country that he owed his selection for his present perilous duty at the extreme outpost. Nevertheless, fatigue had been stronger than resolution and he had fallen asleep. What good or bad angel came in a dream to rouse him from his state of crime, who shall say? Without a movement, without a sound, in the profound silence and the languor of the late afternoon, some invisible messenger of fate touched with unsealing finger the eyes of his consciousness—whispered into the ear of his spirit the mysterious awakening word which no human lips ever have spoken, no human memory ever has recalled. He quietly raised his forehead from his arm and looked between the masking stems of the laurels, instinctively closing his right hand about the stock of his rifle.

His first feeling was a keen artistic delight. On a colossal pedestal, the cliff—motionless at the extreme edge of the capping rock and sharply outlined against the sky—was an equestrian statue of impressive dignity. The figure of the man sat the figure of the horse, straight and soldierly, but with the repose of a Grecian god carved in the marble which limits the suggestion of activity. The gray costume harmonized with its aerial background; the metal of accouterment and caparison [5] was softened and subdued by

the shadow; the animal's skin had no points of high light. A carbine strikingly foreshortened lay across the pommel of the saddle, kept in place by the right hand grasping it at the "grip"; the left hand, holding the bridle rein, was invisible. In silhouette against the sky the profile of the horse was cut with the sharpness of a cameo; it looked across the heights of air to the confronting cliffs beyond. The face of the rider, turned slightly away, showed only an outline of temple and beard; he was looking downward to the bottom of the valley. Magnified by its lift against the sky and by the soldier's testifying sense of the formidableness of a near enemy the group appeared of heroic, almost colossal, size.

For an instant Druse had a strange, half-defined feeling that he had slept to the end of the war and was looking upon a noble work of art reared upon that eminence to commemorate the deeds of an heroic past of which he had been an inglorious part. The feeling was dispelled by a slight movement of the group: the horse, without moving its feet, had drawn its body slightly backward from the verge; the man remained immobile as before. Broad awake and keenly alive to the significance of the situation, Druse now brought the butt of his rifle against his cheek by cautiously pushing the barrel forward through the bushes, cocked the piece, and glancing through the sights covered a vital spot of the horseman's breast. A touch upon the trigger and all would have been well with Carter Druse. At that instant the horseman turned his head and looked in the direction of his concealed foeman—seemed to look into his very face, into his eyes, into his brave, compassionate heart.

Is it then so terrible to kill an enemy in war—an enemy who has surprised a secret vital to the safety of one's self and

[5] ACCOUTERMENT ($\ddot{a}\cdot k\overline{oo}'t\bar{e}r\cdot m\breve{e}nt$) AND CAPARISON ($k\dot{a}\cdot p\breve{a}r'\breve{i}\cdot s'n$)—The first refers to the sword and other trappings of a soldier aside from his uniform and weapons; the second to the trappings of a horse.

comrades—an enemy more formidable for his knowledge than all his army for its numbers? Carter Druse grew pale; he shook in every limb, turned faint, and saw the statuesque group before him as black figures, rising, falling, moving unsteadily in arcs of circles in a fiery sky. His hand fell away from his weapon, his head slowly dropped until his face rested on the leaves in which he lay. This courageous gentleman and hardy soldier was near swooning from intensity of emotion.

It was not for long; in another moment his face was raised from the earth, his hands resumed their places on the rifle, his forefinger sought the trigger; mind, heart, and eyes were clear, conscience and reason sound. He could not hope to capture that enemy; to alarm him would but send him dashing to his camp with his fatal news. The duty of the soldier was plain: the man must be shot dead from ambush—without warning, without a moment's spiritual preparation, with never so much as an unspoken prayer, he must be sent to his account. But no—there is a hope; he may have discovered nothing—perhaps he is but admiring the sublimity of the landscape. If permitted, he may turn and ride carelessly away in the direction whence he came. Surely it will be possible to judge at the instant of his withdrawing whether he knows. It may well be that his fixity of attention—Druse turned his head and looked through the deeps of air downward, as from the surface to the bottom of a translucent sea. He saw creeping across the green meadow a sinuous line of figures of men and horses—some foolish commander was permitting the soldiers of his escort to water their beasts in the open, in plain view from a dozen summits!

Druse withdrew his eyes from the valley and fixed them again upon the group of man and horse in the sky, and again it was through the sights of his rifle. But this time his aim was at the horse. In his memory, as if they were a divine mandate, rang the words of his father at their parting: "Whatever may occur, do what you conceive to be your duty." He was calm now. His teeth were firmly but not rigidly closed; his nerves were as tranquil as a sleeping babe's—not a tremor affected any muscle of his body; his breathing, until suspended in the act of taking aim, was regular and slow. Duty had conquered; the spirit had said to the body: "Peace, be still." He fired.

An officer of the Federal force, who in a spirit of adventure or in quest of knowledge had left the hidden *bivouac* in the valley, and with aimless feet had made his way to the lower edge of a small open space near the foot of the cliff, was considering what he had to gain by pushing his exploration further. At a distance of a quarter-mile before him, but apparently at a stone's throw, rose from its fringe of pines the gigantic face of rock, towering to so great a height above him that it made him giddy to look up to where its edge cut a sharp, rugged line against the sky. It presented a clean, vertical profile against a background of blue sky to a point half the way down, and of distant hills, hardly less blue, thence to the tops of the trees at its base. Lifting his eyes to the dizzy altitude of its summit, the officer saw an astonishing sight—a man on horseback riding down into the valley through the air!

Straight upright sat the rider, in military fashion, with a firm seat in the saddle, a strong clutch upon the rein to hold his charger from too impetuous a plunge. From his bare head his long hair streamed upward, waving like a plume. His hands were concealed in the cloud of the horse's lifted mane. The animal's body was as level as if every hoofstroke encountered the resistant earth. Its motions were those of a wild gallop, but even as the officer looked they ceased, with all the legs thrown sharply forward as in the act of alighting from a leap. But this was a flight!

Filled with amazement and terror by this apparition of a horseman in the sky —half believing himself the chosen scribe of some new apocalypse,[6] the officer was overcome by the intensity of his emotions; his legs failed him and he fell. Almost at the same instant he heard a crashing sound in the trees—a sound that died without an echo—and all was still.

The officer rose to his feet, trembling. The familiar sensation of an abraded shin recalled his dazed faculties. Pulling himself together he ran rapidly obliquely away from the cliff to a point distant from its foot; thereabout he expected to find his man; and thereabout he naturally failed. In the fleeting instant of his vision his imagination had been so wrought upon by the apparent grace and ease and intention of the marvelous performance that it did not occur to him that the line of march of aerial cavalry is directed downward, and that he could find the objects of his search at the very foot of the cliff. A half hour later he returned to camp.

[6] APOCALYPSE (*à·pŏk′à·lĭps*)—A description of supernatural wonders, as the Apocalypse or Book of Revelations in the New Testament.

This officer was a wise man; he knew better than to tell an incredible truth. He said nothing of what he had seen. But when the commander asked him if in his scout he had learned anything of advantage to the expedition he answered:

"Yes, sir; there is no road leading down into this valley from the southward."

The commander, knowing better, smiled.

After firing his shot, Private Carter Druse reloaded his rifle and resumed his watch. Ten minutes had hardly passed when a Federal sergeant crept cautiously to him on hands and knees. Druse neither turned his head nor looked at him, but lay without motion or sign of recognition.

"Did you fire?" the sergeant whispered.

"Yes."

"At what?"

"A horse. It was standing on yonder rock—pretty far out. You see it is no longer there. It went over the cliff."

The man's face was white, but he showed no other sign of emotion. Having answered, he turned away his eyes and said no more. The sergeant did not understand.

"See here, Druse," he said, after a moment's silence, "it's no use making a mystery. I order you to report. Was there anybody on the horse?"

"Yes."

"Well?"

"My father."

The sergeant rose to his feet and walked away. "Good God!" he said.

◇◇◇◇◇◇◇◇◇◇◇◇◇◇◇◇◇◇◇◇◇◇◇◇◇◇◇◇

FOR UNDERSTANDING

1. Explain why Carter Druse's act was both a noble and a terrible one.

2. Because the horseman has seen the Federal regiments in the valley below, it is necessary to kill him at once—not try to capture him and take the risk that he will escape to spread the alarm. Explain why Druse did not try to stop the horseman *before* he reached the lookout point from which he could see the troops. If the enemy discovers the presence of the troops and attacks them, whose fault will it be?

3. Before firing, Druse has already discovered who the horseman is. This explains why he decides to fire at the horse, not the rider. Find the passage in which Druse's behavior and actions reveal (now that we have read the whole story) that he recognizes the rider. Why is it certain that shooting the horse will kill the rider?

4. What words by Druse's father, on the day the young man left home to enlist in the Northern Army, seem to justify Druse's action in this story?

FOR BROADER MEANINGS

1. How does this story suggest, better than most war stories, what an unnatural and terrible thing war is? Why is it easier to realize this when we read about a war between sections of a country than when we read about war against a foreign nation?

2. Because of our more deadly weapons, modern war is more horrible than wars earlier in history. Do you think that, in addition, people today have a different attitude toward war than did people at the time of this story or in still earlier times? That is, can you give evidence that in early periods people accepted war more readily, and glorified it more?

3. Carter Druse made a great sacrifice in order to perform his duty toward his fellow soldiers—and in fact acted contrary to the feelings any person would naturally have toward the members of his own family. Druse's stern and high-minded father— could he have known of the situation— would have disapproved of his son's acting in any other way. In history and literature there are many examples of similar devotion to duty which required great sacrifice,

though not in the same way. Give examples, if you can, and in each case explain why the sacrifice was necessary, not just a foolhardy act.

THE WRITER'S CRAFT

1. To make a story more effective, sometimes an author does not tell it in the most "natural" way. He may *change the chronological order*, perhaps starting at a halfway point in the story and going back afterward to tell the beginning. Or he may *withhold some details from the reader*—hinting at them, but not actually revealing them until the end. Why would "A Horseman in the Sky" be a less dramatic story if the reader knew from the very beginning who the horseman was?

2. Although Bierce's stories are often thrilling, they have been criticized as being somewhat artificial. You will understand what the critics mean if you will reread the description of the man and horse sailing two thousand feet through the air into the valley below, and the account of the officer in the valley who saw the sight. Do you find there anything that is theatrical, that is, overly dramatic? Why would the story of Carter Druse and his father have been even more powerful *without* the spectacular passages?

FOR YOUR VOCABULARY

See how many of the following italicized words you can explain. Afterward, check your answers with a dictionary.

1. No country is so wild and difficult but men will make it a *theater* of war.

2. Half a hundred men in possession of the exits might have starved an army to *submission*.

3. The father lifted his *leonine* head.

4. In the profound silence and the *languor* of the late afternoon, some invisible messenger of fate . . . whispered . . . into the ear of his spirit.

5. On a colossal pedestal, the cliff, . . . was an *equestrian* statue of impressive dignity.

6. The profile of the horse was cut with the sharpness of a *cameo*.

7. The man remained *immobile* as before.

8. The man must be shot dead from *ambush*—without warning.

9. He ran rapidly *obliquely* from the cliff.

AMBROSE BIERCE (1842–1914?)

Ambrose Bierce was born in Ohio and was mainly self-educated. As a young man he served four years in the War Between the States, rising from drummer boy to major in the Union forces. From this experience he was later to draw material for a number of his most famous short stories. He drifted to California where he had a brilliant career as a journalist, to England where he worked on several magazines, then to California again. Tragedy in his immediate family, and memory of the waste and horror of war, helped to disillusion Bierce with life. For his sarcastic wit he was known as "Bitter Bierce." One book, *The Devil's Dictionary*, consists of "definitions" which savagely make fun of humanity and human ideals. The following are samples:

> BORE, *n.* A person who talks when you wish him to listen.
>
> FAMOUS, *adj.* Conspicuously miserable.

Most of Bierce's war stories were published in his volume *Tales of Soldiers and Civilians*, 1891. Their plots are usually melodramatic, showing men's behavior in the face of danger or violent death. The end of Bierce's life is a mystery. In 1913 he disappeared into Mexico, a country which was then undergoing a series of revolutions. It is believed that he was killed by the soldiers of the guerrilla chieftain Pancho Villa.

O Captain! My Captain!

WALT WHITMAN

In April, 1865, came the happiest news Lincoln had ever received as President
—that the war was over. Now the work of reconciliation between North and
South—and the work of recovery—could begin. Less than a week later,
President Lincoln was dead, struck down by an assassin's bullet as he sat in
his box at the theater. Rejoicing turned to sorrow as people mourned the
leader they had learned to love and trust. Walt Whitman expressed their
feelings in "O Captain! My Captain!"

O Captain! my Captain! our fearful trip is done;
The ship has weathered every rack, the prize we sought is won;
The port is near, the bells I hear, the people all exulting,
While follow eyes the steady keel, the vessel grim and daring:
  But O heart! heart! heart!   5
    O the bleeding drops of red,
      Where on the deck my Captain lies,
        Fallen cold and dead.

O Captain! my Captain! rise up and hear the bells;
Rise up—for you the flag is flung—for you the bugle trills;   10
For you bouquets and ribboned wreaths—for you the shores a-crowding;
For you they call, the swaying mass, their eager faces turning;
  Here Captain! dear father!
    This arm beneath your head;
      It is some dream that on the deck,   15
        You've fallen cold and dead.

My Captain does not answer, his lips are pale and still;
My father does not feel my arm, he has no pulse nor will;
The ship is anchored safe and sound, its voyage closed and done;
From fearful trip the victor ship comes in with object won: 20
  Exult, O shores, and ring, O bells!
    But I, with mournful tread,
      Walk the deck my Captain lies,
        Fallen cold and dead.

2. EVERY RACK—Every strain caused by storm.

FOR UNDERSTANDING

1. The "Captain" in this poem is President Lincoln. What is his "ship"? What "fearful trip" is referred to in line 1? Explain "The ship is anchor'd safe and sound," in line 19.

2. In this poem Whitman makes a comparison between *ship* and *nation*. What do the *storms at sea* represent? How is the *strength* of the ship described? What attitude does the poet take toward the *future survival* of the ship?

3. Is Whitman's own attitude one of joy or sorrow? Quote a passage which suggests that Lincoln himself should receive much of the credit for the successful conclusion of the War Between the States.

FOR FURTHER READING

1. Whitman wrote another poem in memory of Lincoln, "When Lilacs Last in the Dooryard Bloom'd," which is difficult to read but contains some very fine passages. The title refers to the season of the year—spring—when Lincoln died. Your teacher may wish to appoint one student to read parts of this poem to the class, explaining them. Sections 5, 6, 10, and 11 are especially good ones to use for this purpose.

2. If your library has Carl Sandburg's famous biography of Lincoln, read in it the account of the solemn funeral train that carried the President's body from Washington to Springfield, Illinois. The story is told in the last chapter of Sandburg's *Abraham Lincoln: The War Years*, Vol. IV, pages 387–413. As you read this chapter, notice the appropriateness of its title, "Vast Pageant, Then Great Quiet."

3. For a detailed account of the last day of Lincoln's life, read *The Day Lincoln Was Shot* (Harper) by Jim Bishop. The conspirators are pictured with skill and accuracy.

FOR BRIEF REPORTS TO
THE CLASS

1. Using the encyclopedia, and biographies of Lincoln, give the details of Lincoln's assassination. Who was the murderer, and what became of him?

2. Make a report to the class on why Lincoln's death was harmful to the nation. That is, how might our history immediately after the War Between the States have been different if he had lived? Use textbooks and other works on American history to find the answer.

◇◇◇◇◇

The Conquered Banner

ABRAM JOSEPH RYAN

This poem expresses the sorrow of the South when their gallant fight ended in defeat. It became the best known of Father Ryan's works. It is remarkable that the poem hardly touches on the bitterness felt in the South over the harm done by invading armies and by vengeful Reconstruction laws. Father Ryan himself gave his best efforts to promoting good will between the states that had once been foes.

Furl that Banner, for 'tis weary;
Round its staff 'tis drooping dreary:
  Furl it, fold it—it is best;
For there's not a man to wave it,
And there's not a sword to save it,   5
And there's not one left to lave it
In the blood which heroes gave it,
And its foes now scorn and brave it:
  Furl it, hide it—let it rest!

Take that Banner down! 'tis tattered;   10
Broken is its staff and shattered;
And the valiant hosts are scattered,
  Over whom it floated high.
Oh, 'tis hard for us to fold it,
Hard to think there's none to hold it, 15
Hard that those who once unrolled it
  Now must furl it with a sigh!

Furl that Banner—furl it sadly!
Once ten thousands hailed it gladly,
And ten thousands wildly, madly,   20
  Swore it should forever wave;
Swore that foeman's sword should never
Hearts like theirs entwined dissever,
Till that flag should float forever
  O'er their freedom or their grave!   25
    6. LAVE (lāv)—To wash.

Furl it! for the hands that grasped it,
And the hearts that fondly clasped it,
  Cold and dead are lying low;
And that Banner—it is trailing,
While around it sounds the wailing   30
  Of its people in their woe.

For, though conquered, they adore it—
Love the cold, dead hands that bore it,
Weep for those who fell before it,
Pardon those who trailed and tore it;   35
And oh, wildly they deplore it,
  Now to furl and fold it so!

Furl that Banner! True, 'tis gory,
Yet 'tis wreathed around with glory,
And 'twill live in song and story   40
  Though its folds are in the dust!
For its fame on brightest pages,
Penned by poets and by sages,
Shall go sounding down the ages—
  Furl its folds though now we must.   45

Furl that Banner, softly, slowly!
Treat it gently—it is holy,
  For it droops above the dead.
Touch it not—unfold it never,
Let it droop there, furled forever—   50
  For its people's hopes are fled!

FOR UNDERSTANDING

1. This poem is constructed around the metaphor of a flag. Every thought grows out of direct contemplation of the Banner itself. For instance, in the first stanza *furling the Banner* is made to mean *ceasing to fight.*

In stanza 2, how is the Banner connected with the memory of the Confederate Army, now disbanded? In stanza 3, how is the Banner connected with the enthusiasm and determination with which the South fought the war? In stanza 4, how is the Banner connected with the men who have fallen in battle?

2. Is it true, as prophesied in the next-to-last stanza, that the fame of the stand made by the Southern States has been recorded in literature? Give as many examples as you can of works dealing with this subject.

3. Give reasons for thinking that the last thought expressed in the poem has proved to be too gloomy.

ABRAM JOSEPH RYAN (1838–1886)

Abram Ryan was a Maryland poet. He had been ordained to the Roman Catholic priesthood a few years before the war, and he served as a chaplain in the Confederate Army. His postwar lyrics reflect the despair of the South at her tremendous losses; there is in them also his manly courage and faith. In the South, his patriotic lyrics became the most widely known of his works. They are published in the book *Father Ryan's Poems*. He is the author of a later volume of religious poetry, *A Crown for Our Queen*.

✧✧✧✧✧

Ode

SUNG AT THE OCCASION OF DECORATING THE GRAVES OF THE CONFEDERATE DEAD, AT MAGNOLIA CEMETERY, CHARLESTON, S. C., 1867

HENRY TIMROD

This poem is intended to express not only the feelings of the poet toward men who fell in the Southern cause, but the feelings of the people who have gathered to do them honor.

Sleep sweetly in your humble graves,
  Sleep, martyrs of a fallen cause;
Though yet no marble column craves
  The pilgrim here to pause.

In seeds of laurel in the earth   5
  The blossom of your fame is blown,
And somewhere, waiting for its birth,
  The shaft is in the stone!

Meanwhile, behalf the tardy years
  Which keep in trust your storied
    tombs,   10

Behold! your sisters bring their tears,
  And these memorial blooms.

Small tributes! but your shades will smile
  More proudly on these wreaths today,
Than when some cannon-molded
    pile   15
  Shall overlook this bay.

Stoop, angels, hither from the skies!
  There is no holier spot of ground
Than where defeated valor lies,
  By mourning beauty crowned.   20

3-4. NO MARBLE COLUMN CRAVES THE PILGRIM HERE TO PAUSE—No monument has yet been erected to attract the notice of those who visit the burial ground.
9. BEHALF THE TARDY YEARS—Temporarily taking the place of the people of later years.

10. STORIED TOMBS—Monuments that will tell in sculpture the story of the dead.
13. SHADES—Spirits.
15. SOME CANNON-MOLDED PILE—Monument made out of cannon metal.

✧✧✧

FOR UNDERSTANDING

1. Stanza 1 mentions that a permanent monument is still lacking. Explain what is meant by the statement in Stanza 2 that somewhere "the shaft is in the stone." In the same stanza the poet mentions a *blossom* which, though fallen, is now a *seed*. What is he saying about the present and future fame of the dead? Use a dictionary

to find out the meaning that has been traditionally associated with the leaves of the *laurel* plant.

2. Quote the words which show that flowers have been placed in the cemetery just before the singing of this ode. What expression shows that the flowers were placed there by a group of maidens?

3. Explain the expressions *defeated valor* and *mourning beauty* in the last stanza.

FOR FURTHER INVESTIGATION

1. Look up and explain the purpose of Memorial Day, sometimes called Decoration Day. On what date is it observed in different regions of the United States?

2. Look up *ode* in the Glossary, and explain why Timrod's poem is correctly called an ode.

3. Explain the following details in the poem: *what the occasion is; who is supposed to be speaking; who are being honored; who is being addressed.*

4. Explain how Timrod's "Ode" and Ryan's "The Conquered Banner" are alike in that the subject is *the actual scene at which the poem is supposed to be recited.*

HENRY TIMROD (1828–1867)

Timrod's patriotic poems earned him the title of "the Laureate of the Confederacy." He was one of a number of talented young Southern writers whose careers were ruined or shortened by the war. After leaving college, he read law, taught in a country school, and began contributing poems to the *Southern Literary Messenger.* He was also a member of a literary group that met at John Russell's bookstore in Charleston, South Carolina, and that for three years published its own magazine.

In 1860 Timrod published the one volume of his poems to appear during his lifetime. They were a young man's writings, partly imitative of classic literature and sometimes sweetly sentimental. Then he volunteered for army service, but soon contracted the tuberculosis of which he later died. His last years were a time of suffering and poverty. Yet the war which brought an end to all his hopes was also the inspiration for his finest work—warmly patriotic, but mature and restrained. The "Ode on the Confederate Dead" and "The Cotton Boll" are two of his best known poems.

⟨⟨⟨⟨⟩

The Marshes of Glynn

SIDNEY LANIER

Like many other poets, Lanier finds that some natural scenes awaken emotions which are like a religious vision. Standing at the edge of the salt marshes in Glynn County, Georgia, and looking eastward to where the great marshes merge with the still greater sea, the poet has a sense of benevolent peace; a reliance on God's generous bounty. "The Marshes of Glynn," a lyric of over a hundred lines, is the best loved of all Lanier's poems. The central portion of the poem is reprinted here.

Vanishing, swerving, evermore curving again into sight,
Softly the sand-beach wavers away to a dim gray looping of light.
And what if behind me to westward the wall of the woods stands high?
The world lies east: how ample, the marsh and the sea and the sky!
A league and a league of marsh grass, waist-high, broad in the blade, 5
Green, and all of a height, and unflecked with a light or a shade,
Stretch leisurely off, in a pleasant plain,
To the terminal blue of the main.
Oh, what is abroad in the marsh and the terminal sea?
    Somehow my soul seems suddenly free 10
From the weighing of fate and the sad discussion of sin,
By the length and the breadth and the sweep of the marshes of Glynn.

Ye marshes, how candid and simple and nothing withholding and free
Ye publish yourselves to the sky and offer yourselves to the sea!
Tolerant plains, that suffer the sea and the rains and the sun, 15
Ye spread and span like the catholic man who hath mightily won
God out of knowledge and good out of infinite pain
And sight out of blindness and purity out of a stain.

As the marsh hen secretly builds on the watery sod,
Behold I will build me a nest on the greatness of God: 20
I will fly in the greatness of God as the marsh hen flies
In the freedom that fills all the space 'twixt the marsh and the skies:
By so many roots as the marsh grass sends in the sod
I will heartily lay me a-hold on the greatness of God:
Oh, like to the greatness of God is the greatness within 25
The range of the marshes, the liberal marshes of Glynn.

8. THE TERMINAL BLUE OF THE MAIN—The "main" is the sea. Its blue color can be seen as the "terminal" or farthest boundary of the horizon.

◇◇

FOR UNDERSTANDING

1. The word "ample" in line 4 means *large, plentiful*. What three things does the poet describe as "ample"? Find two or more additional lines which call attention to the spaciousness of the scene gazed on by the poet.

2. Consult a dictionary for meanings of the following words—meanings which will fit their use in lines 13–16: *candid, publish, tolerant, catholic*.

3. Lines 16–18 mean that the poet has caught a glimpse of a broader, nobler conception of God—one that causes him to reject narrow, gloomy creeds. Explain why he speaks of this faith as a winning of good out of pain and sight out of blindness. That is, what *pain* and *blindness* does he mean?

4. It should be noticed that in the last stanza quoted here Lanier does not *draw a lesson* from the marsh hen and the marsh grass. It is the view of marsh, sea, and sky which produces a surge of religious feeling in Lanier; he mentions the marsh hen and the marsh grass merely as illustrations of his new state of mind. In what *two* ways is he now like the marsh hen? How is he like the marsh grass? What more important comparison is the underlying thought of the entire selection?

SIDNEY LANIER (1842–1881)

Lanier was educated at Oglethorpe University in Georgia. He fought in the War Between the States, and was captured by the Federal troops and imprisoned for several months. When the struggle ended, penniless and sick he tramped five hundred miles back home. Soon he published a novel, *Tiger-Lilies*, based on his war experiences. He determined to devote the remainder of his life to the two things he loved most—poetry and music. He could play any instrument, and his flute had been his best companion during his years as a soldier. He became a flutist in the Baltimore symphony orchestra. Then came the hindrance of failing health. From 1873 until his death, he tried to find a climate and a cure for tuberculosis, the aftermath of his camp life. Even in his sickness, he continued to write and to work. He was appointed lecturer on English literature at Johns Hopkins University. At the last, he addressed his classes from a wheel chair. He died before reaching the age of forty.

Lanier's most important prose work is *The Science of English Verse*. It is an attempt to explore the connections between poetry and music. In some of the poems he had time to write before his early death, Lanier tried to put his theories into practice. "The Symphony" is a complex discussion of social and industrial problems, in which different sections of the poem represent different instruments in an orchestral composition. All his poetry has a distinctive singing quality, and it often shows great skill in the use of sound-effects like alliteration and the frequent repetition of rhymes. Among the best known of his poems are "Song of the Chattahoochee," "A Ballad of Trees and the Master," and "The Marshes of Glynn."

❖❖❖❖❖

For Broader Understanding

1. What were the main points of dispute between North and South? Explain the arguments that you think are strongest and most convincing *on each side.*

2. What events, after the secession of the Confederate States, made armed conflict unavoidable? How long did the war last?

3. What characteristics were (and are) admired in Abraham Lincoln? in Robert E. Lee? What were the most difficult problems faced by each man? Name three works of literature, by three different authors, dealing with Lincoln, and tell what particular phase of his life or character is stressed in each.

4. What works by modern authors, other than the ones reproduced in this book, do you know of that deal in some way with the War Between the States? See how many books the class as a whole can think of. Give reasons why the war has always been a fascinating topic to authors and readers.

5. Name two famous literary selections by Northern authors, and two by Southern authors, which were written about the time of the War Between the States. State the central idea of each.

6. The war affected not only the lives of soldiers but those of nearly all Americans. Explain how Whitman's "Beat! Beat! Drums!" expresses *civilians'* experiences of the war. Why could we also assume that the speaker in Whitman's "As Toilsome I Wander'd Virginia's Woods" may be a civilian? How does Abram Ryan's "The Conquered Banner" reflect a very different experience of the war from that of Whitman? Why would we guess that the author of "A Horseman in the Sky" had probably had actual military experience?

7. See whether class members can reach agreement on the one work of literature, or if that is impossible the two or three works of literature, of the war period that are

"most worth knowing." In class discussion try to define the particular excellent qualities of the literary work which have caused you to prefer it.

SPEAKING ACTIVITIES

1. *Family War Memories.* Make a report to the class on any stories of the War Between the States that have been handed down in your family. What do your parents know about the experiences of any of their ancestors during the war, whether as soldiers or civilians? Give all the details you can find.

2. *War Memories in Your Community.* Select several students to report on whether the war is remembered in your town. Are there any plaques or other memorials? Are there soldiers' graves that recall the war? If there are annual observances such as decorating graves, give full details in your report. What incidents in the history of your city or town during the war are known?

READING AND WRITING ACTIVITIES

Look up one of the following topics and write a report on it.

"Stonewall" Jackson. In what battles did this Southern hero win his greatest victories? See if you can find out how his method of fighting was especially effective.

Philip Sheridan. Give the details of the battle which Sheridan won by his famous twenty-mile ride.

The Underground Railroad. What does this expression mean, and how did the "railroad" operate?

The Fugitive Slave Law. Explain why Northerners thought that this law would extend slavery into free territory.

President Andrew Johnson. When he became president after Lincoln's death, what policies did Johnson try to follow, and what difficulties did he have?

John Greenleaf Whittier, Abolitionist Poet. Find and read at least three of Whittier's antislavery poems, and give the central

idea of each. Tell which you think is most effective, and what its good qualities are.

Joel Chandler Harris. Harris' "Uncle Remus" stories are valuable contributions to our knowledge of American folklore. Read several of the stories, and tell what kind of character "Brer Rabbit" is and how he wins his victories. Explain how Harris' writings give a favorable impression of the life of Negroes under slavery.

FOR FURTHER READING

GEORGE W. CABLE, *The Cavalier* (Scribner). Here are the experiences of Richard Smith who, at the age of nineteen, becomes a scout for the Southern Army. Swift action and an easy style of writing contribute to the story's interest.

BRUCE CATTON, *A Stillness at Appomattox* (Doubleday). The last year of the War Between the States was a cruel one, and in Mr. Catton's narrative the heartbreak and desperation are caught with brilliance. Mr. *Lincoln's Army* and *Glory Road* are forerunners of this work.

ALFRED L. CRABB, *Mockingbird Sang at Chickamauga* (Bobbs-Merrill). General Bedford Forrest is a central figure, the Battle of Chickamauga a central episode, and Chattanooga the location of this fine story.

SCOTT HART, *Eight April Days* (Coward-McCann). This small volume encompasses those days of the Confederate retreat from Petersburg to Appomattox. The woman peddler, Old Pine, tells a moving story.

BURTON J. HENDRICKS, *Lincoln's War Cabinet* (Little). Each of Lincoln's cabinet members is introduced and his part in the War Between the States discussed. This is not merely a history book but a book alive and full of entertaining reading.

ROBERT SYLPH HENRY, *The Story of the Confederacy* (Bobbs-Merrill). This account of the war is told dramatically and with understanding. Of special interest are the first fourteen chapters and the last nine chapters.

MARY JOHNSTON, *The Long Roll* (Houghton). Richard Cleave, a Confederate officer, finds himself the innocent victim of treachery. His fight to clear his name forms the plot.

MACKINLAY KANTOR, *Long Remember* (Coward-McCann). A well-known writer tells an exciting story of the War Between the States. Dan Beale takes no interest in the war that rages around him, but the Battle of Gettysburg changes his mind.

WALTER LORD, editor, *The Fremantle Diary* (Little). Lt. Col. Arthur Fremantle was a British officer who spent a leave from the army traveling through the Confederate States. His account of people, places, and activities is filled with humor and sympathy. Present at the Battle of Gettysburg, he has recorded that event impressively.

CARL SANDBURG, *Abraham Lincoln: The Prairie Years* and *The War Years* (Harcourt). These volumes make a full and intensely interesting biography of a great president. *Storm Over the Land* by the same author concerns the War Between the States.

JAMES STREET, *By Valour of Arms* (Dial). The iron ship Arkansas was instrumental in the destruction of Farragut's fleet and in delaying the capture of Vicksburg.

Here are biographies of important persons at the time of the War Between the States.

WILLIAM E. BROOKS, *Lee of Virginia* (Bobbs-Merrill).

BURKE DAVIS, *They Called Him Stonewall* (Rinehart).

J. J. ECKENRODE, *Jefferson Davis: President of the South* (Macmillan).

W. H. HALE, *Horace Greeley: Voice of the People* (Harper).

LOUIS HOWLAND, *Stephen A. Douglas* (Scribner).

E. B. LONG, editor, *Personal Memoirs of U. S. Grant* (Bobbs-Merrill).

❖❖❖❖❖

HISTORY IN REVIEW

MILESTONES	TRENDS IN AMERICAN LIFE	LITERATURE
1858—Lincoln-Douglas Debates		1846–1860—*Voices of Freedom,* antislavery poems by Whittier; Emerson's antislavery essays; Harriet Beecher Stowe's *Uncle Tom's Cabin;* Walt Whitman's first edition of *Leaves of Grass;* "Dixie"; Lincoln's Cooper Union Address
1859—John Brown's raid on Harper's Ferry	The Abolitionists dominate public opinion in the North. Lincoln's election convinces Southerners that the North will control the federal government	
1860—Abraham Lincoln elected president		
1861—Secession of ten Southern States; organization of the Southern Confederacy, Jefferson Davis, president; attack on Fort Sumter begins the war		
1862—Battles of Shiloh and Antietam; naval battle between *Monitor* and *Merrimac*	After their early victories, the outnumbered Southern armies slowly begin to lose the war	
1863—Emancipation Proclamation; Battle of Gettysburg; surrender of Vicksburg	By its support, and eventually its re-election, of Lincoln the North shows that it is determined to see the war through to the end	1863—Lincoln's Gettysburg Address
1864—Sherman takes Atlanta and Savannah; Lincoln re-elected		
1865—End of the War Between the States; Lincoln assassinated	Extremists in Congress abandon Lincoln's moderate policies. "Carpetbaggers" from the North plunder Southern states by their control of Negro votes. Devastated by war and "Reconstruction," the South slowly makes economic recovery	1865—Lincoln's Second Inaugural Address; Walt Whitman's war poems *Drum-Taps*
1867—"Reconstruction" Acts impose military rule on South		
1869–1877—Ulysses S. Grant is president		1878–1879—Sidney Lanier's "The Marshes of Glynn"; *Father Ryan's Poems* by Abram Joseph Ryan

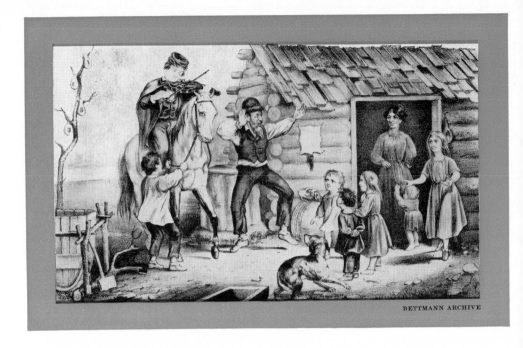

FOLKLORE, AMERICAN STYLE

In a nation's folklore the characteristics of the common people, that is, *the general population*, show themselves. Formerly, the education of most people all over the world consisted of the beliefs, the ideals, the habits of mind, that were handed down through the generations by word of mouth. Each nation's particular kind of *folk ideas* set it apart from all other nations. Even today, in our age of universal education, all of us have been shaped not only by our regular schooling but also by the simple verses, proverbs, even games, that we knew in childhood. The tricks of thought, the attitudes, that grew up in our land have entered into us and made us Americans.

At first, the different kinds of people who settled in America had few characteristics in common. In Colonial times we were a conglomerate—English, Dutch, German, French, Swedish. But soon the War for Independence, the westward extension of the frontier—all the distinctive American experiences—made us one nation. A sure sign that this unification had occurred was the development of our own folklore— a new kind which reflected American life. Throughout the nineteenth century the memory of the "old countries" faded, and their folk literature was replaced by tales and traditions firmly rooted in our own soil.

Folklore comes down to us as literature, whether oral or written, but the growth of an American folklore was more than a literary event. Before the *folk literature* came the *folk ideas* which were the cause of the literature. The springing up of a whole new folk tradition was really a historical event—a "cultural change"—as important as political, physical, or economic changes in the story of the United States.

Today our folklore comes from every part of the map of America. We sing mournful mountain ballads, and lonesome cowboy songs. We repeat "tall tales" of stalwart heroes like Paul Bunyan. We are familiar with backwoods superstitions; with scornfully humorous remarks like "Everybody's out of step but George"; and with picturesque exaggerations like "That horse"—or that car—"can turn on a dime with a nickel to spare." The imagination of the people has created a rich body of tradition which could only have been "made in the U.S.A."

Games, Play Parties, and Sayings

Some things we Americans do and say are so habitual that we hardly think about them. They seem as natural as eating or breathing. Yet they are a part of the culture that we have inherited from earlier generations. There are the verses that go with children's games, and the "play party" songs— some of which, perhaps, were children's songs originally. In many American communities dancing was frowned on as being sinful; so there developed the neighborhood frolic called the "play party." Instead of the forbidden fiddle music, there was singing by the young people. Hand in hand, each couple stepped briskly through the movements the songs called for. These "play party" songs are relics of the "quilting-bee," "house-raising," "pie supper" period of the American past. Finally, there are our folk sayings —the vivid, racy expressions which all of us learn and use without really noticing them.

The Needle's Eye

Two persons join hands and hold them up to make an arch. The others pass under the arch in single file while the two sing:

The needle's eye	A-many a beau
That doth supply	Have I let go
The thread that runs so true.	Because I wanted—you!

At the last word, YOU! the singers drop their arms, catching whoever is going through the "needle's eye" at that moment. Still encircling him with their arms, they lead him off a few feet and in a whisper ask him a question like "Which do you like, vanilla or chocolate ice cream?" All the "chocolates" are sent to stand in one place, and the "vanillas" are sent to another. The process is repeated until all are divided into two groups, ready to play whatever competitive game will follow.

◇◇◇◇◇

Skip to My Lou

In "Skip to My Lou," one player stands inside the circle of couples. Everybody sings as the one who is "it" skips around the circle and finally chooses a partner. The boy and girl are then pursued by the person whose partner has been stolen—all three keeping step to the music. The pursuit ends if the couple succeeds in getting around the circle to the gap that has been left in it. One player is left without a partner, so the procedure can start all over again.

I lost my partner, what'll I do?
I lost my partner, what'll I do?
I lost my partner, what'll I do?
   Skip to my Lou, my darling.

I'll get another one prettier than you,
I'll get another one prettier than you,
I'll get another one prettier than you,
   Skip to my Lou, my darling.

Gone again, skip to my Lou,
Gone again, skip to my Lou,

Gone again, skip to my Lou,
   Skip to my Lou, my darling.

Flies in the buttermilk, shoo fly, shoo,
Flies in the buttermilk, shoo fly, shoo,
Flies in the buttermilk, shoo fly, shoo,
   Skip to my Lou, my darling.

Cat in the cream jar, what'll I do?
Cat in the cream jar, what'll I do?
Cat in the cream jar, what'll I do?
   Skip to my Lou, my darling.

◇◇◇◇◇

The Miller Boy

The couples move in a circle, keeping step to the rhythm of their song. As they begin the final line, they reverse their direction.

    The miller boy, he lives by the mill,
    And the mill turns round with a free good will;
    One hand on the hopper and the other on the sack—
    You turn right around and you go right back.

"Skip to My Lou" from *A Treasury of Folk Songs.* Reprinted by permission of Sylvia and John Kolb.

FOR UNDERSTANDING

1. Read the directions for "The Needle's Eye" and explain "The thread that runs so true." What action makes it appropriate for the players to sing "A-many a beau have I let go"?

2. In the first three stanzas of "Skip to My Lou," how does *the meaning of the words* fit *the actions of the players*? How do the fourth and fifth stanzas suggest an old-fashioned country or small-town scene rather than a city environment?

3. Songs like "Skip to My Lou," and the actions that accompanied them, provided an easy, relaxing way for young people to be sociable and to have the fun of participating in a group activity. "Skip to My Lou" had an added appeal. It symbolized and suggested "going steady" and also the rivalry between boys who are interested in the same girl. Explain how this is true.

4. "The Miller Boy" is a song that might sometimes have been introduced suddenly during the playing of such a game as "Skip to My Lou." That is, on impulse someone might start to sing "The Miller Boy," and then the rest would join in. In such a situation, explain how there actually would be a player to represent the "miller boy." What would be the "mill"?

5. In one of the several versions of "The Miller Boy" the last line goes, "The girls step forward and the men step back." At this point, each boy lets go of his girl's arm and tries to take a new partner—the girl who is just behind him. This action gives the "miller" a chance to steal a partner. When it is played this way, point out the similarities between this game and "Skip to My Lou."

6. Try the game of "Skip to My Lou." A little practice may be necessary to fit your steps to the rhythm of the song. If no one knows the tune, you should be able to find it in any book of American folk songs.

◇◇◇◇◇

From # The People, Yes

CARL SANDBURG

In THE PEOPLE, YES, *a book of poetry about American democracy, Carl Sandburg includes some sayings, yarns, and riddles which he gives in the colorful but down-to-earth language of the people who originated them. They are folk literature because they have no known author but come from the people; and because they reflect the varied patterns of living and the characteristic attitudes of 150,000,000 citizens of a great nation.*

He has an automobile thirst and a wheelbarrow income.
I don't know where I'm going but I'm on my way. . . .
It's a slow burg—I spent a couple of weeks there one day.
He bit off more than he could chew. . . .
Let's take it apart to see how it ticks.

If we had a little ham we could have some ham and eggs if we had some eggs.
He always takes off his hat when he mentions his own name. . . .
"Why didn't you zigzag your car and miss him?" "He was zigzagging himself and outguessed me."

They have yarns

Of a skyscraper so tall they had to put hinges
On the two top stories so to let the moon go by,
Of one corn crop in Missouri when the roots
Went so deep and drew off so much water
The Mississippi riverbed that year was dry,
Of pancakes so thin they had only one side,
Of "a fog so thick we shingled the barn and six feet out on the fog,"
Of Pecos Pete straddling a cyclone in Texas and riding it to the west coast where "it rained out under him,"
Of the man who drove a swarm of bees across the Rocky Mountains and the Desert "and didn't lose a bee,"
Of a mountain railroad curve where the engineer in his cab can touch the caboose and spit in the conductor's eye,
Of the boy who climbed a cornstalk growing so fast he would have starved to death if they hadn't shot biscuits up to him,
Of the old man's whiskers: "When the wind was with him his whiskers arrived a day before he did.". . .

"Do tell!"
"I want to know!"
"You don't say so!"
"For the land's sake!"
"Gosh all fish-hooks!"
"Tell me some more.". . .

A high pressure salesman jumped off the Brooklyn Bridge and was saved by a policeman. But it didn't take him long to sell the idea to the policeman. So together they jumped off the bridge. . . .
An Ohio man bundled up the tin roof of a summer kitchen and sent it to a motor car maker with a complaint of his car not giving service. In three weeks a new car arrived for him and a letter: "We regret delay in shipment but your car was received in a very bad order."
A Dakota cousin of this Ohio man sent six years of tin can accumulations to the same works, asking them to overhaul his car. Two weeks later came a rebuilt car, five old tin cans, and a letter: "We are also forwarding you five parts not necessary in our new model.". . .
They have riddles, good and bad conundrums:
Which goes through the plank first, the bullet or the hole?
Where does the music go when the fiddle is put in the box?

Where does your lap go when you stand up?   The same place your fist goes when you open your hand.

What are the two smallest things mentioned in the Bible?   The widow's mite and the wicked flee.

Who are the shortest people mentioned in the Bible?   Bildad the Shuhite, Knee-high-miah, and the man who had nothing but from whom even that which he had was taken away.

What was the last thing Paul Revere said to his horse on the famous ride? "Whoa!"

"Did you hear about the empty barrel of flour?"   "No."   "Nothing in it."

What is there more of in the world than anything else?   Ends.

◇◇◇

FOR UNDERSTANDING

1. Which of the sayings in the first eight lines seem to you most typically American? Show how the ones you selected suggest some common American trait, habit, or way of looking at life.   Which are merely humorous "wisecracks"?

2. Exaggerated yarns or "tall tales" are a favorite form of American folk humor.   In telling completely unbelievable stories, the storytellers seem to be poking good-natured fun at the American's tendency to boast or brag about his own section of the country, or to value things merely because of their size.   Which of the yarns told here seem to you the most original?   Which sections of the country are represented?   Which specific occupations or industries are made fun of?

3. The author says of the American people: "They have riddles, good and bad conundrums."   Point out those you consider good.   If there are some you think are bad, tell why you think so.

WHAT MAKES POETRY?

Some people might say that this selection is not poetry, since the lines are irregular in beat and unrhymed.   However, if you try reading it aloud, you will discover that even in the jokes and anecdotes there are poetic rhythms beneath the apparently unpoetic language.   Another characteristic of poetry besides rhythm is effective use of figurative language.   See how many imaginative comparisons you can find.   They may be *similes*, that is, stated comparisons; or *metaphors*, comparisons that are merely suggested.

◇◇◇◇◇

Mountain Ballads and Dance Songs

Like most folk ballads each of the following mountain songs has several versions.   For example, the "falsehearted lover" in "On Top of Old Smoky" is sometimes a man and sometimes a girl.   Additional stanzas of "Down in the Valley" place the letter-writer in various jails, the name of the jail depending upon the location of the singer.   However, the universally popular theme of the rejected lover remains unchanged.

On Top of Old Smoky

On top of old Smoky,
All cover'd with snow,
I lost my true lover,
Come a-courtin' too slow.

A-courtin's a pleasure,   5
A-flirtin's a grief,
A falsehearted lover,
Is worse than a thief.

For a thief, he will rob you,
And take what you have,   10
But a falsehearted lover
Will send you to your grave.

She'll hug you and kiss you
And tell you more lies,
Than the crossties on the railroad,
Or the stars in the skies.   16

On top of old Smoky,
All covered with snow,
I lost my true lover,
A-courtin' too slow.   20

◇◇◇◇◇

Down in the Valley

Down in the valley, the valley so low,
Hang your head over, hear the wind blow.
Hear the wind blow, dear, hear the wind
    blow,
Hang your head over, hear the wind blow.

Writing this letter, containing three lines,
Answer my question, will you be mine?
Will you be mine, dear, will you be mine?
Answer my question, will you be mine?

Roses love sunshine, violets love dew,
Angels in heaven know I love you.
Know I love you, dear, know I love you,
Angels in heaven know I love you.

THE BALLAD-MAKER'S CRAFT

1. Do you think the singer in this version of "On Top of Old Smoky" is a boy or a girl? Point out the lines on which you base your opinion. What story is suggested by the statement "I lost my true lover a-courtin' too slow" and the later lines about "a falsehearted lover"? Explain the difference between "a-courtin'" and "a-flirtin'."

2. "Down in the Valley" provides many good examples of the ballad-maker's use of the poetic device of repetition to create musical sound effects. In any one stanza find as many examples as you can of the

repetition of words or phrases. Are there any expressions which occur more than twice?

3. Both these mournful love songs come from the Kentucky mountains. Which is the more typical ballad because it comes closer to telling a story? Which is purely lyric because it expresses the feelings or emotions of the singer? Which do you consider more musical?

4. Point out in both songs references to nature or to scenery which must have been familiar to the singers. Which seems to you most original or poetic?

◇◇◇◇◇

Turkey in the Straw

This song—known in some of its versions by the title "Zip Coon"—comes from Southern plantation life in frontier days. In the 1830's, minstrel singers spread it throughout the country. Its lively tune made it a favorite for square dancing.

As I was a-gwine on down the road,
With a tired team and a heavy load,
I cracked my whip and the leader sprung;
I says day-day to the wagon tongue.

CHORUS: *Turkey in the straw, (whistle) turkey in the hay,*   5
    (whistle)
Roll 'em up and twist 'em up a high tuckahaw,
And hit 'em up a tune called Turkey in the Straw.

Went out to milk and I didn't know how,
I milked the goat instead of the cow.
A monkey sittin' on a pile of straw   10
A-winkin' at his mother-in-law.

Met Mr. Catfish comin' down stream,
Says Mr. Catfish, "What does you mean?"
Caught Mr. Catfish by the snout
And turned Mr. Catfish wrong side out.   15

Came to the river and I couldn't get across,
Paid five dollars for an old blind hoss

3. LEADER—One of the front horses of a four- or six-horse team.
15. TURNED MR. CATFISH . . . OUT—This may be a reference to dressing the fish for frying.

EWING GALLOWAY

Wouldn't go ahead, nor he wouldn't stand still,
So he went up and down like an old saw mill.

As I came down the new cut road   20
Met Mr. Bullfrog, met Miss Toad,
And every time Miss Toad would sing
Ole Bullfrog cut a pigeon wing.

CHORUS: *Turkey in the straw, (whistle) turkey in the hay,*
                    (whistle)
                    Roll 'em up and twist 'em up a high tuckahaw,
                    And hit 'em up a tune called Turkey in the Straw.   25

20–24. NEW CUT ROAD . . . PIGEON WING—A pigeon wing is a fancy dance step made by leaping into the air and striking the legs together. The damp earth of a "new cut road" would be a
natural place to meet "Mr. Bullfrog."

◇◇◇

FOR UNDERSTANDING

1. The gay, nonsensical words of this song would be enjoyed by plantation people gathered together at a barn dance or other scene of merrymaking. The first stanza tells humorously about an accident with a team of horses. Apparently a sudden lurch of the wagon spilled the driver out of his seat. What caused the wagon to lurch? Where did the driver fall, judging from the fact that he found himself saying "Day-day" —"Good day" or "How d'y' do"—to the wagon tongue?

2. A later stanza says that Mr. Bullfrog "cut a pigeon wing." Why is this particular dance step appropriate to him?

3. Mention all the details you can find in the song which suggest plantation or country life.

4. To really enjoy "Turkey in the Straw" you should hear it sung, preferably to the accompaniment of an old-time fiddler. If a recording is not available, some member of the class might be able to play the tune on a violin, accordion, or harmonica to provide appropriate atmosphere for a soloist or a quartet from the class.

Go Down, Moses

In the Book of Exodus in the Old Testament, Moses is a leader of the Israelites who are held in bondage by Pharaoh, king of Egypt. Repeatedly, God commands Moses, "Go unto Pharaoh, and say unto him, Thus saith the Lord, let my people go, that they may serve me." Naturally, God's command to Moses had particular appeal to the Negro people, who were also in bondage. In this slow, solemn Negro "spiritual," singers and hearers could apply the Bible story to their own lives.

When Israel was in Egypt Land,	Thus spoke the Lord, bold Moses said,	
Let my people go,	Let my people go,	10
Oppressed so hard they could not stand,	If not I'll smite your first-born dead,	
Let my people go.	Let my people go.	

Go down, Moses,	5	Go down, Moses,	
Way down in Egypt Land,		Way down in Egypt Land,	
Tell old Pharaoh		Tell old Pharaoh	15
To let my people go.		To let my people go.	

11. I'LL SMITE YOUR FIRST-BORN DEAD—Each time he receives the message, Pharaoh promises to set the Israelites free—but he breaks the promise. At last Moses prophesies that the Lord will kill the first-born child in every Egyptian family.

◇◇◇

FOR UNDERSTANDING

1. By the devout people chanting this song, the command "Let *my* people go" would at once be understood as a reference to the people of Israel who were under the special protection of God. Nevertheless, the first actual mention of God in the song comes as a sort of climax. What is the line in which this occurs?

2. Point out two different types of *repetition* in the song which help to make the warning emphatic.

3. Read the song aloud. What particular vowel sound is repeated many times, giving a solemn effect?

THE BIBLE STORY OF MOSES

1. Appoint one student to read the entire story of the dealings between Moses and Pharaoh and summarize it in an oral report. Each of the plagues with which God punished the Egyptians should be mentioned. The story begins in Chapter VII of the Book of Exodus, and ends in Chapter XII, verse 42.

2. What does the name *Exodus* mean?

Nobody Knows de Trouble I See

The sincerity and directness of this song have made it one of the best loved of all spirituals.

Nobody knows de trouble I see,
Nobody knows but Jesus;
Nobody knows de trouble I see,
Glory hallelujah!

Sometimes I'm up, sometimes I'm 5
down,
Oh, yes, Lord;
Sometimes I'm almost to de groun',
Oh, yes, Lord.

Altho' you see me goin' 'long so,
Oh, yes, Lord; 10
I have my trials here below,
Oh, yes, Lord.

Nobody knows de trouble I see,
Nobody knows but Jesus;
Nobody knows de trouble I see, 15
Glory hallelujah!

FOR UNDERSTANDING
This song, like "Go Down, Moses," is about trouble and unhappiness. What similarity can you see in the two songs in *the thought that consoles the singers* in their troubles?

Swing Low, Sweet Chariot

One of the dramatic passages from the Old Testament is the first part of the second chapter of the second book of Kings which tells how chariots from heaven appeared to carry up the Prophet Elijah when his work on earth was finished. The old man with his follower Elisha walked away from the palace of the king to the River Jordan and beyond it, "And it came to pass as they still went on and talked, that behold there appeared a chariot of fire and horses of fire, which parted them both asunder; and Elijah went up by a whirlwind into heaven. And Elisha saw it and he cried, 'My father, my father, the chariots of Israel and the horsemen thereof!'"

In the mind of an oppressed race, what a glorious leave-taking from the trials of earth! The early spiritual, "Swing low, sweet chariot, comin' for to carry me home," became a hope and a prayer sung by the Negroes everywhere.

512

CHORUS

Swing low, sweet char - i - ot, Com - in' for to car - ry me home!

Swing low, sweet char- i - ot, Com - in' for to car - ry me home!

STANZA

I looked o - ver Jor - dan an' what did I see,

Com - in' for to car - ry me home! A band of an - gels

com - in' af - ter me, Com - in' for to car - ry me home!

Refrain: LEADER: *Swing low, sweet chariot,*
                CHORUS: *Comin' for to carry me home,*
                LEADER: *Swing low, sweet chariot,*
                CHORUS: *Comin' for to carry me home.*

                LEADER: I looked over Jordan and what did I see,
                CHORUS: Comin' for to carry me home,
                LEADER: A band of angels comin' after me,
                CHORUS: Comin' for to carry me home.

Refrain: *Swing low, etc.*

                LEADER: If you get there before I do,
                CHORUS: Comin' for to carry me home,
                LEADER: Tell all my friends I'm comin' too,
                CHORUS: Comin' for to carry me home.

Refrain: *Swing low, etc.*

                LEADER: The brightest day that ever I saw,
                CHORUS: Comin' for to carry me home,
                LEADER: When Jesus wash'd my sins away,
                CHORUS: Comin' for to carry me home.

Refrain: *Swing low, etc.*

                LEADER: I'm sometimes up and sometimes down,
                CHORUS: Comin' for to carry me home,
                LEADER: But still my soul feels heav'nly bound,
                CHORUS: Comin' for to carry me home.

FOR UNDERSTANDING

1. Where is *home?* Explain why this song would be comforting to people who were unhappy or unfortunate.

2. In the spiritual, words and music are so much a part of one another that real appreciation comes only as we sing the words or hear them sung. The music for "Swing Low, Sweet Chariot" is so well known that most of us can sing the words in our minds as we read. Notice how the song lifts death from a frightening experience to a thing of triumph. Why do you think so many of the spirituals deal with the theme of death? Why do the songs about death have a feeling of joy in them?

3. The joyous line *Comin' for to carry me home* attains wonderful power as the song proceeds. The repeated singing of the line makes the heavenly gates of pearl and the golden streets seem very near. To experience the full appeal of this spiritual, let the entire class sing it vigorously.

◇◇◇◇◇

My Old Kentucky Home

STEPHEN FOSTER

Because we know the poet-composer of "My Old Kentucky Home," it is not a true folk song. However, like many other Stephen Foster songs, it has most of the characteristics of folk literature. It presents a colorful, though somewhat romantic, picture of Negro life in the Old South. It has the simple rhythm and the swing of folk music. And, most important, it is universally loved and sung.

> The sun shines bright in the old Kentucky home,
> 'Tis summer, the darkies are gay,
> The corn top's ripe and the meadow's in the bloom,
> While the birds make music all the day.
> The young folks roll on the little cabin floor,   5
> All merry, all happy and bright:
> By'n by hard times comes a-knocking at the door,
> Then my old Kentucky home, good night!

> CHORUS: *Weep no more, my lady,*
>   *O! weep no more today!*   10
>   *We will sing one song for the old Kentucky home,*
>   *For the old Kentucky home, far away.*

They hunt no more for the 'possum and the coon
On the meadow, the hill, and the shore;
They sing no more by the glimmer of the moon,   15
On the bench by the old cabin door.
The day goes by like a shadow o'er the heart,
With sorrow where all was delight;
The time has come when the darkies have to part,
Then my old Kentucky home, good night!   20

The head must bow and the back will have to bend,
Wherever the darky may go:
A few more days, and the trouble all will end
In the field where the sugar canes grow.
A few more days for to tote the weary load,   25
No matter 'twill never be light;
A few more days till we totter on the road,
Then my old Kentucky home, good night!

LIFE ON THE OLD PLANTATION

1. What story do you think lies behind the sadness of this song? Who seems to be speaking? What has happened to change the happy situation described in the first six lines?

2. What details suggest a romantic picture of an old Southern plantation? Was the song written of pre-war or post-war days? Tell why you think so. Check your answer with the dates of Foster's life.

3. Who is the "lady" referred to in the chorus? How does Foster suggest here an affectionate relationship between the Negro and his white folks?

STEPHEN COLLINS FOSTER

(1826–1864)

We are likely to think of Stephen Foster as a Southerner because he discovered and preserved for us so much of the charm of plantation singing. Actually, he was born in a suburb of Pittsburgh, Pennsylvania; and he spent the last years of his life in New York City. But there are no local boundaries to the appeal of his songs. They are sung wherever the English language is known.

His was not a happy life. His family, who were prosperous enough, could not understand a dreamer who preferred music to business. He married Jane McDowell; and she too lost patience with a husband who could not settle down to a conventional, prosperous routine of living. With his music he was not successful financially. He wrote "Old Folks at Home" in 1850, and its popularity helped the sale of other songs. Though he sold many of them for shamefully little, there were years when he realized a fair income. But unhappiness at home, dislike for business, general discontent sent him from a comfortable home to an uncertain, then wretched, existence in New York. He died in poverty in 1864. Appreciation has grown with the years. His heirs realized a considerable fortune in royalties; but more important, his songs have found their way into every American home and heart.

The cowboys of the West and Southwest made little use of books but they composed their own literature in the form of ballads. Two of the best known are given here. "Old Paint" used to be sung at social gatherings in town—after the last dance, and before the cowboys went to get their horses and ride away to the ranches where they worked. The song was their farewell to the girls they had been dancing with. Many extra verses were made up, in order to prolong the leave-taking. "The Cowboy's Lament" was supposed to teach a lesson to "dashing" young fellows who were tempted to drink and gamble.

❖❖❖❖❖

Good-by, Old Paint

My foot in the stirrup, my pony won't stan',
Good-by, old Paint, I'm a-leavin' Cheyenne.
I'm a-leavin' Cheyenne, I'm off for Montan';
Good-by, old Paint, I'm a-leavin' Cheyenne.

I'm a-ridin' old Paint, I'm a-leadin' old Dan;   5
Good-by, old Paint, I'm a-leavin' Cheyenne.
With my feet in the stirrups, my bridle in my hand;
Good-by, old Paint, I'm a-leavin' Cheyenne.

Old Paint's a good pony, he paces when he can;
Good-by, little Annie, I'm off for Cheyenne.   10
Oh, hitch up your horses and feed 'em some hay,
And seat yourself by me as long as you stay.

My hosses ain't hungry, they won't eat your hay;
My wagon is loaded and rollin' away.
I'm a-ridin' old Paint, I'm a-leadin' old Dan,   15
I'm a-goin' to Montan' to throw the hoolihan. . . .

Oh, when I die take my saddle from the wall,
Put it on my pony, lead him from the stall,
Tie my bones to his back, turn our faces to the west,
And we'll ride the prairie that we love the best.   20

16. TO THROW THE HOOLIHAN—To throw the lasso in a special way so that the loop sails through the air horizontally and does not frighten the horses near by. If they use the "hoolihan" or "hooley-ann" throw, several men can rope their horses in a corral at the same time. Therefore, as used here the expression means "to catch my horse in the morning"—that is, "to go to work."

The Cowboy's Lament

As I walked out in the streets of Laredo,
As I walked out in Laredo one day,
I spied a poor cowboy wrapped up in white linen,
Wrapped up in white linen as cold as the clay.

"Oh, beat the drum slowly and play the fife lowly,   5
Play the dead march as you carry me along;
Take me to the green valley, there lay the sod o'er me,
For I'm a young cowboy and I know I've done wrong."

"I see by your outfit that you are a cowboy"—
These words he did say as I boldly stepped by.   10
"Come sit down beside me and hear my sad story;
I am shot in the breast and I know I must die. . . .

"It was once in the saddle I used to go dashing,
It was once in the saddle I used to go gay;
First to the dram-house and then to the card-house;   15
Got shot in the breast and I am dying today.

"Get six jolly cowboys to carry my coffin;
Get six pretty maidens to bear up my pall.
Put bunches of roses all over my coffin,
Put roses to deaden the sods as they fall.   20

"Then swing your rope slowly and rattle your spurs lowly,
And give a wild whoop as you carry me along;
And in the grave throw me and roll the sod o'er me
For I'm a young cowboy and I know I've done wrong.". . .

We beat the drum slowly and played the fife lowly,   25
And bitterly wept as we bore him along;
For we all loved our comrade, so brave, young, and handsome,
We all loved our comrade although he'd done wrong.

15. DRAM-HOUSE—Saloon or barroom. A dram is a drink of liquor.
18. PALL—The black cloth used to cover a coffin; or, in a figurative sense, the coffin itself.

"The Cowboy's Lament" from *Cowboy Songs and Other Frontier Ballads* by John A. and Alan Lomax. Reprinted by permission of Mrs. Ruby Terrill Lomax.

FOR UNDERSTANDING

1. In "Good-by, Old Paint" what details of *riding* emphasize the fact that the singer is in the act of leaving?

2. Which lines are an invitation from one of the girls to stay a while longer? Is the invitation accepted?

3. In "The Cowboy's Lament" the dying man has "done wrong" by getting into a

fight. What is he dying of? How is it suggested that the fight was a quarrel over a game of cards?

4. In spite of its mournful "lesson," this ballad was sung just for fun. Which details of the cowboy's last requests suggest youth and high spirits? To appreciate the not-very-sad rhythm of the ballad, read aloud the first stanza and the last three—speaking the lines somewhat rapidly.

◇◇◇◇◇

Jesse James

One of the earliest of the bad men who have become famous in American story and song was Jesse James, leader of a notorious outlaw gang. He seems to have had many friends of the kind who would ordinarily be considered decent people. They admired his coolness in the face of danger, and his success in evading capture. When he was finally killed in 1882 it was not by officers of the law but by one of his own followers, who shot him in order to receive the large reward that was offered. Afterward, a generation of Americans sang the following ballad in praise of Jesse James' "great" deeds.

To understand the ballad you need to know that James sometimes lived among unsuspecting, law-abiding citizens under the name of "Thomas Howard." Legend has it that "Mister Howard" was occasionally a member of a sheriff's posse which was out hunting for Jesse James.

Jesse James was a lad that killed a-many a man;
He robbed the Danville train.
But that dirty little coward that shot Mister Howard
Has laid poor Jesse in his grave.

CHORUS: *Poor Jesse had a wife to mourn for his life,*   5
Three children, they were brave;
But that dirty little coward that shot Mister Howard
Has laid poor Jesse in his grave.

It was Robert Ford, that dirty little coward,
I wonder how does he feel,   10
For he ate of Jesse's bread and he slept in Jesse's bed,
Then laid poor Jesse in his grave.

"Jesse James" from *American Ballads and Folk Songs* by John A. and Alan Lomax. Reprinted by permission of Mrs. Ruby Terrill Lomax.

Jesse was a man, a friend to the poor,
He never would see a man suffer pain;
And with his brother Frank he robbed the Chicago bank,   15
And stopped the Glendale train.

It was his brother Frank that robbed the Glendale bank,
And carried the money from the town;
It was in this very place that they had a little race,
For they shot Captain Sheets to the ground.   20

It was on a Wednesday night, the moon was shining bright,
They robbed the Glendale train;
The people, they did say, for many miles away,
It was robbed by Frank and Jesse James.

It was on a Saturday night, Jesse was at home,   25
Talking with his family brave,
Robert Ford came along like a thief in the night
And laid poor Jesse in his grave.

The people held their breath when they heard of Jesse's death,
And wondered how he ever came to die.   30
It was one of the gang called little Robert Ford,
He shot poor Jesse on the sly.

This song was made by Billy Gashade,
As soon as the news did arrive;
He said there was no man with the law in his hand,   35
Who could take Jesse James when alive.

<hr>

WHO IS A HERO?

1. Quote lines telling of Jesse's deeds which, among civilized people, are considered wicked. What good characteristics does the ballad-maker assign to his hero? Which lines suggest his reasons for feeling sorry for "poor Jesse"?

2. The author admires Jesse James though he "killed a-many a man." Why, then, does he despise Robert Ford who killed Jesse? What was there about Ford's act that made it seem particularly cowardly and mean to the man who composed the ballad and to the people who sang it?

3. Like many other ballads and folk songs, "Jesse James" makes use of repetition. List expressions that occur more than once in the ballad. What other characteristics of ballads does this poem have?

4. The author of this ballad has managed to put his own name into the last stanza. What is his name? How would you rate him as a poet? Point out specific passages to support your opinion. In the last two lines of this final stanza, he evidently feels that he is offering a reason for admiring the "hero." Explain what the reason is.

Casey Jones

The railroads stretched out longer and the trains ran faster in America than in other lands. Many a saying and humorous tale exists to show what an important place in our consciousness the railroad holds. Casey Jones was only one of a number of "brave engineers" whose deaths are lamented in song. It is said that "Wash" Sanders, an engine wiper in the roundhouse at Canton, Mississippi, made the ballad out of a still older song after Casey's last run on the fast "Cannonball."

Come all you rounders that want to hear
The story of a brave engineer.
Casey Jones was the rounder's name,
On a big eight wheeler, boys, he won his fame.
The caller called Casey at half-past four,   5
He kissed his wife at the station door,
He mounted to the cabin with the orders in his hand,
And he took his farewell trip to that promis'd land.

CHORUS: *Casey Jones—mounted to his cabin,*
            Casey Jones—with his orders in his hand.   10
            Casey Jones—mounted to his cabin,
            And he took his farewell trip to that promis'd land.

When he pulled up that Reno hill,
He whistled for the crossing with an awful shrill;
The switchman knew by the engine's moans   15
That the man at the throttle was Casey Jones.
He looked at his water and his water was low;

He looked at his watch and his watch was slow;
He turned to his fireman and this is what he said,
"Boy, we're going to reach Frisco, but we'll all be dead."   20

CHORUS: *Casey Jones—going to reach Frisco,*
           Casey Jones—but we'll all be dead,
           Casey Jones—going to reach Frisco,
           We're going to reach Frisco, but we'll all be dead.

"So turn on your water and shovel in your coal,   25
Stick your head out the window, watch those drivers roll;
I'll drive her till she leaves the rail,
For I'm eight hours late by that Western Mail."
When he was within six miles of the place,
There number four stared him straight in the face.   30
He turned to his fireman, said, "Jim, you'd better jump,
For there're two locomotives that are going to bump."

CHORUS: *Casey Jones—two locomotives,*
           Casey Jones—going to bump,
           Casey Jones—two locomotives,   35
           There're two locomotives that are going to bump.

Casey said just before he died,
"There're two more roads I would like to ride."
The fireman said, "Which ones can they be?"
"Oh, the Northern Pacific and the Santa Fe."   40
Mrs. Jones sat at her bed a-sighing
Just to hear the news that her Casey was dying.
"Hush up children, and quit your cryin',
For you've got another poppa on the Salt Lake Line."

CHORUS: *Casey Jones—got another poppa.*   45
           Casey Jones—on the Salt Lake Line,
           Casey Jones—got another poppa,
           For you've got another poppa on the Salt Lake Line.

26. DRIVERS—The large wheels of steam locomotives, which are connected together by coupling rods so that all of them help "drive" the locomotive forward.

◇◇◇

FOR UNDERSTANDING

1. Where in the song are we told that Casey Jones had a premonition, or forewarning, of his own death?

2. What was his reason for driving the train at breakneck speed on this particular occasion? Can you find a hint that he was often a hard-driving engineer?

3. The cause of the wreck is given in the line "There number four stared him straight in the face." What was the cause?

4. Excessive speed was indirectly responsible for the tragedy—yet the song seems to

praise Casey, rather than condemn him, for his foolhardiness. What line or lines stand out as glorifying the tremendous speed and power of the big locomotive?

5. Sing, or recite in songlike rhythm, at least a part of "Casey Jones." Let two persons give the stanzas in duet, with everybody joining in on the choruses.

John Henry

John Henry was the greatest steel-driving man ever known. But in his day—that is, in the period in which this ballad was composed—mechanical power was beginning to win out over human muscle. In a gallant last stand, John Henry tried to prove that no machine could beat him and his hammer in drilling for the C. & O. railroad tunnel. As one version of the story has it, it was "de flesh ag'in de steam." But then he died—and the machine still goes on. In the memories of laboring men, John Henry was cherished as one of their fallen champions.

When John Henry was a little fellow,
    You could hold him in the palm of
        your hand,
He said to his pa, "When I grow up
I'm gonna be a steel-driving man.
        Gonna be a steel-driving man."   5

When John Henry was a little baby,
    Setting on his mammy's knee,
He said "The Big Bend Tunnel on the
        C. & O. Road
Is gonna be the death of me,
        Gonna be the death of me."   10

One day his captain told him,
    How he had bet a man
That John Henry would beat his steam
        drill down,
    Cause John Henry was the best in the
        land,
    John Henry was the best in the
        land.   15

John Henry kissed his hammer,
    White man turned on steam,
Shaker held John Henry's trusty steel,
    Was the biggest race the world had
        ever seen,
    Lord, the biggest race the world ever
        seen.   20

John Henry on the right side,
    The steam drill on the left,
"Before I'll let your steam drill beat me
        down,
    I'll hammer my fool self to death,
        Hammer my fool self to death."   25

Captain heard a mighty rumbling,
    Said "The mountain must be caving
        in,"
John Henry said to the captain,   28
    "It's my hammer swinging in de wind,
        My hammer swinging in de wind."

18. SHAKER—The assistant who held the drill for John Henry, and rotated it slightly after each hammer blow so it would bite deeper.

"John Henry" from John Henry: Tracking Down a Negro Legend by Guy B. Johnson, reprinted by permission of Mr. Johnson and the University of North Carolina Press.

522

John Henry said to his shaker,
"Shaker, you'd better pray;
For if ever I miss this piece of steel,
    Tomorrow'll be your burial day,   34
    Tomorrow'll be your burial day.". . .

John Henry said to his captain,
"Before I ever leave town,
Gimme a twelve-pound hammer wid a
    whale-bone handle,
    And I'll hammer dat steam driver down,
    I'll hammer dat steam drill on
        down."   40

John Henry said to his captain,
"A man ain't nothin' but a man,
But before I'll let dat steam drill beat me
    down
    I'll die wid my hammer in my hand,
    Die wid my hammer in my
        hand."   45

The man that invented the steam drill
He thought he was mighty fine,
John Henry drove down fourteen feet,
    While the steam drill only made nine,
    Steam drill only made nine.   50

"Oh, look away over yonder, captain,
You can't see like me,"
He gave a long and loud and lonesome cry,
    "Lawd, a hammer be the death of me,
    A hammer be the death of
        me!". . . .   55

John Henry hammering on the mountain
As the whistle blew for half-past two,
The last words his captain heard him say,
    "I've done hammered my insides in
        two,
    Lawd, I've hammered my insides in
        two."   60

The hammer that John Henry swung
It weighed over twelve pound,
He broke a rib in his left hand side   63
    And his intrels fell on the ground,
    And his intrels fell on the ground.

John Henry, O, John Henry,
His blood is running red,
Fell right down with his hammer to the
    ground
    Said, "I beat him to the bottom but
        I'm dead,
    Lawd, beat him to the bottom but
        I'm dead."   70

When John Henry was laying there dying,
The people all by his side,
The very last words they heard him say,
    "Give me a cool drink of water 'fore I
        die,
    Cool drink of water 'fore I die." 75

John Henry had a little woman,
The dress she wore was red,
She went down the track, and she never
    looked back,
    Going where her man fell dead,   79
    Going where her man fell dead. . . .

They carried him down by the river,
And buried him in the sand,
And everybody that passed that way,
    Said, "There lies that steel-driving man,
    There lies a steel-driving man."   85

They took John Henry to the river,
And buried him in the sand,
And every locomotive come a-roaring by,
    Says, "There lies that steel-drivin' man,
    Lawd, there lies a *steel*-drivin' man."

FOR UNDERSTANDING

1. In tragic ballads there is sometimes a sense of fate, a feeling that the tragic event could not be escaped. Does John Henry (like Casey Jones) have a glimpse of the fate that is in store for him?

2. How does the captain show that he has great confidence in John Henry's pow-

ers? Quote two passages that express John Henry's pride in himself. In what lines are we told that he actually beats the steam drill?

3. Ballads about death often dwell on the dying person's last words, or on the attitudes of surviving relatives and friends. What were John Henry's last words? How did his wife show her grief?

4. The feeling that in his day John Henry had done great things for the railroad is expressed in the next-to-last stanza. What is his "epitaph," pronounced again and again by the trains that roar over the road John Henry helped to build?

REPETITION IN BALLADS

Being brief and not at all elaborate, folk ballads cannot use many poetic devices for beauty and emphasis. One of the few that are often used is *repetition*. As sung or told in the South, by means of repetition the story of John Henry created an almost religious intensity in the listeners—caused them to think hard every moment about his determination and endurance.

Describe the very simple kind of repetition that occurs within each stanza. What is the *refrain* of the ballad—that is, what expression is often repeated in the story?

❖❖❖❖❖

STORIES OF PAUL BUNYAN

There may have been a real "Paul Bunyon," a French Canadian who was chief of a logging camp in the 1840's. Many true tales, or what were supposed to be true tales, were told of his strength and ability. Later, when the stories reached logging camps in the United States, they were transformed into tales of wild, exaggerated humor. To some extent, they got mixed with old Scandinavian hero legends. When the tales were finally written down in English, the French "Bunyon" was changed to "Bunyan." In the logging camps, when an unusually big or awkward man was hired his fellow workmen made fun of him by calling him a "Paul Bunyan." And when a man bragged about the great deeds he had done, someone would say, "That's nothing. In Paul Bunyan's outfit they used to—"

In Paul Bunyan's outfit they used to get out bigger logs, and get them out faster, than any other logging crew in the woods. One reason was that they had the help of Paul's powerful Blue Ox, Babe. The ox measured twenty-four ax handles and a plug of Star tobacco between the eyes. The measurement is sometimes given as forty-two ax handles and a plug of Star tobacco, but this figure is thought to be an exaggeration.

Once Paul Bunyan's crew was using a logging road which was unusually crooked. Paul hitched Babe to the road to straighten it out. The Blue Ox pulled it straight, but there were several miles of road left over. Paul gave the remainder to the city of Minneapolis as a boulevard —or, according to another version, laid it around a circular lake as a highway.

To get ready to cut down a stand of timber, Paul Bunyan would make only

of the way, and the cement mixer dumped batter on the griddle. Other boys on roller skates traveled up and down the center of the table delivering the pancakes.

◇◇◇◇◇◇◇◇◇◇◇◇◇◇◇◇◇◇◇◇◇◇◇◇◇◇◇◇◇◇◇◇◇

FOR UNDERSTANDING

1. Every person who made up a story about Paul Bunyan seems to have tried to outdo all earlier storytellers. Which of the yarns given here seem most exaggerated? Which do you think are most clever, or show most originality and imagination?

2. What other exploits of Paul or his Blue Ox do you know? Tell some of them.

SPIN YOUR OWN YARNS

1. There is a tendency for the Paul Bunyan stories to go on multiplying. Some of the later tales take him out of the lumberjack business and into pipeline construction in the Southwest, or telegraph construction work. In the latter trade Paul put up telegraph lines so fast that the men of the ground crew could keep up only by shooting the insulators to him with a machine gun.

Make up some original stories to illustrate Paul's cleverness and superior ability, using such subjects as Paul Bunyan on the Football Field; Paul Bunyan, Automobile Manufacturer; and Paul Bunyan Helps Overcome the Housing Shortage.

2. Mention at least two remarkable incidents in *The People, Yes*, by Carl Sandburg, which resemble some of the surprising things done by Paul Bunyan. See if members of the class can think of other humorous "whoppers" which are told in America —fish stories, or hunting stories, or some of the prize-winning stories of the organization known as the "Liars' Club."

3. Some heroes of television, movies, and comic strips who have fantastic powers are Mighty Mouse, Superman, and Fearless Fosdick. Summarize one or more of their adventures which are so amazing as to be worthy of being compared with the achievements of Paul Bunyan.

four cuts in each tree, one on each side. Then he would take an ax with a special rope handle, swing it around his head, and fall all the trees at once.

Paul dug the Columbia River so he would have a way to get his logs to market at Astoria on the west coast. First he plowed out the river, then filled it with water so he could float the logs down.

One year it rained so long and hard in the North Woods that Paul decided to do something about it. A column of water was pouring straight down out of the sky. Paul swam up this column of water clear to the top, and turned it off.

Paul Bunyan had the biggest logging crew in the world. At meal time, his men were fed at a table over a mile long. The cooks used a pancake griddle about an acre in size. To grease it, a boy was hired to fasten a side of bacon to each foot and skate over the hot griddle. At one side stood a big cement mixer full of pancake batter. When everything was ready a whistle blew, the boy skipped out

For Broader Understanding

1. What is folklore? How has it been preserved and passed on from one generation to another? It is sometimes said that we can understand a nation better through its folk literature than through other kinds of literature. What arguments might be given in support of this idea?

2. When might a song be considered a piece of folk literature even though the author is known? Give one example of such a song.

3. Thinking over the folklore selections that you have read, explain how they reveal some of the distinctive characteristics of Americans. In your answer mention some specific folk songs or other folk literature, and tell what American qualities are illustrated in each.

4. "Tall tales"—that is, stories about unusual deeds or unusual adventures—are especially prominent in American folklore. Give at least three examples of tall tales in the selections you have read.

5. Name several of the best known folk heroes of America. Explain what each one was famous for. Do the different heroes have any characteristics in common? If so, tell what they are.

6. Name four regions of the United States that are represented in the folklore of our land. Give at least one example of folklore from each region. How might a person reading the folk selection be able to guess what region produced it?

7. Give as many examples as possible of folklore connected with specific happenings or periods in the historical development of America. Some may refer to occupations or industries that were prominent at a particular time in the past.

8. In your opinion, which one of the folk songs in this book is *most musical?* Compare your choice with that of other members of the class.

CLASS PROJECTS: FOLKLORE IN YOUR COMMUNITY

1. Make a collection of local superstitions and other folk beliefs which class members have heard of. One example might be throwing a pinch of salt over the left shoulder. Others might be certain acts which are considered lucky or unlucky. Include such practices as planting crops at a particular "time of the moon." Give the full details of each one, exactly as you have heard them. Tell the origin or the reason for each belief if you can.

2. Make a collection of traditions about places in your community, past events, and past residents. Don't overlook well-known humorous yarns. Of course, if these stories are true they are a part of local *history*. But if most people know them, or if you often hear them mentioned, they are also part of a body of local *tradition*.

READING, SPEAKING, AND WRITING ACTIVITIES

Use encyclopedias, American history books, and books from the Further Reading list at the end of this unit in preparing these reports. Your librarian may be able to help you find additional sources of information.

1. Davy Crockett. Explain the chief characteristics of this famous frontier figure. Give the main events of his life, including his political career. Tell at least two humorous things he is supposed to have done or said.

2. Read aloud, and explain, the traditional ballad called "The Erie Canal," with its chorus of "Low bridge, everybody down!"

3. One student who is fond of cowboy stories should read aloud the humorous broncho-busting ballad "Strawberry Roan."

4. Describe the traditions that have be-

come established in political cartoons. What does "Uncle Sam" look like? Are there certain accepted ways of picturing other nations? How is the American Congress pictured? Try to find cartoons that show the character named "John Q. Public." What does he look like?

5. Write a brief report on verses and riddles you learned in childhood. There should be five or six in all. Give the answers to the riddles, and explain the situations in which the verses would be sung or recited. Use only the ones you learned by hearing them—not ones you have read. If you can, tell *how long ago* you first heard each one.

6. Give eight examples of humorous sayings and colorful slangy expressions you often hear. These should be expressions that are used in your own community— whether or not they are also known all over the country. Use the local version of each. Explain the meaning of the ones that are not completely clear.

7. Write a report on two details of modern life which are standard subjects for jokes and humorous cartoons. One example would be *fathers playing with their children's toys.* Do not use this example, but think of two other favorite topics for jokes. You should be able to think of specific topics concerning motorists, or concerning the activities of school-age people. Explain what belief is expressed in each, and for each one give examples of cartoons or jokes. Tell whether you think the beliefs are well founded, or just bits of folklore which we all accept even though mainly fictitious.

8. Western movies have built up a body of folklore surrounding the cowboy—who in real life probably was not much like the notion given in the movies. Describe him as he is pictured—his dress, his speech, his character, what he can do, and how he spends his time.

FOR FURTHER READING

Stephen Vincent Benét, *The Devil and Daniel Webster* (Countryman). Here is a modern version of the old Faust legend. Benét's Faust, a poor New Hampshire farmer who sells his soul for personal gain, wins his freedom through the efforts of Daniel Webster.

Walter Blair, *Tall Tale America: A Legendary History of Our Humorous Heroes* (Coward). This is an excellent retelling of stories about Captain Stormalong, Jonathan Slick, Mike Fink, Mose, the New York fireman, and Paul Bunyan.

Mody C. Boatright, editor, *Folk Travelers: Ballads, Tales, and Talk* (Southern University Press). The folklore of the Southwest is stressed here. The editor shows how anecdotes, folk ballads, cattle brands, street cries, and the like change as they pass from one part of the country to another.

B. A. Botkin, editor, *A Treasury of New England Folklore* (Crown). Sea chanteys, ghost stories, and graveyard epitaphs appear in this collection of Yankee lore.

James Cloyd Bowman, *Pecos Bill* (Whitman). Here are tall tales about a cowboy and his horse "Widow Maker."

James Daugherty, editor, *Their Weight in Wildcats* (Houghton). In this collection of stories, legendary heroes like Mike Fink, Johnny Appleseed, Davy Crockett, Kit Carson, John Henry, and Paul Bunyan "lick their weight in wildcats."

Maria Leach, *Soup Stone* (Funk). The origin of such things as forks, bedsteads, responses to sneezes, and headache remedies is told here.

Vance Randolph, *We Always Lie to Strangers* (Columbia University Press). These tall tales from the Ozarks tell about oversize and undersize crops, fantastic animals, and unusual weather conditions.

Irwin Shapiro, *Joe Magarac and His USA Citizenship Papers* (Messner). This story tells how "the greatest steelman that ever was" got his citizenship papers.

Louis Untermeyer, *The Wonderful Adventures of Paul Bunyan* (Heritage). This author gives some new twists to the Paul Bunyan fable. The book is well written in a clear, rhythmic style.

527

MASTERS OF AMERICAN LITERATURE

AN AMERICAN "RENAISSANCE"

By the 1820's an active, vigorous literary life was beginning in eastern America. The wilderness had been tamed and the Revolutionary War fought and won. With freedom and security, the American people could begin to enjoy the things they had fought for—among them prosperity, leisure, and acquaintance with books and art. Graduates of Harvard, Yale, Princeton, and newer colleges were interested in scholarship and fine literature. In thriving cities like Boston and Philadelphia there was a growing number of people who valued books and who would buy them. In half a dozen places, literary magazines were founded. Of course, America had had newspapers since early Colonial times. But these new publications with their verse, stories, and essays helped to develop a more cultured reading public.

Under these conditions, fine poetry and other excellent literature began to be written. The period from about 1830 to the War Between the States has been called by some commentators a "flowering," and by others a "renaissance" (new birth) in which the American spirit expressed itself fully for the first time. A large body of literature was built up rather rapidly. Some of it, especially the earlier works, imitated English literature in style and language. This was natural because all authors imitate, and learn from, each other to some extent—and at first there were no good models except in European books. However, each author was trying to find ways to adapt his writing to his surroundings and to his public. As more books were published, a distinctively American tradition began to take form. Younger writers came along who were influenced more by their countrymen than by Europeans. The true masterpieces of the "American Renaissance" are as unmistakably American as a hickory nut or an Indian summer day.

Nearly all these writers dealt with American subject matter. They wrote about the past—old colonial days, and heroic deeds during the Revolutionary War; or they looked at the scene around them and wrote of the new ideas that were suddenly bubbling up everywhere in the young republic. It was a time of many religious movements; of reformers' schemes; of unheard-of notions like vegetarianism and women's rights; of experiments in "perfect" communities like Brook Farm and Fruitlands in Massachusetts, and the Oneida Community in New York State. It is no wonder that the literature of the period had a hopeful, idealistic ring—as if just now the world were beginning all over again.

The same hopeful spirit persisted even after the sad, bitter years of the War Between the States. A number of the writers of the 1830's and 1840's were still living and still publishing after the war—and most younger men had been formed in the same tradition. The idealism of the "American Renaissance" set the tone of our literature throughout the nineteenth century.

MAIN LITERARY TRENDS

Three successive stages can be distinguished in American literature of this period. Among the first important writers were Bryant, Hawthorne, and Emerson—founders of the "New England school." From a background of stern Puritanism came the devotion of the New England writers to "plain living and high thinking." They were studious, educated men who had strong admiration for the older culture of Europe— and also for the noble principles of their ancestors who had cast off British rule.

A little later, writers in other states along the eastern seaboard, especially New York, added their influence to that of the New England school. Washington Irving was one of the earliest of these. Then came Edgar Allan Poe in the South; and Herman Melville and Walt Whitman. New England was no longer the only source of American literature. Whitman, with his enthusiasm for the rapidly developing West, deliberately aimed to become the poet of the whole continent—welcoming, in his songs, vigorous new currents in American life; and Melville, in his tales of the sea, introduced a cosmopolitan or world-minded attitude.

Still later, in the 1860's, the West itself began to produce a literature. It was colorful and breezy, like the frontier talk from which it sprang. Its writers learned their craft not in colleges or in libraries, but by working on Western newspapers. Slang, broad humor, and astounding tales of adventure—these were some of the things readers found in this new type of writing. New England and the Old World were very far away; the subject of the Western writers was life in mining camps, on the prairies, or along the great inland waterways of America. In 1868, *The Overland Monthly* magazine was founded in San Francisco as a kind of far-off rival of *The Atlantic Monthly* in Boston. Its first editor, Bret Harte, soon became a famous author. A much greater man also got his start in literature as a California journalist. This was Mark Twain, whose sketches of the Pacific coast region first made his genius known.

Hand in hand with these regional changes in American literature there occurred a change in outlook: the gradual movement from *romanticism* toward *realism*. Romanticism was a literary trend which was predominant in both Europe and America during the first forty years of the nineteenth century. Romantic authors—usually poets —expressed in their works the dreams and aspirations of mankind. Often they were rebellious when life failed to measure up to their ideals. They were *individualists*. That is, each one was determined to live a rich, full life—like Henry David Thoreau, who told his readers that every man should "advance confidently in the direction of his dreams." They delighted in the unusual, the mysterious and rare, as may be seen in the strange tales of Edgar Allan Poe. A favorite subject in romantic literature is the inspiring beauty of untouched natural scenes—and again, Bryant, Emerson, Thoreau, and many other Americans dealt with this theme.

Realism, as the name suggests, was not a concern with men's hopes and desires but with the outer details of their lives—how they talked, how they worked, the conditions under which they lived. The movement began in Europe among certain authors who felt that romanticism failed, in a sense, to present the true facts about the world. However, realism in America was not influenced by this European movement until very late in the nineteenth century. It was a native American tendency, coming partly from the realistic jokes, songs, and stories of the frontier. Among the first American authors whose works showed signs of realism were Melville, Whitman, and Mark Twain. These men were partly romantic in attitude—as nearly all authors are, and for that matter nearly all human beings. But the poems of Whitman often have a realistic flavor because of his enthusiasm for describing the sights and sounds of his environment; and the books of Melville and Twain are, in part, factual reports of life on board sailing vessels, and in the Far West and the Mississippi Valley. The high admiration in which Twain was held helped to make realism popular in America—but it never completely displaced romanticism. The two opposite ways of looking at the world are still to be found—often in the same author—in American literature today.

A HIGH WATER MARK IN AMERICAN CULTURE

One of the astonishingly rich moments in the literary history of our country, or any country, was the period from 1850 to 1855. In those few years, four of our greatest books were published. These were *The Scarlet Letter*, by Nathaniel Hawthorne; *Moby Dick*, by Herman Melville; *Walden*, by Henry David Thoreau; and *Leaves of Grass*, by Walt Whitman. Still other important books appeared during the same six-year period. But the ones named above are four of the five American works now recognized as being among the truly great books of the entire world. (The fifth is *The Adventures of Huckleberry Finn*, by Mark Twain, which appeared in 1884.) The achievements of these authors are better understood when we remember that 1850 was approximately one generation after the first fine examples of American literature began to appear. The literature of the new nation had had time to grow and develop; in 1850 it had reached its first maturity.

The main value of these great authors, and of other masters of American literature who are represented in the following pages, is not that their writings give us a fuller understanding of American history. Most of their works have this value—but more important, they are masterpieces of creative imagination. Like all high art, for instance great painting or great music, these essays, stories, and poems can enrich and enlarge our lives. Their ability to do so is heightened by the fact that the authors are of our own land. Basically, Thoreau's environment, or Whitman's or Twain's, is our own. Wherever their thoughts carry them, they start from the same feelings and ideas that are within each of us; and reading them, we not only discover the life and thought of our country's past, but we also gain a new insight into human nature generally, and consequently come to a better understanding of ourselves.

WILLIAM CULLEN BRYANT (1794-1878)

Most pictures of William Cullen Bryant show him with long white hair and a beard, for the poet lived to be eighty-four years old. When he was a young man, however, he believed that he had only a few years to live, and he was generally discouraged about his future. That was the situation when he wrote several of his best-remembered poems.

Bryant was born in the Berkshire Hills of Massachusetts, and grew up in a stern religious atmosphere. At fifteen he was ready for college, but after one year he had to drop out because his father had no more money to give him. This was the period when he was most depressed. He wanted to write, but he decided to study law instead because he knew that he could not make a living by writing poetry. Meantime he had written "Thanatopsis," a poem expressing his thoughts on death, and had left the paper in his desk where it lay forgotten. Six years later his father found the poem and sent it to the *North American Review*. It became the most talked-of poem in America.

During the next few years while Bryant was practicing law in Massachusetts, he gradually became an established contributor to several magazines. At the age of twenty-seven he published his first collection of poems. Soon he resolved to abandon the profession of law altogether and make his living by writing. He went to New

York and after several months took a job on the *Evening Post*, a daily newspaper. Eventually he became editor-in-chief, a position he held nearly half a century.

All his life Bryant continued to write poetry, even finding time in later years to make new and excellent translations of *The Iliad* and *The Odyssey*. His long career was a prosperous and happy one. As a prominent New Yorker he took part in such civic projects as the founding of the Metropolitan Museum of Art, and the establishing of Central Park. However, today he is famous chiefly for his poems.

AMERICA'S FIRST IMPORTANT NATURE POET

Although Bryant wrote on many topics that were of public interest in his own day, his most distinguished poems deal with two subjects—nature and God. To Bryant the two were closely related. That is, he felt God's presence in the majesty and beauty of nature. His religious upbringing had given him a solemn consciousness of God's influence in all things. When he could escape to quiet scenes, away from the noise and distraction of city life, human affairs seemed insignificant as compared to the grandeur of the earth and of the higher power that had formed it. His solemn, dignified poems describe the calmness of soul that came to him at such times. They tell us that to know and love the unspoiled forests and fields is to worship their creator.

◇◇◇◇◇

Thanatopsis

When Bryant was sixteen, it was believed that he had contracted tuberculosis and did not have long to live. We know what his thoughts were in this time of despondency, for it was then that he wrote "Thanatopsis." The title means "a view of death." Later he made several changes in the poem —for example, adding the first seventeen lines, and the last sixteen, beginning "As the long train. . . ."

"Thanatopsis" tells us that if we listen to Nature's teachings we will realize that death is a normal part of all life—that it is one episode in the vast drama of the earth. To Bryant this was a consoling thought. See if you agree.

The long dignified sentences are suited to the solemn and lofty thoughts of the poem. However, they may cause some difficulty in reading. Frequently, words are not in their natural order, and sometimes it is not immediately clear what the pronouns stand for. For example, in the very first sentence To HIM means "to anyone" who loves and observes nature. HER and SHE refer to Nature. Try turning the first sentence around—SHE (or Nature) SPEAKS A VARIOUS LANGUAGE TO HIM WHO. . . .

> To him who in the love of Nature holds
> Communion with her visible forms, she speaks
> A various language; for his gayer hours
> She has a voice of gladness, and a smile
> And eloquence of beauty, and she glides   5
> Into his darker musings with a mild
> And healing sympathy that steals away
> Their sharpness, ere he is aware. When thoughts
> Of the last bitter hour come like a blight
> Over thy spirit, and sad images   10
> Of the stern agony, and shroud, and pall,
> And breathless darkness, and the narrow house,
> Make thee to shudder and grow sick at heart—
> Go forth, under the open sky, and list
> To Nature's teachings, while from all around—   15
> Earth and her waters, and the depths of air—
> Comes a still voice—
>   Yet a few days, and thee
> The all-beholding sun shall see no more
> In all his course; nor yet in the cold ground,
> Where thy pale form was laid with many tears,   20
> Nor in the embrace of ocean, shall exist
> Thy image. Earth, that nourished thee, shall claim
> Thy growth, to be resolved to earth again,
> And, lost each human trace, surrendering up
> Thine individual being, shalt thou go   25
> To mix forever with the elements,
> To be a brother to the insensible rock
> And to the sluggish clod, which the rude swain
> Turns with his share, and treads upon. The oak
> Shall send his roots abroad, and pierce thy mold.   30
>
> Yet not to thine eternal resting place
> Shalt thou retire alone, nor couldst thou wish
> Couch more magnificent. Thou shalt lie down
> With patriarchs of the infant world—with kings,

17. COMES A STILL VOICE—That is, the voice of Nature.
17. YET A FEW DAYS . . . SEE NO MORE—The subject of this sentence is *sun*, and *thee* is the object. In prose the sentence would read: "In a few days the all-beholding sun shall see thee no more."

The powerful of the earth—the wise, the good,   35
Fair forms, and hoary seers of ages past,
All in one mighty sepulcher. The hills
Rock-ribbed and ancient as the sun—the vales
Stretching in pensive quietness between;
The venerable woods—rivers that move   40
In majesty, and the complaining brooks
That make the meadows green; and, poured round all,
Old Ocean's gray and melancholy waste—
Are but the solemn decorations all
Of the great tomb of man. The golden sun,   45
The planets, all the infinite host of heaven,
Are shining on the sad abodes of death
Through the still lapse of ages. All that tread
The globe are but a handful to the tribes
That slumber in its bosom.—Take the wings   50
Of morning, pierce the Barcan wilderness,
Or lose thyself in the continuous woods
Where rolls the Oregon, and hears no sound,
Save his own dashings—yet the dead are there;
And millions in those solitudes, since first   55
The flight of years began, have laid them down
In their last sleep—the dead reign there alone.
So shalt thou rest, and what if thou withdraw
In silence from the living, and no friend
Take note of thy departure? All that breathe   60
Will share thy destiny. The gay will laugh
When thou art gone, the solemn brood of care
Plod on, and each one as before will chase
His favorite phantom; yet all these shall leave
Their mirth and their employments, and shall come   65
And make their bed with thee. As the long train
Of ages glides away, the sons of men,
The youth in life's green spring, and he who goes
In the full strength of years, matron and maid,
The speechless babe, and the gray-headed man—   70
Shall one by one be gathered to thy side,
By those who in their turn shall follow them.

So live, that when thy summons comes to join
The innumerable caravan which moves
To that mysterious realm where each shall take   75
His chamber in the silent halls of death,

44. ARE BUT THE SOLEMN DECORATIONS ALL—All these are only the solemn decorations.
51. BARCAN—Barca is a desert in northern Africa.
53. OREGON—The Columbia River was formerly called the Oregon River.
73. SO LIVE—Live so, or live in such a way.

Thou go not, like the quarry-slave at night,
Scourged to his dungeon, but, sustained and soothed
By an unfaltering trust, approach thy grave
Like one who wraps the drapery of his couch   80
About him, and lies down to pleasant dreams.

◇◇

FOR UNDERSTANDING

1. What does the poet mean by saying that Nature speaks "a various language"—that is, says different things at different times? What advice does the poet give to anyone saddened by thoughts of death? Whose is the "still voice" which is represented as speaking the remainder of the poem?

2. In a single sentence, state the main thought of lines 17–30. How do these lines connect *man* with the *earth?*

3. In lines 31–57, how does the poet show that one individual's life and death is only a small episode in the long history of the earth? What is the "one mighty sepulcher," the "great tomb of man"? What are the "solemn decorations" that adorn this tomb?

4. In lines 58–72, what thought does the poet express about the future which makes death seem more acceptable?

5. What idea, new to the poem, is developed in lines 73–81? Why do you think the lines were added? What poetic comparisons does Bryant use to express two very different ways of meeting death? Which words describe the mood of the poem?

6. Read once through the main body of the poem—that is, from line 17 to 72. This is almost exactly the form in which Bryant originally wrote it. Then read the poem with the introduction and conclusion. What important change do you notice in the meaning and tone of the poem?

7. Explain why the consoling view of death expressed in "Thanatopsis" is more likely to come *when one is surrounded by scenes of nature* than at other times.

A POEM OF SOLEMN DIGNITY

1. It seems almost impossible that a boy of sixteen could have written the sonorous lines of "Thanatopsis." However, coming from a family of New England Puritan background, Bryant was brought up with a close acquaintance with the Bible. In its elevated thought and language "Thanatopsis" shows a general resemblance to the Book of Job and Ecclesiastes. A less important but more obvious resemblance to the Bible is the use of terms like "thee"—word forms which poets have often used for their lofty, dignified effect. Point out all the Biblical words you can find in the poem.

2. Another influence on Bryant was the blank verse of English poems like Milton's noble *Paradise Lost.* Blank verse does not rhyme, but the lines have a definite beat or rhythm when read aloud. Read lines 31–32, emphasizing the rhythm. Then tell how many stressed or accented syllables are in each line. How many unstressed syllables are there?

3. The poem contains a number of picture-making phrases that seem to seize hold of the reader's imagination. A very brief one is "the all-beholding sun," in line 18. It is truly descriptive because the sun actually does shine on the entire surface of the earth. Point out at least two other very striking passages in the poem. For instance, look for a passage which expresses the great age of the earth; a passage which emphasizes the wildness of the unsettled parts of the American continent; and a passage which makes us realize how many multitudes of people have died and been buried since the beginning of history.

◇◇◇◇◇◇◇◇◇

To a Waterfowl

One evening while Bryant was still uncertain and unhappy about his future he saw a northbound bird, perhaps a wild duck, soaring against the sky. The sure flight of the bird as it pursued its long migratory journey across the land reassured the poet about his own life.

Whither, midst falling dew,
While glow the heavens with the last
    steps of day,
Far, through their rosy depths, dost thou
    pursue
    Thy solitary way?

Vainly the fowler's eye   5
Might mark thy distant flight to do thee
    wrong,

1. WHITHER—"Where," or "to what place."
5–6. VAINLY THE FOWLER'S . . . DISTANT FLIGHT—In vain the hunter's eye might observe your distant flight.

As, darkly seen against the crimson sky,
    Thy figure floats along.

Seek'st thou the plashy brink   9
Of weedy lake, or marge of river wide,
Or where the rocking billows rise and
    sink
    On the chafed oceanside?

There is a Power whose care
Teaches thy way along that pathless
    coast—
The desert and illimitable air—   15
    Lone wandering, but not lost.

9. PLASHY BRINK—Marshy edge.
10. MARGE—Margin, edge.

All day thy wings have fanned,
At that far height, the cold thin atmos-
      phere,
Yet stoop not, weary, to the welcome
      land,
Though the dark night is near.   20

And soon that toil shall end;
Soon shalt thou find a summer home,
      and rest,
And scream among thy fellows; reeds
      shall bend
Soon, o'er thy sheltered nest.

Thou'rt gone, the abyss of heaven   25
Hath swallowed up thy form; yet, on my
      heart
Deeply has sunk the lesson thou hast
      given,
And shall not soon depart.

He who, from zone to zone,
Guides through the boundless sky thy
      certain flight,   30
In the long way that I must tread
      alone,
Will lead my steps aright.

FOR UNDERSTANDING

where are they going?

1. What question does the poet ask the bird in the first stanza? How is the same question made more specific in the third stanza?

2. Find an expression that tells the time of day. How does the sixth stanza tell us that the bird must be flying north?

3. This poem, like "Thanatopsis," has many accurate bits of nature-description. Give three or more examples of descriptive details that show Bryant's careful observation of nature.

4. The fourth stanza says the bird is "lone wandering, but not lost." What expression in the same stanza says that God is helping the bird? What favorable prediction is made in a later stanza about the outcome of the bird's long, lonely journey?

5. Bryant felt that he, too, was "lone wandering," for he was not sure what occupation he should go into, or whether he could succeed in the one he chose. How does the last stanza apply the lesson of the bird to Bryant's own life?

6. In both "Thanatopsis" and "To a Waterfowl," by his observation of nature Bryant finds comforting answers to his own life problems. "To a Waterfowl" is the later of the two poems. Explain how it expresses a *stronger faith* than "Thanatopsis" does.

WASHINGTON IRVING (1783-1859)

As Bryant was the earliest important literary figure to appear in New England, Irving was the earliest in New York. Because he was the youngest child of a well-to-do merchant family, he did not need to concern himself seriously about making a living. His health was delicate, and he did not work very hard as a law student. Instead, he wandered about the country, visiting with the Dutch-descended farmers. And it was just as well that he did. When the family hardware business went bankrupt, Irving turned to writing. It was the knowledge of old Dutch legends and customs which he had picked up on his rambles that gave him some of his best material. The works that endeared him to the American public—"Rip Van Winkle," *Knickerbocker's History of New York*, "The Legend of Sleepy Hollow"—all have their setting in picturesque old New York State where he was born.

When Irving was twenty, he was sent abroad for his health. He liked Europe, and felt at home there. In 1818, he again visited in England and on the continent. This time he stayed for seventeen years. It was in England that he published *The Sketch Book* and *Bracebridge Hall*, collections of essays and tales—most of them about English life. They were very popular among both British and American readers. In Germany and Italy, too, he found ideas for stories. Some of the legends and sketches in *Tales of a Traveler* have a German setting.

Off and on, Irving spent considerable time in Spain. His studies there gave him the material for three of his books, *History of the Life and Voyages of Christopher Columbus*, *A Chronicle of the Conquest of Granada*, and *The Alhambra*—the last a

539

mixture of descriptive sketches and strange old legendary tales. He served as ambassador to Spain from 1842 to 1846. When his term expired, he returned to his home at Tarrytown on the Hudson. He is buried there in Sleepy Hollow Cemetery.

A TELLER OF ENTERTAINING TALES

Two characteristics are outstanding in Irving's tales. The first is the *manner* he adopts in his writing. He tells his story in a pleasant, mellow style, using long, leisurely sentences. Usually the story is humorous, but the fun is never boisterous enough to interrupt the smooth, even flow of the narrative. Irving is a quiet, gentlemanly entertainer.

The other characteristic is Irving's novel *use of old European legends*. In his day, literary men in both Europe and America were fascinated by picturesque, romantic old traditions—especially those that dealt with supernatural events. There were few such traditions to write about in America, which was still a brand-new country. But everywhere Irving went in the Old World, he collected legends for his books. Sometimes he changed the tales so they would seem to be authentic *American* folklore. "Rip Van Winkle" and "The Legend of Sleepy Hollow"—both rather spooky—were originally weird old German legends which Irving retold in a new way, supplying them with American scenery and American characters. The fact that most of us have read and enjoyed these two stories, and in our minds associate them with the early Dutch communities along the Hudson, is evidence that he was very successful.

◇◇◇◇◇

THE DEVIL AND TOM WALKER

Stories about people who made bargains with the Devil were handed down for centuries in Europe. The most famous of these is the German tale of Faust, who sold his soul in exchange for earthly wealth and power. For twenty-four years he was given great magical powers but upon his death he was carried off to Hell.

In the following story Irving turns the Faust legend into a yarn about a miserly American moneylender named Tom Walker. As a New Yorker, perhaps Irving was poking some good-natured fun at New England when he chose to make his "hero" a scheming Yankee businessman.

A few miles from Boston in Massachusetts, there is a deep inlet, winding several miles into the interior of the country from Charles Bay, and terminating in a thickly wooded swamp or morass. On one side of this inlet is a beautiful dark grove; on the opposite side the land rises abruptly from the water's edge into a high ridge, on which grow a few scattered oaks of great age and immense size. Under one of the gigantic trees, according to old stories, there was a great amount of treasure buried by Kidd the pirate. The inlet allowed a facility to bring the money in a boat secretly and at night to the very foot of the hill; the elevation of the place permitted a good lookout to be kept that no one was at hand; while the remarkable trees formed good landmarks by which the place might easily be found again. The old stories add, moreover, that the Devil presided at the hiding of the money, and took it under his guardianship; but this, it is well known, he always does with buried treasure, particularly when it has been ill-gotten. Be that as it may, Kidd never returned to recover his wealth; being shortly after seized at Boston, sent out to England, and there hanged for a pirate.

About the year 1727, just at the time that earthquakes were prevalent in New England, and shook many tall sinners down upon their knees, there lived near this place a meager, miserly fellow of the name of Tom Walker. He had a wife as miserly as himself: they were so miserly that they even conspired to cheat each other. Whatever the woman could lay hands on, she hid away; a hen could not cackle but she was on the alert to secure the new-laid egg. Her husband was continually prying about to detect her secret hoards, and many and fierce were the conflicts that took place about what ought to have been common property.

They lived in a forlorn-looking house that stood alone, and had an air of starvation. A few straggling savin trees,[1] emblems of sterility, grew near it; no smoke ever curled from its chimney; no traveler stopped at its door. A miserable horse, whose ribs were as articulate as the bars of a gridiron, stalked about a field, where a thin carpet of moss, scarcely covering the ragged beds of pudding stone, tantalized and balked his hunger; and sometimes he would lean his head over the fence, look piteously at the passer-by, and seem to petition deliverance from this land of famine.

The house and its inmates had altogether a bad name. Tom's wife was a tall termagant, fierce of temper, loud of tongue, and strong of arm. Her voice was often heard in wordy warfare with her husband; and his face sometimes showed signs that their conflicts were not confined to words. No one ventured, however, to interfere between them. The lonely wayfarer shrunk within himself at the horrid clamor and clapperclawing; eyed the den of discord askance; and hurried on his way, rejoicing, if a bachelor, in his celibacy.

One day that Tom Walker had been to a distant part of the neighborhood, he took what he considered a short cut homeward, through the swamp. Like most short cuts, it was an ill-chosen route. The swamp was thickly grown with great gloomy pines and hemlocks, some of them ninety feet high, which made it dark at noonday and a retreat for all the owls of the neighborhood. It was full of pits and quagmires, partly covered with weeds and mosses, where the green surface often betrayed the traveler into a gulf of black, smothering mud; there were also dark and stagnant pools, the abodes of the tadpole, the bullfrog, and the wa-

[1] SAVIN (săv′ĭn) TREES—Juniper trees.

ter snake; where the trunks of pines and hemlocks lay half drowned, half rotting, looking like alligators sleeping in the mire.

Tom had long been picking his way cautiously through this treacherous forest; stepping from tuft to tuft of rushes and roots, which afforded precarious footholds among deep sloughs; or pacing carefully, like a cat, along the prostrate trunks of trees; startled now and then by the sudden screaming of the bittern, or the quacking of a wild duck rising on the wing from some solitary pool. At length he arrived at a firm piece of ground, which ran out like a peninsula into the deep bosom of the swamp. It had been one of the strongholds of the Indians during their wars with the first colonists. Here they had thrown up a kind of fort, which they had looked upon as almost impregnable, and had used as a place of refuge for their squaws and children. Nothing remained of the old Indian fort but a few embankments, gradually sinking to the level of the surrounding earth, and already overgrown in part by oaks and other forest trees, the foliage of which formed a contrast to the dark pines and hemlocks of the swamp.

It was late in the dusk of evening when Tom Walker reached the old fort, and he paused there awhile to rest himself. Anyone but he would have felt unwilling to linger in this lonely, melancholy place, for the common people had a bad opinion of it, from the stories handed down from the time of the Indian wars, when it was asserted that the savages held incantations here, and made sacrifices to the evil spirit.

Tom Walker, however, was not a man to be troubled with any fears of the kind. He reposed himself for some time on the trunk of a fallen hemlock, listening to the boding cry of the tree toad, and delving with his walking staff into a mound of black mold at his feet. As he turned up the soil unconsciously, his staff struck against something hard. He raked it out of the vegetable mold and lo! a cloven skull, with an Indian tomahawk buried deep in it, lay before him. The rust on the weapon showed the time that had elapsed since this deathblow had been given. It was a dreary memento of the fierce struggle that had taken place in this last foothold of the Indian warriors.

"Humph!" said Tom Walker, as he gave it a kick to shake the dirt from it.

"Let that skull alone!" said a gruff voice. Tom lifted up his eyes and beheld a great black man seated directly opposite him, on the stump of a tree. He was exceedingly surprised, having neither heard nor seen anyone approach; and he was still more perplexed on observing, as well as the gathering gloom would permit, that the stranger was neither Negro nor Indian. It is true he was dressed in a rude half-Indian garb and had a red belt or sash swathed round his body; but his face was neither black nor copper color, but swarthy and dingy, and begrimed with soot, as if he had been accustomed to toil among fires and forges. He had a shock of coarse black hair that stood out from his head in all directions, and bore an ax on his shoulder.

He scowled for a moment at Tom with a pair of great red eyes.

"What are you doing on my grounds?" said the black man, with a hoarse growling voice.

"Your grounds!" said Tom, with a sneer, "no more your grounds than mine; they belong to Deacon Peabody."

"Deacon Peabody!" said the stranger, "let him look more into his own sins and less to those of his neighbors. Look yonder, and see how Deacon Peabody is faring."

Tom looked in the direction that the stranger pointed and beheld one of the great trees, fair and flourishing without, but rotten at the core, and saw that it had been nearly hewn through, so that the first high wind was likely to blow it down. On the bark of the tree was scored the name of Deacon Peabody, an eminent man, who had waxed wealthy by driving shrewd bargains with the Indians. He now looked around and found most of the tall trees marked with the name of some great man of the colony, and all more or less scored by the ax. The one on which he had been seated, and which had evidently just been hewn down, bore the name of Crowninshield; and he recollected a mighty rich man of that name, who made a vulgar display of wealth, which it was whispered he had acquired by buccaneering.

"He's just ready for burning!" said the black man, with a growl of triumph. "You see I am likely to have a good stock of firewood for winter."

"But what right have you," said Tom, "to cut down Deacon Peabody's timber?"

"The right of a prior claim," said the other. "This woodland belonged to me long before one of your white-faced race put foot upon the soil."

"And pray, who are you, if I may be so bold?" said Tom.

"Oh, I go by various names. I am the wild huntsman in some countries; the black miner in others. In this neighborhood I am known by the name of the black woodsman. I am he to whom the red men consecrated this spot, and in honor of whom they now and then roasted a white man, by way of sweet-smelling sacrifice. Since the red men have been exterminated by you white savages, I amuse myself by presiding at the persecutions of Quakers and Anabaptists;[2] I

[2] PERSECUTIONS OF QUAKERS AND ANABAP-TISTS—Although the Puritans came to America for the sake of religious freedom, they sometimes persecuted other sects like the Quakers and Anabaptists.

am the great patron and prompter of slave dealers, and the grand master of the Salem witches."

"The upshot of all which is, that, if I mistake not," said Tom, sturdily, "you are he commonly called Old Scratch." [3]

"The same, at your service!" replied the black man, with a half-civil nod.

Such was the opening of this interview, according to the old story; though it has almost too familiar an air to be credited. One would think that to meet with such a singular personage in this wild, lonely place would have shaken any man's nerves; but Tom was a hard-minded fellow, not easily daunted, and he had lived so long with a termagant wife that he did not even fear the Devil.

It is said that after this commencement they had a long and earnest conversation together, as Tom returned homeward. The black man told him of great sums of money buried by Kidd the pirate, under the oak trees on the high ridge, not far from the morass. All these were under his command and protected by his power, so that none could find them but such as propitiated his favor. These he offered to place within Tom Walker's reach, having conceived an especial kindness for him; but they were to be had only on certain conditions. What these conditions were may be easily surmised, though Tom never disclosed them publicly. They must have been very hard, for he required time to think of them, and he was not a man to stick at trifles when money was in view. When they had reached the edge of the swamp, the stranger paused. "What proof have I that all you have been telling me is true?" said Tom. "There's my signature," said the black man, pressing his finger on Tom's forehead. So saying, he turned off among the thickets of

[3] OLD SCRATCH—Another term for the Devil.

the swamp and seemed, as Tom said, to go down, down, down, into the earth, until nothing but his head and shoulders could be seen, and so on, until he totally disappeared.

When Tom reached home, he found the black print of a finger burnt, as it were, into his forehead, which nothing could obliterate. The first news his wife had to tell him was the sudden death of Absalom Crowninshield, the rich buccaneer. It was announced in the papers with the usual flourish, that "A great man had fallen in Israel." [4]

Tom recollected the tree which his black friend had just hewn down, and which was ready for burning. "Let the freebooter roast," said Tom, "who cares!" He now felt convinced that all he had heard and seen was no illusion.

He was not prone to let his wife into his confidence; but as this was an uneasy secret, he willingly shared it with her. All her avarice was awakened at the mention of hidden gold, and she urged her husband to comply with the black man's terms and secure what would make them wealthy for life. However Tom might have felt disposed to sell himself to the Devil, he was determined not to do so to oblige his wife; so he flatly refused, out of the mere spirit of contradiction. Many and bitter were the quarrels they had on the subject; but the more she talked, the more was Tom opposed to please her.

At length she determined to drive the bargain on her own account, and if she succeeded, to keep all the gain to herself. Being of the same fearless temper as her husband, she set off for the old Indian fort towards the close of a summer's day.

[4] "A GREAT MAN HAD FALLEN IN ISRAEL"— The quotation means "The community had lost one of its most prominent citizens." Because the man was rich, he was praised in spite of his misdeeds.

She was many hours absent. When she came back, she was reserved and sullen in her replies. She spoke something of a black man, whom she had met about twilight hewing at the root of a tall tree. He was sulky, however, and would not come to terms; she was to go again with a propitiatory offering, but what it was she forbore to say.

The next evening she set off for the swamp, with her apron heavily laden. Tom waited and waited for her, but in vain; midnight came, but she did not make her appearance; morning, noon, night returned, but still she did not come. Tom now grew uneasy for her safety, especially as he found she had carried off in her apron the silver teapot and spoons, and every portable article of value. Another night elapsed, another morning came, but no wife. In a word, she was never heard of more.

What was her real fate nobody knows, in consequence of so many pretending to know. It is one of those facts which have become confounded by a variety of historians. Some asserted that she lost her way among the tangled mazes of the swamp and sank into some pit or slough; others, more uncharitable, hinted that she had eloped with the household booty, and made off to some other province; while others surmised that the tempter had decoyed her into a dismal quagmire, on the top of which her hat was found lying. In confirmation of this, it was said a great black man, with an ax on his shoulder, was seen late that very evening coming out of the swamp, carrying a bundle tied in a checked apron, with an air of surly triumph.

The most current and probable story, however, observes that Tom Walker grew so anxious about the fate of his wife and his property that he set out at length to seek them both at the Indian fort. During a long summer's afternoon he searched about the gloomy place, but no wife was to be seen. He called her name repeatedly, but she was nowhere to be heard. The bittern alone responded to his voice, as he flew screaming by; or the bullfrog croaked dolefully from a neighboring pool. At length, it is said, just in the brown hour of twilight, when the owls began to hoot and the bats to flit about, his attention was attracted by the clamor of carrion crows hovering about a cypress tree. He looked up and beheld a bundle tied in a checked apron and hanging in the branches of the tree, with a great vulture perched hard by, as if keeping watch upon it. He leaped with joy; for he recognized his wife's apron and supposed it to contain the household valuables.

"Let us get hold of the property," said he, consolingly to himself, "and we will endeavor to do without the woman."

As he scrambled up the tree, the vulture spread its wide wings and sailed off, screaming, into the deep shadows of the forest. Tom seized the checked apron, but, woeful sight! found nothing but a heart and liver tied up in it!

Such, according to this most authentic old story, was all that was to be found of Tom's wife. She had probably attempted to deal with the black man as she had been accustomed to deal with her husband; but though a female scold is generally considered a match for the Devil, yet in this instance she appears to have had the worst of it. She must have died game, however; for it is said Tom noticed many prints of cloven feet deeply stamped about the tree, and found handfuls of hair that looked as if they had been plucked from the coarse black shock of the woodsman. Tom knew his wife's prowess by experience. He shrugged his shoulders, as he looked at the signs of a fierce clapperclawing. "Egad," said he to himself, "Old Scratch must have had a tough time of it!"

Tom consoled himself for the loss of his property with the loss of his wife, for he was a man of fortitude. He even felt something like gratitude towards the black woodsman, who, he considered, had done him a kindness. He sought, therefore, to cultivate a further acquaintance with him, but for some time without success; the old blacklegs played shy, for whatever people may think, he is not always to be had for calling for; he knows how to play his cards when pretty sure of his game.

At length, it is said, when delay had whetted Tom's eagerness to the quick and prepared him to agree to anything rather than not gain the promised treasure, he met the black man one evening in his usual woodsman's dress, with his ax on his shoulder, sauntering along the swamp, and humming a tune. He affected to receive Tom's advances with great indifference, made brief replies, and went on humming his tune.

By degrees, however, Tom brought him to business, and they began to haggle about the terms on which the former was to have the pirate's treasure. There was one condition which need not be mentioned, being generally understood in all cases where the Devil grants favors; but there were others about which, though of less importance, he was inflexibly obstinate. He insisted that the money found through his means should be employed in his service. He proposed, therefore, that Tom should employ it in the black traffic; that is to say, that he should fit out a slave ship. This, however, Tom resolutely refused; he was bad enough in all conscience; but the Devil himself could not tempt him to turn slave trader. Finding Tom so squeamish on this point, he did not insist upon it, but proposed, instead, that he should turn usurer; [5] the Devil being extremely anxious for the increase of usurers, looking upon them as his peculiar people.

To this no objections were made, for it was just to Tom's taste.

"You shall open a broker's shop in Boston next month," said the black man.

"I'll do it tomorrow, if you wish," said Tom Walker.

"You shall lend money at two per cent a month."

"Egad, I'll charge four!" replied Tom Walker.

"You shall extort bonds, foreclose mortgages, drive the merchants to bankruptcy—"

"I'll drive them to the Devil," cried Tom Walker.

"You are the usurer for my money!" said blacklegs with delight. "When will you want the rhino?" [6]

"This very night."

"Done!" said the Devil.

"Done!" said Tom Walker. So they shook hands and struck a bargain.

A few days' time saw Tom Walker seated behind his desk in a counting-house in Boston.

His reputation for a ready-moneyed man, who would lend money out for a good consideration, soon spread abroad. Everybody remembers the time of Governor Belcher, when money was particularly scarce. It was a time of paper credit. The country had been deluged with government bills, the famous Land Bank had been established; there had been a rage for speculating; the people had run mad with schemes for new settlements, for building cities in the wilderness; land-

[5] USURER (ū′zhŏŏ·rēr)—A moneylender, especially one who charges excessive interest on loans.

[6] RHINO—Slang for *money*.

jobbers went about with maps of grants and townships and Eldorados,[7] lying nobody knew where, but which everybody was ready to purchase. In a word, the great speculating fever which breaks out every now and then in the country had raged to an alarming degree, and everybody was dreaming of making sudden fortunes from nothing. As usual the fever had subsided; the dream had gone off, and the imaginary fortunes with it; the patients were left in doleful plight, and the whole country resounded with the consequent cry of "hard times."

At this propitious time of public distress did Tom Walker set up as usurer in Boston. His door was soon thronged by customers. The needy and adventurous; the gambling speculator; the dreaming land-jobber; the thriftless tradesman; the merchant with cracked credit; in short, everyone driven to raise money by desperate means and desperate sacrifices hurried to Tom Walker.

Thus Tom was the universal friend of the needy and acted like a "friend in need"; that is to say, he always exacted good pay and good security. In proportion to the distress of the applicant was the highness of his terms. He accumulated bonds and mortgages, gradually squeezed his customers closer and closer, and sent them at length, dry as a sponge, from his door.

In this way he made money hand over hand, became a rich and mighty man, and exalted his cocked hat upon 'Change.[8] He built himself, as usual, a vast house, out of ostentation; but left the greater part of it unfinished and unfurnished, out of parsimony. He even set up a carriage in the fullness of his vainglory, though he nearly starved the horses which drew it; and as the ungreased wheels groaned and screeched on the axletrees, you would have thought you heard the souls of the poor debtors he was squeezing.

As Tom waxed old, however, he grew thoughtful. Having secured the good things of this world, he began to feel anxious about those of the next. He thought with regret on the bargain he had made with his black friend and set his wits to work to cheat him out of the conditions. He became, therefore, all of a sudden, a violent churchgoer. He prayed loudly and strenuously, as if heaven were to be taken by force of lungs. Indeed, one might always tell when he

---

[7] ELDORADOS (ĕl'dȯ·rä'dōz)—Imaginary kingdoms abounding in gold; hence, any lands that people imagine it would be profitable to invest in.

[8] UPON 'CHANGE—Upon the Exchange, the center for financial transactions in Boston.

had sinned most during the week, by the clamor of his Sunday devotion. The quiet Christians who had been modestly and steadfastly traveling Zionward were struck with self-reproach at seeing themselves so suddenly outstripped in their career by this new-made convert. Tom was as rigid in religious as in money matters; he was a stern supervisor and censurer of his neighbors, and seemed to think every sin entered up to their account became a credit on his own side of the page. He even talked of the expediency of reviving the persecution of Quakers and Anabaptists. In a word, Tom's zeal became as notorious as his riches.

Still, in spite of all this strenuous attention to forms, Tom had a lurking dread that the Devil, after all, would have his due. That he might not be taken unawares, therefore, it is said he always carried a small Bible in his coat pocket. He had also a great folio Bible on his countinghouse desk, and would frequently be found reading it when people called on business; on such occasions he would lay his green spectacles in the book to mark the place, while he turned round to drive some usurious bargain.

Some say that Tom grew a little crack-brained in his old days and that, fancying his end approaching, he had his horse new-shod, saddled and bridled, and buried with his feet uppermost; because he supposed that at the last day the world would be turned upside down; in which case he should find his horse standing ready for mounting, and he was determined at the worst to give his old friend a run for it. This, however, is probably a mere old wives' fable. If he really did take such a precaution, it was totally superfluous; at least so says the authentic old legend, which closes this story in the following manner.

One hot summer afternoon in the dog days, just as a terrible black thunder-gust was coming up, Tom sat in his counting-house, in his white linen cap and India silk morning gown. He was on the point of foreclosing a mortgage by which he would complete the ruin of an unlucky land-speculator for whom he had professed the greatest friendship. The poor land-jobber begged him to grant a few months' indulgence. Tom had grown testy and irritated, and refused another day.

"My family will be ruined and brought upon the parish," said the land-jobber.

"Charity begins at home," replied Tom; "I must take care of myself in these hard times."

"You have made so much money out of me," said the speculator.

Tom lost his patience and his piety. "The Devil take me," said he, "if I have made a farthing!"

Just then there were three loud knocks at the street door. He stepped out to see who was there. A black man was holding a black horse, which neighed and stamped with impatience.

"Tom, you're come for," said the black fellow, gruffly. Tom shrank back, but too late. He had left his little Bible at the bottom of his coat pocket, and his big Bible on the desk buried under the mortgage he was about to foreclose: never was sinner taken more unawares. The black man whisked him like a child into the saddle, gave the horse the lash, and away he galloped, with Tom on his back, in the midst of the thunderstorm. The clerks stuck their pens behind their ears and stared after him from the windows. Away went Tom Walker, dashing down the streets; his white cap bobbing up and down; his morning gown fluttering in the wind, and his steed striking fire out of the pavement at every bound. When the clerks turned to look for the black man, he had disappeared.

Tom Walker never returned to foreclose the mortgage. A countryman, who lived on the border of the swamp, reported that in the height of the thundergust he had heard a great clattering of hoofs and a howling along the road, and running to the window caught sight of a figure, such as I have described, on a horse that galloped like mad across the fields, over the hills, and down into the black hemlock swamp towards the old Indian fort; and that shortly after, a thunderbolt falling in that direction seemed to set the whole forest in a blaze.

The good people of Boston shook their heads and shrugged their shoulders, but had been so much accustomed to witches and goblins, and tricks of the Devil, in all kinds of shapes, from the first settlement of the colony, that they were not so much horror-struck as might have been expected. Trustees were appointed to take charge of Tom's effects. There was nothing, however, to administer upon. On searching his coffers, all his bonds and mortgages were found reduced to cinders. In place of gold and silver, his iron chest was filled with chips and shavings; two skeletons lay in his stable instead of his half-starved horses, and the very next day his great house took fire and was burnt to the ground.

Such was the end of Tom Walker and his ill-gotten wealth. Let all griping money brokers lay this story to heart. The truth of it is not to be doubted. The very hole under the oak trees, whence he dug Kidd's money, is to be seen to this day; and the neighboring swamp and the old Indian fort are often haunted on stormy nights by a figure on horseback, in morning gown and white cap, which is doubtless the troubled spirit of the usurer. In fact, the story has resolved itself into a proverb, and is the origin of that popular saying, so prevalent throughout New England, of "The Devil and Tom Walker."

◇◇◇◇◇◇◇◇◇◇◇◇◇◇◇◇◇◇◇◇◇◇◇◇◇◇◇◇◇◇◇◇

FOR UNDERSTANDING

1. Without turning back to the story, give your impression of the appearance of the woods where Tom first met the stranger. In what ways are these surroundings appropriate to the plot? How are we supposed to interpret the black complexion of the stranger?

2. What was the result of the dealings of Tom's wife with the stranger? How does this episode hint at the outcome of the main story?

3. In older times some people believed, as Tom Walker did, that anyone who had a copy of the Bible with him would be protected against the Evil One. In his story Irving pretends to accept this belief as being perfectly true. How does he arrange things so Tom does *not* have a Bible with him at the moment the black man comes to get him?

4. Stories about bargains with the Devil have been popular ever since the Middle Ages. Although such tales are fantastic and unreal, they are suggestive of a true idea. Any person who acts wickedly to get what he wants is, figuratively speaking, selling his soul to the Devil. Show how this fundamental truth is present in "The Devil and Tom Walker." For example, at the outset of his career of wealth Tom bargains away his soul just as in the old stories. Explain how he serves the Devil constantly in his everyday business life. How is the concluding event of the story figuratively true?

AMERICANIZING EUROPEAN LEGENDS

The basic plot of "The Devil and Tom Walker" is centuries old, but Irving makes it "old" in a different sense. He pretends that the tale is American rather than European, and that it has come down from Colonial times in Massachusetts—a period when people were superstitious, believing in witchcraft and in the frequent appearance of ghosts and demons.

1. Notice the care with which Irving connects the story with American scenery and American history. The opening sentence takes us to a spot "a few miles from Boston," where there is a deep inlet from Charles Bay. What *actual* person buried a treasure here—according to Irving's story? When Tom sets up his moneylending business, Irving talks about Governor Belcher and the Land Bank. What *actual* place in the city of Boston is named in this part of the story? What two *actual* religious sects are mentioned?

2. To make his tale seem a legend that grew up in America, Irving inserts remarks like "Such was the opening of this interview, *according to the old story*," and "*It is said* that after this commencement they had a long and earnest conversation together." What very doubtful yarn does Irving tell us grew up concerning Tom's scheme to escape the Devil on the last day of the world? What two proofs—according to Irving—do people still offer that the legend is true? What do you think of the soundness of such proofs?

3. Irving knew how to flavor his tales with typical American expressions, as when he said Tom's wife "must have died game." What does the remark mean? What quaint, homely expression does the Devil use in announcing that he has come to take

Tom away? Explain how at the end of the story Irving connects the entire tale with an actual proverbial saying in New England.

IRVING'S LEISURELY, EASY-GOING TALES

Irving was the first great American author to write brief works of fiction. His writings are often called *tales* to distinguish them from the *short stories* which were developed by later authors. The difference is that short stories usually build up rather quickly to a dramatic climax and then end abruptly. Irving's tales, on the other hand, jog along at an easy pace, with many descriptive details. The reader surrenders himself to the restful, dreamy atmosphere that Irving creates, and doesn't care very much whether anything important happens or not. Eventually the tale reaches a climax, but afterward it may "taper off" slowly. Irving does not try to write forceful, exciting stories. His aim is to provide a quiet half hour of enjoyment.

In "The Devil and Tom Walker," the important action of the story does not begin until Irving has told us about the countryside; about a superstitious legend concerning the pirate Kidd; about Tom and his wife; and about the gloomy swamp in which Tom first meets the stranger. Even after we find out what finally happens to Tom, Irving adds three more paragraphs. Explain how these last paragraphs direct our attention to *the quaint old superstitions of the community* rather than to *Tom Walker himself.*

⬦⬦⬦⬦⬦

THE STOUT GENTLEMAN

The traveler was forced to stay indoors, during a long rainy day, in a small-town British inn. He was half sick, and lonely. There was nothing to do, and everything he looked at depressed him. But then he began to get interested in the mysterious occupant of Room No. 13.

It was a rainy Sunday in the gloomy month of November. I had been detained, in the course of a journey, by a slight indisposition, from which I was recovering; but was still feverish and obliged to keep within doors all day in an inn of the small town of Derby. A wet Sunday in a country inn—whoever has had the luck to experience one can alone judge of my situation. The rain pattered against the casements; the bells tolled for church with a melancholy sound. I went to the windows in quest of something to amuse the eye, but it seemed as if I had been placed completely out of the reach of all amusement. The windows of my bedroom looked out among tiled roofs and stacks of chimneys, while those of my sitting room commanded a full view of the stable yard. I know of nothing more calculated to make a man sick of this world than a stable yard on a rainy day. The place was littered with wet straw that had been kicked about by travelers and stable boys. In one corner was a stagnant pool of water, surrounding an island of muck; there were several half-drowned fowls crowded together under a cart, among which was a miserable, crestfallen cock, drenched out of all life and spirit, his drooping tail matted, as it were, into a single feather, along which the water trickled from his back; near the cart was a half-dozing cow, chewing the cud, and standing patiently to be rained on, with wreaths of vapor rising from her reeking hide; a wall-eyed horse, tired of the loneliness of the stable, was poking his spectral head out of a window, with the rain dripping on it from the eaves; an unhappy cur, chained to a doghouse hard by, uttered something, every now and then, between a bark and a yelp; a drab of a kitchen wench tramped backwards and forwards through the yard in pattens,[1] looking as sulky as the weather itself; everything, in short, was comfortless and forlorn, excepting a crew of hardened ducks, assembled like boon companions round a puddle, and making a riotous noise over their liquor.

I was lonely and listless, and wanted amusement. My room soon became insupportable. I abandoned it and sought what is technically called the travelers' room. This is a public room set apart at most inns for the accommodation of a class of wayfarers called travelers, or riders; a kind of commercial knights-errant,[2] who are incessantly scouring the kingdom in gigs, on horseback, or by coach. They are the only successors that I know of at the present day to the knights-errant of yore. They lead the same kind of roving, adventurous life, only changing the lance for a driving whip, the buckler for a pattern-card, and the coat of mail for an upper Benjamin.[3] Instead of vindicating the charms of peerless beauty, they rove about, spreading the fame and standing of some substantial tradesman or manufacturer, and are ready at any time to bargain in his name; it being the fashion nowadays to trade, instead of fight, with one another. As the room of the hostel, in the good old fighting times, would be hung round at night with the armor of wayworn warriors, such as coats of mail, falchions,[4] and yawning helmets, so the travelers' room is garnished with the harnessing of their successors, with box coats, whips of all kinds, and

[1] PATTENS—A type of footwear; wooden shoes, clogs.
[2] KNIGHTS-ERRANT—Wandering knights. In medieval times, knights were supposed to ride through the world seeking adventure. Each knight announced that the woman he loved was of unequaled beauty, and he would demand a combat with anyone who would not agree with him.
[3] UPPER BENJAMIN—Slang for "overcoat."
[4] FALCHIONS (fôl'chŭnz)—Swords.

spurs, gaiters,[5] and oilcloth-covered hats.

I was in hopes of finding some of these worthies to talk with, but was disappointed. There were, indeed, two or three in the room; but I could make nothing of them. One was just finishing his breakfast, quarreling with his bread and butter, and huffing the waiter; another buttoned on a pair of gaiters, with many execrations at Boots [6] for not having cleaned his shoes well; a third sat drumming on the table with his fingers and looking at the rain as it streamed down the window glass; they all appeared infected by the weather, and disappeared, one after the other, without exchanging a word.

I sauntered to the window and stood gazing at the people picking their way to church, with petticoats hoisted midleg high, and dripping umbrellas. The bell ceased to toll, and the streets became silent. I then amused myself with watching the daughters of a tradesman opposite; who, being confined to the house for fear of wetting their Sunday finery, played off their charms at the front windows, to fascinate the chance tenants of the inn. They at length were summoned away by a vigilant vinegar-faced mother, and I had nothing further from without to amuse me.

What was I to do to pass away the long-lived day? I was sadly nervous and lonely; and everything about an inn seems calculated to make a dull day ten times duller. Old newspapers, smelling of beer and tobacco smoke, and which I had already read a dozen times. Good-for-nothing books, that were worse than rainy weather. I bored myself to death with an old volume of the *Lady's Maga-*

zine. I read all the commonplace names of ambitious travelers scrawled on the panes of glass; the eternal families of the Smiths, and the Browns, and the Jacksons, and the Johnsons, and all the other sons; and I deciphered several scraps of fatiguing inn-window poetry which I have met with in all parts of the world.

The day continued lowering and gloomy; the slovenly, ragged, spongy cloud drifted heavily along; there was no variety even in the rain: it was one dull, continued, monotonous patter—patter— patter, excepting that now and then I was enlivened by the idea of a brisk shower, from the rattling of the drops upon a passing umbrella.

It was quite *refreshing* (if I may be allowed a hackneyed phrase of the day) when, in the course of the morning, a horn blew and a stagecoach whirled through the street, with outside passengers stuck all over it, cowering under cotton umbrellas, and seethed together, and reeking with the steams of wet box coats and upper Benjamins.

The sound brought out from their lurking places a crew of vagabond boys, and vagabond dogs, and the carroty-headed hostler, and the nondescript animal ycleped [7] Boots, and all the other vagabond race that infest the purlieus [8] of an inn; but the bustle was transient; the coach again whirled on its way; and boy and dog, and hostler and Boots, all slunk back again to their holes; the street again became silent, and the rain continued to rain on. In fact, there was no hope of its clearing up; the barometer pointed to rainy weather; mine hostess' tortoise-shell cat sat by the fire washing her face and rubbing her paws over her ears; and on, referring to the Almanac, I found a dire-

---

[5] GAITERS—Leggings, formerly a normal part of outdoor costume.

[6] BOOTS—The hotel servant who cleaned shoes.

[7] YCLEPED (ĭ·klĕpt′)—Called; named.

[8] PURLIEUS (pûr′lūz)—Limits; confines; boundaries.

ful prediction stretching from the top of the page to the bottom through the whole month, "expect—much—rain—about—this—time!"

I was dreadfully hipped.[9] The hours seemed as if they would never creep by. The very ticking of the clock became irksome. At length the stillness of the house was interrupted by the ringing of a bell. Shortly after I heard the voice of a waiter at the bar: "The stout gentleman in No. 13 wants his breakfast. Tea and bread and butter, with ham and eggs; the eggs not to be too much done."

In such a situation as mine, every incident is of importance. Here was a subject of speculation presented to my mind, and ample exercise for my imagination. I am prone to paint pictures to myself, and on this occasion I had some materials to work upon. Had the guest upstairs been mentioned as Mr. Smith, or Mr. Brown, or Mr. Jackson, or Mr. Johnson, or merely as "the gentleman in No. 13," it would have been a perfect blank to me. I should have thought nothing of it; but "the stout gentleman!"—the very name had something in it of the picturesque. It at once gave the size; it embodied the personage to my mind's eye, and my fancy did the rest.

He was stout, or, as some term it, lusty; in all probability, therefore, he was advanced in life, some people expanding as they grow old. By his breakfasting rather late, and in his own room, he must be a man accustomed to live at his ease, and above the necessity of early rising; no doubt a round, rosy, lusty old gentleman.

There was another violent ringing. The stout gentleman was impatient for his breakfast. He was evidently a man of importance; "well-to-do in the world"; accustomed to be promptly waited upon; of a keen appetite, and a little cross when

[9] HIPPED—"Blue" or depressed.

hungry; "perhaps," thought I, "he may be some London Alderman; or who knows but he may be a Member of Parliament?"

The breakfast was sent up, and there was a short interval of silence; he was, doubtless, making the tea. Presently there was a violent ringing; and before it could be answered, another ringing still more violent. "Bless me! what a choleric [10] old gentleman!" The waiter came down in a huff. The butter was rancid, the eggs were overdone, the ham was too salt—the stout gentleman was evidently nice in his eating; one of those who eat and growl, and keep the waiter on the trot, and live in a state militant with the household.

The hostess got into a fume. I should observe that she was a brisk, coquettish woman; a little of a shrew,[11] and something of a slammerkin,[12] but very pretty withal; with a nincompoop for a husband, as shrews are apt to have. She rated the servants roundly for their negligence in sending up so bad a breakfast, but said not a word against the stout gentleman; by which I clearly perceived that he must be a man of consequence, entitled to make a noise and to give trouble at a country inn. Other eggs, and ham, and bread and butter were sent up. They appeared to be more graciously received; at least there was no further complaint.

I had not made many turns about the travelers' room, when there was another ringing. Shortly afterwards there was a stir and an inquest about the house. The stout gentleman wanted the *Times* or the *Chronicle* newspaper. I set him down, therefore, for a Whig;[13] or rather,

[10] CHOLERIC (kŏl'ĕr·ĭk)—Quick-tempered; peevish.
[11] SHREW—A nagging woman.
[12] SLAMMERKIN—Slang for an untidily dressed woman.
[13] A WHIG—A member of the liberal party in English politics.

553

from his being so absolute and lordly, where he had a chance, I suspected him of being a radical. Hunt,[14] I had heard, was a large man; "Who knows," thought I, "but it is Hunt himself!"

My curiosity began to be awakened. I inquired of the waiter who was this stout gentleman that was making all this stir; but I could get no information: nobody seemed to know his name. The landlords of bustling inns seldom trouble their heads about the names or occupations of their transient guests. The color of a coat, the shape or size of the person, is enough to suggest a traveling name. It is either the tall gentleman, or the short gentleman, or the gentleman in black, or the gentleman in snuff color; or, as in the present instance, the stout gentleman. A designation of the kind once hit

[14] HUNT—Leigh Hunt, a prominent writer, was a leader of the radical party which wished to overthrow the British monarchy and establish a republic.

on, answers every purpose, and saves all further inquiry.

Rain—rain—rain! pitiless, ceaseless rain! No such thing as putting a foot out of doors, and no occupation nor amusement within. By and by I heard someone walking overhead. It was in the stout gentleman's room. He evidently was a large man by the heaviness of his tread; and an old man from his wearing such creaking soles. "He is doubtless," thought I, "some rich old square-toes of regular habits, and is now taking exercise after breakfast."

I now read all the advertisements of coaches and hotels that were stuck about the mantelpiece. The *Lady's Magazine* had become an abomination to me; it was as tedious as the day itself. I wandered out, not knowing what to do, and ascended again to my room. I had not been there long, when there was a squall from a neighboring bedroom. A door opened and slammed violently; a chambermaid, that I had remarked for having a ruddy, good-humored face, went downstairs in a violent flurry. The stout gentleman had been rude to her!

This sent a whole host of my deductions to the deuce in a moment. This unknown personage could not be an old gentleman; for old gentlemen are not apt to be so obstreperous to chambermaids. He could not be a young gentleman; for young gentlemen are not apt to inspire such indignation. He must be a middle-aged man, and confounded ugly into the bargain, or the girl would not have taken the matter in such terrible dudgeon. I confess I was sorely puzzled.

In a few minutes I heard the voice of my landlady. I caught a glance of her as she came tramping upstairs—her face glowing, her cap flaring, her tongue wagging the whole way. "She'd have no such doings in her house, she'd warrant. If gentlemen did spend money freely, it was no rule. She'd have no servant maids of hers treated in that way, when they were about their work, that's what she wouldn't."

As I hate squabbles, particularly with women, and above all with pretty women, I slunk back into my room and partly closed the door; but my curiosity was too much excited not to listen. The landlady marched intrepidly to the enemy's citadel and entered it with a storm: the door closed after her. I heard her voice in high windy clamor for a moment or two. Then it gradually subsided, like a gust of wind in a garret; then there was a laugh; then I heard nothing more.

After a little while my landlady came out with an odd smile on her face, adjusting her cap, which was a little on one side. As she went downstairs, I heard the landlord ask her what was the matter; she said, "Nothing at all, only the girl's a fool"— I was more than ever perplexed

what to make of this unaccountable personage, who could put a good-natured chambermaid in a passion, and send away a termagant landlady in smiles. He could not be so old, nor cross, nor ugly either.

I had to go to work at his picture again, and to paint him entirely different. I now set him down for one of those stout gentlemen that are frequently met with swaggering about the doors of country inns. Moist, merry fellows, whose bulk is a little assisted by malt liquors. Men who have seen the world; who are used to tavern life. . . .

Dinnertime came. I hoped the stout gentleman might dine in the travelers' room, and that I might at length get a view of his person; but no—he had dinner served in his own room. What could be the meaning of this solitude and mystery? He could not be a radical; there was something too aristocratical in thus keeping himself apart from the rest of the world and condemning himself to his own dull company throughout a rainy day. And then, too, he lived too well for a discontented politician. He seemed to expatiate on a variety of dishes and to sit over his wine like a jolly friend of good living. Indeed, my doubts on this head were soon at an end; for he could not have finished his first bottle before I could faintly hear him humming a tune; and on listening I found it to be "God Save the King." 'Twas plain, then, he was no radical, but a faithful subject; one who grew loyal over his bottle and was ready to stand by king and constitution, when he could stand by nothing else. But who could he be? My conjectures began to run wild. Was he not some personage of distinction traveling incog.? [15]

[15] INCOG—Abbreviation of *incognito*; a device used by a person to conceal his true identity; *i.e.* traveling under a false name.

"God knows!" said I, at my wit's end; "it may be one of the royal family for aught I know, for they are all stout gentlemen!" [16]

The weather continued rainy. The mysterious unknown kept his room, and, as far as I could judge, his chair, for I did not hear him move. In the meantime, as the day advanced, the travelers' room began to be frequented. Some, who had just arrived, came in buttoned up in box coats; others came home who had been dispersed about the town; some took their dinners, and some their tea. Had I been in a different mood, I should have found entertainment in studying this peculiar class of men. There were two especially, who were regular wags of the road, and up to all the standing jokes of travelers. They had a thousand sly things to say to the waiting maid, whom they called Louisa, and Ethelinda, and a dozen other fine names, changing the name every time, and chuckling amazingly at their own waggery. My mind, however, had

[16] ONE OF THE ROYAL FAMILY . . . FOR THEY ARE ALL STOUT GENTLEMEN—This is a quip at the royal House of Hanover, which was very unpopular. George IV had just become king at the age of 58. He was a heavy, beefy-looking man. So were the eight princes, his brothers, all of whom were over 40 years old.

been completely engrossed by the stout gentleman. He had kept my fancy in chase during a long day, and it was not now to be diverted from the scent.

The evening gradually wore away. The travelers read the papers two or three times over. Some drew round the fire and told long stories about their horses, about their adventures, their overturns, and breakings-down. They discussed the credit of different merchants and different inns; and the two wags told several choice anecdotes of pretty chambermaids and kind landladies. All this passed as they were quietly taking what they called their nightcaps, that is to say, strong glasses of brandy and water and sugar, or some other mixture of the kind; after which they one after another rang for Boots and the chambermaid, and walked off to bed in old shoes cut down into marvelously uncomfortable slippers. . . .

The church bells chimed midnight. All at once the stout gentleman began to walk overhead, pacing slowly backwards and forwards. There was something extremely awful in all this, especially to one in my state of nerves. These ghastly greatcoats, these guttural breathings, and the creaking footsteps of this mysterious being. His steps grew fainter and fainter,

and at length died away. I could bear it no longer. I was wound up to the desperation of a hero of romance. "Be he who or what he may," said I to myself, "I'll have a sight of him!" I seized a chamber candle, and hurried up to No. 13. The door stood ajar. I hesitated—I entered; the room was deserted. There stood a large, broad-bottomed elbowchair at a table, on which was an empty tumbler and a *Times* newspaper, and the room smelt powerfully of Stilton cheese.

The mysterious stranger had evidently but just retired.[17] I turned off, sorely disappointed, to my room, which had been changed to the front of the house. As I went along the corridor, I saw a large pair of boots, with dirty, waxed tops, standing at the door of a bedchamber. They doubtless belonged to the unknown; but it would not do to disturb so redoubtable a personage in his den: he might discharge a pistol, or something worse, at my head. I went to bed, therefore, and lay awake half the night in a terribly nervous state; and even when I fell asleep, I was still haunted in my dreams by the idea of the stout gentleman and his waxtopped boots.

I slept rather late the next morning and was awakened by some stir and bustle in the house, which I could not at first comprehend; until getting more awake, I found there was a mailcoach starting from the door. Suddenly there was a cry from below, "The gentleman has forgot his umbrella! Look for the gentleman's umbrella in No. 13!" I heard an immediate scampering of a chambermaid along the passage and a shrill reply as she ran, "Here it is! Here's the gentleman's umbrella!"

The mysterious stranger then was on

[17] HAD EVIDENTLY BUT JUST RETIRED—Lodgings consisted of *two* rooms. The stranger had gone to his bedchamber, leaving his sitting room empty.

the point of setting off. This was the only chance I should ever have of knowing him. I sprang out of bed, scrambled to the window, snatched aside the curtains, and just caught a glimpse of the rear of a person getting in at the coach door. The skirts of a brown coat parted behind and gave me a full view of the broad disk of a pair of drab breeches. The door closed—"All right!" was the word—the coach whirled off—and that was all I ever saw of the stout gentleman!

FOR UNDERSTANDING

1. The second sentence explains that the author was slightly ill, and had to pass the time away as best he could inside the house. Mention three ways he tried to amuse himself. Why is his boredom a good introduction for the "mystery" of the stout gentleman?

2. The "travelers' room" mentioned in the second paragraph is for the use of traveling salesmen, or, as they were called in England, "commercial travelers." Explain how, in Irving's imagination, these men are like the *knights-errant* of olden times. Whose fame do the salesmen spread through the world, just as each knight used to praise the beauty of the woman he loved? What do the salesmen do that corresponds to the *fighting* of the knights? What does the salesman carry that corresponds to the knight's *buckler*, or shield? What other equipment does he have that may be compared to the equipment of a knight?

3. Find the place in the story where the "stout gentleman" is first mentioned. Can you explain why Irving tells of the arrival of the coach in the paragraphs *just preceding* the first mention of the stranger?

4. Explain why the reader's curiosity about the stout gentleman gets stronger and stronger as the story progresses. Mention several guesses made by the author as to what the gentleman is like. On what does he base these guesses?

5. This story takes place in a small English town in 1821. In an American town today, instead of by stagecoach how would the stout gentleman leave his hotel? What other differences between past and present can you point out? What similarities or differences between people then and now can you mention?

THE WRITER'S CRAFT

IRVING'S REALISTIC PICTURE OF A RAINY DAY

Some writers are inclined to forget that dreary or ugly scenes are just as real as more agreeable sights, and can be as interesting to describe. One of the best parts of "The Stout Gentleman" is the long opening paragraph which tells what is to be seen through the window on a wet day. The "wet straw that had been kicked about," and the soggy-looking chickens standing under the cart for shelter, are good descriptive details.

Irving's vivid, precise language helps us "see" the scene more completely. He does not use big words, but for each detail he chooses expressions that will make that detail stand out clearly. Explain the picture that is created by the italicized expressions in the following quotations. Use a dictionary, if some words are unfamiliar.

". . . a miserable, *crestfallen* cock, *drenched* out of all life and spirit."

". . . a half-dozing cow, chewing the cud, and standing patiently to be rained on, with *wreaths of vapor* rising from her *reeking hide.*"

". . . a *wall-eyed* horse, tired of the loneliness of the stable, was poking his *spectral* head out of a window."

". . . a crew of hardened ducks, assembled like *boon companions* round a puddle, and making a riotous noise over their liquor."

BUILDING UP FOR A LET-DOWN

Explain why this story is a joke on the reader. Mention some of the things the reader might have expected would happen at the end. Irving's story is more typical of actual life than of fiction because, after all, no unusual event takes place. In contrast, in most stories in popular magazines something remarkable happens to the hero. Summarize the plots of two such stories you have read which end with a "big" event instead of a let-down.

WRITING PROJECTS

1. Write a short description of an *unpleasing* scene which you have observed closely. Put in many exact details, and describe the more important ones very carefully so that your reader will get the same feeling you had when you were looking at the scene. Here are some possible subjects: a littered, untidy back yard; an alley in the business district of town; a city dump, or any other place where trash is thrown; a dreary, deserted playground on a wet, disagreeable day; the banks of a weedy, marshy ditch. For a longer theme, you might like to use your description as part of a story—following the suggestion below.

2. Imitate Irving by writing a brief story that *could* actually have happened to you. Build up suspense by telling about the fear or expectation in your mind, but end the story with a "let-down." Be sure to mention several dramatic conclusions which you imagined would be the outcome of your "adventure." Then, finish with one sentence like "When I handed it to him, he didn't say a word," or "When we finally got the door pried open, there it was, still safe and sound."

FOR FURTHER READING

LAURA BENÉT, *Washington Irving: Explorer of American Legend*, (Dodd). Washington Irving's early life is reconstructed with imagination.

SAXE COMMINS, ed., *Selected Writings of Washington Irving*, (Modern Library). This volume includes *Knickerbocker's History of New York*, selections from *The Sketch Book, Bracebridge Hall, Tales of a Traveller, The Alhambra,* and *Wolfert's Roost and Other Papers.*

EDGAR ALLAN POE (1809-1849)

Poe led a strange, disordered, and tragic life, but he was both a genius and a painstaking student of literary art. His father and mother, who were traveling actors, died in his early childhood and he was brought up by the Allans, a wealthy family in Richmond, Virginia. Repeated quarrels with his foster father embittered his life as a boy. Mr. Allan took him out of the University of Virginia because of a gambling escapade, and during a temporary reconciliation obtained an appointment for him at West Point. After another quarrel, Poe deliberately neglected his military duties and was dismissed. From then on, he was without support.

In the meantime he had published three books of poems, all of them before he was twenty-three. They brought him little money. He turned to writing stories, and won a hundred-dollar prize contest with "MS. Found in a Bottle." He found editorial positions on the *Southern Literary Messenger* and other publications. During the next few years his literary reputation grew rapidly. He wrote many short stories, and some of his finest poems. His book reviews in the magazines that he helped to edit were the most intelligent that had appeared in America, and the magazines gained in circulation.

But Poe was unstable and quarrelsome, and often failed to keep to his schedule of work as an editor. He lost one job after another, and suffered the most extreme poverty. He had married his young cousin Virginia Clemm—a frail girl who developed tuberculosis. In his anxiety, Poe began to drink. He did not drink heavily, but the smallest amount of liquor seemed to craze him. More than ever, he was unfit for regular work. Virginia died, and a few years later Poe himself died suddenly in Baltimore.

AMERICA'S FIRST "FINE ARTIST" IN LITERATURE

In his poetry, Poe was an artist rather than a thinker. His mind turned naturally toward melancholy subjects, and especially to the thought of death. He offered no new insights into his subjects, but tried to make each poem a perfect piece of art—as a jeweler polishes a strange, rare stone. He often used foreign names and unusual expressions—*Nicean, of yore, Porphyrogene*—for their exotic flavor. He studied the emotional effects of different word-sounds, and knew how to intensify these effects by using repetition. All his poems are strange, haunting, and melodious.

Poe was also an artist in his stories. Their wildly imaginative quality is suggested by the title Poe gave to his collection, *Tales of the Grotesque and Arabesque.* Each one is carefully planned to develop a particular feeling in the reader—often a feeling of dread or suspense. Poe declares that the very first sentence of a story must begin to create the feeling the author intends to produce, and says, "In the whole composition there should be no word written, of which the tendency, direct or indirect, is not to the one pre-established design." As a result, the reader enters more and more intensely into the mood of the story, his interest rising to its highest point as the tale reaches its dramatic conclusion.

Besides tales of terror, Poe wrote tales about a master-mind French detective called Monsieur Dupin. By his brilliant powers of reasoning, Dupin could solve crimes that baffled the Paris police. These stories show the originality of Poe's talent, for in creating Monsieur Dupin, Poe became the inventor of the modern detective story.

◇◇◇◇◇

To Helen

Poe has told us that "Helen" is his name for a lovely and sympathetic woman, Mrs. Jane Stanard, whom he idolized in boyhood. She died when Poe was fifteen. This poem was written some years later in her memory. It is like Poe to portray her, not as a Virginia gentlewoman, but as a vision of classic grace.

560

Helen, thy beauty is to me
  Like those Nicean barks of yore,
That gently, o'er a perfumed sea,
  The weary, wayworn wanderer bore
  To his own native shore.   5

On desperate seas long wont to roam,
  Thy hyacinth hair, thy classic face,
Thy Naiad airs have brought me home
  To the glory that was Greece,
  And the grandeur that was Rome.   10

Lo! in yon brilliant window niche
How statuelike I see thee stand,
The agate lamp within thy hand!
Ah, Psyche, from the regions which
Are Holy Land!   15

2. NICEAN (nī·sē'ăn)—Perhaps a misspelling of "Nyseian," referring to the beautiful island of Nysa in ancient mythology.
7. HYACINTH HAIR—Imitated from the adjective "hyacinthine," which is often used in Homer's poems to describe golden-colored hair.
8. NAIAD (nā'ăd)—In Greek mythology, naiads were spirits represented as beautiful maidens who dwelt in streams, lakes, and springs.
13. AGATE LAMP—A lamp made of semi-precious stone.
14. PSYCHE (sī'kē)—Goddess of the soul, personified as a lovely maiden.

◇◇

FOR UNDERSTANDING

1. The first stanza suggests the beauty of classical Greece and Rome by the word "Nicean" and also by the phrase about the "wayworn wanderer," reminding us of Ulysses' dangerous voyage home from the Trojan War. How does the name "Helen" also remind us of ancient times?

2. In the second stanza, Helen's loveliness has given the poet a glimpse of beauty which he has not found elsewhere in his unhappy life. Point out all the words in this stanza which remind us of the ancient world. How does this stanza continue the comparison which was begun in stanza 1?

3. To understand the third stanza we must recall that Helen is dead. The lighted "window niche" is in the poet's memory and imagination, where she stands forever. Classic perfection is hinted again in "statuelike"—but figures of saints, also, are enshrined in lighted niches. What words suggest this further comparison to saints?

4. What does Poe's use of alliteration add to the effect of the poem?

◇◇◇◇◇

Israfel

Here is a poem that tells how the poet feels about his own art. When he published "Israfel," Poe placed these lines at the beginning:

"And the angel Israfel, whose heartstrings are a lute, and who has the sweetest voice of all God's creatures." KORAN.*

This introductory note expresses one of the main ideas of the poem—that the best poet is he whose songs come truly from the heart.

In Heaven a spirit doth dwell,
 "Whose heartstrings are a lute."
None sing so wildly well
As the angel Israfel,
And the giddy stars (so legends tell)   5
Ceasing their hymns, attend the spell
 Of his voice, all mute.

Tottering above,
 In her highest noon,
 The enamored moon   10
Blushes with love,
 While, to listen, the red levin
 (With the rapid Pleiads, even,
 Which were seven)
Pauses in Heaven.   15

And they say (the starry choir
 And the other listening things)
That Israfeli's fire
Is owing to that lyre
 By which he sits and sings—   20
The trembling living wire
 Of those unusual strings.

But the skies that angel trod,
 Where deep thoughts are a duty—
Where Love's a grown-up God—   25
 Where the Houri glances are
Imbued with all the beauty
 Which we worship in a star.

Therefore, thou art not wrong,
 Israfeli, who despisest   30
An unimpassioned song;
To thee the laurels belong,
 Best bard, because the wisest!
Merrily live, and long!

The ecstasies above   35
 With thy burning measures suit—
Thy grief, thy joy, thy hate, thy love,
 With the fervor of thy lute—
 Well may the stars be mute!

Yes, Heaven is thine; but this   40
 Is a world of sweets and sours;
 Our flowers are merely—flowers,
And the shadow of thy perfect bliss
 Is the sunshine of ours.

If I could dwell   45
Where Israfel
 Hath dwelt, and he where I,
He might not sing so wildly well
 A mortal melody,
While a bolder note than this might
 swell   50
From my lyre within the sky.

iades. In Greek mythology these were the seven daughters of Atlas who were changed into a group of stars.

23. BUT THE SKIES THAT ANGEL TROD—The expression means "But that angel trod the skies."

26. HOURI (hōō'rĭ)—A nymph possessing perpetual youth and beauty who lives in the Mohammedan paradise.

31. AN UNIMPASSIONED SONG—A song that does not come from deep emotion.

* KORAN—The Koran is the Mohammedan book of scriptures. Actually Poe himself added the notion that Israfel played upon his own heartstrings as a lute.

12. LEVIN—Lightning.

13. PLEIADS (plē'yȧ·dĕz)—Now spelled *ple-*

◇◇◇

FOR UNDERSTANDING

1. The idea that the true poet must express exactly what is *in his heart* is to be found in the third stanza. The key words are "is owing to." In your own words explain what "they say" causes the fire of Israfeli's poetry. Point out a phrase in the fifth stanza that alludes to the same notion.

2. Another main idea in "Israfel" is that it is a splendid thing to make perfect songs. In fact, we get the idea that Poe is envious of the angel. Point out phrases in the early part of the poem which stress the beauty of Israfel's singing.

3. A third main idea is that because a poet sings exactly what is in his heart, his songs will not be perfect unless his own experience—his environment—is superior. Explain what the first two lines of stanza 6 say about the connection between Israfel's *heavenly surroundings* and his *songs*.

What opinion of our own world is indicated by "sweets and sours," and the remark about flowers, in stanza 7?

4. Which of the three ideas mentioned above are woven into the final stanza? For each one that you find, give evidence that the final stanza actually does refer to it.

5. According to Poe, what would be the result if he and Israfel were to exchange dwellings? Why?

6. One of the most striking and imaginative passages in "Israfel" is lines 43–44. Re-read the passage and explain what it means.

◇◇◇◇◇

The Haunted Palace

This poem originally appeared in "The Fall of the House of Usher," a short story in which the main character is on the verge of insanity. Here "palace" is used symbolically to represent a human being. Using the subject of the story as a clue to the interpretation of the poem, see if you can find other symbols. Notice the physical parts of the man that are mentioned, and the changes that come over them after the palace is "haunted."

In the greenest of our valleys
  By good angels tenanted,
Once a fair and stately palace—
  Radiant palace—reared its head.
In the monarch Thought's domin-
    ion— 5
  It stood there!
Never seraph spread a pinion
  Over fabric half so fair!

Banners yellow, glorious, golden,
  On its roof did float and flow, 10
(This—all this—was in the olden
  Time long ago),
And every gentle air that dallied,
  In that sweet day,
Along the ramparts plumed and pallid,
  A wingèd odor went away. 16

Wanderers in that happy valley,
  Through two luminous windows, saw
Spirits moving musically,
  To a lute's well-tunèd law, 20
Round about a throne where, sitting,
  Porphyrogene,
In state his glory well befitting,
  The ruler of the realm was seen.

And all with pearl and ruby glowing 25
  Was the fair palace door,
Through which came flowing, flowing,
    flowing,
  And sparkling evermore,

22. PORPHYROGENE (pòr′fĭ·rô·jēn′)—This is supposed to be the name of the "ruler of the realm." It means "born to the purple"—that is, of royal ancestry.

A troop of Echoes, whose sweet duty
  Was but to sing,   30
In voices of surpassing beauty,
  The wit and wisdom of their king.

But evil things, in robes of sorrow,
  Assailed the monarch's high estate.
(Ah, let us mourn!—for never mor-
    row   35
  Shall dawn upon him, desolate!)
And round about his home the glory
  That blushed and bloomed,

Is but a dim-remembered story
  Of the old time entombed.   40

And travelers, now, within that
    valley,
  Through the red-litten windows see
Vast forms, that move fantastically
  To a discordant melody,
While, like a ghastly rapid river,   45
  Through the pale door
A hideous throng rush out forever
  And laugh—but smile no more.

FOR UNDERSTANDING

1. What are the yellow banners that wave over the roof? What are the two windows? The "spirits" within are pleasing, well-ordered thoughts. What do you think the "ruler" represents?

2. In stanza 4, what are the pearls and rubies of the palace door? Explain why it is when the Echoes *come out* of the palace door that they testify as to the "wit and wisdom of their king."

3. According to Poe's own explanation, in the last two stanzas the man's mind becomes "haunted by phantoms"—that is, by horrible, even insane, ideas. In which line are they first mentioned? "V*ast* forms" in the last stanza suggests that these ideas are terrifying, and perhaps irresistibly strong. What expressions show disorder and confusion? What phrase suggests the strange gleam in a mad person's eyes?

4. In the last four lines of the poem Poe completes his task of describing a man who has gone out of his mind. Compare these lines to stanza 4, and state *all* the differences which have taken place in the victim's speech. Explain the meaning of line 48.

THE MASQUE OF THE RED DEATH

Stories by Poe show that he delighted in picturing scenes of splendor and luxury. Also, his imagination was haunted by the terror of death. In this story the two subjects are combined. As you read, notice how the story exemplifies Poe's theory that mood is the most important element of a short story.

TITLE—A *masque* is a dance where all wear masks and elaborate costumes.

The "Red Death" had long devastated the country. No pestilence had ever been so fatal, or so hideous. Blood was its avatar [1] and its seal—the redness and the horror of blood. There were sharp pains, and sudden dizziness, and then profuse bleeding at the pores, with dissolution. The scarlet stains upon the body, and especially upon the face, of the victim were the pest ban which shut him out from the aid and from the sympathy of his fellow men. And the whole seizure, progress, and termination of the disease were the incidents of half an hour.

But the Prince Prospero was happy and dauntless and sagacious. When his dominions were half depopulated he summoned to his presence a thousand hale and lighthearted friends from among the knights and dames of his court, and with these retired to the deep seclusion of one of his castellated [2] abbeys. This was an extensive and magnificent structure, the creation of the prince's own eccentric yet august taste. A strong and lofty wall girdled it in. This wall had gates of iron. The courtiers, having entered, brought furnaces and massy hammers, and welded the bolts. They resolved to leave means neither of ingress or egress to the sudden impulses of despair or of frenzy from within. The abbey was amply provisioned. With such precautions the courtiers might bid defiance to contagion. The external world could take care of itself. In the meantime it was folly to grieve, or to think. The prince had provided all the appliances of pleasure. There were buffoons,[3] there were improvisatori,[4] there were ballet dancers, there were musicians, there was Beauty, there

[1] AVATAR (ăv′á·tär′)—Embodiment or manifestation.
[2] CASTELLATED—Castlelike.
[3] BUFFOONS—Clowns, merrymakers.
[4] IMPROVISATORI (ĭm′prò·vĭ′zà·tō′rĭ)—Composers of extemporaneous songs or poetry.

was wine. All these and security were within. Without was the Red Death.

It was toward the close of the fifth or sixth month of his seclusion, and while the pestilence raged most furiously abroad, that the Prince Prospero entertained his thousand friends at a masked ball of the most unusual magnificence.

It was a voluptuous scene, that masquerade. But first let me tell of the rooms in which it was held. There were seven—an imperial suite. In many palaces, however, such suites form a long and straight vista, while the folding doors slide back nearly to the walls on either hand, so that the view of the whole extent is scarcely impeded. Here the case was very different, as might have been expected from the prince's love of the bizarre. The apartments were so irregularly disposed that the vision embraced but little more than one at a time. There was a sharp turn at every twenty or thirty yards, and at each turn a novel effect. To the right and left, in the middle of each wall, a tall and narrow Gothic window looked out upon a closed corridor which pursued the windings of the suite. These windows were of stained glass, whose color varied in accordance with the prevailing hue of the decorations of the chamber into which it opened. That at the eastern extremity was hung, for example, in blue—and vividly blue were its windows. The second chamber was purple in its ornaments and tapestries, and here the panes were purple. The third was green throughout, and so were the casements. The fourth was furnished and lighted with orange, the fifth with white, the sixth with violet. The seventh apartment was closely shrouded in black velvet tapestries that hung all over the ceiling and down the walls, falling in heavy folds upon a carpet of the same material and hue. But, in this chamber only, the color of the windows failed to correspond with the decorations. The panes here were scarlet—a deep blood color. Now in no one of the seven apartments was there any lamp or candelabrum, amid the profusion of golden ornaments that lay scattered to and fro or depended from the roof. There was no light of any kind emanating from lamp or candle within the suite of chambers. But in the corridors that followed the suite there stood, opposite to each window, a heavy tripod, bearing a brazier of fire, that projected its rays through the tinted glass and so glaringly illumined the room. And thus were produced a multitude of gaudy and fantastic appearances. But in the western or black chamber the effect of the firelight that streamed upon the dark hangings through the blood-tinted panes was ghastly in the extreme, and produced so wild a look upon the countenances of those who entered that there were few of the company bold enough to set foot within its precincts at all.

It was in this apartment, also, that there stood against the western wall a gigantic clock of ebony. Its pendulum swung to and fro with a dull, heavy, monotonous clang; and when the minute hand made the circuit of the face, and the hour was to be stricken, there came from the brazen lungs of the clock a sound which was clear and loud and deep and exceedingly musical, but of so peculiar a note and emphasis that, at each lapse of an hour, the musicians of the orchestra were constrained to pause, momentarily, in their performance, to hearken to the sound; and thus the waltzers perforce ceased their evolutions; and there was a brief disconcert of the whole gay company; and, while the chimes of the clock yet rang, it was observed that the giddiest grew pale, and the more aged

and sedate passed their hands over their brows as if in confused revery or meditation. But when the echoes had fully ceased, a light laughter at once pervaded the assembly; the musicians looked at each other and smiled as if at their own nervousness and folly, and made whispering vows, each to the other, that the next chiming of the clock should produce in them no similar emotion and then, after the lapse of sixty minutes (which embrace three thousand and six hundred seconds of the Time that flies) there came yet another chiming of the clock, and then were the same disconcert and tremulousness and meditation as before.

But in spite of these things, it was a gay magnificent revel. The tastes of the prince were peculiar. He had a fine eye for colors and effects. He disregarded the *decora* [5] of mere fashion. His plans were bold and fiery, and his conceptions glowed with barbaric luster. There are some who would have thought him mad. His followers felt that he was not. It was necessary to hear and see and touch him to be *sure* that he was not.

He had directed, in great part, the movable embellishments of the seven chambers, upon occasion of this great fête; and it was his own guiding taste which had given character to the masqueraders. Be sure they were grotesque. There were much glare and glitter and piquancy and phantasm [6]—much of what has been since seen in *Hernani*.[7] There were arabesque figures with unsuited [8] limbs and appointments. There were delirious fancies such as the madman fashions. There was much of the beautiful, much of the wan-

---

[5] *Decora* (dĕ·kō′rà)—Fitness.
[6] PIQUANCY AND PHANTASM—Zest and ghostliness.
[7] *Hernani* (ĕr·nä′nĕ)—A tragedy by Victor Hugo in which the actors wear rich costumes.
[8] UNSUITED—Unmatched.

ton, much of the bizarre, something of the terrible, and not a little of that which might have excited disgust. To and fro in the seven chambers there stalked, in fact, a multitude of dreams. And these —the dreams—writhed in and about, taking hue from the rooms, and causing the wild music of the orchestra to seem as the echo of their steps. And, anon, there strikes the ebony clock which stands in the hall of the velvet. And then, for a moment, all is still, and all is silent save the voice of the clock. The dreams are stiff frozen as they stand. But the echoes of the chime die away—they have endured but an instant—and a light, half-subdued laughter floats after them as they depart. And now again the music swells, and the dreams live, and writhe to and fro more merrily than ever, taking hue from the many-tinted windows through which stream the rays from the tripods. But to the chamber which lies most westwardly of the seven, there are now none of the maskers who venture; for the night is waning away, and there flows a ruddier light through the blood-colored panes; and the blackness of the sable drapery appalls; and to him whose foot falls upon the sable carpet, there comes from the near clock of ebony a muffled peal more solemnly emphatic than any which reaches their ears who indulge in the more remote gaieties of the other apartments.

But these other apartments were densely crowded, and in them beat feverishly the heart of life. And the revel went whirlingly on, until at length there commenced the sounding of midnight upon the clock. And then the music ceased, as I have told; and the evolutions of the waltzers were quieted; and there was an uneasy cessation of all things as before. But now there were twelve strokes to be sounded by the bell of the clock; and thus it happened, perhaps, that more of thought crept, with more of time, into the meditations of the thoughtful among those who reveled. And thus too it happened, perhaps, that before the last echoes of the last chime had utterly sunk into silence, there were many individuals in the crowd who had found leisure to become aware of the presence of a masked figure which had arrested the attention of no single individual before. And the rumor of this new presence having spread itself whisperingly around, there arose at length from the whole company a buzz, or murmur, expressive of disapprobation and surprise—then, finally, of terror, of horror, and of disgust.

In an assembly of phantasms such as I have painted, it may well be supposed that no ordinary appearance could have excited such sensation. In truth the masquerade license of the night was nearly unlimited; but the figure in question had out-Heroded Herod,[9] and gone beyond the bound of even the prince's indefinite decorum. There are chords in the hearts of the most reckless which cannot be touched without emotion. Even with the utterly lost, to whom life and death are equally jests, there are matters of which no jest can be made. The whole company, indeed, seemed now deeply to feel that in the costume and bearing of the stranger neither wit nor propriety existed. The figure was tall and gaunt, and shrouded from head to foot in the habiliments of the grave. The mask which concealed the visage was made so nearly to resemble the countenance of a stiffened corpse that the closest scrutiny must have had difficulty in detecting the cheat. And yet all this might have been

[9] HAD OUT-HERODED HEROD—This is an expression from Shakespeare's *Hamlet*. Here it means "was more daring than the most outrageous of the other costumes."

endured, if not approved, by the mad revelers around. But the mummer [10] had gone so far as to assume the type of the Red Death. His vesture was dabbled in *blood*—and his broad brow, with all the features of the face, was besprinkled with the scarlet horror.

When the eyes of Prince Prospero fell upon this spectral image (which with a slow and solemn movement, as if more fully to sustain its rôle, stalked to and fro among the waltzers) he was seen to be convulsed, in the first moment, with a strong shudder either of terror or distaste; but, in the next, his brow reddened with rage.

"Who dares?" he demanded hoarsely of the courtiers who stood near him— "who dares insult us with this blasphemous mockery? Seize him and unmask him—that we may know whom we have to hang at sunrise, from the battlements!"

It was in the eastern or blue chamber

[10] MUMMER—Masquerader.

in which stood the Prince Prospero as he uttered these words. They rang throughout the seven rooms loudly and clearly— for the prince was a bold and robust man, and the music had become hushed at the waving of his hand.

It was in the blue room where stood the prince, with a group of pale courtiers by his side. At first, as he spoke, there was a slight rushing movement of this group in the direction of the intruder, who at the moment was also near at hand, and now, with deliberate and stately step, made closer approach to the speaker. But from a certain nameless awe with which the mad assumptions of the mummer had inspired the whole party, there were found none who put forth hand to seize him; so that, unimpeded, he passed within a yard of the prince's person; and while the vast assembly, as if with one impulse, shrank from the centers of the rooms to the walls, he made his way uninterruptedly, but with the same solemn and measured step which had distinguished him from the first, through the blue chamber to the purple—through the purple to the green—through the green to the orange —through this again to the white—and even thence to the violet, ere a decided movement had been made to arrest him. It was then, however, that the Prince Prospero, maddening with rage and the shame of his own momentary cowardice, rushed hurriedly through the six chambers, while none followed him on account of a deadly terror that had seized upon all. He bore aloft a drawn dagger, and had approached, in rapid impetuosity, to within three or four feet of the retreating figure, when the latter, having attained the extremity of the velvet apartment, turned suddenly and confronted his pursuer. There was a sharp cry—and the dagger dropped gleaming upon the sable carpet, upon which, instantly afterwards, fell prostrate in death the Prince Prospero. Then, summoning the wild courage of despair, a throng of the revelers at once threw themselves into the black apartment, and, seizing the mummer, whose tall figure stood erect and motionless within the shadow of the ebony clock, gasped in unutterable horror at finding the grave-cerements and corpselike mask, which they handled with so violent a rudeness, untenanted by any tangible form.

And now was acknowledged the presence of the Red Death. He had come like a thief in the night. And one by one dropped the revelers in the blood-bedewed halls of their revel, and died each in the despairing posture of his fall. And the life of the ebony clock went out with that of the last of the gay. And the flames of the tripods expired. And Darkness and Decay and the Red Death held illimitable dominion over all.

FOR UNDERSTANDING

1. Why do you think the reader is not told in what country or at what time of history this story is supposed to have taken place? Decide what countries and periods would be appropriate, and explain why.

2. Which details of the disease called the "Red Death" were most frightening? How did the prince try to protect himself and his friends? Why were the gates sealed shut?

3. What colors were the tapestries that covered each of the walls of the seven apartments? Explain the unusual way in which each apartment was lighted. What was different about the lighting of the seventh apartment?

4. We are supposed to imagine the dance as a scene of wild, reckless revelry. From time to time, what sound stilled the musicians and the revelers for a little while? Why would they pause longest of all when the hour of midnight came?

5. What was particularly shocking about the costume of the stranger who entered at midnight? Where did the Prince Prospero pursue him, and where did the pursuit come to an end? What did the revelers find when they seized the stranger? What does the stranger represent?

THE STORYTELLER'S CRAFT

1. At the very beginning of the first paragraph, Poe introduces the sense of horror that is to dominate his story. In contrast, the second paragraph tells of the actions of the "happy and dauntless" Prince Prospero. What is the purpose of this deliberate contrast? Explain why the life Prospero and his friends live in the palace seems shocking to us. Which sentence in the second paragraph shows their *selfishness*? What suspicion about their safety is suggested by the last two sentences of this paragraph?

2. Glance through the description of the seven apartments. Which one is described *last*? Notice that the account of this last apartment rises to a climax in the descrip-

tion of the strange effect the room had on the people who entered it.

3. Explain how the description of the clock also rises to a climax.

4. Reread the paragraph beginning "He had directed, in great part, the movable embellishments of the seven chambers." In this paragraph, again, Poe begins in an ordinary descriptive tone and builds up to a climax. Explain how this paragraph *combines* details from the other two paragraphs.

5. The *passing of time*—and the fearful reactions of the dancers each time the clock strikes—has already been emphasized several times when the story reaches the hour of midnight. By describing the stranger, and by turning our attention to Prince Prospero, Poe halts the rising action of the story for a while. When the stranger begins to move forward, how does the route he takes produce once more a feeling of climax? Reread the long sentence in which the revelers seize hold of the stranger. How is this sentence arranged so that the *last* detail given in it is a climax?

6. After the stranger has been seized, Poe adds only a brief closing paragraph to his story. Read this paragraph aloud. Why is almost the last phrase of all "the Red Death"? What gives this paragraph its *chant-like* effect?

FOR BROADER MEANINGS

"The Masque of the Red Death" might be taken as a picture of *all* human beings, for death must eventually come to everyone. Poe makes this thought as frightening as possible by using a horrible disease, with ghastly symptoms, as a symbol of death.

1. If Prince Prospero's guests are supposed to be ourselves, explain what the clock represents. Do you believe that people in general are as frightened by the "clock" as the people in the story?

2. The story suggests that all of life is a sort of frenzied dance—that we try to shut out the fear of death, as long as we can, by noise and gaiety. Discuss the accuracy of this description of life. What kinds of activity does it leave out?

3. Normally, we pay little attention to the thought of death. Since it is such an important fact in human existence, do you think it is a good thing that we have poets and other writers to remind us of it? Poe's rather morbid imagination causes him to think of death in ways that most people would reject. Contrast Poe's view of death with the view expressed in either "Thanatopsis," by Bryant or "Nature," by Longfellow.

❖❖❖❖❖

THE CASK OF AMONTILLADO

This story is an attempt to picture a perfect revenge—at least, a perfect revenge according to the queer, warped mentality of the speaker.

The thousand injuries of Fortunato I had borne as I best could, but when he ventured upon insult, I vowed revenge. You, who so well know the nature of my soul, will not suppose, however, that I gave utterance to a threat. *At length* I

TITLE—Amontillado (á·mŏn′tĭ·l(y)ä′dō) is a pale, dry Spanish wine.

would be avenged; this was a point definitively settled—but the very definitiveness with which it was resolved precluded the idea of risk. I must not only punish, but punish with impunity.[1] A wrong is unredressed[2] when retribution overtakes

[1] IMPUNITY—Without being punished.
[2] UNREDRESSED—Not repaid.

its redresser. It is equally unredressed when the avenger fails to make himself felt as such to him who has done the wrong.

It must be understood that neither by word nor deed had I given Fortunato cause to doubt my good will. I continued, as was my wont, to smile in his face, and he did not perceive that my smile *now* was at the thought of his immolation.[3]

He had a weak point—this Fortunato —although in other regards he was a man to be respected and even feared. He prided himself on his connoisseurship in wine. Few Italians have the true virtuoso spirit. For the most part their enthusiasm is adopted to suit the time and opportunity to practice imposture upon the British and Austrian millionaires. In painting and gemmary[4] Fortunato, like his countrymen, was a quack, but in the matter of old wines he was sincere. In this respect I did not differ from him materially; I was skillful in the Italian vintages myself, and bought largely whenever I could.

It was about dusk, one evening during the supreme madness of the carnival season,[5] that I encountered my friend. He accosted me with excessive warmth, for he had been drinking much. The man wore motley.[6] He had on a tight-fitting parti-striped dress, and his head was surmounted by a conical cap and bells. I was so pleased to see him that I thought I should never have done wringing his hand.

I said to him, "My dear Fortunato, you are luckily met. How remarkably well you are looking today! But I have received a pipe[7] of what passes for Amontillado, and I have my doubts."

"How?" said he. "Amontillado? A pipe? Impossible! And in the middle of the carnival?"

"I have my doubts," I replied; "and I was silly enough to pay the full Amontillado price without consulting you in the matter. You were not to be found, and I was fearful of losing a bargain."

"Amontillado!"

"I have my doubts."

"Amontillado!"

"And I must satisfy them."

"Amontillado!"

"As you are engaged, I am on my way to Luchresi. If any one has a critical turn, it is he. He will tell me—"

"Luchresi cannot tell Amontillado from Sherry."

"And yet some fools will have it that his taste is a match for your own."

"Come, let us go."

"Whither?"

"To your vaults."

"My friend, no; I will not impose upon your good nature. I perceive you have an engagement. Luchresi—"

"I have no engagement; come."

"My friend, no. It is not the engagement, but the severe cold with which I perceive you are afflicted. The vaults are insufferably damp. They are incrusted with niter."[8]

"Let us go, nevertheless. The cold is merely nothing. Amontillado! You have been imposed upon; and as for Luchresi, he cannot distinguish Sherry from Amontillado."

---

[3] HIS IMMOLATION—His sacrifice, or death.

[4] GEMMARY—The art of the jeweler; the cutting, polishing, and setting of precious stones so that their beauty is best displayed.

[5] CARNIVAL SEASON—The time of feasting and merrymaking just before Lent. The yearly carnival in Rome, where this story takes place, has long been famous for its gorgeousness.

[6] MOTLEY—A woolen cloth which is woven of many colors and which is the traditional costume of a court fool.

[7] PIPE—A barrel.

[8] NITER—Potassium nitrate, which forms on the rock walls of caves and cellars.

Thus speaking, Fortunato possessed himself of my arm. Putting on a mask of black silk, and drawing a *roquelaure* [9] closely about my person, I suffered him to hurry me to my palazzo.

There were no attendants at home; they had absconded to make merry in honor of the time. I had told them that I should not return until the morning and had given them explicit orders not to stir from the house. These orders were sufficient, I well knew, to insure their immediate disappearance, one and all, as soon as my back was turned.

I took from their sconces two flambeaus,[10] and giving one to Fortunato, bowed him through several suites of rooms to the archway that led into the vaults. I passed down a long and winding staircase, requesting him to be cautious as he followed. We came at length to the foot of the descent and stood together on the damp ground of the catacombs of the Montresors.[11]

The gait of my friend was unsteady, and the bells upon his cap jingled as he strode.

"The pipe," said he.

"It is farther on," said I; "but observe the white webwork which gleams from these cavern walls."

He turned towards me and looked into my eyes with two filmy orbs that distilled the rheum of intoxication.

"Niter?" he asked, at length.

"Niter," I replied. "How long have you had that cough?"

"Ugh! ugh! ugh!—ugh! ugh! ugh!— ugh! ugh! ugh!—ugh! ugh! ugh!—ugh! ugh! ugh!"

My poor friend found it impossible to reply for many minutes.

"It is nothing," he said, at last.

"Come," I said, with decision, "we will go back; your health is precious. You are rich, respected, admired, beloved; you are happy, as once I was. You are a man to be missed. For me it is no matter. We will go back; you will be ill, and I cannot be responsible. Besides, there is Luchresi—"

"Enough," he said; "the cough is a mere nothing: it will not kill me. I shall not die of a cough."

"True—true," I replied; "and, indeed, I had no intention of alarming you unnecessarily—but you should use all proper caution. A small draught of this Medoc [12] will defend us from the damps."

Here I knocked off the neck of a bottle which I drew from a long row of its fellows that lay upon the mold.

"Drink," I said, presenting him the wine.

He raised it to his lips with a leer. He paused and nodded to me familiarly, while his bells jingled.

"I drink," he said, "to the buried that repose around us."

"And I to your long life."

He again took my arm, and we proceeded.

"These vaults," he said, "are extensive."

"The Montresor," I replied, "were a great and numerous family."

"I forget your arms." [13]

"A huge human foot d'or, in a field azure; [14] the foot crushes a serpent ramp-

---

[9] *Roquelaure* (rŏk'ĕ·lōr)—A short cloak.

[10] TOOK FROM THEIR SCONCES TWO FLAMBEAUS—Took two torches from their holders.

[11] CATACOMBS OF THE MONTRESORS—Underground burial chambers of the Montresor family.

[12] MEDOC (mȧ·dŏk')—Wine from the district of Medoc in southwest France.

[13] ARMS—Family coat of arms.

[14] FOOT D'OR IN A FIELD AZURE—On the coat of arms, the picture of the human foot is gold colored. The field, or background, is blue

ant [15] whose fangs are imbedded in the heel."

"And the motto?"

"*Nemo me impune lacessit.*" [16]

"Good!" he said.

The wine sparkled in his eyes and the bells jingled. My own fancy grew warm with the Medoc. We had passed through walls of piled bones, with casks and puncheons intermingling, into the inmost recesses of the catacombs. I paused again, and this time I made bold to seize Fortunato by an arm above the elbow.

"The niter!" I said; "see it increases. It hangs like moss upon the vaults. We are below the river's bed. The drops of moisture trickle among the bones.

Come, we will go back ere it is too late. Your cough—"

"It is nothing," he said; "let us go on. But first, another draught of the Medoc."

I broke and reached him a flagon of De Grave.[17] He emptied it at a breath. His eyes flashed with a fierce light. He laughed and threw the bottle upwards with a gesticulation I did not understand.

I looked at him in surprise. He repeated the movement—a grotesque one.

"You do not comprehend?" he said.

"Not I," I replied.

"Then you are not of the brotherhood."

"How?"

"You are not of the masons."

"Yes, yes," I said, "yes, yes."

"You? Impossible! A mason?"

[15] A serpent rampant—A picture of a serpent raised in a position to strike.

[16] *Nemo me impune lacessit* (nā′mō mā ĭm·pū′nâ lă·chĕs′sĭt)—No one attacks me with impunity.

[17] A flagon of de grave—A large bottle of wine that came from the district of Graves, in France.

"A mason," I replied.

"A sign," he said.

"It is this," I answered, producing a trowel from beneath the folds of my *roquelaure.*

"You jest," he exclaimed, recoiling a few paces. "But let us proceed to the Amontillado."

"Be it so," I said, replacing the tool beneath the cloak, and again offering him my arm. He leaned upon it heavily. We continued our route in search of the Amontillado. We passed through a range of low arches, descended, passed on, and descending again, arrived at a deep crypt,[18] in which the foulness of the air caused our flambeaus rather to glow than flame.

At the most remote end of the crypt there appeared another less spacious. Its walls had been lined with human remains piled to the vault overhead, in the fashion of the great catacombs of Paris. Three sides of this interior crypt were still ornamented in this manner. From the fourth the bones had been thrown down, and lay promiscuously upon the earth, forming at one point a mound of some size. Within the wall thus exposed by the displacing of the bones, we perceived a still interior recess, in depth about four feet, in width three, in height six or seven. It seemed to have been constructed for no especial use within itself, but formed merely the interval between two of the colossal supports of the roof of the catacombs, and was backed by one of their circumscribing walls of solid granite.

It was in vain that Fortunato, uplifting his dull torch, endeavored to pry into the depths of the recess. Its termination the feeble light did not enable us to see.

"Proceed," I said; "herein is the Amontillado. As for Luchresi—"

18 CRYPT—An underground chamber.

"He is an ignoramus," interrupted my friend, as he stepped unsteadily forward, while I followed immediately at his heels. In an instant he had reached the extremity of the niche, and finding his progress arrested by the rock, stood stupidly bewildered. A moment more and I had fettered him to the granite. In its surface were two iron staples, distant from each other about two feet, horizontally. From one of these depended a short chain, from the other a padlock. Throwing the links about his waist, it was but the work of a few seconds to secure it. He was too much astounded to resist. Withdrawing the key I stepped back from the recess.

"Pass your hand," I said, "over the wall; you cannot help feeling the niter. Indeed it is *very* damp. Once more let me *implore* you to return. No? Then I must positively leave you. But I must first render you all the little attentions in my power."

"The Amontillado!" ejaculated my friend, not yet recovered from his astonishment.

"True," I replied; "the Amontillado."

As I said these words I busied myself among the pile of bones of which I have before spoken. Throwing them aside, I soon uncovered a quantity of building stone and mortar. With these materials and with the aid of my trowel, I began vigorously to wall up the entrance of the niche.

I had scarcely laid the first tier of the masonry when I discovered that the intoxication of Fortunato had in a great measure worn off. The earliest indication I had of this was a low moaning cry from the depth of the recess. It was *not* the cry of a drunken man. There was then a long and obstinate silence. I laid the second tier, and the third, and the fourth; and then I heard the furious vibrations of the chain. The noise lasted for several minutes, during which, that I might hearken to it with the more satisfaction, I ceased my labors and sat down upon the bones. When at last the clanking subsided, I resumed the trowel and finished without interruption the fifth, the sixth, and the seventh tier. The wall was now nearly upon a level with my breast. I again paused, and holding the flambeaus over the mason work, threw a few feeble rays upon the figure within.

A succession of loud and shrill screams, bursting suddenly from the throat of the chained form, seemed to thrust me violently back. For a brief moment I hesitated—I trembled. Unsheathing my rapier, I began to grope with it about the recess; but the thought of an instant reassured me. I placed my hand upon the solid fabric of the catacombs and felt satisfied. I reapproached the wall. I replied to the yells of him who clamored. I re-echoed—I aided—I surpassed them in volume and in strength. I did this, and the clamorer grew still.

It was now midnight, and my task was drawing to a close. I had completed the eighth, the ninth, and the tenth tier. I had finished a portion of the last and the eleventh; there remained but a single stone to be fitted and plastered in. I struggled with its weight; I placed it partially in its destined position. But now there came from out the niche a low laugh that erected the hairs upon my head. It was succeeded by a sad voice, which I had difficulty in recognizing as that of the noble Fortunato. The voice said—

"Ha! ha! ha!—he! he! he!—a very good joke indeed—an excellent jest. We will have many a rich laugh about it at the palazzo—he! he! he!—over our wine—he! he! he!"

"The Amontillado!" I said.

"He! he! he!—he! he! he!—yes, the Amontillado. But is it not getting late? Will not they be awaiting us at the palazzo, the Lady Fortunato and the rest? Let us be gone."

"Yes," I said, "let us be gone."

"*For the love of God, Montresor!*"

"Yes," I said, "for the love of God!"

But to these words I hearkened in vain for a reply. I grew impatient. I called aloud—

"Fortunato!"

No answer. I called again—

"Fortunato!"

No answer still. I thrust a torch through the remaining aperture [19] and let it fall within. There came forth in re-

[19] APERTURE—An opening in the wall.

turn only a jingling of the bells. My heart grew sick—on account of the dampness of the catacombs. I hastened to make an end of my labor. I forced the last stone into its position; I plastered it up. Against the new masonry I re-erected the old rampart of bones. For the half of a century no mortal has disturbed them. *In pace requiescat!* [20]

[20] *In pace requiescat* (ĭn pä'chä rå'kwē·ĕs' kät)—May he rest in peace.

◇◇◇◇◇◇◇◇◇◇◇◇◇◇◇◇◇◇◇◇◇◇◇◇◇◇◇◇

FOR UNDERSTANDING

1. Montresor, the speaker, tells us that he is in no hurry to get revenge on Fortunato—but that when he does, his revenge must meet two requirements. What are they?

2. We are told that the "weak point" of Fortunato is his pride in being an expert judge of wines. Explain how Montresor is able to take advantage of this pride in putting his scheme into effect. How does the carnival season provide a favorable opportunity for his plan?

3. Montresor needed an isolated spot to which he could lure his enemy—and the wine vaults and ancient burial vaults deep under his own palace were such a place. However, we should also notice that such surroundings are the kind that Poe's imagination often dwells on. What details in this story seem particularly characteristic of Poe's writings?

4. Explain what the revenge was. How did it fulfill the requirements for a perfect revenge which were stated at the beginning? With what attitude do you think Montresor uttered the Latin words at the end of the story?

POE'S SUBTLE WAY OF
REVEALING CHARACTER

Because this story is told in the first person, we readily fall in with the speaker's way of looking at everything. However, a moment's thought will remind us that a man who broods and schemes over revenge is wicked, if not partly insane.

1. Early in the story, when Montresor meets his victim he pretends to be very friendly. What would most people think of a man who does evil under pretense of friendship, and who takes advantage of an enemy's drunkenness or other unfit condition? Which is punished more severely by law—a *premeditated* crime, or a crime *committed in sudden anger?* Explain how this distinction affects our opinion of Montresor.

2. One cruel detail of the revenge is Fortunato's gradual discovery, as he comes to himself after his intoxication, of the situation he is in. Explain the unusual horror of this situation.

3. Besides being cruel, Montresor is extremely clever. By what clever means does he keep Fortunato interested in going farther into the catacombs?

4. Explain why Montresor repeatedly begs his enemy to turn back—telling him that the dampness of the vaults will injure his health. What do these requests tell us about Montresor's nature? What has he done just *before* he repeats the request for the last time?

5. We may suspect that the main character is insane not only because of his fiendish cruelty, but because it seems likely he has only *imagined* that Fortunato has injured him. How is such a possibility suggested by Fortunato's manner toward the main character? In general, what kind of person does Fortunato appear to be?

6. In stories in which one of the characters is the narrator, sometimes the author makes the story richer and more interesting by having the narrator reveal things *that he does not realize himself.* In "The Cask of Amontillado" it is clear that the speaker is proud of his deeds. Do you think he would be surprised to overhear readers criticizing his character? Another story of this type is Ring Lardner's "I Can't Breathe," which appears in this text. What things does the girl *unconsciously* tell us about herself?

Students who have read Mark Twain's *Huckleberry Finn* should try to recall, and explain to the class, some of the remarks Huck makes that cause us to laugh at his simple-mindedness—although he is shrewd and sensible in most situations. Students who enjoy reading subtle, rather difficult modern novels will like J. P. Marquand's *The Late George Apley*, in which the narrator, not too bright, tells us a story which we understand far better than he does.

7. As a class project, plan a narrative in which the speaker shows himself to be the opposite kind of person from what he thinks he is. He might consider himself to be generous and thoughtful of others, when in fact he is selfish. Or he might talk about how conscientiously he is fulfilling his responsibilities, when in reality he is shiftless and self-indulgent. What incidents would you have him talk about? What would he say? How would the reader find out his real character?

POE'S MASTERY OF SUSPENSE

Suspense begins in "The Cask of Amontillado" when we wonder what the revenge is to be. It rises as we puzzle ourselves about how the strange underground journey will conclude. What hint of the outcome, although it only mystifies us, does Poe give when the victim happens to mention the secret society of Freemasons? How does Montresor's "cat-and-mouse" game with the victim—urging him to turn back—tantalize us further?

Poe arranges his story so as to keep us guessing about what will happen until it actually does happen, at the end. Even when Fortunato is chained to the stone wall, we are not certain why. What purposes might the narrator have had besides the one he finally reveals? Did you guess exactly what his intention was when he lifted the last stone to cement it in place? Which sentence in the story is the climax—that is, which sentence at last makes

us realize the full horror of the revenge?

Compare this story with Irving's "The Devil and Tom Walker" in dramatic power. In which one do we seem to be "right there" with the characters? Which story do we mainly *hear about* instead of seeming to see it happen? How do the two authors differ in their ways of beginning and concluding a story?

FOR YOUR VOCABULARY

The main character of "The Cask of Amontillado" is so intent on getting revenge that he could be described as having a *monomania*. That is, on *one* subject (*mono-* means *one*) he has an *insane attitude* (*-mania*). Use this information in defining the following words. Try them first without using a dictionary.

monotone	kleptomania
monotony	dipsomania
monarch	megalomania
monocle	maniac
monotheism	bibliomania
monogamy	Anglomania

FOR FURTHER READING

HERVEY ALLEN, ed., *The Complete Tales and Poems of Edgar Allan Poe* (Modern Library). Hervey Allen, a well-known novelist, wrote the introduction to this collection. Among the stories are "The Gold Bug," "The Murders in the Rue Morgue," "The Purloined Letter," "The Pit and the Pendulum," and "The Fall of the House of Usher."

Among Poe's best known poems are these: "The Raven," "Annabel Lee," "The Bells," "The City in the Sea," and "Lenore."

LAURA BENÉT, *Young Edgar Allan Poe* (Dodd). Poe's best qualities are brought out in this biographical sketch describing his home, his trip to Great Britain, and his college career.

NATHANIEL HAWTHORNE (1804-1864)

Nathaniel Hawthorne determined very early in life to become an author. After his graduation from Bowdoin College, he settled down in his mother's house in Salem, Massachusetts, to read and write. His ancestors had been prominent men in Salem in Puritan times, and that period of history fascinated Hawthorne. In the 1830's he published many short stories and essays about the stern, gloomy Puritans. Later a number of these were collected in a book called *Twice-Told Tales*. To earn money enough to get married, he worked in the Boston Custom House for two years. Then he and his wife moved to the Old Manse, a former parsonage, in Concord, Massachusetts, where he again turned to literature. In 1846 he published a second collection of his writings as *Mosses from an Old Manse*.

Hawthorne's greatest achievement was his novel *The Scarlet Letter*, which appeared in 1850. It is a historical novel that deals with the old Puritan custom of forcing sinners to wear a badge or other distinguishing mark to proclaim their shame to the world. But the real subject of this harsh, somber book is the effects of sin on the secret thoughts and emotions of the sinner. Hawthorne was an acute student of human nature, and he examined and probed into the minds of his characters with the concentration of a scientist. Some people today consider *The Scarlet Letter* the greatest book in American literature.

The House of the Seven Gables was Hawthorne's second novel. It is a comparatively cheerful story that traces the history of a Salem family from the seventeenth century down to the nineteenth, and shows the influence of past generations on the present. Hawthorne's remaining books are less well known today. In later life he served four years as United States consul in Liverpool, and then traveled in France and Italy. His health began to fail shortly after his return to America, and he died in 1864.

LITERARY ARTIST, AND STUDENT OF HUMAN NATURE

Hawthorne organized his stories with great care, and sometimes they produce a single, concentrated dramatic effect like those of Poe. For this reason, Poe and Hawthorne are given joint credit for developing the earliest *short stories* out of the looser, more leisurely *tales* that had been written by men like Irving. By their example, Poe and Hawthorne taught literary men in both America and Europe how to write short stories as we know them today.

However, there is an important difference between Hawthorne and Poe. Hawthorne was a wiser man, and saw more deeply into human life. He was a moralist and a keen psychologist. Poe is more skillful at making us share the unbelievable adventures of his characters, but in the long run Hawthorne's stories make a more profound impression because they *tell us important things about ourselves.*

❖❖❖❖❖

FEATHERTOP

In the late seventeenth century many New England colonists believed in witches, who were supposedly able to do miraculous things through the help of evil spirits. Salem, Massachusetts, in 1692, was the scene of shameful witchcraft trials during which many "witches" were cruelly treated and some were put to death.

Nearly a century and a half later Nathaniel Hawthorne, a native of Salem, wrote a number of tales about Puritan times—some of them dealing with the superstitious belief in witches. In "Feathertop" Hawthorne pretends that witchcraft really existed. It is a cheerful, humorous story which also carries a deeper thought. Although Feathertop, the old witch's puppet, is only a scarecrow with a pumpkin for a head, his imposing manner fools almost everyone.

"Dickon," cried Mother Rigby, "a coal for my pipe!"

The pipe was in the old dame's mouth when she said these words. She had thrust it there after filling it with tobacco but without stooping to light it at the hearth where, indeed, there was no appearance of a fire having been kindled that morning. Forthwith, however, as soon as the order was given, there was an intense red glow out of the bowl of the pipe, and a whiff of smoke came from Mother Rigby's lips. Whence the coal came, and how brought thither by an invisible hand, I have never been able to discover.

"Good!" quoth Mother Rigby, with a nod of her head. "Thank ye, Dickon! And now for making this scarecrow. Be within call, Dickon, in case I need you again."

The good woman had risen thus early (for as yet it was scarcely sunrise) in order to set about making a scarecrow, which she intended to put in the middle of her cornpatch. It was now the latter week of May, and the crows and blackbirds had already discovered the little, green, rolled-up leaf of the Indian corn just peeping out of the soil. She was determined, therefore, to contrive as lifelike a scarecrow as ever was seen, and to finish it immediately from top to toe, so that it should begin its sentinel's duty that very morning. Now Mother Rigby (as everybody must have heard) was one of the most cunning and potent witches in New England, and might, with very little trouble, have made a scarecrow ugly enough to frighten the minister himself. But on this occasion, as she had awakened in an uncommonly pleasant humor, and was further dulcified [1] by her pipe of tobacco, she resolved to produce something fine, beautiful, and splendid, rather than hideous and horrible.

"I don't want to set up a hobgoblin in my own cornpatch, and almost at my own doorstep," said Mother Rigby to herself, puffing out a whiff of smoke; "I could do it if I pleased, but I'm tired of doing marvelous things, and so I'll keep within the bounds of everyday business just for variety's sake. Besides, there is no use in scaring the little children for a mile roundabout, though 'tis true I'm a witch." It was settled, therefore, in her own mind, that the scarecrow should represent a fine gentleman of the period, so far as the materials at hand would allow. Perhaps it may be as well to enumerate the chief of the articles that went to the composition of this figure.

The most important item of all, probably, although it made so little show, was a certain broomstick on which Mother Rigby had taken many an airy gallop at midnight, and which now served the scarecrow by way of a spinal column or, as the unlearned phrase it, a backbone. One of its arms was a disabled flail which used to be wielded by Goodman Rigby before his spouse worried him out of this troublesome world; the other, if I mistake not, was composed of the pudding stick and a broken rung of a chair, tied loosely together at the elbow. As for its legs, the right was a hoe handle, and the left an undistinguished and miscellaneous stick from the woodpile. Its lungs, stomach, and other affairs of that kind, were nothing better than a mealbag stuffed with straw. Thus we have made out the skeleton and entire corporosity [2] of the scarecrow, with the exception of its head; and this was admirably supplied by a somewhat withered and shriveled pumpkin, in which Mother Rigby cut

[1] DULCIFIED—Sweetened, made agreeable.

[2] CORPOROSITY—A humorous word meaning "body."

two holes for the eyes and a slit for the mouth, leaving a bluish-colored knob in the middle to pass for a nose. It was really quite a respectable face.

"I've seen worse ones on human shoulders, at any rate," said Mother Rigby. "And many a fine gentleman has a pumpkin head, as well as my scarecrow."

But the clothes, in this case, were to be the making of the man. So the good old woman took down from a peg an ancient plum-colored coat of London make, and with relics of embroidery on its seams, cuffs, pocket-flaps, and button-holes, but lamentably worn and faded, patched at the elbows, tattered at the skirts, and threadbare all over. On the left breast was a round hole, whence either a star of nobility had been rent away, or else the hot heart of some former wearer had scorched it through and through. The neighbors said that this rich garment belonged to the Black Man's[3] wardrobe, and that he kept it at Mother Rigby's cottage for the convenience of slipping it on whenever he wished to make a grand appearance at the governor's table. To match the coat there was a velvet waistcoat of very ample size, and formerly embroidered with foliage that had been as brightly golden as the maple leaves in October, but which had now quite vanished out of the substance of the velvet. Next came a pair of scarlet breeches once worn by the French governor of Louisbourg, and the knees of which had touched the lower step of the throne of Louis le Grand. The Frenchman had given these smallclothes to an Indian pow-wow, who parted with them to the old witch for a gill of strong waters at one of their dances in the forest. Furthermore, Mother Rigby produced a pair of silk stockings and put them on the figure's legs, where they showed as unsub-

[3] BLACK MAN'S—The Devil's.

stantial as a dream, with the wooden reality of the two sticks making itself miserably apparent through the holes. Lastly, she put her dead husband's wig on the bare scalp of the pumpkin, and surmounted the whole with a dusty three-cornered hat, in which was stuck the longest tailfeather of a rooster.

Then the old dame stood the figure up in a corner of her cottage and chuckled to behold its yellow semblance of a visage, with its nobby little nose thrust into the air. It had a strangely self-satisfied aspect, and seemed to say, "Come, look at me!"

"And you are well worth looking at, that's a fact!" quoth Mother Rigby, in admiration at her own handiwork. "I've made many a puppet since I've been a witch, but methinks this the finest of them all. 'Tis almost too good for a scarecrow. And, by the by, I'll just fill a fresh pipe of tobacco and then take him out to the cornpatch."

While filling her pipe the old woman continued to gaze with almost motherly affection at the figure in the corner. To say the truth, whether it were chance, or skill, or downright witchcraft, there was something wonderfully human in this ridiculous shape, bedizened with its tattered finery; and as for the countenance, it appeared to shrivel its yellow surface into a grin—a funny kind of expression betwixt scorn and merriment, as if it understood itself to be a jest at mankind. The more Mother Rigby looked, the better she was pleased.

"Dickon," cried she, sharply, "another coal for my pipe!"

Hardly had she spoken than, just as before, there was a red-glowing coal on the top of the tobacco. She drew in a long whiff and puffed it forth again into the bar of morning sunshine which struggled through the one dusty pane of her cottage window. Mother Rigby always liked to flavor her pipe with a coal of fire from the particular chimney corner whence this had been brought. But where that chimney corner might be, or who brought the coal from it—further than that the invisible messenger seemed to respond to the name of Dickon—I cannot tell.

"That puppet yonder," thought Mother Rigby, still with her eyes fixed on the scarecrow, "is too good a piece of work to stand all summer in a cornpatch frightening away the crows and blackbirds. He's capable of better things. Why, I've danced with a worse one, when partners happened to be scarce, at our witch meetings in the forests! What if I should let him take his chance among the other men of straw and empty fellows who go bustling about the world?"

The old witch took three or four more whiffs of her pipe and smiled.

"He'll meet plenty of his brethren at every street corner!" continued she. "Well, I didn't mean to dabble in witchcraft today, further than the lighting of my pipe, but a witch I am, and a witch I'm likely to be, and there's no use trying to shirk it. I'll make a man of my scarecrow, were it only for the joke's sake!"

While muttering these words, Mother Rigby took the pipe from her own mouth and thrust it into the crevice which represented the same feature in the pumpkin visage of the scarecrow.

"Puff, darling, puff!" said she. "Puff away, my fine fellow! Your life depends on it!"

This was a strange exhortation,[4] undoubtedly, to be addressed to a mere thing of sticks, straw, and old clothes, with nothing better than a shriveled pumpkin for a head, as we know to have been the scarecrow's case. Nevertheless,

as we must carefully hold in remembrance, Mother Rigby was a witch of singular power and dexterity; and, keeping this fact duly before our minds, we shall see nothing beyond credibility in the remarkable incidents of our story. Indeed, the great difficulty will be at once got over if we can only bring ourselves to believe that as soon as the old dame bade him puff there came a whiff of smoke from the scarecrow's mouth. It was the very feeblest of whiffs, to be sure; but it was followed by another and another, each more decided than the preceding one.

"Puff away, my pet! Puff away, my pretty one!" Mother Rigby kept repeating, with her pleasantest smile. "It is the breath of life to ye, and that you may take my word for."

Beyond all question, the pipe was bewitched. There must have been a spell either in the tobacco or in the fiercely glowing coal that so mysteriously burned on top of it, or in the pungently aromatic smoke which exhaled from the kindled weed. The figure, after a few doubtful attempts, at length blew forth a volley of smoke extending all the way from the obscure corner into the bar of sunshine. There it eddied and melted away among the motes of dust. It seemed a convulsive effort, for the two or three next whiffs were fainter, although the coal still glowed and threw a gleam over the scarecrow's visage. The old witch clapped her skinny hands together and smiled encouragingly upon her handiwork. She saw that the charm had worked well. The shriveled yellow face, which heretofore had been no face at all, had already a thin, fantastic haze, as it were, of human likeness, shifting to and fro across it, sometimes vanishing entirely, but growing more perceptible than ever with the next whiff from the pipe. The whole fig-

[4] EXHORTATION—Encouragement or advice.

ure, in like manner, assumed a show of life such as we impart to ill-defined shapes among the clouds, and half deceive ourselves with the pastime of our own fancy.

If we must needs pry closely into the matter, it may be doubted whether there was any real change, after all, in the sordid, worn-out, worthless, and ill-jointed substance of the scarecrow, but merely a spectral illusion and a cunning effect of light and shade, so colored and contrived as to delude the eyes of most men. The miracles of witchcraft seem always to have had a very shallow subtlety and, at least, if the above explanations do not hit the truth of the process, I can suggest no better.

"Well puffed, my pretty lad!" still cried old Mother Rigby. "Come, another good stout whiff, and let it be with might and main. Puff for thy life, I tell thee! Puff out of the very bottom of thy heart, if any heart thou hast, or any bottom to

it! Well done, again! Thou didst suck in that mouthful as if for the pure love of it."

And then the witch beckoned to the scarecrow, throwing so much magnetic potency into her gesture that it seemed as if it must inevitably be obeyed, like the mystic call of the lodestone [5] when it summons the iron.

"Why lurkest thou in the corner, lazy one?" said she. "Step forth! Thou hast the world before thee!"

Upon my word, if the legend were not one which I heard on my grandmother's knee, and which had established its place among things credible before my childish judgment could analyze its probability, I question whether I should have the face to tell it now.

In obedience to Mother Rigby's word, and extending its arm as if to reach her

[5] LODESTONE—A magnet.

outstretched hand, the figure made a step forward—a kind of hitch and jerk, however, rather than a step—then tottered and almost lost its balance. What could the witch expect? It was nothing, after all, but a scarecrow stuck upon two sticks. But the strong-willed old beldam [6] scowled and beckoned and flung the energy of her purpose so forcibly at this poor combination of rotten wood and musty straw and ragged garments that it was compelled to show itself a man, in spite of the reality of things. So it stepped into the bar of sunshine. There it stood—poor devil of a contrivance that it was—with only the thinnest vesture of human similitude about it, through which was evident the stiff, rickety, incongruous, faded, tattered, good-for-nothing patchwork of its substance, ready to sink in a heap upon the floor, as conscious of its own unworthiness to be erect. Shall I confess the truth? At its present point of vivification, the scarecrow reminds me of some of the lukewarm and abortive [7] characters composed of heterogeneous materials used for the thousandth time, and never worth using, with which romance writers (and myself, no doubt, among the rest) have so overpeopled the world of fiction.

But the fierce old hag began to get angry and show a glimpse of her diabolic nature, like a snake's head peeping with a hiss out of her bosom, at this pusillanimous [8] behavior of the thing which she had taken the trouble to put together.

"Puff away, wretch!" cried she, wrathfully. "Puff, puff, puff, thou thing of straw and emptiness! thou rag or two! thou mealbag! thou pumpkin head! thou nothing! Where shall I find a name vile

enough to call thee by? Puff, I say, and suck in thy fantastic life with the smoke, else I snatch the pipe from thy mouth and hurl thee where that red coal came from."

Thus threatened, the unhappy scarecrow had nothing for it but to puff away for dear life. As need was, therefore, it applied itself lustily to the pipe and sent forth such abundant volleys of tobacco smoke that the small cottage kitchen became all vaporous. The one sunbeam struggled mistily through and could but imperfectly define the image of the cracked and dusty windowpane on the opposite wall. Mother Rigby, meanwhile, with one brown arm akimbo and the other stretched toward the figure, loomed grimly amid the obscurity with such port and expression as when she was wont to heave a ponderous nightmare on her victims and stand at the bedside to enjoy their agony. In fear and trembling did this poor scarecrow puff. But its efforts, it must be acknowledged, served an excellent purpose, for with each successive whiff the figure lost more and more of its dizzy and perplexing tenuity and seemed to take denser substance. Its very garments, moreover, partook of the magical change, and shone with the gloss of novelty, and glistened with the skillfully embroidered gold that had long ago been rent away. And, half revealed among the smoke, a yellow visage bent its lusterless eyes on Mother Rigby.

At last the old witch clenched her fist and shook it at the figure. Not that she was postively angry, but merely acting on the principle—perhaps untrue, or not the only truth, though as high a one as Mother Rigby could be expected to attain—that feeble and torpid natures, being incapable of better inspiration, must be stirred up by fear. But here was the crisis. Should she fail in what she now

[6] BELDAM—Ugly old woman.
[7] ABORTIVE—Ineffective or unsuccessful.
[8] PUSILLANIMOUS (pū'sĭl·lăn'ĭ·mŭs)—Cowardly.

584

sought to effect, it was her ruthless purpose to scatter the miserable simulacre[9] into its original elements.

"Thou hast a man's aspect," said she, sternly. "Have also the echo and mockery of a voice! I bid thee speak!"

The scarecrow gasped, struggled, and at length emitted a murmur which was so incorporated with its smoky breath that you could scarcely tell whether it were indeed a voice or only a whiff of tobacco. Some narrators of this legend held the opinion that Mother Rigby's conjurations and the fierceness of her will had compelled a familiar spirit into the figure, and that the voice was his.

"Mother," mumbled the poor stifled voice, "be not so awful with me! I would fain speak, but, being without wits, what can I say?"

"Thou canst speak, darling, canst thou?" cried Mother Rigby, relaxing her grim countenance into a smile. "And what shalt thou say, quotha![10] Say, indeed! Art thou of the brotherhood of the empty skull, and demandest of me what thou shalt say? Thou shalt say a thousand things, and saying them a thousand times over, thou shalt still have said nothing! Be not afraid, I tell thee! When thou comest into the world—whither I purpose sending thee forthwith—thou shalt not lack the wherewithal to talk. Talk! Why, thou shalt babble like a millstream, if thou wilt. Thou hast brains enough for that, I trow!"

"At your service, Mother," responded the figure.

"And that was well said, my pretty one," answered Mother Rigby. "Then thou spakest like thyself and meant nothing. Thou shalt have a hundred such set

phrases, and five hundred to the boot of them. And now, darling, I have taken so much pains with thee and thou art so beautiful that, by my troth, I love thee better than any witch's puppet in the world; and I've made them of all sorts—clay, wax, straw, sticks, night fog, morning mist, sea foam, and chimney smoke. But thou art the very best. So give heed to what I say."

"Yes, kind mother," said the figure, "with all my heart!"

"With all thy heart!" cried the old witch, setting her hands to her sides and laughing loudly. "Thou hast such a pretty way of speaking! With all thy heart! And thou didst put thy hand to the left side of thy waistcoat, as if thou really hadst one!"

So, now in high good humor with this fantastic contrivance of hers, Mother Rigby told the scarecrow that it must go and play its part in the great world, where not one man in a hundred, she affirmed, was gifted with more real substance than itself. And, that he might hold up his head with the best of them, she endowed him on the spot with an unreckonable amount of wealth. It consisted partly of a gold mine in Eldorado, and of ten thousand shares in a broken bubble, and of half a million acres of vineyard at the North Pole, and of a castle in the air, and a château in Spain, together with all the rents and income therefrom accruing. She further made over to him the cargo of a certain ship laden with salt of Cadiz which she herself by her necromantic arts had caused to founder ten years before in the deepest part of mid-ocean. If the salt were not dissolved and could be brought to market, it would fetch a pretty penny among the fishermen. That he might not lack ready money, she gave him a copper farthing of Birmingham manufacture, being all the coin she had about her,

[9] SIMULACRE (sĭm′ū·lā′kẽr)—Imitation.
[10] QUOTHA—An exclamation of contempt, from *quoth he* ("said he"). The meaning is "indeed!" or "for goodness' sake!"

and likewise a great deal of brass, which she applied to his forehead, thus making it yellower than ever.

"With that brass alone," quoth Mother Rigby, "thou canst pay thy way all over the earth. Kiss me, pretty darling! I have done my best for thee."

Furthermore, that the adventurer might lack no possible advantage toward a fair start in life, this excellent old dame gave him a token by which he was to introduce himself to a certain magistrate, member of the council, merchant, and elder of the church (the four capacities constituting but one man) who stood at the head of society in the neighboring metropolis. The token was neither more nor less than a single word, which Mother Rigby whispered to the scarecrow, and which the scarecrow was to whisper to the merchant.

"Gouty[11] as the old fellow is, he'll run thy errands for thee when once thou hast given him that word in his ear," said the old witch. "Mother Rigby knows the worshipful justice Gookin, and the worshipful justice knows Mother Rigby!"

Here the witch thrust her wrinkled face close to the puppet's, chuckling irrepressibly, and fidgeting all through her system with delight at the idea which she meant to communicate.

"The worshipful Master Gookin," whispered she, "hath a comely maiden to his daughter. And hear me, my pet! Thou hast a fair outside and a pretty wit enough of thine own. Yea, a pretty wit enough! Thou wilt think better of it when thou hast seen more of other people's wits. Now, with thy outside and thy inside, thou art the very man to win a young girl's heart. Never doubt it! I

tell thee it shall be so. Put but a bold face on the matter, sigh, smile, flourish thy hat, thrust forth thy leg like a dancing master, put thy right hand to the left side of thy waistcoat, and pretty Polly Gookin is thine own!"

All this while the new creature had been sucking in and exhaling the vapory fragrance of his pipe and seemed now to continue this occupation as much for the enjoyment it afforded as because it was an essential condition of his existence. It was wonderful to see how exceedingly like a human being it behaved. Its eyes (for it appeared to possess a pair) were bent on Mother Rigby, and at suitable junctures it nodded or shook its head. Neither did it lack words proper for the occasion—"Really!"—"Indeed!"—"Pray tell me!"—"Is it possible!"—"Upon my word!"—"By no means!"—"Oh!"—"Ah!"—"Hem!" and other such weighty utterances as imply attention, inquiry, acquiescence, or dissent on the part of the auditor. Even had you stood by and seen the scarecrow made, you could scarcely have resisted the conviction that it perfectly understood the cunning counsels which the old witch poured into its counterfeit of an ear. The more earnestly it applied its lips to the pipe, the more distinctly was its human likeness stamped among visible realities, the more sagacious[12] grew its expression, the more lifelike its gestures and movements, and the more intelligibly audible its voice. Its garments, too, glistened so much the brighter with an illusory magnificence. The very pipe in which burned the spell of all this wonderwork ceased to appear as a smoke-blackened earthen stump, and became a meerschaum[13] with painted bowl and amber mouthpiece.

[11] GOUTY—Afflicted with a painful swelling of the joints, especially those of the feet or the big toe. Gout is traditionally supposed to come from overindulgence in rich foods or wine.

[12] SAGACIOUS (să·gā′shŭs)—Shrewd.
[13] MEERSCHAUM (mēr′shŭm)—A pipe made of a costly claylike mineral.

It might be apprehended, however, that, as the life of the illusion seemed identical with the vapor of the pipe, it would terminate simultaneously with the reduction of the tobacco to ashes. But the beldam foresaw the difficulty.

"Hold thou the pipe, my precious one," said she, "while I fill it for thee again."

It was sorrowful to behold how the fine gentleman began to fade back into a scarecrow while Mother Rigby shook the ashes out of the pipe and proceeded to replenish it from her tobacco box.

"Dickon," cried she, in her high, sharp tone, "another coal for this pipe!"

No sooner said than the intensely red speck of fire was glowing within the pipe bowl; and the scarecrow, without waiting for the witch's bidding, applied the tube to his lips and drew in a few short, convulsive whiffs, which soon, however, became regular and equable.

"Now, mine own heart's darling," quoth Mother Rigby, "whatever may happen to thee, thou must stick to thy pipe. Thy life is in it; and that, at least, thou knowest well, if thou knowest nought besides. Stick to thy pipe, I say! Smoke, puff, blow thy cloud; and tell the people, if any question be made, that it is for thy health, and that so the physician orders thee to do. And, sweet one, when thou shalt find thy pipe getting low, go apart into some corner, and—first filling thyself with smoke—cry sharply, 'Dickon, a fresh pipe of tobacco!' and, 'Dickon, another coal for my pipe!' and have it into thy pretty mouth as speedily as may be, else instead of a gallant gentleman in a gold-laced coat, thou wilt be but a jumble of sticks and tattered clothes, and a bag of straw, and a withered pumpkin! Now depart, my treasure, and good luck go with thee!"

"Never fear, Mother!" said the figure, in a stout voice, and sending forth a courageous whiff of smoke, "I will thrive, if an honest man and a gentleman may!"

"Oh, thou wilt be the death of me!" cried the old witch, convulsed with laughter. "That was well said! If an honest man and a gentleman may! Thou playest thy part to perfection. Get along with thee for a smart fellow; and I will wager on thy head, as a man of pith and substance, with a brain and what they call a heart, and all else that a man should have, against any other thing on two legs. I hold myself a better witch than yesterday, for thy sake. Did not I make thee? And I defy any witch in New England to make such another! Here! take my staff along with thee!"

The staff, though it was but a plain oaken stick, immediately took the aspect of a gold-headed cane.

"That gold head has as much sense in it as thine own," said Mother Rigby, "and it will guide thee straight to worshipful Master Gookin's door. Get thee gone, my pretty pet, my darling, my precious one, my treasure; and if any ask thy name, it is 'Feathertop,' for thou hast a feather in thy hat, and I have thrust a handful of feathers into the hollow of thy head. And thy wig, too, is of the fashion they call 'feathertop'; so be 'Feathertop' thy name!"

And, issuing from the cottage, Feathertop strode manfully towards town. Mother Rigby stood at the threshold, well pleased to see how the sunbeams glistened on him, as if all his magnificence were real, and how diligently and lovingly he smoked his pipe, and how handsomely he walked in spite of a little stiffness of his legs. She watched him until out of sight and threw a witch benediction after her darling when a turn of the road snatched him from her view.

Betimes in the forenoon, when the principal street of the neighboring town was just at its acme of life and bustle, a stranger of very distinguished figure was seen on the sidewalk. His port as well as his garments betokened nothing short of nobility. He wore a richly-embroidered plum-colored coat, a waistcoat of costly velvet, magnificently adorned with golden foliage, a pair of splendid scarlet breeches, and the finest and glossiest of white silk stockings. His head was covered with a peruke [14] so daintily powdered and adjusted that it would have been sacrilege to disorder it with a hat, which, therefore (and it was a gold-laced hat set off with a snowy feather), he carried beneath his arm. On the breast of his coat glistened a star. He managed his gold-headed cane with an airy grace peculiar to the fine gentlemen of the period; and, to give the highest possible finish to his equipment, he had lace ruffles at his wrist of a most ethereal delicacy, sufficiently avouching how idle and aristocratic must be the hands which they half concealed.

It was a remarkable point in the accouterment of this brilliant personage that he held in his left hand a fantastic kind of pipe with an exquisitely painted bowl and an amber mouthpiece. This he applied to his lips as often as every five or six paces and inhaled a deep whiff of smoke, which, after being retained a moment in his lungs, might be seen to eddy gracefully from his mouth and nostrils.

As may well be supposed, the street was all astir to find out the stranger's name.

"It is some great nobleman, beyond question," said one of the townspeople. "Do you see the star at his breast?"

"Nay, it is too bright to be seen," said another. "Yes, he must needs be a nobleman, as you say. But by what conveyance, think you, can his Lordship have voyaged or traveled hither? There has

been no vessel from the old country for a month past; and if he has arrived overland from the southward, pray where are his attendants and equipage?"

"He needs no equipage to set off his rank," remarked a third. "If he came among us in rags, nobility would shine through a hole in his elbow. I never saw such dignity of aspect. He has the old Norman blood in his veins, I warrant him."

"I rather take him to be a Dutchman or one of your high Germans," said another citizen. "The men of those countries have always the pipe at their mouths."

"And so has a Turk," answered his companion. "But in my judgment, this stranger hath been bred at the French court and hath there learned politeness and grace of manner, which none understand so well as the nobility of France. That gait, now! A vulgar spectator might deem it stiff—he might call it a hitch and jerk—but, to my eye, it hath an unspeakable majesty and must have been acquired by constant observation of the deportment of the Grand Monarque. The stranger's character and office are evident enough. He is a French ambassador come to treat with our rulers about the cession of Canada."

"More probably a Spaniard," said another, "and hence his yellow complexion; or, most likely, he is from the Havana or from some port on the Spanish main and comes to make investigation about the piracies which our government is thought to connive at. Those settlers in Peru and Mexico have skins as yellow as the gold which they dig out of their mines."

"Yellow or not," cried a lady, "he is a beautiful man! So tall, so slender! Such a fine, noble face, with so well-shaped a nose, and all that delicacy of expression about the mouth! And, bless me, how

[14] PERUKE—A wig.

bright his star is! It positively shoots out flames!"

"So do your eyes, fair lady," said the stranger, with a bow and a flourish of his pipe, for he was just passing at the instant. "Upon my honor, they have quite dazzled me!"

"Was ever so original and exquisite a compliment?" murmured the lady, in an ecstasy of delight.

Amid the general admiration excited by the stranger's appearance there were only two dissenting voices. One was that of an impertinent cur which, after snuffing at the heels of the glistening figure, put its tail between its legs and skulked into its master's backyard, vociferating an execrable howl. The other dissentient was a young child who squalled at the fullest stretch of his lungs and babbled some unintelligible nonsense about a pumpkin.

Feathertop, meanwhile, pursued his way along the street. Except for the few complimentary words to the lady, and now and then a slight inclination of the head in requital of the profound reverences of the bystanders, he seemed wholly absorbed in his pipe. There needed no other proof of his rank and consequence than the perfect equanimity [15] with which

[15] EQUANIMITY (ē′kwà·nĭm′ĭ·tĭ)—Calm or unruffled attitude.

he comported himself, while the curiosity and admiration of the town swelled almost into clamor around him. With a crowd gathering behind his footsteps, he finally reached the mansion house of the worshipful Justice Gookin, entered the gate, ascended the steps of the front door, and knocked. In the interim, before his summons was answered the stranger was observed to shake the ashes out of his pipe.

"What did he say in that sharp voice?" inquired one of the spectators.

"Nay, I know not," answered his friend. "But the sun dazzles my eyes strangely. How dim and faded His Lordship looks all of a sudden! Bless my wits, what is the matter with me?"

"The wonder is," said the other, "that his pipe, which was out only an instant ago, should be all alight again, and with the reddest coal I ever saw. There is something mysterious about this stranger. What a whiff of smoke was that! 'Dim and faded,' did you call him? Why, as he turns about the star on his breast is all ablaze."

"It is, indeed," said his companion; "and it will go near to dazzle pretty Polly Gookin, whom I see peeping at it out of the chamber window."

The door being now opened, Feathertop turned to the crowd, made a stately

bend of his body like a great man acknowledging the reverence of the meaner sort, and vanished into the house. There was a mysterious kind of smile, if it might not better be called a grin or grimace, upon his visage, but of all the throng that beheld him not an individual appears to have possessed insight enough to detect the illusive character of the stranger, except a little child and a cur dog.

Our legend here loses somewhat of its continuity, and, passing over the preliminary explanation between Feathertop and the merchant, goes in quest of the pretty Polly Gookin. She was a damsel of a soft, round figure with light hair and blue eyes, and a fair rosy face which seemed neither very shrewd nor very simple. This young lady had caught a glimpse of the glistening stranger while standing on the threshold and had forthwith put on a laced cap, a string of beads, her finest kerchief, and her stiffest damask petticoat in preparation for the interview. Hurrying from her chamber to the parlor, she had ever since been viewing herself in the large looking glass and practicing pretty airs—now a smile, now a ceremonious dignity of aspect, and now a softer smile than the former, kissing her hand likewise, tossing her head, and managing her fan, while within the mirror an unsubstantial little maid repeated every gesture and did all the foolish things that Polly did, but without making her ashamed of them. In short, it was the fault of pretty Polly's ability, rather than her will, if she failed to be as complete an artifice as the illustrious Feathertop himself; and when she thus tampered with her own simplicity, the witch's phantom might well hope to win her.

No sooner did Polly hear her father's gouty footsteps approaching the parlor door, accompanied with the stiff clatter of Feathertop's high-heeled shoes, than she seated herself bolt upright and innocently began warbling a song.

"Polly! Daughter Polly!" cried the old merchant. "Come hither, child."

Master Gookin's aspect, as he opened the door, was doubtful and troubled.

"This gentleman," continued he, presenting the stranger, "is the Chevalier Feathertop—nay, I beg his pardon, My Lord Feathertop—who hath brought me a token of remembrance from an ancient friend of mine. Pay your duty to His Lordship, child, and honor him as his quality deserves."

After these few words of introduction, the worshipful magistrate immediately quitted the room. But, even in that brief moment, had the fair Polly glanced aside at her father instead of devoting herself wholly to the brilliant guest, she might have taken warning of some mischief nigh at hand. The old man was nervous, fidgety, and very pale. Purposing a smile of courtesy, he had deformed his face with a sort of galvanic grin which, when Feathertop's back was turned, he exchanged for a scowl, at the same time shaking his fist and stamping his gouty foot—an incivility which brought its retribution along with it. The truth appears to have been that Mother Rigby's word of introduction, whatever it might be, had operated far more on the rich merchant's fears than on his good will. Moreover, being a man of wonderfully acute observation, he had noticed that the painted figures on the bowl of Feathertop's pipe were in motion. Looking more closely, he became convinced that these figures were a party of little demons, each duly provided with horns and a tail, and dancing hand in hand with gestures of diabolical merriment round the circumference of the pipe bowl. As if to confirm his suspicions, while Master Gookin ushered his guest along a dusky passage from his private room to the parlor, the star on Feathertop's breast had scintillated actual flames, and threw a flickering gleam upon the wall, the ceiling, and the floor.

With such sinister prognostics [16] manifesting themselves on all hands, it is not to be marveled at that the merchant should have felt that he was committing his daughter to a very questionable acquaintance. He cursed in his secret soul the insinuating elegance of Feathertop's manners as this brilliant personage bowed, smiled, put his hand on his heart, inhaled a long whiff from his pipe, and enriched the atmosphere with the smoky vapor of a fragrant and visible sigh. Gladly would poor Master Gookin have thrust his dangerous guest into the street, but there was a restraint and terror within him. This respectable old gentleman, we fear, at an earlier period of life, had given some pledge or other to the Evil Principle, and perhaps was now to redeem it by the sacrifice of his daughter.

It so happened that the parlor door was partly of glass shaded by a silken curtain, the folds of which hung a little awry. So strong was the merchant's interest in witnessing what was to ensue between the fair Polly and the gallant Feathertop that, after quitting the room, he could by no means refrain from peeping through the crevice of the curtain.

But there was nothing very miraculous to be seen; nothing—except the trifles previously noticed—to confirm the idea of a supernatural peril environing the pretty Polly. The stranger, it is true, was evidently a thorough and practiced man of the world, systematic and self-possessed, and therefore the sort of person to whom a parent ought not to confide a simple young girl without due watchfulness for the result. The worthy magis-

[16] PROGNOSTICS—Signs; omens.

trate, who had been conversant with all degrees and qualities of mankind, could not but perceive every motion and gesture of the distinguished Feathertop came in its proper place. Nothing had been left rude or native in him; a well-digested conventionalism had incorporated itself thoroughly with his substance and transformed him into a work of art. Perhaps it was this peculiarity that invested him with a species of ghastliness and awe. It is the effect of anything completely and consummately artificial in human shape that the person impresses us as an unreality, and as having hardly pith enough to cast a shadow upon the floor. As regarded Feathertop, all this resulted in a wild, extravagant, and fantastical impression, as if his life and being were akin to the smoke that curled upward from his pipe.

But pretty Polly Gookin felt not thus. The pair were now promenading the room—Feathertop with his dainty stride, and no less dainty grimace, the girl with a native maidenly grace just touched, not spoiled, by a slightly affected manner which seemed caught from the perfect artifice of her companion. The longer the interview continued, the more charmed was pretty Polly, until, within the first quarter of an hour (as the old magistrate noted by his watch), she was evidently beginning to be in love. Nor need it have been witchcraft that subdued her in such a hurry; the poor child's heart, it may be, was so very fervent that it melted her with its own warmth, as reflected from the hollow semblance of a lover. No matter what Feathertop said, his words found depth and reverberation in her ear; no matter what he did, his action was heroic to her eye. And by this time, it is to be supposed, there was a blush on Polly's cheek, a tender smile about her mouth, and a liquid softness in her glance, while the star kept coruscating [17] on Feathertop's breast, and the little demons careered with more frantic merriment than ever about the circumference of his pipe bowl. Oh, pretty Polly Gookin! Why should these imps rejoice so madly that a silly maiden's heart was about to be given to a shadow? Is it so unusual a misfortune—so rare a triumph?

By and by Feathertop paused and, throwing himself into an imposing attitude, seemed to summon the fair girl to survey his figure and resist him longer if she could. His star, his embroidery, his buckles glowed at that instant with unutterable splendor; the picturesque hues of his attire took a richer depth of coloring; there was a gleam and polish over his whole presence betokening the perfect witchery of well-ordered manners. The maiden raised her eyes and suffered them to linger upon her companion with a bashful and admiring gaze. Then, as if desirous of judging what value her own simple comeliness might have side by side with so much brilliancy, she cast a glance toward the full-length looking glass in front of which they happened to be standing. It was one of the truest plates in the world and incapable of flattery. No sooner did the images therein reflected meet Polly's eye than she shrieked, shrank from the stranger's side, gazed at him for a moment in the wildest dismay, and sank insensible upon the floor. Feathertop, likewise, had looked towards the mirror, and there beheld, not the glittering mockery of his outside show, but a picture of the sordid patchwork of his real composition, stripped of all witchcraft.

The wretched simulacrum! We almost pity him. He threw up his arms with an expression of despair that went farther than any of his previous manifes-

[17] CORUSCATING—Glittering; flashing.

tations towards vindicating his claims to be reckoned human. For perchance the only time since this so often empty and deceptive life of mortals began its course, an illusion had seen and fully recognized itself.

Mother Rigby was seated by her kitchen hearth in the twilight of this eventful day, and had just shaken the ashes out of a new pipe, when she heard a hurried tramp along the road. Yet it did not seem so much the tramp of human footsteps as the clatter of sticks or the rattling of dry bones.

"Ha!" thought the old witch, "what step is that? Whose skeleton is out of its grave now, I wonder?"

A figure burst headlong into the cottage door. It was Feathertop! His pipe was still alight, the star still flamed upon his breast, the embroidery still glowed upon his garments, nor had he lost in any degree or manner that could be estimated the aspect that assimilated him with our mortal brotherhood. But yet, in some indescribable way (as is the case with all that has deluded us when once found out), the poor reality was felt beneath the cunning artifice.

"What has gone wrong?" demanded the witch. "Did yonder sniffling hypocrite thrust my darling from his door? The villain! I'll set twenty fiends to torment him till he offer thee his daughter on his bended knees!"

"No, Mother," said Feathertop despondingly; "it was not that."

"Did the girl scorn my precious one?" asked Mother Rigby, her fierce eyes glowing like two coals of Tophet. "I'll cover her face with pimples! Her nose shall be as red as the coal in thy pipe! Her front teeth shall drop out! In a week hence she shall not be worth thy having."

"Let her alone, Mother," answered poor Feathertop. "The girl was half won;

and methinks a kiss from her sweet lips might have made me altogether human. But," he added after a brief pause and then a howl of self-contempt, "I've seen myself, Mother! I've seen myself for the wretched, ragged, empty thing I am! I'll exist no longer!"

Snatching the pipe from his mouth, he flung it with all his might against the chimney, and at the same instant sank upon the floor, a medley of straw and tattered garments, with some sticks protruding from the heap and a shriveled pumpkin in the midst. The eyeholes were now lusterless, but the rudely-carved gap that just before had been a mouth still seemed to twist itself into a despairing grin, and was so far human.

"Poor fellow!" quoth Mother Rigby, with a rueful glance at the relics of her ill-fated contrivance. "My poor, dear, pretty Feathertop! There are thousands upon thousands of coxcombs and charlatans [18] in the world made up of just such a jumble of wornout, forgotten, and good-for-nothing trash as he was, yet they live in fair repute, and never see themselves for what they are. And why should my poor puppet be the only one to know himself and perish for it?"

While thus muttering the witch had filled a fresh pipe of tobacco, and held the stem between her fingers, as doubtful whether to thrust it into her own mouth or Feathertop's.

"Poor Feathertop!" she continued. "I could easily give him another chance, and send him forth again tomorrow. But no! His feelings are too tender, his sensibilities too deep. He seems to have too much heart to bustle for his own advantage in such an empty and heartless world. Well, well! I'll make a scarecrow of him, after all. 'Tis an innocent

[18] COXCOMBS AND CHARLATANS—Conceited fools and impostors.

and useful vocation, and will suit my darling well; and if each of his human brethren had as fit a one, 't would be the better for mankind. And as for this pipe of tobacco, I need it more than he."

So saying, Mother Rigby put the stem between her lips. "Dickon!" cried she, in her high, sharp tone, "another coal for my pipe!"

❖❖❖❖❖❖❖❖❖❖❖❖❖❖❖❖❖❖❖❖❖❖❖❖❖❖❖❖

FOR UNDERSTANDING

1. An important element of this story is *satire*—that is, scornful fun directed at fools or villains. What idea about affected and pretentious people is suggested by the name given the scarecrow? How is the account of the way he is constructed a satirical hit at vain and overdressed people? What sort of conversational remarks does Feathertop practice before going out into the world to make his fortune?

2. Explain why the people in the street are impressed by the scarecrow. What does their attitude suggest as to the wisdom of people in general? Give one example of how their imaginations turn Feathertop's defects into good qualities. Summarize in your own words the author's satirical view of fashionable young girls, as shown in Polly Gookin's feelings toward the stranger.

3. Who are we supposed to think lights Mother Rigby's pipe? What "chimney corner" is referred to in the sentence, "Mother Rigby always liked to flavor her pipe with a coal of fire from the particular chimney corner whence this had been brought"? What other character in the story besides Mother Rigby seems to have something to do with evil spirits? What does he do for Feathertop, although unwillingly?

4. What spoiled Feathertop's attempt to make a fine impression on Polly Gookin? At the end of the story, what "career" is being planned for him, instead of that of an elegant gentleman?

5. The only ones who were not fooled by Feathertop were an "impertinent" cur and

a young child. Why do you suppose the author named these particular individuals as being more clear-sighted than the others? If you know the tale of "The Emperor's New Clothes," or can easily find a copy to read, explain its similarity to the story of Feathertop.

READING BENEATH THE SURFACE

1. Reread the paragraph in which Mother Rigby endows Feathertop with riches. "Eldorado" is the name given to an imaginary land supposed to be rich in gold and precious stones. A "bubble" is any worthless project, such as a fraudulent investment scheme. "A château in Spain" (from the French expression "les chateaux en Espagne") is exactly the same thing as "a castle in the air." What does this last expression mean? Explain how this whole paragraph is a satire on the actual situation of some seemingly prosperous prominent people. How do you interpret Mother Rigby's comment on the "great deal of brass" which she gave Feathertop?

2. Reread the last part of the story, which tells of Feathertop's downfall. If this were *only* a fairy tale, the mirror's reflection of a scarecrow instead of a fine gentleman might not be so important. In many old legends, supernatural creatures are not able to produce any effect on natural objects. Ghosts do not cast a shadow, and they do not leave footprints. Correspondingly, in "Feathertop" the mirror reflects the exact reality instead of the illusion.

However, the author seems to lay great emphasis on the fact that Feathertop *sees himself* for what he really is. How does this put an end to his career? Quote the remark by Mother Rigby which shows how his experience can be applied to preten-

tious people in actual life. Give an imaginary example showing how young persons might easily form an exaggerated idea of their own superiority or importance.

3. What deeper meaning might be symbolized by the old folk tale of Cinderella and her two proud sisters? by the tale of the Three Little Pigs and their adventures with the wolf?

THREE FAMOUS STORYTELLERS

"Feathertop" is not as intense and gripping as most of Poe's tales. Although some of Hawthorne's stories create suspense in the reader, this one arouses only mild curiosity about the outcome of Feathertop's adventures. Furthermore, the outcome is revealed several paragraphs before the end— and the rest of the story consists of discussion and explanation.

The story might better be compared to Irving's tales than to Poe's. Hawthorne's "Feathertop" and Irving's "The Devil and Tom Walker" both deal with supernatural happenings. Both stories are supposed to take place in Colonial times, when many people believed in witches and magic. However, there is a difference in their flavor. Irving seems to be saying, "Isn't this odd and amusing? This is the kind of queer belief people used to have in the old days." Hawthorne seems to be saying, "This yarn about old times is amusing—but maybe it contains a serious idea, too. If we examine these old superstitions closely, we might find out something about *ourselves*." Which of the three writers is mainly interested in *providing humorous entertainment?* Which writer is interested in *making us more thoughtful about human nature?* Which writer is chiefly interested in *producing stories of great dramatic power?* What other stories by these authors have you read which show these same individual purposes?

DR. HEIDEGGER'S EXPERIMENT

In "Feathertop," a witch plays the trick of passing off a scarecrow as a fine gentleman—and almost gets away with it. In the following story, the mysterious Dr. Heidegger tries an equally strange experiment. He attempts to find out how old people would behave if by some miracle they could live their lives again.

That very singular man, old Dr. Heidegger, once invited four venerable friends to meet him in his study. There were three white-bearded gentlemen, Mr. Medbourne, Colonel Killigrew, and Mr. Gascoigne, and a withered gentlewoman, whose name was the Widow Wycherly. They were all melancholy old creatures, who had been unfortunate in life, and whose greatest misfortune it was that they were not long ago in their graves. Mr. Medbourne, in the vigor of his age, had been a prosperous merchant, and had lost his all by a frantic speculation, and was now little better than a mendicant.[1] Colonel Killigrew had wasted his best years, and his health and substance, in the pursuit of sinful pleasures, which had given birth to a brood of pains, such as the gout and divers other torments of soul and body. Mr. Gascoigne was a ruined politician, a man of evil fame, or at least had been so, till time had buried him from the knowledge of the present generation and made him obscure instead of infamous. As for the Widow Wycherly, tradition tells us that she was a great beauty in her day; but, for a long while past, she had lived in deep seclusion on account of certain scandalous stories, which had prejudiced the gentry of the town against her. It is a circumstance worth mentioning, that each of these three old gentlemen, Mr. Medbourne, Colonel Killigrew, and Mr. Gascoigne, were early lovers of the Widow Wycherly and had once been on the point of cutting each other's throats for her sake. And, before proceeding farther, I will merely hint that Dr. Heidegger and all his four guests were sometimes thought to be a little beside themselves; as is not unfrequently the case with old people, when worried either by present troubles or woeful recollections.

"My dear old friends," said Dr. Heidegger, motioning them to be seated, "I am desirous of your assistance in one of those little experiments with which I amuse myself here in my study."

If all stories were true, Dr. Heidegger's study must have been a very curious place. It was a dim, old-fashioned chamber, festooned with cobwebs and besprinkled with antique dust. Around the walls stood several oaken bookcases, the lower shelves of which were filled with rows of gigantic folios and black-letter quartos, and the upper with little parchment-covered duodecimos.[2] Over the

[1] MENDICANT—Beggar.

[2] FOLIOS, QUARTOS, DUODECIMOS—Different sizes of books; the folio page is half of a very large sheet; the quarto, a fourth; the duodecimo, a twelfth.

central bookcase was a bronze bust of Hippocrates,[3] with which, according to some authorities, Dr. Heidegger was accustomed to hold consultations in all difficult cases of his practice. In the obscurest corner of the room stood a tall and narrow oaken closet, with its door ajar, within which doubtfully appeared a skeleton. Between two of the bookcases hung a looking glass, presenting its high and dusty plate within a tarnished gilt frame. Among many wonderful stories related of this mirror, it was fabled that the spirits of all the doctor's deceased patients dwelt within its verge and would stare him in the face whenever he looked thitherward. The opposite side of the chamber was ornamented with the full-length portrait of a young lady, arrayed in the faded magnificence of silk, satin, and brocade, and with a visage as faded as her dress. Above half a century ago, Dr. Heidegger had been on the point of marriage with this young lady; but being affected with some slight disorder, she had swallowed one of her lover's prescriptions and died on the bridal evening. The greatest curiosity of the study remains to be mentioned; it was a ponderous folio volume, bound in black leather, with massive silver clasps. There were no letters on the back, and nobody could tell the title of the book. But it was well known to be a book of magic; and once, when a chambermaid had lifted it, merely to brush away the dust, the skeleton had rattled in its closet, the picture of the young lady had stepped one foot upon the floor, and several ghastly faces had peeped forth from the mirror; while the brazen head of Hippocrates frowned and said, "Forbear!"

Such was Dr. Heidegger's study. On the summer afternoon of our tale, a small round table, as black as ebony,[4] stood in the center of the room, sustaining a cut-glass vase of beautiful form and elaborate workmanship. The sunshine came through the window between the heavy festoons of two faded damask curtains, and fell directly across this vase; so that a mild splendor was reflected from it on the ashen visages of the five old people who sat around. Four champagne glasses were also on the table.

"My dear old friends," repeated Dr. Heidegger, "may I reckon on your aid in performing an exceedingly curious experiment?"

Now Dr. Heidegger was a very strange old gentleman, whose eccentricity had become the nucleus for a thousand fantastic stories. Some of these fables, to my shame be it spoken, might possibly be traced back to mine own veracious self; and if any passages of the present tale should startle the reader's faith, I must be content to bear the stigma of a fiction-monger.

When the doctor's four guests heard him talk of his proposed experiment, they anticipated nothing more wonderful than the murder of a mouse in an air-pump, or the examination of a cobweb by the microscope, or some similar nonsense, with which he was constantly in the habit of pestering his intimates. But without waiting for a reply, Dr. Heidegger hobbled across the chamber and returned with the same ponderous folio, bound in black leather, which common report affirmed to be a book of magic. Undoing the silver clasps, he opened the volume and took from among its black-letter pages a rose, or what was once a rose, though now the green leaves and crimson petals had assumed one brownish hue, and the ancient flower seemed ready to

---

[3] HIPPOCRATES (hĭ·pŏk′rà·tēz)—A Greek physician of the fourth century B.C.; known as the Father of Medicine.

[4] EBONY—A hard, black wood.

crumble to dust in the doctor's hands.

"This rose," said Dr. Heidegger, with a sigh, "this same withered and crumbling flower, blossomed five-and-fifty years ago. It was given to me by Sylvia Ward, whose portrait hangs yonder; and I meant to wear it in my bosom at our wedding. Five-and-fifty years it has been treasured between the leaves of this old volume. Now, would you deem it possible that this rose of half a century could ever bloom again?"

"Nonsense!" said the Widow Wycherly, with a peevish toss of her head. "You might as well ask whether an old woman's wrinkled face could ever bloom again."

"See!" answered Dr. Heidegger.

He uncovered the vase and threw the faded rose into the water which it contained. At first it lay lightly on the surface of the fluid, appearing to imbibe none of its moisture. Soon, however, a singular change began to be visible. The crushed and dried petals stirred and assumed a deepening tinge of crimson, as if the flower were reviving from a death-like slumber; the slender stalk and twigs of foliage became green; and there was the rose of half a century, looking as fresh as when Sylvia Ward had first given it to her lover. It was scarcely full-blown; for some of its delicate red leaves curled modestly around its moist bosom, within which two or three dewdrops were sparkling.

"That is certainly a very pretty deception," said the doctor's friends, carelessly, however, for they had witnessed greater miracles at a conjuror's show; "pray how was it effected?"

"Did you never hear of the 'Fountain of Youth,'" asked Dr. Heidegger, "which Ponce de León, the Spanish adventurer, went in search of two or three centuries ago?"

"But did Ponce de León ever find it?" said the Widow Wycherly.

"No," answered Dr. Heidegger, "for he never sought it in the right place. The famous Fountain of Youth, if I am rightly informed, is situated in the southern part of the Floridian peninsula, not far from Lake Macaco. Its source is overshadowed by several gigantic magnolias, which, though numberless centuries old, have been kept as fresh as violets by the virtues of this wonderful water. An acquaintance of mine, knowing my curiosity in such matters, has sent me what you see in the vase."

"Ahem!" said Colonel Killigrew, who believed not a word of the doctor's story; "and what may be the effect of this fluid on the human frame?"

"You shall judge for yourself, my dear Colonel," replied Dr. Heidegger; "and all of you, my respected friends, are welcome to so much of this admirable fluid as may restore to you the bloom of youth. For my own part, having had much trouble in growing old, I am in no hurry to grow young again. With your permission, therefore, I will merely watch the progress of the experiment."

While he spoke, Dr. Heidegger had been filling the four champagne glasses with the water of the Fountain of Youth. It was apparently impregnated [5] with an effervescent [6] gas, for little bubbles were continually ascending from the depths of the glasses and bursting in silvery spray at the surface. As the liquor diffused a pleasant perfume, the old people doubted not that it possessed cordial and comfortable properties; and, though utter skeptics as to its rejuvenescent [7] power, they were inclined to swallow it at once.

[5] IMPREGNATED—Saturated, filled through and through.
[6] EFFERVESCENT—Pertaining to a liquid which continuously gives off little bubbles of gas.
[7] REJUVENESCENT—Restoring youth.

But Dr. Heidegger besought them to stay a moment.

"Before you drink, my respectable old friends," said he, "it would be well that, with the experience of a lifetime to direct you, you should draw up a few general rules for your guidance in passing a second time through the perils of youth. Think what a sin and shame it would be, if, with your peculiar advantages, you should not become patterns of virtue and wisdom to all the young people of the age."

The doctor's four venerable friends made him no answer, except by a feeble and tremulous laugh, so very ridiculous was the idea, that, knowing how closely repentance treads behind the steps of error, they should ever go astray again.

"Drink, then," said the doctor, bowing. "I rejoice that I have so well selected the subjects of my experiment."

With palsied hands, they raised the glasses to their lips. The liquor, if it really possessed such virtues as Dr. Heidegger imputed to it, could not have been bestowed on four human beings who needed it more woefully. They looked as if they had never known what youth or pleasure was, but had been the offspring of Nature's dotage, and always the gray, decrepit, sapless, miserable creatures who now sat stooping round the doctor's table, without life enough in their souls or bodies to be animated even by the prospect of growing young again. They drank off the water and replaced their glasses on the table.

Assuredly there was an almost immediate improvement in the aspect of the party, not unlike what might have been produced by a glass of generous wine, together with a sudden glow of cheerful sunshine, brightening over all their visages at once. There was a healthful suffusion on their cheeks, instead of the ashen hue that had made them look so corpse-like. They gazed at one another and fancied that some magic power had really begun to smooth away the deep and sad inscriptions which Father Time had been so long engraving on their brows. The Widow Wycherly adjusted her cap, for she felt almost like a woman again.

"Give us more of this wonderful water!" cried they, eagerly.

"We are younger—but we are still too old! Quick—give us more!"

"Patience, patience!" quoth Dr. Heidegger, who sat watching the experiment with philosophic coolness. "You have been a long time growing old. Surely, you might be content to grow young in half an hour! But the water is at your service."

Again he filled their glasses with the liquor of youth, enough of which still remained in the vase to turn half the old people in the city to the age of their own grandchildren. While the bubbles were yet sparkling on the brim, the doctor's four guests snatched their glasses from the table, and swallowed the contents in a single gulp. Was it delusion? Even while the draft was passing down their throats, it seemed to have wrought a change on their whole systems. Their eyes grew clear and bright; a dark shade deepened among their silvery locks; they sat around the table, three gentlemen of middle age and a woman hardly beyond her buxom prime.

"My dear widow, you are charming!" cried Colonel Killigrew, whose eyes had been fixed upon her face while the shadows of age were flitting from it like darkness from the crimson daybreak.

The fair widow knew, of old, that Colonel Killigrew's compliments were not always measured by sober truth; so she started up and ran to the mirror, still dreading that the ugly visage of an old

woman would meet her gaze. Meanwhile, the three gentlemen behaved in such a manner as proved that the water of the Fountain of Youth possessed some intoxicating qualities; unless, indeed, their exhilaration of spirits were merely a lightsome dizziness caused by the sudden removal of the weight of years. Mr. Gascoigne's mind seemed to run on political topics, but whether relating to the past, present, or future, could not easily be determined, since the same ideas and phrases have been in vogue these fifty years. Now he rattled forth full-throated sentences about patriotism, national glory, and the people's right; now he muttered some perilous stuff or other, in a sly and doubtful whisper, so cautiously that even his own conscience could scarcely catch the secret; and now, again, he spoke in measured accents and a

deeply deferential [8] tone, as if a royal ear [9] were listening to his well-turned periods. Colonel Killigrew all this time had been trolling forth a jolly bottle-song and ringing his glass in symphony with the chorus, while his eyes wandered toward the buxom figure of the Widow Wycherly. On the other side of the table, Mr. Medbourne was involved in a calculation of dollars and cents, with which was strangely intermingled a project for supplying the East Indies with ice by harnessing a team of whales to the polar icebergs.

As for the Widow Wycherly, she stood before the mirror curtsying and simpering to her own image and greeting it as

[8] DEFERENTIAL—Respectful.
[9] A ROYAL EAR—We are to assume that at the time of Mr. Gascoigne's political career, America was still ruled by the king of England.

the friend whom she loved better than all the world beside. She thrust her face close to the glass to see whether some long-remembered wrinkle or crow's-foot [10] had indeed vanished. She examined whether the snow had so entirely melted from her hair that the venerable cap could be safely thrown aside. At last, turning briskly away, she came with a sort of dancing step to the table.

"My dear old doctor," cried she, "pray favor me with another glass!"

"Certainly, my dear madam, certainly!" replied the complaisant doctor; "see! I have already filled the glasses."

There, in fact, stood the four glasses, brimful of this wonderful water, the delicate spray of which, as it effervesced from the surface, resembled the tremulous glitter of diamonds. It was now so nearly sunset that the chamber had grown duskier than ever; but a mild and moon-like splendor gleamed from within the vase and rested alike on the four guests and on the doctor's venerable figure. He sat in a high-backed, elaborately-carved oaken armchair, with a gray dignity of aspect that might have well befitted that very Father Time, whose power had never been disputed save by this fortunate company. Even while quaffing the third draft of the Fountain of Youth, they were almost awed by the expression of his mysterious visage.

But, the next moment, the exhilarating gush of young life shot through their veins. They were now in the happy prime of youth. Age, with its miserable train of cares and sorrows and diseases was remembered only as the trouble of a dream from which they had joyously awoke. The fresh gloss of the soul, so early lost, and without which the world's

successive scenes had been but a gallery of faded pictures, again threw its enchantment over all their prospects. They felt like new-created beings in a new-created universe.

"We are young! We are young!" they cried exultingly. Youth, like the extremity of age, had effaced the strongly marked characteristics of middle life and mutually assimilated [11] them all. They were a group of merry youngsters, almost maddened with the exuberant frolicsomeness of their years. The most singular effect on their gaiety was an impulse to mock the infirmity and decrepitude of which they had so lately been the victims. They laughed loudly at their old-fashioned attire, the wide-skirted coats and flapped waistcoats of the young men, and the ancient cap and gown of the blooming girl. One limped across the floor like a gouty grandfather; one set a pair of spectacles astride of his nose and pretended to pore over the black-letter pages of the book of magic; a third seated himself in an armchair and strove to imitate the venerable dignity of Dr. Heidegger. Then all shouted mirthfully and leaped about the room. The Widow Wycherly—if so fresh a damsel could be called a widow—tripped up to the doctor's chair, with a mischievous merriment in her rosy face.

"Doctor, you dear old soul," cried she, "get up and dance with me!" And then the four young people laughed louder than ever to think what a queer figure the poor old doctor would cut.

"Pray excuse me," answered the doctor, quietly. "I am old and rheumatic, and my dancing days were over long ago. But either of these gay young gentlemen will be glad of so pretty a partner."

"Dance with me, Clara!" cried Colonel Killigrew.

[10] CROW'S-FOOT—The wrinkles radiating from the outer corner of the eye, often noticed in aged people.

[11] ASSIMILATED—Made alike.

"No, no, I will be her partner!" shouted Mr. Gascoigne.

"She promised me her hand fifty years ago!" exclaimed Mr. Medbourne.

They all gathered round her. One caught both her hands in his passionate grasp—another threw his arm about her waist—the third buried his hand among the glossy curls that clustered beneath the widow's cap. Blushing, panting, struggling, chiding, laughing, her warm breath fanning each of their faces by turns, she strove to disengage herself, yet still remained in their triple embrace. Never was there a livelier picture of youthful rivalship, with bewitching beauty for the prize. Yet, by a strange deception, owing to the duskiness of the chamber and the antique dresses which they still wore, the tall mirror is said to have reflected the figures of the three old, gray, withered grandsires, ridiculously contending for the skinny ugliness of a shriveled grandam.

But they were young, their burning passions proved them so. Inflamed to madness by the coquetry of the girl-widow, who neither granted nor quite withheld her favors, the three rivals began to interchange threatening glances. Still keeping hold of the fair prize, they grappled fiercely at one another's throats. As they struggled to and fro, the table was overturned and the vase dashed into a thousand fragments. The precious Water of Youth flowed in a bright stream across the floor, moistening the wings of a butterfly, which, grown old in the decline of summer, had alighted there to die. The insect fluttered lightly through the chamber and settled on the snowy head of Dr. Heidegger.

"Come, come, gentlemen!—come, Madam Wycherly," exclaimed the doctor, "I really must protest against this riot."

They stood still and shivered; for it seemed as if gray Time were calling them back from their sunny youth, far down into the chill and darksome vale of years. They looked at old Dr. Heidegger, who sat in his carved armchair, holding the rose of half a century, which he had rescued from among the fragments of the shattered vase. At the motion of his hand, the four rioters resumed their seats, the more readily because their violent exertions had wearied them, youthful though they were.

"My poor Sylvia's rose!" ejaculated

Dr. Heidegger, holding it in the light of the sunset clouds; "it appears to be fading again."

And so it was. Even while the party were looking at it, the flower continued to shrivel up till it became as dry and fragile as when the doctor had first thrown it into the vase. He shook off the few drops of moisture which clung to its petals.

"I love it as well thus, as in its dewy freshness," observed he, pressing the withered rose to his withered lips. While he spoke, the butterfly fluttered down from the doctor's snowy head and fell upon the floor.

His guests shivered again. A strange chillness, whether of the body or spirit they could not tell, was creeping gradually over them all. They gazed at one another and fancied that each fleeting moment snatched away a charm and left a deepening furrow where none had been before. Was it an illusion? [12] Had the changes of a lifetime been crowded into so brief a space, and were they now four aged people, sitting with their old friend, Dr. Heidegger?

"Are we grown old again, so soon!" cried they, dolefully.

In truth, they had. The Water of Youth possessed merely a virtue more transient than that of wine. The delirium which it created had effervesced away. Yes! they were old again. With a shuddering impulse that showed her a woman still, the widow clasped her skinny hands before her face and wished that the coffin-lid were over it, since it could be no longer beautiful.

"Yes, friends, ye are old again," said Dr. Heidegger; "and lo! the Water of Youth is all lavished on the ground. Well—I bemoan it not; for if the fountain gushed at my very doorstep I would

[12] ILLUSION—A false, unreal appearance.

not stoop to bathe my lips in it—no, though its delirium were for years instead of moments. Such is the lesson ye have taught me!"

But the doctor's four friends had taught no such lesson to themselves. They resolved forthwith to make a pilgrimage to Florida and quaff at morning, noon, and night from the Fountain of Youth.

FOR UNDERSTANDING

1. Dr. Heidegger seems almost as uncanny as old Mother Rigby in "Feathertop." His character is a combination of the modern scientist who probes into the secrets of the universe, and the medieval alchemist who tried to concoct a "water of youth" by mixing strange chemicals together while at the same time he mumbled magic words. In the description of the doctor's study, what details build up an atmosphere of old-time magic and mystery? On the other hand, what does the author say that makes us think of Dr. Heidegger as a queer old fellow who, out of curiosity, is always performing little experiments in his laboratory?

2. The author takes his time in getting to the fantastic part of his story—the drinking of the miraculous water and the results that followed. He must first get his readers into a believing mood, so far as that is possible. How does the incident of the rose do this?

3. All four of the old people who drink the water have some discreditable things in their past. For instance, Colonel Killigrew had apparently overindulged himself in rich food and drink. The Widow Wycherly, who in her youth was very attractive to men, had been involved in several scandals. After they drink the water, how do these two show by their actions that the same characteristics have revived once more? How does Mr. Gascoigne show that he is just as much an insincere politician as ever? What scheme comes into the mind of Mr. Medbourne, the merchant-speculator?

4. It seems likely that Dr. Heidegger's intention was not only to find out whether the water had miraculous power, but to find out whether people really would live better lives if they were given a second chance. Does he drink any of the water himself? How do his four friends react to his warning, before they drink the water, that they should draw up rules of conduct that will prevent them from repeating their former mistakes? At the end of the story, what does the doctor say he has learned from the experiment? What have his friends learned?

5. Give an example from your own life of thinking you have "learned a lesson"—and afterward, making the same mistake a second time. Or, if you think Hawthorne's story is not true to human nature, give an example of actually applying the lessons of experience.

FOR BROADER MEANINGS

The plots of Hawthorne's stories stir up in our minds all sorts of questions about life and conduct. Hawthorne seldom states these problems simply and clearly. His aim is to *suggest*—to *stimulate the thinking* of his readers, and let them find in his stories whatever meanings they can. One obvious thought in "Dr. Heidegger's Experiment" is that we should try to profit by our own mistakes—not behave like the foolish people in the story. But the author suggests a number of other ideas as well, and it would be hard to decide which one is his main point.

Hawthorne may have intended to show that it is not really very important to be allowed "a second chance." The characters of the four old people have not improved with age. They have misspent their entire lives—and their actions show that as a result they have gained no wisdom at all. Therefore, what we should be concerned about is our "first chance." We should develop habits and attitudes *now* that will lead to better and happier lives in the years to come. Give examples of (*a*) habits of

conduct in young people that may lead to a worthless adult life unless they are changed; (*b*) good habits which, if they persist, will lead to a useful and respected life.

At the end of the story, two opposite attitudes are expressed toward *youth*. The four old people still think being young is so much better than being old that they want to go to Florida and find the Fountain of Youth. On the other hand, Dr. Heidegger concludes that youth is a "delirium" which he does not want to experience again. Hawthorne probably does not want us to agree altogether with Dr. Heidegger's opinion. For one thing, not all young people act like the characters in this story. What Hawthorne accomplishes by his sharp contrast between youth and age is to make us *think of the whole of human life at once.* When a person thinks of *all* of his life, he can see how ridiculous some of his present actions are. How does the reflection in Dr. Heidegger's mirror suggest such a thought? Give three examples of things that people are very much concerned about in early life, but that might seem ridiculous to them when they reach the age of seventy. Judging from the story, what kind of behavior seems *most* childish and foolish to Hawthorne?

THE STORYTELLER'S CRAFT

1. In many of Hawthorne's stories, as in Poe's, the action builds up higher and higher to the climax, the decisive event. In "Dr. Heidegger's Experiment," this *rising action* begins when we first learn what the experiment is to be. It approaches its highest point when the four people who have drunk the Water of Youth become increasingly wild and noisy. How is their gaiety turned into a quarrel? What accident happens during the struggle?

2. Dr. Heidegger's protest quiets the young people for a moment, but this is not yet the climax of the story. What is the climax? What minor incident, just after the doctor gets the young people to sit

down, prepares us for the climax? Contrast the way Hawthorne ends this story with the way Poe ends "The Cask of Amontillado." Which author focuses his readers' attention most sharply on *action?*

3. Hawthorne often tells stories in which marvelous things happen, but he likes to arrange his plots so that every event can be explained in a perfectly common-sense way, if the reader prefers. Find one or more remarks in the early part of "Dr. Heidegger's Experiment" which suggest that the strange stories about the doctor are mere hearsay, not truth. Near the end, the word "delirium" implants a suspicion that *perhaps* the four characters had not really been made young again but had been under the influence of an intoxicating drug. How is this suspicion strengthened by what Hawthorne says about the *mirror* during the struggle over the Widow Wycherly? What similar use does Hawthorne make of a mirror in "Feathertop"?

FOR YOUR VOCABULARY

1. ". . . a *ponderous* folio volume . . . with *massive* silver clasps." Look up the italicized words in your dictionary. What would be the difference between handling a *ponderous* book and handling a *massive* book?

2. ". . . a sudden glow of cheerful sunshine, brightening over their *visages* at once." Define *visages.*

3. "She stood before the mirror *curtsying* and *simpering* to her own image." What two things was she doing?

4. "Blushing, panting, struggling, *chiding,* laughing." How does the word *chide* differ in meaning from its synonym *scold?*

5. "Inflamed to madness by the *coquetry* of the girl-widow, who neither granted nor quite withheld her favors." What kind of behavior is *coquetry?*

6. "The Water of Youth possessed merely a *virtue* more *transient* than that of wine." In this sentence the word *virtue* means *power.* Explain the word *transient.*

FOR FURTHER READING

MALCOLM COWLEY, ed., *The Portable Hawthorne* (Viking). Besides such stories as "An Old Woman's Tale," "My Kinsman, Major Molineaux," "The Birthmark" and "Ethan Brand," this book contains selections from the author's novels, journals, and letters. Additional stories may be found in *The Complete Novels and Selected Tales of Nathaniel Hawthorne*, edited by Norman Holmes Pearson (Modern Library).

HILDEGARDE HAWTHORNE, *Romantic Rebel: The Story of Nathaniel Hawthorne* (Appleton-Century-Crofts). Here is an intimate story about one of America's great writers as told by his granddaughter.

NATHANIEL HAWTHORNE, *The House of the Seven Gables.* In this novel Hawthorne traces the story of the haughty Pyncheon family which supposedly has lived in Salem since early Puritan times. There is a curse on the family which affects one member of each generation in turn. Young Phoebe Pyncheon, a cousin, comes to Salem to live, bringing sunshine and kindness into the gloomy old family mansion. The events that finally cause the ancestral curse to be lifted make up the plot of this weird, mysterious novel.

MRS. LOUISE (HALL) THARP, *The Peabody Sisters of Salem* (Little). This highly readable biography of three women—one of whom was the wife of Nathaniel Hawthorne—gives a delightful picture of the times and introduces its readers to such intellectual figures as Thoreau and Emerson.

RALPH WALDO EMERSON (1803–1882)

The career of Emerson seemed to have come to an end by his twenty-ninth year. His wife had died after two years of marriage; and Emerson had resigned his position as a minister in Boston because he could not agree with the creeds of his church. But Emerson ended life as a man whose name was honored all over America. He had become the leader of a famous group of writers and thinkers in the little town of Concord, Massachusetts, and he had won esteem as the wisest man of the century he lived in.

To the earnest piety of his New England ancestors Emerson added wide learning. He was educated at Harvard and at the Boston Divinity School. After leaving the ministry he traveled to Europe where he made the acquaintance of the two living writers he most admired, Samuel Coleridge and Thomas Carlyle. Their books—as well as Greek and German philosophy, and the ancient religious writings of India— were influences on his thought.

Back in America, Emerson remarried and settled in Concord. He made his living by lecturing—at first to lyceum audiences in Massachusetts, and later as far west as Wisconsin and Michigan. The literary circle which looked up to him as a leader founded a magazine, *The Dial*, which Emerson helped to edit. He and his associates taught the doctrine known as *transcendentalism*—a term borrowed from German philosophy. Transcendentalism is hard to define because it was a cluster of religious ideas rather than a single easily stated belief. One part of it was the thought that our minds "transcend," go beyond, the knowledge of material objects—that in our deepest instinctive feelings we are in communication with God. Thus religion becomes not only a matter of adhering to an accepted creed, or of recognizing God's design in nature, but a joyous inner experience.

A GUIDE AND COUNSELOR

Emerson's sober, inquiring essays are his most famous works, but he also wrote a few extremely fine poems. In all his writings, his independence of thought reminds one of the individualistic old Puritans—religious men, solid as granite, trusting God and themselves rather than governments, unafraid of either public disapproval or British redcoats. Emerson is a guide; a counselor who seeks to make us aware of our own highest and most worthy desires, and to encourage us to live up to them. From a thousand different texts he preaches that every individual has greater things in him than he realizes. Perhaps the best characterization ever made of Emerson's total work is this: "He is the friend and aider of those who would live in the spirit."

✧✧✧✧✧

Concord Hymn

During the nineteenth century the village of Concord was the home of Emerson, Thoreau, and other noted writers. But Concord was already famous before these men were born. Here and at Lexington, in 1775 the "minutemen" fought the first battle of the Revolutionary War. Sixty-two years later, upon the completion of a new monument at Concord Bridge, Emerson was asked to compose a song for the dedication. Thus its "first edition" was the printed sheet from which the people of Concord sang the hymn. Appropriately, the date was July 4th.

By the rude bridge that arched the flood,
   Their flag to April's breeze unfurled,
Here once the embattled farmers stood,
   And fired the shot heard round the world.

The foe long since in silence slept;   5
   Alike the conqueror silent sleeps;
And Time the ruined bridge has swept
   Down the dark stream which seaward creeps.

On this green bank, by this soft stream,
   We set today a votive stone;   10
That memory may their deed redeem,
   When, like our sires, our sons are gone.

Spirit, that made those heroes dare
   To die, and leave their children free,
Bid Time and Nature gently spare   15
   The shaft we raise to them and thee.

10. VOTIVE (vō′tĭv)—Consecrated by a vow.

FOR UNDERSTANDING

1. This is an "occasional" poem—one written for a particular occasion. The word "here" in the first stanza alludes to the fact that the hymn is actually to be sung at Concord Bridge. What other phrases indicate the place? Find two lines that refer to the people who are singing the hymn.

2. What lines indicate that the original Concord Bridge is no longer there? What reference is made to the people who made the spot famous?

3. What *spirit* do you think is referred to in the last stanza? What request is made of the spirit? Explain what is meant by saying the monument is raised "to *them* and *thee*."

4. The first stanza contains the two most famous lines of the poem. The expression "the shot heard round the world" is *figuratively* true, and has often been praised for saying much in a few words. Explain what it means.

FOR FURTHER INVESTIGATION

1. Look up the Battle of Concord and Lexington, and report to the class (*a*) the purpose of the raid by the British troop (*b*) how the Americans were warned of their approach (*c*) the outcome of the skirmish.

2. Longfellow's familiar poem "Paul Revere's Ride," although not historically accurate in all details, is a vivid expression of the way Americans feel about the historic battle. Appoint one person to explain the events of the poem, and read it aloud.

◇◇◇◇◇

Voluntaries

If this poem were written today it would be called "Volunteers." The title refers to heroes who of their own choice enlisted in the War Between the States.

What causes heroism and self-sacrifice? It is a strange, wonderful fact that men will even give their lives in loyalty to a great cause. Emerson always counsels his readers to act according to their own noblest impulses; in this poem he discusses such action. He also hints at an explanation of it. The following lines are the third stanza of the poem.

In an age of fops and toys,
Wanting wisdom, void of right,
Who shall nerve heroic boys
To hazard all in Freedom's fight—
Break sharply off their jolly games,   5
Forsake their comrades gay
And quit proud homes and youthful
   dames
For famine, toil, and fray?
Yet on the nimble air benign
Speed nimbler messages,   10
That waft the breath of grace divine
To hearts in sloth and ease.
So nigh is grandeur to our dust,
So near is God to man,
When Duty whispers low, *Thou must,*
The youth replies, *I can.*   16

1. FOPS—Vain persons devoted to fine clothes and manners.
1. TOYS—Here the word means ornaments, or other playthings with which *adults* childishly occupy themselves.
2. VOID OF RIGHT—Lacking a sense of right.

FOR UNDERSTANDING

1. What are the pleasant things the young men must give up when they volunteer for war?

2. Notice that line 14 repeats, in plainer language, the thought of line 13 and is therefore a sort of explanation of line 13. Explain why "our dust" can be a synonym for "man." Compare other corresponding expressions in the two lines. Then explain how the language of line 13 is more elevated and rhetorical than that of line 14.

3. In many of his writings Emerson declares that there is a spark of divinity— something godlike—in all of us, and that we should be ruled by it rather than by our selfish appetites. How does this poem suggest that we have something high and noble in us?

4. The last four lines of this stanza are among the most famous of all Emerson's writings. Explain how lines 15–16 are a *completion* of lines 13–14. That is, how do they prove or illustrate that we are *near to* God?

RISING TO HIGH RESPONSI-
   BILITIES

Today and in the past, it has often happened that when duty demands, a person shows unexpected energy and strength of character. This happens in personal and family situations as well as in public life. Sometimes the transformation of the person's character is so great that we say, "I didn't know he had it in him."

Describe an example of such a transformation—in literature, history, or modern life. Make it an example from civilian, not military, life.

◇◇◇◇◇

Forbearance

This poem is made up of five examples of forbearance, or self-control. Those in the first four lines are easy to understand. However, the fifth is less obvious. At first it may seem to you to be out of harmony with the others. Perhaps that is because the ideal expressed by Emerson is so high we have trouble even comprehending it.

As you read, see if you can discover any reason for the order in which the examples are given. Which is least important? Which is most important?

> Hast thou named all the birds without a gun?
> Loved the wood rose, and left it on its stalk?
> At rich men's tables eaten bread and pulse?
> Unarmed, faced danger with a heart of trust?
> And loved so well a high behavior,   5
> In man or maid, that thou from speech refrained,
> Nobility more nobly to repay?
> O, be my friend, and teach me to be thine!

3. PULSE—The edible seeds of various vegetables, symbolic of simple diet.

FOR UNDERSTANDING

1. Explain the first four kinds of forbearance. Tell what is praiseworthy about each.

2. Read lines 5–7, which describe the fifth and last type of forbearance. The phrase "that thou from speech refrained" implies that one would usually feel an impulse to comment on "high behavior." What sort of comment would one be inclined to make?

3. According to ordinary standards, if we fail to praise a noble act it might be supposed that we did not appreciate it. However, to understand Emerson's thought we must realize that when we give such praise we are almost acting *surprised* over the friend's action. Explain how it is a finer compliment to say nothing at all. That is, in paying the compliment of silence, what do we imply as to how we suppose the friend will *always* act?

◇◇◇◇◇

*D*ays

Each new day in your life brings you a whole new set of opportunities—to improve yourself, to attend to your duties, or to fritter away your time aimlessly. In this poem, Emerson pictures the Days as a stately, silent procession of women. As they pass by us they offer gifts of every kind. What will we take?

Daughters of Time, the hypocritic Days,
Muffled and dumb like barefoot dervishes,
And marching single in an endless file,
Bring diadems and fagots in their hands.
To each they offer gifts after his will, 5
Bread, kingdoms, stars, and sky that holds them all.
I, in my pleached garden, watched the pomp,
Forgot my morning wishes, hastily
Took a few herbs and apples, and the Day
Turned and departed silent. I, too late,
Under her solemn fillet saw the scorn. 11

1. HYPOCRITIC (hĭp′ô·krĭt′ĭk)—Insincere; false.
2. DERVISHES (dûr′vĭsh·ĕz)—Holy men of the Moslem religion.
4. DIADEMS (dī′ă·dĕmz)—Crowns.
4. FAGOTS (făg′ŭtz)—Bundles of firewood.
7. PLEACHED (plēcht)—Fenced in by interwoven branches.
11. FILLET (fĭl′ĕt)—Headband.

◇◇◇

FOR UNDERSTANDING

1. The Days offer each man gifts "after his will." Because of their silence they seem completely impartial as to which gifts are valuable. What idea about the gifts is suggested by "diadems and fagots"?

2. What does the expression "took a few herbs and apples" imply about the use the speaker made of his day? What had his earlier intentions been?

3. How is it shown that the speaker had regrets after the day was over? Explain the connection between the *scorn* mentioned in the last line and the word *hypocritic* in the first line.

Ode

INSCRIBED TO W. H. CHANNING

Emerson praised the vigor and the quick, inventive intelligence shown in the growing commercial life of America. Yet he also complained, as in these lines, that in striving for success men often make themselves slaves, not masters.

The horseman serves the horse,
The neatherd serves the neat,
The merchant serves the purse,
The eater serves his meat;
'Tis the day of the chattel,   5
Web to weave, and corn to grind;
Things are in the saddle,
And ride mankind.

There are two laws discrete,
Not reconciled—   10
Law for man, and law for thing;
The last builds town and fleet,
But it runs wild,
And doth the man unking.

2. NEATHERD (nēt′hûrd′) . . . NEAT—The herdsman serves the cattle.
5. CHATTEL (chăt′l)—Property, including goods, money, and livestock.
9. DISCRETE (dĭs·krēt′)—Separate; distinct from one another.

❖❖

FOR UNDERSTANDING

1. List several services to mankind which can be performed by a large manufacturing plant. Then list the ways in which such an enterprise, if it "runs wild," can harm mankind.

2. Which passage in the selection shows that the poet realizes that labor and commerce are useful and important?

3. Emerson seems impressed by the danger that men will *live only for their work.* List several benefits which a person might expect to gain from financial success. Which ones would you name as most precious? Which of these benefits might actually be lost by a person who applied himself too constantly to his work? What other still more precious things in life might be lost?

4. What remark in the poem expresses most dramatically the thought that we can place too high a value on material progress?

THE AMERICAN SCHOLAR

Like a number of Emerson's essays, "The American Scholar" was originally delivered as a lecture. Emerson read it in 1837 to the Harvard chapter of Phi Beta Kappa, the honorary scholarship fraternity. The lecture emphasizes that true scholars must have broad curiosity even though they may be studying in narrowly specialized fields; that they must not shut themselves off from the life around them.

The famous passage given here comes near the beginning of Emerson's lecture, and is really his opening thought. Notice how he attracts and holds the attention of his audience by making an unusual comparison to get his idea across.

It is one of those fables which, out of an unknown antiquity, convey an unlooked-for wisdom, that the gods, in the beginning, divided Man into men, that he might be more helpful to himself; just as the hand was divided into fingers, the better to answer its end.

The old fable covers a doctrine ever new and sublime; that there is One Man—present to all particular men only partially, or through one faculty;[1] and that you must take the whole society to find the whole man. Man is not a farmer, or a professor, or an engineer, but he is all. Man is priest, and scholar, and statesman, and producer, and soldier. In the *divided* or social state these functions are parcelled out to individuals, each of whom aims to do his stint of the joint work, whilst each other performs his. The fable implies that the individual, to possess himself, must sometimes return from his own labor to embrace all the other laborers. But, unfortunately, this original unit, this fountain of power, has been so distributed to multitudes, has been so minutely subdivided and peddled out, that it is spilled into drops and cannot be gathered. The state of society is one in which the members have suffered amputation from the trunk, and strut about so many walking monsters—a good finger, a neck, a stomach, an elbow, but never a man.

Man is thus metamorphosed[2] into a thing, into many things. The planter, who is Man sent out into the field to gather food, is seldom cheered by any idea of the true dignity of his ministry. He sees his bushel and his cart, and nothing beyond, and sinks into the farmer, instead of Man on the farm. The tradesman scarcely ever gives an ideal worth to his work but is ridden by the routine of his craft, and the soul is subject to dollars. The priest becomes a form; the attorney, a statute book; the mechanic, a machine; the sailor, a rope of a ship.

In this distribution of functions the scholar is the delegated[3] intellect. In

[1] FACULTY—One particular natural aptitude or ability.

[2] METAMORPHOSED (mĕt′à·môr′fōz′d)— Changed, transformed.

[3] DELEGATED (dĕl′ê·gâ·tĕd)—Appointed.

611

the right state, he is *Man Thinking*. In the degenerate state, when the victim of society, he tends to become a mere thinker, or, still worse, the parrot of other men's thinking.

FOR UNDERSTANDING

1. Emerson mentions that in the old fable a single creature, *Man*, was divided into many *men* so that he could better provide for himself. Explain why it is advantageous for each of us to work in one field such as engineering, farming, or medicine.

2. According to Emerson, each individual has lost something if he gives up being "Man" and becomes *merely* a specialist. Think of any well-known occupation and explain how if a man concentrates too closely on it for a long time his character or outlook sometimes changes for the worse.

3. In daily life we sometimes hear expressions like "a farm hand," "a factory hand," "This machine shop employs twenty hands." Quote a remark by Emerson in which he could have inserted the word "hand" in exactly this sense. Describe an imaginary situation in which it would be very unfortunate for a manufacturing firm if the men had no more ability than is implied by the word "hands."

4. Explain how the third paragraph of this selection is similar in thought to Emerson's "Ode Inscribed to W. H. Channing."

5. Think about what Emerson has in mind when he distinguishes between "the farmer" and "Man on the farm." How might the farmer be handicapped *in his career* if he were not to some extent a student

of economics? a scientist? a student of politics? Still worse, how might he be a failure *as a human being* if he did not possess other abilities as well?

6. At the end of the selection Emerson contrasts "Man Thinking" with the "mere thinker." Why would experience of life and people be of value to a historian? to a student of literature? Describe the activities of some highly trained person—for instance, a scientist—you have heard or read about who has interests reaching beyond his own specialized profession.

EMERSON'S USE OF COMPARISONS TO PICTURE HIS THOUGHT

In this essay Emerson uses two comparisons:

1. Mankind—hand; individual men—fingers.
2. Mankind—the whole body; men of specialized occupations—parts of the body.

1. Explain how Emerson's use of comparison helps us to understand his thought on the disadvantages of overspecialization. That is, explain *how* a farmer or an attorney might be like an amputated finger or elbow.

2. In the poem "Days," Emerson pictures *a procession of women* to illustrate his thought. Explain how the various details of the picture correspond to actual facts about the days of a person's life.

3. In the study of the human body, the *nervous system* is sometimes compared to a *telephone system*. Explain how the two are alike. Can you think of other comparisons that are used in science to help us picture something that is hard to understand?

SELF-RELIANCE

The title "Self-Reliance" is likely to make us think of such ideas as "Stand on your own feet," and "Don't just drift along; manage your affairs"—sound advice, but rather obvious. Actually, as you will discover when you read this excerpt from his famous essay, Emerson's advice is much bolder.

Emerson kept a journal in which from time to time he wrote down a proverb-like sentence which forcefully expressed some phase of his thinking. Later he incorporated these sentences into his essays. If you can get hold of the two rich nuggets of thought that appear at the beginning of this selection from "Self-Reliance," you will be close to understanding the basic idea of the entire essay.

There is a time in every man's education when he arrives at the conviction that envy is ignorance; that imitation is suicide; that he must take himself for better, for worse, as his portion. . . .

Trust thyself: every heart vibrates to that iron string. Accept the place the Divine Providence has found for you, the society of your contemporaries, the connection of events. Great men have always done so and confided themselves childlike to the genius of their age, betraying their perception that the Eternal was stirring at their heart, working through their hands, predominating in all their being. . . .

What pretty oracles [1] Nature yields us on this text in the face and behavior of children, babes, and even brutes. . . . Infancy conforms to nobody; all conform to it; so that one babe commonly makes four or five out of the adults who prattle and play to it. . . . Do not think the youth has no force, because he cannot speak to you and me. Hark! in the next room his voice is sufficiently clear and emphatic. It seems he knows how to speak to his contemporaries. Bashful or bold then, he will know how to make us seniors very unnecessary.

The nonchalance of boys who are sure of a dinner, and would disdain as much as a lord to do or say aught to conciliate one,[2] is the healthy attitude of human nature. A boy is in the parlor what the pit is in the playhouse;[3] independent, irresponsible, looking out from his corner on such people and facts as pass by; he tries and sentences them on their merits, in the swift, summary way of boys, as good, bad, interesting, silly, eloquent, troublesome. He cumbers himself never about consequences, about interests; he gives an independent, genuine verdict. You must court him; he does not court you. . . .

Society everywhere is in conspiracy against the manhood of every one of its

[1] ORACLES—Revelations; disclosures.

[2] DO OR SAY . . . CONCILIATE ONE—Do or say anything for the sake of winning approval.

[3] PIT . . . IN THE PLAYHOUSE—In the early days of theaters, the pit was the area where the common people stood to watch the play. They behaved just as they pleased, and would even interrupt the play to applaud or jeer at the actors.

members. Society is a joint stock company, in which the members agree, for the better securing of his bread to each shareholder, to surrender the liberty and culture of the eater. The virtue in most request is conformity. Self-reliance is its aversion.[4] It loves not realities and creators, but names and customs.

Whoso would be a man, must be a nonconformist. He who would gather immortal palms must not be hindered by the name of goodness, but must explore if it be goodness. Nothing is at last sacred but the integrity [5] of your own mind. . . . My friend suggested, "But these impulses may be from below, not from above." I replied, "They do not seem to me to be such; but if I am the Devil's child, I will live then from the Devil." No law can be sacred to me but that of my nature. . . . I shun father and mother and wife and brother when my genius calls me. I would write on the lintels of the doorpost, *Whim.* I hope it is somewhat better than whim at last, but we cannot spend the day in explanation. . . .

For nonconformity the world whips you with its displeasure. And therefore a man must know how to estimate a sour face. The bystanders look askance on him in the public street or in the friend's parlor. If this aversion had its origin in contempt and resistance like his own he might well go home with a sad countenance; but the sour faces of the multitude, like their sweet faces, have no deep cause, but are put on and off as the wind blows and a newspaper directs. . . .

The other terror that scares us from self-trust is our consistency; a reverence for our past act or word because the eyes of others have no other data for computing our orbit [6] than our past acts, and we are loath to disappoint them.

But why should you keep your head over your shoulder? Why drag about this corpse of your memory, lest you contradict somewhat you have stated in this or that public place? Suppose you should contradict yourself; what then? It seems to be a rule of wisdom never to rely on your memory alone, scarcely even in acts of pure memory, but to bring the past for judgment into the thousand-eyed present and live ever in a new day. . . .

A foolish consistency is the hobgoblin of little minds,[7] adored by little statesmen and philosophers and divines. With consistency a great soul has simply nothing to do. He may as well concern himself with his shadow on the wall. Speak what you think now in hard words and tomorrow speak what tomorrow thinks in hard words again, though it contradict everything you said today. "Ah, so you shall be sure to be misunderstood!"— Is it so bad then to be misunderstood? Pythagoras was misunderstood, and Socrates, and Jesus, and Luther, and Copernicus, and Galileo, and Newton,[8] and every pure and wise spirit that ever took flesh. To be great is to be misunderstood. . . .

Man is timid and apologetic; he is no longer upright; he dares not say "I think," "I am," but quotes some saint or sage. He is ashamed before the blade of grass or the blowing rose. These roses under my window make no reference to former roses or to better ones; they are for what they are; they exist with God today.

[6] COMPUTING OUR ORBIT—Predicting our future actions, as astronomers predict the paths of heavenly bodies.

[7] A FOOLISH CONSISTENCY . . . LITTLE MINDS—A hobgoblin is any imaginary goblin or bogy of which superstitious people are frightened. The sentence means that mediocre people are afraid of seeming inconsistent.

[8] PYTHAGORAS (pĭ·thăg′ô·răs) . . . NEWTON—All great men—philosophers, scientists, and moral leaders.

[4] AVERSION—Dislike. Society rejects self-reliance.

[5] INTEGRITY—Honesty; uprightness.

There is no time to them. There is simply the rose; it is perfect in every moment of its existence. Before a leaf bud has burst, its whole life acts; in the full-blown flower there is no more; in the leafless root there is no less. Its nature is satisfied and it satisfies nature in all moments alike. But man postpones or remembers; he does not live in the present, but with reverted eye laments the past, or, heedless of the riches that surround him, stands on tiptoe to foresee the future. He cannot be happy and strong until he too lives with nature in the present, above time. . . .

If our young men miscarry in their first enterprises they lose all heart. If the young merchant fails, men say he is *ruined.* If the finest genius studies at one of our colleges, and is not installed in an office within one year afterwards, in the cities or suburbs of Boston or New York, it seems to his friends and to himself that he is right in being disheartened and in complaining the rest of his life. A sturdy lad from New Hampshire or Vermont, who in turn tries all the professions, who teams it, farms it, peddles, keeps a school, preaches, edits a newspaper, goes to Congress, buys a township, and so forth, in successive years, and always like a cat falls on his feet, is worth a hundred of these city dolls. He walks abreast with his days and feels no shame in not "studying a profession," for he does not postpone his life, but lives already. He has not one chance, but a hundred chances. Let a Stoic [9] open the resources of man and tell men they are not leaning willows, but can and must detach themselves; that with the exercise of self-trust, new powers shall appear; that a man is the Word made flesh, born to shed healing to the nations; that he

should be ashamed of our compassion, and that the moment he acts from himself, tossing the books, idolatries, and customs out of the window, we pity him no more but thank and revere him; and that teacher shall restore the life of man to splendor and make his name dear to all history.

All men plume themselves on the improvement of society, and no man improves.

Society never advances. It recedes as fast on one side as it gains on the other. It undergoes continual changes, it is barbarous, it is civilized, it is christianized, it is rich, it is scientific; but this change is not amelioration.[10] For everything that is given something is taken. Society acquires new arts and loses old instincts. What a contrast between the well-clad, reading, writing, thinking American, with a watch, a pencil, and a bill of exchange in his pocket, and the naked New Zealander, whose property is a club, a spear, a mat, and an undivided twentieth of a shed to sleep under! But compare the health of the two men and you shall see that the white man has lost his aboriginal [11] strength. If the traveler tell us truly, strike the savage with a broadax and in a day or two the flesh shall unite and heal as if you struck the blow into soft pitch, and the same blow shall send the white to his grave.

The civilized man has built a coach, but has lost the use of his feet. He is supported on crutches, but lacks so much support of muscle. He has a fine Geneva watch, but he fails of the skill to tell the hour by the sun. A Greenwich nautical almanac he has, and so being sure of the information when he wants it, the man in the street does not know a star in the

---

[9] STOIC—One whose calm attitude is unswayed by good or bad fortune, like the Stoic philosophers of ancient Greece.

[10] AMELIORATION (à·mēl′yò·rā′shŭn)—Improvement; betterment.

[11] ABORIGINAL (ăb′ô·rĭj′ĭ·năl)—Primitive.

sky. The solstice [12] he does not observe; the equinox [13] he knows as little; and the whole bright calendar of the year is without a dial in his mind. His notebooks impair his memory: his libraries overload his wit; the insurance office increases the number of accidents. . . .

A political victory, a rise of rents, the recovery of your sick or the return of your absent friend, or some other favorable event raises your spirits, and you think good days are preparing for you. Do not believe it. It can never be so. Nothing can bring you peace but yourself. Nothing can bring you peace but the triumph of principles.

[12] SOLSTICE (sŏl′stĭs)—The time when the sun is farthest north or farthest south of the equator.

[13] EQUINOX—The time when the sun is directly over the equator and day and night are of equal length.

◇◇◇◇◇◇◇◇◇◇◇◇◇◇◇◇◇◇◇◇◇◇◇◇◇◇

FOR UNDERSTANDING: WHAT EMERSON BELIEVED

Six main topics in Emerson's many-sided essay on "Self-Reliance" are listed below. Your teacher may wish to assign certain ones of these for special study.

1. THE HIGH WORTH OF THE INDIVIDUAL

The opening paragraph of the essay shows one of the literary skills in which Emerson trained himself—the ability to compress a complex idea into a single phrase. In stressing the importance of the individual, he gives us two puzzling remarks to consider.

"*Envy is ignorance.*" To Emerson the most precious thing in the world is each man's individuality, the *self* that is unique in each of us. When we envy other people, what is it that we are *ignorant* of? In what direction should we turn our thoughts in order to overcome our envy of a person who has some ability we can never equal?

"*Imitation is suicide.*" What is wrong with trying to imitate the way other people

dress or talk, even if the imitation is successful? What would Emerson think of fashions in clothes? What do you think Emerson's advice would be on deciding what kind of clothes to wear?

2. BEING A NONCONFORMIST

What do you think is the main reason we are usually *conformists* instead of *nonconformists*? Give an imaginary example of a person standing up stoutly for what he believes is right, even though it is unpopular to do so.

America is founded on the idea of individual freedom—the idea that each person should think and act as he pleases, so long as he does not hamper the freedom of others. However, being *allowed* to be a free man is not enough. Emerson reminds us that freedom exists only when the individual *uses* his freedom. Give an example from history or from modern life of how a strong current of public opinion can sometimes overpower the individual's better judgment and make him fall in with the majority. Give a similar example from school life. Give an example of how public opinion sometimes seems to dictate *how we spend our money*—that is, makes us buy things to "keep up with the Joneses" instead of to supply our real wants.

The principle of nonconformity is easily misunderstood. People sometimes assume that it means you must take pains to be peculiar and different from others. Explain why acting in this way is really being ruled by others rather than by yourself. Explain how a true nonconformist will sometimes agree with other people and sometimes disagree with them.

3. THE FEAR OF INCONSISTENCY

Emerson seems to think that the wise man will change his mind when there is good reason to do so. According to Emerson, what is the main reason we are afraid to be inconsistent with our past actions? Give an example of a situation in which it would be very foolish not to change your former opinion.

Explain this sentence: "But why should you keep your head over your shoulder?"

4. THE FEAR OF "FAILING" IN LIFE

Reread the paragraph beginning "If our young men miscarry in their first enterprises. . . ." What does Emerson think about saying a man is *ruined* when he has lost all his money? Give several reasons why he is *not* ruined. Which reason do you think Emerson would call the most important one?

The "sturdy lad from New Hampshire or Vermont" will probably never be unable to support himself, but he probably will never become rich either. Why does Emerson think him more self-reliant than the "city dolls"? What does Emerson mean by saying that the sturdy lad "does not postpone his life, but lives already"?

Reread the last paragraph in the selection. What is Emerson's final criticism of "success in life" as we ordinarily measure success? Describe a real person or one in literature who has not become rich or risen high in any profession, but who in your opinion has attained true success and happiness. Thinking of your own strongest desires as they now appear to you, explain what sort of life would bring you true happiness—regardless of whether you were prosperous.

5. THE RELIGIOUS BASIS OF SELF-RELIANCE

Basically, Emerson's trust in the Self is trust in God, for he believes that man's inner nature is divine. Of course he does not mean that all our notions and impulses are sacred. He means that the right answers to important questions can be found if one asks himself thoughtfully and sincerely, "Is this what I *really* want?" or "Is this what I *really* think is right?" Emerson's lifelong aim was to learn which of his impulses were the teachings of his inmost soul, and to be true to those teachings.

Reread the paragraph beginning, "Man is timid and apologetic." Explain why we might imagine that *roses*, or other natural living things, illustrate what it means to live

in perfect accordance with God's will. Describe what it would be like for a human being to apply the following principles to his own life: (*a*) "These roses . . . make no reference to former roses or to better ones" (*b*) "They are for what they are; they exist with God today."

Reread Emerson's remarks about *whim*. What does the word mean? What does Emerson mean by "somewhat better than whim at last"? If Emerson acted in a way that his friends thought was odd, why would he not try to justify his actions to them?

It is easier to see why Emerson places little importance on worldly satisfactions when we realize that to him *self-reliance* is *religious happiness*. Quote one or more Bible texts which teach, as Emerson does, that "Nothing can bring you peace but yourself. Nothing can bring you peace but the triumph of principles."

6. THE LAW OF "COMPENSATION"

One of Emerson's most famous ideas is that of "compensation," or "action and reaction." It is his idea that in our physical, outer life we never gain an advantage without a corresponding disadvantage. This thought plays a part in the essay on "Self-Reliance" because Emerson wished to show that *human progress* cannot increase human happiness any more than prosperity or fame can.

Reread Emerson's explanation of why "society never advances." Perhaps his illustration is inaccurate. What kinds of ill health might the savage suffer that the civilized man escapes? On the other hand, what evidence might Emerson give that many people in civilized life are unhappy and maladjusted? What disadvantages have been brought about by our modern, comfortable city life?

What are the *disadvantages* of being a great athlete? an extremely rich man? If you cheated someone and were not found out, what disadvantage would you suffer even though you might not realize it? What *advantages* can come from suffering a great disappointment? from having to work for what you get?

FOR FURTHER INVESTIGATION OF EMERSON'S "LAW OF COMPENSATION"

For a special report to the class, read Emerson's essay "Compensation," or selected passages as assigned by your teacher. In giving your report, quote two or three of the most striking sentences, and explain them. Explain the main idea of the selection, and then read aloud one passage which expresses this idea particularly well.

SELF-RELIANCE IN DAILY LIFE

Smart-aleck, know-it-all attitudes are not self-reliance. It would be absurd for a young man learning the carpenter's trade to insist that his own judgment was as reliable as that of experienced men. His immediate job is to learn all he can under the guidance of others—working toward the time when he knows what he is doing and can be self-reliant.

However, everyone can be self-reliant among his *equals*—although it takes courage and intelligence. Young people sometimes find it painful to examine themselves through Emerson's eyes. Like adults, they are inclined to let "the crowd" make decisions for them.

1. Does Emerson seem to approve of young children being self-assertive and independent on the playground? Do you think it is natural for a healthy child to conduct himself in this way? Explain what a child should learn about the *limits* to such conduct.

2. Emerson would probably look with amusement and pity at high-school students who are concerned about belonging to "cliques" or "gangs." Describe a situation in which such a group actually restricts the individuality of its members—dictating their actions, their choice of amusement, or their way of dressing.

3. Describe an opposite situation in which a group *helps* in the development of an individual by providing an opportunity for him to pursue one of his real interests.

4. A "fad" or "craze" sometimes sweeps over a school like a miniature mass movement. Give one example of such a movement, and explain how an individual student who takes part in it is lacking in self-reliance.

5. The desire for the approval of our fellows is so strong that sometimes we substitute *what is popular* for *what we really want* without even realizing that we are doing so. Name some personal interests or hobbies which a student in your school would be *encouraged* to follow because he would receive the admiration of most of the students. Then name some others, equally worth while, which would get *almost no encouragement* from the attitude of most students.

◇◇◇◇◇

THOREAU

Emerson much admired one of his fellow-citizens of Concord, the brilliant young Henry Thoreau. The two were close friends for twenty-four years, until Thoreau's death in 1862. In a sense Thoreau LIVED what Emerson PREACHED. What such a life was like may be learned from the following essay. Emerson read it as a memorial address at Thoreau's funeral, and it was later printed in the ATLANTIC MONTHLY.

It is notable that the tone of this memorial speech is not sorrowful, as one might expect it to be. Instead, it shows Emerson's delight in his memories of one of the most remarkably original minds America has ever known.

Henry David Thoreau was the last male descendant of a French ancestor who came to this country from the Isle of Guernsey. His character exhibited occasional traits drawn from this blood, in singular combination with a very strong Saxon genius.

He was born in Concord, Massachusetts, on the 12th of July, 1817. He was graduated at Harvard College in 1837, but without any literary distinction. An iconoclast[1] in literature, he seldom thanked colleges for their service to him, holding them in small esteem, whilst yet his debt to them was important. After leaving the University, he joined his brother in teaching a private school, which he soon renounced. His father was a manufacturer of lead pencils, and Henry applied himself for a time to this craft, believing he could make a better pencil than was then in use. After completing his experiments, he exhibited his work to chemists and artists in Boston, and having obtained their certificates to its excellence and to its equality with the best London manufacture, he returned home contented. His friends congratulated him that he had now opened his way to fortune. But he replied, that he should never make another pencil. "Why should I? I would not do again what I have done once." He resumed his endless walks and miscellaneous studies, making every day some new acquaintance with Nature, though as yet never speaking of zoology or botany, since, though very studious of natural facts, he was incurious of technical and textural science. . . .

He was bred to no profession; he never married; he lived alone; he never went to church; he never voted; he refused to pay a tax to the State; he ate no flesh, he drank no wine, he never knew the use of tobacco; and, though a naturalist, he used neither trap nor gun. He chose, wisely no doubt for himself, to be the bachelor of thought and nature. He had no talent for wealth and knew how to be poor without the least hint of squalor or inelegance. Perhaps he fell into his way of living without forecasting it much, but approved it with later wisdom. "I am often reminded," he wrote in his journal, "that if I had bestowed on me the wealth of Croesus,[2] my aims must be still the same, and my means essentially the same." He had no temptations to fight against—no appetites, no passions, no taste for elegant trifles. A fine house, dress, the manners and talk of highly cultivated people were all thrown away on him. He much preferred a good Indian, and considered these refinements as impediments to conversation, wishing to meet his companion on the simplest terms. He declined invitations to dinner parties, because there each was in every one's way, and he could not meet the in-

[1] ICONOCLAST—A breaker of sacred images. Emerson uses the word to show that Thoreau did not follow blindly the "sacred" traditions of literature.

[2] CROESUS (krē′sŭs)—A king of the ancient country of Lydia who was famous for his immense wealth.

dividuals to any purpose. "They make their pride," he said, "in making their dinner cost much; I make my pride in making my dinner cost little." When asked at table what dish he preferred, he answered, "The nearest." He did not like the taste of wine, and never had a vice in his life. He said—"I have a faint recollection of pleasure derived from smoking dried lily stems, before I was a man. I had commonly a supply of these. I have never smoked anything more noxious."

He chose to be rich by making his wants few and supplying them himself. In his travels, he used the railroad only to get over so much country as was unimportant to the present purpose, walking hundreds of miles, avoiding taverns, buying a lodging in farmers' and fishermen's houses, as cheaper, and more agreeable to him, and because there he could better find the men and the information he wanted.

There was somewhat military in his nature, not to be subdued, always manly and able, but rarely tender, as if he did not feel himself except in opposition. He wanted a fallacy[3] to expose, a blunder to pillory,[4] I may say required a little sense of victory, a roll of the drum, to call his powers into full exercise. It cost him nothing to say No; indeed he found it much easier than to say Yes. It seemed as if his first instinct on hearing a proposition was to controvert[5] it, so impatient was he of the limitations of our daily thought. This habit, of course, is a little chilling to the social affections; and

³ FALLACY—A mistaken or false idea.
⁴ PILLORY—A device for punishing wrongdoers. Here it is used figuratively to mean to hold up to public ridicule.
⁵ CONTROVERT—To contradict or oppose by reasoning.

though the companion would in the end acquit him of any malice or untruth, yet it mars conversation. Hence, no equal companion stood in affectionate relations with one so pure and guileless. "I love Henry," said one of his friends, "but I cannot like him; and as for taking his arm, I should as soon think of taking the arm of an elm tree.". . .

He was a speaker and actor of the truth, born such, and was ever running into dramatic situations from this cause. In any circumstance it interested all by-standers to know what part Henry would take, and what he would say; and he did not disappoint expectation, but used an original judgment on each emergency. In 1845 he built himself a small framed house on the shores of Walden Pond and lived there two years alone, a life of labor and study. This action was quite native and fit for him. No one who knew him would tax him with affectation. He was more unlike his neighbors in his thought than in his action. As soon as he had exhausted the advantages of that solitude, he abandoned it. In 1847, not approving some uses to which the public expenditure was applied, he refused to pay his town tax and was put in jail. A friend paid the tax for him, and he was released. The like annoyance was threatened the next year. But, as his friends paid the tax, notwithstanding his protest, I believe he ceased to resist. No opposition or ridicule had any weight with him. . . .

He noted what repeatedly befell him that, after receiving from a distance a rare plant, he would presently find the same in his own haunts. And those pieces of luck which happen only to good players happened to him. One day, walking with a stranger, who inquired where Indian arrowheads could be found, he replied, "Everywhere," and, stooping for-ward, picked one on the instant from the ground. . . .

It was a pleasure and a privilege to walk with him. He knew the country like a fox or a bird and passed through it as freely by paths of his own. He knew every track in the snow or on the ground, and what creature had taken this path before him. One must submit abjectly [6] to such a guide, and the reward was great. Under his arm he carried an old music book to press plants; in his pocket, his diary and pencil, a spy glass for birds, microscope, jackknife, and twine. He wore a straw hat, stout shoes, strong gray trousers, to brave scrub oaks and smilax, and to climb a tree for a hawk's or a squirrel's nest. He waded into the pool for the water plants, and his strong legs were no insignificant part of his armor. . . . He thought that, if waked up from a trance, in this swamp, he could tell by the plants what time of the year it was within two days. . . .

No college ever offered him a diploma or a professor's chair; no academy made him its corresponding secretary, its dis-coverer, or even its member. Perhaps these learned bodies feared the satire of his presence. Yet so much knowledge of Nature's secret and genius few others possessed; none in a more large and re-ligious synthesis. For not a particle of respect had he to the opinions of any man or body of men, but homage solely to the truth itself; and as he discovered everywhere among doctors some leaning of courtesy, it discredited them. He grew to be revered and admired by his townsmen, who had at first known him only as an oddity. The farmers who em-ployed him as a surveyor soon discovered his rare accuracy and skill, his knowledge of their lands, of trees, of birds, of In-dian remains and the like, which enabled

[6] ABJECTLY—Humbly.

him to tell every farmer more than he knew before of his own farm; so that he began to feel a little as if Mr. Thoreau had better rights in his land than he. They felt, too, the superiority of character which addressed all men with a native authority.

Indian relics abound in Concord—arrowheads, stone chisels, pestles, and fragments of pottery; and on the riverbank, large heaps of clam shells and ashes mark spots which the savages frequented. These, and every circumstance touching the Indian, were important in his eyes. His visits to Maine were chiefly for love of the Indian. He had the satisfaction of seeing the manufacture of the bark canoe, as well as of trying his hand in its management on the rapids. He was inquisitive about the making of the stone arrowhead, and in his last days charged a youth setting out for the Rocky Mountains to find an Indian who could tell him that: "It was well worth a visit to California to learn it." Occasionally, a small party of Penobscot Indians would visit Concord and pitch their tents for a few weeks in summer on the riverbank. He failed not to make acquaintance with the best of them; though he well knew that asking questions of Indians is like catechizing beavers and rabbits. In his last visit to Maine he had great satisfaction from Joseph Polis, an intelligent Indian of Oldtown, who was his guide for some weeks. . . .

I subjoin a few sentences taken from his unpublished manuscripts, not only as records of his thought and feeling, but for their power of description and literary excellence—

"The chub is a soft fish, and tastes like boiled brown paper salted."

"The youth gets together his materials to build a bridge to the moon, or, perchance, a palace or temple on the earth,

and, at length the middle-aged man concludes to build a woodshed with them."

"The locust z-ing.". . .

"Sugar is not so sweet to the palate as sound to the healthy ear."

"I put on some hemlock boughs, and the rich salt crackling of their leaves was like mustard to the ear, the crackling of uncountable regiments. Dead trees love the fire."

"The bluebird carries the sky on his back."

"The tanager flies through the green foliage as if it would ignite the leaves."

"Fire is the most tolerable third party."

"Nature made ferns for pure leaves, to show what she could do in that line."

<><><><><><><><><><><><><><><><><><><><><>

FOR UNDERSTANDING

1. Give two facts about Thoreau which show how completely at home he was in the fields and woods.

2. What was Thoreau's reason for deciding to stop manufacturing lead pencils just when he could have become prosperous?

3. Emerson says Thoreau "chose to be rich by making his wants few." Explain how this is being "rich."

4. The things Thoreau wanted above all else were *leisure* to read, write, and think; and the *opportunity to study and enjoy nature.* Explain how he was able to provide for each of these.

5. Judging from the essay "Self-Reliance," what characteristics of Thoreau would Emerson particularly admire? For each one you name, give an example of an *action* by Thoreau which shows he actually had this characteristic.

6. Discuss whether there was anything in Thoreau's life which illustrates the ideas stated in Emerson's "The American Scholar."

7. Which of Thoreau's sentences quoted by Emerson seem to you most striking or original?

HENRY DAVID THOREAU (1817-1862)

Little need be added to Emerson's account of Thoreau except some facts about his writings. When Thoreau graduated from Harvard and came home to Concord, Emerson was already an established writer. Publishers and readers automatically thought of Thoreau as a mere follower of Emerson, and took little interest in his work. Through the older man's influence, many of Thoreau's earliest essays and poems were printed in *The Dial*—but *The Dial* was not a large, popular magazine and could not pay its contributors. In 1849 Thoreau published his first book, *A Week on the Concord and Merrimac Rivers*, describing a trip he had taken with his brother in a small boat. But the *Week* was not well received. Out of 1000 copies, 706 were eventually returned to Thoreau, who had paid for the printing himself. With characteristic tart humor he wrote, "I have now a library of nearly nine hundred volumes, over seven hundred of which I wrote myself. Is it not well that the author should behold the fruits of his labor?"

Walden, or Life in the Woods, is one of the masterpieces of all literature, but like Thoreau's first book it was slow to find readers. Of his remaining works, the best known are two essays, "Civil Disobedience" and "A Plea for Captain John Brown." In both of them Thoreau upholds the rather drastic idea that it is right to defy the government when the laws are unjust. This was a principle that Thoreau himself practiced when, because of his disapproval of the Mexican War, he refused to pay his poll tax and spent a night in the Concord jail. He was forced to leave next morning because, as he said, a relative "interfered, and paid that tax." Thoreau died of tuberculosis before he had made any progress on his third book beyond taking a few notes. It was to have been about the American Indians—a subject that had always fascinated him.

Each generation since Thoreau's death has prized his *Walden* more and more highly. As his reputation grew, there was increased interest in the private journal he had kept. The entire journal was published in fourteen volumes in 1906.

⬥⬥⬥⬥⬥

WALDEN

Thoreau's most valued writings are reports of personal experience. He left it to Emerson to EXPLAIN *Transcendentalist ideas, and to support them by examples from history or from the great books of all ages. Thoreau wrote mainly about what he saw right around him in Concord. He wanted to* REPORT WHAT IT IS LIKE *to try leading a free, natural life.*

It is in this spirit that WALDEN *is written. For two years Thoreau lived in a small hut on the shore of Walden Pond. He supplied his few necessities very easily by raising a garden and by working at odd jobs in the neighborhood. He had almost endless leisure to do what he wished—to read, to write, and to spend hours on the lake or in the woods.* WALDEN *tells the story of a man who "retired" without bothering to spend his whole life earning money to retire on.*

During these two years Thoreau was not a hermit, as some people have supposed. He walked to the village nearly every day, called on his friends, and received callers at his home in the woods. His book is full of the people, as well as the natural sights and sounds, of Concord Township—farmers, hunters, woodchoppers. WALDEN *is a refreshing and original book because Thoreau did an unusual thing. He* SAW *in all its details the world that lay near at hand. Both he and his readers find it a fascinating world.*

ECONOMY

When I wrote the following passages, or rather the bulk of them, I lived alone in the woods, a mile from any neighbor, in a house which I had built myself, on the shore of Walden Pond in Concord, Massachusetts, and earned my living by the labor of my hands only. I lived there two years and two months.

I see young men, my townsmen, whose misfortune it is to have inherited farms, houses, barns, cattle, and farming tools; for these are more easily acquired than got rid of. Better if they had been born in the open pasture and suckled by a wolf, that they might have seen with clearer eyes what field they were called to labor in. Who made them serfs of the soil? Why should they eat their sixty acres, when man is condemned to eat only his peck of dirt?

One farmer says to me, "You cannot live on vegetable food solely, for it furnishes nothing to make bones with"; and so he religiously devotes a part of his day to supplying his system with the raw material of bones, walking all the while he talks behind his oxen, which, with vegetable-made bones, jerk him and his lumbering plough along in spite of every obstacle.

Most of the luxuries, and many of the so-called comforts, of life are not only not indispensable, but positive hindrances to the elevation of mankind. With respect to luxuries and comforts, the wisest have ever lived a more simple and meager life than the poor. The ancient philosophers, Chinese, Hindu, Persian, and Greek, were a class than which none has been poorer in outward riches, none so rich in inward.

When a man is warmed . . . what does he want next? Surely not more warmth of the same kind, as more and richer food, larger and more splendid houses, finer and more abundant clothing, more numerous, incessant, and hot-

ter fires, and the like. When he has obtained those things which are necessary to life, there is another alternative than to obtain the superfluities; and that is, to adventure on life now, his vacation from humbler toil having commenced.

As for Clothing, to come at once to the practical part of the question, perhaps we are led oftener by the love of novelty, and to regard for the opinions of men, in procuring it, than by a true utility. . . . I sometimes try my acquaintances by such tests as this—who could wear a patch, or two extra seams only, over the knee? Most behave as if they believed that their prospects for life would be ruined if they should do it. It would be easier for them to hobble to town with a broken leg than with a broken pantaloon. . . .

When I ask for a garment of a particular form, my tailoress tells me gravely, "They do not make them so now," not emphasizing the "They" at all, as if she quoted an authority as impersonal as the Fates, and I find it difficult to get made what I want. . . . I am inclined to answer her with equal mystery, and without any more emphasis of the "they,"— "It is true, they did not make them so recently, but they do now."

As for a Shelter, I will not deny that this is now a necessary of life, though there are instances of men having done without it for long periods in colder countries than this. . . .

However, if one designs to construct a dwelling house, it behooves him to exercise a little Yankee shrewdness, lest after all he find himself in a workhouse, a labyrinth [1] without a clue, a museum, an

[1] LABYRINTH (lăb'ĭ·rĭnth)—A structure with so many winding passages that it is almost impossible to find your way out of it.

almshouse, a prison, or a splendid mausoleum [2] instead.

The farmer is endeavoring to solve the problem of a livelihood by a formula more complicated than the problem itself. To get his shoestrings he speculates in herds of cattle. . . .

And when the farmer has got his house, he may not be the richer but the poorer for it, and it be the house that has got him.

Near the end of March, 1845, I borrowed an ax and went down to the woods by Walden Pond, nearest to where I intended to build my house, and began to cut down some tall arrowy white pines, still in their youth, for timber. . . . The owner of the ax, as he released his hold on it, said that it was the apple of his eye; [3] but I returned it sharper than I received it.

I intend to build me a house which will surpass any on the main street in Concord in grandeur and luxury, as soon as it pleases me as much and will cost me no more than my present one.

One says to me, "I wonder that you do not lay up money; you love to travel; you might take the cars and go to Fitchburg today and see the country." But I am wiser than that. I have learned that the swiftest traveler is he that goes afoot. I say to my friend, "Suppose we try who will get there first. The distance is thirty miles; the fare ninety cents. That is almost a day's wages. I remember when wages were sixty cents a day for laborers on this very road. Well, I start now on

[2] MAUSOLEUM (mô′sô·lē′ŭm)—A large, magnificent tomb. The word is used humorously to refer to any massive, gloomy house or structure.

[3] SAID THAT IT WAS THE APPLE OF HIS EYE—The lender of the ax praised it highly, as a hint that he was afraid Thoreau might harm it.

foot and get there before night; I have traveled at that rate by the week together. You will in the meanwhile have earned your fare and arrive there sometime to-morrow, or possibly this evening, if you are lucky enough to get a job in season. Instead of going to Fitchburg, you will be working here the greater part of the day. And so, if the railroad reached round the world, I think that I should keep ahead of you; and as for seeing the country and getting experience of that kind, I should have to cut your acquaintance altogether."

My food alone cost me in money about twenty-seven cents a week. It was, for nearly two years after this, rye and Indian meal without yeast, potatoes, rice, a very little salt pork, molasses, and salt, and my drink, water. . . .

Bread I at first made of pure Indian meal and salt, genuine hoecakes, which I baked before my fire out of doors on a shingle or the end of a stick of timber sawed off in building my house; but it was wont to get smoked and to have a piny flavor. I tried flour also; but have at last found a mixture of rye and Indian meal most convenient and agreeable. In cold weather it was no little amusement to bake several small loaves of this in succession, tending and turning them. . . .

For more than five years I maintained myself thus solely by the labor of my hands, and I found that by working about six weeks in a year, I could meet all the expenses of living. The whole of my winters, as well as most of my summers I had free and clear for study. . . .

In short, I am convinced, both by faith and experience, that to maintain one's self on this earth is not a hardship but a pastime, if we will live simply and wisely. . . . It is not necessary that a man should earn his living by the sweat of his brow, unless he sweats easier than I do.

One young man of my acquaintance, who has inherited some acres, told me that he thought he should live as I did, *if he had the means.* I would not have anyone adopt *my* mode of living on any account; for, besides that before he has fairly learned it I may have found out another for myself, I desire that there may be as many different persons in the world as possible; but I would have each one be very careful to find out and pursue *his own* way, and not his father's or his mother's or his neighbor's instead. The youth may build or plant or sail, only let him not be hindered from doing that which he tells me he would like to do.

WHERE I LIVED, AND WHAT I LIVED FOR

When first I took up my abode in the woods, that is, began to spend my nights as well as days there, which, by accident, was on Independence Day, or the Fourth of July, 1845, my house was not finished for winter, but was merely a defense against the rain, without plastering or chimney, the walls being of rough, weather-stained boards, with wide chinks, which made it cool at night. The upright white hewn studs and freshly planed door and window casings gave it a clean and airy look, especially in the morning, when its timbers were saturated with dew, so that I fancied that by noon some sweet gum would exude from them. To my imagination it retained throughout the day more or less of this auroral [4] character, reminding me of a certain house on a mountain which I had visited a year before. This was an airy and unplastered cabin, fit to entertain a travel-

[4] AURORAL (ô·rō′răl)—Fresh, morning-like. The word comes from Aurora, goddess of dawn.

ing god, and where a goddess might trail her garments. . . .

The only house I had been the owner of before, if I except a boat, was a tent, which I used occasionally when making excursions in the summer, and this is still rolled up in my garret; but the boat, after passing from hand to hand, has gone down the stream of time. With this more substantial shelter about me, I had made some progress toward settling in the world. This frame, so slightly clad, was a sort of crystallization around me, and reacted on the builder. It was suggestive somewhat as a picture in outlines. I did not need to go outdoors to take the air, for the atmosphere within had lost none of its freshness. It was not so much within doors as behind a door where I sat, even in the rainiest weather. . . .

Every morning was a cheerful invitation to make my life of equal simplicity, and I may say innocence, with Nature herself. I have been as sincere a worshiper of Aurora as the Greeks. I got up early and bathed in the pond; that was a religious exercise, and one of the best things which I did. . . . Morning brings back the heroic ages. . . . All memorable events, I should say, transpire in morning time and in a morning atmosphere. . . . It matters not what the clocks say or the attitudes and labors of men. Morning is when I am awake and there is a dawn in me. Moral reform [5] is the effort to throw off sleep. . . . The millions are awake enough for physical labor; but only one in a million is awake enough for effective intellectual exertion, only one in a hundred millions to a poetic or divine life. To be awake is to be alive. I have never yet met a man who was quite awake. How could I have looked him in the face? . . .

[5] MORAL REFORM—That is, all efforts to improve one's mind or live more nobly.

I went to the woods because I wished to live deliberately, to front only the essential facts of life, and see if I could not learn what it had to teach, and not, when I came to die, discover that I had not lived. . . . I wanted to live deep and suck out all the marrow of life, to live so sturdily and Spartanlike [6] as to put to rout all that was not life, to cut a broad swath and shave close, to drive life into a corner, and reduce it to its lowest terms, and, if it proved to be mean, why then to get the whole and genuine meanness of it. . . .

BRUTE NEIGHBORS

One day when I went out to my woodpile, or rather my pile of stumps, I observed two large ants, the one red, the other much larger, nearly half an inch long, and black, fiercely contending with one another. Having once got hold they never let go, but struggled and wrestled and rolled on the chips incessantly. Looking farther, I was surprised to find that the chips were covered with such combatants, that it was not a *duellum*, but a *bellum*, [7] a war between two races of ants, the red always pitted against the black, and frequently two red ones to one black. The legions of these Myrmidons [8] covered all the hills and vales in my woodyard, and the ground was already strewn with the dead and dying, both red and black. It was the only battle which I have ever witnessed, the only battlefield I ever trod while the battle was

[6] SPARTANLIKE—Thoreau wishes to imitate the frugal, disciplined lives led by the citizens of the ancient Greek city-state of Sparta. These people were famous for their great courage and powers of endurance.

[7] NOT A *duellum*, BUT *a bellum*—Not a duel between two individuals only, but a war.

[8] MYRMIDONS (mŭr′mĭ·dŏnz)—Warriors from Thessaly who served under Achilles in the Trojan War.

raging; internecine war; [9] the red republicans on the one hand, and the black imperialists on the other. On every side they were engaged in deadly combat, yet without any noise that I could hear, and human soldiers never fought so resolutely. I watched a couple that were fast locked in each other's embraces, in a little sunny valley amid the chips, now at noonday prepared to fight till the sun went down, or life went out. The smaller red champion had fastened himself like a vise to his adversary's front, and through all the tumblings on that field never for an instant ceased to gnaw at one of his feelers near the root, having already caused the other to go by the board; while the stronger black one dashed him from side to side, and, as I saw on looking nearer, had already divested him of several of his members.[10] They fought with more pertinacity than bulldogs. Neither manifested the least disposition to retreat. It was evident that their battle cry was "Conquer or die." In the meanwhile there came along a single red ant on the hillside of this valley, evidently full of excitement, who either had dispatched his foe, or had not yet taken part in the battle; probably the latter, for he had lost none of his limbs; whose mother had charged him to return with his shield or upon it.[11] Or perchance he was some Achilles, who had nourished his wrath apart, and had now come to avenge or rescue his Patroclus.[12] He saw this unequal combat from afar—for the blacks were nearly twice the size of the red—he drew near with rapid pace till he stood on his guard within half an inch of the combatants; then, watching his opportunity, he sprang upon the black warrior and commenced his operations near the root of his right foreleg, leaving the foe to select among his own members; and so there were three united for life, as if a new kind of attraction had been invented which put all other locks and cements to shame. I should not have wondered by this time to find that they had their respective musical bands stationed on some eminent chip, and playing their national airs the while, to excite the slow and cheer the dying combatants. I was myself excited somewhat even as if they had been men. The more you think of it, the less the difference. And certainly there is not the fight recorded in Concord history at least, if in the history of America, that will bear a moment's comparison with this, whether for the numbers engaged in it, or for the patriotism and heroism displayed. . . . I have no doubt that it was a principle they fought for, as much as our ancestors, and not to avoid a three-penny tax on their tea; and the results of this battle will be as important and memorable to those whom it concerns as those of the battle of Bunker Hill, at least.

I took up the chip on which the three I have particularly described were struggling, carried it into my house, and placed it under a tumbler on my window sill, in order to see the issue. Holding a micro-

[9] INTERNECINE (ĭn′tẽr·nē′sĭn) WAR—Deadly, destructive to both sides involved in the fighting.

[10] DIVESTED HIM OF SEVERAL OF HIS MEMBERS—The black ant had destroyed several parts of the red ant's body, such as his limbs and feelers.

[11] WHOSE MOTHER HAD CHARGED HIM TO RETURN WITH HIS SHIELD OR UPON IT—The expression means to return victorious, or be slain. According to legend, mothers in ancient Sparta gave this parting word to their sons before a battle.

[12] ACHILLES (á·kĭl′ēz) . . . PATROCLUS (pá-trō′klŭs)—Achilles, the hero of Homer's *Iliad*, was a leader of the Greeks in the Trojan War. Angered by an insult from his commander, he sulked in his tent and refused to fight. When Patroclus, his best friend, was killed in battle, Achilles returned to the combat to avenge his death.

scope to the first-mentioned red ant, I saw that, though he was assiduously gnawing at the near foreleg of his enemy, having severed his remaining feeler, his own breast was all torn away, exposing what vitals he had there to the jaws of the black warrior, whose breastplate was apparently too thick for him to pierce; and the dark carbuncles [13] of the sufferer's eyes shone with ferocity such as war only could excite. They struggled half an hour longer under the tumbler, and when I looked again the black soldier had severed the heads of his foes from their bodies, and the still living heads were hanging on either side of him like ghastly trophies at his saddle bow, still apparently as firmly fastened as ever, and he was endeavoring with feeble struggles, being without feelers and with only the remnant of a leg, and I know not how many other wounds, to divest himself of them; which at length, after half an hour more, he accomplished. I raised the glass, and he went off over the window sill in that crippled state. Whether he finally survived that combat, and spent the remainder of his days in some Hôtel des Invalides,[14] I do not know; but I thought that his industry would not be worth much thereafter. I never learned which party was victorious, nor the cause of the war; but I felt for the rest of that day as if I had had my feelings excited and harrowed by witnessing the struggle, the ferocity and carnage, of a human battle before my door. . . .

THE POND IN WINTER

. . . Then to my morning work. First I take an ax and pail and go in search of water, if that be not a dream. After a cold and snowy night it needed a divining rod to find it. Every winter the liquid and trembling surface of the pond, which was so sensitive to every breath and reflected every light and shadow, becomes solid to the depth of a foot or a foot and a half, so that it will support the heaviest teams, and perchance the snow covers it to an equal depth, and it is not to be distinguished from any level field. Like the marmots [15] in the surrounding hills, it closes its eyelids and becomes dormant for three months or more. Standing on the snow-covered plain, as if in a pasture amid the hills, I cut my way first through a foot of snow, and then a foot of ice, and open a window under my feet, where, kneeling to drink, I look down into the quiet parlor of the fishes, pervaded by a softened light as through a window of ground glass, with its bright sanded floor the same as in summer; there a perennial waveless serenity reigns as in the amber twilight sky, corresponding to the cool and even temperament of the inhabitants. Heaven is under our feet as well as over our heads.

Early in the morning, while all things are crisp with frost, men come with fishing reels and slender lunch, and let down their fine lines through the snowy field to take pickerel and perch; wild men, who instinctively follow other fashions and trust other authorities than their townsmen, and by their goings and comings stitch towns together in parts where else they would be ripped. They sit and eat their luncheon in stout fearnoughts [16] on the dry oak leaves on the shore, as wise in natural lore as the citizen is in artificial. They never consulted with

[13] CARBUNCLES—Red gems, such as rubies or garnets. Thoreau uses the word as a metaphor or comparison.

[14] HÔTEL DES INVALIDES (ô′tĕl′ dä-zăn′và′-lēd′)—A hospital in Paris for old or disabled soldiers.

[15] MARMOTS—A marmot is a type of rodent; a woodchuck or groundhog.

[16] FEARNOUGHTS—Coats of heavy woolen cloth.

books, and know and can tell much less than they have done. The things which they practice are said not yet to be known. Here is one fishing for pickerel with grown perch for bait. You look into his pail with wonder as into a summer pond, as if he kept summer locked up at home, or knew where she had retreated. How, pray, did he get these in midwinter? Oh, he got worms out of rotten logs since the ground froze, and so he caught them. His life itself passes deeper in nature than the studies of the naturalist penetrate; himself a subject for the naturalist. The latter raises the moss and bark gently with his knife in search of insects; the former lays open logs to their core with his ax, and moss and bark fly far and wide. He gets his living by barking trees. Such a man has some right to fish, and I love to see nature carried out in him. The perch swallows the grubworm, the pickerel swallows the perch, and the fisherman swallows the pickerel; and so all the chinks in the scale of being are filled. . . .

Ah, the pickerel of Walden! When I see them lying on the ice, or in the well which the fisherman cuts in the ice, making a little hole to admit the water, I am always surprised by their rare beauty, as if they were fabulous fishes; they are so foreign to the streets, even to the woods, foreign as Arabia to our Concord life.

They possess a quite dazzling and transcendent beauty which separates them by a wide interval from the cadaverous cod and haddock whose fame is trumpeted in our streets.[17] They are not green like the pines, nor gray like the stones, nor blue like the sky; but they have, to my eyes, if possible, yet rarer colors, like flowers and precious stones, as if they were the pearls, the animalized *nuclei* or crystals of the Walden water. They, of course, are Walden all over and all through; are themselves small Waldens in the animal kingdom, Waldenses. It is surprising that they are caught here—that in this deep and capacious spring, far beneath the rattling teams and chaises and tinkling sleighs that travel the Walden road, this great gold and emerald fish swims. I never chanced to see its kind in any market; it would be the cynosure of all eyes there. Easily, with a few convulsive quirks, they give up their watery ghosts, like a mortal translated before his time to the thin air of heaven. . . .

While yet it is cold January, and snow and ice are thick and solid, the prudent landlord comes from the village to get ice to cool his summer drink; impressively,

[17] THE CADAVEROUS COD AND HADDOCK . . . IN OUR STREETS—Cod and haddock were important products of New England, and were peddled in the streets of the towns. *Cadaverous* means that these fish are gaunt in appearance, like a corpse or cadaver.

even pathetically wise, to foresee the heat and thirst of July now in January—wearing a thick coat and mittens! when so many things are not provided for. It may be that he lays up no treasures in this world which will cool his summer drink in the next. He cuts and saws the solid pond, unroofs the house of fishes, and carts off their very element and air, held fast by chains and stakes like corded wood, through the favoring winter air, to wintry cellars, to underlie the summer there. It looks like solidified azure,[18] as, far off, it is drawn through the streets. . . .

Like the water, the Walden ice, seen near at hand, has a green tint but at a distance is beautifully blue, and you can easily tell it from the white ice of the river, or the merely greenish ice of some ponds, a quarter of a mile off. Sometimes one of those great cakes slips from the iceman's sled into the village street and lies there for a week like a great emerald, an object of interest to all passers. I have noticed that a portion of Walden which in the state of water was green will often, when frozen, appear from the same point of view blue. So the hollows about this pond will, sometimes, in the winter, be filled with a greenish water somewhat like its own, but the next day will have frozen blue. Perhaps the blue color of water and ice is due to the light and air they contain, and the most transparent is the bluest. . . .

CONCLUSION

I left the woods for as good a reason as I went there. Perhaps it seemed to me that I had several more lives to live and could not spare any more time for that one. It is remarkable how easily and insensibly we fall into a particular route

[18] SOLIDIFIED AZURE—Solidified pieces of blue sky.

and make a beaten track for ourselves. I had not lived there a week before my feet wore a path from my door to the pondside; and though it is five or six years since I trod it, it is still quite distinct. It is true, I fear, that others may have fallen into it, and so helped to keep it open. The surface of the earth is soft and impressible by the feet of men; and so with the paths which the mind travels. How worn and dusty, then, must be the highways of the world, how deep the ruts of tradition and conformity! I did not wish to take a cabin passage, but rather to go before the mast and on the deck of the world, for there I could best see the moonlight amid the mountains. I do not wish to go below now.

I learned this, at least, by my experiment: that if one advances confidently in the direction of his dreams and endeavors to live the life which he has imagined, he will meet with a success unexpected in common hours. He will put some things behind, will pass an invisible boundary; new, universal, and more liberal laws will begin to establish themselves around and within him; or the old laws be expanded and interpreted in his favor in a more liberal sense, and he will live with the license [19] of a higher order of beings. In proportion as he simplifies his life, the laws of the universe will appear less complex, and solitude will not be solitude, nor poverty poverty, nor weakness weakness. If you have built castles in the air, your work need not be lost; that is where they should be. Now put the foundations under them.

[19] LICENSE—Freedom.

◇◇◇◇◇◇◇◇◇◇◇◇◇◇◇◇◇◇◇◇◇◇◇◇◇◇◇◇◇◇◇◇

FOR UNDERSTANDING

ECONOMY

1. After reading Thoreau's comments on *clothing, shelter,* and *food,* explain why he

found it very easy to obtain these three main necessities of life.

2. Explain what Thoreau meant by his reply to the tailoress who told him "they" had stopped making suits the way he wanted his suit made. How is his reply an illustration of Emerson's principle of self-reliance? Explain Thoreau's argument that he can get to Fitchburg more quickly on foot than by train.

3. Why does Thoreau wish to spend as little time as possible earning food, clothing, and shelter?

4. At the end of the selection from this chapter Thoreau says he does not recommend that everyone follow his particular way of living. Then what *does* he want everyone to do, in spite of all obstacles?

5. Like many writers of his day, Thoreau had a thorough knowledge of Greek and Roman mythology, and used many classical allusions in his writing. In his chapter on "Economy," Thoreau says one should be careful when he constructs a dwelling house, or he may find himself in "a *labyrinth* without a *clue.*" Nobody knows the original meaning of the word *labyrinth*, but according to Greek legend this was once the name of a strange building on the island of Crete, with many rooms and intricate passageways. The hero Theseus was compelled to enter the Labyrinth, but he escaped by following a thread which he had unwound from a *clew*, or ball, on his way in. Therefore *clew* means not only a ball of thread or yarn, but anything that helps to guide one in a perplexing situation. In this sense, it is spelled *clue.*

   a. Explain what Thoreau means by his remark. That is, how could the owner of a fine house find that he is lost in a labyrinth?

   b. Show the present-day use of the word *clue* by using it in a sentence about a puzzle or an unsolved crime.

WHERE I LIVED, AND WHAT I LIVED FOR

1. Thoreau makes clear that to him *morning* is something more than a certain time of day. Explain in your own words his definition of morning.

2. Why can he claim that unlike most other people he is experiencing only the *essential* facts of life? That is, what superfluous things in life are most of us concerned with, according to Thoreau?

BRUTE NEIGHBORS

1. Thoreau pretends that he thinks the battle of the ants was as important an event as the famous battles of the Revolutionary War. What are his reasons?

2. This selection is made amusing by Thoreau's talking about the ants in the same way we would talk about a human combat. Quote two phrases in which he does this.

3. Most of us have seen ants scurrying about on the ground, but few of us pay as close attention to them as Thoreau did. Mention two details in his description of the battle which reveal his close, thorough observation.

THE POND IN WINTER

1. Read aloud the description of the pickerel of Walden, and choose two phrases which seem to convey best the idea that these fish are strange and wonderful.

2. Name one or more strange things Thoreau brings out about the lake in winter —strange even though they are so familiar that we hardly notice them.

3. What does Thoreau admire about the "wild" men who come to do ice-fishing?

4. Quote a remark which shows that Thoreau is amused at people who cut the ice off Walden Pond and store it up for summer. What do you think his reasons are for considering this an absurd thing to do?

5. What does Thoreau find even in a chunk of ice that arouses his curiosity and interest?

CONCLUSION

1. Interpret the following figurative remark: "I did not wish to take a cabin pas-

sage, but rather to go before the mast and on the deck of the world."

2. Thoreau declares that if one "advances confidently in the direction of his dreams," he will meet with more success than he would have imagined possible. Give an imaginary example of a person who is prevented from doing what he most wants to do by obstacles which he falsely imagines cannot be overcome. Include an explanation of how he could have got what he wanted if he had been sufficiently willing to sacrifice other satisfactions.

THOREAU'S IDEAS AND EMERSON'S

1. A young man of good ability, just out of Harvard College, would be expected by his neighbors and perhaps by his own family to conform to expected standards—both in what he worked at and how he lived. In resisting the pressures of public opinion, Thoreau was an example of what Emerson meant by a *nonconformist*. List all the ways, great and small, in which he refused to conform.

2. Reread Thoreau's remarks on the mistaken notions people have about *shelter*. How are they in agreement with Emerson's statement that "Things are in the saddle, and ride mankind"?

THOREAU TODAY

People who enjoy reading Thoreau today do not praise him as an extremely wise man. They think of him as a rather brash, opinionated young fellow whose stout independence and delight in the outdoors are refreshing, like a clear, cold drink from a spring. Thoreau never married, and his kind of life could not be imitated by anyone with family responsibilities. On the other hand, he never invited other people to imitate *him*,

but to be equally persistent in getting what *they* wanted.

1. Discuss the ways in which a typical city family today could simplify its life so as to have better health, a more leisurely existence, and more money for savings and other really essential things.

2. Discuss the ways in which Americans today follow Thoreau to some extent in their appreciation and enjoyment of outdoor nature.

3. How does the complexity of life in the twentieth century make it difficult to apply Thoreau's ideas about *obtaining a place to live?* about *using mechanical means of transportation?*

ADDITIONAL READING FOR REPORTS

1. In *Walden*, read the account of the loon in the latter part of the chapter "Brute Neighbors." Notice particularly the pains Thoreau took to find out exactly how this bird acted when it was pursued.

2. In *Walden*, read what Thoreau says in "Visitors" about the Canadian woodchopper he met in the woods. What does Thoreau seem to admire about this man, and what does he find amusing about him?

3. Read the chapter entitled "Walden" in E. B. White's book, *One Man's Meat*. Here a brilliant present-day author writes humorously of a journey he made to the site of Thoreau's hut. Of particular interest is White's discussion of how the scenery of Concord has changed since Thoreau's time, and how much his short automobile trip cost him in comparison to how much it cost Thoreau to live there for several months.

4. Read Chapter 14, "Walden Pond," in Henry Seidel Canby's biography *Thoreau*. What did the people of Concord think of Thoreau and of his way of living by Walden Pond?

HERMAN MELVILLE (1819-1891)

Melville was born in New York City. Because of the early death of his father he had only a few years of school, but as a young man he read prodigiously in Shakespeare and in books by great thinkers of the past. First, however, he had a career as a sailor. It began when he shipped on a vessel bound for Liverpool. He was fascinated by the sea, and also repelled by the brutality of ship discipline. Next he went on a whaling voyage to the South Seas. At the Marquesas Islands, with a fellow sailor he deserted the ship and lived for a month among cannibal tribes. On an Australian ship he made his way to Tahiti, where again he saw something of the life of island natives. A whaling ship took him to Honolulu, and at last he came home as a seaman on an American man-of-war.

Now Melville's literary career began. In rapid succession he wrote two novels about adventures among the natives of the Pacific islands, and three about the conditions of life on board military ships and commercial vessels. One of his most popular books was *Typee*. It tells of the peaceful, happy existence of a runaway sailor among South Sea islanders—until he discovers that they intend to tattoo him like themselves, and suspects that they are planning to eat him. These early novels were very successful. The public supposed, rightly, that they were in part reports of the author's actual experiences.

In 1851 Melville published his sixth and most important book, *Moby Dick*. It is a story about a whaling voyage and about Captain Ahab's search for one particular whale—snow white in color, and known by the name Moby Dick. Years earlier, Ahab had had his leg bitten off by this whale, and he has made a vow of revenge. Melville succeeded in making his central character a great tragic figure. Into his long, detailed narrative he poured his knowledge of the sea, and the conclusions about Man and Nature that came to him from his reading. Melville was an admirer of the works of Nathaniel Hawthorne, whose friend he became; and in drawing his picture of the vengeful Ahab he probed into questions about good and evil somewhat as Hawthorne did.

But *Moby Dick* was not well received. Although a few people realized its worth, most readers disliked, or did not understand, the deeper thought of the book. Melville's later works—among them *Billy Budd*, about a sailor who is hanged for killing a cruel officer—were found equally strange and repelling. Melville wrote less and less, and died a forgotten author.

Then, over half a century after it first appeared, *Moby Dick* was rediscovered. Critics published new interpretations of the book and won new readers for it. Biographies of Melville were written. Today, much more attention is paid to him than in his lifetime. All his works are scrutinized for a fuller understanding of his thought—and *Moby Dick* is praised as one of the three greatest American novels.

◇◇◇◇◇

MOBY DICK

There are three main reasons for the fame of MOBY DICK. In the first place, it is A DRAMATIC TALE OF ADVENTURE. Second, its plot seems to symbolize THE PAST AND PRESENT HISTORY OF MANKIND. On board Captain Ahab's ship are men of all races of the world. The broad ocean across which the little vessel finds its way—with the White Whale hidden somewhere in its unknown depths—suggests the immensity of the universe, and man's precarious existence.

Third, the book is filled with LORE OF THE SEA AND OF OLD WHALE-HUNT-ING DAYS. We see the wild-looking seamen who come ashore for a day or two at Massachusetts ports like New Bedford and Nantucket, and then disappear again. We hear the lookout's cry, "There she blows!" and the shout of the oarsmen, "A dead whale or a stove boat!" We share their peril, and shudder at the giant strength of their prey. In the following passages from MOBY DICK notice how Melville paints in bold colors the strangest trade ever followed by men.

THE SPOUTER-INN

The narrator of the story is a sailor named Ishmael. (The name, which is from the Bible, signifies a wanderer or outcast.) He arrives in New Bedford just at nightfall. Where will he sleep? Perhaps he can get a bed at the queer-looking old sailors' hotel called "The Spouter-Inn"—

Upon entering the place I found a number of young seamen gathered about a table, examining by a dim light divers specimens of *skrimshander*.[1] I sought the landlord, and telling him I desired to be accommodated with a room, received for answer that his house was full—not a bed unoccupied. "But avast,"[2] he added, tapping his forehead, "you hain't no objections to sharing a harpooner's blanket, have ye? I s'pose you are goin' a whalin', so you'd better get used to that sort of thing."

I told him that I never liked to sleep two in a bed; that if I should ever do so, it would depend upon who the harpooner might be, and that if he (the landlord) really had no other place for me, and the harpooner was not decidedly objectionable, why rather than wander farther about a strange town on so bitter a night, I would put up with the half of any decent man's blanket.

"I thought so. All right; take a seat. Supper?—you want supper? Supper'll be ready directly."

I sat down on an old wooden settle, carved all over like a bench on the Battery.[3] At one end a ruminating tar[4] was still further adorning it with his jackknife, stooping over and diligently working away at the space between his legs. He was trying his hand at a ship under full sail, but he didn't make much headway, I thought.

At last some four or five of us were summoned to our meal in an adjoining room. It was cold as Iceland—no fire at all—the landlord said he couldn't afford it. Nothing but two dismal tallow candles, each in a winding sheet. We were fain to button up our monkey jackets, and hold to our lips cups of scalding tea with our half frozen fingers. But the fare was of the most substantial kind—not only meat and potatoes, but dumplings; good heavens! dumplings for supper! One young fellow in a green box coat, addressed himself to these dumplings in a most direful manner.

[1] *Skrimshander*—"Skrimshander" or "scrimshaw" is any piece of sailor's handicraft prepared during off-duty hours, such as carved pieces of shell, ivory, or whalebone.

[2] AVAST—"Stop," "wait."

[3] THE BATTERY—The lower tip of Manhattan Island. Battery Park, on the waterfront, is still a favorite place for watching New York harbor traffic. The name is from a "battery" or fort that stood there in Colonial times.

[4] A RUMINATING TAR—A tobacco-chewing sailor.

"My boy," said the landlord, "you'll have the nightmare to a dead sartainty."

"Landlord," I whispered, "that ain't the harpooner, is it?"

"Oh, no," said he, looking a sort of diabolically funny, "the harpooner is a dark-complexioned chap. He never eats dumplings, he don't—he eats nothing but steaks, and likes 'em rare."

"I'll wager he does," says I. "Where is that harpooner? Is he here?"

"He'll be here afore long," was the answer.

I could not help it, but I began to feel suspicious of this "dark-complexioned" harpooner. At any rate, I made up my mind that if it so turned out that we should sleep together, he must undress and get into bed before I did.

Supper over, the company went back to the barroom, when, knowing not what else to do with myself, I resolved to spend the rest of the evening as a looker on.

Presently a rioting noise was heard without. Starting up, the landlord cried, "That's the "Grampus'" crew. I seed her reported in the offing [5] this morning; a three years' voyage, and a full ship. Hurrah, boys; now we'll have the latest news from the Feegees." [6]

A tramping of sea boots was heard in the entry; the door was flung open, and in rolled a wild set of mariners enough. Enveloped in their shaggy watch coats, and with their heads muffled in woolen comforters, all bedarned and ragged, and their beards stiff with icicles, they seemed an eruption of bears from Labrador. They had just landed from their boat, and this was the first house they entered. No wonder, then, that they made a straight wake for the whale's mouth—the bar—where the wrinkled little old Jonah, there officiating, soon poured them out

[5] IN THE OFFING—A short distance off shore —that is, just arriving from a voyage.
[6] THE FEEGEES—The Fiji Islands, in the South Pacific Ocean.

brimmers all round. One complained of a bad cold in his head, upon which Jonah mixed him a pitchlike potion of gin and molasses, which he swore was a sovereign cure for all colds and catarrhs whatsoever, never mind of how long standing, or whether caught off the coast of Labrador, or on the weather side of an ice-island.

The liquor soon mounted into their heads, as it generally does even with the arrantest topers newly landed from sea, and they began capering about most obstreperously.

I observed, however, that one of them held somewhat aloof, and though he seemed desirous not to spoil the hilarity of his shipmates by his own sober face, yet upon the whole he refrained from making as much noise as the rest. This man interested me at once; and since the seagods had ordained that he should soon become my shipmate (though but a sleeping partner one, so far as this narrative is concerned), I will here venture upon a little description of him. He stood full six feet in height, with noble shoulders, and a chest like a cofferdam.[7] I have seldom seen such brawn in a man. His face was deeply brown and burnt, making his white teeth dazzling by the contrast; while in the deep shadows of his eyes floated some reminiscences that did not seem to give him much joy. His voice at once announced that he was a Southerner, and from his fine stature, I thought he must be one of those tall mountaineers from the Alleghenian Ridge in Virginia. When the revelry of his companions had mounted to its height, this man slipped away unobserved, and I saw no more of him till he became my comrade on the sea. In a few minutes, however, he was missed by his shipmates, and being, it seems, for some reason a huge favorite with them, they raised a cry of "Bulkington! Bulkington! where's Bulkington?" and darted out of the house in pursuit of him.

It was now about nine o'clock, and the room seeming almost supernaturally quiet after these orgies,[8] I began to congratulate myself upon a little plan that had occurred to me just previous to the entrance of the seamen.

No man prefers to sleep two in a bed. In fact, you would a good deal rather not sleep with your own brother. I don't know how it is, but people like to be private when they are sleeping. And when it comes to sleeping with an unknown stranger, in a strange inn, in a strange town, and that stranger a harpooner, then your objections indefinitely multiply. Nor was there any earthly reason why I as a sailor should sleep two in a bed, more than anybody else; for sailors no more sleep two in a bed at sea, than bachelor kings do ashore. To be sure they all sleep together in one apartment, but you have your own hammock, and cover yourself with your own blanket, and sleep in your own skin.

The more I pondered over this harpooner, the more I abominated the thought of sleeping with him. It was fair to presume that being a harpooner, his linen or woolens, as the case might be, would not be of the tidiest, certainly none of the finest. I began to twitch all over. Besides, it was getting late, and my decent harpooner ought to be home and going bedwards. Suppose now, he should tumble in upon me at midnight—how could I tell from what vile hole he had been coming?

"Landlord! I've changed my mind about that harpooner. I shan't sleep with him. I'll try the bench here."

"Just as you please; I'm sorry I can't

---

[7] COFFERDAM—A watertight compartment located near the waterline of a ship.

[8] THESE ORGIES—This merrymaking.

spare ye a tablecloth for a mattress, and it's a plaguy rough board here"—feeling of the knots and notches. "But wait a bit, Skrimshander; I've got a carpenter's plane there in the bar—wait, I say, and I'll make ye snug enough." So saying he procured the plane; and with his old silk handkerchief first dusting the bench, vigorously set to planing away at my bed, the while grinning like an ape. The shavings flew right and left; till at last the plane iron came bump against an indestructible knot. The landlord was near spraining his wrist, and I told him for heaven's sake to quit—the bed was soft enough to suit me, and I did not know how all the planing in the world could make eider down of a pine plank. So gathering up the shavings with another grin, and throwing them into the great stove in the middle of the room, he went about his business, and left me in a brown study.

I now took the measure of the bench, and found that it was a foot too short; but that could be mended with a chair. But it was a foot too narrow, and the other bench in the room was about four inches higher than the planed one—so there was no yoking them. I then placed the first bench lengthwise along the only clear space against the wall, leaving a little interval between, for my back to settle down in. But I soon found that there came such a draft of cold air over me from under the sill of the window, that this plan would never do at all, especially as another current from the rickety door met the one from the window, and both together formed a series of small whirlwinds in the immediate vicinity of the spot where I had thought to spend the night.

The devil fetch that harpooner, thought I, but stop, couldn't I steal a march on him—bolt his door inside, and jump into his bed, not to be wakened by the most violent knockings? It seemed no bad idea; but upon second thoughts I dismissed it. For who could tell but what the next morning, so soon as I popped out of the room, the harpooner might be standing in the entry, all ready to knock me down!

Still, looking round me again, and seeing no possible chance of spending a sufferable night unless in some other person's bed, I began to think that after all I might be cherishing unwarrantable prejudices against this unknown harpooner. Thinks I, I'll wait awhile; he must be dropping in before long. I'll have a good look at him then, and perhaps we may become jolly good bedfellows after all—there's no telling.

But though the other boarders kept coming in by ones, twos, and threes, and going to bed, yet no sign of my harpooner.

"Landlord!" said I, "what sort of a chap is he—does he always keep such late hours?" It was now hard upon twelve o'clock.

The landlord chuckled again with his lean chuckle, and seemed to be mightily tickled at something beyond my comprehension. "No," he answered, "generally he's an early bird—airley to bed and airley to rise—yea, he's the bird what catches the worm. But tonight he went out a peddling, you see, and I don't see what on airth keeps him so late, unless, may be, he can't sell his head."

"Can't sell his head?—What sort of a bamboozling story is this you are telling me?" getting into a towering rage. "Do you pretend to say, landlord, that this harpooner is actually engaged this blessed Saturday night, or rather Sunday morning, in peddling his head around this town?"

"That's precisely it," said the landlord,

"and I told him he couldn't sell it here, the market's overstocked."

"With what?" shouted I.

"With heads to be sure; ain't there too many heads in the world?"

"I tell you what it is, landlord," said I, quite calmly, "you'd better stop spinning that yarn to me—I'm not green."

"Maybe not," taking out a stick and whittling a toothpick, "but I rayther guess you'll be done *brown* if that ere harpooner hears you a slanderin' his head."

"I'll break it for him," said I, now flying into a passion again at this unaccountable farrago [9] of the landlord's.

"It's broke a'ready," said he.

"Broke," said I—"*broke*, do you mean?"

"Sartain, and that's the very reason he can't sell it, I guess."

"Landlord," said I, going up to him as cool as Mt. Hecla [10] in a snowstorm—"landlord, stop whittling. You and I must understand one another, and that too without delay. I come to your house and want a bed; you tell me you can only give me half a one; that the other half belongs to a certain harpooner. And about this harpooner, whom I have not yet seen, you persist in telling me the most mystifying and exasperating stories, tending to beget in me an uncomfortable feeling towards the man whom you design for my bedfellow—a sort of connection, landlord, which is an intimate and confidential one in the highest degree. I now demand of you to speak out and tell me who and what this harpooner is, and whether I shall be in all respects safe to spend the night with him. And in the first place, you will be so good as to unsay that story about selling his head,

which if true I take to be good evidence that this harpooner is stark mad, and I've no idea of sleeping with a madman; and you, sir, *you* I mean, landlord, *you*, sir, by trying to induce me to do so knowingly, would thereby render yourself liable to a criminal prosecution."

"Wall," said the landlord, fetching a long breath, "that's a purty long sarmon for a chap that rips a little now and then. But be easy, be easy, this here harpooner I have been tellin' you of has just arrived from the South Seas, where he bought up a lot of 'balmed New Zealand heads [11] (great curios, you know), and he's sold all on 'em but one, and that one he's trying to sell tonight, cause tomorrow's Sunday, and it would not do to be sellin' human heads about the streets when folks is goin' to churches. He wanted to, last Sunday, but I stopped him just as he was goin' out of the door with four heads strung on a string, for all the airth like a string of inions." [12]

This account cleared up the otherwise unaccountable mystery and showed that the landlord, after all, had no idea of fooling me—but at the same time what could I think of a harpooner who stayed out of a Saturday night clean into the Sabbath, engaged in such a cannibal business as selling heads of dead idolaters? [13]

"Depend upon it, landlord, that harpooner is a dangerous man."

"He pays reg'lar," was the rejoinder. "But come, it's getting dreadful late, you had better be turning flukes [14]—it's a

[9] FARRAGO (fă·rā′gō)—A mixture or hodge-podge.
[10] MT. HECLA—A volcano in Iceland. Like the volcano, Ishmael is hot inside but his manner is cold.
[11] 'BALMED NEW ZEALAND HEADS—Embalmed, or preserved, heads of New Zealand natives. The savage tribes of the Pacific formerly collected their victims' heads as trophies, and sometimes sold them as ornaments.
[12] INIONS—Onions.
[13] IDOLATERS (ī·dŏl′ȧ·tẽrz)—Idol-worshipers.
[14] TURNING FLUKES—Going to bed. A whale "turns flukes"—that is, flips his tail into the air—when he dives straight down. The expression means "go under," and is slang for "go to bed."

nice bed. Come along here, I'll give ye a glim [15] in a jiffy"; and so saying he lighted a candle and held it towards me, offering to lead the way. But I stood irresolute; when looking at a clock in the corner, he exclaimed "I vum [16] it's Sunday—you won't see that harpooner tonight; he's come to anchor somewhere—come along then; *do* come; *won't* ye come?"

I considered the matter a moment, and then upstairs we went, and I was ushered into a small room, cold as a clam, and furnished, sure enough, with a prodigious bed, almost big enough indeed for any four harpooners to sleep abreast.

"There," said the landlord, placing the candle on a crazy old sea chest that did double duty as a washstand and center table; "there, make yourself comfortable now, and good night to ye." I turned round from eyeing the bed, but he had disappeared.

Folding back the counterpane, I stooped over the bed. Though none of the most elegant, it yet stood the scrutiny tolerably well. I then glanced round the room; and besides the bedstead and center table, could see no other furniture belonging to the place, but a rude shelf, the four walls, and a papered fireboard [17] representing a man striking a whale. Of things not properly belonging to the room, there was a hammock lashed up, and thrown upon the floor in one corner; also a large seaman's bag, containing the harpooner's wardrobe, no doubt in lieu of a land trunk. Likewise, there was a parcel of outlandish bone fishhooks on the shelf over the fireplace, and a tall harpoon standing at the head of the bed.

But what is this on the chest? I took it up, and held it close to the light, and felt it, and smelled it, and tried every way possible to arrive at some satisfactory conclusion concerning it. I can compare it to nothing but a large door mat, ornamented at the edges with little tinkling tags something like the stained porcupine quills round an Indian moccasin. There was a hole or slit in the middle of this mat, as you see the same in South American ponchos. But could it be possible that any sober harpooneer would get into a door mat, and parade the streets of any Christian town in that sort of guise? I put it on, to try it, and it weighed me down like a hamper, being uncommonly shaggy and thick, and I thought a little damp, as though this mysterious harpooner had been wearing it of a rainy day. I went up in it to a bit of glass stuck against the wall, and I never saw such a sight in my life. I tore myself out of it in such a hurry that I gave myself a kink in the neck.

I sat down on the side of the bed, and commenced thinking about this head-peddling harpooner, and his door mat. After thinking some time on the bedside, I got up and took off my monkey jacket, and then stood in the middle of the room thinking. I then took off my coat, and thought a little more in my shirt sleeves. But beginning to feel very cold now, half undressed as I was, and remembering what the landlord said about the harpooner's not coming home at all that night, it being so very late, I made no more ado, but jumped out of my pantaloons and boots, and then blowing out the light tumbled into bed, and commended myself to the care of heaven.

Whether that mattress was stuffed with corncobs or broken crockery, there is no telling, but I rolled about a good deal, and could not sleep for a long time. At

---

[15] A GLIM—Slang for "a light."

[16] I VUM—The landlord speaks New England dialect. This is his pronunciation of "I affirm" or "I vow"—that is, "I declare."

[17] FIREBOARD—A board, often ornamental, used to close up a fireplace in summer.

last I slid off into a light doze, and had pretty nearly made a good offing towards the land of Nod, when I heard a heavy footfall in the passage, and saw a glimmer of light come into the room from under the door.

Lord save me, thinks I, that must be the harpooner, the infernal head-peddler. But I lay perfectly still, and resolved not to say a word till spoken to. Holding a light in one hand, and that identical New Zealand head in the other, the stranger entered the room, and without looking towards the bed, placed his candle a good way off from me on the floor in one corner, and then began working away at the knotted cords of the large bag I before spoke of as being in the room. I was all eagerness to see his face, but he kept it averted for some time while employed in unlacing the bag's mouth. This accomplished, however, he turned round—when, good heavens! what a sight! such a face! It was of a dark, purplish, yellow color, here and there stuck over with large, blackish-looking squares. Yes, it's just as I thought, he's a terrible bedfellow; he's been in a fight, got dreadfully cut, and here he is, just from the surgeon. But at that moment he chanced to turn his face towards the light, that I plainly saw they could not be sticking-plasters at all, those black squares on his cheeks. They were stains of some sort or other. At first I knew not what to make of this; but soon an inkling of the truth occurred to me. I remembered a story of a white man—a whaleman too—who, falling among the cannibals, had been tatooed by them. I concluded that this harpooner, in the course of his distant voyages, must have met with a similar adventure. And what is it, thought I, after all? It's only his outside; a man can be honest in any sort of skin. But then, what to make of his unearthly complexion, that part of it, I mean, lying round about, and completely independent of the squares of tattooing. To be sure, it might be nothing but a good coat of tropical tanning; but I never heard of a hot sun's tanning a white man into a purplish yellow one. However, I had never been in the South Seas; and perhaps the sun there produced these extraordinary effects upon the skin. Now, while all these ideas were passing through me like lightning, this harpooner never noticed me at all. But, after some difficulty having opened his bag, he commenced fumbling in it, and presently pulled out a sort of tomahawk, and a sealskin wallet with the hair on. Placing these on the old chest in the middle of the room, he then took the New Zealand head—a ghastly thing enough—and crammed it down into the bag. He now took off his hat—a new beaver hat—when I came nigh singing out with fresh surprise. There was no hair on his head —none to speak of at least—nothing but a small scalp knot twisted up on his forehead. His bald purplish head now looked for all the world like a mildewed skull. Had not the stranger stood between me and the door, I would have bolted out of it quicker than ever I bolted a dinner.

Even as it was, I thought something of slipping out of the window, but it was the second floor back. I am no coward, but what to make of this head-peddling purple rascal altogether passed my comprehension. Ignorance is the parent of fear, and being completely nonplussed and confounded about the stranger, I confess I was now as much afraid of him as if it was the devil himself who had thus broken into my room at the dead of night. In fact, I was so afraid of him that I was not game enough then to address him, and demand a satisfactory answer concerning what seemed inexplicable in him.

Meanwhile, he continued the business of undressing, and at last showed his chest and arms. As I live, these covered parts of him were checkered with the same squares as his face; his back, too, was all over the same dark squares; he seemed to have been in a Thirty Years' War, and just escaped from it with a sticking-plaster shirt. Still more, his very legs were marked, as if a parcel of dark green frogs were running up the trunks of young palms. It was now quite plain that he must be some abominable savage or other shipped aboard of a whaleman in the South Seas, and so landed in this Christian country. I quaked to think of it. A peddler of heads too—perhaps the heads of his own brothers. He might take a fancy to mine—heavens! look at that tomahawk!

But there was no time for shuddering, for now the savage went about something that completely fascinated my attention, and convinced me that he must indeed be a heathen. Going to his heavy grego, or wrapall, or dreadnaught,[18] which he had previously hung on a chair, he fumbled in the pockets, and produced at length a curious little deformed image with a hunch on its back, and exactly the color of a three days' old Congo baby. Remembering the embalmed head, at first I almost thought that this black manikin[19] was a real baby preserved in some similar manner. But seeing that it was not at all limber, and that it glistened a good deal like polished ebony, I concluded that it must be nothing but a wooden idol, which indeed it proved to be. For now the savage goes up to the empty fireplace, and removing the papered fireboard, sets up this little hunch-backed image, like a tenpin, between the

andirons. The chimney jambs and all the bricks inside were very sooty, so that I thought this fireplace made a very appropriate little shrine for his Congo idol.

I now screwed my eyes hard towards the half hidden image, feeling but ill at ease meantime—to see what was next to follow. First he takes about a double handful of shavings out of his grego pocket, and places them carefully before the idol; then laying a bit of ship biscuit on top and applying the flame from the lamp, he kindled the shavings into a sacrificial blaze. Presently, after many hasty snatches into the fire, and still hastier withdrawals of his fingers (whereby he seemed to be scorching them badly), he at last succeeded in drawing out the biscuit; then blowing off the heat and ashes a little, he made a polite offer of it to the little Negro. But the little idol did not seem to fancy such dry sort of fare at all; he never moved his lips. All these strange antics were accompanied by still stranger guttural noises from the devotee, who seemed to be praying in a singsong or else singing some pagan psalmody[20] or other, during which his face twitched about in the most unnatural manner. At last extinguishing the fire, he took the idol up very unceremoniously, and bagged it again in his grego pocket as carelessly as if he were a sportsman bagging a dead woodcock.

All these queer proceedings increased my uncomfortableness, and seeing him now exhibiting strong symptoms of concluding his business operations, and jumping into bed with me, I thought it was high time, now or never, before the light was put out, to break the spell in which I had so long been bound.

But the interval I spent in deliberating what to say was a fatal one. Taking up

---

[18] GREGO, OR WRAPALL, OR DREADNAUGHT—These are names for a warm, heavy coat.

[19] MANIKIN—A little image of a man.

[20] PAGAN PSALMODY (săl'mô·dĭ)—Heathen hymn.

his tomahawk from the table, he examined the head of it for an instant, and then holding it to the light, with his mouth at the handle, he puffed out great clouds of tobacco smoke. The next moment the light was extinguished, and this wild cannibal, tomahawk between his teeth, sprang into bed with me. I sang out, I could not help it now; and giving a sudden grunt of astonishment he began to touch me.

Stammering out something, I knew not what, I rolled away from him against the wall, and then conjured him,[21] whoever or whatever he might be, to keep quiet, and let me get up and light the lamp again. But his guttural responses satisfied me at once that he but ill comprehended my meaning.

"Who-e you?"—he at last said—"you no speak-e, I kill-e." And so saying the lighted tomahawk began flourishing about me in the dark.

"Landlord, help, Peter Coffin!"[22] shouted I. "Landlord! Watch! Coffin! Angels! Save me!"

"Speak-e! tell-ee me who-ee be, or I kill-e!" again growled the cannibal, while his horrid flourishings of the tomahawk scattered the hot tobacco ashes about me till I thought my linen would get on fire. But thank heaven, at that moment the landlord came into the room, light in hand, and leaping from the bed I ran up to him.

"Don't be afraid now," said he, grinning again. "Queequeg here wouldn't harm a hair of your head."

"Stop your grinning," shouted I, "and why didn't you tell me that that infernal harpooner was a cannibal?"

"I thought ye know'd it—didn't I tell ye, he was a peddlin' heads around town? —but turn flukes again and go to sleep.

[21] CONJURED HIM—Earnestly requested him.
[22] PETER COFFIN—The landlord's name.

Queequeg, look here—you sabbee[23] me, I sabbee you—this man sleepe you—you sabbee?"

"Me sabbee plenty"—grunted Queequeg, puffing away and sitting up in bed.

"You gettee in," he added, motioning to me with his tomahawk, and throwing the clothes to one side. He really did this in not only a civil but a really kind and charitable way. I stood looking at him a moment. For all his tattooings he was on the whole a clean, comely looking cannibal. What's all this fuss I have been making about, thought I to myself —the man's a human being just as I am: he has just as much reason to fear me, as I have to be afraid of him. Better sleep with a sober cannibal than a drunken Christian.

"Landlord," said I, "tell him to stash his tomahawk there, or pipe, or whatever you call it; tell him to stop smoking, in short, and I will turn in with him. But I don't fancy having a man smoking in bed with me. It's dangerous. Besides, I ain't insured."

This being told to Queequeg, he at

[23] SABBEE—Know, understand. The word comes from the Spanish expression *sabe usted* (you know).

once complied, and again politely motioned me to get into bed—rolling over to one side as much as to say—I won't touch a leg of ye.

"Good night, landlord," said I, "you may go."

I turned in, and never slept better in my life.

THE QUARTER-DECK

Ishmael and Queequeg become friends, and together they sign up for a voyage on a whaling vessel, the "Pequod." During the first part of the voyage, Ishmael catches only an occasional glimpse of the mysterious captain of the ship, Ahab, stumping about the deck with his artificial leg. At last, one day Ahab suddenly gives the order to call the whole crew together—

"Sir!" said the mate, astonished at an order seldom or never given on shipboard except in some extraordinary case.

"Send everybody aft," repeated Ahab. "Mastheads, there! come down!"

When the entire ship's company were assembled, and with curious and not wholly unapprehensive faces, were eyeing him, for he looked not unlike the weather horizon when a storm is coming up, Ahab, after rapidly glancing over the bulwarks, and then darting his eyes among the crew, started from his standpoint; and as though not a soul were nigh him resumed his heavy turns upon the deck. With bent head and half-slouched hat he continued to pace, unmindful of the wondering whispering among the men; till Stubb cautiously whispered to Flask [24] that Ahab must have summoned them there for the purpose of witnessing a pedestrian feat. But this did not last long. Vehemently pausing, he cried:

"What do ye do when ye see a whale, men?"

"Sing out for him!" was the impulsive rejoinder from a score of clubbed voices.

"Good!" cried Ahab, with a wild approval in his tones, observing the hearty animation into which his unexpected question had so magnetically thrown them.

"And what do ye next, men?"

"Lower away, and after him!"

"And what tune is it ye pull to, men?"

"A dead whale or a stove boat!" [25]

More and more strangely and fiercely glad and approving grew the countenance of the old man at every shout; while the mariners began to gaze curiously at each other, as if marveling how it was that they themselves became so excited at such seemingly purposeless questions.

But they were all eagerness again, as Ahab, now half-revolving in his pivot hole,[26] with one hand reaching high up a shroud, and tightly, almost convulsively grasping it, addressed them thus:

"All ye mastheaders have before now heard me give orders about a white whale. Look ye! D'ye see this Spanish ounce of gold?"—holding up a broad bright coin to the sun—"it is a sixteen dollar piece, men. D'ye see it? Mr. Starbuck, hand me yon top maul."

While the mate was getting the hammer, Ahab, without speaking, was slowly rubbing the gold piece against the skirts

[25] A STOVE BOAT—A smashed boat.

[26] PIVOT-HOLE—Ahab had caused shallow holes to be bored in the quarter-deck where he could steady himself on his peg-leg.

[24] STUBB . . . FLASK—These are the second mate and third mate, both Massachusetts men.

of his jacket, as if to heighten its luster, and without using any words was meanwhile lowly humming to himself, producing a sound so strangely muffled and inarticulate that it seemed the mechanical humming of the wheels of his vitality in him.

Receiving the top maul from Starbuck, he advanced towards the mainmast with the hammer uplifted in one hand, exhibiting the gold with the other, and with a high, raised voice exclaiming: "Whosoever of ye raises me [27] a white-headed whale with a wrinkled brow and a crooked jaw; whosoever of ye raises me that white-headed whale with three holes punctured in his starboard fluke [28]—look ye, whosoever of ye raises me that same white whale, he shall have this gold ounce, my boys!"

"Huzza! huzza!" cried the seamen, as with swinging tarpaulins they hailed the act of nailing the gold to the mast.

"It's a white whale, I say," resumed Ahab, as he threw down the top maul: "a white whale. Skin your eyes for him, men; look sharp for white water; if ye see but a bubble, sing out."

All this while Tashtego, Daggoo, and Queequeg [29] had looked on with even more intense interest and surprise than the rest, and at the mention of the wrinkled brow and crooked jaw they had started as if each was separately touched by some specific recollection.

"Captain Ahab," said Tashtego, "that white whale must be the same that some call Moby Dick."

"Moby Dick?" shouted Ahab. "Do ye know the white whale then, Tash?"

"Does he fan-tail a little curious, sir, before he goes down?" said the Gay-Header deliberately.

"And has he a curious spout, too," said Daggoo, "very bushy, even for a parmacetty,[30] and mighty quick, Captain Ahab?"

"And he have one, two, tree—oh! good many iron in him hide,[31] too, Captain," cried Queequeg disjointedly, "all twisketee betwisk, like him—him—" faltering

---

[27] WHOSOEVER OF YE RAISES ME—Whoever first sees the whale and gives the signal.

[28] HIS STARBOARD FLUKE—The right-hand lobe of his tail.

[29] TASHTEGO, DAGGOO, AND QUEEQUEG—These are the harpooners. Their different nationalities help to suggest that the "Pequod's" crew symbolizes the entire human race. Tashtego is an American Indian from Gay Head, on the island Martha's Vineyard near Cape Cod; Daggoo is a native of Africa; and Queequeg is from an island in the southwestern Pacific.

[30] PARMACETTY—This is Daggoo's pronunciation of *spermaceti*, meaning *sperm whale*—the largest of the whale species.

[31] GOOD MANY IRON IN HIM HIDE—Moby Dick has often been harpooned, but has always broken loose.

hard for a word, and screwing his hand round and round as though uncorking a bottle—"like him—him—"

"Corkscrew!" cried Ahab, "aye, Queequeg, the harpoons lie all twisted and wrenched in him; aye, Daggoo, his spout is a big one, like a whole shock of wheat, and white as a pile of our Nantucket wool after the great annual sheepshearing; aye, Tashtego, and he fan-tails like a split jib in a squall. Death and devils! men, it is Moby Dick ye have seen—Moby Dick—Moby Dick!"

"Captain Ahab," said Starbuck, who, with Stubb and Flask, had thus far been eyeing his superior with increasing surprise, but at last seemed struck with a thought which somewhat explained all the wonder. "Captain Ahab, I have heard of Moby Dick—but it was not Moby Dick that took off thy leg?"

"Who told thee that?" cried Ahab; then pausing, "Aye, Starbuck; aye, my hearties all round; it was Moby Dick that dismasted me; Moby Dick that brought me to this dead stump I stand on now. Aye, aye," he shouted with a terrific, loud, animal sob, like that of a heart-stricken moose; "Aye, aye! it was that accursed white whale that razeed [32] me; made a poor begging lubber of me for ever and a day!" Then tossing both arms, with measureless imprecations he shouted out: "Aye, aye! and I'll chase him round Good Hope, and round the Horn, and round the Norway Maelstrom, and round perdition's flames before I give him up. And this is what ye have shipped for, men! to chase that white whale on both sides of land, and over all sides of earth, till he spouts black blood and rolls fin out. What say ye, men, will ye splice hands on it, now? I think ye do look brave."

"Aye, aye!" shouted the harpooners and seamen, running closer to the excited old man: "A sharp eye for the white whale; a sharp lance for Moby Dick!"

"God bless ye," he seemed to half sob and half shout. "God bless ye, men. Steward! go draw the great measure of grog." [33]

---

[32] RAZEED—To razee a ship is to cut down its size by removing the upper deck or decks.

[33] GROG—A slang term for liquor, especially when served to a ship's crew as a treat or reward.

THE LINE

After many weeks, the "Pequod" reaches the Indian Ocean. Only once have whales been sighted—and on that occasion a squall of wind prevents the crew from making a kill. Ishmael describes the long, tedious journey, and tells his readers many facts about whales and whaling—

With reference to the whaling scene shortly to be described, as well as for the better understanding of all similar scenes elsewhere presented, I have here to speak of the magical, sometimes horrible whale line. . . .

The whale line is only two-thirds of an inch in thickness. At first sight, you would not think it so strong as it really is. By experiment its one and fifty yarns will each suspend a weight of one hundred and twenty pounds; so the whole rope will bear a strain nearly equal to three tons. In length, the common sperm whale line measures something over two hundred fathoms. Towards the

stern of the boat it is spirally coiled away in the tub, not like the worm-pipe of a still [34] though, but so as to form one round, cheese-shaped mass of densely bedded "sheaves," or layers of concentric spiralizations, without any hollow but the "heart," or minute vertical tube formed at the axis of the cheese. As the least tangle or kink in the coiling would, in running out, infallibly take somebody's arm, leg, or entire body off, the utmost precaution is used in stowing the line in its tub. Some harpooners will consume almost an entire morning in this business, carrying the line high aloft and then reeving it downwards through a block [35] towards the tub, so as in the act of coiling to free it from all possible wrinkles and twists.

Before lowering the boat for the chase, the upper end of the line is taken aft from the tub, and passing round the loggerhead there, is again carried forward [36] the entire length of the boat, resting crosswise upon the loom or handle of every man's oar, so that it jogs against his wrist in rowing; and also passing between the men, as they alternately sit at the op-

[34] THE WORM-PIPE OF A STILL—The spiral tube of a distilling apparatus, in which the liquid is cooled as it passes through.
[35] REEVING IT DOWNWARDS THROUGH A BLOCK —Passing it through a pulley.
[36] THE UPPER END OF THE LINE IS TAKEN AFT FROM THE TUB, AND . . . IS AGAIN CARRIED FORWARD—That is, the line goes from the tub to the rear of the boat, and then clear to the front where the harpooner is stationed.

posite gunwales, to the leaded chocks or grooves in the extreme pointed prow of the boat, where a wooden pin or skewer the size of a common quill, prevents it from slipping out. From the chocks it hangs in a slight festoon over the bows, and is then passed inside the boat again; and some ten or twenty fathoms (called box line) being coiled upon the box in the bows, it continues its way to the gunwale still a little further aft, and is then attached to the short-warp—the rope which is immediately connected with the harpoon; but previous to that connection, the short-warp goes through sundry mystifications too tedious to detail.

Thus the whale line folds the whole boat in its complicated coils, twisting and writhing around it in almost every direction. All the oarsmen are involved in its perilous contortions; so that to the timid eye of the landsman, they seem as Indian jugglers, with the deadliest snakes sportively festooning their limbs. Nor can any son of mortal woman, for the first time, seat himself amid those hempen intricacies, and while straining his utmost at the oar, bethink him that at any unknown instant the harpoon may be darted, and all these horrible contortions be put in play like ringed lightnings; he cannot be thus circumstanced without a shudder that makes the very marrow in his bones to quiver in him like a shaken jelly. Yet habit—strange thing! what cannot habit accomplish?—Gayer sallies, more merry mirth, better jokes, and brighter repartees, you never heard over your mahogany, than you will hear over the half-inch white cedar of the whaleboat, when thus hung in hangman's nooses; and six men composing the crew pull into the jaws of death, with a halter around every neck, as you may say.

Perhaps a very little thought will now

enable you to account for those repeated whaling disasters—some few of which are casually chronicled—of this man or that man being taken out of the boat by the line, and lost. For, when the line is darting out, to be seated then in the boat, is like being seated in the midst of the manifold whizzings of a steam engine in full play, when every flying beam, and shaft, and wheel, is grazing you. It is worse; for you cannot sit motionless in the heart of these perils, because the boat is rocking like a cradle, and you are pitched one way and the other, without the slightest warning; and only by a certain self-adjusting buoyancy and simultaneousness of volition and action, can you escape being run away with where the all-seeing sun himself could never pierce you out.

Again: as the profound calm, which only apparently precedes and prophesies of the storm, is perhaps more awful than the storm itself; for, indeed, the calm is but the wrapper and envelope of the storm; and contains it in itself, as the seemingly harmless rifle holds the fatal powder, and the ball, and the explosion; so the graceful repose of the line, as it silently serpentines about the oarsmen before being brought into actual play—this is a thing which carries more of true terror than any other aspect of this dangerous affair. But why say more? All men live enveloped in whale lines. All are born with halters round their necks; but it is only when caught in the swift, sudden turn of death, that mortals realize the silent, subtle, ever-present perils of life. And if you be a philosopher, though seated in the whaleboat, you would not at heart feel one whit more of terror, than though seated before your evening fire with a poker, and not a harpoon, by your side.

STUBB KILLS A WHALE

From his knowledge of the sea, Queequeg is sure that whales are near. However, next day there seems no sign of life. The air is still and sultry. The sea is quiet. Ishmael is standing watch, but like everybody else on board the "Pequod," he is half asleep—

It was my turn to stand at the foremast-head;[37] and with my shoulders leaning against the slackened royal shrouds,[38] to and fro I idly swayed in what seemed an enchanted air. No resolution could withstand it; in that dreamy mood losing all consciousness, at last my soul went out of my body; though my body still continued to sway as a pendulum will, long after the power which first moved it is withdrawn.

Ere forgetfulness altogether came over me, I had noticed that the seamen at the main and mizzen mastheads [39] were already drowsy. So that at last all three of us lifelessly swung from the spars, and for every swing that we made there was a nod from below from the slumbering helmsman. The waves, too, nodded their indolent crests; and across the wide trance of the sea, east nodded to west, and the sun over all.

[37] STAND AT THE FOREMAST-HEAD—That is, keep a lookout for whales from a platform high up on the front mast of the ship.

[38] ROYAL SHROUDS—These are ropes running from the ship's sides to the "royal mast"—that is, to a portion of the mast above where the lookout is standing.

[39] AT THE MAIN AND MIZZEN MASTHEADS—Perched on the second and third masts.

Suddenly bubbles seemed bursting beneath my closed eyes; like vises my hands grasped the shrouds; some invisible, gracious agency preserved me; with a shock I came back to life. And lo! close under our lee, not forty fathoms off, a gigantic sperm whale lay rolling in the water like the capsized hull of a frigate, his broad, glossy back, of an Ethiopian hue, glistening in the sun's rays like a mirror. But lazily undulating in the trough of the sea, and ever and anon tranquilly spouting his vapory jet, the whale looked like a portly burgher smoking his pipe of a warm afternoon.[40] But that pipe, poor whale, was thy last. As if struck by some enchanter's wand, the sleepy ship and every sleeper in it all at once started into wakefulness; and more than a score of voices from all parts of the vessel, simultaneously with the three notes from aloft, shouted forth the accustomed cry, as the great fish slowly and regularly spouted the sparkling brine into the air.

"Clear away the boats! Luff!"[41] cried Ahab. And obeying his own order, he dashed the helm down before the helmsman could handle the spokes.

The sudden exclamations of the crew must have alarmed the whale; and ere the boats were down, majestically turning, he swam away to the leeward, but with such a steady tranquillity, and making so few ripples as he swam, that thinking after all he might not as yet be alarmed, Ahab gave orders that not an oar should be used, and no man must speak but in whispers. So seated like Ontario Indians on the gunwales of the boats, we swiftly but silently paddled along; the calm not admitting of the noiseless sails being set. Presently, as we thus glided in chase, the monster perpendicularly flitted his tail forty feet into the air, and then sank out of sight like a tower swallowed up.

"There go flukes!" was the cry, an announcement immediately followed by Stubb's producing his match and igniting his pipe, for now a respite[42] was granted. After the full interval of his sounding had elapsed, the whale rose again, and being now in advance of the smoker's boat, and much nearer to it than to any of the others, Stubb counted upon the honor of the capture. It was obvious, now, that the whale had at length become aware of his pursuers. All silence of cautiousness was therefore no longer of use. Paddles were dropped, and oars came loudly into play. And still puffing at his pipe, Stubb cheered on his crew to the assault.

Yes, a mighty change had come over the fish. All alive to his jeopardy, he was going "head out," that part obliquely projecting from the mad yeast which he brewed.

"Start her, start her, my men! Don't hurry yourselves; take plenty of time—but start her; start her like thunderclaps, that's all," cried Stubb, spluttering out the smoke as he spoke. "Start her, now; give 'em the long and strong stroke, Tashtego. Start her, Tash, my boy—start her, all; but keep cool, keep cool—cucumbers is the word—easy, easy—only start her like grim death and grinning devils, and raise the buried dead perpendicular out of their graves, boys—that's all. Start her!"

"Woo-hoo! Wa-hee!" screamed the

[40] LIKE A PORTLY BURGHER SMOKING HIS PIPE—Burgher is a Dutch word meaning *citizen of a town*. The suggestion is that the huge whale, lazily spouting vapor into the air, looks like a fat Dutch merchant puffing tobacco smoke.

[41] LUFF!—"Turn into the wind!" The command is given because Ahab wants to stop the ship immediately.

[42] A RESPITE (rĕs'pĭt)—A relief or rest from work. The men have nothing to do until the whale is forced to come to the surface again for air.

Gay-Header in reply, raising some old war whoop to the skies; as every oarsman in the strained boat involuntarily bounced forward with the one tremendous leading stroke which the eager Indian gave.

But his wild screams were answered by others quite as wild. "Kee-hee! Kee-hee!" yelled Daggoo, straining forwards and backwards on his seat, like a pacing tiger in his cage.

"Ka-la! Koo-loo!" howled Queequeg, as if smacking his lips over a mouthful of grenadier's steak.[43] And thus with oars and yells the keels cut the sea. Meanwhile, Stubb retaining his place in the van, still encouraged his men to the onset, all the while puffing the smoke from his mouth. Like desperadoes they tugged and they strained, till the welcome cry was heard—"Stand up, Tashtego! give it to him!" The harpoon was hurled. "Stern all!" The oarsmen backed water; the same moment something went hot and hissing along every one of their wrists. It was the magical line. An instant before, Stubb had swiftly caught two additional turns with it round the loggerhead, whence, by reason of its increased rapid circlings, a hempen blue smoke now jetted up and mingled with the steady fumes from his pipe. As the line passed round and round the loggerhead; so also, just before reaching that point, it blisteringly passed through and through both of Stubb's hands, from which the handcloths, or squares of quilted canvas sometimes worn at these times, had accidentally dropped. It was like holding an enemy's sharp two-edged sword by the blade, and that enemy all the time striving to wrest it out of your clutch.

"Wet the line! wet the line!" cried Stubb to the tub oarsman (him seated by the tub) who, snatching off his hat, dashed the sea water into it. More turns were taken, so that the line began holding its place. The boat now flew through the boiling water like a shark all fins. Stubb and Tashtego here changed places [44]—stem for stern—a staggering business truly in that rocking commotion.

From the vibrating line extending the entire length of the upper part of the boat, and from its now being more tight than a harpstring, you would have thought the craft had two keels—one cleaving the water, the other the air—as the boat churned on through both opposing elements at once. A continual cascade played at the bows; a ceaseless whirling eddy in her wake; and at the slightest motion from within, even but of a little finger, the vibrating, cracking craft canted over her spasmodic gunwale [45] into the sea. Thus they rushed; each man with might and main clinging to his seat, to prevent being tossed to the foam; and the tall form of Tashtego at the steering oar crouching almost double, in order to bring down his center of gravity. Whole Atlantics and Pacifics seemed passed as they shot on their way, till at length the whale somewhat slackened his flight.

"Haul in—haul in!" cried Stubb to the bowsman! and, facing round towards the whale, all hands began pulling the boat up to him, while yet the boat was being towed on. Soon ranging up by his flank, Stubb, firmly planting his knee in the clumsy cleat, darted dart after dart into the flying fish; at the word of command, the boat alternately sterning out of the way of the whale's horrible wallow, and then ranging up for another fling.

[44] STUBB AND TASHTEGO HERE CHANGED PLACES—Having thrown his harpoon, Tashtego moves to the stern. Stubb comes to the front of the boat to spear the whale to death.

[45] CANTED OVER HER SPASMODIC GUNWALE— Tilted over the violently shaking gunwale.

[43] GRENADIER'S STEAK—*Grenadier* is the name of a kind of deep-sea fish.

The red tide now poured from all sides of the monster like brooks down a hill. His tormented body rolled not in brine but in blood, which bubbled and seethed for furlongs behind in their wake. The slanting sun playing upon this crimson pond in the sea, sent back its reflection into every face, so that they all glowed to each other like red men. And all the while, jet after jet of white smoke was agonizingly shot from the spiracle of the whale,[46] and vehement puff after puff from the mouth of the excited headsman;[47] as at every dart, hauling in upon his crooked lance (by the line attached to it), Stubb straightened it again and again, by a few rapid blows against the gunwale, then again and again sent it into the whale.

"Pull up—pull up!" he now cried to the bowsman, as the waning whale relaxed in his wrath. "Pull up—close to!" and the boat ranged along the fish's flank. When reaching far over the bow, Stubb slowly churned his long sharp lance into the fish, and kept it there, carefully churning and

[46] JET AFTER JET OF WHITE SMOKE . . . FROM THE SPIRACLE OF THE WHALE—Vapor shoots from the "nose" of the whale as it breathes.

[47] VEHEMENT PUFF AFTER PUFF FROM THE MOUTH OF THE EXCITED HEADSMAN—Stubb smokes his pipe harder and harder as he strikes.

churning, as if cautiously seeking to feel after some gold watch that the whale might have swallowed, and which he was fearful of breaking ere he could hook it out. But that gold watch he sought was the innermost life of the fish. And now it is struck; for, starting from his trance into that unspeakable thing called his "flurry," the monster horribly wallowed in his blood, over-wrapped himself in impenetrable, mad, boiling spray, so that the imperiled craft, instantly dropping astern, had much ado blindly to struggle out from that frenzied twilight into the clear air of the day.

And now abating in his flurry, the whale once more rolled out into view; surging from side to side; spasmodically dilating and contracting his spout hole, with sharp, cracking, agonized respirations. At last, gush after gush of clotted red gore, as if it had been the purple lees of red wine, shot into the frighted air; and falling back again, ran dripping down his motionless flanks into the sea. His heart had burst!

"He's dead, Mr. Stubb," said Daggoo.

"Yes; both pipes smoked out!" and withdrawing his own from his mouth, Stubb scattered the dead ashes over the water; and, for a moment, stood thoughtfully eyeing the vast corpse he had made.

THE CHASE—THIRD DAY

The dead whale is towed to the side of the ship, and Ishmael describes the process of "cutting in"—peeling off the whale's thick outer layer of blubber, and stowing the strips below deck. As more whales are killed in the following weeks, Ahab becomes more and more frantic in his desire to find Moby Dick. Whenever the "Pequod" meets another whaling vessel, Ahab hails her with "Hast seen the White Whale?" One ship, the "Rachel," is searching for a missing whaleboat, with the captain's own son aboard—but Ahab refuses to turn aside even for a few hours to aid in the search.

At last, one morning, Moby Dick is sighted. Ahab himself sees him first, and gives the cry. For three days, driven by the captain's wild enthusiasm, the crew of the "Pequod" fight the great whale. On the first day, Moby Dick bites a whaleboat in two. On the second day, he capsizes one of the boats, and Ahab's ivory leg is broken off. But the carpenter makes a new leg from the wood of the wrecked boat—and all night Ahab stands on deck, waiting "for the earliest sun."

On the afternoon of the third day, Ahab again catches sight of the whale, and cries, "Forehead to forehead I meet thee, this third time, Moby Dick!" The men lower the boats once more—and discover that the sea is full of sharks. Unafraid, they push toward their prey. Moby Dick disappears—

Suddenly the waters around them slowly swelled in broad circles; then quickly upheaved, as if sideways sliding from a submerged berg of ice, swiftly rising to the surface. A low rumbling sound was heard; a subterraneous hum; [48] and then all held their breaths; as bedraggled with trailing ropes, and harpoons, and lances, a vast form shot lengthwise, but obliquely from the sea. Shrouded in a thin drooping veil of mist, it hovered for a moment in the rainbowed air; and then fell swamping back into the deep. Crushed thirty feet upwards, the waters flashed for an instant like heaps of fountains, then brokenly sank in a shower of flakes, leaving the circling surface creamed like new milk round the marble trunk of the whale.

"Give way!" cried Ahab to the oarsmen, and the boats darted forward to the attack; but maddened by yesterday's fresh irons that corroded in him, Moby Dick seemed combinedly possessed by all the angels that fell from heaven. The wide tiers of welded tendons overspreading his broad white forehead, beneath the transparent skin, looked knitted together; as head on, he came churning his tail among

the boats and once more flailed them apart, spilling out the irons and lances from the two mates' boats and dashing in one side of their bows, but leaving Ahab's almost without a scar. . . .

The harpoon dropped from his hand.

"Away, mates, to the ship! those boats are useless now; repair them if ye can in time, and return to me; if not, Ahab is enough to die—Down, men! the first thing that but offers to jump from this boat I stand in, that thing I harpoon. Ye are not other men, but my arms and my legs; and so obey me. Where's the whale? gone down again?"

But he looked too nigh the boat; for as if bent upon escaping . . . Moby Dick was now again steadily swimming forward and had almost passed the ship— which thus far had been sailing in the contrary direction to him, though for the present her headway had been stopped. He seemed swimming with his utmost velocity, and now only intent upon pursuing his own straight path in the sea.

"Oh! Ahab," cried Starbuck,[49] "not

[48] A SUBTERRANEOUS HUM—A noise from the depths.

[49] STARBUCK—Starbuck is the chief mate. He is a brave man of prudent common sense who has tried several times to get Ahab to give up his mad determination to kill Moby Dick.

too late is it, even now, the third day, to desist. See! Moby Dick seeks thee not. It is thou, thou, that madly seekest him!"

Setting sail to the rising wind, the lonely boat was swiftly impelled to leeward by both oars and canvas. And at last when Ahab was sliding by the vessel, so near as plainly to distinguish Starbuck's face as he leaned over the rail, he hailed him to turn the vessel about, and follow him, not too swiftly, at a judicious interval. Glancing upwards he saw Tashtego, Queequeg, and Daggoo, eagerly mounting to the three mastheads; while the oarsmen were rocking in the two staved boats which had just been hoisted to the side, and were busily at work in repairing them. One after the other, through the portholes, as he sped, he also caught flying glimpses of Stubb and Flask, busying themselves on deck among bundles of new irons and lances. As he saw all this; as he heard the hammers in the broken boats; far other hammers seemed driving a nail into his heart. But he rallied. And now marking that the vane or flag was gone from the main masthead, he shouted to Tashtego, who had just gained that perch, to descend again for another flag, and a hammer and nails, and so nail it to the mast.

Whether fagged by the three days' running chase, or whether it was some latent deceitfulness and malice in him: whichever was true, the White Whale's way now began to abate, as it seemed, from the boat so rapidly nearing him once more; though indeed the whale's last start had not been so long a one as before. And still as Ahab glided over the waves the unpitying sharks accompanied him; and so pertinaciously stuck to the boat, and so continually bit at the plying oars that the blades became jagged and crunched, and left small splinters in the sea, at almost every dip.

"Heed them not! those teeth but give new rowlocks to your oars. Pull on! 'tis the better rest, the shark's jaw than the yielding water."

"But at every bite, sir, the thin blades grow smaller and smaller!"

"They will last long enough! pull on— But who can tell"—he muttered—"whether these sharks swim to feast on the whale or on Ahab? But pull on! Aye, all alive, now—we near him. The helm! take the helm! let me pass"—and so saying, two of the oarsmen helped him forward to the bows of the still flying boat.

At length as the craft was cast to one side, and ran ranging along with the White Whale's flank, he seemed strangely oblivious of its advance—as the whale sometimes will—and Ahab was fairly within the smoky mountain mist, which, thrown off from the whale's spout, curled round his great Monadnock [50] hump; he was even thus close to him; when, with body arched back, and both arms lengthwise high-lifted to the poise, he darted his fierce iron and his far fiercer curse into the hated whale. As both steel and curse sank to the socket, as if sucked into a morass, [51] Moby Dick sideways writhed; spasmodically rolled his nigh flank against the bow, and, without staving a hole in it, so suddenly canted the boat over, that had it not been for the elevated part of the gunwale to which he then clung, Ahab would once more have been tossed into the sea. As it was, three of the oarsmen—who foreknew not the precise instant of the dart, and were therefore unprepared for its effects—these were flung out; but so fell, that, in an instant two of them clutched the gunwale again, and rising to its level on a combing

[50] MONADNOCK (mȯ·năd′nŏk). A mountain in New Hampshire.
[51] MORASS—Marsh.

wave, hurled themselves bodily inboard again; the third man helplessly dropping astern, but still afloat and swimming.

Almost simultaneously, with a mighty volition of ungraduated, instantaneous swiftness, the White Whale darted through the weltering sea.[52] But when Ahab cried out to the steersman to take new turns with the line, and hold it so; and commanded the crew to turn round on their seats, and tow the boat up to the mark; the moment the treacherous line felt that double strain and tug, it snapped in the empty air!

"What breaks in me? Some sinew cracks! 'tis whole again; oars! oars! Burst in upon him!"

Hearing the tremendous rush of the sea-crashing boat, the whale wheeled round to present his blank forehead at

[52] THE WELTERING SEA—The heaving sea. The water is in a turmoil because of the struggle.

bay; but in that evolution, catching sight of the nearing black hull of the ship; seemingly seeing in it the source of all his persecutions; bethinking it—it may be—a larger and nobler foe; of a sudden, he bore down upon its advancing prow, smiting his jaws amid fiery showers of foam.

Ahab staggered; his hand smote his forehead. "I grow blind; hands! stretch out before me that I may yet grope my way. It's night?"

"The whale! The ship!" cried the cringing oarsmen.

"Oars! oars! Slope downwards to thy depths, O sea, that ere it be forever too late, Ahab may slide this last, last time upon his mark! I see: the ship! the ship! Dash on, my men! will ye not save my ship?"

But as the oarsmen violently forced their boat through the sledge-hammering seas, the before whale-smitten bow-ends of two planks burst through, and in an instant almost, the temporarily disabled boat lay nearly level with the waves; its half-wading, splashing crew trying hard to stop the gap and bail out the pouring water.

Meantime, for that one beholding instant, Tashtego's masthead hammer remained suspended in his hand; and the red flag, half-wrapping him as with a plaid,[53] then streamed itself straight out from him, as his own forward-flowing heart; while Starbuck and Stubb, standing upon the bowsprit beneath, caught sight of the downcoming monster just as soon as he.

"The whale, the whale![54] Up helm, up helm! Oh, all ye sweet powers of air, now hug me close! Let not Starbuck die, if die he must, in a woman's fainting fit. Up helm, I say—ye fools, the jaw! the jaw! Is this the end of all my bursting prayers? all my lifelong fidelities? Oh, Ahab, Ahab, lo, thy work. Steady! helmsman, steady. Nay, nay! Up helm again! He turns to meet us! Oh, his unappeasable brow drives on towards one, whose duty tells him he cannot depart. My God, stand by me now!"

"Stand not by me,[55] but stand under me, whoever you are that will now help Stubb; for Stubb, too, sticks here. I grin at thee, thou grinning whale! Whoever helped Stubb, or kept Stubb awake, but Stubb's own unwinking eye? And now poor Stubb goes to bed upon a mattress that is all too soft; would it were stuffed with brushwood! I grin at thee, thou grinning whale! Look ye, sun, moon, and stars! I call ye assassins of as good a

fellow as ever spouted up his ghost. For all that, I would yet ring glasses with thee, would ye but hand the cup! Oh, oh! oh, oh! thou grinning whale, but there'll be plenty of gulping soon! Why fly ye not, O Ahab! For me, off shoes and jacket to it; let Stubb die in his drawers! A most moldy and over-salted death, though—cherries! cherries! cherries! Oh, Flask, for one red cherry ere we die!"

"Cherries? I only wish that we were where they grow. Oh, Stubb, I hope my poor mother's drawn my part-pay[56] ere this; if not, few coppers will now come to her, for the voyage is up."

From the ship's bows, nearly all the seamen now hung inactive; hammers, bits of plank, lances, and harpoons, mechanically retained in their hands, just as they had darted from their various employments; all their enchanted eyes intent upon the whale, which from side to side strangely vibrating his predestinating[57] head, sent a broad band of overspreading semicircular foam before him as he rushed. Retribution,[58] swift vengeance, eternal malice were in his whole aspect, and spite of all that mortal man could do, the solid white buttress of his forehead smote the ship's starboard bow, till men and timbers reeled. Some fell flat upon their faces. Like dislodged trucks, the heads of the harpooners aloft shook on their bull-like necks. Through the breach, they heard the waters pour, as mountain torrents down a flume.

Diving beneath the settling ship, the

---

[53] A PLAID—A blanket.

[54] "THE WHALE, THE WHALE! . . ."—In this paragraph Starbuck is speaking.

[55] "STAND NOT BY ME, . . ."—This paragraph is spoken by Stubb; the next paragraph is Starbuck's reply.

[56] PART-PAY—Funds advanced to a sailor's family, and deducted from the salary due him at the end of the voyage.

[57] PREDESTINATING—This word means "deciding in advance." Here it suggests both that Moby Dick's own head, or brain, will decide what he does next, and that he cannot be prevented from doing it.

[58] RETRIBUTION—Punishment, "getting even."

whale ran quivering along its keel; but turning under water, swiftly shot to the surface again, far off the other bow, but within a few yards of Ahab's boat, where, for a time, he lay quiescent.

"I turn my body from the sun. What ho, Tashtego! let me hear thy hammer. Oh! ye three unsurrendered spires of mine; thou uncracked keel; thou firm deck, and haughty helm, and Pole-pointed prow—death-glorious ship! must ye then perish, and without me? Am I cut off from the last fond pride of meanest shipwrecked captains? Oh, lonely death on lonely life! Oh, now I feel my topmost greatness lies in my top-most grief. Ho, ho! from all your farthest bounds, pour ye now in, ye bold billows of my whole foregone life, and top this one piled comber [59] of my death! To-wards thee I roll, thou all-destroying but unconquering whale; to the last I grapple with thee. Let me then tow to pieces, while still chasing thee, though tied to thee, thou cursed whale! *Thus,* I give up the spear!"

The harpoon was darted; the stricken whale flew forward; with igniting velocity the line ran through the groove—ran foul. Ahab stooped to clear it; he did clear it; but the flying turn caught him round the neck, and voicelessly as Turkish mutes bowstring their victim,[60] he was shot out of the boat, ere the crew knew he was gone. Next instant, the heavy eye splice in the rope's final end flew out of the stark-empty tub, knocked down an oars-man, and smiting the sea, disappeared in its depths.

For an instant, the tranced boat's crew stood still; then turned. "The ship? Great God, where is the ship?" Soon they through dim, bewildering mediums saw her sidelong fading phantom,[61] as in the gaseous Fata Morgana;[62] only the uppermost masts out of the water; while fixed by infatuation, or fidelity, or fate, to their once lofty perches, the pagan har-pooners still maintained their sinking lookouts on the sea. And now, concen-tric circles seized the lone boat itself, and all its crew, and each floating oar, and every lance-pole, and spinning animate and inanimate all round and round in one vortex, carried the smallest chip of the "Pequod" out of sight.

But as the last whelmings [63] intermix-ingly poured themselves over the sunken head of the Indian at the mainmast, leaving a few inches of the erect spar [64] yet visible, together with long streaming yards of the flag, which calmly undulated, with ironical coincidings,[65] over the de-stroying billows they almost touched—at that instant, a red arm and a hammer hovered backwardly uplifted in the open air, in the act of nailing the flag faster and yet faster to the subsiding spar. A sky hawk that tauntingly had followed the main-truck downwards from its nat-ural home among the stars, pecking at

[59] COMBER—A long curling wave.

[60] VOICELESSLY AS TURKISH MUTES BOW-STRING THEIR VICTIM—In early times, Turkish sultans put offenders to death by strangling them with bowstrings. The victim was unable to cry out, and the executioners were silent too because they were "mutes"—that is, men who were un-able to speak.

[61] HER SIDELONG FADING PHANTOM—The ship has been rammed head-on by Moby Dick, and has already sunk below the surface. For a moment the men can see it dimly in the water as it goes down.

[62] FATA MORGANA—A mirage which is fre-quently seen in the sea between Sicily and Italy. Formerly it was believed to have been created by fairies. The name means "the fairy Morgana."

[63] WHELMINGS—Overwhelming waves.

[64] SPAR—A spar is any pole on a ship which helps support the sails. Here the word refers to the mainmast.

[65] IRONICAL COINCIDINGS—The flag "coin-cides" with the surface just below by rising and falling when the billows do—as if making fun of them.

the flag, and incommoding[66] Tashtego there; this bird now chanced to intercept its broad fluttering wing between the hammer and the wood; and simultaneously feeling that etherial[67] thrill, the submerged savage beneath, in his death gasp, kept his hammer frozen there; and so the bird of heaven, with archangelic[68] shrieks, and his imperial beak thrust up-wards, and his whole captive form folded in the flag of Ahab, went down with his ship, which, like Satan, would not sink to hell till she had dragged a living part of heaven along with her, and helmeted herself with it.

Now small fowls flew screaming over the yet yawning gulf; a sullen white surf beat against its steep sides; then all collapsed, and the great shroud[69] of the sea rolled on as it rolled five thousand years ago.

[66] INCOMMODING—Interfering with.
[67] ETHERIAL—Heavenly, celestial. Melville uses the word here because the hawk lives in the air.
[68] ARCHANGELIC—Like one of the chief angels.
[69] SHROUD—Garment or winding sheet for the dead.

EPILOGUE

"AND I ONLY AM ESCAPED ALONE TO TELL THEE"
—Job.

THE DRAMA'S DONE. *Why then here does anyone step forth? Because one did survive the wreck.*

It so chanced that I was he who, when on the last day the three men were tossed from out of the rocking boat, was dropped astern. So, floating on the margin of the ensuing scene, and in full sight of it, when the half-spent suction of the sunk ship reached me, I was then, but slowly, drawn towards the closing vortex. When I reached it, it had subsided to a creamy pool. Round and round, then, and ever contracting towards the button-like black bubble at the axis of that slowly wheeling circle, I did revolve. Till, gaining that vital center, the black bubble upward burst; and now, owing to its great buoyancy, rising with great force, a life buoy shot lengthwise from the sea, fell over, and floated by my side. Buoyed up by that for almost one whole day and night, I floated on a soft and dirgelike main.[70] The unharming sharks, they glided by as if with padlocks on their mouths; the savage sea hawks sailed with sheathed beaks. On the second day, a sail drew near, nearer, and picked me up at last. It was the devious-cruising "Rachel,"[71] that in her retracing search after her missing children, only found another orphan.

[70] *Main*—Sea.
[71] *Devious-cruising Rachel*—A devious route is winding, or crooked. The "Rachel," which the "Pequod" had met several days earlier, is still cruising back and forth in search of her missing whaleboat and its crew.

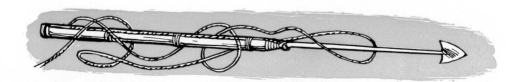

FOR UNDERSTANDING

A STORY OF ADVENTURE

Ishmael, the narrator of the tale, is not a principal character, but by reading about his adventures, we become acquainted with the crew and captain of the "Pequod," and follow them to the end of the story.

1. In "The Spouter-Inn," what puzzling hints are given to Ishmael about the man he is to sleep with? When he finally sees Queequeg, why is he afraid of him? Explain how the scene between Queequeg, the frightened narrator, and later the landlord, is partly a humorous one. Is Queequeg really a dangerous person?

2. In "The Quarter-Deck," how does Ahab get the crew to support him enthusiastically in his search for Moby Dick? How does the conversation in this scene bring out the fact that Moby Dick is well known to experienced whaling men? Point out one or more passages that show Ahab's intense desire to find this particular whale.

3. In the chapter called "Stubb Kills a Whale," how does the author make us realize the eagerness and excitement of the men in the whaleboats? Explain Stubb's final remark, "Yes; both pipes smoked out." Like scenes of danger or excitement in real life, this one ends rather quietly and soberly. What *details* does the author use to emphasize the quietness of the moment after the death of the whale?

4. The climax of the novel comes on the third day of the fight with Moby Dick. What advice does Ahab receive about continuing the fight? How do the sharks hamper the oarsmen in Ahab's boat? Describe the picture we get of Ahab's boat and the men in it, just after it breaks apart. Does Ahab's attempt to kill Moby Dick end in success or failure? Find the last place Ahab is mentioned, and explain what finally becomes of him.

5. Why does the ship sink? Just as it goes down, what is Tashtego doing? Explain how a hawk gets carried down with the sinking ship. Reread the dramatic final paragraph beginning "Now small fowls flew screaming . . ." The author says the surface of the sea looks just as it did five thousand years ago—unchanged since the dawn of history.

6. An *epilogue* is a final comment or explanation, a sort of "second ending." Explain why the author is forced to add an epilogue to this story. How is Ishmael saved?

AHAB, A TRAGIC HERO

A work of literature is called a *tragedy* when it ends in disaster for the hero. Of course, the author must succeed in making the readers interested in this person, so that his fate will be important to them. In addition, the tragic ending must ring true. Readers must feel, "That's right. That's the way this story would probably end."

1. Why are we inclined to sympathize with Ahab's desire to kill the White Whale? What admirable qualities does Ahab have? Does his enemy, the whale, seem to have vicious qualities, or does he merely defend himself?

2. What details in the story make disaster seem unavoidable—that is, what details give us a feeling that Moby Dick is so powerful that it is impossible to defeat him?

3. In tragedies, often the hero is partly the cause of his own downfall, through some terrible mistake or some defect in his character. Explain how the tragic ending of *Moby Dick* comes partly from Ahab's own actions and partly from other causes. Looking back, do you think Ahab *started* the series of events that finally ended in disaster? How is it emphasized in the last chapter that he still has an opportunity to prevent the tragedy? What does Ahab's last command to Tashtego—to nail the flag to the mast of the sinking ship—show about his state of mind?

4. In ancient Greek tragedies and in Shakespeare's tragedies, the hero is nearly always a king or a great leader—so his downfall affects not only himself but a whole nation. How is Ahab in a similar position? His determination to seek and kill Moby Dick is wild, and almost insane.

How is it also *wicked*, when we consider his responsibility to others?

5. Explain how, in the final chapter, one event is piled on another to build up a sense of terror—impressing on us the greatness of the catastrophe.

MAN AGAINST NATURE

A frequent subject in literature is some kind of struggle between man and the forces of nature. *Moby Dick* is one of the most famous books ever written on this inexhaustible subject.

1. If the class has already read "To Build a Fire," by Jack London, point out details in it that are similar to events in *Moby Dick*. Explain how the book *Robinson Crusoe*, by Daniel Defoe, might be considered another example of this type of story. Have you read other books, or seen movies, dealing with this subject? For each, explain what the struggle is.

2. Judging from what we know about prehistoric man, what *living* creatures were a menace to him, and what was his protection? Give several examples of living creatures that are seriously harmful to human life today. On the other hand, how is mankind dependent on living creatures for his survival?

3. In *Moby Dick*, the whale might be considered a symbol of the great ocean that is its home. Looked at from this point of view, the whole book suggests the struggle against the sea that has gone on ever since men invented the first boats. What dangers are still encountered in navigation today? Explain why men are not likely ever to stop their continual contest with the sea.

4. To some readers, Ahab and his crew suggest *the whole human race*, and the danger that threatens them is a reminder of *man's situation in the universe*. Mention one or more *natural* changes that might endanger mankind—whether among the stars and planets, or on the earth itself. What *man-made* events might destroy us? Reread the last paragraph of the chapter called "The Line," and explain how Melville is justified in comparing *a man seated in a tossing whaleboat* to *a man seated comfortably by his own fireplace*.

5. Ahab, in his determined war against Moby Dick, is overproud, even wicked. It is sometimes argued that man, by recklessly interfering with nature, can bring destruction on himself. Can you think of scientific inventions, startling medical discoveries, or great engineering projects that might seem too bold—as if man thought there were no limits to his power? What dangerous consequences have come, or might come, from such tampering with nature?

On the other hand, most of the familiar details of civilized life are the result of such "interference." If we did not seek to control nature, what are some common *foods* that we would have to do without? some kinds of *medical care?* some forms of *transportation?* In what ways did even comparatively uncivilized peoples like the American Indians "interfere" with nature?

MELVILLE'S PICTURE OF THE WHALING INDUSTRY

Moby Dick is almost like an encyclopedia of whaling in story form. Even a brief selection from the book gives many facts about the way whales were hunted, and about the men who hunted them, a hundred years ago.

1. In "The Spouter-Inn," how does Melville show us that the sailors are rather boisterous and untamed in their behavior? When Queequeg finally appears, which details of his appearance and actions seem particularly outlandish? In "Stubb Kills a Whale," how does Melville impress us with the wildness of the three harpooners, Queequeg, Tashtego, and Daggoo?

2. From Melville's description of whale-hunting, explain how the people on the ship go about finding a whale in the first place. Explain what they do when they begin the actual chase. The whale is not a true fish but an *animal*, and must come to the surface at regular intervals for air. How is this fact of great importance in trying to

get close enough to the whale to harpoon him? Explain the process of harpooning the whale, and why this brings the men one step closer to killing their prey. How is the whale finally killed?

3. Describe the various kinds of danger the men in the whaleboat are exposed to—from the whale, and from the whale line.

NAUTICAL EXPRESSIONS

For the most part it is not necessary to understand the sailors' lingo in *Moby Dick* —except temporarily, to know what is happening in the story. However, a few of the expressions used should be a part of everyone's knowledge.

Melville often speaks of *fore* and *aft*— meaning toward the front of the ship, and toward the rear. The two ends of the ship are the *stern* and the *bow* (pronounced to rhyme with *now*). Which end—stern or bow—is *fore*, and which is *aft*?

What is the *wake* of a ship? Which is the *leeward side*?

In chasing one of the whales, the men are ordered to *paddle* the boats instead of *rowing* them, so the whale won't hear them coming. Although these are everyday expressions, not everyone understands them completely. Explain the difference. Why is paddling less noisy than rowing?

REPORTS ON WHALES AND WHALING

1. From encyclopedias, find information for a written or oral report on one of the following topics:

The size and characteristics of whales.

Parts of the whale having commercial value.

2. Make a report on *modern* methods of hunting whales. Use encyclopedias—and also, if possible, the picture-article "Antarctic Whaling," in *Life* magazine for Sep-

tember 30, 1946. There are also many interesting and informative books on the subject of whaling.

FURTHER READING—MELVILLE, WHALES, AND THE SEA

RACHEL CARSON, *The Sea Around Us.* This popular book is fascinating to people who have never even seen the ocean. Written for the general reader, it tells what scientists have learned about tides, ocean depths, and the geological changes that formed seas and continents.

R. H. DANA, *Two Years Before the Mast.* In 1834, to cure himself of serious eye trouble, Dana shipped as a common sailor on a merchant vessel. The voyage took him around South America to the little-known coast of California. In his book, which was much admired by Melville, he describes his experiences.

HERMAN MELVILLE, *Moby Dick.* Some students will enjoy reading the entire story of Moby Dick, perhaps in a shortened version. If no abridged edition is available, read the first 22 chapters and the last 33— that is, from Chapter 103 to the end.

HERMAN MELVILLE, *Typee. Typee* is a short novel about cannibals on an island in the Pacific. It was Melville's first and most popular book.

HERMAN MELVILLE, *Omoo.* In *Omoo* Melville continues the story of the preceding book, telling of adventures on other islands and on board ship.

R. B. ROBERTSON, *Of Whales and Men.* In 1950 Dr. Robertson went as chief medical officer on a whaling cruise. His book tells about modern whaling equipment— including radar, and harpoons fired from cannons; about drawing 100-foot whales on board ship to be butchered; about Scottish and Norwegian seamen; and about the dangers and hardships that are still a part of whaling life.

HENRY WADSWORTH LONGFELLOW
(1807-1882)

Longfellow was the "household poet" of the nineteenth century. He wrote a great many simply worded, easily read poems—"A Psalm of Life," *Hiawatha*, "The Skeleton in Armor." His countrymen loved them.

Born in Maine, Longfellow was a classmate of Hawthorne's at Bowdoin College. He was offered a position at Bowdoin as professor of modern languages if he would prepare himself for it. He did so by three years of travel and study in France, Spain, Italy, and Germany. He made an excellent teacher, and after another period of study abroad he became Professor of French and Spanish literature at Harvard.

Both in the classroom and in his writing, Longfellow was a sort of interpreter of foreign culture to Americans. He was a lifelong student of all the styles and types of poetry that had been developed in older civilizations, and he made Americans familiar with them by imitating them in his own writing. He translated famous European poems, and wrote many tales in verse which dealt with European history. But the poems his public liked best were those on American history—"Paul Revere's Ride," *The Courtship of Miles Standish*—and short poems on daily life that always ended with an easily understood moral.

Longfellow was a friendly, kindhearted man. His beautiful home in Cambridge, Massachusetts, became a meeting place for the literary men of New England. Perhaps his popularity was bad for him. It made him write too rapidly; and it made him content to find and adapt material from earlier writers rather than try to produce original masterpieces. He is not as highly admired now as during his own lifetime—but perhaps the pendulum of critical opinion has swung too far. It is true that many of Longfellow's poems are oversentimental, and that their thought is too obvious to be of interest to experienced readers. But he has introduced millions of children to the pleasure of reading poetry, and his collected works contain many poems in which his genuinely fine talent shows itself.

◇◇◇◇◇

The Building of the Ship

Longfellow's long poem "The Building of the Ship" gives an accurate picture of nineteenth-century shipmaking. But in the last lines of the poem, quoted here, the poet turned to a greater topic—a more important "ship." He made his praise of the splendid vessel, and his prayer for her safety, into a song about the "Ship of State"—America. See how well you can follow his comparison.

Thou, too, sail on, O Ship of State!
Sail on, O Union, strong and great!
Humanity with all its fears,
With all the hopes of future years,
Is hanging breathless on thy fate! 5
We know what Master laid thy keel,
What Workmen wrought thy ribs of steel,
Who made each mast, and sail, and rope,
What anvils rang, what hammers beat,
In what forge and what a heat 10
Were shaped the anchors of thy hope!

Fear not each sudden sound and shock,
'Tis of the wave and not the rock;
'Tis but the flapping of the sail,
And not a rent made by the gale! 15
In spite of rock and tempest's roar,
In spite of false lights on the shore,
Sail on, nor fear to breast the sea!
Our hearts, our hopes, are all with thee,
Our hearts, our hopes, our prayers, our tears, 20
Our faith triumphant o'er our fears,
Are all with thee—are all with thee!

FOR UNDERSTANDING

1. What arguments could be given for the idea that lines 3–5 are true, not just poetic exaggeration?

2. Explain the real meaning of lines 12–15. Give two or more examples of "sound and shock" in the history of our country, and explain how each one turned out to be "of the wave and not the rock."

METAPHORS OF THE SEA

When Longfellow speaks of a nation as if it were a ship, he is using a figure of speech called a *metaphor*. He is able to express his ideas more vividly by making us picture the United States as a mighty ship plowing forward through the sea to unknown adventures. One reason he is able to do so is that there have been sailors ever since the beginning of history, and metaphors from sailing have become embedded in our language and thought.

1. Describe an imaginary situation in which each of the following phrases might be used as metaphors: (a) to set sail; (b) to set a course; (c) with so-and-so at the helm; (d) to lie at anchor; (e) my ship has come in; (f) "any port in a storm."

2. Name at least one other American poem based on a metaphor between ship and nation.

The Arsenal at Springfield

An arsenal is a storehouse of weapons and other military equipment. At one time when the Longfellows were visiting the United States Arsenal at Springfield, Massachusetts, Mrs. Longfellow remarked that the guns stacked row on row were like the pipes of an organ. The poet wove the fancy of his wife into a prayer for peace.

This is the Arsenal. From floor to ceiling,
 Like a huge organ, rise the burnished arms;
But from their silent pipes no anthem pealing
 Startles the villages with strange alarms.

Ah! what a sound will rise, how wild and dreary,   5
 When the death angel touches those swift keys!
What loud lament and dismal Miserere
 Will mingle with their awful symphonies!

I hear even now the infinite fierce chorus,
 The cries of agony, the endless groan,   10
Which, through the ages that have gone before us,
 In long reverberations reach our own.

On helm and harness rings the Saxon hammer,
 Through Cimbric forest roars the Norseman's song,
And loud, amid the universal clamor,   15
 O'er distant deserts sounds the Tartar gong.

I hear the Florentine, who from his palace
 Wheels out his battle bell with dreadful din,
And Aztec priests upon their teocallis
 Beat the wild war drums made of serpent's skin;   20

The tumult of each sacked and burning village;
 The shout that every prayer for mercy drowns;
The soldiers' revels in the midst of pillage;
 The wail of famine in beleaguered towns;

The bursting shell, the gateway wrenched asunder,   25
 The rattling musketry, the clashing blade;
And ever and anon, in tones of thunder,
 The diapason of the cannonade.

Is it, O man, with such discordant noises,
 With such accursèd instruments as these,   30
Thou drownest Nature's sweet and kindly voices,
 And jarrest the celestial harmonies?

---

 7. MISERERE (mĭz′ĕ·rē′rĕ)—A psalm for mercy.
 14. CIMBRIC (sĭm′brĭk)—The Cimbri were an ancient tribe living in what is now northern Germany.
 19. TEOCALLIS (tē′ô·kăl′ĭz)—The teocallis was a flat-topped pyramid used by the Aztecs as a place of worship.
 28. DIAPASON (dī′à·pā′zŭn)—The basal melodic tone of a pipe organ; the complete range of tone in a musical instrument.

Were half the power that fills the world with terror,
    Were half the wealth bestowed on camps and courts,
Given to redeem the human mind from error,   35
    There were no need of arsenals and forts:

The warrior's name would be a name abhorrèd!
    And every nation, that should lift again
Its hand against a brother, on its forehead
    Would wear forevermore the curse of Cain!   40

Down the dark future, through long generations,
    The echoing sounds grow fainter and then cease;
And like a bell, with solemn, sweet vibrations,
    I hear once more the voice of Christ say, "Peace!"

Peace! and no longer from its brazen portals   45
    The blast of War's great organ shakes the skies!
But beautiful as songs of the immortals,
    The holy melodies of love arise.

40. CURSE OF CAIN—A curse was placed upon Cain, the first murderer, for slaying his brother Abel. See Genesis 4:11–12.

FOR UNDERSTANDING

1. Try to form a mental picture of the sight that inspired this poem. Would the masses of stacked guns be placed horizontally or vertically? Why does the second line compare them to a *huge* organ?

2. How is the second stanza an imaginative extension of the idea that the guns look like organ pipes?

3. Lines 9–28 summarize *sounds* created by all civilizations throughout history. What do the sounds have in common? What louder burst of sound ends this section of the poem? Explain how it is true as stated in stanza 3 that the cries of agony in past ages "in long reverberations reach our own."

4. Explain the method suggested by the poet in lines 33–36 for banishing war. What do you think of the suggestion in lines 37–40 that it should be considered as wicked for a nation to make war as for an individual to commit murder? How is it possible to agree with the poet's view of this matter and still be in favor of maintaining war plants and arsenals of weapons?

5. Reread the last two stanzas, which are a prophecy of the future. Discuss the extent to which the prophecy has come true in the history of our country since 1845, when this poem was written. If the prophecy ever comes true completely, what means do you think will have been successful in bringing about such a change?

667

The Rainy Day

In this poem Longfellow starts with a description of a familiar scene and then uses the scene to illustrate a fact about human life.

The day is cold, and dark, and dreary;
It rains, and the wind is never weary;
The vine still clings to the moldering wall,
But at every gust the dead leaves fall,
    And the day is dark and dreary.   5

My life is cold, and dark, and dreary;
It rains, and the wind is never weary;
My thoughts still cling to the moldering
    Past,

But the hopes of youth fall thick in the
    blast,
    And the days are dark and dreary.   10

Be still, sad heart! and cease repining;
Behind the clouds is the sun still
    shining;
Thy fate is the common fate of all,
Into each life some rain must fall,   14
    Some days must be dark and dreary.

FOR UNDERSTANDING

1. What is the "rain" that is referred to in stanzas 2 and 3?

2. The word *day* in the first stanza has been changed to *life* in the second stanza. What does Longfellow compare to the vine? to the wall? to the falling leaves? Discuss whether in making this very complete and detailed comparison Longfellow made his poem *more* or *less* effective.

3. Although many readers find comfort and encouragement in the line "Into each life some rain must fall," the real strength of the poem is in the first stanza. That is, the first stanza *produces* the mood of dejection and gloom which the rest of the poem merely comments on. Point out all details in the stanza, besides those in the opening line, which help build up this mood.

Nature

In this poem Longfellow uses a comparison from everyday experience to picture his idea that as we advance into old age, Life gently prepares us for the further experience of Death.

As a fond mother, when the day is o'er,
Leads by the hand her little child to bed,
Half willing, half reluctant to be led,
And leave his broken playthings on the floor,
Still gazing at them through the open door,   5
Nor wholly reassured and comforted
By promises of others in their stead,
Which, though more splendid, may not please him more;
So Nature deals with us, and takes away
Our playthings, one by one, and by the hand   10
Leads us to rest so gently, that we go
Scarce knowing if we wish to go or stay,
Being too full of sleep to understand
How far the unknown transcends the what-we-know.

FOR UNDERSTANDING

1. The first part of the poem shows us the small boy at bedtime. The last part, beginning "So Nature . . ." goes on to make a comparison with the last years of a person's life. Explain two or more resemblances noted in the poem.

2. In this poem *Nature* does not mean outdoor nature, but the natural changes that take place in our own bodies and minds. What are some of the "playthings" that one by one are taken from an aging person? Why might they be called "broken"?

3. What line suggests that in old age we feel almost willing to die? What reason is given for our not being *completely* willing?

4. Explain the word *transcends* in the last line. In using it, what does the poet indicate about the other world, after death? How does the thought in this poem differ from that in Bryant's "Thanatopsis," which is also a view of death?

THE SONNET FORM

1. This poem is written in a form called the *sonnet*. Sonnets have fourteen lines, and are divided into two "movements." How many lines are in the first part?

2. The first part or *octave* must follow a set rhyme scheme. It begins by rhyming *a b b a*, and then goes on to repeat the same rhyme sounds—*a b b a* again. Just as the same rhyme scheme is repeated twice in the octave, the thought is more or less repeated. How could lines 5–8 of this poem be said to discuss the same thing as lines 1–4? However, the subject has shifted slightly. How so?

3. The second movement or *sestet* is a sort of comment on the first movement, or an application of it. Explain how this rule is followed in the sestet of "Nature."

The Day Is Done

The gentle, almost pleasurable melancholy of this simple poem makes it a good example of Longfellow's writing. It expresses a mood that sometimes comes at the end of a day, when we are tired and are grateful for the peace and rest of home.

The day is done, and the darkness
  Falls from the wings of Night,
As a feather is wafted downward
  From an eagle in his flight.

I see the lights of the village   5
  Gleam through the rain and the mist,
And a feeling of sadness comes o'er me,
  That my soul cannot resist;

A feeling of sadness and longing
  That is not akin to pain,   10
And resembles sorrow only
  As the mist resembles the rain.

Come, read to me some poem,
  Some simple and heartfelt lay,   14
That shall soothe this restless feeling,
  And banish the thoughts of day.

Not from the grand old masters,
  Not from the bards sublime,
Whose distant footsteps echo
  Through the corridors of Time.   20

For, like strains of martial music,
  Their mighty thoughts suggest
Life's endless toil and endeavor;
  And tonight I long for rest.

Read from some humbler poet,   25
  Whose songs gushed from his heart,
As showers from the clouds of summer,
  Or tears from the eyelids start;

Who, through long days of labor,
  And nights devoid of ease,   30
Still heard in his soul the music
  Of wonderful melodies.

Such songs have power to quiet
  The restless pulse of care,

And come like the benediction   35
  That follows after prayer.

Then read from the treasured volume
  The poem of thy choice,
And lend to the rhyme of the poet
  The beauty of thy voice.   40

And the night shall be filled with music,
  And the cares that infest the day,
Shall fold their tents, like the Arabs,
  And as silently steal away.

FOR UNDERSTANDING

1. The poet does not explain the reason for his sadness, for there does not seem to be any particular reason for it. What lines best express the idea that it is only a very slight sadness?

2. In such moods as this, we do not care for strenuous kinds of enjoyment. What quiet activity does the poet think will comfort him? Explain why the "grand old masters" would not be right for this purpose.

3. This poem was first printed as an introduction to *The Waif*, which was a collection Longfellow had made of the works of lesser known poets. Explain all the reasons why it would make an appropriate introduction to such a book.

FIGURES OF SPEECH

1. In the first stanza, the full night has not yet come. For that reason, Longfellow compares the early darkness to a *single* feather dropped by an eagle. Explain how, in the last stanza, he finds a reason to compare *cares* to a wandering band of *Arabs*.

2. These two figures of speech at the be-ginning and end are like bits of decoration, and do not add much to the thought of the poem. However, lines 16–20 contain a powerful and imaginative figure of speech, one that impresses us as "just right." Why does Longfellow call the great poets—such men as Shakespeare, Milton, and Dante—"distant"? Reread the stanza. Then tell whether you get the impression that their footsteps are loud and confident, or soft and hesitant.

3. One of the "grand old masters" might be Shakespeare. He wrote his poetry more than three centuries ago, and it has been read, imitated, and discussed endlessly ever since. Explain why it is appropriate to say Shakespeare's poetry *echoes* through the corridors of Time.

FOR FURTHER READING

Tales of a Wayside Inn are stories in verse supposed to have been told at the Red Horse Inn, Sudbury, Massachusetts. Among the many selections in this book are, "The Bell of Atri," "Challenge of Thor," "King Robert of Sicily," "The Legend Beautiful," "Paul Revere's Ride," and "The Saga of King Olaf."

OLIVER WENDELL HOLMES (1809–1894)

Because of his sparkling, witty conversation Holmes has been called the official jester of Boston. He loved his prosperous, cultured city, and Boston loved him. Once he said, in mock-admiration which nevertheless reflected his real admiration, "Boston State-house is the hub of the solar system." The wisecrack has turned into the popular saying, "Boston is the hub of the universe." Holmes was fond of puns and quips of all kinds. He was in great demand as a lecturer. Whenever his Harvard class gathered for a reunion, he was expected to produce a humorously sentimental poem in honor of the occasion.

Added to his popularity as an entertainer was Holmes's solid achievement as a medical scientist. He served as professor of anatomy and physiology at Harvard for thirty-five years. He was one of the first great physicians in America, and he wrote some influential books on medicine. During his lifetime the germ theory of disease was just beginning to be understood, and Dr. Holmes helped to establish the sterilization of medical instruments as standard practice in hospitals.

A CLEVER ESSAYIST AND POET

When Holmes was twenty-one, to save the gallant ship "Constitution" from being scrapped, he wrote "Old Ironsides," one of his few serious poems. The verses saved the ship and made Holmes famous. When the *Atlantic Monthly* magazine was founded in 1857, it was Holmes who suggested its title. He contributed to the new magazine his first series of whimsical essays, entitled *The Autocrat of the Breakfast Table*. Later series were called *The Professor at the Breakfast Table, The Poet at the Breakfast Table,* and *Over the Teacups.* Into these chatty papers Holmes inserted some of his best poems. He is famous in literature mainly for the *Autocrat* essays and for his humorous verse.

◇◇◇◇◇

The Last Leaf

This poem might have been subtitled "Thoughts of a young man while looking at an old one." Poor old Major Melville, hobbling along the streets of Boston in the 1830's, was a queer-looking sight. For one thing, he wore the old-fashioned knee breeches of Colonial and Revolutionary times. Young Holmes could not resist turning out a whimsical verse on the old Major.

I saw him once before,
As he passed by the door,
  And again
The pavement stones resound,
As he totters o'er the ground   5
  With his cane.

They say that in his prime,
Ere the pruning knife of Time
  Cut him down,
Not a better man was found   10
By the Crier on his round
  Through the town.

But now he walks the streets,
And he looks at all he meets
  Sad and wan,   15
And he shakes his feeble head,
That it seems as if he said,
  "They are gone!"

The mossy marbles rest
On the lips that he has pressed   20
  In their bloom,
And the names he loved to hear
Have been carved for many a year
  On the tomb.

My grandmamma has said—   25
Poor old lady, she is dead
  Long ago—
That he had a Roman nose,
And his cheek was like a rose
  In the snow;   30

But now his nose is thin,
And it rests upon his chin
  Like a staff,
And a crook is in his back,
And a melancholy crack   35
  In his laugh.

I know it is a sin
For me to sit and grin
  At him here;
But the old three-cornered hat,   40
And the breeches, and all that,
  Are so queer!

And if I should live to be
The last leaf upon the tree
  In the spring,   45
Let them smile, as I do now,
At the old forsaken bough
  Where I cling.

FOR UNDERSTANDING

This poem hovers between sentimentality and humor. It could easily have become oversentimental, but the humor saves it from that. On the other hand, the poet's genuine sympathy for the old man prevents the humor from being cruel. This mixture of feelings enriches the poem—and corresponds very closely to the way we might have felt in Holmes's place.

1. The odd but pleasing stanza form contributes to the humor. Describe the way each stanza rhymes, and the arrangement of long and short lines.

2. Find the first *comparison* that is made in the poem. Explain why it is appropriate, and discuss whether it has a sentimental or humorous effect. Point out later lines which are obviously humorous.

3. What is meant by "Not a *better man* was found"? In your opinion, what passage most dramatically suggests that the old man has lived on long past the time when he played an active part in life?

4. Elderly persons ought to be treated with respect, as the poet admits in the next-to-last stanza. What *two* excuses does he offer for himself in the last two stanzas?

5. For better enjoyment of the gentle humor and the rather pleasing melancholy of "The Last Leaf," read it aloud.

◇◇◇◇◇

Contentment

At the beginning of this poem Holmes placed the quotation, "MAN WANTS BUT LITTLE HERE BELOW." The imaginary speaker seems to be a man of modest desires, very easily satisfied. But when he begins to explain these desires more fully, we get a different impression.

Little I ask; my wants are few;
    I only wish a hut of stone,
(A *very plain* brown stone will do)
    That I may call my own—
And close at hand is such a one,   5
In yonder street that fronts the sun.

Plain food is quite enough for me;
    Three courses are as good as ten—
If Nature can subsist on three,
    Thank Heaven for three. Amen!   10
I always thought cold victual nice—
My *choice* would be vanilla ice.

I care not much for gold or land—
    Give me a mortgage here and there—
Some good bank stock, some note of
        hand,
    Or trifling railroad share—   15

I only ask that Fortune send
A *little* more than I shall spend.

Honors are silly toys, I know,
    And titles are but empty names;   20
I would, *perhaps*, be Plenipo—
    But only near St. James;
I'm very sure I should not care
To fill our Gubernator's chair.

Jewels are baubles; 'tis a sin   25
    To care for such unfruitful things—
One good-sized diamond in a pin—
    Some, *not so large*, in rings—
A ruby, and a pearl, or so,
Will do for me—I laugh at show.   30

21. PLENIPO—Minister Plenipotentiary. A foreign ambassador or diplomat.
22. ST. JAMES—England; the Court of St. James.

My dame should dress in cheap attire;
  (Good, heavy silks are never dear);
I own perhaps I *might* desire
  Some shawls of true cashmere—
Some marrowy crapes of China silk,   35
Like wrinkled skins on scalded milk.

I would not have the horse I drive
  So fast that folks must stop and stare;
An easy gait—two forty-five—
  Suits me; I do not care—   40
Perhaps, for just a *single spurt*,
Some seconds less would do no hurt.

Of pictures, I should like to own
  Titians and Raphaels three or four—
I love so much their style and tone,   45
  One Turner, and no more,
(A landscape—foreground golden dirt—
The sunshine painted with a squirt).

Of books but few—some fifty score
  For daily use, and bound for wear;   50
The rest upon an upper floor—
  Some *little* luxury *there*
Of red morocco's gilded gleam
And vellum rich as country cream.

44. TITIANS (tĭsh'ănz) AND RAPHAELS (răf'-ȧ·ĕlz)—Valuable works of art by great Italian painters. Turner, mentioned in line 46, was a famous English painter.

Busts, cameos, gems—such things as these,   55
  Which others often show for pride,
I value for their power to please,
  And selfish churls deride—
One Stradivarius, I confess,   59
Two Meerschaums, I would fain possess.

Wealth's wasteful tricks I will not learn,
  Nor ape the glittering upstart fool—
Shall not carved tables serve my turn,
  But *all* must be of buhl?
Give grasping pomp its double share—
I ask but *one* recumbent chair.   66

Thus humble let me live and die,
  Nor long for Midas' golden touch;
If Heaven more generous gifts deny,
  I shall not miss them *much*—   70
Too grateful for the blessing lent
Of simple tastes and mind content!

53–54. OF RED MOROCCO'S . . . CREAM—Morocco and vellum are soft, fine-grained leathers used for rich bindings of books.
  59. STRADIVARIUS (străd'ĭ·vâr'ĭ·ŭs)—A priceless violin made by Antonio Stradivari.
  60. MEERSCHAUMS (mẽr'chŭmz)—Tobacco pipes made of a fine white material.
  64. BUHL (bōōl)—Decorative inlaid work of tortoise shell and rare metals.
  68. MIDAS—A legendary Greek king whose wish that everything he touched be turned to gold was granted.

FOR UNDERSTANDING

1. The willingness of the speaker to live in "a hut of stone" is the first joke in the poem. It turns out that he means a *brownstone house*—an expensive type of residence that was the fashion in Holmes's day. Explain the joke in the next stanza about living on "cold victual." What do you think of the speaker's willingness to do without ten-course meals?

2. Why is it tremendously funny to declare that the only wealth you desire is "a little more" than you will spend?

3. To enjoy lines 37–42 we should remember that before automobiles were made, it was fashionable to drive a fast horse—and a horse that could do a mile in two minutes and forty-five seconds was fast. In these lines the humor is given an added twist, for we unexpectedly learn that the speaker would like a horse that could sometimes go *even faster* than the pace mentioned. Point out a similar unexpected turn in lines 49–54.

4. Holmes had a talent for descriptive phrases that delight us with their cleverness and accuracy. One of these occurs in the lines about pictures. Turner was a great nineteenth-century English painter whose landscapes seemed to glow with brilliant sunlight. In two witty lines Holmes seems almost to make us catch a glimpse of one of these pictures. Discuss the accuracy of his description of China silk in lines 35–36.

5. What would you call the real subject of this poem, instead of contentment? What one hint is given that the speaker is even envious of other people's possessions? Explain how the word "*much*" in the last stanza suddenly opens up visions of even larger desires on the part of the speaker.

◇◇◇◇◇

THE AUTOCRAT OF THE BREAKFAST TABLE

Holmes was famous for his conversational powers, and according to gossip, he seldom permitted anyone else to get in a word. Each month, subscribers to the new magazine, the ATLANTIC MONTHLY, *opened it eagerly to "hear" Dr. Holmes talk—for in the "Autocrat" essays he skipped along from one topic to another as he might do at a small social gathering.*

An AUTOCRAT *is a monarch, one who rules. As we read this essay, we are to imagine a genteel boardinghouse where, at breakfast each morning, the Autocrat talks and talks. He very much resembles Dr. Holmes—well educated, full of lively ideas, and well satisfied with himself. Once in a while the other boarders seem to rebel a little, but the Autocrat cheerfully assumes that on the whole they are happy to hear about anything that pops into his head.*

——I never saw an author in my life—saving, perhaps, one—that did not purr as audibly as a full-grown domestic cat (*Felis Catus*, LINN.) [1] on having his fur smoothed in the right way by a skillful hand.

But let me give you a caution. Be very careful how you tell an author he is *droll*. Ten to one he will hate you; and if he does, be sure he can do you a mischief, and very probably will. Say you *cried* over his romance or his verses, and he will love you and send you a copy. You can laugh over that as much as you like—in private.

——Wonder why authors and actors are ashamed of being funny?—Why, there are obvious reasons, and deep philosophical ones. The clown knows very well that the women are not in love with him, but with Hamlet, the fellow in the black cloak and plumed hat. Passion never laughs. The wit knows that his place is at the tail of a procession.

If you want the deep underlying reason, I must take more time to tell it. There is a perfect consciousness in every form of wit—using that term in its general sense—that its essence consists in a partial and incomplete view of whatever it touches. It throws a single ray, separated from the rest—red, yellow, blue, or any intermediate shade—upon an object; never white light; that is the province of wisdom. We get beautiful effects from wit—all the prismatic colors—but never the object as it is in fair daylight. A pun, which is a kind of wit, is a different and much shallower trick in mental optics; throwing the *shadows* of two objects so that one overlies the other. Poetry uses the rainbow tints for special effects, but always keeps its essential object in the

purest white light of truth.—Will you allow me to pursue this subject a little farther?

[They didn't allow me at that time, for somebody happened to scrape the floor with his chair just then; which accidental sound, as all must have noticed, has the instantaneous effect that the cutting of the yellow hair by Iris had upon infelix Dido.[2] It broke the charm, and that breakfast was over.]

——Don't flatter yourselves that friendship authorizes you to say disagreeable things to your intimates. On the contrary, the nearer you come into relation with a person, the more necessary do tact and courtesy become. Except in cases of necessity, which are rare, leave your friend to learn unpleasant truths from his enemies; they are ready enough to tell them. Good breeding *never* forgets that *amour-propre*[3] is universal. When you read the story of the Archbishop and Gil Blas,[4] you may laugh, if you will, at the poor old man's delusion; but don't forget that the youth was the greater fool of the two, and that his master served such a booby rightly in turning him out of doors.

Neither make too much of flaws and occasional overstatements. Some persons seem to think that absolute truth, in the form of rigidly stated propositions, is all that conversation admits. But remember that talking is one of the fine arts—

---

[1] *Felis Catus*—This is the name of the cat in the internationally accepted system of classifying plants and animals. LINN. is Linnaeus, the great Swedish scientist who devised the system.

[2] IRIS . . . DIDO (dĭ'dō)—In Virgil's poem, the *Aeneid*, when Queen Dido was dying, the goddess Iris came to cut off a lock of her hair, thus releasing her soul. Dido is called *infelix*, or unhappy, because her lover, Aeneas, left her.

[3] *Amour-propre* (à'mōōr' prŏ'pr'). Self-love.

[4] GIL BLAS (zhēl bläs). The Archbishop was a vain clergyman and Gil Blas his flattering servant. The Archbishop had promised Gil a pension if he would warn his master that he was losing power as a preacher. Instead, when the time came for Gil to give the warning, he lost his job.

the noblest, the most important, and the most difficult—and that its fluent harmonies may be spoiled by the intrusion of a single harsh note. Therefore conversation which is suggestive rather than argumentative, which lets out the most of each talker's results of thought, is commonly the pleasantest and the most profitable. It is not easy, at the best, for two persons talking together to make the most of each other's thoughts, there are so many of them.

[The company looked as if they wanted an explanation.]

When John and Thomas, for instance, are talking together, it is natural enough that among the six there should be more or less confusion and misapprehension.

[Our landlady turned pale—no doubt she thought there was a screw loose in my intellects—and that involved the probable loss of a boarder. A severe-looking person, who wears a Spanish cloak and a sad cheek, fluted by the passions of the melodrama, whom I understand to be the professional ruffian of the neighboring theater, alluded, with a certain lifting of the brow, drawing down of the corners of the mouth, and somewhat rasping *voce di petto*,[5] to Falstaff's nine men in buckram.[6] Everybody looked up. I believe the old gentleman opposite was afraid I should seize the carving knife; at any rate, he slid it to one side, as it were carelessly.]

I think, I said, I can make it plain to Benjamin Franklin[7] here, that there are at least six personalities distinctly to be

recognized as taking part in that dialogue between John and Thomas.

Three Johns.
1. The real John; known only to his Maker.
2. John's ideal John; never the real one, and often very unlike him.
3. Thomas' ideal John; never the real John, nor John's John, but often very unlike either.

Three Thomases.
1. The real Thomas.
2. Thomas' ideal Thomas.
3. John's ideal Thomas.

Only one of the three Johns is taxed; only one can be weighed on a platform balance; but the other two are just as important in the conversation. Let us suppose the real John to be old, dull, and ill-looking. But as the Higher Powers have not conferred on men the gift of seeing themselves in the true light, John very possibly conceives himself to be youthful, witty, and fascinating, and talks from the point of view of his ideal. Thomas, again, believes him to be an artful rogue, though really simple and stupid. The same conditions apply to the three Thomases. It follows, that, until a man can be found who knows himself as his Maker knows him, or who sees himself as others see him, there must be at least six persons engaged in every dialogue between two. Of these, the least important, philosophically speaking, is the one that we have called the real person. No wonder two disputants often get angry, when there are six of them talking and listening all at the same time.

[A very unphilosophical application of the above remarks was made by a young fellow, answering to the name of John, who sits near me at table. A certain basket of peaches, a rare vegetable, little known to boardinghouses, was on its way to me *via* this unlettered Johannes. He appropriated the three that remained in

[5] *Voce di petto* (vō′chä dē pĕt′tŏ)—Deep voice.

[6] FALSTAFF'S NINE MEN IN BUCKRAM—Falstaff, the comic fat man in Shakespeare's *Henry IV*, ran away from a fight. Telling about it later, he said that he had killed two men in buckram suits. Each time he told the tale, he increased the number of men he had "killed."

[7] BENJAMIN FRANKLIN—The landlady of the boardinghouse had named her son after the famous Revolutionary statesman.

678

the basket, remarking that there was just one apiece for him. I convinced him that his practical inference was hasty and illogical, but in the meantime he had eaten the peaches.]

◇◇◇◇◇◇◇◇◇◇◇◇◇◇◇◇◇◇◇◇◇◇◇◇◇◇◇◇◇

FOR UNDERSTANDING

Although Holmes makes *The Autocrat of the Breakfast Table* as light and entertaining as possible, we realize that the *ideas* expressed are those he seriously believes in himself. As he "talks," he thinks of all sorts of clever analogies or comparisons which make his main points better understood.

1. What does the word *droll* mean? Instead of telling an author that his works are droll, what should we tell him?

2. In the third paragraph, the Autocrat explains why, in the long run, people value *wit* less highly than *seriousness*. A witty remark shows us only a part of the truth—although it may show us a part that we hadn't thought of before, and therefore may have *some* value. To illustrate, take the witty proverb, "Don't cross a bridge before you come to it." What *partial* truth does the proverb suggest? Describe a situation in which the proverb would be good advice. Then describe a situation in which it would be bad advice.

3. According to the science of physics, how do *white* rays of light differ from other rays? (If necessary, look up *prismatic colors* in a science text or reference book.) How does the analogy of *light rays* apply to the difference between *wit* and *truth?*

4. Which paragraph discusses the importance of "saving the face" of those with whom we talk? The Autocrat does not use the term "face-saving"; in which sentence does he use a term that means the same thing?

5. According to the Autocrat's theory of the three Johns, which John plays the *least*

important part in conversation with the three Thomases? Explain why. Apply the theory by telling about a typical misunderstanding between a boy and his father. Make sure your story fits the theory—that is, make sure the misunderstanding arises because there are "more than one" boy and "more than one" father.

6. One way Holmes makes the essay seem more like *talk* is by punctuation. What does the long dash at the beginning of a paragraph indicate? What does the shorter dash before a sentence within a paragraph indicate?

7. For humorous effect, Holmes occasionally says something about the long-suffering fellow boarders, who seem to talk very little. Perhaps they are busy eating. Find the first reference to them—enclosed in brackets, just after the remarks about wit and truth. At this point, what seems to be their attitude toward the Autocrat's lecture? Find the second reference to them, and explain how the sentence could be interpreted humorously. At the end of the selection, how does "the young fellow answering to the name of John" demonstrate in an unexpected way that he has been listening to the Autocrat? Why is his *name* important? What very clever remark does he make?

FOR FURTHER READING

"My Aunt" and "Dorothy Q" are word pictures of two members of Holmes's family. The first is the humorous, half-pathetic picture of his maiden aunt, the second a portrait of one of his forebears.

Two other humorous poems by Holmes are "The Deacon's Masterpiece" and "How the Old Horse Won the Bet." "The Chambered Nautilus" is an example of his more serious work.

HILDEGARDE HAWTHORNE, *Happy Autocrat: A Life of Oliver Wendell Holmes* (Longmans). This biography of the famous physician and author is a good choice.

JAMES RUSSELL LOWELL (1819-1891)

Lowell seems to have been destined from the beginning for a career either in one of the learned professions or in literature. He was born in Cambridge, of parents interested in books and music, and was educated at Harvard and abroad. Soon he was trying his hand at poetry and journalism. Under the encouragement of his first wife he joined the Abolitionists in their crusade against slavery. This was a radical step for a young man of conservative Cambridge society. Lowell's antislavery poems were written in Yankee dialect—the *spoken* language of New England farms and small towns. They were hard-hitting satirical verses, often directed against local politicians. Because they were supposedly written by a backwoods lad named "Hosea Biglow," they were called *The Biglow Papers*.

In 1855, Harvard University offered Lowell the honor of succeeding Longfellow when the older man retired from his professorship of foreign literature. Lowell now became more of a critic than a poet and wrote many magazine essays, later collected in book form, in which he discussed and explained the great books of the world. His purpose was to encourage better understanding of the masterpieces of world literature, and to establish a higher standard of performance among American writers. During this same period he served four years as the first editor of the *Atlantic Monthly*. In this magazine, which was splendidly successful, appeared the works of famous men like Emerson and Longfellow. In addition, Lowell helped to spread the popularity of the new, distinctively American form of fiction—the short story—by searching for talent among young, unknown writers, and publishing their stories.

Lowell's dignified Cambridge acquaintances might be scandalized to learn that to-day the "Biglow" verses are considered some of the best things he wrote. Lowell himself would not be shocked. He was a pioneer scholar in the study of dialect, and he defended colorful Yankee talk because of its "life and vigor and originality." Of his writings in "literary" English, those most admired today are his odes—powerful, sober poems that occasionally attain the grandeur of organ music.

◇◇◇◇◇

The Courtin'

"The Courtin' " is one of Lowell's most pleasing dialect poems. It shows us the speech of Yankees who had not had book learning, and it also shows us the interior of a New England farmhouse. More important, it makes us know and like the two persons in the story—Ezekiel, a fine, stalwart fellow who is too bashful to make love; and Hilda, a prim, pretty girl who knows how to give a tart answer when she is annoyed.

God makes sech nights, all white an' still
  Fur'z you can look or listen,
Moonshine an' snow on field an' hill,
  All silence an' all glisten.

Zekle crep' up quite unbeknown   5
  An' peeked in thru' the winder,
An' there sot Huldy all alone,
  'ith no one nigh to hender.

A fireplace filled the room's one side
  With half a cord o' wood in—   10
There warn't no stoves (tell comfort died)
  To bake ye to a puddin'.

The wa'nut logs shot sparkles out
  Towards the pootiest, bless her,
An' leetle flames danced all about   15
  The chiny on the dresser.

Agin the chimbley crooknecks hung,
  An' in amongst 'em rusted
The ole queen's arm thet gran'ther Young   19
  Fetched back f'om Concord busted.

The very room, coz she was in,
  Seemed warm f'om floor to ceilin',
An' she looked full ez rosy agin
  Ez the apples she was peelin'.

'Twas kin' o' kingdom come to look
  On sech a blessed cretur,   26
A dog rose blushin' to a brook
  Ain't modester nor sweeter.

He was six foot o' man, A 1,
  Clear grit an' human natur',   30
None couldn't quicker pitch a ton
  Nor dror a furrer straighter.

11. TELL COMFORT DIED—Until comfort died. Many people in Lowell's time preferred cheerful fireplaces to the newfangled stoves.

17. CROOKNECKS—Gourds.
19. THE OLE QUEEN'S ARM—The old musket.

He'd sparked it with full twenty gals,
  He'd squired 'em, danced 'em, druv
    'em,
Fust this one, an' then thet, by spells—
  All is, he couldn't love 'em.   36

But long o' her his veins 'ould run
  All crinkly like curled maple,
The side she breshed felt full o' sun
  Ez a south slope in Ap'il.   40

She thought no v'ice hed sech a swing
  Ez hisn in the choir;
My! when he made Ole Hunderd ring,
  She *knowed* the Lord was nigher.

An' she'd blush scarlit, right in prayer,
  When her new meetin'-bunnet   46
Felt somehow thru' its crown a pair
  O' blue eyes sot upun it.

Thet night, I tell ye, she looked *some!*
  She seemed to 've gut a new soul,   50
For she felt sartin-sure he'd come,
  Down to her very shoe-sole.

She heered a foot, an' knowed it tu,
  A-raspin' on the scraper—
All ways to once her feelins flew   55
  Like sparks in burnt-up paper.

He kin' o' l'itered on the mat,
  Some doubtfle o' the sekle,
His heart kep' goin' pity-pat,
  But hern went pity Zekle.   60

An' yit she gin her cheer a jerk
  Ez though she wished him furder,

43. OLE HUNDERD—A favorite hymn in New England churches. Its words are a revision of the hundredth Psalm.

54. THE SCRAPER—The metal foot-scraper fastened to the porch or to the walk in front of country homes.

57. L'ITERED ON THE MAT—Loitered on the door mat, hesitating to enter.

58. THE SEKLE—The sequel; that is, the outcome of his visit.

An' on her apples kep' to work,
  Parin' away like murder.

"You want to see my Pa, I s'pose?"   65
  "Wal . . . no . . . I come dasignin' "—
"To see my Ma? She's sprinklin' clo'es
  Agin tomorrer's i'nin'."

To say why gals acts so or so,
  Or don't, 'ould be persumin';   70
Mebby to mean *yes* an' say *no*
  Comes nateral to women.

He stood a spell on one foot fust,
  Then stood a spell on t'other,
An' on which one he felt the wust   75
  He couldn't ha' told ye nuther.

Says he, "I'd better call agin";
  Says she, "Think likely, Mister":
Thet last word pricked him like a pin,
  An' . . . Wal, he up an' kist her.   80

When Ma bimeby upon 'em slips,
  Huldy sot pale ez ashes,
All kin' o' smily roun' the lips
  An' teary roun' the lashes.

For she was jes' the quiet kind   85
  Whose naturs never vary,
Like streams that keep a summer mind
  Snowhid in Jenooary.

The blood clost roun' her heart felt glued
  Too tight for all expressin',   90
Tell Mother see how metters stood,
  An' gin' em both her blessin'.

Then her red come back like the tide
  Down to the Bay o' Fundy,
An' all I know is they was cried   95
  In meetin' come nex' Sunday.

94. THE TIDE DOWN TO THE BAY O' FUNDY— The funnel-shaped Bay of Fundy, along the Nova Scotia coast, is famous for its huge tides.

95. THEY WAS CRIED—Their intention to marry was formally announced in church.

FOR UNDERSTANDING

1. Many words in "The Courtin'" are spelled to correspond to New England pronunciation. Wherever they are hard to understand, reading the whole stanza aloud will help. Some quaint, characteristic phrases are used for picturesque effect. Explain "An' she looked *full ez rosy agin* ez the apples she was peelin'." Explain what Huldy says her "Ma" is doing.

2. Point out two or more comparisons drawn from everyday or local New England scenes.

3. How do we know that in reality Huldy is fond of Zekle? Why do you think she treats him in such a standoffish way?

4. The story has a happy ending. How does Zekle finally solve his problem of making his feelings known? Explain why the remark made by Huldy just before this would increase his desperation.

5. An equally humorous account might be given of boy-girl relationships today. Give an example of a typical stratagem used by a high-school girl to increase a boy's interest or to bewilder him. Or, explain the strategy sometimes used by a boy.

◇◇◇◇◇

Lincoln

These lines are from Lowell's long poem, "Harvard Commemoration Ode," written in 1865. The ode was recited in honor of Harvard men who had died in the War Between the States, but one section was devoted to President Lincoln whose death had occurred three months before.

The lines preceding this tribute to Lincoln were written in praise of all men who fight stoutly in a good cause.

Such was he, our Martyr-Chief,
  Whom late the Nation he had led,
  With ashes on her head,
Wept with the passion of an angry grief:
Forgive me, if from present things I turn   5
To speak what in my heart will beat and burn,
And hang my wreath on his world-honored urn.
  Nature, they say, doth dote,
  And cannot make a man
  Save on some worn-out plan,   10
  Repeating us by rote:
For him her Old-World molds aside she threw,

And choosing sweet clay from the breast
  Of the unexhausted West,   14
With stuff untainted shaped a hero new,
Wise, steadfast in the strength of God, and true.
  How beautiful to see
Once more a shepherd of mankind indeed,
Who loved his charge, but never loved to lead;
One whose meek flock the people joyed to be,   20
  Not lured by any cheat of birth,
  But by his clear-grained human worth,
And brave old wisdom of sincerity!

They knew that outward grace is dust;
   They could not choose but trust   25
In that sure-footed mind's unfaltering
   skill,
   And supple-tempered will
That bent like perfect steel to spring
   again and thrust.
   His was no lonely mountain peak of
     mind,
   Thrusting to thin air o'er our cloudy
     bars,   30
   A seamark now, now lost in vapors
     blind;
   Broad prairie rather, genial, level-
     lined,
   Fruitful and friendly for all human
     kind,
Yet also nigh to heaven and loved of
   loftiest stars.
   Nothing of Europe here,   35
Or, then, of Europe fronting mornward
   still,
   Ere any names of Serf and Peer
   Could Nature's equal scheme deface
   And thwart her genial will;
   Here was a type of the true elder
     race,   40

And one of Plutarch's men talked with
   us face to face.
   I praise him not; it were too late;
And some innative weakness there must
   be
In him who condescends to victory
Such as the Present gives, and cannot
   wait,   45
   Safe in himself as in a fate.
     So always firmly he:
     He knew to bide his time,
     And can his fame abide,
Still patient in his simple faith sublime,
     Till the wise years decide.   51
Great captains, with their guns and
   drums,
   Disturb our judgment for the hour,
   But at last silence comes;
These all are gone, and standing like a
   tower,   55
Our children shall behold his fame,
   The kindly, earnest, brave, foresee-
     ing man,
Sagacious, patient, dreading praise, not
   blame,
   New birth of our new soil, the first
     American.

41. ONE OF PLUTARCH'S MEN—The Greek biographer, Plutarch (plōō'tärk), wrote the lives of the famous heroes of ancient Greece and Rome. Therefore, this phrase compares Lincoln to such men as Julius Caesar.

◇◇

FOR UNDERSTANDING

1. Why does line 4 say the nation mourned Lincoln with "an angry grief"?

2. When the poet speaks of Lincoln as being formed out of "stuff untainted" he is declaring that this was a new kind of great man, a kind that the world had never seen before. What difference is mentioned in lines 21–22, which refer to the people's reason for trusting Lincoln? From what you know of Lincoln, explain line 24, which hints at another difference.

3. What comparison is being made when the poet says we have seen *"once more a shepherd of mankind"*?

4. Lincoln was not yet regarded as a hero

when this poem was written. Lines 48–51 are a recognition of this fact. Read Lowell's prophecy in lines 52–56, and discuss its accuracy. With what other great American leaders is Lincoln usually classed nowadays?

5. In the last line it is suggested that Lincoln's qualities were purely American, owing nothing to older nations of the world. This is an idea that is emphasized throughout the selection. Point out two other places where it occurs. What arguments can you give in support of such an idea?

6. Reread the metaphor about "mountain peak" as contrasted to "broad prairie" (lines 29–34). Explain all the ways in which this thought can be applied to Lincoln's character.

JOHN GREENLEAF WHITTIER (1807-1892)

Whittier, the Quaker poet, was born in Massachusetts on a farm which his great-great-grandfather had cleared in the wilderness. He had opportunity for only a little education, and not much encouragement for writing. His parents had no literary interests, and the farm was poor. After some country schooling, he had two terms at the academy in nearby Haverhill, where he paid his own way by making and selling slippers. Early and late, he was busy on the farm. However, he liked farm work, and, on the side, he was developing an interest in reading and writing poetry. His father disapproved of his writing, but a sister sent some of the poems to the country newspaper. When they began appearing in print, Whittier experienced his first thrill of encouragement.

He was still a young man when he became interested in the Abolitionist movement. People considered the antislavery leaders as troublemakers, and Whittier realized that he was helping an unpopular cause. He had wanted to be a writer who would show his countrymen the romance of early American history and the picturesqueness of American rural life. Instead, for thirty years he sacrificed everything else to the Abolitionist cause—editing antislavery newspapers, and turning out poems and articles in support of his views. Engaging in rough-and-tumble political agitation was a strange activity for a peaceful, deeply religious man. As Lowell wrote—

"There is Whittier, whose swelling and vehement heart
Strains the strait-breasted drab of the Quaker apart . . .
Our Quaker leads off metaphorical fights
For reform and whatever they call human rights,
Both singing and striking in front of the war,
And hitting his foes with the mallet of Thor."

That the issue had to be settled by war was a great sorrow to him. After the struggle was over, he settled back to peaceful living at Amesbury, Massachusetts, where a favorite niece kept house for him.

A POET OF HOMELY SCENES AND OF EARNEST FAITH

In the remaining years of his life Whittier wrote his best poems—most of them New England idylls and lyrics reminiscent of his youth. He knew and loved the flavor of simple domestic life and of the plain, wholesome ways of neighborhood and village. It is in the homelike scenes of "Telling the Bees" and "Snowbound" and in the strong, sure faith of his hymns that we see Whittier at his best.

⬦⬦⬦⬦⬦

Telling the Bees

The speaker in this poem is gazing at a farm home and recalling the last time he looked at this scene, a year before. As he stands looking, and remembering details, we learn the purpose of that earlier visit—and its sad conclusion.

Knowledge of an old rural custom is necessary in order to understand the end of the poem. Whenever a death had occurred in a farmhouse, a bit of mourning crepe was placed on each beehive. It was believed that if the bees were not informed of the death they would swarm and leave the farm.

Here is the place; right over the hill
  Runs the path I took;
You can see the gap in the old wall
  still,
  And the stepping stones in the shallow
  brook.

There is the house with the gate red-
  barred,   5
  And the poplars tall;

And the barn's brown length, and the
  cattle yard,
  And the white horns tossing above the
  wall.

There are the beehives ranged in the sun;
  And down by the brink   10
Of the brook are her poor flowers, weed-
  o'errun,
  Pansy and daffodil, rose and pink.

A year has gone, as the tortoise goes,
  Heavy and slow;
And the same rose blows, and the same
    sun glows,   15
  And the same brook sings of a year ago.

There's the same sweet clover smell in
    the breeze;
  And the June sun warm
Tangles his wings of fire in the trees,
  Setting, as then, over Fernside farm.

I mind me how, with a lover's care,   21
  From my Sunday coat
I brushed off the burrs, and smoothed my
    hair,
  And cooled at the brookside my brow
    and throat.

Since we parted, a month had passed—
  To love, a year;   26
Down through the beeches I looked at
    last
  On the little red gate and the well-
    sweep near.

I can see it all now—the slantwise rain
  Of light through the leaves,   30
The sundown's blaze on her window-
    pane,
  The bloom of her roses under the eaves.

Just the same as a month before—
  The house and the trees,

The barn's brown gable, the vine by the
    door—   35
  Nothing changed but the hives of bees.

Before them, under the garden wall,
  Forward and back,
Went, drearily singing, the chore girl
    small,
  Draping each hive with a shred of
    black.   40

Trembling, I listened; the summer sun
  Had the chill of snow;
For I knew she was telling the bees of
    one
  Gone on the journey we all must go!

Then I said to myself, "My Mary weeps
  For the dead today;   46
Haply her blind old grandsire sleeps
  The fret and the pain of his age away."

But her dog whined low; on the doorway
    sill,
  With his cane to his chin,   50
The old man sat; and the chore girl still
  Sang to the bees stealing out and in.

And the song she was singing ever since
  In my ear sounds on:
"Stay at home, pretty bees, fly not hence!
  Mistress Mary is dead and gone!"   56

47. HAPLY—Perhaps.

FOR UNDERSTANDING

1. The word "her" in the third stanza is the earliest hint as to why the speaker was interested in the farm home. Where do we learn that he has been absent a year? Why, on that earlier visit, did he brush off his coat and smooth his hair? At the time of that visit, he had been gone only a month. What is the meaning of lines 25–26?

2. Reread the last six stanzas. How did the young man first learn that someone was dead? How does line 41 show that he immediately feared it was his sweetheart that had died? What other explanation does he make up which immediately proves mistaken?

3. Turn back to the fourth stanza and explain why the speaker says the past year has gone "heavy and slow." This is a

hint of the tragedy which the reader will not understand until he has read the whole poem. What still earlier hint can the reader now detect in the description of the flowers, in the third stanza?

4. All the way through the poem, the story slowly becomes clearer. How can we be almost certain, in the next-to-last stanza, of who has died? Reread the final stanza carefully, and explain how in it the time-order has been reversed so as to save the climax to the very end.

Dear Lord and Father of Mankind

The language in Whittier's religious poetry shows an ease and perfection which is sometimes lacking in his other works. His deeply reverent nature, drawn from a mixed Puritan and Quaker ancestry, made it possible for devotional poems like this one to flow naturally from his pen. The stanzas that make up this hymn were taken from a longer poem.

Dear Lord and Father of mankind,
  Forgive our feverish ways!
Reclothe us in our rightful mind,
In purer lives thy service find,
  In deeper reverence, praise. 5

In simple trust like theirs who heard
  Beside the Syrian sea
The gracious calling of the Lord,
Let us, like them, without a word,
  Rise up and follow thee. 10

O Sabbath rest by Galilee!
  O calm of hills above,
Where Jesus knelt to share with thee
The silence of eternity
  Interpreted by love! 15

Drop thy still dews of quietness,
  Till all our strivings cease;
Take from our souls the strain and stress,
And let our ordered lives confess
  The beauty of thy peace. 20

Breathe through the heats of our desire
  Thy coolness and thy balm;
Let sense be dumb, let flesh retire;
Speak through the earthquake, wind, and fire,
  O still, small voice of calm! 25

FOR UNDERSTANDING

1. The first line so perfectly expresses trust and devotion that it seems an obvious line to write—after someone has done it! Give as many instances as you can from the Bible to show that God as a loving *father* is a familiar idea in the Christian faith.

2. Who were those who heard "the gracious calling of the Lord" beside the Syrian sea? In what way should we be like them?

3. Whittier's Quaker faith made him a zealous reformer, and he was a prominent figure in the New England antislavery

movement. At the same time he was opposed to angry, violent disputes. In the first and fourth stanzas, what expressions seem to refer to conflicts in public affairs? What disputes in America might Whittier object to if he were living today?

4. According to the last two stanzas, the effect of religion on our lives should be to stop our quarrels, and to cool down our heated passions. Make a list of words in the hymn which are suggestive of peacefulness and quiet.

Snowbound

Whittier much admired the works of Robert Burns, the Scottish farmer-poet who wrote "To a Mouse" and "Auld Lang Syne." His ambition as a young man was to be the American Burns, picturing rural New England life as unforgettably as Burns had depicted the life of Scottish peasants. Whittier had no such genius for song as the man he admired, but in his later years he produced one exceptionally fine poem—"Snowbound." In making us experience the storm, the sight of the high snowdrifts, and the coziness of the shut-in family around the fireplace, Whittier has given us a picture of a time gone by and has almost equaled Burns's famous "Cotter's Saturday Night." The lines below are selected passages from the long poem.

The sun that brief December day
Rose cheerless over hills of gray,
And, darkly circled, gave at noon
A sadder light than waning moon.
Slow tracing down the thickening sky   5
Its mute and ominous prophecy;
A portent seeming less than threat,
It sank from sight before it set.
A chill no coat, however stout,
Of homespun stuff could quite shut out,
A hard, dull bitterness of cold,   11
   That checked, mid-vein, the circling race
   Of lifeblood in the sharpened face,
The coming of the snowstorm told.
The wind blew east; we heard the roar
Of Ocean on his wintry shore,   16
And felt the strong pulse throbbing there
Beat with low rhythm our inland air.

Meanwhile we did our nightly chores—
Brought in the wood from out of
   doors,   20
Littered the stalls, and from the mows
Raked down the herd's-grass for the cows:
Heard the horse whinnying for his corn;
And, sharply clashing horn on horn,
Impatient down the stanchion rows   25
The cattle shake their walnut bows;
While, peering from his early perch
Upon the scaffold's pole of birch,
The cock his crested helmet bent   29
And down his querulous challenge sent.

Unwarmed by any sunset light
The gray day darkened into night,
A night made hoary with the swarm
And whirl-dance of the blinding storm,
As zigzag wavering to and fro   35

Crossed and recrossed the wingèd snow:
And ere the early bedtime came
The white drift piled the window frame,
And through the glass the clothesline
    posts   39
Looked in like tall and sheeted ghosts.
So all night long the storm roared on:
The morning broke without a sun;
In tiny spherule traced with lines
Of Nature's geometric signs,
In starry flake and pellicle   45
All day the hoary meteor fell;
And, when the second morning shone,
We looked upon a world unknown,
On nothing we could call our own.
Around the glistening wonder bent   50
The blue walls of the firmament,
No cloud above, no earth below—
A universe of sky and snow!
The old familiar sights of ours
Took marvelous shapes; strange domes
    and towers   55
Rose up where sty or corncrib stood,
Or gardenwall or belt of wood;
A smooth white mound the brush pile
    showed,
A fenceless drift what once was road;
The bridle post an old man sat   60
With loose-flung coat and high cocked
    hat;
The wellcurb had a Chinese roof;
And even the long sweep, high aloof,
In its slant splendor, seemed to tell
Of Pisa's leaning miracle.   65

A prompt, decisive man, no breath
Our father wasted: "Boys, a path!"

43. SPHERULE—Little sphere.
46. METEOR—Here the meaning is "snow."
A meteor is anything in the atmosphere.
62. WELLCURB—The enclosing structure around the top of a well.
63. SWEEP—The long pole pivoted to the top of a post, to raise and lower the bucket for drawing water from the well.
65. PISA'S LEANING MIRACLE—A famous bell tower in the city of Pisa, Italy. It is 180 feet high and leans 14 feet from the perpendicular position.

Well pleased (for when did farmer boy
Count such a summons less than joy?)
Our buskins on our feet we drew;   70
    With mittened hands, and caps drawn
    low,
        To guard our necks and ears from
        snow,
We cut the solid whiteness through;
And, where the drift was deepest, made
A tunnel walled and overlaid   75
With dazzling crystal: we had read
Of rare Aladdin's wondrous cave,
And to our own his name we gave,
With many a wish the luck were ours
To test his lamp's supernal powers.   80
We reached the barn with merry din,
And roused the prisoned brutes within.
The old horse thrust his long head out,
And grave with wonder gazed about.
The cock his lusty greeting said,   85
And forth his speckled harem led;
The oxen lashed their tails, and hooked,
And mild reproach of hunger looked;
The hornèd patriarch of the sheep,   89
Like Egypt's Amun roused from sleep,
Shook his sage head with gesture mute,
And emphasized with stamp of foot.

All day the gusty north wind bore
The loosening drift its breath before;
Low circling round its southern zone,   95
The sun through dazzling snow-mist
    shone.
No church bell lent its Christian tone
To the savage air, no social smoke
Curled over woods of snow-hung oak.
A solitude made more intense   100
By dreary-voicèd elements,

80. SUPERNAL—Coming from above, divine. In *The Arabian Nights* stories, when Aladdin rubbed his wonderful lamp a spirit would appear and carry out any command that was given.
89. THE HORNÈD PATRIARCH OF THE SHEEP—The male sheep which was the leader of the flock. His stately, rather surly manner reminds Whittier of the Egyptian god Amun or Ammon, who was pictured as having a sheep's head with curving horns.

The shrieking of the mindless wind,
The moaning tree boughs swaying blind,
And on the glass the unmeaning beat
Of ghostly finger tips of sleet.   105
Beyond the circle of our hearth
No welcome sound of toil or mirth
Unbound the spell, and testified
Of human life and thought outside.
We minded that the sharpest ear   110
The buried brooklet could not hear,
The music of whose liquid lip
Had been to us companionship,
And, in our lonely life, had grown
To have an almost human tone.   115

As night drew on, and, from the crest
Of wooded knolls that ridged the west,
The sun, a snow-blown traveler, sank
From sight beneath the smothering
     bank,   119
We piled, with care, our nightly stack
Of wood against the chimney back—
The oaken log, green, huge, and thick,

And on its top the stout backstick;
The knotty forestick laid apart,
And filled between with curious art   125
The ragged brush; then, hovering near,
We watched the first red blaze appear,
Heard the sharp crackle, caught the
     gleam
On whitewashed wall and sagging beam,
Until the old, rude-furnished room   130
Burst, flowerlike, into rosy bloom;
While radiant with a mimic flame
Outside the sparkling drift became,
And through the bare-boughed lilac tree
Our own warm hearth seemed blazing
     free.   135
The crane and pendent trammels showed,
The Turks' heads on the andirons glowed;
While childish fancy, prompt to tell
The meaning of the miracle,
Whispered the old rhyme: *"Under the
     tree,*   140
When the fire outdoors burns merrily,
There the witches are making tea." . . .

Shut in from all the world without,
We sat the clean-winged hearth about,
Content to let the north wind roar   145
In baffled rage at pane and door,
While the red logs before us beat
The frost line back with tropic heat;
And ever, when a louder blast
Shook beam and rafter as it passed,   150
The merrier up its roaring draft
The great throat of the chimney laughed.
The house dog on his paws outspread
Laid to the fire his drowsy head,
The cat's dark silhouette on the wall
A couchant tiger's seemed to fall;   156
And, for the winter fireside meet,
Between the andirons' straddling feet,
The mug of cider simmered slow,
The apples sputtered in a row,   160
And, close at hand, the basket stood
With nuts from brown October's
    wood. . . .

Within our beds awhile we heard
The wind that round the gables roared,
With now and then a ruder shock,   165
Which made our very bedsteads rock.
We heard the loosened clapboards tossed,
The board nails snapping in the frost;
And on us, through the unplastered wall,
Felt the light-sifted snowflakes fall;   170
But sleep stole on, as sleep will do
When hearts are light and life is new;
Faint and more faint the murmurs grew,
'Till in the summerland of dreams
They softened to the sound of streams,
Low stir of leaves, and dip of oars,   176
And lapsing waves on quiet shores.

Next morn we wakened with the shout
Of merry voices high and clear;
And saw the teamsters drawing near   180
To break the drifted highways out.
Down the long hillside treading slow
We saw the half-buried oxen go,
Shaking the snow from heads uptossed,
Their straining nostrils white with frost.

Before our door the straggling train   186
Drew up, an added team to gain.
The elders threshed their hands a-cold,
    Passed, with the cider mug, their jokes
    From lip to lip; the younger folks   190
Down the loose snowbanks, wrestling,
    rolled,
Then toiled again the cavalcade
    O'er windy hill, through clogged ravine,
    And woodland paths that wound be-
    tween
Low drooping pine boughs winter-
    weighed.   195
From every barn a team afoot,
At every house a new recruit,
Where, drawn by Nature's subtlest law,
Haply the watchful young men saw
Sweet doorway pictures of the curls   200
And curious eyes of merry girls,
Lifting their hands in mock defense
Against the snowball's compliments,
And reading in each missive tossed
The charm which Eden never lost.   205

We heard once more the sleigh bell's
    sound;
    And, following where the teamsters led,
The wise old Doctor went his round,
Just pausing at our door to say,
In the brief autocratic way   210
Of one who, prompt at Duty's call,
Was free to urge her claim on all,
    That some poor neighbor sick abed
    At night our mother's aid would
    need. . . .

So days went on; a week had passed   215
Since the great world was heard from last.
The Almanac we studied o'er,
Read and reread our little store
Of books and pamphlets, scarce a score,
One harmless novel, mostly hid   220
From younger eyes, a book forbid,
And poetry, (or good or bad,
A single book was all we had). . . .

212. HER CLAIM—That is, Duty's claim.

At last the floundering carrier bore
The village paper to our door.   225
Lo! broadening outward as we read,
To warmer zones the horizon spread;
In panoramic length unrolled
We saw the marvels that it told. . . .
We felt the stir of hall and street,   230
The pulse of life that round us beat;
The chill embargo of the snow
Was melted in the genial glow;   233
Wide swung again our ice-locked door,
And all the world was ours once more!

227. TO WARMER ZONES—The village paper contained news from other parts of the world than wintry New England.

◇◇◇◇◇◇◇◇◇◇◇◇◇◇◇◇◇◇◇◇◇◇◇◇◇◇◇◇◇◇

FOR UNDERSTANDING

1. Explain why the sun, according to line 8, "sank from sight before it set." In this first part of the poem, which lines do you think are most successful in conveying to us the severity of the winter storm?

2. Explain the passage about the "fire" seen outside the house. What superstitious idea—not really believed in—was connected with such a sight?

3. "Snowbound" is the very opposite of a difficult or complex piece of writing. The author's only intention is to tell, in simple, straightforward narrative, "what it was like." Do you feel he has succeeded? What short passage would you choose as best making us feel the good cheer of the fireside scene? What one or two descriptive bits about the outdoors, or the interior of the barn, stand out sharply—remaining in the reader's mind as a minor detail in a photograph sometimes does?

4. What was the first contact the family had with the outside world again—that is, whom did they first meet, and what was happening? The second contact was with the doctor, who had come to get help for a sick neighbor. Find the expression that tells how he had earned the right almost to *command* such help.

5. The poet evidently does not feel that his story is over until after the mail carrier has arrived with the village newspaper. What does he mean by saying that "as we read, . . . the horizon spread"? Explain the figurative truth contained in the last two lines of the selection.

THEN AND NOW

1. Mention a few of the facts about farm life in an earlier time—concerning equipment, household furnishings, or customs—that are recorded in "Snowbound." In our day, what replaces the "breaking out" of the drifted roads—that is, beating a track through them with teams?

2. A modern farm family, even when "snowed in," would seldom be so wholly alone. For one thing, roads would be passable much sooner. What other differences would there be? On the other hand, in Whittier's time the individual family was much more self-sufficient than now. Name *all* the necessities a modern household would be deprived of if gas and electric power failed completely. How did the household described by Whittier supply each of these things?

3. To be completely shut off from the world is an increasingly rare experience, limited mainly to explorers and campers. Try to recall and describe the longest time you were isolated from the rest of civilization—either alone or in a small group. Try to remember exactly which details of the experience made you feel most strongly the sense of isolation.

FOR FURTHER READING

Other works of Whittier you may enjoy include *Mogg Megone*, a prose account of Indian life in Colonial days, *Legends of New England in Prose and Verse*, and poems like "Skipper Ireson's Ride" and "The Poor Voter on Election Day."

◇◇◇◇◇◇◇◇◇◇

WALT WHITMAN (1819-1892)

It was Whitman's great ambition to express the American spirit perfectly in poetry. He even tried to shape his own character into what he thought an American should be—a hearty, cheerful, outdoor fellow, self-confident and even boastful. He loved the bustle of city crowds, the stir of great national events—and the peacefulness of the seashore or the countryside at night.

In his childhood Whitman spent many hours, in every season of the year, playing alone on the untouched beaches of Long Island. He grew up to be a sort of vagabond, with no regular job and no family to support. He had only elementary school education, but at sixteen he was teaching in a rural school and writing for newspapers. He dabbled at other professions, but stuck to journalism for fifteen years, editing papers from Brooklyn to New Orleans. He had a vast appetite for books, for plays and operas, for sightseeing, and for loafing. He was not at all concerned about making money. And then when he was thirty-six he published a book of unrhymed verse, *Leaves of Grass*. At first the book was utterly condemned, but it was read. Whitman continually revised his poems, and added new ones. Every few years he published his enlarged collection—always with the title *Leaves of Grass*. His "free verse" became more and more famous, and he eventually gained many staunch friends and bitter adversaries.

Through it all, Whitman seemed uninfluenced either by praise or blame. In his writing and in his life, he put into practice Emerson's principles of self-reliance and individualism. He admitted obligations to no one. Even when the War Between the States began, he felt no call to fight. But a brother was in the Union Army, and in 1862 was wounded. Walt went to Washington to visit him. What he saw in the army hospital stirred him to volunteer in the hardest, most unselfish service of his life—months of duty as a nurse to the sick and wounded men. He was wonderfully tender with them, and they loved him. When the war ended, he was offered a clerkship in a government office. In the meantime he continued to write. In 1873 a stroke of paralysis ended his physical activity, and most of his remaining years were spent quietly at Camden, New Jersey. From England, where his poetry was much admired, came praise from famous writers. The cottage at Camden became a shrine which was visited by friends and admirers from every sort of life. Among his friends were many of the great literary men of the century.

Whitman's poetry was like nothing ever written before. It was never sweet and tinkling, like some European poetry. At its worst, it was like the hoarse shouting of an auctioneer or a side show barker. At its best, as one modern writer has declared, it was like a strong wind that "roared in the pines."

To understand Whitman's thought we should remember his desire to be the spokesman of America—the *poet of the New World*. In the first place, he sang in praise of *democracy*. This meant that he loved both the tradition of freedom and the millions of "average" Americans—the stalwart workmen and mothers—whose daily life *was* American freedom.

Second, Whitman sang of *the glorious future of America*. He was thrilled by the thought of immigrants pouring into the New World; by the expansion of our country into former Mexican territory; by our swift progress in inventions, in industry and commerce, in the building of railroads. In his poems he prophesied many times that the United States would become the leader of all nations.

Third, he praised the huge, rugged *American continent*. The New England poets examined fields and ponds, but Whitman's imagination was stirred by mighty rivers, endless prairies, and giant salt oceans pressing in on thousand-mile coastlines. More than any other poet, he learned to express the idea of *bigness*.

Whitman's vigorous poetry sometimes becomes awkward and longwinded. Words tumble out of him in a reckless torrent. In most of his war poems he kept a uniformly high quality of expression, but on more casual subjects he sometimes wrote alternate passages of noble poetry and commonplace prose. Yet in spite of these inconsistencies he has come very near achieving his ambition, for today he is generally honored as America's one great poet.

I Hear America Singing

Wherever life throbbed Whitman found inspiration. In the singing of different kinds of people at work he heard the great chorus of America itself.

I hear America singing, the varied carols I hear;
Those of mechanics—each one singing his, as it should be, blithe and strong;
The carpenter singing his, as he measures his plank or beam,
The mason singing his, as he makes ready for work, or leaves off work;
The boatman singing what belongs to him in his boat—the deckhand singing on the
    steamboat deck;   5
The shoemaker singing as he sits on his bench—the hatter singing as he stands;
The woodcutter's song—the ploughboy's, on his way in the morning, or at the noon
    intermission, or at sundown;
The delicious singing of the mother—or of the young wife at work—or of the girl sew-
    ing or washing;
Each singing what belongs to him or her, and to none else;
The day what belongs to the day—at night, the party of young fellows, robust,
    friendly,   10
Singing, with open mouths, their strong melodious songs.

FOR UNDERSTANDING

1. Point out phrases in the poem that are suggestive of health and vigor.

2. Explain how Whitman's choice of workers named in the poem is also suggestive of an active, healthy life. Name some less active occupations that are completely omitted. How are the mother, wife, and girl suited to Whitman's list?

3. Boatmen in Whitman's time actually did have songs that were specifically about their kind of life. What ones can you name? What songs might the mother or wife sing that probably would not be sung by male workers? Name several songs more likely to be sung by a "party of young fellows" in the evening than during working hours.

4. Whitman was so heartily in love with all the different sights, sounds, and experiences of life that he even declared that everything on earth is perfect. In line 5, "singing what belongs to him" is a hint of this same feeling. It means that to Whitman, it is right for the boatman to sing whatever song *is characteristic* of boatmen. In the same way, Whitman would admire a man who acted in a manly way, and he would be equally pleased with a wild animal that acted just like a wild animal. Find two other places in the poem where the phrase "what belongs to" occurs. How does line 2 express this same idea?

THE SPIRIT OF THE AGE

1. This poem was written in 1860 or shortly before—a period of American energy and optimism, when it might well seem appropriate to imagine everyone in the nation caroling "strong melodious songs." Whitman, more than any other poet, caught the spirit of this expansive, vigorous age. What conditions, or what historical events, contributed to such a spirit?

2. The poem would be interesting

enough if it had no more meaning than appears on the surface. But to Whitman, the various songs probably suggested something further—the ways of life, the feelings and attitudes, of all the different kinds of people who make up the whole of America. To some people, such a heterogeneous mixture of classes and interests, scattered over a great continent, is somewhat frightening; the "songs" of such people might create a giant discord. To Whitman, they made a mighty harmony which he found exciting.

When have Americans shown their ability to unite in one aim? When have they shown signs of disagreeing so bitterly among themselves as to harm the nation? How could the mixed nature of our population sometimes save the whole country from making a disastrous mistake? What arguments might Whitman use to prove that in time of crisis our mixed population could be a cause of strength?

A NEW KIND OF POETRY

Whitman declared that the new land of America should have a totally new kind of literature. In his ambition to become the literary spokesman for the nation, he turned to "American" subjects—praise of friendship between the states; descriptions of the rich, cultivated farmlands and the brand-new cities of our land; and descriptions of everyday work and activities instead of the love songs and tales of war and adventure which filled the literature of European nations.

"I Hear America Singing" is a good example of this new subject matter. It is also an example of the new *poetic form* invented by Whitman. He refused to be bound by the requirement of rhyme. Usually he did not divide his poems into equal stanza units. And instead of set meter, he used long, swinging rhythms which he varied whenever it pleased him. Many later poets, partly because of Whitman's influence, have allowed themselves a similar freedom. Their poetry is called *free verse*.

However, Whitman's poetry is not formless. The following suggested activities will introduce you to the techniques Whitman used in place of the ones he discarded.

1. *Parallelism.* Whitman's lines often give an effect of repetition by expressing a series of parallel thoughts, using the same kind of sentence structure each time. Thus when the lines are read aloud they turn into a sort of chant.

Find a series of parallel statements in "I Hear America Singing." Explain how *each part* of the first line is similar to the corresponding parts of the remaining lines.

2. *Division of Line.* Very often Whitman's long lines fall naturally into two parts with a slight pause between. The second part often consists of explanatory material which modifies or rounds out the first part. When the verses are read aloud we quickly get into the habit of expecting to hear these "pairs," and are pleased when they occur.

Find several lines in this poem that break into pairs. (Not all of them break into *two* parts.) Tell where the division occurs in each line. To find it read the line aloud as if it were prose, and *listen* to see what happens.

3. *Phrase Rhythm.* Although Whitman does not worry about the exact meter of his lines, within each *half line* there is usually strong emphasis near the beginning and again near the end. Thus, after a bold beginning each half line falls away somewhat and then rises again, as in this line:

sing´ ing with open mouths´ their strong´

melodious so´ngs

This rise, fall, and rise is a sort of *phrase rhythm* that is more easy-going than the *precise meter* of conventional poetry. On which words does emphasis fall in lines 1, 3, and 5?

4. Have one person read "I Hear America Singing" aloud, while other members of the class watch for the three features just discussed. Do not expect all lines to follow the pattern, for Whitman varies them enough to avoid monotony.

5. For added enjoyment in reading the remaining Whitman selections in this book, notice how he has used these three features.

697

For You, O Democracy

To Walt Whitman democracy was almost like a religion. He not only accepted the theory that all men are equal but actually lived as if all men were his brothers. "For You, O Democracy" is one of the many lyrics in which he expresses his love of America and his faith in her future.

Come, I will make the continent indissoluble,
I will make the most splendid race the sun ever shone upon,
I will make divine magnetic lands,
    With the love of comrades,
      With the lifelong love of comrades.   5

I will plant companionship thick as trees all along the rivers of America,
    and along the shores of the great lakes, and all over the prairies,
I will make inseparable cities with their arms about each other's necks,
    By the love of comrades,
      By the manly love of comrades.

For you these from me, O Democracy, to serve you, *ma femme!*   10
For you, for you I am trilling these songs.

10. *Ma femme*—French for "my lady" or "my woman."

◇◇

FOR UNDERSTANDING

1. A key word in this poem is *indissoluble*. What does it mean? Today we sometimes forget that America is really a *union* of states—that is, of nations. In Whitman's time people were much more aware of this fact, but Whitman was eager to see the states cemented together more and more firmly. How does the phrasing of line 3 show that Whitman was conscious of the separateness of our states? What *eastern* states once actually conducted themselves as independent nations, only loosely associated with each other? What *western* state was once completely independent? What national situation would have been in Whitman's mind in 1860 as he wrote this poem?

2. When Whitman says "I" will make the states inseparable, and "I" will plant companionship, what means does he intend to use? Explain how his activities might contribute toward such a result.

3. To Whitman the basic ingredient of democracy was the practice of brotherhood. How many times does the poem mention brotherly attitudes between Americans?

4. Give examples of different parts of the country treating each other in a brotherly way, through governmental action or otherwise.

WHITMAN'S USE OF PARALLELISM

1. Even in this brief poem Whitman is able to use his favorite device of parallelism. In the first section, how many cases

do you find in which two or more lines resemble each other in thought and wording?

2. There is further parallelism in this poem, for the second section resembles the first almost line by line. Explain how lines 6–7 are parallel to lines 1–2. Lines 8–9 correspond to lines 4–5. Their chief similarity is the repetition of the phrase "love of comrades." What are the differences between the two pairs?

◇◇◇◇◇

Thick-Sprinkled Bunting

Bunting is the material from which flags are made, and the title of this poem refers to the Stars and Stripes. But it is what our flag symbolizes—both present and future—that interests Whitman.

Thick-sprinkled bunting! flag of stars!
Long yet your road, fateful flag—long yet your road, and lined with bloody death,
For the prize I see at issue at last is the world,
All its ships and shores I see interwoven with your threads, greedy banner;
Dreamed again the flag of kings, highest borne, to flaunt unrivalled?   5
O hasten flag of man—O with sure steady step, passing highest flag of kings,
Walk supreme to the heavens, mighty symbol—run up above them all,
Flag of stars! thick-sprinkled bunting!

FOR UNDERSTANDING

1. With what is our flag *sprinkled?* Remembering Whitman's fervent patriotism, explain why he would be pleased that the flag is *thickly* sprinkled.

2. Explain how history has proved the accuracy of Whitman's prophecy in the second line.

3. In lines 5 and 6, the "flag of man" is contrasted with the "flag of kings." What right do we have to call our flag the "flag of man" in so far as our country's internal affairs are concerned? in the part we have played in foreign wars?

4. Notice that the opening and closing lines of this poem are almost identical. How are they different? What expression is given most prominence by the order in which the phrases occur?

AMERICA'S CONNECTIONS WITH THE REST OF THE WORLD

Whitman states that all the ships and shores of the world are interwoven with the threads of the American flag. Judging from his other patriotic poems, he was thinking of some—probably all—of the following matters. Explain how his statement could be applied to each.

1. The origin of our country.

2. Immigration in the nineteenth century.

3. The example held up by our form of government.

4. America's military strength.

❖❖❖❖❖

There Was a Child Went Forth

This poem might be called "Early Surroundings of a Poet," for in it Whitman, looking back, mentions many of the things he observed and experienced as a child. He feels that all these things played some part, however slight, in shaping his personality. The outdoor scenes are from the fields and farms on Long Island where the poet roamed in childhood. His mother, mentioned in lines 20–21, was a cheerful, deeply religious woman of Quaker ancestry.

There was a child went forth every day;
And the first object he looked upon, that object he became;
And that object became part of him for the day, or a certain part of the day, or for
    many years, or stretching cycles of years.

The early lilacs became part of this child,
And grass, and white and red morning glories, and white and red clover, and the song
    of the phoebe bird, 5
And the Third-month lambs, and the sow's pink-faint litter, and the mare's foal, and
    the cow's calf,
And the noisy brood of the barnyard, or by the mire of the pondside,

6. THIRD-MONTH LAMBS—Lambs born in March. Imitating the custom of the Quakers, Whitman often says "Third-month," or "Fourth-month," instead of the ordinary names of the months.

And the fish suspending themselves so curiously below there—and the beautiful curious liquid,
And the water plants with their graceful flat heads—all became part of him.

The field sprouts of Fourth-month and Fifth-month became part of him;   10
Winter grain sprouts, and those of the light yellow corn, and the esculent roots of the garden,
And the apple trees covered with blossoms, and the fruit afterward, and wood berries, and the commonest weeds by the road. . . .
And the schoolmistress that passed on her way to the school,
And the friendly boys that passed—and the quarrelsome boys,
And the tidy and fresh-cheeked girls—and the barefoot Negro boy and girl,   15
And all the changes of city and country, wherever he went.

His own parents, he that had fathered him, and she that had conceived him in her womb, and birthed him,
They gave this child more of themselves than that;
They gave him afterward every day—they became part of him. . . .
The mother at home, quietly placing the dishes on the supper table;   20
The mother with mild words—clean her cap and gown, a wholesome odor falling off her person and clothes as she walks by;
The father, strong, self-sufficient, manly, mean, angered, unjust;
The blow, the quick loud word, the tight bargain, the crafty lure,
The family usages, the language, the company, the furniture—the yearning and swelling heart,
Affection that will not be gainsay'd—the sense of what is real—the thought if, after all, it should prove unreal,   25
The doubts of day-time and the doubts of night-time—the curious whether and how,
Whether that which appears so is so, or is it all flashes and specks?
Men and women crowding fast in the streets—if they are not flashes and specks, what are they?
The streets themselves, and the façades of houses, and goods in the windows,
Vehicles, teams, the heavy-planked wharves—the huge crossing at the ferries,   30
The village on the highland, seen from afar at sunset—the river between,
Shadows, aureola and mist, the light falling on roofs and gables of white or brown, three miles off,
The schooner near by, sleepily dropping down the tide—the little boat slack-towed astern,
The hurrying tumbling waves, quick-broken crests, slapping,
The strata of color'd clouds, the long bar of maroon tint, away solitary by itself—the spread of purity it lies motionless in,   35
The horizon's edge, the flying sea crow, the fragrance of salt marsh and shore mud;
These became part of that child who went forth every day, and who now goes, and will always go forth every day.

11. ESCULENT—Edible.
32. AUREOLA—The shining area around the sun when seen through mist.

701

FOR UNDERSTANDING

1. As very young children we hardly have distinct personalities. Therefore, it seems there is some truth in Whitman's suggestion that we become "us" as a result of our surroundings and experiences. Give examples of several *different* ways in which early experiences could become a permanent "part of" a person—whether this "part" is visible to others or not.

2. Can you trace the effect *in his poetry* of any of the objects "look'd upon" by the poet in his childhood?

3. A number of details in this poem show Whitman's close and appreciative observation. In line 8, what does he mean by "the fish *suspending* themselves"? Unlike most of us, Whitman realizes that when we look down into a pool we not only see *through* the water but also see the "beautiful curious liquid" itself. What color or other characteristics of the water does this phrase bring to mind?

OBSERVATION OF ONE'S OWN
    MEMORY

This poem demonstrates a fact which we are hardly aware of—that even as children we led rich, crowded lives, full of discovery. Test your memory by jotting down your *earliest* half-dozen experiences which were connected with your brothers and sisters. If you are an only child, substitute your earliest memories of your parents.

WHITMAN'S CATALOGUES

Critics of Whitman sometimes make fun of his *catalogues*—the long lists that frequently appear in his poems. If the reader wished to be unkind he might say writing poems is rather easy if all one has to do is to list all the things he remembers, and then tie them together by saying "These became a part of me"; or list everything he sees, and then say "These are what make America wonderful." However, when Whitman's lists do not grow so long as to be tedious they are very effective—expressing Whitman's healthy delight in experience.

1. Explain how Whitman's tendency to use catalogues is well suited to his favorite poetic device of parallelism.

2. Explain why this tendency is well suited to a poet to whom all the shapes, colors, and sounds of the world are exciting and wonderful.

◇◇◇◇◇

Miracles

We think of a miracle as an event or an object which SURPRISES US, *one which* WE CANNOT EXPLAIN. *Whitman would agree perfectly with this definition, but he interprets it in a new way.*

WHY! who makes much of a miracle?
As to me, I know of nothing else but miracles,
Whether I walk the streets of Manhattan,
Or dart my sight over the roofs of houses toward the sky,
Or wade with naked feet along the beach, just in the edge of the water,   5
Or stand under trees in the woods,
Or talk by day with anyone I love—or sleep in the bed at night with anyone I love,
Or sit at table at dinner with my mother,
Or look at strangers opposite me riding in the car,

Or watch honeybees busy around the hive, of a summer forenoon,   10
Or animals feeding in the fields,
Or birds—or the wonderfulness of insects in the air,
Or the wonderfulness of the sundown—or of stars shining so quiet and bright,
Or the exquisite, delicate, thin curve of the new moon in spring;
Or whether I go among those I like best, and that like me best—mechanics, boat-
    men, farmers,   15
Or among the savants—or to the soiree—or to the opera,
Or stand a long while looking at the movements of machinery,
Or behold children at their sports,
Or the admirable sight of the perfect old man, or the perfect old woman,
Or the sick in hospitals, or the dead carried to burial,   20
Or my own eyes and figure in the glass;
These, with the rest, one and all, are to me miracles,
The whole referring—yet each distinct, and in its place.

To me, every hour of the light and dark is a miracle,
Every cubic inch of space is a miracle,   25
Every square yard of the surface of the earth is spread with the same,
Every foot of the interior swarms with the same;
Every spear of grass—the frames, limbs, organs, of men and women, and all that con-
    cerns them,
All these to me are unspeakably perfect miracles.

To me the sea is a continual miracle;   30
The fishes that swim—the rocks—the motion of the waves—the ships, with men in
    them.
What stranger miracles are there?

16. SAVANTS (să·vänz′)—Men of learning.
16. SOIREE (swä·rā′)—A social gathering.
23. THE WHOLE REFERRING—Each object being connected in some way with all the other objects in the world as, for instance, there is a connection between "children at their sports" and "the
perfect old man, or the perfect old woman."

❖❖

FOR UNDERSTANDING

1. What "miracles" could Whitman mention that all of us see every spring, but pay little attention to? Give examples of "miracles" of *weather*; of *growth*.

2. Whitman would say that all the *changes* mentioned in question 1 are surprising and ought to be called miracles. But to him, *unchanging* things like hills and stones are also miraculous. What reason could he give?

3. How does a very young child show, by his manner toward the objects near him, that, like Whitman, he regards them as miracles?

4. We think of miracles as being *exciting and pleasing* as well as *astonishing*. Give examples of statements in other poems by Whitman which show, as this one does, that he finds excitement and pleasure in all sorts of everyday experiences.

5. Point out two examples of *parallelism* in this poem.

6. Turn back to the beginning of Thoreau's chapter on "The Pond in Winter" (page 630). How is his opening description of the solidly frozen ice similar to the thought expressed in Whitman's "Miracles"?

◇◇◇◇◇

When I Heard the Learn'd Astronomer

This poem does not state any opinion or attitude, but it SUGGESTS *one. Explain what it is.*

When I heard the learn'd astronomer,
When the proofs, the figures, were ranged in columns before me,
When I was shown the charts and diagrams, to add, divide, and measure them,
When I sitting heard the astronomer where he lectured with much applause in the
  lecture room,
How soon unaccountable I became tired and sick,
Till rising and gliding out I wandered off by myself,
In the mystical moist night air, and from time to time,
Look'd up in perfect silence at the stars.

◇◇

FOR UNDERSTANDING

Many poets cherish an attitude toward nature which they think brings them closer to it than does the scientist's probing and dissecting. Few poets in the nineteenth century were more enthusiastic about science than Walt Whitman was, yet here he voices a rather typical poet's complaint against science.

1. What does Whitman think the astronomer missed in his study of the stars?

2. Compare the thought of this poem with Thoreau's remarks about the naturalist (biologist) *versus* the fisherman, in the second paragraph of "The Pond in Winter." State the idea that both writers seem to have about the right way to know and understand nature.

3. Turn back to Whitman's "I Hear America Singing" and notice the kinds of *workers* he mentions. Why would the "learn'd astronomer" seem out of place in this list of the kinds of people Whitman admires?

CHANGING RHYTHM WITHIN A POEM

1. Most of the lines of this poem have a pause near the middle, but the last line flows along without a break. In the first four lines, where do the pauses occur? Decide by reading the lines aloud. Notice how different the last line sounds when it is read.

2. Throughout most of the poem, the unequal rhythm is fairly typical of Whit-

man's verse. That is, in most cases *each half* of the line rises, falls, and rises again. Line 2 is a good example:

When the proófs, the figúres, were rangéd

in columns befóre me.

But the final line smooths out into placid, regular meter which matches the serenity of the thought.

Read lines 2–4 aloud several times to become aware of this rhythm pattern. Then read the last line, noticing the contrast.

❖❖❖❖❖

To a Locomotive in Winter

A locomotive seems a rather unpoetic topic, and up to the present most poets have avoided writing about machinery. However, Whitman was just the man to do it.

Thee for my recitative!
Thee in the driving storm, even as now—the snow—the winter day declining;
Thee in thy panoply, thy measured dual throbbing, and thy beat convulsive;
Thy black cylindric body, golden brass, and silvery steel;
Thy ponderous side bars, parallel and connecting rods, gyrating, shuttling at thy
 sides;   5

1. RECITATIVE (rĕs′ĭ·tȧ·tēv′)—A musical *recitation*, rather than a *song*, used in the prose parts of operas. Operatic recitatives were an influence on Whitman's poetry.
3. PANOPLY (păn′ô·plĭ)—A complete suit of armor. Here the word may be a reference to a crust of snow or ice on the locomotive.

Thy metrical, now swelling pant and roar, now tapering in the distance;
Thy great protruding headlight, fixed in front;
Thy long, pale, floating vapor pennants, tinged with delicate purple;
The dense and murky clouds out-belching from thy smokestack;
Thy knitted frame—thy springs and valves—the tremulous twinkle of thy wheels;   10
Thy train of cars behind, obedient, merrily following,
Through gale or calm, now swift, now slack, yet steadily careering:
Type of the modern! emblem of motion and power! pulse of the continent!
For once, come serve the Muse, and merge in verse, even as here I see thee,
With storm, and buffeting gusts of wind, and falling snow;   15
By day, thy warning, ringing bell to sound its notes,
By night, thy silent signal lamps to swing.

Fierce-throated beauty!
Roll through my chant, with all thy lawless music! thy swinging lamps at night;
Thy piercing, madly whistled laughter! thy echoes, rumbling like an earthquake,
   rousing all!   20
Law of thyself complete, thine own track firmly holding;
(No sweetness debonair of tearful harp or glib piano thine)
Thy trills of shrieks by rocks and hills returned,
Launched o'er the prairies wide—across the lakes,
To the free skies, unpent, and glad, and strong.   25

14. THE MUSE—The spirit supposed to inspire poets and artists. According to Greek mythology the Muses were nine goddesses, one presiding over each art.

◇◇

FOR UNDERSTANDING

1. The poem begins with many specific descriptive details. Quote a line that gives a quick glimpse of the *colors* of the locomotive. Quote a line that calls attention to its visible *moving parts*. If you have ever observed a steam locomotive closely, see if you can decide what is meant by "dual throbbing" in line 3.

2. What phrase in line 14 shows that Whitman realizes he is doing an unusual thing in making a poem on such a subject? Name one mechanical means of transportation which is so ancient and familiar that poets very often write about it. What tools or other hand-operated instruments can you name that are sometimes mentioned in poetry?

3. In line 13 we see some of the reasons Whitman is interested in locomotives. In many of his other poems he praises the *modern* era, the era of progress. To him, *motion* and *power* were two important characteristics of the American nation, so the locomotive could be an *emblem* or symbol of our country. Explain the appropriateness of his figure of speech, *pulse of the continent*.

4. The last section of the poem emphasizes the noise made by the speeding locomotive—that is, its "whistling," a weak name for the noise it designates. In discussing *sound* how does Whitman at the same time manage to suggest *immense power*? Can you give any evidence as to which part of the country the locomotive is traveling in? The final line is a kind of summary of Whitman's feelings about the locomotive. Give examples from other poems of his admiration for the qualities mentioned in this line.

SAMUEL L. CLEMENS (1835-1910)

In the stories of Samuel Clemens, the voice of the West was heard in literature for the first time. Earlier American works—even those of Walt Whitman, whose imagination soared out across the continent—were products of Atlantic seaboard civilization. It was Clemens who brought to the world the rich, masculine humor of the West—and who was the first writer to get into his books the adventurous, roving freedom of boyhood.

At Hannibal, Missouri, like the boys in *Tom Sawyer*, young Sam Clemens played hooky to go swimming and fishing in the Mississippi River. When his father died he was apprenticed to the printer's trade, and afterward wrote for his brother Orion's newspaper. For a year or two he drifted about, finding employment as a journeyman printer. Then he returned to the Mississippi to become a steamboat pilot. When the War Between the States closed river navigation, Sam and Orion Clemens traveled to Nevada, where Orion had been appointed Secretary of the Territory. Soon, Sam was prospecting for gold and silver, but he had little luck.

The turning point in his life came when he tried the newspaper trade again, in Nevada and California. In competition with other journalists he learned the Western tricks of wild, exaggerated humor; picturesque descriptive expressions; and tall tales. Recalling river days, he adopted the pen name "Mark Twain," which was the leadsman's cry meaning "two fathoms of water." From his gold-mining friends he heard the hilarious story which he made into "The Celebrated Jumping Frog of Calaveras County." It was reprinted in a New York newspaper, and retold everywhere. Sam Clemens suddenly found himself a famous man.

Clemens stayed only a little longer in California, developing a reputation as a humorous public speaker, then he set out to try his fortune in New York. Easterners crowded the lecture halls to hear his funny stories and his drawling, not-too-truthful accounts of life in the Wild West. Two newspapers paid him to go on a tour of Europe and the Mediterranean, and send descriptive letters home. In his characteristic humorous style, Twain made fun of palaces, art masterpieces, and foreigners in general. Readers enjoyed his Western irreverence toward the Old World. When his sketches were later collected under the title *The Innocents Abroad*, they proved to be immensely popular.

Thereafter, book followed book, and Clemens became rich. He married and settled in Hartford, Connecticut, but continued to travel and lecture. His vigorous, realistic tales invaded even the hallowed pages of the *Atlantic Monthly*. He became acquainted with many of the prominent Americans of his time. Because of his buoyant, sunny disposition he made hundreds of friends wherever he went. On the other hand, there was a pessimistic strain in him which came to the fore when, through unwise speculations, he was financially ruined in 1894. By lecturing, and by turning out another half-dozen books, he paid his debts and rebuilt his fortune. But the change that had come over him is shown in bitter, brooding tales like "The Man That Corrupted Hadleyburg" and *The Mysterious Stranger*.

Of Twain's short stories, the finest is probably the "Jumping Frog" yarn. Young readers enjoy it, but the full flavor of its inspired tomfoolery can only be appreciated by adults. Of the books, *The Adventures of Tom Sawyer* and *The Prince and the Pauper* are children's novels, but both are enjoyed by older readers so unfortunate as to have missed them earlier. *The Innocents Abroad*, in spite of its one-sidedness, is a very funny debunking of the places in Europe so admired by gaping tourists. In *A Connecticut Yankee in King Arthur's Court*, Twain extends his debunking to the age of knighthood and chivalry. The Yankee hero is transported back to the Middle Ages, where his pistol and his scientific knowledge make him superior to Sir Lancelot and all the other famous Knights of the Round Table.

The greatest of all Twain's books are the two that picture most fully his own early environment—*The Adventures of Huckleberry Finn* and *Life on the Mississippi*. *Huckleberry Finn* is a novel in which Huck himself tells about his journey down-river on a raft. It is full of adventures, both on the great river itself, and among the rascals and the good people who travel it or live on its shores. *Life on the Mississippi* is a mixture of reminiscence, history, and travelogue. It contains Twain's own story of how he was trained to be a river pilot. Both books spring from intimate knowledge of small-town life deep in the interior of America—and of the colorful pageantry of steamboat travel which fascinated Samuel Clemens as boy and man.

THE ADVENTURES OF HUCKLEBERRY FINN

The hero and narrator of THE ADVENTURES OF HUCKLEBERRY FINN *is the town "bad boy." Huck doesn't like clean clothes, he resists going to school, and he tells fibs when he gets into a scrape. His father is a loafer and drunkard, and Huck decides to run away from him. To avoid being pursued, Huck plants "evidence" that he has been murdered by robbers. He shoots a wild hog and sprinkles its blood around the shack his father lives in. Then he skips out in a drift-canoe to Jackson's Island, a few miles down the river. There he meets Jim—a runaway slave. The two fugitives decide to do their hiding together.*

HUCK FINN IN DISGUISE

The following selection is one of the famous comic episodes of the novel. This kind of nonsense—a contest between two sharp-witted opponents—is typical of Western humor. On the one side we have the clever Huck Finn trying to pass himself off as a girl. On the other we have Mrs. Loftus, who wasn't born yesterday.

Next morning I said it was getting slow and dull, and I wanted to get a stirring-up some way. I said I reckoned I would slip over the river [1] and find out what was going on. Jim liked that notion; but he said I must go in the dark and look sharp. Then he studied it over and said, couldn't I put on some of them old things and dress up like a girl? That was a good notion, too. So we shortened up one of the calico gowns,[2] and I turned up my trouser-legs to my knees and got into it. Jim

[1] I WOULD SLIP OVER THE RIVER—That is, to the town Huck and Jim had run away from.
[2] ONE OF THE CALICO GOWNS—These had been found in a house that came floating down the Mississippi at flood stage.

hitched it behind with the hooks, and it was a fair fit. I put on the sunbonnet and tied it under my chin, and then for a body to look in and see my face was like looking down a joint of stovepipe. Jim said nobody would know me, even in the daytime, hardly. I practiced around all day to get the hang of the things, and by and by I could do pretty well in them, only Jim said I didn't walk like a girl; and he said I must quit pulling up my gown to get at my britches-pocket. I took notice, and done better.

I started up the Illinois shore in the canoe just after dark.

I started across to the town from a little below the ferry-landing, and the drift of the current fetched me in at the bottom of the town. I tied up and started along the bank. There was a light burning in a little shanty that hadn't been lived in for a long time, and I wondered who had took up quarters there. I slipped up and peeped in at the window. There was a woman about forty year old in there knitting by a candle that was on a pine table. I didn't know her face; she was a stranger, for you couldn't start a face in that town that I didn't know. Now this was lucky, because I was weakening; I was getting afraid I had come; people might know my voice and find me out. But if this woman had been in such a little town two days she could tell me all I wanted to know; so I knocked at the door, and made up my mind I wouldn't forget I was a girl.

"Come in," says the woman, and I did. She says: "Take a cheer."

I done it. She looked me all over with her little shiny eyes, and says:

"What might your name be?"

"Sarah Williams."

"Where'bouts do you live? In this neighborhood?"

"No'm. In Hookerville, seven mile below. I've walked all the way and I'm all tired out."

"Hungry, too, I reckon. I'll find you something."

"No'm, I ain't hungry. I was so hungry I had to stop two miles below here at a farm; so I ain't hungry no more. It's what makes me so late. My mother's down sick, and out of money and everything, and I come to tell my uncle Abner Moore. He lives at the upper end of the town, she says. I hain't ever been here before. Do you know him?"

"No; but I don't know everybody yet. I haven't lived here quite two weeks. It's a considerable ways to the upper end of the town. You better stay here all night. Take off your bonnet."

"No," I says; "I'll rest awhile, I reckon, and go on. I ain't afeard of the dark."

She said she wouldn't let me go by myself, but her husband would be in by and by, maybe in a hour and a half, and she'd send him along with me. Then she got to talking about her husband, and about her relations up the river, and her relations down the river, and about how much better off they used to was, and how they didn't know but they'd made a mistake coming to our town, instead of letting well alone—and so on and so on, till I was afeard I had made a mistake coming to her to find out what was going on in the town; but by and by she dropped on to Pap and the murder, and then I was pretty willing to let her chatter right along. She told about me and Tom Sawyer finding the twelve thousand dollars [3] (only she got it twenty) and all about Pap and what a hard lot he was, and what a hard lot I was, and at last she got down to where I was murdered. I says:

"Who done it? We've heard considerable about these goings-on down in Hookerville, but we don't know who 'twas that killed Huck Finn."

"Well, I reckon there's a right smart chance of people *here* that'd like to know who killed him. Some think old Finn done it himself.". . .

I had got so uneasy I couldn't set still. I had to do something with my hands; so I took up a needle off of the table and went to threading it. My hands shook, and I was making a bad job of it. When the woman stopped talking I looked up, and she was looking at me pretty curious and smiling a little. . . . I didn't feel a

[3] THE TWELVE THOUSAND DOLLARS—In Twain's earlier novel, *The Adventures of Tom Sawyer*, Huck and his friend Tom had discovered a hoard of gold coins.

bit comfortable. Pretty soon she says:

"What did you say your name was, honey?"

"M—Mary Williams."

Somehow it didn't seem to me that I said it was Mary before, so I didn't look up—seemed to me I said it was Sarah; so I felt sort of cornered, and was afeard maybe I was looking it, too. I wished the woman would say something more; the longer she set still the uneasier I was. But now she says:

"Honey, I thought you said it was Sarah when you first come in?"

"Oh, yes'm, I did. Sarah Mary Williams. Sarah's my first name. Some calls me Sarah, some calls me Mary."

"Oh, that's the way of it?"

"Yes'm."

I was feeling better then, but I wished I was out of there, anyway. I couldn't look up yet.

Well, the woman fell to talking about how hard times was, and how poor they had to live, and how the rats was as free as if they owned the place, and so forth and so on, and then I got easy again. She was right about the rats. You'd see one stick his nose out of a hole in the corner every little while. She said she had to have things handy to throw at them when she was alone, or they wouldn't give her no peace. She showed me a bar of lead twisted up into a knot, and said she was a good shot with it generly, but she'd wrenched her arm a day or two ago, and didn't know whether she could throw true now. But she watched for a chance, and directly banged away at a rat; but she missed him wide, and said, "Ouch!" it hurt her arm so. Then she told me to try for the next one. I wanted to be getting away before the old man got back, but of course I didn't let on. I got the thing, and the first rat that showed his nose I let drive, and if he'd

'a' stayed where he was he'd 'a' been a tolerable sick rat. She said that was first-rate, and she reckoned I would hive the next one. She went and got the lump of lead and fetched it back, and brought along a hank of yarn which she wanted me to help her with. I held up my two hands and she put the hank over them, and went on talking about her and her husband's matters. But she broke off to say:

"Keep your eye on the rats. You better have the lead in your lap, handy."

So she dropped the lump into my lap just at that moment, and I clapped my legs together on it and she went on talking. But only about a minute. Then she took off the hank and looked me straight in the face, and very pleasant, and says:

"Come, now, what's your real name?"

"Wh-hat, mum?"

"What's your real name? Is it Bill, or Tom, or Bob?—or what is it?"

I reckon I shook like a leaf, and I didn't know hardly what to do. But I says:

"Please to don't poke fun at a poor girl like me, mum. If I'm in the way here, I'll—"

"No, you won't. Set down and stay where you are. I ain't going to hurt you, and I ain't going to tell on you, nuther. You just tell me your secret, and trust me. I'll keep it; and what's more, I'll help you. So'll my old man if you want him to. You see, you're a runaway 'prentice,[4] that's all. It ain't anything. There ain't no harm in it. You've been treated bad, and you made up your mind to cut. Bless you, child, I wouldn't tell on you. Tell me all about it, that's a good boy."

[4] A RUNAWAY 'PRENTICE—A boy who has been "bound" legally to work a certain number of years as an apprentice without pay, but has run away from his master.

So I said it wouldn't be no use to try to play it any longer, and I would just make a clean breast and tell her everything, but she mustn't go back on her promise. Then I told her my father and mother was dead, and the law had bound me out to a mean old farmer in the country thirty mile back from the river, and he treated me so bad I couldn't stand it no longer; he went away to be gone a couple of days, and so I took my chance and stole some of his daughter's old clothes and cleared out, and I had been three nights coming the thirty miles. I traveled nights, and hid daytimes and slept, and the bag of bread and meat I carried from home lasted me all the way, and I had a-plenty. I said I believed my uncle Abner Moore would take care of me, and so that was why I struck out for this town of Goshen.

"Goshen, child? This ain't Goshen. This is St. Petersburg. Goshen's ten mile further up the river. Who told you this was Goshen?"

"Why, a man I met at daybreak this morning, just as I was going to turn into the woods for my regular sleep. He told me when the roads forked I must take the right hand, and five mile would fetch me to Goshen."

"He was drunk, I reckon. He told you just exactly wrong."

"Well, he did act like he was drunk, but it ain't no matter now. I got to be moving along. I'll fetch Goshen before daylight."

"Hold on a minute. I'll put you up a snack to eat. You might want it."

So she put me up a snack, and says:

"Say, when a cow's laying down, which end of her gets up first? Answer up prompt now—don't stop to study over it. Which end gets up first?"

"The hind end, mum."

"Well, then, a horse?"

"The for'rard end, mum."

"Which side of a tree does the moss grow on?"

"North side."

712

"If fifteen cows is browsing on a hillside, how many of them eats with their heads pointed the same direction?"

"The whole fifteen, mum."

"Well, I reckon you *have* lived in the country. I thought maybe you was trying to hocus me again. What's your real name, now?"

"George Peters, mum."

"Well, try to remember it, George. Don't forget and tell me it's Elexander before you go, and then get out by saying it's George Elexander when I catch you. And don't go about women in that old calico. You do a girl tolerable poor, but you might fool men, maybe. Bless you, child, when you set out to thread a needle don't hold the thread still and fetch the needle up to it; hold the needle still and poke the thread at it; that's the way a woman most always does, but a man always does t'other way. And when you throw at a rat or anything, hitch yourself up a-tiptoe and fetch your hand up over your head as awkward as you can, and miss your rat about six or seven foot. Throw stiff-armed from the shoulder, like there was a pivot there for it to turn on, like a girl; not from the wrist and elbow, with your arm out to one side, like a boy. And, mind you, when a girl tries to catch anything in her lap she throws her knees apart; she don't clap them together, the way you did when you catched the lump of lead. Why, I spotted you for a boy when you was threading the needle; and I contrived the other things just to make certain. Now trot along to your uncle, Sarah Mary Williams George Elexander Peters, and if you get into trouble you send word to Mrs. Judith Loftus, which is me, and I'll do what I can to get you out of it. Keep the river road all the way, and next time you tramp take shoes and socks with you. The river road's a rocky one, and your feet'll be in a condition when you get up to Goshen, I reckon."

I went up the bank about fifty yards, and then I doubled on my tracks and slipped back to where my canoe was, a good piece below the house. I jumped in, and was off in a hurry. . . .

FOR UNDERSTANDING

1. Huck naturally thinks it safer to talk to somebody who has never seen him before. What is humorous about his remark that "if this woman had been in such a little town two days she could tell me all I wanted to know"?

2. When Huck first meets the woman, he immediately invents details to explain why a "girl" is wandering around alone after dark. This is an example of his way of making up a plausible story whenever he is in difficulties. Why isn't the "girl" willing to take off her bonnet?

3. Explain why Huck's way of threading a needle arouses Mrs. Loftus' suspicion that he is a boy. In talking to her, what mistake does he make that adds to her suspicion?

4. Explain the two tests Mrs. Loftus uses to test the "girl" further. How does Huck fail the tests? What is her reason for putting the hank of yarn over Huck's hands?

5. How does Huck's sharp observation of animals help him to convince Mrs. Loftus that he is from a farm, as he says? In what way is Huck a winner in the contest of wits, even though Mrs. Loftus finds out that he is a boy?

6. Both Huck Finn and Mrs. Loftus talk in backwoods dialect. Give two examples of *mispronunciation of words*, and two examples of *words or expressions not used in literary English*.

THE FUN IN MATCHING WITS

If some members of the class know Twain's "The Celebrated Jumping Frog of Calaveras County," have them tell how it is another example of a story in which one person outwits another. Others may be able to give additional examples of such stories—old, humorous yarns they have heard, or read.

Mrs. Loftus might be considered an ama-teur detective. Give examples from fiction or from real life of similar incidents in which a clever investigator thinks of a way to test whether his suspicions are accurate.

HUCK'S ADVENTURES WITH THE GRANGERFORDS

This episode is one of the many experiences Huck Finn has as he and Jim journey down the Mississippi on a raft. The two runaways evade notice by traveling after dark, until one night a steamboat smashes full speed into their raft. In the excitement Jim disappears, but Huck manages to swim ashore. He lands near "a big old-fashioned double log house"—and halts when a pack of dogs rush out from the house barking at him.

What happens next gives Mark Twain an opportunity to show us a plantation household of the 1840's. Huck admires everything—it is like a whole new world to him—but sometimes Twain's typical humor creeps into the story. On the other hand, there is nothing humorous about the fight that breaks out between the Grangerford family and their enemies, the Shepherdsons. In telling about it, Twain pictures the violence that was still characteristic of the Mississippi region in his youth.

In about a minute somebody spoke out of a window without putting his head out, and says:

"Be done, boys![1] Who's there?"

I says: "It's me."

"Who's me?"

"George Jackson, sir."

"What do you want?"

"I don't want nothing, sir. I only want to go along by, but the dogs won't let me."

"What are you prowling around here this time of night for—hey?"

"I warn't prowling around, sir; I fell overboard off of the steamboat."

"Oh, you did, did you? Strike a light there, somebody. What did you say your name was?"

"George Jackson, sir. I'm only a boy."

"Look here, if you're telling the truth

---
[1] BE DONE, BOYS!—Be quiet, dogs!

you needn't be afraid—nobody'll hurt you. But don't try to budge; stand right where you are. Rouse out Bob and Tom, some of you, and fetch the guns. George Jackson, is there anybody with you?"

"No, sir, nobody."

I heard the people stirring around in the house now, and see a light. The man sung out:

"Snatch that light away, Betsy, you old fool—ain't you got any sense? Put it on the floor behind the front door. Bob, if you and Tom are ready, take your places."

"All ready."

"Now, George Jackson, do you know the Shepherdsons?"

"No, sir; I never heard of them."

"Well, that may be so, and it mayn't. Now, all ready. Step forward, George Jackson. And mind, don't you hurry—come mighty slow. If there's anybody with you, let him keep back—if he shows himself he'll be shot. Come along now. Come slow; push the door open yourself —just enough to squeeze in, d'you hear?"

I didn't hurry; I couldn't if I'd a-wanted to. I took one slow step at a time and there warn't a sound, only I thought I could hear my heart. The dogs were still as the humans, but they followed a little behind me. When I got to the three log doorsteps I heard them unlocking and unbarring and unbolting. I put my hand on the door and pushed it a little and a little more till somebody said, "There, that's enough—put your head in." I done it, but I judged they would take it off.

The candle was on the floor, and there they all was, looking at me, and me at them, for about a quarter of a minute: Three big men with guns pointed at me, which made me wince, I tell you; the oldest, gray and about sixty, the other two thirty or more—all of them fine and handsome—and the sweetest old gray-headed lady, and back of her two young women which I couldn't see right well. The old gentleman says:

"There; I reckon it's all right. Come in."

As soon as I was in, the old gentleman he locked the door and barred it and bolted it, and told the young men to come in with their guns, and they all went in a big parlor that had a new rag carpet on the floor, and got together in a corner that was out of the range of the front windows—there warn't none on the side. They held the candle, and took a good look at me, and all said, "Why, *he* ain't a Shepherdson—no, there ain't any Shepherdson about him." Then the old man said he hoped I wouldn't mind being searched for arms, because he didn't mean no harm by it—it was only to make sure. So he didn't pry into my pockets, but only felt outside with his hands, and said it was all right. He told me to make myself easy and at home, and tell all about myself; but the old lady says:

"Why, bless you, Saul, the poor thing's as wet as he can be; and don't you reckon it may be he's hungry?"

"True for you, Rachel—I forgot."

So the old lady says:

"Betsy" (one of the servants), "you fly around and get him something to eat as quick as you can, poor thing; and one of you girls go and wake up Buck and tell him—oh, here he is himself. Buck, take this little stranger and get the wet clothes off from him and dress him in some of yours that's dry."

Buck looked about as old as me—thirteen or fourteen or along there, though he was a little bigger than me. He hadn't on anything but a shirt, and he was very frowzy-headed. He came in gaping and digging one fist into his eyes, and he was dragging a gun along with the other one. He says:

"Ain't they no Shepherdsons around?"

They said no, 'twas a false alarm.

"Well," he says, "if they'd 'a' ben some, I reckon I'd 'a' got one."

They all laughed, and Bob says:

"Why, Buck, they might have scalped us all, you've been so slow in coming."

"Well, nobody come after me, and it ain't right. I'm always kept down; I don't get no show."

"Never mind, Buck, my boy," says the old man, "you'll have show enough, all in good time, don't you fret about that. Go 'long with you now, and do as your mother told you."

When we got upstairs to his room he got me a coarse shirt and a roundabout [2] and pants of his, and I put them on. While I was at it he asked me what my

[2] A ROUNDABOUT—A type of short jacket formerly worn by young boys.

name was, but before I could tell him he started to tell me about a bluejay and a young rabbit he had catched in the woods day before yesterday, and he asked me where Moses was when the candle went out. I said I didn't know; I hadn't heard about it before, no way.

"Well, guess," he says.

"How'm I going to guess," says I, "when I never heard tell of it before?"

"But you can guess, can't you? It's just as easy."

"*Which* candle?" I says.

"Why, any candle," he says.

"I don't know where he was," says I; "where was he?"

"Why, he was in the *dark!* That's where he was!"

"Well, if you knowed where he was, what did you ask me for?"

"Why, blame it, it's a riddle, don't you see? Say, how long are you going to stay here? You got to stay always. We can just have booming times—they don't have no school now. Do you own a dog? I've got a dog—and he'll go in the river and bring out chips that you throw in. Do you like to comb up Sundays, and all that kind of foolishness? You bet I don't, but Ma she makes me. Confound these ole britches! I reckon I'd better put 'em on, but I'd ruther not, it's so warm. Are you all ready? All right. Come along, old hoss."

Cold corn pone, cold corn beef, butter and buttermilk—that is what they had for me down there, and there ain't nothing better that ever I've come across yet. Buck and his ma and all of them smoked cob pipes, except Betsy, who was gone, and the two young women. They all smoked and talked, and I eat and talked. The young women had quilts around them, and their hair down their backs. They all asked me questions, and I told them how Pap and me and all the family

was living on a little farm down at the bottom of Arkansaw, and my sister Mary Ann run off and got married and never was heard of no more, and Bill went to hunt them and he warn't heard of no more, and Tom and Mort died, and then there warn't nobody but just me and Pap left, and he was just trimmed down to nothing, on account of his troubles; so when he died I took what there was left, because the farm didn't belong to us, and started up the river, deck passage,[3] and fell overboard; and that was how I come to be here. So they said I could have a home there as long as I wanted it. Then it was most daylight and everybody went to bed, and I went to bed with Buck, and when I waked up in the morning, drat it all, I had forgot what my name was. So I laid there about an hour trying to think, and when Buck waked up I says:

"Can you spell, Buck?"

"Yes," he says.

"I bet you can't spell my name," says I.

"I bet you what you dare I can," says he.

"All right," says I, "go ahead."

"G-e-o-r-g-e J-a-x-o-n—there now," he says.

"Well," says I, "you done it, but I didn't think you could. It ain't no slouch of a name to spell—right off without studying."

I set it down, private, because somebody might want *me* to spell it next, and so I wanted to be handy with it and rattle it off like I was used to it.

It was a mighty nice family, and a mighty nice house, too. I hadn't seen no house out in the country before that was so nice and had so much style. It didn't have an iron latch on the front

[3] DECK PASSAGE—An inexpensive way of traveling since the passenger did not have a cabin, but spent the entire trip on the deck of the boat.

door, nor a wooden one with a buckskin string, but a brass knob to turn, the same as houses in town. There warn't no bed in the parlor, nor a sign of a bed; but heaps of parlors in towns has beds in them. There was a big fireplace that was bricked on the bottom, and the bricks was kept clean and red by pouring water on them and scrubbing them with another brick; sometimes they wash them over with red water paint that they call Spanish-brown, same as they do in town. They had big brass dog irons that could hold up a saw log. There was a clock on the middle of the mantlepiece, with a picture of a town painted on the bottom half of the glass front, and a round place in the middle of it for the sun, and you could see the pendulum swinging behind it. It was beautiful to hear that clock tick; and sometimes when one of these peddlers had been along and scoured her up and got her in good shape, she would start in and strike a hundred and fifty before she got tuckered out. They wouldn't took any money for her.

Well, there was a big outlandish parrot on each side of the clock, made out of something like chalk, and painted up gaudy. By one of the parrots was a cat made of crockery, and a crockery dog by the other; and when you pressed down on them they squeaked, but didn't open their mouths nor look different nor interested. They squeaked through underneath. There was a couple of big wild-turkey-wing fans spread out behind those things. On the table in the middle of the room was a kind of a lovely crockery basket that had apples and oranges and peaches and grapes piled up in it, which was much redder and yellower and prettier than real ones is, but they warn't real because you could see where pieces had got chipped off and showed the white chalk, or whatever it was, underneath.

This table had a cover made out of beautiful oilcloth, with a red and blue spread-eagle painted on it, and a painted border all around. It come all the way from Philadelphia, they said. There was some books, too, piled up perfectly exact, on each corner of the table. One was a big family Bible full of pictures. One was *Pilgrim's Progress*, about a man that left his family, it didn't say why. I read considerable in it now and then. The statements was interesting, but tough. Another was *Friendship's Offering*, full of beautiful stuff and poetry; but I didn't read the poetry. Another was Henry Clay's Speeches, and another was Dr. Gunn's *Family Medicine*, which told you all about what to do if a body was sick or dead. There was a hymnbook, and a lot of other books. And there was nice split-bottom chairs, and perfectly sound, too—not bagged down in the middle and busted, like an old basket.

They had pictures hung on the walls—mainly Washingtons and Lafayettes, and battles, and Highland Marys,[4] and one called "Signing the Declaration." There was some that they called crayons, which one of the daughters which was dead made her own self when she was only fifteen years old. They was different from any pictures I ever see before—blacker, mostly, than is common. One was a woman in a slim black dress, belted small under the armpits, with bulges like a cabbage in the middle of the sleeves, and a large black scoop-shovel bonnet with a black veil, and white slim ankles crossed about with black tape, and very wee black slippers, like a chisel, and she was leaning pensive on a tombstone on her right elbow, under a weeping willow, and her other hand hanging down her

side holding a white handkerchief and a reticule,[5] and underneath the picture it said "Shall I Never See Thee More Alas." Another one was a young lady with her hair all combed up straight to the top of her head, and knotted there in front of a comb like a chair-back, and she was crying into a handkerchief and had a dead bird laying on its back in her other hand with its heels up, and underneath the picture it said "I Shall Never Hear Thy Sweet Chirrup More Alas." There was one where a young lady was at a window looking up at the moon, and tears running down her cheeks; and she had an open letter in one hand with black sealing wax showing on one edge of it, and she was mashing a locket with a chain to it against her mouth, and underneath the picture it said, "And Art Thou Gone Yes Thou Art Gone Alas."

These was all nice pictures, I reckon, but I didn't somehow seem to take to them, because if ever I was down a little they always give me the fan-tods.[6] Everybody was sorry she died, because she had laid out a lot more of these pictures to do, and a body could see by what she had done what they had lost. But I reckoned that with her disposition she was having a better time in the graveyard. She was at work on what they said was her greatest picture when she took sick, and every day and every night it was her prayer to be allowed to live till she got it done, but she never got the chance. It was a picture of a young woman in a long white gown, standing on the rail of a bridge all ready to jump off, with her hair all down her back, and looking up to the moon, with the tears running down her face, and she had two arms folded across her

[4] HIGHLAND MARYS—Highland Mary was Mary Campbell, a sweetheart of Robert Burns, the Scotch poet. He is supposed to have written many of his most beautiful poems about her.

[5] RETICULE (rĕt′ĭ·kūl)—A woman's handbag made of network.

[6] THEY ALWAYS GIVE ME THE FAN-TODS—They always made me nervous.

breast, and two arms stretched out in front, and two more reaching up toward the moon—and the idea was to see which pair would look best, and then scratch out all the other arms; but, as I was saying, she died before she got her mind made up, and now they kept this picture over the head of the bed in her room, and every time her birthday come they hung flowers on it. Other times it was hid with a little curtain. The young woman in the picture had a kind of a nice sweet face, but there was so many arms it made her look too spidery, seemed to me.

This young girl kept a scrapbook when she was alive, and used to paste obituaries and accidents and cases of patient suffering in it out of the *Presbyterian Observer*, and write poetry after them out of her own head. It was very good poetry. This is what she wrote about a boy by the name of Stephen Dowling Bots that fell down a well and was drownded:

ODE TO STEPHEN DOWLING
BOTS, DEC'D [7]

And did young Stephen sicken,
  And did young Stephen die?
And did the sad hearts thicken,
  And did the mourners cry?

No; such was not the fate of
  Young Stephen Dowling Bots;
Though sad hearts round him thickened,
  'Twas not from sickness' shots.

No whooping cough did rack his frame,
  Nor measles drear with spots;
Not these impaired the sacred name
  Of Stephen Dowling Bots.

Despised love struck not with woe
  That head of curly knots,
Nor stomach troubles laid him low,
  Young Stephen Dowling Bots.

[7] DEC'D—Deceased, dead.

O no. Then list with tearful eye,
  Whilst I his fate do tell.
His soul did from this cold world fly
  By falling down a well.

They got him out and emptied him;
  Alas it was too late;
His spirit was gone for to sport aloft
  In the realms of the good and great.

If Emmeline Grangerford could make poetry like that before she was fourteen, there ain't no telling what she could 'a' done by and by. Buck said she could rattle off poetry like nothing. She didn't ever have to stop to think. He said she would slap down a line, and if she couldn't find anything to rhyme with it would just scratch it out and slap down another one, and go ahead. She warn't particular; she could write about anything you choose to give her to write about just so it was sadful. Every time a man died, or a woman died, or a child died, she would be on hand with her "tribute" before he was cold. She called them tributes. The neighbors said it was the doctor first, then Emmeline, then the undertaker—the undertaker never got in ahead of Emmeline but once, and then she hung fire on a rhyme for the dead person's name, which was Whistler. She warn't ever the same after that; she never complained, but she kinder pined away and did not live long. Poor thing, many's the time I made myself go up to the little room that used to be hers and get out her poor old scrapbook and read in it when her pictures had been aggravating me and I had soured on her a little. I liked all that family, dead ones and all, and warn't going to let anything come between us. Poor Emmeline made poetry about all the dead people when she was alive, and it didn't seem right that there warn't nobody to make some about her now she was gone; so I tried to sweat out a verse or two myself, but I couldn't seem to make it go somehow. They kept Emmeline's room trim and nice, and all the things fixed in it just the way she liked to have them when she was alive, and nobody ever slept there. The old lady took care of the room herself, though there were plenty of servants, and she sewed there a good deal and read her Bible there mostly.

Well, as I was saying about the parlor, there was beautiful curtains on the windows: white, with pictures painted on them of castles with vines all down the walls, and cattle coming down to drink. There was a little old piano, too, that had tin pans in it, I reckon, and nothing was ever so lovely as to hear the young ladies sing "The Last Link Is Broken" and play "The Battle of Prague" on it. The walls of all the rooms was plastered, and most had carpets on the floors, and the whole house was whitewashed on the outside.

It was a double house, and the big open place betwixt them was roofed and floored, and sometimes the table was set there in the middle of the day, and it was a cool, comfortable place. Nothing couldn't be better. And warn't the cooking good, and just bushels of it too!

Col. Grangerford was a gentleman, you see. He was a gentleman all over; and so was his family. He was wellborn, as the saying is, and that's worth as much in a man as it is in a horse. . . . Col. Grangerford was very tall and very slim, and had a darkish-paly complexion, not a sign of red in it anywheres; he was clean-shaved every morning all over his thin face, and he had the thinnest kind of lips, and the thinnest kind of nostrils, and a high nose, and heavy eyebrows, and the blackest kind of eyes, sunk so deep back that they seemed like they was looking out of caverns at you, as you may say. His forehead was high, and his hair was gray and straight and hung to his shoulders. His hands was long and thin, and every day of his life he put on a clean shirt and a full suit from head to foot made out of linen so white it hurt your eyes to look at it; and on Sundays he wore a blue tail coat with brass buttons on it. He carried a mahogany cane with a silver head to it. There warn't no frivolishness about him, not a bit, and he warn't ever loud. He was as kind as he could be—you could feel that, you know, and so you had confidence. Sometimes he smiled, and it was good to see; but when he straightened himself up like a liberty pole, and the lightning begun to flicker out from under his eyebrows, you wanted to climb a tree first, and find out what the matter was afterwards. He didn't ever have to tell anybody to mind their manners—everybody was always good-mannered where he was. Everybody loved to have him around, too; he was sunshine most always—I mean he made it seem like good weather. When he turned into a cloud bank it was awful dark for half a minute, and that was enough; there wouldn't nothing go wrong again for a week.

When him and the old lady come down in the morning all the family got up out of their chairs and give them good day, and didn't set down again till they had set down. Then Tom and Bob went to the sideboard where the decanter was, and mixed a glass of bitters and handed it to him, and he held it in his hand and waited till Tom's and Bob's was mixed, and then they bowed and said, "Our duty to you, sir, and madam"; and *they* bowed the least bit in the world and said thank you, and so they drank, all three, and Bob and Tom poured a spoonful of water on the sugar and the mite of whisky or apple brandy in the bottom of their tumblers, and give it to me and Buck, and we drank to the old people too.

Bob was the oldest and Tom next—tall, beautiful men with very broad shoulders and brown faces, and long black hair and black eyes. They dressed in white linen from head to foot, like the old gentleman, and wore broad Panama hats.

Then there was Miss Charlotte; she was twenty-five, and tall and proud and grand, but as good as she could be when she warn't stirred up; but when she was she had a look that would make you wilt in your tracks, like her father. She was beautiful.

So was her sister, Miss Sophia, but it was a different kind. She was gentle and sweet like a dove, and she was only twenty.

Each person had their own servant to wait on them—Buck too. Mine had a monstrous easy time, because I warn't used to having anybody do anything for me, but Buck's was on the jump most of the time.

This was all there was of the family now, but there used to be more—three sons; they got killed; and Emmeline that died.

The old gentleman had a lot a farms and over a hundred hands. Sometimes a stack of people would come there, horseback, from ten or fifteen miles around, and stay five or six days, and have such junketings round about and on the river, and dances and picnics in the woods daytimes, and balls at the house nights. These people was mostly kinfolks of the family. The men brought their guns with them. It was a handsome lot of quality, I tell you.

There was another clan of aristocracy around there—five or six families—mostly of the name of Shepherdson. They was as high-toned and wellborn and rich and grand as the tribe of Grangerfords. The Shepherdsons and Grangerfords used the same steamboat landing, which was about two mile above our house; so sometimes when I went up there with a lot of our folks I used to see a lot of the Shepherdsons there on their fine horses.

One day Buck and me was away out in the woods hunting, and heard a horse coming. We was crossing the road. Buck says:

"Quick! Jump for the woods!"

We done it, and then peeped down the woods through the leaves. Pretty soon a splendid young man came galloping down the road, setting his horse easy and looking like a soldier. He had his gun across his pommel.[8] I had seen him before. It was young Harney Shepherdson. I heard Buck's gun go off at my ear, and Harney's hat tumbled off from his head. He grabbed his gun and rode straight to the place where we was hid. But we didn't wait. We started through the woods on a run. The woods warn't thick, so I looked over my shoulder to dodge the bullet, and twice I seen Harney cover Buck with his gun; and then he rode away the way he come—to get his hat, I reckon, but I couldn't see. We never stopped running till we got home. The old gentleman's eyes blazed a minute—'twas pleasure, mainly, I judged—then his face sort of smoothed down, and he says, kind of gentle:

"I don't like that shooting from behind a bush. Why didn't you step into the road, my boy?"

"The Shepherdsons don't, Father. They always take advantage."

Miss Charlotte she held her head up like a queen while Buck was telling his tale, and her nostrils spread and her eyes snapped. The two young men looked dark, but never said nothing. Miss Sophia she turned pale, but the color come

[8] POMMEL—The knob at the front of a saddle.

back when she found the man warn't hurt.

Soon as I could get Buck down by the corncribs under the trees by ourselves, I says:

"Did you want to kill him, Buck?"

"Well, I bet I did."

"What did he do to you?"

"Him? He never done nothing to me."

"Well, then, what did you want to kill him for?"

"Why, nothing—only it's on account of the feud."

"What's a feud?"

"Why, where was you raised? Don't you know what a feud is?"

"Never heard of it before—tell me about it."

"Well," says Buck, "a feud is this way: A man has a quarrel with another man, and kills him; then that other man's brother kills *him*; then the other brothers, on both sides, goes for one another; then the *cousins* chip in—and by and by everybody's killed off, and there ain't no more feud. But it's kind of slow, and takes a long time."

"Has this one been going on long, Buck?"

"Well, I should *reckon!* It started thirty year ago, or som'ers along there. There was trouble 'bout something, and then a lawsuit to settle it; and the suit went agin one of the men, and so he up and shot the man that won the suit—which he would naturally do, of course. Anybody would."

"What was the trouble about, Buck?—land?"

"I reckon maybe—I don't know."

"Well, who done the shooting? Was it a Grangerford or a Shepherdson?"

"Laws, how do *I* know? It was so long ago."

"Don't anybody know?"

"Oh, yes, Pa knows, I reckon, and some

of the other old people; but they don't know now what the row was about in the first place."

"Has there been many killed, Buck?"

"Yes; right smart chance of funerals. But they don't always kill. Pa's got a few buckshot in him; but he don't mind it 'cuz he don't weigh much, anyway. Bob's been carved up some with a bowie, and Tom's been hurt once or twice."

"Has anybody been killed this year, Buck?"

"Yes; we got one and they got one. 'Bout three months ago my cousin Bud, fourteen year old, was riding through the woods on t'other side of the river, and didn't have no weapon with him, which was blame' foolishness, and in a lonesome place he hears a horse a-coming behind him, and see old Baldy Shepherdson a-linkin' after him with his gun in his hand and his white hair a-flying in the wind; and 'stead of jumping off and taking to the brush, Bud 'lowed he could outrun him; so they had it, nip and tuck, for five mile or more, the old man a-gaining all the time; so at last Bud seen it warn't any use, so he stopped and faced around so as to have the bullet-holes in front, you know, and the old man he rode up and shot him down. But he didn't git much chance to enjoy his luck, for inside of a week our folks laid *him* out."

"I reckon that old man was a coward, Buck."

"I reckon he *warn't* a coward. Not by a blame' sight. There ain't a coward amongst them Shepherdsons—not a one. And there ain't no cowards amongst the Grangerfords either. Why, that old man kep' up his end in a fight one day for half an hour against three Grangerfords, and come out winner. They was all a-horseback; he lit off of his horse and got behind a little woodpile, and kep' his horse before him to stop the bullets; but the Grangerfords stayed on their horses and capered around the old man, and peppered away at him, and he peppered away at them. Him and his horse both went home pretty leaky and crippled, but the Grangerfords had to be *fetched* home— and one of 'em was dead, and another died the next day. No, sir; if a body's out hunting for cowards he don't want to fool away any time amongst them Shepherdsons, becuz they don't breed any of that *kind*."

Next Sunday we all went to church, about three mile, everybody a-horseback. The men took their guns along, so did Buck, and kept them between their knees or stood them handy against the wall. The Shepherdsons done the same. It was pretty ornery preaching—all about brotherly love, and such-like tiresomeness; but everybody said it was a good sermon, and they all talked it over going home, and had such a powerful lot to say about faith and good works and free grace and preforeordestination,[9] and I don't know what all, that it did seem to me to be one of the roughest Sundays I had run across yet.

About an hour after dinner everybody was dozing around, some in their chairs and some in their rooms, and it got to be pretty dull. Buck and a dog was stretched out on the grass in the sun sound asleep. I went up to our room, and judged I would take a nap myself. I found that sweet Miss Sophia standing in her door, which was next to ours, and she took me in her room and shut the door very soft, and asked me if I liked her, and I said I did; and she asked me if

[9] PREFOREORDESTINATION—This is a combination of the words "predestination" and "foreordination," both of which mean the same thing—a religious doctrine which states that, by God's will, rather than by their own actions, certain men are destined for eternal happiness and others are doomed to eternal damnation.

I would do something for her and not tell anybody, and I said I would. Then she said she'd forgot her Testament, and left it in the seat at church between two other books, and would I slip out quiet and go there and fetch it to her, and not say nothing to nobody. I said I would. So I slid out and slipped off up the road, and there warn't anybody at the church, except maybe a hog or two, for there warn't any lock on the door, and hogs likes a puncheon floor [10] in summertime because it's cool. If you notice, most folks don't go to church only when they've got to; but a hog is different.

Says I to myself, something's up; it ain't natural for a girl to be in such a sweat about a Testament. So I give it a shake, and out drops a little piece of paper with "Half past two" wrote on it with a pencil. I ransacked it, but couldn't find anything else. I couldn't make anything out of that, so I put the paper in the book again, and when I got home and upstairs there was Miss Sophia in her door waiting for me. She pulled me in and shut the door; then she looked in the Testament till she found the paper, and as soon as she read it she looked glad; and before a body could think she grabbed me and give me a squeeze, and said I was the best boy in the world, and not to tell anybody. She was mighty red in the face for a minute, and her eyes lighted up, and it made her powerful pretty. I was a good deal astonished, but when I got my breath I asked her what the paper was about, and she asked me if I had read it, and I said no, and she asked me if I could read writing, and I told her "no, only coarse-hand," and then she said the paper warn't anything but a bookmark to keep her place, and I might go and play now.

[10] A PUNCHEON FLOOR—A floor made of heavy slabs of wood.

I went off down to the river, studying over this thing, and pretty soon I noticed that my servant was following along behind. When we was out of sight of the house he looked back and around a second, and then comes a-running, and says:

". . . If you'll come down into de swamp I'll show you a whole stack o' water moccasins."

Thinks I, that's mighty curious; he said that yesterday. He oughter know a body don't love water moccasins enough to go around hunting for them. What is he up to, anyway? So I says:

"All right; trot ahead."

I followed a half a mile; then he struck out over the swamp, and waded ankle-deep as much as another half mile. We come to a little flat piece of land which was dry and very thick with trees and bushes and vines, and he says:

"You shove right in dah jist a few steps . . . ; dah's whah dey is. I's seed 'm befo'; I don't k'yer to see 'em no mo'."

Then he slopped right along and went away, and pretty soon the trees hid him. I poked into the place a ways and come to a little open patch as big as a bedroom all hung around with vines, and found a man laying there asleep—and, by jings, it was my old Jim!

I waked him up, and I reckoned it was going to be a grand surprise to him to see me again, but it warn't. He nearly cried he was so glad, but he warn't surprised. Said he swum along behind me that night, and heard me yell every time, but dasn't answer, because he didn't want nobody to pick him up and take him into slavery again. Says he:

"I got hurt a little, en couldn't swim fas', so I wuz a considerable ways behine you towards de las'; when you landed I reck'ned I could ketch up wid you on de lan' 'dout havin' to shout at you, but when I see dat house I begin to go slow.

I 'uz off too fur to hear what dey say to you—I wuz 'fraid o' de dogs; but when it 'uz all quiet ag'in I knowed you's in de house, so I struck out for de woods to wait for day. Early in de mawnin' some er de help come along, gwyne to de fields, en dey tuk me en showed me dis place, whah de dogs can't track me on accounts o' de water, en dey brings me truck to eat every night, en tells me how you's a-gitten' along."

"Why didn't you tell my Jack to fetch me here sooner, Jim?"

"Well, 'twarn't no use to 'sturb you, Huck, tell we could do sumfn—but we's all right now. I ben a-buyin' pots en pans en vittles, as I got a chanst, en a-patchin' up de raf' nights when—"

"What raft, Jim?"

"Our ole raf'."

"You mean to say our old raft warn't smashed all to flinders?"

"No, she warn't. She was tore up a good deal—one en' of her was; but dey warn't no great harm done, on'y our traps was mos' all los'. Ef we hadn' dive' so deep en swum so fur under water, en de night hadn' ben so dark, en we warn't so sk'yerd, en ben sich punkinheads, as de sayin' is, we'd a seed de raf'. But it's jis' as well we didn't, 'kase now she's all fixed up ag'in mos' as good as new, en we's got a new lot o' stuff, in de place o' what 'uz los'."

"Why, how did you get hold of the raft again, Jim—did you catch her?"

"How I gwyne to ketch her en I out in de woods? No; some er de hands foun' her ketched on a snag along heah in de ben', en dey hid her in a crick 'mongst de willows, en dey wuz so much jawin' 'bout which un 'um she b'long to de mos' dat I come to heah 'bout it pooty soon, so I ups en settles de trouble by tellin' 'um she don't b'long to none uv 'um, but to you en me; en I ast 'm if dey

gwyne to grab a young . . . genlman's propaty, en git a hid'n for it? Den I gin 'm ten cents apiece, en dey 'uz mighty well satisfied, en wisht some mo' raf's 'ud come along en make 'm rich ag'in. Dey's mighty good to me, . . . en whatever I wants 'm to do fur me I doan' have to ast 'm twice, honey. Dat Jack's a good boy, en pooty smart."

"Yes, he is. He ain't ever told me you was here; told me to come, and he'd show me a lot of water moccasins. If anything happens, *he* ain't mixed up in it. He can say he never seen us together, and it'll be the truth."

I don't want to talk much about the next day. I reckon I'll cut it pretty short. I waked up about dawn, and was a-going to turn over and go to sleep again when I noticed how still it was—didn't seem to be anybody stirring. That warn't usual. Next I noticed that Buck was up and gone. Well, I gets up, a-wondering, and goes downstairs—nobody around; everything still as a mouse. Just the same outside. Thinks I, what does it mean? Down by the woodpile I comes across my Jack, and says:

"What's it all about?"

Says he: "Don't you know . . . ?"

"No," says I, "I don't."

"Well, den, Miss Sophia's run off! 'deed she has. She run off in de night some time—nobody don't know jis' when; run off to get married to dat young Harney Shepherdson, you know—leastways, so dey 'spec. De fambly foun' it out 'bout half an hour ago—maybe a little mo'—en' I *tell* you dey warn't no time los'. Sich another hurryin' up guns en hosses *you* never see! De women folks has gone for to stir up de relations, en de ole genlman en de boys tuck dey guns en rode up de river road for to try to ketch dat young man en kill him 'fo' he kin git acrost de river wid Miss Sophia. I reck'n dey's gwyne to be mighty rough times."

"Buck went off 'thout waking me up."

"Well, I reck'n he *did!* Dey warn't gwyne to mix you up in it. Buck he loaded up his gun en 'lowed he's gwyne to fetch home a Shepherdson or bust. Well, dey'll be plenty un 'm dah, I reck'n, en you bet you he'll fetch one ef he gits a chanst."

I took up the river road as hard as I could put. By and by I begin to hear guns a good ways off. When I came in sight of the log store and the woodpile where the steamboats lands I worked along under the trees and brush till I got to a good place, and then I clumb up into the forks of a cottonwood that was out of reach, and watched. There was a wood-rank [11] four foot high a little ways in front of the tree, and first I was going to hide behind that; but maybe it was luckier I didn't.

There was four or five men cavorting around on their horses in the open place before the log store, cussing and yelling, and trying to get at a couple of young chaps that was behind the wood-rank alongside of the steamboat landing; but they couldn't come it. Every time one of them showed himself on the river side of the woodpile he got shot at. The two boys was squatting back to back behind the pile, so they could watch both ways.

By and by the men stopped cavorting around and yelling. They started riding towards the store; then up gets one of the boys, draws a steady bead over the wood-rank, and drops one of them out of his saddle. All the men jumped off of their horses and grabbed the hurt one and started to carry him to the store; and that minute the two boys started on the run. They got halfway to the tree I was in

[11] WOOD-RANK—A cord of wood which is arranged in a pile four feet high, four feet wide, and eight feet long.

before the men noticed. Then the men see them, and jumped on their horses and took out after them. They gained on the boys, but it didn't do no good, the boys had too good a start; they got to the woodpile that was in front of my tree, and slipped in behind it, and so they had the bulge on the men again. One of the boys was Buck, and the other was a slim young chap about nineteen years old.

The men ripped around awhile, and then rode away. As soon as they was out of sight I sung out to Buck and told him. He didn't know what to make of my voice coming out of the tree at first. He was awful surprised. He told me to watch out sharp and let him know when the men come in sight again; said they was up to some devilment or other—wouldn't be gone long. I wished I was out of that tree, but I dasn't come down. Buck begun to cry and rip, and 'lowed that him and his cousin Joe (that was the other young chap) would make up for this day yet. He said his father and his two brothers was killed, and two or three of the enemy. Said the Shepherdsons laid for them in ambush. Buck said his father and brothers ought to waited for their relations—the Shepherdsons was too strong for them. I asked him what was become of young Harney and Miss Sophia. He said they'd got across the river and was safe. I was glad of that; but the way Buck did take on because he didn't manage to kill Harney that day he shot at him—I hain't ever heard anything like it.

All of a sudden, bang! bang! bang! goes three or four guns—the men had slipped around through the woods and come in from behind without their horses! The boys jumped for the river—both of them hurt—and as they swum down the current the men run along the bank shooting at them and singing out, "Kill them, kill them!" It made me so sick I most fell out of the tree. I ain't a-going to tell *all* that happened—it would make me sick again if I was to do that. I wished I hadn't ever come ashore that night to see such things. I ain't ever going to get shut of them—lots of times I dream about them.

I stayed in the tree till it begun to get dark, afraid to come down. Sometimes I heard guns away off in the woods; and twice I seen little gangs of men gallop past the log store with guns; so I reckoned the trouble was still a-going on. I was mighty downhearted; so I made up my mind I wouldn't ever go anear that house again, because I reckoned I was to blame, somehow. I judged that that piece of paper meant that Miss Sophia was to meet Harney somewheres at half past two and run off; and I judged I ought to told her father about that paper and the curious way she acted, and then maybe he would 'a' locked her up, and this awful mess wouldn't ever happened.

When I got down out of the tree I crept along down the riverbank a piece, and found the two bodies laying in the edge of the water, and tugged at them till I got them ashore; then I covered up their faces, and got away as quick as I could. I cried a little when I was covering up Buck's face, for he was mighty good to me.

It was just dark now. I never went near the house, but struck through the woods and made for the swamp. Jim warn't on his island, so I tramped off in a hurry for the crick, and crowded through the willows, red-hot to jump aboard and get out of that awful country. The raft was gone! My souls, but I was scared! I couldn't get my breath for most a minute. Then I raised a yell. A voice not twenty-five foot from me says:

"Good lan'! is dat you, honey? Doan' make no noise."

It was Jim's voice—nothing ever sounded so good before. I run along the bank a piece and got aboard, and Jim he grabbed me and hugged me, he was so glad to see me. He says:

"Laws bless you, chile, I 'uz right down sho' you's dead ag'in. Jack's been heah; he says he reck'n you's ben shot, kase you didn' come home no mo'; so I's jes' dis minute a-startin' de raf' down towards de mouf er de crick, so's to be all ready for to shove out en leave soon as Jack comes ag'in en tells me for certain you *is* dead. Lawsy, I's mighty glad to get you back ag'in, honey."

I says: "All right—that's mighty good; they won't find me, and they'll think I've been killed, and floated down the river— there's something up there that'll help them think so—so don't you lose no time, Jim, but just shove off for the big water

just as fast as ever you possibly can."

I never felt easy till the raft was two mile below there and out in the middle of the Mississippi. Then we hung up our signal lantern, and judged that we was free and safe once more. I hadn't had a bite to eat since yesterday, so Jim he got out some corndodgers and buttermilk, and pork and cabbage and greens—there ain't nothing in the world so good when it's cooked right—and whilst I eat my supper we talked and had a good time. I was powerful glad to get away from the feuds, and so was Jim to get away from the swamp. We said there warn't no home like a raft, after all. Other places do seem so cramped up and smothery, but a raft don't. You feel mighty free and easy and comfortable on a raft.

◇◇◇◇◇◇◇◇◇◇◇◇◇◇◇◇◇◇◇◇◇◇◇◇◇◇◇◇◇

FOR UNDERSTANDING

1. It is natural that Huck would be badly scared by the manner in which the Grangerfords receive him when he first enters their house. How do they show their kindness and friendliness as soon as they decide he is not a dangerous person?

2. How does Huck show a tendency to overdo the job of making up a story about himself to tell to the Grangerfords? What difficulty does he get into about his name, and how does he get out of it?

3. Huck seems to observe every detail about the Grangerfords' handsome parlor. Which of the parlor ornaments would seem very odd in a modern home? How does Twain suggest that the books on the parlor table don't really mean very much to Huck? How does he suggest that the Grangerfords themselves regard the books as ornaments rather than as reading material?

4. The description of the sad, sentimental pictures on the walls is one of Twain's famous pieces of humor. Even if readers were not told, how could they guess that the pictures were painted by a young lady? Why is the *unfinished* picture the funniest of all? What justification is there for Huck's remark about the artist, now dead, that "with her disposition she was having a better time in the graveyard"?

5. The "Ode to Stephen Dowling Bots, Dec'd" is a *parody*, or humorous imitation, of the sentimental poetry that was popular in the nineteenth century—and which Mark Twain detested. Why is the *title* of the poem funny? What ridiculous expressions can you find within the poem? Explain the fun in the account of Emmeline Grangerford's career as a poet.

6. Twain builds up a picture of the Grangerfords as a proud, fine family. Colonel Grangerford is a typical gentleman of the period. Would you say he is severe and unfriendly, or the opposite? What details about the clothes of the Grangerford men impress Huck? What impresses him about the behavior of the younger Grangerfords toward their parents? What information is given about the way the Grangerfords sometimes entertain "quality" families?

7. In the 1840's, which is the period of Huck's adventures, *clothes* were an important outward sign of the difference between respectable people and shiftless people. The former took great pride in their appearance, and "dressed up" more than we do today—to distinguish themselves from loafers and ne'er-do-wells, who didn't care how they looked. Nowadays most people do not place such a high value on fine clothes. However, in what ways are clothes and general appearance an indication of character even today?

8. What incident, while Huck and Buck Grangerford are out hunting in the woods, causes Huck to learn about the feud? Why does Miss Sophia's elopement cause a new outbreak of fighting between the Grangerfords and Shepherdsons? How is Huck partly responsible for the elopement? What happens to Huck's friend, Buck, during the fighting?

9. How does Huck happen to find Jim hiding in the swamp near the Grangerford home? How has Jim managed to get hold

of the raft again? Huck's getaway with Jim forms a natural conclusion to the story of the Grangerfords. What are Huck's reasons for wanting to leave?

MARK TWAIN'S TREATMENT OF FEUDS

1. In the fights between the Grangerfords and Shepherdsons, as Buck Grangerford describes them to Huck, what do both sides do that seem unworthy of such people? Why do you suppose Twain has Buck say that the Shepherdsons are a fine family, like his own?

2. How does the conversation between the two boys about the *cause* of the feud suggest the senselessness of such an affair? Explain how the description of the Sunday morning church service suggests the same thought.

3. Why does it seem particularly horrifying that all the Grangerfords are eager to kill young Harney Shepherdson? What do you consider the most sickening thing about the fight at the woodpile, beside the steamboat landing?

4. One of Twain's purposes in describing the feud is to tell an exciting story—for almost any story of danger is interesting, no matter how terrible it is. A deeper purpose of Twain's was to expose, in all its ugliness, a savage custom that still existed in the Mississippi region in his lifetime. We can congratulate ourselves that feuds are a thing of the past. Even so, what arguments could Twain give to prove that mankind still shows very little more sense than the Grangerfords and Shepherdsons did?

THE CHARACTER OF HUCK FINN

1. Until Mark Twain came along, few authors had written sympathetically about boys. Nearly all young people's stories told their readers that they should behave nicely, do their duty, and in general imitate adults as closely as possible. But the boys in Twain's stories try to escape disagreeable tasks, they get into mischief, and sometimes they do things that are actually wrong like telling lies. Twain seems to think that with all their faults, these boys are pretty good fellows. Huck Finn has many good qualities. He is friendly; he is always ready to do a kind deed; in emergencies he is brave and capable; and in matters of injustice or cruelty he *instinctively stands up for what is right*. In the brief selections from *The Adventures of Huckleberry Finn* that are given in this text, how are Huck's good qualities shown? The novel was written for adults, not children, and many people think that boys and girls should not read it because it might have a bad influence. What do you think? In your answer, be fair—that is, give full consideration to the arguments on both sides.

2. There is much more to a person's character than the question of whether we approve or disapprove of it. In Huck, Twain pictures a boy who is sometimes shrewd, sometimes naïve. Huck can watch out for himself, and can size up other people's motives and actions—but some of his ideas are ignorant and rather simple-minded. Although he is perfectly serious in his praise of the clock in the Grangerfords' parlor, to the reader his remarks about it are humorous. Why? *Huck's ideas* are not always the same as *Mark Twain's ideas*. For instance, Huck doesn't really like Emmeline Grangerford's paintings very well, but he doesn't fully realize this fact. He naïvely accepts the notion that they are masterpieces of art. Can you find any *unconsciously humorous* remarks that he makes about the paintings or about Emmeline? Reread the story of how Emmeline used to write "tributes" whenever anyone died. Does Huck know the story is funny?

THE STORYTELLER'S CRAFT

1. Mark Twain gives us a hint of the feud when Huck first arrives at the Grangerford home. Looking back, we can see that their first suspicious attitude when the bark-

ing dogs wake them up is true to life. They act as anyone would who might be attacked any time by enemies. Then, as Huck settles down to live with the Grangerfords, most readers temporarily forget this opening scene—but it helps prepare them for the scenes of violence that occur later on. This kind of careful planning—putting in incidents that will seem much more significant at a later point in the story—is called *foreshadowing*.

2. While Huck is getting acquainted with the Grangerfords, his companion Jim seems to have disappeared from the story. However, after a while Mark Twain provides a scene in which Huck wades out into the swamp and discovers that Jim is alive and has saved the raft. The next event is the day of the shooting. When that day is over, Huck is eager to get away from feuds and killings. Jim and the raft are waiting for him—and the novel can go on to Huck's further adventures.

3. One reason why the story of the feud is excellent is that it is told with almost no comment. The author does almost nothing to indicate his point of view, except that he has Huck make one or two remarks such as anyone would naturally make under the same circumstances. The whole story is told very briefly. By making us *see* what a terrible story it is, instead of *telling* us, Twain gets his point across more effectively.

FOR FURTHER READING OF MARK TWAIN

The Adventures of Huckleberry Finn is recognized today as one of the world's great stories. It is a rich, many-sided book which every American should know.

The Adventures of Tom Sawyer is a lighter book based on Mark Twain's memories of his own boyhood in Missouri. Here Tom and his friend Huck Finn have many exciting times together and life is full of fun. Some students will want to read *Tom Sawyer* and follow it with *Huckleberry Finn*.

A Connecticut Yankee in King Arthur's Court is Twain's third greatest novel. It is a funny, imaginative story about a modern American who in a fight is struck over the head so hard that he wakes up in the year 528 A.D.

Pudd'nhead Wilson is a strange, tragic novel about early days in the South. It is a good book for students who have read the novels listed above and would like to know more about Twain's works.

The Innocents Abroad is the most amusing of Twain's nonfiction works. Because it is rambling and disconnected, it is a good book to read for idle enjoyment, a half-hour at a time.

Life on the Mississippi is the most valuable of Twain's nonfiction because it is an eyewitness description of an important era in history. Part I might be considered an entire book in itself—and it is more colorful than Part II. To see whether you would like it, try the sample called "Scenes on the Mississippi," pages 417–427 in this textbook.

Roughing It tells about Twain's adventures during the gold rush days in the West. Don't accept all the episodes as the exact truth, for some of them are probably "whoppers."

EMILY DICKINSON (1830-1886)

Emily Dickinson was born in Amherst, a little town in Massachusetts which she hardly ever left after her return from a year of college at Mount Holyoke "Female Seminary." Her father was a well-to-do lawyer whose house was full of books, and who knew a number of the important writers of the time. Many prominent people who came to lecture at Amherst were entertained in the Dickinson home. Emily talked easily and brilliantly with whatever guests appeared. She had a quick wit, and she developed a startlingly different way of expressing herself. Words fascinated her, and she pored over the dictionary as if it were a novel. She loved every detail of the New England landscape near her home—orchards, familiar flowers, sunrises, and summer days. She was more interested in such things than in human beings—except for her family and a few close friends.

After 1862, Emily mingled very little even with the people in her own community. She became more and more absorbed in writing poetry, but she showed no desire to publish her poems. She enclosed some of them with letters. Some went with flowers to a friend, or with some little gift to a neighbor. Fortunately her family realized the unusual quality of her work, and after her death arranged to have it collected and published. Today over a thousand of her lyrics are in print. Biographers have tried without success to learn her reason for shutting herself off from the world. It may be that there was no definite reason, but that she fell gradually into a way of living which suited her own disposition. The true explanation will probably never be known with certainty.

What is certain is the brilliant originality of Miss Dickinson's mind. Somewhat like Emerson, she has a power of seeing *into* experiences and revealing new things about them. Again like Emerson, she can compress a subtle idea into a single witty phrase. At first glance her little poems seem odd, charming, and simple. When they are reread, they are still odd and charming—but each is seen to be richer in thought than a half-dozen pages by some poets. They are careful explorations of her own emotions, and of those features of the outdoors that were within her range of observation. With her high intelligence, her quiet sense of fun, and her sense of wonder, she enjoyed a lifetime of adventure at home in Amherst.

◇◇◇◇◇

I Like to See It Lap the Miles

In her collected works, the poems of Emily Dickinson have no titles; they are merely numbered. What well-known thing does the following poem describe?

I like to see it lap the miles,
And lick the valleys up,
And stop to feed itself at tanks;
And then, prodigious, step

Around a pile of mountains,　　　　5
And, supercilious, peer
In shanties by the side of roads;
And then a quarry pare

To fit its sides, and crawl between,
Complaining all the while　　　　10
In horrid, hooting stanza;
Then chase itself down hill

And neigh like Boanerges;
Then, punctual as a star,
Stop—docile and omnipotent—　　　　15
At its own stable door.

13. BOANERGES (bō′à·nûr′jēz)—A name from the Bible meaning "Sons of Thunder"; it is sometimes applied to any loud-speaking orator.

The poems on the following pages are selected from *The Poems of Emily Dickinson*, edited by Martha Dickinson Bianchi and Alfred Leete Hampson, and are reprinted by permission of Little, Brown & Co. The poems include: "I Like to See It Lap the Miles"; "The Bustle in a House"; "The Soul Selects Her Own Society"; "My Life Closed Twice"; "I'm Nobody"; "The Snake"; "He Ate and Drank the Precious Words."

◇◇

FOR UNDERSTANDING

1. A part of the pleasure of reading this poem comes from slowly beginning to understand what it is about, and then becoming increasingly certain. Which detail in the first stanza gives a good clue? What characteristics make you more sure?

2. By telling us what the subject of the poem *is like* instead of *what its name is*, Miss Dickinson achieves one of the aims of good poetry—to make us "see" things freshly instead of ignoring them because they seem so familiar. One of the remarkable things about the object described here is summed up in the phrase "docile and omnipotent." What do these two adjectives mean, and how are they somewhat contradictory? Point out all the details in the poem that seem to fit the idea of *omnipotence* and *docility*.

3. Give the literal meaning of "complaining all the while in horrid, hooting stanza" and "at its own stable door."

4. It takes acute intelligence to capture, in a word or two, the exact way something looks or acts. Emily Dickinson had a gift for this kind of writing. Explain how "lap the miles" is just right for the thing being described. In what way is the picture created by "lick the valleys up" different?

5. What *animal* does the poet seem to have in mind in the last stanza? How are the main ideas stressed in this poem different from the main ideas of Whitman's "To a Locomotive in Winter"?

USE OF IMPERFECT RHYME

Emily Dickinson is a sophisticated writer who *almost* makes her lines rhyme but does not quite do so. This element of surprise can make a brief poem more interesting.

1. Name all the pairs of rhyme words in "I Like to See It Lap the Miles." For instance, what does "up" rhyme with in the first stanza? Are all the rhymes *imperfect*, or are there some *perfect* rhymes?

2. Examine the pairs of rhyme words carefully. Are the *consonant sounds* exactly alike in each pair? Are the *vowel sounds* completely different each time, or only partly different?

UNUSUAL CHOICE OF WORDS

Like her rhymes, Emily Dickinson's vocabulary is often arresting and unusual. She startles us into paying closer attention to what she is saying.

1. What is the meaning of *prodigious*? Explain how it is suitable as used here.

2. Explain *supercilious*. Why could the train be called supercilious?

3. The word *quarry* usually means an excavation from which rock is obtained for buildings or for other purposes. In this poem it means *a narrow cut*, perhaps along the side of a mountain, which *looks like* a quarry because of its steep, rocky sides. The word *pare*, meaning *cut*, is probably intended to suggest that from a distance the "quarry" is invisible. As a result, each time the train passes, it appears to be cutting its way right through. Can you explain why the train would *crawl* when it reaches this point in its journey, instead of dashing through in a hurry?

4. We expect a train to be *punctual*, but how do you explain the phrase *as a star*?

◇◇◇◇◇

The Bustle in a House

Just as Emily Dickinson's descriptive poems center on scenes observed near at hand, so her deeper poems examine with microscopic care the emotional experiences met while living quietly at home. What is it like within a family just after a death? Such an experience comes to everyone, but it takes a poet with the keen perception and the detachment of Emily Dickinson to analyze and tell how she feels.

The bustle in a house
The morning after death
Is solemnest of industries
Enacted upon earth—

The sweeping up the heart,
And putting love away
We shall not want to use again
Until eternity.

FOR UNDERSTANDING

1. Think over the meaning of the second stanza. It is a thoughtful description of what we often speak of as "readjustment" after a death in the family. Why is there love that is not needed? Why is it being saved "until eternity"?

2. Much of the poem's force comes from the imaginative metaphor of putting a house in order. There is solemnity in such an activity when arrangements of some permanence are being made—for instance, in preparation for an absence of even a few months. What expressions in the second stanza are a part of the metaphor?

OF FORM AND STYLE

1. Give examples of imperfect rhyme in this poem.

2. Explain how the second stanza fulfills and completes the first. That is, how does the first stanza, after beginning the discussion of a topic, leave it incomplete? How does the second stanza complete it?

The Soul Selects Her Own Society

Some biographers of Emily Dickinson believe her reason for living almost as a recluse in the last twenty-five years of her life was that she had fallen in love with a man who could not return her affection. Whether or not this is correct, "The Soul Selects" makes us realize the strange way the human mind can concentrate itself exclusively on one subject.

The soul selects her own society,
Then shuts the door;
On her divine majority
Obtrude no more.

Unmoved, she notes the chariot's pausing
At her low gate;
Unmoved, an emperor is kneeling
Upon her mat.

I've known her from an ample nation
Choose one;
Then close the valves of her attention
Like stone.

734

FOR UNDERSTANDING

1. The second stanza makes us think automatically that this poem is intended to represent a person who has fallen in love and will never love again. However, the attachment need not be to a person of the opposite sex. For instance, it could be a follower-leader relationship, or the love of a parent for a child. As another possibility, give an imaginary example of a person devoting his whole life to one great idea, one cause that he works for.

2. The thought of the poem has been fully introduced by the end of the first stanza. It is emphasized by the stanza about the chariot and the kneeling emperor.

Then the thought rises to a climax in the third stanza. "Close the valves" seems more final than the earlier phrase "shuts the door." Explain why the final line "Like stone" suggests even more strongly a permanent decision.

OF FORM AND STYLE

In this poem, lines of medium length alternate with short lines. Examine the short lines of the first two stanzas. How many syllables do they contain? What change in the number of syllables do you find in the short lines of the last stanza? Why does this change seem appropriate to the climax of this particular poem?

◇◇◇◇◇

My Life Closed Twice

If we are to take this poem as actual autobiography, two very tragic experiences happened to Emily Dickinson. She does not bother to tell us what they were, but concentrates on making us realize how important they seem to her when she thinks about her entire life.

My life closed twice before its close;
  It yet remains to see
If Immortality unveil
  A third event to me,

So huge, so hopeless to conceive,
  As these that twice befell.
Parting is all we know of heaven,
  And all we need of hell.

FOR UNDERSTANDING

1. Reread the first line and think about its meaning. It makes a perfectly calm statement, and trips along so swiftly that it almost seems lighthearted. Yet it tells us how shattering the speaker's two experiences were. Explain the ways in which the word "close" is used in this line.

2. The first statement hints that the two events are the most tremendous things that

will happen to the speaker up to her death. The second statement—lines 2–6—carries her thoughts *beyond* death. She wonders how any future event—even in the other world—can be as important to her as what has already happened. Which *word* makes clear that she is referring to what happens after death? Which *line* emphasizes again how importantly the two experiences loom up in her mind?

3. The third statement—the last two

lines—is the climax of the poem, and has been much admired. It is an explanation of the preceding statement. That is, the speaker suggests that already, here on earth, she has experienced both heaven and hell. Name one kind of *parting* the poet may have in mind, judging from the poem "The Bustle in a House." What other kinds of parting could she mean?

4. The remark that parting "is all we need of hell" is the poet's final statement on how tragic it is to be separated from a loved one. The parallel remark that "parting is all we know of heaven" is harder to understand. The poet certainly does not mean that the parting itself is heaven. See if you can explain what the sentence means.

❖❖❖❖❖

I'm Nobody

Here the poet explores one of the more cheerful corners of her mind. She has a little fun at the expense of people who are "somebody"—but at the same time she probably means what she says.

I'm nobody! Who are you?
　Are you nobody too?
Then there's a pair of us—don't tell!
　They'd banish us, you know.

How dreary to be somebody!
　How public like a frog
To tell your name the livelong day
　To an admiring bog!

FOR UNDERSTANDING

1. Literally speaking, it is impossible for any person to be *nobody*, just as, literally speaking, every person is *somebody*. Exactly what do these two words mean in the familiar, slangy sense used here?

2. Explain what the poet means by saying in the second stanza that a frog tells his name all day long. Is the thought in this stanza the same as that in the saying "He's a big frog in a small puddle"? Explain the saying. In the saying and the poem, what rather undesirable quality is hinted at?

3. Give some reasons why it might be dreary to "be somebody." Give an example of how a noted public figure might be urged to express his opinions on some current question, whether he knew anything about the subject or not. Even though a famous person might have "admiring" followers, how might his life still be "dreary"?

HUMOROUS "MISUNDER-STANDINGS"

Humorists sometimes have fun with well-known figurative expressions by taking them *literally*—that is, by paying attention to what they actually say instead of what they mean. For instance, a cartoon might show a headless man walking along, and another man explaining, "He lost his head during an argument this afternoon." In lines 3–4 of "I'm Nobody," Emily Dickinson uses just a touch of this kind of humor. If you literally were *nobody*, you would be banished from the world—that is, you couldn't get people to speak to you, couldn't buy food to eat, and so on.

1. What does a person *say*, but not actually *mean*, when he remarks, "You're not yourself this morning"? Suppose you have gone to the bank to cash a check. Why would it be very inconvenient if the cashier made this remark, and intended it literally?

The Snake

This is another poem in which Emily Dickinson amazes us with the penetrating accuracy of her description. She sets herself the task of expressing not only what we see when we happen upon a snake, but also how we feel.

A narrow fellow in the grass
Occasionally rides;
You may have met him—did you not?
His notice sudden is.

The grass divides as with a comb,   5
A spotted shaft is seen;
And then it closes at your feet
And opens further on.

He likes a boggy acre,
A floor too cool for corn.   10
Yet when a child, and barefoot,
I more than once, at morn,

Have passed, I thought, a whiplash
Unbraiding in the sun—
When, stooping to secure it,   15
It wrinkled, and was gone.

Several of nature's people
I know, and they know me;
I feel for them a transport
Of cordiality;   20

But never met this fellow,
Attended or alone,
Without a tighter breathing,
And zero at the bone.

FOR UNDERSTANDING

1. What is meant by saying the grass "divides as with a comb"? by saying it "closes at your feet and opens further on"?

2. What *two* things happened, suddenly, when the snake "wrinkled, and was gone"?

3. The last line of the poem catches perfectly the feeling many people have when they just miss stepping on a snake. What is the more familiar, and therefore less effective, expression for the same feeling?

Where else in the poem is the idea of *being startled* touched on?

4. The next-to-last stanza digresses a moment from the main subject. Explain in your own words what it says. How does it lead up to the climax in the last line and make it all the more emphatic?

5. Emily Dickinson's poetry and Whitman's are extremely different in a great many ways. Point out one similarity in *what interested* the two writers. What difference can be seen even in their interests?

737

He Ate and Drank the Precious Words

This poem begins as a sort of riddle. How could one "eat and drink" words? You will need to read the entire poem to find out.

He ate and drank the precious words,
His spirit grew robust;
He knew no more that he was poor,
Nor that his frame was dust.

He danced along the dingy days,
And this bequest of wings
Was but a book. What liberty
A loosened spirit brings!

◇◇

FOR UNDERSTANDING

This tribute to the power of books will seem odd to some readers. For us, books and other media of information are so readily available that we forget how precious they are—just as we never think of our dependence on water and air. One way to get the full force of this poem is to imagine what a few books could mean to the uneducated villagers of India or South Africa, or to people under Communist governments which seek to control their sources of knowledge. Another way is to imagine how little *you* would know if you had never learned to read.

1. "He knew no more that he was poor/ Nor that his frame was dust." Why not? Explain the lines.

2. What one or two books would you name that especially stimulated or delighted you—either recently or in your childhood? Explain what you found particularly absorbing in each.

3. The "loosened spirit" might be produced by any one of many different types of books. For example, a person brought up in ignorance of religion might find his whole life transformed by such a book as the Bible. In a book of American history, what one type of information do you think would cause the greatest change in the outlook of an uneducated person? in a book of science?

4. The figure of speech in the first line of the poem startles us into realizing how much the book meant to the reader. The second line tells us that it was his *spirit* that was hungry. Point out contrasts in the remaining lines between the mental and the physical side of life.

5. Accounts of the life of Abraham Lincoln show that he was one whose spirit was "loosened" by a few precious books. Do you know any other famous men or women whose lives were enriched by books? Do you have any personal friends to whom books are very important?

FOR YOUR VOCABULARY

Define *robust*, *dingy*, and *bequest*. If any of these words are unfamiliar, guess at their meanings from the way they are used in the poem. Write down your guesses, then check them with a dictionary.

738

conformity (kŏn·fôr′mĭ·tĭ). The act of following the established patterns of behavior and thought.

confounded (kŏn·found′ĕd). Confused.

confute (kŏn·fūt′). To overcome by argument.

conjure (kŏn·jōōr′). 1. To plead. 2. To call forth, supposedly by the use of magic.

connive (kŏ·nīv′). To act as if ignorant of a wrongdoing.

connoisseurship (kŏn·ĭ·sûr′shĭp). The ability to judge the excellence of wine, food, etc.

connotation (kŏn′ŏ·tā′shŭn). A thought or meaning which comes to the mind upon hearing a word, even though not related to the exact meaning of the word.

conscientious (kŏn′shĭ·ĕn′shŭs). Faithful; performing one's duty as well as possible.

consecrate (kŏn′sē·krāt). To dedicate; to make sacred.

consequence (kŏn′sē·kwĕns). Importance; dignity.

consign (kŏn·sīn′). To assign; to order.

consolidate (kŏn·sŏl′ĭ·dāt). To collect together and strengthen.

consternation (kŏn′stēr·nā′shŭn). Fearful wonderment and confusion.

constrain (kŏn·strān′). To force; to make necessary.

consummate (kŏn·sŭm′ĭt). At the highest point or climax; complete or perfect.

consumptive (kŏn·sŭmp′tĭv). One whose body is wasted away by disease; one suffering from tuberculosis.

contemplation (kŏn′tĕm·plā′shŭn). Meditation or attentive thought; consideration.

contemporary (kŏn·tĕm′pō·rēr′ĭ). Existing in the same period or time.

contend (kŏn·tĕnd′). 1. To struggle. 2. To argue.

contrite (kŏn′trīt). Ashamed and sorry for wrong done.

contrive (kŏn·trīv′). To plan; to plot.

controversy (kŏn′trō·vûr′sĭ). An argument.

convey (kŏn·vā′). 1. To carry; to send. 2. To communicate.

conveyance (kŏn·vā′ăns). That which is used for transporting.

conviction (kŏn·vĭk′shŭn). The state of being convinced or sure of something.

convulsive (kŏn·vŭl′sĭv). 1. Afflicted with intense and sudden contractions or cramps. 2. Undergoing a disturbance.

cope (kōp). To match; to fight on equal terms.

correspondence (kŏr′ē·spŏn′dĕns). 1. A similarity between persons or things. 2. Communication.

corrode (kŏ·rōd′). To rust.

couchant (kouch′ănt). Lying down; reclining with the head raised.

counseling (koun′sĕl·ĭng). Advising.

countenance (koun′tē·năns). 1. The face. 2. Facial expression.

countermand (koun′tēr·mănd′). To cancel an order by giving a contrary order.

counterpart (koun′tēr·pärt′). A copy; that which corresponds to another.

couple (kŭp′l). To join; to connect.

covert (kŭv′ērt). 1. -adj. Private; secret. 2. -n. A sheltered or hidden place.

crag (krăg). A steep, rough cliff or rock.

craven (krā′vĕn). Cowardly; fearful.

crevice (krĕv′ĭs). An opening; a crack.

crypt (krĭpt). A deeply hidden spot; an underground chamber.

crystallization (krĭs′tăl·ĭ·zā′shŭn). An idea which has taken definite shape.

culminate (kŭl′mĭ·nāt). To reach a climax.

cultivation (kŭl′tĭ·vā′shŭn). Development of the mind; refinement.

culverin (kŭl′vēr·ĭn). A kind of gun, used especially of cannon.

cumber (kŭm′bēr). To bother.

cutler (kŭt′lēr). One who makes or repairs knives or other cutlery.

cylindric (sĭ·lĭn′drĭk). Like a cylinder; circular and long.

cynosure (sī′nō·shōōr). Center of attention.

D

dank (dăngk). Wet and vaporous.

dappled (dăp′l′d). Spotted.

debauch (dē·bôch′). An excessive indulgence in pleasures of the senses.

debonair (dĕb′ō·nâr′). Gentle; lighthearted.

declaim (dē·klām′). To announce formally.

declamation (dĕk′la·mā′shŭn). Oratory.

declination (dĕk′lĭ·nā′shŭn). A refusal.

decorum (dē·kō′rŭm). Knowledge of what is proper.

deem (dēm). To suppose; to think.

defection (dē·fĕk′shŭn). Abandonment.

defer (dē·fûr′). To postpone; to put aside.

deference (dĕf′ēr·ĕns). Regard or respect for another's desires.

definitiveness (dē·fĭn′ĭ·tĭv·nĕs). Having the quality of being definite or exact.

degenerate (dē·jĕn′ēr·ĭt). 1. Having less hardiness or courage. 2. Broken down; worthless.

deliberate (dē·lĭb′ēr·āt). To think over.

delude (dē·lūd′). To mislead; to deceive.

deluge (dĕl′ûj). To flood.

delusive (dē·lū′sĭv). Deceitful; false.

delve (dĕlv). To dig; to make a hole.

demean (dē·mēn′). To conduct oneself; to behave.

demeanor (dē·mēn′ēr). Appearance.

demigod (dĕm′ĭ·gŏd′). 1. One supposedly half god and half man. 2. A hero.

denominate (dē·nŏm′ĭ·nāt). To name.

denounce (dē·nouns′). 1. To condemn or accuse. 2. To proclaim or make known in a solemn and formal manner.

denunciation (dē·nŭn′sĭ·ā′shŭn). A warning of evil or punishment to come.

depict (dē·pĭkt′). To portray; to picture.

deplore (dē·plōr′). To sorrow over; to dislike.

deprecate (dĕp′rē·kāt). To show disapproval.

depreciate (dē·prē′shĭ·āt). To lower in value.

derange (dē·rānj′). To disturb; to embarrass.

cōol, cŏŏk; our, boil; cūte, ŭnite, bûrn, cŭt, ŭnless, menü; check; goat, sing, ~~this~~, thick, scriptŭre, verdŭre.

741

deride (dĕ·rīd′). To ridicule; to scorn.
derivation (dĕr′ĭ·vā′shŭn). Beginning; origin.
derive (dĕ·rīv′). To obtain; to receive.
design (dĕ·zīn′). An aim or plan.
designate (dĕz′ĭg·nāt). To point out.
desist (dĕ·zĭst′). To quit; to stop.
desolate (dĕs′ō·lĭt). Forsaken; unhappy.
detachment (dĕ·tăch′mĕnt). A group of soldiers which has been sent on a special mission.
detain (dĕ·tān′). To stop or delay.
detract (dĕ·trăkt′). To take away; to withdraw.
devastating (dĕv′ăs·tāt′ĭng). 1. Overpowering. 2. Destructive.
devoid (dĕ·void′). Empty; without.
dexterity (dĕks·tĕr′ĭ·tĭ). Skill; cleverness.
diabolical (dī′a·bŏl′ĭ·kăl). Devilish; evil.
diffusion (dĭ·fū′zhŭn). A spreading; an extension.
dilate (dī′lāt). To grow wide.
diligent (dĭl′ĭ·jĕnt). Steady; hard working.
diminutive (dĭ·mĭn′ŭ·tĭv). Very small; tiny.
direful (dīr′fool). Bad or dreadful.
dirgelike (dûrj′līk′). Like a funeral lament.
disapprobation (dĭs′ăp·rō·bā′shŭn). Disapproval.
disavow (dĭs′a·vou′). To refuse to give approval of; to deny responsibility for.
discern (dĭ·zûrn′). To discover; to see or distinguish finely between things.
disconcert (dĭs·kŏn′sûrt). Disturbance.
disconsolate (dĭs·kŏn′sō·lĭt). Sad and downhearted; not able to be consoled.
discordant (dĭs·kôr′dănt). Out of tune.
discourse (dĭs·kōrs′). Speech or sermon.
discreet (dĭs·krēt′). Wise; reserved.
disdainful (dĭs·dān′fool). Scornful.
disembark (dĭs′ĕm·bärk′). To leave a ship to go ashore.
disfranchised (dĭs·frăn′chīzed). Deprived of or forbidden the rights of citizenship.
disgorge (dĭs·gôrj′). To send out with great force.
disinterested (dĭs·ĭn′tĕr·ĕs·tĕd). Unprejudiced; not influenced by selfish desires.
dispel (dĭs·pĕl′). To drive away.
disperse (dĭs·pûrs′). To scatter or separate.
disposed (dĭs·pōzd′). Willing; inclined.
disposition (dĭs′pō·zĭsh′ŭn). 1. State of mind; inclination. 2. Arrangement.
disputatious (dĭs′pŭ·tā′shŭs). Inclined to argue.
dissension (dĭ·sĕn′shŭn). Open disagreement.
dissever (dĭ·sĕv′ēr). To separate; to cut apart.
dissipated (dĭs′ĭ·pāt′ĕd). Wasted; immoral.
dissolution (dĭs·ō·lū′shŭn). Death; ending.
distend (dĭs·tĕnd′). To stretch or spread apart.
distill (dĭs·tĭl′). To let fall in drops.
distraught (dĭs·trôt′). Mentally upset.
divers (dī′vĕrz). Several; various.
diversity (dĭ·vûr′sĭ·tĭ). Variety.
divest (dĭ·vĕst′). To take away from; to strip.
docile (dŏs′ĭl). Gentle.
doleful (dōl′fool). Full of sadness or grief.
dominion (dō·mĭn′yŭn). 1. The right to rule. 2. Ruled territory.
dormant (dôr′mănt). Asleep; inactive.

dote (dōt). To be extremely fond of.
drab (drăb). 1. Woolen cloth, a dull brown or yellow in color. 2. An untidy, lazy woman.
draft (dráft). To draw up, as a plan or outline.
dray (drā). A wagon for hauling heavy loads.
dreadnaught (drĕd′nôt′). A large battleship.
dudgeon (dŭj′ŭn). Anger.
duly (dū′lĭ). As it should be done; properly.
duplex (dū′plĕks). A suite of rooms on two floors of an apartment house.

E

eccentricity (ĕk′sĕn·trĭs′ĭ·tĭ). Oddness; a personal habit varying from usual behavior.
ecstasy (ĕk′sta·sĭ). Joy; rapture.
eddy (ĕd′ĭ). 1. -n. A whirlpool. 2. -v. To move or flow rapidly, as a whirlpool.
edifice (ĕd′ĭ·fĭs). A large structure or building.
effect (ĕ·fĕkt′). To bring about.
egress (ē′grĕs). Exit.
ejaculation (ĕ·jăk′ŭ·lā′shŭn). An exclamation.
eloquence (ĕl′ō·kwĕns). Quality of being intensely moving.
emaciation (ĕ·mā′sĭ·ā′shŭn). Extreme thinness.
emanate (ĕm′a·nāt). To give forth; send out.
embark (ĕm·bärk′). To go on board a ship for a voyage.
embattled (ĕm·băt′′ld). Drawn up in a battle position.
embellishment (ĕm·bĕl′ĭsh·mĕnt). Decoration.
embody (ĕm·bŏd′ĭ). 1. To make more obvious by collecting in one place or form. 2. To give form or shape to an idea.
emerge (ĕ·mûrj′). To come forth into view.
eminence (ĕm′ĭ·nĕns). A high place.
enamored (ĕn·ăm′ĕrd). Charmed; full of love.
encompass (ĕn·kŭm′păs). 1. To accomplish. 2. To enclose or surround.
encounter (ĕn·koun′tĕr). To meet face to face.
encroach (ĕn·krōch′). To intrude or trespass.
endeavor (ĕn·dĕv′ĕr). To try or attempt.
endow (ĕn·dou′). To give a gift; to present.
engross (ĕn·grōs′). To take up entirely; to monopolize.
enigma (ĕ·nĭg′ma). A mystery.
enjoin (ĕn·join′). To command; to order.
ensemble (än·sŏm′b′l). A musical chorus.
ensue (ĕn·sū′). To follow.
entail (ĕn·tāl′). To involve; to result in.
enterprise (ĕn′tĕr·prīz). Initiative or energy which enables one to take part in activities requiring boldness and courage.
entreaty (ĕn·trēt′ĭ). A plea; a request.
entree (än′trā). Freedom of entrance.
enumerate (ĕ·nū′mĕr·āt). To list; to count.
environing (ĕn·vī′rŭn·ĭng). Surrounding.
epitomize (ĕ·pĭt′ō·mīz). To make brief.
equable (ĕk′wa·b′l). Even; steady.
equanimity (ē′kwa·nĭm′ĭ·tĭ). Even-temper.
equestrian (ĕ·kwĕs′trĭ·ăn). On horseback.
equipage (ĕk′wĭ·pĭj). 1. A carriage. 2. A train of servants.
equity (ĕk′wĭ·tĭ). Fairness; justice.

āte, chăotic, dâre, ădd, ăccuse, bär, càsk, afar; ēat, dẹar, ĕlude, ĕgg, quiĕt, centēr; īdle, ĭf, activĭty; ōpen, ōbey, ôr, ŏrange, ŏffer, ŏccur.

equivocate (ê·kwĭv′ô·kāt). To deceive through use of double meaning; to lie.

ere (âr). Before.

essay (ĕ·sā′). To try; to make an attempt.

esteem (ĕs·tēm′). To honor or hold in high regard.

ethereal (ê·thēr′ê·ăl). Heavenly; delicate.

ethical (ĕth′ĭ·kăl). Morally correct.

euphony (ū′fô·nĭ). A harmonious arrangement of words.

eventual (ê·vĕn′tŭ·ăl). In the end or at the final outcome.

evince (ê·vĭns′). To make clear; to show plainly.

evolution (ĕv′ô·lū′shŭn). A movement forming part of an intricate pattern.

exalt (ĕg·zôlt′). To raise up; to inspire.

excerpt (ĕk′sûrpt). A selection from the whole.

execrable (ĕk′sē·krȧ·b′l). Horrifying.

execration (ĕk·sē·krā′shŭn). A curse or protest.

exhilaration (ĕg·zĭl·ȧ·rā′shŭn). Gaiety; cheerfulness; merriment.

exorbitant (ĕg·zôr′bĭ·tănt). Excessive.

exotic (ĕks·ŏt′ĭk). Strange; foreign.

expatiate (ĕks·pā′shĭ·āt). To enlarge upon.

expatriated (ĕks·pā′trĭ·āt′ĕd). Banished; exiled.

expedient (ĕks·pē′dĭ·ĕnt). A practical method devised to solve a problem.

expiration (ĕk′spĭ·rā′shŭn). An end or finish.

expletive (ĕks′plē·tĭv). An oath; exclamation.

explicit (ĕks·plĭs′ĭt). Clear, definite and exact.

exploit (ĕks′ploit). -*n*. 1. Achievement; success. 2. A deed of daring.

exploit (ĕks′ploit). -*v*. To use for personal gain.

expostulation (ĕks·pŏs′tŭ·lā′shŭn). The act of reasoning with a person about an action which is considered wrong.

exquisite (ĕks′kwĭ·zĭt). Intense; keen; sharp.

extemporize (ĕks·tĕm′pô·rīz). To make up without notice or special preparation.

extenuate (ĕks·tĕn′ŭ·āt). To lessen; to treat as a matter of small importance.

extort (ĕks·tôrt′). To obtain by force.

extremity (ĕks·trĕm′ĭ·tĭ). The highest degree of danger or necessity.

exuberant (ĕg·zū′bēr·ănt). Overflowing with happiness.

exude (ĕks·ūd′). To discharge or give off.

F

façade (fȧ·säd′). The front or outward face.

facetious (fȧ·sē′shŭs). Amusing; humorous.

facilitate (fȧ·sĭl′ĭ·tāt). To make easy.

faction (făk′shŭn). A group or party.

faculty (făk′ŭl·tĭ). An ability or talent.

fain (fān). With joy; gladly.

falsetto (fôl·sĕt′ō). A human voice raised above its proper tone or range.

fanatical (fȧ·năt′ĭ·kăl). Excessively enthusiastic and single-minded; unreasonably fervent.

farthing (fär′thĭng). Something of little value.

fastness (fȧst′nĕs). A place that is hard to get to; a stronghold.

fathom (făth′ŭm). 1. -*n*. Unit used to measure the depth of water. 2. -*v*. To understand.

fawn (fôn). To seek favor by flattery.

feasible (fē′zĭ·b′l). Likely; able to be done.

felicity (fê·lĭs′ĭ·tĭ). Success; good fortune.

felonious (fē·lō′nĭ·ŭs). Wicked; intentionally criminal.

firmament (fûr′mȧ·mĕnt). The heavens.

fluent (flōō′ĕnt). Flowing.

foreshorten (fōr·shôr′t'n). To decrease the size of objects to give the effect of distance.

formidable (fôr′mĭ·dȧ·b'l). Arousing fear.

forthwith (fōrth′wĭth′). Immediately; promptly.

fortitude (fôr′tĭ·tūd). Strength; firmness.

fratricidal (frăt′rĭ·sīd′ăl). Pertaining to the murder of men by their blood brothers.

fray (frā). An attack or fight.

freshet (frĕsh′ĕt). A flood caused by melting snow or heavy rains.

friction (frĭk′shŭn). Disagreement; tension.

fume (fūm). A fit of anger.

furbish (fûr′bĭsh). To make like new or fix up.

furl (fûrl). To roll or wrap up.

furlong (fûr′lŏng). One-eighth of a mile.

furore (fū′rōr). 1. Great enthusiasm. 2. A rage.

furtive (fûr′tĭv). Secretive; sly.

G

gainsay (gān′sā′). To speak against.

gait (gāt). Way; course.

galvanic (găl·văn′ĭk). Quick, as if from a shock.

garish (gâr′ĭsh). Gaudy; showy.

gesticulation (jĕs·tĭk′ŭ·lā′shŭn). Making expressive movements with the body.

gilded (gĭl′dĕd). Painted with gold color.

gory (gōr′ĭ). Bloody.

gross (grōs). 1. Entire; whole. 2. Large; bulky.

grotesque (grô·tĕsk′). Awkward; out of proportion; strange.

guileless (gīl′lĕs). Not deceitful; sincere.

guinea (gĭn′ĭ). A British coin, discontinued in 1813, worth a little over five dollars.

guise (gīz). 1. Appearance. 2. Disguise.

guttural (gŭt′ēr·ăl). Throaty sounds.

gyrate (jī′rāt). Whirl around; revolve.

H

habiliment (hȧ·bĭl′ĭ·mĕnt). Dress; equipment.

hallowed (hăl′ōd). Sacred; blessed.

harbinger (här′bĭn·jēr). A forerunner.

hard (härd). Near to; almost.

hazard (hăz′ērd). To risk; to take a chance.

heel (hēl). To roll or tip to one side.

heterogeneous (hĕt′ēr·ô·jē′nê·ŭs). Made up of different kinds.

hoary (hōr′ĭ). White or gray, as hoary beards.

homage (hŏm′ĭj). Tribute; praise.

host (hōst). 1. A great crowd. 2. An army.

huff (hŭf). To bully another.

husbanded (hŭz′bănd·ĕd). Carefully saved.

husbandman (hŭz′bănd·măn). A farmer.

hybrid (hī′brĭd). Made of different elements.

hypocrite (hĭp′ô·krĭt). A person who does not practice what he preaches.

hypothesis (hī·pŏth′ê·sĭs). Theory.

cōōl, cŏŏk; our, boil; cūte, ûnite, bûrn, cŭt, ŭnless, menü; check; goat, sing, this, thick, scriptŭre, verdŭre.

GLOSSARY

I

idyll (ī′dĭl). Poetry or prose about country life.
illimitable (ĭl·lĭm′ĭt·a·b'l). Unlimited.
illusion (ĭ·lū′zhŭn). A false mental picture.
imbue (ĭm·bū′). To fill with something.
immedicable (ĭm·mĕd′ĭ·ka·b'l). Incurable.
impair (ĭm·pâr′). To weaken or damage.
impassive (ĭm·păs′ĭv). Unemotional; calm.
impeccable (ĭm·pĕk′a·b'l). Without fault.
impede (ĭm·pēd′). To hinder or obstruct.
impel (ĭm·pĕl′). 1. To force. 2. To drive.
impenetrable (ĭm·pĕn′ê·tra·b'l). Unable to be pierced; dense.
imperative (ĭm·pĕr′a·tĭv). Necessary; urgent.
imperceptible (ĭm′pĕr·sĕp′tĭ·b'l). Not able to be noticed; very slight.
imperial (ĭm·pēr′ĭ·al). Kingly; warlike.
impetuous (ĭm·pĕt′ū·ŭs). Acting without thought.
implicate (ĭm′plĭ·kāt). To involve another in something.
implication (ĭm′plĭ·kā′shŭn). A suggestion or hint.
import (ĭm′pōrt). Meaning.
importune (ĭm′pôr·tūn′). To plead with or urge.
imposing (ĭm·pōz′ĭng). Awe-inspiring.
imposition (ĭm′pô·zĭsh′ŭn). 1. A deception. 2. Unfair treatment of another.
impoverished (ĭm·pŏv′ĕr·ĭsht). Very poor.
imprecation (ĭm′prê·kā′shŭn). A curse.
impregnable (ĭm·prĕg′na·b'l). Not able to be conquered.
impregnate (ĭm·prĕg′nāt). To fill; to inject into.
inalienable (ĭn·āl′yĕn·a·b'l). Rightfully belonging to one's nature.
inarticulate (ĭn′är·tĭk′ū·lāt). Not expressed clearly.
incantation (ĭn′kăn·tā′shŭn). A calling forth of spirits; a magic ritual.
incarnate (ĭn·kär′nāt). To give form or body to; to make real and alive.
incessant (ĭn·sĕs′ănt). Without interruption.
incivility (ĭn′sĭ·vĭl′ĭ·tĭ). Rudeness.
incompatible (ĭn′kŏm·păt′ĭ·b'l). Incapable of joining or agreeing with.
incomprehensible (ĭn′kŏm·prê·hĕn′sĭ·b'l). Not able to be understood by the human mind.
inconceivable (ĭn′kŏn·sēv′a·b'l). Unbelievable.
incongruous (ĭn·kŏng′groō·ŭs). Out of place and unsuitable.
inconsequential (ĭn·kŏn′sê·kwĕn′shăl). Not important or related to the given situation.
incorrigible (ĭn·kŏr′ĭ·jĭ·b'l). Incurable.
incredulity (ĭn′krê·dū′lĭ·tĭ). Disbelief.
indemnity (ĭn·dĕm′nĭ·tĭ). Repayment or return for injury or loss suffered.
indisposition (ĭn′dĭs·pô·zĭsh′ŭn). An illness.
indissoluble (ĭn·dĭs′ô·lû·b'l). Not capable of being destroyed or dissolved.
indolent (ĭn′dô·lĕnt). Lazy; sluggish.
indubitable (ĭn·dū′bĭ·ta·b'l). Without a doubt.

induce (ĭn·dūs′). To urge; to influence.
indulge (ĭn·dŭlj′). To yield or give in to.
indulgent (ĭn·dŭl′jĕnt). Overly generous.
inestimable (ĭn·ĕs′tĭ·ma·b'l). Too great or valuable to be measured; priceless.
inevitable (ĭn·ĕv′ĭ·ta·b'l). Unavoidable.
inexplicable (ĭn·ĕks′plĭ·ka·b'l). Puzzling.
infallible (ĭn·făl′ĭ·b'l). Without mistake.
infamy (ĭn′fa·mĭ). A crime, or wicked act.
infatuation (ĭn·făt′ū·ā′shŭn). Lack of judgment; foolishness.
inference (ĭn′fēr·ĕns). Conclusion; judgment.
infernal (ĭn·fûr′năl). Pestlike; annoying.
infest (ĭn·fĕst′). 1. To annoy. 2. To overrun.
infidelity (ĭn′fĭ·dĕl′ĭ·tĭ). Unfaithfulness.
infinite (ĭn′fĭ·nĭt). Endless; without limits.
inflexible (ĭn·flĕk′sĭ·b'l). Firm; unbending.
infuse (ĭn·fūz′). To suggest; to pour into.
ingenious (ĭn·jēn′yŭs). Intelligent; talented.
ingress (ĭn′grĕs). Entrance.
innative (ĭn·nā′tĭv). Innate; inborn.
innovation (ĭn′ô·vā′shŭn). A change; something new.
inquest (ĭn′kwĕst). An official inquiry.
inscrutable (ĭn·skroō′ta·b'l). Incapable of being understood or known thoroughly.
insensible (ĭn·sĕn′sĭ·b'l). 1. Unconscious; without feelings. 2. Lacking sense perception.
insidious (ĭn·sĭd′ĭ·ŭs). Sly and deceitful.
insight (ĭn′sīt′). The ability to understand clearly the inner nature of things.
insinuating (ĭn·sĭn′ū·āt′ĭng). Hinting in an indirect and stealthy way.
insolence (ĭn′sô·lĕns). Rudeness which comes from a feeling of superiority.
instigate (ĭn′stĭ·gāt). To urge; to bring on.
insupportable (ĭn′sŭ·pōr′ta·b'l). Unbearable.
insurgent (ĭn·sûr′jĕnt). One who rebels.
intangible (ĭn·tăn′jĭ·b'l). That which is real but cannot be touched or felt.
integrity (ĭn·tĕg′rĭ·tĭ). Truthfulness; honesty.
intemperate (ĭn·tĕm′pĕr·ĭt). Lacking control.
interim (ĭn′tēr·ĭm). The meantime; interval.
intermittent (ĭn′tēr·mĭt′ĕnt). Stopping and starting; disconnected; periodic.
interposition (ĭn′tēr·pô·zĭsh′ŭn). Coming between; intervention; mediation.
intersperse (ĭn′tēr·spûrs′). To insert here and there.
interval (ĭn′tēr·văl). A short space of time.
intervene (ĭn′tēr·vēn′). To come between.
intimate (ĭn′tĭ·māt). 1. To declare; to make known. 2. To suggest indirectly.
intimation (ĭn′tĭ·mā′shŭn). Notice; announcement.
intimidation (ĭn·tĭm′ĭ·dā′shŭn). Act of frightening or making fearful and timid.
intrepid (ĭn·trĕp′ĭd). Without fear; bold.
inure (ĭn·ūr′). To become used to.
invariable (ĭn·vâr′ĭ·a·b'l). 1. Not changing; constant. 2. Without fail; always.
inventory (ĭn′vĕn·tō′rĭ). An account or list of all available goods.
inveterate (ĭn·vĕt′ĕr·ĭt). Long-established; old.

āte, châotic, dâre, ădd, ăccuse, bär, càsk, afar; ēat, dẹar, ĕlude, ĕgg, quiĕt, centēr; īdle, ĭf, activĭty; ōpen, ôbey, ôr, ŏrange, ŏffer, ŏccur.

invincible (ĭn·vĭn′sĭ·b'l). Not able to be defeated or overcome.

inviolate (ĭn·vī′ô·lăt). Unbroken; uninjured.

irascible (ĭ·răs′ĭ·b'l). Hot-tempered; impatient.

ironical (ĭ·rŏn′ĭ·kăl). Having a meaning opposite from the stated one.

irrelevance (ĭr′rĕl′ê·văns). Lack of relationship; having no connection with.

irrepressible (ĭr′rê·prĕs′ĭ·b'l). Not able to be controlled or subdued.

irresolute (ĭ·rĕz′ô·lūt). Undecided.

irreverence (ĭ·rĕv′ēr·ĕns). Lack of respect.

issue (ĭsh′ū). 1. The reason for an argument. 2. Final outcome.

J

jeopardy (jĕp′ēr·dĭ). Danger.

judicious (jōō·dĭsh′ŭs). Showing wise judgment.

jurisdiction (jōōr′ĭs·dĭk′shŭn). Authority or power to govern or legislate.

K

keel (kēl). 1. A main timber extending along the bottom of a ship. 2. Poetically, "a ship."

kersey (kûr′zĭ). Coarse, ribbed woolen cloth.

kilometer (kĭl′ô·mē′tēr). About five-eighths of a mile.

kindred (kĭn′drĕd). Sharing the same feelings with another.

klaxon (klăk′sŭn). A type of automobile horn.

L

lamentable (lăm′ĕn·tá·b'l). Sad; sorrowful.

lapse (lăps). A gradual passing of time.

latent (lā′tĕnt). 1. Hidden. 2. Undeveloped.

lay (lā). Poem or song.

league (lēg). A measure of about three miles.

lee (lē). 1. The side opposite that from which the wind blows. 2. Dregs; sediment.

legitimate (lê·jĭt′ĭ·mĭt). Lawful; not wrong.

leonine (lē′ô·nīn). Lionlike.

lethargy (lĕth′ēr·jĭ). Unhealthy sleepiness; indifference.

levy (lĕv′ĭ). 1. To make. 2. To collect.

libel (lī′bĕl). An unjust attack on a person either by speech or in writing.

liberal (lĭb′ēr·ăl). Free and unrestricted.

libretto (lĭ·brĕt′ō). The play, or words for an opera.

lieu (lū). Instead of.

lore (lōr). Learning; knowledge.

lubber (lŭb′ēr). One who is clumsy.

ludicrous (lū′dĭ·krŭs). Ridiculous; laughable.

lurid (lū′rĭd). 1. Violent. 2. Brilliant; glaring.

lustrous (lŭs′trŭs). Shining; gleaming.

lusty (lŭs′tĭ). Healthy; vigorous.

lute (lūt). A mandolinlike stringed instrument.

lyre (līr). An instrument of the harp class.

M

magnanimity (măg′ná·nĭm′ĭ·tĭ). Nobleness of soul; greatness and courage of spirit.

malediction (măl′ê·dĭk′shŭn). A curse.

malevolence (má·lĕv′ô·lĕns). Hatred; ill will.

malice (măl′ĭs). Ill-will; enmity; evil.

mandate (măn′dāt). An order or command.

manifest (măn′ĭ·fĕst). To show; make visible.

manifold (măn′ĭ·fōld). Numerous and varied.

marauder (má·rôd′ēr). A robber or thief.

marital (măr′ĭ·tăl). Pertaining to marriage.

marrow (măr′ō). 1. A tissue in the hollow part of bones. 2. The life giving part.

martial (mär′shăl). Military.

masque (másk). 1. Masquerade. 2. A type of drama.

maudlin (môd′lĭn). Overly sentimental.

maxim (măk′sĭm). A truth given as a proverb.

mazy (mā′zĭ). Winding and bewildering.

mediator (mē′dĭ·ā′tēr). One who attempts to reunite those who are quarreling.

melodramatic (mĕl′ô·drá·măt′ĭk). Arousing temporarily deep emotion; sensational.

meridian (mê·rĭd′ĭ·ăn). The highest visible point.

microscopic (mī′krô·skŏp′ĭk). Very small; tiny.

migratory (mī′grá·tō′rĭ). 1. Moving from one area or climate to another. 2. Roving.

millennial (mĭ·lĕn′ĭ·ăl). Pertaining to a thousand years.

minion (mĭn′yŭn). A servant; a dependent.

minute (mĭ·nūt′). Very small; tiny.

misdemeanor (mĭs′dê·mēn′ēr). Bad behavior.

mitigate (mĭt′ĭ·gāt). To make less severe.

modification (mŏd′ĭ·fĭ·kā′shŭn). A change.

modish (mōd′ĭsh). Fashionable.

moldering (mōl′dēr·ĭng). Decaying; crumbling.

mollify (mŏl′ĭ·fī). To soothe or calm.

morbid (môr′bĭd). Unhealthy; diseased.

mote (mōt). A small piece; anything very tiny.

murky (mûr′kĭ). Dark and thick, as of mist.

muse (mūz). To meditate; to think deeply.

muster (mŭs′tēr). 1. -n. An assembly; a collection. 2. -v. To call together.

mute (mūt). Silent; speechless.

N

naïve (nä·ēv′). Simple and unsophisticated.

necromantic (nĕk′rô·măn′tĭk). Magical.

niche (nĭch). A hollowed out space in a wall.

nocturne (nŏk′tûrn). In painting, a night scene.

nomenclature (nō′mĕn·klā′tŭr). A classification or list of names.

nonce (nŏns). For the time being.

nondescript (nŏn′dê·skrĭpt). Belonging to no particular class or type; an ordinary person.

nonplussed (nŏn′plŭst). Puzzled.

notorious (nô·tō′rĭ·ŭs). Very well-known, usually for evil or unacceptable actions.

novel (nŏv′ĕl). New; fresh.

noxious (nŏk′shŭs). Poisonous; harmful.

nucleus (nū′klê·ŭs). The central part; core.

O

oblique (ŏb·lēk′). Slanting; not in a straight line.

obliterate (ŏb·lĭt′ēr·āt). To blot out; to erase.

oblivious (ŏb·lĭv′ĭ·ŭs). 1. Forgotten. 2. Unaware or unconscious of.

cōol, cŏŏk; our, boil; cūte, ûnite, bûrn, cŭt, ŭnless, menü; check; goat, sing, ~~this~~, thick, scriptŭre, verdŭre.

obsessive (ŏb·sĕs'ĭv). Pertaining to the constant dwelling upon a single idea.

obsolescent (ŏb'sŏ·lĕs'ĕnt). Slowly becoming outmoded or out of style.

obstreperous (ŏb·strĕp'ēr·ŭs). Noisy; unruly.

obtrude (ŏb·trōōd'). To intrude.

obviate (ŏb'vĭ·āt). To put a stop to.

occult (ŏ·kŭlt'). Not clearly known; hidden.

ode (ōd). A lyric poem which can be set to music and has dignity of style and thought.

omen (ō'mĕn). A sign; a happening which supposedly foretells a future event.

ominous (ŏm'ĭ·nŭs). Predicting evil; foretelling something bad.

omnipotence (ŏm·nĭp'ŏ·tĕns). 1. Unlimited power. 2. Presence in all places at all times.

onslaught (ŏn'slôt'). A violent, heavy attack.

ordinance (ôr'dĭ·nǎns). A governmental decree.

orgy (ôr'jĭ). Wild and unrestrained ceremony.

ostentation (ŏs'tĕn·tā'shǔn). Unnecessary show of wealth.

own (ōn). To admit.

P

pall (pôl). The heavy black cloth laid over a coffin; hence, figuratively, a coffin.

panoramic (păn'ō·răm'ĭk). Widespread; not cut off from view.

pantomime (păn'tô·mīme). A dramatic performance in which the story is told by the actions, without the use of words.

parcel (pär'sĕl). To divide.

parch (pärch). To become hot and dry.

parley (pär'lĭ). A conference or discussion.

parsimony (pär'sĭ·mō'nĭ). Stinginess.

partiality (pär'shĭ·ăl'ĭ·tĭ). Preference; tendency to favor a thing or person.

passive (păs'ĭv). Enduring and patient; being acted upon without resistance.

patent (păt'ĕnt). Evident or obvious.

pathos (pā'thŏs). Tender and sympathetic feeling aroused by the suffering of others.

peculiar (pê·kūl'yēr). Belonging to one only; singular and distinctive.

peer (pēr). Match; equal.

pellicle (pĕl'ĭ·k'l). A thin film.

pendent (pĕn'dĕnt). Hanging.

pending (pĕnd'ĭng). 1. In the process of being decided or concluded. 2. Occurring almost immediately.

pensive (pĕn'sĭv). Seriously thoughtful.

pent (pĕnt). Imprisoned; confined.

perceive (pēr·sēv'). 1. To understand completely. 2. To notice; to recognize.

perceptible (pēr·sĕp'tĭ·b'l). Able to be seen.

perception (pēr·sĕp'shǔn). Act of knowing or being aware of something.

peremptory (pēr·ĕmp'tô·rĭ). Commanding; positive; allowing no possibility of denial.

perennial (pēr·ĕn'ĭ·ǎl). Regularly; permanently.

perfidious (pēr·fĭd'ĭ·ŭs). Treacherous; dishonorable.

perforce (pēr·fôrs'). By force.

perfunctory (pēr·fŭngk'tô·rĭ). Done mechanically or merely as a duty.

permeate (pûr'mê·āt). To seep through and fill thoroughly; to penetrate.

perpetuate (pēr·pĕt'ū·āt). To cause to last.

perplexity (pēr·plĕk'sĭ·tĭ). Confusion; bewilderment and uncertainty.

perspective (pēr·spĕk'tĭv). A scenic view or picture giving an impression of distance.

perspicuity (pûr'spĭ·kū'ĭ·tĭ). Having the ability to make one's meaning clear.

pertinacity (pûr'tĭ·nǎs'ĭ·tĭ). Stubbornness; determination.

pervade (pēr·vād'). To spread throughout.

perverseness (pēr·vûrs'nĕs). Willfulness; stubbornness; contrariness.

pervert (pēr·vûrt'). To corrupt; to turn away from what is right.

pestilence (pĕs'tĭ·lĕns). Widespread disease or death.

phantasm (făn'tăs'm). A weird looking object.

phantom (făn'tǔm). Illusion; false belief.

phenomenal (fê·nŏm'ê·nǎl). Unusual.

pinion (pĭn'yǔn). A wing.

pique (pēk). To make angry or resentful.

pith (pĭth). Substance; strength of purpose.

pithy (pĭth'ĭ). Brief and full of meaning.

plaintive (plān'tĭv). Sad and melancholy.

plausible (plô'zĭ·b'l). Seemingly worthy of belief or consideration; reasonable.

plume (plōōm). To take pride in or credit for.

plunder (plŭn'dēr). To take by force; to rob.

pneumatic (nū·măt'ĭk). Using compressed air.

poach (pōch). To trespass in order to steal game or fish.

poignant (poin'yǎnt). Emotionally moving; calling forth pity and sympathy.

pomp (pŏmp). Ceremony; magnificent display.

ponder (pŏn'dēr). To consider carefully.

ponderous (pŏn'dēr·ŭs). Heavy; bulky.

porous (pō'rŭs). Filled with tiny openings through which liquid can be absorbed.

portal (pōr'tǎl). A gate or door.

portent (pōr'tĕnt). A sign; an omen.

portray (pōr·trā'). To describe or draw a picture of; to represent.

posture (pŏs'tǔr). 1. Condition. 2. Pose or attitude of body or mind.

potent (pō'tĕnt). 1. Strong; powerful. 2. Full of unused power.

pound (pound). The British unit of money, at present worth about $2.80.

precarious (prê·kâr'ĭ·ŭs). Unstable; insecure; in a dangerous position.

precedent (prĕs'ê·dĕnt). That which sets the pattern for future action.

precipitous (prê·sĭp'ĭ·tŭs). Steep and rocky.

precise (prê·sīs). Strict; exact; accurate.

preclude (prê·klōōd'). To hinder; to shut out.

predisposing (prê'dĭs·pōz'ĭng). Making favorable; supplying a tendency towards.

prehistoric (prê'hĭs·tŏr'ĭk). Belonging to a time before history began.

premeditation (prê'mĕd·ĭ·tā'shǔn). Forethought; planning ahead of time.

āte, châotic, dâre, ădd, ǎccuse, bär, càsk, afar; ēat, dēar, ĕlude, ĕgg, quiĕt, centēr; īdle, ĭf, activĭty; ōpen, ŏbey, ôr, ŏrange, ŏffer, ǒccur.

---

preoccupied (prē·ŏk'û·pīd). Absorbed in thought.
preside (prē·zīd'). To exercise authority.
pretext (prē'tĕkst). A pretense.
prevail (prē·vāl'). To win or be victorious.
prime (prīm). The point when all a man's powers are at their greatest height.
primeval (prī·mē'văl). In its original state.
proclaim (prō·klām'). To declare; to make known widely.
proclivity (prō·klĭv'ĭ·tĭ). Natural inclination.
procure (prō·kūr'). To obtain; to secure.
prodigious (prō·dĭj'ŭs). Immense in size or amount.
profound (prō·found'). 1. Deep. 2. Full of knowledge.
profuse (prō·fūs'). Overflowing; abundant.
prohibition (prō'ĭ·bĭsh'ŭn). Act of forbidding something.
promiscuous (prō·mĭs'kû·ŭs). Made up of a haphazard assortment.
proneness (prōn'nĕs). Tendency; inclination.
propitiate (prō·pĭsh'ĭ·āt). To seek to make favorable or promising.
propitiatory (prō·pĭsh'ĭ·a·tō'rĭ). That which is offered as satisfaction for a wrong done.
protracted (prō·trăk'tĕd). Extended over a long period of time.
providence (prŏv'ĭ·dĕns). Guidance; interest and care.
provocation (prŏv'ô·kā'shŭn). That which arouses anger or strong feeling.
prudence (prōō'dĕns). Caution; practical wisdom.
puncheon (pŭn'chŭn). A large cask for wine.
pungent (pŭn'jĕnt). Penetrating; tart.

Q

quagmire (kwăg'mīr). Quicksand; a bog.
quell (kwĕl). To finish or put a stop to.
querulous (kwĕr'û·lŭs). Cross; complaining.
quiescent (kwĭ·ĕs'ĕnt). At rest; free from motion.
quirk (kwûrk). Twist or turn.

R

rail (rāl). To reproach; to scold harshly.
raiment (rā'mĕnt). Clothing.
rakish (rāk'ĭsh). At an angle; in a jaunty or sporty manner.
rampart (răm'pärt). A protecting wall; a barrier.
rancor, rancour (răng'kĕr). Bitterness; hatred.
rapture (răp'tûr). Ecstacy; an intense feeling of love.
rate (rāt). To scold.
ravening (răv'ĕn·ĭng). Seizing by violence; devouring; preying.
ravish (răv'ĭsh). 1. To carry away with intense emotion. 2. To seize by violence.
rebus (rē'bŭs). Using a picture to represent a word.
recess (rē·sĕs'). An indented space; a niche.
reciprocal (rē·sĭp'rō·kăl). Mutually shared or felt; jointly; equally.

recitative (rĕs'ĭ·ta·tēv'). A musical recitation, used in narrative parts of an opera.
recompense (rĕk'ŏm·pĕns). 1. A reward for suffering. 2. Payment for services done.
reconcile (rĕk'ŏn·sĭl). To bring to agreement.
recount (rē·kount'). To tell; to narrate.
recourse (rē·kōrs'). To turn to for assistance.
rectitude (rĕk'tĭ·tūd). Honesty; righteousness.
recumbent (rē·kŭm'bĕnt). Lying down; resting.
recur (rē·kûr'). To happen again.
redoubtable (rē·dout'a·b'l). Worthy of respect.
redress (rē·drĕs'). Making right a wrong.
regenerating (rē·jĕn'ĕr·āt'ĭng). Changing for the better; being spiritually reborn.
reiterate (rē·ĭt'ĕr·āt). To say again or repeat.
rejoinder (rē·join'dĕr). Reply; answer.
relief (rē·lēf'). A sharp outline in contrast to a softer background.
relish (rĕl'ĭsh). To enjoy; to take delight in.
remonstrate (rē·mŏn'strāt). To urge against.
render (rĕn'dĕr). 1. To make. 2. To give.
renowned (rē·nound'). Famous; well-known.
rent (rĕnt). A tear or rip; a split.
repair (rē·pâr'). To go.
repartee (rĕp'ĕr·tē'). A witty response.
repine (rē·pīn'). To complain or feel sad.
repose (rē·pōz'). 1. *n.* Ease and dignity; rest; lack of movement. 2. *-v.* To lie at rest; to lie buried.
reproof (rē·prōof'). A rebuke; a scolding.
requisite (rĕk'wĭ·zĭt). That which is essential or absolutely necessary.
requital (rē·kwī'tăl). In return; in acknowledgment.
resolve (rē·sŏlv'). 1. To reduce something to its simplest form. 2. To decide.
resort (rē·zôrt'). To go; to repair.
retain (rē·tān'). To keep or hold in a fixed condition.
retard (rē·tärd'). To slow down; to hold back.
retraction (rē·trăk'shŭn). The removal or taking back of a statement one has made.
retribution (rĕt'rĭ·bū'shŭn). 1. Punishment. 2. Reward.
retrospection (rĕt'rō·spĕk'shŭn). A remembrance or a looking back at past events.
revel (rĕv'ĕl). A party; a festive gathering.
reverberation (rē·vûr'bĕr·ā'shŭn). An echo.
revere (rē·vēr'). To regard or honor highly.
revert (rē·vûrt'). To return; to go back.
rheum (rōōm). A watery discharge from the eyes.
rift (rĭft). A break or opening.
rigor (rĭg'ĕr). Hardness or severity of life.
rivet (rĭv'ĕt). To fasten tightly.
roseate (rō'zĕ·āt). Rose-tinted; figuratively, pleasing.
rote (rōt). Memory; mechanical repetition of something learned.
rout (rout). A disorderly retreat.
rude (rōōd). 1. Crude. 2. Simple; rustic.
rueful (rōō'fool). Woeful; arousing pity.
ruthless (rōōth'lĕs). Cruel; without pity.

cōol, cŏŏk; our, boil; cūte, ŭnite, bûrn, cŭt, *ŭ*nless, menü; check; goat, sing, ~~this~~, thick, scriptûre, verdûre.

747

S

sable (sā'b'l). Black.

sack (săk). To ruin; to strip of valuables.

sagacious (să·gā'shŭs). Having wise judgment.

sage (sāj). 1. *adj.* Wise. 2. *-n.* A scholar.

sardonic (sär·dŏn'ĭk). Mocking; scornfully amused.

saturate (săt'ŭ·rāt). To fill or soak completely.

score (skōr). The original music, as for an opera.

scourge (skûrj). 1. *-n.* A punishment; an affliction. 2. *-v.* To whip; to beat.

scribe (skrīb). One who copies manuscripts or who writes from dictation.

scrupulous (skrōō'pŭ·lŭs). Strict; careful in doing what is right.

scrutiny (skrōō'tĭ·nĭ). Close and careful inspection.

scurvy (skûr'vĭ). A disease caused by a lack of certain foods.

seer (sēr). A prophet.

selfless (sĕlf'lĕs). Completely unselfish.

sensible (sĕn'sĭ·b'l). Aware; conscious.

sententious (sĕn·tĕn'shŭs). Brief; to the point.

sepal (sē'păl). A leaf.

sepulcher (sĕp'ŭl·kēr). A grave; a tomb.

seraphim (sĕr'á·fĭm). An order of angels.

serpentine (sûr'pĕn·tēn). Winding in a snakelike manner; twisting.

share (shâr). A plowshare.

sheer (shēr). Perpendicular; straight.

sibyl (sĭb'ĭl). A prophetess of ancient times, to whom people came to ask advice.

similitude (sĭ·mĭl'ĭ·tūd). Resemblance.

simultaneous (sī'mŭl·tā'nê·ŭs). Happening at the same time.

singular (sĭng'gŭ·lēr). Strange; different.

sinuous (sĭn'ŭ·ŭs). Moving in a winding or snakelike manner.

sloth (slōth). Laziness; inactivity.

slough (slōō). Marshland; wet, muddy land.

slovenly (slŭv'ĕn·lĭ). Untidy; disorderly.

smote (smōt). Hit or struck.

snare (snâr). A trap.

solace (sŏl'ĭs). Consolation in sorrow.

solicitude (sô·lĭs'ĭ·tūd). Concern; anxiety.

sovereignty (sŏv'ēr·ĭn·tĭ). Right or power of ruling; supremacy in matters of government.

spasmodical (spăz·mŏd'ĭ·kăl). 1. Occurring irregularly. 2. Pertaining to a violent effort of short duration.

speculative (spĕk'ŭ·lā'tĭv). Curious; inquiring.

spur (spûr). A projection from the main part.

squalor (skwăl'ēr). Deep poverty.

stalwart (stôl'wērt). 1. Brave. 2. Strong; firm.

stark (stärk). Harsh and unadorned.

stead (stĕd). Place; in place of.

steadfast (stĕd'fást). Firm; steady; constant.

sterility (stĕ·rĭl'ĭ·tĭ). Barrenness; unproductivity.

sterling (stûr'lĭng). Of real value; genuine.

stigma (stĭg'má). Mark of disgrace.

stimulus (stĭm'ŭ·lŭs). Something that arouses action.

stint (stĭnt). Allowance; quantity; portion.

stipulate (stĭp'ŭ·lāt). To order; to specify or ask for certain items.

stolidity (stô·lĭd'ĭ·tĭ). Great emotional calm.

straitened (strāt'nd). Limited; not plentiful.

strata (strā'tá). Layers.

strategy (străt'ê·jĭ). Careful planning; intrigue.

suave (swäv). Worldly; sophisticated.

subjoin (sŭb·join'). To add on immediately following the written or oral matter.

subjugation (sŭb'jōō·gā'shŭn). State of being conquered and forced under another's rule.

sublimity (sŭb·lĭm'ĭ·tĭ). Nobility; grandeur.

subsequent (sŭb'sê·kwĕnt). Following; coming later.

subsist (sŭb·sĭst'). To exist; to be.

substantial (sŭb·stăn'shăl). Solidly established; actual; real.

subterranean (sŭb'tĕ·rā'nê·ăn). Underground.

subtle (sŭt'l). Shrewd and delicate.

subvert (sŭb·vûrt'). To corrupt; to overthrow.

suffer (sŭf'ēr). To allow; to permit.

sufferance (sŭf'ēr·áns). Endurance; patient forbearance.

suffusion (sŭ·fū'zhŭn). Flush or blush.

sundry (sŭn'drĭ). Several and varied.

supercilious (sû·pēr·sĭl'ĭ·ŭs). Haughty; proud.

superfluous (sû·pûr'flōō·ŭs). Extra; unnecessary.

supine (sû·pīn'). Unalert; indifferent.

supple (sŭp'l). Bending with ease; elastic.

supplement (sŭp'lê·mĕnt). To add to in order to complete; to fill an empty space.

supplication (sŭp'li·kā'shŭn). Act of pleading humbly.

surmount (sûr·mount'). To top; to crown.

survey (sûr'vā). An inspection; an examination.

sustain (sŭs·tān'). 1. To support or hold up. 2. To keep one's spirits up.

swain (swān). A young peasant.

sylvan (sĭl'văn). Pertaining to the forest.

syncopated (sĭng'kô·pāt'ĕd). Having irregular or changing rhythm.

synthesis (sĭn'thê·sĭs). The process of combining separate parts.

T

talisman (tăl'ĭs·măn). A magic charm.

tangible (tăn'jĭ·b'l). Real; able to be touched.

taper (tā'pēr). To gradually decrease in size.

tattoo (tă·tōō'). A drum call sounded in a military camp shortly before taps.

taut (tôt). Stretched tightly.

tedious (tē'dĭ·ŭs). Tiresome; boring.

teeming (tēm'ĭng). Overflowing; crowded.

temper (tĕm'pēr). To regulate or adjust by softening or lessening.

tender (tĕn'dēr). To offer.

tenuity (tĕn·ū'ĭ·tĭ). Slimness; flimsiness.

termagant (tûr'má·gănt). A quarrelsome woman.

testy (tĕs'tĭ). Snappish; irritable.

tippet (tĭp'ĕt). A garment made like a scarf.

toil (toil). A net or trap.

topographical (tŏp'ô·grăf'ĭ·kăl). Descriptive of the physical features of a region.

āte, chăotic, dâre, ădd, ŏccuse, bär, càsk, áfar; ēat, dĕar, ĕlude, ĕgg, quĭĕt, centēr; īdle, ĭf, activĭty; ōpen, ôbey, ôr, ŏrange, ŏffer, ŏccur.

torpid (tôr′pĭd). Lazy; inactive.
torrential (tŏ·rĕn′shăl). Violent; overwhelming.
tossing (tŏs′ĭng). Disturbed; in a state of commotion.
trammel (trăm′ĕl). A pothook.
transcend (trăn·sĕnd′). To go beyond or above.
transient (trăn′shĕnt). Temporary; quickly passing.
translucent (trăns·lū′sĕnt). Partially transparent.
transport (trăns′pōrt). A strong emotion.
travail (trăv′āl). 1. Suffering. 2. Hard labor.
traverse (trăv′ērs). To pass over.
treble (trĕb′'l). A high-pitched sound.
tremulous (trĕm′ŭ·lŭs). Shaking; trembling.
trestle (trĕs′'l). A wooden support, as for a board or a table.
tribute (trĭb′ūt). Honor or respect that is deserved or earned.
trivial (trĭv′ĭ·ăl). Of little value; small; paltry.
turmoil (tûr′moil). Great unrest and confusion.
turret (tûr′ĕt). A small tower.

U

unappeasable (ŭn·ȧ·pēz′ȧ·b′l). Not able to be calmed or soothed.
unapprehensive (ŭn′ăp·rė·hĕn′sĭv). Not worried.
undulate (ŭn′dṳ·lāt). To move gently up and down.
unfaltering (ŭn·fôl′tēr·ĭng). Unwavering; unhesitating.
unique (ṳ·nēk′). Only one of its kind.
unrequited (ŭn′rė·kwīt′ĕd). Not repaid; unavenged.
unverified (ŭn·vĕr′ĭ·fīd). Not officially established as being true.
unwarrantable (ŭn·wŏr′ăn·tȧ·b′l). Not able to be defended; groundless; not justifiable.
unwieldy (ŭn·wēl′dĭ). Awkward; clumsy; hard to move or handle.
unwonted (ŭn·wŭn′tĕd). Unusual; not customary.
urn (ûrn). Vessel for holding the ashes of one who has died; figuratively, any burial place.
usurpation (ū′zēr·pā′shŭn). Illegal seizure of power.
utilitarian (ṳ·tĭl′ĭ·târ′ĭ·ȧn). Useful; practical.

V

vainglory (văn′glō′rĭ). Great pride in one's accomplishments; boasting.
vanguard (văn′gärd′). 1. That which goes in front. 2. The advance part of an army.
variable (vâr′ĭ·ȧ·b′l). Changeable.
vault (vôlt). 1. -n. An underground storage room with an arched ceiling. 2. -v. To leap.
vehemence (vē′ȧ·mĕns). Violence; force.
velocity (vė·lŏs′ĭ·tĭ). Speed.
venerable (vĕn′ēr·ȧ·b′l). Worthy of honor and respect by reason of age and dignity.
vengeance (vĕn′jăns). Revenge; punishment.
venomous (vĕn′ŭm·ŭs). Poisonous.

vent (vĕnt). To pour forth; to express.
venture (vĕn′tṳr). 1. -n. A dangerous undertaking. 2. -v. To dare to engage in.
veracious (vė·rā′shŭs). Truthful.
verbal (vûr′băl). Given by spoken words, rather than written down.
veritable (vĕr′ĭ·tȧ·b′l). Real; genuine; true.
vernacular (vēr·năk′ṳ·lēr). The everyday language of the greatest number of people.
vesture (vĕs′tṳr). 1. Appearance. 2. Clothing.
vexation (vĕks·ā′shŭn). Trouble; disquiet.
vicissitude (vĭ·sĭs′ĭ·tūd). Irregular change; change of fortune.
vigilant (vĭj′ĭ lănt). Alert; watchful.
vindicate (vĭn′dĭ·kāt). To defend the honor of; to free from unjust accusations.
vindictive (vĭn·dĭk′tĭv). Desiring revenge.
virtual (vûr′tṳ·ăl). Real; actual, although not carried out in fact.
virtuoso (vûr′tṳ·ō′sō). One who has exquisite taste in the fine arts; a connoisseur.
visage (vĭz′ĭj). The face or facial expression.
vista (vĭs′tȧ). An extensive view.
vital (vī′tăl). 1. Flourishing and full of life. 2. Essential; basic or necessary for life.
vituperative (vī·tū′pēr·ā′tĭv). Scolding.
vivacious (vī·vā′shŭs). Lively and gay.
vivification (vĭv′ĭ·fĭ·kā′shŭn). Restoration to life; revival.
vixen (vĭk′s′n). An ill-tempered woman.
vociferation (vō·sĭf′ēr·ā′shŭn). Shouting and clamor; noise.
void (void). A large, empty space.
volition (vō·lĭsh′ŭn). Will.
voluble (vŏl′ṳ·b′l). Talkative.
voluptuous (vō·lŭp′tṳ·ŭs). Full of pleasure; luxurious.
vortex (vôr′tĕks). A whirlpool.
vouchsafe (vouch·sāf′). To guarantee safety.
vying (vī′ĭng). Competing for superiority.

W

waft (wȧft). To bear or carry along; to move through the air.
waif (wāf). A homeless child.
wake (wāk). The track left by a ship moving through the water.
waning (wān′ĭng). Drawing to an end; closing.
wanton (wŏn′tŭn). 1. Unrestrained. 2. Reckless.
warrant (wŏr′ănt). To declare without fear of being wrong.
weal (wēl). Welfare; healthy condition.
whimsical (hwĭm′zĭ·kăl). Fanciful.
wont (wŭnt). Habit or custom.
wrought (rôt). Formed or shaped.

Z

zeal (zēl). 1. Ardent and enthusiastic devotion to a cause. 2. Eagerness.
zest (zĕst). That which gives relish or flavor to aid in the enjoyment of something.

cōōl, cŏŏk; our, boil; cūte, ŭnite, bûrn, cŭt, ŭnless, menü; check; goat, sing, ~~th~~is, thick, scriptṳre, verdṳre

INDEX